P9-ARG-237

Donation.

William M. Anderson Library
West Shore Community College
3000 N. Stiles Road
Scottville, MI 49454
231-843-5529
library@westshore.edu

The Western Heritage

Combined Volume

Twelfth Edition

Donald Kagan
Yale University

Steven Ozment
Harvard University

Frank M. Turner
Yale University

with
Gregory F. Viggiano
Sacred Heart University

Pearson

Portfolio Manager: Ed Parsons
Content Developer: Judy O'Neill
Content Developer Manager: Darcy Betts
Portfolio Manager Assistant: Andy Maldonado
Content Producer: Rob DeGeorge
Field Marketer: Alexa Macri
Product Marketer: Nicholas Bolt
Content Producer Manager: Ken Volcjak
Digital Studio Course Producer: Heather Pagano
Cover Credit: Combined Volume: Petrus Christus, A Goldsmith in His Shop (1449) – Credit: age fotostock/Alamy Stock Photo; Volume 1: Minoan Bull-Leaping, Great Palace

Knossos – Credit: Peter Horree/Alamy Stock Photo; Volume 2: Augustus Leopold Egg, Travelling Companions (1862) – Credit: Peter Barritt/Alamy Stock Photo
Cover Design: Pearson CSC
Cartographer: International Mapping
Full Service Project Managers: Mohamed Hameed and Ronard Imperial, Pearson CSC
Compositor: Pearson CSC
Printer/Binder: LSC Communications
Cover Printer: LSC Communications
Text Font: Palatino LT Pro 9.5/13

Brief Contents

Contents

The Source Collection at the end of each chapter is available only in the Revel version of *The Western Heritage*, Twelfth Edition.

Maps

Features

Three distinctive features of *The Western Heritage* put special focus on topics, artifacts, and text-based primary sources that offer historical accounts of how material artifacts represent a culture and its time.

Compare and Connect

Encountering the Past

A Closer Look

Revel™ Source Collection Documents

The following documents are available in the Revel version of *The Western Heritage*, Twelfth Edition, at the end of each chapter. They do not appear in the print version of the book.

Hammurabi, Code of Hammurabi [epilogue] (ca. 1750 B.C.E.)

Hammurabi, Code of Hammurabi [laws] (ca. 1750 B.C.E.)

Taram-Kubi, An Assyrian Woman Writes to Her Husband (ca. 1800 B.C.E.)

Epic of Gilgamesh, Excerpt from Book X [at the Edge of the World] (ca. 2000 B.C.E.)

Epic of Gilgamesh, Excerpt from Book XI [Immortality Denied] (ca. 2000 B.C.E.)

Excerpt from Genesis

Excerpt from Exodus

Homer, Husband and Wife in Homer's Troy, Excerpt from the *Iliad* (ca. 760 B.C.E.)

Homer, Quarrel of Achilles and Agamemnon, Excerpt from the *Iliad* (ca. 760 B.C.E.)

Homer, Hector and Andromache, Excerpt from the *Iliad* (ca. 760 B.C.E.)

Homer, Embassy to Achilles, Excerpt from the *Iliad* (ca. 760 B.C.E.)

Homer, Glaukos and Sarpedon, Excerpt from the *Iliad* (ca. 760 B.C.E.)

Aristotle, On the Polis, Excerpt from *Politics* (ca. 335 B.C.E.)

Tyrtaeus, On Sparta (ca. 600 B.C.E.)

Plutarch, Life of Lycurgus, Excerpt from *Lives of the Noble Grecians and Romans* (Second Century C.E.)

Euripides, Medea Bemoans the Condition of Women, Excerpt from *Medea* (431 B.C.E.)

Plato, On the Role of Women in His Utopian Republic, Excerpt from the *Republic* (ca. 380 B.C.E.)

Plutarch, On Archimedes and Hellenistic Science, Excerpt from *Lives of the Noble Grecians and Romans* (Second Century C.E.)

Thucydides, Funeral Speech of Pericles, Excerpt from *History of the Peloponnesian War* (431–404 B.C.E.)

Thucydides, Melian Dialogue, Excerpt from History of the Peloponnesian War (431–404 B.C.E.)

Thucydides, Speech of the Corinthians to Sparta, Excerpt from *History of the Peloponnesian War* (431–404 B.C.E.)

Aristophanes, Excerpt from *Clouds* (423 B.C.E.)

Plato, *Apology of Socrates* (ca. 390 B.C.E.)

Plato, Allegory of the Cave, Excerpt from the *Republic* (ca. 380 B.C.E.)

Plato, Myth of Er, Excerpt from the *Republic* (ca. 380 B.C.E.)

Livy, On Rome's Treatment of Conquered Italian Cities, Excerpt from *History of Rome* (ca. 27 B.C.E.)

Plutarch, A Description of a Roman Triumph, Excerpt from *Lives of the Noble Grecians and Romans* (Second Century C.E.)

Plutarch, On the Ruin of the Roman Family Farm and the Gracchan Reforms, Excerpt from *Lives of the Noble Grecians and Romans* (Second Century C.E.)

Vergil, The Theme of the Poem, Excerpt from the *Aeneid* (Book 1) (29–19 B.C.E.)

Livy, Excerpt from *History of Rome* (Late First Century B.C.E.)

Law of the Twelve Tables (ca. 450 B.C.E.)

Polybius, Preface on Political Constitutions, Excerpt from *Histories* (ca. 150 B.C.E.)

Cicero, Excerpt from *On the Commonwealth* (ca. 54 B.C.E.)

Cicero, Excerpt from *On the Laws* (ca. 52 B.C.E.)

Cicero, Excerpt from *On Moral Duties* (44. B.C.E.)

Cicero, "Scipio's Dream," Excerpt from *On the Commonwealth* (ca. 54 B.C.E.)

Soranus, Excerpt from *Gynecology* (Second Century C.E.)

Ovid, Excerpt from *Amores* (ca. 20 B.C.E.)

Mark, On the Resurrection of Jesus, Excerpt from the Gospel of Mark (ca. 70 C.E.)

Augustus, Deeds of the Divine Augustus (14 C.E.)

Vergil, Descent into the Underworld, Excerpt from the *Aeneid* (29–19 B.C.E.)

Matthew, Sermon on the Mount (Matt. 5:1–48) (ca. 100 C.E.)

Pliny and Trajan, Letters on Christianity (ca. 113 C.E.)

St. Augustine, Excerpts from *The City of God* (Early Fifth Century C.E.)

Benedict of Nursia, On Good Works, Obedience, and Silence, Excerpts from the *Rule of St. Benedict* (ca. 530)

Benedict of Nursia, On Humility, Excerpt from the *Rule of St. Benedict* (ca. 530)

Corpus Juris Civilis, Justinian on Slavery (533)

Procopius, The Character and "Innovations" of Justinian and Theodora (ca. 550)

De Villis, On the Carolingian Manor (ca. 770)

Anonymous, Donation of Constantine (ca. 775)

Boethius, Excerpts from *Consolation of Philosophy* (ca. 524 C.E.)

Pope Gregory VII, Declaration of the Power of the Pope, Excerpt from the *Dictatus Papae* (1075)

Magna Carta [brief excerpt] (1215)

Magna Carta [in full] (1215)

Revel™ Videos

The following videos are available in the Revel version of *The Western Heritage*, Twelfth Edition. They do not appear in the print version of the book.

History 360 Experiences

History 360 STONEHENGE

History 360 PYRAMIDS AND SPHINX AT GIZA

History 360 ATHENIAN ACROPOLIS

History 360 AMPHITHEATER AND TEMPLE COMPLEX AT DELPHI

History 360 ROMAN AQUEDUCTS AT SEGOVIA, SPAIN

History 360 HADRIAN'S WALL

History 360 ROMAN COLOSSEUM

History 360 HAGIA SOPHIA

History 360 MOSQUE-CATHEDRAL OF CÓRDOBA

History 360 VIKING SHIP *HUGIN*

History 360 CHARTRES CATHEDRAL

History 360 CRUSADER CASTLE (Krak des Chevalier, Syria)

History 360 VENICE (Maritime Power and Wealth)

History 360 PISA CATHEDRAL, BAPTISTERY, AND TOWER

History 360 PIAZZA SAN MARCO (Venice)

History 360 SISTINE CHAPEL

History 360 ALHAMBRA PALACE

History 360 CARAVEL *MATTHEW*

History 360 GLOBE THEATER

History 360 PALACE OF VERSAILLES

History 360 ISAAC NEWTON'S WOOLSTHORPE MANOR

History 360 PALACE OF VERSAILLES

History 360 EIGHTEENTH-CENTURY VIENNA

History 360 MASSON MILL TEXTILE FACTORY

History 360 NINETEENTH-CENTURY PARIS

History 360 ANTONI GAUDÍ'S PARC GÜELL

History 360 WORLD WAR I TRENCH

History 360 AUSCHWITZ

History 360 PRAGUE SPRING, WENCESLAS SQUARE

History 360 REUNIFICATION OF BERLIN

History 360 RED SQUARE

History 360 CALAIS "JUNGLE"

History 360 CHERNOBYL

History 360 BREXIT VOTE

Artifacts as Evidence

Artifacts as Evidence FLOOD TABLET

Artifacts as Evidence MINOAN BULL-LEAPER

Artifacts as Evidence COIN WITH HEAD OF ALEXANDER

Artifacts as Evidence BASSE YUTZ FLAGON

Artifacts as Evidence HINTON ST. MARY MOSAIC

Artifacts as Evidence LOTHAIR CRYSTAL

Artifacts as Evidence HEDWIG GLASS BEAKER

Artifacts as Evidence BACKGAMMON PIECE

Artifacts as Evidence PENDANT RELIQUARY CROSS

Artifacts as Evidence DURER'S RHINOCEROS

Artifacts as Evidence *A BRIEFE TREATISE OF DIVERS PLAINE AND SURE WAIES TO FINDE OUT THE TRUTH*

Artifacts as Evidence THE HENEAGE JEWEL

Artifacts as Evidence CHINESE FIGURINE OF LOUIS XIV

Artifacts as Evidence *NOVA REPERTA* (NEW INVENTIONS OF MODERN TIMES)

Artifacts as Evidence EARLY VICTORIAN TEA SET

Artifacts as Evidence AKAN DRUM

Artifacts as Evidence NO STAMP ACT TEAPOT

Artifacts as Evidence BUST OF HANS SLOANE

Artifacts as Evidence REVOLUTIONARY PLAYING CARDS

Artifacts as Evidence BUST OF JOHN WESLEY

Artifacts as Evidence HENRY "ORATOR" HUNT BEAKER

Artifacts as Evidence FREED SLAVE FIGURINE

Artifacts as Evidence SLAVE SHIP MANIFEST (from Schooner *Lafayette*)

Artifacts as Evidence MINIATURE BUGLE

Artifacts as Evidence *THE SUFFRAGETTE*

Artifacts as Evidence HMS *BEAGLE* CHRONOMETER

Artifacts as Evidence COMMODORE MATTHEW PERRY SCROLL

Artifacts as Evidence *LUSITANIA* MEDAL

Artifacts as Evidence SOVIET SHOCK WORKER BADGE

Artifacts as Evidence *THEY FIGHT BY NIGHT*

Artifacts as Evidence KOREAN WAR COLD WEATHER GEAR

Artifacts as Evidence SUEZ CRISIS FILMS

Artifacts as Evidence U-2 SPY PLANE

Artifacts as Evidence *YOUR BRITAIN, FIGHT FOR IT NOW*

Artifacts as Evidence APPLE II PERSONAL COMPUTER

Preface

The years since the publication of the eleventh edition of *The Western Heritage* have produced significant changes that present new and serious challenges to the West and the rest of the world. The most striking of these changes is in the economy. In 2008, a serious financial crisis produced a deep recession that diminished the widespread economic growth and prosperity of the West and much of the world and threatened to produce the political instability that usually accompanies economic upheaval. By 2012, the European Union, long an economic powerhouse, felt the threat to its currency and the solvency of its weaker members. The United States also suffered a severe setback, and the recovery from its recession was the slowest in decades. After a decade of slow growth and mixed results from attempts at fiscal austerity and loose monetary policy, the global economy appears to be returning to expansion.

In the realms of international relations and politics, the United States and its European friends and allies pursued mixed policies. The war in Iraq, which some had thought lost, took a turn in 2008 when the Americans changed their approach by introducing a sharply increased military force, popularly called "the surge," and a new counter-insurgence strategy. It was so successful that the western allies chose to withdraw their combat troops and leave the remaining fighting to the new Iraqi government. With fewer troops and a less clear commitment, the Americans undertook a similar "surge" in Afghanistan. The effort met with considerable success, but the prospect of continued fighting and diminishing support by the engaged Western powers left the future of their efforts to clear the region of terrorist bases uncertain. The reduced commitment of American forces led to the rise of new waves of threats from terrorism in the form of militant organizations such as the Islamic State of Iraq and the Levant and in protracted war in Syria.

New challenges arose in still another area involving important Western interests: North Africa and the Middle East. Insurrections against well-established autocracies in Libya and Egypt drew support in different degrees from members of NATO. Both nations succeeded in removing dictatorial rulers, but the character of the new regimes and their relationship with the West remains uncertain. The war in Syria and the migration crisis it has fueled add to these difficulties.

The authors of this volume continue to believe that the heritage of Western civilization remains a major point of departure for understanding and defining the challenges of our time. The spread of its interests and influence throughout the world has made the West a crucial part of the world's economy and a major player on the international scene. This book aims to introduce its readers to the Western heritage so that they may be better-informed and more culturally sensitive citizens of the increasingly troubled and challenging global age.

Since *The Western Heritage* first appeared, we have sought to provide our readers with a work that does justice to the richness and variety of Western civilization and its many complexities. We hope that such an understanding of the West will foster lively debate about its character, values, institutions, and global influence. Indeed, we believe such a critical outlook on their own culture has characterized the peoples of the West since the dawn of history. Through such debates we define ourselves and the values of our culture. Consequently, we welcome the debate and hope that *The Western Heritage* can help foster an informed discussion through its history of the West's strengths and weaknesses and the controversies surrounding Western history.

We also believe that any course addressing the experience of the West must also look beyond its historical European borders. Students reading this book come from a wide variety of cultures and experiences. They live in a world of highly interconnected economies and instant communication between cultures. In this emerging multicultural society, it seems both appropriate and necessary to recognize how Western civilization has interacted with other cultures throughout its history, both influencing and being influenced by them. For this reason, there is a chapter that focuses on the nineteenth-century European age of imperialism. Further examples of Western interaction with other parts of the world, such as with Islam, appear throughout the text. To further highlight the theme of cultural interaction, *The Western Heritage* includes a series of comparative essays, "The West and the World," which fall at the end of every part.

What Is the Western Heritage?

This book invites students and instructors to explore the Western heritage. What is that heritage? The Western heritage emerges from an evolved and evolving story of human actions and interactions, peaceful and violent, that arose in the eastern Mediterranean, then spread across the western Mediterranean into northern Europe, and eventually to the American continents, and in their broadest impact, to the peoples of Africa and Asia as well.

The Western heritage as a distinct portion of world history descends from the ancient Greeks. They saw their own political life based on open discussion of law and policy as different from that of Mesopotamia, Persia, and Egypt, where kings ruled without regard to public opinion. The Greeks invented the concept of citizenship, defining it as engagement in some form of self-government. Furthermore, through their literature and philosophy, the Greeks established the conviction that became characteristic of the West, that reason can shape and analyze physical nature, politics, and morality.

The city of Rome, spreading its authority through military conquest across the Mediterranean world, embraced Greek literature and philosophy. Through their conquests and imposition of their law, the Romans created the Western world as a vast empire stretching from Egypt and Syria in the east to Britain in the west. Although the Roman Republic, governed by a senate and popular political institutions, gave way after civil wars to the autocratic rule of the Roman Empire, the idea of a free republic of engaged citizens governed by public law and constitutional arrangements limiting political authority survived centuries of arbitrary rule by emperors. As in the rest of the world, the Greeks, the Romans, and virtually all other ancient peoples excluded women and slaves from political life and tolerated considerable social inequality.

In the early fourth century C.E., the emperor Constantine reorganized the Roman Empire in two fundamental ways that reshaped the West. First, he moved the imperial capital from Rome to Constantinople (Istanbul), establishing separate emperors in the east and west. Thereafter, large portions of the Western empire became subject to the rulers of Germanic tribes. In the confusion of these times, most of the texts embodying ancient philosophy, literature, and history became lost in the West, and for centuries Western Europeans were intellectually severed from that ancient heritage, which would later be recovered in a series of renaissances, or cultural rebirths, beginning in the eighth century.

Constantine's second fateful major reshaping of the West was his recognition of Christianity as the official religion of the empire. Christianity had grown out of the ancient monotheistic religion of the Hebrew people living in ancient Palestine. With the ministry of Jesus of Nazareth and the spread of his teachings by the Apostle Paul, Christianity had established itself as one of many religions in the empire. Because Christianity was monotheistic, Constantine's official embrace of it led to the eradication of pagan polytheism. Thereafter, the West became more or less coterminous with Latin Christianity, or that portion of the Christian church acknowledging the Bishop of Rome as its head.

As the emperors' rule broke down, bishops became the effective political rulers in many parts of Western Europe. But the Christian church in the West never governed without negotiation or conflict with secular rulers, and religious law never replaced secular law. Nor could secular rulers govern if they ignored the influence of the church. Hence from the fourth century C.E. to the present day, rival claims to political and moral authority between ecclesiastical and political officials have characterized the West.

In the seventh century the Christian West faced a new challenge from the rise of Islam. This new monotheistic religion originating in the teachings of the prophet Muhammad arose on the Arabian Peninsula and spread through rapid conquests across North Africa and eventually into Spain, turning the Mediterranean into what one historian has termed "a Muslim lake." Between the eleventh and thirteenth centuries, Christians attempted to reclaim the Holy Land from Muslim control in church-inspired military Crusades that still resonate negatively in the Islamic world.

It was, however, in the Muslim world that most of the texts of ancient Greek and Latin learning survived and were studied, while intellectual life languished in the West. Commencing in the twelfth century, knowledge of those texts began to work its way back into Western Europe. By the fourteenth century, European thinkers redefined themselves and their intellectual ambitions by recovering the literature and science from the ancient world, reuniting Europe with its Greco-Roman past.

From the twelfth through the eighteenth centuries, a new European political system slowly arose, based on centralized monarchies characterized by large armies, navies, and bureaucracies loyal to the monarch, and by the capacity to raise revenues. Whatever the personal ambitions of individual rulers, for the most part these monarchies recognized both the political role of local or national assemblies drawn from the propertied elites and the binding power of constitutional law on themselves. Also, in each of these monarchies, church officials and church law played important roles in public life. The monarchies, their military, and their expanding commercial economies became the basis for the extension of European and Western influence around the globe.

In the late fifteenth and early sixteenth centuries, two transforming events occurred. The firs t was the European discovery and conquest of the American continents, thus opening the Americas to Western institutions, religion, and economic exploitation. Over time, the labor shortages of the Americas led to the forced migration of millions of Africans as slaves to the New World. By the mid-seventeenth century, the West consequently embraced the entire transatlantic world and its multiracial societies.

Second, shortly after the American encounter, a religious schism erupted within Latin Christianity. Reformers rejecting both many medieval Christian doctrines as unbiblical and the primacy of the pope in Rome established Protestant churches across much of northern Europe. As a consequence, for almost two centuries religious warfare between Protestants and Roman Catholics overwhelmed the continent as monarchies chose to defend one side or the other. This religious turmoil meant that the Europeans who conquered and settled the Americas carried with them particularly energized religious convictions, with Roman Catholics dominating Latin America, and English Protestants most of North America.

By the late eighteenth century, the idea of the West denoted a culture increasingly dominated by two new forces. First, science arising from a new understanding of nature achieved during the sixteenth and seventeenth centuries persuaded growing numbers of the educated elite that human beings can rationally master nature for ever-expanding productive purposes improving the health and well-being of humankind. From this era to the present, the West has been associated with advances in technology, medicine, and scientific research. Second, during the eighteenth century, a drive for economic improvement that vastly increased agricultural production and then industrial manufacturing transformed economic life, especially in Western Europe and later the United States. Both of these economic developments went hand in hand with urbanization and the movement of the industrial economy into cities where the new urban populations experienced major social dislocation.

During these decades, certain West European elites came to regard advances in agricultural and manufacturing economies that were based on science and tied to commercial expansion as "civilized" in contrast to cultures that lacked those characteristics. From these ideas emerged the concept of "Western Civilization" defined to suggest that peoples dwelling outside Europe or inside Europe east of the Elbe River were less than civilized. Whereas Europeans had once defined themselves against the rest of the world as free citizens and then later as Christians, they now defined themselves as "civilized." Europeans would carry this self-assured superiority into their nineteenth- and early twentieth-century encounters with the peoples of Asia, Africa, and the Pacific.

During the last quarter of the eighteenth century, political revolution erupted across the transatlantic world. The British colonies of North America revolted. Then revolution occurred in France and spread across much of Europe. From 1791 through 1830, the Wars of Independence liberated Latin America from its European conquerors. These revolutions created bold new modes of political life, rooting the legitimacy of the state in some form of popular government and generally written constitutions. Thereafter, despite the presence of authoritarian governments on the European continent, the idea of the West, now including the new republics of the United States and Latin America, became associated with liberal democratic governments.

Furthermore, during the nineteenth century, most major European states came to identify themselves in terms of nationality—language, history, and ethnicity—rather than loyalty to a monarch. Nationalism eventually inflamed popular opinion and unloosed unprecedented political ambition by European governments.

These ambitions led to imperialism and the creation of new overseas European empires in the late nineteenth century. For the peoples living in European-administered Asian and African colonies, the idea and reality of the West embodied foreign domination and often disadvantageous involvement in a world economy. When in 1945 the close of World War II led to a sharp decline in European imperial authority, colonial peoples around the globe challenged that authority and gained independence. These former colonial peoples, however, often still suspected the West of seeking to control them. Hence, anticolonialism, like colonialism before it, redefined definitions of the West far from its borders.

Late nineteenth-century nationalism and imperialism also unleashed with World War I in 1914 unprecedented military hostilities among European nations that spread around the globe, followed a quarter-century later by an even greater world war. As one result of World War I, revolution occurred in Russia with the establishment of the Communist Soviet Union. During the interwar years a Fascist Party seized power in Italy and a Nazi Party took control of Germany. In response to these new authoritarian regimes, West European powers and the United States identified themselves with liberal democratic constitutionalism, individual freedom, commercial capitalism, science and learning freely pursued, and religious liberty, all of which they defined as the Western heritage. During the Cold War, conceived of as an East versus West, democratic versus Communist struggle that concluded with the collapse of the Soviet Union in 1991, the Western powers led by the United States continued to embrace those values in conscious opposition to the Soviet government, which since 1945 had also dominated much of Eastern Europe.

Since 1991 the West has again become redefined in the minds of many people as a world political and economic order dominated by the United States. Europe clearly remains the West, but political leadership has moved to North America. That American domination and recent American foreign policy have led throughout the West and elsewhere to much criticism of the United States.

Such self-criticism itself embodies one of the most important and persistent parts of the Western heritage. From the Hebrew prophets and Socrates to the critics of European imperialism, American foreign policy, social inequality, and environmental devastation, voices in the West have again and again been raised to criticize often in the most strident manner the policies of Western governments and the thought, values, social conditions, and inequalities of Western societies.

Consequently, we study the Western heritage not because the subject always or even primarily presents an admirable picture, but because the study of the Western heritage, like the study of all history, calls us to an integrity of research, observation, and analysis that clarifies our minds and challenges our moral sensibilities. The challenge of history is the challenge of thinking, and it is to that challenge that this book invites its readers.

Content Highlights

In this edition, as in past editions, our goal has been to present Western civilization fairly, accurately, and in a way that does justice to this great, diverse legacy of human enterprise. History has many facets, no single one of which can alone account for the others. Any attempt to tell the story of the West from a single overarching perspective, no matter how timely, is bound to neglect or suppress some important parts of this story. Like all other authors of introductory texts, we have had to make choices, but we have attempted to provide the broadest possible introduction to Western civilization.

Goals of the Text

Our primary goal has been to present a strong, clear, narrative account of the central developments in Western history. We have also sought to call attention to certain critical themes:

- The capacity of Western civilization, from the time of the Greeks to the present, to transform itself through self-criticism.

- The development in the West of political freedom, constitutional government, and concern for the rule of law and individual rights.

- The shifting relations among religion, society, and the state.

- The development of science and technology and their expanding impact on Western thought, social institutions, and everyday life.

- The major religious and intellectual currents that have shaped Western culture.

We believe that these themes have been fundamental in Western civilization, shaping the past and exerting a continuing influence on the present.

Flexible Presentation

The Western Heritage is designed to accommodate a variety of approaches to a course in Western civilization, allowing instructors to stress what is most important to them. Some instructors will ask students to read all the chapters. Others will select from among them to reinforce assigned readings and lectures. We believe the "Compare and Connect" documents, as well as the "Encountering the Past," and "A Closer Look" features may also be adopted selectively by instructors for purposes of classroom presentation and debate and as the basis for short written assignments.

Integrated Social, Cultural, and Political History

The Western Heritage provides one of the richest accounts of the social history of the West available today, with strong coverage of family life, the changing roles of women, and the place of the family in relation to broader economic, political, and social developments. This coverage reflects the explosive growth in social historical research in the past half-century, which has enriched virtually all areas of historical study.

We have also been told repeatedly by instructors that no matter what their own historical specialization, they believe that a political narrative gives students an effective tool to begin to understand the past. Consequently, we have sought to integrate such a strong political narrative with our treatment of the social, cultural, and intellectual factors in Western history.

We also believe that religious faith and religious institutions have been fundamental to the development of the West. No other survey text presents so full an account of the religious and intellectual development of the West. People may be political and social beings, but they are also reasoning and spiritual beings. What they think and believe are among the most important things we can know about them. Their ideas about God, society, law, gender, human nature, and the physical world have changed over the centuries and continue to change. We cannot fully grasp our own approach to the world without understanding the religious and intellectual currents of the past and how they have influenced our thoughts and conceptual categories. We seek to recognize the impact of religion in the expansion of the West, including the settlement of the Americas in the sixteenth century and the role of missionaries in nineteenth-century Western imperialism.

Clarity and Accessibility

Good narrative history requires clear, vigorous prose. As with earlier editions, we have paid careful attention to our writing, subjecting every paragraph to critical scrutiny. Our goal has been to make the history of the West accessible to students without compromising vocabulary or conceptual level. We hope this effort will benefit both instructors and students.

A Note on Dates and Transliterations

This edition of *The Western Heritage* continues the practice of using B.C.E. (before the common era) and C.E. (common era) instead of B.C. (before Christ) and A.D. (*anno Domini*, in the year of our Lord) to designate dates. We also follow the most accurate currently accepted English transliterations of Arabic words. For example, today *Koran* has been replaced by the more accurate *Qur'an;* similarly *Muhammad* is preferable to *Moham-med* and *Muslim* to *Moslem.*

New to This Edition

Here are just some of the changes, updates, and refinements that can be found throughout this new edition of *The Western Heritage.*

Improved Structure

To improve narrative structure and accessibility, chapters have been divided, wherever pertinent, into shorter subsections. Each new subsection carries its own heading, designed to reach readers and draw them in, in addition to aiding them in the skimming and scanning of pages for relevant information and insights. Explicit attention, also, has been paid to shortening passages for clarity.

New Illustrations

Images of historical figures, events, objects, sites, and period art and architecture can be as striking and informative as the ideas they represent. Over a third of the more than 400 images in *The Western Heritage* are new to this edition.

New Key Terms

To encourage and facilitate comprehension and review, each chapter now ends with an expanded list of key terms and definitions.

New Content

Every opportunity to provide additional context for shifts in the evolving story of human actions and interactions within the larger history of Western civilization has been energetically pursued. For example, in Chapter 29, the section on the resurgence of Russia under Putin has been expanded to include the invasions of Crimea and Ukraine. New content about the rise of ISIS, as well as the Arab Spring protests, has been added. In Chapter 30, the section on the papacy since the death of John Paul II has been updated with relevant details. New material on recent developments in the European Union, including the migration crisis and Brexit, and on changes marking the start of the Trump presidency has been written. Also new to this edition is an exploration of the future of renewable energy.

In particular, new content has been written for many of our popular "Compare and Connect" and "Encountering the Past" sidebars— all in the service of good storytelling—to make them even more responsive to students' interests:

Chapter 2—Encountering the Past: Marriage in Ancient Athens

Chapter 4—Compare and Connect: Why Did Rome Win the Punic Wars?

Chapter 5—Encountering the Past: The Roman Love of Bathing

Chapter 6—Encountering the Past: Medieval Cooking

Chapter 7—Compare and Connect: Anti-Jewish Violence and the First Crusade

Chapter 8—Compare and Connect: What Do Kings Have to Do with Universities?

Chapter 9—Compare and Connect: Peasant Revolts in England and France

Chapter 11—Compare and Connect: Can Anyone Understand the Word of God?

Chapter 11—Encountering the Past: Pictures, Preachers, and Songs

Chapter 13—Compare and Connect: The World Turned Upside Down

Chapter 14—Encountering the Past: The Science of Healthy Eating

Chapter 15—Encountering the Past: Brewing Becomes a Man's Profession

Chapter 18—Compare and Connect: What Did the National Assembly Accomplish?

Chapter 18—Encountering the Past: "La Marseillaise"

Chapter 21—Compare and Connect: From Republic to Empire, Again

Chapter 21—Encountering the Past: Opera and Italian Nationalism

Chapter 24—Compare and Connect: Charles Darwin's Christian Critics

Chapter 25—Encountering the Past: Hiram Maxim and the Maxim Gun

Chapter 26—Compare and Connect: War Poets on the Western Front

Chapter 29—Encountering the Past: Blood in the Water

Streamlined Timelines

The histories of key events, publications, dates, campaigns, and dynasties rendered as timelines in *The Western Heritage* have been judiciously edited to cover only the essentials.

Revel™ for *The Western Heritage*

Revel is an interactive learning environment that deeply engages students and prepares them for class. Media and assessment integrated directly within the authors' narrative lets students read, explore interactive content, and practice in one continuous learning path. Thanks to the dynamic reading experience in Revel, students come to class prepared to discuss, apply, and learn from instructors and from each other.

Learn more about Revel

www.pearson.com/revel

In Revel, *The Western Heritage* expresses many of the forms that make digital publishing dynamic, interactive, and better than print.

History 360 Experiences

Embedded History 360 experiences allow students to learn about history through the exploration of historical sites, including Stonehenge, the pyramids at Giza, the Athenian Acropolis, Hadrian's Wall, the Colosseum in Rome, Hagia Sophia, the Mosque-Cathedral of Córdoba, Chartres Cathedral, the Sistine Chapel, the Globe Theatre, Isaac Newton's Woolsthorpe Manor, the Palace of Versailles, nineteenth-century Paris, Auschwitz, Red Square, Chernobyl, and the Calais refugee camp. Each immersive experience combines 360-degree photographs and videos with sound, images, and text to help bring the past to life.

Artifacts as Evidence Videos

Created in partnership with the British Museum, the Imperial War Museums, the Smithsonian Institution, and the Victoria and Albert Museum, these videos focus on a wide range of unique artifacts that explain and illuminate the Western heritage.

Interactive Maps

Custom-built interactive maps and diagrams, with clickable layers, panning and zooming, rollover annotations, storytelling progressions, and related functionality provide students with multiple ways of engaging with visual content.

Source Collections

An end-of-chapter source collection includes a selection of primary source documents relevant to chapter content. Each document includes header notes, questions, and audio. Students can highlight and make notes on the documents.

Integrated Writing Opportunities

To help students reason more logically and write more clearly, each chapter of *The Western Heritage* offers varieties of writing prompts to elicit opinions and feedback, confirm knowledge and understanding, engage in historical analysis, and produce evidence-based arguments.

- *Journal Prompts*—Interspersed throughout chapters, journal prompts are designed to obtain free-form responses from students on topics that address each chapter's focus questions as well as each "Compare and Connect" excerpted primary source, each "Closer Look" historical artifact, and each "Encountering the Past" themed essay.

- *Shared Writing Prompts*—Found at the close of every chapter, shared writing prompts encourage students to consider multiple sides of issues by sharing their own views and responding to each other's viewpoints in a structured discussion-board-type environment that encourages critical thinking and collaboration.

- *Essay Prompts*—Focused on major themes in *The Western Heritage*, essay prompts appear in Pearson's Writing Space and can be assigned and graded by instructors.

Integrated Assessments

Multiple-choice quizzes appear at the end of every major section, allowing instructors and students to track progress and get immediate feedback as they progress through chapters. At the end of every chapter, lengthier quizzes measure the extent to which students have achieved desired learning outcomes.

Tools for Review

Every chapter includes an array of useful tools that allow students to check understanding and consolidate knowledge.

- *The Chapter in Perspective*—Chapter summaries encapsulate key chapter content, not only to aid review but also to articulate what historians perceive as essential to the study of the period.

- *Learn the Key Terms*—From Act of Supremacy to Zionism, more than 600 key terms central to the study of Western civilization allow students to engage with the lexicon of history.

- *Browse the Media Galleries*—Images and videos from the chapter, arranged together in one end-of-chapter carousel, form extensive digital collections of the photographic and videographic content in *The Western Heritage*. Each gallery reinforces comprehension and serves as an all-in-one reminder of the people, events, topics, and policies visually documented within the chapter.

Revel Combo Card

The Revel Combo Card provides an all-in-one access code and loose-leaf print reference (delivered by mail).

Ancillary Instructional Materials

Make more time for your students with instructor resources that offer effective learning assessments and classroom engagement. Pearson's partnership with educators does not end with the delivery of course materials; Pearson is there with you on the first day of class and beyond. A dedicated team of local Pearson representatives will work with you to not only choose course materials but also integrate them into your class and assess their effectiveness. Our goal is your goal—to improve instruction with each semester.

Pearson is pleased to offer the following resources to qualified adopters of *The Western Heritage*. Several of these supplements are available to instantly download on the Instructor Resource Center (IRC); please visit the IRC at www.pearsonhighered.com/irc to register for access.

Test Bank

Evaluate learning at every level. Reviewed for clarity and accuracy, the Test Bank measures this book's learning objectives with multiple-choice, short-answer, and essay questions. The large pool of multiple-choice questions for each chapter includes factual, conceptual, and analytical questions, so that instructors may assess students on basic information as well as critical thinking. You can easily customize the assessment to work in any major learning management system and to match what is covered in your course.

Pearson MyTest

This powerful assessment generation program includes all of the questions in the Test Bank. Quizzes and exams can be easily authored and saved online and then printed for classroom use, giving you ultimate flexibility to manage assessments anytime and anywhere. To learn more, visit www.pearsonhighered.com/mytest.

Instructor's Resource Manual

Create a comprehensive roadmap for teaching classroom, online, or hybrid courses. Designed for new and experienced instructors, the Instructor's Manual includes *An Introduction to Revel* section that walks users through the Revel product using screen shots that identify and explain the numerous Revel features, chapter summaries, learning objectives, discussion questions, lecture topics, Revel assessment questions, and information on audiovisual resources that can be used in developing and preparing lecture presentations.

PowerPoint Presentation

Make lectures more enriching for students. The PowerPoint presentation includes a full lecture outline, photos, and figures from the book. All PowerPoints are ADA compliant.

About the Authors

DONALD KAGAN is Sterling Professor of History and Classics at Yale University, where he has taught since 1969. He received his A.B. degree in history from Brooklyn College, his M.A. in classics from Brown University, and his Ph.D. in history from Ohio State University. During 1958 to 1959 he studied at the American School of Classical Studies as a Fulbright Scholar. He has received three awards for undergraduate teaching at Cornell and Yale. He is the author of a history of Greek political thought, *The Great Dialogue* (1965); a four-volume history of the Peloponnesian war, *The Origins of the Peloponnesian War* (1969); *The Archidamian War* (1974); *The Peace of Nicias and the Sicilian Expedition* (1981); *The Fall of the Athenian Empire* (1987); a biography of Pericles, *Pericles of Athens and the Birth of Democracy* (1991); *On the Origins of War* (1995); and *The Peloponnesian War* (2003). He is the coauthor, with Frederick W. Kagan, of *While America Sleeps* (2000). With Brian Tierney and L. Pearce Williams, he is the editor of *Great Issues in Western Civilization*, a collection of readings. He was awarded the National Humanities Medal for 2002 and was chosen by the National Endowment for the Humanities to deliver the Jefferson Lecture in 2004.

STEVEN OZMENT is McLean Professor of Ancient and Modern History at Harvard University. He has taught Western Civilization at Yale, Stanford, and Harvard. He is the author of twelve books, including *When Fathers Ruled: Family Life in Reformation Europe* (1983). *The Age of Reform, 1250–1550* (1980) won the Schaff Prize and was nominated for the 1981 National Book Award. Five of his books have been selections of the History Book Club: *Magdalena and Balthasar: An Intimate Portrait of Life in Sixteenth Century Europe* (1986), *Three Behaim Boys: Growing Up in Early Modern Germany* (1990), *Protestants: The Birth of a Revolution* (1992), *The Burgermeister's Daughter: Scandal in a Sixteenth Century German Town* (1996), and *Flesh and Spirit: Private Life in Early Modern Germany* (1999). His most recent publications are *Ancestors: The Loving Family of Old Europe* (2001), *A Mighty Fortress: A New History of the German People* (2004), "Why We Study Western Civ," *The Public Interest*, *158* (2005), and *The Serpent and the Lamb: Cranach, Luther, and the Making of the Reformation* (2011).

FRANK M. TURNER was John Hay Whitney Professor of History at Yale University and Director of the Beinecke Rare Book and Manuscript Library at Yale University, where he served as University Provost from 1988 to 1992. He received his B.A. degree from the College of William and Mary and his Ph.D. from Yale. He received the Yale College Award for Distinguished Undergraduate Teaching. He directed a National Endowment for the Humanities Summer Institute. His scholarly research received the support of fellowships from the National Endowment for the Humanities, the Guggenheim Foundation, and the Woodrow Wilson Center. He is the author of *Between Science and Religion: The Reaction to Scientific Naturalism in Late Victorian England* (1974); *The Greek Heritage in Victorian Britain* (1981), which received the British Council Prize of the Conference on British Studies and the Yale Press Governors Award; *Contesting Cultural Authority: Essays in Victorian Intellectual Life* (1993); and *John Henry Newman: The Challenge to Evangelical Religion* (2002). He also contributed numerous articles to journals and served on the editorial advisory boards of *The Journal of Modern History*, *Isis*, and *Victorian Studies*. He edited *The Idea of a University*, by John Henry Newman (1996), *Reflections on the Revolution in France by Edmund Burke* (2003), and *Apologia Pro Vita Sua and Six Sermons* by John Henry Newman (2008). He served as a Trustee of Connecticut College from 1996–2006. In 2003, Professor Turner was appointed Director of the Beinecke Rare Book and Manuscript Library at Yale University.

About the Contributor

GREGORY F. VIGGIANO received his Ph.D. in classics from Yale University and is Associate Professor of History at Sacred Heart University in Fairfield, Connecticut, where he teaches courses on ancient Greece and Rome and Western civilization. With Donald Kagan, he authored of *Problems in the History of Ancient Greece* (2009) and edited *Men of Bronze: Hoplite Warfare in Ancient Greece* (2013), which has been translated into Spanish (2017). He has published chapters and articles on ancient Greek history and is currently editing *A Cultural History of War in Antiquity*. He joined the authorship team of *The Western Heritage* during preparation of the twelfth edition for publication.

Acknowledgments

We are grateful to the scholars and instructors whose thoughtful and often detailed comments helped shape this revision: Jeffrey Auerbach, California State University, Northridge; Robert Brennan, Cape Fear Community College; Michael Broyles, Macomb Community College; Kevin Caldwell, Blue Ridge Community College; Geoffrey Clark, SUNY Potsdam; Dolores Davison, Foothill College; Robert Genter, Nassau Community College; Christian Griggs, Dalton State College; David Halahmy, Cypress College; Jeffrey Hardy, Brigham Young University; Nichola Harris, SUNY Ulster; Robin Hermann, University of Louisiana Lafayette; Martha Kinney, SUNY Suffolk; Frederic Krome, Clermont College; Sofia Laurein, San Diego City College; Susan Maurer, Nassau Community College; Bruce Nye, Front Range Community College, Westminster; Jason Ripper, Everett Community College; Jim Rogers, Louisiana State University, Alexandria; Michael Rutz, University of Wisconsin Oshkosh; Mark Spencer, Southeastern Oklahoma State University; David Tengwall, Anne Arundel Community College; Lisa Tran, California State University, Fullerton; Laura Trauth, Community College of Baltimore County; David Valone, Quinnipiac University.

We want especially to thank Lisa Tran, of California State University, Fullerton, who researched many new images for inclusion in this edition with uncommon care and intelligence and provided the accompanying captions.

Chapter 1
The Birth of Civilization

THE PHARAOH TUTANKHAMUN (r. 1336–1327 B.C.E.) With his "ka" (life force) in attendance, the Pharaoh Tutankhamun embraces Osiris, god of the Afterlife. This wall painting is from Tutankhamun's tomb, which was discovered in the 1920s. "King Tut" died at the age of eighteen.
SOURCE: François Guenet/Art Resource, NY

 ## Contents and Focus Questions

The Chapter in Brief

HISTORY, IN ITS TWO SENSES—as the events of the past that make up the human experience on earth and as the written record of those events—is a subject of both interest and importance. We naturally want to know how we came to be who we are, and how the world we live in came to be what it is. But beyond its intrinsic interest, history provides crucial insight into present human behavior. To understand who we are now, we need to know the record of the past and to try to understand the people and forces that shaped it.

For hundreds of thousands of years after the human species emerged, people lived by hunting, fishing, and collecting wild plants. Only some 10,000 years ago did they learn to cultivate plants, herd animals, and make airtight pottery for storage. These discoveries transformed people from gatherers to producers and allowed them to grow in number and to lead a settled life. About 5,000 years ago humans learned how to control the waters of great river valleys, making possible much richer harvests and supporting a further increase in population. The peoples of these river valley societies created the earliest civilizations. They invented writing, which, among other things, enabled them to keep inventories of food and other resources. They discovered the secret of smelting metal to make tools and weapons of bronze far superior to the stone implements of earlier times. They came together in towns and cities, where industry and commerce flourished. Complex religions took form, and social divisions increased. Kings—considered to be representatives of the gods or to be themselves divine—emerged as rulers, assisted by priests and defended by well-organized armies.

The first of these civilizations appeared among the Sumerians before 3500 B.C.E. in the Tigris-Euphrates Valley we call Mesopotamia. From the Sumerians to the Assyrians and Babylonians, a series of peoples ruled Mesopotamia, each shaping and passing along its distinctive culture, before the region fell under the control of great foreign empires. A second early civilization emerged in the Nile Valley around 3100 B.C.E. Egyptian civilization developed a remarkably continuous pattern, in part because Egypt was largely protected from invasion by the formidable deserts surrounding the valley. The essential character of Egyptian civilization changed little for nearly 3,000 years. Influences from other areas, however, especially Nubia to the south, Syria-Palestine to the northeast, and the Aegean to the north, may be seen during many periods of Egyptian history.

By the fourteenth century B.C.E., several powerful empires had arisen and were vying for dominance in regions that included Egypt, Mesopotamia, and Asia Minor. Northern warrior peoples, such as the Hittites who dominated Asia Minor, conquered and ruled peoples in various areas.

For two centuries, the Hittite and Egyptian empires struggled with each other for control of Syria-Palestine. By about 1200 B.C.E., however, both these empires had collapsed. Beginning about 850 B.C.E., the Assyrians arose in northern Mesopotamia and ultimately established a mighty new empire, even invading Egypt in the early seventh century B.C.E. The Assyrians were dominant until the late seventh century B.C.E., when they fell to a combination of enemies. Their vast empire was overtaken by the Babylonians, but these people, too, would soon become only a small, though important, part of the enormous empire of Persia.

Among all these great empires nestled a people called the Israelites, who maintained a small, independent kingdom in the region between Egypt and Syria for several centuries. This kingdom ultimately fell to the Assyrians and later remained subject to other conquerors. The Israelites possessed little worldly power or wealth, but they created a powerful religion, Judaism, the first certain and lasting worship of a single god in a world of polytheism. Judaism was the seedbed of two other religions that have played a mighty role in the history of the world: Christianity and Islam. The great empires have collapsed, forgotten for millennia until the tools of archaeologists uncovered their remains, but the religion of the Israelites, itself and through its offshoots, has endured as a powerful force.

1.1 Early Humans and Their Culture

How did life in the Neolithic Age differ from the Paleolithic?

Scientists estimate that creatures very much like humans appeared perhaps three to five million years ago, probably in Africa. Some one to two million years ago, erect and tool-using early humans spread throughout much of Africa, Europe, and Asia. Our own species, *Homo sapiens*, meaning "wise man," probably emerged some 200,000 years ago, and the earliest remains of fully modern humans date to about 90,000 years ago.

Humans, unlike other animals, are cultural beings. **Culture** may be defined as the ways of living built up by a group and passed on from one generation to another. It includes behavior such as courtship or childrearing practices; material things such as tools, clothing, and shelter; and ideas, institutions, and beliefs. Language, apparently a uniquely human trait, lies behind our ability to create ideas and institutions and to transmit culture from one generation to another. Our flexible and dexterous hands enable us to hold and make tools and so to create the material artifacts of culture. Because culture is learned and not inherited, it permits rapid adaptation to changing conditions, making possible the spread of humanity to almost all the lands of the globe.

1.1.1 The Paleolithic Age

Anthropologists designate early human cultures by their tools. The earliest period—the **Paleolithic Age** (from Greek, "old stone")—dates from the first use of stone tools some one million years ago to about 10000 B.C.E. During this immensely long period, people were hunters, fishers, and gatherers, but not producers, of food. They learned to make and use increasingly sophisticated tools of stone and perishable materials like wood; they learned to make and control fire; and they acquired language and the ability to use it to pass on what they had learned.

These early humans, dependent on nature for food and vulnerable to wild beasts and natural disasters, may have developed responses to a world rooted in fear of the unknown—of the uncertainties of human life or the overpowering forces of nature. Religious and magical beliefs and practices may have emerged in an effort to propitiate or coerce the superhuman forces thought to animate or direct the natural world. Evidence of religious faith and practice, as well as of magic, goes as far back as archaeology can take us. Fear or awe, exaltation, gratitude, and empathy with the natural world must all have figured into the cave art and into the ritual practices, such as burial, that we find at Paleolithic sites around the globe. The sense that there is more to the world than meets the eye—in other words, the religious response to the world—seems to be as old as humankind.

The style of life and the level of technology of the Paleolithic period could support only a sparsely settled society. If hunters were too numerous, game would not suffice. In Paleolithic times, people were subject to the same natural and ecological constraints that today maintain a balance between wolves and deer in Alaska.

Evidence from Paleolithic art and from modern hunter-gatherer societies suggests that human life in the Paleolithic Age was probably characterized by a division of labor by sex. Men engaged in hunting, fishing, making tools and weapons, and fighting against other families, clans, and tribes. Women, less mobile because of childbearing, gathered nuts, berries, and wild grains, wove baskets, and made clothing. Women gathering food probably discovered how to plant and care for seeds. This knowledge eventually made possible the development of agriculture and animal husbandry.

1.1.2 The Neolithic Age

Only a few Paleolithic societies made the initial shift from hunting and gathering to agriculture. Some 10,000 years ago parts of what we now call the Near East began to change from a nomadic hunter-gatherer culture to a more settled agricultural one. Because the shift to agriculture coincided with advances in stone tool technology, this period is called the **Neolithic Age** (from Greek, "new stone," the later period in the Stone Age). Productive animals, such as sheep and goats, and food crops, such as wheat and barley, were first domesticated in the mountain foothills. Once domestication had taken place, people could move to new areas, such as the river valleys of the Near East. The invention of pottery during the Neolithic Age enabled people to store surplus foods and liquids and to transport them, as well as to cook agricultural products. The invention of the wheel and its use for making pottery made it possible to create bowls and plates more efficiently. Cloth was made from flax and wool. Crops required constant care from planting to harvest, so Neolithic farmers built permanent dwellings. Houses in a Neolithic village were normally all the same size and were built on the same plan, suggesting that most Neolithic villagers had about the same level of wealth and social status. Neolithic villages tended to be self-sufficient.

PALEOLITHIC CAVE PAINTING Cave paintings discovered in Lascaux in southwestern France in 1940 suggest that early humans had developed beliefs and practices that helped them to understand and control their world. In this Paleolithic painting, a bird-headed man, an arrow at his feet, is surrounded by a bison, a small bird, and the partial outline of another animal.
SOURCE: Glasshouse Images/Alamy Stock Photo

Two larger Neolithic settlements do not fit this village pattern. One was found at Çatal Höyük, in a fertile agricultural region about 150 miles south of Ankara, the capital of present-day Turkey. This was a large town covering more than fifteen acres, with a population probably well over 6,000 people. The site of Jericho, an oasis around a spring near the Dead Sea, was occupied as early as 12,000 B.C.E. Around 8000 B.C.E., a town of eight to ten acres grew up, surrounded by a massive stone wall with at least one tower against the inner face. The inhabitants of Neolithic Jericho had a mixed agricultural, herding, and hunting economy and may have traded salt. They had no pottery but plastered the skulls of their dead to make realistic memorial portraits of them. Over time, in the regions where agriculture and animal husbandry appeared, the number of human beings grew at an unprecedented rate. One reason for this is that farmers usually had larger families than hunters. When animals and plants were domesticated and brought to the river valleys, the relationship between human beings and nature was changed forever. People had learned to control nature, a vital prerequisite for the emergence of civilization. But farmers had to work harder and longer than hunters did, and they had to stay in one place. Herders, in contrast, often moved from place to place in search of pasture and water, returning to their villages in the spring. Some scholars refer to the dramatic changes in subsistence, settlement, technology, and population of this time as the *Neolithic Revolution*. The earliest Neolithic societies appeared in the Mideast about 8000 B.C.E., in China about 4000 B.C.E., and in India about 3600 B.C.E. Neolithic agriculture was based on wheat and barley in the Mideast, on millet and rice in China, and on corn in Mesoamerica, several millennia later.

1.1.3 The Bronze Age and the Birth of Civilization

Neolithic agricultural villages and herding cultures gradually replaced Paleolithic culture in much of the world. Then another major shift occurred, first in the plains along the Tigris and Euphrates Rivers in the region the Greeks and Romans called **Mesopotamia** (modern Iraq), later in the Nile River valley in Egypt, and somewhat later in India and the Yellow River basin in China. This shift was associated initially with the growth of towns alongside villages, creating a hierarchy of larger and smaller settlements in the same region. Some towns then grew into much larger urban centers and often drew populations to them, so that nearby villages and towns declined. The urban centers, or cities, usually had monumental buildings, such as temples and fortifications. These were vastly larger than individual houses and could be built only by the sustained effort of hundreds and even thousands of people over many years. Elaborate representational artwork appeared, sometimes made of rare and imported materials. New technologies,

such as smelting and the manufacture of metal tools and weapons, were characteristic of urban life. Commodities, like pottery and textiles that had been made in individual houses in villages, were mass produced in cities. Cities were characterized by social stratification; that is, the grouping of people into classes based on factors such as control of resources; family, religious or political authority; and personal wealth. The development of wheeled vehicles helped promote long-distance trade. The earliest writing is also associated with the growth of cities. Writing, like representational art, was a powerful means of communicating over space and time and was probably invented to deal with urban problems of management and record keeping.

These attributes—urbanism; technological, industrial, and social change; long-distance trade; and new methods of symbolic communication—are defining characteristics of the form of human culture called **civilization**. At about the time the earliest civilizations were emerging, someone discovered how to combine tin and copper to make a stronger and more useful material—bronze. Archaeologists coined the term **Bronze Age** to refer to this period.

1.2 Early Civilizations to ca. 1000 B.C.E.

Why did the first cities develop?

By 4000 B.C.E., people had settled in large numbers in the river-watered lowlands of Mesopotamia and Egypt. By about 3000 B.C.E., when the invention of writing gave birth to history, urban life and the organization of society into centralized states were well established in the valleys of the Tigris and Euphrates Rivers in Mesopotamia and of the Nile River in Egypt.

Much of the population of cities consists of people who do not grow their own food, so urban life is possible only where farmers and stockbreeders can be made to produce a substantial surplus beyond their own needs. Also, a process has to be in place so this surplus can be collected and redeployed to sustain city dwellers. Efficient farming of plains alongside rivers, moreover, requires intelligent management of water resources for irrigation. In Mesopotamia, irrigation was essential because, in the south (later Babylonia), there was not enough rainfall to sustain crops. Furthermore, the rivers, fed by melting snows in Armenia, rose to flood the fields in the spring, about the time for harvest, when water was not needed. When water was needed for the autumn planting, less was available. This meant that people had to build dikes to keep the rivers from flooding the fields in the spring and had to devise a means to store water for use in the autumn. The Mesopotamians became skilled at that activity early on. In Egypt, however, the Nile River flooded at the right moment for cultivation, so irrigation was simply a matter of directing the water to the fields. In Mesopotamia, villages, towns, and cities tended to be strung along natural watercourses and, eventually, man-made canal systems. Thus, control of water could be important in warfare because an enemy could cut off water upstream of a city to force it to submit. Since the Mesopotamian plain was flat, branches of the rivers often changed their courses, and people would have to abandon their cities and move to new locations. Large-scale irrigation appeared only long after urban civilization had already developed, so major waterworks were a *consequence* of urbanism, not a cause of it.

1.2.1 Mesopotamian Civilization

The first civilization appears to have arisen in Mesopotamia. The region is divided into two ecological zones, roughly north and south of modern Baghdad. In the south (Babylonia), irrigation is vital; in the north (later Assyria), agriculture is possible with rainfall and wells. The south has high yields from irrigated lands, whereas the north has lower yields, but much more land under cultivation, so it can produce more than the south. The oldest Mesopotamian cities seem to have been founded by a people called the Sumerians during the fourth millennium B.C.E. in the land of Sumer, which is the southern half of Babylonia. By 3000 B.C.E., the Sumerian city of Uruk was the largest city in the world. (See Map 1–1.)

From about 2800 to 2370 B.C.E., in what is called the Early Dynastic period, several Sumerian city-states, independent political units consisting of a major city and its surrounding territory, existed in southern Mesopotamia, arranged in north–south lines along the major watercourses. Among these cities were Uruk, Ur, Nippur, Shuruppak, and Lagash. Some of the city-states formed leagues among themselves that apparently had both political and religious significance. Quarrels over water and agricultural land led to incessant warfare, and in time, stronger towns and leagues conquered weaker ones and expanded to form kingdoms ruling several city-states.

Map 1–1 THE ANCIENT NEAR EAST

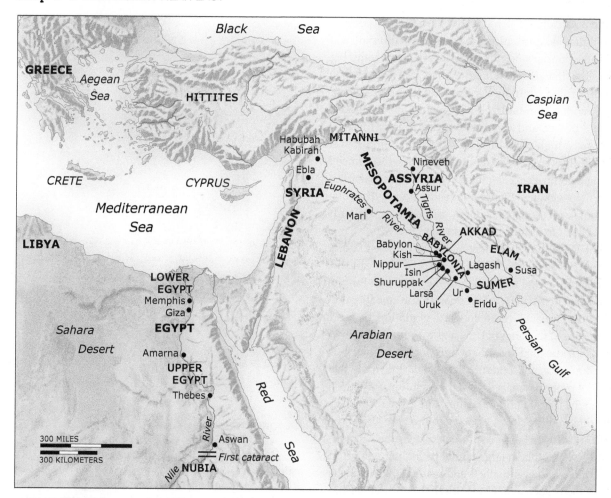

There were two ancient river valley civilizations. Egypt was united into a single state, and Mesopotamia was long divided into a number of city-states.

KEY EVENTS IN MESOPOTAMIAN HISTORY	
ca. 3500 B.C.E.	Development of Sumerian cities, especially Uruk
ca. 2800–2370 B.C.E.	Early Dynastic period of Sumerian city-states
ca. 2370 B.C.E.	Sargon establishes Akkadian dynasty and Akkadian Empire
ca. 2125–2027 B.C.E.	Third Dynasty of Ur
ca. 2000–1800 B.C.E.	Establishment of Amorites in Mesopotamia
ca. 1792–1750 B.C.E.	Reign of Hammurabi

Peoples who, unlike the Sumerians, mostly spoke Semitic languages (that is, languages in the same family as Arabic and Hebrew) occupied northern Mesopotamia and Syria. The Sumerian language is not related to any language known today. Many of these Semitic peoples absorbed aspects of Sumerian culture, especially writing. In northern Babylonia, the Mesopotamians believed that the large city of Kish had the first kings in history. Far east of this territory, not far from modern Baghdad, a people known as the Akkadians established their own kingdom at a capital city called Akkade under their first king, Sargon, who had been a servant of the king of Kish.

The Akkadians conquered all the Sumerian city-states and invaded southwestern Iran and northern Syria. This was the first empire in history, with a heartland, provinces, and an absolute ruler. It included numerous peoples, cities, languages, and cultures, as well as different ecological zones, under one rule. Sargon's name became legendary as the first great conqueror of history. His grandson, **Naram-Sin**, ruled from the Persian Gulf to the Mediterranean Sea, with a standardized administration, unheard-of wealth and power, and a grand style that to later Mesopotamians was a high point of their history. Naram-Sin even declared himself a god and had temples built to himself, something no Sumerian ruler had ever done. External attack and internal weakness eventually destroyed the Akkadian Empire, but several smaller states flourished independently, notably Lagash in Sumer, under its ruler Gudea.

About 2125 B.C.E., the Sumerian city of Ur rose to dominance, and the rulers of the **Third Dynasty of Ur** established an empire built on the foundation of the Akkadian Empire, but far smaller. In this period, Sumerian culture and literature flourished. Epic poems were composed, glorifying the deeds of the ancestors of the kings of Ur. A highly centralized administration kept detailed records of agriculture, animal husbandry, commerce, and other matters. After little more than a century of prominence, however, the kingdom of Ur disintegrated in the face of famine and invasion. From the east, the Elamites attacked the city of Ur and captured the king. From the north and west, a Semitic-speaking people, the Amorites, invaded Mesopotamia in large numbers, settling around the Sumerian cities and eventually founding their own dynasties in some of them, such as at Uruk, Babylon, Isin, and Larsa.

The fall of the Third Dynasty of Ur put an end to Sumerian rule, and the Sumerians gradually disappeared as an identifiable group. The Sumerian language survived only in writing as the learned language of Babylonia taught in schools and used by priests and scholars. So great was the respect for the Sumerian language that seventeen centuries after the fall of Ur, when Alexander the Great arrived in Babylon in 331 B.C.E., Sumerian was still used as a scholarly and religious language there.

For some time after the fall of Ur, there was relative peace in Babylonia under the Amorite kings of Isin, who used the Sumerian language at their court and considered themselves the successors of the kings of Ur. Eventually, another Amorite dynasty at the city of Larsa contested control of Babylonia, and a period of warfare began, consisting mostly of attacks on strategic points on waterways. A powerful new dynasty at Babylon defeated Isin, Larsa, and other rivals and dominated Mesopotamia for nearly 300 years. Its high point was the reign of its most famous king, **Hammurabi** (r. ca. 1792–1750 B.C.E.), best known today for the collection

VICTORY STELE OF NARAM-SIN, KING OF AKKAD This carved stone slab, or stele, commemorates the Akkadian king Naram-Sin's campaign against the Lullubi (c. 2230 B.C.E.), a people living in the northern Zagros Mountains, along the eastern frontier of Mesopotamia. Kings set up monuments like this one in the courtyards of temples to record their deeds. They were also left in remote corners of the empire to warn distant peoples of the death and enslavement awaiting the king's enemies.
SOURCE: Louvre, Paris, France/Bridgeman Images

of laws that bears his name. Hammurabi destroyed the great city of Mari on the Euphrates and created a kingdom embracing most of Mesopotamia.

Collections of laws existed as early as the Third Dynasty of Ur, and Hammurabi's owed much to earlier models and different legal traditions. His collection of laws, now referred to as the Code of Hammurabi, revealed a society divided by class. There were nobles, commoners, and slaves, and the law did not treat all of them equally. In general, punishments were harsh, based literally on the principle of "an eye for an eye, a tooth for a tooth," whereas Sumerian law often levied fines instead of bodily mutilation or death. Disputes over property and other complaints were heard first by local city assemblies of leading citizens and heads of families. Professional judges heard cases for a fee and held court near the city gate. In Mesopotamian trials, witnesses and written evidence had to be produced and a written verdict issued. False testimony was punishable by death. Sometimes the contesting parties would submit to an oath before the gods, based on the theory that no one would risk swearing a false oath. In cases where evidence or oath could not establish the truth, the contesting parties might take an ordeal, such as being thrown into the river for the god to decide who was telling the truth. Cases of capital punishment could be appealed to the king. Hammurabi was closely involved with the details of his kingdom, and his surviving letters often deal with minor local disputes.

About 1600 B.C.E., the Babylonian kingdom fell apart under the impact of invasions from the north by the Hittites, Hurrians, and Kassites, all non-Mesopotamian peoples.

1.2.1.1 GOVERNMENT From the earliest historical records, it is clear the Sumerians were ruled by monarchs in some form. The type of rule varied at different times and places. In later Assyria, for example, the king served as chief priest; in Babylonia, the priesthood was separate from royalty. Royal princesses were sometimes appointed as priestesses of important gods. One of the most famous of these was Enheduanna, daughter of Sargon of Akkad. She is the first author in history whose writings can be identified with a real person. Although she was an Akkadian, she wrote complicated, passionate, and intensely personal poetry in the Sumerian language, in which she tells of important historical events that she experienced. In one passage, she compares the agony of writing a poem to giving birth.

The government and the temples cultivated large areas of land to support their staffs and retinue. Laborers of low social status who were given rations of raw foods and other commodities to sustain them and their families did some of the work on this land. Citizens leased some land for a share of the crop and a cash payment. The government and temples owned large herds of sheep, goats, cattle, and donkeys. The Sumerian city-states exported wool and textiles to buy metals, such as copper, that were not available in Mesopotamia. Families and private individuals often owned their own farmland or houses in the cities, which they bought and sold as they liked.

1.2.1.2 WRITING AND MATHEMATICS Government, business, and scholarship required a good system of writing. The Sumerians invented the writing system now known as **cuneiform** (from the Latin *cuneus*, "wedge") because of the wedge-shaped marks made by writing on clay tablets with a cut reed stylus. The Sumerian writing system used several thousand characters, some of which stood for words and some for sounds. Some characters stood for many different sounds or words, and some sounds could be written using a choice of many different characters. The result was a writing system that was difficult to learn. Sumerian students were fond of complaining about their unfair teachers, how hard their schoolwork was, and their too-short vacations. Sumerian and Babylonian schools emphasized language and literature, accounting, legal practice, and mathematics, especially geometry, along with memorization of much abstract knowledge that had no relevance to everyday life. The ability to read and write was restricted to an elite who could afford to go to school. Success in school, however, and factors such as good family connections, meant a literate Sumerian could find employment as a clerk, surveyor, teacher, diplomat, or administrator.

The Sumerians also began the development of mathematics. The earliest Sumerian records suggest that before 3000 B.C.E. people had not yet thought of the concept of "number" independently of counting specific things. Therefore, the earliest writing used different numerals for counting different things, and the numerals had no independent value. (The same sign could be ten or eighteen, for example, depending on what was counted.) Once an independent concept of number was established, mathematics developed rapidly. The Sumerian system was based on the number sixty ("sexagesimal"), rather than the number ten ("decimal"), the system in general use today. Sumerian counting survives in the modern sixty-minute hour and the circle of 360 degrees. By the time of Hammurabi, the Mesopotamians were expert in many types of mathematics, including mathematical astronomy. The calendar the Mesopotamians used had twelve lunar months of thirty days each. To keep the calendar synched with the solar year and the seasons, the Mesopotamians occasionally introduced a thirteenth month.

1.2.1.3 RELIGION The Sumerians and their successors worshiped many gods and goddesses. Most of the gods were identified with some natural phenomenon such as the sky, fresh water, or storms. They were visualized in human form, with human needs and weaknesses, but they differed from humans in their greater power, sublime position in the universe, and immortality. The Mesopotamians believed humans were created to serve the gods and to relieve the gods of the necessity of providing for themselves. The gods were considered universal, but also residing in specific places—usually one important god or goddess in each city. Mesopotamian temples were run like great households where the gods were fed lavish meals, entertained with music, and honored with devotion and ritual. There were gardens for their pleasure and bedrooms to retire to at night. The images of the gods were dressed and adorned with the finest materials. Theologians organized the gods into families and generations. Human social institutions like kingship, or crafts like carpentry, were associated with specific gods, so the boundaries between human and divine society were not always clearly drawn. Because the great gods were visualized as human rulers, remote from the common people and their concerns, the Mesopotamians imagined another, more personal, intercessor god to look after a person, rather like a guardian spirit. The public festivals of the gods were important holidays, with parades, ceremonies, and special foods. People wore their best clothes and celebrated their city and its gods. The Mesopotamians were religiously tolerant and readily accepted the possibility that different people might have different gods.

The Mesopotamians had a vague and gloomy picture of the afterworld. The winged spirits of the dead were recognizable as individuals. They were confined to a dusty, dark netherworld, doomed to perpetual hunger and thirst unless someone offered them food and drink. Some spirits escaped to haunt human beings. There was no preferential treatment in the afterlife for those who had led religious or virtuous lives—everyone was equally miserable.

Mesopotamian families often had ceremonies to remember and honor their dead. People were usually buried together with goods such as pottery and ornaments. In the Early Dynastic period, certain kings were buried with a large retinue of attendants, including soldiers and musicians, who apparently took poison during the funeral ceremony and were buried where they fell. But this practice soon disappeared. Children were sometimes buried under the floors of houses. Some families used burial vaults; others, large cemeteries. No tombstones or inscriptions identified the deceased. Mesopotamian religion focused on problems of this world and how to lead a good life before dying.

The ancient Mesopotamians also put much thought and effort into discovering signs that they believed would indicate future events, interpreting the meaning of these signs, and taking steps to avert evil. Mesopotamians believed in divination the way many people today put their trust in science. (See the "Encountering the Past" sidebar, which follows below, on divination in ancient Mesopotamia.)

Encountering the Past

Divination in Ancient Mesopotamia

DIVINATION ATTEMPTS TO foretell the future using magic or occult practices. One of the earliest divination methods the Mesopotamians used involved the sacrifice of sheep and goats. Seers examined the entrails of the sacrificed animals for deformations that could foretell the future. Clay tablets recorded particular deformations and the historical events they had foretold. The search for omens in the innards of sacrificial animals was especially important to Mesopotamian kings, who always performed that ceremony before undertaking important affairs of state.

MESOPOTAMIAN CLAY HUMBABA DEMON MASK
In the *Epic of Gilgamesh*, the oldest surviving work of literature in the world, the grimacing demon Humbaba (also spelled Huwawa) guards a forest of cedars. This clay mask of Humbaba comes from the city of Sippar in southern Iraq and dates from around 1800–1600 B.C.E.
SOURCE: www.BibleLandPictures.com/Alamy Stock Photo

But animal sacrifice was expensive. Most Mesopotamians, therefore, used other devices for divination. They burned incense and examined the shape of the smoke that arose. They poured oil into water and studied the resulting patterns for signs. They found omens in how people answered questions or in what they overheard strangers say. They collected clay tablets—their books—that described people's appearance and what it might tell them about the future.

The heavens were another source of omens. Astrologers recorded and interpreted the movements of the stars, planets, comets, and other heavenly bodies. Mesopotamia's great progress in astronomy derived in large part from this practice. The study of dreams and of unusual births, both human and animal, was also important. Troubled dreams and strange offspring had frightening implications for human affairs.

These practices all derived from the belief that the gods sent omens to warn human beings. Once the omens had been interpreted, Mesopotamians sought to avert danger with magic and prayers.

Questions

1. How did Mesopotamians try to predict the future, and what did they attempt to do about what they learned?
2. How would Mesopotamians explain their great interest in omens?

Religion played a large part in the literature and art of Mesopotamia. Epic poems told of the deeds of the gods, such as how the world was created and organized, of a great flood the gods sent to wipe out humanity, and of the hero-king Gilgamesh, who tried to escape death by going on a fantastic journey to find the sole survivor of a great flood. (See the "Compare and Connect" sidebar on two ancient stories of great floods.) Religious architecture

Compare and Connect

The Great Flood

STORIES OF A GREAT deluge appeared in many cultures at various times in the ancient world. In the Mesopotamian world, the earliest known story of a great flood sent by the gods to destroy mankind appeared in the Sumerian civilization. Later the story was included in the *Epic of Gilgamesh* in a Semitic language. The great flood of Noah's time appears in the book of Genesis in the Hebrew Bible.

THE FLOOD TABLET (TABLET XI) The Flood Tablet, the eleventh tablet in a series that relates the *Epic of Gilgamesh*, describes the meeting of Gilgamesh and Utnapishtim who, along with his wife, survived a great flood that destroyed the rest of humankind.

SOURCE: The Trustees of the British Museum/Art Resource, NY

Before Reading

- In the Babylonian story of the flood, notice how Enlil sends the deluge to destroy mankind.
- In the story of the flood from Genesis, think about why God makes a covenant with Noah.

Questions

1. In what ways is the story from the *Epic of Gilgamesh* similar to the story of Noah in the Hebrew Bible?
2. How is the account of a great flood in the story of Noah different from that in the *Epic of Gilgamesh*?
3. What is the significance of the similarities and differences between the two accounts?

I. THE BABYLONIAN STORY OF THE FLOOD

The passage that follows is part of the Babylonian Epic of Gilgamesh. *An earlier independent Babylonian Story of the Flood suggested that the gods sent a flood because there were too many people on the earth. A version of this story was later combined with the* Epic of Gilgamesh, *a legendary king who became terrified of death when his best friend and companion died. After many adventures, Gilgamesh crossed the distant ocean and the "waters of death" to ask Utnapishtim, who, with his wife, was the only survivor of the great flood, the secret of eternal life. In response, Utnapishtim narrated the story of the great flood to show that his own immortality derived from a onetime event in the past, so Gilgamesh could not share his destiny.*

For six days and [seven] nights the wind blew, and the flood and the storm swept the land. But the seventh day arriving did the rainstorm subside and the flood which had heaved like a woman in travail; there quieted the sea, and the storm-wind stood still, the flood stayed her flowing. I opened a vent and the fresh air moved over my cheek-bones. And I looked at the sea; there was silence, the tide-way lay flat as a roof-top—but the whole of mankind had returned unto clay. I bowed low: I sat and I wept: o'er my cheek-bones my tears kept on running.

When I looked out again in the directions, across the expanse of the sea, mountain ranges had emerged in twelve places and on Mount Nisir the vessel had grounded. Mount Nisir held the vessel fast nor allowed any movement. For a first day and a second, fast Mount Nisir held the vessel nor allowed of any movement. For a third day and a fourth day, fast Mount Nisir held the vessel nor allowed of any movement. For a fifth and a sixth day, held Mount Nisir fast the vessel nor allowed of any movement.

On the seventh day's arriving, I freed a dove and did release him. Forth went the dove but came back to me: there was not yet a resting-place and he came returning. Then I set free a swallow and did release him. Forth went the swallow but came back to me: there was not yet a resting-place and he came returning. So I set free a raven and did release him. Forth went the raven— and he saw again the natural flowing of the waters, and he ate and he flew about and he croaked, and came not returning.

So all set I free to the four winds of heaven, and I poured a libation, and scattered a food-offering, on the height of the mountain. Seven and seven did I lay the vessels, heaped into their incense-basins sweet cane, cedarwood and myrtle. And the gods smelled the savour, the gods smelled the sweet savour, the gods gathered like flies about the priest of the offering.

Then, as soon as the Mother-goddess arrived, she lifted up the great jewels which (in childhood, her father) Anu had made as a plaything for her: "O ye gods here present, as I still do not forget these lapis stones of my neck, so shall I remember these days—shall not forever forget them! If it please now the gods to come here to the offering, never shall Enlil come here to the offering, for without any discrimination he brought on the deluge, even (the whole of) my people consigned to destruction."

But as soon as Enlil arrived, he saw only the vessel—and furious was Enlil, he was filled with anger against the (heaven-) gods, the Igigi: "Has aught of livingkind escaped? Not a man should have survived the destruction!"

Ninurta opened his mouth and spake unto warrior Enlil: "Who except Ea could have designed such a craft? For Ea doth know every skill of invention."

Then Ea opened his mouth and spake unto warrior Enlil: "O warrior, thou wisest among gods, how thus indiscriminately couldst thou bring about this deluge? (Had thou counselled): On the sinner lay his sin, on the transgressor lay his transgression: loosen (the rope) that his life be not cut off, yet pull tight (on the rope) that he do not [escape]: then instead of thy sending a Flood would that the lion had come and diminished mankind: instead of thy sending a Flood would that the wolf had come and diminished mankind; instead of thy sending a Flood would that a famine had occurred and impoverished mankind; instead of thy sending a Flood would that a pestilence had come and smitten mankind. And I, since I could not oppose the decision of the great gods, did reveal unto the Exceeding-Wise a (magic) dream, and thus did he hear the gods' decision. Wherefore now take thee counsel concerning him."

Thereupon Enlil went up into the vessel: he took hold of my hand and made me go aboard, he bade my wife go aboard and made her kneel at my side. Standing between us, he touched our foreheads and did bless us, saying: "Hitherto Utnapishti has been but a man; but now Utnapishti and his wife shall be as gods like ourselves. In the Far Distance, at the mouth of the Rivers, Utnapishti shall dwell."

So they took me and did make me to dwell in the Far Distance, at the mouth of the Rivers. . . .

II. NOAH'S FLOOD

In Genesis, Noah is the hero of a different kind of creation story.

In the six hundredth year of Noah's life, in the second month, on the seventeenth day of the month, on that day all the fountains of the great deep burst forth, and the windows of the heavens were opened. The rain fell on the earth forty days and forty nights. . . .

At the end of forty days Noah opened the window of the ark that he had made and sent out the raven; and it went to and fro until the waters were dried up from the earth. Then he sent out the dove from him, to see if the waters had subsided from the face of the ground; but the dove found no place to set its foot, and it returned to him to the ark, for the waters were still on the face of the whole earth. So he put out his hand and took it and brought it into the ark with him. He waited another seven days, and again he sent out the dove from the ark; and the dove came back to him in the evening, and there in its beak was a freshly plucked olive leaf; so Noah knew that the waters had subsided from the earth. Then he waited another seven days, and sent out the dove; and it did not return to him any more. . . .

Then God said to Noah and to his sons with him, "As for me, I am establishing my covenant with you and your descendants after you, and with every living creature that is with you, the birds, the domestic animals, and every animal of the earth with you, as many as came out of the ark. I establish my covenant with you, that never again shall all flesh be cut off by the waters of a flood, and never again shall there be a flood to destroy the earth."

SOURCES: (I) "The Babylonian Story of the Flood" from *Documents from Old Testament Times*, D. Winton Thomas, editor and translator (Harper Torchbook Series, 1958), pp. 22–24. (II) Genesis 7.11–9.11.

took the form of great temple complexes in the major cities. The most imposing religious structure was the **ziggurat**, a tower in stages, sometimes with a small chamber on top. The terraces may have been planted with trees to resemble a mountain. Poetry about ziggurats often compares them to mountains, with their peaks in the sky and their roots in the netherworld, linking heaven to earth, but their precise purpose is not known. Eroded remains of many of these monumental structures still dot the Iraqi landscape. Through the Bible, ziggurats have entered Western tradition as "the tower of Babel."

1.2.1.4 SOCIETY Hundreds of thousands of cuneiform texts from the early third millennium B.C.E. until the third century B.C.E. give us a detailed picture of how peoples in ancient Mesopotamia conducted their lives and of the social conditions in which they lived. From the time of Hammurabi, for example, there are many royal letters to and from various rulers of the age, letters from the king to his subordinates, administrative records from many different cities, and numerous letters and documents belonging to private families.

Categorizing the laws of Hammurabi according to the aspects of life with which they deal reveals much about Babylonian life in his time. The third largest category of laws deals with commerce, relating to such issues as contracts, debts, rates of interest, security, and default. Business documents of Hammurabi's time show how people invested their money in land, money lending, government contracts, and international trade. Some of these laws regulate professionals, such as builders, judges, and surgeons. The second largest category of laws deals with land tenure, especially land given by the king to soldiers and marines in return for their service. The letters of Hammurabi that deal with land tenure show he was concerned with upholding the individual rights of landholders against powerful officials who tried to take their land from them. The largest category of laws relates to the family and its maintenance and protection, including marriage, inheritance, and adoption.

Parents usually arranged marriages, and betrothal was followed by the signing of a marriage contract. The bride usually left her own family to join her husband's. The husband-to-be could make a bridal payment, and the father of the bride-to-be provided a dowry for his daughter in money, land, or objects. A marriage began as monogamous, but a husband whose wife was childless or sickly could take a second wife. Sometimes husbands also sired children from domestic slave women. Women divorced by their husbands without good cause could get their dowry back, and a woman seeking divorce could also recover her dowry if her husband could not convict her of wrongdoing. A married woman's place was thought to be in the home, but women could possess their own property and do business on their own. Hundreds of letters between

Mesopotamian wives and husbands show them as equal partners in the ventures of life. Single women who were not part of families could set up business on their own, often as tavern owners or moneylenders, or could be associated with temples, sometimes working as midwives and wet nurses, or taking care of orphaned children.

1.2.1.5 SLAVERY: CHATTEL SLAVES AND DEBT SLAVES There were two main types of slavery in Mesopotamia: chattel and debt slavery. Chattel slaves were bought like any other piece of property and had no legal rights. They had to wear their hair in a certain way and were sometimes branded or tattooed on their hands. They were often non-Mesopotamians bought from slave merchants. Prisoners of war could also be enslaved. Chattel slaves were expensive luxuries during most of Mesopotamian history. They were used in domestic service rather than in production, such as fieldwork. A wealthy household might have five or six chattel slaves, male and female. True chattel slavery did not become common until the Neo-Babylonian period (612–539 B.C.E.).

Debt slavery was more common than chattel slavery. Rates of interest were high, as much as 33.3 percent, so people often defaulted on loans. One reason the interest rates were so high was that the government periodically canceled certain types of debts, debt slavery, and obligations, so lenders ran the risk of losing their money. If debtors had pledged themselves or members of their families as surety for a loan, they became the debt slave of the creditor; their labor paid the interest on the loan. Debt slaves could not be sold but could redeem their freedom by paying off the loan.

Although laws against fugitive slaves or slaves who denied their masters were harsh, Mesopotamian slavery appears enlightened compared with other slave systems in history. Slaves were generally of the same people as their masters. They had been enslaved because of misfortune from which their masters were not immune, and they generally labored alongside them. Slaves could engage in business and, with certain restrictions, hold property. They could marry free men or women, and the resulting children would normally be free. A slave who acquired the means could buy his or her freedom. Children of a slave by a master might be allowed to share his property after his death. Nevertheless, slaves were property, subject to an owner's will, and had little legal protection.

1.2.2 Egyptian Civilization

As Mesopotamian civilization arose in the valley of the Tigris and Euphrates, another great civilization emerged in Egypt, centered on the Nile River. From its sources in Lake Victoria and the Ethiopian highlands, the Nile flows north some 4,000 miles to the Mediterranean Sea. Ancient Egypt included the 750-mile stretch of smooth, navigable river from Aswan to the sea. South of Aswan the river's course is interrupted by several cataracts—rocky areas of rapids and whirlpools.

The Egyptians recognized two sets of geographical divisions in their country. **Upper** (southern) **Egypt** consisted of the narrow valley of the Nile. **Lower** (northern) **Egypt** referred to the broad triangular area, named by the Greeks after their letter "delta," formed by the Nile as it branches out to empty into the Mediterranean. (See Map 1–2.) Egyptians also made a distinction between what they termed the "black land," the dark fertile fields along the Nile, and the "red land," the desert cliffs and plateaus bordering the valley.

The Nile alone made agriculture possible in Egypt's desert environment. Each year the rains of central Africa caused the river to rise over its floodplain, cresting in September and October. In places, the plain extended several miles on either side; elsewhere the cliffs sloped down to the water's edge. When the floodwaters receded, they left a rich layer of organically fertile silt. The construction and maintenance of canals, dams, and irrigation ditches to control the river's water, together with careful planning and organization of planting and harvesting, produced an agricultural prosperity unmatched in the ancient world.

The Nile served as the major highway connecting Upper and Lower Egypt. There was also a network of desert roads running north and south, as well as routes across the eastern desert to the Sinai and the Red Sea. Other tracks led to oases

Map 1–2 THE NEAR EAST AND GREECE ABOUT 1400 B.C.E.

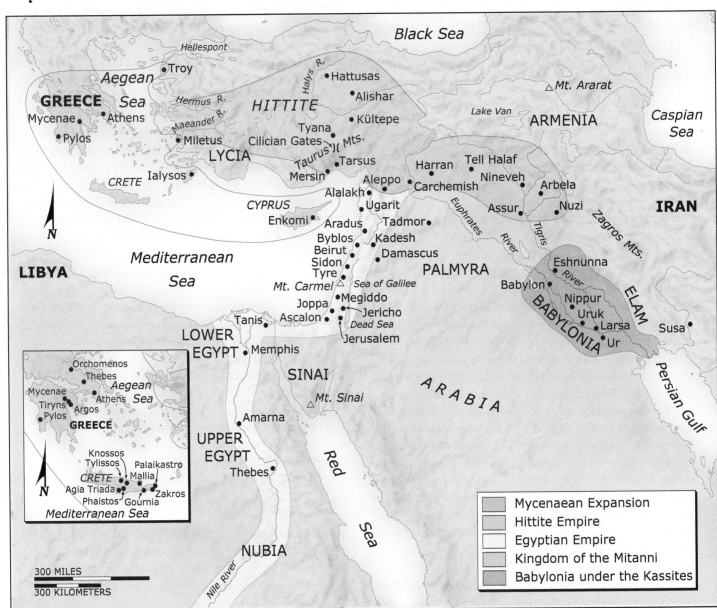

About 1400 B.C.E., the Near East was divided among four empires. Egypt extended south to Nubia and north through Palestine and Phoenicia. The Kassites ruled in Mesopotamia, the Hittites in Asia Minor, and the Mitannians in Assyrian lands. In the Aegean, the Mycenaean kingdoms were at their height.

MAJOR PERIODS IN ANCIENT EGYPTIAN HISTORY		
	Dynastic Period	*Dynastic Number*
3100–2700 B.C.E.	Early Dynastic Period	(1–2)
2700–2200 B.C.E.	Old Kingdom	(3–6)
2200–2052 B.C.E.	First Intermediate Period	(7–11)
2052–1630 B.C.E.	Middle Kingdom	(12–13)
1630–1550 B.C.E.	Second Intermediate Period	(14–17)
1550–1075 B.C.E.	New Kingdom	(18–20)

in the western desert. Thanks to geography and climate, Egypt was more isolated and enjoyed far more security than Mesopotamia. This security, along with the predictable flood calendar, gave Egyptian civilization a more optimistic outlook than the civilizations of the Tigris and Euphrates, which were more prone to storms, flash floods, and invasions.

The 3,000-year span of ancient Egyptian history is traditionally divided into thirty-one royal dynasties. The first was said to have been founded by Menes, the king who originally united Upper and Lower Egypt, while the last was established by Alexander the Great, who conquered Egypt in 332 B.C.E. Ptolemy, one of Alexander's generals, founded the Ptolemaic dynasty, whose last ruler was Cleopatra. In 30 B.C.E., the Romans defeated Egypt, effectively ending the independent existence of a civilization that had lasted three millennia.

The unification of Upper and Lower Egypt was vital, for it meant the entire river valley could benefit from an unimpeded distribution of resources. Three times in its history, Egypt experienced a century or more of political and social disintegration, known as Intermediate Periods. During these eras, rival dynasties often set up separate power bases in Upper and Lower Egypt until a strong leader reunified the land.

1.2.2.1 THE OLD KINGDOM (2700–2200 B.C.E.) The Old Kingdom represents the culmination of the cultural and historical developments of the Early Dynastic period. For more than 400 years, Egypt enjoyed internal stability and great prosperity. During this period, the pharaoh was a king who was also a god. From his capital at Memphis, the god-king administered Egypt according to set principles, prime among them being *maat*, an ideal of order, justice, and truth. In return for the king's building and maintaining temples, the gods preserved the equilibrium of the state and ensured the king's continuing power, which was absolute. Since the king was obligated to act infallibly in a benign and beneficent manner, the welfare of the people of Egypt was automatically guaranteed and safeguarded.

Nothing better illustrates the nature of Old Kingdom royal power than the pyramids built as pharaonic tombs. Beginning in the Early Dynastic period, kings constructed increasingly elaborate burial complexes in Upper Egypt. Djoser, a Third Dynasty king, was the first

to erect a monumental six-step pyramid of hard stone. Subsequent pharaohs built other stepped pyramids until Snefru, the founder of the Fourth Dynasty, converted a stepped to a true pyramid over the course of putting up three monuments.

His son Khufu (Cheops in the Greek version of his name) chose the desert plateau of Giza, south of Memphis, as the site for the largest pyramid ever constructed. Its dimensions are prodigious: 481 feet high, 756 feet long on each side, and its base covering 13.1 acres. The pyramid is made of 2.3 million stone blocks averaging 2.5 tons each. It is also a geometrical wonder, deviating from absolutely level and square only by the most minute measurements using the latest modern devices. Khufu's successors, Khafre (Chephren) and Menkaure (Mycerinus), built equally perfect pyramids at Giza, and together, the three constitute one of the most extraordinary achievements in human history. Khafre also built the huge composite creature, part lion and part human, that the Greeks named the Sphinx. Recent research has shown that the Great Sphinx played a crucial role in the solar cult aspects of the pyramid complex.

The pyramids are remarkable, not only for the great technical skill they demonstrate, but also for the concentration of resources they represent. They are evidence that the pharaohs controlled vast wealth and had the power to focus and organize enormous human effort over the years it took to build each pyramid. They also provide a visible indication of the nature of the Egyptian state: the pyramids, like the pharaohs, tower above the land; the low tombs at their base, like the officials buried there, seem to huddle in relative unimportance.

THE GREAT SPHINX With the body of a lion and the head of a man, the Great Sphinx was carved at Giza in the reign of the pharaoh Khafre (c. 2570–2544 B.C.E.).
SOURCE: Joana Kruse/Alamy Stock Photo

Originally, the pyramids and their associated cult buildings contained statuary, offerings, and all the pharaoh needed for the afterlife. Despite great precautions and ingenious concealment methods, tomb robbers took nearly everything. Several full-size wooden boats have been found, however, still in their own graves at the base of the pyramids, ready for the pharaoh's journeys in the next world. Recent excavations have uncovered remains of the large town built to house the thousands of pyramid builders, including the farmers who worked at Giza during the annual flooding of their fields.

Numerous officials, both members of the royal family and nonroyal men of ability, aided the god-kings. The highest office was the *vizier* (a modern term from Arabic). Central offices dealing with granaries, surveys, assessments, taxes, and salaries administered the land. Water management was local rather than on a national level. Upper and Lower Egypt were divided into *nomes*, or districts, each governed by a *nomarch*, or governor, and his local officials. The kings could also appoint royal officials to oversee groups of nomes or to supervise pharaonic landholdings throughout Egypt.

1.2.2.2 THE FIRST INTERMEDIATE PERIOD AND MIDDLE KINGDOM (2200–1630 B.C.E.)

Toward the end of the Old Kingdom absolute pharaonic power waned as the nomarchs and other officials became more independent and influential. About 2200 B.C.E., the Old Kingdom collapsed and gave way to the decentralization and disorder of the First Intermediate Period, which lasted until about 2052 B.C.E. Eventually, the kings of Dynasty 11, based in Thebes in Upper Egypt, defeated the rival Dynasty 10, based in a city south of Giza.

Amunemhet I, the founder of Dynasty 12 and the Middle Kingdom, probably began his career as a successful vizier under an Eleventh Dynasty king. After reuniting Upper and Lower Egypt, he turned his attention to making three important and long-lasting administrative changes. First, he moved his royal residence from Thebes to a brand-new town, just south of the old capital at Memphis, signaling a fresh start rooted in past glories. Second, he reorganized the nome structure by more clearly defining the nomarchs' duties to the state, granting them some local autonomy within the royal structure. Third, he established a co-regency system to smooth transitions from one reign to another.

Amunemhet I and the other Middle Kingdom pharaohs sought to evoke the past by building pyramid complexes like those of the later Old Kingdom rulers. Yet the events of the First Intermediate Period had irrevocably changed the nature of Egyptian kingship. Gone was the absolute, distant god-king; the king was now more directly concerned with his people. In art, instead of the supremely confident faces of the Old Kingdom pharaohs, the Middle Kingdom rulers seemed thoughtful, careworn, and brooding.

Egypt's relations with its neighbors became more aggressive during the Middle Kingdom. To the south, royal fortresses were built to control Nubia and the growing trade in African resources. To the north and east, Syria and Palestine increasingly came under Egyptian influence, even as fortifications sought to prevent settlers from the Levant from moving into the Delta.

1.2.2.3 THE SECOND INTERMEDIATE PERIOD AND THE NEW KINGDOM (1630–1075 B.C.E.)

During Dynasty 13, the kingship changed hands rapidly and the western Delta established itself as an independent Dynasty 14, ushering in the Second Intermediate Period. The eastern Delta, with its expanding Asiatic populations, came under the control of the **Hyksos** (Dynasty 15) and minor Asiatic kings (Dynasty 16). Meanwhile, the Dynasty 13 kings left their northern capital and regrouped in Thebes (Dynasty 17).

Though much later sources describe the Hyksos ("chief of foreign lands" in Egyptian) as ruthless invaders from parts unknown, they were almost certainly Amorites from the Levant, part of the gradual infiltration of the Delta during the Middle Kingdom. After nearly a century of rule, the Hyksos were expelled, a process begun by Kamose, the last king of Dynasty 17, and completed by his brother Ahmose, the first king of the Eighteenth Dynasty and the founder of the New Kingdom.

During Dynasty 18, Egypt pursued foreign expansion with renewed vigor. Military expeditions reached as far north as the Euphrates in Syria, with frequent campaigns in the Levant. To the south, major Egyptian temples were built in the Sudan, almost 1,300 miles from Memphis. Egypt's economic and political power was at its height.

Egypt's position was reflected in the unprecedented luxury and cosmopolitanism of the royal court and in the ambitious palace and temple projects undertaken throughout the country. Perhaps to foil tomb robbers, the Dynasty 18 pharaohs were the first to cut their tombs deep into the rock cliffs of a desolate valley in Thebes, known today as the Valley of the Kings. To date, only one intact royal tomb has been discovered there, that of the young Dynasty 18 king, Tutankhamun, and even it had been disturbed shortly after his death. The thousands of goods buried with him, many of them marvels of craftsmanship, give an idea of Egypt's material wealth during this period.

Following the premature death of Tutankhamun in 1323 B.C.E., a military commander named Horemheb assumed the kingship, which passed in turn to his own army commander, Ramses I. The pharaohs Ramessides of Dynasty 19 undertook numerous monumental projects, among them Ramses II's rock-cut temples at Abu Simbel, south of the First Cataract. There and elsewhere, Ramses II left textual and pictorial accounts of the **Battle of Kadesh** in 1285 B.C.E. against the Hittites on the Orontes in Syria. Sixteen years later, the Egyptians and Hittites signed a formal peace treaty, forging an alliance against an increasingly volatile political situation in the Mideast and eastern Mediterranean during the thirteenth century B.C.E.

Merneptah, one of the hundred offspring of Ramses II, held off a hostile Libyan attack, as well as incursions by the

Sea Peoples, a loose coalition of Mediterranean raiders who seem to have provoked and taken advantage of unsettled conditions. One of Merneptah's inscriptions commemorating his military triumphs contains the first known mention of Israel.

Despite Merneptah's efforts, by the end of Dynasty 20, Egypt's period of imperial glory had passed. The next thousand years witnessed a Third Intermediate Period, a Saite Renaissance, Persian domination, conquest by Alexander the Great, the Ptolemaic period, and finally, defeat at the hands of Octavian in 30 B.C.E.

1.2.2.4 LANGUAGE AND LITERATURE Writing first appears in Egypt about 3000 B.C.E. The writing system, dubbed **hieroglyphics** ("sacred carvings") by the Greeks, was highly sophisticated, involving hundreds of picture signs that remained relatively constant in the way they were rendered for over 3,000 years. A cursive version of hieroglyphics was used for business documents and literary texts, which were penned rapidly in black and red ink. The Egyptian language, part of the Afro-Asiatic (or Hamito-Semitic) family, evolved through several stages—Old, Middle, and Late Egyptian, Demotic, and Coptic—thus giving it a history of continuous recorded use well into the medieval period.

Egyptian literature includes narratives, myths, books of instruction in wisdom, letters, religious texts, and poetry, written on papyri, limestone flakes, and potsherds. Unfortunately, only a small fraction of this enormous literature has survived, and many texts are incomplete.

1.2.2.5 RELIGION: GODS AND TEMPLES Egyptian religion encompasses a multitude of concepts that often seem mutually contradictory to us. Three separate explanations for the origin of the universe were formulated, each based in the philosophical traditions of a venerable Egyptian city. The cosmogony of Heliopolis, north of Memphis, held that the creator sun god Atum (also identified as Re) emerged from the darkness of a vast sea to stand upon a primeval mound, containing within himself the life force of the gods he was to create. At Memphis, it was the god Ptah who created the other gods by uttering their names. Further south, at Hermopolis, eight male and female entities within a primordial slime suddenly exploded, and the energy that resulted created the sun and Atum, from which the rest came.

Amun, one of the eight entities in the Hermopolitan cosmogony, provides a good example. Thebes, Amun's cult center, rose to prominence in the Middle Kingdom. In the New Kingdom, Amun was elevated above his seven cohorts and took on aspects of the sun god Re to become Amun-Re.

Not surprisingly in a nearly rainless land, solar cults and mythologies were highly developed. Much thought was devoted to conceptualizing what happened as the sun god made his perilous way through the underworld in the night hours between sunset and sunrise.

The Eighteenth Dynasty was one of several periods during which solar cults were in ascendancy. Early in his reign,

SEATED EGYPTIAN SCRIBE, FIFTH DYNASTY, ca. 2510–2460 B.C.E. One of the hallmarks of the early river valley civilizations was the development of writing. Ancient Egyptian scribes such as this one had to undergo rigorous training but were rewarded with a position of respect and privilege.
SOURCE: Erich Lessing/Art Resource, NY

Amunhotep IV promoted a single, previously minor aspect of the sun, the Aten ("disk"), above Re himself and the rest of the gods. He declared that the Aten was the creator god who brought life to humankind and all living beings, with himself and his queen Nefertiti as the sole mediators between the Aten and the people. Amunhotep went further, changing his name to Akhenaten ("the effective spirit of the Aten"), building a new capital called Akhetaten ("the horizon of the Aten") near Amarna north of Thebes, and chiseling out the name of Amun from inscriptions everywhere. Shortly after his death, Amarna was abandoned and partially razed. During the reigns of Akhenaten's successors, Tutankhamun (born Tutankhaten) and Horemheb, Amun was restored to his former position, and Akhenaten's monuments were defaced and even demolished.

In representations, Egyptian gods have human bodies, possess human or animal heads, and wear crowns, celestial disks, or thorns. The lone exception is the Aten, made nearly abstract by Akhenaten, who altered its image to a plain disk with solar rays ending in small hands holding the hieroglyphic sign for life to the nostrils of Akhenaten and Nefertiti. The gods were thought to reside in their cult centers, where, from the New Kingdom on, increasingly ostentatious temples were built, staffed by full-time priests. Though the ordinary person could not enter a temple precinct, great festivals took place for all to see. During Amun's major festival of Opet, the statue of the god traveled in a divine boat along the Nile, whose banks were thronged with spectators.

1.2.2.6 WORSHIP AND THE AFTERLIFE   For most Egyptians, worship took place at small local shrines. They left offerings to the chosen gods, as well as votive inscriptions with simple prayers. Private houses often had niches containing busts for ancestor worship and statues of household deities. The Egyptians strongly believed in the power of magic, dreams, and oracles, and they possessed a wide variety of amulets to ward off evil.

The Egyptians thought the afterlife was full of dangers, which could be overcome by magical means, among them the spells in the *Book of the Dead*. The goals were to join and be identified with the gods, especially Osiris, or to sail in the "boat of millions." Originally only the king could hope to enjoy immortality with the gods, but gradually this became available to all. Since the Egyptians believed the preservation of the body was essential for continued existence in the afterlife, early on they developed mummification, a process that took seventy days by the New Kingdom. How lavishly tombs were prepared and decorated varied over the course of Egyptian history and in accordance with the wealth of a family. A high-ranking Dynasty 18 official, for example, typically had a Theban rock-cut tomb of several rooms embellished with scenes from daily life and funerary texts, as well as provisions and equipment for the afterlife, statuettes of workers, and a place for descendants to leave offerings.

1.2.2.7 WOMEN IN EGYPTIAN SOCIETY   It is difficult to assess the position of women in Egyptian society, because our pictorial and textual evidence comes almost entirely from male sources. Women's primary roles were related to management of the household. They could not hold office, go to scribal schools, or become artisans. Nevertheless, women could own and control property, sue for divorce, and, at least in theory, enjoy equal legal protection.

Royal women often wielded considerable influence, particularly in the Eighteenth Dynasty. The most remarkable was **Hatshepsut**, daughter of Thutmose I and widow of Thutmose II, who ruled as pharaoh for nearly twenty years. Having acted as queen regent for seven years, she assumed the royal title of king of Egypt contrary to the tradition that only men could hold this revered position. She emphasized her role as divine king by representing herself with male dress and male body in statues and portraits. During her extraordinary reign, Hatshepsut engaged in ambitious building projects and trading expeditions. Her great naval voyage opened new ways of access to Punt and expanded trade in the region. Several successful military campaigns won her a reputation as a warrior. In addition to the exceptional reign of Hatshepsut, many Egyptian queens held the title "god's wife of Amun," a power base of great importance.

In Egyptian art, royal and nonroyal women are conventionally depicted smaller in size than their husbands or sons. Yet it is probably of greater significance that women are so frequently depicted in a wide variety of contexts. Much care was lavished on details of their gestures, clothing, and hairstyles. With their husbands, they attend banquets, boat in the papyrus marshes, make and receive offerings, and supervise the myriad affairs of daily life.

THE EGYPTIAN AFTERLIFE   The Egyptians believed in the possibility of life after death through the god Osiris. Aspects of each person's life had to be tested by forty-two assessor-gods before the person could be presented to Osiris. In this scene from a papyrus manuscript of the *Book of the Dead*, the deceased and his wife (on the left) watch the scales of justice weighing his heart (on the left side of the scales) against the feather of truth. The jackal-headed god Anubis also watches the scales, and the ibis-headed god Thoth keeps the record.

SOURCE: British Museum, London, UK/Bridgeman Art Library

1.2.2.8 SLAVES Slaves did not become numerous in Egypt until the growth of Egyptian imperial power in the Middle Kingdom (2052–1786 B.C.E.). During that period, black Africans from Nubia to the south and Asians from the east were captured in war and brought back to Egypt as slaves. The great period of Egyptian imperial expansion, the New Kingdom (1550–1075 B.C.E.), vastly increased the number of slaves and captives in Egypt. Sometimes an entire people was enslaved, as the Bible says the Hebrews were.

Slaves in Egypt performed many tasks. They labored in the fields with the peasants, in the shops of artisans, and as domestic servants. Others worked as policemen and soldiers. Many slaves labored to erect the great temples, obelisks, and other huge monuments of Egypt's imperial age. As in Mesopotamia, slaves were branded for identification and to help prevent their escape. Slaves could be freed in Egypt, but manumission seems to have been rare. Nonetheless, former slaves were not set apart and could expect to be assimilated into the mass of the population.

1.3 Ancient Near Eastern Empires

What were the great empires of the ancient Near East?

KEY EVENTS IN THE HISTORY OF ANCIENT NEAR EASTERN EMPIRES	
ca. 1400–1200 B.C.E.	Hittite Empire
ca. 1100 B.C.E.	Rise of Assyrian power
732–722 B.C.E.	Assyrian conquest of Syria-Palestine
671 B.C.E.	Assyrian conquest of Egypt
612 B.C.E.	Destruction of Assyrian capital at Nineveh
612–539 B.C.E.	Neo-Babylonian (Chaldean) Empire

In the time of Dynasty 18 in Egypt, new groups of peoples had established themselves in the Near East: the Kassites in Babylonia, the Hittites in Asia Minor, and the Mitannians in northern Syria and Mesopotamia. (See Map 1–2.) The Kassites and Mitannians were warrior peoples who ruled as a minority over more civilized folk and absorbed their culture. The Hittites established a kingdom of their own and forged an empire that lasted some 200 years.

1.3.1 The Hittites

The Hittites were an Indo-European people, speaking a language related to Greek and Sanskrit. By about 1500 B.C.E., they established a strong, centralized government with a capital at Hattusas (near Ankara, the capital of modern Turkey). Between 1400 and 1200 B.C.E., they emerged as a leading military power in the Mideast and contested Egypt's ambitions to control Palestine and Syria. This struggle culminated in a great battle between the Egyptian and Hittite armies at Kadesh in northern Syria (1285 B.C.E.) and ended as a standoff. The Hittites adopted Mesopotamian writing and many aspects of Mesopotamian culture, especially

through the Hurrian peoples of northern Syria and southern Anatolia. Their extensive historical records are the first to mention the Greeks, whom the Hittites called Ahhiyawa (the Achaeans of Homer). The Hittite kingdom disappeared by 1200 B.C.E., swept away in the general invasions and collapse of the Mideastern states at that time.

1.3.1.1 THE DISCOVERY OF IRON An important technological change took place in northern Anatolia, somewhat earlier than the creation of the Hittite kingdom, but perhaps within its region. This was the discovery of how to smelt iron and the decision to use it to manufacture weapons and tools in preference to copper or bronze. Archaeologists refer to the period after 1100 B.C.E. as the Iron Age.

1.3.2 The Assyrians

The Assyrians were originally a people living in Assur, a city in northern Mesopotamia on the Tigris River. They spoke a Semitic language closely related to Babylonian. They had a proud, independent culture heavily influenced by Babylonia. Assur had been an early center for trade but emerged as a political power during the fourteenth century B.C.E. The first Assyrian Empire spread north and west but ended in the general collapse of Near Eastern states at the end of the second millennium. A people called the Arameans, a Semitic nomadic and agricultural people originally from northern Syria who spoke a language called Aramaic, invaded Assyria. Aramaic is still used in parts of the Near East and is one of the languages of medieval Jewish and Mideastern Christian culture.

1.3.3 The Second Assyrian Empire

After 1000 B.C.E., the Assyrians began a second period of expansion, and by 665 B.C.E., they controlled all of Mesopotamia, much of southern Asia Minor, Syria, Palestine, and Egypt to its southern frontier. They succeeded, thanks to a large, well-disciplined army and a society that valued military skills. Some Assyrian kings boasted of their atrocities, so their names inspired terror throughout the Near East. They constructed magnificent palaces at Nineveh and Nimrud (near modern Mosul, Iraq), surrounded by parks and gardens.

The Assyrians organized their empire into provinces with governors, military garrisons, and administration for taxation, communications, and intelligence. Important officers were assigned large areas of land throughout the empire, and agricultural colonies were set up in key regions to store supplies for military actions beyond the frontiers. Vassal kings had to send tribute and delegations to the Assyrian capital every year. Tens of thousands of people were forcibly displaced from their homes and resettled in other areas of the empire, partly to populate sparsely inhabited regions, partly to diminish resistance to Assyrian rule. People of the kingdom of Israel, which the Assyrians invaded and destroyed, were among them.

The empire became too large to govern efficiently. The Medes, a powerful people from western and central Iran, had been expanding across the Iranian plateau. The Medes attacked Assyria and were joined by the Babylonians, who had always been restive under Assyrian rule, under the leadership of a general named Nebuchadnezzar. They eventually destroyed the Assyrian cities, including Nineveh in 612 B.C.E., so thoroughly that Assyria never recovered.

1.3.4 The Neo-Babylonians

The Medes did not follow up on their conquests, so Nebuchadnezzar took over much of the Assyrian Empire. Under him and his successors, Babylon grew into one of the greatest cities of the world. Nebuchadnezzar's dynasty did not last long, and the government passed to various

men in rapid succession. The last independent king of Babylon set up a second capital in the Arabian desert and tried to force the Babylonians to honor the Moon-god above all other gods. He allowed dishonest or incompetent speculators to lease huge areas of temple land for their personal profit. These policies proved unpopular—some said that the king was insane—and many Babylonians may have welcomed the Persian conquest that came in 539 B.C.E. After that, Babylonia began another, even more prosperous phase of its history as one of the most important provinces of another great Eastern empire, that of the Persians. Cartography was among the many intellectual achievements of the Babylonians (see the "Closer Look," which follows below, to learn more.)

A Closer Look

Babylonian World Map

THE MAP ILLUSTRATED here, inscribed on a clay tablet about 600 B.C.E., is thought to be the earliest surviving map of the world. The Babylonians did not intend this map to be a precise or literal picture of the universe or even of the land on which human beings lived, as they did not represent such important and numerous peoples as the Egyptians and Persians, whom they knew very well.

The cuneiform inscription above the picture and on the back of the tablet helps make its identification as a map secure.

Beyond an encircling "Bitter River," seven islands are arranged to form a seven-pointed star.

The tablet shows the world from a Babylonian point of view as flat and round, with Babylon sitting at its center on the Euphrates River.

Cities and lands, including Armenia and Assyria, surround Babylon.

INSCRIBED MAP OF BABYLON AND THE WORLD
SOURCE: World History Archive/Alamy Stock Photo

Questions

1. Why do you think this map locates some of the Babylonians' neighbors but ignores other important neighboring cultures?
2. Why has cartography remained so important throughout the ages?
3. Is the subjectivity reflected in this map unique, or is it a general characteristic of cartography throughout history?

1.4 The Persian Empire

What were the Persian rulers' attitudes toward the cultures they ruled?

The great Persian Empire arose in the region now called Iran. The ancestors of the people who would rule it spoke a language from the Aryan branch of the family of Indo-European languages, related to the Greek spoken by the Hellenic peoples and the Latin of the Romans. The most important collections of tribes among them were the Medes and the Persians, peoples so similar in language and customs that the Greeks used both names interchangeably.

KEY EVENTS IN THE HISTORY OF THE PERSIAN EMPIRE	
550 B.C.E.	Cyrus the Great unites Persians and Medes
546 B.C.E.	Persia conquers Lydia
521–486 B.C.E.	Reign of Darius the Great

The Medes were the first Iranian people to organize their tribes into a union. They were aggressive enough to build a force that challenged the great empires of Mesopotamia. With the help of the ruler of Babylon, they defeated the mighty Assyrian Empire in 612 B.C.E. Until the middle of the sixth century, the Persians were subordinate to the Medes, but when Cyrus II (called the Great) became King of the Persians (r. 559–530 B.C.E.), their positions were reversed. About 550 B.C.E., Cyrus captured the capital at Ecbatana and united the Medes and Persians under his own rule.

1.4.1 Cyrus the Great

Cyrus quickly expanded his power. The territory he inherited from the Medes touched on Lydia, ruled by the rich and powerful king Croesus. Croesus controlled western Asia Minor, having conquered the Greek cities of the coast about 560 B.C.E. Made confident by his victories, by alliances with Egypt and Babylon, and by what he thought was a favorable signal from the Greek oracle of Apollo at Delphi, he invaded Persian territory in 546 B.C.E. Cyrus achieved a decisive victory, capturing Croesus and his capital city of Sardis. By 539 B.C.E. Cyrus had conquered the Greek cities and extended his power as far to the east as the Indus valley and modern Afghanistan.

In that same year, he captured Babylon. Unlike the harsh Babylonian and Assyrian conquerors who preceded him, Cyrus pursued a policy of toleration and restoration. He did not impose the Persian religion but claimed to rule by the favor of the Babylonian god. Instead of deporting defeated peoples from their native lands and destroying their cities, he rebuilt their cities and allowed the exiles to return. The conquest of the Babylonian Empire had brought Palestine under Persian rule, so Cyrus permitted the Hebrews, taken into captivity by King Nebuchadnezzar in 586 B.C.E., to return to their native land of Judah. This policy, followed by that of his successors, was effective but not as gentle as it might seem. Wherever they ruled, Cyrus the Great and his successors demanded tribute from their subjects and military service, enforcing these requirements strictly and sometimes brutally.

1.4.2 Darius the Great

Cyrus's son Cambyses succeeded to the throne in 529 B.C.E. His great achievement was the conquest of Egypt, establishing it as a satrapy (province) that ran as far west as Libya and as far south as Ethiopia. The Persians ruled, as the Bible puts it, "from India to Ethiopia, one hundred and twenty-seven provinces" (Esther 1:1). (See Map 1–3.) On Cambyses's death in 522 B.C.E., a civil war roiled much of the Persian Empire. Darius emerged as the new emperor in 521 B.C.E.

On a great rock hundreds of feet in the air near the mountain Iranian village of Behistun, Darius the Great had carved an inscription in three languages—Babylonian, Old Persian, and Elamite—all in the cuneiform script. It boasted of his victories and the greatness of his rule and, discovered almost 2,000 years later, greatly helped scholars decipher all three languages. Darius's long and prosperous reign lasted until 486 B.C.E., during which he brought the empire to its greatest extent. To the east he added new conquests in northern India. In the west, Darius sought to conquer the nomadic people called Scythians who roamed around the Black Sea. For this purpose, he crossed into Europe over the Hellespont (Dardanelles) to the Danube River and beyond, taking possession of Thrace and Macedonia on the fringes of the Greek mainland. In 499 B.C.E., the Ionian Greeks of western Asia Minor rebelled, launching the wars between Greeks and Persians that would not end until two decades later.

1.4.3 Government and Administration

Like the Mesopotamian kingdoms, the Persian Empire was a hereditary monarchy that claimed divine sanction from the god Ahura Mazda. The ruler's title was *Shahanshah*, "king of kings." In theory, all the land and the peoples in the empire belonged to him as absolute monarch, and he demanded tribute and service for the use of his property. In practice, he depended on the advice and administrative service of aristocratic courtiers, ministers, and provincial governors, the satraps. He was expected, as Ahura Mazda's chosen representative, to rule with justice, in accordance with established custom and the precedents in the Law of the Medes and Persians. Still, the king ruled as a semi-divine autocrat; anyone approaching him prostrated himself as before a god who could demand their wealth, labor, and military service and had the power of life and death. The Greeks would see him as the model of a despot or tyrant who regarded his people as slaves.

Map 1–3 THE ACHAEMENID PERSIAN EMPIRE

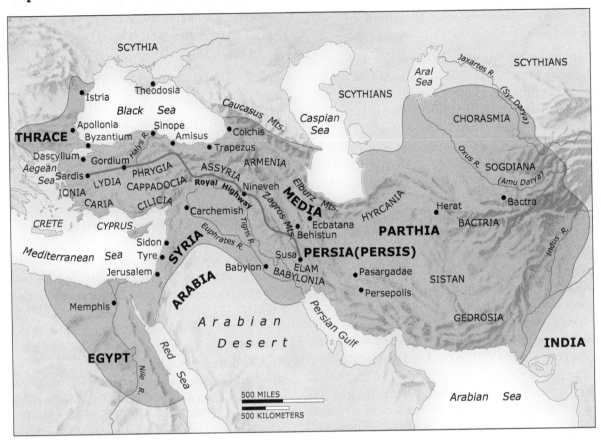

The empire created by Cyrus had reached its fullest extent under Darius when Persia attacked Greece in 490 B.C.E. It extended from India to the Aegean, and even into Europe, encompassing the lands formerly ruled by the Egyptians, Hittites, Babylonians, and Assyrians. A system of excellent royal roads, including the 1,500-mile route from Sardis in Lydia to the Persian capital at Susa, facilitated travel and communication.

The empire was divided into twenty-nine satrapies. The satraps were allowed considerable autonomy. They ruled over civil affairs and commanded the army in war, but the king exercised several means of control. In each satrapy, he appointed a secretary and a military commander. He also chose inspectors called "the eyes and ears of the king" who traveled throughout the empire reporting on what they learned in each satrapy. Their travels and those of royal couriers were made swifter and easier by a system of excellent royal roads. The royal postal system was served by a kind of "pony express" that placed men mounted on fast horses at stations along the way. It normally took three months to travel the 1,500 miles from Sardis in Lydia to the Persian capital at Susa. The royal postal service made the trip in less than two weeks. Ruling over a vast empire whose people spoke countless different languages, the Persians did not try to impose their own, but instead adopted Aramaic, the most common language of Middle-Eastern commerce, as the imperial tongue. This practical decision simplified both civil and military administration.

Medes and Persians made up the core of the army. Royal schools trained aristocratic Median and Persian boys as military officers and imperial administrators. The officers commanded not only the Iranian troops but also drafted large numbers of subject armies when needed. A large Persian army, such as the one that invaded Greece in 490 B.C.E., included hundreds of thousands of non-Iranian soldiers organized by ethnic group, each dressed in its own uniforms, taking orders from Iranian officers.

1.4.4 Religion

Persia's religion was different from that of its neighbors and subjects. Its roots lay in the Indo-European traditions of the Vedic religion that Aryan peoples brought into India about 1500 B.C.E. Their religious practices included animal sacrifices and a reverence for fire. Although the religion was polytheistic, its chief god Ahura Mazda, the "Wise Lord," placed an unusual emphasis on a stern ethical code. It took a new turn with the appearance of Zarathustra, a Mede whom the Greeks called Zoroaster, perhaps as early as 1000 B.C.E., as tradition states, although some scholars place him about 600 B.C.E. He was a great religious prophet and teacher who changed the traditional Aryan worship.

RELIEF OF DARIUS Persian nobles pay homage to King Darius in this relief from the treasury at the Persian capital of Persepolis. Darius is seated on the throne; his son and successor Xerxes stands behind him. Darius and Xerxes are carved in larger scale to indicate their royal status.
SOURCE: Courtesy of the Oriental Institute of the University of Chicago

Zarathustra's reform made Ahura Mazda the only god, dismissing the others as demons not to be worshipped but fought. There would be no more polytheism and no sacrifices. The old sacrificial fire was converted into a symbol of goodness and light. Zarathustra insisted that the people reject the "Lie" (*druj*) and speak only the "Truth" (*asha*), portraying life as an unending struggle between two great forces: Ahura Mazda, the creator and only god, representing goodness and light, and Ahriman, a demon, representing darkness and evil. He urged human beings to fight for the good, with the expectation that the good would be rewarded with glory and the evil punished with suffering.

Traditions and legends about Zarathustra as well as law, liturgy, and the teachings of the prophet are contained in the *Avesta*, the sacred book of the Persians. By the middle of the sixth century B.C.E., Zoroastrianism had become the chief religion of the Persians. On the great inscribed monument at Behistun, Darius the Great paid public homage to the god of Zarathustra and his teachings: "On this account Ahura Mazda brought me help . . . because I was not wicked, nor was I a liar, nor was I a tyrant, neither I nor any of my line. I have ruled according to righteousness."[1]

1.4.5 Art and Culture

The Persians learned much from the people they encountered and those they conquered, especially from Mesopotamia and Egypt, but they shaped this knowledge to fit comfortably in Persian society. A good example is the Persian system of writing: the Aramaic alphabet of the Semites was adapted to create a Persian alphabet, and the cuneiform symbols of Babylon to write the old Persian language they spoke. The Persians also borrowed their calendar from Egypt.

Persian art and architecture contain elements of styles borrowed from other societies and blended with Persian traditions to serve Persian purposes.

Probably the most magnificent of Persian remains are those of the Royal Palace at Persepolis, built by Darius and his son and successor Xerxes (r. 485–465 B.C.E.). Its foundation was a high platform supported on three sides by a stone wall 20 or 30 feet high. This could be reached by a grand stairway whose sides were covered with carvings.

The complex contained the Hall of a Hundred Columns where the kings did their judicial duties. More than any other tangible objects, the columns, stairway, and the gateway with winged bulls reveal the grandeur of the ancient Persian Empire.

1.5 Palestine

How was Hebrew monotheism different from Mesopotamian and Egyptian polytheism?

None of the powerful kingdoms of the ancient Near East had as much influence on the future of Western civilization as the small stretch of land between Syria and Egypt, the land called Palestine for much of its history. The three great religions of the modern world outside the Far East—Judaism, Christianity, and Islam—trace their origins, at least in part, to the people who arrived there a little before 1200 B.C.E. The book that recounts their experiences is the Hebrew Bible.

1.5.1 The Canaanites and the Phoenicians

Before the Israelites arrived in their promised land, it was inhabited by groups of people speaking a Semitic language called Canaanite. The Canaanites lived in walled cities and were farmers and seafarers. Instead of the hundreds of characters required to read Egyptian or cuneiform, their alphabet used between twenty and thirty characters. The Canaanites, like the other peoples of Syria-Palestine, worshipped many gods, especially gods of weather and fertility, whom they thought resided in the clouds atop the high mountains of northern Syria. The invading Israelites destroyed various Canaanite cities and holy places, and may have forced some of the population to move north and west, though Canaanite and Israelite culture also intermingled.

The **Phoenicians** were the descendants of the Canaanites and other peoples of Syria-Palestine, especially those who lived along the coast. They played an important role in Mediterranean trade, sailing to ports in Cyprus, Asia Minor, Greece, Italy, France, Spain, Egypt, and North Africa, as far as Gibraltar and possibly beyond. They founded colonies throughout the Mediterranean as far west as Spain. The most famous of these colonies was Carthage, near modern Tunis in North Africa. Sitting astride the trade routes, the Phoenician cities were important sites for the transmission of culture from east to west. The Greeks, who had long forgotten their older writing system of the Bronze Age, adopted a Phoenician version of the Canaanite alphabet that is the origin of our present alphabet.

1.5.2 The Israelites

The Israelites are mentioned only rarely in the records of their neighbors, so we must rely chiefly on their own account, the Hebrew Bible. This is not a history in our sense, but a complicated collection of historical narrative, pieces of wisdom, poetry, law, and religious witness. Scholars of an earlier time tended to discard it as a historical source, but the most recent trend is to take it seriously while using it with caution.

KEY EVENTS IN THE HISTORY OF THE ISRAELITES	
ca. 1000–961 B.C.E.	Reign of King David
ca. 961–922 B.C.E.	Reign of King Solomon
722 B.C.E.	Assyrian conquest of Israel (northern kingdom)
586 B.C.E.	Destruction of Jerusalem; fall of Judah (southern kingdom); Babylonian captivity
539 B.C.E.	Restoration of temple; return of exiles

According to tradition, the patriarch Abraham came from Ur and wandered west to tend his flocks in the land of the Canaanites. Some of his people settled there, and others wandered into Egypt. By the thirteenth century B.C.E., led by Moses, they had left Egypt and wandered in the desert until they reached and conquered Canaan. They established a united kingdom that reached its peak under David and Solomon in the tenth century B.C.E. The sons of Solomon could not maintain the unity of the kingdom, and it split into two parts: Israel in the north and Judah, with its capital at Jerusalem, in the south. (See Map 1–4.) The rise

of the great empires brought disaster to the Israelites. The northern kingdom fell to the Assyrians in 722 B.C.E., and its people—the **ten lost tribes**—were scattered and lost forever. Only the kingdom of Judah remained. It is from this time that we may call the Israelites Jews.

In 586 B.C.E., Judah was defeated by the Neo-Babylonian king Nebuchadnezzar II. He destroyed the great temple built by Solomon and took thousands of hostages to Babylon. When the Persians defeated Babylonia, they ended this Babylonian captivity of the Jews and allowed them to return to their homeland. After that, the area of the old kingdom of the Jews in Palestine was dominated by foreign peoples for some 2,500 years, until the establishment of the State of Israel in 1948 C.E.

Map 1–4 ANCIENT PALESTINE

The Hebrews established a unified kingdom under Kings David and Solomon in the tenth century B.C.E. After Solomon, the kingdom was divided into Israel in the north and Judah, with its capital, Jerusalem, in the south. North of Israel were the great commercial cities of Phoenicia, Tyre, and Sidon.

1.5.3 The Jewish Religion

The fate of the small nation of Israel would be of little interest were it not for its unique religious achievement. The great contribution of the Jews is the development of **monotheism**—the belief in one universal God, the creator and ruler of the universe. The Jewish God is neither a natural force nor like human beings or any other creatures; he is so elevated that those who believe in him may not picture him in any form. The faith of the Jews is given special strength by their belief that God made a covenant with Abraham that his progeny would be a chosen people who would be rewarded for following God's commandments and the law he revealed to Moses.

Like the teachings of Zarathustra in Iran, Jewish religious thought included a powerful ethical element. God is a severe, but just, judge. Ritual and sacrifice are not enough to achieve his approval. People must be righteous, and God himself appears to be bound to act righteously. The Jewish prophetic tradition was a powerful ethical force. The prophets constantly criticized any falling away from the law and the path of righteousness. They placed God in history, blaming the misfortunes of the Jews on God's righteous and necessary intervention to punish the people for their misdeeds. The prophets also promised the redemption of the Jews if they repented. However, the prophetic tradition expected the redemption to come in the form of a Messiah who would restore the house of David. Christianity, emerging from this tradition, holds that Jesus of Nazareth was that Messiah.

Jewish religious ideas influenced the future development of the West, both directly and indirectly. The Jews'

belief in an all-powerful creator (who is righteous himself and demands righteousness and obedience from humankind) and a universal God (who is the father and ruler of all peoples) is a critical part of Western heritage.

1.6 General Outlook of Mideastern Cultures

How did the worldview of the Egyptians, Babylonians and Hebrews compare with that of the emerging culture of the Greeks?

Our brief account of the history of the ancient Mideast so far reveals that its various peoples and cultures were different in many ways. Yet the distance between all of them and the emerging culture of the Greeks is striking. We can see this distance best by comparing the approach of the other cultures to several fundamental human problems with that of the Greeks: what is the relationship of humans to nature? to the gods? to each other? These questions involve attitudes toward religion, philosophy, science, law, politics, and government. Unlike the Greeks, the civilizations of the Mideast seem to have these features in common: once established, they tended toward cultural uniformity and stability. Reason, though employed for practical and intellectual purposes, lacked independence from religion and the high status to challenge the most basic received ideas. The standard form of government was a monarchy; republics were unknown. Rulers were considered divine or the appointed spokesmen for divinity. Religious and political institutions and beliefs were thoroughly intertwined. Government was not subject to secular, reasoned analysis but rested on religious authority, tradition, and power. Individual freedom had no importance.

1.6.1 Humans and Nature

For the peoples of the Mideast, there was no simple separation between humans and nature or even between animate creatures and inanimate objects. Humanity was part of a natural continuum, and all things partook of life and spirit. These peoples imagined that gods more or less in the shape of humans ruled a world that was irregular and unpredictable, subject to divine whims. The gods were capricious because nature seemed capricious.

TEMPLE MOUNT, JERUSALEM A place of worship for both Jews and Muslims, the Temple Mount is a walled religious complex in Jerusalem. The oldest parts date as far back as the late first century B.C.E. In the seventh century, Jerusalem came under Muslim control. Muslims refer to the Temple Mount as Haram al-Sharif.
SOURCE: domonabikeIsrael/Alamy Stock Photo

ISHTAR GATE, BABYLON, MESOPOTAMIA The Ishtar Gate marked the main entrance to the city of Babylon. Commissioned by Nebuchadnezzar II, brightly colored glazed bricks and images of animals and mythical creatures decorated it. A reproduction of the gate, shown here, is on display at the Pergamon Museum in Berlin, Germany.
SOURCE: imageBROKER/Alamy Stock Photo

A Babylonian story of creation makes it clear that humanity's function is merely to serve the gods. The creator Marduk says,

> I shall compact blood, I shall cause bones to be,
> I shall make stand a human being, let "Man" be its name.
> I shall create humankind,
> They shall bear the gods' burden that those may rest.[2]

In a world ruled by powerful deities of this kind, human existence was precarious. Disasters that we would think human in origin, the Mesopotamians saw as the product of divine will.

Both the Egyptian and the Babylonian versions of the destruction of humankind clearly show human vulnerability in the face of divine powers. In one Egyptian tale, Re, the god who had created humans, decided to destroy them because they were plotting evil against him. He sent the goddess Sekhmet to accomplish the deed, and she was resting in the midst of her task, having enjoyed the work and wading in a sea of blood, when Re changed his mind. He ordered 7,000 barrels of blood-colored beer poured in Sekhmet's path. She quickly became too drunk to continue the slaughter and thus humanity was preserved. In the Babylonian story of the flood, the motive for the destruction of humanity is given as follows:

> The land had grown numerous, the peoples had increased,
> The land was bellowing like a bull.
> The god was disturbed by their uproar,

> The god Enlil heard their clamor.
> He said to the great gods,
> "The clamor of mankind has become burdensome to me,
> "I am losing sleep to their uproar!"[3]

Utnapishtim and his wife survived because he was friendly with Enki, the god of wisdom, who helped him to pull through by a trick.

In such a universe, humans could not hope to understand nature, much less control it. At best, they could try by magic to use uncanny forces against others.

> [So] may the curse, something evil, revenge, interrogation,
> The sickness of my suffering, wrong-doing, crime, misdeed, sin
> The sickness which is in my body, flesh, and sinews
> Be peeled off like this garlic.[4]

1.6.2 Humans and the Gods, Law, and Justice

Human relationships to the gods were equally humble. There was no doubt that the gods could destroy human beings and might do so at any time for no good reason. Humans could—and, indeed, had to—try to win the gods over through prayers and sacrifices, but there was no guarantee of success. The gods were bound by no laws and no morality. The best behavior and the greatest devotion to the cult of the gods were no defense against the divine and cosmic caprice.

In the earliest civilizations, human relations were guided by laws, often set down in written codes. The basic question about law concerned its legitimacy: why, apart from the lawgiver's power to coerce obedience, should anyone obey the law? For Old Kingdom Egyptians, the answer was simple: the king was bound to act in accordance with maat, the Egyptian concept of truth, balance, order, and harmony, and so his laws were righteous. For the Mesopotamians, the answer was almost the same: the king was a representative of the gods, so the laws he set forth were authoritative. The prologue to the most famous legal document in antiquity, the Code of Hammurabi, makes this plain:

> I am the king who is preeminent among kings;
> my words are choice; my ability has no equal.
> By the order of Sharnash, the great judge of heaven and earth,
> may my justice prevail in the land;
> by the word of Marduk, my lord,
> may my statutes have no one to rescind them.[5]

The Hebrews introduced some important new ideas. Their unique God was capable of great anger and destruction, but he was open to persuasion and subject to morality. He was therefore more predictable and comforting, for all the terror of his wrath. The biblical version of the flood story, for instance, reveals the great difference between the Hebrew God and the Babylonian deities. The Hebrew God was powerful and wrathful, but he was not arbitrary. He chose to destroy his creatures for their moral failures:

> the wickedness of man was great in the earth, and that every imagination of the thought of his heart was evil continually . . . the earth was corrupt in God's sight and the earth was filled with violence.[6]

When he repented and wanted to save someone, he chose Noah because "Noah was a righteous man, blameless in his generation."[7]

The biblical story of Sodom and Gomorrah shows that God was bound by his own definition of righteousness. He had chosen to destroy these wicked cities but felt obliged by his covenant to inform Abraham first.[8] Abraham called on God to abide by his own moral principles, and God saw Abraham's point.

Such a world offered the possibility of order in the universe and on this earth. There was also the possibility of justice among human beings, for the Hebrew God had provided his people with law. Through his prophet Moses, he had provided humans with regulations that would enable them to live in peace and justice. If they would abide by the law and live upright lives, they and their descendants could expect happy and prosperous lives. This idea was different from the uncertainty of the Babylonian view, but like it and its Egyptian partner, it left no doubt of the certainty of the divine. Cosmic order, human survival, and justice all depended on God.

1.7 Toward the Greeks and Western Thought

Why was Greek rationalism such an important break with earlier intellectual traditions?

Greek thought offered different approaches and answers to many of the concerns we have been discussing. Calling attention to some of those differences will help convey the distinctive outlook of the Greeks and the later cultures within Western civilization that have drawn heavily on Greek influence.

Greek ideas had much in common with the ideas of earlier peoples. The Greek gods had most of the characteristics of the Mesopotamian deities. Magic and incantations played a part in the lives of most Greeks, and Greek law, like that of earlier peoples, was usually connected with divinity. Many, if not most, Greeks in the ancient world must have lived with notions similar to those other peoples held. It is surprising that some Greeks developed ideas that were strikingly different and, in so doing, set part of humankind on an entirely new path.

As early as the sixth century B.C.E., some Greeks living in the Ionian cities of Asia Minor raised questions and suggested answers about the nature of the world that produced an intellectual revolution. In their speculations, they made guesses that were completely naturalistic and made no reference to supernatural powers. One historian of Greek thought, discussing the views of Thales, the first Greek philosopher, put the case particularly well:

> In one of the Babylonian legends it says: "All the lands were sea. . . . Marduk bound a rush mat upon the face of the waters, he made dirt and piled it beside the rush mat." What Thales did was to leave Marduk out. He, too, said that everything was once water. But he thought that earth and everything else had been formed out of water by a natural process, like the silting up of the Delta of the Nile. . . . It is an admirable beginning, the whole point of which is that it gathers into a coherent picture a number of observed facts without letting Marduk in.[9]

By putting the question of the world's origin in a naturalistic form, Thales, in the sixth century B.C.E., may have begun the unreservedly rational investigation of the universe and, in so doing, initiated both philosophy and science.

The same relentlessly rational approach was used even in regard to the gods themselves. In the same century as Thales, Xenophanes of Colophon expressed the opinion that humans think

THE LION GATE OF MYCENAE Constructed in the thirteenth century B.C.E., the Lion Gate marked the entrance to the citadel of Mycenae in southern Greece. The upright bodies of two lions flank a column set atop an altar. Some scholars view the Lion Gate as a symbol of royal power or as an expression of divinity; others, as protectors of the royal house.
SOURCE: Rob Cole Photography/Alamy Stock Photo

of the gods as resembling themselves: that they were born, that they wear clothes like theirs, and that they have voices and bodies like theirs. If oxen, horses, and lions had hands and could paint like humans, Xenophanes argued, they would paint gods in their own image; the oxen would draw gods like oxen and the horses like horses. Thus, Africans believed in flat-nosed, black-faced gods, and the Thracians in gods with blue eyes and red hair.[10] In the fifth century B.C.E., Protagoras of Abdera went so far toward agnosticism as to say, "I cannot say whether or not the gods exist or what is their nature"[11]

This rationalistic, skeptical way of thinking carried over into practical matters. The school of medicine led by Hippocrates of Cos (about 400 B.C.E.) attempted to understand, diagnose, and cure disease without any attention to supernatural forces.

By the fifth century B.C.E., the historian Thucydides could analyze and explain human behavior completely in terms of human nature and chance, leaving no place for the gods or supernatural forces.

The same absence of divine or supernatural forces characterized Greek views of law and justice. Most Greeks, of course, liked to think that, in a vague way, law came ultimately from the gods. In practice, however, and especially in the democratic states, they knew that laws were made by humans and should be obeyed because they represented the expressed consent of the citizens.

The Chapter in Perspective

The questions that follow, so different from any that came before the Greeks, open up a discussion about most of the important issues in the long history of Western civilization that remain major concerns in the modern world. What is the nature of the universe, and how can it be controlled? Are there divine powers, and, if so, what is humanity's relationship to them? Are law and justice human, divine, or both? What is the place in human society of freedom, obedience, and reverence? These and many other matters were either first considered or first elaborated on by the Greeks.

The Greeks' sharp departure from the thinking of earlier cultures marked the beginning of the unusual experience that we call Western civilization. Nonetheless, they built on a foundation of lore that people in the Near East had painstakingly accumulated. From ancient Mesopotamia and Egypt, they borrowed important knowledge and skills in mathematics, astronomy, art, and literature. From Phoenicia, they learned the art of writing. The discontinuities, however, are more striking than the continuities.

Hereditary monarchies, often elevated by the aura of divinity, ruled the great civilizations of the river valleys. Powerful priesthoods presented yet another bastion of privilege that stood between the ordinary person and the knowledge and opportunity needed for freedom and autonomy. Religion was an integral part of the world of the ancient Near East, in the kingdoms and city-states of Palestine, Phoenicia, and Syria, just as in the great empires of Egypt, Mesopotamia, and Persia. The secular, reasoned questioning that sought to understand the world in which people lived—that sought explanations in the natural order of things rather than in the supernatural acts of the gods—was not characteristic of the older cultures. Nor would it appear in similar societies at other times in other parts of the world. The new way of looking at things was uniquely the product of the Greeks. We now need to understand why they raised fundamental questions in the way that they did.

The Chapter in Review

Review Questions

1. How was life during the Paleolithic Age different from that in the Neolithic Age? What advancements in agriculture and human development had taken place by the end of the Neolithic era? Is it valid to speak of a Neolithic Revolution?

2. What were the political and intellectual outlooks of the civilizations of Egypt and Mesopotamia? How did geography influence the religious outlooks of these two civilizations?

3. To what extent did the Hebrew faith bind the Jews politically? Why was the concept of monotheism so radical for Near Eastern civilizations?

4. How did the Assyrian Empire differ from that of the Hittites or Egyptians? Why did the Assyrian Empire ultimately fail to survive? Why was the Persian Empire so successful?

5. What were the main teachings of Zarathustra? How did his concept of the divine compare to that of the Jews?

6. In what ways did Greek thought develop along different lines from that of Near Eastern civilizations? What new questions about human society did the Greeks ask?

Key Terms

Amunhotep IV (r. 1353–1336 B.C.E.) Pharaoh of the Eighteenth Dynasty of Egypt, who promoted the worship of the Aten or "disk" of the sun above Re himself and the rest of the gods.

Battle of Kadesh Thirteenth-century battle in which the Egyptian Empire fought the Hittite kingdom to a draw in a massive chariot contest at the city of Kadesh on the Orontes River.

Bronze Age The name given to the earliest civilized era, ca. 4000 to 1000 B.C.E. Reflects the importance of the metal bronze, a mixture of tin and copper, for the peoples of this age for use as weapons and tools.

civilization A form of human culture marked by urbanism, metallurgy, and writing.

culture The ways of living built up by a group and passed on from one generation to another.

cuneiform (Q-nee-i-form) A writing system invented by the Sumerians that used a wedge-shaped stylus, or pointed tool, to write on wet clay tablets that were then baked or dried (*cuneus* means "wedge" in Latin). The writing was also cut into stone.

Hammurabi (r. ca. 1792–1750 B.C.E.) The sixth and most famous king of the First Babylonian dynasty, best known for the collection of laws that bears his name.

Hatshepsut (r. 1479–1458 B.C.E.) The fifth pharaoh of the Eighteenth Dynasty and one of Egypt's most successful monarchs.

hieroglyphics (HI-er-o-gli-phicks) Meaning "sacred carvings" in Greek. The complicated writing script of ancient Egypt. Combined picture writing with pictographs and sound signs.

Homo sapiens **(HO-mo say-pee-ans)** Meaning "wise man." The scientific name for human beings. Emerged some 200,000 years ago.

Hyksos A group of Asiatic invaders that took over the eastern Nile Delta to rule Egypt for nearly a century. Expelled by Ahmose, the first king of the Eighteenth Dynasty and founder of the New Kingdom.

Lower Egypt The Nile Delta.

maat The Egyptian concept of truth, order, justice, law, and harmony, personified as a goddess.

Mesopotamia (MEZ-o-po-tay-me-a) Modern Iraq. The land between the Tigris and Euphrates Rivers where the first civilization appeared around 3000 B.C.E.

monotheism The worship of one universal God.

Naram-Sin (r. ca. 2254–2218 B.C.E.) The grandson of Sargon, the world's first emperor, who took the title "god of Akkad." The first Mesopotamian king to claim to be a living deity.

Neolithic Age (NEE-o-lith-ick) Meaning "new stone" in Greek. Also called the Age of Agriculture. The shift beginning 10,000 years ago from hunter-gatherer societies to settled communities of farmers and artisans. Included the invention of farming, the domestication of plants and animals, and the development of technologies such as pottery and weaving. First appeared in the Near East about 8000 B.C.E.

nomes Regions or provinces of ancient Egypt governed by officials called *nomarchs*.

Paleolithic Age (PAY-lee-o-lith-ick) Meaning "old stone" in Greek. The earliest period when stone tools were used, from about 1,000,000 to 10000 B.C.E.

pharaoh (FAY-row) Meaning "great house" or palace. The god-kings of ancient Egypt.

Phoenicians (FA-nee-shi-ans) The ancient inhabitants of modern Lebanon. A trading people who established colonies throughout the Mediterranean.

ten lost tribes The Israelites who were scattered and lost to history when the northern kingdom of Israel fell to the Assyrians in 722 B.C.E.

Third Dynasty of Ur (ca. 2125–2004 B.C.E.) The last ruling Sumerian dynasty based in the city Ur. Based on the foundations of the old Akkadian Empire, but much smaller. Produced earliest collections of laws.

Upper Egypt The part of Egypt that runs from the Nile Delta to the Sudanese border.

ziggurat The most impressive religious structure in Mesopotamia. Consisted of a rectangular stepped tower meant to resemble mountains. Most likely inspired the biblical story of "the tower of Babel."

Notes

1. J. H. Breasted, *Ancient Times: A History of the Early World*, 2nd ed. (Boston: Ginn & Co., 1935), p. 277.
2. Benjamin R. Foster, *From Distant Days, Myths, Tales, and Poetry of Ancient Mesopotamia* (Bethesda, MD: CDL Press, 1999), p. 38.
3. Foster, *From Distant Days, Myths, Tales, and Poetry of Ancient Mesopotamia*, pp. 170–171.
4. Foster, *From Distant Days, Myths, Tales, and Poetry of Ancient Mesopotamia*, p. 412.
5. James B. Pritchard, *Ancient Near Eastern Texts Related to the Old Testament*, 3rd ed. (Princeton, NJ: Princeton University Press, 1969), p. 164.
6. King James Version, Genesis 6:5 and 11.
7. Genesis 6:9.
8. Genesis 18:20–33.
9. Benjamin Farrington, *Greek Science* (London: Penguin, 1953), p. 37.
10. Henri Frankfort et al., *Before Philosophy* (Baltimore: Penguin, 1949), pp. 14–16.
11. Hermann Diels, *Fragmente der Vorsokratiker*, 5th ed., ed. by Walter Krantz (Berlin: Weidmann, 1934–1938), Fig. 4, translated by Donald Kagan.

Chapter 2
The Rise of Greek Civilization

RIACE BRONZE In 1972, this striking statue was found off the coast of Riace, southern Italy. Possibly a votive statue from the sanctuary of Delphi in Greece, it may have been the work of the sculptor Phidias (ca. 490–430 B.C.E.).
SOURCE: Erich Lessing/Art Resource, Inc.

 ## Contents and Focus Questions

The Chapter in Brief

ABOUT 2000 B.C.E., GREEK-SPEAKING PEOPLES settled the lands surrounding the Aegean Sea and established a style of life and formed a set of ideas, values, and institutions that spread far beyond the Aegean corner of the Mediterranean Sea. Preserved and adapted by the Romans, Greek culture powerfully influenced the society of Western Europe in the Middle Ages and dominated the Byzantine Empire in the same period. It would ultimately spread across Europe and cross the Atlantic to the Western Hemisphere.

At some time in their history, the Greeks of the ancient world founded cities on every shore of the Mediterranean Sea. Pushing on through the Dardanelles, they settled on the coasts of the Black Sea in southern Russia and as far east as the approaches to the Caucasus Mountains. The center of Greek life, however, has always been the Aegean Sea and the islands in and around it. This location at the eastern end of the Mediterranean soon put the Greeks in touch with the more advanced civilizations of Mesopotamia, Egypt, Asia Minor, and Syria-Palestine.

The Greeks acknowledged the influence of these predecessors. A character in one of Plato's dialogues says, "Whatever the Greeks have acquired from foreigners they have, in the end, turned into something finer."[1] This is a proud statement, but it also shows that the Greeks were aware of how much they had learned from other civilizations.

The Bronze Age Minoan culture of Crete contributed to Greek civilization; and the mainland Mycenaean culture, which conquered Minoan Crete, contributed even more. Both these cultures, however, had more in common with the cultures of the Near East than with the new Hellenic culture established by the Greeks in the centuries after the end of the Bronze Age in the twelfth century B.C.E.

The rugged geography of the Greek peninsula and its nearby islands isolated the Greeks of the early Iron Age from their richer and more culturally advanced neighbors, shaping, in part, their way of life and permitting them to develop that way of life on their own. The aristocratic world of the Greek Dark Ages (1150–750 B.C.E.) produced impressive artistic achievements, especially in the development of painted pottery and most magnificently, in the epic poems of Homer. In the eighth century B.C.E., social, economic, and military changes profoundly influenced the organization of Greek political life; the Greek city-state, the *polis*, came into being and thereafter dominated the cultural development of the Greek people.

This change came in the midst of turmoil, for the pressure of a growing population led many Greeks to leave home and establish colonies far away. Those who remained often fell into political conflict, from which tyrannies sometimes emerged. These tyrannies, however, were transitory, and the Greek cities emerged from them as self-governing polities, usually ruled by an oligarchy, broad or narrow. The two most important states, Athens and Sparta, moved in different directions. Sparta formed a mixed constitution in which a small part of the population dominated the vast majority, and Athens developed the world's first democracy.

2.1 The Bronze Age on Crete and on the Mainland to ca. 1150 B.C.E.

In what ways were the Minoan and Mycenaean civilizations different?

The Bronze Age civilizations in the region the Greeks would rule arose on the island of Crete, on the islands of the Aegean Sea, and on the mainland of Greece. Crete was the site of the earliest Bronze Age settlements, and modern scholars have called the civilization that arose there **Minoan**, after Minos, the legendary king of Crete. A later Bronze Age civilization was centered at the mainland site of Mycenae and is called **Mycenaean**.

2.1.1 The Minoans

With Greece to the north, Egypt to the south, and Asia to the east, Crete was a cultural bridge between the older civilizations and the new one of the Greeks. The Bronze Age came to Crete not long after 3000 B.C.E., and the Minoan civilization, which powerfully influenced the islands of the Aegean and the mainland of Greece, arose in the third and second millennia B.C.E.

Scholars have established links between stratigraphic layers at archaeological sites on Crete and specific styles of pottery and other artifacts found in the layers. On this basis they have divided the Bronze Age on Crete into three major periods—Early, Middle, and Late Minoan—with some subdivisions. Dates for Bronze Age settlements on the Greek mainland, for which the term *Helladic* is used, are derived from the same chronological scheme.

During the Middle and Late Minoan periods in the cities of eastern and central Crete, a civilization developed that was new and unique in its character and beauty. Its most striking creations are the palaces uncovered at such sites as Phaestus, Haghia Triada, and, most important, Cnossus. Each of these palaces was built around a central court surrounded by a labyrinth of rooms. Some sections of the palace at Cnossus were four stories high. The basement contained many storage rooms for oil and grain, apparently paid as taxes to the king. The main and upper floors contained living quarters, and workshops for making pottery and jewelry. There were sitting rooms and even bathrooms, to which water was piped through excellent plumbing. Lovely columns, which tapered downward, supported the ceilings, and many of the walls carried murals showing landscapes and seascapes, festivals, and sports. The palace design and the paintings show the influence of Syria, Asia Minor, and Egypt, but the style and quality are unique to Crete.

In contrast to the Mycenaean cities on the mainland of Greece, Minoan palaces and settlements lacked strong defensive walls. This evidence that the Minoans built without defense in mind has raised questions and encouraged speculation. Some scholars, pointing also to evidence that Minoan religion was more matriarchal than the patriarchal religion of the Mycenaeans and their Greek descendants, have argued that the civilizations of Crete, perhaps reflecting the importance of women, were inherently more tranquil and pacific than others. An earlier and different explanation for the absence of Minoan fortifications was that the protection provided by the sea made them unnecessary. The evidence is not strong enough to support either explanation, and the mystery remains.

Along with palaces, paintings, pottery, jewelry, and other valuable objects, Minoan excavations have revealed clay writing tablets like those found in Mesopotamia. The tablets, preserved accidentally when a great fire that destroyed the royal palace at Cnossus hardened them, have three distinct kinds of writing on them: a kind of picture writing called *hieroglyphic*, and two different linear scripts called Linear A and Linear B. The languages of the two other scripts remain unknown, but Linear B proved to be an early form of Greek. The contents of the tablets, primarily inventories, reveal an organization centered on the palace and ruled by a king who was supported by an extensive bureaucracy that kept remarkably detailed records.

This sort of organization is typical of early civilizations in the Near East, but as we shall see, is nothing like that of the Greeks after the Bronze Age. Yet the inventories were written in a form of Greek. If they controlled Crete throughout the Bronze Age, why should the Minoans, who were not Greek, have written in a language not their own? This question raises the larger one of what the relationship was between Crete and the Greek mainland in the Bronze Age and leads us to an examination of mainland culture.

2.1.2 The Mycenaeans

In the third millennium B.C.E.—the Early Helladic Period—most of the Greek mainland, including many of the sites of later Greek cities, was settled by people who used metal, built some impressive houses, and traded with Crete and the islands of the Aegean. The names they gave to places, names that were sometimes preserved by later invaders, make it clear they were not Greeks: they spoke a language that was not Indo-European (the language family to which Greek belongs).

Not long after the year 2000 B.C.E., many of these Early Helladic sites were destroyed by fire, some were abandoned, and still others appear to have yielded peacefully to

MINOAN FRESCO The palace of Knossos on the Greek island of Crete offers a glimpse into a highly developed civilization. Dating from about 1450 B.C.E., this fresco fragment of a young woman reflects the style and tastes of late Minoan art.
SOURCE: INTERFOTO/Alamy Stock Photo

an invading people. These signs of invasion probably signal the arrival of the Greeks.

All over Greece, there was a smooth transition between the Middle and Late Helladic periods. The invaders succeeded in establishing control of the entire mainland. The shaft graves cut into the rock at the royal palace-fortress of Mycenae show that they prospered and sometimes became rich. At Mycenae, the richest finds come from the period after 1600 B.C.E. The city's wealth and power reached their peak during this time, and the culture of the whole mainland during the Late Helladic Period goes by the name *Mycenaean*.

The presence of the Greek Linear B tablets at Cnossus suggests that Greek invaders also established themselves in Crete, and there is good reason to believe that at the height of Mycenaean power (1400–1200 B.C.E.), Crete was part of the Mycenaean world. Although their dating is still controversial, the Linear B tablets at Cnossus seem to belong to Late Minoan III. Thus, what is called the great "palace period" at Cnossus would have followed an invasion by the Mycenaeans in 1400 B.C.E. These Greek invaders ruled Crete until the end of the Bronze Age.

2.1.2.1 MYCENAEAN CULTURE The excavation of Mycenae, Pylos, and other Mycenaean sites reveals a culture influenced by, but different from, the Minoan culture. Mycenae and Pylos, like Cnossus, were built some distance from the sea, but defense against attack was foremost in the minds of the founders of these Mycenaean cities. Both Mycenae and Pylos were built on hills in a position commanding the neighboring territory. The Mycenaean people were warriors, as their art, architecture, and weapons reveal. The success of their campaigns and the defense of their territory required strong central authority, and all available evidence shows that the kings provided it. Mycenaean palaces, in which the royal family and its retainers lived, were located within the walls; most of the population lived outside the walls. As on Crete, paintings usually covered the palace walls, but instead of peaceful landscapes and games, the Mycenaean murals depicted scenes of war and boar hunting.

About 1500 B.C.E., the already impressive shaft graves were abandoned in favor of *tholos* tombs. These large, beehive-like chambers were built of enormous well-cut and fitted stones and were approached by an unroofed passage (*dromos*) cut horizontally into the side of the hill. The lintel block alone of one of these tombs weighs more than one hundred tons. Only a strong king whose wealth was great, whose power was unquestioned, and who commanded the labor of many people could undertake such a project. His wealth probably came from plundering raids, piracy, and trade. Some of this trade went westward to Italy and Sicily, but most of it was with the islands of the Aegean, the coastal towns of Asia Minor, and the cities of Syria, Egypt, and Crete. The Mycenaeans sent pottery, olive oil, and animal hides in exchange for jewels and other luxuries.

Tablets containing the Mycenaean Linear B writing have been found all over the mainland; the largest and most useful collection was found at Pylos. These tablets reveal a world similar to the one the records at Cnossus show. The king, whose title was *wanax*, held a royal domain, appointed officials, commanded servants, and kept a close record of what he owned and what was owed to him. This evidence confirms all the rest; the Mycenaean world was made up of several independent, powerful, and well-organized monarchies.

2.1.2.2 THE RISE AND FALL OF MYCENAEAN POWER At the height of their power (1400–1200 B.C.E.), the Mycenaeans were prosperous and active. They enlarged their cities, expanded their trade, and even established commercial colonies in the East. The archives of the Hittite kings of Asia Minor mention them, and Egyptian records name them as marauders of the Nile Delta. Sometime about 1250 B.C.E., they probably sacked Troy, on the coast of northwestern Asia Minor, giving rise to the epic poems of Homer—the

CITADEL OF MYCENAE The citadel of Mycenae, a major center of the Greek civilization of the Bronze Age, was built of enormously heavy stones. The Lion Gate at its entrance was built in the thirteenth century B.C.E.
SOURCE: Constantinos Iliopoulos/Alamy Stock Photo

Iliad and the *Odyssey*. (See Map 2–1.) Around 1200 B.C.E., however, the Mycenaean world showed signs of trouble, and by 1100 B.C.E., it was gone. Its palaces were destroyed, many of its cities were abandoned, and its art, way of life, and system of writing were buried and forgotten.

What happened? Some recent scholars, noting evidence that the Aegean island of Thera (modern Santorini) suffered a massive volcanic explosion in the middle to late second millennium B.C.E., have suggested that this natural disaster was responsible. The Mycenaean towns were not destroyed all at once; many fell around 1200 B.C.E., but some flourished for another century, and the Athens of the period was never destroyed or abandoned. No theory of natural disaster can account for this pattern, leaving us to seek less dramatic explanations for the end of Mycenaean civilization.

2.1.2.3 THE DORIAN INVASION Some scholars have suggested that piratical sea raiders destroyed Pylos and, perhaps, other sites on the mainland. The Greeks themselves believed in a legend that told of the Dorians, a rude people from the north who spoke a Greek dialect different from that of the Mycenaean peoples. According to the legend, the Dorians joined with one of the Greek tribes, the Heraclidae, in an attack on the southern Greek peninsula of **Peloponnesus**, which was repulsed. One hundred years later, they returned and gained full control. Some historians have identified this legend of "the return of the Heraclidae" with the **Dorian invasion**.

Archaeology has not provided material evidence of whether there was a single Dorian invasion or a series of them, and it is impossible to say with any certainty what happened at the end of the Bronze Age in the Aegean area. The chances are good, however, that Mycenaean civilization ended gradually during the century between 1200 B.C.E. and

Map 2–1 THE AEGEAN AREA IN THE BRONZE AGE

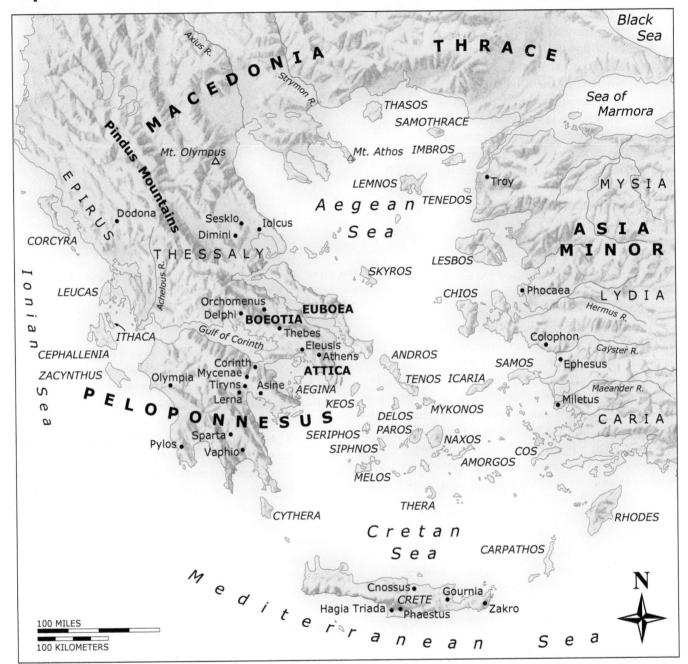

The Bronze Age in the Aegean area lasted from ca. 1900 to ca. 1100 B.C.E. Its culture on Crete is called Minoan and was at its height from ca. 1900 to 1400 B.C.E. Bronze Age Helladic culture on the mainland flourished from ca. 1600 to 1200 B.C.E.

1100 B.C.E. Its end may have been the result of internal conflicts among the Mycenaean kings combined with continuous pressure from outsiders, who raided, infiltrated, and eventually dominated Greece and its neighboring islands. There is reason to believe that Mycenaean society suffered internal weaknesses due to its organization around the centralized control of military force and agricultural production. This rigid organization may have deprived Mycenaean society of flexibility and vitality, leaving it vulnerable to outside challengers. In any case, Cnossus, Mycenae, and Pylos were abandoned, their secrets to be kept for more than 3,000 years.

2.2 The Greek Middle Ages to ca. 750 B.C.E.

What were the Greek Dark Ages?

The immediate effects of the Dorian invasion were disastrous for the inhabitants of the Mycenaean world. The palaces and the kings and bureaucrats who managed them were destroyed. The wealth and organization that had supported the artists and merchants were likewise swept away by a

COMBAT SCENE FROM *THE ILIAD* Dating from about 530 B.C.E., this Attic black-figure calyx krater depicts a battle scene, possibly from Homer's *Iliad*. The slain man on the ground is believed to be Patroclus, a friend to Achilles.
SOURCE: The History Collection/Alamy Stock Photo

barbarous people who did not have the knowledge or social organization to maintain them. Many villages were abandoned and never resettled. Some of their inhabitants probably turned to a nomadic life, and many perished. The chaos resulting from the collapse of the rigidly controlled palace culture produced severe depopulation and widespread poverty that lasted for a long time.

2.2.1 Greek Migrations

Another result of the invasion was the spread of the Greek people eastward from the mainland to the Aegean islands and the coast of Asia Minor. The Dorians themselves, after occupying most of the Peloponnesus, occupied the southern Aegean islands and the southern part of the Anatolian coast.

These migrations made the Aegean Sea a Greek lake. The fall of the advanced Minoan and Mycenaean civilizations, however, virtually ended trade with the old civilizations of the Near East; nor was there much internal trade among the different parts of Greece. The Greeks were forced to turn inward, and each community was left largely to its own devices. The Near East was also in disarray at this time, and no great power arose to impose its ways and its will on the helpless people who lived about the Aegean. The Greeks were allowed time to recover from their disaster, however, and to create their own unique style of life.

Our knowledge of this period in Greek history rests on limited sources. Writing disappeared after the fall of Mycenae, and no new script appeared until about 750 B.C.E., so we have no contemporary author to shed light on the period. Excavation reveals no architecture, sculpture, or painting until after 750 B.C.E.

2.2.2 The Age of Homer

For a picture of society in these "Dark Ages," the best source is Homer. His epic poems, the *Iliad* and the *Odyssey*, emerged from a tradition of oral poetry whose roots extend into the Mycenaean Age. Through the centuries bards had sung tales of the heroes who had fought at Troy, using verse arranged in rhythmic formulas to aid the memory. In this way some old material was preserved into the eighth century B.C.E., when the poems attributed to Homer were finally written down. Although the poems tell of the deeds of Mycenaean Age heroes, the world they describe clearly differs from the Mycenaean world. Homer's heroes are not buried in tholos tombs but are cremated; they worship gods in temples, whereas the Mycenaeans had no temples; they have chariots but do not know their proper use in warfare. Certain aspects of the society described in the poems appear instead to resemble the world of the tenth and ninth centuries B.C.E., and other aspects appear to belong to the poet's own time, when population was growing at a swift pace and prosperity was returning, thanks to changes in Greek agriculture, society, and government.

2.2.2.1 GOVERNMENT In the Homeric poems, kings had much less power than Mycenaean rulers. Homeric kings had to consult a council of nobles before they made important decisions. The nobles felt free to discuss matters in vigorous language and in opposition to the king's wishes. In the *Iliad*, Achilles does not hesitate to address Agamemnon, the "most kingly" commander of the Trojan expedition, with these words: "you with a dog's face and a deer's heart." Such language may have been impolite, but it was not treasonous. The king could ignore the council's advice, but it was risky for him to do so.

Only noblemen had the right to speak in council, but the common people could not be entirely ignored. If a king planned a war or a major change of policy during a campaign, he would not fail to call the common soldiers to an assembly; they could listen and express their feelings by acclamation, though they could not take part in the debate. Homer shows that even in these early times the Greeks, unlike their predecessors and contemporaries, practiced some forms of limited constitutional government.

2.2.2.2 SOCIETY Homeric society, nevertheless, was sharply divided into classes, the most important division being the one between nobles and everyone else. We do not know the origin of this distinction, but we cannot doubt that at this time Greek society was aristocratic. Birth determined noble status, and wealth usually accompanied it. Below the nobles were three other classes: *thetes*, landless laborers, and slaves. We do not know whether the thetes owned the land they worked outright (and so were free to sell it) or worked a hereditary plot that belonged to their clan (and was, therefore, not theirs to dispose of as they chose).

The worst condition was that of the free, but landless, hired agricultural laborer. The slave, at least, was attached to a family household and so was protected and fed. In a world where membership in a settled group gave the only security, the free laborers were desperately vulnerable. Slaves were few and were mostly women, who served as maids and concubines. Some male slaves worked as shepherds. Few, if any, worked in agriculture, which depended on free labor throughout Greek history.

2.2.2.3 HOMERIC VALUES The Homeric poems reflect an aristocratic code of values that powerfully influenced all future Greek thought. In classical times, Homer was the schoolbook of the Greeks. They memorized his texts, settled diplomatic disputes by citing passages in them, and emulated the behavior and cherished the values they found in them. Those values were physical prowess; courage; fierce protection of one's family, friends, and property; and, above all, personal honor and reputation. Speed of foot, strength, and most of all, excellence at fighting made a man great, and all these attributes promoted personal honor. Achilles, the great hero of the *Iliad*, refused to fight in battle, allowing his fellow Greeks to be slain and almost defeated, because Agamemnon had wounded his honor by taking away his battle prize. He returns not out of a sense of duty to the army, but to avenge the death of his dear friend Patroclus. Odysseus, the hero of the *Odyssey*, returning home after his wanderings, ruthlessly kills the many suitors who had, in his long absence, sought to marry his wife Penelope; they had dishonored him by consuming his wealth, wooing Penelope, and scorning his son.

The highest virtue in Homeric society was *arete*— manliness, courage in the most general sense, and the excellence proper to a hero. This quality was best revealed in a contest, or *agon*. Homeric battles were not primarily group combats, but a series of individual contests between great champions. One of the prime forms of entertainment was the athletic contest, and such a contest celebrated the funeral of Patroclus.

The central ethical idea in Homer can be found in the instructions that Achilles's father gives him when he sends him off to fight at Troy: "Always be the best and distinguished above others." The father of another Homeric hero had given his son exactly the same orders and added to them the injunction: "Do not bring shame on the family of your fathers who were by far the best in Ephyre and in wide Lycia." In a nutshell, the chief values of the aristocrats of Homer's world are: to vie for individual supremacy in arete and to defend and increase the honor of the family. These would remain prominent aristocratic values long after Homeric society was only a memory.

2.2.2.4 WOMEN IN HOMERIC SOCIETY In the world described by Homer, the role of women was chiefly to bear and raise children, but the wives of the heroes also had a respected position, presiding over the household, overseeing the servants, and safeguarding the family property. They were prized for their beauty, constancy, and skill at weaving. All these fine qualities are combined in Penelope, the wife of Odysseus, probably the ideal Homeric woman. For the twenty years of her husband's absence, she put off the many suitors who sought to marry her and take his place, remained faithful to him, preserved his property, and protected the future of their son.

Far different was the reputation of Agamemnon's wife, Clytemnestra, who betrayed her husband while he was off fighting at Troy and murdered him on his return. Homer contrasts her with the virtuous Penelope in a passage that reveals a streak of hostility to women that can be found throughout the ancient history of the Greeks:

> Not so did the daughter of Tyndareus fashion her evil deeds, when she killed her wedded lord, and a song of loathing will be hers among men, to make evil the reputation of womankind, even for those whose acts are virtuous.[2]

Unlike Greek women in later centuries, the women of the higher class depicted in Homer are seen moving freely about their communities in town and country. They have a place alongside their husbands at the banquets in the great halls and take part in the conversation. In the *Odyssey*'s land of Phaeacia, admittedly a kind of fairyland, the wise queen Arete can decide the fate of suppliants and sometimes is asked to settle disputes even between men. A good marriage is viewed as essential, admirable, and desirable. The shipwrecked Odysseus tries to win the sympathy of Arete's young daughter by wishing for her "all that you desire in your heart":

> A husband and a home and the accompanying unity of mind and feeling
> Which is so desirable, for there is nothing nobler or better than this,
> When two people, who think alike, keep house
> As man and wife; causing pain to their enemies,
> And joy to their well-wishers, as they themselves know best.[3]

2.3 The *Polis*

*Describe the **polis** and how it affected society and government.*

The characteristic Greek institution was the *polis* (plural *poleis*). The common translation of that word as "city-state" is misleading, for it says both too much and too little. All Greek poleis began as little more than agricultural villages or towns, and many stayed that way, so the word "city" is inappropriate. All of them were states, in the sense of being independent political units, but they were much more than that. The polis was thought of as a community of relatives; all its citizens, who were theoretically descended from a common ancestor, belonged to subgroups, such as fighting brotherhoods or *phratries*, clans, and tribes, and worshipped the gods in common ceremonies.

Aristotle argued that the polis was a natural growth and the human being was by nature "an animal who lives in a polis." Humans alone have the power of speech and from it derive the ability to distinguish good from bad and right from wrong, "and the sharing of these things is what makes a household and a polis." Therefore, humans who are incapable of sharing these things or who are so self-sufficient that they have no need of them are not humans at all, but either wild beasts or gods. Without law and justice, human beings are the worst and most dangerous of the animals. With them, humans can be the best, and justice exists only in the polis. These high claims were made in the fourth century B.C.E., hundreds of years after the polis came into existence, but they accurately reflect an attitude that was present from the first.

2.3.1 Development of the *Polis*

Originally the word *polis* referred only to a citadel—an elevated, defensible rock to which the farmers of the neighboring area could retreat in case of attack. The **Acropolis** in Athens and the hill called Acrocorinth in Corinth are examples. For some time, such high places and the adjacent farms made up the polis. The towns grew gradually and without planning, as their narrow, winding, and disorderly streets show. For centuries, they had no walls. Unlike the city-states of the Near East, they were not placed for commercial convenience on rivers or the sea. Nor did they grow up around a temple to serve the needs of priests and to benefit from the needs of worshippers. The availability of farmland and of a natural fortress determined their location. They were placed either well inland or far enough from the sea to avoid piratical raids. Only later and gradually did the *agora*—a marketplace and civic center—appear within the polis. The agora was to become the heart of the Greeks' remarkable social life, distinguished by conversation and argument carried on in the open air.

Some poleis probably came into existence early in the eighth century B.C.E. The institution was certainly common by the middle of the century, for all the colonies that were established by the Greeks in the years after 750 B.C.E. took the form of the polis. Once the new institution had been fully established, true monarchy disappeared. Vestigial kings survived in some places, but they were almost always only ceremonial figures without power. The original form of the polis was an aristocratic republic dominated by the nobility through its council of nobles and its monopoly of the magistracies.

About 750 B.C.E., coincident with the development of the polis, the Greeks borrowed a writing system from one of the Semitic scripts and added vowels to create the first true alphabet. This new Greek alphabet was easier to learn than any earlier writing system, leading to much wider literacy.

2.3.2 The *Hoplite* Phalanx

A new military technique was crucial to the development of the polis. In earlier times, small troops of cavalry and individual "champions" who first threw their spears and then came to close quarters with swords may have borne the brunt of fighting. Toward the end of the eighth century B.C.E., however, the *hoplite* **phalanx** emerged and remained the basis of Greek warfare thereafter.

The hoplite was a heavily armed infantryman who fought with a spear and a large shield. Most scholars believe that these soldiers were formed into a phalanx in close order, usually at least eight ranks deep, although some argue for a looser formation. If the *hoplites* fought bravely and held their ground, there would be few casualties and no defeat, but if they gave way, the result was usually a rout. All depended on the discipline, strength, and courage of the individual soldier. At its best, the phalanx could withstand cavalry charges and defeat infantries not as well protected or disciplined. Until defeated by the Roman legion, it was the dominant military force in the eastern Mediterranean.

The usual hoplite battle in Greece was between the armies of two poleis quarreling over land. One army invaded the territory of the other when the crops were almost ready for harvest. The defending army had to protect its fields. If an army was beaten, its fields were captured or destroyed and its people might starve. In every way, the phalanx was a communal effort that relied not on the extraordinary actions of the individual, but on the courage of a considerable portion

THE PHALANX This detail from the Protocorinthian "Chigi" vase, produced sometime around 640 B.C.E., features an early hoplite phalanx.
SOURCE: World History Archive/Alamy Stock Photo

of the citizenry. This style of fighting produced a single, decisive battle that reduced the time lost in fighting other kinds of warfare; it spared the houses, livestock, and other capital of the farmer-soldiers who made up the phalanx; and it also reduced the number of casualties. The phalanx perfectly suited the farmer-soldier-citizen, who was the backbone of the polis, and, by keeping wars short and limiting their destructiveness and expense, it helped the polis prosper.

The phalanx and the polis arose together, and both heralded the decline of the kings. The phalanx, however, was not made up only of aristocrats. Most of the hoplites were farmers working small holdings. The immediate beneficiaries of the royal decline were the aristocrats, but because the existence of the polis depended on small farmers, their wishes could not be wholly ignored. The rise of the hoplite phalanx created a bond between the aristocrats and the yeoman family farmers who fought in it. This bond helps explain why class conflicts were muted for some time. It also guaranteed, however, that the aristocrats, who dominated at first, would not always be unchallenged.

2.4 Expansion of the Greek World

How and why did the Greeks colonize large parts of the Mediterranean?

From the middle of the eighth century B.C.E. until well into the sixth century B.C.E., the Greeks vastly expanded their territory, their wealth, and their contacts with other peoples. A burst of colonizing activity placed poleis from Spain to the Black Sea. A century earlier, a few Greeks had established trading posts in Syria. There they had learned new techniques in the arts and crafts and much more from the older civilizations of the Near East.

KEY EVENTS IN THE RISE OF GREECE	
ca. 2900–1150 B.C.E.	Minoan period
ca. 1900 B.C.E.	Probable date of the arrival of the Greeks on the mainland
ca. 1600–1200 B.C.E.	Mycenaean period
ca. 1250 B.C.E.	Sack of Troy
ca. 1200–1100 B.C.E.	Destruction of Mycenaean centers in Greece
ca. 1100–750 B.C.E.	Greek Dark Ages
ca. 750–600 B.C.E.	Major period of Greek colonization
ca. 750 B.C.E.	Probable date when Homer flourished
ca. 700 B.C.E.	Probable date when Hesiod flourished
ca. 700–500 B.C.E.	Major period of Greek tyranny

2.4.1 *Magna Graecia*

Syria and its neighboring territory were too strong to penetrate, so the Greeks settled the southern coast of Macedonia. This region was sparsely settled, and the natives were not organized well enough to resist the Greek colonists. Southern Italy and eastern Sicily were even more inviting areas. Before long, there were so many Greek colonies in Italy and Sicily that the Romans called the whole region *Magna Graecia*, "Great Greece." The Greeks also established colonies in Spain and southern France. In the seventh century B.C.E., Greek colonists settled the coasts of the northeastern Mediterranean, the Black Sea, and the straits connecting them. About the same time, they established settlements on the eastern part of the North African coast. The Greeks now had outposts throughout the Mediterranean world. (See Map 2–2.)

2.4.2 The Greek Colony

The Greeks did not lightly leave home to join a colony. The voyage by sea was dangerous and uncomfortable, and at the end of it were uncertainty and danger. Only powerful pressures like overpopulation and hunger for land drove thousands from their homes to establish new poleis.

The colony, although sponsored by the mother city, was established for the good of the colonists rather than for the benefit of those they left behind. The colonists tended to divide the land they settled into equal shares, reflecting an egalitarian tendency inherent in the ethical system of the yeoman farmers in the mother cities. They often copied their home constitution, worshipped the same gods as the people of the mother city at the same festivals in the same way, and carried on a busy trade with the mother city. Most colonies, though independent, were friendly with their mother cities. Each might ask the other for aid in times of trouble and expect to receive a friendly hearing, although neither was obligated to help the other.

The Athenians had colonies of this typical kind but introduced innovations during their imperial period (478–404 B.C.E.). At one point, they began to treat all the colonies of their empire as though they were Athenian settlements, requiring them to bring an offering of a cow and a suit of armor to the Great Panathenaic festival, just like true Athenian colonies. The goal may have been to cloak imperial rule in the more friendly garb of colonial family attachment.

The best-known exception to the rule of friendly relations between colony and mother city was the case of Corinth and its colony Corcyra, which quarreled and fought for more than two centuries. Thucydides tells of a fateful conflict between them that played a major role in causing the Peloponnesian War.

Colonization had a powerful influence on Greek life. By relieving the pressure of a growing population, it provided a safety valve that allowed the poleis to escape civil wars. By confronting the Greeks with the differences between themselves and the new peoples they met, colonization gave them a sense of cultural identity and fostered a **Panhellenic** ("all-Greek") spirit that led to the establishment

Map 2–2 GREEK COLONIZATION

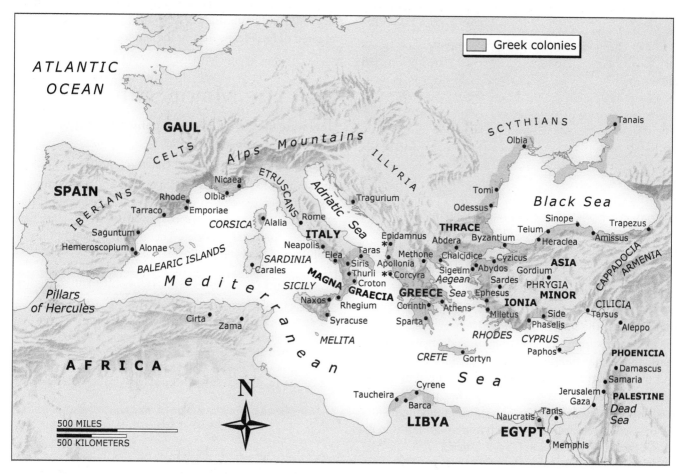

The height of Greek colonization was between about 750 and 550 B.C.E. Greek colonies stretched from the Mediterranean coasts of Spain and Gaul (modern France) in the west to the Black Sea and Asia Minor in the east.

of common religious festivals. The most important ones were at Olympia, Delphi, Corinth, and Nemea.

Colonization also encouraged trade and industry. The influx of new wealth from abroad and the increased demand for goods from the homeland stimulated a more intensive use of the land and an emphasis on crops for export, chiefly the olive and the wine grape. The manufacture of pottery, tools, weapons, and fine artistic metalwork, as well as perfumed oil, the soap of the ancient Mediterranean world, was likewise encouraged. New opportunities allowed some men, sometimes outside the nobility, to become wealthy and important. The new rich became a troublesome element in the aristocratic poleis, for, although they were increasingly important in the life of their states, the ruling aristocrats barred them from political power, religious privileges, and social acceptance. These conditions soon created a crisis in many states.

2.4.3 The Tyrants (ca. 700–500 B.C.E.)

In some cities—perhaps only a small percentage of the more than 1,000 Greek poleis—the crisis produced by new economic and social conditions led to or intensified

factional divisions within the ruling aristocracy. Between 700 and 500 B.C.E., the result was often the establishment of a tyranny.

2.4.3.1 THE RISE OF TYRANNY A tyrant was a monarch who had gained power in an unorthodox or unconstitutional, but not necessarily wicked, way and who exercised a strong one-man rule that might well be beneficent and popular.

The founding tyrant was usually a member of the ruling aristocracy who either had a personal grievance or led an unsuccessful faction. He often rose to power because of his military ability and support from the hoplites. He generally had the support of the politically powerless group of the newly wealthy and of the poor farmers. When he took power, a tyrant often expelled many of his aristocratic opponents and divided at least some of their land among his supporters. He pleased his commercial and industrial supporters by destroying the privileges of the old aristocracy and by fostering trade and colonization.

The tyrants presided over a period of population growth that saw an increase especially in the number of city dwellers. They responded with a program of public works

THE *DIOLKOS* CONSTRUCTED BY PERIANDER The tyrant Periander ruled Corinth from about 627 to 587 B.C.E. Under his rule, Corinth became a bustling commercial center. Periander is credited with the construction of the *diolkos* ("portage way"), a paved road across the Isthmus of Corinth.
SOURCE: Erin Babnik/Alamy Stock Photo

that included the improvement of drainage systems, care for the water supply, the construction and organization of marketplaces, the building and strengthening of city walls, and the erection of temples. Tyrants introduced new local festivals and elaborated the old ones. They patronized the arts, supporting poets and artisans with gratifying results. All this activity contributed to the tyrant's popularity, to the prosperity of his city, and to his self-esteem.

In most cases, the tyrant's rule was secured by a personal bodyguard and by mercenary soldiers. An armed citizenry, necessary for an aggressive foreign policy, would have been dangerous, so tyrants usually sought peaceful alliances with other tyrants abroad and avoided war.

2.4.3.2 THE END OF THE TYRANTS By the end of the sixth century B.C.E., tyranny had disappeared from the Greek states and did not return in the same form or for the same reasons. The last tyrants were universally hated for their cruelty and repression. They left bitter memories in their own states and became objects of fear and hatred everywhere.

Besides the outrages individual tyrants committed, the very concept of tyranny was inimical to the idea of the polis. The notion of the polis as a community to which every member must be responsible, the importance of justice within that community, and the natural aristocratic hatred of monarchy all made tyranny alien and offensive. The rule of a tyrant, however beneficent, was arbitrary and unpredictable. Tyranny came into being in defiance of tradition and law, yet the tyrant governed without either. He was not answerable in any way to his fellow citizens.

From a longer perspective, however, the tyrants made important contributions to the development of Greek civilization. They encouraged economic changes that helped secure the future prosperity of Greece. They increased communication with the rest of the Mediterranean world and

cultivated crafts and technology, as well as arts and literature. Most important, tyrants broke the grip of the aristocracy and put the productive powers of the most active and talented of its citizens fully at the service of the polis.

2.5 The Major States

How were the government and politics of Athens different from those of Sparta?

Generalization of the polis became difficult shortly after its appearance, for although the states had much in common, some of them developed in unique ways. Sparta and Athens, which became the two most powerful Greek states, had especially unusual histories. The geography and political evolution of each state make this clear.

KEY EVENTS IN THE EARLY HISTORY OF SPARTA AND ATHENS	
ca. 725–710 B.C.E.	First Messenian War
ca. 650–625 B.C.E.	Second Messenian War
632 B.C.E.	Cylon tries to establish a tyranny at Athens
621 B.C.E.	Draco publishes legal code at Athens
594 B.C.E.	Solon institutes reforms at Athens
ca. 560–550 B.C.E.	Sparta defeats Tegea: Beginning of Peloponnesian League
546–527 B.C.E.	Pisistratus reigns as tyrant at Athens (main period)
510 B.C.E.	Hippias, son of Pisistratus, deposed as tyrant of Athens
ca. 508–501 B.C.E.	Clisthenes institutes reforms at Athens

2.5.1 Sparta

At first Sparta—located on the Peloponnesus, the southern peninsula of Greece—seems not to have been strikingly different from other poleis. About 725 B.C.E., however, the pressure of population and hunger led the Spartans to

RUINS OF THE TEMPLE OF ARTEMIS ON THE SPARTAN ACROPOLIS The Sanctuary of Artemis Orthia sits on the west bank of the Eurotas River. Established in the ninth century B.C.E., it was an important religious site in Sparta. The temple was built later. Today, only a section remains.
SOURCE: Peter Brown/Alamy Stock Photo

Map 2–3 THE PELOPONNESUS

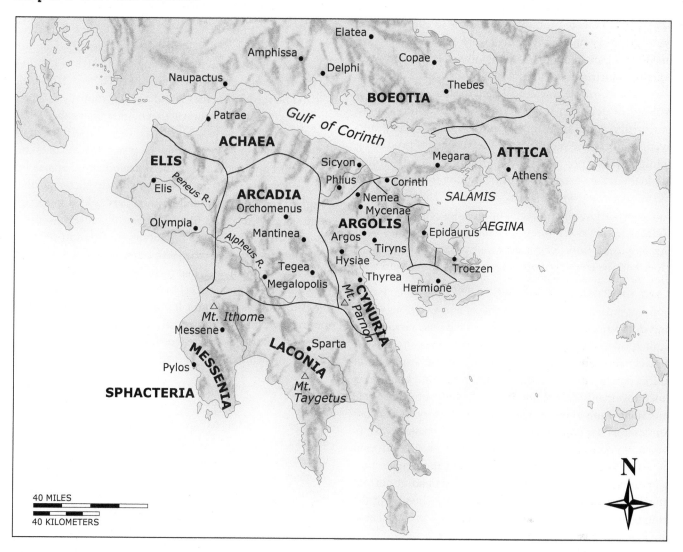

Sparta's region, Laconia, was in the Peloponnesus. Most nearby states were members of the Peloponnesian League under Sparta's leadership.

launch a war of conquest against their western neighbor, Messenia. (See Map 2–3.) The First Messenian War gave the Spartans as much land as they would ever need. The reduction of the Messenians to the status of serfs, or **Helots**, meant the Spartans did not even need to work the land that supported them.

The turning point in Spartan history came about 650 B.C.E., when, in the Second Messenian War, the Helots rebelled with the help of Argos and other Peloponnesian cities. The war was long and bitter and at one point threatened the existence of Sparta. After they had suppressed the revolt, the Spartans were forced to reconsider their way of life. They could not expect to keep down the Helots, who outnumbered them perhaps ten to one, and still maintain the old free and easy habits typical of most Greeks. Faced with the choice of making drastic changes and sacrifices or abandoning their control of Messenia, the Spartans chose to turn their city forever after into a military academy and camp.

2.5.1.1 SPARTAN SOCIETY The new system that emerged late in the sixth century B.C.E. exerted control over each Spartan from birth, when officials of the state decided which infants were physically fit to survive. At the age of seven, the Spartan boy was taken from his mother and turned over to young instructors. He was trained in athletics and the military arts and taught to endure privation, to bear physical pain, and to live off the country, by theft if necessary. At twenty, the Spartan youth was enrolled in the army, where he lived in barracks with his companions until the age of thirty. Marriage was permitted, but a strange sort of marriage it was, for the Spartan male could visit his wife only infrequently and by stealth. At thirty, he became a full citizen, an "equal." He took his meals at a public mess in the company of fifteen comrades. His own plot of land, worked by Helots, provided his food, a simple diet without much meat or wine. Military service was required until the age of sixty; only then could the Spartan retire to his home and family.

This educational program extended to women, too, although they were not given military training. Like males, female infants were examined for fitness to survive. Girls were given gymnastic training, were permitted greater freedom of movement than among other Greeks, and were equally indoctrinated with the idea of service to Sparta.

The entire system was designed to change the natural feelings of devotion to family and children into a more powerful commitment to the polis. Privacy, luxury, and even comfort were sacrificed for the purpose of producing soldiers whose physical powers, training, and discipline made them the best in the world. Nothing that might turn the mind away from duty was permitted. The very use of coins was forbidden lest it corrupt the desires of Spartans. Neither family nor money was allowed to interfere with the only ambition permitted to a Spartan male: to win glory and the respect of his peers through bravery in war.

2.5.1.2 SPARTAN GOVERNMENT The Spartan constitution was mixed, containing elements of monarchy, oligarchy, and democracy. There were two kings, whose power was limited by law and also by the rivalry that usually existed between the two royal houses. The origins and explanation of this unusual dual kingship are unknown, but both kings ruled together in Sparta and exercised equal powers. Their functions were chiefly religious and military. A Spartan army rarely left home without a king in command.

A council of elders, consisting of twenty-eight men over the age of sixty elected for life, and the kings represented the oligarchic element. These elders had important judicial functions, sitting as a court in cases involving the kings. They also were consulted before any proposal was put before the assembly of Spartan citizens.

The Spartan assembly consisted of all males over thirty. This was thought to be the democratic element in the constitution, but its membership included only a small percentage of the entire population. Theoretically, they were the final authority, but in practice, only magistrates, elders, and kings participated in debate, and voting was usually by acclamation. Therefore, the assembly's real function was to ratify decisions already made or to decide between positions favored by the leading figures. Sparta also had a unique institution, the board of *ephors*. This consisted of five men elected annually by the assembly. Originally, boards of ephors appear to have been intended to check the power of the kings, but gradually they gained other important functions. They controlled foreign policy, oversaw the generalship of the kings on campaign, presided at the assembly, and guarded against rebellions by the Helots.

The whole system was remarkable both for how it combined participation by the citizenry with significant checks on its power and for its unmatched stability. Most Greeks admired the Spartan state for these qualities and also for its ability to mold citizens so thoroughly to an ideal. Many political philosophers, from Plato to modern times, have based utopian schemes on a version of Sparta's constitution and educational system.

2.5.1.3 THE PELOPONNESIAN LEAGUE By about 550 B.C.E., the Spartan system was well established, and its limitations were plain. Suppression of the Helots required all the effort and energy that Sparta had. The Spartans could expand no further, but they could not allow unruly independent neighbors to cause unrest that might inflame the Helots.

When the Spartans defeated Tegea, their northern neighbor, they imposed an unusual peace. Instead of taking away land and subjugating the defeated state, Sparta left the Tegeans their land and their freedom. In exchange, they required the Tegeans to follow the Spartan lead in foreign affairs and to supply a fixed number of soldiers to Sparta on demand. This became the model for Spartan relations with the other states in the Peloponnesus. Soon Sparta was the leader of an alliance that included every Peloponnesian state but Argos; modern scholars have named this alliance the Peloponnesian League. It provided Sparta with security and made it the most powerful polis in Hellenic history. By 500 B.C.E., Sparta and the league had given the Greeks a force capable of facing mighty threats from abroad.

2.5.2 Athens

Athens—located in **Attica**—was slow to come into prominence and to join in the new activities that were changing the more advanced states. The reasons were several: Athens was not situated on the most favored trade routes of the eighth and seventh centuries B.C.E.; its large area (about 1,000 square miles) allowed population growth without great pressure; and the many villages and districts within this territory were not fully united into a single polis until the seventh century B.C.E. (See Map 2–4.)

2.5.2.1 ARISTOCRATIC RULE In the seventh century B.C.E., Athens was a typical aristocratic polis. Its people were divided into four tribes and into several clans and brotherhoods (*phratries*). The aristocrats held the most land and the best land, and dominated religious and political life. There was no written law, and powerful nobles rendered decisions on the basis of tradition and, most likely, self-interest. The **Areopagus**, a council of nobles deriving its name from the hill where it held its sessions, governed the state. Annually the council elected nine magistrates, called *archons*, who joined the Areopagus after their year in office. Because the archons served for only a year, were checked by their colleagues, and looked forward to a lifetime as members of the Areopagus, the aristocratic Areopagus, not the archons, was the true master of the state.

2.5.2.2 PRESSURE FOR CHANGE In the seventh century B.C.E., the peaceful life of Athens was disturbed, in part by quarrels within the nobility and in part by the beginnings of an agrarian crisis. In 632 B.C.E., a nobleman named Cylon

Map 2–4 ATTICA AND VICINITY

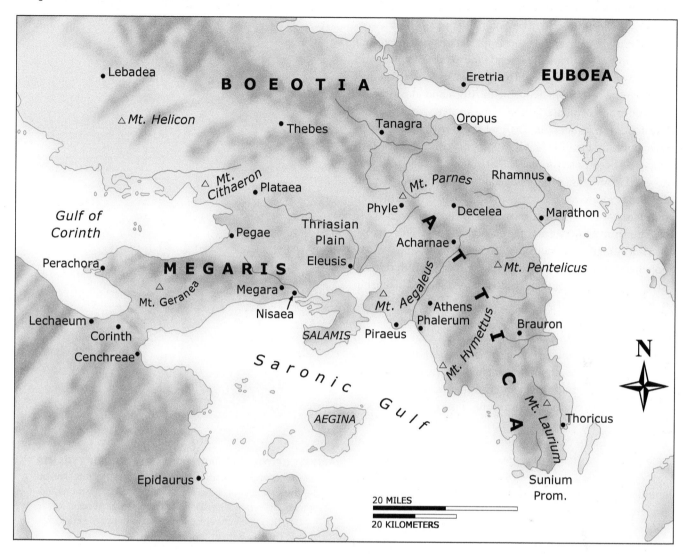

Citizens of all towns in Attica were also citizens of Athens.

attempted a coup to establish himself as tyrant. He was thwarted, but the unrest continued.

In 621 B.C.E., a man named Draco was given special authority to codify and publish laws for the first time. In later years penalties framed by Draco were thought to be harsh—hence the saying that his laws were written in blood. (We still speak of unusually harsh penalties as Draconian.) Draco's work was probably limited to laws concerning homicide and was aimed at ending blood feuds between clans, but it set an important precedent: The publication of laws strengthened the hand of the state against the local power of the nobles.

The root of Athens's troubles was agricultural. Many Athenians worked family farms, from which they obtained most of their living. It appears that they planted wheat, the staple crop, year after year without rotating fields or using enough fertilizer. Shifting to more intensive agricultural techniques and to the planting of fruit and olive trees and grapevines required capital, leading the less successful farmers to acquire excessive debt. To survive, some farmers had

to borrow from wealthy neighbors to get through the year. In return, they promised one-sixth of the next year's crop. The deposit of an inscribed stone on the entailed farms marked the arrangement. As their troubles persisted, debtors had to pledge their wives, their children, and themselves as surety for new loans. Inevitably, many Athenians defaulted and were enslaved. Some were even sold abroad. Revolutionary pressures grew among the poor, who began to demand the abolition of debt and a redistribution of the land.

2.5.2.3 REFORMS OF SOLON In the year 594 B.C.E., as tradition has it, the Athenians elected **Solon** as the only archon with extraordinary powers to legislate and revise the constitution. Immediately, he attacked the agrarian problem by canceling current debts and forbidding future loans secured by the person of the borrower. He helped bring back many Athenians enslaved abroad and freed those in Athens enslaved for debt. This program was called the "shaking off of burdens." It did not, however, solve the fundamental economic problem, and Solon did not redistribute the land.

In the short run, therefore, Solon did not resolve the economic crisis, but his other economic actions had profound success in the long run. He forbade the export of wheat and encouraged that of olive oil. This policy had the initial effect of making wheat more available in Attica and encouraging the cultivation of olive oil (used in the ancient world not only as a food, but as soap and as fuel for lamps) and wine as cash crops. By the fifth century B.C.E., the cultivation of cash crops had become so profitable that much Athenian land was diverted from grain production, and Athens became dependent on imported wheat. Solon also changed the Athenian standards of weights and measures to conform with those of Corinth and Euboea and the cities of the east. This change also encouraged commerce and moved Athens in the direction that would lead it to great prosperity in the fifth century B.C.E. Solon also encouraged industry by offering citizenship to foreign artisans, and the development of the outstanding Attic pottery of the sixth century reflects his success.

Solon also changed the constitution. Citizenship had previously been the privilege of all male adults whose fathers were citizens; to their number he added those immigrants who were tradesmen and merchants. All these Athenian citizens were divided into four classes on the basis of wealth, measured by annual agricultural production. The two highest classes alone could hold the archonship, the chief magistracy in Athens, and sit on the Areopagus.

Men of the third class could serve as hoplites. They could be elected to a council of 400 chosen by all the citizens, one hundred from each tribe. Solon seems to have meant this council to serve as a check on the Areopagus and to prepare business that needed to be put before the traditional assembly of all adult male citizens. The thetes made up the last class. They voted in the assembly for the archons and the council members and on any other business brought before them by the archons and the council. They also sat on a new popular court established by Solon. This new court was recognized as a court of appeal, and by the fifth century B.C.E., almost all cases came before it. In Solon's Athens, as everywhere in the world before the twentieth century, women took no part in the political or judicial process.

2.5.2.4 PISISTRATUS THE TYRANT

Solon's efforts to avoid factional strife failed. Within a few years contention reached such a degree that no archons could be chosen. Out of this turmoil emerged the first Athenian tyranny. **Pisistratus**—a nobleman, leader of a faction, and military hero—briefly seized power in 560 B.C.E. and again in 556 B.C.E., but each time his support was inadequate, and he was driven out. Finally, in 546 B.C.E., he came back at the head of a mercenary army from abroad and established a successful tyranny. It lasted beyond Pisistratus's death, in 527 B.C.E., until the expulsion of his son Hippias in 510 B.C.E.

ARISTOGEITON AND HARMODIUS, SLAYERS OF TYRANTS
Aristogeiton and Harmodius were Athenian aristocrats slain in 514 B.C.E. after assassinating Hipparchus, son of Pisistratus and brother of the tyrant Hippias. After Hippias was overthrown in 510 B.C.E., the Athenians erected a statue to honor the aristocrats' memory. This is a Roman copy.
SOURCE: Scala/Art Resource, NY

In many respects, Pisistratus resembled the other Greek tyrants. His rule rested on the force provided by mercenary soldiers. He engaged in great programs of public works, urban improvement, and religious piety. Temples were built, and religious centers were expanded and improved. Poets and artists were supported to add cultural luster to the court of the tyrant.

Pisistratus sought to increase the power of the central government at the expense of the nobles. The newly introduced festival of the god Dionysus and the improved and expanded Great Panathenaic festival helped fix attention on the capital city, as did the new temples and the reconstruction of the agora as the center of public life. Circuit judges were sent out into the country to hear cases, weakening the power of the local barons. All this time Pisistratus made no formal change in the Solonian constitution. The assembly, councils, and courts met; the magistrates and councils were elected. Pisistratus merely saw to it that his supporters dominated these bodies. The intended effect was to blunt the sharp edge of tyranny with the appearance of a constitutional government, and it worked. The rule of Pisistratus was remembered as popular and mild. The unintended effect was to give the Athenians more experience in the procedures of self-government and a growing taste for it.

2.5.2.5 SPARTAN INTERVENTION Pisistratus was succeeded by his oldest son, Hippias, who followed his father's ways at first. In 514 B.C.E., however, his brother Hipparchus was murdered as a result of a private quarrel. Hippias became nervous, suspicious, and harsh. The Alcmaeonids, one of the noble clans that Hippias and Hipparchus had exiled, won favor with the influential oracle at Delphi and used its support to persuade Sparta to attack the Athenian tyranny. Led by their ambitious king, Cleomenes I, the Spartans marched into Athenian territory in 510 B.C.E. and deposed Hippias, who went into exile to the Persian court. The tyranny was over.

The Spartans must have hoped to leave Athens in friendly hands, and indeed Cleomenes' friend Isagoras, a rival of the Alcmaeonids, held the leading position in Athens after the withdrawal of the Spartan army. Isagoras, however, faced competitors, chief among them **Clisthenes** of the restored Alcmaeonid clan. Clisthenes lost out in the initial political struggle among the noble factions. Isagoras seems then to have tried to restore a version of the pre-Solonian aristocratic state. As part of his plan, he removed from the citizen lists those whom Solon or Pisistratus had added and any others thought to have a doubtful claim.

Clisthenes then took an unprecedented action: He turned to the people for political support and won it with a program of great popular appeal. In response, Isagoras called in the Spartans again. The people refused to tolerate an aristocratic restoration and drove out the Spartans and Isagoras with them. Clisthenes and his allies returned, ready to put their program into effect.

2.5.2.6 CLISTHENES, THE FOUNDER OF DEMOCRACY A central aim of Clisthenes's reforms was to diminish the influence of traditional localities and regions in Athenian life, for these were an important source of power for the nobility and of factions in the state. He immediately restored to citizenship those Athenians who had supported him whom Isagoras had disenfranchised, and he added new citizens to the rolls. In 508 B.C.E., he made the *deme*, the equivalent of a small town in the country or a ward in the city, the basic unit of civic life. The deme was a purely political unit that elected its own officers. The distribution of demes in each tribe guaranteed that no region would dominate any of them. Because the tribes had common religious activities and fought as regimental units, this new organization also increased devotion to the polis and diminished regional divisions and personal loyalty to local barons.

A new council of 500 replaced the Solonian council of 400. The council's main responsibility was to prepare legislation for the assembly to discuss, but it also had important financial duties and received foreign emissaries. Final authority in all things rested with the assembly of all adult male Athenian citizens. Debate in the assembly was free and open; any Athenian could submit legislation, offer amendments, or argue the merits of any question. In practice, political leaders did most of the talking.

It is fair to call Clisthenes the father of Athenian democracy. He did not alter the property qualifications of Solon, but his enlargement of the citizen rolls, his diminution of the power of the aristocrats, and his elevation of the role of the assembly, with its effective and manageable council, all give him a firm claim to that title.

As a result of the work of Solon, Pisistratus, and Clisthenes, Athens entered the fifth century B.C.E. well on the way to prosperity and democracy. It was much more centralized and united than it had been, and it was ready to take its place among the major states that would lead the defense of Greece against the dangers that lay ahead.

2.6 Life in Archaic Greece

What role did religion play in the lives of ordinary Greeks?

Despite the growing presence of the artisan and merchant, the independent farmer citizen soldier made up the heart of the emerging Greek polis in the archaic period. The small farmer's life of toil contrasted with the leisure available to the aristocrat who employed slaves to work his land. The free time that defined the life of the aristocracy allowed the well born to display their virtue and compete for prizes in the symposium and in athletic contests.

Religious worship played a central role in the lives of all citizens of the polis. Religious practices reflected the Greek emphasis on the values of justice and moderation. On the other hand, the poetry of the sixth century displayed a new individualism and the increasing tension between the social classes. The traditional aristocracy of birth lamented its declining status as the small farmers and the commercial class asserted their newfound confidence.

2.6.1 Society

As the Dark Ages ended, the features that would distinguish Greek society thereafter took shape. The artisan and the merchant grew more important as contact with the non-Hellenic world became easier. Most people, however, continued to make their living from the land. Wealthy aristocrats with large estates, powerful households, families, and clans led different lives from those of the poorer countryfolk and the independent farmers who had smaller and less fertile fields.

2.6.1.1 FARMERS Ordinary country people rarely leave a written record of their thoughts or activities, and we

THE WATER BEARERS Greek houses had no running water. The scene painted on this sixth-century B.C.E. hydria—a pot for collecting and carrying water—shows five women taking water home from a fountain.

SOURCE: DEA/G. NIMATALLAH/Getty Images

have no such record from ancient Greece. The poet Hesiod (ca. 700 B.C.E.), however, was certainly no aristocrat. He presented himself as a small farmer, and his *Works and Days* gives some idea of the life of such a farmer. The crops included grain, chiefly barley, but also wheat; grapes for making wine; olives for food and oil; green vegetables, especially the bean; and some fruit. Sheep and goats provided milk and cheese. The Homeric heroes had great herds of cattle and ate lots of meat, but by Hesiod's time land fertile enough to provide fodder for cattle was needed to grow grain. He and small farmers like him tasted meat chiefly from sacrificial animals at festivals.

These farmers worked hard to make a living. Although Hesiod had the help of oxen and mules and one or two hired helpers for occasional labor, his life was one of continuous toil. The hardest work came in October, at the start of the rainy season, the time for the first plowing. The plow was light and easily broken, and the work of forcing the iron tip into the earth was backbreaking, even with the help of a team of oxen. For the less fortunate farmer, the cry of the crane that announced the time of year to plow "bites the heart of the man without oxen." Autumn and winter were the time for cutting wood, building wagons, and making tools. Late winter was the time to tend to the vines, May

Encountering the Past

Marriage in Ancient Athens

AS IN THE REST of the ancient world, Athenian marriages were arranged affairs. Athenian law did not allow women to choose their marriage partners, and this responsibility usually fell to the bride-to-be's male guardian. A variety of considerations went into the selection of marriage partners, but the choice was usually made within a relatively small social circle that included relatives, family friends, and business associates. Marriages between first cousins was common, and unions of uncles and nieces and even between siblings of the same father but of different mothers were considered acceptable. Brides were typically fourteen to sixteen years old, while grooms were usually in their late twenties or early thirties.

MARRIAGE PROCESSION A bride is led to her new home by friends and relatives.

SOURCE: Chronicle/Alamy Stock Photo

The first step towards arranging a marriage was the *engue*. The engue was a verbal contract between the bride's guardian and the groom. The two men agreed on a dowry, and the bride's guardian sealed their bargain with the traditional phrase, "I hand over this woman to you for the ploughing of legitimate children," a reflection of the agricultural nature of Athenian society.

With these formalities out of the way, a series of religious rituals and ceremonies could take place. The bride's father made a sacrifice to the gods. The bride cut off her hair and consecrated a girdle she had worn since puberty as a guarantee of her virginity. She was then given a ritual bath with water from a sacred spring that had been carried to her home in a special vessel called a *loutrophoros*. This same vessel was used to carry water to funerals, and it may be that it's use in bridal baths signified the end of one life and the beginning of another.

Weddings began in the early evening. The bride, her face hidden behind a veil, was carried to her future home in a torch-lit procession, while wedding guests sung special hymns. Once they arrived at their destination, the bride was greeted by her mother-in-law, who took her to the hearth in her new home. The hearth was the symbolic center of an Athenian home and the focal point of female domestic duties. A wedding feast then commenced, where guests ate, drank, and sang and threw nuts and dried fruit, emblems of fertility and prosperity, at the bride and groom. The evening came to an end when the groom led his new wife to the bridal chamber, while the guests once again sang hymns. The following day the couple were presented with gifts for their household, and the marriage ceremony was complete. The bride had been transferred from one male guardian to another, and was ready to take on her new responsibilities of maintaining her husband's household and producing children.

SOURCES: Stephanie Lynn Budin and Jean MacIntosh Turfa, eds., *Women in Antiquity: Real Women Across the Ancient World* (New York: Routledge, 2016); Sue Blundell, *Women in Ancient Greece* (Cambridge: Harvard University Press, 1991).

Questions

1. How were marriages arranged in ancient Athens?
2. What do Athenian marriage customs tell us about the purpose of marriage in ancient Athens?

---

was the time to harvest the grain, July to winnow and store it. Only at the height of summer's heat did Hesiod allow for rest, but when September came, it was time to harvest the grapes. As soon as that task was done the cycle started again.

2.6.1.2 ARISTOCRATS Most aristocrats were rich enough to employ many hired laborers, sometimes sharecroppers, and sometimes even slaves, to work their extensive lands. They could therefore enjoy leisure for other activities. The center of aristocratic social life was the drinking party, or *symposium*. This activity was not a mere drinking bout meant to remove inhibitions and produce oblivion. The Greeks, in fact, almost always mixed their wine with water, and one of the goals of the participants was to drink as much as the others without becoming drunk.

The symposium was a carefully organized occasion, with a "king" chosen to set the order of events and to determine that night's mixture of wine and water. Only men took part; they ate and drank as they reclined on couches along the walls of the room. The sessions began with prayers and libations to the gods. Usually there were games, such as dice or *kottabos*, in which wine was flicked from the cups at different targets. Sometimes dancing girls or flute girls offered entertainment. Frequently the aristocratic participants provided their own amusements with songs, poetry, or even philosophical disputes. Characteristically, these took the form of contests, with a prize for the winner, for aristocratic values continued to emphasize competition and the need to excel, whatever the arena.

This aspect of aristocratic life appears in the athletic contests that became widespread early in the sixth century. The games included running events; the long jump; the discus and javelin throws; the pentathlon, which included

all of these; boxing; wrestling; and the chariot race. Only the rich could afford to raise, train, and race horses, so the chariot race was a special preserve of aristocracy. The nobility also especially favored wrestling, and the *palaestra*, or fields, where they practiced became an important social center for the aristocracy. The contrast between the hard, drab life of the farmers and the leisured and lively one of the aristocrats could hardly have been greater.

2.6.2 Religion

Like most ancient peoples, the Greeks were **polytheists**, and religion played an important part in their lives. Much of Greek art and literature was closely connected with religion, as was the life of the polis in general.

2.6.2.1 OLYMPIAN GODS The Greek pantheon consisted of the twelve gods who lived on Mount Olympus. These were:

- Zeus, the father of the gods
- Hera, his wife

Zeus's siblings:

- Poseidon, his brother, god of the seas and earthquakes
- Hestia, his sister, goddess of the hearth
  Demeter, his sister, goddess of agriculture and marriage

Zeus's children:

- Aphrodite, goddess of love and beauty
- Apollo, god of the sun, music, poetry, and prophecy
- Ares, god of war
- Artemis, goddess of the moon and the hunt

- Athena, goddess of wisdom and the arts
- Hephaestus, god of fire and metallurgy
- Hermes, messenger of the gods, connected with commerce and cunning

These gods were viewed as behaving much like mortals, with all the foibles of humans, except they were superhuman in these as well as in their strength and immortality. In contrast, Zeus, at least, was seen as a source of human justice, and even the Olympians were understood to be subordinate to the Fates. Each polis had one of the Olympians as its guardian deity and worshipped that god in its own special way, but all the gods were Panhellenic. In the eighth and seventh centuries B.C.E., common shrines were established at Olympia for the worship of Zeus, at Delphi for Apollo, at the Isthmus of Corinth for Poseidon, and at Nemea once again for Zeus. Each held athletic contests in honor of its deity, to which all Greeks were invited and for which a sacred truce was declared.

2.6.2.2 IMMORTALITY AND MORALITY Besides the Olympians, the Greeks also worshipped countless lesser deities connected with local shrines. They even worshipped human heroes, real or legendary, who had accomplished great deeds and had earned immortality and divine status. The worship of these deities was not a very emotional experience. It was a matter of offering prayer, libations, and gifts in return for protection and favors from the god during the lifetime of the worshipper. The average human had no hope of immortality, and these devotions involved little moral teaching.

Most Greeks seem to have believed in the commonsense notion that justice lay in paying one's debts. They thought civic virtue consisted of worshipping the state deities in the traditional way, performing required public services, and fighting in defense of the state. To them, private morality meant to do good to one's friends and harm to one's enemies.

2.6.2.3 THE CULT OF DELPHIAN APOLLO In the sixth century B.C.E., the influence of the cult of Apollo at Delphi and of his oracle there became great. Apollo's oracle was the most important of several that helped satisfy the human craving for a clue to the future. The priests of Apollo preached moderation; the two famous sayings identified with Apollo: "Know thyself" and "Nothing in excess" exemplified their advice. Humans needed self-control (*sophrosyneē*). Its opposite was arrogance (*hubris*), brought on by excessive wealth or good fortune. Hubris led to moral blindness and, finally, to divine vengeance. This theme of moderation and the dire consequences of its absence was central to Greek popular morality and appears frequently in Greek literature.

2.6.2.4 THE CULT OF DIONYSUS AND THE ORPHIC CULT The somewhat cold religion of the Olympian gods and of the cult of Apollo did little to assuage human fears or satisfy human hopes and passions. For these needs, the Greeks turned to other deities and rites. Of these deities, the most popular was Dionysus, a god of nature and fertility, of the grapevine, drunkenness, and sexual abandon. In some of his rites, this god was followed by *maenads*, female devotees who cavorted by night, ate raw flesh, and were reputed to tear to pieces any creature they came across.

The Orphic cult, named after its supposed founder, the mythical poet **Orpheus**, provided its followers with more hope than did the worship of the twelve Olympians. Cult followers are thought to have refused to kill animals or eat their flesh and to have believed in the transmigration of souls, which offered the prospect of some form of life after death.

2.6.3 Poetry

The poetry of the sixth century B.C.E. also reflected the great changes sweeping through the Greek world. The lyric style—poetry meant to be sung, either by a chorus or by one person—predominated. Sappho of Lesbos, Anacreon of Teos, and Simonides of Cos composed personal poetry, often relating the pleasure and agony of love. Alcaeus of Mytilene, an aristocrat driven from his city by a tyrant, wrote bitter invective.

Perhaps the most interesting poet of the century from a political point of view was Theognis of Megara. Theognis was the spokesperson for the old, defeated aristocracy of birth. He divided everyone into two classes, the noble and the base; the former were the good, the latter bad. Those nobly born, he wrote, must associate only with others like themselves if

ATTIC CUP FROM LESBOS, WITH SAPPHO AND ALCAEUS This cup from the fifth century B.C.E. shows the two great poets from the island of Lesbos, Sappho (right) and Alcaeus of Mytilene.
SOURCE: INTERFOTO/Alamy Stock Photo

they were to preserve their virtue; if they mingled with the base, they became base. Those born base, however, could never become noble. Only nobles could aspire to virtue and possessed the critical moral and intellectual qualities—respect or honor and judgment. These qualities could not be taught; they were innate. Even so, they had to be carefully guarded against corruption by wealth or by mingling with the base. Intermarriage between the noble and the base was especially condemned. Theognis's ideas were those of the unreconstructed nobility, whose power had been destroyed or reduced in most Greek states by this time. Such ideas remained alive in aristocratic hearts throughout the next century and greatly influenced later thinkers, Plato among them.

2.7 The Persian Wars

What was the significance of the wars between the Greeks and the Persians?

The Greeks' period of fortunate isolation and freedom ended in the sixth century B.C.E. They had established colonies along most of the coast of Asia Minor from as early as the eleventh century B.C.E. The colonies maintained friendly relations with the mainland but developed a flourishing economic and cultural life independent of their mother cities and of their eastern neighbors. In the middle of the sixth century B.C.E., however, these Greek cities of Asia Minor came under the control of Lydia and its king, **Croesus** (r. ca. 560–546 B.C.E.). Lydian rule seems not to have been harsh, but the Persian conquest of Lydia in 546 B.C.E. brought a less pleasant subjugation.

THE GREEK WARS AGAINST PERSIA	
ca. 560–546 B.C.E.	Greek cities of Asia Minor conquered by Croesus of Lydia
546 B.C.E.	Cyrus of Persia conquers Lydia and gains control of Greek cities
499–494 B.C.E.	Greek cities rebel (Ionian rebellion)
490 B.C.E.	Battle of Marathon
480–479 B.C.E.	Xerxes's invasion of Greece
480 B.C.E.	Battles of Thermopylae, Artemisium, and Salamis
479 B.C.E.	Battles of Plataea and Mycale

2.7.1 The Ionian Rebellion

The Ionian Greeks (those living on the central part of the west coast of Asia Minor and nearby islands) had been moving toward democracy and were not pleased to find themselves under the monarchical rule of Persia. That rule, however, was not overly burdensome at first. The Persians required their subjects to pay tribute and to serve in the Persian army. They ruled the Greek cities through local individuals, who governed their cities as "tyrants." Most of the tyrants, however, were not harsh, the Persian tribute was not excessive, and the Greeks enjoyed general prosperity. Neither the death of the Persian king Cyrus the Great fighting on a distant frontier in

530 B.C.E., nor the suicide of his successor Cambyses, nor the civil war that followed it in 522–521 B.C.E. produced any disturbance in the Greek cities. When Darius emerged as Great King in 521 B.C.E., he found **Ionia** perfectly obedient.

The private troubles of the ambitious tyrant of Miletus, Aristagoras, ended this calm. He had urged a Persian expedition against the island of Naxos; when it failed, he feared the consequences and organized the Ionian rebellion of 499 B.C.E. To gain support, Aristagoras overthrew the tyrannies and proclaimed democratic constitutions. Then he turned to the mainland states for help, petitioning first Sparta, the most powerful Greek state. The Spartans, however, would have none of Aristagoras's promises of easy victory and great wealth. They had no close ties with the Ionians and no national interest in the region. Furthermore, the thought of leaving their homeland undefended against the Helots while their army was far off terrified them.

Aristagoras next sought help from the Athenians, who were related to the Ionians and had close ties of religion and tradition with them. Besides, Hippias, the deposed tyrant of Athens, was an honored guest at the court of Darius, who had already made it plain that he favored the tyrant's restoration. The Persians, moreover, controlled both sides of the Hellespont, the route to the grain fields beyond the Black Sea that were increasingly vital to Athens. Perhaps some Athenians already feared that a Persian attempt to conquer the Greek mainland was only a matter of time. The Athenian assembly agreed to send a fleet of twenty ships to help the rebels. The Athenian expedition was strengthened by five ships from Eretria in Euboea, which participated out of gratitude for past favors.

In 498 B.C.E., the Athenians and their allies made a surprise attack on Sardis, the old capital of Lydia and now the seat of the satrap, and burned it. This action caused the revolt to spread throughout the Greek cities of Asia Minor outside Ionia, but the Ionians could not follow it up. The Athenians withdrew and took no further part. Gradually the Persians reimposed their will. In 495 B.C.E., they defeated the Ionian fleet at Lade, and in the next year they wiped out Miletus. The Ionian rebellion was over.

2.7.2 The War in Greece

In 490 B.C.E., the Persians launched an expedition directly across the Aegean to punish Eretria and Athens, to restore Hippias, and to gain control of the Aegean Sea. (See Map 2–5.) They landed their infantry and cavalry forces first at Naxos, destroying it for its successful resistance in 499 B.C.E. Then they destroyed Eretria and deported its people deep into the interior of Persia.

2.7.2.1 BATTLE OF MARATHON Rather than submit and accept the restoration of the hated tyranny of Hippias, the Athenians chose to resist the Persian forces bearing down on them and risk the same fate that had just befallen Eretria. Miltiades, an Athenian who had fled from Persian service,

Map 2–5 THE PERSIAN INVASION OF GREECE

This map traces the route taken by the Persian king Xerxes in his invasion of Greece in 480 B.C.E. The gray arrows show movements of Xerxes's army, the purple arrows show movements of his navy, and the green arrows show movements of the Greek army and navy.

led the city's army to confront the Persians at the **Battle of Marathon**. There some 10,000 Athenians, and their allies from the Plataea, defeated two or three times their number, killing thousands of the enemy while losing only 192 of their own men.

A Persian victory at Marathon would have destroyed Athenian freedom and led to the conquest of all the mainland Greeks. The greatest achievements of Greek culture, most of which lay in the future, would never have occurred. But the Athenians won a decisive victory, instilling them with a sense of confidence and pride in their polis, their unique form of government, and themselves.

2.7.2.2 THE GREAT INVASION Internal troubles prevented the Persians from taking swift revenge for their loss at Marathon. Almost ten years elapsed before Darius's successor, Xerxes, in 481 B.C.E., gathered an army of at least 150,000 men and a navy of more than 600 ships to conquer Greece. In Athens, Themistocles, who favored making Athens into a naval power, had become the leading politician. During his archonship in 493 B.C.E., Athens had already built a fortified port at Piraeus. A decade later, the Athenians came upon a rich vein of silver in the state mines, and Themistocles persuaded them to use the profits to increase their fleet. By 480 B.C.E., Athens had more than 200 ships, the backbone of a navy that was to defeat the Persians. The key to their naval supremacy, their dominant warship, the trireme, can be examined in detail in the "Closer Look" sidebar, which follows below.

A Closer Look

The Trireme

THE GREEKS OF the Classical Period owed their prosperity and their freedom to the control of the seas that surrounded their lands. Without the navies that defeated the Persian invaders in 480/479 B.C.E., their cities would have been conquered and their distinctive civilization smothered before it had reached its peak. The trireme was the combat vessel that dominated naval warfare in the Mediterranean in the fifth and fourth centuries B.C.E. The naval battles of the Persian Wars and the Peloponnesian War were fought between fleets of triremes—light, fast, and maneuverable ships powered by oars. During combat operations, a ship's complement of spearmen and bowmen carried out boarding actions or could be landed to fight on shore. This is a picture of the *Olympias*, a modern reconstruction of an ancient trireme commissioned by the Greek navy.

The trireme was propelled by rowers, usually free citizens of the lower classes, in three tiers along each side of the vessel: thirty-one in the top tier, twenty-seven in the middle, and twenty-seven in the bottom.

The mast supported a sail that could help propel the ship when the wind was favorable. During battle, however, the mast was taken down, and the trireme maneuvered by oars alone.

The principal armament of the trireme was a bronze-clad ram, which extended from the keel at or below the waterline and was designed to pierce the light hulls of enemy warships.

A trireme was about 120 feet long and 18 feet wide, with a hull that was made of a thin shell of planks joined edge-to-edge and then stiffened by a keel and light transverse ribs.

TRIREME CREW AND EQUIPMENT
SOURCE: AAAC/Topham/The Image Works

Questions

1. What advantages do you think the trireme had over other kinds of warships? What disadvantages?
2. What is the significance, military and political, of having these ships rowed by free citizens?

Of the hundreds of Greek states, only thirty-one—led by Sparta, Athens, Corinth, and Aegina—were willing to fight as the Persian army gathered south of the Hellespont. In the spring of 480 B.C.E., Xerxes launched his invasion. The Persian strategy was to march into Greece, destroy Athens, defeat the Greek army, and add the Greeks to the number of Persian subjects. The huge Persian army needed to keep in touch with the fleet for supplies. If the Greeks could defeat the Persian navy, the army could not remain in Greece long. Themistocles knew that the Aegean Sea was subject to sudden devastating storms. His strategy was to delay the Persian army and then to bring on the kind of naval battle he might hope to win. (See the "Compare and Connect" sidebar on the Greek strategy, which follows below.)

Severe storms wrecked many Persian ships while the Greek fleet waited safely in a protected harbor. Then Xerxes attacked Thermopylae, and for two days the Greeks butchered his best troops without serious loss to themselves. On the third day, however, a traitor showed the Persians a mountain trail that permitted them to attack the Greeks from behind. Many allies escaped, but Leonidas and his 300 Spartans all died fighting. At about the same time, the Greek

Compare and Connect

Greek Strategy in the Persian War

IN THE SUMMER of 480 B.C.E., Xerxes, king of Persia, led an enormous invading army into Greece. During the previous year, those Greeks who meant to resist met to plan a defense. After abandoning an attempt to make a stand at Tempe in Thessaly,

they fell back to central Greece, at Thermopylae on land and Artemisium at sea. Herodotus is our main source, and his account of Greek military strategy is not clear. How did the Greeks hope to defeat the Persians? Did they hope to halt the Persians at Thermopylae, or was the plan to force a sea battle at Artemisium? Were both the army and the fleet intended only to fight holding actions until the Athenians fled to Salamis and the Peloponnesus? Scholars have long argued these questions, which have been sharpened by the discovery of the "Themistocles Decree," an inscription from the third century B.C.E. that purports to be an Athenian decree passed in 480 B.C.E. before the Battle of Artemisium. The authenticity of the decree is still in question, but if it reflects a reliable tradition, it must influence our view in important ways.

ATTACK ON PERSIAN SOLDIER BY GREEK HOPLITE The contrast between the Greek's metal body armor, large shield, and long spear and the Persian's cloth and leather garments indicates one reason the Greeks won. This Attic vase was found on Rhodes and dates from ca. 475 B.C.E. Greece.
SOURCE: The Metropolitan Museum of Art/Image source/Art Resource, NY

Before Reading

- Examine why, according to Herodotus, the situation become so critical in Athens after the defeat at Thermopylae.
- Think about why families were removed from Athens so hastily.

Questions

1. In Herodotus's account, what was the state of Athenian preparation for war?
2. What does this account reveal about the original Greek strategy for the war?
3. Was the "Themistocles Decree" passed before or after the battle at Thermopylae? What light does this decree shed on Greek military strategy?
4. How do the two documents compare? Are they compatible with each other?

I. THE ACCOUNT OF HERODOTUS

In this passage, Herodotus describes Athens after the Greek defeat at Thermopylae.

Meanwhile, the Grecian fleet, which had left Artemisium, proceeded to Salamis, at the request of the Athenians, and there cast anchor. The Athenians had begged them to take up this position, in order that they might convey their women and children out of Attica, and further might deliberate upon the course which it now behooved them to follow. Disappointed in the hopes which they had previously entertained, they were about to hold a council concerning the present posture of their affairs. For they had looked to see the Peloponnesians drawn up in full force to resist the enemy in Boeotia, but found nothing of what they had expected; nay, they learnt that the Greeks of those parts, only concerning themselves about their own safety, were building a wall across the Isthmus, and intended to guard the Peloponnese, and let the rest of Greece take its chance. These tidings caused them to make the request whereof I spoke, that the combined fleet should anchor at Salamis.

So while the rest of the fleet lay off this island, the Athenians cast anchor along their own coast. Immediately upon their arrival, proclamation was made, that every Athenian should save his children and household as he best could; whereupon some sent their families to Aegina, some to Salamis, but the greater number to Troezen. This removal was made with all possible haste, partly from a desire to obey the advice of the oracle, but still more for another reason. The Athenians say they have in their acropolis a huge serpent which lives in the temple, and is the guardian of the whole place. Nor do they only say this, but, as if the serpent really dwelt there, every month they lay out its food, which consists of a honey-cake. Up to this time the honey-cake had always been consumed; but now it lay untouched. So the priestess told the people what had happened; whereupon they left Athens the more readily, since they believed that the goddess had abandoned the citadel.

II. THE "THEMISTOCLES DECREE"

Remember, scholars question the authenticity of the "Themistocles Decree."

By the Council and the People

Themistocles, son of Neokles, of Phrearroi, made the motion:

To entrust the city to Athena the Mistress of Athens and to all the other Gods to guard and defend from the Barbarian for the sake of the land. The Athenians themselves and the foreigners who live in Athens are to send their children and women to safety in Troizen, their protector being Pittheus, the founding hero of the land. They are to send the old men and their movable possessions to safety on Salamis. The treasurers and priestesses are to remain on the acropolis guarding the property of the gods.

All the other Athenians and foreigners of military age are to embark on the 200 ships that are ready and defend against the Barbarian for the sake of their own freedom and that of the rest of the Greeks along with the Lakedaimonians, the Korinthians, the Aiginetans, and all others who wish to share the danger.

The generals are to appoint, starting tomorrow, 200 trierarchs [captains], one to a ship, from among those who have land and house in Athens and legitimate children and who are not older than fifty; to these men the ships are to be assigned by lot. They are to enlist marines, 10 to each ship, from men between the ages of twenty and thirty, and four archers. They are to distribute the servicemen [the marines and archers] by lot at the same time as they assign the trierarchs to the ships by lot. The generals are to write up the rest ship by ship on white boards, (taking) the Athenians from the lexiarchic registers, the foreigners from those registered with the polemarch. They are to write them up assigning them by divisions, 200 of about one hundred (men) each, and to write above each division the name of the trireme and of the trierarch and the servicemen, so that they may know on which trireme each division is to embark. When all the divisions have been composed and allotted to the triremes, the Council and the generals are to man all the 200 ships, after sacrificing a placatory offering to Zeus the Almighty and Athena and Nike and Poseidon the Securer.

When the ships have been manned, with 100 of them they are to meet the enemy at Artemision in Euboia, and with the other 100 they are to lie off Salamis and the coast of Attica and keep guard over the land. In order that all Athenians may be united in their defense against the Barbarian those who have been sent into exile for ten years are to go to Salamis and to stay there until the People come to some decision about them, while those who have been deprived of citizen rights are to have their rights restored. . . .

The Greek League, founded specifically to resist this Persian invasion, met at Corinth as the Persians were ready to cross the Hellespont. They chose Sparta as leader and first confronted the Persians at Thermopylae, the "hot gates," on land and off Artemisium at sea. The opening between the mountains and the sea at Thermopylae was so narrow that a small army could hold it against a much larger one. The Spartans sent their king, Leonidas, with 300 of their own citizens and enough allies to make a total of about 9,000.

SOURCES: (I) From Herodotus, *Histories* 8.40.41, trans. by George Rawlinson. (II) From "Waiting for the Barbarian," *Greece and Rome*, second series, trans. by Michael H. Jameson (Oxford, UK: Oxford University Press, 1961), pp. 5–18. By permission of the Oxford University Press.

and Persian fleets fought an indecisive battle at Artemisium. The fall of Thermopylae, however, forced the Greek navy to withdraw.

After Thermopylae, the Persian army moved into Attica and burned Athens. If an inscription discovered in 1959 is authentic, Themistocles had foreseen this possibility before the fall of Thermopylae, and the Athenians had begun to evacuate their homeland before they sent their fleet north to fight at Artemisium.

2.7.2.3 DEFEATING THE PERSIANS The **Battle of Salamis**, a sea battle in the narrow waters to the east of the island of Salamis, to which the Greek fleet withdrew after the battle at Artemisium, decided the fate of Greece. The Peloponnesians were reluctant to confront the Persian fleet at this spot, but Themistocles persuaded them to stay by threatening to resettle all the Athenians in Italy. The Spartans knew that they and the other Greeks could not hope to win without the aid of the Athenians. Because Greek ships were fewer, slower, and less maneuverable than those of the Persians, the Greeks put soldiers on their ships and relied chiefly on hand-to-hand combat. In the ensuing battle, the Persians lost more than one-half of their ships and retreated to Asia with a good part of their army, but the danger was not over yet.

The Persian general Mardonius spent the winter in central Greece, and in the spring, he unsuccessfully tried to win the Athenians away from the Greek League. The Spartan regent, Pausanias, then led the largest Greek army up to that time to confront Mardonius in Boeotia. At Plataea, in the summer of 479 B.C.E., the Persians suffered a decisive defeat. Mardonius died in battle, and his army fled.

Meanwhile, the Ionian Greeks urged King Leotychidas, the Spartan commander of the fleet, to fight the Persian fleet. At Mycale, on the coast of Samos, Leotychidas destroyed the Persian camp and its fleet. The Persians fled the Aegean and Ionia. For the moment, at least, the Persian threat was gone.

The Chapter in Perspective

Hellenic civilization, that unique cultural experience at the root of Western civilization, has powerfully influenced the peoples of the modern world. It was itself influenced by the great Bronze Age Minoan civilization of Crete and emerged from the collapse of the Bronze Age civilization on the Greek mainland called Mycenaean. These earlier Aegean civilizations more closely resembled other early civilizations in Egypt, Mesopotamia, Syria-Palestine, and elsewhere than the Hellenic civilization that sprang from them. They had highly developed cities; a system of writing; a strong, centralized monarchical government with tightly organized, large bureaucracies; hierarchical social systems; professional standing armies; and a regular system of taxation to support it all. To a greater or lesser degree, these early civilizations tended toward cultural stability—changing little over time—and uniformity, all sharing many structural features. The striking thing about the emergence of the Hellenic civilization is its sharp departure from this pattern.

The collapse of the Mycenaean world produced a harsh material and cultural decline for the Greeks. Small farm villages replaced cities. Trade all but ended, and communication among the Greeks themselves, and between them and other peoples was sharply curtailed. The art of writing was lost for more than three centuries. During this "Dark Age," the rest of the world ignored the Greeks—poor, few in number, isolated, and illiterate—and left them alone to develop their own society and the matrix of Hellenic civilization.

During the three-and-a-half centuries from about 1100 to 750 B.C.E., the Greeks set the foundations for their great achievements. The crucial unit in the new Greek way of life was the polis, the Hellenic city-state. There were hundreds of them, and each evoked a kind of loyalty and attachment by its citizens that made the idea of dissolving one's own polis into a larger unit unthinkable. The result was a dynamic, many-faceted, competitive, sometimes chaotic world in which rivalry for excellence and victory had the highest value. This agonistic, or competitive, quality marks Greek life throughout its history. Its negative aspect was constant warfare among the states. Its positive side was an extraordinary achievement in literature and art; competition, sometimes formal and organized, spurred on poets and artists.

Kings had been swept away with the Mycenaean world, and the poleis were republics. Since the Greeks were so poor, the differences in wealth among them were relatively small. Therefore, class distinctions were less marked and important than in other civilizations. The introduction of a new mode of fighting, the hoplite phalanx, had further leveling effects, for it placed the safety of the state in the hands of the average farmer. Armies were made up of citizen-soldiers, who were not paid and who returned to their farms after a campaign. As a result, a relatively large portion of the people shared political control, and participation in political life was highly valued. There was no bureaucracy, for there were no kings and not much economic surplus to support bureaucrats. Most states imposed no regular taxation. There was no separate caste of priests and little concern with life after death. In this varied, dynamic, secular, and remarkably free context, speculative natural philosophy developed based on observation and reason, the root of modern natural science and philosophy.

Contact with the rest of the world increased trade and wealth and brought in valuable new information and ideas. Egyptian and Near Eastern models that were always adapted and changed, rather than copied, powerfully shaped Greek art. Changes often produced social and economic strain, leading to the overthrow of traditional aristocratic regimes by tyrants. But monarchic rule was anathema to the Greeks, and these regimes were temporary. In Athens, the destruction of tyranny brought the world's first democracy. Sparta, in contrast, developed a uniquely stable government that avoided tyranny and impressed the other Greeks.

The Greeks' time of independent development, untroubled by external forces, ended in the sixth century, when Persia conquered the Greek cities of Asia Minor. When the Persian kings tried to conquer the Greek mainland, however, the leading states managed to put their quarrels aside and unite against the common enemy. Their determination to preserve their freedom carried them to victory against tremendous odds.

The Chapter in Review

Review Questions

1. How did the later Bronze Age Mycenaean civilization differ from the Minoan civilization of Crete in political organization, art motifs, and military posture?
2. What are the most important historical sources for the Minoan and Mycenaean civilizations? Is it Linear B, and if so, what problems does it raise for the reconstruction of Bronze Age history? How valuable are the Homeric epics as sources of early Greek history?
3. What were the fundamental political, social, and economic institutions of Athens and Sparta in about 500 B.C.E.? Why did Sparta develop its unique form of government?
4. What were the main stages in the transformation of Athens from an aristocratic state to a democracy between 600 and 500 B.C.E.? In what ways did Draco, Solon, Pisistratus, and Clisthenes each contribute to the process?
5. Why did the Greeks and Persians go to war in 490 and 480 B.C.E.? Why did the Persians want to conquer Greece? Why were the Greeks able to defeat the Persians, and how did they benefit from the victory?

Key Terms

Acropolis (ACK-row-po-lis) The religious and civic center of Athens. It is the site of the Parthenon.

agora **(AG-o-rah)** The Greek marketplace and civic center. It was the heart of the social life of the polis.

Areopagus The governing council of Athens, originally open only to the nobility. Named after the hill on which it met.

arete **(AH-ray-tay)** Manliness, courage, and the excellence appropriate to a hero. Was considered the highest virtue of Homeric society.

Attica The region of Greece where Athens is located.

Battle of Marathon A critical victory of the Athenians and the Plataeans over the forces of Persia in 490 B.C.E.

Battle of Salamis The naval contest in the narrow waters to the east of the island of Salamis that decided the fate of the victorious Greeks in 480 B.C.E.

Clisthenes The father of Athenian democracy who in 508 B.C.E. made the deme the basic unit of civic life and established the council of 500.

Croesus The king of Lydia (r. ca. 560–546 B.C.E.) who subjected the Greek cities of Asia Minor under his rule.

deme **(DEEM)** A small town in Attica or a ward in Athens that became the basic unit of Athenian civic life under the democratic reforms of Clisthenes in 508 B.C.E.

Dorian invasion A group of Greek speakers that the Greeks themselves believed to have attacked the southern peninsula of the Peloponnesus at the end of the Bronze Age.

Helots (HELL-ots) Hereditary Spartan serfs.

hoplite **phalanx (FAY-lanks)** The basic unit of Greek warfare in which infantrymen fought in close order, shield to shield, usually eight ranks deep that perfectly suited the farmer-soldier-citizen who was the backbone of the polis.

hubris **(WHO-bris)** Arrogance brought on by excessive wealth or good fortune. Believed by the Greeks to lead to moral blindness and divine vengeance.

Iliad and the *Odyssey* **(ILL-ee-ad) (O-dis-see)** Epic poems by Homer about the "Dark Age" heroes of Greece who fought at Troy, and written down in the eighth century B.C.E. after centuries of being sung by bards.

Ionia (I-o-knee-a) The part of western Asia Minor heavily colonized by the Greeks.

Magna Graecia The area of southern Italy and eastern Sicily colonized by the Greeks starting in the eighth century and named "Great Greece" by the Romans.

Minoan (MIN-o-an) The Bronze Age civilization that arose in Crete in the third and second millennia B.C.E.

Mycenaean (MY-cen-a-an) The Bronze Age civilization of mainland Greece that was centered at Mycenae.

Orpheus The mythical poet and founder of the Orphic cult that believed in the transmigration of souls and life after death.

Panhellenic (PAN-hell-en-ick) Meaning "all-Greek." The sense of cultural identity that all Greeks felt in common with one another.

Peloponnesus (PELL-o-po-knee-sus) The southern peninsula of Greece where Sparta was located.

Pisistratus The first tyrant in Athens (r. 546–527 B.C.E.) whose popular and mild rule lead to a golden age for the polis.

polis **(PO-lis)** (plural, poleis) The basic Greek political unit. Usually, but incompletely, translated as "city-state." Thought of by the Greeks as a community of citizens theoretically descended from a common ancestor.

polytheists (PAH-lee-thee-ists) Those who worship many gods.

Solon The great statesman and lawgiver elected sole archon in Athens in 594 B.C.E. to reform the constitution.

symposium **(SIM-po-see-um)** The carefully organized drinking party that was the center of Greek aristocratic social life and featured games, songs, poetry, and even philosophical disputation.

tholos A large beehive-like chamber built of enormous well-cut and fitted stones and used as a burial chamber for kings in Late Bronze Age Mycenae.

Notes

1. Plato, *Epinomis* 987 d.
2. Homer, *Odyssey* 24.199–202, trans. by Richmond Lattimore (Chicago: University of Chicago Press, 1965).
3. Homer, *Odyssey* 6.181–185, in *Ancient Greece*, trans. by M. Dillon and L. Garland (London: Routledge, 2000).

Chapter 3
Classical and Hellenistic Greece

WINGED VICTORY OF SAMOTHRACE One of the great masterpieces of Hellenistic sculpture, the *Winged Victory of Samothrace* appears to be the work of the Rhodian sculptor Pythokritos, ca. 200 B.C.E. The statue stood in the sanctuary of the Great Gods on the Aegean island of Samothrace on a base made in the shape of a ship's prow. The goddess is seen landing on the ship to crown its victorious commander and crew.
SOURCE: Erich Lessing/Art Resource, Inc

⌄ Contents and Focus Questions

The Chapter in Brief

THE GREEKS' REMARKABLE victory over the Persians
in 480–479 B.C.E. won them another period of freedom
and autonomy. They used this time to carry their political and cultural achievement to its height. In Athens,
especially, it produced a great sense of confidence and
ambition.

Spartan withdrawal from active leadership against the
Persians left a vacuum that was filled by the Delian League,
which soon turned into the Athenian Empire. At the same
time as it tightened its hold over the Greek cities in and
around the Aegean Sea, Athens developed an extraordinarily democratic constitution at home. Fears and jealousies
of this new kind of state and empire created a split in the
Greek world that led to major wars impoverishing Greece
and leaving it vulnerable to conquest. In 338 B.C.E., Philip
of Macedon conquered the Greek states, putting an end to
the age of the polis.

3.1 The Aftermath of Victory

What led to the formation of the Delian League?

The unity of the Greeks had weakened even in the life-
and-death struggle against the Persians. Within two years
of the Persian retreat, it gave way almost completely, leading to a division of the Greek world into two spheres of
influence, dominated by Sparta and Athens. The Ionian
Greeks' need to obtain and defend their freedom from
Persia and the desire of many Greeks to gain revenge and
financial reparation for the Persian attack brought on the
split. (See Map 3–1.)

3.1.1 The Delian League

Sparta had led the Greeks to victory, and it was natural
to look to the Spartans to continue the campaign against
Persia. But Sparta was ill-suited to the task, which required
both a long-term commitment far from the Peloponnesus
and continuous naval action.

Athens had become the leading naval power in Greece,
and the same motives that led the Athenians to support the
Ionian revolt prompted them to try to drive the Persians from
the Aegean and the Hellespont. The Ionians were at least as
eager for the Athenians to take the helm as the Athenians
were to accept the responsibility and opportunity.

In the winter of 478–477 B.C.E., the islanders and the
Greeks from the coast of Asia Minor and other Greek cities
on the Aegean met with the Athenians on the sacred island
of Delos and swore oaths of alliance. The aims of this new
Delian League were to free those Greeks who were under Persian rule, to protect all against a Persian return, and to obtain
compensation from the Persians by attacking their lands and
taking booty. An assembly in which each state, including Athens, had one vote was supposed to determine league policy.
Athens, however, was clearly designated the leader.

From the first, the league was remarkably successful.
The Persians were driven from Europe and the Hellespont,
and the Aegean was cleared of pirates. Some states were
forced into the league or were prevented from leaving.
The members approved coercion because it was necessary
for the common safety. In 467 B.C.E., a great victory at the
Eurymedon River in Asia Minor routed the Persians and
added several cities to the league.

3.1.2 The Rise of Cimon

Cimon, son of Miltiades, hero of the Battle of Marathon,
became the leading Athenian soldier and statesman soon
after the war with Persia. A coalition of his enemies drove
Themistocles from power. Ironically, the leader of the Greek
victory over Persia of 480 B.C.E. was exiled and ended his
days at the court of the Persian king. Cimon, who was to
dominate Athenian politics for almost two decades, pursued a policy of aggressive attacks on Persia and friendly
relations with Sparta. In domestic affairs Cimon was
conservative. He accepted the democratic constitution
of Clisthenes, which appears to have become somewhat
more limited after the Persian War. Defending this constitution and his interventionist foreign policy, Cimon led the
Athenians and the Delian League to victory after victory,
and his own popularity grew with his successes.

Map 3–1 CLASSICAL GREECE

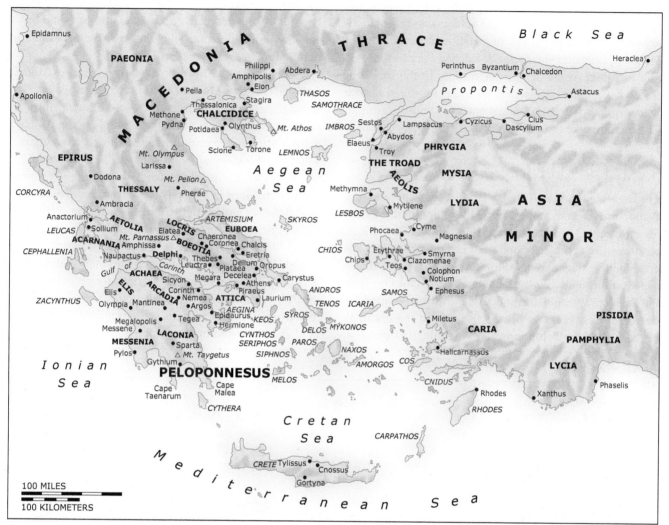

Greece in the Classical period (ca. 480–338 B.C.E.) centered on the Aegean Sea. Although there were important Greek settlements in Italy, Sicily, and all around the Black Sea, the area shown in this general reference map embraced the vast majority of Greek states.

3.2 The First Peloponnesian War: Athens Against Sparta

What was the cause of the Peloponnesian War, and what was the end result?

In 465 B.C.E., the island of Thasos rebelled against the Delian League, and Cimon put it down after a siege of more than two years. The Thasian revolt is the first recorded instance in which Athenian interests alone seemed to determine league policy, a significant step in the league's evolution into the Athenian Empire.

When Cimon returned to Athens from Thasos, he was charged with taking bribes for having refrained from conquering Macedonia, although conquering Macedonia had not been part of his assignment. He was acquitted; the trial was only a device by which his political opponents tried to reduce his influence. Their program at home was to undo

the gains made by the Areopagus and bring about further democratic changes. In foreign policy, Cimon's enemies wanted to break with Sparta and contest its claim to leadership over the Greeks. They intended at least to establish the independence of Athens and its alliance. The head of this faction was Ephialtes. His supporter, and the person chosen to be the public prosecutor of Cimon, was Pericles, a member of a distinguished Athenian family. He was still young, and his defeat in court did not do lasting damage to his career.

3.2.1 The Breach with Sparta

When the Thasians began their rebellion, they asked Sparta to invade Athens the next spring, and the *ephors*, the annual magistrates responsible for Sparta's foreign policy, agreed. An earthquake, however, accompanied by a rebellion of the Helots that threatened the survival of Sparta, prevented the invasion. The Spartans asked their allies, the Athenians among them, for help, and Cimon persuaded the Athenians to send it. This policy was disastrous for Cimon and his faction.

While Cimon was in the Peloponnesus helping the Spartans, Ephialtes stripped the Areopagus of almost all its power. The Spartans, meanwhile, fearing "the boldness and revolutionary spirit of the Athenians," ultimately sent them home. In 462 B.C.E., Ephialtes was assassinated, and Pericles replaced him as leader of the democratic faction. In the spring of 461 B.C.E., Cimon was ostracized, and Athens made an alliance with Argos, Sparta's traditional enemy. Almost overnight, Cimon's domestic and foreign policies had been overturned.

3.2.2 The Division of Greece

The new regime at Athens, led by Pericles and the democratic faction, was confident and ambitious. When Megara, getting the worst of a border dispute with Corinth, withdrew from the Peloponnesian League, the Athenians accepted the Megarians as allies. This alliance gave Athens a great strategic advantage, for Megara barred the way from the Peloponnesus to Athens. Sparta, however, resented the defection of Megara to Athens, leading to the outbreak of the first of the **Peloponnesian Wars**, the first phase in a protracted struggle between Athens and Sparta, with the Athenians conquering Aegina and gaining control of Boeotia. At this moment Athens was supreme and apparently invulnerable, controlling the states on its borders and dominating the sea. (See Map 3–2.)

About 455 B.C.E., however, the tide turned. An Athenian fleet that had gone to aid an Egyptian rebellion against Persia met a disastrous defeat. The great loss of men, ships, and prestige caused rebellions in the empire, forcing Athens to make a truce in Greece to subdue its allies in the Aegean. In 449 B.C.E., the Athenians ended the war against Persia.

In 446 B.C.E., the war on the Greek mainland broke out again. Rebellions in Boeotia and Megara removed Athens' land defenses and brought a Spartan invasion. Rather than fight, Pericles, the commander of the Athenian army, agreed to the **Thirty Years' Peace** by the terms of which he abandoned all Athenian possessions on the Greek mainland outside of Attica. In return, the Spartans formally recognized the Athenian Empire. From then on, Greece was divided into two power blocs: Sparta with its alliance on the mainland and Athens ruling its empire in the Aegean.

Map 3–2 THE ATHENIAN EMPIRE ABOUT 450 B.C.E.

The Athenian Empire at its fullest extent shortly before 450 B.C.E. Shown here are Athens and the independent states that provided manned ships for the imperial fleet but paid no tribute; dependent states that paid tribute; and states allied to, but not actually in, the empire.

THE PARTHENON Construction of the Parthenon began in 447 B.C.E., when the Athenian Empire was at its peak, and took fifteen years to complete. A symbol of Athens' imperial power, the Parthenon also exemplifies classical Greek architecture.

SOURCE: funkyfood London - Paul Williams/Alamy Stock Photo

3.3 Classical Greece

How did democracy work in fifth-century B.C.E. Athens?

The transition from alliance to empire and the expansion of the democracy were two of the main changes of the fifth century B.C.E. in Athens. Both developments point to the rise of the landless poor who rowed the ships of the league fleet as a political force and the decisive influence of Pericles. Athenian culture reached its zenith during this period. However, the outright tyrannical rule of Athens created resentment not only among its subject states. The growing power of the Athenians also inspired fear and suspicion at Sparta and among her allies.

KEY EVENTS IN ATHENIAN HISTORY BETWEEN THE PERSIAN WAR AND THE GREAT PELOPONNESIAN WAR	
478–477 B.C.E.	Delian League founded
ca. 474–462 B.C.E.	Cimon becomes leading politician
467 B.C.E.	Victory over Persians at Eurymedon River
465–463 B.C.E.	Rebellion of Thasos
462 B.C.E.	Ephialtes murdered; Pericles rises to leadership
461 B.C.E.	Cimon ostracized
461 B.C.E.	Reform of Areopagus
ca. 460 B.C.E.	First Peloponnesian War begins
454 B.C.E.	Athens defeated in Egypt; crisis in the Delian League
449 B.C.E.	Peace with Persia
445 B.C.E.	Thirty Years' Peace ends First Peloponnesian War

3.3.1 The Athenian Empire

After the Egyptian disaster, the Athenians moved the Delian League's treasury to Athens and began to keep one-sixtieth

of the annual revenues for themselves. Because of the peace with Persia, there seemed no further reason for the allies to pay tribute, so the Athenians were compelled to find a new justification for their empire. They called for a Panhellenic congress to meet at Athens to discuss rebuilding the temples the Persians had destroyed and to consider how to maintain freedom of the seas. When Sparta's reluctance to participate prevented the congress, Athens felt free to continue to collect funds from the allies, both to maintain its navy and to rebuild the Athenian temples. Athenian propaganda suggested that henceforth the allies would be treated as colonies and Athens as their mother city, held together by good feeling and common religious observances.

There is little reason, however, to believe the allies were taken in or were truly content with their lot. Nothing could cloak the fact that Athens was becoming the master and its allies mere subjects. By 445 B.C.E., when the Thirty Years' Peace gave formal recognition to an Athenian Empire, only Chios, Lesbos, and Samos were autonomous and provided ships. All the other states paid tribute. The change from alliance to empire came about because of the pressure of war and rebellion and largely because the allies were unwilling to see to their own defense. Although the empire had many friends among the lower classes and the democratic politicians in the subject cities, it was seen more and more as a tyranny. Athenian prosperity and security, however, had come to depend on the empire, and the Athenians were determined to defend it.

3.3.2 Athenian Democracy

Even as the Athenians were tightening their control over their empire, they were expanding democracy at home. Under the leadership of Pericles, they evolved the freest government the world had yet seen.

3.3.2.1 DEMOCRATIC LEGISLATION Legislation was passed making the hoplite class eligible for the archonship, and, in practice, no one was thereafter prevented from serving in this office on the basis of property class. Pericles himself proposed a law introducing pay for jury members, opening that important duty to the poor. Circuit judges were reintroduced, a policy making swift impartial justice available even to the poorest residents in the countryside.

Finally, Pericles himself introduced a bill limiting citizenship to those who had two citizen parents. Democracy was

ATHENIAN TETRADRACHM An Athenian four-drachma silver coin (*tetradrachm*) from the fifth century B.C.E. (440–430 B.C.E.). On the front (left) is the profile of Athena and on the back (right) is her symbol of wisdom, the owl. The silver from which the coins were struck came chiefly from the state mines at Sunium in southern Attica.
SOURCE: INTERFOTO/Alamy Stock Photo, Eddie Gerald/Alamy Stock Photo

defined as the privilege of those who held citizenship, making citizenship a valuable commodity. Limiting it increased its value. Women, resident aliens, and slaves were also denied participation in government in all the Greek states.

3.3.2.2 HOW DID THE DEMOCRACY WORK? Within the citizen body, the extent of Athenian democracy was remarkable. The popular assembly—a collection of the people, not their representatives—had to approve every decision of the state. Every judicial decision was subject to appeal to a popular court of not fewer than 51 and as many as 1,501 citizens, chosen from an annual panel of jurors widely representative of the Athenian population. (See the "Encountering the Past" sidebar about going to court in Athens, which follows below.) Most officials were selected by lot without regard to class. The main elected officials, such as the ten generals (the generalship was an office that had both political and military significance) and the imperial treasurers, were usually nobles and almost always rich men, but the people were free to choose otherwise. All public officials were subject to scrutiny before taking office and could be called to account or to be removed from office during their tenure. They were subject to compulsory examination and accounting at the end of their term. There was no standing army; no police force, open or secret; and no way to coerce the people.

Pericles was elected to the generalship fifteen years in a row and thirty times in all, not because he was a dictator, but because he was a persuasive speaker, a skillful politician, a respected military leader, an acknowledged patriot, and patently incorruptible. When he lost the people's

confidence, they did not hesitate to depose him from office. In 443 B.C.E., however, he stood at the height of his power. The defeat of the Athenian fleet in the Egyptian campaign and the failure of Athens' continental campaigns had persuaded Pericles to favor a conservative policy, seeking to retain the empire in the Aegean and live at peace with the Spartans. It was in this direction that Pericles led Athens' imperial democracy in the years after the First Peloponnesian War. (See the "Compare and Connect" sidebar, which follows below, on the pros and cons of Athenian democracy.)

3.3.3 The Women of Athens: Legal Status and Everyday Life

Men dominated Greek society, as in most other societies all over the world throughout history. This was true of the democratic city of Athens in the great days of Pericles in the fifth century B.C.E., no less than of any other Greek city. The actual position of women in classical Athens, however, has been the subject of much controversy.

The bulk of the evidence—coming from the law, from philosophical and moral writings, and from information about the conditions of daily life and the organization of society—shows that women were excluded from most aspects of public life. They could not vote, could not take part in politics or join political assemblies, and could not hold public office. Since Athens was one of the few places in the ancient world where male citizens of all classes had these public responsibilities and opportunities, the exclusion of women was even more significant.

Encountering the Past

Going to Court in Athens

THE ATHENIANS PLACED the administration of justice directly in the hands of their fellow citizens, including the poorest ones. Each year 6,000 Athenian males, between one-quarter and one-fifth of the citizen body, signed on to a panel. (Because women were not considered citizens, they were not allowed to sit on juries or sue in the courts.) From this panel on any given day, jurors were assigned to specific courts and cases. The usual size of a jury was 501, although there were juries of from 51 to as many as 1,501 members.

WATER-CLOCK Participants in an Athenian trial could speak for only a limited time. A water-clock (or *clepsydra*) like this one from ancient Greece dating from the fifth century B.C.E. kept the time by measuring the gradual flow of water through an escape hold at the bottom of the vessel.
SOURCE: DEA/G. NIMATALLAH/Getty Images

Unlike in a modern American court, there was no public prosecutor, no lawyers, and no judge. The jury was everything. Private citizens registered complaints and argued their own cases. In deciding fundamental matters of justice and fairness, the Athenian democrat put little faith in experts.

In the courtroom, the plaintiff and defendant would each present his case for himself, rebut his opponent, cite the relevant laws and precedents, produce witnesses, and sum up. No trial lasted more than a day. The jury did not deliberate but voted by secret ballot, and a simple majority decided the verdict. If a penalty was called for and not prescribed by law (as few were), the plaintiff proposed one penalty, and the defendant a different one. The jury then voted to choose one of these penalties but could not propose any other. Normally, this process led both sides to suggest moderate penalties, as an unreasonable suggestion would alienate the jury. To further deter frivolous lawsuits, the plaintiff had to pay a large fine if he did not win a stated percentage of the jurors' votes.

The Athenian system of justice had obvious flaws. Decisions could be quirky and unpredictable because they were unchecked by precedent. Juries could be prejudiced, and jurors had no defense except their own intelligence and knowledge against speakers who cited laws incorrectly and distorted history. Speeches—unhampered by rules of evidence and relevance, and without the discipline judges impose—could be fanciful, false, and deceptive.

For all its flaws, however, the Athenian system was simple, speedy, open, and easily understood by the citizens. It counted, as always, on the common sense of the ordinary Athenian and contained provisions aimed at producing moderate penalties and deterring unreasonable lawsuits. No legal technicalities or experts came between the citizens and their laws.

Questions

1. What were the advantages and disadvantages of the Athenian justice system?
2. Do you think this system would lead to fair and just results?

In the private aspects of life women were always under the control of a male guardian—a father, a husband, or some other male relative. Women married young, usually between age twelve and eighteen, whereas their husbands were typically more than thirty. In many ways, women's relationships with men were like father-daughter relationships. Marriages were arranged; women normally had no choice of husband, and male relatives controlled their dowries. To obtain a divorce, women needed the approval of a male relative who was willing to serve as guardian after the dissolution of the marriage. In case of divorce, the dowry returned with the woman, but her father or the appropriate male relative controlled it.

The main function and responsibility of a respectable Athenian woman of a citizen family was to produce male heirs for the *oikos*, or household, of her husband. If, however, her father's oikos lacked a male heir, the daughter became an *epikleros*, the "heiress" to the family property. In that case, she was required by law to marry a relative on her father's side to produce the desired male offspring. In the Athenian way of thinking, one household "lent" a woman to another for bearing and raising a male heir to ensure the existence of the *oikos*.

Because the pure and legitimate lineage of the offspring was important, women were carefully segregated from men outside the family and were confined to the

Compare and Connect

Athenian Democracy—Pro and Con

THE FIRST DEMOCRACY in the world's history appeared in Athens at the end of the sixth century B.C.E. By the middle of the fifth century B.C.E., the Athenian constitution had broadened to give all adult males participation in all aspects of government.

Although most Greek states remained oligarchic, some adopted the Athenian model and became democratic, but democracy was harshly criticized by members of the upper classes, traditionalists, and philosophers. In the following documents, Pericles, the most famous Athenian political leader, and an anonymous pamphleteer present contrasting evaluations of the Athenian democracy.

PERICLES Pericles (ca. 495–429 B.C.E.) was the leading statesman of Athens for much of the fifth century B.C.E. This is a Roman copy in marble of the Greek bronze bust that was probably cast in the last decade of Pericles's life.
SOURCE: Library of Congress

Before Reading

- Notice the features of democracy that Pericles praises.
- Examine how these elements compare with the Spartan constitution.
- Make note of points in the Old Oligarch's text that agree and disagree with Pericles's points.

Questions

1. What virtues does Pericles find in the Athenian constitution?
2. What criticisms of Athenian democracy does Pericles defend against?
3. What are the anonymous author's objections to democracy? How would a defender of the Athenian constitution and way of life answer his complaints?
4. To what extent do these two descriptions of Athenian democracy agree? In what ways do they disagree?

I. PERICLES'S FUNERAL ORATION

In 431 B.C.E., the first year of the Peloponnesian War, Pericles delivered a speech to honor and commemorate the Athenian soldiers who had died in the war. A key part of his speech was the praise of the Athenian democratic constitution, which, he argued, justified the sacrifice these soldiers had made.

Our constitution does not copy the laws of neighbouring states; we are rather a pattern to others than imitators ourselves. Its administration favours the many instead of the few; this is why it is called a democracy. If we look to the laws, they afford equal justice to all in their private differences; if to social standing, advancement in public life falls to reputation for capacity, class considerations not being allowed to interfere with merit; nor again does poverty bar the way, if a man is able to serve the state, he is not hindered by the obscurity of his condition. The freedom which we enjoy in our government extends also to our ordinary life. There, far from exercising a jealous surveillance over each other, we do not feel called upon to be angry with our neighbour for doing what he likes, or even to indulge in those injurious looks which cannot fail to be offensive, although they inflict no positive penalty. But all this ease in our private relations does not make us lawless as citizens. Against this fear is our chief safeguard, teaching us to obey the magistrates and the laws, particularly such as regard the protection of the injured, whether they are actually on the statute book, or belong to that code which, although unwritten, yet cannot be broken without acknowledged disgrace.

II. ATHENIAN DEMOCRACY: AN UNFRIENDLY VIEW

The following selection comes from an anonymous pamphlet thought to have been written during the Peloponnesian War. Because it came down to us among the works of Xenophon but cannot be his work, it is sometimes called "The Constitution of the Athenians" by Pseudo-Xenophon. It is also common to refer to the unknown author as "The Old Oligarch"—although neither his age nor his purpose is known—because of the obviously antidemocratic tone of the work. Such opinions were common among members of the upper classes in Athens in the late fifth century B.C.E. and thereafter.

As for the constitution of the Athenians, their choice of this type of constitution I do not approve, for in choosing thus they chose that rascals should fare better than good citizens. This then is why I do not approve. However this being their decision, I shall show how well they preserve their constitution, and how well otherwise they are acting where the rest of Greece thinks that they are going wrong.

First of all, then, I shall say that at Athens the poor and the commons seem justly to have the advantage over the well-born and the wealthy; for it is the commons which mans the fleet and has brought the state her power, and the steersmen and the boatswains and the ship-masters and the lookout-men and the ship-builders—these have brought the state her power much rather than the infantry and the well-born and the good citizens. This being so it seems just that all should have a share in offices filled by lot or by election, and that any citizen who wishes should be allowed to speak. Then, in those offices which bring security to the whole commons, if they are in the hands of good citizens, but if not ruin, the commons desires to have no share. They do not think that they ought to have a share through the lot in the supreme commands or in the cavalry commands, for the commons realises that it reaps greater benefit by not having these offices in its own hands, but by allowing men of standing to hold them. All those offices, however, whose end is pay and family benefits, the commons does seek to hold.

Secondly some folk are surprised that everywhere they give the advantage to rascals, the poor, and the democrats rather than to good citizens. This is just where they will be seen to be preserving the democracy. For if the poor and the common folk and the worse elements are treated well, the growth of these classes will exalt the democracy; whereas, if the rich and the good citizens are treated well, the democrats strengthen their own opponents. In every land, the best element is opposed to democracy. Among the best elements, there is very little license and injustice, very great discrimination as to what is worthy; while among the commons, there is very great ignorance, disorderliness and rascality; for poverty tends to lead them to what is disgraceful, as does lack of education and the ignorance which befalls some men as a result of lack of means.

It may be said that they ought not to have allowed everyone in turn to make speeches or sit on the Council, but only those of the highest capability and quality. But in allowing even rascals to speak, they are also very well advised. For if the good citizens made speeches and joined in deliberations, good would result to those like themselves and ill to the democrats. As it is, anyone who wants, a rascally fellow maybe, gets up and makes a speech, and devises what is to the advantage of himself and those like him. Someone may ask how such a fellow would know what is to the advantage of himself or the commons. They know that this man's ignorance, rascality, and goodwill are more beneficial than the good citizen's worth, wisdom, and ill-will. From such procedure, then, a city would not attain the ideal, but the democracy would be best preserved thus. For it is the wish of the commons not that the state should be well ordered and the commons itself in complete subjection, but that the commons should have its freedom and be in control; disorderliness is of little consequence to it. From what you consider lack of order, come the strength and the liberty of the commons itself.

SOURCES: (I) From Richard Crawley, trans., *Thucydides, History of the Peloponnesian War, Done in English by Richard Crawley* (London: J. M. Dent and Sons, 1914), pp. 121–122. (II) From James A. Petch, trans., *The Old Oligarch: Being the Constitution of the Athenians Ascribed to Xenophon* (Oxford: Basil Blackwell, 1900), pp. 15–17.

THE ACROPOLIS, ATHENS The Acropolis was both the religious and civic center of Athens. It was completed during the rule of Pericles and his successors in the late fifth century B.C.E. This photograph shows the Parthenon and to its left the Erechtheum, two structures of great architectural and historical significance on the Acropolis.

SOURCE: nagelestock.com/Alamy Stock Photo

women's quarters in the house. Men might seek sexual gratification outside the house with prostitutes of high or low style, frequently recruited from abroad. Respectable women stayed home to raise the children, cook, weave cloth, and oversee the management of the household. The only public function of women—an important one—was in the various rituals and festivals of the state religion. Apart from these activities, Athenian women were expected to remain at home out of sight, quiet, and unnoticed. Pericles told the widows and mothers of the Athenian men who died in the first year of the Peloponnesian War only this: "Your great glory is not to fall short of your natural character, and the greatest glory of women is to be least talked about by men, whether for good or bad."

This picture of the legal status of women derived from these sources is largely accurate. It does not fit well, however, with other evidence from mythology, from pictorial art, and from the tragedies and comedies by the great Athenian dramatists. These often show women as central characters and powerful figures in both the public and the private spheres, suggesting that Athenian women may have played a more complex role than their legal status suggests. In

Aeschylus's tragedy *Agamemnon*, for example, Clytemnestra arranges the murder of her royal husband and establishes the tyranny of her lover, whom she dominates.

As a famous speech in Euripides's tragedy *Medea* makes clear, we are left with an apparent contradiction. In this speech, Medea paints a bleak picture of the subjugation of women as dictated by their legal status. Yet Medea, as Euripides depicted her, is a powerful figure who negotiates with kings. She is the central character in a tragedy bearing her name, produced at state expense before most of the Athenian population and written by one of Athens' greatest poets and dramatists. Medea inspires terror in the audience and, at the same time, is an object of their pity and sympathy as a victim of injustice. She is certainly not, as Pericles recommended in his *Funeral Oration*, "least talked about by men, whether for good or for bad." It is also important to remember that she is a foreigner with magical powers, by no means a typical Athenian woman.

3.3.3.1 AN EXCEPTIONAL WOMAN: ASPASIA Pericles's life did not conform to his own prescription. After divorcing his first wife, he entered into a liaison that was unique for his time, to a woman who was, in her own way, as remarkable as the great Athenian leader. His companion was Aspasia, a young woman who had left her native Miletus and come to live in Athens. The ancient writers refer to her as a *hetaira*, a kind of high-class courtesan who provided men with both erotic and other kinds of entertainment. She clearly had a keen and lively intellect and may well have been trained in the latest ideas and techniques of discussion in her native city, the home of the Greek Enlightenment. Socrates thought it was worth his time to talk with her in the company of his followers and friends. In the dialogue *Menexenus*, Plato jokingly gives her credit for writing Pericles's speeches, including the *Funeral Oration*. There should be no doubt that both Pericles and the men in his circle took Aspasia seriously.

Aspasia represented something completely different from Athenian women. She was not a child, not a sheltered and repressed creature confined to the narrow world of slave women, children, and female relatives. She was a beautiful, independent, brilliantly witty young woman capable of holding her own in conversation with the best minds in Greece and of discussing and illuminating any question with her husband. There can be no doubt that Pericles loved her passionately. He took her into his house, and whether they were formally and legally married or not, he treated her as his one and only beloved wife.

For an Athenian to consort with courtesans was normal—to take one into his house and treat her as a concubine, perhaps only a little less so. What was shocking and, to many, offensive, was Pericles's treatment of such a woman, a foreigner, as a wife, lavishing affection on her as few Athenian wives enjoyed, involving her regularly in conversation with other men, discussing important matters with her, and treating her opinions with respect. The scandal was immense, and the comic poets made the most of it. Enemies claimed that Pericles was enslaved to a foreign woman who was using her power over him for political purposes of her own. The Samian War, which arose over a quarrel between Aspasia's native Miletus and Samos, intensified these allegations, for the story spread that Pericles had launched the war at her bidding. After Pericles's death, Aristophanes would reuse these old accusations comically to blame Aspasia for the Peloponnesian War as well.

To some degree, the reality of women's lives in ancient Greece must have depended on their social and economic status. Poorer women necessarily worked hard at household as well as agricultural tasks and in shops. They also fetched water from the wells and fountains, and both vase paintings and literature show women gathering and chatting at these places. Aristotle asks, "How would it be possible to prevent the wives of the poor from going out of doors?"[1] Women of the better classes, however, had no such duties or opportunities. They were more easily and closely supervised. Our knowledge of the experience of women, however, comes from limited sources that do not always agree. Different scholars arrive at conflicting pictures by emphasizing one kind of a source rather than another. Although the legal subordination of women cannot be doubted, the reality of their place in Greek society remains a lively topic of debate.

3.3.4 Slavery

The Greeks had some form of slavery from the earliest times, but true chattel slavery was initially rare. The most common forms of bondage were different kinds of serfdom in relatively backward areas such as Crete, Thessaly, and Sparta. Another early form of bondage involving a severe, but rarely permanent, loss of freedom resulted from default in debt. In Athens, however, at about 600 B.C.E., such bondsmen, called *hektemoroi*, were sold outside their native land as true slaves until the reforms of Solon put an end to debt bondage entirely.

True chattel slavery began to increase about 500 B.C.E. and remained important to Greek society thereafter. The main sources of slaves were war captives and the captives of pirates. Like the Chinese, Egyptians, and many other peoples, the Greeks regarded foreigners as inferior, and most slaves working for the Greeks were foreigners. Greeks sometimes enslaved Greeks, but not to serve in their home territories.

The chief occupation of the Greeks, as of most of the world before the twenty-first century, was agriculture. Most Greek farmers worked small farms too poor to support even one slave, but some had one or two slaves to work alongside them. The upper classes had larger farms that were let out to free tenant farmers or were worked by slaves, generally under an overseer who was himself a slave. Large landowners generally did not have a single great estate but possessed several smaller farms scattered about the polis. This arrangement did not lend itself to a great numbers of agricultural slaves such as those who would later work on the cotton and sugar plantations of the New World. Industry, however, was different.

Larger numbers of slaves labored in industry, especially in mining. Nicias, a wealthy Athenian of the fifth century B.C.E., owned 1,000 slaves he rented to a mining contractor for profit, but this is by far the largest number known. Most manufacturing was on a small scale, with shops using one, two, or a handful of slaves. Slaves worked as craftsmen in almost every trade, and, like agricultural slaves on small farms, they worked alongside their masters. Many slaves were domestic servants or shepherds. Publicly held slaves served as policemen, prison attendants, clerks, and secretaries.

The number of slaves in ancient Greece and their importance to Greek society are subjects of controversy. We have no useful figures of the absolute number of slaves or their percentage of the free population in the classical period (fifth and fourth centuries B.C.E.), and estimates range from 20,000 to 100,000. Accepting the mean between the extremes, 60,000, and estimating the free population at its height at about 40,000 households, would yield a figure of fewer than two slaves per family. Estimates suggest that only one-quarter to one-third of free Athenians owned any slaves at all.

Some historians have noted that in the American South during the period before the Civil War—where slaves made up less than one-third of the total population and three-quarters of free Southerners had no slaves—the proportion of slaves to free citizens was similar to that of ancient Athens. Because slavery was so important to the economy of the South, these historians suggest, it may have been equally important and similarly oppressive in ancient Athens. This argument has several problems.[2] First, in the cotton states of the American South before the Civil War, a single cash crop, well suited for exploitation by large groups of slaves, dominated the economy and society. In Athens, in contrast, the economy was mixed, the crops varied, and the land and its distribution were poorly suited to massive slavery.

Different, too, was the likelihood that a slave would become free. Americans rarely freed their slaves, but in Greece liberation was common. The most famous example is that of the Athenian slave Pasion, who began as a bank clerk, earned his freedom, became Athens' richest banker, and was awarded Athenian citizenship. Such cases were certainly rare, but gaining one's freedom was not.

It is important also to distinguish the American South, where skin color separated slaves from their masters, from the different society of classical Athens. Southern masters were increasingly hostile to freeing slaves and afraid of slave rebellions, but in Athens slaves walked the streets with such ease that it offended class-conscious Athenians.

Even more remarkable, the Athenians sometimes considered freeing all their slaves. In 406 B.C.E., when their city was facing defeat in the Peloponnesian War, Athenians freed all slaves of military age and granted citizenship to those who rowed the ships that won the battle of Arginusae. Twice more at crucial moments, similar proposals were made, although without success.

3.3.5 Religion in Public Life

In Athens, as in the other Greek states, religion was more a civic than a private matter. Participation in the rituals of the state religion was not a matter of faith, but of patriotism and good citizenship. In its most basic form, it had little to do with morality. Over time poets and philosophers put forth ethical and moral ideas that among other peoples, like the Hebrews and Persians, were the work of religious prophets and basic to their religious beliefs. Greek religion, however, emphasized not moral conduct or orthodox belief, but the faithful practice of rituals meant to win the favor of the gods. To fail to carry out these duties or to attack the gods in any way were blows against the state and were severely punished.

Famous examples of such blasphemies and their punishment occurred in the late fifth and in the early fourth centuries B.C.E. In 415 B.C.E., some men mutilated the statues of Hermes found on every street in Athens. Others were accused of mocking the sacred mysteries of the worship of the goddesses Demeter and Persephone. Suspicions arose at once that the purpose of these sacrilegious acts was to overthrow the Athenian democracy, and the perpetrators were put to death. In 399 B.C.E., the philosopher Socrates was convicted of not honoring the state's gods and of introducing new divinities. Connected to this conviction, he was also charged with corrupting Athenian youth. Because his actions were believed to have done harm to the well-being of Athens, he was put to death. In ancient Greece, there was no thought of separating religion from civic and political life.

3.4 The Great Peloponnesian War

How did the Peloponnesian War affect the faith in the polis?

During the first decade after the Thirty Years' Peace of 445 B.C.E., the willingness of each side to respect the new arrangements was tested and not found wanting. About 435 B.C.E., however, a dispute in a remote and unimportant part of the Greek world ignited a long and disastrous war that shook the foundations of Greek civilization.

KEY EVENTS IN THE GREAT PELOPONNESIAN WAR	
435 B.C.E.	Civil war at Epidamnus
432 B.C.E.	Sparta declares war on Athens
431 B.C.E.	Peloponnesian invasion of Athens
421 B.C.E.	Peace of Nicias
415–413 B.C.E.	Athenian invasion of Syracuse
405 B.C.E.	Battle of Aegospotami
404 B.C.E.	Athens surrenders

3.4.1 Causes of the Great Peloponnesian War

The spark that ignited the conflict was a civil war at Epidamnus, a Corcyraean colony on the Adriatic. This civil war caused a quarrel between Corcyra (modern Corfu) and its mother city and traditional enemy, Corinth, an ally of Sparta. The Corcyraean fleet was second in size only to that of Athens, and the Athenians feared that its capture by Corinth would threaten Athenian security. As a result, the Athenians made an alliance with the previously neutral Corcyra, angering Corinth and leading to a series of crises in 433–432 B.C.E. that threatened to bring the Athenian Empire into conflict with the Peloponnesian League.

In the summer of 432 B.C.E., the Spartans met to consider the grievances of their allies. Persuaded, chiefly by the Corinthians, that Athens was an insatiably aggressive power seeking to enslave all the Greeks, they voted for war. The peace of 445 B.C.E. specifically provided that all differences be submitted to arbitration, and Athens repeatedly offered to arbitrate any question. Pericles insisted that the Athenians refuse to yield to threats or commands and to uphold the peace and the arbitration clause. Sparta refused to arbitrate, and in the spring of 431 B.C.E., its army marched into Attica, the Athenian homeland.

3.4.2 Strategic Stalemate

The Spartan strategy was traditional: to invade the enemy's country and threaten the crops, forcing the enemy to defend them in a hoplite battle. The Spartans were sure to win such a battle because they had the better army and they outnumbered the Athenians at least two to one. Any ordinary polis would have yielded or fought and lost. Athens, however, had an enormous navy, an annual income from the empire, a vast reserve fund, and long walls that connected the fortified city with the fortified port of Piraeus.

The Athenians' strategy was to allow devastation of their own land to prove that Spartan invasions could not hurt Athens. At the same time, the Athenians launched seaborne raids on the Peloponnesian coast to hurt Sparta's allies. Pericles expected that within a year or two—three at most—the Peloponnesians would become discouraged and make peace, having learned their lesson.

The plan required restraint and the leadership only Pericles could provide. In 429 B.C.E., however, after a devastating plague and a political crisis that had challenged his authority, Pericles died. After his death, no dominant leader emerged to hold the Athenians to a consistent policy. Two factions vied for influence: One, led by Nicias, wanted to continue the defensive policy, and the other, led by Cleon, preferred a more aggressive strategy. In 425 B.C.E., the aggressive faction won a victory that changed the course of the war. Four hundred Spartans surrendered. Sparta offered peace at once to get them back. The great victory and the prestige it brought Athens made it safe to raise the imperial tribute, without which Athens could not continue to fight. The Athenians indeed wanted to continue, for the Spartan peace offer gave no adequate guarantee of Athenian security.

In 424 B.C.E., the Athenians undertook a more aggressive policy. They sought to make Athens safe by conquering Megara and Boeotia. Both attempts failed, and defeat helped discredit the aggressive policy, leading to a truce in 423 B.C.E. Meanwhile, Sparta's ablest general, Brasidas, took a small army to Thrace and Macedonia. He captured Amphipolis, the most important Athenian colony in the region. Thucydides led the Athenian fleet in those waters

and was held responsible for the city's loss. He was exiled and was thereby given the time and opportunity to write his famous history of the Great Peloponnesian War. In 422 B.C.E., Cleon led an expedition to undo the work of Brasidas. At Amphipolis, both he and Brasidas died in battle. The removal of these two leaders of the aggressive factions in their respective cities paved the way for the Peace of Nicias, named for its chief negotiator, which was ratified in the spring of 421 B.C.E.

3.4.3 The Fall of Athens

The peace, officially supposed to last fifty years and, with a few exceptions, guarantee the status quo, was in fact fragile. Neither side carried out all its commitments, and several of Sparta's allies refused ratification. In 415 B.C.E., Alcibiades persuaded the Athenians to attack Syracuse to bring it under Athenian control. This ambitious and unnecessary undertaking ended in disaster in 413 B.C.E., when the entire expedition was destroyed. The Athenians lost some 200 ships, about 4,500 of their own men, and almost ten times as many allies. It shook Athens' prestige, reduced its power, provoked rebellions, and brought the wealth and power of Persia into the war on Sparta's side.

It is remarkable that the Athenians could continue fighting despite the disaster. They survived a brief oligarchic coup in 411 B.C.E. and won several important victories at sea as the war shifted to the Aegean. Their allies rebelled, however, and Persia paid for fleets to sustain them. Athenian financial resources shrank and finally disappeared. When its fleet was caught napping and was destroyed at Aegospotami in 405 B.C.E., Athens could not build another. The Spartans, under Lysander, a clever and ambitious general who was responsible for obtaining Persian support, cut off the food supply through the Hellespont, and the Athenians were starved into submission. In 404 B.C.E., they surrendered unconditionally; the city walls were dismantled, Athens was permitted no fleet, and the empire was gone. The Great Peloponnesian War was over.

3.5 Competition for Leadership in the Fourth Century B.C.E.

How did Athens and Sparta compete for leadership in the Greek world?

Athens' defeat did not bring domination to the Spartans. Instead, the period from 404 B.C.E. until the Macedonian conquest of Greece in 338 B.C.E. was a time of intense rivalry among the Greek cities, each seeking to achieve leadership and control over the others. Sparta, a recovered Athens, and a newly powerful Thebes were the main competitors in a struggle that ultimately weakened all the Greeks and left them vulnerable to outside influence and control.

3.5.1 The Hegemony of Sparta

The collapse of the Athenian Empire created a vacuum of power in the Aegean and opened the way for Spartan leadership or hegemony. Fulfilling the contract that had brought them the funds to win the war, the Spartans handed the Greek cities of Asia Minor back to Persia. Under the leadership of Lysander, the Spartans made a mockery of their promise to free the Greeks by stepping into the imperial role of Athens in the cities along the European coast and the islands of the Aegean. In most of the cities, Lysander installed a board of ten local oligarchs loyal to him and supported them with a Spartan garrison. Tribute brought in an annual revenue almost as great as that the Athenians had collected.

Limited population, the Helot problem, and traditional conservatism all made Sparta a less than ideal state to rule a maritime empire. The increasing arrogance of Sparta's policies alienated some of its allies, especially Thebes and Corinth. In 404 B.C.E., Lysander installed an oligarchic government in Athens, and its leaders' outrageous behavior earned them the title "**Thirty Tyrants.**" Democratic exiles took refuge in Thebes and Corinth and raised an army to challenge the oligarchy. Sparta's conservative king, Pausanias, replaced Lysander, arranging a peaceful settlement and, ultimately, the restoration of democracy. Thereafter, Athenian foreign policy remained under Spartan control, but otherwise Athens was free.

In 405 B.C.E., Darius II of Persia died and was succeeded by Artaxerxes II. His younger brother, Cyrus, received Spartan help in recruiting a Greek mercenary army to help him contest the throne. The Greeks marched inland as far as Mesopotamia, where they defeated the Persians at Cunaxa in 401 B.C.E., but Cyrus was killed in the battle. The Greeks were able to march back to the Black Sea and safety; their success revealed the potential weakness of the Persian Empire.

The Greeks of Asia Minor had supported Cyrus and were now afraid of Artaxerxes's revenge. The Spartans accepted their request for aid and sent an army into Asia, attracted by the prospect of prestige, power, and money. In 396 B.C.E., the command of Sparta's army was given to a new king, Agesilaus, who dominated Sparta until his death in 360 B.C.E. His consistent advocacy of aggressive policies that provided him opportunities to display his bravery in battle may have been motivated by a psychological need to compensate for his physical lameness and his disputed claim to the throne.

Agesilaus collected much booty and frightened the Persians. They sent a messenger with money and promises of further support to friendly factions in all the Greek states likely to help them against Sparta. By 395 B.C.E., Thebes was able to organize an alliance that included Argos, Corinth, and a resurgent Athens. The result was the Corinthian War (395–387 B.C.E.), which put an end to Sparta's Asian adventure. In 394 B.C.E., the Persian fleet destroyed Sparta's maritime empire. Meanwhile, the Athenians rebuilt their walls, enlarged their navy, and even recovered some of their lost empire in the Aegean. The war ended when the exhausted Greek states accepted a peace dictated by the great king of Persia.

The Persians, frightened now by the recovery of Athens, turned the management of Greece over to Sparta. Agesilaus broke up all alliances except the Peloponnesian League. He used or threatened to use the Spartan army to interfere with other poleis and put friends of Sparta in power within them. Sparta reached a new level of lawless arrogance in 382 B.C.E., when it seized Thebes during peacetime without warning or pretext. In 379 B.C.E., a Spartan army made a similar attempt on Athens. That action persuaded the Athenians to join with Thebes, which had rebelled against Sparta a few months earlier, to wage war on the Spartans.

In 371 B.C.E., the Thebans, led by their great generals Pelopidas and Epaminondas, defeated the Spartans at Leuctra. The Thebans encouraged the Arcadian cities of the central Peloponnesus to form a league, freed the Helots, and helped them found a city of their own. They deprived Sparta of much of its farmland and of the people who worked it and hemmed Sparta in with hostile neighbors. Sparta's population had shrunk so it could put fewer than 2,000 men into the field at Leuctra. Its aggressive policies had led to ruin. The Theban victory brought the end of Sparta as a power of the first rank.

3.5.2 The Hegemony of Thebes: The Second Athenian Empire

Thebes' power after its victory at Leuctra lay in its democratic constitution, its control over Boeotia, and its two outstanding and popular generals. One of these generals, Pelopidas, died in a successful attempt to gain control of Thessaly. The other, Epaminondas, made Thebes dominant over all of Greece north of Athens and the Corinthian Gulf and challenged the reborn Athenian Empire in the Aegean. All this activity provoked resistance, and by 362 B.C.E., Thebes faced a Peloponnesian coalition as well as Athens. Epaminondas, once again leading a Boeotian army into the Peloponnesus, confronted this coalition at the Battle of Mantinea. His army was victorious, but Epaminondas himself was killed, and Theban dominance died with him.

The **Second Athenian Confederation**, which Athens had organized in 378 B.C.E., was aimed at resisting Spartan aggression in the Aegean. Its constitution avoided the abuses of the Delian League, but the Athenians soon began to repeat them anyway. This time, however, they did not have the power to suppress resistance. When the collapse of Sparta and Thebes and the restraint of Persia removed any reason for voluntary membership, Athens' allies revolted. By 355 B.C.E., Athens had to abandon most of the empire. After two centuries of almost continuous warfare, the Greeks returned to the chaotic disorganization that characterized the time before the founding of the Peloponnesian League.

3.6 The Culture of Classical Greece

What are the achievements of Classical Greece?

The repulse of the Persian invasion created a flood of creative activity in Greece that was rarely, if ever, matched anywhere at any time. The century and a half between the Persian retreat and the conquest of Greece by **Philip II of Macedon** (479–338 B.C.E.) produced achievements of such quality as to justify the designation of that era as the Classical Period.

STORAGE JAR (AMPHORA) Made about 540 B.C.E., this storage jar is attributed to the anonymous Athenian master artist called the Amasis Painter. It shows Dionysus, the god of wine, revelry, and fertility, with two of his ecstatic female worshippers called maenads.
SOURCE: Bibliotheque Nationale, Cabinet de Medailles, Paris/Bridgeman Images

Ironically, we often use the term *classical* to suggest calm and serenity, but the word that best describes Greek life, thought, art, and literature in this period is *tension*.

3.6.1 The Fifth Century B.C.E.

Two sources of tension contributed to the artistic outpouring of fifth-century B.C.E. Greece. One arose from the conflict between the Greeks' pride in their accomplishments and their concern that overreaching would bring retribution. Friction among the poleis intensified during this period, as Athens and Sparta gathered most of them into two competing and menacing blocs. The victory over the Persians brought a sense of exultation in the capacity of humans to accomplish great things and a sense of confidence in the divine justice that had brought low the arrogant pride of Xerxes. But the Greeks recognized that Xerxes's fate awaited all those who reached too far, creating a sense of unease. The second source of tension was the conflict between the soaring hopes and achievements of individuals and the claims and limits their fellow citizens in the polis put on them. These tensions were felt throughout Greece. They had the most spectacular consequences, however, in Athens in its Golden Age, the time between the Persian and the Peloponnesian wars.

3.6.1.1 ATTIC TRAGEDY Nothing reflects Athens' concerns better than Attic tragedy, which emerged as a major form of Greek poetry in the fifth century B.C.E. The tragedies were presented in a contest as part of the public religious observations in honor of the god Dionysus. The festivals in which they were shown were civic occasions.

Each poet who wished to compete submitted his work to the archon. Each offered three tragedies (which might or might not have a common subject) and a satyr play, or comic choral dialogue with Dionysus, to close. The three best competitors were each awarded three actors and a chorus. The state paid the actors. The state selected a wealthy citizen to provide the chorus as *choregos*, for the Athenians had no direct taxation to support such activities. Most of the tragedies were performed in the theater of Dionysus on the south side of the Acropolis, and as many as 30,000 Athenians could attend. A jury of Athenians chosen by lot voted prizes and honors to the best author, actor, and choregos.

Attic tragedy served as a forum in which the poets raised vital issues of the day, enabling the Athenian audience to think about them in a serious, yet exciting, context. On rare occasions, the subject of a play might be a contemporary or historic event, but almost always it was chosen from mythology. Until late in the century, the tragedies always dealt solemnly with difficult questions of religion, politics, ethics, morality, or some combination of these. The plays of the dramatists Aeschylus and Sophocles, for example, follow this pattern. The plays of Euripides, written toward the end of the century, are less solemn and more concerned with individual psychology.

3.6.1.2 OLD COMEDY Comedy was introduced into the Dionysian festival early in the fifth century B.C.E. Cratinus, Eupolis, and the great master of the genre called Old Comedy, Aristophanes (ca. 450–385 B.C.E.), the only one from whom we have complete plays, wrote political comedies. They were filled with scathing invective and satire against such contemporary figures as Pericles, Cleon, Socrates, and Euripides.

3.6.1.3 ARCHITECTURE AND SCULPTURE The great architectural achievements of Periclean Athens, as much as Athenian tragedy, illustrate the magnificent results of the union of and tension between religious and civic responsibilities, on the one hand, and the transcendent genius of the individual artist, on the other. Beginning in 448 B.C.E. and continuing to the outbreak of the Great Peloponnesian War, Pericles undertook a great building program on the Acropolis. (See Map 3–3.) The income from the empire paid for it. The new buildings included temples to honor the city's gods and a fitting gateway to the temples. Pericles's main purpose seems to have been to represent visually the greatness and power of Athens, by emphasizing intellectual and artistic achievement—civilization rather than military and naval power. It was as though these buildings were tangible proof of Pericles's claim that Athens was "the school of Hellas"—that is, the intellectual center of all Greece. (For more information about Greek temple architecture of the

Map 3–3 ANCIENT ATHENS

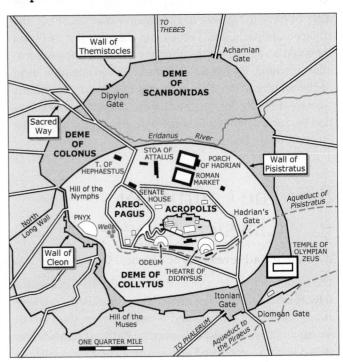

This map locates some of the major features of the ancient city of Athens that have been excavated and are visible today. It includes monuments ranging in age from the earliest times to the period of the Roman Empire. The geographical relation of the Acropolis to the rest of the city is apparent, as is that of the Agora, the Areopagus (where the early council of aristocrats met), and the Pnyx (site of assembly for the larger, more democratic meetings of the entire people).

time, see the "Closer Look" sidebar, which follows below, on the Erechtheum and its distinctive Porch of the Maidens.)

3.6.1.4 PHILOSOPHY The tragic dramas, architecture, and sculpture of the fifth century B.C.E. all indicate an extraordinary concern with human beings—their capacities, their limits, their nature, and their place in the universe. The same concern is clear in the development of philosophy.

To be sure, some philosophers continued the speculation about the nature of the cosmos (as opposed to human nature) that began with Thales in the sixth century B.C.E. **Parmenides of Elea** and his pupil Zeno, in opposition to the earlier philosopher Heraclitus, argued that change was only an illusion of the senses. Reason and reflection showed that reality was fixed and unchanging because it seemed evident that nothing could be created out of nothingness. Empedocles of Acragas further advanced such fundamental speculations by identifying four basic elements: fire, water, earth, and air. Like Parmenides, he thought that reality was permanent, but he thought it was not immobile; two primary forces, he contended, love and strife—or, as we might say, attraction and repulsion—moved the four elements.

Empedocles's theory is clearly a step toward the **atomist** theory of Leucippus of Miletus and Democritus

THE THREE ORDERS OF GREEK ARCHITECTURE The three orders of Greek architecture, Doric, Ionic, and Corinthian, have had an enduring impact on Western architecture. They figure prominently in the neoclassical architecture of the second half of the eighteenth century.
SOURCE: Antiqueimages/Alamy Stock Photo

A Closer Look

The Erechtheum: Porch of the Maidens

THE ERECHTHEUM, LOCATED on the north side of the Acropolis of Athens, was a temple to the goddess Athena in her oldest form as Athena Polias, the protector of the city. It was built between 421 and 407 B.C.E., probably to replace an older temple the Persians had destroyed in 480.

The new temple included the sites of some of the most ancient and holy relics of the Athenians: a small olive wood statue of Athena Polias; the tombs of Cecrops and Erechtheus, legendary early kings of Athens; the marks of the sea god Poseidon's trident; and the saltwater well (the "salt sea") that legend said resulted from Poseidon's strike. In the courtyard, according to the myth, Athena caused an olive tree to grow when she was contesting Poseidon for the honor of being the patron divinity of Athens. Poseidon created a saltwater spring on the Acropolis, but Athena's olive tree won over the judges, and she was victorious. Sculpture in the west pediment of the Parthenon depicted this contest.

Within the foundations, the sacred snake of the temple, whose well-being was thought essential for the safety of the city, was thought to live.

The famous "porch of the maidens" has six draped female figures (or caryatids) that support the entablature instead of columns.

The need to preserve the many sacred precincts likely explains this complex design.

ERECHTHEUM
SOURCE: Steve Allen/Getty Images

ERECHTHEUM CARYATIDS, FROM THE PORCH OF THE MAIDENS
SOURCE: Roy Rainford/robertharding/Getty Images

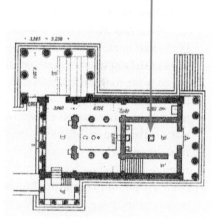

ARCHITECTURAL PLAN OF ERECHTHEUM CELLA AND PORTICO
SOURCE: Buyenlarge/Getty Images

Questions

1. What is the significance of the competition between the two gods honored by the Erechtheum temple and of the victory of Athena?
2. Why is the design of the Erechtheum so different from other Greek temples such as the Parthenon?
3. What does its date of construction indicate about the role of religion in Athenian life?

of Abdera. According to this theory, the world consists of innumerable tiny, solid, indivisible, and unchangeable particles—or "atoms"—that move about in the void. The size of the atoms and the arrangements they form when joined produce the secondary qualities that our senses perceive, such as color and shape. These secondary qualities are merely conventional—the result of human interpretation and agreement—unlike the atoms themselves, which are natural.

Previous to the atomists, Anaxagoras of Clazomenae, an older contemporary and a friend of Pericles, had spoken of tiny fundamental particles called *seeds*, which were put together on a rational basis by a force called *nous*, or "mind." Anaxagoras was thus suggesting a distinction between matter and mind. The atomists, however, regarded "soul," or mind, as material and believed purely physical laws guided everything. These conflicting positions were the beginning of the enduring philosophical debate between materialism and idealism.

These speculations were of interest to few people, and, in fact, most Greeks were suspicious of them. A group of professional teachers who emerged in the mid-fifth century B.C.E. began a far more influential debate. Called *Sophists*, they traveled about and received pay for teaching such practical techniques of persuasion as rhetoric, dialectic, and argumentation. (Persuasive skills were much valued in democracies like Athens, where so many issues were resolved through open debate.) Some Sophists claimed to teach wisdom and even virtue. Reflecting the human focus characteristic of fifth-century B.C.E. thought, they refrained from speculations about the physical universe, instead applying reasoned analysis to human beliefs and institutions. In doing so, the Sophists identified a central problem of human social life and the life of the polis: the conflict between nature and custom, or law. The more traditional Sophists argued that law itself was in accord with nature and was of divine origin, a view that fortified the traditional beliefs of the polis.

Others argued, however, that laws were merely the result of convention—an agreement among people—and not in accord with nature. The laws could not pretend to be a positive moral force but merely had the negative function of preventing people from harming one another. The most extreme Sophists argued that law was contrary to nature, a trick whereby the weak control the strong. **Critias**, an Athenian oligarch and one of the more extreme Sophists, even said that some clever person had invented the gods themselves to deter people from doing what they wished. Such ideas attacked the theoretical foundations of the polis and helped provoke the philosophical responses of Plato and Aristotle in the next century.

3.6.1.5 HISTORY The first prose literature in the form of history was Herodotus's account of the Persian War. "The father of history," as he has been deservedly called, was born shortly before the outbreak of the war. His account goes far beyond all previous chronicles, genealogies, and geographical studies and attempts to explain human actions and to draw instruction from them.

Although his work was completed about 425 B.C.E. and shows a few traces of Sophist influence, its spirit is that of an earlier time. Herodotus accepted the evidence of legends and oracles, although not uncritically, and often explained human events in terms of divine intervention. Human arrogance and divine vengeance are key forces that help explain the defeat of Croesus by Cyrus, as well as Xerxes's defeat by the Greeks. Yet the *History* is typical of its time in celebrating the crucial role of human intelligence as exemplified by Miltiades at Marathon and Themistocles at Salamis. Nor was Herodotus unaware of the importance of institutions. His pride in the superiority of the Greek polis, in the discipline it inspired in its citizen soldiers, and in the superiority of the Greeks' voluntary obedience to law over the Persians' fear of punishment is unmistakable.

Thucydides, the historian of the Peloponnesian War, was born about 460 B.C.E. and died a few years after the end of the Great Peloponnesian War. He was very much a product of the late fifth century B.C.E. His work, which was influenced by the secular, human-centered, skeptical rationalism of the Sophists, also reflects the scientific attitude of the school of medicine named for his contemporary, Hippocrates of Cos.

The Hippocratic school, known for its pioneering work in medicine and scientific theory, emphasized an approach to the understanding, diagnosis, and treatment of disease that combined careful observation with reason. In the same way, Thucydides took pains to achieve factual accuracy and tried to use his evidence to discover meaningful patterns of human behavior. He believed human nature was essentially unchanging, so a wise person equipped with the understanding history provided might accurately foresee events and thus help to guide them. Thucydides believed, however, that only a few had the ability to understand history and to put its lessons to good use. He thought that the intervention of chance, which played a great role in human affairs, could foil even the wisest. Thucydides focused his interest on politics, and in that area his assumptions about human nature do not seem unwarranted. His work has proved to be, as he hoped, "a possession forever." Its description of the terrible civil war between the two basic kinds of poleis is a final and fitting example of the tension that was the source of both the greatness and the decline of Classical Greece.

3.6.2 The Fourth Century B.C.E.

Historians often speak of the Peloponnesian War as the crisis of the polis and of the fourth century B.C.E. as the period of its decline. The war did bring powerfully important changes: the impoverishment of some Greek cities and, with it, an intensification of class conflict; the development of professionalism in the army; and demographic shifts that sometimes reduced the citizen population and increased the numbers of resident aliens. The Greeks of the fourth century B.C.E. did not know, however, that their traditional way of life was on the verge of destruction. Still, thinkers recognized that they lived in a time of troubles, and they

responded in various ways. Some looked to the past and tried to shore up the weakened structure of the polis; others tended toward despair and looked for new solutions; and still others averted their gaze from the public arena altogether. All these responses are apparent in the literature, philosophy, and art of the period.

3.6.2.1 DRAMA The tendency of some to turn away from the life of the polis and inward to everyday life, the family, and their own individuality is apparent in the poetry of the fourth century B.C.E. A new genre, called Middle Comedy, replaced the political subjects and personal invective of the Old Comedy with a comic-realistic depiction of daily life, plots of intrigue, and a mild satire of domestic situations. Significantly, the role of the chorus, which in some way represented the polis, was diminished quite a bit. These trends all continued and were carried even further in the New Comedy. Its leading playwright, **Menander** (342–291 B.C.E.), completely abandoned mythological subjects in favor of domestic tragicomedy. His gentle satire of the foibles of ordinary people and his tales of lovers temporarily thwarted before a happy and proper ending would not be unfamiliar to viewers of modern situation comedies.

Tragedy faded as a robust and original form. It became common to revive the great plays of the previous century.

THEATER AT EPIDAURUS Named after the god of medicine, the Sanctuary of Asclepius was an important center of healing. Among the structures that dotted the sanctuary was a theater, which drew many visitors during religious festivals.
SOURCE: Giannis Katsaros/Alamy Stock Photo

No tragedies written in the fourth century B.C.E. have been preserved. The plays of Euripides, which rarely won first prize when first produced for Dionysian festival competitions, became increasingly popular in the fourth century and after. Euripides was less interested in cosmic confrontations of conflicting principles than in the psychology and behavior of individual human beings. Some of his late plays, in fact, are less like the tragedies of Aeschylus and Sophocles than forerunners of later forms such as the New Comedy. Plays like *Helena*, *Andromeda*, and *Iphigenia in Tauris* are more like fairy-tales, tales of adventure, or love stories than tragedies.

3.6.2.2 SCULPTURE   The same movement away from the grand, the ideal, and the general, and toward the ordinary, the real, and the individual is apparent in the development of Greek sculpture. To see these developments, one has only to compare the statue of the striding god from Artemisium (ca. 460 B.C.E.), thought to be either Zeus on the point of releasing a thunderbolt or Poseidon about to throw his trident, or the Doryphoros of Polycleitus (ca. 450–440 B.C.E.)

STRIDING GOD FROM ARTEMISIUM This bronze statue of the striding god from Artemisium dates from about 460 B.C.E. It was found in the sea near Artemisium, the northern tip of the large Greek island of Euboea, and is now on display in the Athens Archaeological Museum. Exactly whom the striding god represents is not known. Some have thought him to be Poseidon holding a trident; others believe he is Zeus hurling a thunderbolt. In either case, it is a splendid representative of early Greek sculpture.
SOURCE: Erich Lessing/Art Resource, NY

with the Hermes of Praxiteles (ca. 340–330 B.C.E.), or the Apoxyomenos attributed to Lysippus (ca. 330 B.C.E.).

3.6.3 Philosophy and the Crisis of the Polis

The Great War, the fall of Athens, and the ensuing struggle for hegemony shook the remarkable confidence the Greeks placed in the polis to provide freedom and justice for its citizens. This crisis inspired a profound response from several Athenian philosophers.

3.6.3.1 SOCRATES   Probably the most complicated response to the crisis of the polis may be found in the life and teachings of Socrates (469–399 B.C.E.). Because he wrote nothing, our knowledge of Socrates comes chiefly from his disciples Plato and Xenophon and from later tradition. Although as a young man Socrates was interested in speculations about the physical world, he later turned to the investigation of ethics and morality; as the Roman writer and statesman Cicero put it, he brought philosophy down from the heavens. Socrates was committed to the search for truth and for the knowledge about human affairs that he believed reason could discover. His method was to question and cross-examine men, particularly those reputed to know something, such as craftsmen, poets, and politicians.

The result was always the same. Those Socrates questioned might have technical information and skills but seldom had any knowledge of the fundamental principles of human behavior. It is understandable that Athenians so exposed should be angry with their examiner, and it is not surprising they thought Socrates was undermining the beliefs and values of the polis. Socrates's unconcealed contempt for democracy, which seemingly relied on ignorant amateurs to make important political decisions without any knowledge, created further hostility. Moreover, his insistence on the primacy of his own individualism and his determination to pursue philosophy even against the wishes of his fellow citizens reinforced this hostility and the prejudice that went with it.

But Socrates, unlike the Sophists, did not accept pay for his teaching; he professed ignorance and denied that he taught at all. His individualism, moreover, was unlike the worldly hedonism of some of the Sophists. It was not wealth or pleasure or power that he urged people to seek, but "the greatest improvement of the soul." Unlike the more radical Sophists, he also denied that the polis and its laws were merely conventional. Socrates thought, on the contrary, that they had a legitimate claim on the citizen, and he proved it in the most convincing fashion.

In 399 B.C.E., an Athenian jury condemned Socrates to death on the charges of bringing new gods into the city and of corrupting the youth. His dialectical inquiries had angered many important people. His criticism of democracy must have been viewed with suspicion, especially since Critias and Charmides, who were members of the Thirty Tyrants, and the traitor Alcibiades, who had gone over to the Spartans, had been among his disciples. He was given a chance to escape but, as Plato's *Crito* tells us, he refused to do so because of his veneration of the laws. Socrates's career set the stage for later responses to the travail of the polis. He recognized its difficulties and criticized its shortcomings, and he turned away from an active political life, but he did not abandon the idea of the polis. He fought as a soldier in its defense, obeyed its laws, and sought to solidify its values through reason.

3.6.3.2 PLATO

Plato (429–347 B.C.E.) was by far the most important of Socrates's associates and is a perfect example of the pupil who becomes greater than his master. He was the first systematic philosopher and therefore the first to place political ideas in their full philosophical context. He was also a writer of genius, leaving us twenty-six philosophical discussions. Almost all are in the form of dialogues, which somehow make the examination of difficult and complicated philosophical problems seem dramatic and entertaining. Plato came from a noble Athenian family, and he looked forward to an active political career until the excesses of the Thirty Tyrants and the execution of Socrates discouraged him from that pursuit. Twice he made trips to Sicily in the hope of producing a model state at Syracuse under the tyrants Dionysius I and II, but without success.

In 386 B.C.E., Plato founded the **Academy**, a center of philosophical investigation and a school for training statesmen and citizens. It had a powerful impact on Greek thought and lasted until the emperor Justinian closed it in the sixth century C.E.

Like Socrates, Plato firmly believed in the polis and its values. Its virtues were order, harmony, and justice, and one of its main objects was to produce good people. Like his master, and unlike the radical Sophists, Plato thought the polis was in accord with nature. He accepted Socrates's doctrine of the identity of virtue and knowledge. He made it plain what that knowledge was: *episteme*—science—a body of true and unchanging wisdom open to only a few philosophers whose training, character, and intellect allowed them to see reality. Only such people were qualified to rule; they would prefer the life of pure contemplation, but would accept their responsibility as philosopher kings. The training of such an individual required a specialization of function and a subordination of that individual to the community even greater than that at Sparta. This specialization would lead to Plato's definition of justice: Each person should do only that one thing to which his or her nature is best suited.

Plato understood that the polis of his day suffered from terrible internal stress, class struggle, and factional divisions. His solution, however, was not that of some Greeks— that is, conquest and resulting economic prosperity. For Plato, the answer was in moral and political reform. The way to harmony was to destroy the causes of strife: private property, the family—anything, in short, that stood between the individual citizen and devotion to the polis.

Concern for the redemption of the polis was at the heart of Plato's system of philosophy. He began by asking the traditional questions: What is a good man, and how is he made? The goodness of a human being belonged to moral philosophy, and when goodness became a function of the state, it became political philosophy. Because goodness depended on knowledge of the good, it required a theory of knowledge and an investigation of what kind of knowledge goodness required. The answer must be metaphysical and so required a full examination of metaphysics. Even when the philosopher knew the good, however, the question remained how the state could bring its citizens to the necessary comprehension of that knowledge. The answer required a theory of education. Even purely logical and metaphysical questions, therefore, were subordinate to the overriding political questions. In this way, Plato's need to find a satisfactory foundation for the beleaguered polis contributed to the birth of systematic philosophy.

3.6.3.3 ARISTOTLE

Aristotle (384–322 B.C.E.) was a pupil of Plato's and owed much to the thought of his master, but his different experience and cast of mind led him in new directions. He was born at Stagirus, the son of the court doctor of neighboring Macedon. As a young man, he went to Athens to study at the Academy, where he stayed until Plato's death. Then he joined a Platonic colony at Assos in Asia Minor, and from there he moved to Mytilene. In both places, he did research in marine biology, and biological interests played a large part in all his thoughts. In 342 B.C.E., Philip, the king of Macedon, appointed him tutor to his son, the young Alexander.

In 336 B.C.E., Aristotle returned to Athens, where he founded his own school, the **Lyceum**, or the Peripatos, as it was also called because of the covered walk within it. In later years its members were called *Peripatetics*. On the death of Alexander the Great in 323 B.C.E., the Athenians rebelled against Macedonian rule, and Aristotle found it wise to leave. He died the following year.

Unlike the Academy, the members of the Lyceum took little interest in mathematics and were concerned with gathering, ordering, and analyzing all human knowledge. Aristotle wrote dialogues on the Platonic model, but none survive. He and his students also prepared many collections of information to serve as the basis for scientific works. Of these, only the *Constitution of the Athenians*, one of 158 constitutional treatises, remains. Almost all that we possess is in the form of philosophical and scientific studies, whose loose organization and style suggest they were lecture notes. The range of subjects treated is astonishing, including logic, physics, astronomy, biology, ethics, rhetoric, literary criticism, and politics.

In each field, the method is the same. Aristotle began with observation of the empirical evidence, which in some cases was physical and in others was common opinion. To this body of information, he applied reason and discovered inconsistencies or difficulties. To deal with these, he introduced metaphysical principles to explain the problems or to reconcile the inconsistencies.

His view on all subjects, like Plato's, was teleological; that is, both Plato and Aristotle recognized purposes apart from and greater than the will of the individual human being. Plato's purposes, however, were contained in ideas, or forms that were transcendental concepts outside the experience of most people. For Aristotle, the purposes of most things were easily inferred by observation of their behavior in the world. Aristotle's most striking characteristics are his moderation and his common sense. His epistemology finds room for both reason and experience; his metaphysics gives meaning and reality to both mind and body; his ethics aims at the good life, which is the contemplative life, but recognizes the necessity for moderate wealth, comfort, and pleasure.

All these qualities are evident in Aristotle's political thought. Like Plato, he opposed the Sophists' assertion that the polis was contrary to nature and the result of mere convention. His response was to apply to politics the teleology he saw in all nature. In Aristotle's view, matter existed to achieve an end, and it developed until it achieved its form, which was its end. There was constant development from matter to form, from potential to actual. Therefore, human primitive instincts could be viewed as the matter out of which the human's potential as a political being could be realized. The polis made individuals self-sufficient and allowed the full realization of their potentiality. It was therefore natural.

According to Aristotle, the realization of human potential was also the highest point in the evolution of the social institutions that serve the human need to continue the species—marriage, household, village, and, finally, polis. For Aristotle, the purpose of the polis was neither economic nor military, but moral. According to Aristotle, "The end of the state is the good life" (*Politics* 1280b), the life lived "for the sake of noble actions" (1281a), a life of virtue and morality.

Characteristically, Aristotle was less interested in the best state—the utopia that required philosophers to rule it—than in the best state that was practically possible, one that would combine justice with stability. The constitution for that state he called *politeia*, not the best constitution, but the next best, the one most suited to, and most possible, for most states. Its quality was moderation, and it naturally gave power to neither the rich nor the poor, but to the middle class, which must also be the most numerous. The middle class possessed many virtues; because of its moderate wealth, it was free of the arrogance of the rich and the malice of the poor. For this reason, it was the most stable class.

The stability of the constitution also came from its being a mixed constitution, blending in some way the laws of democracy and of oligarchy. Aristotle's scheme was unique because of its realism and the breadth of its vision. All political thinkers of the fourth century B.C.E. recognized that the polis was in danger, and all hoped to save it. All recognized the economic and social troubles that threatened it. Isocrates, a contemporary of Plato and Aristotle, urged a program of imperial conquest as a cure for poverty and revolution. Plato saw the folly of solving a political and moral problem by purely economic means and resorted to the creation of utopias. Aristotle combined the practical analysis of political and economic realities with the moral and political purposes of the traditional defenders of the polis. The result was a passionate confidence in the virtues of moderation and of the middle class, and the proposal of a constitution that would give it power. It is ironic that the best defense of the polis came soon before its demise.

3.7 The Hellenistic World

Who was Alexander the Great, and what was his legacy?

The term *Hellenistic* was coined in the nineteenth century to describe the period of three centuries during which Greek culture spread far from its homeland to Egypt and deep into Asia. The new civilization formed in this expansion was a mixture of Greek and Near Eastern elements, although the degree of mixture varied from time to time and place to place. The Hellenistic world was larger than the world of Classical Greece, and its major political units were much larger than the city-states, though these persisted in different forms. The new political and cultural order had its roots in the rise to power of a Macedonian dynasty that conquered Greece and the Persian Empire in two generations.

3.7.1 The Macedonian Conquest of Greece

The quarrels among the Greeks brought on defeat and conquest by a new power that suddenly rose to eminence in the fourth century B.C.E.: the kingdom of Macedon. The Macedonians inhabited the land to the north of Thessaly (see Map 3–1), and through the centuries they had unknowingly served the vital purpose of protecting the Greek states from the barbarian tribes further to the north.

By Greek standards, Macedon was a backward, semi-barbaric land. It had no poleis and was ruled loosely by a king in a rather Homeric fashion. He was chosen partly based on descent, but the acclamation of the army gathered in assembly was required to make him legitimate. Quarrels among pretenders to the throne and even murder to secure it were not uncommon. A council of nobles

CHARIOTEER OF DELPHI This freestanding statue of the *Charioteer of Delphi* is one of the few full-scale bronze sculptures that survive from the fifth century B.C.E. Polyzalos, the tyrant of the Greek city of Gela in Sicily, dedicated it after winning a victory in the chariot race in the Pythian games, either in 478 or 474 B.C.E. The games were held at the sacred shrine of the god Apollo at Delphi, and the statue was placed within the god's sanctuary, not far from Apollo's temple.
SOURCE: Nimatallah/Art Resource, NY

checked the royal power and could reject a weak or incompetent king. Hampered by constant wars with the barbarians, internal strife, loose organization, and lack of money, Macedon played no great part in Greek affairs up to the fourth century B.C.E.

The Macedonians were of the same stock as the Greeks and spoke a Greek dialect, and the nobles, at least, thought of themselves as Greeks. The kings claimed descent from Heracles and the royal house of Argos. They tried to bring Greek culture to their court and won acceptance at the Olympic games. If a king could be found to unify this nation, it was bound to play a greater part in Greek affairs.

KEY EVENTS IN THE RISE OF MACEDON	
359–336 B.C.E.	Reign of Philip II
338 B.C.E.	Battle of Chaeronea; Philip conquers Greece
338 B.C.E.	Founding of League of Corinth
336–323 B.C.E.	Reign of Alexander III (the Great)
334 B.C.E.	Alexander invades Asia
333 B.C.E.	Battle of Issus
331 B.C.E.	Battle of Gaugamela
330 B.C.E.	Fall of Persepolis
327 B.C.E.	Alexander reaches Indus Valley
323 B.C.E.	Death of Alexander

3.7.1.1 PHILIP OF MACEDON That king was Philip II (r. 359–336 B.C.E.), who, although still under thirty, took advantage of his appointment as regent to overthrow his infant nephew and proclaim himself king. Like many of his predecessors, he admired Greek culture. Between 367 and 364 B.C.E., he had been a hostage in Thebes, where he learned much about Greek politics and warfare from Epaminondas. His talents for war and diplomacy and his boundless ambition made him the ablest king in Macedonian history. Using both diplomatic and military means, he pacified the tribes on his frontiers and strengthened his own hold on the throne. Then he began to undermine Athenian control of the northern Aegean. He took control of Amphipolis, which gave him control of gold and silver mines. The income allowed him to found new cities, to bribe politicians in foreign towns, and to reorganize his army into the finest fighting force in the world.

3.7.1.2 THE MACEDONIAN ARMY Philip put to good use what he had learned in Thebes and combined it with the advantages afforded by Macedonian society and tradition. His genius created a versatile and powerful army that was at once national and professional, unlike the amateur armies of citizen-soldiers who fought for the individual poleis.

The infantry was drawn from among Macedonian farmers and the frequently rebellious Macedonian hill people. In time, these two elements were integrated to form a loyal and effective national force. Infantrymen were armed with thirteen-foot pikes instead of the more common nine-foot pikes and stood in a more open phalanx formation than the hoplite phalanx of the poleis. The effectiveness of this formation depended more on the skillful use of the pike than the weight of the charge. In Macedonian tactics, the role of the phalanx was not to be the decisive force, but to hold the enemy until a massed cavalry charge could strike a winning blow on the flank or into a gap. The cavalry was made up of Macedonian nobles and clan leaders, called Companions, who lived closely with the king and developed a special loyalty to him.

Philip also employed mercenaries who knew the latest tactics used by mobile light-armed Greek troops and were familiar with the most sophisticated siege machinery known to the Greeks. With these mercenaries, and with draft forces from among his allies, he could expand on his native Macedonian army of as many as 40,000 men.

3.7.1.3 THE INVASION OF GREECE

So-armed, Philip turned south toward central Greece. Since 355 B.C.E., the Phocians had been fighting against Thebes and Thessaly. Philip gladly accepted the request of the Thessalians to be their general, defeated Phocis, and treacherously took control of Thessaly. Swiftly he turned northward again to Thrace and gained domination over the northern Aegean coast and the European side of the straits to the Black Sea. This conquest threatened the vital interests of Athens, which still had a formidable fleet of 300 ships.

The Athens of 350 B.C.E. was not the Athens of Pericles. It had neither imperial revenue nor allies to share the burden of war, and its own population was smaller than in the fifth century B.C.E. The Athenians, therefore, were reluctant to go on expeditions themselves or even to send out mercenary armies under Athenian generals, for they had to be paid out of taxes or contributions from Athenian citizens.

The leading spokesman against this cautious foreign policy was Demosthenes (384–322 B.C.E.), one of the greatest orators in Greek history. He was convinced that Philip was a dangerous enemy to Athens and the other Greeks. He spent most of his career urging the Athenians to resist Philip's encroachments. He was right, for beginning in 349 B.C.E., Philip attacked several cities in northern and central Greece and firmly planted Macedonian power in those regions. The king of "barbarian" Macedon was elected president of the Pythian Games at Delphi, and the Athenians were forced to concur in the election.

In these difficult times, it was Athens' misfortune not to have the kind of consistent political leadership that Cimon or Pericles had offered a century earlier. Many, perhaps most, Athenians accepted Demosthenes's view of Philip, but few were willing to run the risks and make the sacrifices necessary to stop him. Others, like Eubulus, an outstanding financial official and conservative political leader, favored a cautious policy of cooperation with Philip in the hope that his aims were limited and were no real threat to Athens.

Not all Athenians feared Philip. Isocrates (436–338 B.C.E.), the head of an important rhetorical and philosophical school in Athens, looked to him to provide the unity and leadership needed for a Panhellenic campaign against Persia. He and other orators had long urged such a campaign. They saw the conquest of Asia Minor as the solution to the economic, social, and political problems that had brought poverty and civil war to the Greek cities ever since the Peloponnesian War. Finally, there seem to have been some Athenians who were paid by Philip, for he used money lavishly to win support.

The years between 346 B.C.E. and 340 B.C.E. were spent in diplomatic maneuvering, with each side trying to win useful allies. At last, Philip attacked Perinthus and Byzantium, the lifeline of Athenian commerce; in 340 B.C.E., he besieged both cities and declared war. The Athenian fleet saved both, and so in the following year, Philip marched into Greece. Demosthenes performed wonders in rallying the Athenians and winning Thebes over to the Athenian side. In 338 B.C.E.,

however, Philip defeated the allied forces at Chaeronea in Boeotia. The decisive blow in this great battle was a cavalry charge led by Alexander, the eighteen-year-old son of Philip.

3.7.1.4 THE MACEDONIAN GOVERNMENT OF GREECE

The Macedonian settlement of Greek affairs was not as harsh as many had feared, although in some cities the friends of Macedon came to power and killed or exiled their enemies. Demosthenes remained free to engage in politics. Athens was spared from attack on the condition that it give up what was left of its empire and follow the lead of Macedon. The rest of Greece was arranged to remove all dangers to Philip's rule. To guarantee his security, Philip placed garrisons at Thebes, Chalcis, and Corinth.

In 338 B.C.E., Philip called a meeting of the Greek states to form the federal **League of Corinth**. The constitution of the league provided for autonomy, freedom from tribute and garrisons, and suppression of piracy and civil war. The league delegates would make foreign policy in theory without consulting their home governments or Philip. All this was a façade; not only was Philip of Macedon president of the league, but he was also its ruler. The defeat at Chaeronea ended Greek freedom and autonomy. Although it maintained its form and way of life for some time, the polis had lost control of its own affairs and the special conditions that had made it unique.

Philip did not choose Corinth as the seat of his new confederacy simply out of convenience or by accident. It was at Corinth that the Greeks had gathered to resist a Persian invasion almost 150 years earlier. And it was there in 337 B.C.E. that Philip announced his intention to invade Persia in a war of liberation and revenge, as leader of the new league. In the spring of 336 B.C.E., however, as he prepared to begin the campaign, Philip was assassinated.

In 1977, a mound was excavated at the Macedonian village of Vergina. The structures revealed and the extraordinarily rich finds associated with them have led many scholars to conclude this is the royal tomb of Philip II, and the evidence seems persuasive. Philip certainly deserved so distinguished a resting place. He found Macedon a disunited kingdom of semibarbarians, despised and exploited by the Greeks. He left it a united kingdom, master and leader of the Greeks, rich, powerful, and ready to undertake the invasion of Asia.

3.7.2 Alexander the Great

Philip's first son, Alexander III (356–323 B.C.E.), later called Alexander the Great, succeeded his father at the age of twenty. The young king also inherited his father's daring plans to conquer Persia.

3.7.2.1 THE CONQUEST OF THE PERSIAN EMPIRE

The Persian Empire was vast and its resources enormous. The usurper Cyrus and his Greek mercenaries, however, had shown it to be vulnerable when they penetrated deep into its interior in the fourth century B.C.E. Its size and disparate nature made it hard to control and exploit. Its rulers faced constant troubles on its far-flung frontiers and intrigues within the royal palace. Throughout the fourth century B.C.E., they had used Greek mercenaries to suppress uprisings. At the time of Philip II's death in 336 B.C.E., a new and inexperienced king, Darius III, was ruling Persia. Yet with a navy that dominated the sea, a huge army, and vast wealth, it remained a formidable opponent.

In 334 B.C.E., Alexander crossed the Hellespont into Asia. His army consisted of about 30,000 infantry and 5,000 cavalry; he had no navy and little money. These facts determined his early strategy: to seek quick and decisive battles to gain money and supplies from the conquered territory, and to move along the coast to neutralize the Persian navy by depriving it of ports.

Alexander met the Persian forces of Asia Minor at the Granicus River, where he won a smashing victory in characteristic style. (See Map 3–4.) He led a cavalry charge across the river into the teeth of the enemy on the opposite bank. He almost lost his life in the process, but he won the devotion of his soldiers. That victory left the coast of Asia Minor open. Alexander captured the coastal cities, thus denying them to the Persian fleet.

In 333 B.C.E., Alexander marched inland to Syria, where he met the main Persian army under King Darius at Issus. Alexander himself led the cavalry charge that broke the Persian line and sent Darius fleeing into central Asia Minor. He continued along the coast and captured previously impregnable Tyre after a long and ingenious siege, putting an end to the threat of the Persian navy. He took Egypt with little trouble and was greeted as liberator, pharaoh, and son of Re (an Egyptian god whose Greek equivalent was Zeus). At Tyre, Darius sent Alexander a peace offer, yielding his entire empire west of the Euphrates River and his daughter in exchange for an alliance and an end to the invasion. But Alexander aimed at conquering the whole empire and probably whatever lay beyond.

In the spring of 331 B.C.E., Alexander marched into Mesopotamia. At the **Battle of Gaugamela**, near the ancient Assyrian city of Nineveh, he met Darius, ready for a last stand. Once again, Alexander's tactical genius and personal leadership carried the day. The Persians were broken, and Darius fled once more. Alexander entered Babylon, again hailed as liberator and king.

In January of 330 B.C.E., he came to Persepolis, the Persian capital, which held splendid palaces and the royal treasury. This bonanza ended Alexander's financial troubles and put a vast sum of money into circulation, with economic consequences that lasted for centuries. After a stay of several months, Alexander burned Persepolis to dramatize the destruction of the native Persian dynasty and the completion of Hellenic revenge for the earlier Persian invasion of Greece.

The new regime could not be secure while Darius lived, so Alexander pursued him eastward. Just south of the Caspian Sea, he came on the corpse of Darius, killed by his relative Bessus. The Persian nobles around Darius had lost faith in him and had joined in the plot. The murder

removed Darius from Alexander's path, but now he had to catch Bessus, who proclaimed himself successor to Darius. The pursuit of Bessus (who was soon caught), combined with his own great curiosity and longing to go to the most distant places, took Alexander to the frontier of India.

Near Samarkand, in the land of the Scythians, he founded Alexandria Eschate ("Furthest Alexandria"), one of the many cities bearing his name that he founded as he traveled. As part of his grand scheme of amalgamation and conquest, Alexander married the Bactrian princess Roxane and enrolled 30,000 young Bactrians into his army. These were to be trained and sent back to the center of the empire for later use.

In 327 B.C.E., Alexander took his army through the Khyber Pass in an attempt to conquer the lands around the Indus River (modern Pakistan). He reduced the king of these lands, Porus, to vassalage but pushed on in the hope of reaching the river called Ocean that the Greeks believed encircled the world. Finally, his weary men refused to go on. By the spring of 324 B.C.E., the army was back at the Persian Gulf and celebrated in the Macedonian style, with a wild spree of drinking.

3.7.2.2 THE DEATH OF ALEXANDER Alexander was filled with plans for the future: for the consolidation and organization of his empire; for geographical exploration; for building new cities, roads, and harbors; and perhaps for further conquests in the west. There is even some evidence that he asked to be deified and worshipped as a god, although we cannot be sure if he really did so or why. In June 323 B.C.E., however, he was overcome by a fever and died in Babylon at the age of thirty-two.

Alexander's memory has never faded, and he soon became the subject of myth, legend, and romance. From the beginning, estimates of him have varied. Some have seen in him a man of grand and noble vision who transcended the narrow limits of Greek and Macedonian ethnocentrism and sought to realize the solidarity of humankind in a great world state. Others have seen him as a calculating despot, given to drunken brawls, brutality, and murder.

The truth is probably somewhere in between. Alexander was one of the greatest generals the world has seen; he never lost a battle or failed in a siege, and with a modest army he conquered a vast empire. He had rare organizational talents, and his plan for creating a multinational empire was the only intelligent way to consolidate his conquests. He established many new cities—seventy, according to tradition—mostly along trade routes. These cities encouraged commerce and prosperity and introduced Hellenic civilization to new areas. It is hard to know if even Alexander could have held together the vast new empire he had created, but his death proved that only he would have had a chance to succeed.

3.7.3 The Successors

Nobody was prepared for Alexander's sudden death, and a weak succession further complicated affairs: Roxane's unborn child and Alexander's weak-minded half brother. His able

Map 3–4 ALEXANDER'S CAMPAIGNS

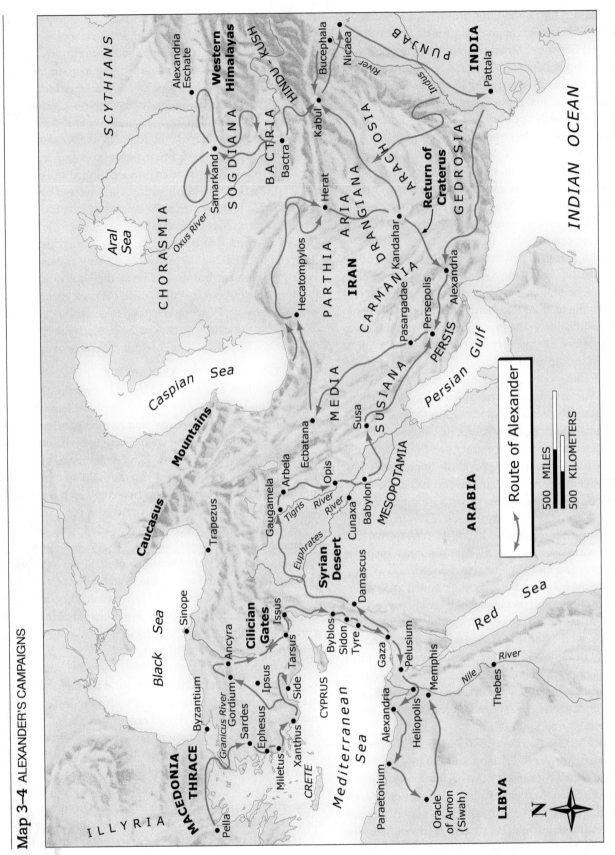

The route taken by Alexander the Great in his conquest of the Persian Empire, 334 to 323 B.C.E. Starting from the Macedonian capital at Pella, he reached the Indus Valley before being turned back by his own restive troops. He died of fever in Mesopotamia.

and loyal Macedonian generals at first hoped to preserve the empire for the Macedonian royal house, and to this end they appointed themselves governors of the various provinces of the empire. The conflicting ambitions of these strong-willed men, however, led to prolonged warfare among them. In these conflicts three of the original number were killed, and all the direct members of the Macedonian royal house were either executed or murdered. With the murder of Roxane and her son in 310 B.C.E., there was no longer any focus for the enormous empire; and in 306 and 305 B.C.E., the surviving governors proclaimed themselves kings of their various holdings.

Three of these Macedonian generals founded dynasties of significance in the spread of Hellenistic culture:

- Ptolemy I, 367–283 B.C.E.; founder of Dynasty 31 in Egypt, the Ptolemies, of whom Cleopatra, who died in 30 B.C.E., was the last active ruler

- Seleucus I, 358–280 B.C.E.; founder of the Seleucid Dynasty in Mesopotamia

- Antigonus I, 382–301 B.C.E.; founder of the Antigonid Dynasty in Asia Minor and Macedon

For the first seventy-five years or so after the death of Alexander, the world ruled by his successors enjoyed considerable prosperity. The vast sums of money that he and they put into circulation greatly increased the level of economic activity. The opportunities for service and profit in the East attracted many Greeks and relieved their native cities of some of the pressure of the poor. The opening of vast new territories to Greek trade, the increased demand for Greek products, and the new availability of desired goods, as well as the conscious policies of the Hellenistic kings, all helped the growth of commerce.

The new prosperity, however, was not evenly distributed. The urban Greeks, the Macedonians, and the Hellenized natives who made up the upper and middle classes lived in comfort and even luxury, but the rural native peasants did not. Unlike the independent men who owned and worked the relatively small and equal lots of the polis in earlier times, Hellenistic farmers were reduced to subordinate, dependent peasant status, working on large plantations of decreasing efficiency. During prosperous times, these class distinctions were bearable, although even then there was tension between the two groups. After a while, however, the costs of continuing wars, inflation, and a gradual lessening of the positive effects of the introduction of Persian wealth all led to economic crisis. The kings bore down heavily on the middle classes, who were skilled at avoiding their responsibilities. The pressure on the peasants and the city laborers became great too, and they responded by slowing down their work and even by striking. In Greece, economic pressures brought clashes between rich and poor, demands for the abolition of debt and the redistribution of land, and even, on occasion, civil war.

These internal divisions, along with international wars, weakened the capacity of the Hellenistic kingdoms to resist

outside attack. By the middle of the second century B.C.E., they had all, except for Egypt, succumbed to an expanding Italian power, Rome. The two centuries between Alexander and the Roman conquest, however, were of great and lasting importance. They saw the entire eastern Mediterranean coast, Greece, Egypt, Mesopotamia, and the old Persian Empire formed into a single political, economic, and cultural unit.

3.8 Hellenistic Culture

How did Hellenistic culture differ from the culture of Classical Greece?

The career of Alexander the Great marked a significant turning point in Greek thought as it was represented in literature, philosophy, religion, and art. His conquests and the establishment of the successor kingdoms put an end to the central role of the polis in Greek life and thought. Some scholars disagree about the end of the polis, denying that Philip's victory at Chaeronea marked its demise. They point to the persistence of poleis throughout the Hellenistic period and even see a continuation of them in the Roman *municipia*. These were, however, only a shadow of the vital reality that had been the true polis.

Deprived of control of their foreign affairs, and with a foreign monarch determining their important internal

THE *LAOCOÖN* This is a Roman copy of one of the masterpieces of Hellenistic sculpture, the *Laocoön*. According to legend, Laocoön was a priest who warned the Trojans not to accept the Greeks' wooden horse into their city. This sculpture depicts his punishment. Great serpents sent by the goddess Athena, who sided with the Greeks, devoured Laocoön and his sons before the horrified people of Troy.
SOURCE: INTERFOTO/Alamy Stock Photo

arrangements, the post-Classical cities lost the political freedom that was basic to the old outlook. They were cities, perhaps—in a sense, even city-states—but not poleis. As time passed, they changed from sovereign states to municipal towns merged into military empires. Never again in antiquity would there be either a serious attack on or defense of the polis, for its importance was gone. For the most part, the Greeks after Alexander turned away from political solutions for their problems. Instead, they sought personal responses to their hopes and fears, particularly in religion, philosophy, and magic. The confident, sometimes arrogant, humanism of the fifth century B.C.E. gave way to a kind of resignation to fate, a recognition of helplessness before forces too great for humans to manage.

3.8.1 Philosophy

These developments are noticeable in the changes that overtook the established schools of philosophy as well as in the emergence of two new and influential groups of philosophers: the **Epicureans** and the **Stoics**. Athens' position as the center of philosophical studies was reinforced, for the Academy and the Lyceum continued in operation, and the new schools were also located in Athens. The Lyceum turned gradually away from the universal investigations of its founder Aristotle, even from his scientific interests, to become a center chiefly of literary and especially historical studies.

The Academy turned even further away from its tradition. It adopted the systematic Skepticism of Pyrrho of Elis. Under the leadership of Arcesilaus and Carneades, the Skeptics of the Academy became skilled at pointing out fallacies and weaknesses in the philosophies of the rival schools. They thought that nothing could be known and consoled themselves and their followers by suggesting that nothing mattered. It was easy for them, therefore, to accept conventional morality and the world as it was.

3.8.1.1 THE EPICUREANS Epicurus of Athens (342–271 B.C.E.) formulated a new teaching, embodied in the school he founded in his native city in 306 B.C.E. His philosophy conformed to the mood of the times in that its goal was not knowledge but human happiness, which he believed a style of life based on reason could achieve. He viewed sense perception as the basis of all human knowledge. The reality and reliability of sense perception rested on the acceptance of the physical universe described by the atomists, Democritus and Leucippus. The **Epicureans** proclaimed atoms were continually falling through the void and giving off images that were in direct contact with the senses. These falling atoms could swerve in an arbitrary, unpredictable way to produce the combinations seen in the world.

Epicurus thereby removed an element of determinism that existed in the Democritean system. When a person died, the atoms that composed the body dispersed, so the person had no further existence or perception and therefore nothing to fear after death. Epicurus believed the gods existed, but that they took no interest in human affairs. This belief amounted to a practical atheism, and Epicureans were often thought to be atheists.

The purpose of Epicurean physics was to liberate people from their fear of death, of the gods, and of all nonmaterial or supernatural powers. Epicurean ethics were hedonistic, that is, based on the acceptance of pleasure as true happiness. But pleasure for Epicurus was chiefly negative: the absence of pain and trouble. The goal of the Epicureans was *ataraxia*, the condition of being undisturbed, without trouble, pain, or responsibility. Ideally, a man should have enough means to allow him to withdraw from the world and avoid business and public life. Epicurus even advised against marriage and children. He preached a life of genteel, restrained selfishness that might appeal to intellectual men of means but was not calculated to be widely attractive.

3.8.1.2 THE STOICS Soon after Epicurus began teaching in his garden in Athens, Zeno of Citium in Cyprus (335–263 B.C.E.) established the Stoic school. It derived its name from the *stoa poikile*, or painted portico, in the Athenian *agora*, where Zeno and his disciples walked and talked beginning about 300 B.C.E. From then until about the middle of the second century B.C.E., Zeno and his successors preached a philosophy that owed a good deal to Socrates, by way of the Cynics. It was also fed by a stream of Eastern thought. Zeno, of course, came from Phoenician Cyprus; Chrysippus, one of his successors, came from Cilicia in southern Asia Minor; and other early Stoics came from such places as Carthage, Tarsus, and Babylon.

Like the Epicureans, the Stoics sought the happiness of the individual. But unlike them, the Stoics proposed a philosophy almost indistinguishable from religion. They believed humans must live in harmony within themselves and with nature; for the Stoics, God and nature were the same. The guiding principle in nature was *Logos*, divine reason, or fire. Every human had a spark of this divinity, and after death it returned to the eternal divine spirit. From time to time the world was destroyed by fire, from which a new world arose.

The aim of humans, and the definition of human happiness, was the virtuous life: a life lived in accordance with natural law, "when all actions promote the harmony of the spirit dwelling in the individual man with the will of him who orders the universe."[3] To live such a life required the knowledge only the wise possessed. They knew what was good, what was evil, and what was neither, but "indifferent." According to the Stoics, good and evil were dispositions of the mind or soul: prudence, justice, courage, temperance, and so on, were good; folly, injustice, cowardice, and the like, were evil. Life, health, pleasure, beauty, strength, wealth, and so on, were neutral—morally indifferent—for they did not contribute either to happiness or to misery. Human misery came from an irrational mental contraction—from passion, which was a disease of the soul. The wise sought *apatheia*, or freedom from passion, because passion arose from things that were morally indifferent.

Politically, the Stoics fit well with the new world. They thought of it as a single polis in which all people were children of the same God. Although they did not forbid political activity, and many Stoics took part in political life, withdrawal was obviously preferable because the usual subjects of political argument were indifferent. Because the Stoics strove for inner harmony of the individual, their aim was a life lived in accordance with the divine will, their attitude fatalistic, and their goal a form of apathy. They fit in well with the reality of post-Alexandrian life. In fact, Stoicism facilitated the creation of a new political system that relied not on the active participation of the governed but merely on their docile submission.

3.8.2 Literature

Hellenistic literature reflects the new intellectual currents, the new conditions of literary life, and the new institutions created in that period. The center of literary life in the third and second centuries B.C.E. was the new city of Alexandria in Egypt. There the Ptolemies, the monarchs of Egypt during that time, founded the museum—a great research institute where royal funds supported scientists and scholars—and the library, which contained almost half a million papyrus scrolls.

The library contained much of the great body of past Greek literature, most of which has since been lost. Alexandrian scholars made copies of what they judged to be the best works. They edited and criticized these works from the point of view of language, form, and content, and wrote biographies of the authors. Their work is responsible for the preservation of most of what remains of ancient literature.

The scholarly atmosphere of Alexandria naturally gave rise to work in history and chronology. Eratosthenes (ca. 275–195 B.C.E.) established a chronology of important events dating from the Trojan War, and others undertook similar tasks. Contemporaries of Alexander, such as Ptolemy I, Aristobulus, and Nearchus, wrote what were apparently sober and essentially factual accounts of his career. We know most of the work of Hellenistic historians only in fragments that later writers cited. It seems, in general, to have emphasized sensational and biographical detail over the kind of rigorous, impersonal analysis that marked the work of Thucydides.

3.8.3 Architecture and Sculpture

The advent of the Hellenistic monarchies greatly increased the opportunities open to architects and sculptors. Money was plentiful, rulers sought outlets for conspicuous display, new cities needed to be built

and beautified, and the well-to-do wanted objects of art. The new cities were usually laid out on the grid plan introduced in the fifth century B.C.E. by Hippodamus of Miletus. Temples were built on the classical model, and the covered portico, or *stoa*, became a popular addition to the agoras of the Hellenistic towns.

Reflecting the cosmopolitan nature of the Hellenistic world, leading sculptors accepted commissions wherever they were attractive. The result was a certain uniformity of style, although Alexandria, Rhodes, and the kingdom of Pergamum in Asia Minor developed their own distinctive characteristics. For the most part, Hellenistic sculpture moved away from the balanced tension and idealism of the fifth century B.C.E. toward the sentimental, emotional, and realistic mode of the fourth century B.C.E. These qualities are readily apparent in the marble statue called the Laocoön, carved at Rhodes in the second century B.C.E. and afterward taken to Rome.

3.8.4 Mathematics and Science

Among the most spectacular and remarkable intellectual developments of the Hellenistic Age were those in mathematics and science. The burst of activity in these subjects drew their inspiration from several sources. The work of Plato and Aristotle sparked intellectual curiosity that should not be ignored. Alexander's interest in science, evidenced by the scientists he took with him on his expedition and the aid he gave them in collecting data, provided further impetus.

The expansion of Greek horizons geographically and the consequent contacts with Egyptian and Babylonian knowledge were also helpful. Finally, the patronage of the

HIDDEN MANUSCRIPT OF ARCHIMEDES A page from *On Floating Bodies*. Archimedes's work was covered by a tenth-century manuscript, but ultraviolet radiation reveals the original text and drawings underneath.
SOURCE: Greek School/Private Collection/Photo © Christie's Images/Bridgeman Images

Ptolemies and the opportunity for many scientists to work with one another at the museum at Alexandria provided a unique opportunity for scientific work. The work the Alexandrians did formed the greater part of the scientific knowledge available to the Western world until the scientific revolution of the sixteenth and seventeenth centuries C.E.

Euclid's *Elements* (written early in the third century B.C.E.) remained the textbook of plane and solid geometry until recent times. Archimedes of Syracuse (ca. 287–212 B.C.E.) made further progress in geometry, established the theory of the lever in mechanics, and invented hydrostatics.

These advances in mathematics, once they were applied to the Babylonian astronomical tables available to the Hellenistic world, spurred great progress in astronomy. As early as the fourth century B.C.E., Heraclides of Pontus (ca. 390–310 B.C.E.) had argued that Mercury and Venus circle around the sun and not the earth. He appears to have made other suggestions leading to a **heliocentric theory** of the universe. Most scholars, however, give credit for that theory to Aristarchus of Samos (ca. 310–230 B.C.E.), who asserted that the sun, along with the other fixed stars, did not move and that the earth revolved around the sun in a circular orbit and rotated on its axis while doing so. The heliocentric theory ran contrary not only to the traditional view codified by Aristotle but also to what seemed to be common sense.

Hellenistic technology was not up to proving the theory, and, of course, the planetary orbits are not circular. The heliocentric theory did not, therefore, take hold. Hipparchus of Nicea (b. ca. 190 B.C.E.) constructed a model of the universe on the geocentric theory; his ingenious and complicated model did a good job of accounting for the movements of the sun, the moon, and the planets. Ptolemy of Alexandria (second century C.E.) improved Hipparchus's system, which remained dominant until the work of Copernicus, in the sixteenth century C.E.

Hellenistic scientists mapped the earth as well as the sky. Eratosthenes of Cyrene (ca. 275–195 B.C.E.) calculated the circumference of the earth to within about 200 miles. He wrote a treatise on geography based on mathematical and physical reasoning and the reports of travelers. Despite the new data that were available to later geographers, Eratosthenes's map was in many ways more accurate than the one Ptolemy of Alexandria constructed, which became standard in the Middle Ages. (See Map 3–5.)

The Hellenistic Age contributed little to the life sciences, such as biology, zoology, and medicine. Even the sciences that had such impressive achievements in the third century B.C.E. made little progress thereafter. In fact, to some extent, there was a retreat from science. Astrology and magic became subjects of great interest as scientific advance lagged.

Map 3–5 THE WORLD ACCORDING TO ERATOSTHENES

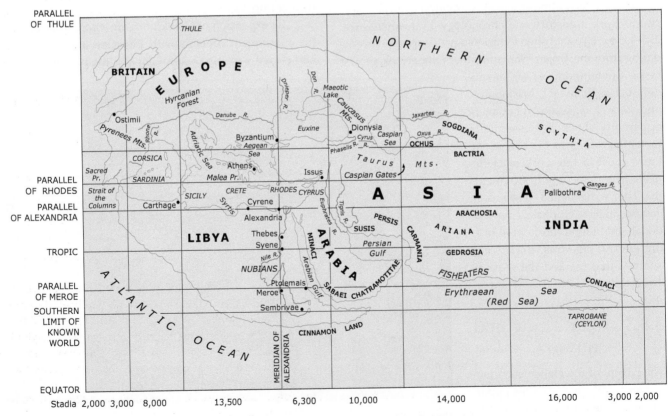

Eratosthenes of Cyrene (ca. 275–195 B.C.E.) was a Hellenistic geographer. His map, reconstructed here, was remarkably accurate for its time. The world was divided by lines of "latitude" and "longitude," thus anticipating modern global divisions.

The Chapter in Perspective

The Classical Age of Greece was a period of unparalleled achievement. Whereas monarchical, hierarchical, command societies continued to characterize the rest of the world, in Athens democracy was carried as far as it would go before modern times. Although Athenian citizenship was limited to adult males of native parentage, citizens were granted full and active participation in every decision of the state without regard to wealth or class. Democracy disappeared late in the fourth century B.C.E. with the end of Greek autonomy. When it returned in the modern world more than two millennia later, it was broader, but shallower. Democratic citizenship did not again imply the active, direct participation of every citizen in the government of the state.

It was in this democratic, imperial Athens that the greatest artistic, literary, and philosophical achievements of Classical Greece took place. Analytical, secular history, tragedy and comedy, the philosophical dialogue, an organized system of logic, and the logical philosophical treatise were among the achievements of the Classical Age. The tradition of rational, secular speculation in natural philosophy and science was carried forward, but more attention was devoted to human questions in medicine and ethical and political philosophy. A naturalistic style of art evolved that showed human beings first as they ideally might look and then as they really looked, an approach that dominated Greek and Roman art until the late stages of the Roman Empire. This naturalistic style had a powerful effect on the Italian Renaissance and, through it, the modern world.

These Hellenic developments, it should be clear, diverge sharply from the experience of previous cultures and of contemporary ones in the rest of the world.

To a great degree, they sprang from the unique political experience of the Greeks, based on the independent city-states. That unique experience and the Classical period ended with the Macedonian conquest, which introduced the Hellenistic Age and ultimately made the Greeks subject to, or part of, a great national state or empire.

The Hellenistic Age speaks to us less fully and vividly than the age of Classical Greece, chiefly because it had no historian to compare with Herodotus and Thucydides. We lack the clear picture that a continuous, rich, lively, and meaningful narrative provides. This deficiency should not obscure the great achievements of the age. Its literature, art, scholarship, and science deserve attention in their own right.

The Hellenistic Age did perform a vital civilizing function. It spread Greek culture over a remarkably wide area and made a significant and lasting impression on much of it. Greek culture also adjusted to its new surroundings, unifying and simplifying its cultural cargo to make it more accessible to outsiders. The various Greek dialects gave way to a version of the Attic tongue, the koine, or common language.

In the same way, the scholarship of Alexandria established canons of literary excellence and the scholarly tools with which to make the great treasures of Greek culture understandable to later generations. The syncretism of thought and belief introduced in this period also made understanding and accord more likely among different peoples. When the Romans encountered Hellenism, it impressed them powerfully. When they conquered the Hellenistic world, they became, as their poet Horace said, captives of its culture.

The Chapter in Review

Review Questions

1. How was the Delian League transformed into the Athenian Empire during the fifth century B.C.E.? Did the empire offer any advantages to its subjects?
2. Why did Athens and Sparta come to blows in the Great Peloponnesian War? What was each side's strategy for victory? Why did Sparta win the war?
3. Give examples from art, literature, and philosophy of the tension that characterized Greek life and thought in the Classical Age. How does Hellenistic art differ from that of the Classical Age?
4. Between 431 and 362 B.C.E., why did Athens, Sparta, and Thebes each fail to impose hegemony over the city-states of Greece? What does your analysis tell you about the components of successful rule?
5. How and why did Philip II conquer Greece between 359 and 338 B.C.E.? How was he able to turn Macedon into a formidable military and political power? Why was Athens unable to defend itself against Macedon? Where does more of the credit for Philip's success lie—in Macedon's strength or in the weakness of the Greek city-states?
6. What were the major consequences of Alexander's death? What did he achieve? Was he a conscious promoter of Greek civilization or just an egomaniac drunk with the lust for conquest?

Key Terms

Academy   Center of philosophical investigation and a school for training statesmen and citizens that was founded by Plato in 386 b.c.e.

atomist   School of ancient Greek philosophy founded in the fifth century b.c.e. by Leucippus of Miletus and Democritus of Abdera. Believed that the world consisted of innumerable, tiny, solid, indivisible, and unchangeable particles called *atoms*.

Battle of Gaugamela   The decisive contest in 331 b.c.e. through which Alexander the Great beat Darius and proclaimed himself king of the Persian Empire.

Cimon   The son of Miltiades, the hero of the Battle of Marathon, who dominated Athenian politics for nearly two decades after the Persian Wars. The leading general of the Delian League, he pursued a policy of aggressive attacks on Persia and friendship with Sparta.

Critias   An Athenian oligarch and one of the more extreme Sophists whose ideas attacked the theoretical foundations of the polis. Member of the Thirty Tyrants.

Delian League (DEE-li-an)   An alliance of Greek states under the leadership of Athens that was formed in 478–477 b.c.e. to resist the Persians and, in time, was transformed into the Athenian Empire.

Epicureans (EP-i-cure-ee-ans)   School of philosophy founded by Epicurus of Athens (342–271 b.c.e.). Sought to liberate people from fear of death and the supernatural by teaching that the gods took no interest in human affairs and that true happiness consisted in pleasure, defined as the absence of pain. Defined *ataraxia* as freedom from trouble, pain, and responsibility by withdrawing from business and public life.

heliocentric theory (HE-li-o-cen-trick)   The theory, now universally accepted, that the earth and the other planets revolve around the sun. First proposed by Aristarchos of Samos (310–230 b.c.e.). Opposed the geocentric theory, dominant until the sixteenth century c.e., which held that the sun and the planets revolved around the earth.

Hellenistic   A term coined in the nineteenth century to describe the period of three centuries during which Greek culture spread far from its homeland to Egypt and deep into Asia.

League of Corinth   The federation of Greek states formed by Philip II in 338 b.c.e. to dominate Greece.

Logos **(LOW-goz)**   Divine reason, or fire, which according to the Stoics was the guiding principle in nature and meant that every human had a spark of this divinity, which returned to the eternal divine spirit after death.

Lyceum   The name of the school founded by Aristotle when he returned to Athens in 336 b.c.e.

Menander   (342–291 b.c.e.) The leading playwright of New Comedy in Athens, who, in contrast with writers of drama in the fifth century b.c.e., abandoned mythological subjects in favor of domestic tragicomedy.

Parmenides of Elea   A philosopher of Elea who argued that change was only an illusion of the senses.

Peloponnesian Wars (PELL-o-po-knees-ee-an)   The protracted struggle between Athens and Sparta to dominate Greece between 460 b.c.e. and Athens' final defeat in 404 b.c.e.

Philip II of Macedon   (r. 359–336 b.c.e) The king who united Macedon into a powerful state through both diplomatic and military means and who created a national and professional army with which he conquered the Greek world.

Second Athenian Confederation   Organized by Athens in 378 b.c.e. Sought to resist Spartan aggression in the Aegean and avoid the abuses of the Delian League.

Stoics (STOW-icks)   A philosophical school founded by Zeno of Citium (335–263 b.c.e.) that taught that humans could only be happy with natural law; human misery was caused by passion, which was a disease of the soul; and that the wise sought *apatheia*, freedom from passion.

Thirty Tyrants   The oligarchic government that the Spartan Lysander installed after the Peloponnesian War in Athens, whose outrageous behavior, which included the slaughter of hundreds of Athenian citizens, earned them their name.

Thirty Years' Peace   Treaty struck between Athens and Sparta in 445 b.c.e. that gave formal recognition of the Athenian Empire. An important clause in the agreement required that all disputes be resolved through arbitration.

Notes

1. Aristotle, *Politics* 1300a.
2. M. I. Finley, "Was Greek Civilization Based on Slave Labor?" *Historia* 8 (1959), p. 151.
3. Diogenes Laertius, *Life of Antisthenes* 6.11.

Chapter 4
Rome: From Republic to Empire

THE PONT DU GARD An aqueduct and bridge, the Pont du Gard was built in the first century B.C.E. in southern France in Rome's first province beyond the Alps.
SOURCE: Walter S. Clark/Photo Researchers, Inc.

∨ Contents and Focus Questions

The Chapter in Brief

THE ACHIEVEMENT OF the Romans was one of the most remarkable in human history. Descendants of the inhabitants of a small village in central Italy, the Romans came eventually to rule the entire Italian peninsula and then the entire Mediterranean coastline. They conquered most of the Near East and finally, much of continental Europe. They ruled this vast empire under a single government that provided considerable peace and prosperity for centuries. Neither before the Romans nor since has that area been united, and rarely, if ever, has it enjoyed a stable peace. But Rome's legacy was not merely military excellence and political organization. The Romans adopted and transformed the intellectual and cultural achievements of the Greeks and combined them with their own outlook and historical experience. The resulting Greco-Roman tradition in literature, philosophy, and art became the core of learning for the Middle Ages and paved the way to the new paths taken in the Renaissance. It remains at the heart of Western civilization to this day.

4.1 Prehistoric Italy

How did the arrival of the Italic peoples affect the culture of Italy?

The culture of Italy developed late. Paleolithic settlements gave way to the Neolithic mode of life only around 2500 B.C.E. The Bronze Age began around 1500 B.C.E. About 1000 B.C.E., bands of new arrivals—warlike peoples speaking a set of closely related languages we call *Italic*—began to infiltrate Italy from across the Adriatic Sea and around its northern end. These invaders cremated their dead and put the ashes in tombs stocked with weapons and armor. Their bronzework was of a higher quality than that of the people they displaced, and they were soon making weapons, armor, and tools of iron. By 800 B.C.E., they had occupied the highland pastures of the Apennines, and within a short time, they began to challenge the earlier settlers for control of the tempting western plains. It would be the descendants of these tough mountain people—Umbrians, Sabines, Samnites, and Latins—together with others soon to arrive—Etruscans, Greeks, and Celts—who would shape the future of Italy.

4.2 The Etruscans

Who were the Etruscans, and how did they influence Rome?

The **Etruscans** exerted the most powerful external influence on the Romans. Their civilization arose in Etruria (now Tuscany), west of the Apennines between the Arno and Tiber Rivers, about 800 B.C.E. (See Map 4–1.) Since antiquity their origin has been debated, some arguing that they were indigenous and others that they came from the east. The evidence does not permit any certainty, and scholarship today focuses on the formation of a people rather than its origins.

4.2.1 Government

The Etruscans brought civilization with them. Their settlements were self-governing, fortified city-states, of which

APOLLO OF VEII Attributed to the sixth-century B.C.E. Etruscan artist Vulca, the Apollo of Veii is a terracotta statue standing at nearly six feet tall. It was found at the Sanctuary of Portonaccio north of Rome and is regarded as a fine example of Etruscan art.
SOURCE: De Agostini Picture Library/Getty Images

Map 4–1 ANCIENT ITALY

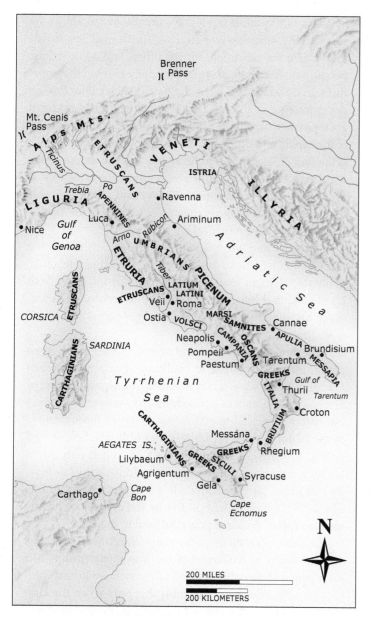

This map of ancient Italy and its neighbors before the expansion of Rome shows major cities and towns as well as several geographical regions and the locations of some of the Italic and non-Italic peoples.

twelve formed a loose religious confederation. At first, kings ruled these cities, but they were replaced by an agrarian aristocracy, which ruled through a council and elected annual magistrates. The Etruscans were a military ruling class that exploited the native Italians (the predecessors of the later Italic speakers), who worked the Etruscans' land and mines and served as infantry in Etruscan armies. This aristocracy accumulated wealth through agriculture, industry, piracy, and commerce with the Carthaginians and the Greeks.

4.2.2 Religion

The Etruscans' greatest influence on the Romans was in religion. They imagined a world filled with gods and spirits, many of them evil. To deal with such demons, the Etruscans developed complicated rituals and powerful priesthoods. Divination by sacrifice and omens in nature helped discover the divine will, and careful attention to precise rituals directed by priests helped please the gods. After a while the Etruscans, influenced by the Greeks, worshipped gods in the shape of humans and built temples for them.

4.2.3 Women

Etruscan women had a more significant role in family and society than did Greek women in the world of the polis. Etruscan wives appeared in public, in religious festivals, and at public banquets together with their husbands. Many of them were literate, and women both took part in athletic contests and watched them as spectators alongside men. Inscriptions on tombs and paintings on coffins mention both father and mother of the deceased and often depict husbands and wives together as respectful and loving couples.

4.2.4 Dominion

The Etruscan aristocracy remained aggressive and skillful in the use of horses and war chariots. In the seventh and sixth centuries B.C.E., they expanded their power in Italy and across the sea to Corsica and Elba. They conquered **Latium** (a region that included the small town of Rome) and Campania, where they became neighbors of the Greeks of Naples. In the north, they got as far as the Po Valley.

ETRUSCAN SARCOPHAGUS OF A COUPLE This elaborate coffin was discovered in a tomb at Cerveteri in the Italian region of Tuscany, the heart of ancient Etruria. Dated to about 520 B.C.E. and made of terracotta, it shows wife and husband reclining affectionately together.
SOURCE: Erich Lessing/Art Resource, NY

Etruscan power reached its height some time before 500 B.C.E. and then rapidly declined. About 400 B.C.E., Celtic peoples from the area the Romans called **Gaul** (modern France) broke into the Po Valley and drove out the Etruscans. They settled this land so firmly that the Romans thereafter called it *Cisalpine Gaul* (Gaul on this side of the Alps). Eventually, even the Etruscan heartland in Etruria lost its independence and was incorporated into Roman Italy. The Etruscan language was forgotten, and Etruscan culture gradually became only a memory, but its influence on the Romans remained.

4.3   Royal Rome

How did ideas about the family influence society and government in early Rome?

Rome was an unimportant town in Latium until the Etruscans conquered it, but its location—fifteen miles from the mouth of the Tiber River, at the point where hills made further navigation impossible—gave it advantages over its Latin neighbors. The island in the Tiber southwest of the Capitoline Hill made the river fordable, so Rome was naturally a center for communication and trade, both east–west and north–south.

4.3.1   Government

In the sixth century B.C.E., Rome came under Etruscan control. Led by Etruscan kings, the Roman army, equipped and organized like the Greek phalanx, gained control of most of Latium. This success was made possible by an effective political and social order that gave extraordinary power to the ruling figures in both public and private life. To their kings, the Romans gave the awesome power of

HUT OF ROMULUS Romulus was the legendary founder of the city of Rome. The purported remains of his hut on the Palatine Hill, built in the eighth century B.C.E., offer glimpses into early architectural techniques.
SOURCE: Valery Rokhin/Shutterstock

imperium—the right to issue commands and to enforce them by fines, arrests, and corporal, or even capital, punishment. Although it tended apparently to remain in the same family, kingship was elective. The Roman Senate had to approve the candidate for the office, and a vote of the people gathered in an assembly formally granted the imperium. In this structure, a basic characteristic of later Roman government was already apparent, namely, the granting of great power to executive officers contingent on the approval of the Senate and ultimately the people. The word *imperium* is the root of *imperator*, a military title and the source of our word *emperor*, which would eventually become the title of Rome's rulers. This union of military and political power would be a major theme in the transformation of the Roman Republic into a monarchical empire.

In theory and law, the king was the commander of the army, the chief priest, and the supreme judge. He could make decisions in foreign affairs, call out the army, lead it in battle, and impose discipline on his troops, all by virtue of his imperium. In practice, the royal power was much more limited.

The Senate was the second branch of the early Roman government. According to tradition, it originated when Romulus, Rome's legendary first king, chose one hundred of Rome's leading men to advise him. The number of senators ultimately increased to 300, where it stayed through most of the history of the republic. Ostensibly, the Senate had neither executive nor legislative power; it met only when the king summoned it to advise him. In reality, its authority was great, for the senators, like the king, served for life. The Senate, therefore, had continuity and experience, and its members were the most powerful men in the state.

The third branch of government, the curiate assembly, was made up of citizens divided into thirty groups. (In early Rome, citizenship required descent from Roman parents on both sides.) The assembly met only when the king summoned it; he determined the agenda, made proposals, and recognized other speakers, if any. Usually, the assembly was called to listen and approve. Voting was not by head, but by group; a majority within each group determined its vote, and the majority vote of all groups determined decisions. Group voting would be typical of all future forms of Roman assembly.

4.3.2   Family

The center of Roman life was the family. At its head stood the father (*paterfamilias*), whose power and authority within the family resembled those of the king within the state. Over his children, the father held broad powers analogous to imperium in the state; he had the right to sell his children into slavery, and he even had the power of life and death over them. Over his wife, he had less power; he could not sell or kill her. In practice, consultation within the family, public opinion, and most of all, tradition limited his power to dispose of his children. The father was also the chief priest of the family. He led his family in daily prayers to the dead, which reflected the ancestor worship central to the Roman family and state.

4.3.3 Women

Early Roman society was hierarchical and dominated by males. Throughout her life, a woman was under the control of some adult male. Before her marriage it was her father, afterward her husband, or when neither was available, a guardian chosen from one of their male relatives. One of them had to approve her right to buy or sell property or make contracts. Roman law gave control of a woman from father to husband by the right of *manus* (hand). This was conferred by one of two formal marriage ceremonies that were typical in early Rome. Over time, however, a third form of marriage became popular that left the power of manus in the hands of the woman's father, even after her marriage. This kind of union was similar to what we would call common-law marriage, in which a woman could stay out of her husband's control and regain her dowry by leaving her husband's home for at least three consecutive nights each year. This gave her greater rights of inheritance in her father's family and greater independence in her marriage.

In early Rome, marriage with manus was most common, but women of the upper classes had a position of influence and respect greater than that of the classical Greeks and more like what appears to have been true of the Etruscans. Just as the husband was *paterfamilias,* the wife was *materfamilias.* She was mistress within the home, controlling access to the storerooms, keeping the accounts, and supervising the slaves and the raising of the children. She also was part of the family council and a respected adviser on all questions concerning the family. Divorce was difficult and rare and limited to a few specific transgressions by the wife, one of which was drunkenness. Even when divorced for cause, the wife retained her dowry.

4.3.4 Clientage

One of Rome's most important institutions was **clientage.** The client was "an inferior entrusted, by custom or by himself, to the protection of a stranger more powerful than he, and rendering certain services and observances in return for this protection."[1] The Romans spoke of a client as being in the *fides,* or trust, of his patron, and so the relationship always had moral implications. The patron provided his client with protection, both physical and legal. He gave him economic assistance in the form of a land grant, the opportunity to work as a tenant farmer or a laborer on the

patron's land, or simply handouts. In return, the client would fight for his patron, work his land, and support him politically. Public opinion and tradition reinforced these mutual obligations. When early custom was codified in the mid-fifth century B.C.E., one of the twelve tablets of laws announced, "Let the patron who has defrauded his client be accursed."

In the early history of Rome, patrons were rich and powerful, whereas clients were poor and weak, but as time passed, rich and powerful members of the upper classes became clients of even more powerful men, chiefly for political purposes. Because the client–patron relationship was hereditary and sanctioned by religion and custom, it played an important part in the life of the Roman Republic.

4.3.5 Patricians and Plebeians

In the royal period, a class distinction based on birth divided Roman society in two. The wealthy **patrician** upper class held a monopoly of power and influence. Its members alone could conduct state religious ceremonies, sit in the Senate, or hold office. They formed a closed caste by forbidding marriage outside their own group.

The **plebeian** lower class must have consisted originally of poor, dependent small farmers, laborers, and artisans—the clients of the nobility. As Rome and its population grew, plebeian families who were rich, but outside the charmed circle of patricians, grew wealthy. From early times, therefore, there were rich plebeians, whereas incompetence and bad luck may have created some poor patricians. The line between the classes and the monopoly of privileges remained firm, nevertheless, and the struggle of the plebeians to gain equality lasted more than two centuries in republican history.

4.4 The Republic

What role did consuls, the Senate, and the assembly play in republican government?

Roman tradition tells us that the outrageous behavior of the last kings led the noble families to revolt in 509 B.C.E., bringing the monarchy to a sudden close and leading to the creation of the Roman Republic. During the next three centuries two major developments took place in Rome. First, the power struggle between the patricians and the plebeians resulted in a mixed constitution. Second, a series of wars with their neighbors made Rome the dominant state in Italy. The need for internal cohesion and stability in the face of their enemies inspired the Romans to overcome the limitations found in the Greek polis. Rome demonstrated its superiority once it became involved in the affairs of the wider Mediterranean.

BUSTS OF A ROMAN COUPLE FROM THE PERIOD OF THE REPUBLIC Although some have identified the individuals on these busts as Cato the Younger and his daughter Porcia, there is no evidence that confirms this claim.
SOURCE: Scala/Art Resource, NY

4.4.1 Constitution

One of the hallmarks of the Roman Republic was its mixed constitution. Unlike the poleis of the Greek world such as Athens or Sparta, the Romans did not name a great lawgiver as the source of their government. Instead they believed that their state evolved through a natural process that balanced the interests of the different classes in society.

4.4.1.1 THE CONSULS The Roman constitution was an unwritten accumulation of laws and customs. The Romans were a conservative people and were never willing to deprive their chief magistrates of the great powers the monarchs had exercised. They elected two patricians to the office of consul and endowed them with imperium. Two financial officials called *quaestors*, whose number ultimately reached eight, assisted them. Like the kings, the **consuls** led the army, fulfilled religious duties, and served as judges. They retained the visible symbols of royalty: the purple robe, the ivory chair, and the *lictors* (minor officials, whose role in Roman affairs is considered in the "Closer Look" sidebar, which follows), who accompanied them bearing rods and axe. The power of the consuls, however, was limited legally and institutionally as well as by custom.

The power of the consulship was granted not for life but for only a year. Each consul could prevent any action of his colleague simply by objecting to his proposal. Their religious powers were also shared with others. Even the imperium was limited. Although the consuls had full powers of life and death while leading an army, within the sacred boundary of

the city of Rome, the citizens had the right to appeal all cases involving capital punishment to the popular assembly. Besides, after their year in office, the consuls would spend the rest of their lives as members of the Senate. Only a reckless consul would fail to ask the advice of the Senate or to follow it when there was general agreement.

These many checks on consular action tended to prevent initiative, swift action, and change, but this was just what a conservative, traditional, aristocratic republic wanted. Only in the military sphere did divided counsel and a short term of office create important problems. The Romans tried to get around these difficulties by sending only one consul into the field or, when this was impossible, allowing each consul sole command on alternate days. In serious crises, the consuls, with the advice of the Senate, could appoint a dictator to the command and could retire in his favor. The dictator's term of office was limited to six months, but his imperium was valid both inside and outside the city without appeal.

These devices worked well enough in the early years of the republic when Rome's battles were near home. Longer wars and more sophisticated opponents, however, revealed the system's weaknesses, which required significant changes. Long campaigns prompted the invention of the **proconsulship** in 325 B.C.E., whereby the term of a consul serving in the field was extended. This innovation planted the seeds of many troubles for the constitution.

The creation of the office of praetor also helped provide commanders for Rome's many campaigns. The basic function of the praetors was judicial, but they also had imperium and served as generals. Praetors' terms were also for one year. By the end of the republic, there were eight praetors, whose annual terms, like the consuls', could be extended for military commands when necessary.

At first, the consuls identified citizens and classified them according to age and property. After the middle of the fifth century B.C.E., this job was delegated to a new office, that of the **censor**. The Senate elected two censors every five years. They conducted a census and drew up the citizen rolls. Their task was not just clerical; the classification of citizens fixed their taxation and status, so the censors had to be men of fine reputation, former consuls. They soon acquired additional powers. By the fourth century B.C.E., they compiled the roll of senators and could strike senators from that roll not only for financial but also for moral reasons. As the prestige of the office grew, it became the most desirable prize in Roman politics.

A Closer Look

Lictors

THE LICTORS WERE ATTENDANTS of the Roman magistrates who held the power of imperium, or the right to command. In republican times, these magistrates were the consuls, praetors, and proconsuls. The lictors were men from the lower classes—some even former slaves—who attended the magistrates when they appeared in public. The lictors cleared a magistrate's way in crowds, and summoned, arrested, and punished offenders for him. They also served as their magistrate's house guard.

After the establishment of the Roman republic, the lictor and his fasces and axe were the symbols of those magistrates that held imperium. Twelve lictors accompanied each consul; a praetor had six. When a dictator was appointed during a crisis, he was escorted by twenty-four lictors to show that he was more powerful than both consuls.

The axe carried by the man on the left is a symbol of the magistrate's power, when he was acting as a military commander outside the city, to put a Roman citizen to death.

The bundle of sticks, called fasces, the other two lictors carry indicates the magistrates' right to employ corporal punishment, but their bindings symbolize the right of citizens not on military duty not to be punished without a trial.

The traditional dress of a lictor was a toga when in Rome, and a red coat called a sagum when outside the city or when taking part in a triumph.

LICTORS, ROME'S MAGISTERIAL ATTENDANTS
SOURCE: Alinari/Art Resource, NY

Questions

1. Why do you think Roman magistrates required bodyguards?
2. What does the use of lictors indicate about the nature of early Roman public life?

4.4.1.2 THE SENATE AND THE ASSEMBLY With the end of the monarchy, the Senate became the single continuous, deliberative body in the Roman state, greatly increasing its influence and power. Its members were prominent patricians, often leaders of clans and patrons of many clients. The Senate soon gained control of the state's finances and of foreign policy. Neither magistrates nor popular assemblies could lightly ignore its formal advice.

The most important assembly in the early republic was the *centuriate assembly*, which was, in a sense, the Roman army acting in a political capacity. Its basic unit was the *century*, theoretically one hundred fighting men classified according to their weapons, armor, and equipment. Because each man equipped himself, this meant the organization was by classes according to wealth.

Voting was by century and proceeded in order of classification from the cavalry down. The assembly elected the consuls and several other magistrates, voted on bills put before it, made decisions of war and peace, and also served as the court of appeal against decisions of the magistrates affecting the life or property of a citizen. In theory, the assembly had final authority, but the Senate exercised great, if informal, influence.

4.4.1.3 THE STRUGGLE OF THE ORDERS The laws and constitution of the early republic gave to the patricians almost a monopoly of power and privilege. Plebeians were barred from public office, from priesthoods, and from other public religious offices. They could not serve as judges and could not even know the law, for there was no published legal code. The only law was traditional practice, and that existed only in the minds and actions of patrician magistrates. Plebeians were subject to the imperium but could not exercise its power. They were not allowed to marry patricians. When Rome gained new land by conquest, patrician magistrates distributed it in a way that favored patricians. The patricians dominated the assemblies and the Senate. The plebeians undertook a campaign to achieve political, legal, and social equality: This attempt, which succeeded after two centuries of intermittent effort, is called the Struggle of the Orders.

The most important source of plebeian success was the need for their military service. According to tradition, the plebeians, angered by patrician resistance to their demands, withdrew from the city and camped on the Sacred Mount. There they formed a plebeian tribal assembly and elected plebeian **tribunes** to protect them from the arbitrary power of the magistrates. Plebeians declared the tribune inviolate and sacrosanct; anyone laying violent hands on him was accursed and liable to death without trial. By extension of his right to protect the plebeians, the tribune gained the power to veto any action of a magistrate or any bill in a Roman assembly or the Senate. The plebeian assembly voted by tribe, and a vote of the assembly was binding on plebeians. They tried to make their decisions binding on all Romans, but could not do so until 287 B.C.E.

Next, the plebeians obtained access to the laws, when early Roman custom in all its harshness and simplicity was codified in the Twelve Tables around 450 B.C.E. In 445 B.C.E., plebeians gained the right to marry patricians. The main prize, the consulship, the patricians did not yield easily. Not until 367 B.C.E. did legislation—the Licinian-Sextian Laws—allow that at least one consul could be a plebeian. Before long, plebeians held other offices—even the dictatorship and the censorship. In 300 B.C.E., they were admitted to the most important priesthoods, the last religious barrier to equality. In 287 B.C.E., the plebeians were finally triumphant. They once again withdrew from the city and secured the passage of a law whereby decisions of the plebeian assembly bound all Romans and did not require the approval of the Senate.

It might seem that the Roman aristocracy had given way under the pressure of the lower class. Yet the victory of the plebeians did not bring democracy. An aristocracy based strictly on birth had given way to an aristocracy more subtle, but no less restricted, based on a combination of wealth and birth. A relatively small group of rich and powerful families, both patrician and plebeian, known as *nobiles*, attained the highest offices in the state. The significant distinction was no longer between patrician and plebeian but between the *nobiles* and everyone else.

The absence of the secret ballot in the assemblies enabled the *nobiles* to control most decisions and elections through intimidation and bribery. The leading families constantly competed with one another for office, power, and prestige, but they often joined in marriage and less formal alliances to keep the political plums within their own group. In the century from 233 to 133 B.C.E., for instance, twenty-six families provided 80 percent of the consuls, and only ten families accounted for almost 50 percent. These same families dominated the Senate, whose power became ever greater. Rome's success brought the Senate prestige, increased control of policy, and greater confidence in its capacity to rule. The end of the Struggle of the Orders brought domestic peace under a republican constitution dominated by a capable, if narrow, senatorial aristocracy. This outcome satisfied most Romans outside the ruling group because Rome conquered Italy and brought many benefits to its citizens.

4.4.2 The Conquest of Italy

Not long after the fall of the monarchy in 509 B.C.E., a coalition of Romans, Latins, and Italian Greeks drove the Etruscans out of Latium for good. Throughout the fifth century B.C.E., the

LATIN WARRIOR, FOURTH CENTURY B.C.E. The Samnites fought the Roman Republic in three separate wars from the fourth to the third centuries B.C.E. This bronze of a Samnite warrior dates from the third century B.C.E.
SOURCE: De Agostini Picture Library/Getty Images

powerful Etruscan city of Veii, only twelve miles north of the Tiber River, raided Roman territory. After a hard struggle and a long siege, the Romans took Veii in 392 B.C.E., more than doubling the size of Rome.

Roman policy toward defeated enemies used both the carrot and the stick. When the Romans made friendly alliances with some, they gained new soldiers for their army. When they treated others more harshly by annexing their land, they achieved a similar end. Service in the Roman army was based on property, and the distribution to poor Romans of conquered land made soldiers of previously useless men. It also gave the poor a stake in Rome and reduced the pressure against its aristocratic regime. From that time on, the Romans paid their soldiers, thus giving their army greater flexibility and a more professional quality.

4.4.2.1 GALLIC INVASION AND ROMAN REACTION At the beginning of the fourth century B.C.E., a disaster struck. In 387 B.C.E., the Gauls, barbaric Celtic tribes from across the Alps, defeated the Roman army and burned Rome. The Gauls sought plunder, not conquest, so they extorted a ransom from the Romans and returned to the north. Rome's power appeared to be wiped out.

By about 350 B.C.E., however, the Romans were more dominant than ever. Their success in turning back new Gallic raids added to their power and prestige. As the Romans tightened their grip on Latium, the Latins became resentful. In 340 B.C.E., they demanded independence from Rome or full equality and launched a war of independence that lasted until 338 B.C.E. The victorious Romans dissolved the Latin League, and their treatment of the defeated opponents provided a model for the settlement of Italy.

4.4.2.2 ROMAN POLICY TOWARD THE CONQUERED The Romans did not destroy any of the Latin cities or their people, nor did they treat them all alike. Some near Rome received full Roman citizenship. Others farther away gained municipal status, which gave them the private rights of intermarriage and commerce with Romans, but not the public rights of voting and holding office in Rome. They retained the rights of local self-government and could obtain full Roman citizenship if they moved to Rome. They followed Rome in foreign policy and provided soldiers to serve in the Roman legions.

Still other states became allies of Rome based on treaties, which differed from city to city. Some were given the private rights of intermarriage and commerce with Romans, and some were not; the allied states were always forbidden to exercise these rights with one another. Some, but not all, were allowed local autonomy. Land was taken from some states, but not from others, nor was the percentage taken always the same. All the allies supplied troops to the army, in which they fought in auxiliary battalions under Roman officers, but they did not pay taxes to Rome.

On some of the conquered land, the Romans set up colonies, permanent settlements of veteran soldiers in the territory of recently defeated enemies. The colonists retained their Roman citizenship and enjoyed home rule; in return for the land they had been given, they were a kind of permanent garrison to deter or suppress rebellion. These colonies were usually connected to Rome by a network of military roads built as straight as possible and so durable that some are used even today. The roads guaranteed that a Roman army could swiftly reinforce an embattled colony or put down an uprising in any weather.

The Roman settlement of Latium reveals even more clearly than before the principles by which Rome could conquer and dominate Italy. The excellent army and the diplomatic skill that allowed Rome to separate its enemies help explain its conquests. The reputation for harsh punishment of rebels, and the sure promise that such punishment would be delivered, was made unmistakably clear: both the colonies and military roads help explain the reluctance to revolt. But the more positive side, represented by Rome's organization of the defeated states, is at least as important. The Romans did not regard the status given each newly conquered city as permanent. They held out to loyal allies the prospect of improving their status—even of achieving the ultimate prize, full Roman citizenship. In so doing, the Romans gave their allies a stake in Rome's future success and a sense of being colleagues, though subordinate ones, rather than subjects. The result, in general, was that most of Rome's allies remained loyal even when put to the severest test.

4.4.2.3 DEFEATED SAMNITES The next great challenge to Roman arms came in a series of wars with a tough mountain people of the southern Apennines, the Samnites. Some of Rome's allies rebelled, and soon the Etruscans and Gauls joined in the war against Rome. But most of the allies remained loyal. In 295 B.C.E., at Sentinum, the Romans defeated an Italian coalition, and by 280 B.C.E., they were masters of central Italy. Their power extended from the Po Valley south to Apulia and Lucania.

Now the Romans were in direct contact with the Greek cities of southern Italy. Roman intervention in a quarrel between Greek cities brought them face to face with Pyrrhus, king of Epirus. Pyrrhus, probably the best general of his time, commanded a well-disciplined and experienced mercenary army, which he hired out for profit, and a new weapon: twenty war elephants. He defeated the Romans twice but suffered many casualties. When one of his officers rejoiced at the victory, Pyrrhus told him, "If we win one more battle against the Romans, we shall be completely ruined." This "Pyrrhic victory" led him to withdraw to Sicily in 275 B.C.E. The Greek cities that had hired him were forced to join the Roman confederation.

KEY EVENTS IN THE ROMAN EXPANSION IN ITALY

392 B.C.E.	Fall of Veii; Etruscans defeated
387 B.C.E.	Gauls burn Rome
338 B.C.E.	Latin League defeated
295 B.C.E.	Battle of Sentinum; Samnites and allies defeated
275 B.C.E.	Pyrrhus driven from Italy

By 265 B.C.E., Rome ruled all Italy as far north as the Po River, an area of 47,200 square miles. The year after the defeat of Pyrrhus, Ptolemy Philadelphus, king of Egypt, sent a message of congratulations to establish friendly relations with Rome. This act recognized Rome's new status as a power in the Hellenistic world.

4.4.3 Rome and Carthage

The conquest of southern Italy brought the Romans face to face with the great naval power of the western Mediterranean, Carthage. (See Map 4–2.) Late in the ninth century B.C.E., the Phoenician city of Tyre had planted a colony on the coast of northern Africa near modern Tunis, calling it the New City, or Carthage. The city was located on a defensible site and commanded an excellent harbor that encouraged commerce. The coastal plain grew abundant grains, fruits, and vegetables, and an inland plain allowed sheepherding. The Phoenician settlers conquered the native inhabitants and used them to work the land.

Beginning in the sixth century B.C.E., the Carthaginians expanded their domain to include the coast of northern Africa west beyond the Straits of Gibraltar and eastward into Libya. Overseas, they came to control the southern part of Spain, Sardinia, Corsica, Malta, the Balearic Islands, and western Sicily. The people of these territories, though originally allies, were all subjected like the natives of the Carthaginian home territory. They all served in the Carthaginian army or navy and paid tribute. Carthage also profited greatly from the mines of Spain and from an absolute monopoly of trade imposed on the western Mediterranean.

An attack by Hiero, tyrant of Syracuse, on the Sicilian city of Messana just across from Italy, first caused trouble between Rome and Carthage. Messana had been seized by a group of Italian mercenary soldiers who called themselves *Mamertines*, the sons of the war god Mars. When Hiero defeated the Mamertines, some of them called on the Carthaginians to help save their city. Carthage agreed and sent a garrison, for the Carthaginians wanted to prevent

Map 4–2 WESTERN MEDITERRANEAN AREA DURING THE RISE OF ROME

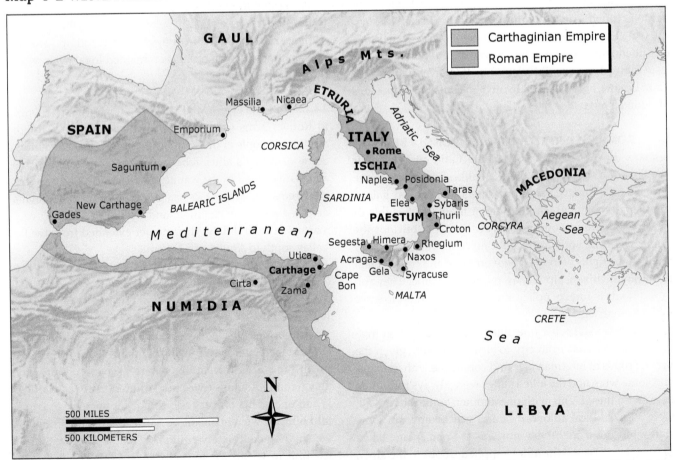

This map depicts the theater of conflict between the growing Roman dominions and those of Carthage in the third century B.C.E. The Carthaginian Empire stretched westward from the city of Carthage (near modern Tunis) along the North African coast and into southern Spain.

Syracuse from dominating the straits. One Mamertine faction, however, fearing that Carthage might take undue advantage of the opportunity, asked Rome for help.

In 264 B.C.E., the request came to the Senate. Because a Punic garrison (the Romans called the Carthaginians *Phoenicians*; in Latin the word is *Poeni* or *Puni*—hence the adjective *Punic*) was in place at Messana, any intervention would not be against Syracuse, but against the mighty empire of Carthage. Unless Rome intervened, however, Carthage would gain control of all of Sicily and the straits. The assembly voted to send an army to Messana and expelled the Punic garrison. The First Punic War was on.

Compare and Connect

Why Did Rome Win the Punic Wars?

THE PUNIC WARS WERE A TURNING POINT in Roman history. Having conquered southern Italy, the Romans now had to contend with the Carthaginians, a powerful rival, for control of the western Mediterranean. Like the Romans, the Carthaginians were an expansionist power. Over the centuries proceeding the Punic Wars, they had used their formidable army and navy to gain control of much of North Africa and Spain. In the excerpts from Polybius's *Histories* included below, the Greek historian seeks to explain Rome's eventual victory by comparing the combatants' governments. In his view, all other factors that influenced the outcome of the war were secondary to the excellence of Roman government.

Before Reading

- Think about Polybius's ideas about the nature of historical change.
- Ask yourself how the Romans saw their victory over the Carthaginians.
- Note the aspects of government which are most important to Polybius.

Questions:

1. According to Polybius, what are the different types of government? What kind was Rome?
2. What advantages did Polybius see in Roman government?
3. How did Polybius connect Roman government to Rome's victory over Carthage in the Punic Wars?

I. AN ANALYSIS OF THE ROMAN GOVERNMENT

The three kinds of government, monarchy, aristocracy and democracy, were all found united in the commonwealth of Rome. And so even was the balance between them all, and so regular the administration that resulted from their union, that it was no easy thing to determine with assurance, whether the entire state was to be estimated an aristocracy, a democracy, or a monarchy. . . .

The consuls, when they remain in Rome, before they lead out the armies into the field, are the masters of all public affairs. For all other magistrates, the tribunes alone excepted, are subject to them, and bound to obey their commands. They introduce ambassadors into the senate. They propose also to the senate the subjects of debates; and direct all forms that are observed in making the decrees. . . .

To the senate belongs, in the first place, the sole care and management of the public money. For all returns that are brought into the treasury, as well as all the payments that are issued from it, are directed by their orders. Nor is it allowed to the quaestors to apply any part of the revenue to particular occasions as they arise, without a decree of the senate; those sums alone excepted, which are expended in the service of the consuls. And even those more general, as well as greatest disbursements, which are employed at the return every five years, in building and repairing the public edifices, are assigned to the censors for that purpose, by the express permission of the senate. To the senate also is referred the cognizance of all the crimes, committed in any part of Italy, that demand a public examination and inquiry: such as treasons, conspiracies, poisonings, and assassinations. Add to this, that when any controversies arise, either between private men, or any of the cities of Italy, it is the part of the senate to adjust all disputes; to censure those that are deserving of blame: and to yield assistance to those who stand in need of protection and defense. When any embassies are sent out of Italy; either to reconcile contending states; to offer exhortations and advice; or even, as it sometimes happens, to impose commands; to propose conditions of a treaty; or to make a denunciation of war; the care and conduct of all these transactions is entrusted wholly to the senate. When any ambassadors also arrive in Rome, it is the senate likewise that determines how they shall be received and treated, and what answer shall be given to their demands.

In all these things that have now been mentioned, the people [have] no share. To those, therefore, who come to reside in Rome during the absence of the consuls, the government appears to be purely aristocratic.

II. ROME AND CARTHAGE COMPARED

The government of Carthage seems also to have been originally well contrived with regard to those general forms that have been mentioned. For there were kings in this government, together with a senate, which was vested with aristocratic authority. The people likewise enjoy the exercise of certain powers that were appropriated to them. In a word, the entire frame of the republic very much resembled those of Rome and Sparta. But at the time of the war of Hannibal the Carthaginian constitution was worse in its condition than the Roman. For as nature has assigned to every body, every government, and every action, three successive periods; the first, of growth; the second, of perfection; and that which follows, of decay; and as the period of perfection is the time in which they severally display their greatest strength; from hence arose the difference that was then found between the two republics. For the government of Carthage, having reached the highest point of vigor and perfection much sooner than that of Rome, had now declined from it in the same proportion: whereas the Romans, at this very time, had just raised their constitution to the most flourishing and perfect state. The effect of this difference was, that among the Carthaginians the people possessed the greatest sway in all deliberations, but the senate among the Romans. And as, in the one republic, all measures were determined by the multitude; and, in the other, by the most eminent citizens; of so great force was this advantage in the conduct of affairs, that the Romans, though brought by repeated losses into the greatest danger, became, through the wisdom of their counsels, superior to the Carthaginians in the war.

SOURCES: (I) From Oliver J. Thatcher, ed., *The Library of Original Sources* (Milwaukee: University Research Extension Co., 1907), Vol. III: *The Roman World*, p. 166. (II) From Oliver J. Thatcher, ed., *The Library of Original Sources* (Milwaukee: University Research Extension Co., 1907), Vol. III: *The Roman World*, p. 186.

4.4.3.1 THE FIRST PUNIC WAR (264–241 B.C.E.)   The war in Sicily soon settled into a stalemate until the Romans built a fleet to cut off supplies to the besieged Carthaginian cities at the western end of Sicily. When Carthage sent its own fleet to raise the siege, the Romans destroyed it. In 241 B.C.E., Carthage signed a treaty giving up Sicily and the islands between Italy and Sicily; it also agreed to pay a war indemnity in ten annual installments. Neither side was to attack the allies of the other. The peace was realistic and not unduly harsh; Rome had earned Sicily, and Carthage could well afford the indemnity. If it had been carried out in good faith, it might have brought lasting peace.

A rebellion, however, broke out in Carthage among the mercenaries newly recruited from Sicily, who now demanded their pay. In 238 B.C.E., while Carthage was still preoccupied with the rebellion, Rome seized Sardinia and Corsica and demanded that Carthage pay an additional indemnity. This was a harsh and cynical action by the Romans; even the historian Polybius, a great champion of Rome, could find no justification for it. It undid the calming effects of the peace of 241 B.C.E. without preventing the Carthaginians from recovering their strength to seek vengeance in the future.

The conquest of overseas territory presented the Romans with new administrative problems. Instead of following the policy they had pursued in Italy, they made Sicily a province and Sardinia and Corsica another. It became common to extend the term of the governors of these provinces beyond a year. The governors were unchecked by colleagues and exercised full imperium. New magistracies, in effect, were thus created free of the limits constraining the power of officials in Rome.

The new populations were neither Roman citizens nor allies; they were subjects who did not serve in the army but paid tribute instead. The old practice of extending citizenship and, with it, loyalty to Rome thus stopped at the borders of Italy. Rome collected taxes on these subjects by "farming" them out at auction to the highest bidder. These innovations were the basis for Rome's imperial organization in the future. In time, such tactics strained the constitution and traditions and threatened the existence of the republic.

After the First Punic War, campaigns against the Gauls and across the Adriatic Sea distracted Rome. Meanwhile, Hamilcar Barca, the Carthaginian governor of Spain from 237 B.C.E. until his death in 229 B.C.E., was leading Carthage on the road to recovery. Hamilcar sought to build a Punic Empire in Spain. He improved the ports and the commerce conducted in them, exploited the mines, gained control of the hinterland, won over many of the conquered tribes, and built a strong and disciplined army.

Hamilcar's successor, his son-in-law Hasdrubal, pursued the same policies. His success alarmed the Romans. They imposed a treaty in which Hasdrubal promised not to take an army north across the Ebro River in Spain, although Punic expansion in Spain was well south of that river at the time. Though the agreement appeared to put Rome in the position of giving orders to an inferior, it benefited both sides equally. If the Carthaginians accepted the limit of the Ebro on their expansion in Spain, the Romans would not interfere with that expansion.

4.4.3.2 THE SECOND PUNIC WAR (218–202 B.C.E.)   Upon Hasdrubal's assassination in 221 B.C.E., the army chose as his successor the son of Hamilcar Barca, Hannibal, who was twenty-five years old at the time. He quickly consolidated and extended the Punic Empire in Spain. A few years before his accession, Rome had received an offer of alliance

ROMAN NAVAL POWER Late in its history, Rome became a naval power to defeat Carthage in the First Punic War (264–241 B.C.E.). This sculpture in low relief shows a Roman ship propelled by oars, with both ram and soldiers, ready to either ram or board an enemy ship.

SOURCE: Museo Pio Clementino, Vatican Museums, Vatican State/Scala/Art Resource, NY

from the people of Saguntum, a Spanish town about one hundred miles south of the Ebro. The Romans accepted the friendship and the responsibilities it entailed, despite the Ebro treaty. At first, Hannibal avoided any action against Saguntum, but the Saguntines, confident of Rome's protection, began to interfere with some of the Spanish tribes allied with Hannibal. When the Romans sent an embassy to Hannibal warning him to let Saguntum alone and repeating the injunction not to cross the Ebro, he ignored the warning and captured the town. The Romans sent an ultimatum to Carthage demanding the surrender of Hannibal. Carthage refused, and Rome declared war in 218 B.C.E.

Between the close of the First Punic War and the outbreak of the Second, Rome had repeatedly provoked Carthage, taking Sardinia in 238 B.C.E. and interfering with Spain, but had not prevented Carthage from building a powerful and dangerous empire in Spain. Hannibal saw to it that the Romans paid the price for these blunders. By September 218 B.C.E., he was across the Alps, in Italy and among the friendly Gauls.

Hannibal defeated the Romans at the Ticinus River and crushed the joint consular armies at the Trebia River. In 217 B.C.E., he outmaneuvered and trapped another army at Lake Trasimene. The key to success, however, would be defection by Rome's allies. Hannibal released Italian prisoners without harm or ransom and moved his army south of Rome to encourage rebellion. But the allies remained firm.

Sobered by their defeats, the Romans elected Quintus Fabius Maximus as dictator. His strategy was to avoid battle while harassing Hannibal's army. He would fight only when his army had recovered and then only on favorable ground.

At the **Battle of Cannae**, in 216 B.C.E., Hannibal marched to Cannae in Apulia to tempt the Romans, under different generals, into another open fight. The Romans sent an army of some 80,000 men to meet him. Almost the entire Roman army was wiped out in the worst defeat in Roman history. Rome's prestige was shattered, and most of its allies in southern Italy, as well as Syracuse in Sicily, aligned themselves with Hannibal. For more than a decade, no Roman army would dare face Hannibal in the field.

Hannibal, however, had neither the numbers nor the supplies to besiege walled cities, nor did he have the equipment to take them by assault. The Romans appointed Publius Cornelius Scipio (237–183 B.C.E.), later called Africanus, to the command in Spain with proconsular imperium. Scipio was not yet twenty-five and had held no high office, but he was a general almost as talented as Hannibal. Within a few years, young Scipio had conquered all of Spain and had deprived Hannibal of any hope of help from that region.

In 204 B.C.E., Scipio landed in Africa and forced the Carthaginians to accept a peace, which included the withdrawal of Hannibal and his army from Italy. Hannibal had won every battle but lost the war, for he had not counted on the determination of Rome and the loyalty of its allies. Hannibal's return inspired Carthage to break the peace and to risk all in battle. In 202 B.C.E., Scipio and Hannibal faced each other at the Battle of Zama. The generalship of Scipio and the desertion of Hannibal's mercenaries gave the victory to Rome. The new peace terms reduced Carthage to the status of a dependent ally of Rome. The Second Punic War ended the Carthaginian command of the western Mediterranean and Carthage's term as a great power. Rome ruled the seas and the entire Mediterranean coast from Italy westward.

4.4.4 The Republic's Conquest of the Hellenistic World

At first Rome was reluctant to become involved in Greek affairs in the east, but the actions of Philip V of Macedon and his alliance with Carthage during the war with Hannibal dictated Rome's response. The conflict with Macedon soon included the Seleucid king, Antiochus III, and eventually Perseus, the successor of Philip. Rome's ultimate victory brought great wealth to the city and transformed its foreign policy.

4.4.4.1 THE EAST By the middle of the third century B.C.E., the eastern Mediterranean had reached a condition of stability based on a balance of power among the three great Hellenistic kingdoms that allowed an established place even for lesser states. Two aggressive monarchs, Philip V of Macedon (221–179 B.C.E.) and Antiochus III of the Seleucid kingdom (223–187 B.C.E.), threatened this equilibrium, however. Philip and Antiochus moved swiftly, the latter against Syria and Palestine, the former against cities in the Aegean, in the Hellespontine region, and on the coast of Asia Minor.

The threat that a more powerful Macedon might pose to Rome's friends and perhaps even to Italy persuaded the Romans to intervene. Philip had already attempted to meddle in Roman affairs when he formed an alliance with Carthage during the Second Punic War, provoking a conflict known as the First Macedonian War (215–205 B.C.E.). In 200 B.C.E., in an action that began the Second Macedonian War, the Romans sent an ultimatum to Philip ordering him not to attack any Greek city and to pay reparations to Pergamum. These orders were meant to provoke, not avoid, war, and Philip refused to obey. Two years later, the Romans sent out a talented young general, Flamininus, who demanded that Philip withdraw from Greece entirely. In 197 B.C.E., with Greek support, Flamininus defeated Philip at Cynoscephalae, ending the war. The Greek cities freed from Philip were made autonomous, and in 196 B.C.E., Flamininus proclaimed the freedom of the Greeks.

Soon after the Romans withdrew from Greece, they came into conflict with Antiochus, who was expanding his power in Asia and on the European side of the Hellespont. On the pretext of freeing the Greeks from Roman domination, he landed an army on the Greek mainland. The Romans routed Antiochus at Thermopylae and quickly drove him from Greece. In 189 B.C.E., they crushed his army at the Battle of Magnesia in Asia Minor. The peace of Apamia in the next year deprived Antiochus of his elephants and his navy and imposed a huge indemnity on him. Once again, the Romans took no territory for themselves and left several Greek cities in Asia free. They regarded Greece, and now Asia Minor, as a kind of protectorate in which they could or could not intervene as they chose.

This relatively mild policy was destined to end as the stern and businesslike policies of the conservative censor Cato gained favor in Rome. A new harshness was to be applied to allies and bystanders, as well as to defeated opponents.

In 179 B.C.E., Perseus succeeded Philip V as king of Macedon. He tried to gain popularity in Greece by favoring the democratic and revolutionary forces in the cities. The Romans, troubled by his threat to stability, launched the Third Macedonian War (172–168 B.C.E.), and in 168 B.C.E. Aemilius Paulus defeated Perseus at Pydna. The peace that followed this war, reflecting the changed attitude at Rome, was harsh. It divided Macedon into four separate republics, whose citizens were forbidden to intermarry or even to do business across the new national boundaries. Anti-Roman factions in the Greek cities were punished severely.

When Aemilius Paulus returned from his victory, he celebrated his triumph for three days by parading the spoils of war, royal prisoners, and great wealth through the streets of Rome. The public treasury benefited to such a degree that the direct property tax on Roman citizens was abolished. Part of the booty went to the general and part to his soldiers. New motives were thereby introduced into Roman foreign policy, or perhaps old motives were given new prominence. Foreign campaigns could bring profit to the state; rewards to the army; and wealth, fame, honor, and political power to the general.

4.4.4.2 THE WEST Harsh as the Romans had become toward the Greeks, they treated the people of the Iberian Peninsula (Spain and Portugal), whom they considered barbarians, even worse. They committed dreadful atrocities, lied, cheated, and broke treaties to exploit and pacify the natives, who fought back fiercely in guerrilla style. From 154 to 133 B.C.E., the fighting waxed, and it became hard to recruit Roman soldiers to participate in the increasingly ugly war. At last, in 134 B.C.E., Scipio Aemilianus took the key city of Numantia by siege and burned it to the ground. This put an end to the war in Spain.

Roman treatment of Carthage was no better. Although Carthage lived up to its treaty with Rome faithfully and posed no threat, some Romans refused to abandon their hatred of the traditional enemy. Cato is said to have ended all his speeches in the Senate with the same sentence: "Ceterum censeo delendam esse Carthaginem" ("Besides, I think that Carthage must be destroyed"). Finally, the Romans took advantage of a technical breach of the peace to destroy Carthage. In 146 B.C.E., during a third Punic war, Scipio Aemilianus took the city, plowed up its land, and put salt in the furrows as a symbol of the permanent abandonment of the site. The Romans incorporated it as the province of Africa, one of six Roman provinces, including Sicily, Sardinia-Corsica, Macedonia, Hither Spain, and Further Spain.

KEY EVENTS OF THE PUNIC WARS	
264–241 B.C.E.	First Punic War
238 B.C.E.	Rome seizes Sardinia and Corsica
221 B.C.E.	Hannibal takes command of Punic army in Spain
218–202 B.C.E.	Second Punic War
216 B.C.E.	Battle of Cannae
209 B.C.E.	Scipio takes New Carthage
202 B.C.E.	Battle of Zama
149–146 B.C.E.	Third Punic War
146 B.C.E.	Destruction of Carthage

4.5 Civilization in the Early Roman Republic

How did contact with the Hellenistic world affect Rome?

Close and continued association with the Greeks of the Hellenistic world brought important changes in the Roman style of life and thought. The Roman attitude toward the Greeks ranged from admiration for their culture and history to contempt for their constant squabbling, their commercial practices, and their weakness. Conservatives such as Cato might speak contemptuously of the Greeks as "Greeklings" (*Graeculi*), but even he learned Greek and absorbed Greek culture.

Before long, the education of the Roman upper classes was bilingual. Young Roman nobles studied Greek rhetoric, literature, and sometimes philosophy. These studies even affected education and the Latin language. As early as the third century B.C.E., Livius Andronicus, a liberated Greek slave, translated the *Odyssey* into Latin. It became a primer for young Romans and set Latin on the road to becoming a literary language.

4.5.1 Religion

The Greeks influenced Roman religion almost from the beginning. The Romans identified their own gods with Greek equivalents and incorporated Greek mythology into their own. Mostly, however, Roman religious practice remained autochthonous, until the third century B.C.E. brought important new influences from the East.

4.5.1.1 TRADITIONAL RELIGION AND CHARACTER
In early Rome, the family was at the center of religious observance, and gods of the household and farm were most important. The *Lares* protected the family property, the *Penates* guarded what was inside the household, and the *Genius* protected the life of the family. In the early days, before they were influenced by the Etruscans and Greeks,

Roman religion incorporated little mythology: their gods were impersonal forces, *numina*, rather than deities in human or superhuman form. To win their favor and protection the Romans developed a detailed and rigid set of rituals that used ceremony as a kind of magical bargain with which they could win and bind the benevolence of divinity. The Roman image of an afterlife was vague and insubstantial. Rome had no priestly caste, so the father (*paterfamilias*) was the family's priest. In the same way, in the republic, the head of the state's board of chief priests, the *pontifex maximus*, was elected by the popular assembly. Morality played little role in Roman religion but, since failure to perform the necessary rites correctly could bring harm on the entire state, everyone had to participate in religious observance as a civic duty and evidence of patriotism. (See the "Encountering the Past" sidebar on two Roman festivals, which follows below.)

In 205 B.C.E., the Senate approved the public worship of Cybele, the Great Mother goddess from Phrygia in Asia Minor. Hers was a fertility cult accompanied by ecstatic, frenzied, and sensual rites that so outraged conservative Romans that they soon banned the cult. Similarly, the Senate banned the worship of Dionysus, or Bacchus, in 186 B.C.E. In the second century B.C.E., interest in Babylonian astrology also grew, and the Senate's attempt in 139 B.C.E. to expel the "Chaldaeans," as the astrologers were called, did not prevent the continued influence of their superstition.

4.5.2 Education

Education in the early republic reflected the limited, conservative, and practical nature of that community of plain farmers and soldiers. Education was entirely the responsibility of the family, with the father teaching his own son at home. It is not clear whether in these early times girls received any education, though they certainly did later. The boys learned how to read, write, calculate, and farm. They memorized the laws of the Twelve Tables, learned how to perform religious rites, heard stories of the great deeds of

ROMAN SCHOOLMASTER AND PUPILS This carved relief from the second century C.E. shows a schoolmaster and his pupils. The pupil at the right is arriving late.
SOURCE: Alinari/Art Resource, NY

Encountering the Past

Two Roman Festivals: The Saturnalia and Lupercalia

THE ROMANS LOVED festivals, and their calendar contained many of them. The most famous celebrations were the Lupercalia, on February 15, and the Saturnalia, which took place from December 17 to 24. Both festivals were so popular that the Christian Church later adopted them under different names for its own religious calendar.

FAUNUS The Romans identified the ancient Italian rural deity Faunus (often depicted as half man, half goat) with the Greek god Pan, who was associated with merriment. People prayed to Faunus to increase the fertility of their land and livestock.
SOURCE: Lanmas/Alamy Stock Photo

The Saturnalia celebrated Saturn, an agricultural god. (Our Saturday is named after him.) During this festival, all public and private business gave way to feasting, gambling, wild dancing, and the kind of revelry that still occurs today during Mardi Gras in cities like New Orleans and Rio de Janeiro.

During the Saturnalia, masters permitted slaves to say and do what they liked; moral restrictions were eased; and Romans exchanged presents. Rather than try to abolish the Saturnalia, the Christian Church established December 25 as the birth date of Jesus, and the irrepressible Roman holiday, including the giving of presents, parties, and elaborate meals, became the celebration of Christmas.

The Lupercalia was dedicated, in part, to Faunus, the ancient Italian god of the countryside. Worshipped as the bringer of fertility to fields and flocks, Faunus was typically represented in art as half man, half goat, and was associated with merriment similar to the Greek god Pan.

On the day of the Lupercalia, young male priests called Luperci sacrificed goats and a dog to Faunus. The Luperci then ran naked around the city, striking any woman who came near them with a thong cut from the skins of the sacrificed goats to render her fertile. Women who had not conceived or who wanted more children made sure that the Luperci struck them. It was at the Lupercalia of 44 B.C.E. that the consul Marcus Antonius (Shakespeare's Mark Antony) offered a royal crown to Julius Caesar. In 494 C.E., the Christian church converted the festival into the Feast of the Purification of the Virgin Mary.

Questions

1. Why do you think the Romans loved festivals such as the Saturnalia and Lupercalia?
2. Why might the Christian Church have chosen to adapt pagan customs instead of trying to abolish them?

early Roman history and particularly those of their ancestors, and engaged in the physical training appropriate for potential soldiers. This course of study was practical, vocational, and moral; it aimed to make the boys moral, pious, patriotic, law abiding, and respectful of tradition.

4.5.2.1 HELLENIZED EDUCATION In the third century B.C.E., the Romans encountered the Greeks of southern Italy, and this contact changed Roman education. Greek teachers introduced the study of language, literature, and philosophy, as well as the idea of a liberal education, or what the Romans called *humanitas*, the root of our concept of the humanities. The goal of education changed from the mastery of practical, vocational skills to broad intellectual training, critical thinking, an interest in ideas, and the development of a well-rounded person.

The new emphasis required students to learn Greek, for Rome did not yet have a literature of its own. Hereafter, educated Romans were expected to be bilingual. Schools were established in which a teacher, called a *grammaticus*, taught students the Greek language and its literature, especially the poets and particularly Homer. After the completion of this elementary education, Roman boys of the upper classes studied rhetoric—the art of speaking and writing well. Although for the Greeks rhetoric was less important than philosophy, the more practical Romans took to it avidly, for it was of great use in legal disputes and political life.

Some Romans were attracted to Greek literature and philosophy whereas others were not. Scipio Aemilianus, who finally defeated and destroyed Carthage, surrounded himself and his friends with such Greek thinkers as the historian Polybius and the philosopher Panaetius. Equally outstanding Romans, such as Cato the Elder, were more conservative and opposed the new learning on the grounds that it would weaken Roman moral fiber. On more than one occasion, the Romans passed laws expelling philosophers and teachers of rhetoric. But these attempts to go back to older ways failed. The new education suited the needs of the Romans of the second century B.C.E. They found themselves changing from a rural to an urban society and were being thrust into the sophisticated world of Hellenistic Greeks.

By the last century of the Roman Republic, the new Hellenized education had become dominant. Latin literature had come into being and, along with Latin translations of Greek poets, formed part of the course of study. But Roman gentlemen still were expected to be bilingual, and Greek language and literature were still central to the curriculum. Many schools were established, and the number of educated people increased.

In the late republic, Roman education, though still entirely private, became more formal and organized. From the ages of seven to twelve, boys went to elementary school accompanied by a Greek slave called a *paedagogus* (hence our term *pedagogue*), who looked after their physical well-being and their manners and helped improve their ability to converse in Greek. At school, the boys learned to read and write, using a wax tablet and a stylus, and to do simple arithmetic with an abacus and pebbles (*calculi*). Discipline was harsh and corporal punishment frequent. From twelve to sixteen, boys went to a higher school, where the grammaticus provided a liberal education, using Greek and Latin literature as his subject matter. He also taught dialectic, arithmetic, geometry, astronomy, and music. Sometimes he included the elements of rhetoric, especially for those boys who would not go on to a higher education.

At sixteen, some boys went on to advanced study in rhetoric. The instructors were usually Greek. They trained their charges by studying models of fine speech of the past and by having them write, memorize, and declaim speeches suitable for different occasions. Sometimes the serious student attached himself to some famous public speaker to learn from him. At times, a rich Roman would support a Greek philosopher in his own home. His son could converse with the philosopher and acquire the learning and polished thought necessary for a fully cultured gentleman. Some, like the great orator Cicero, undertook what we might call postgraduate study by traveling abroad to study with great teachers of rhetoric and philosophy in the Greek world.

This style of education broadened the Romans' understanding through the careful study of a foreign language and culture. It made them a part of the older and wider culture of the Hellenistic world, a world they had come to dominate and needed to understand.

4.5.2.2 EDUCATION OF WOMEN Though the evidence is limited, we can be sure that girls of the upper classes received an education equivalent at least to the early stages of a boy's education. They were probably taught by tutors at home rather than going to school, as was increasingly the fashion among boys in the late republic. Young women did not study with philosophers and rhetoricians, for they were usually married by the age at which men were pursuing their higher education. Still, some women continued their education and became prose writers or poets. By the first century C.E., there were apparently enough learned women to provoke the complaints of a crotchety and conservative satirist:

> Still more exasperating is the woman who begs as soon as she sits down to dinner, to discourse on poets and poetry, comparing Virgil with Homer; professors, critics, lawyers, auctioneers—even another woman—can't get a word in. She rattles on at such a rate that you'd think that all the pots and pans in the kitchen were crashing to the floor or that every bell in town was clanging. All by herself she makes as much noise as some primitive tribe chasing away an eclipse. She should learn the philosopher's lesson: "moderation is necessary even for intellectuals." And, if she still wants to appear educated and eloquent, let her dress as a man, sacrifice to men's gods and bathe in the men's baths. Wives shouldn't try to be public speakers; they shouldn't use rhetorical devices; they shouldn't read all the classics—there should be some things women don't understand. I myself cannot understand a woman who can quote the rules of grammar and never make a mistake and cites obscure, long-forgotten poets—as if men cared about such things. If she has to correct somebody let her correct her girl friends and leave her husband alone.[2]

4.5.3 Slavery

Like most ancient peoples, the Romans had slaves from early in their history. Slavery became a basic element in the Roman economy and society only during the second century B.C.E., after the Romans had conquered most of the lands bordering the Mediterranean. In the time between the beginning of Rome's first war against Carthage (264 B.C.E.)

and the conquest of Spain (133 B.C.E.), the Romans enslaved some 250,000 prisoners of war, greatly increasing the availability of slave labor and reducing its price. Many slaves worked as domestic servants, feeding the growing appetite for luxury of the Roman upper class; at the other end of the spectrum, many worked in the mines of Spain and Sardinia. Some worked as artisans in small factories and shops or as public clerks. Slaves were permitted to marry, and they produced sizable families. As in Greece, domestic slaves and those used in crafts and commerce could earn money, keep it, and, in some cases, use it to purchase their own freedom. *Manumission* (the freeing of slaves) was common among the Romans. After a time, a considerable proportion of the Roman people included freedmen who had been slaves themselves or whose ancestors had been bondsmen. It was not uncommon to see the son or grandson of a slave become wealthy as a freedman and the slave himself or his son become a Roman citizen.

A unique development in the Roman world was the emergence of an agricultural system that employed and depended on a vast number of slaves. By the time of Jesus, there were between two and three million slaves in Italy, about 35–40 percent of the total population, most of them part of great slave gangs that worked the vast plantations the Romans called *latifundia*. Latifundia owners sought maximum profits and treated their slaves simply as means to that end. The slaves often worked in chains, were oppressed by brutal foremen, and lived in underground prisons.

Such harsh treatment led to serious slave rebellions of a kind we do not hear of in other ancient societies. A rebellion in Sicily in 134 B.C.E. kept the island in turmoil for more than two years, and the rebellion of the gladiators led by Spartacus in 73 B.C.E. produced an army of 70,000 slaves that repeatedly defeated the Roman legions and overran southern Italy before it was brutally crushed.

Slavery retained its economic and social importance in the first century of the imperial period, but its centrality began to decline in the second. The institution was never abolished, nor did it disappear while the Roman Empire lasted, but over time it became less important. The reasons for this decline are rather obscure. A rise in the cost of slaves and a consequent reduction in their economic value seem to have been factors. More important, it appears, was a general economic decline that permitted increasing pressure on the free lower classes. More and more they were employed as **coloni**—tenant farmers—tied by imperial law to the land they worked, ostensibly free, but bonded and obligated. Over centuries, these increasingly serf-like coloni replaced most agricultural slave labor. Pockets of slave labor remained as late as the eighth century C.E., but the system of ancient slavery had essentially been replaced by the time the Roman Empire fell in the West.

4.6 Roman Imperialism: The Late Republic

How did the expansion of Rome change the republic?

Rome's expansion in Italy and overseas was accomplished without a grand general plan. (See Map 4–3.) The Romans gained the new territories as a result of wars that they believed were either defensive or preventive. Their foreign policy was aimed at providing security for Rome on Rome's terms, but these terms were often unacceptable to other nations and led to continued conflict. Whether intended or not, Rome's expansion brought the Romans an empire and, with it, power, wealth, and responsibilities. The need to govern an empire beyond the seas would severely test the republican constitution that had served Rome well during its years as a city-state and that had been well adapted to the mastery of Italy. Roman society and the Roman character had maintained their integrity through the period of expansion in Italy, but the temptations and strains that wealth and the complicated problems of an overseas empire presented would test them.

4.6.1 The Aftermath of Conquest

War and expansion changed the economic, social, and political life of Italy. Before the Punic Wars, most Italians owned their own farms, which provided the greater part of the family's needs. Some families owned larger holdings, but their lands chiefly grew grain, and they used the labor of clients, tenants, and hired workers rather than slaves. Fourteen years of fighting in the Second Punic War damaged Italian farmland terribly. Many veterans returning from the wars found it impossible or unprofitable to go back to their farms. Some moved to Rome, where they could find work as laborers, but most stayed in the country as tenant farmers or hired hands. Often, the wealthy converted the abandoned land into latifundia for growing cash crops—grain, olives, and grapes for wine—or into cattle ranches.

The upper classes had plenty of capital to operate these estates because of profits from the war and from exploiting the provinces. Land was cheap, and so was slave labor. By fair means and foul, large landholders obtained great quantities of public land and forced small farmers from it. These changes separated the people of Rome and Italy more sharply into rich and poor, landed and landless, privileged and deprived. The result was political, social, and, ultimately, constitutional conflict that threatened the existence of the republic.

4.6.2 The Gracchi

By the middle of the second century B.C.E., the problems caused by Rome's rapid expansion troubled perceptive

Map 4–3 ROMAN DOMINIONS OF THE LATE REPUBLIC

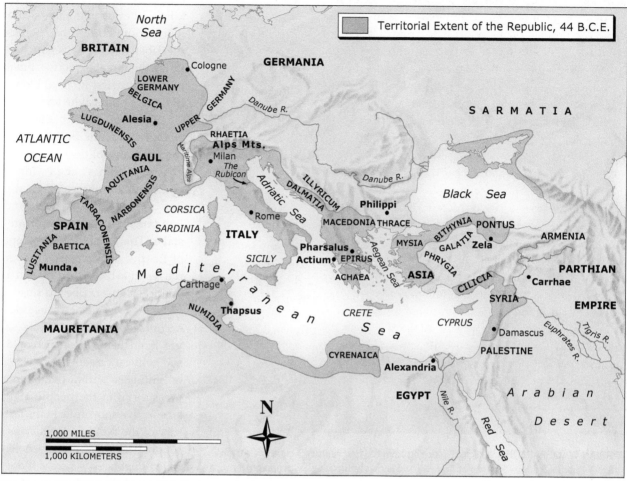

The Roman Republic's conquest of Mediterranean lands—and beyond—until the death of Julius Caesar is shown here. Areas conquered before the time of Tiberius Gracchus (ca. 133 B.C.E.) are distinguished from later ones and from client areas owing allegiance to Rome.

Roman nobles. The fall in status of peasant farmers made it harder to recruit soldiers and came to present a political threat as well. The patron's traditional control over his clients was weakened when they fled from their land. Even those former landowners who worked on the land of their patrons as tenants or hired hands were less reliable. The introduction of the secret ballot in the 130s B.C.E. made them even more independent.

4.6.2.1 TIBERIUS GRACCHUS In 133 B.C.E., Tiberius Gracchus tried to solve these problems. He became tribune for a year in 133 B.C.E. on a program of land reform; some of the most powerful members of the Roman aristocracy helped him draft the bill. Meant to be a moderate attempt at solving Rome's problems, the bill's target was public land that had been acquired and held illegally, some of it for many years. The bill allowed holders of this land to retain as many as 500 iugera (approximately 320 acres), but the state would reclaim anything more than that and redistribute it in small lots to the poor, who would pay a small rent to the state and could not sell what they had received.

The bill aroused great hostility. Its passage would hurt many senators who held vast estates. Others thought it would be a bad precedent to allow any interference with property rights, even if they involved illegally held public land. Still others feared the political gains that Tiberius and his associates would make if the beneficiaries of their law were properly grateful to its drafters.

When Tiberius put the bill before the tribal assembly, one of the tribunes, M. Octavius, interposed his veto. Tiberius went to the Senate to discuss his proposal, but the senators continued their opposition. Tiberius now had to choose between dropping the matter and undertaking a revolutionary course. Unwilling to give up, he put his bill before the tribal assembly again. Again Octavius vetoed. So Tiberius, strongly supported by the people, had Octavius removed from office, violating the constitution. The assembly's removal of a magistrate implied a fundamental shift of power from the Senate to the people. If the assembly could pass laws that the Senate opposed and a tribune vetoed, and if they could remove magistrates, then Rome would become a democracy like Athens instead of

POMPEIAN WALL PAINTING This wall painting from the first century B.C.E. comes from the villa of Publius Fannius Synistor at Pompeii and shows an upper-class woman playing a cithara.
SOURCE: The Metropolitan Museum of Art/Art Resource, NY

At the elections a riot broke out, and a mob of senators and their clients killed Tiberius and some 300 of his followers and threw their bodies into the Tiber River. The Senate had put down the threat to its rule, but at the price of the first internal bloodshed in Roman political history.

The tribunate of Tiberius Gracchus changed Roman politics. Heretofore Roman political struggles had generally been struggles for honor and reputation between great families or coalitions of such families. Fundamental issues were rarely at stake. The revolutionary proposals of Tiberius, however, and the senatorial resort to bloodshed created a new political climate. Tiberius's use of the tribunate to challenge senatorial rule encouraged imitation despite his failure. From then on, Romans could pursue political careers not based solely on influence within the aristocracy; pressure from the people might be an effective substitute. In the last century of the republic, politicians who sought backing from the people were called *populares*, whereas those who supported the traditional role of the Senate were called *optimates*, or "the best men."

These groups were not political parties with formal programs and party discipline, but they were more than merely vehicles for the political ambitions of unorthodox politicians. Fundamental questions—such as those about land reform, the treatment of the Italian allies, the power of the assemblies versus the power of the Senate, and other problems—divided the Roman people, from the time of Tiberius Gracchus to the fall of the republic. Some popular leaders, of course, were cynical self-seekers who used the issues only for their own ambitions, while a few may have been sincere advocates of a principled position. Most, no doubt, were a mixture of the two, like most politicians throughout history.

4.6.2.2 GAIUS GRACCHUS The tribunate of Gaius Gracchus (brother of Tiberius) was much more dangerous than that of Tiberius. All the tribunes of 123 B.C.E. were his supporters, so there could be no veto, and a recent law had permitted the reelection of tribunes. Gaius's program appealed to a variety of groups. First, he revived the agrarian commission, which had been allowed to lapse. Because there was not enough good public land left to meet the

a traditional oligarchy. At this point, many of Tiberius's senatorial allies deserted him.

Tiberius proposed a second bill, harsher than the first and more appealing to the people, for he had given up hope of conciliating the Senate. This bill, which passed the assembly, provided for a commission to carry it out. When King Attalus of Pergamum died and left his kingdom to Rome, Tiberius proposed using the Pergamene revenue to finance the commission. This proposal challenged the Senate's control of both finances and foreign affairs. Thereafter there could be no compromise: either Tiberius or the Roman constitution would go under.

Tiberius understood the danger he would face if he stepped down from the tribunate, so he announced his candidacy for a second successive term, striking another blow at tradition. His opponents feared he might go on to hold office indefinitely, to dominate Rome in what appeared to them a demagogic tyranny. They concentrated their fire on the constitutional issue, the deposition of the tribune. They appear to have had some success, for many of Tiberius's supporters did not come out to vote.

demand, he proposed establishing new colonies: two in Italy and one on the old site of Carthage. Among other popular acts, he passed a law stabilizing the price of grain in Rome, which involved building granaries to guarantee an adequate supply.

Gaius broke new ground in appealing to the equestrian order in his struggle against the Senate. The **equestrians** (so called because they served in the Roman cavalry) were neither peasants nor senators. Some were businesspeople who supplied goods and services to the Roman state and collected its taxes. Almost continuous warfare and the need for tax collection in the provinces had made many of the equestrians rich. Most of the time, these wealthy men had the same outlook as the Senate; generally, they used their profits to purchase land and to try to reach senatorial rank themselves. Still, they had a special interest in Roman expansion and in the exploitation of the provinces. In the late second century B.C.E., they developed a clear sense of group interest and exerted political influence.

In 129 B.C.E., Pergamum became the new province of Asia. Gaius put through a law giving the equestrian order the privilege of collecting Pergamum's revenue. He also barred senators from serving as jurors on the courts that tried provincial governors charged with extortion. The combination was a wonderful gift for wealthy equestrian businessmen, who were now free to squeeze profits out of the rich province of Asia without much fear of interference from the governors. The results for Roman provincial administration were bad, but the immediate political consequences for Gaius were excellent. The equestrians were now truly a class; as a political unit, they might be set against the Senate or formed into a coalition to serve Gaius's purposes.

Gaius easily won reelection as tribune for 122 B.C.E. His goal was to grant citizenship to the Italians, both to resolve their dissatisfaction and to add them to his political coalition. But the common people did not want to share the advantages of Roman citizenship. The Senate seized on this proposal to drive a wedge between Gaius and his supporters.

The Romans did not reelect Gaius for 121 B.C.E., leaving him vulnerable to his enemies. A hostile consul provoked an incident that led to violence. The Senate decreed that the consuls see to it that no harm came to the republic; in effect, this decree established martial law. Gaius was hunted down and killed, and a senatorial court condemned and put to death some 3,000 of his followers without a trial.

4.6.3 Marius and Sulla

For the moment, the senatorial oligarchy had fought off the challenge to its traditional position. Before long, it faced several serious threats arising from troubles abroad. The first grew out of a dispute over the succession to the throne of Numidia, a client kingdom of Rome's near Carthage.

4.6.3.1 THE REFORMS OF MARIUS

The victory of Jugurtha, who became king of Numidia, and his massacre of Roman and Italian businessmen in the province gained Roman attention. Although the Senate was reluctant to become involved, pressure from the equestrians and the people forced the declaration of what became known as the Jugurthine War in 111 B.C.E.

As the war dragged on, the people, sometimes with good reason, suspected the Senate of taking bribes from Jugurtha. They elected C. **Marius** (157–86 B.C.E.) to the consulship for 107 B.C.E. The assembly, usurping the role of the Senate, assigned Marius to Numidia. This action was significant in several ways. Marius was a *novus homo*, a "new man"—that is, the first in the history of his family to reach the consulship. Although a wealthy equestrian, he had been born in the town of Arpinum and was outside the closed circle of the old Roman aristocracy. His earlier career had won him a reputation as an outstanding soldier and a political maverick.

Marius quickly defeated Jugurtha, but Jugurtha escaped, and guerrilla warfare continued. Finally, Marius's subordinate, L. Cornelius Sulla (138–78 B.C.E.), trapped Jugurtha and brought the war to an end. Marius celebrated the victory, but Sulla, an ambitious though impoverished descendant of an old Roman family, resented being cheated of the credit he thought he deserved. Rumors credited Sulla with the victory and diminished Marius's role. Thus, the seeds were planted for a mutual hostility that would last until Marius's death.

While the Romans were fighting Jugurtha, a far greater danger threatened Rome from the north. In 105 B.C.E., two barbaric tribes, the Cimbri and the Teutones, had come down the Rhone Valley and crushed a Roman army at Arausio (Orange) in southern France. When these tribes threatened again, the Romans elected Marius to his second consulship to meet the danger. He served five consecutive terms until 100 B.C.E., when the crisis was over.

While the barbarians were occupied elsewhere, Marius used the time to make important changes in the army. He began using volunteers for the army, mostly the dispossessed farmers and rural proletarians whose problems the Gracchi had not solved. They enlisted for a long term of service and viewed the army not as an unwelcome duty but as an opportunity and a career. These volunteers became semiprofessional clients of their general and sought guaranteed food, clothing, shelter, and booty from victories. They came to expect a piece of land as a form of mustering-out pay, or veteran's bonus, when they retired.

Volunteers were most likely to enlist with a man who was a capable soldier and influential enough to obtain what they needed from him. They looked to him rather than to the state for their rewards. He, however, had to obtain these favors from the Senate if he was to maintain his power and reputation. Marius's innovation created both the opportunity and the necessity for military leaders to gain enough power to challenge civilian authority. The promise of rewards won these leaders the personal loyalty of their troops, and that loyalty allowed them to intimidate the Senate into granting their demands.

4.6.3.2 THE WARS AGAINST THE ITALIANS (90–88 B.C.E.)

For a decade, Rome avoided serious troubles, but in that time the Senate took no action to deal with Italian discontent. The Italians were excluded from the land bill for Marius's veterans. Their discontent caused the Senate to expel all Italians from Rome in 95 B.C.E. Four years later, the tribune M. Livius Drusus put forward a bill to enfranchise the Italians. Drusus seems to have been a sincere aristocratic reformer, but he was assassinated in 90 B.C.E. Frustrated, the Italians revolted and established a separate confederation with its own capital and coinage.

Employing the traditional device of divide and conquer, the Romans immediately offered citizenship to those cities that remained loyal and soon made the same offer to the rebels if they laid down their arms. Even then, hard fighting was needed to put down the uprising, but by 88 B.C.E., the war against the allies was over. All the Italians became Roman citizens with the protections that citizenship offered. However, they retained local self-government and a dedication to their own municipalities that made Italy flourish. The passage of time blurred the distinction between Romans and Italians and forged them into a single nation.

4.6.3.3 SULLA'S DICTATORSHIP

During the war against the allies, Sulla had performed well. He was elected consul for 88 B.C.E. and was given command of the war against Mithridates, who was leading a major rebellion in Asia. At this point, the seventy-year-old Marius emerged from obscurity and sought the command for himself. With popular and equestrian support, he persuaded the assembly to transfer the command to him. But Sulla, defending the rights of the Senate and his own interests, marched his army against Rome. This was the first time a Roman general had used his army against fellow citizens. Marius and his men fled, and Sulla regained the command. As soon as Sulla left again for Asia, however, Marius joined with the consul Cinna and seized Rome, outlawing Sulla and doing away with senatorial opposition. Marius died soon after his election to a seventh consulship, for 86 B.C.E.

Cinna now was the chief man at Rome. Supported by Marius's men, he held the consulship from 87 to 84 B.C.E. His future depended on Sulla's fortunes in the East.

By 85 B.C.E., Sulla had driven Mithridates from Greece and had crossed over to Asia Minor. Eager to regain control of Rome, he negotiated a compromise peace. In 83 B.C.E., he returned to Italy and fought a civil war that lasted for more than a year. Sulla won the war and drove the followers of Marius from Italy. He had himself appointed dictator, not in the traditional sense, but to remake the state.

Sulla's first step was to wipe out the opposition. The names of those proscribed were posted in public. As outlaws, anyone could kill them and receive a reward. Sulla proscribed not only political opponents but also his personal enemies and men whose only crime was their wealth. With the proceeds from the confiscations, Sulla rewarded his veterans, perhaps as many as 100,000 men, thereby building a solid base of support.

Sulla had enough power to make himself the permanent ruler of Rome. He was traditional enough to want to restore senatorial government, but reformed enough to prevent the misfortunes of the past. To deal with the decimation of the Senate caused by the proscriptions and the civil war, Sulla enrolled 300 new members, many of them from the equestrian order and the upper classes of the Italian cities. The office of tribune, which the Gracchi had used to attack senatorial rule, was transformed into a political dead end.

Sulla's most valuable reforms improved the quality of the courts and the entire legal system. He created new courts to deal with specified crimes, bringing the number of courts to eight. Because both judge and jurors were senators, the courts, too, enhanced senatorial power. These actions were the most permanent of Sulla's reforms, laying the foundation for Roman criminal law.

Sulla retired to a life of ease and luxury in 79 B.C.E. He could not, however, undo the effect of his own example: a general using the loyalty of his troops to take power and to massacre his opponents, as well as innocent men. These actions proved to be more significant than his constitutional reforms.

4.7 The Fall of the Republic

What events led to the fall of the republic?

Within a year of Sulla's death, his constitution came under assault. To deal with an armed threat to its powers, the Senate violated the very procedures meant to defend them. These actions furthered the political trends that had become manifest from the time of the Gracchi. For example, instead of relying on their moral authority and the traditions of the republic to rule the state, the senate entrusted an ambitious figure, Pompey, with extraordinary commands.

KEY EVENTS IN THE FALL OF THE ROMAN REPUBLIC

133 B.C.E.	Tribunate of Tiberius Gracchus
123–122 B.C.E.	Tribunate of Gaius Gracchus
111–105 B.C.E.	Jugurthine War
104–100 B.C.E.	Consecutive consulships of Marius
90–88 B.C.E.	War against the Italian allies
88 B.C.E.	Sulla's march on Rome
82 B.C.E.	Sulla assumes dictatorship
71 B.C.E.	Crassus crushes rebellion of Spartacus
71 B.C.E.	Pompey defeats Sertorius in Spain
70 B.C.E.	Consulship of Crassus and Pompey
60 B.C.E.	Formation of First Triumvirate
58–50 B.C.E.	Caesar in Gaul
53 B.C.E.	Crassus killed in Battle of Carrhae
49 B.C.E.	Caesar crosses Rubicon; civil war begins
48 B.C.E.	Pompey defeated at Pharsalus; killed in Egypt
46–44 B.C.E.	Caesar's dictatorship
45 B.C.E.	End of civil war
43 B.C.E.	Formation of Second Triumvirate
42 B.C.E.	Triumvirs defeat Brutus and Cassius at Philippi
31 B.C.E.	Octavian and Agrippa defeat Antony at Actium

THEATER OF POMPEY The Theater of Pompey was situated in the southern part of ancient Rome's Campus Martius, the Field of Mars. It was built in 55 B.C.E. and was Rome's first permanent theater. This detail of a model of ancient Rome shows what the theater looked like. **SOURCE:** DEA/A. DAGLI ORTI/Getty Images

4.7.1 Pompey, Crassus, Caesar, and Cicero

The Senate gave the command of the army to Pompey (106–48 B.C.E.), who was only twenty-eight and had never been elected to a magistracy. Then, when Sertorius, a Marian general, resisted senatorial control, the Senate appointed Pompey proconsul in Spain in 77 B.C.E. These actions ignored Sulla's rigid rules for office holding, which had been meant to guarantee experienced, loyal, and safe commanders. In 71 B.C.E., Pompey returned to Rome with new glory, having put down the rebellion of Sertorius.

In 73 B.C.E., the Senate made another extraordinary appointment to end a great slave rebellion led by the gladiator Spartacus. Marcus Licinius Crassus, a rich and ambitious senator, was given command of almost all of Italy. Together with the newly returned Pompey, he crushed the rebellion in 71 B.C.E. Extraordinary commands of this sort proved to be the ruin of the republic.

Crassus and Pompey were both ambitious men whom the Senate feared. Both demanded special honors and election to the consulship for the year 70 B.C.E. Pompey was legally ineligible because he had never gone through the strict course of offices Sulla's constitution prescribed, and Crassus needed Pompey's help. They joined forces, though they disliked and were jealous of each other. They gained popular support by promising to restore the full powers of the tribunes, which Sulla had curtailed, and they gained equestrian backing by promising to restore equestrians to the extortion court juries. Crassus and Pompey both won election and repealed most of Sulla's constitution. This paved the way for further attacks on senatorial control and for collaboration between ambitious generals and demagogic tribunes.

In 67 B.C.E., a special law gave Pompey imperium for three years over the entire Mediterranean and fifty miles in from the coast. It also gave him the power to raise troops and money to rid the area of pirates. The assembly passed the law over senatorial opposition, and in three months Pompey cleared the seas of piracy. Meanwhile, a new war had broken out with Mithridates. In 66 B.C.E., the assembly transferred the command to Pompey, giving him unprecedented powers. He held imperium over all Asia, with the right to make war and peace at will. His imperium was superior to that of any proconsul in the field.

Once again, Pompey justified his appointment. He defeated Mithridates and drove him to suicide. By 62 B.C.E., Pompey had extended Rome's frontier to the Euphrates River and had organized the territories of Asia so well that his arrangements remained the basis of Roman rule well into the imperial period. When Pompey returned to Rome in 62 B.C.E., he had more power, prestige, and popular support than any Roman in history. The Senate and his personal enemies had reason to fear he might emulate Sulla and establish his own rule.

Rome had not been quiet in Pompey's absence. Crassus was the foremost among those who had reason to fear Pompey's return. Although rich and influential, Crassus did not have the confidence of the Senate, a firm political base of his own, or the kind of military glory needed to rival

Pompey. During the 60s B.C.E., therefore, he allied himself with various popular leaders.

The ablest of these men was Gaius Julius Caesar (100–44 B.C.E.). He was a descendant of an old, but politically obscure, patrician family that claimed descent from the kings and even from the goddess Venus. Despite this noble lineage, Caesar was connected to the popular party through his aunt, the wife of Marius, and through his own wife, Cornelia, the daughter of Cinna. Caesar was an ambitious young politician whose daring and rhetorical skill made him a valuable ally in winning the discontented of every class to the cause of the *populares*. Though Crassus was the senior partner, each needed the other to achieve what both wanted: significant military commands with which to build a reputation, a political following, and a military force to compete with Pompey's.

The chief opposition to Crassus's candidates for the consulship for 63 B.C.E. came from Cicero (106–43 B.C.E.), a *novus homo*, from Marius's hometown of Arpinum. He had made a spectacular name as the leading lawyer in Rome. Cicero, though he came from outside the senatorial aristocracy, was no *popularis*. His program was to preserve the republic against demagogues and ambitious generals by making the government more liberal. He wanted to unite the stable elements of the state—the Senate and the equestrians—in a harmony of the orders. This program did not appeal to the senatorial oligarchy, but the Senate preferred Cicero to Catiline, a dangerous and popular politician thought to be linked with Crassus. Cicero and Antonius were elected consuls for 63 B.C.E., with Catiline running third.

Cicero soon learned of a plot hatched by Catiline. Catiline had run in the previous election on a platform of cancellation of debts; this appealed to discontented elements in general, but especially to the heavily indebted nobles and their many clients. Made desperate by defeat, Catiline planned to stir up rebellions around Italy, to cause confusion in the city, and to take it by force. Quick action by Cicero defeated Catiline.

4.7.2 The First Triumvirate

Toward the end of 62 B.C.E., Pompey landed at Brundisium. Surprisingly, he disbanded his army, celebrated a great triumph, and returned to private life. He had delayed his return in the hope of finding Italy in such a state as to justify his keeping the army and dominating the scene. But Cicero's quick suppression of Catiline prevented Pompey's plan, and he had to either act illegally or lay down his arms. Because he had not considered monarchy or revolution, but merely wanted to be recognized and treated as the greatest Roman, Pompey chose the latter course.

Pompey had achieved amazing things for Rome and simply wanted the Senate to approve his excellent arrangements in the East and to make land allotments to his veterans. Pompey's demands were far from unreasonable, and a prudent Senate would have granted them and tried to employ his power in defense of the constitution. But the Senate was jealous and fearful of overmighty individuals and refused his requests. Pompey was driven to an alliance with his natural enemies, Crassus and Caesar, because the Senate blocked what all three wanted.

In 60 B.C.E., Caesar returned to Rome from his governorship of Spain. He wanted to celebrate a triumph, the great victory procession that the Senate granted certain generals to honor especially great achievements, and to run for consul. The law did not allow him to do either, however, requiring Caesar to stay outside the city with his army but demanding that he canvass for votes personally within the city. He asked for a special dispensation, but the Senate refused. Caesar then performed a political miracle. He reconciled Crassus with Pompey and gained the support of both for his own ambitions. So was born the First Triumvirate, an informal agreement among three Roman politicians, each seeking his own private goals, which further undermined the republic.

4.7.3 Julius Caesar and His Government of Rome

Though he was forced to forgo his triumph, Caesar was elected to the consulship for 59 B.C.E. His fellow consul was M. Calpernius Bibulus, the son-in-law of Cato and a conservative hostile to Caesar and the other *populares*. Caesar did not hesitate to override his colleague. The triumvirs' program was quickly enacted. Caesar received the extraordinary command that would give him a chance to earn the glory and power with which to rival Pompey: the governorship of Illyricum and Gaul for five years. A land bill settled Pompey's veterans comfortably, and his eastern settlement was ratified. Crassus, much of whose influence came from his position as champion of the equestrians, won for them a great windfall by having the government renegotiate a tax contract in their favor. To safeguard against any reversal of these actions, the triumvirs continued their informal but effective collaboration, arranging for the election of friendly consuls and the departure of potential opponents.

Caesar was now free to seek the military success he craved. His province included Cisalpine Gaul in the Po Valley (by now occupied by many Italian settlers as well as Gauls) and Narbonese Gaul beyond the Alps (modern Provence).

Relying first on the excellent quality of his army and the experience of his officers and then on his own growing military ability, Caesar made great progress. By 56 B.C.E., he had conquered most of Gaul, but he had not yet consolidated his victories firmly. He therefore sought an extension of his command, but quarrels between Crassus and Pompey

JULIUS CAESAR (100–44 B.C.E.) Gaius Julius Caesar (100–44 B.C.E.).
He was a descendant of an old, but politically obscure, patrician
family that claimed descent from the kings and even from the
goddess Venus.
SOURCE: Scala/Art Resource, NY

so weakened the Triumvirate that the Senate was prepared
to order Caesar's recall.

To prevent the dissolution of his base of power, Caesar
persuaded Crassus and Pompey to meet with him at Lucca
in northern Italy to renew the coalition. They agreed that
Caesar would get another five-year command in Gaul,
and Crassus and Pompey would become consuls again in
55 B.C.E. After that, they would each receive an army and a
five-year command. Caesar was free to return to Gaul and
finish the job. The capture of Alesia in 51 B.C.E. marked the
end of the serious Gallic resistance and of Gallic liberty. For
Caesar, it brought the wealth, fame, and military power he
wanted. He commanded thirteen loyal legions, a match for
his enemies as well as for his allies.

By the time Caesar was ready to return to Rome, the
Triumvirate had dissolved and a crisis was at hand. At
Carrhae, in 53 B.C.E., Crassus died trying to conquer the
Parthians, successors to the Persian Empire. His death
broke one link between Pompey and Caesar. The death

of Caesar's daughter Julia, who had been Pompey's wife,
dissolved another.

As Caesar's star rose, Pompey became jealous and
fearful. He did not leave Rome but governed his province
through a subordinate. In the late 50s B.C.E., political rioting at Rome caused the Senate to appoint Pompey sole
consul. This grant of unprecedented power and responsibility brought Pompey closer to the senatorial aristocracy in mutual fear of, and hostility to, Caesar. The Senate
wanted to bring Caesar back to Rome as a private citizen
after his proconsular command expired. He would then
be open to attack for past illegalities. Caesar tried to avoid
the trap by asking permission to stand for the consulship
in absentia.

Early in January of 49 B.C.E., the more extreme faction
in the Senate had its way. It ordered Pompey to defend the
state and Caesar to lay down his command by a specified
day. For Caesar, this meant exile or death, so he ordered
his legions to cross the Rubicon River, the boundary of his
province. (See Map 4–4.) This action started a civil war.
In 45 B.C.E., Caesar defeated the last forces of his enemies
under Pompey's sons at Munda in Spain. The war was over,
and Caesar, in Shakespeare's words, bestrode "the narrow
world like a Colossus."

From the beginning of the civil war until his death in
44 B.C.E., Caesar spent less than a year and a half in Rome,
and many of his actions were attempts to deal with immediate problems between campaigns. His innovations generally
sought to make rational and orderly what was traditional
and chaotic. An excellent example is Caesar's reform of
the calendar. By 46 B.C.E., it was eighty days ahead of the
proper season, because the official year was lunar, with only
355 days. Using the best scientific advice, Caesar instituted a
new calendar, now known as the *Julian Calendar:* With minor
changes by Pope Gregory XIII in the sixteenth century, it is
the calendar in use today.

Caesar's reforms in the political area included the
elevation of the role of Italians and even provincials at the
expense of the old Roman families, most of whom were his
political enemies. He raised the number of senators to 900
and filled the Senate's depleted ranks with Italians and even
Gauls. He was free with grants of Roman citizenship, giving the franchise to Cisalpine Gaul as a whole and to many
individuals of various regions.

Caesar made few changes in the government of Rome.
The Senate continued to play its role, in theory. But its
increased size, packed with supporters of Caesar, and
Caesar's monopoly of military power made the whole thing
a sham. He treated the Senate as his creature, sometimes
with disdain.

Caesar's legal position rested on several powers. In
46 B.C.E., he was appointed dictator for ten years, and in
the next year he was appointed for life. Caesar also held
the consulship, the immunity of a tribune (although, being

Map 4–4 THE CIVIL WARS OF THE LATE ROMAN REPUBLIC

This map shows the extent of the territory controlled by Rome at the time of Julius Caesar's death and the sites of the major battles of the civil wars of the late republic.

a patrician, he had never been a tribune), the chief priesthood of the state, and—a new position—prefect of morals, which gave him censorial power. Usurping the elective power of the assemblies, Caesar even named the magistrates for the next few years because he expected to be away in the East.

The enemies of Caesar were quick to accuse him of aiming at monarchy. A conspiracy under the leadership of Gaius Cassius Longinus and Marcus Junius Brutus included some sixty senators. On 15 March 44 B.C.E., Caesar entered the Senate, characteristically without a bodyguard, and was stabbed to death. The assassins regarded themselves as heroes but did not have a clear plan of action to follow the tyrant's death. No doubt they simply expected the republic to be restored in the old way, but things had gone too far for that. There followed instead thirteen more years of civil war, at the end of which the republic received its final burial.

4.7.4 The Second Triumvirate and the Triumph of Octavian

Caesar had had legions of followers, and he had a capable successor in Mark Antony. But the dictator had named his eighteen-year-old grandnephew, Gaius Octavius (63 B.C.E.– 14 C.E.), as his heir and had left him three-quarters of his vast wealth. To everyone's surprise, Octavius, a sickly and inexperienced young man, came to Rome to claim his legacy. He gathered an army, won the support of many of Caesar's veterans, and became a figure of importance—the future Augustus.

At first, the Senate tried to use Octavius against Antony, but when the conservatives rejected his request for the consulship, Octavius broke with them. Following Sulla's grim precedent, he took his army and marched on Rome. There he finally assumed his adopted name, C. Julius Caesar Octavianus. Modern historians refer to him at this stage in his career as Octavian, although he insisted on being called Caesar. In August 43 B.C.E., he became consul and declared the assassins of Caesar outlaws. Brutus and Cassius had an army of their own, so Octavian made a pact with Mark Antony and M. Aemilius Lepidus, a Caesarean governor of the western provinces. They took control of Rome and had themselves appointed "triumvirs to put the republic in order," with great powers. This was the Second Triumvirate, and, unlike the first, it was legally empowered to rule almost dictatorially.

The need to pay their troops, their own greed, and the passion that always emerges in civil wars led the triumvirs to start a wave of proscriptions that outdid even those of Sulla. In 42 B.C.E., the triumviral army defeated Brutus and Cassius at Philippi in Macedonia, and the last hope of republican restoration died with the tyrannicides. Each of the triumvirs received a command: The junior partner, Lepidus, was given Africa, Antony took the rich and inviting East, and Octavian got the West and the many troubles that went with it.

Octavian had to fight a war against Sextus, the son of Pompey, who held Sicily. He also had to settle 100,000 veterans in Italy, confiscating much property and making many enemies. Helped by his friend Agrippa, he defeated Sextus Pompey in 36 B.C.E. Among Octavian's close associates was Maecenas, who served him as adviser and diplomatic agent. Maecenas helped manage the delicate relations with Antony and Lepidus, but perhaps equally important was his role as a patron of the arts. Among his clients were the poets Vergil and Horace, both of whom did important work for Octavian. They painted him as a restorer of Roman values, as a man of ancient Roman lineage and of traditional Roman virtues, and as the culmination of Roman destiny. More and more Octavian was identified with Italy and the West, as well as with order, justice, and virtue.

Meanwhile, Antony was in the East, chiefly at Alexandria with Cleopatra, the queen of Egypt. In 36 B.C.E., he attacked Parthia, with disastrous results. Octavian had promised to send troops to support Antony's Parthian campaign but never sent them. Antony was forced to depend on the East for support, and this meant reliance on Cleopatra. Octavian understood the advantage of representing himself as the champion of the West, Italy, and Rome. Meanwhile, he represented Antony as the man of the East and the dupe of Cleopatra, her tool in establishing Alexandria as the center of an empire and herself as its ruler. Such propaganda made it easier for Caesareans to abandon Antony in favor of the young heir of Caesar. It did not help Antony's cause that he agreed to a public festival at Alexandria in 34 B.C.E., where he and Cleopatra sat on golden thrones. She was proclaimed "Queen of Kings," her son by Julius Caesar was named "King of Kings," and her other children received parts of the Roman Empire.

By 32 B.C.E., all pretense of cooperation ended. Octavian and Antony each tried to put the best face on what was essentially a struggle for power. Lepidus had been put aside some years earlier. Antony sought senatorial support and promised to restore the republican constitution. Octavian seized and published what was alleged to be the will of Antony, revealing his gifts of provinces to the children of Cleopatra. This caused the conflict to take the form of East against West, Rome against Alexandria.

In 31 B.C.E., the matter was settled at Actium in western Greece. Agrippa, Octavian's best general, cut off the enemy by land and sea, forcing and winning a naval battle. Octavian pursued Antony and Cleopatra to Alexandria, where both committed suicide. The civil wars were over, and at the age of thirty-two, Octavian was absolute master of the Mediterranean world. His power was enormous, but he had to restore peace, prosperity, and confidence. This required establishing a constitution that would reflect the new realities without offending unduly the traditional republican prejudices that still had so firm a grip on Rome and Italy.

The Chapter in Perspective

The history of the Roman Republic was almost as sharp a departure from the common experiences of ancient civilizations as that of the Greek city-states. A monarchy in its earliest known form, Rome not long thereafter expelled its king and established an aristocratic republic somewhat like the poleis of the Greek "Dark Ages." But unlike the Greeks, the Romans continued to be in touch with foreign neighbors, including the far more civilized urban monarchies of the Etruscans. Nonetheless, the Romans clung to their republican institutions. For a long time, the Romans remained a nation of farmers and herdsmen, to whom trade was relatively unimportant, especially outside of Italy.

Over time, the caste distinctions between patricians and plebeians were replaced by distinctions based on wealth and, even more important, aristocracy, wherein the significant distinction was between noble families, who held the highest elected offices in the state, and those outside the nobility. The Roman Republic from the first found itself engaged in almost continuous warfare with its neighbors—either in defense of its own territory, in fights over disputed territory, or in defense of other cities or states who were friends and allies of Rome.

Both internally and in their foreign relations, the Romans were a legalistic people, placing great importance on traditional behavior encoded into laws. Although backed by the powerful authority of the magistrates at home and the potent Roman army abroad, the laws were based on experience, common sense, and equity. Roman law aimed at stability and fairness, and it succeeded well enough that few people who lived under it wanted to do away with it. It lived on and grew during the imperial period and beyond. During the European Middle Ages, it played an important part in the revival of the West and continued to exert an influence into modern times.

The force of Roman arms, the high quality of Roman roads and bridges, and the pragmatic character of Roman law helped create something unique: an empire ruled by a republic, first a large one on land that included all of Italy and later one that commanded the shores of the entire Mediterranean and extended far inland in many places. Rome controlled an area that bears comparison with some of the empires of the East. It acquired that territory, wealth, and

power in a state managed by annual magistrates elected by the male Roman citizens and by an aristocratic Senate, which had to take notice of popular assemblies and a published, impersonal code of law. It achieved its greatness with an army of citizens and allies, without a monarchy or a regular bureaucracy.

The temptations and responsibilities of governing a vast and rich empire, however, finally proved too much for the republican constitution. Trade grew, and with it a class of merchants and financiers—equestrians—that was neither aristocratic nor agricultural, but increasingly powerful. The influx of masses of slaves captured in war undermined the small farmers who had been the backbone of the Roman state and its army. As many of them were forced to leave their farms, they moved to the cities, chiefly to Rome, where they had no productive role. Conscripted armies of farmers serving relatively short terms gave way to volunteer armies of landless men serving as professionals and expecting to be rewarded for their services with gifts of land or money. The generals of these armies were not annual magistrates whom the Senate and the constitution controlled, but ambitious military leaders seeking glory and political advantage.

The result was civil war and the destruction of the republic. The conquest of a vast empire moved the Romans away from their unusual historical traditions toward the more familiar path of an empire that older rulers in Egypt and Mesopotamia had trodden.

The Chapter in Review

Review Questions

1. How did the institutions of family and clientage and the establishment of patrician and plebeian classes contribute to the stability of the early Roman Republic? How important were education and slavery to the success of the republic?

2. What was the Struggle of the Orders? How did plebeians get what they wanted? How was Roman society different after the struggle ended?

3. How was Rome able to conquer and control Italy? In their relations with Greece and Asia Minor in the second century B.C.E., were the Romans looking for security? Wealth? Power? Fame?

4. Why did the Romans and the Carthaginians clash in the First and Second Punic Wars? Could the wars

have been avoided? How did Rome benefit from its victory over Carthage? What problems did this victory create?

5. What social, economic, and political problems did Italy have in the second century B.C.E.? What were the main proposals of Tiberius and Gaius Gracchus? What questions about Roman society did they raise? Why did their proposals fail?

6. What problems plagued the Roman Republic in its last century? To what extent was the republic destroyed by ambitious generals who loved power more than Rome itself?

Key Terms

Battle of Cannae (216 B.C.E.) Battle of the Second Punic War at Cannae in Apulia, in which Hannibal inflicted the worst defeat ever suffered by the Romans.

censor Official of the Roman Republic charged with conducting the census and compiling the lists of citizens

and members of the Senate and who could expel senators for financial or moral reasons. Two censors elected every five years.

clientage (KLI-ent-age) The custom in ancient Rome whereby men became supporters of more powerful men in return for legal and physical protection and economic benefits.

coloni (CO-loan-ee) Farmers or sharecroppers on the estates of wealthy Romans.

consuls (CON-suls) The two chief magistrates of the Roman state.

equestrians (EE-quest-ree-ans) Meaning "cavalrymen" or "knights." In the earliest years of the Roman Republic those who could afford to serve as mounted warriors. Evolved into a social rank of well-to-do businessmen and middle-ranking officials, many of whom supported the Gracchi.

Etruscans (EE-trus-cans) A people of central Italy who exerted the most powerful external influence on the early Romans and whose kings ruled Rome until 509 B.C.E.

Gaul (GAWL) Modern France.

humanitas **(HEW-man-i-tas)** The Roman name for a liberal arts education.

imperium **(IM-pear-ee-um)** In ancient Rome, the right to issue commands and to enforce them with fines, arrests, and even corporal and capital punishment.

latifundia **(LAT-ee-fun-dee-a)** Large plantations for growing cash crops owned by wealthy Romans.

Latium A region that included the small town of Rome, conquered by the Etruscan aristocracy in sixth century B.C.E.

Marius (157–86 B.C.E.) Roman general and consul who made important reforms to the Roman army.

optimates **(OP-tee-ma-tes)** Meaning "the best men." Roman politicians who supported the traditional role of the Senate.

paedagogus A Greek slave who accompanied Roman boys from the ages of seven to twelve to school in the late republic and looked after their physical well-being and their manners.

patrician (PA-tri-she-an) The hereditary upper class of early republican Rome.

plebeian (PLEB-bee-an) The hereditary lower class of early republican Rome.

populares **(PO-pew-lar-es)** Roman politicians who pursued a political career based on the support of the people rather than just the aristocracy.

proconsulship (PRO-con-sul-ship) In republican Rome, the extension of a consul's imperium beyond the end of his term of office to allow him to continue to command an army in the field.

tribunes (TRIB-unes) Roman plebeian officials elected by the plebeian assembly to protect plebeians from the arbitrary power of the magistrates.

Notes

1. E. Badian, *Foreign Clientelae* (264–70 B.C.E.) (Oxford, UK: Clarendon Press, 1958), p. 1.

2. Juvenal, *Satires* 6.434–456, trans. by Roger Killian, Richard Lynch, Robert J. Rowland, and John Sims, cited by Sarah B. Pomeroy in *Goddesses, Whores, Wives, and Slaves* (New York: Schocken Books, 1975), p. 172.

Chapter 5
The Roman Empire

EMPEROR AUGUSTUS (r. 27 B.C.E.–14 C.E.) This statue of Emperor Augustus, now in the Vatican, stood in the villa of Augustus's wife Livia. The figures on the elaborate breastplate all have symbolic significance. At the top, for example, Dawn in her chariot celebrates a new day under the protective mantle of the sky god; in the center, Tiberius, Augustus's future successor, accepts the return of captured Roman army standards from a barbarian prince; and at the bottom, Mother Earth offers a horn of plenty.
SOURCE: Scala / Art Resource

Contents and Focus Questions

The Chapter in Brief

THE VICTORY OF Augustus put an end to the deadly period of civil strife that had begun with the murder of Tiberius Gracchus. The establishment of a monarchy, at first concealed in republican forms but gradually more obvious, brought a long period of peace. Rome's unquestioned control of the entire Mediterranean permitted the growth of trade and a prosperity in the first two centuries of the Roman Empire not to be equaled for more than a millennium.

Management of the empire outside Italy became more benign and efficient. With shared citizenship, the provinces usually accepted Roman rule readily and even enthusiastically. Latin became the official language of the western part of the empire and Greek the official language in the east. This permitted the growth and spread of a common culture, today called *classical civilization*, throughout the empire, with a great outburst of activity and excellence in the arts. The loss of political freedom, however, brought a decline in the vitality of the great Roman genre of rhetoric.

Christianity emerged in the first century C.E. as one of many competing Eastern cults. It continued to spread and attract converts, winning toleration and finally dominance in the fourth century. The world of imperial Rome powerfully shaped Christianity, which absorbed and used classical culture even while fighting it.

The third century C.E. brought serious attacks on Rome's frontiers, causing political and economic chaos. For a time, such emperors as Diocletian (r. 284–305 C.E.) and Constantine (r. 306–337 C.E.) took heroic measures to restore order. Their solutions involved increased centralization, militarization, and attempts to control every aspect of life. The emperors became more exalted and remote and the people increasingly burdened with heavy taxes even as the loss of economic freedom reduced their ability to pay. At last a new wave of barbarian attacks proved irresistible, and the Roman Empire in the West ended in the second half of the fifth century.

5.1 The Augustan Principate

How did Augustus transform Roman politics and government?

If the problems facing Octavian after the Battle of Actium in 31 B.C.E. were great, so were his resources for addressing them. He was the master of a vast military force, the only one in the Roman world, and he had loyal and capable assistants. Of enormous importance was the rich treasury of Egypt, which Octavian treated as his personal property. The people of Italy were eager for an end to civil war and a return to peace, order, and prosperity. In exchange for these, most were prepared to accept a considerable abandonment of republican practices and to give power to an able ruler. The memory of Julius Caesar's fate, however, was still fresh in Octavian's mind. Its lesson was that it was dangerous to flaunt unprecedented powers and to disregard all republican traditions.

Octavian did not devise his constitutional solution in a single stroke. It developed gradually as he tried new devices to fit his perception of changing conditions. Behind all the republican trappings and the apparent sharing of authority with the Senate, the government of Octavian, like that of his successors, was a monarchy. All real power, both civil and military, lay with the ruler—whether he was called by the unofficial title of *princeps*, or "first citizen," like Octavian, or the founder of the regime or imperator, "emperor," like those who followed. During the civil war, Octavian's powers came from his triumviral status, whose dubious legality and unrepublican character were an embarrassment. From 31 B.C.E. on, he held the consulship each year, but this circumstance was neither strictly legal nor satisfactory.

On 13 January 27 B.C.E., Octavian proposed a new plan in dramatic style, coming before the Senate to give up all his powers and provinces. In what was surely a rehearsed response, the Senate begged him to reconsider. At last, Octavian agreed to accept the provinces of Spain, Gaul, and Syria as proconsular powers for military command, and to retain the consulship in Rome. The other provinces would be governed by the Senate as before. Because the provinces retained by Octavian were border provinces that contained twenty of Rome's twenty-six legions, his true power was undiminished. The Senate, however, responded with almost hysterical gratitude, voting him many honors. Among them was the semireligious title *Augustus*, which implied veneration, majesty, and holiness. From this time on, historians speak of Rome's first emperor as Augustus and of his regime as the *principate*. This would have pleased

Octavian, for the terms help conceal the novel, unrepublican nature of his regime and the naked power on which it rested.

In 23 B.C.E., Augustus resigned his consulship and held that office rarely thereafter. Instead, he was voted two powers that were to be the basis of his rule thereafter: the proconsular *imperium maius* and the *tribunician power*. The former made Augustus's proconsular power greater than that of any other proconsul and permitted him to exercise it even within the city of Rome. The latter gave him the right to conduct public business in the assemblies and the Senate, the power of the veto, the *tribunician sacrosanctity* (immunity from arrest and punishment), and a connection with the Roman popular tradition. From that day forward, Augustus's powers remained, with only minor changes, as those conferred in 23 B.C.E.

5.1.1 Administration

Augustus made important changes in the government of Rome, Italy, and the provinces. Most of his reforms reduced inefficiency and corruption; ended the threat to peace and order from ambitious individuals; and lessened the distinction between Romans and Italians, senators and equestrians. The assemblies lost their significance as a working part of the constitution, and the Senate took on most of the functions of the assemblies. Augustus purged the old Senate of undesirable members and fixed its number at 600. He recruited its members from wealthy men of good character, who joined after serving as lesser magistrates. Augustus controlled the elections and ensured that promising young men, whatever their origin, served the state as administrators and provincial governors. In this way, many equestrians and Italians who had no connection with the Roman aristocracy became members of the Senate. Regardless of his power, Augustus was always careful to treat the Senate with respect and honor.

Augustus divided Rome into regions and wards with elected local officials. He gave the city, with its rickety wooden tenements, its first public fire department and police force. He carefully controlled grain distribution to the poor and created organizations to provide an adequate water supply. The Augustan period was one of great prosperity, based on the wealth brought in by the conquest of Egypt, on the great increase in commerce and industry made possible by general peace, on a vast program of public works, and on the revival of small farming by Augustus's resettled veterans.

The union of political and military power in the hands of the princeps enabled Augustus to install rational, efficient, and stable government in the provinces for the first time. The emperor, in effect, chose the governors, removed the incompetent or rapacious, and allowed the effective ones to keep their provinces for longer periods. Also, Augustus allowed much greater local autonomy, giving considerable responsibility to the upper classes in the provincial cities and towns and to the tribal leaders in less civilized areas.

ARA PACIS (ALTAR OF PEACE) This scene from Augustus's Altar of Peace in Rome shows the general Marcus Agrippa (63–12 B.C.E.) in procession with the imperial family. Agrippa was a powerful deputy, close friend, and son-in-law of Augustus. He was chiefly responsible for the victory over Mark Antony at the Battle of Actium in 31 B.C.E.

SOURCE: Nimatallah/Art Resource, NY

5.1.2 The Army and Defense

The main external problem facing Augustus—and one that haunted all his successors—was the northern frontier. (See Map 5–1.) Rome needed to pacify the regions to the north and the northeast of Italy and to find defensible frontiers against the recurring waves of barbarians. Augustus's plan was to push forward into central Europe to create the shortest possible defensive line. The eastern part of the plan succeeded, and the campaign in the West started well. In 9 C.E., however, the German tribal leader Herrmann, or Arminius, as the Romans called him, ambushed and destroyed three Roman legions, and the aged Augustus abandoned the campaign, leaving a problem of border defense that bedeviled his successors.

Under Augustus, the armed forces achieved professional status. Enlistment, chiefly by Italians, was for twenty years, but the pay was good, with occasional bonuses and the promise of a pension upon retirement in the form of money or a plot of land. Together with the auxiliaries from the provinces, these forces formed a frontier army of about 300,000 men. In normal times, this was barely enough to hold the line.

The army permanently based in the provinces brought Roman culture to the natives. The soldiers spread their language and customs, often marrying local women and settling down in the area of their service. The army attracted merchants, as new towns and cities that grew into centers of Roman civilization formed around the military camps. As time passed, the provincials on the frontiers became Roman citizens who helped strengthen Rome's defenses against the barbarians outside.

5.1.3 Religion and Morality

A century of political strife and civil war had undermined many of the foundations of traditional Roman society. To repair the damage, Augustus sought to preserve and restore the traditional values of the family and religion in Rome and Italy. He introduced laws curbing adultery and divorce and encouraging early marriage and the procreation of legitimate children. He set an example of austere behavior in his own household and even banished his daughter, Julia, whose immoral behavior had become public knowledge.

Map 5–1 THE ROMAN EMPIRE, 14 C.E.

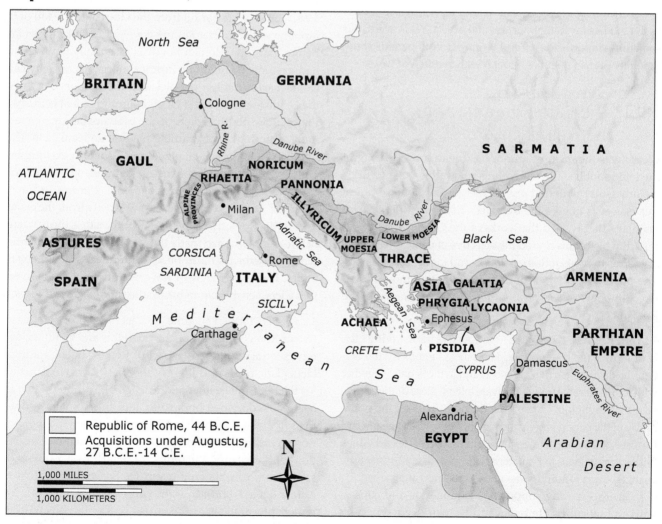

This map shows the growth of the Roman empire under Augustus and its extent at his death in 14 C.E.

Augustus's attempts at restoring the dignity of formal Roman religion included building many temples, reviving old cults, invigorating the priestly colleges, and banning the worship of newly introduced foreign gods. Writers such as Vergil, whom Augustus patronized, pointed out his family's legendary connection with Venus. During his lifetime, Augustus did not accept divine honors, though he was deified after his death. As with Julius Caesar, a state cult was dedicated to his worship.

5.2 Civilization of the Ciceronian and Augustan Ages

How did political developments shape the culture of the Ciceronian and Augustan ages?

The high point of Roman culture came in the last century of the republic and during the principate of Augustus. Both periods reflected the dominant influence of Greek culture, especially its Hellenistic mode. Upper-class Romans were educated in Greek rhetoric, philosophy, and literature, which also served as the models for Roman writers and artists. Yet in spirit and sometimes in form, the art and writing of both periods show uniquely Roman qualities, though each in different ways.

5.2.1 The Late Republic and the Age of Cicero

Cicero was the greatest author of Roman prose writing of the late republic. The overriding goal of his major works, including his public and private speeches and philosophical treatises, was to give the Romans a literature in their own language that rivaled the works of the Greeks. Cicero and the Latin historians shared the objective of using Greek literary forms to present Roman values and models of behavior. The poets of the late republic also adopted and adapted Greek models of composition for the Latin language and Roman tastes.

5.2.1.1 CICERO Cicero (106–43 B.C.E.) was the towering literary figure of the late republic. He is most famous for the orations he delivered in the law courts and in the Senate. Together with a considerable body of private letters, these orations give us great insight into Cicero's mind, and help us see the political life of the period largely through his eyes. Cicero also wrote treatises on rhetoric, ethics, and politics that expressed Greek philosophical ideas in Latin terminology and at the same time changed them to suit Roman conditions and values.

Cicero's writing supported his moderate and conservative practicality. He believed in a world governed by divine and natural law that human reason could perceive and human institutions could reflect. He looked to law, custom, and tradition as sources of both stability and liberty. Cicero's literary style, as well as his values and ideas, were an important legacy for the Middle Ages and, reinterpreted, for the Renaissance. He was killed at the order of Mark Antony, whose political opponent he had been during the civil wars after the death of Julius Caesar.

5.2.1.2 HISTORY The last century of the republic produced some historical writing, much of which is lost to us. Sallust (86–35 B.C.E.) wrote a history of the years 78 to 67 B.C.E., but only a few fragments remain to remind us of his reputation as the greatest of republican historians. His surviving work consists of two pamphlets on the Jugurthine War and on the conspiracy of Catiline of 63 B.C.E. They reveal his Caesarean and antisenatorial prejudices and the stylistic influence of Thucydides.

Julius Caesar wrote important treatises on the Gallic and civil wars. They are not fully rounded historical accounts, but chiefly military narratives written from Caesar's point of view and to enhance his reputation. Their objective manner (Caesar always referred to himself in the third person) and their direct, simple, and vigorous style make these narratives persuasive even today.

5.2.1.3 LAW The period from the Gracchi to the fall of the republic was important in the development of Roman law. Before that time, Roman law was essentially national and had developed chiefly by juridical decisions, case by case. Contact with foreign peoples and the influence of Greek ideas, however, forced a change. From the last century of the republic on, the edicts of the praetors became increasingly important in developing the Roman legal code. They interpreted and even changed and added to existing law. Quite early, the edicts of the magistrates who dealt with foreigners developed the idea of the *jus gentium*, or "law of peoples," as opposed to that arising strictly from the experience of the Romans. In the first century B.C.E., the influence of Greek thought had made the idea of jus gentium identical with that of the *jus naturale*, or "natural law," taught by the Stoics. It was this view of a world ruled by divine reason that Cicero enshrined in his treatise on the law, *De Legibus*.

5.2.1.4 POETRY The time of Cicero also encompassed two of Rome's greatest poets, Lucretius and Catullus, each representing a different aspect of Rome's poetic tradition. Hellenistic poets and literary theorists saw two functions for the poet: entertainer and teacher. They thought that the best poet combined both roles, and the Romans adopted the same view. When Naevius and Ennius wrote epics on Roman history, they combined historical and moral instruction with pleasure. Lucretius (ca. 99–55 B.C.E.) pursued a similar path in his epic poem *De Rerum Natura* (*On the Nature of the World*). In it, he presented the scientific and philosophical ideas of Epicurus and Democritus with the zeal of a missionary trying to save society from fear and superstition. He knew his doctrine might be bitter medicine to the reader: "That is why I have tried to administer it to you in the dulcet strain of poesy, coated with the sweet honey of the Muses."[1]

Catullus (ca. 84–54 B.C.E.) was a thoroughly different kind of poet. He wrote poems that were personal—even autobiographical. Imitating the Alexandrians, he wrote short poems filled with learned allusions to mythology, but he far surpassed his models in intensity of feeling. He wrote of the joys and pains of love, he hurled invective at contemporaries like Julius Caesar, and he amused himself in witty poetic exchanges with others. Catullus offered no moral lessons and was not interested in Rome's glorious history or in contemporary politics. In a sense, he is an example of the proud, independent, pleasure-seeking nobleman who characterized part of the aristocracy at the end of the republic.

5.2.2 The Age of Augustus

The spirit of the Augustan Age, the Golden Age of Roman literature, was different, reflecting the new conditions of society. The old aristocratic order, with its independent nobles following their own particular interests, was gone. So was the world of poets of the lower orders, who received patronage from individual aristocrats. Under Augustus, all patronage flowed from the princeps, usually through his chief cultural adviser, Maecenas.

The major poets of this time, Vergil and Horace, had lost their property during the civil wars. The patronage of the princeps allowed them the leisure and the security to write poetry, but it also made them dependent on him and limited their freedom of expression. They wrote on subjects that were useful for his policies and glorified him and his family. These poets were not mere propagandists, however. It seems clear that mostly they believed in the virtues of Augustus and his reign and sang his praises with some degree of sincerity. Because they were poets of genius, they were also able to maintain a measure of independence in their work.

5.2.2.1 VERGIL Vergil (70–19 B.C.E.) was the most important of the Augustan poets. His greatest work is the *Aeneid*, a long national epic that placed the history of Rome in the great tradition of the Greeks and the Trojan War. Its hero, the Trojan warrior Aeneas, personifies the ideal Roman qualities of duty, responsibility, serious purpose, and patriotism. As the Romans' equivalent of Homer, Vergil glorified not the personal honor and excellence of the Greek epic heroes but the civic greatness, peace, and prosperity that Augustus and the Julian family had given to imperial Rome.

5.2.2.2 HORACE Horace (65–8 B.C.E.) was the son of a freedman and fought on the republican side until its defeat at Philippi. The patronage of Maecenas and the attractions of the Augustan reforms won him over to the Augustan side. His *Satires* are genial and humorous. His *Odes*, which are ingenious in their adaptation of Greek meters to the requirements of Latin verse, best reveal his great skills as

ROMAN MOSAIC Found in Tunisia, this mosaic shows the poet Vergil reading from his *Aeneid* to the Muses of Epic and Tragedy.
SOURCE: DEA/G. ROLI/Getty Images

a lyric poet. Two of the *Odes* directly praise Augustus, and many of them glorify the new Augustan order, the imperial family, and the empire.

5.2.2.3 PROPERTIUS Sextus Propertius lived in Rome in the second half of the first century B.C.E., a contemporary of Vergil and Horace. Like them, he was part of the poetic circle surrounding Augustus's adviser Maecenas. He wrote witty and graceful elegies.

5.2.2.4 OVID The career of Ovid (43 B.C.E.–18 C.E.) exhibits the darker side of Augustan influence on the arts. Ovid wrote light and entertaining love elegies that revealed the loose sexual code of a notorious sector of the Roman aristocracy whose values and amusements undermined the serious, family-centered life Augustus tried to foster. Ovid's *Ars Amatoria*, a poetic textbook on the art of seduction, angered Augustus and was partly responsible for the poet's exile in 8 C.E. His most popular work is the *Metamorphoses*, a kind of mythological epic that turned Greek myths into charming stories in a graceful and lively style.

5.2.2.5 HISTORY The achievements of Augustus, his emphasis on tradition, and the continuity of his regime with the glorious history of Rome encouraged both historical and antiquarian prose works. Some Augustan writers wrote scholarly treatises on history and geography in Greek. By far the most important and influential prose writer of the time, however, was Titus Livius, known as Livy (59 B.C.E.–17 C.E.), an Italian from Padua. His *History of Rome* was written in Latin and treated the period from the legendary origins of Rome until 9 B.C.E. Its purpose was moral, and Livy presented historical models as examples of good and bad behavior and, above all, patriotism. Livy glorified Rome's greatness and connected it with Rome's past, as Augustus tried to do.

5.2.2.6 ARCHITECTURE AND SCULPTURE
Augustus was as great a patron of the visual arts as he was of literature. His building program beautified Rome, glorified his reign, and contributed to the general prosperity and his own popularity. He filled the Campus Martius with beautiful new buildings, theaters, baths, and basilicas; rebuilt the Roman Forum; and built a forum of his own. At its heart was the temple of Mars the Avenger, which commemorated Augustus's victory and the greatness of his ancestors. On Rome's Palatine Hill, Augustus built a splendid temple to his patron god, Apollo, to further his religious policy.

The Greek classical style, which aimed at serenity and the ideal type, influenced most Augustan architecture. These same classical features were visible in the portrait sculpture of Augustus and his family. The greatest monument of the age is the *Ara Pacis*, or "Altar of Peace," dedicated in 9 B.C.E. Part of it shows a procession in which Augustus and his family appear to move forward, followed in order by the magistrates, the Senate, and the people of Rome. There is no better symbol of the new order.

5.3 Imperial Rome, 14 to 180 C.E.

How was imperial Rome governed, and what was life like for its people?

The central problem for Augustus's successors was the position of the ruler and his relationship to the ruled.

RULERS OF THE EARLY ROMAN EMPIRE	
27 B.C.E.–14 C.E.	Augustus
The Julio-Claudian Dynasty	
14–37 C.E.	Tiberius
37–41 C.E.	Gaius (Caligula)
41–54 C.E.	Claudius
54–68 C.E.	Nero
69 C.E.	Year of the Four Emperors
The Flavian Dynasty	
69–79 C.E.	Vespasian
79–81 C.E.	Titus
81–96 C.E.	Domitian
The "Good Emperors"	
96–98 C.E.	Nerva
98–117 C.E.	Trajan
117–138 C.E.	Hadrian
138–161 C.E.	Antoninus Pius
161–180 C.E.	Marcus Aurelius

Augustus tried to cloak the monarchical nature of his government, but his successors soon abandoned all pretense. The ruler came to be called imperator—from which comes our word "emperor"—as well as Caesar. The latter title signified connection with the imperial house, and the former indicated the military power on which everything was based.

5.3.1 The Emperors

Because Augustus was ostensibly only the "first citizen" of a restored republic and the Senate and the people theoretically voted him his powers, he could not legally name his successor. In fact, he plainly designated his heirs by lavishing favors on them and giving them a share in the imperial power and responsibility. Tiberius (r. 14–37 C.E.),[2] his immediate successor, was at first embarrassed by the ambiguity of his new role, but soon the monarchical and hereditary nature of the regime became clear. Gaius (Caligula, r. 37–41 C.E.), Claudius (r. 41–54 C.E.), and Nero (r. 54–68 C.E.) were all descended from either Augustus or his wife, Livia, and all were elevated because of that fact.

MARCUS AURELIUS Emperor of Rome from 161 to 180 C.E., Marcus Aurelius was one of the five "good emperors" who brought a period of relative peace and prosperity to the empire. This is the only Roman bronze equestrian statue that has survived.
SOURCE: Stefano Politi Markovina/Alamy Stock Photo

Gaius Caesar Germanicus succeeded Tiberius in 37 C.E. at the age of twenty-five. When he was a boy, the soldiers of his father's legions gave him the nickname Caligula (little boot), which stayed with him for the rest of his life. Recovered from a severe illness that struck him soon after becoming emperor, Caligula launched a series of wild, tyrannical actions. He restored the use of trials for treason that had darkened the reign of Tiberius and was vicious and cruel. He claimed to be divine even while alive and was thought to desire a despotic monarchy like that of the Ptolemies in Egypt. Caligula spent the large amount of money in the state treasury and tried to get more by seizing the property of wealthy Romans. He was widely thought to be insane.

In 41 C.E., the naked military basis of imperial rule was revealed when the Praetorian Guard, having assassinated Caligula, dragged the lame, stammering, and frightened Claudius from behind a curtain and made him emperor. In 68 C.E., the frontier legions learned what the historian Tacitus (ca. 55–120 C.E.) called "the secret of Empire . . . that an emperor could be made elsewhere than at Rome." Nero's incompetence and unpopularity, and especially his inability to control his armies, led to a serious rebellion in Gaul in 68 C.E. The year 69 C.E. saw four different emperors assume power in quick succession as different Roman armies took turns placing their commanders on the throne.

Vespasian (r. 69–79 C.E.) emerged victorious from the chaos, and his sons, Titus (r. 79–81 C.E.) and Domitian (r. 81–96 C.E.), carried forward his line, the Flavian dynasty. Vespasian, a tough soldier from the Italian middle class, was the first emperor who did not come from the old Roman nobility. A good administrator and a hardheaded realist of rough wit, he resisted all attempts by flatterers to find noble ancestors for him. On his deathbed, he is said to have ridiculed the practice of deifying emperors by saying, "Alas, I think I am becoming a god."

The assassination of Domitian put an end to the Flavian dynasty. Because Domitian had no close relative who had been designated as successor, the Senate put Nerva (r. 96–98 C.E.) on the throne to avoid chaos. He was the first of the five "good emperors," who included Trajan (r. 98–117 C.E.), Hadrian (r. 117–138 C.E.), Antoninus Pius (r. 138–161 C.E.), and Marcus Aurelius (r. 161–180 C.E.). Until Marcus Aurelius, none of these emperors had sons, so they each followed the example set by Nerva of adopting an able senator and establishing him as successor. This rare solution to the problem of monarchical succession was, therefore, only a historical accident. The result, nonetheless, was almost a century of peaceful succession and competent rule, which ended when Marcus Aurelius allowed his incompetent son, Commodus (r. 180–192 C.E.), to succeed him, with unfortunate results.

The genius of the Augustan settlement lay in its capacity to enlist the active cooperation of the upper classes and their effective organ, the Senate. The election of magistrates was taken from the assemblies and given to the Senate, which became the major center for legislation and exercised important judicial functions. This semblance of power persuaded some contemporaries and even some modern scholars that Augustus had established a *dyarchy*—a system of joint rule by princeps and Senate. That was never true.

The hollowness of the senatorial role became more apparent as time passed. Some emperors, like Vespasian, took pains to maintain, increase, and display the prestige and dignity of the Senate. Others, like Caligula, Nero, and Domitian, degraded the Senate and paraded their own despotic power. But from the first, the Senate's powers were illusory. The emperors controlled magisterial elections, and the Senate's legislative function quickly degenerated into mere assent to what the emperor or his representatives put before it. The true function of the Senate was to be a legislative and administrative extension of the emperor's rule.

Real opposition to imperial rule sometimes took the form of plots against the life of the emperor. Plots and the suspicion of plots led to repression, the use of spies and paid informers, book burning, and executions. The opposition consisted chiefly of senators who looked back to republican liberty for their class and who found justification in the Greek and Roman traditions of tyrannicide as well as in the precepts of Stoicism. Plots and repression were most common under Nero and Domitian. From Nerva to Marcus Aurelius, however, the emperors, without yielding any power, again learned to enlist the cooperation of the upper class by courteous and modest deportment.

5.3.2 The Administration of the Empire

The provinces flourished economically and generally accepted Roman rule easily. (See Map 5–2.) In the eastern provinces, the emperor was worshipped as a god; even in Italy, most emperors were deified after their death as long as the imperial cult established by Augustus continued. Imperial policy usually combined an attempt to unify the empire and its various peoples with a respect for local customs and differences. Roman citizenship was spread ever more widely, and by 212 C.E., almost every free inhabitant of the empire was a citizen. Latin became the language of the western provinces. Although the East remained essentially Greek in language and culture, even it adopted many aspects of Roman life. The spread of **Romanitas**, or "Roman-ness," was more than nominal, for senators and even emperors began to be chosen from provincial families.

5.3.2.1 LOCAL MUNICIPALITIES From an administrative and cultural standpoint, the empire was a collection of cities and towns and had little to do with the countryside. Roman policy during the principate was to raise urban centers to the status of Roman municipalities, with the rights

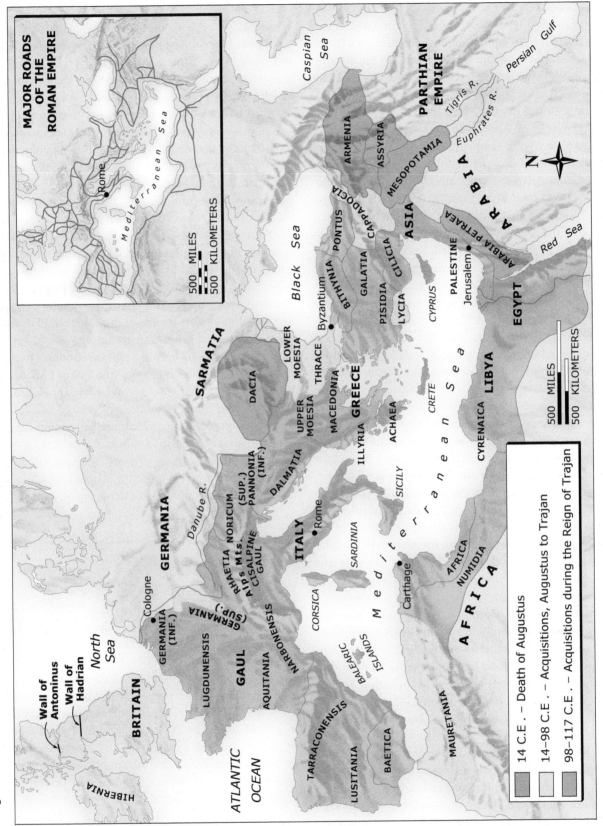

Map 5–2 PROVINCES OF THE ROMAN EMPIRE TO 117 C.E.

MAJOR ROADS OF THE ROMAN EMPIRE

14 C.E. – Death of Augustus

14–98 C.E. – Acquisitions, Augustus to Trajan

98–117 C.E. – Acquisitions during the Reign of Trajan

The growth of the empire to its greatest extent is shown here in three stages—at the death of Augustus in 14 C.E., at the death of Nerva in 98 C.E., and at the death of Trajan in 117 C.E. The division into provinces is also shown. The inset shows the major roads that tied the far-flung empire together.

LEPTIS MAGNA, LIBYA The largest city of the ancient region of Tripolitania, Leptis Magna was located sixty-two miles southeast of Tripoli on the Mediterranean coast of Libya in North Africa. In its heyday, it was one of the richest cities in the Roman Empire, and it contains some of the finest remains of Roman architecture. The city was lavishly rebuilt by the emperor Septimius Severus (r. 193–211 C.E.), who was born at Leptis in 146 C.E.
SOURCE: Peter Wilson/DK Images

and privileges attached to them. A typical municipal charter left much responsibility in the hands of local councils and magistrates elected from the local aristocracy. Moreover, the holding of a magistracy, and later a seat on the council, carried Roman citizenship with it. Therefore, the Romans enlisted the upper classes of the provinces in government, spread Roman law and culture, and won the loyalty of the influential people.

There were exceptions to this picture of success. The Jews found their religion incompatible with Roman demands and were savagely repressed when they rebelled in 66–70, 115–117, and 132–135 C.E. (as the "Closer Look," which follows below, explains). In Egypt, the Romans exploited the peasants with exceptional ruthlessness and did not pursue a policy of urbanization.

As the efficiency of the bureaucracy grew, so did the number and scope of its functions and therefore its size. The emperors came to take a broader view of their responsibilities for the welfare of their subjects than before. Nerva conceived and Trajan introduced the *alimenta*, a program of public assistance for the children of the poor. More and more, the emperors intervened when municipalities had difficulties, usually financial, sending imperial troubleshooters to deal with problems. The importance and autonomy of the municipalities shrank as the central administration took a greater part in local affairs. The provincial aristocracy came to regard public service in its own cities as a burden rather than an opportunity. The price paid for the increased efficiency that centralized control offered was the loss of the vitality of the cities throughout the empire.

The success of Roman civilization also came at great cost to the farmers who lived outside of Italy. Taxes, rents, mandatory gifts, and military service drew capital away from the countryside to the cities on a scale not previously seen in the Greco-Roman world. More and more, the rich life of the urban elite came at the expense of millions of previously stable farmers.

5.3.2.2 FOREIGN POLICY Augustus's successors, for the most part, accepted his conservative and defensive foreign policy. Trajan was the first emperor to take the offensive in a sustained way. Between 101 and 106 C.E., he crossed the Danube and, after hard fighting, established the new province of Dacia between the Danube and the Carpathian Mountains. He was tempted, no doubt, by its gold mines, but he probably was also pursuing a new general strategy: to defend the empire more aggressively by driving wedges into the territory of threatening barbarians. This same strategy dictated the invasion of the Parthian Empire in the East (113–117 C.E.). Trajan's early success was astonishing, and he established three new provinces in Armenia, Assyria, and Mesopotamia. But his lines were overextended, rebellions sprang up, and the campaign crumbled. Trajan was forced to retreat, and he died before getting back to Rome.

Hadrian's reign marked an important shift in Rome's frontier policy. Previously, Rome had been on the offensive against the barbarians. Although the Romans rarely gained new territory, they launched frequent attacks to chastise and pacify troublesome tribes. Hadrian hardened the Roman defenses, building a stone wall in the south of Scotland and a wooden one across the Rhine-Danube triangle.

The Roman defense became rigid, and initiative passed to the barbarians. Marcus Aurelius was compelled to spend most of his reign resisting dangerous attacks in the East and on the Danube frontier.

5.3.2.3 AGRICULTURE: THE DECLINE OF SLAVERY AND THE RISE OF THE COLONI The defense of its frontiers put enormous pressure on the human and financial resources of the empire, but the effect of these pressures was not immediately felt. The empire generally experienced considerable economic growth well into the reigns of the "good emperors." Internal peace and efficient administration benefited agriculture as well as trade and industry. Farming and trade developed together as political conditions made it easier to sell farm products at a distance.

Small farms continued to exist, but the large estate, managed by an absentee owner and growing cash crops,

A Closer Look

Spoils from Jerusalem on the Arch of Titus in Rome

THE ARCH OF the Emperor Titus (r. 79–81 C.E.) stands at the highest point of the ancient Sacred Way that leads to the Roman Forum. It commemorates Titus's conquest of Judea, which ended the Jewish Wars (66–70 C.E.).

Flavius Josephus, a first-century C.E. historian and eyewitness to the event, described Titus's triumph: "The spoils in general were borne in promiscuous heaps; but conspicuous above all stood out those captured in the Temple at Jerusalem. These consisted of a golden table, many talents in weight, and a lampstand, likewise made of gold, but constructed on a different pattern from those we use in ordinary life. Affixed to a pedestal was a central shaft, from which there extended slender branches, arranged trident-fashion, a wrought lamp being attached to the extremity of each branch; of these there were seven, indicating the honor paid to the number among the Jews. After these, and last of all the spoils, was carried a copy of the Jewish Law" (*The Jewish War* 7.148–50).

Carved on one of the internal faces of the passageway is a scene showing the triumphal procession with the booty from the Temple at Jerusalem—the sacred Menorah, the Table of the Shewbread shown at an angle, and the silver trumpets that called the Jews to celebrate the holy days of Rosh Hashanah.

THE ARCH OF TITUS
SOURCE: Werner Forman / Art Resource

The bearers of the booty wear laurel crowns and those carrying the candlestick have pillows on their shoulders. Placards in the background explain the spoils and the victories Titus won. These few figures, standing for hundreds in the actual procession, move toward the carved arch at the right.

Questions

1. Why did the Jews repeatedly revolt against the Romans?
2. Why did the Romans take the specific items they did? What was the significance of the items apart from their material value?

dominated agriculture. At first, as in the republican period, slaves mostly worked these estates, but in the first century, this began to change. Economic pressures forced many of the free lower classes to become tenant farmers, or coloni, and eventually the coloni replaced slaves as the mainstay of agricultural labor. Typically, these sharecroppers paid rent in labor or in kind, though sometimes they made cash payments. Eventually, they were tied to the land they worked, much as were the manorial serfs of the Middle Ages. Whatever its social costs, the system was economically efficient, however, and contributed to the general prosperity.

5.3.3 Women of the Upper Classes

By the late years of the Roman republic, women of the upper classes had achieved considerable independence and influence. Some of them had become wealthy through inheritance and were well educated. Women conducted literary salons and took part in literary groups. Marriage without the husband's right of manus became common, and some women conducted their sexual lives as freely as men. (The notorious Clodia, from one of Rome's noblest and most powerful families, is described as conducting many affairs, the most famous with the poet Catullus, who reviles her even as he describes the pangs of his love.) Such women were reluctant to have children and increasingly employed contraception and abortion to avoid childbirth. Augustus tried to restore Rome to an earlier ideal of decency and family integrity that reduced the power and sexual freedom of women. He also introduced legislation to encourage the procreation of children, but the new laws seem to have had little effect.

In the first imperial century, several powerful women played important, if unofficial, political roles. Augustus's wife Livia had great power during his reign, and he honored her with the title Augusta in his will. Even during the reign of her son (and Augustus's stepson) Tiberius, she exercised great influence, and it was said that he fled Rome to live in Capri to escape her domination. The Emperor Claudius's wife Messalina took part in a plot to overthrow him. The Elder Agrippina, wife of the general Germanicus, was active in opposition to Tiberius, and her daughter, also called Agrippina, helped bring her son Nero to the throne. In later centuries, women were permitted to make wills and inherit from children. At the turn of the first century, the emperor Domitian freed women from the need for guardianship.

5.3.4 Life in Imperial Rome: The Apartment House

The civilization of the Roman Empire depended on the vitality of its cities. The typical city had about 20,000 inhabitants, and perhaps only three or four had a population of more than 75,000. The population of Rome, however, was certainly greater than 500,000, perhaps more than a million.

People coming to Rome for the first time found it overwhelming and its size, bustle, and noise either thrilled or horrified them. (The graffiti left on the walls of Pompeii at the time of its destruction by Vesuvius provide us with unusually rich glimpse into ordinary Roman life.

The rich lived in elegant homes called *domūs*. These were single-storied houses with plenty of space; an open central courtyard; and rooms designed for specific and different purposes, such as dining, sitting, or sleeping, in privacy and relative quiet. Though only a small portion of Rome's population lived in them, domūs took up as much as one-third of the city's space. Public space for temples, markets, baths, gymnasiums, theaters, circuses, forums, and governmental buildings took up another quarter of Rome's territory.

This left less than half of Rome's area to house the mass of its inhabitants, who were squeezed into multiple dwellings that grew increasingly tall. Most Romans during the imperial period lived in apartment buildings called **insulae**, or "islands," that rose to a height of five or six stories and sometimes even more. The most famous of them, the Insula of Febiala, seems to have "towered above the Rome of the Antonines like a skyscraper."[3]

These buildings were divided into separate apartments (cenicula) of undifferentiated rooms, the same plan on each floor. The apartments were cramped and uncomfortable. They had neither central heating nor open fireplaces; heat and fire for cooking came from small portable stoves. The apartments were hot in summer, cold in winter, and stuffy and smoky when the stoves were lit. There was no plumbing, so tenants needed to go into the streets to wells or fountains for water and to public baths and latrines, or to less regulated places. The higher up one lived, the more difficult were these trips, so chamber pots and commodes were kept in the rooms. These receptacles were emptied into vats on the staircase landings or in the alleys outside; on occasion, the contents, and even the containers, were tossed out the window. Roman satirists complained of the discomforts and dangers of walking the streets beneath such windows. Roman law tried to find ways to assign responsibilities for the injuries done to dignity and person.

Despite these difficulties, the attractions of the city and the shortage of space caused rents to rise, making life in the insulae buildings expensive, uncomfortable, and dangerous. The houses were lightly built of concrete and brick and were far too high for the limited area of their foundations, and so they often collapsed. Laws limiting the height of buildings were not always obeyed and did not, in any case, always prevent disaster. The satirist Juvenal did not exaggerate much when he wrote, "We inhabit a city held up chiefly by slats, for that is how the landlord patches up the cracks in the old wall, telling the tenants to sleep peacefully under the ruin that hangs over their heads."

Even more serious was the threat of fire. Wooden beams supported the floors, and torches, candles, and oil lamps lit the rooms and braziers heated them. Fires broke out easily and, without running water, they usually led to disaster.

When we compare these apartments with the attractive public places in the city, we can understand why the Romans spent most of their time out of doors.

5.3.5 The Culture of the Early Empire

The years from 14 to 180 C.E. were a time of general prosperity and a flourishing material and artistic culture, but not as brilliant and original as in the Age of Augustus.

5.3.5.1 LITERATURE In Latin literature, the period between the death of Augustus and the time of Marcus Aurelius is known as the Silver Age. In contrast to the hopeful, positive optimists of the Augustans, the writers of the Silver Age were gloomy, negative, and pessimistic. In the works of the former period, praise of the emperor, his achievements, and the world abounds; in the latter, criticism and satire lurk everywhere. Some of the most important writers of the Silver Age came from the Stoic opposition and reflected its hostility to the growing power and personal excesses of the emperors.

The writers of the second century C.E. appear to have turned away from contemporary affairs and even recent history. Historical writing was about remote periods so there would be less danger of irritating imperial sensibilities. Scholarship was encouraged, but we hear little of poetry, especially that dealing with dangerous subjects. In the third century C.E., romances written in Greek became popular and offer further evidence of the tendency of writers of the time to seek and offer escape from contemporary realities.

5.3.5.2 ARCHITECTURE The main contribution of the Romans lay in two new kinds of buildings—the great public bath and a new freestanding kind of amphitheater—and in the advances in engineering that made these large structures possible. While keeping the basic post-and-lintel construction used by the Greeks, the Romans added to it the principle of the semicircular arch, borrowed from the Etruscans. They also made good use of concrete, a building material the Hellenistic Greeks first used and the Romans fully developed. The arch, combined with the post and lintel, produced the great Colosseum built by the Flavian emperors. When used internally in the form of vaults and domes, the arch permitted great buildings like the baths, of which the most famous and best preserved are those of the later emperors Caracalla (r. 211–217) and Diocletian (r. 284–305). (See Map 5–3.)

Map 5–3 ANCIENT ROME

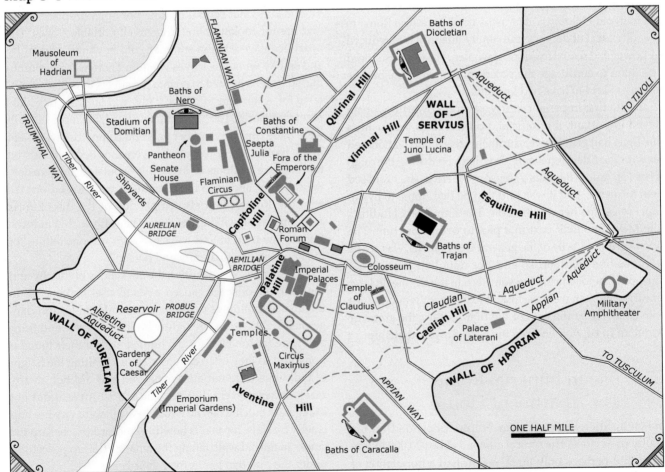

This map of Rome during the late empire shows the seven hills on and around which the city was built, as well as the major walls, bridges, and other public sites and buildings.

One of Rome's most famous buildings, the Pantheon, begun by Augustus's friend Agrippa and rebuilt by Hadrian, combined all these elements. Its portico of Corinthian columns is of Greek origin, but its rotunda of brick-faced concrete with its domed ceiling and relieving arches is thoroughly Roman. The new engineering also made possible the construction of more mundane, but useful, structures like bridges and aqueducts and baths (see the "Encountering the Past" sidebar on Roman baths, which follows below).

5.3.5.3 SOCIETY One of the dark sides of Roman society, at least since the third century B.C.E., had been its increasing addiction to the brutal contests involving gladiators. By the end of the first century C.E., emperors regularly appealed to this barbaric entertainment as a way of winning the acclaim of their people. Over the centuries politicians of the republic and, later, emperors of Rome, also provided other free entertainments for the Roman public, such as trick riding displays and exhibitions of and hunts for wild animals, but the chariot races were the most popular.

Encountering the Past

The Roman Love of Bathing

ROMANS OF ALL CLASSES bathed frequently, and bathing played a significant role in Roman culture. For most people, bathing was not a private activity. While the wealthy often had private bathing facilities within their own homes, most Romans used communal baths called *thermae*. Even Romans who could afford their own baths frequented public baths to relax, socialize,

ROMAN BATHS IN SOMERSET, ENGLAND The Roman baths in Bath, Somerset, England, take advantage of natural hot springs, and continue to draw visitors to this day.
SOURCE: Robert Estall photo agency / Alamy Stock Photo

and conduct business. By the fourth century C.E., there were almost a thousand public baths of various sizes in the city of Rome alone. The largest public bath in Rome could accommodate 3,000 bathers at a time.

Roman baths were, in many ways, like modern spas. In addition to the actual baths, they featured food booths, libraries, and reading rooms. Some baths had attached stages for theatrical performances, and others had stadiums for exercise and athletic competitions. The most luxurious baths featured fine marble floors, exquisite decorations, and a full range of upscale amenities.

Bathers were normally segregated by sex, although mixed bathing grew more common from the first century C.E. Since elites brought their slaves with them to assist in their bathing, most baths had three entrances: one for men, one for women, and one for slaves.

Taking a bath in Rome was a complex process. After disrobing, the bather proceeded to the *frigidarium*, or cold room. There, he or she bathed in a tank of cold water. The bather then moved on to the *tepidarium*, or warm room, and then finally to the *caldarium*, the hot room. The *caldarium* was heated by charcoal fires under the floor. Once the bather had worked up a sweat in the *caldarium*, he or she returned to the *tepidarium* for a massage and to have his or her skin scraped free of dirt and oil with special metal instruments.

The Romans exported their love of bathing to their colonies, building bathing complexes in many colonial urban centers. In some places, such as Bath in Britain and Vichy in Gaul, the Romans took advantage of natural hot springs to build particularly impressive bathing complexes.

Questions

1. What role did bathing play in Roman life?
2. What was it like to visit a Roman bath?

LOW-RELIEF SCULPTURE OF CHARIOT RACES Romans bet heavily on the kind of chariot races shown on this low relief and were fanatically loyal to their favorite riders and stables.
SOURCE: DEA/L. PEDICINI/De Agostini/Getty Images

On other fronts in Roman society, by the second century C.E., troubles were brewing that foreshadowed the difficult times ahead. The literary efforts of the time reveal an escape from the present, from reality, and from the public realm to the past, to romance, and to private pursuits. Some of the same aspects may be seen in everyday life, especially in the decline of vitality in the local government.

In the first century C.E., members of the upper classes vied with each other for election to municipal office and for the honor of doing service to their communities. By the second century C.E., the emperors had to intervene to correct abuses in local affairs and even to force unwilling members of the ruling classes to accept public office. Magistrates and council members were held personally and collectively responsible for the revenues due. Some magistrates even fled to avoid their office, a practice that became widespread in later centuries.

These difficulties also reflected more basic problems. The prosperity that the end of civil war and the influx of wealth from the East brought could not sustain itself beyond the first half of the second century C.E. Population also appears to have declined for reasons that remain mysterious. The cost of government kept rising. The emperors were required to maintain a standing army, minimal in size but costly, to keep the people in Rome happy with "bread and circuses," to pay for an increasingly numerous bureaucracy, and to wage expensive wars to defend the frontiers against dangerous and determined barbarian enemies. The ever-increasing need for money compelled the emperors to raise taxes, to pressure their subjects, and to bring on inflation by debasing the coinage. These elements brought about the desperate crises that ultimately destroyed the empire.

5.4 The Rise of Christianity

Who was Jesus of Nazareth?

Christianity emerged, spread, survived, and ultimately conquered the Roman Empire despite its origin among poor

JESUS, THE GOOD SHEPHERD This second-century statue in the Lateran Museum in Rome shows Jesus as the biblical Good Shepherd.
SOURCE: Scala/Art Resource, NY

people from an unimportant and remote province of the empire. Christianity faced the hostility of the established religious institutions of its native Judea. It also had to compete against the official cults of Rome and the highly sophisticated philosophies of the educated classes and against such other "mystery" religions as the cults of Mithras, Isis, and Osiris. The Christians also faced the opposition of the imperial government and formal persecution. Yet Christianity achieved toleration and finally became the exclusive official religion of the empire.

5.4.1 Jesus of Nazareth

To understand this amazing outcome, one must begin with the story of Jesus of Nazareth. The most important evidence about Jesus's life is in the Gospel accounts, all of them written well after his death. The earliest, by Mark, is dated about 70 C.E. and the latest, by John, about 100 C.E. These accounts were not, moreover, attempts at simply describing the life of Jesus with historical accuracy. Rather, they were statements of faith by true believers. The authors of the Gospels believed that Jesus was the son of God and that he had come into the world to redeem humanity and to bring immortality to those who believed in him and followed his way. To the Gospel writers, Jesus's resurrection was striking proof of his teachings. At the same time, the Gospels regarded Jesus as a historical figure, and they recounted events in his life as well as his sayings.

Jesus was born in the province of Judea in the time of Augustus, and he was an effective teacher in the tradition of the prophets. This tradition promised the coming of a **Messiah** (in Greek, *christos*—so Jesus Christ means "Jesus the Messiah"), the redeemer who would help Israel triumph over its enemies and establish the kingdom of God on earth. In fact, Jesus seems to have insisted the Messiah would not establish an earthly kingdom but would bring an end to the world as human beings knew it at the Day of Judgment. On that day, God would reward the righteous with immortality and happiness in heaven and condemn the wicked to eternal suffering in hell. Until then (a day his followers believed would come soon), Jesus taught the faithful to abandon sin and worldly concerns; to follow him and his way; to follow the moral code described in the Sermon on the Mount, which preached love, charity, and humility; and to believe in him and his divine mission.

Jesus won a considerable following, especially among the poor, which caused great suspicion among the upper classes. His novel message and his criticism of the religious practices at the temple at Jerusalem and of its priests provoked the hostility of the religious establishment. A misunderstanding of the movement made it easy to convince the Roman governor, Pontius Pilate, that Jesus and his followers might be dangerous revolutionaries. Jesus was put to death in Jerusalem by the cruel and degrading device of crucifixion, probably in 30 C.E. His followers believed he was resurrected on the third day after his death, and that belief became a critical element in the religion they propagated throughout the Roman Empire and beyond.

This new belief spread quickly to the Jewish communities of Syria and Asia Minor. It might, however, have had only a short life as a despised Jewish heresy were it not for the conversion and career of Paul.

5.4.2 Paul of Tarsus

Paul was born Saul, a citizen of the Cilician city of Tarsus in Asia Minor. He had been trained in Hellenistic culture and was a Roman citizen. But he was also a zealous member of the Jewish sect known as the **Pharisees**, the group that was most strict in its adherence to Jewish law. He took part in the persecution of the early Christians until his own conversion outside Damascus about 35 C.E., after which he changed his name from Saul to Paul.

The great problem facing the early Christians was resolving their relationship to Judaism. If the new faith was a version of Judaism, then it must adhere to the Jewish law and seek converts only among Jews. James, called the brother of Jesus, was a conservative who held to that view, whereas the Hellenist Jews tended to see Christianity as a new and universal religion. To force all converts to follow Jewish law would have been fatal to the growth of the new sect. Jewish law's many technicalities and dietary prohibitions were strange to Gentiles, and the necessity of circumcision—a frightening, painful, and dangerous operation for adults—would have been a tremendous deterrent to conversion. Paul supported the position of the Hellenists and soon found many converts among the Gentiles. After some conflict within the sect, Paul won out. Consequently, Paul, the "apostle to the Gentiles" deserves recognition as a crucial contributor to the success of Christianity.

Paul believed that the followers of Jesus should be *evangelists* (messengers), to spread the gospel, or "good news," of God's gracious gift. He taught that Jesus would soon return for the Day of Judgment, and that all who would, should believe in him and accept his way. Faith in Jesus as the Christ was necessary, but not sufficient, for salvation, nor could good deeds alone achieve it. That final blessing of salvation was a gift of God's grace that would be granted to all who asked for it.

5.4.3 Organization

Paul and the other apostles did their work well. The new religion spread throughout the Roman Empire and even beyond its borders. Christianity had its greatest success in the cities and among the poor and uneducated. The rites of the early communities appear to have been simple and few. Baptism by water removed original sin and permitted participation in the community and its activities. The central ritual was a common meal called the *agape*, or "love feast," followed by the ceremony of the **Eucharist**, or "thanksgiving," a celebration of the Lord's Supper in which unleavened bread was eaten and unfermented wine was drunk. There were also prayers, hymns, or readings from the Gospels.

Not all the early Christians were poor, and the rich provided for the poor at the common meals. The sense of common love fostered in these ways focused the community's attention on the needs of the weak, the sick, the unfortunate, and the unprotected. This concern for others gave the early Christian communities a warmth and a human appeal that stood in marked contrast to the coldness and impersonality of the pagan cults. No less attractive were the promise of salvation, the importance to God of each human soul, and the spiritual equality of all in the new faith. As Paul put it, "There is neither Jew nor Greek, there is neither slave nor free, there is neither male nor female; for you are all one in Christ Jesus."[4] The future of Christianity depended on its communities finding an organization that would preserve unity within the group and help protect it against enemies outside. At first, the churches had little formal organization. Soon, it appears, affairs were placed in the hands of boards of presbyters "elders," and **deacons**, or "those who serve." By the second century C.E., as their numbers grew, the Christians of each city tended to accept the authority and leadership of **bishops** (*episkopoi*, or "overseers"). The congregations elected bishops to lead them in worship and to supervise funds. As time passed, the bishops extended their authority over the Christian communities in outlying towns and the countryside. The power and almost monarchical authority of the bishops were soon enhanced by the doctrine of **Apostolic Succession**, which asserted that ordination passed on the powers Jesus had given his original disciples from bishop to bishop.

The bishops kept in touch with each other, maintained communications among different Christian communities, and prevented doctrinal and sectarian splintering, which would have destroyed Christian unity. They maintained internal discipline and dealt with the civil authorities. After a time, the bishops began coming together in councils to settle difficult questions, to establish orthodox opinion, and even to expel as **heretics** those who would not accept it. It is unlikely that Christianity could have survived the travails of its early years without such strong internal organization and government.

5.4.4 The Persecution of Christians

The new faith soon incurred the distrust of the pagan world and of the imperial government. At first, Christians were thought of as a Jewish sect and were therefore protected by Roman law. It soon became clear, however, that they were different, both mysterious and dangerous. They denied the existence of the pagan gods and were accused of atheism, and their refusal to worship the emperor was judged treasonous. Because Christians kept mostly to themselves, took no part in civic affairs, engaged in secret rites, and had an organized network of local associations, they were misunderstood and suspected. Their love feasts were erroneously reported to be scenes of sexual scandal. The alarming doctrine of the actual presence of Jesus's body in the Eucharist was distorted into an accusation of cannibalism.

The privacy and secrecy of Christian life and worship ran counter to a traditional Roman dislike of any private association, especially any of a religious nature. Christians thus earned the reputation of being "haters of humanity." Claudius expelled them from Rome, and Nero tried to make them scapegoats for the great fire that struck the city in 64 C.E. By the end of the first century, "the name alone"—that is, simple membership in the Christian community—was a crime.

But, for the most part, the Roman government did not take the initiative in attacking Christians in the first two centuries. When one governor requested instructions for dealing with the Christians, the emperor Trajan urged moderation. Christians were not to be sought out, anonymous accusations were to be disregarded, and anyone denounced could be acquitted merely by renouncing Christ and sacrificing to the emperor. (See "Compare and Connect" sidebar on the persecution of Christians in the Roman Empire, which follows below.) Unfortunately, no true Christian could meet the conditions, and so there were martyrdoms.

5.4.5 The Emergence of Catholicism

Division within the Christian church may have been an even greater threat to its existence than persecution from outside. Most Christians never accepted complex, intellectualized opinions but held to what even then were traditional, simple, conservative beliefs. This body of majority opinion, considered to be universal, or **catholic**, was enshrined by the church that came to be called Catholic. The Catholic Church's doctrines were deemed **orthodox**, that is, "holding the right opinions," whereas those holding contrary opinions were heretics.

The need to combat heretics, however, compelled the orthodox to formulate their own views more clearly and firmly. By the end of the second century C.E., an orthodox canon included the Old Testament, the Gospels, and the Epistles of Paul, among other writings. This was a vitally important start to a process of creating a standard set of holy books that was not completed for at least two more centuries. The orthodox declared the Catholic Church itself to be the depository of Christian teaching and the bishops to be its receivers. They also drew up a **creed** or brief statements of faith to which true Christians must adhere.

Compare and Connect

Christianity in the Roman Empire—Why Did the Romans Persecute the Christians?

THE RISE OF Christianity and its spread throughout the Mediterranean presented a serious problem to the magistrates of the Roman Empire. Like most other pagans, the Romans were tolerant of most religious beliefs. Persecution on religious grounds was unusual among the Romans. The Christians, however, were very different from votaries of Isis, Mithras, Magna Mater, even from the Jews, and the Romans did, in fact, persecute them with varying degrees of severity. The following passages focus on the persecution of Christians during the reigns of Nero and Trajan and shed light on the character of and reasons for these persecutions.

ST. MAMAI Thrown to the lions in 275 C.E. by the Romans for refusing to recant his Christian beliefs, St. Mamai is an important martyr in the iconography of Georgia, a Caucasian kingdom that embraced Christianity early in the fourth century C.E. This gilded silver medallion, made in Georgia in the eleventh century C.E., depicts the saint astride a lion while he bears a cross in one hand, symbolizing his triumphant victory over death and ignorance.
SOURCE: Library of Congress

Before Reading

- Consider how the beliefs of the Christians differed from those of other groups.
- Explain how the nature of Christian faith may have influenced Nero's actions.
- Think about why Trajan might have adopted his policy toward the Christians.

Questions

1. Why did Nero blame the Christians for the fire in Rome?
2. On what grounds did Pliny the Younger punish the Christians?
3. What was the reaction of Trajan to Pliny's letter describing his policies toward Christians?
4. How were the approaches of Nero and Trajan to persecution of the Christians similar or different?

I. THE PERSECUTION BY NERO

In 64 C.E., a terrible fire broke out in Rome that destroyed a good part of the city. Here the historian Tacitus tells us how the emperor Nero dealt with its aftermath.

The next thing was to seek means of propitiating the gods, and recourse was had to the Sibylline books, by the direction of which prayers were offered to Vulcanus, Ceres, and Proserpina. Juno, too, was entreated by the matrons, first, in the Capitol, then on the nearest part of the coast, whence water was procured to sprinkle the fane [temple] and image of the goddess. And there were sacred banquets and nightly vigils celebrated by married women. But all human efforts, all the lavish gifts of the emperor, and the propitiations of the gods, did not banish the sinister belief that the conflagration was the result of an order. Consequently, to get rid of the report, Nero fastened the guilt and inflicted the most exquisite tortures on a class hated for their abominations, called Christians by the populace. Christus, from whom the name had its origin, suffered the extreme penalty during the reign of Tiberius at the hands of one of our procurators, Pontius Pilatus, and a most mischievous superstition, thus checked for the moment, again broke out not only in Judaea, the first source of the evil, but even in Rome, where all things hideous and shameful from every part of the world find their centre and become popular. Accordingly, an arrest was first made of all who pleaded guilty; then, upon their information, an immense multitude was convicted, not so much of the crime of firing the city, as of hatred against mankind. Mockery of every sort was added to their deaths. Covered with the skins of beasts, they were torn by dogs and perished, or were nailed to crosses, or were doomed to the flames and burnt, to serve as a nightly illumination, when daylight had expired.

Nero offered his gardens for the spectacle, and was exhibiting a show in the circus, while he mingled with the people in the dress of a charioteer or stood aloft on a car. Hence, even for criminals who deserved extreme and exemplary punishment, there arose a feeling of compassion; for it was not, as it seemed, for the public good, but to glut one man's cruelty, that they were being destroyed.

II. THE EMPEROR TRAJAN AND THE CHRISTIANS

Pliny the Younger was governor of the Roman province of Bithynia in Asia Minor about 112 C.E. Confronted by problems caused by Christians, he wrote to the emperor Trajan to report his policies and to ask for advice. The following exchange between governor and emperor is evidence of the challenge Christianity posed to Rome and the Roman response.

TO THE EMPEROR TRAJAN

Having never been present at any trials of the Christians, I am unacquainted with the method and limits to be observed either in examining or punishing them.

In the meanwhile, the method I have observed towards those who have been denounced to me as Christians is this: I interrogated them whether they were Christians; if they confessed it, I repeated the question twice again, adding the threat of capital punishment; if they still persevered, I ordered them to be executed. For whatever the nature of their creed might be, I could at least feel no doubt that contumacy and inflexible obstinacy deserved chastisement. There were others also possessed with the same infatuation, but being citizens of Rome, I directed them to be carried thither. . . .

TRAJAN TO PLINY

The method you have pursued, my dear Pliny, in sifting the cases of those denounced to you as Christians is extremely proper. It is not possible to lay down any general rule which can be applied as the fixed standard in all cases of this nature. No search should be made for these people, when they are denounced and found guilty they must be punished; with the restriction, how-ever, that when the party denies himself to be a Christian, and shall give proof that he is not (that is, by adoring our Gods) he shall be pardoned on the ground of repentance even though he may have formerly incurred suspicion. Informations without the accuser's name subscribed must not be admitted in evidence against anyone, as it is introducing a very dangerous precedent, and by no means agreeable to the spirit of the age.

SOURCES: (I) From Tacitus, *Annals of Tacitus* 15.44, trans. Alfred J. Church and William J. Brodribb (London: Macmillan, 1895), pp. 304–305. (II) From Pliny the Younger, *Letters*, trans. by W. Melmoth, rev. by W. M. Hutchinson (London: William Heinemann, Ltd.; Cambridge, MA: Harvard University Press, 1925).

In the first century, all that was required to become a Christian was to be baptized, to partake of the Eucharist, and to call Jesus the Lord. By the end of the second century, an orthodox Christian—that is, a member of the Catholic Church—was required to accept its creed, its canon of holy writings, and the authority of the bishops. The loose structure of the apostolic church had given way to an organized religious body with recognized leaders able to define its faith and to exclude those who did not accept it.

5.4.6 Rome as a Center of the Early Church

During this same period, the church in Rome came to have special prominence. As the center of communications and the capital of the empire, Rome had natural advantages. After the Roman destruction of Jerusalem in 135 C.E., no other city had any convincing claim to primacy in the church. Besides having the largest single congregation of Christians, Rome also benefited from the tradition that Jesus's apostles Peter and Paul were martyred there.

Peter, moreover, was thought to be the first bishop of Rome. The Gospel of Matthew (16:18) reported Jesus's statement to Peter: "Thou art Peter [in Greek, *Petros*] and upon this rock [in Greek, *petra*] I will build my church." Eastern Christians might later point out that Peter had been the leader of the Christian community at Antioch before he went to Rome. But in the second century, the church at Antioch, along with the other Christian churches of Asia Minor, was fading in influence, and by 200 C.E., Rome was the most important center of Christianity. Because of the city's early influence and the Petrine doctrine derived from the Gospel of Matthew, later bishops of Rome claimed supremacy in the Catholic Church. But as the era of the "good emperors" came to a close, this controversy was far in the future.

5.5 The Crisis of the Third Century

How did economic developments lead to the political and military crisis of the third century?

Dio Cassius, a historian of the third century C.E., described the Roman Empire after the death of Marcus Aurelius as declining from "a kingdom of gold into one of iron and rust." Although we have seen that the gold contained more than a little impurity, there is no reason to quarrel with Dio's assessment of his own time. Commodus (r. 180–192 C.E.), the son of Marcus Aurelius, unfortunately proved the "good emperors's" notion about successors correct: He was a successor selected for family ties rather than for his talents. Commodus was incompetent and autocratic, he reduced the respect of the imperial office, and his assassination brought the return of civil war.

5.5.1 Barbarian Invasions

The pressure on Rome's frontiers reached massive proportions in the third century C.E. In the East, a new power threatened the frontiers. In the third century B.C.E., the Parthians had made the Iranians independent of the Hellenistic kings and had established an empire of their own on the old foundations of the Persian Empire. Roman attempts to conquer them had failed, but as late as 198 C.E., the Romans could reach and destroy the Parthian capital and bring at least northern Mesopotamia under their rule.

In 224 C.E., however, a new Iranian dynasty, the **Sassanians**, seized control from the Parthians and brought new vitality to Persia. They soon recovered Mesopotamia in 260 C.E. and humiliated the Romans by taking the emperor Valerian (r. 253–260 C.E.) prisoner; he died in captivity.

On the western and northern frontiers, the pressure came not from a well-organized rival empire, but from an ever-increasing number of German tribes. Though the Germans had been in contact with the Romans at least since the second century B.C.E., civilization had not much affected them. The men did no agricultural work, but confined their activities to hunting, drinking, and fighting. They were organized on a family basis by clans, hundreds, and tribes. Their leaders were chiefs, usually from a royal family, elected by the assembly of fighting men. The king was surrounded by a collection of warriors, whom the Romans called his *comitatus*. Always eager for plunder, these tough barbarians were attracted by the civilized delights they knew existed beyond the frontier of the Rhine and Danube Rivers.

The most aggressive of the Germans in the third century C.E. were the Goths. Centuries earlier they had wandered from their ancestral home near the Baltic Sea into southern Russia. In the 220s and 230s C.E., they began to put pressure on the Danube frontier. By about 250 C.E., they were able to penetrate the empire and overrun the Balkans. The need to meet this threat and the one the Persian Sassanians posed in the East forced the Romans to weaken their western frontiers, and other Germanic peoples—the Franks and the Alemanni—broke through in those regions. There was danger that Rome would be unable to meet this challenge.

The unprecedentedly numerous and simultaneous attacks, no doubt, caused Rome's perils, but its internal weakness encouraged these attacks. The Roman army was not what it had been in its best days. By the second century C.E., it was made up mostly of romanized provincials. The pressure on the frontiers and epidemics of plague in the time of Marcus Aurelius forced the emperor to conscript slaves, gladiators, barbarians, and brigands. The training and discipline with which the Romans had conquered the Mediterranean world had declined. The Romans also failed to respond to the new conditions of constant pressure on all the frontiers. A strong, mobile reserve that could meet a threat in one place without causing a weakness elsewhere might have helped, but no such unit was created.

Septimius Severus (r. 193–211 C.E.) and his successors transformed the character of the Roman army. Septimius was a military usurper who owed everything to the support of his soldiers. He meant to establish a family dynasty, in contrast to the policy of the "good emperors" of the second century, and he was prepared to make Rome into an undisguised military monarchy. Septimius drew recruits for the army increasingly from peasants of the less civilized provinces.

5.5.2 Economic Difficulties

The financial burdens caused by the barbarian attacks led to greater economic difficulties. Inflation had forced Commodus to raise the soldiers' pay. Yet the Severan emperors had to double it to keep up with prices, which increased the imperial budget by as much as 25 percent. To raise money, the emperors invented new taxes, debased the coinage, and even sold the palace furniture. But it was still difficult to recruit troops. The new style of military life Septimius introduced—with its laxer discipline, more pleasant duties, and greater opportunity for advancement, not only in the army but also in Roman society—was needed to attract men into the army. The policy proved effective for a short time but could not prevent the chaos of the late third century.

The same issues that caused problems for the army damaged society at large. The shortage of workers for the large farms, which had all but wiped out the independent family farm, reduced agricultural production. Distracted by external threats, the emperors were less able to preserve domestic peace. Piracy, brigandage, and the neglect of roads and harbors hampered trade, as well as the debasement of the coinage and inflation in general. Imperial taxation and confiscations of the property of the rich removed badly needed capital from productive use.

More and more, the government had to demand services that had been given gladly in the past. Because the empire lived hand to mouth, with no significant reserve fund and no system of credit financing, the emperors had to force people to provide food, supplies, money, and labor. The upper classes in the cities were made to serve as administrators without pay and to fill deficits in revenue out of their own pockets. Sometimes these demands caused provincial rebellions, as in Egypt and Gaul. More typically, they caused peasants and even town administrators to flee to escape their burdens. All these difficulties weakened Rome's economic strength when it was most needed.

5.5.3 The Social Order

The new conditions caused important changes in the social order. Hostile emperors and economic losses decimated the Senate and the traditional ruling class, and men coming up through the army took their places. The whole state began to take on an increasingly military appearance. Distinctions among the classes by dress had been traditional since the republic; in the third and fourth centuries C.E., the people's everyday clothing became a kind of uniform that precisely revealed status. Titles were assigned to ranks in society similar to ranks in the army. The most important distinction, formally established by Septimius Severus, drew a sharp line between the *honestiores* (senators, equestrians, the municipal aristocracy, and the soldiers) and the lower classes, or *humiliores*. Septimius gave the *honestiores* a privileged position before the law: They were given lighter punishments, could not be tortured, and alone had the right of appeal to the emperor.

As time passed, it became more difficult to move from the lower order to the higher, another example of the growing rigidity of the late Roman Empire. Peasants were tied to their lands, artisans to their crafts, soldiers to the army, merchants and shipowners to the needs of the state, and citizens of the municipal upper class to the collection and payment of increasingly burdensome taxes. Freedom and private initiative gave way to the needs of the state and its ever-expanding control of its citizens.

5.5.4 Civil Disorder

Commodus was killed on the last day of 192 C.E. The succeeding year was similar to the year 69. Three emperors ruled in swift succession, with Septimius Severus emerging, as we have seen, to establish firm rule and a dynasty. The murder of Alexander Severus, the last of the dynasty, in 235 C.E., brought on a half-century of internal anarchy and foreign invasion.

The empire seemed at the point of collapse. But the two conspirators who overthrew and succeeded the emperor Gallienus (r. 253–268) proved to be able soldiers. Claudius II Gothicus (r. 268–270 C.E.) and Aurelian (r. 270–275 C.E.) drove back the barbarians and stamped out internal disorder. The soldiers who followed Aurelian on the throne were good fighters who made significant changes in Rome's system of defense. Around Rome, Athens, and other cities, they built heavy walls that could resist barbarian attack. They drew back their best troops from the frontiers, relying chiefly on a newly organized heavy cavalry and a mobile army near the emperor's own residence.

Thereafter, mercenaries, who came from among the least civilized provincials and even from among the Germans, largely made up the army. These officers, loyal to the emperor rather than to the empire, became a foreign, hereditary caste of aristocrats that increasingly filled positions of high administrators and even emperors. In effect, the Roman people hired an army of mercenaries, who were only technically Roman, to protect them.

5.6 The Late Empire

What factors contributed to the decline and eventual fall of Rome?

During the fourth and fifth centuries, the Romans strove to meet the many challenges, internal and external, that threatened the survival of their empire. Growing pressure from barbarian tribes pushing against its frontier intensified the empire's tendency to smother individuality, freedom, and initiative, in favor of an intrusive and autocratic centralized monarchy. Economic and military weakness increased, and it became even harder to keep the vast empire together.

Hard and dangerous times may well have helped the rise of Christianity, encouraging people to turn away from the troubles of this world to concern about the next.

REIGNS OF SELECTED LATE EMPIRE RULERS (ALL DATES ARE C.E.)	
180–192	Commodus
193–211	Septimius Severus
222–235	Alexander Severus
249–251	Decius
253–259	Valerian
259 (253)–268	Gallienus
268–270	Claudius II Gothicus
270–275	Aurelian
284–305	Diocletian
306–337	Constantine (sole emperor after 324)
337–361	Constantius II
361–363	Julian the Apostate
364–375	Valentinian I
364–378	Valens
379–395	Theodosius I

5.6.1 The Fourth Century and Imperial Reorganization

The period from Diocletian (r. 284–305 C.E.) to Constantine (r. 306–337 C.E.) was one of reconstruction and reorganization after a time of civil war and turmoil. Diocletian

THE TETRARCHS This porphyry sculpture on the corner of the church of San Marco in Venice shows the tetrarchs, Emperor Diocletian (r. 284–305 C.E.) and his three imperial colleagues. Dressed for battle, they clasp each other to express their mutual solidarity.
SOURCE: John Heseltine/DK Images

was from Illyria (the former Yugoslavia of the twentieth century). A man of undistinguished birth, he rose to the throne through the ranks of the army. He knew that the job of defending and governing the entire empire was too great for one individual.

Diocletian therefore decreed the introduction of the **tetrarchy**, the rule of the empire by four men with power divided territorially. (See Map 5–4.) He allotted the provinces of Thrace, Asia, and Egypt to himself. His co-emperor, Maximian, shared with him the title of Augustus and governed Italy, Africa, and Spain. In addition, two men were given the subordinate title of Caesar: Galerius, who ruled the Danube frontier and the Balkans, and Constantius, who governed Britain and Gaul. This arrangement not only afforded a good solution to the military problem but also provided for a peaceful succession.

Diocletian was the senior Augustus, but each tetrarch was supreme in his own sphere. The Caesars were recognized as successors to each half of the empire, and marriages to daughters of the Augusti enhanced their loyalty. It was a return, in a way, to the precedent of the "good emperors" of 96 to 180 C.E., who chose their successors from the ranks of the ablest men. It seemed to promise orderly and peaceful transitions instead of assassinations, chaos, and civil war.

Each man established his residence and capital at a place convenient for frontier defense, and none chose Rome. The effective capital of Italy became the northern city of Milan. Diocletian beautified Rome by constructing his monumental baths, but he visited the city only once and made his own capital at Nicomedia in Asia Minor. This was another step in the long leveling process that had reduced the eminence of Rome and Italy. It was also evidence of the growing importance of the East.

In 305 C.E., Diocletian retired and compelled his co-emperor to do the same. But his plan for a smooth succession failed. In 310, there were five Augusti and no Caesars. Out of this chaos, Constantine, son of Constantius, produced order. In 324, he defeated his last opponent and made himself sole emperor, uniting the empire once again; he reigned until 337. For the most part, Constantine carried forward the policies of Diocletian. He supported Christianity, however, which Diocletian had tried to suppress.

5.6.1.1 DEVELOPMENT OF AUTOCRACY

Under Diocletian and Constantine, the imperial office developed into an **autocracy.** The emperor ruled by decree, consulting only a few high officials whom

Map 5–4 DIVISIONS OF THE ROMAN EMPIRE UNDER DIOCLETIAN, 284–305 C.E.

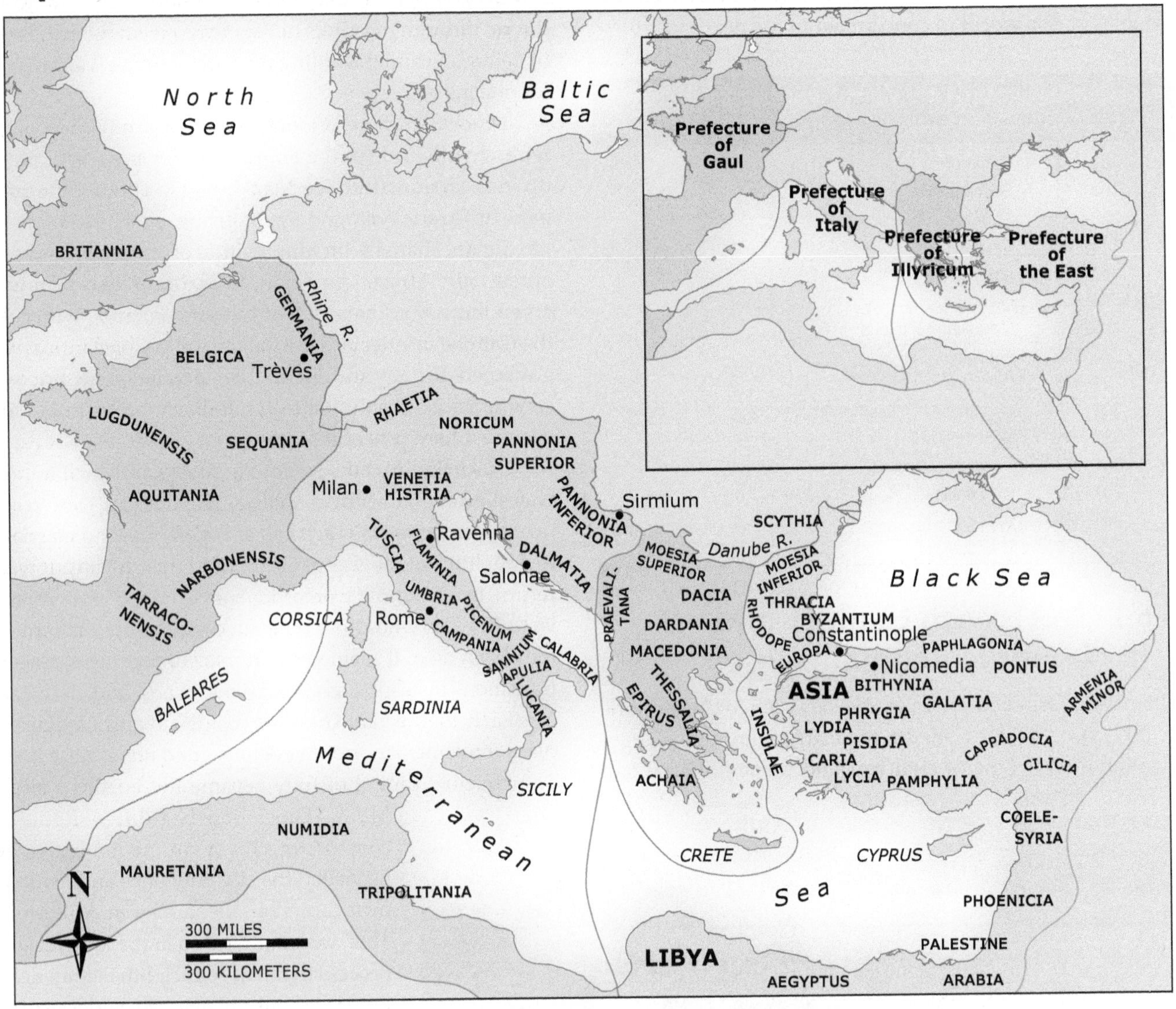

Diocletian divided the sprawling empire into four prefectures for more effective government and defense. The inset map shows their boundaries, and the larger map details some regions and provinces. The major division between the East and the West, shown here, was along the line running south between Pannonia and Moesia.

he himself appointed. The Senate had no role whatsoever, and the elimination of all distinctions between senator and equestrian further diminished its dignity.

The emperor was a remote figure surrounded by carefully chosen high officials. He lived in a great palace and was almost unapproachable. Those admitted into his presence had to prostrate themselves before him and kiss the hem of his robe, which was purple with golden threads woven through it. The emperor was addressed as *dominus*, or "lord," and his right to rule was not derived from the Roman people but from heaven. This distance and ceremony had a double purpose: to enhance the dignity of the emperor and to safeguard him against assassination.

Constantine erected the new city of Constantinople on the site of ancient Byzantium on the Bosporus, which leads to both the Aegean and Black Seas, and made it the new capital of the empire. Its strategic location was excellent

for protecting the eastern and Danubian frontiers, and surrounded on three sides by water, it was easily defended. This location also made it easier to continue the policies that fostered autocracy and Christianity. Rome was full of tradition, the center of senatorial and even republican memories, and of pagan worship, whereas Constantinople was free of both. Its dedication in 330 C.E. marked the beginning of a new era. Until its fall to the Turks in 1453, it served as a bastion of civilization, the preserver of classical culture, a bulwark against barbarian attack, and the greatest city in Christendom.

A civilian bureaucracy, carefully separated from the military to reduce the chances of rebellion by anyone combining these two kinds of power, carried out the autocratic rule of the emperors. Below the emperor's court, the most important officials were the praetorian prefects, each of whom administered one of the four major areas into which the empire was divided: Gaul, Italy, Illyricum, and the Orient. The four prefectures were subdivided into twelve territorial units called *dioceses*, each under a vicar subordinate to the prefect. The dioceses were further divided into almost hundred provinces, each under a provincial governor.

A vast system of spies and secret police, without whom the increasingly rigid organization could not be trusted to perform, supervised the entire system. Despite these efforts, the system was corrupt and inefficient.

The cost of maintaining a 400,000-man army, as well as the vast civilian bureaucracy, the expensive imperial court, and the imperial taste for splendid buildings strained an already weak economy. Diocletian's attempts to establish a reliable currency failed, leading instead to increased inflation. To deal with it, he resorted to price control with his Edict of Maximum Prices in 301 C.E.: For each product and each kind of labor, a maximum price was set, and violations were punishable by death. The edict still failed.

Peasants unable to pay their taxes and officials unable to collect them tried to escape. Diocletian resorted to stern regimentation to keep all in their places and at the service of the government. The terror of the third century forced many peasants to seek protection in the villas, or "country estates," of large and powerful landowners and to become tenant farmers. As social boundaries hardened, these coloni and their descendants became increasingly tied to their estates.

5.6.1.2 DIVISION OF THE EMPIRE The peace and unity Constantine established did not last long. Constantius II (r. 337–361 C.E.) won the struggle for succession after

THE ARCH OF CONSTANTINE Built in 315 C.E., the Arch of Constantine represents a transition from classical to medieval, pagan to Christian. Many of the sculptures incorporated in the arch were taken from earlier works dating to the first and second centuries C.E. Others, contemporary with the arch, reflect new, less refined style.
SOURCE: DEA PICTURE LIBRARY/De Agostini/Getty Images

his death. Constantius's death, in turn, left the empire in the hands of his young cousin Julian (r. 361–363 C.E.), whom Christians called **Julian the Apostate** because of his attempt to stamp out Christianity and restore paganism. Julian undertook a campaign against Persia to put a Roman on the throne of the Sassanids and end the Persian menace once and for all. He penetrated deep into Persia but was killed in battle. His death ended the expedition and the pagan revival.

The Germans in the West took advantage of the eastern campaign to attack along the Rhine and upper Danube Rivers. But even greater trouble was brewing along the middle and upper Danube. (See Map 5–5.) The eastern Goths, known as the Ostrogoths, occupied that territory. They were being pushed hard by their western cousins, the Visigoths, who in turn had been driven from their home in the Ukraine by the fierce Huns, a nomadic people from central Asia.

The emperor Valentinian I (r. 364–375 C.E.) recognized that he could not defend the empire alone and appointed his brother Valens (r. 364–378 C.E.) as co-ruler. Valentinian made his own headquarters at Milan and spent the rest of his life fighting and defeating the Franks and the Alemanni in the West. Valens was given control of the East. The empire was once again divided in two. The two emperors maintained their own courts, and the halves of the empire became increasingly separate and different. Latin was the language of the West and Greek of the East.

In 376, the Visigoths, pursued by the Huns, won rights of settlement and material assistance within the empire from Valens, in exchange for defending the eastern frontier as foederati, or special allies of the empire. The Visigoths, however, did not keep their bargain with the Romans and plundered the Balkan provinces. Nor did the Romans comply. They treated the Visigoths cruelly, even forcing them to trade their children for dogs to eat. Valens attacked the Goths and died, along with most of his army, at Adrianople in Thrace in 378.

Theodosius I (r. 379–395 C.E.), an able and experienced general, was named co-ruler in the East. Through a combination of military and diplomatic skills, he pacified the Goths, giving them land and autonomy and enrolling many of them in his army. He made important military reforms, putting greater emphasis on the cavalry. Theodosius tried to unify the empire again, but his death in 395 left it divided and weak.

5.6.2 The Triumph of Christianity

The rise of Christianity to dominance in the empire was closely connected with the political and cultural experiences of the third and fourth centuries C.E. Political chaos and decentralization had religious and cultural consequences.

Map 5–5 THE EMPIRE'S NEIGHBORS

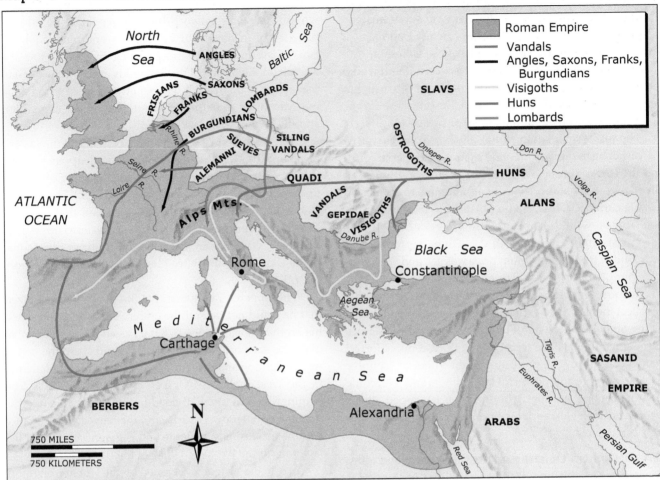

In the fourth century C.E., the Roman Empire was nearly surrounded by threatening neighbors. This map identifies the various so-called barbarians and where they lived before their armed contact with the Romans.

THE TRIUMPH OF CHRISTIANITY	
ca. 4 B.C.E.	Birth of Jesus of Nazareth
ca. 30 C.E.	Crucifixion of Jesus
64 C.E.	Fire at Rome; persecution by Nero
ca. 70–100 C.E.	Gospels written
ca. 250–260 C.E.	Severe persecutions by Decius and Valerian
303 C.E.	Persecution by Diocletian
311 C.E.	Galerius issues Edict of Toleration
312 C.E.	Battle of Milvian Bridge; conversion of Constantine to Christianity
325 C.E.	Council of Nicaea
395 C.E.	Christianity becomes official religion of Roman Empire

5.6.2.1 RELIGIOUS CURRENTS IN THE EMPIRE In some provinces, native languages replaced Latin and Greek, sometimes even for official purposes. The classical tradition that had been the basis of imperial life belonged exclusively to a small, educated aristocracy. In religion, the public cults had grown up in an urban environment and were largely political in character. As the importance of the cities diminished, so did the significance of their gods. People might still take comfort in the worship of the friendly, intimate deities of family, field, hearth, storehouse, and craft, but these gods were too petty to serve their needs in a confused and frightening world. The only universal worship was that of the emperor, but he was far off, and obeisance to his cult was more a political than a religious act.

In the troubled fourth and fifth centuries, people sought powerful, personal deities who would bring them safety and prosperity in this world and immortality in the next. Paganism was open and tolerant. Many people worshiped new deities alongside the old and even intertwined elements of several gods to form a new amalgam by the cult called **syncretism**.

Manichaeism was an especially potent rival of Christianity. Named for its founder, Mani, a Persian who lived in the third century C.E., this movement contained aspects of various religious traditions, including Zoroastrianism from Persia and both Judaism and Christianity. The Manichaeans pictured a world in which light and darkness, good and evil, were constantly at war. Good was spiritual and evil was material. Because human beings were made of matter, their bodies were prisons of evil and darkness, but they also contained an element of light and good. The "Father of Goodness" had sent Mani, among other prophets, to free humanity and gain its salvation. To achieve salvation, humans must aspire to reach the realm of light and abandon all physical desires. Manichaeans led an ascetic life and practiced a simple worship guided by a well-organized church. The movement reached its greatest strength in the fourth and fifth centuries, and some of its central ideas persisted into the Middle Ages.

Christianity had some aspects in common with these cults and answered many of the same needs their devotees had. None of these movements, however, attained Christianity's universality, and none appears to have given the early Christians as much competition as the ancient philosophies or the state religion.

5.6.2.2 IMPERIAL PERSECUTION By the third century, Christianity had taken firm hold in the eastern provinces and in Italy. It had not made much headway in the West, however. (See Map 5–6.) Christian apologists pointed out that Christians were good citizens who differed from others only in not worshipping the public gods. Until the middle of the third century C.E., the emperors tacitly accepted this view, without granting official toleration. As times became difficult and the Christians became more numerous and visible, that policy changed. Popular opinion blamed disasters, natural and military, on the Christians.

About 250 C.E., the emperor Decius (r. 249–251 C.E.) invoked the aid of the gods in his war against the Goths and required all citizens to worship the state gods publicly. True Christians could not obey, and Decius started a major persecution. Many Christians—even some bishops—yielded to threats and torture, but others held out and were killed. Valerian (r. 253–260 C.E.) resumed the persecutions, partly to confiscate the wealth of rich Christians. His successors, however, found other matters more pressing, and the persecution lapsed until the end of the century.

By the time of Diocletian, the increasing number of Christians included high officials. But hostility to the Christians had also grown on every level. Diocletian's own effort to bolster imperial power with the aura of divinity boded ill for the church, and in 303 C.E., he launched the most serious persecution inflicted on the Christians in the Roman Empire. He confiscated church property and destroyed churches and their sacred books. He deprived upper-class Christians of public office and judicial rights, imprisoned clergy, and enslaved Christians of the lower classes. He fined anyone refusing to sacrifice to the public gods. A final decree required public sacrifices and libations. The persecution horrified many pagans, and the plight and the demeanor of the martyrs aroused pity and sympathy.

Ancient states could not carry out a program of terror with the thoroughness of modern totalitarian governments,

Map 5–6 THE SPREAD OF CHRISTIANITY

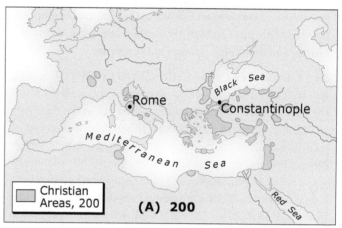

(A) 200

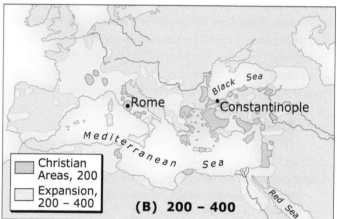

(B) 200 – 400

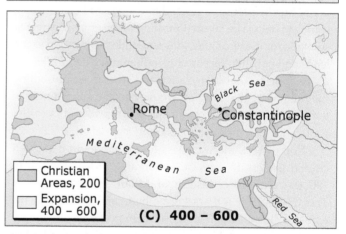

(C) 400 – 600

Christianity grew swiftly in the third, fourth, fifth, and sixth centuries C.E.—especially after the conversion of the emperors in the fourth century C.E. By 600 C.E., on the eve of the birth of the new religion of Islam, Christianity was dominant throughout the Mediterranean world and most of Western Europe.

so the Christians and their church survived to enjoy what they must have considered a miraculous change of fortune. In 311 C.E., Galerius, who had been one of the most vigorous persecutors, was influenced, perhaps by his Christian wife, to issue the Edict of Toleration, permitting Christian worship.

The victory of Constantine and his emergence as sole ruler of the empire changed the condition of Christianity from a precariously tolerated sect to the religion the emperor favored. This put Christianity on the path to becoming the official and only legal religion in the empire.

5.6.2.3 EMERGENCE OF CHRISTIANITY AS THE STATE RELIGION The sons of Constantine continued to favor the new religion, but the succession of Julian the Apostate in 360 C.E. posed a new threat. Julian was a devotee of traditional classical pagan culture and, as a believer in **Neoplatonism**, an opponent of Christianity. Neoplatonism was a religious philosophy, or a philosophical religion, whose connection with Platonic teachings was distant. Its chief formulator was Plotinus (205–270 C.E.), who tried to combine classical and rational philosophical speculation with the mystical spirit of his time. Plotinus's successors were bitter critics of Christianity, and their views influenced Julian. Though he refrained from persecution, Julian tried to undo the work of Constantine by withdrawing the privileges of the church, removing Christians from high offices, and introducing a new form of pagan worship. His reign, however, was short, and his work did not last.

In 394 C.E., Theodosius forbade the celebration of pagan cults and abolished the pagan religious calendar. At his death, Christianity was the official religion of the Roman Empire.

The establishment of Christianity as the state religion did not put an end to the troubles of the Christians and their church; instead, it created new ones and complicated some old ones. The favored position of the church attracted converts for the wrong reasons and diluted the moral excellence and spiritual fervor of its adherents. The problem of the relationship between church and state arose, presenting the possibility that religion would become subordinate to the state, as it had been in the classical world and in earlier civilizations. In the East, that largely happened.

In the West, the weakness of the emperors permitted church leaders to exercise remarkable independence. In 390 C.E., Ambrose, bishop of Milan, excommunicated Theodosius I for a massacre he had carried out, and the emperor did penance. This act set an important precedent for future assertions of the church's autonomy and authority, but it did not end secular interference and influence in the church.

5.6.2.4 ARIANISM AND THE COUNCIL OF NICAEA Internal divisions proved to be even more troubling as new heresies emerged. Because they threatened the unity of an empire that was now Christian, they inevitably involved the emperor and the powers of the state. Before long, the world would see Christians persecuting other Christians with a zeal at least as great as the most fanatical pagans had displayed against them.

Among the many controversial views that arose, the most important and the most threatening was **Arianism**, founded by a priest named Arius of Alexandria (ca. 280–336 C.E.). The issue creating difficulty was the relation of God the Father to God the Son. Arius argued that Jesus was a created being, unlike God the Father. He was, therefore, not made of the substance of God and was not eternal. "The Son has a beginning," he said, "but God is without beginning." For Arius, Jesus was neither fully man nor fully God, but something in between. Arius's view did away with the mysterious concept of the Trinity, the difficult doctrine that holds that God is three persons (the Father, the Son, and the Holy Spirit) and also one in substance and essence.

The Arian concept appeared simple, rational, and philosophically acceptable. To its ablest opponent, Athanasius, however, it had serious shortcomings. Athanasius (ca. 293–373 C.E.), later bishop of Alexandria, saw the Arian view as an impediment to any acceptable theory of salvation, to him the most important religious question. He adhered to the old Greek idea of salvation as the transformation of sinful mortality into divine immortality through the gift of "life." Only if Jesus were both fully human and fully God could the transformation of humanity to divinity have taken place in him and be transmitted by him to his disciples. "Christ was made man," he said, "that we might be made divine."

To deal with the controversy, Constantine called a council of Christian bishops at Nicaea, not far from Constantinople, in 325 C.E. For the emperor, the question was essentially political, but for the disputants, salvation was at stake. At Nicaea, Athanasius's view won out, became orthodox, and was embodied in the Nicene Creed. But Arianism persisted and spread. Some later emperors were either Arians or sympathetic to that view. Some of the most successful missionaries to the barbarians were Arians; as a result, many of the German tribes that overran the empire were Arians. The Christian emperors hoped to bring unity to their increasingly decentralized realms by imposing a single religion. Over time Christianity did prove to be a unifying force, but it also introduced divisions where none had previously existed.

5.7 Arts and Letters in the Late Empire

How did arts and letters in late Rome reflect the developing relationship between pagan and Christian ideas?

The art and literature of the late empire reflect the confluence of pagan and Christian ideas and traditions and the conflict between them. Much of the literature is polemical and much of the art is propaganda.

THE PASSION OF CHRIST This late-Roman ivory plaque (420 C.E.) shows a scene from Christ's Passion. The art of the late empire was transitional from the classical past to the medieval future.
SOURCE: British Museum, London, UK/Bridgeman Art Library

A military revolution led by provincials whose origins were in the lower classes saved the empire from the chaos of the third century. Yet the new ruling class was not interested in leveling; it wanted instead to establish itself as a new aristocracy. It thought of itself as effecting a great restoration rather than a revolution and sought to restore classical culture and absorb it. The comfort of Christianity tempered the confusion and uncertainty of the times. But the new ruling class also sought order and stability—ethical, literary, and artistic—in the classical tradition.

5.7.1 The Preservation of Classical Culture

One of the main requirements and accomplishments of this period was the preservation of classical culture. Ways were discovered to make it available and useful to the newly arrived ruling class. Works of the great classical authors were reproduced in many copies and were transferred from perishable and inconvenient papyrus rolls to sturdier codices, bound volumes that were as easy to use as modern

books. Scholars also digested long works like Livy's *History of Rome* into shorter versions, wrote learned commentaries, and compiled grammars. Original works by pagan writers of the late empire were neither numerous nor especially distinguished.

5.7.2 Christian Writers

The late empire saw a great outpouring of Christian writings, including many examples of Christian apologetics, in poetry and prose, and sermons, hymns, and biblical commentaries. Christianity could also boast important scholars. Jerome (348–420 C.E.), thoroughly trained in classical Latin literature and rhetoric, produced a revised version of the Bible in Latin. Commonly called the **Vulgate**, it became the Bible the Catholic Church used. Probably the most important eastern scholar was Eusebius of Caesarea (ca. 260–340 C.E.). He wrote apologetics, an idealized biography of Constantine, and a valuable chronology of important events in the past. His most important contribution, however, was his *Ecclesiastical History*, an attempt to present the Christian view of history. Eusebius saw all history as the working out of God's will. History, therefore, had a purpose and a direction, and Constantine's victory and the subsequent unity of empire and church were its culmination.

The closeness and the complexity of the relationship between classical pagan culture and that of Christianity of the late empire are nowhere better displayed than in the career and writings of Augustine (354–430 C.E.), bishop of Hippo in North Africa. He was born at Carthage and was trained as a teacher of rhetoric. His father was a pagan, but his mother was a Christian, and hers was ultimately the stronger influence. Augustine passed through several intellectual way stations—skepticism and Neoplatonism among others—before his conversion to Christianity. His training and skill in pagan rhetoric and philosophy made him peerless among his contemporaries as a defender of Christianity and as a theologian.

His greatest works are his *Confessions*, an autobiography describing the road to his conversion, and *The City of God*. The latter was a response to the pagan charge that the abandonment of the old gods and the advent of Christianity caused the Visigoths' sack of Rome in 410 C.E. The optimistic view some Christians held that God's will worked its way in history and was easily comprehensible needed further support in the face of this calamity. Augustine sought to separate the fate of Christianity from that of the Roman Empire. He contrasted the secular world, the City of Man, with the spiritual, the City of God. The former was selfish, the latter unselfish; the former evil, the latter good.

Augustine argued that history was moving forward, in the spiritual sense, to the Day of Judgment, but there was no reason to expect improvement before then in the secular sphere. The fall of Rome was neither surprising nor important. All states, even a Christian Rome, were part of the City of Man and were therefore corrupt and mortal. Only the City of God was immortal, and it, consisting of all the saints on earth and in heaven, was untouched by earthly calamities.

Though the *Confessions* and *The City of God* are Augustine's most famous works, they emphasize only a part of his thought. His treatises *On the Trinity* and *On Christian Education* reveal the great skill with which he supported Christian belief with the learning, logic, and philosophy of the pagan classics. Augustine believed faith is essential and primary (a thoroughly Christian view) but not a substitute for reason (the foundation of classical thought). Instead, faith is the starting point for, and liberator of, human reason, which continues to be the way people can understand what faith reveals. His writings consistently reveal the presence of both Christian faith and pagan reason, as well as the tension between them, a legacy he left to the Middle Ages.

5.8 The Problem of the Decline and Fall of the Empire in the West

Why were new conquests so important to the vitality of the Roman Empire?

Whether important to Augustine or not, the massive barbarian invasions of the fifth century put an end to effective imperial government in the West. For centuries people have speculated about the causes of the collapse of the ancient world. Every kind of reason has been proposed, and some suggestions seem to have nothing to do with reason at all. Exhaustion of the soil, plague, climatic change, and even poisoning by lead water pipes have been suggested as reasons for Rome's decline in population, vigor, and the capacity to defend itself. Some blame slavery and a resulting failure to make advances in science and technology. Others blame excessive government interference in the economic life of the empire and still others the destruction of the urban middle class, the carrier of classical culture.

A simpler and more obvious explanation might begin with the observation that the growth of so mighty an empire as Rome's was by no means inevitable. Rome's greatness had come from conquests that provided the Romans with the means to expand still further, until there were not enough Romans to conquer and govern any more peoples and territory. When pressure from outsiders grew, the Romans lacked the resources to advance and defeat the enemy as in the past. The tenacity and success of their resistance for so long were remarkable. But without new conquests to provide the immense wealth needed to defend and maintain internal prosperity, the Romans finally yielded to unprecedented onslaughts by fierce and numerous attackers.

To blame the ancients and slavery for the failure to produce an industrial and economic revolution like that of the later Western world (one capable of producing wealth without taking it from another) is to stand the problem on its head. No one yet has a satisfactory explanation for those industrial and economic revolutions, so it is improper to blame any institution or society for not achieving what has been achieved only once in human history. Perhaps we should think of the problem as did Edward Gibbon, the author of the great eighteenth-century study of Rome's collapse and transformation:

> The decline of Rome was the natural and inevitable effect of immoderate greatness. Prosperity ripened the principle of decay; the cause of the destruction multiplied with the extent of conquest; and, as soon as time or accident had removed the artificial supports, the stupendous fabric yielded to the pressure of its own weight. The story of the ruin is simple and obvious; and instead of inquiring why the Roman Empire was destroyed, we should rather be surprised that it had subsisted so long.[5]

The Chapter in Perspective

Out of the civil wars and chaos that brought down the republic, Augustus brought unity, peace, order, and prosperity. As a result, he was regarded with almost religious awe and attained more military and political power than any Roman before him. Augustus ruled firmly but with moderation. He tried to limit military adventures and the costs they incurred. His public works encouraged trade and communications. He tried to restore and invigorate the old civic pride, and in this he had much success. He was less successful in promoting private morality based on family values. Augustus patronized the arts to beautify Rome and glorify his reign. On his death, Augustus was able to pass on the regime to his family, the Julio-Claudians.

For almost 200 years, with a few brief interruptions, the empire was generally prosperous, peaceful, and well run. But problems grew. Management of the many responsibilities the government assumed required the growth of a large bureaucracy that placed a heavy and increasing burden on the treasury, required higher taxes, and stifled both civic spirit and private enterprise. Pressure from barbarians on the frontiers required a large standing army, which led to further taxation.

In the late empire, Rome's rulers resorted to many devices for dealing with their problems. More and more, the emperors' rule and their safety depended on the loyalty of the army, so they courted the soldiers' favor with gifts. This only increased the burden of taxes; the rich and powerful found ways to avoid their obligations, increasing the load on everyone else. The government's control over the lives of its people became ever greater and the society more rigid as people tried to flee to escape the crushing load of taxes. Expedients were tried, including inflating the currency, fixing farmers to the soil as serfs or coloni, building walls to keep the barbarians out, and bribing barbarian tribes to fight for Rome against other barbarians. Ultimately, all these measures failed. The Roman Empire in the west fell, leaving disunity, insecurity, disorder, and poverty. Like similar empires in the ancient world, it had been unable to sustain its "immoderate greatness."

The Chapter in Review

Review Questions

1. What solutions did Augustus have for the political problems that had plagued the Roman Republic? Why was the Roman population willing to accept Augustus as head of the state?
2. How was the Roman Empire organized, and why did it function smoothly? What role did the emperor play in maintaining political stability?
3. How did the literature in the Golden Age of Augustus differ from that of the Silver Age during the first and second centuries C.E.? How did the poetry of Vergil and Horace contribute to Augustus's rule?
4. Why did the Roman authorities persecute Christians? What were the more important reasons for Christianity's success?
5. What political, social, and economic problems beset Rome in the third and fourth centuries C.E.? How did Diocletian and Constantine deal with them? Were they effective in stemming the tide of decline and disintegration in the Roman Empire? What problems were they unable to solve?
6. What theories have scholars advanced to explain the decline and fall of the Roman Empire?

Key Terms

agape (AG-a-pay)   Meaning "love feast." A common meal that was part of the central ritual of early Christian worship.

Apostolic Succession   The Christian doctrine that the powers given by Jesus to his original disciples have been handed down from bishop to bishop through ordination.

Arianism (AIR-ee-an-ism)   The belief formulated by Arius of Alexandria (ca. 280–336 C.E.) that Jesus was a created being, neither fully man nor fully God, but something in between. It did away with the doctrine of the Trinity.

autocracy (AW-to-kra-see)   Government in which the ruler has absolute power.

bishop   Originally a person elected by early Christian congregations to lead them in worship and supervise their funds. In time, became the religious and even political authorities for Christian communities within large geographical areas.

catholic   Meaning "universal." The body of belief held by most Christians enshrined within the church.

creed   A brief statement of faith to which true Christians should adhere.

deacon   Meaning "those who serve." In early Christian congregations, assisted the presbyters, or elders.

dioceses   The twelve territorial units into which Diocletian subdivided the four prefectures of the Roman empire, each under a vicar subordinate to the prefect; in turn divided into a hundred provinces, each under a provincial governor.

Eucharist (YOU-ka-rist)   Meaning "thanksgiving." The celebration of the Lord's Supper. Considered the central ritual of worship by most Christians. Also called *Holy Communion*.

heretics (HAIR-i-ticks)   People whose beliefs were contrary to those of the Catholic Church.

honestiores **(HON-est-ee-or-ez)**   The Roman term formalized from the beginning of the third century C.E. to denote the privileged classes: senators, equestrians, the municipal aristocracy, and soldiers.

humiliores **(HEW-mi-lee-orez)**   The Roman term formalized at the beginning of the third century C.E. for the lower classes.

insulae **(IN-sul-lay)**   Meaning "islands." The multistoried apartment buildings of Rome in which most of the inhabitants of the city lived.

Julian the Apostate   (r. 361-363 C.E.) Roman emperor who attempted to stamp out Christianity and restore traditional pagan worship.

jus gentium **(YUZ GEN-tee-um)**   Meaning "law of peoples." The body of Roman law that dealt with foreigners.

jus naturale **(YUZ NAH-tu-rah-lay)**   Meaning "natural law." The Stoic concept of a world ruled by divine reason.

Manichaeism   A syncretic religion named after its founder, Mani, a Persian who lived in the third century. Contained aspects of Zoroastrianism, and both Judaism and Christianity.

Messiah (MESS-eye-a)   The redeemer whose coming Jews believed would establish the kingdom of God on earth. Jesus considered to be the Messiah by Christians (*Christ* means *Messiah* in Greek).

Neoplatonism (KNEE-o-play-ton-ism)   A religious philosophy that tried to combine mysticism with classical and rationalist speculation. Chief formulator was Plotinus (205–270 C.E.).

orthodox   Meaning "holding the right opinions." Applied to the doctrines of the Catholic Church.

Pharisees (FAIR-i-sees)   The group that was most strict in its adherence to Jewish law.

Romanitas **(row-MAN-ee-tas)**   Meaning "Roman-ness." The spread of the Roman way of life and the sense of identifying with Rome across the Roman Empire.

Sassanians   An Iranian dynasty that seized control of Persia from the Parthians in 224 C.E. Recovered Mesopotamia in 260 C.E. and took the Roman emperor Valerian prisoner.

syncretism (SIN-cret-ism)   The intermingling of different religions to form an amalgam that contained elements from each.

tetrarchy (TET-rar-key)   Diocletian's (r. 306–337 C.E.) system for ruling the Roman Empire by four men with power divided territorially.

Vulgate   The Latin translation of the Bible by Jerome (348–420 C.E.) that became the standard bible used by the Catholic Church.

Notes

1. Lucretius, *De Rerum Natura*, lines 931 ff.
2. Dates for emperors give the years of their reigns, indicated by *r*.
3. J. Carcopino, *Daily Life in Ancient Rome* (New Haven, CT: Yale University Press, 1940), p. 26.
4. Galatians 3:28, Revised Standard Version of the Bible.
5. Edward Gibbon, *The History of the Decline and Fall of the Roman Empire*, 2nd ed., Vol. 4, ed. by J. B. Bury (London: McThuen & Co., 1909), pp. 173–174.

The West and the World
Ancient Warfare

WAR HAS BEEN a persistent part of human experience since before the birth of civilization.[1] Organized warfare goes back to the Stone Age. There may be evidence of it as early as the late Paleolithic Age, but clearly it was a significant human activity by the Neolithic Age. The earliest civilizations of Egypt and Mesopotamia added powerful new elements to the character of warfare and were from the first occupied with war, as were later Bronze and Iron Age cultures all over the world.

The earliest literary work in the Western tradition, Homer's *Iliad*, describes a long, bitter war and the men who fought it. The Rigvedic hymns of the ancient culture of India tell of the warrior god Indra, who smashes the fortifications of his enemies. The earliest civilizations of China were established by armies armed with spears, composite bows, and war chariots. The evidence is plentiful that war is one of the oldest and most continuous activities of the human species.

The Causes of War

Ancient philosophers like Plato and Aristotle took all this for granted. They believed men (they never thought of women in this context) were naturally acquisitive and aggressive, and that governments and laws existed to curb those tendencies. The ancient Greeks, wracked by perpetual war, were eager to investigate its causes. Thucydides, writing at the end of the fifth century B.C.E., carefully described the quarrels between the Athenians and the Peloponnesians and explained why they broke their treaty: "so that no one may ever have to seek the cause that led to the outbreak of so great a war among the Greeks." He provided a profound and helpful understanding of the causes of wars and of the motives of those going to war. He understood war as the armed competition for power, but he believed that wise and capable leaders could limit their own fears and desires—and those of their people— and choose to gain and defend only as much power as was needed for their purposes.

In this struggle, whether for a rational need or for the insatiable drive for power, Thucydides found that people go to war because of "fear, honor, and interest."[2] That trio

of motives illuminates the understanding of the origins of wars throughout history. Fear and interest as causes of war will not surprise the modern reader, but concern for honor as a motivation may seem strange. If we understand honor to mean "fame," "glory," "renown," or "splendor," it may appear applicable to war in the premodern world alone. If, however, we understand its significance as "deference," "esteem," "just due," "regard," "respect," or "prestige," honor proves to be an important motive of nations in the modern world as well.

Wars are made by human beings who may choose different courses of action. Sometimes decisions are made by a single individual or a small group, sometimes by a very large number. Their choices are always limited and affected by circumstances, and the closer the outbreak of a war, the more limited the choices seem. Those who decide to make war always think they have good reason to fight. Although impersonal forces play a role, and the reasons publicly given are not necessarily the true ones, the reasons must be taken seriously, for

> the conflicts between states which have usually led to war have normally arisen, not from any irrational and emotional drives, but from almost a superabundance of analytic rationality. . . . [I]n general men have fought during the past two hundred years neither because they are aggressive nor because they are acquisitive animals, but because they are reasoning ones: because they discern, or believe that they can discern, dangers before they become immediate, and thus the possibility of threats before they are made.[3]

Throughout history, there has been widespread agreement that some things are desirable and worth fighting for. Liberty, autonomy, the freedom to exercise one's religion, and the search for wealth have been among the most common through the ages. Fear of their opposites—slavery, subordination, religious suppression, and poverty—has probably been an even greater cause of wars. All causes, however, depend on power, for the distribution of power determines who can and cannot impose his or her will on others. In one sense, there are a myriad of causes for war. But in another sense, there is only one cause: Wars have rarely happened by accident or because of honest misunderstandings; most of them have resulted from calculations of power, which is valued because it provides security, reputation, and material advantage.

In the sixth century B.C.E., the Greek philosopher Heracleitus observed that "war is the father of all things." In 1968, Will and Ariel Durant calculated that in the previous 3,421 years, only 268 were free of war. There have been none since, suggesting, in that respect, that little has changed in more than three millennia. The causes that led to war in the past have seemingly not disappeared.

Human beings, organized into nations and states, continue to compete for a limited supply of desirable things, to seek honor and advantage, and to fear others. All too often, the result has been war.

War and Technology

The nature of war is shaped at the deepest level by the character of the societies involved, their values, their needs, and their organization, but from the beginning, technology has played a vital role. Weapons and other necessities of war are the products of technological development, and war and technology have had similar effects on one another: From the earliest times, new technologies have helped shape the character of war, and the needs of armies have provoked technological advance.

Fortress Walls

Jericho, built about 7000 B.C.E. in the Neolithic Age, already reveals the importance of warfare and the development of technology that accompanied it. Jericho was surrounded by a stone wall 700 yards around, 10 feet thick, and 13 feet high, protected by a moat 10 feet deep and 30 feet wide. This barrier made the city a powerful fortress that could be defeated only by an enemy who could besiege it long enough to starve it out. The expense and effort to build such a structure would not have been undertaken unless war was a relatively common danger.

Not many years after the rise of civilization in Mesopotamia (ca. 3000 B.C.E.), fortified Sumerian cities appeared in the

WALLS OF JERICHO This mound of ruins marks the ancient city of Jericho. Thought by some to be the earliest Neolithic site in the Near East, it sprang up around an oasis about 7000 B.C.E. Surrounded by thick stone walls and a moat, Jericho was meant to be a fortress that could resist sieges, confirming that warfare was common at least as early as the construction of this city.
SOURCE: Robert Hoetink/Alamy Stock Photo

south. A thousand years later, the pharaohs of Dynasty 12 in Egypt devised a strategic defense system of fortresses on their southern frontier with Nubia. In early China, the towns had no walls because the surrounding plains lacked both trees and stone. During the Shang dynasty (ca. 1766–1050 B.C.E.), however, towns with walls made of beaten earth appeared. Once the techniques needed to build fortresses strong enough to withstand attack were mastered, kingdoms could expand into empires that could defend their conquered lands.

The history of warfare and military technology is a story of continued change caused by a permanent competition between defense and offense. In time, construction of fortified strongholds led to new devices and techniques for besieging them. Excavations in Egypt and Mesopotamia have uncovered scaling ladders, battering rams, siege towers (some of them mobile), and mines burrowing under fortress walls. Catapults capable of hurling stones against an enemy's walls appeared in Greece in the fourth century B.C.E.; this weapon was brought to greater perfection and power by the Romans centuries later. Alexander the Great and some of his Hellenistic successors were skilled in storming fortified cities with the aid of such technology, but throughout ancient history, successful defeat of a fortified place was usually the result of starvation and surrender after a long siege. Not until the invention of gunpowder and powerful cannons did offensive technology overcome the defensive strength of fortification.

Army Against Army

A different kind of warfare, of army against army in the open field, appeared as early as the Stone Age. Scholars disagree as to whether it emerged in the Paleolithic Age or in Neolithic times, but we know that warriors used such weapons as wooden or stone clubs, spears and axes with sharpened stone heads, and simple bows with stone-tipped arrows. The discovery of metallurgy brought the Bronze Age to Mesopotamia, perhaps as early as 3500 B.C.E., providing armies with weapons that were sharper and sturdier than stone and with body armor and helmets that brought greater safety to warriors. The Mesopotamian rulers already had wealth, a sizable population, a civilized organization, and substantial fortress walls. Now, with bronze weapons, Mesopotamian rulers could expand their empires far beyond their early frontiers. When, not much later, the Bronze Age came to Egypt, its rulers, too, used this new technology to expand and defend their wealthy kingdom.

The Chariot and the Bow

The next great revolution in warfare occurred with the inventions of the chariot and the composite bow. When these came together by about 1800 B.C.E., their users defeated all before them, conquering both Egypt and Mesopotamia. The chariot was a light vehicle, a platform on two wheels pulled by a team of two or four horses that could move swiftly on a battlefield. It was strong enough to hold two men—a driver and a warrior—as it sped along on an open field. The wheels were of wood—not solid, but with spokes and a hub—and were attached to an axle; building them required great skill and experience. The warrior on the chariot wielded a new weapon: the composite bow, more powerful by far than anything that had come before it. Made of thin strips of wood glued together and fastened with animal tendons and horn, the bow was short and easy to use from a moving chariot. It could shoot a light arrow accurately for 300 yards and penetrate the armor of the day at about 100. A warrior on a chariot on a flat enough field, using a composite bow with a quiver full of light arrows, could devastate an army of foot soldiers. "Circling at a distance of 100 or 200 yards from the herds of unarmored foot soldiers, a chariot crew—one to drive, one to shoot—might have transfixed six men a minute. Ten minutes' work by ten chariots would cause 500 casualties or more."[4]

For several centuries, beginning about 1800 B.C.E., peoples from the north using such weapons smashed into Mesopotamia and conquered the kingdoms they attacked. In India, the Aryans, who also spoke an Indo-European language, crushed the indigenous Indus civilization. In Egypt, the Hyksos, speakers of a Semitic language, conquered the northern kingdom. In China, the chariot-riding Shang dynasty established an aristocratic rule based on the new weapons. In Europe, the Mycenaean Greeks used chariots, although it is not clear if they had the composite bow and used the tactics that had brought such great success elsewhere.

The most sophisticated users of ancient military technology before Alexander the Great were the Assyrians. They had a wide range of devices for siege warfare and took them along on all their campaigns. But new weapons made of new materials with new techniques do not in themselves constitute a revolution in military affairs. To use them effectively, armies require appropriate operational plans and training for their soldiers in the necessary skills and technology.

The Assyrian annals suggest that by the eighth century B.C.E., their kings had turned their chariot forces into

> a weapon of shock and terror, manipulated by the driver to charge at breakneck speed behind a team of perfectly schooled horses and used by the archer as a platform from which to launch a hail of arrows; squadrons of chariots, their drivers trained to act in mutual support, might have clashed much

as armored vehicles have done in our time, success going to the side that could disable the larger opposing number, while the footmen unlucky or foolhardy enough to stand in their way would have been scattered like chaff.[5]

Mounted Cavalry

In 612 B.C.E., the great Assyrian Empire fell before a coalition of opponents, but it had already been weakened by enemies who commanded a new military technique: mounted cavalry. Ironically, the Assyrians may have been the first to develop the critical skills of riding astride a horse while keeping both hands free to shoot with a bow.

The first peoples to use the new cavalry technology to great effect were nomads from the steppes of northern Eurasia. About 690 B.C.E., a people the Greeks called Cimmerians flooded into Asia Minor on their warhorses, shaking the established order. Later in that century they were followed by another group of steppe nomads called the Scythians, who came from the Altay mountains in central Asia. The Scythians overthrew the Cimmerians and then joined with more settled peoples in the battles that destroyed the Assyrian Empire. This was the beginning of a series of attacks by horse-riding nomads from the steppes against the settled lands to their south that lasted for two millennia. In China, no clear evidence exists for such attacks before the fourth century B.C.E., but it is possible that attacks from Mongolia and nearby areas may have brought down the western Chou dynasty in 771 B.C.E.

In the Middle East, the Babylonian Empire had succeeded the Assyrian but was soon replaced by the Persian Empire. The Persians had no other way of preventing the nomads' devastating raids than to pay other nomads to defend their frontiers, and the Chinese emperors did the same. The Chinese also developed a cavalry that carried the crossbow, more powerful than the composite bow. The Great Wall of China was a fortress built during the Ch'in dynasty (256–206 B.C.E.), designed to keep invaders with their ravaging horsemen out. But this, too, proved ineffective. Despite endless disturbances in the political and military relationships between grassland and plowland, peoples of the steppe enjoyed a consistent advantage because of their superior mobility and the cheapness of their military equipment. This produced a pattern of recurrent nomad conquests of civilized lands.[6]

GREAT WALL OF CHINA Originally built during the Ch'in dynasty (256–206 B.C.E.), what can be seen today is a section of the Great Wall as it was completely rebuilt during the Ming dynasty (1368–1644 C.E.).
SOURCE: Paolo Koch/Science Source

Iron-Wielding Warriors

As the chariot and the warhorse were having a great impact on the nature of ancient warfare, a far more fundamental revolution in military affairs was under way. Bronze is an alloy of copper and tin, but the latter is a rather rare metal, so it was expensive. Horses also were costly to keep, so warfare that depended on bronze weapons and horses was necessarily limited to a relatively small number of men. About 1400 B.C.E. in Asia Minor, however, a technique was discovered that made iron so hard and durable that tools and weapons made of it were clearly superior to those of bronze. Iron was also far more abundant than the components of bronze, easier to work with, and much less expensive. For the first time, it became possible for common people to own and use metal. Now a much larger part of the population could own arms and armor, and

> [o]rdinary farmers and herdsmen thereby achieved a new formidability in battle, and the narrowly aristocratic structure of society characteristic of the

chariot age altered abruptly. A more democratic era dawned as iron-wielding invaders overthrew ruling elites that had based their power on a monopoly of chariotry.[7]

Within two centuries, the new technology spread over the Middle East and into Europe. A new round of invasions by iron-wielding warriors swept away kingdoms and empires and brought new peoples to power. The Assyrians, combining the bureaucratic organizational skills of Mesopotamian civilization with a warrior spirit and an ability to assimilate new techniques, achieved control of their own region with the aid of iron weapons. But many indigenous rulers of civilized lands were subdued or swept away. For example, in Europe, a Greek-speaking people called the Mycenaeans had ruled the Greek peninsula and the Aegean Sea with a Bronze Age civilization similar to those of the Middle East. Between 1200 B.C.E. and 1100 B.C.E., however, the Mycenaeans were overthrown by a new wave of Greeks with iron weapons who obliterated the old civilization and brought a new culture based on new ways of fighting.

ALEXANDER AND DARIUS This mosaic of Alexander battling Darius was found on a wall of the House of the Faun at Pompeii. It is believed to be a copy of a painting by Philoxenus of Eretria in the fourth century B.C.E. Alexander is the mounted hatless man on the left and King Darius wears a headdress as he stands on a chariot on the right.
SOURCE: Erich Lessing/Art Resource, NY

The Shield and the Phalanx

The heart of this new Greek civilization, which is called *Hellenic*, was the city-state, or polis, hundreds of which emerged toward the end of the eighth century B.C.E. Their armies consisted of independent yeoman farmers who produced enough wealth to supply their own iron weapons and body armor, made cheap enough by the revolution in metallurgy. But again, these would have been of little value without organizational change. Now, a new kind of warfare, which made infantry the dominant fighting force on land for centuries, permitted an alliance of poor Greek states to defeat the mighty and wealthy Persian Empire. The soldiers, wearing helmets, body armor, and a heavy, large round shield for protection, carried short iron swords but used iron-tipped wooden pikes as their chief weapon. Arrayed in compact blocks called phalanxes, usually eight men deep, these freemen, well disciplined and highly motivated, defeated lesser infantries, archers, and cavalry. Adapted by the Macedonians under King Philip II and his son Alexander the Great, the hoplite phalanx remained the dominant infantry force until it was defeated by the Roman legion in the second century B.C.E.

Trireme Warfare

The Greeks also achieved supremacy at sea by improving an existing technological innovation and providing it with an effective operational plan. Oared galleys were known at Cyprus as early as about 1000 B.C.E., and the Phoenicians improved their speed and maneuverability by superimposing a second and then a third bank of rowers over the first to produce a ship the Greeks called a trireme. The Greeks added outriggers for the top rowers, and it is possible this permitted their rowers to use the full power of their strongest leg muscles by sliding back and forth as they rowed. At first, the main mode of trireme warfare was for one ship to come alongside another, grapple it, and send marines to board the enemy ship. In time, however, the Greeks placed a strong ram at the prow of each ship and learned how to row with great bursts of speed and to make sharp turns that allowed them to ram and disable their opponents by striking them in the side or rear. With such ships and tactics, the Greek triremes repeatedly sank fleets of the Egyptians and Phoenicians who rowed for the Persian Empire, thus gaining complete naval mastery.

The Macedonians came to dominate the Greek world, to conquer the Persian Empire, and to rule its successor states in the Hellenistic period (323–31 B.C.E.), but technological innovation in military affairs played only a small part in their success. Military victories came chiefly from the quality of their leaders, the number, spirit, and discipline of their troops, and the ability to combine infantry, cavalry, and light-armed troops to win battles. Alexander's engineers also brought unprecedented skill to the use of siege weapons.

Roman Legions

The armies of the Roman Republic defeated Macedon in a series of wars in the third and second centuries B.C.E. and brought the entire Mediterranean world under Roman sway by the end of the second century. This conquest was achieved almost entirely by the power of the infantry. In time, the Roman army moved from the phalanx formation to a looser, more open order of battle based on the legion, which was divided into smaller, self-sufficient units. The Romans abandoned the pike as the chief infantry weapon, using instead the pilum, a heavy iron javelin that was thrown to cause disarray in the enemy line and permit the Romans to use their short double-edged swords at close quarters. In the imperial period, beginning especially in the third century C.E., nomadic barbarian tribes began applying severe pressure on Rome's frontiers that would ultimately bring down the empire. Like the Chinese, the Romans built walls in some places to ease the burden of defending their extensive borders. In the empire's last years, the Romans began to use heavily armored horses ridden by knights in heavy armor, carrying lances and capable of charging an enemy with great force and effect. These armored cavalrymen, called *cataphracts* in Greek, would develop into a major new system of fighting in the Western Middle Ages, but they were too few to take a significant role in the final, futile defense of the empire.

Questions

1. How early is the evidence for warfare among human beings?

2. According to Thucydides, what was the definition of war? For what purposes did he think people went to war?

3. Consider the impact of war on technology and vice versa. Is war a rational or irrational action? Can you think of a good reason for fighting a war?

Notes

1. Arther Ferrill, *The Origins of War* (London, Thames and Hudson, 1985), p. 13, says "organized warfare appeared at least by the end of the Paleolithic Age," but Richard A. Gabriel argues that true warfare did not come until the Bronze Age and the invention of the state and the social structure that came with it. No one, however, doubts that war is at least as old as civilization.

2. 1.75.3.

3. Michael Howard, *The Lessons of History* (New Haven, CT: Yale University Press, 1991), p. 81.

4. John Keegan, *A History of Warfare* (New York: Vintage Books, 1993), p. 166.

5. Ibid., pp. 176–177.

6. William H. McNeill, *The Pursuit of Power* (Chicago: University of Chicago Press, 1982), p. 16.

7. Ibid., p. 12.

Chapter 6
Late Antiquity and the Early Middle Ages: Creating a New European Society and Culture (476–1000)

OUR LADY OF VLADIMIR The veneration of icons was central to Byzantine religious life, and Byzantine missionaries brought this practice with them as they spread Christianity throughout Eastern Europe from the ninth century C.E. onward. A masterpiece of Byzantine art, the icon of *Our Lady of Vladimir* was sent from Constantinople to Kiev (Ukraine) in the early twelfth century and was later transferred to Moscow in 1395 to protect the city from Mongol attacks. It depicts a sorrowful Virgin Mary gazing intently at the viewer while the infant Jesus raises his head to his mother's cheek.
SOURCE: Heritage Image Partnership Ltd/Alamy Stock Photo

 ## Contents and Focus Questions

6.4 Western Society and the Developing
Christian Church
*How did the developing Christian church
influence Western society during the early
Middle Ages?*

6.5 The Kingdom of the Franks: From Clovis to
Charlemagne
*How did the reign of Clovis differ from that of
Charlemagne?*

6.6 Feudal Society
What were the characteristics of a feudal society?

The Chapter in Brief

SCHOLARS INCREASINGLY VIEW the six centuries between 250 and 800 C.E. as a single world bounded by the Roman and Persian empires, spreading from Rome to Baghdad. Embracing Late Antiquity and the early Middle Ages, this epoch saw the Western and Eastern empires of Rome alternately decline and recover, separate and mingle, while never succumbing culturally to barbarian and Muslim invaders.

The two parts of the empire went their different ways. The West became increasingly rural as barbarian invasions intensified. The new world emerging in the West by the fifth century and afterward was increasingly made up of isolated units of rural aristocrats and their dependent laborers. Over time, however, a new power established itself in the crumbling empire's northwestern corner. There the Merovingian and Carolingian Franks would weave their own Germanic barbarian heritage together with Judeo-Christian religion, Roman language and law, and Greco-Byzantine administration and culture, creating a Western civilization of their own. The reign of Charlemagne (r. 768–814) saw a modest renaissance of classical antiquity. The peculiar Western social and political forms that emerged at this time—the manor and feudalism—not only coped with unprecedented chaos but also proved to be fertile seedbeds from which distinctive Western political institutions were in time to grow.

In the East, Constantinople—the "New Rome"—became the center of a vital and flourishing culture, which we call **Byzantine**. Many Byzantine cities continued to prosper, and the emperors made their will good over the nobles in the countryside. A strong navy allowed commerce to flourish in the eastern Mediterranean and, in good times, far beyond. When we contemplate the decline and fall of the Roman Empire in the fourth and fifth centuries, we are speaking only of the West. A form of classical culture, shaped by the Christian religion, Roman law, and Eastern artistic influences, persisted in the Byzantine East for a thousand years more.

Further still to the east, an Iranian dynasty, the Sassanians, came to power in Persia and Mesopotamia in the third century, overthrowing the Parthians and creating a powerful empire. For three hundred years, the Sassanians and their Roman/Byzantine neighbors launched repeated outbreaks of bitter warfare against each other in a protracted struggle that left both empires ill-equipped to deal with the emergence of Islam in the early seventh century. Within roughly a century, the successors of Muhammad would overthrow the Sassanians, lay siege to Constantinople, and extend Muslim influence across the Middle East and North Africa into Europe and eventually as far as northern Spain.

* * * * *

The centuries before and after the fall of Rome (476 C.E.) were a vibrant period of self-discovery and self-definition for the peoples just described. Many scholars have called this period—between the end of the ancient world and the birth of the Middle Ages—**Late Antiquity** (250–800). It witnessed a new appropriation of ancient history by Jews, Christians, Muslims, and pagan Germanic and eastern tribes, each of whom competed with one another for their roots in the past (from which they drew authority) and their place in the future (where they would exercise power). In the process, each borrowed the best features of the other. The Jews had long adopted the attractive myths of the ancient Mesopotamians and the Christians the prophecies of the Jews, while the Muslims subordinated both the Jewish and Christian scriptures to God's final, seventh-century revelations to Muhammad, the last of the prophets. The Christian Franks, the most eclectic and enterprising of all, claimed ancestors among the ancient Trojans of Greek myth and Homer's *Iliad*.

In Late Antiquity, these various peoples and their religions borrowed from and bumped into each other for several centuries, as the ancient world evolved into the medieval. In government, religion, language, as well as geography, the Christian West ultimately grew apart from the Byzantine East and the Islamic Arab world. Although divided by states and cultures that became increasingly rigid and competitive over time, the world these peoples inhabited between 250 and 800 was a cohesive one, a world together as well as a world moving apart.

6.1 The Byzantine Empire

How did the Byzantine Empire continue the legacy of Rome?

As we have already seen, by the late third century C.E., the Roman Empire had become too large for a single emperor to govern and was beginning to fail. The emperor Diocletian (r. 284–305) tried to strengthen the empire by dividing it between himself and a co-emperor. The result was a dual empire with an eastern and a western half, each with its own emperor and, eventually, imperial bureaucracy and army. A critical shift of the empire's resources and orientation to the eastern half accompanied these changes. As imperial rule weakened in the West and strengthened in the East, it also became increasingly autocratic.

Diocletian's reign was followed by factional strife. His eventual successor, Constantine the Great (r. 306–337), briefly reunited the empire by conquest (his three sons and their successors would divide it again) and ruled as sole emperor of the eastern and western halves after 324. In that year, he moved the capital of the empire from Rome to Byzantium, an ancient Greek city that stood at the crossroads of the major sea and land routes between Europe and Asia Minor. Here, Constantine built the new city of Constantinople (modern-day Istanbul), which he dedicated in 330. As the imperial residence and the new administrative center of the empire, Constantinople gradually became a "new Rome."

Because of its defensible location, the skill of its emperors, and the firmness and strength of its base in Asia Minor, Constantinople could deflect and repulse barbarian attacks. It remained the sole imperial capital until the close of the eighth century, when the Frankish ruler Charlemagne (r. 768–814) revived the Western empire and reclaimed its imperial title. While in historical usage, the term *Byzantine* indicates the Hellenistic Greek, Roman, and Judaic monotheistic elements that distinguish the culture of the East from the Latin West, the Byzantines continued to refer to themselves and their civilization as "Roman" until its collapse.

Between 324 and 1453, the Byzantine Empire moved from an early period of expansion and splendor to a time of sustained contraction, splintering, and finally catastrophic defeat. Historians divide its history into three distinct periods:

1. From the rebuilding of Byzantium as Constantinople in 324 to the beginning of the Arab expansion and the spread of Islam in 632

2. From 632 to the conquest of Asia Minor by the Seljuk Turks in 1071 or, as some believe, to the fall of Constantinople to the Western Crusaders in 1204

3. From either 1071 or 1204 to the fall of Constantinople to the Ottoman Turks in 1453, the end of the empire

6.1.1 The Reign of Justinian

In terms of territory, political power, and cultural achievement, the first period of Byzantine history (324–632 C.E.) was by far the greatest. (See Map 6–1.) Its pinnacle was the reign of Emperor Justinian (r. 527–565) and his like-minded wife, Empress Theodora (d. 548). A strongman ruler who expected all his subjects—clergy and laity, high and low—to submit absolutely to his hierarchical control, Justinian spent, built, and destroyed on a grand scale. Theodora, the daughter of a circus bear trainer, had been an entertainer in her youth and, if Justinian's tell-all court historian, Procopius, is believed, a prostitute as well. Whatever her background, she possessed an intelligence and toughness that matched and might even have exceeded that of her husband. Theodora was a true co-ruler.

6.1.1.1 CITIES During Justinian's thirty-eight-year reign, the empire's strength lay in its more than 1,500 cities. Constantinople, with perhaps 350,000 inhabitants, was the largest city and the cultural crossroads of Asian and European civilizations. The dominant provincial cities had populations of 50,000. The most popular entertainments were the theater, where, according to clerical critics, nudity and immorality were on display, and the chariot races at the Hippodrome.

Between the fourth and fifth centuries, urban councils of roughly two hundred members known as *decurions*, all local, wealthy landowners, governed the cities. The intellectual and economic elite of the empire, the decurions were heavily taxed, which did not make them the emperor's most docile or loyal servants. By the sixth century, fidelity to the throne had become the coin of the realm, and special governors, lay and clerical, chosen from the landholding classes, replaced the decurion councils as more reliable instruments of the emperor's sovereign will. As the sixth and seventh centuries saw the beginning of new barbarian invasions of the empire from the north and the east, such political tightening was imperative.

6.1.1.2 LAW The imperial goal—as reflected in Justinian's policy of "one God, one empire, one religion"—was to centralize government by imposing legal and doctrinal conformity throughout. To this end, the emperor ordered a collation and revision of Roman law. What Justinian wanted was loyal and docile subjects guided by clear and enforceable laws.

The result was the ***Corpus Juris Civilis*** ("body of civil law"), a three-part compilation undertaken by a committee of the most learned lawyers. The first compilation, known as the *Code*, was completed in 529 and revised in 534; it consisted of imperial edicts issued since the reign of Hadrian (r. 117–138). The second compilation, the *Digest*, gathered the major opinions of the old legal experts. The goal of the third compilation, the *Institutes*, was to put into the hands of young scholars a practical textbook that drew

Map 6–1 THE BYZANTINE EMPIRE AT THE TIME OF JUSTINIAN'S DEATH

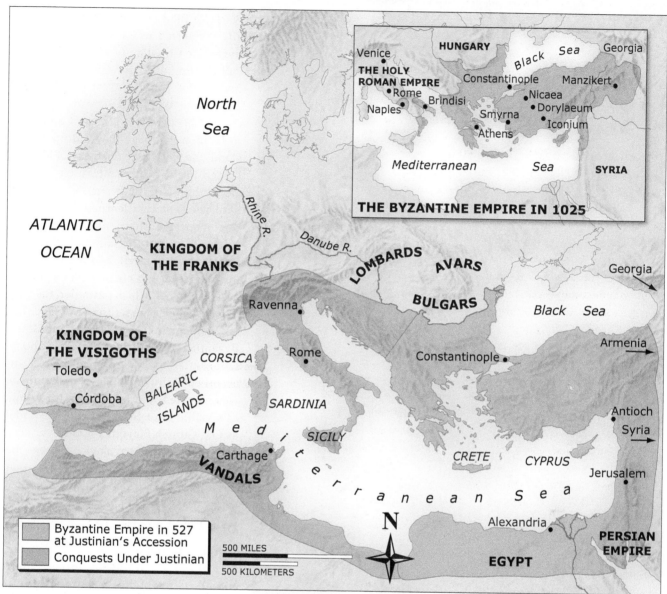

The inset shows the empire in 1025, before its losses to the Seljuk Turks.

its lessons from the *Code* and the *Digest*. Decrees issued by Justinian and his immediate successors after 534 were later assembled in a compilation known as the *Novellae*, or "new things."

In the twelfth century, the *Corpus* began to be actively studied in the West, especially at Bologna in Italy, and gradually laid the foundation for much subsequent European law. Because bringing subjects under the authority of a single sovereign was a fundamental goal of Roman law, rulers seeking to centralize their states especially benefited from Justinian's legal legacy.

6.1.1.3 HAGIA SOPHIA Justinian was also a great builder. At his command and expense, fortifications, churches, monasteries, and palaces arose across the empire. His most famous and enduring monument in stone is the Hagia Sophia (Church of Holy Wisdom) completed in Constantinople in 537. Its key feature is a massive dome, 112 feet in diameter, that, together with the church's many windows, gives the interior a remarkable airiness and luminosity.

6.1.1.4 RECONQUEST IN THE WEST Justinian sought to reconquer the imperial provinces lost to the barbarians in the West. Beginning in 533 c.e., his armies overran the Vandal kingdom in North Africa and Sicily, the Ostrogothic kingdom in Italy, and part of Spain. But the price paid in blood and treasure was enormous, particularly in Italy, where prolonged resistance by the Ostrogoths did not end until 554. By Justinian's death, his empire was financially exhausted, and plague had ravaged the population of Constantinople and much of the East. Although Byzantine rule survived in Sicily and parts of southern Italy until the eleventh century, most

CHURCH OF HAGIA SOPHIA (HOLY WISDOM) Built during the reign of Justinian, Hagia Sophia (Church of Holy Wisdom) is a masterpiece of Byzantine and world architecture. After the Turkish conquest of Constantinople in 1453, Hagia Sophia was transformed into a mosque with four minarets, still visible today.
SOURCE: Steve Vidler/Alamy Stock Photo

of Justinian's Western and North African conquests were soon lost to Lombard invaders from north of the Alps and to the Muslim Arabs.

6.1.2 The Spread of Byzantine Christianity

In the late sixth and seventh centuries, nomadic, pagan tribes of Avars, Slavs, and Bulgars invaded and occupied the Balkan provinces of the Eastern empire, threatening a "dark age" there. More than once, these fierce raiders menaced Constantinople itself. Yet after almost two centuries of intermittent warfare, the Slavs and Bulgars eventually converted to Eastern Orthodoxy or Byzantine Christianity. Hoping to build a cultural-linguistic firewall against menacing Franks from the West who had conquered the Avars and were attempting to convert his people to Roman Catholicism in Latin, a language they did not understand, the Slav Duke Rastislav of Moravia turned in the ninth century C.E. to Constantinople for help. In response, the emperor sent two learned missionaries to convert the Moravians: the brothers, priests, and future saints Constantine, later known as Cyril, and Methodius. In Moravia, the two created a new, Greek-based alphabet, which permitted the Slavs to devise their own written language. That language gave the Christian gospels and Byzantine theology a lasting Slavic home. Later, after the Bulgars conquered and absorbed many of the Slavs, that alphabet was elevated to a broader script known as Cyrillic after St. Cyril. Known today as Old Church Slavonic, it has ever since been the international Slavic language that allowed Byzantine Christianity to penetrate eastern Europe.

6.1.3 Persians and Muslims

During the reign of Emperor Heraclius (r. 610–641 C.E.), the Byzantine Empire turned its attention eastward. Heraclius spent his entire reign resisting Persian and Islamic invasions, the former successfully, the latter in vain. In 628 he defeated the Persian Sassanid king Khosro II and took back one of Western Christendom's great lost relics: a piece of Christ's Cross that Khosro had carried off when he captured Jerusalem in 614. After 632, however, Islamic armies overran much of the empire, directly attacking Constantinople for the first time in the mid-670s. Not until Leo III of the Isaurian dynasty (r. 717–740) did the Byzantines succeed in repelling Arab armies and regaining most of Asia Minor, having lost forever Syria, Egypt, and North Africa. The setback was traumatic and forced a major restructuring of the diminished empire, creating a new system of provincial government under the direct authority of imperial generals.

Following these reforms, a reinvigorated Byzantium went on the offensive, pushing back the Muslims in Armenia and northern Syria. Bulgarian advances into

COURT OF EMPRESS THEODORA Early Byzantine Christian mosaic showing the union of political and spiritual authority in the empress Theodora.
SOURCE: Scala/Art Resource, NY

6.2 Islam and the Islamic World

How did Islamic culture influence the West?

In the seventh century C.E., a drama began to unfold with a new rival far more dangerous to both Byzantium and the West than any had been before: the new faith of **Islam**. By the time of Muhammad's death in 632, Islamic armies were beginning to absorb the attention and the resources of the emperors in Constantinople and the rulers in the West.

At first, the Muslims were both open and cautious. They borrowed and integrated elements of Persian and Greek culture into their own. The new religion of Islam adopted elements of Christian, Jewish, and Arab pagan religious beliefs and practices. Muslims tolerated religious minorities within the territories they conquered as long as those minorities recognized Islamic political rule, refrained from trying to convert Muslims, and paid their taxes. Nonetheless, the Muslims were keen to protect the purity and integrity of Islamic religion, language, and law from any corrupting foreign influence. Over time and after increased conflict with Eastern and Western Christians, this protective tendency grew stronger. Despite significant contacts and exchanges, Islamic culture did not take root as creatively in the West as barbarian and Byzantine cultures did, leaving Islam a strange and threatening religion to many Westerners.

6.2.1 Muhammad's Religion

Muhammad (570–632 C.E.), an orphan, was raised by a family of modest means. As a youth, he worked as a merchant's assistant, traveling the major trade routes. When he was twenty-five, he married a wealthy widow from the city of Mecca, the religious and commercial center of Arabia. Now a wealthy man, Muhammad became a kind of social activist, criticizing Meccan materialism, paganism, and unjust treatment of the poor and needy. At about age forty, a deep religious experience heightened his commitment to reform, and it transformed his life. He began to receive revelations from the angel Gabriel, who recited God's word to him at irregular intervals. These revelations were collected after Muhammad's death into the Islamic holy book, the *Qur'an* (literally, a "reciting"), which his followers compiled between 650 and 651. The basic message Muhammad had received was a summons to all Arabs to submit to God's will. Followers of Muhammad's religion came to be called *Muslim* ("submissive" or "surrendering"); *Islam* itself means "submission."

Byzantium's western provinces were brought to a halt by the fiercest emperor of the dynasty, Basil II (r. 976–1025), known as the "Bulgar-slayer." The internal stability resulting from these military victories led to a flourishing age of art, culture, and literature, personified by the period's philosopher-king, Emperor Constantine VII *Porphyrogenitus* (i.e., born in the "imperial purple"), sole ruler from 945 to 959. But as with Justinian's conquests in the sixth century C.E., the rapid territorial expansion may have overtaxed the empire's strength. In the eleventh century, Byzantine fortunes rapidly reversed. After inflicting a devastating defeat on the Byzantine army at Manzikert in Armenia in 1071, Muslim Seljuk Turks overran most of Asia Minor, from which the Byzantines had drawn most of their tax revenue and troops.

The empire never fully recovered, yet its end—which came when the Seljuks' cousins, the Ottoman Turks, captured Constantinople in 1453—was still almost four centuries away. In 1092, after two decades of steady Turkish advance, the Eastern emperor Alexius I Comnenus (r. 1081–1118) called for Western aid, which helped spark the First Crusade. It also heightened tensions between Latin West and Greek East and exposed the riches of Constantinople to predatory Western eyes. A century later (1204), the Fourth Crusade was diverted from Jerusalem to Constantinople, not, however, to rescue the city, but rather to inflict more damage on it and on the Byzantine Empire than all non-Christian invaders had done before. When the Byzantines eventually recovered the city in 1261, Byzantine power was a shadow of its former self, the empire was impoverished, and the Turks had become a constant threat.

GREAT MOSQUE OF CÓRDOBA The ecclesiastical name of the mosque-cathedral of Córdoba is the Cathedral of Our Lady of the Assumption. Now a Catholic church in the Spanish region of Andalusia, the original structure, known as Great Mosque of Córdoba, was built in 784 under the order of Abd al-Rahman I, the first Emir of Córdoba. Later Muslim rulers expanded this masterpiece of Moorish architecture, doubling its size. It was converted to a Roman Catholic cathedral in 1236 when control of Córdoba returned to Christian Spain after more than 500 years of Muslim rule.
SOURCE: Wim Wiskerk/Alamy Stock Photo

Muhammad's message was not a new one. A long line of Jewish prophets going back to Noah had reiterated it. According to Muslims, however, this line ended with Muhammad who, as the last of God's chosen prophets, became "the Prophet." The *Qur'an* also recognized Jesus Christ as a prophet but denied that he was God's co-eternal and co-equal son. Like Judaism, Islam was a monotheistic and theocentric religion, not a trinitarian one like Christianity.

Mecca was a major pagan pilgrimage site. The *Ka'ba* ("the cube"), which became Islam's holiest shrine, housed a sacred black meteorite that was originally a pagan object of worship. Muhammad's condemnation of idolatry and immorality threatened the trade that flowed from the pilgrims, enraging the merchants of Mecca. Persecuted for their attacks on traditional religion, Muhammad and his followers fled Mecca in 622 for Medina, 240 miles to the north. This event came to be known as the *Hegira* ("flight") and marks the beginning of the Islamic calendar.

In Medina, Muhammad organized his forces and drew throngs of devoted followers. He raided caravans going back and forth to Mecca. He also had his first conflicts with Medina's Jews, who were involved in trade with Mecca. By 624, he was able to conquer Mecca and made it the center of the new religion.

During these years, the basic rules of Islamic practice evolved. True Muslims were expected (1) to be honest and modest in all their dealings and behavior; (2) to be unquestionably loyal to the Islamic community; (3) to abstain from pork and alcohol at all times; (4) to wash and pray facing Mecca five times a day; (5) to contribute to the support of the poor and needy; (6) to fast during daylight hours for one month each year; and (7) to make a pilgrimage to Mecca and visit the Ka'ba at least once in a lifetime. The last requirement reflects the degree to which Islam was an assimilationist religion: It "Islamicized" a major pagan religious practice.

Islam also permitted Muslim men to have up to four wives—provided they treated them all justly and gave each equal attention—and as many concubines as they wished. A husband could divorce a wife with a simple declaration, whereas to divorce her husband, a wife had to show good cause before a religious judge. A wife was expected to be totally loyal and devoted to her husband and to show her face to no man but him. (See the "Compare and Connect" sidebar, which follows below, on the issue of husbands and wives in Christianity and Islam.)

In contrast to Christianity, Islam drew no rigid distinction between the clergy and the laity. A lay scholarly elite developed, however, and held moral authority within Islamic society in domestic and religious matters. This elite, known as the *ulema*, or "persons with correct knowledge," served a social function similar to that of a professional priesthood or rabbinate. Its members were men of great piety and obvious learning whose opinions came to have the force of law in Muslim society. They also ensured that Muslim rulers adhered to the letter of the *Qur'an*.

6.2.2 Islamic Diversity

The success of Islam lay in its ability to unify and inspire tribal Arabs and other non-Jewish and non-Christian people. Islam also appealed to Arab pride, for it deemed Muhammad to be history's major religious figure and his followers to be God's chosen people.

As early as the seventh century c.e., however, disputes arose among Muslims over the nature of Islamic society and authority within it that left permanent divisions. Disagreement over the true line of succession to Muhammad—the **caliphate**—was one source of discord. Another related disagreement was over doctrinal issues involving the extent

Compare and Connect

The Battle of the Sexes in Christianity and Islam

IN EARLY CHRISTIANITY man and woman were viewed as one and the same offspring, Eve born of Adam—the reason they were drawn irresistibly to one another forever. They were so tightly bound that what one did to the other, one also did to oneself.

DISPUTING HUSBAND AND WIFE Muslims are enjoined to live by the *Shari'a*, or divine law, and have the right to have disputes settled by an arbiter of the Shari'a. Here we see a husband complaining about his wife before the *qadi*, the state-appointed judge. The wife, backed by two other women, points an accusing finger at her husband. In such cases, the first duty of the qadi, who should be a learned person of faith, is to try to effect a reconciliation before the husband divorces his wife or the wife herself seeks a divorce.

SOURCE: Bibliothèque Nationale de France, Paris

This special bond between husband and wife made their relationship caring and charitable.

Muhammad's role as a husband was by all accounts exemplary: a spouse who dealt shrewdly and fairly with his wives and a splendid role model for Muslim men. According to the *Qur'an*, conflict between husband and wife must first be resolved by talking, and that failing, by the husband's departure from the marital bed. Heeding the example of the Prophet and the teachings of the *Qur'an*, devout Muslim men viewed hitting their wives as a last resort in resolving conflict. Yet, when a wife flagrantly disobeyed her husband (called *nashiz*) or, much worse, was unfaithful to him, hitting often became the husband's, and society's condoned, first response.

Before Reading

- Highlight the details that confirm or negate St. John Chrysostom's view that the bond between husband and wife in Christian marriage is reciprocal.
- Compare the statements about Muslim marriage cited by the chronicler al-Ghazali.
- Consider why more emphasis is placed on the husband's behavior toward his wife in the Muslim marriage source.

Questions

1. How does the marriage bond differ in the Christian and Muslim faiths? What does it mean to Christians to say that husband and wife are one flesh? Is that also the way spouses are perceived in Islam?

2. How successful is male discipline of himself and of his wife in Islam? Is Christian marriage too egalitarian, and hence more vulnerable to failure?

3. If marriage is a mirror of religion, what does it reveal about Christianity and Islam?

I. CHRISTIAN MARRIAGE

St. John Chrysostom (347–407) elaborated the relationship between Christian spouses in his Homily on Christian Spouses: *"Wives, be subject to your husbands, as to the Lord. . . . Husbands, love your wives as Christ loved the Church" (Ephesians 5:22–25).*

There is no relationship between human beings so close as that of husband and wife, if they are united as they ought to be. . . . God did not fashion woman independently from man. . . . [N]or did He enable woman to bear children without man. . . . He made the one man Adam to be the origin of all mankind, both male and female, and made it impossible for men and women to be self-sufficient [without one another]. . . .

The love of husband and wife is [thus] the force that wields society together. . . . Why else would [God] say, "Wives, be subject to your husbands?" Because when harmony prevails, the children are raised well, the household is kept in order . . . and great benefits, both for families and for states, results. . . .

Having seen the amount of obedience necessary, hear now about the amount of love that is needed. [If] you want your wife to be obedient to you . . . then be responsible for the same providential care of her as Christ has for the Church. Even if you see her belittling you, or despising and mocking you . . . subject her to yourself through affection, kindness, and your great regard for her. . . . One's partner for life, the mother of one's children, the source of one's every joy, should never be fettered with fear and threats, but with love and patience. . . . What sort of satisfaction could a husband have, if he lives with his wife as if she were a slave and not a woman [there] by her own free will. [So] suffer anything for her sake, but never disgrace her, for Christ never did this with the Church. . . .

A wife should never nag her husband [saying] "You lazy coward, you have no ambition! Look at our relatives and neighbors; they have plenty of money. Their wives have far more than I do." Let no wife say any such thing; she is her husband's body, and it is not for her to dictate to her head, but rather to submit and obey. . . . Likewise, if a husband has a wife who behaves this way, he must never exercise his authority by insulting and abusing her.

II. MUSLIM MARRIAGE

Chronicler Abu Hamid al-Ghazali (1058–1111), writing in Ihya'Ulum *(2:34–35), in the eleventh century, elaborates the teaching of Qur'an (4:34): "Men are the protectors and maintainers of women because God has given [men] more strength. . . . and because they support [women] from their means."*

Treating women well and bearing their ill treatment [is] required for marriage. . . . God said, "keep them good company." [Among] the last things the Messenger [Muhammad] recommended was to take care of your slaves. Do not burden them with things beyond their capacity, and observe God's exhortations relating to your wives, for they are like slaves in your hands. You took them in trust from God and made them your wives by His words. . . .

One should know that treating one's wife well does not only mean not harming her; it also means to endure ill treatment and be patient when she gets angry and loses her temper, a [method] the Messenger used to forgive his wives who argued with him and turned away from him for the whole day. . . .

'A'ishah [a wife of the Prophet] once got angry and said to the Prophet . . . "You, who claims to be the Prophet of God!" The Messenger of God smiled and tolerated her in the spirit of forgiveness and generosity. . . . It is believed that the first love story in Islam was that of Prophet Muhammad and 'A'ishah. The Prophet used to say to his other wives: "Do not upset me by saying bad things about 'A'ishah, for she is the only woman in whose company I have received the revelation [of God]! Anas [Ibn Malik, a ninth-century chronicler] reported that the Prophet was the most compassionate person in matters concerning women and children. . . .

Respond to [as he did to women's] harshness by teasing, joking, and kidding them, for it is certain this softens women's hearts. The Prophet said, "The people with the most perfect faith are those with the best ethics and those who are the kindest toward their families." Umar [a companion of the Prophet and the second caliph of Islam] once said: "One should always be like a child with his family, but when they need him they should find [in him] a man."

SOURCES: (I) From Don S. Browning et al., *Sex, Marriage, and Family in World Religions* (New York: Columbia University Press, 2009), pp. 106–108. (II) From Browning, *Sex, Marriage, and Family,* pp. 190–91, 194–95.

to which Islam was an inclusive religion, open to sinners as well as to the virtuous. Several groups emerged from these disputes. The most radical was the Kharijites, whose leaders seceded from the camp of the caliph Ali (656–661) because Ali compromised with his enemies on a matter of principle. Righteous and judgmental, the Kharijites wanted all but the most rigorously virtuous Muslims excluded from the community of the faithful. In 661, a Kharijite assassinated Ali.

Another, more influential group was the *Shi'a*, or "partisans of Ali" (*Shi'at Ali*). The Shi'a looked on Ali and his descendants as the rightful successors of Muhammad not only by kinship but also by the expressed will of the

PLAYING THE LUTE Picture of a Muslim and a Christian playing the *ud*, or lute, together, displayed in the thirteenth-century *Book of Chants* in the Escorial Monastery of Madrid. Medieval Europe was deeply influenced by Arab–Islamic culture, transmitted particularly from Spain. Some of the many Arabic works on musical theory were translated into Latin and Hebrew, but the main Islamic influence on music came from the singing and playing spread by minstrels.

SOURCE: Monasterio de El Escorial, El Escorial, Spain/Index/Bridgeman Art Library

Prophet himself. To the Shi'a, Ali's assassination revealed the most basic truth of a devout Muslim life: A true *imam*, or "ruler," must expect to suffer unjustly even unto death in the world and so, too, must his followers. A distinctive theology of martyrdom has ever since been a mark of Shi'a teaching. And the Shi'a, until modern times, have been an embattled minority within mainstream Islamic society.

A third group, which has been dominant for most of Islamic history, was the majority centrist **Sunnis** (followers of *sunna*, or "tradition"). Sunnis have always placed loyalty to the community of Islam above all else and have spurned the exclusivism and purism of the Kharijites and the Shi'a.

6.2.3 Islamic Empires

Under Muhammad's first three successors—the caliphs Abu Bakr (r. 632–634 C.E.), Umar (r. 634–644), and Uthman (r. 644–655)—Islam expanded by conquest throughout the southern and eastern Mediterranean into territories mostly still held today by Islamic states. In the eighth century, Muslim armies occupied parts of Spain in the West and of India in the East, producing a truly vast empire. (See Map 6–2.) The capital of this empire moved, first from Mecca to Damascus in Syria and then, in 750, to Baghdad in Iraq after the Abbasid dynasty replaced the Umayyads in a struggle for the caliphate. Thereafter, the huge Muslim Empire gradually broke up into separate states, some with their own line of caliphs claiming to be the true successors of Muhammad.

The early Muslim conquests would not have been so rapid and thorough had the contemporary Byzantine and Persian empires not been exhausted by decades of war. The Muslims struck at both empires in the 630s, completely overrunning the Persian Empire by 651. Most of the inhabitants in Byzantine Syria and Palestine, although Christian, were Semites like the Arabs. Any religious unity they felt with the Byzantine Greeks may have been offset by hatred of the Byzantine army of occupation and by resentment of Constantinople's efforts to impose Greek "orthodox" beliefs on the Monophysite churches of Egypt and Syria. As a result, many Egyptian and Syrian Christians, hoping for deliverance from Byzantine oppression, appear to have welcomed the Islamic conquerors.

Although Islam gained converts from among the Christians in the Near East, North Africa, and Spain, its efforts to invade northern Europe were rebuffed. The ruler of the Franks, Charles Martel, defeated a raiding party of Arabs on the western frontier of Europe at Poitiers (today in central France) in 732. This victory and the failure to capture Constantinople ended any Arab effort to expand into Western or central Europe.

Map 6–2 MUSLIM CONQUESTS AND DOMINATION OF THE MEDITERRANEAN TO ABOUT 750 C.E.

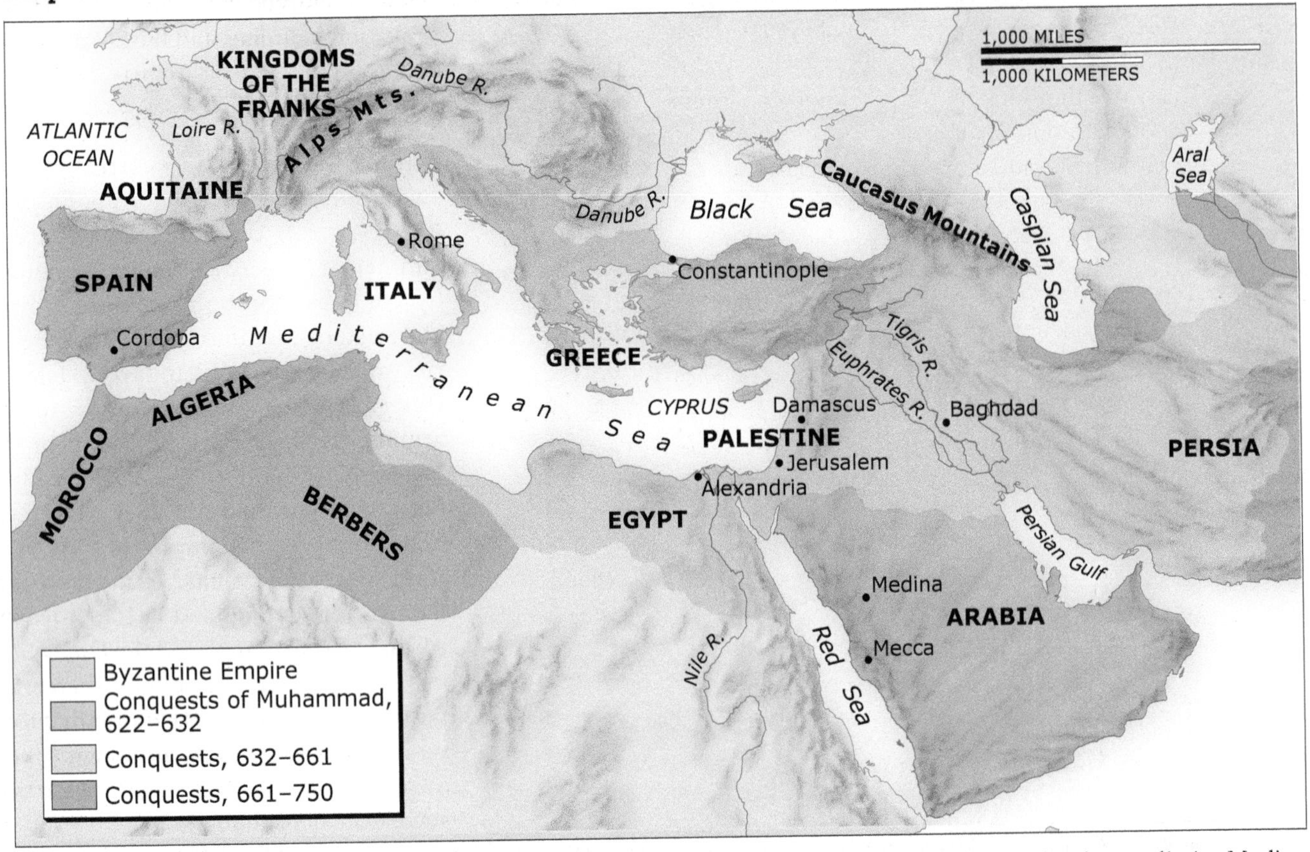

The rapid spread of Islam (both as a religion and as a political-military power) is shown here. Within 125 years of Muhammad's rise, Muslims came to dominate Spain and all areas south and east of the Mediterranean.

6.2.4 Byzantium's Contribution to Islamic Civilization

With the slowdown of Muslim expansion, commerce and exchange with Byzantium intensified. The caliphates of Islam regarded Byzantium as a model. The splendor of court culture and ceremony was adopted from the Byzantines with the intent to intimidate and impress. Byzantine architecture and craftsmanship were much admired, and Byzantine art and iconography formed a foundation for later Arab illuminations and artwork.

Arab empire builders were curious about earlier peoples and wished to associate themselves with an older tradition of authority. In the Byzantines, they saw the greatest challenge to the legitimacy of the Islamic Empire. The Muslims also wanted to understand their faith in intellectual terms. From these diverse motives there developed considerable interest in Ancient Greek learning, particularly in works on logic, philosophy, and medicine. A great deal of translation was underway by the ninth century C.E., facilitated by such learned figures as the Caliph Ma'mun (r. 813–833). Texts were acquired from Byzantium; commentaries by Arab scholars noted that Christianity had suppressed the study of these same works for religious reasons.

6.2.5 The European Debt to Islam

Arab invasions and their presence in the Mediterranean area during the early Middle Ages contributed both directly and indirectly to the formation of Western Europe. They did so indirectly by driving Western Europeans back to their native tribal and inherited Judeo-Christian, Greco-Roman, and Byzantine elements, from which they had created a Western culture of their own. Also, by diverting the attention and energies of the Byzantine Empire during the formative centuries, the Arabs may have prevented it from expanding into and reconquering Western Europe. That allowed two Germanic peoples to gain ascendancy: first the Franks and then the Lombards, who invaded Italy in the sixth century C.E. and settled in the Po valley around the city of Milan.

Despite the hostility of the Christian West to the Islamic world, there was nonetheless much creative interchange between these two different cultures, and the West profited greatly and directly from it. At this time, Arab civilizations were the more advanced, enjoying their golden age, and they had much to teach a toddling West. Between the eighth and tenth centuries, Córdoba, the capital of Muslim Spain, was a model multicultural city embracing Arabs, Berbers from North Africa, Christian converts to Islam, and Jews. Córdoba was a conduit for the finest Arabian tableware, leather, silks, dyes, aromatic ointments, and perfumes into the West. The Arabs taught Western farmers how to irrigate fields and Western artisans how to tan leather and refine silk. The West also gained from its contacts with Arabic scholars. Thanks to the skills of Islamic scholars, ancient Greek works on astronomy, mathematics, and medicine became available in Latin to Westerners. Down to the sixteenth century, the basic gynecological and child-care manuals guiding the work of Western midwives and physicians were compilations by the Baghdad physician Al-Razi (Rhazes, ca 854–935)., the philosopher and physician Ibn Sina (Avicenna, 980–1037), and Ibn Rushd (known in the West as Averroës, 1126–1198), who was also Islam's greatest authority on Aristotle. Jewish scholars also thrived amid the intellectual culture Islamic scholars created. The greatest of them, Moses Maimonides (1135–1204), wrote in both Arabic and Hebrew.

6.3 On the Eve of the Frankish Ascendancy

How did Germanic migrations contribute to the fall of the Roman Empire?

The city of Rome and the Western empire were already in decline in the late third and fourth centuries, well before the barbarian invasions in the West began. Suffering from internal political and religious quarrels and geographically distant from the crucial military fronts in Syria and along the Danube River, Rome declined in importance, and was even replaced as the imperial residence in 286 C.E. by Milan in northern Italy. In 402, the seat of Western government would be moved to another northern Italian city, Ravenna, a seaport on the Adriatic that was protected on the landward side by impenetrable marshes. When the barbarian invasions of non-Roman Germanic and eastern peoples began in the late fourth century, the West was in political and economic disarray, and imperial power and prestige had shifted decisively to Constantinople and the East.

Facing barbarian invasions from the north and east and a strong Islamic presence in the Mediterranean, the West found itself in decline during the fifth and sixth centuries. As trade waned, cities rapidly fell on hard times, depriving the West of centers for the exchange of goods and ideas that might enable it to look and live beyond itself. As Western shipping declined in the Mediterranean, urban populations that otherwise would have engaged in trade-related work left the cities for the countryside in ever greater numbers. The **villa**, a fortified country estate, became the basic unit of life. There, *coloni*, or tenant farmers, gave their services to the local magnate in return for economic assistance and protection from both barbarians and imperial officials. Many

cities shrank to no more than tiny walled fortresses ruled by military commanders and bishops. The upper classes moved to the country and asserted an ever-greater independence from imperial authority. The failure of the central authority to maintain the roads and the constant danger from bands of robbers curtailed trade and communications, forcing greater self-reliance and a more primitive lifestyle.

Furthermore, in the seventh century, the Byzantine emperors had their hands full with the Islamic threat in the East and were unable to assert themselves in the West, leaving most of the region to the Franks and the Lombards. As a result, Western Europeans now had to rely on their native Greco-Roman, Judeo-Christian, and barbarian heritages as they put together a distinctive culture of their own.

6.3.1 Germanic Migrations

Before the massive migrations from the north and the east, Roman and Germanic cultures had commingled peacefully for centuries. The Romans had "imported" barbarians as servants, slaves, and soldiers. Barbarian soldiers commanded Roman legions.

Beginning in 376 C.E. with a great influx of Visigoths, or "west Goths," into the empire, this peaceful coexistence ended. The Visigoths, accomplished horsemen and fierce warriors, were themselves pushed into the empire by the emergence of a notoriously violent people, the Huns, from what is now Mongolia. The Visigoths ultimately reached southern Gaul and Spain. Soon to be Christianized, they won rights of settlement and material assistance within the empire from the Eastern emperor Valens (r. 364–378) in exchange for defending the eastern frontier as *foederati*, or the emperor's "special" allies. Instead of the promised assistance, however, the Visigoths received harsh treatment from their new allies. After repeated conflicts, the Visigoths rebelled and overwhelmed Valens at the Battle of Adrianople in 378.

Thereafter, the Romans passively permitted the settlement of barbarians within the heart of the Western empire. The Vandals crossed the Rhine in 406 and within three decades gained control of northwest Africa and much of the Mediterranean. The Burgundians, who came on the heels of the Vandals, settled in Gaul. Most important for subsequent Western history were the Franks, who settled northern and central Gaul, some along the seacoast (the Salian Franks) and others along the Rhine, Seine, and Loire Rivers (the Ripuarian Franks).

Why was there so little Roman resistance to these Germanic tribes, whose numbers—at most 100,000 people in the largest of them—were comparatively small? The invaders were successful because they came in rapid succession upon a badly overextended Western empire divided politically by ambitious military commanders and weakened by decades of famine, pestilence, and overtaxation. By the second half of the fourth century, Roman frontiers had become too vast to manage. Efforts to do so by "barbarizing" the Roman army, that is, by recruiting many peasants into it and by making the Germanic tribes key Roman allies, only weakened it further. The Eastern empire retained enough wealth and vitality to field new armies or to buy off the invaders. The Western empire, in contrast, succumbed not so much because of moral decay and materialism, as was once believed, but because of a combination of military rivalry, political and economic mismanagement, and disease.

6.3.2 New Western Masters

In the early fifth century C.E., Italy and the "eternal city" of Rome suffered devastating blows. In 410 the Visigoths, under Alaric (ca. 370–410), sacked Rome. In 452, the Huns, led by Attila—the "scourge of God"—invaded Italy. Rome was sacked still again, in 455—this time by the Vandals.

By the mid-fifth century, power in Western Europe had passed decisively from the hands of the Roman emperors to those of barbarian chieftains. In 476, the traditional date historians give for the fall of the Roman Empire, the barbarian Odoacer (ca. 434–493) deposed the last Western emperor Romulus Augustulus. The Eastern emperor Zeno (r. 474–491) recognized Odoacer's authority in the West, and

Odoacer acknowledged Zeno as sole emperor, content to serve as Zeno's Western viceroy. In a later coup in 493, Theodoric (ca. 454–526), king of the Ostrogoths, or "east Goths," replaced Odoacer. Theodoric then governed with the full acceptance of the Roman people, the emperor in Constantinople, and the Christian church.

By the end of the fifth century, the barbarians from west and east had saturated the Western empire. The Ostrogoths settled in Italy, the Franks in northern Gaul, the Burgundians in Provence, the Visigoths in southern Gaul and Spain, the Vandals in Africa and the western Mediterranean, and the Angles and Saxons in England. (See Map 6–3.)

These barbarian military victories did not, however, obliterate Roman culture; Western Europe's new masters were willing to learn from the people they had conquered. They admired Roman culture and had no desire to destroy it. Except in Britain and northern Gaul, Roman law; Roman government; and Latin, the Roman language; coexisted with the new Germanic institutions. In Italy under Theodoric, tribal custom gradually gave way to Roman law. Only the Vandals and the pagan Anglo-Saxons—and, after 466, the Visigoths—refused to profess at least titular obedience to the emperor in Constantinople.

Map 6–3 BARBARIAN MIGRATIONS INTO THE WEST IN THE FOURTH AND FIFTH CENTURIES

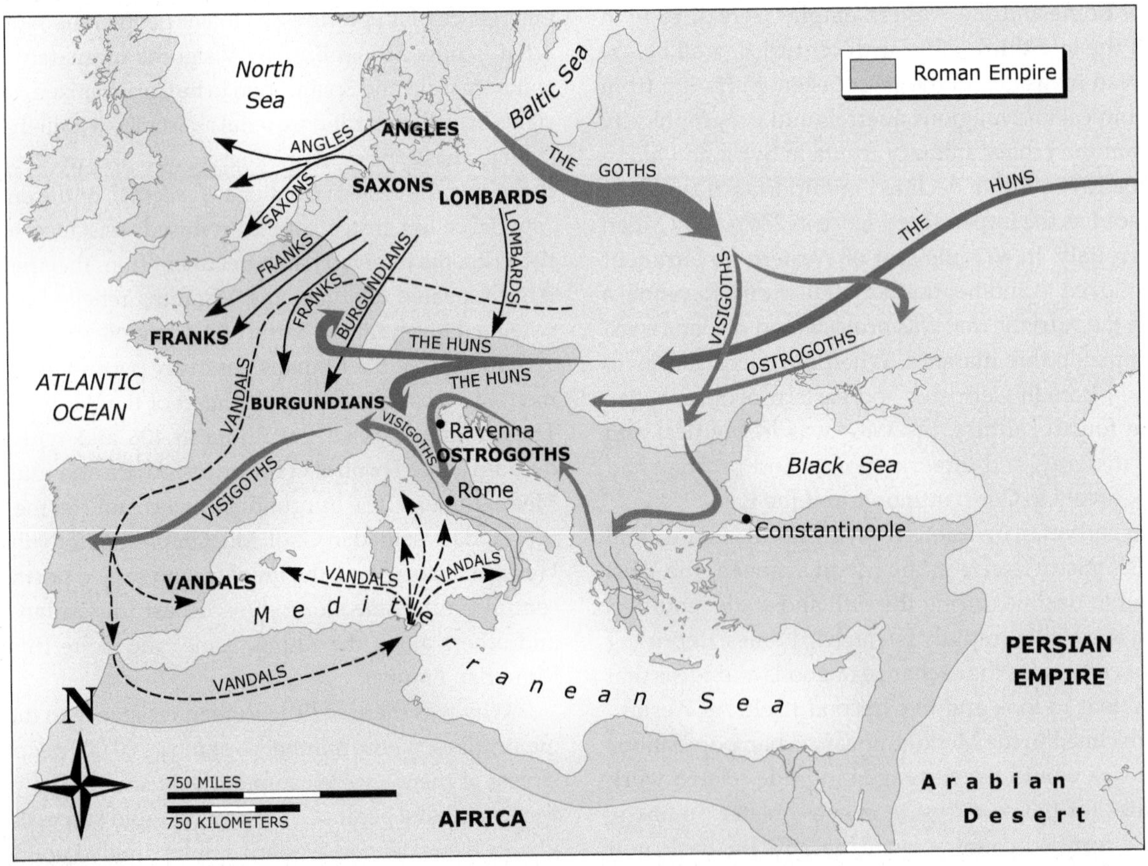

The forceful intrusion of Germanic and non-Germanic barbarians into the Roman Empire from the last quarter of the fourth century through the fifth century created a constantly changing pattern of movement and relations. The map shows the major routes taken by the usually unwelcome newcomers and the areas most deeply affected by the main groups.

The Visigoths, the Ostrogoths, and the Vandals had entered the West as Christians, which helped them accommodate to Roman culture. They were, however, Arians, followers of a version of Christianity that had been condemned as heresy at the Council of Nicaea in 325. Later, around 500, the Franks, who had settled in Gaul, would convert to the Nicene, or "Catholic," form of Christianity supported by the bishops of Rome. As we will see, the Franks ultimately dominated most of Western Europe, helping convert the Goths and other barbarians to Roman Christianity.

A gradual interpenetration of two strong cultures—a creative tension—marked the period of the Germanic migrations. Despite Western military defeat, many Roman cultural traditions remained powerfully entrenched, and the Goths and the Franks became far more romanized than the Romans were germanized. The Latin language, Nicene Catholic Christianity, and eventually Roman law and government would triumph in the West during the Middle Ages.

6.4 Western Society and the Developing Christian Church

How did the developing Christian church influence Western society during the early Middle Ages?

One institution remained firmly entrenched and increasingly powerful within the declining cities of the waning Western Roman Empire: the Christian church. The church had long modeled its own structure on that of the imperial Roman administration. Like the imperial government, church government was centralized and hierarchical. Strategically placed "generals" (bishops) in European cities looked for spiritual direction to their leader, the bishop of Rome. As the Western empire crumbled, Roman governors withdrew and populations emigrated to the countryside, where the resulting vacuum of authority was filled by local bishops and cathedral chapters. The local cathedral became the center of urban life and the local bishop the highest authority for those who remained in the cities. In Rome, on a larger and more fateful scale, the pope took control of the city as the Western emperors gradually departed and died out. Left to its own devices, Western Europe soon discovered that the Christian church was its best repository of Roman administrative skills and classical culture.

Challenged by Rome's decline to become a major political force, the Christian church survived the period of Germanic and Islamic invasions as a somewhat spiritually weakened and compromised institution. Yet it remained a potent civilizing and unifying force. The church had a

religious message of providential purpose and individual worth that could give solace and meaning to life at its worst. It had a ritual of baptism and a creed, or statement of belief, that united people beyond the traditional barriers of social class, education, and gender. Alone in the West, the church retained an effective hierarchical administration, scattered throughout the old empire, staffed by the best educated minds in Europe, and centered in emperor-less Rome.

6.4.1 Monastic Culture

Throughout Late Antiquity the Christian church gained the services of growing numbers of monks, who were not only loyal to its mission but also objects of great popular respect. Monastic culture proved again and again to be the peculiar strength of the church during the Middle Ages.

The first monks were hermits who had withdrawn from society to pursue a more perfect way of life. Inspired by Christian ideals, they led a life of complete self-denial in imitation of Christ. The popularity of **monasticism** began to grow as Roman persecution of Christians waned and Christianity became the favored religion of the empire during the fourth century. Monasticism replaced martyrdom as the most perfect way to imitate Christ and to confess one's faith.

Christians came to view monastic life—embracing, as it did, the biblical "counsels of perfection" (chastity, poverty, and obedience)—as the purest form of religious practice, going beyond the baptism and creed that identified ordinary believers. This view evolved during the Middle Ages into a belief in the general superiority of the clergy and in the church's mission over the laity and the state. That belief served the papacy in later confrontations with secular rulers.

Anthony of Egypt (ca. 251–356 C.E.), the father of hermit monasticism, was inspired by Jesus's command in the Gospels to the rich young ruler: "If you will be perfect, sell all that you have, give it to the poor, and follow me" (Matthew 19:21). Anthony went into the desert to pray and work, setting an example followed by hundreds in Egypt, Syria, and Palestine in the fourth and fifth centuries.

Hermit monasticism was soon joined by the development of communal monasticism. In the first quarter of the fourth century, Pachomius (ca. 286–346) organized monks in southern Egypt into a highly regimented community in which monks shared a life of labor, order, and discipline enforced by a strict penal code. Such monastic communities grew to contain a thousand or more inhabitants. They were little "cities of God," trying to separate themselves from the collapsing Roman Empire and the nominal Christian world. Basil the Great (329–379) popularized communal monasticism throughout the East, providing a less severe rule than Pachomius, one that directed monks into such worldly services as caring for orphans, widows, and the infirm in surrounding communities.

Athanasius (ca. 293–373) and Martin of Tours (ca. 315–399) introduced monasticism to the West. The teachings of John Cassian (ca. 360–435) and Jerome (ca. 340–420) then helped shape the basic values and practices of Western monasticism. The great organizer of Western monasticism, however, was Benedict of Nursia (ca. 480–547). In 529, he established a monastery at Monte Cassino in Italy, founding the form of monasticism—Benedictine—that bears his name and quickly came to dominate in the West. It eventually replaced an Irish, non-Benedictine monasticism that was common until the 600s in the British Isles and Gaul.

Benedict wrote a *Rule of St. Benedict*, a sophisticated and comprehensive plan for every activity of the monks, even detailing the manner in which they were to sleep. His *Rule* opposed the severities of earlier monasticism that tortured the body and anguished the mind. Benedict insisted on good food and even some wine, adequate clothing, and proper amounts of sleep and relaxation. Periods of devotion (about four hours each day) were set aside for the "work of God." That is, regular prayers, liturgical activities, and study alternated with manual labor (farming). This program permitted not a moment's idleness and carefully nurtured the religious, intellectual, and physical well-being of the cloistered monks. The monastery was directed by an abbot, whose command the monks had to obey unquestioningly.

Individual Benedictine monasteries remained autonomous until the later Middle Ages, when the Benedictines became a unified order of the church. During the early Middle Ages, Benedictine missionaries Christianized both England and Germany. Their disciplined organization and devotion to hard work made the Benedictines an economic and political power as well as a spiritual force wherever they settled.

6.4.2 The Doctrine of Papal Primacy

Constantine and his successors, especially the Eastern emperors, ruled religious life with an iron hand and consistently looked on the church as little more than a department of the state. Such political assumption of spiritual power involved the emperor directly in the church's affairs, allowing him to play the theologian and to summon councils to resolve its doctrinal quarrels. At first, state control of religion was also the rule in the West. Most of the early popes were mediocre and not very influential. To increase their influence, in the fifth and sixth centuries, they took advantage of imperial weakness and distraction to develop a new defense: the powerful weaponry of papal primacy. This doctrine raised the Roman pope, or pontiff, to unassailable supremacy within the church when it came to defining church doctrine. It also put him in a position to make important secular claims, paving the way to repeated conflicts between church and state, pope and emperor, throughout the Middle Ages.

Papal primacy was first asserted as a response to the decline of imperial Rome. It was also a response to the claims of the patriarchs of the Eastern church, who, after imperial power was transferred to Constantinople, looked on the bishop of Rome as an equal, but no superior. In 381 C.E., the ecumenical Council of Constantinople declared the bishop of Constantinople to be of first rank after the bishop of Rome "because Constantinople is the new Rome." In 451, the ecumenical Council of Chalcedon recognized Constantinople as having the same religious primacy in the East as Rome had possessed in the West. By the mid-sixth century, the bishop of Constantinople described himself in his correspondence as a "universal" patriarch.

Roman pontiffs, understandably jealous of such claims and resentful of the political interference of Eastern emperors, launched a counteroffensive. Pope Damasus I (r. 366–384)[1] took the first of several major steps in the rise of the Roman church when he declared a Roman "apostolic" primacy. Pointing to Jesus's words to Peter in the Gospel of Matthew (16:18), "Thou art Peter, and upon this rock I will build my church," he claimed himself and all other popes to be Peter's direct successors as the unique "rock" on which the Christian church was built. Pope Leo I (r. 440–461) took still another fateful step by assuming the title *pontifex maximus,* or "supreme priest." He further proclaimed himself to be endowed with a "plenitude of power," thereby establishing the supremacy of the bishop of Rome over all other bishops. During Leo's reign, an imperial decree recognized his exclusive jurisdiction over the Western church. At the end of the fifth century, Pope Gelasius I (r. 492–496) proclaimed the authority of the clergy to be "more weighty" than the power of kings because priests had charge of divine affairs and the means of salvation.

Events as well as ideology favored the papacy. As barbarian and Islamic invasions isolated the West by diverting the attention of the Byzantine Empire, they also prevented both emperors and the Eastern patriarchs from interfering in the affairs of the Western church. Islam may even be said to have "saved" the Western church from Eastern domination. At the same time, the Franks became a new political ally of the church. Eastern episcopal competition with Rome ended as bishopric after bishopric fell to Islamic armies in the East. The power of the exarch of Ravenna—the Byzantine emperor's viceroy in the West—was eclipsed in the late sixth century by invading Lombards who conquered most of Italy. Thanks to Frankish prodding, the Lombards became Nicene Christians loyal to Rome and a new counterpart to Eastern power and influence in the West. In an unprecedented act, Pope Gregory I, "the Great" (r. 590–604), instead of looking for protection to the emperor in Constantinople, negotiated an independent peace treaty with the Lombards.

6.4.3 The Religious Division of Christendom

In both East and West, religious belief alternately served and undermined imperial political unity. Since the fifth century C.E., the patriarch of Constantinople had blessed Byzantine emperors in that city (the "second Rome"), attesting to the close ties between rulers and the Eastern church. In 391, Christianity became the official faith of the Eastern empire, while all other religions and sects were deemed "demented and insane."[2] Between the fourth and sixth centuries, the patriarchs of Constantinople, Alexandria, Antioch, and Jerusalem received generous endowments of land and gold from rich, pious donors, empowering the church to act as the state's welfare agency.

While orthodox Christianity was the religion that mattered most, it was not the only religion in the empire with a significant following. Nor did Byzantine rulers view religion as merely a political tool. From time to time, Christian heresies also received imperial support. Moreover, with imperial encouragement, Christianity absorbed pagan religious practices and beliefs that were too deeply rooted in rural and urban cultures to be eradicated, thus turning local gods and their shrines into Christian saints and holy places. (See "Encountering the Past: Two Roman Festivals" in Chapter 4.)

The empire was also home, albeit inhospitably, to large numbers of Jews. Pagan Romans viewed Jews as narrow, dogmatic, and intolerant but tolerated Judaism as an ancient and acceptable form of worship. When Rome adopted Christianity, Jews continued to have legal protection as long as they did not attempt to convert Christians, build new synagogues, or try to hold certain official positions or enter some professions. Whereas Justinian, the emperor most intent on religious conformity within the empire, encouraged Jews to convert voluntarily, later emperors commanded them to be baptized and gave them tax breaks as incentives to become Christians. However, neither persuasion nor coercion succeeded in converting the empire's Jews.

The differences between Eastern and Western Christianity grew. One issue even divided Justinian and his wife Theodora. Whereas Justinian remained strictly orthodox in his Christian beliefs, Theodora supported a divisive Eastern teaching that the Council of Chalcedon in 451 had condemned as heresy: namely, that Christ had a single, immortal nature and was not both eternal God and mortal man in one and the same person. In reaction to this controversy, orthodox Christianity became even more determined to protect the sovereignty of God. This concern is apparent in Byzantine art, which portrays Christ as impassive and transcendent, as united in his personhood with God, not as a suffering mortal man. In the sixth century, despite imperial persecution, the **Monophysites** became a

separate church in the East where many Christians adhere to it still today.

A similar dispute appeared in Eastern debates over the relationship among the members of the Trinity, specifically whether the Holy Spirit proceeded only from the Father, as the Nicene-Constantinopolitan Creed taught, or from the Father and the Son (*filioque* in Latin), an idea that became increasingly popular in the West and was eventually adopted by the Western church and inserted into its creed. These disputes, which appear trivial and are almost unintelligible to many people today, were vitally important to many Christians at the time. Eastern theologians argued that adding filioque to the creed not only diminished God's majesty by seeming to subordinate the Holy Spirit but also weakened a core Christian belief—the divine unity and dignity of all three persons of the Trinity. Some perceive here a hidden political concern important in the East. By protecting the unity and majesty of God the Father, Eastern theology also safeguarded the unity and majesty of the emperor himself, from whom all power on earth was believed properly to flow. The idea of a divisible Godhead, no matter how abstract and subtle, was unacceptable to Eastern Christians and the imperial government because it also suggested the divisibility of imperial power—not a tenet for an emperor who closely associated himself with God.

Another major rift between the Christian East and West was over the veneration of images in worship. In 726, Emperor Leo III (r. 717–741) forbade the use of images and icons that portrayed Christ, the Virgin Mary, and the saints throughout Christendom. As the veneration of images had been commonplace for centuries, the decree came as a shock, especially to the West, where it was rejected as heresy: **iconoclasm**, as the change in policy was called, drove the popes into the camp of the Franks, where they found in Charlemagne an effective protector against the Byzantine world. Although images were eventually restored in the Eastern churches, many masterpieces were lost during a near century of theology-inspired destruction.

A third difference between East and West was the Eastern emperors' pretension to absolute sovereignty, both secular and religious. Expressing their sense of sacred mission, the emperors presented themselves in the trappings of holiness and directly interfered in matters of church and religion: This is called **Caesaropapism**, or the emperor acting as if he were pope as well as caesar. To a degree unknown in the West, Eastern emperors appointed and manipulated the clergy, convening church councils and enforcing church decrees. By comparison, the West nurtured a distinction between church and state that became visible in the eleventh century.

The Eastern church also rejected several disputed requirements of Roman Christianity. It denied the existence of Purgatory; permitted lay divorce and remarriage; allowed

ICONOCLASM This page from the "Chludov' Psalter"—a book of psalms—was illuminated by an anonymous monk in the middle of the ninth century. It is one of only three Byzantine psalters to survive from the ninth century. This illustration, perhaps the target of an iconoclastic purge, appears to have been deliberately defaced. **SOURCE:** Heritage Image Partnership Ltd/Alamy Stock Photo

priests, but not bishops, to marry; and conducted religious services in the languages that people in a given locality actually spoke (the so-called "vernacular" languages) instead of Greek and Latin. In these matters, Eastern Christians gained opportunities and rights that Christians in the West would not enjoy, and then only in part, until the Protestant Reformation in the sixteenth century.

Having piled up over the centuries, these differences between East and West ultimately resulted in a schism between the two churches in 1054. In that year, a Western envoy of the pope, Cardinal Humbertus, visited the Patriarch of Constantinople, Michael Cerularius, in the hope of overcoming the differences that divided Christendom. The patriarch was not, however, welcoming. Relations between the two men quickly deteriorated, and cardinal and patriarch engaged in mutual recriminations and insults. Before leaving the city, Humbertus left a bull of excommunication on the altar of Hagia Sophia. In response, the patriarch proclaimed all Western popes to have been heretics since

the sixth century! Nine hundred and eleven years would pass before this breach was repaired. In a belated ecumenical gesture in 1965, a Roman pope met with the patriarch of Constantinople to revoke the mutual condemnations of 1054.

6.5 The Kingdom of the Franks: From Clovis to Charlemagne

How did the reign of Clovis differ from that of Charlemagne?

A warrior chieftain, Clovis (ca. 466–511 C.E.), who converted to Catholic Christianity around 496, founded the first Frankish dynasty: the Merovingians, named for Merovich, an early leader of one branch of the Franks. Clovis and his successors united the Salian and Ripuarian Franks, subdued the Arian Burgundians and Visigoths, and established the kingdom of the Franks within ancient Gaul, making the Franks and the Merovingian kings a significant force in Western Europe. The Franks themselves occupied a broad belt of territory that extended throughout modern France, Belgium, the Netherlands, and western Germany, and their loyalties remained strictly tribal and local.

KEY POLITICAL AND RELIGIOUS DEVELOPMENTS OF THE EARLY MIDDLE AGES	
313	Emperor Constantine issues the Edict of Milan
325	Council of Nicaea defines Christian doctrine
451	Council of Chalcedon further defines Christian doctrine
451–453	Europe is invaded by the Huns under Attila
476	Odoacer deposes last Western emperor and rules as king of the Romans
489–493	Theodoric establishes kingdom of Ostrogoths in Italy
529	Benedict founds monastery at Monte Cassino
533	Justinian codifies Roman law
533–554	Byzantines reconquer parts of the Western empire
622	Muhammad flees Mecca (Hegira)
711	Muslims invade Spain
732	Charles Martel defeats Muslims at Poitiers
754	Pope Stephen II and Pepin III ally

6.5.1 Governing the Franks

In attempting to govern their sprawling kingdom, the Merovingians encountered what proved to be the most persistent problem of medieval political history—the competing claims of the "one" and the "many." On the one hand, the king struggled for a centralized government and transregional loyalty, and on the other, powerful local magnates strove to preserve their regional autonomy and traditions.

The Merovingian kings addressed this problem by making pacts with the landed nobility and by creating the royal office of counts. The counts were men without possessions to whom the king gave great lands in the expectation that they would be, as the landed aristocrats often were not, loyal officers of the kingdom. Like local aristocrats, however, the Merovingian counts also let their immediate self-interest gain the upper hand. Once established in office for a period of time, they, too, became territorial rulers in their own right, so the Frankish kingdom progressively fragmented into independent regions and tiny principalities. The Frankish custom of dividing the kingdom equally among the king's legitimate male heirs furthered this fragmentation.

Rather than purchasing allegiance and unity within the kingdom, the Merovingian largess simply occasioned the rise of competing magnates and petty tyrants, who became laws unto themselves within their regions. By the seventh century, the Frankish king was king in title only and had no effective executive power. Real power became concentrated in the office of the "mayor of the palace," spokesperson at the king's court for the great landowners of the three regions into which the Frankish kingdom was divided: Neustria, Austrasia, and Burgundy. Through this office, the Carolingian dynasty rose to power.

The Carolingians controlled the office of the mayor of the palace from the time that Pepin I of Austrasia (d. 639) rose to the position until 751, when, with the enterprising connivance of the pope, they simply seized the Frankish crown. Pepin II (d. 714) ruled in fact, if not in title, over the Frankish kingdom. His illegitimate son, Charles Martel ("the Hammer," d. 741), created a great cavalry by bestowing lands known as **benefices**, or **fiefs**, on powerful noblemen. In return, they agreed to be ready to serve as the king's army. This army defeated the Muslims at Poitiers in 732.

The fiefs so generously bestowed by Charles Martel to create his army came in large part from landed property he usurped from the church. His alliance with the landed aristocracy in this grand manner permitted the Carolingians to have some measure of political success where the Merovingians had failed. The Carolingians created counts almost entirely from among the same landed nobility from which the Carolingians themselves had risen. The Merovingians, in contrast, had tried to compete directly with these great aristocrats by raising landless men to power. By playing to strength rather than challenging it, the Carolingians strengthened themselves, at least for the short term. The church, by this time dependent on the protection of the Franks against the Eastern emperor and the Lombards, could only suffer the loss of its lands in silence. Later, the Franks partially compensated the church for these lands, although they never returned them.

The church came to play a large and enterprising role in the Frankish government. By Carolingian times, monasteries were a dominant force. Their intellectual achievements made them respected centers of culture. Their religious teaching and example imposed order on surrounding populations. Their relics and rituals made them magical shrines to which pilgrims came in great numbers. Also, thanks to their many gifts and internal discipline and industry, many monasteries had become profitable farms and landed estates, their abbots rich and powerful magnates. Already in Merovingian times, the higher clergy were employed along with counts as royal agents.

AACHEN CATHEDRAL The Aachen Cathedral is a Roman Catholic church in Aachen, Germany, and one of the oldest cathedrals in Europe. The building uses two main architectural styles, Carolingian-Romanesque and Gothic. It contains the tomb of the Emperor Charlemagne (742–814), who ordered its construction. The work on the central part of the cathedral, the Palatine Chapel, began around 796. After the canonization of Charlemagne by Frederick Barbarossa in 1165, the cathedral became an important site of pilgrimage.
SOURCE: Andrew Moss/Alamy Stock Photo

It was the policy of the Carolingians, perfected by Charles Martel and his successor, Pepin III ("the Short," d. 768), to use the church to pacify conquered neighboring tribes—Frisians, Thüringians, Bavarians, and especially the Franks' archenemies, the Saxons. Conversion to Nicene Christianity became an integral part of the successful annexation of conquered lands and people. Christian bishops in missionary districts and elsewhere became lords, appointed by and subject to the king. This ominous integration of secular and religious policy planted the seeds of the investiture controversy of the eleventh and twelfth centuries.

The church served more than Carolingian territorial expansion. Pope Zacharias (r. 741–752) also sanctioned Pepin the Short's termination of the Merovingian dynasty and supported the Carolingian accession to outright kingship of the Franks. With the pope's public blessing, Pepin was proclaimed king by the nobility in council in 751.

Zacharias's successor, Pope Stephen II (r. 752–757), did not let Pepin forget the favor of his predecessor. In 753, when the Lombards besieged Rome, Pope Stephen crossed the Alps and appealed directly to Pepin to cast out the invaders and to guarantee papal claims to central Italy, largely dominated at this time by the Eastern emperor. As already noted, in 754 during the controversy over icons, the Franks and the church formed an alliance against the Lombards and the Eastern emperor. Carolingian kings became the protectors of the Catholic Church and thereby "kings by the grace of God." Pepin gained the title *patricius Romanorum*, "patrician of the Romans," a title first borne by the ruling families of Rome and heretofore applied to the representative of the Eastern emperor. In 755, the Franks defeated the Lombards and gave the pope the lands surrounding Rome, creating what came to be known as the **Papal States**.

The papacy had looked to the Franks for an ally strong enough to protect it from the Eastern emperors. Ironically, the church found in the Carolingian dynasty a Western imperial government that drew almost as slight a boundary between state and church and between secular and religious policy as did Eastern emperors. Although Carolingian patronage was eminently preferable to Eastern domination for the popes, it proved in its own way to be no less constraining.

THE CAROLINGIAN DYNASTY (751–987 C.E.)	
751	Pepin III "the Short" becomes king of the Franks
755	Franks protect church against Lombards and create the Papal States
768–814	Charlemagne rules as king of the Franks
774	Charlemagne defeats Lombards in northern Italy
ca. 775	Donation of Constantine protests Frankish domination of church
800	Pope Leo III crowns Charlemagne emperor
814–840	Louis the Pious succeeds Charlemagne as emperor
843	Treaty of Verdun partitions the Carolingian Empire
911	Last Carolingian emperor (Louis the Child) dies
962	Saxons under Otto I established as successors to Carolingians in Germany

6.5.2 The Reign of Charlemagne (768–814)

Charlemagne, the son of Pepin the Short, continued the role of his father as papal protector in Italy and his policy of territorial conquest in the north. After decisively defeating King Desiderius and the Lombards of northern Italy in 774 C.E., Charlemagne took upon himself the title "King of the Lombards." He widened the frontiers of his kingdom further by subjugating surrounding pagan tribes, foremost among them the Saxons, whom the Franks brutally Christianized and dispersed in small groups throughout Frankish lands. The Muslims were chased beyond the Pyrenees, and the Avars (a tribe related to the Huns) were practically annihilated, bringing the Danubian plains into the Frankish orbit.

CHARLEMAGNE ENTHRONED This image in high-relief of Charlemagne is part of the *Karlsschrein* (Shrine of Charlemagne), located in the Palatine Chapel of Aachen Cathedral. An expensive reliquary commissioned by Frederick II, Emperor of the Holy Roman Empire, it was completed in 1215. The composition is highly symbolic: Charlemagne is seated on his royal throne directly below Christ, the source of his regal authority, with Pope Leo III on his right and Archbishop Turpin of Rheims on his left.
SOURCE: Steve Vidler/Alamy Stock Photo

By the time of his death on January 28, 814, Charlemagne's kingdom embraced modern France, Belgium, Holland, Switzerland, almost the whole of western Germany, much of Italy, a portion of Spain, and the island of Corsica. (See Map 6–4.)

6.5.2.1 THE NEW EMPIRE Encouraged by his ambitious advisers, Charlemagne came to harbor imperial designs. He desired to be not only king of all the Franks but a universal emperor as well. He had his sacred palace city, Aachen (in French, Aix-la-Chapelle), near the modern border between Germany and France, constructed to imitate the courts of the ancient Roman and contemporary Eastern emperors. Although he permitted the church its independence, he looked after it with a paternalism almost as

great as that of any Eastern emperor. He used the church, above all, to promote social stability and hierarchical order throughout the kingdom—as an aid in the creation of a great Frankish Christian Empire. Frankish Christians were ceremoniously baptized, professed the Nicene Creed (with the *filioque* clause), and learned in church to revere Charlemagne.

The formation of a distinctive Carolingian Christendom was made clear in the 790s C.E., when Charlemagne issued the so-called *Libri Carolini*. These documents attacked the Second Council of Nicaea, which, in what was actually a friendly gesture to the West, had met in 787 to formulate a new, more accommodating position for the Eastern church on the use of icons in worship. "No compromise" was Charlemagne's message to the East.

Map 6–4 THE EMPIRE OF CHARLEMAGNE TO 814

Building on the successes of his predecessors, Charlemagne greatly increased the Frankish domains. Such traditional enemies as the Saxons and the Lombards fell under his sway.

Charlemagne fulfilled his imperial pretensions on Christmas Day, 800, when Pope Leo III (r. 795–816) crowned him emperor in Rome. This event began what would come to be known as the **Holy Roman Empire**, a revival of the old Roman Empire in the West, based in Germany after 870.

In 799, Pope Leo III had been imprisoned by the Roman aristocracy but escaped to the protection of Charlemagne, who restored him as pope. The fateful coronation of Charlemagne was thus, in part, an effort by the pope to enhance the church's stature and to gain some leverage over this powerful king. It was, however, no papal coup d'état; Charlemagne's control over the church remained as strong after as before the event. If the coronation benefited the church, as it certainly did, it also served Charlemagne's purposes.

Before his coronation, Charlemagne had been a minor Western potentate in the eyes of Eastern emperors. After the coronation, Eastern emperors reluctantly recognized his new imperial dignity, and Charlemagne even found it necessary to disclaim ambitions to rule as emperor over the East.

6.5.2.2 THE NEW EMPEROR

Charlemagne stood a majestic six feet three and a half inches tall—a fact confirmed when his tomb was opened and exact measurements of his remains were taken in 1861. He was restless, ever ready for a hunt. Informal and gregarious, he insisted on the presence of friends even when he bathed. He was widely known for his practical jokes, lusty good humor, and warm hospitality. Aachen was a festive palace city to which people and gifts came from all over the world. In 802 C.E., Charlemagne even received from the caliph of Baghdad, Harun-al-Rashid, a white elephant, whose transport across the Alps was as great a wonder as the creature itself.

Charlemagne had five official wives in succession, as well as many mistresses and concubines, and he sired numerous children. This connubial variety created special problems. His oldest son by his first marriage, Pepin, jealous of the attention shown by his father to the sons of his second wife and fearing the loss of paternal favor, joined noble enemies in a conspiracy against his father. He spent the rest of his life in confinement in a monastery after the plot was exposed.

6.5.2.3 PROBLEMS OF GOVERNMENT

Charlemagne governed his kingdom through counts, of whom there were perhaps as many as 250, strategically located within the administrative districts into which the kingdom was divided. Carolingian counts tended to be local magnates who possessed the armed might and the self-interest to enforce the will of a generous king. Counts had three main duties: to maintain a local army loyal to the king, to collect tribute and dues, and to administer justice throughout their districts.

This last responsibility a count undertook through a district law court known as the *mallus*. The mallus received testimony from witnesses familiar with the parties involved in a dispute or criminal case, much as a modern court does. Through such testimony, the mallus sought to discover the character and believability of each side. On occasion, in difficult cases where the testimony was insufficient to determine guilt or innocence, recourse would be taken through judicial duels or a variety of "divine" tests or ordeals. Among these was the length of time it took a defendant's hand to heal after immersion in boiling water. In another, a defendant was thrown with his hands and feet bound into a river or pond that a priest had blessed. If he floated, he was pronounced guilty because the pure water had obviously rejected him; if, however, the water received him and he sank, he was deemed innocent and quickly retrieved.

In such ordeals God was believed to render a verdict. Once guilt had been made clear to the mallus, either by testimony or by ordeal, it assessed a monetary compensation to be paid to the injured party. This most popular way of settling grievances usually ended hostilities between individuals and families.

As in Merovingian times, many counts used their official position and new judicial powers to their own advantage and became little despots within their districts. As the strong became stronger, they also became more independent. They began to look on the land grants with which they were paid as hereditary possessions rather than generous royal donations—a development that began to fragment Charlemagne's kingdom. Charlemagne tried to oversee his overseers and improve local justice by creating special royal envoys. Known as *missi dominici*, these were lay and clerical agents (counts, archbishops, and bishops) who made annual visits to districts other than their own. Yet their impact was marginal. Permanent provincial governors, bearing the title of prefect, duke, or margrave, were created in yet another attempt to supervise the counts and organize the outlying regions of the kingdom. Yet as these governors became established in their areas, they proved no less corruptible than the others.

Charlemagne never solved the problem of creating a loyal bureaucracy. Ecclesiastical agents proved no better than secular ones in this regard. Landowning bishops had not only the same responsibilities but also the same secular lifestyles and aspirations as the royal counts. Save for their attendance to the liturgy and to church prayers, they were largely indistinguishable from the lay nobility. *Capitularies*, or royal decrees, discouraged the more outrageous behavior of the clergy. However, Charlemagne also sensed, and rightly so as the Gregorian reform of the eleventh century would prove, that the emergence of a distinctive, reform-minded class of ecclesiastical landowners would be a danger to royal government. He purposefully treated his bishops as he treated his counts, that is, as **vassals** who served at the king's pleasure.

To be a Christian in this period was more a matter of ritual and doctrine (being baptized and reciting the creed) than of following rules for ethical behavior and social service. Both clergy and laity were more concerned with contests over the most basic kinds of social protections than with more elevated ethical issues. An important legislative achievement of Charlemagne's reign, for example, was to give a free vassal the right to break his oath of loyalty to his lord if the lord tried to kill him, reduce him to an unfree **serf**, withhold promised protection in time of need, or seduce his wife.

6.5.2.4 ALCUIN AND THE CAROLINGIAN RENAISSANCE
Charlemagne accumulated great wealth in the form of loot and land from conquered tribes. He used part of this booty to attract Europe's best scholars to Aachen, where they developed court culture and education. By making scholarship materially as well as intellectually rewarding, Charlemagne attracted such scholars as Theodulf of Orleans, Angilbert, his own biographer Einhard, and the renowned Anglo-Saxon master Alcuin of York (735–804 c.e.). In 782, at almost fifty years of age, Alcuin became director of the king's palace school. He brought classical and Christian learning to Aachen in schools run by the monasteries. Alcuin was handsomely rewarded for his efforts with several monastic estates, including that of Saint Martin of Tours, the wealthiest in the kingdom.

Although Charlemagne also appreciated learning for its own sake, his grand palace school was not created simply for the love of classical scholarship. Charlemagne wanted to upgrade the administrative skills of the clerics and officials who staffed the royal bureaucracy. By preparing the sons of the nobility to run the religious and secular offices of the realm, court scholarship served kingdom building. The school provided basic instruction in the seven liberal arts, with special concentration on grammar, logic, rhetoric, and the basic mathematical arts. It therefore provided training in reading, writing, speaking, sound reasoning, and counting—the basic tools of bureaucracy.

Among the results of this intellectual activity was the appearance of a more accurate Latin in official documents and the development of a clear style of handwriting known as *Carolingian minuscule*. By making reading both easier and more pleasurable, Carolingian minuscule helped lay the foundations of subsequent Latin scholarship. It also increased lay literacy.

A modest renaissance of antiquity occurred in the palace school as scholars collected and preserved ancient manuscripts for a more curious posterity. Alcuin worked on a correct text of the Bible and made editions of the works of Gregory the Great and the monastic *Rule of St. Benedict*. These scholarly activities aimed at concrete reforms and helped bring uniformity to church law and liturgy, educate the clergy, and improve monastic morals. Through personal correspondence and visitations, Alcuin created a genuine, if limited, community of scholars and clerics at court. He did much to infuse the highest administrative levels with a sense of comradeship and common purpose.

6.5.3 Breakup of the Carolingian Kingdom

In his last years, an ailing Charlemagne knew his empire was ungovernable. The seeds of dissolution lay in regionalism, that is, the determination of each region, no matter how small, to look first—and often only—to its own self-interest. Despite his skill and resolve, Charlemagne's realm became too fragmented among powerful regional magnates. Although they were Charlemagne's vassals, they were also landholders and lords in their own right. They knew their sovereignty lessened as Charlemagne's increased, and accordingly they became reluctant royal servants. In feudal society, a direct relationship existed between physical proximity to authority and loyalty to authority. Local people obeyed local lords more readily than they obeyed a glorious, but distant, king.

Charlemagne had been forced to recognize and even to enhance the power of regional magnates to gain needed financial and military support. But as in the Merovingian kingdom, the tail came increasingly to wag the dog in the Carolingian.

6.5.3.1 LOUIS THE PIOUS
The Carolingian kings did not give up easily, however. Charlemagne's only surviving son and successor was Louis the Pious (r. 814–840 c.e.), so-called because of his close alliance with the church and his promotion of puritanical reforms. Before his death, Charlemagne secured the imperial succession for Louis by raising him to "co-emperor" in a grand public ceremony. After Charlemagne's death, Louis no longer referred to himself as king of the Franks. He bore instead the single title of emperor. The assumption of this title reflected not only the Carolingian pretense to be an imperial dynasty but also Louis's determination to unify his kingdom and raise its people above mere regional and tribal loyalties.

A Closer Look

The *Lindau Gospels*: A Multicultural Book Cover

CAROLINGIAN EDUCATION, ART, and architecture served royal efforts to unify the kingdom by fusing inherited Celtic–Germanic and Greco–Roman–Byzantine cultures. Charlemagne, his son, and grandsons decorated their churches with a variety of art forms, among them illuminated manuscripts, such as the bejeweled metalwork that became the binding of the *Lindau Gospels* (ca. 870).

On surrounding panels, angels in heaven and Christ's mortal followers on earth writhe with grief

The Christ seen here reflects early Christian art and Byzantine theology, which did not endow divinity with human suffering. So impassive is this Christ that he seems almost to smile on the cross.

Precious stones are set on tiny pedestals to maximize the luster illuminating the crucified Christ

JEWELED BINDING OF THE *LINDAU GOSPELS*
SOURCE: The Morgan Library & Museum/Art Resource, NY

Questions

1. Does the inclusiveness exhibited on the *Lindau Gospels'* book cover suggest a shared heritage among Celts, Germans, Greeks, Romans, and Byzantines?
2. How does the composite of ancient cultures on the book cover compare with actual historical relations in the ninth century?
3. Since the nonsuffering Christ on the book cover presents a distinctive Byzantine icon, does it imply a common heritage among the Celts, Germans, Greeks, Romans, and Byzantines? Do the agonizing figures on the book cover (both angels and humans) represent other religious traditions that prefer a suffering Christ upon the cross?

Unfortunately, Louis's own fertility joined with Salic, or Frankish, law and custom to prevent the attainment of this high goal. Louis had three sons by his first wife. According to Salic law, a ruler partitioned his kingdom equally among his surviving sons. (Salic law forbade women to inherit the throne.) Louis, who saw himself as an emperor and no mere king, recognized that a tripartite kingdom would hardly be an empire and acted early in his reign, in 817, to break this legal tradition. This he did by making his eldest son, Lothar (d. 855), co-regent and sole imperial heir by royal decree. To Lothar's brothers he gave important, but much lesser, *appanages*, or assigned hereditary lands: Pepin (d. 838) became king of Aquitaine, and Louis II, known as "the German" (d. 876), became king of Bavaria, over the eastern Franks.

In 823, Louis's second wife, Judith of Bavaria, bore him a fourth son, Charles, later called "the Bald" (d. 877). Mindful of Frankish law and custom, and determined her son should receive more than just a nominal inheritance, the queen incited the brothers Pepin and Louis against Lothar, who fled for refuge to the pope. More important, Judith was instrumental in persuading Louis to adhere to tradition and divide the kingdom equally among his four living sons. As their stepmother and the young Charles rose in their father's favor, the three brothers, fearing still further reversals, decided to act against their father. Supported by the pope, they joined forces and defeated their father in a battle near Colmar in 833.

As the bestower of crowns on emperors, the pope had an important stake in the preservation of the revived Western empire and the imperial title. Louis's belated agreement to an equal partition of his kingdom threatened to weaken the pope as well as the royal family. Therefore, the pope condemned Louis and restored Lothar to his original inheritance. But Lothar's regained imperial dignity only stirred anew the resentments of his brothers, including his stepbrother, Charles, who joined in renewed warfare against him.

6.5.3.2 THE TREATY OF VERDUN AND ITS AFTERMATH

In 843 c.e., with the Treaty of Verdun, peace finally came to the surviving heirs of Louis the Pious. (Pepin had died in 838.) The great Carolingian Empire was divided into three equal parts. Lothar received a middle section, known as Lotharingia, which embraced roughly modern Holland, Belgium, Switzerland, Alsace-Lorraine, and Italy. Charles the Bald acquired the western part of the kingdom, or roughly modern France. And Louis the German took the eastern part, or roughly modern Germany. (See Map 6–5.)

Although Lothar retained the imperial title, the universal empire of Charlemagne and Louis the Pious ceased to exist after Verdun. Not until the sixteenth century, with the election in 1519 of Charles I of Spain as Holy Roman emperor Charles V, would the Western world again see a kingdom as vast as Charlemagne's.

The Treaty of Verdun proved to be only the beginning of Carolingian fragmentation. When Lothar died in 855, his middle kingdom was divided equally among his three surviving sons, the eldest of whom, Louis II, retained Italy and the imperial title. This partition of the partition sealed the dissolution of the great empire of Charlemagne.

Map 6–5 THE TREATY OF VERDUN, 843, AND THE TREATY OF MERSEN, 870

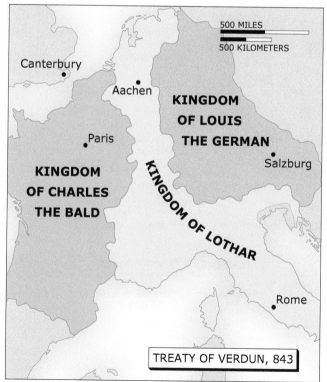

TREATY OF VERDUN, 843

TREATY OF MERSEN, 870

The Treaty of Verdun divided the kingdom of Louis the Pious among his three feuding children: Charles the Bald, Lothar, and Louis the German. After Lothar's death in 855, his lands and titles were divided among his three sons: Louis, Charles, and Lothar II. When Lothar II, who had received his father's northern kingdom, died in 870, Charles the Bald and Louis the German claimed the middle kingdom and divided it between themselves in the Treaty of Mersen.

Henceforth, Western Europe saw an eastern and a western Frankish kingdom—roughly Germany and France—at war over parts of the middle kingdom, a contest that continued into modern times.

In Italy, the demise of the Carolingian emperors enhanced for the moment the power of the popes, who had become adept at filling vacuums. The popes were now strong enough to excommunicate weak emperors and override their wishes. In a major church crackdown on the polygyny of the Germans, Pope Nicholas I (r. 858–867) excommunicated Lothar II for divorcing his wife. After the death of the childless emperor Louis II in 876, Pope John VIII (r. 872–882) installed Charles the Bald as emperor against the express last wishes of Louis II.

When Charles the Bald died in 877, both the papal and the imperial thrones suffered defeat. They became pawns in the hands of powerful Italian and German magnates, respectively. The last Carolingian emperor died in 911. This internal political breakdown of the empire and the papacy coincided with new barbarian attacks. Neither pope nor emperor knew dignity and power again until a new Western imperial dynasty—the Saxons—attained dominance during the reign of Otto I (r. 962–973).

6.5.3.3 VIKINGS, MAGYARS, AND MUSLIMS Late ninth- and tenth-century Europe saw successive waves of Normans (North-men), better known as Vikings, from Scandinavia; Magyars, or Hungarians, the great horsemen from the eastern plains; and Muslims from the south. (See Map 6–6.) The political breakdown of the Carolingian Empire coincided with these new external threats, probably set off by overpopulation and famine in northern and eastern Europe. Taking to the sea in rugged longboats of doubled-hulled construction, the Vikings terrified their neighbors to the south, invading and occupying English and European coastal and river towns. In the 880s, the Vikings even penetrated to Aachen and besieged Paris.

In the ninth century, the Vikings transformed York in northern England into a major trading post for their woolens, jewelry, and ornamental wares. Erik the Red made it to Greenland, and his son, Leif Erikson, wintered in Newfoundland and may even have reached New England 500 years before Columbus. In the eleventh century, Christian conversions and the English defeat of the Danes and Norwegians effectively restricted the Vikings to their Scandinavian homelands.

Map 6–6 VIKING, MAGYAR, AND MUSLIM INVASIONS TO THE ELEVENTH CENTURY

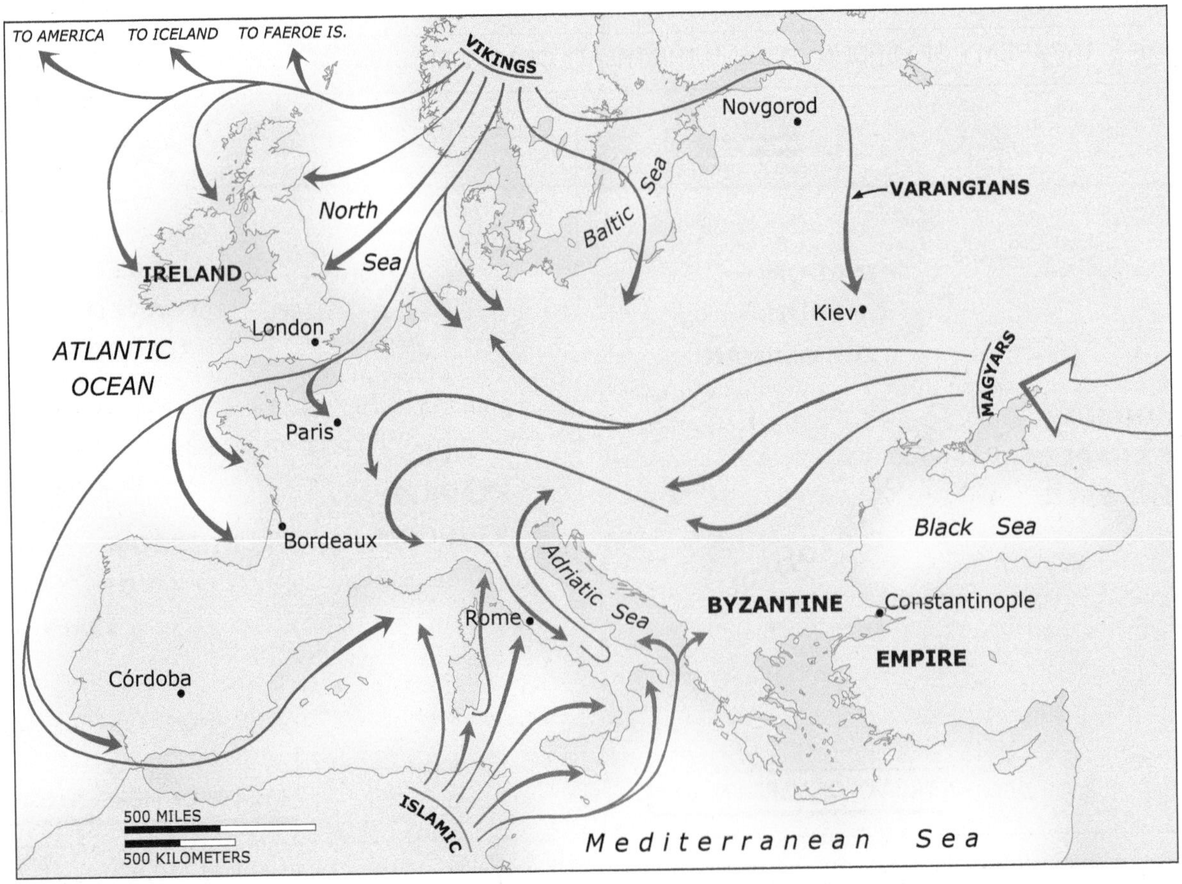

Western Europe was sorely beset by new waves of outsiders from the ninth to the eleventh centuries. From north, east, and south, a stream of invading Vikings, Magyars, and Muslims brought the West at times to near collapse and, of course, gravely affected institutions within Europe.

VIKING BURIAL SHIP This 75-foot-long Viking burial ship from the early ninth century is decorated with beastly figures. It bore a dead queen, her servant, and assorted sacrificed animals to the afterlife. The bodies of the passengers were confined within a burial cabin at midship surrounded with a treasure trove of jewels and tapestries.
SOURCE: Greg Balfour Evans/Alamy Stock Photo

Magyars, the ancestors of the modern Hungarians, swept into Western Europe from the eastern plains, while Muslims made incursions across the Mediterranean from North Africa. The Franks built fortified towns and castles in strategic locations, and when they could, they bought off the invaders with grants of land and payments of silver. In the resulting turmoil, local populations became more dependent than ever on local strongmen for life, limb, and livelihood—the essential precondition for the maturation of feudal society.

6.6 Feudal Society

What were the characteristics of a feudal society?

The Middle Ages were characterized by a chronic absence of effective central government and the constant threat of famine, disease, and foreign invasion. In this state of affairs, the weaker sought the protection of the stronger, and the true lords and masters became those who could guarantee immediate security from violence and starvation. The term **feudal society** refers to the social, political, military, and economic system that emerged from these conditions.

The feudal society of the Middle Ages was dominated by warlords. What people needed most was the assurance that others could be depended on in time of dire need. Lesser men pledged themselves to powerful individuals—warlords or princes—recognizing them as personal superiors and promising them faithful service. Large warrior groups of vassals sprang up and ultimately developed into a prominent professional military class with its own code of knightly conduct. The result was a network of relationships based on mutual loyalty that enabled warlords to acquire armies and to rule over territory, whether they owned land or had a royal title. The emergence of these extensive military organizations—warlords and their groups of professional military vassals—was an adaptation to the absence of strong central government and the predominance of a noncommercial, rural economy.

6.6.1 Origins

Following the modern authority on the subject, the late French historian Marc Bloch, historians distinguish the cruder forms of feudal government that evolved during the early Middle Ages from the sophisticated institutional arrangements by which princes and kings consolidated their territories and established royal rule during the High Middle Ages (the so-called second feudal age).

The origins of feudal government can be found in the divisions and conflicts of Merovingian society. In the sixth and seventh centuries C.E., it became customary for individual freemen who did not already belong to families or groups that could protect them to place themselves under the protection of more powerful freemen. In this way, the latter built up armies and became local magnates, and the former solved the problem of simple survival. Freemen who so entrusted themselves to others came to be described as **vassals**, *vassi* or "those who serve," from which evolved the term *vassalage*, meaning the placement of oneself in the personal service of another who promises protection in return.

Landed nobles, like kings, tried to acquire as many such vassals as they could because military strength in the early Middle Ages lay in numbers. Because it proved impossible to maintain these growing armies within the lord's own household (as was the original custom) or to support them by special monetary payments, the practice evolved of simply granting them land as a "tenement." Vassals were expected to dwell on these benefices, or fiefs, and maintain horses, armor, and weapons in good order. Originally, vassals therefore were little more than gangs-in-waiting.

6.6.2 Vassalage and the Fief

Vassalage involved "fealty" to the lord. To swear **fealty** was to promise to refrain from action that might in any way threaten the lord's well-being and to perform personal services for him on his request. Chief among the expected services of a vassal was military duty as a mounted knight. This could involve a variety of activities: a short or long military expedition, escort duty, standing castle guard, or placing his own fortress at the lord's disposal, if the vassal had one. Continuous bargaining and bickering occurred over the terms of service. Limitations were placed on the number of days a lord could require services from a vassal. In France in the eleventh century, about forty days of service a year were considered sufficient. It also became possible for vassals to buy their way out of military service by a monetary payment, known as **scutage**. The lord, in turn, could use this payment to hire mercenaries, who often proved more efficient than contract-conscious vassals.

Beyond military duty, the vassal was also expected to advise his lord upon request and to sit as a member of his court when it was in session. The vassal also owed his lord financial assistance when his lord was in obvious need or distress: for example, if his lord were captured and needed to be ransomed or when he was outfitting himself for a crusade or a major military campaign. Also, gifts of money might be expected when the lord's daughters married or when his sons became knights.

Beginning with the reign of Louis the Pious (r. 814–840 C.E.), bishops and abbots swore fealty to the king and received their offices from him as a benefice. The king formally "invested" these clerics in their offices during a special ceremony in which he presented them with a ring and a staff, the symbols of high spiritual office. Earlier, Louis's Frankish predecessors had confiscated church lands with only modest and belated compensation to the church. This practice was long a sore point with the church, and lay investiture of the clergy provoked a serious confrontation of church and state in the late tenth and eleventh centuries. At that time, reform-minded clergy rebelled against what they then believed to be a kind of involuntary clerical vassalage. Even reform-minded clerics, however, welcomed Louis's grants of land and power to the clergy.

The lord's obligations to his vassals were specific. First, he was obligated to protect the vassal from physical harm and to stand as his advocate in public court. After fealty was sworn and homage paid, the lord ensured the vassal's physical maintenance by the bestowal of a benefice or fief. The fief was simply the physical or material wherewithal to meet the vassal's military and other obligations. It could take the form of liquid wealth, as well as the more common grant of real property. There were so-called money fiefs, which empowered a vassal to receive regular payments from the lord's treasury. Such fiefs created potential conflicts because they made it possible for a nobleman in one land to acquire vassals among the nobility in another. Normally, the fief consisted of a landed estate of anywhere from a few to several thousand acres. It could also take the form of a castle.

In Carolingian times, a benefice varied in size from one or more small villas to several *mansi*, agricultural holdings of twenty-five to forty-eight acres. The king's vassals are known to have received benefices of at least thirty and as many as two hundred such mansi, truly a vast estate. Royal vassalage with a benefice understandably came to be widely sought by the highest classes of Carolingian society. As a royal policy, however, it ultimately proved deadly to the king. Although Carolingian kings jealously guarded their rights over property granted in benefice to vassals, resident vassals could dispose of their benefices as they pleased. Vassals of the king, strengthened by his donations, in turn created their own vassals. These, in turn, created still further vassals of their own—vassals of vassals of vassals—in a pyramid effect that fragmented land and authority from the highest to the lowest levels by the late ninth century.

6.6.3 Daily Life and Religion

Daily life in the early Middle Ages centered on the manor. The relationship between peasants and their lords defined all aspects of social, economic, and religious life. This set of mutual obligations offered a degree of centralized order otherwise absent in the period.

6.6.3.1 THE HUMBLE CAROLINGIAN MANOR The agrarian economy of the early Middle Ages was organized and controlled through village farms known as **manors**. On these, peasants labored as tenants for a lord, that is, a more powerful landowner who allotted them land and tenements in exchange for their services and a portion of their crops. The part of the land tended for the lord was the *demesne*, on average about one-quarter to one-third of the arable land. All crops grown there were harvested for the lord. The manor also included common meadows for grazing animals and forests reserved exclusively for the lord to hunt in.

Peasants were treated according to their personal status and the size of their tenements. A freeman, that is, a peasant with his own modest *allodial*, or hereditary property (property free from the claims of an overlord), became a serf by surrendering his property to a greater landowner—a lord—in exchange for protection and assistance. The freeman received his land back from the lord with a clear definition of his economic and legal rights. Although the land was no longer his property, he had full possession and use of it, and the services and amount of goods he was to supply to the lord were carefully spelled out.

Peasants with little real property (perhaps only a few farm implements and animals) ended up as unfree serfs.

Such serfs were far more vulnerable to the lord's demands, often spending up to three days a week working the lord's fields. Peasants who had nothing to offer a lord except their hands had the lowest status and were the least protected from excessive demands on their labor.

All classes of serfs were subject to various dues: firewood in return for cutting the lord's wood, sheep for being allowed to graze their sheep on the lord's land, and the like. Thus the lord, who furnished the serfs with shacks and small plots of land from his vast domain, had at his disposal an army of servants of varying status who provided him with everything from eggs to boots. Weak serfs often fled to monasteries rather than continue their servitude. That many serfs were discontented is reflected in the high number of recorded escapes, and in an astrological calendar from the period that even marked the days most favorable for escaping. Escaped serfs roamed as beggars and vagabonds, searching for better masters.

By the time of Charlemagne, the moldboard plow and the **three-field system** of land cultivation were coming into use. The moldboard plow cut deep into the soil, turning it to form a ridge, which provided a natural drainage system and permitted the deep planting of seeds. This made cultivation possible in the regions north of the Mediterranean, where soils were dense and waterlogged from heavy precipitation. The three-field system alternated fallow with planted fields each year, and this increased the amount of cultivated land by leaving only one-third fallow in a given year. It also better adjusted crops to seasons. In fall, one field was planted with winter crops of wheat or rye, to be harvested in early summer. In late spring, a second field was planted with summer crops of oats, barley, and beans. The third field was left fallow, to be planted in its turn with winter and summer crops. The new summer crops, especially beans, restored nitrogen to the soil and helped increase yields. (See the "Encountering the Past" sidebar on medieval cookery, which follows below.)

Encountering the Past

Medieval Cooking

SEVERAL ELEMENTS DISTINGUISH THE MEDIEVAL DIET from modern eating practices. First, instead of today's standard three meals a day, almost everyone consumed only two meals: a dinner, between 10 and 11 a.m. in the morning, and a late afternoon supper, at about 4 or 5 p.m. Second, all society, including monarchs, had to follow strict rules about eating. Above all, the church forbade consuming meat on Wednesday, Friday, Saturday, and throughout Lent and Advent—more than half the year. Third, the seasonal availability of various foods affected the medieval diet. Fruit was fresher in autumn, white bread pie and flans were more common at harvest time, and the availability of garden produce depended on the time of year. In general, the times of day, the days of the week, and the seasons of the year mattered much more then than now. Finally, the social class of diners had a decisive impact on their eating practices.

THE LORD OF THE MANOR AT TABLE (above) AND HIS COOKS (below)

SOURCE: Robana Picture Library/AGE Fotostock [Top] Dining. British Library, London, UK © British Library Board. All Rights Reserved//Bridgeman Art Library [Bottom] Kitchen Scene; Chopping Meat.

Meat, the main food of the rich, was desired by all. Although yeomen and townsmen might strive to emulate the lifestyle of well-to-do nobles and clergy, in practice, however, those at the bottom of the social scale consumed much less meat than those at the top. Restrictions on hunting further limited the diet of the lower classes. The poor man's sparse table would even include food ordinarily fed to animals, depending on scarcity. Bread made up the most important part of the medieval peasant's diet. Not fine white bread, however. The bread of the poor was coarse dark rye or wheat and rye or, perhaps, bread made from barley or oats or a mixture of oats and wheat.

At the top of the social scale, the lords of noble households enjoyed the best food, the best cuisine, and the greatest variety of food, especially when they entertained companions. Lords also consumed three meals a day, not two, which were distinct in both quality and quantity, ranging from small portions of pottage to the elaborate, lavish in color, spice, and construction: Live birds, for example, might be baked into a pie and fly out when sliced open.

Complex rules and regulations about status also governed the medieval table. For example, certain laws restricted the quantity of food one might consume. A lord was limited to five dishes, a gentlemen to three dishes, and grooms to two dishes. At a lord's table, the first course involved boiled or baked meats in sauces, brawn (boar meat) with mustard, or a meat stew. Dinner was extensive and the meal usually went on for up to two hours, with each course separated by a small intervening course of fruit and nuts. A second meat course consisted of roasted flesh and exotic carved meats, despite the no-meat rules set by the church, which bound the nobility as much as the peasantry. During Advent and Lent meals of fish were equally elaborately prepared. Notwithstanding religious prohibition, the nobility and gentry of England ate to culinary excess. The lord's house came well-stocked with wine, consumed only by the nobility, and with ale, which lords, servants, and staff all drank—first-, second- and third-best ale, respectively.

The rules for the provision of food and drink in the monasteries was as complicated as those of the nobleman's household. To the abbot, the only figure allowed to eat breakfast, the best food was reserved. Most remarkable, and unique to the monastery, the *Rule of St. Benedict* forbade eating the meat of four-legged animals. Many monks, however, who tended to come from well-off families accustomed to splendid dining, found ways to circumvent this rule. For instance, since the rule stated that monks not eat meat in the *refectory*, or dining hall, many monasteries built second dining rooms, or *misericords* (places of mercy), where beef, lamb, and pork were consumed, provided it was not Wednesday, Friday, Saturday, Lent, or Advent. Most monks consumed 400 meat dishes a year. They also drank very fine ale. Wine, on the other hand, could be drunk only on a saint's feast day, but there were, thankfully, about sixty to seventy feast days a year.

Question

1. How did medieval meals reflect the essential characteristics of feudalism?

SOURCES: *Food in the Middle Ages: A Book of Essays*, ed. by Melitta Weiss Adamson (New York: Greenwood Press, 1995); *Regional Cuisines of Medieval Europe: A Book of Essays*, ed. by Melitta Weiss Adamson (New York: Routledge, 2002); Terrence Scully, *The Art of Cookery in the Middle Ages* (Woodbridge, UK: Boydell Press, 1995).

These developments in land cultivation made possible what has been called the "expansion of Europe within Europe." They permitted the old lands formerly occupied by barbarians to be tended and filled with farms and towns. This, in turn, led to major population growth in the north and ultimately a shift of political power from the Mediterranean to northern Europe.

6.6.3.2 THE CARE OF CAROLINGIAN SOULS
The lower clergy lived among, and were drawn from, peasant ranks. They fared hardly better than peasants in Carolingian times. As owners of the churches on their lands, lords had the right to promote chosen serfs to the post of parish priest, placing them in charge of the churches on the lords' estates. Church law directed a lord to set a serf free before he entered the clergy. Lords, however, were reluctant to do this and thereby risk a possible later challenge to their jurisdiction over the ecclesiastical property with which the serf, as priest, was invested. Lords preferred a "serf priest," one who not only said the Mass on Sundays and holidays but who also continued to serve his lord during the week, waiting on the lord's table and tending his steeds. Like Charlemagne with his bishops, Frankish lords cultivated a docile parish clergy.

The ordinary people looked to religion for comfort and consolation. They especially associated religion with the major Christian holidays and festivals, such as Christmas and Easter. They baptized their children, attended mass, tried to learn the Lord's Prayer and the Apostles' Creed, and received the last rites from the priest as death approached. Because local priests on the manors were no better educated than their congregations, religious instruction in the meaning of Christian doctrine and practice remained minimal. The church sponsored street dramas in accordance with the church calendar. These were designed to teach onlookers the highlights of the Bible and church history and to instill in them basic Christian moral values.

People understandably became particularly attached in this period to the more tangible veneration of saints and relics. The Virgin Mary was also widely revered, although a true cult of Mary would not develop until the eleventh and twelfth centuries. Religious devotion to saints has been compared to subjection to powerful lords in the secular world. Both the saint and the lord were protectors whose honor the serfs were bound to defend and whose help they hoped to receive in time of need. Veneration of saints was also rooted in old tribal customs, to which the common folk were still attached. Indeed, Charlemagne, who was devoted to veneration of saints, enforced laws against witchcraft, sorcery, and the ritual sacrifice of animals by monks.

But religion also had an intrinsic appeal and special meaning to the masses of medieval men and women burdened, fearful, and with little hope of material betterment on this side of eternity. Charlemagne shared many of the religious beliefs of his ordinary subjects. He collected and venerated relics, made pilgrimages to Rome, and frequented the Church of Saint Mary in Aachen several times a day. In his last will and testament, he directed that all but a fraction of his great treasure be spent to endow masses and prayers for his departed soul.

6.6.4 Fragmentation and Divided Loyalty

In addition to the fragmentation brought about by the multiplication of vassalage, effective occupation of land gradually led to claims of hereditary possession. Hereditary possession became a legally recognized principle in the ninth century and laid the basis for claims to real ownership. Fiefs given as royal donations became hereditary possessions and, over time, sometimes even the actual property of the possessor.

Furthermore, vassal obligations increased in still another way as enterprising freemen sought to accumulate as much land as possible: One man could be a vassal to several different lords. This led in the ninth century to the development of the "liege lord"—the lord a vassal must obey should a direct conflict arise among several of his lords.

The problem of loyalty was reflected both in the literature of the period, which praised the virtues of honor and fidelity, and in the development of the ceremonial act of commendation by which a freeman became a vassal. In the mid-eighth century, an oath of fealty highlighted the ceremony. A vassal reinforced his promise of fidelity to the lord by swearing a special oath with his hand on a sacred relic or the Bible. In the tenth and eleventh centuries, paying homage to the lord involved not only swearing such an oath but also placing the vassal's hands between the lord's and sealing the ceremony with a kiss.

As the centuries passed, personal loyalty and service became secondary to the acquisition of property. In developments that signaled the waning of feudal society in the tenth century, the fief came to overshadow fealty, the benefice became more important than vassalage, and freemen would swear allegiance to the highest bidder.

Feudal arrangements nonetheless provided stability throughout the early Middle Ages and aided the difficult process of political centralization during the High Middle Ages (ca. 1000–1300 C.E.). The genius of feudal government lay in its adaptability. Contracts of different kinds could be made with almost anybody, as circumstances required. Feudal arrangements embraced a wide spectrum of people, from the king at the top to the lowliest vassal in the remotest part of the kingdom. The foundations of the modern nation-state would emerge in France and England from the fine-tuning of essentially feudal arrangements as kings sought to adapt their goal of centralized government to the reality of local power and control.

The Chapter in Perspective

The centuries between 476 and 1000 C.E. saw both the decline of classical civilization and the birth of a new European civilization in the regions that had been the Western Roman Empire. Beginning in the fifth century, barbarian invasions separated Western Europe culturally from much of its classical past. Although some important works and concepts from antiquity survived and the church preserved major features of Roman government, the West would be recovering its classical heritage in "renaissances" that stretched into the sixteenth century. Out of this mix of barbarian and surviving or recovered classical culture, a distinct Western culture was born. Aided and abetted by the church, the Franks created a new imperial tradition and shaped basic Western political and social institutions for centuries to come.

The early Middle Ages also saw the emergence of a rift between Eastern and Western Christianity. Evolving from the initial division of the Roman Empire into eastern and western parts, this rift resulted in bitter conflict between popes and patriarchs.

During this period, the capital of the Byzantine Empire, Constantinople, far exceeded in population and culture any city of the West. Serving both as a buffer against Persian, Arab, and Turkish invasions of the West and as a major repository of classical learning and science for Western scholars, the Byzantine Empire made possible the development of Western Europe as a distinctive political and cultural entity. Islam, another cultural and religious rival of the West, also saw its golden age during these centuries. Like the Byzantine world, the Muslim world preserved ancient scholarship and, especially through Muslim Spain, retransmitted it to the West. But despite such examples of coexistence and even friendship, the cultures of the Western and Muslim worlds were too different and their peoples too estranged from one another for them to become good neighbors.

The early Middle Ages were not centuries of great ambition in the West. It was a time when modest foundations were laid. Despite a somewhat common religious culture, Western society remained more primitive and fragmented than probably anywhere else in the contemporary world. Two distinctive social institutions developed in response to this fragmentation: the manor and feudal bonds. The manor ensured that all would be fed and cared for; feudal bonds provided protection from outside predators. Western people were concerned primarily about satisfying basic needs; great cultural ambition would come later.

The Chapter in Review

Review Questions

1. How and why was the history of the eastern half of the Roman Empire so different from that of the western half? What role did emperors play in the Eastern church?
2. What were the tenets of Islam, and how were the Muslims suddenly able to build an empire? How did Islamic civilization influence Western Europe?
3. What role did the church play in the West after the fall of the Roman Empire? Why did Christianity split into eastern and western branches?
4. What role did the nobility play during Charlemagne's rule? Why did Charlemagne encourage learning at his court? How could the Carolingian renaissance have been dangerous to Charlemagne's rule? Why did his empire break apart?

Key Terms

benefices   Church offices granted by the ruler of a state or the pope to an individual. It also meant *fiefs* in the Middle Ages.

Byzantine   Refers to the culture that flourished in the East, was centered at Constantinople, and was known as the "New Rome."

Caesaropapism   The direct involvement of a ruler in religious doctrine and practice, giving him powers of church as well as state.

caliphate (KAH-li-fate)   The true line of succession to Muhammad.

Corpus Juris Civilis   Meaning "body of civil law." Three-part compilation and revision of Roman law ordered by Justinian.

fealty   An oath of loyalty by a vassal to a lord, promising to perform specified services.

feudal society   The social, political, military, and economic system that prevailed in the Middle Ages and beyond in some parts of Europe.

fiefs   Land granted to a vassal in exchange for services, usually military.

foederati **(FAY-der-ah-tee)**   Meaning "special allies." Barbarian tribes that enlisted as allies of the Roman Empire, in exchange for rights of settlement and material assistance.

Hegira **(HEJ-ear-a)**   Meaning "flight." The flight of Muhammad and his followers from Mecca to Medina in 622, marking the beginning of the Islamic calendar.

Holy Roman Empire   The revival of the old Roman Empire in the West, based mainly in Germany and northern Italy, that endured from 800 to 1806.

iconoclasm (i-KON-o-kla-zoom)   A heresy in Eastern Christianity that sought to ban the veneration of sacred images, or icons, in worship.

Islam (IZ-lahm)   Meaning "submission." The religion founded by the prophet Muhammad.

Ka'ba **(KAH-bah)**   Meaning "the cube." Islam's holiest shrine in the city of Mecca that houses a sacred black meteorite.

Late Antiquity   The multicultural period between the end of the ancient world and the birth of the Middle Ages, 250–800 C.E.

manors   Village farms owned by a lord, on which peasants labored.

monasticism   Movement in the Christian church that arose first in the East in the third and fourth centuries in which individual hermits and later organized communities of monks and nuns separated themselves from the world to lead lives in imitation of Christ. In the West, dictated by the *Rule of St. Benedict* (c. 480–547).

Monophysites (ma-NO-fiz-its)   Adherents to the theory that Jesus had only one nature.

Papal States   Territory in central Italy given by the Franks to the pope in 755 and ruled by the pope until 1870.

pontifex maximus **(PON-ti-feks MAK-suh-muss)**   Meaning "supreme priest." The chief priest of ancient Rome. The title was later assumed by the popes.

Qur'an **(kuh-RAN)**   Meaning "a reciting." The Islamic bible, which Muslims believe God revealed to the prophet Muhammad.

scutage   Monetary payments by a vassal to a lord in place of required military service.

serf   A peasant tied to the land he tilled, and subject to dues to a lord.

Shi'a **(SHE-ah)**   Meaning "partisans of Ali." The minority of Muslims who trace their beliefs to the caliph Ali who was assassinated in 661.

Sunnis   Those who follow the "tradition" (*sunna*) of the prophet Muhammad. The dominant movement within Islam to which the majority of Muslims adhere.

three-field system   A medieval innovation that increased the amount of land under cultivation by leaving only one-third of land fallow in a given year.

ulema **(oo-LEE-mah)**   Meaning "persons with correct knowledge." The Islamic scholarly elite who served a social function similar to the professional priesthood or rabbinate.

vassals   Meaning "those who serve." Persons granted an estate or cash payments in return for accepting the obligation to render services to a lord.

villa   A fortified country estate that became the basic unit of life in the West during the fifth and sixth centuries.

Notes

1. Dates after popes' names are the years of each reign.

2. Cyril Mango, *Byzantium: The Empire of New Rome* (New York: Charles Scribner's Sons, 1980), p. 88.

Chapter 7
The High Middle Ages: The Rise of European Empires and States (1000–1300)

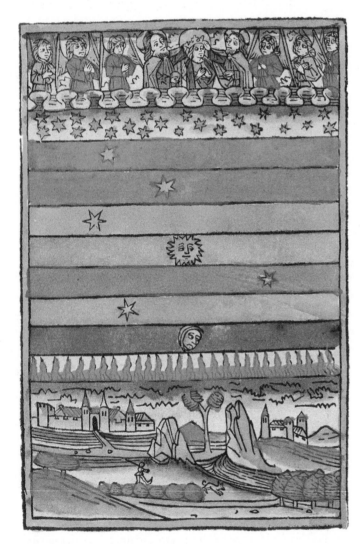

EARTH-CENTERED UNIVERSE OF MEDIEVAL EUROPE
In medieval Europe, the traditional geocentric or earth-centered universe was usually depicted by concentric circles. In this popular German work on natural history, medicine, and science, Konrad von Megenberg (1309–1374 c.e.) depicted the universe in a most unusual but effective manner. The seven known planets are contained within straight horizontal lines separating the earth below from heaven above, populated by saints and angels.
SOURCE: Library of Congress Prints and Photographs Division

 Contents and Focus Questions

The Chapter in Brief

THE HIGH MIDDLE Ages were a period of political expansion and consolidation accompanied by an intellectual flowering. Medievalist Joseph Strayer called it an age that saw "the full development of all the potentialities of medieval civilization."[1] For not a few historians it was a more creative period than even the Italian Renaissance and the German Reformation. In the High Middle Ages, the borders of Western Europe were largely secured against foreign invaders. Although intermittent Muslim aggression continued well into the sixteenth century, fear of war diminished. After being the prey of enemies and outsiders for so many centuries, Western Europe was able to become the feared hunter for both the eastern Byzantine and Muslim worlds, thanks to the Christian Crusades and the foreign trade they opened in the late eleventh and twelfth centuries.

In this period, "national" monarchies emerged. Rulers in England and France successfully adapted feudal principles of government to create new, centralized political realms. At the same time, parliaments and popular assemblies emerged to secure the rights and customs of the privileged—the nobility, clergy, and propertied townspeople—against the wishes of kings. In the process, the foundations of modern European states were being laid. The Holy Roman Empire proved to be the great exception to this centralizing trend. Despite a revival of the empire under the Ottonians and their immediate successors, the events of these centuries left the empire weak and fragmented until modern times.

The High Middle Ages also saw the Latin, or Western, church establish itself in concept and law as a spiritual authority independent of secular, monarchical government, thereby sowing the seeds of the distinctive Western separation of church and state. During the so-called **investiture controversy**, a bitter confrontation between popes and emperors begun in the late eleventh century and lasting through the twelfth, a reformed papacy overcame its long subservience to the Carolingian and Ottonian kings. In this great struggle over the authority of rulers to designate bishops and other high clergy by investing them with the symbols of royal authority, the papacy, under Pope Gregory VII and his immediate successors, won out. It did so, however, by itself becoming a monarchy among the secular world's new emerging monarchies, thereby paving the way for still more lethal confrontations between popes and monarchs. In the eyes of religious reformers, the Gregorian papacy of the High Middle Ages betrayed the church's spiritual mission while declaring its independence from secular power.

In mid-twelfth-century France, Gothic architecture began to replace the unadorned and ponderous Romanesque style, which had been preferred in highly fortified Europe during the early Middle Ages. The grace and beauty of the new architecture—its soaring arches, bold flying buttresses, dazzling light, and stained glass—were a testament to the vitality of humankind as well as to the glory of God in this unique period.

7.1 Otto I and the Revival of the Empire

How was Otto able to secure the power of his Saxon dynasty?

The fortunes of both the old empire and the papacy revived after the dark period of the late ninth and early tenth centuries. In 918, the Saxon Henry I ("the Fowler," d. 936), the strongest of the German dukes, became the first non-Frankish king of Germany.

7.1.1 Unifying Germany

It was Henry who rebuilt royal power by forcibly combining the duchies of Swabia, Bavaria, Saxony, Franconia, and Lotharingia. In doing so he secured the imperial borders by checking the invasions of the Hungarians and the Danes. Although much smaller an empire than Charlemagne's, the new German kingdom Henry created gave his son and successor, **Otto I** (r. 936–973), a strong territorial position.

Otto wisely refused to recognize the duchies as independent, hereditary entities. Rather, he treated each as a subordinate member of a unified kingdom. In a truly imperial gesture, he invaded Italy and proclaimed himself its king in 951. But Otto's most magnificent victory was the defeat of the Hungarians at Lechfeld, a victory that secured German borders, unified the German duchies, and earned

Otto the well-deserved title of "Otto the Great." In defining the boundaries of Western Europe, Otto's conquest was comparable to Charles Martel's earlier triumph over the Saracens at Poitiers in 732.

7.1.2 Embracing the Church

As part of a careful rebuilding program, Otto followed his predecessors in enlisting the church. Bishops and abbots possessed a keen sense of universal empire, but as clergy they could not marry nor found competitive dynasties. They became the king's congenial princes and agents, and as royal bureaucrats, they received great landholdings and immunity from local counts and dukes, and looked on their vassalage to the king as a blessing. The medieval church evidently did not become a great territorial power reluctantly. It appreciated the blessings of taking and receiving, while teaching the blessedness of giving.

In 961, Otto, who aspired to the imperial crown, responded to a call for help from Pope John XII (r. 955–964), who was then being bullied by an Italian enemy of the German king. In exchange for his rescue, Pope John crowned Otto emperor on February 2, 962. For his part, Otto recognized the existence of the Papal States and proclaimed himself their protector. Over time, such close cooperation between emperor and pope put the church more than ever under royal control. Its bishops and abbots became Otto's faithful appointees and bureaucrats, and the pope reigned in Rome under the protection of the emperor's sword.

Recognizing the royal web in which the church was slowly becoming entangled, Pope John joined the Italian opposition to the new emperor. This turnabout brought Otto's swift revenge. At an ecclesiastical synod over which he presided, Otto deposed Pope John and proclaimed that no pope could take office thereafter without first swearing an oath of allegiance to the emperor. Under Otto I, popes would rule at the emperor's pleasure.

As these events show, Otto had shifted the royal focus from Germany to Italy. His imperial successors—Otto II (r. 973–983) and Otto III (r. 983–1002)—also became so preoccupied with running the affairs of Italy that their German base disintegrated, sacrificed to imperial dreams. They might have learned a lesson from the contemporary Capetian kings, the successor dynasty to the Carolingians in France. Those kings, perhaps more by circumstance than by design, pursued a different course than the Ottonians. They mended local fences and concentrated their limited resources on securing the royal domain, never neglecting it for the lure of foreign adventure.

But the Ottonians, in contrast, reached far beyond their grasp when they tried to subdue Italy. As the briefly revived empire began to crumble in the first quarter of the eleventh century, the church, long unhappy with Carolingian and Ottonian domination, prepared to declare its independence.

7.2 The Reviving Catholic Church

What explains the popularity of the Cluniac reform movement?

During the late ninth and early tenth centuries, the clergy became tools of kings and magnates, and the papacy a toy of the Italian nobles. The church now had to regain its lost respect and authority. The failing fortunes of the overextended Ottonian empire gave them the opportunity not only to strike but also to force long-needed reform upon the church itself. Popular support in the form of lay piety and noble patronage allowed the Cluniac movement to become one of the major religious forces in Europe.

7.2.1 The Cluny Reform Movement

The great monastery in Cluny in east-central France had long been poised to lead a monastic reform movement that could win the support of secular lords and German kings. The real Christianization of Europe began with this resolve. As both successful reform initiatives and the growth of heresy attested, a new atmosphere of change and reform engulfed the church, enabling it to challenge royal authority at both the local episcopal and papal levels.

The **Cluny reform movement** was also helped by the widespread popular respect for the church, which found expression in lay religious fervor and generous baronial patronage of the religious houses. One reason so many lay people admired the clerics and monks was that the church was medieval society's most democratic institution as far as they were concerned. In the Middle Ages, any man could theoretically rise to the position of pope, an office one was elected to by "the people and the clergy." All people were candidates for the church's grace and salvation, and the church promised a better life to the masses of ordinary people, who found present-day life brutish and hopeless.

Since the fall of the Roman Empire, popular support for the church had been especially inspired by the example set by the monks. Monks remained the least secularized and most spiritual of the church's clergy. Their cultural achievements were widely admired, their relics and rituals deemed transformative, and their high religious ideals and sacrifices were eagerly imitated by the laity.

The tenth and eleventh centuries also saw an unprecedented boom in the construction of new monasteries. William the Pious, duke of Aquitaine, founded the great monastery of Cluny in 910. It was a Benedictine monastery devoted to the strictest observance of Benedict of Nursia's *Rule of Saint Benedict*, with a special emphasis on liturgical purity. Although the reformers who emerged at Cluny were loosely organized and their demands not always consistent, they shared a determination to maintain a spiritual church.

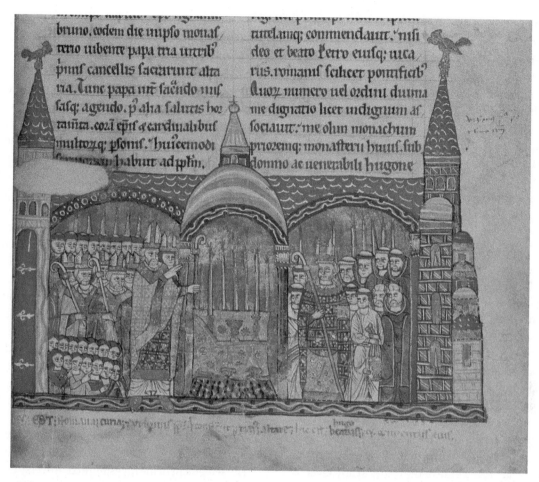

ABBEY OF CLUNY The consecration of the Abbey of Cluny by Pope Urban II, from a twelfth-century manuscript.
SOURCE: Bibliotheque Nationale, Paris, France/Bridgeman Art Library

They absolutely rejected the subservience of the clergy, especially that of the German bishops, to royal authority anywhere and taught that the pope in Rome was the sole ruler over all the clergy. Local secular rulers could no longer have control over Cluny's monasteries.

The monastic life of the reformers was strict from beginning to end. They denounced the sins of the flesh of the "secular" parish clergy, who maintained concubines in a relationship akin to marriage. The Cluny reformers resolved to free the clergy from both kings and "wives"—to create an independent and chaste clergy throughout Christendom. The church alone would now be the clergy's lord and spouse. Thus, the distinctive Western separation of church and state and strict rule of celibacy, both of which continue today, are still faithful to their tenth-century creed dating back to the Cluny reform movement.

Under very aggressive abbots, Cluny grew to embrace almost 1,500 dependent cloisters, each devoted to monastic and church reform. In the latter half of the eleventh century, the Cluny reformers reached their summit when the papacy embraced their reform program.

In the late ninth and early tenth centuries the proclamation of a series of church decrees, called the Peace of God, reflected the influence of the Cluny movement. The result of a cooperative venture between the clergy and the higher nobility, these decrees were intended to lessen the endemic warfare of medieval society by threatening excommunication for those who harmed members of vulnerable groups, such as women, peasants, merchants, and the clergy. The Peace of God was subsequently reinforced by the Truce of God, a church order proclaiming that all men must abstain from violence and warfare during a certain part of each week (from Wednesday night until Monday morning) and in all holy seasons.

Popes devoted to Cluny's reforms came to power during the reign of Emperor Henry III (r. 1039–1056). Pope Leo IX (r. 1049–1054) empowered regional synods to oppose *simony* (the selling of spiritual things, especially church offices) and clerical marriage (in as much as celibacy had not been strictly enforced). Pope Leo also placed Cluny reformers in key administrative posts in Rome. However, imperial influence over the papacy was still strong during Henry's reign, and helped control the great aristocratic families who manipulated the elections of popes for their own gain. Before Leo IX's papacy, Henry had deposed three such popes, each a pawn of a Roman noble faction, and had installed a German bishop of his own choosing who ruled as Pope Clement II (r. 1046–1047).

Such high-handed practices ended soon after Henry's death. To prevent local factional control of papal elections, Pope Nicholas II (r. 1059–1061) decreed that a body of high church officials and advisers, known as the College of Cardinals, would choose the pope and establish the procedures for papal succession, which the Catholic Church still follows today. With this decree, the papacy declared its full independence from both local Italian and distant royal interference. Nevertheless, rulers continued to have considerable indirect influence on the election of popes.

7.2.2 The Investiture Struggle: Gregory VII and Henry IV

Pope Gregory VII (r. 1073–1085) was another fervent advocate of Cluny's reforms who had entered the papal bureaucracy a quarter of a century earlier during the pontificate of Leo IX. It was he who put the church's declaration of independence to the test. Cluny reformers had repeatedly inveighed against simony. Cardinal Humbert, a prominent reformer, argued that lay investiture of the clergy—that is, the appointment of bishops and other church officials by secular officials and rulers—was the worst form of this evil practice. In 1075, Pope Gregory embraced these arguments and condemned, under penalty of excommunication, lay investiture of the clergy at any level.

After Gregory's ruling, emperors were no more able to install bishops than they were to install popes. As popes were elected by the College of Cardinals, and no longer appointed by kings or nobles, bishops would also be installed in their offices by high ecclesiastical authority empowered by the pope. The spiritual origins and allegiance of the episcopal office were thereby made clear to all.

Gregory's prohibition came as a jolt to royal authority. Since the days of Charlemagne, emperors would award rich bishoprics to their favorite members of the clergy. Bishops who received such royal estates were appointees of the emperors and servants of the state. Henry IV's Carolingian and Ottonian predecessors had carefully nurtured the theocratic character of the empire in both concept and its administrative bureaucracy. The church and religion had become integral parts of government.

Now the emperor Henry IV was suddenly ordered to secularize the empire by drawing distinct lines between the emporal and spiritual, the royal and ecclesiastical, and authority and jurisdiction. Henry considered Gregory's action a direct challenge to his authority.

The territorial princes, however, eager to see the emperor weakened, were quick to understand the advantages of Gregory's ruling. If a weak emperor could not gain a bishop's ear, then a strong prince might, thus bringing the offices of the church into his orbit of power. In the hope of gaining an advantage over both the emperor and the clergy in their territory, the German princes fully supported Gregory's edict.

The lines of battle were quickly drawn. Prince Henry assembled his loyal German bishops at Worms in January 1076 and had them proclaim their independence from Gregory. The pope promptly responded with the church's heavy artillery: he excommunicated Henry and absolved all of Henry's subjects from loyalty to him. This turn of events delighted the German princes, and Henry found himself facing a general revolt led by the duchy of Saxony. He had no recourse but to come to terms with Gregory. In a famous scene, Henry prostrated himself outside Gregory's castle retreat at Canossa on January 25, 1077. There he reportedly stood barefoot in the snow off and on for three days before the pope agreed to absolve him. Papal power had at this moment reached a pinnacle. But Gregory's power, as he must have known when he restored Henry to power, would soon be challenged.

Henry regrouped his forces, regained much of his power within the empire, and soon acted as if the humiliation at Canossa had never occurred. In March 1080, Gregory excommunicated Henry once again, but this time the action was ineffectual. In 1084, Henry, absolutely dominant, installed his own antipope, Clement III, and forced Gregory into exile, where he died the following year. It appeared as if the old practice of kings controlling popes had been restored—with a vengeance. Clement, however, was never recognized within the church, and Gregory's followers, who retained wide popular support, later regained power.

The settlement of the investiture controversy came in 1122 with the Concordat of Worms. Emperor Henry V (r. 1106–1125), having early abandoned his predecessors' practice of nominating popes and raising up antipopes, formally renounced his power to invest bishops with ring and staff. In exchange, Pope Calixtus II (r. 1119–1124) recognized the emperor's right to be present and to invest bishops with fiefs before and after their investment with ring and staff by the church. The old church-and-state dickering continued in this way, but now on different terms. The clergy received their offices and attendant religious powers solely from ecclesiastical authority and no longer from kings and emperors. Rulers continued to bestow lands and worldly goods on high clergy in the hope of influencing them. The Concordat of Worms thus made the clergy more independent, but not necessarily less worldly.

The Gregorian party may have won the independence of the clergy, but the price it paid was division among the feudal forces within the empire. The pope made himself strong by making imperial authority weak. In the end, those who profited most from the investiture controversy were the German princes.

The new Gregorian fence between temporal and spiritual power did not prevent kings and popes from being good neighbors if each was willing. In succeeding centuries, however, the aspirations of kings were too often in conflict with those of popes for peaceful coexistence to endure. The most bitter clash between church and state was still to come. It would occur during the late thirteenth and early fourteenth centuries in the confrontation between Pope Boniface VIII and King Philip IV of France.

7.2.3 The Crusades

The **Crusades** opened new avenues for commerce and provided an outlet for the religious zeal, some of it fanatical, of the late eleventh and twelfth centuries. As such, they stand as a symbol of popular piety and support for the pope in the High Middle Ages.

Late in the eleventh century, when the Byzantine Empire was under severe pressure from the Seljuk Turks, the Eastern emperor, Alexius I Comnenus (r. 1081–1118), appealed for Western aid. At the Council of Clermont in 1095, Pope Urban II (r. 1088–1099) responded positively to that appeal, setting the First Crusade in motion. This event has puzzled some historians because the First Crusade was a risky venture. Yet the pope, the nobility, and Western society at large had much to gain by removing large numbers of noblemen temporarily from Europe. Too many idle, restless noble youths spent too great a part of their lives feuding with each other and raiding other people's lands. The pope believed that peace and tranquility might more easily be gained at home by sending these quarrelsome aristocrats abroad, 100,000 of whom marched off with the First Crusade. The nobility, in turn, believed that fortunes could be made in foreign wars. That was especially true for the younger sons of noblemen, who, in an age of growing population and shrinking landed wealth, saw in crusading the opportunity to become landowners. Pope Urban may have believed that the Crusade would reconcile and reunite Western and Eastern Christianity.

Unlike the later Crusades, which were undertaken for mercenary reasons, the piety of the early Crusaders was carefully orchestrated by a revived papacy. In case of death on the battlefield, popes promised the first Crusaders a plenary indulgence, or full remission of the temporal punishment attached to all unexpiated sins, as well as full release from purgatory. In addition to this spiritual reward, the Crusaders were also motivated by the prospect of a Holy War against the Muslim infidel, and by the sheer romance of a pilgrimage to the Holy Land. All these motives combined to make the First Crusade a Christian success.

En route to the Holy Land, the Crusaders also began a general cleansing of Christendom that would intensify during the thirteenth-century papacy of Pope Innocent III. Accompanied by the new mendicant orders of Dominicans and Franciscans, Christian knights attempted to rid Europe of Jews as well as Muslims. Along the Crusaders' routes, especially in the Rhineland, Jewish communities were subjected to pogroms. (See the "Compare and Connect" sidebar, which follows below, on anti-Jewish violence and the First Crusade.)

Compare and Connect

Anti-Jewish Violence and the First Crusade

AS BANDS OF WOULD-BE CRUSADERS made their way to Italian ports, they did not wait until they arrived in the Holy Land to begin their attack on those they saw as enemies of Christendom. Urban II's call for a crusade brought with it a wave of anti-Jewish violence. In cities and towns across Europe, Jewish communities found themselves under siege. In some cases, they found Christian allies who helped protect them, but all too often they were left to fend for themselves. From the perspective of their attackers, the Jews of Europe were "the other." Both Jews and Muslims were regarded with suspicion, and often with

hatred and disdain, for very different reasons: the former for the practice of usury and the latter for the practice of impaling their enemies in war. In the excerpts included below, two Christian observers, Albert of Aix and Ekkehard of Aura, comment on the wave of anti-Jewish violence that accompanied the First Crusade, focusing on the atrocities committed by Count Emico, a nobleman from the Rhineland.

THE EXPULSION OF THE JEWS FROM FRANCE IN 1182
The First Crusade set off a wave of anti-Jewish violence in France. In March 1181, King Philip Augustus ordered the arrest of all Jews in France and the confiscation of their money and investments. The following year, he ordered the expulsion of the Jews from the kingdom.
SOURCE: Heritage Image Partnership Ltd/Alamy Stock Photo

Before Reading

- Consider the history of anti-Semitism in Europe prior to the Crusades. Think about the attitudes and beliefs that might help explain the violence the commentators describe.
- Take note of the participants. Identify the events that prompted each group of participants to join in the attacks against Jews.
- Think about the commentators' response to the violence. Ask yourself how you might expect medieval commentators to respond to the events described below.

Questions

1. What do the excerpts reveal about the motives of the Crusaders?
2. What are the most important differences between the two accounts of the deeds of Count Emico?
3. How would you explain the anti-Jewish violence described in these accounts?

I. ALBERT OF AIX

At the beginning of summer in the same year in which Peter, and Gottschalk, after collecting an army, had set out, there assembled in like fashion a large and innumerable host of Christians from diverse kingdoms and lands; namely, from the realms of France, England, Flanders, and Lorraine. . . . I know not whether by a judgment of the Lord, or by some error of mind, they rose in a spirit of cruelty against the Jewish people scattered throughout these cities and slaughtered them without mercy, especially in the Kingdom of Lorraine, asserting it to be the beginning of their expedition and their duty against the enemies of the Christian faith. This slaughter of Jews was done first by citizens of Cologne. These suddenly fell upon a small band of Jews and severely wounded and killed many; they destroyed the houses and synagogues of the Jews and divided among themselves a very large, amount of money. . . .

Not long after this, they started upon their journey, as they had vowed, and arrived in a great multitude at the city of Mainz. There, Count Emico, a nobleman and a very mighty man in this region, was awaiting with a large band of Teutons the arrival of the pilgrims, who were coming thither from diverse lands by the King's highway.

The Jews of this city, knowing of the slaughter of their brethren, and that they themselves could not escape the hands of so many, fled in hope of safety to Bishop Rothard. They put an infinite treasure in his guard and trust, having much faith in his protection, because he was Bishop of the city. Then that excellent Bishop of the city cautiously set aside the incredible amount of money received from them. He placed the Jews in the very spacious hall of his own house, away from the sight of Count Emico and his followers, that they might remain safe and sound in a very secure and strong place.

But Emico and the rest of his band held a council and, after sunrise, attacked the Jews in the hall with arrows and lances. Breaking the bolts and doors, they killed the Jews, about seven hundred in number, who in vain resisted the force and attack of so many thousands. They killed the women, also, and with their swords pierced tender children of whatever age and sex. The Jews, seeing that their Christian enemies were attacking them and their children, and that they were sparing no age, likewise fell upon one another, brother, children, wives, and sisters, and thus they perished at each other's hands. Horrible to say, mothers cut the throats of nursing children with knives and stabbed others, preferring them to perish thus by their own hands rather than to be killed by the weapons of the uncircumcised.

II. EKKEHARD OF AURA

Just at that time, there appeared a certain soldier, Emico, Count of the lands around the Rhine, a man long of very ill repute on account of his tyrannical mode of life. Called by divine revelation, like another Saul, as he maintained, to the practice of religion of this kind, he usurped to himself the command of almost twelve thousand cross bearers. As they were led through the cities of the Rhine and the Main and also the Danube, they either utterly destroyed the execrable race of the Jews wherever they found them (being even in this matter zealously devoted to the Christian religion) or forced them into the bosom of the Church. When their forces, already increased by a great number of men and women, reached the boundary of Pannonia, they were prevented by well fortified garrisons from entering that kingdom, which is surrounded partly by swamps and partly by woods. For rumor had reached and forewarned the ears of King Coloman; a rumor that, to the minds of the Teutons, there was no difference between killing pagans and Hungarians. And so, for six weeks they besieged the fortress Wieselburg and suffered many hardships there; yet, during this very time, they were in the throes of a most foolish civil quarrel over which one of them should be King of Pannonia. Moreover, while engaged in the final assault, although the walls had already been broken through, and the citizens were fleeing, and the army of the besieged were setting fire to their own town, yet, through the wonderful providence of Almighty God, the army of pilgrims, though victorious, fled. And they left behind them all their equipment, for no one carried away any reward except his wretched life.

And thus the men of our race, zealous, doubtless, for God, though not according to the knowledge of God, began to persecute other Christians while yet upon the expedition which Christ had provided for freeing Christians. They were kept from fraternal bloodshed only by divine mercy; and the Hungarians also were freed. This is the reason why some of the more guileless brethren, ignorant of the matter, and too hasty in their judgement were scandalized and concluded that the whole expedition was vain and foolish.

SOURCES: (I) August. C. Krey, *The First Crusade: The Accounts of Eyewitnesses and Participants* (Princeton: Princeton University Press, 1921), pp. 54–56. (II) Krey, *The First Crusade*, pp. 53–54.

7.2.3.1 THE FIRST VICTORY The Eastern emperor welcomed Western aid against advancing Islamic armies. However, the Crusaders had not assembled merely to defend Europe's outermost borders against Muslim aggression. Their goal was rather to rescue the holy city of Jerusalem, which had been in the hands of the Muslims since the seventh century. To this end, three great armies—tens of thousands of Crusaders—gathered in France, Germany, and Italy and, taking different routes, reassembled in Constantinople in 1097. (See Map 7–1.)

The convergence of the Crusaders on the Eastern capital was a cultural shock that deepened antipathy toward the West. The Eastern emperor suspected their motives, and the common people, whose villages the Crusaders plundered and suppressed, did not consider them to be Christian brothers in a common cause. Nonetheless, the Crusaders accomplished what no Byzantine army had been able to do. They soundly defeated one Muslim army after another in a steady advance toward Jerusalem, which was captured on July 15, 1099. The Crusaders owed their victory to superior military discipline and weaponry, but they were also helped by the deep political divisions within the Islamic world that prevented unified Muslim resistance.

The victorious Crusaders divided the conquered territories into the feudal states of Jerusalem, Edessa, and Antioch, which were given to them as fiefs from the pope. But the Crusaders were like small islands within a great sea of Muslims, who looked on the Western invaders as savages to be slain or driven out. Once settled in the Holy Land, the Crusaders found themselves increasingly on the defensive. Now an occupying rather than a conquering army, they became obsessed with fortification, building castles and forts throughout the Holy Land, the ruins of which can still be seen today.

Once secure within their new enclaves, the Crusaders ceased to live off the land, as they had done since departing

Map 7–1 THE EARLY CRUSADES

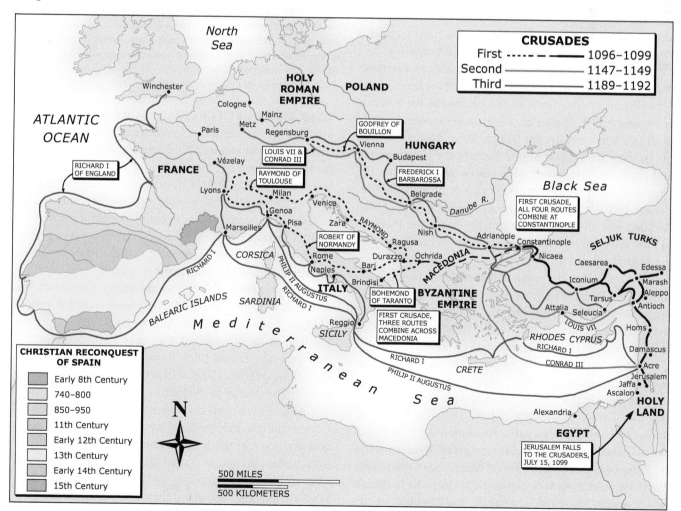

This map shows the routes of several leaders of the Crusades during the first century of the movement. The names shown do not include all the great nobles who went on the First Crusade. The even greater array of monarchs of the Second and Third Crusades were still ineffective in achieving the goals of the Crusades.

Europe, and increasingly relied on imports from home. As they developed the economic resources of their new lands, the once-fierce warriors were transformed into international traders and businessmen. The Knights Templar, originally a military-religious order, became castle stewards and escorts for Western pilgrims going to and from the Holy Land. Through such endeavors the Crusaders became rich, ending up as wealthy bankers and moneylenders.

7.2.3.2 THE SECOND AND THIRD CRUSADES Native resistance broke the Crusaders' resolve around mid-century, and the forty-year-plus Latin presence in the East began to crumble. Edessa fell to Islamic armies in 1144. A Second Crusade, preached by Christendom's most eminent religious leader, the Cistercian monk Bernard of Clairvaux (1091–1153), attempted a rescue but was a dismal failure. In October 1187, Saladin (1138–1193), king of Egypt and Syria, reconquered Jerusalem. Except for a brief interlude in the thirteenth century, the holiest of cities remained in Islamic hands until the twentieth century.

A Third Crusade in the twelfth century (1189–1192) attempted yet another rescue, led by the most powerful Western rulers: Hohenstaufen emperor Frederick Barbarossa; Richard the Lion-Hearted, the king of England; and Philip Augustus, the king of France. It became instead a tragicomic commentary on the passing of the original crusading spirit. Frederick Barbarossa drowned while fording a small stream, the Saleph River, near the end of his journey across Asia Minor. Richard the Lion-Hearted and Philip Augustus reached Palestine only to shatter the Crusaders' unity and chances of victory by their intense personal rivalry. Philip Augustus returned to France and declared war on Richard's continental territories. Richard, in turn, fell captive to the Emperor Henry VI while returning to England.

The English paid a handsome ransom for their adventurous king Richard's release. Popular resentment of taxes levied for that ransom was one reason for the revolt against the English monarchy that led to royal recognition of English freedoms in the Magna Carta of 1215.

The long-term results of the first three Crusades had little to do with their original purpose. Politically and religiously they were a failure, and the Holy Land reverted firmly to Muslim hands. The Crusades had, however, been a safety valve for violence-prone Europeans. More important, they stimulated Western trade with the East, as Venetian, Pisan, and Genoan merchants followed the Crusaders across Byzantium to lucrative new markets. The need to resupply the Christian settlements in the Near East also created new trade routes and reopened old ones long closed by Islamic supremacy over the Mediterranean.

CRUSADERS FROM VENICE Venetian Crusaders sailing toward the Holy Land, from a twelfth-century gilded silver and enamel panel from the Pala d'Oro in the Basilica of St. Mark, Venice. The city-state of Venice, which dominated eastern Mediterranean shipping, profited enormously from the Crusades.
SOURCE: San Marco, Venice, Italy/Brigdeman Art Library

7.2.3.3 THE FOURTH CRUSADE A sad comment on both the degeneration of the original crusading ideal and the Crusaders' true historical importance, a Fourth Crusade became a piratical, commercial venture controlled by the Venetians. In 1202, 30,000 Crusaders arrived in Venice to set sail for Egypt. When they could not pay for transport, the Venetians negotiated another venture: the conquest of Zara, a rival Christian port on the Adriatic. Zara, however, proved to be only their first digression; in 1204, they besieged, captured, and sacked Constantinople itself.

This stunning victory brought Venice new lands and maritime rights that ensured its domination of the eastern Mediterranean. Constantinople was now the center for Western trade throughout the Near East. Although its capture embarrassed Pope Innocent III, the papacy was soon sharing the spoils, gleeful at the prospect of extending Roman Christianity to the East.

A confidant of the pope became patriarch of Constantinople and launched a mission to win the Greeks and the Slavs to the Roman Church. Western control of Constantinople continued until 1261, when eastern emperor Michael Palaeologus (r. 1261–1282), helped by the Genoese, who envied their Venetian rival's windfall in the East, finally recaptured the city. This fifty-seven-year occupation of Constantinople did nothing to heal the political and religious divisions between East and West.

A Closer Look

Europeans Embrace a Black Saint

ST. MAURICE, PATRON saint of Magdeburg, Germany, was a third-century Egyptian Christian who commanded the Egyptian legion of the Roman army in Gaul. In 286 C.E. he and his soldiers were executed for impiety after refusing to worship Roman gods. Maurice's cult began in 515, and he became a favorite saint of Charlemagne and other pious, warring German kings.

Portrayed as a white man for centuries, St. Maurice was first depicted as a black man in the mid-thirteenth century. In the era of the Crusades, rulers had their eyes on new possessions in the Orient. Maurice, an Eastern-looking patron saint, seemed the perfect talisman as Western merchants and armies headed east to trade and conquer. At this time, artists also began to paint a black man as one of the three Magi who visited baby Jesus on his birthday. His name, Maurice, came from Latin "Mauri, -orum" (the Moors, inhabitants of Mauritania) and "Maurus, -a, -um" (Moorish, poet, African, Carthaginian). The German word for Moors ("Mohren") also reflects this etymological origin.

The third-century saint continued to be portrayed as a black African. By the fifteenth and sixteenth centuries, Maurice's head adorned the coats of arms of leading Nuremberg families who traded in the Near East: among them were the Tuchers, Nuremberg's great cloth merchants, and Albrecht Dürer, Germany's most famous Renaissance artist.

Europeans apparently believed that representations of St. Maurice as a black African, when carried with them on their travels east as traders and occupiers, would help gain the trust of the people who inhabited Eastern lands.

The simplicity of the saint, and his plain suit of chain mail, suggests that a living model may have posed for the artist who rendered this realistic-looking hero.

ST. MAURICE
SOURCE: Foto Marburg/Art Resource, NY

Questions

1. Did Charlemagne and other German kings embrace Maurice as their favorite saint for mercenary, religious, or military motives?

2. Was racism the reason for the portrayal of Maurice as a white man for eleven centuries, before painters correctly presented him as a dark-skinned saint?

3. Why would some of Nuremberg's leading families adorn their coats of arms with the head of an African saint?

7.2.4 The Pontificate of Innocent III

Pope Innocent III (r. 1198–1216) was a papal monarch who ruled in the Gregorian tradition of papal independence from secular domination. He practiced the doctrine of the plenitude of papal power like no previous pope had done. In a famous statement, Innocent likened the relationship of the pope to the emperor—and the church to the state—to that of the sun to the moon. Like the moon that received its light from the sun, the emperor received his brilliance (i.e., his crown) from the hand of the pope—an allusion to the famous precedent set on Christmas Day, 800, when Pope Leo III crowned Charlemagne.

Although this pretentious theory greatly exceeded Innocent's ability to practice it, he and his successors did not hesitate to act on the ambitions it reflected. When Philip II, the king of France, tried unlawfully to annul his marriage, Innocent placed France under interdict, suspending all church services save baptism and the last rites. England received the same punishment with even greater force when King John refused to accept Innocent's nominee for archbishop of Canterbury. Innocent also intervened frequently and forcefully in the political affairs of the Holy Roman Empire.

7.2.4.1 THE NEW PAPAL MONARCHY Innocent made the papacy a great secular power, with financial resources and a bureaucracy equal to those of contemporary monarchs. During his reign, the papacy was transformed, in effect, into an efficient ecclesio-commercial complex, which reformers would attack throughout the later Middle Ages. Innocent consolidated and expanded ecclesiastical taxes on the laity, the chief of which was "Peter's pence." In England, that tax, long a levy on all but the poorest houses, became a lump-sum payment by the English crown during Innocent's reign. Innocent also imposed an income tax of 2.5 percent on the clergy. *Annates* (the payment of a portion or all of the first year's income received by the holder of a new *benefice*) and fees for the *pallium* (an archbishop's symbol of office) became especially favored revenue-gathering devices.

Innocent also reserved to the pope the absolution of many sins and religious crimes, requiring those wanting pardons or exemptions to bargain directly with Rome. This was a measure of the degree to which the papacy had embraced the new money economy, since it now employed Lombard merchants and bankers to collect the growing papal revenues.

7.2.4.2 CRUSADES IN FRANCE AND THE EAST Innocent's predilection for power politics was also expressed in his embrace of the Crusade, the traditional weapon of the church against Islam, to suppress internal dissent and heresy. Heresy had grown under the influence of native religious reform movements that tried, often naively, to disassociate the church from the growing materialism of the age and to purify it of political scheming. Heresy also stemmed from anticlericalism fed by real clerical abuses that the laity resented, such as immorality, greed, and poor pastoral service.

The idealism of these movements was too extreme for the papacy. In 1209, Innocent launched a Crusade against the **Albigensians**, also known as Cathars, or "pure ones." These advocates of an ascetic, dualist religion were concentrated in the area of Albi in Languedoc in southern France, but they also had adherents among the laity in Italy and Spain. The Albigensians generally sought a pure and simple religious life, claiming to follow the model of the apostles of Jesus in the New Testament. Yet they denied the Old Testament and its God of wrath, as well as God's incarnation in Jesus Christ. Despite certain Christian-influenced ideas, they were non-Christians; their idea of a church was an invisible spiritual force, not a real-world institution.

The more radical Cathars opposed human procreation, believing that to reproduce corporeal bodies was to prolong the imprisonment of immortal souls in dying matter. They avoided it either through extreme sexual asceticism or the use of contraceptives (sponges and acidic ointments) and even abortion. The Cathars' strong dualism, however, also gave latitude in sexual behavior to ordinary believers, based on the idea that the flesh and the spirit were so fundamentally different that the flesh mattered little. It was in opposition to such beliefs that the church developed its strict social teachings condemning contraception and abortion.

The Crusades against the Albigensians were carried out by powerful noblemen from northern France. These great magnates, led by Simon de Montfort, were as much attracted by the great wealth of the area of Languedoc as they were moved by a Christian conscience to stamp out heresy. The Crusades also allowed the northerners to extend their political power into the south. This resulted in a succession of massacres and ended with a special Crusade led by King Louis VIII of France from 1225 to 1226, which destroyed the Albigensians as a political entity. Pope Gregory IX (r. 1227–1241) introduced the **Inquisition** into the region to complete the work of the Crusaders. This institution, a formal tribunal to detect and punish heresy, had been used by the church since the mid-twelfth century as a way for bishops to maintain diocesan discipline. During Innocent's pontificate, it became centralized in the papacy. Papal legates were dispatched to chosen regions to conduct interrogations, trials, and executions.

7.2.4.3 THE FOURTH LATERAN COUNCIL Under Innocent's direction, the **Fourth Lateran Council** met in 1215 to formalize church discipline throughout the hierarchy, from pope to parish priest. The council enacted important ecclesiastical legislation that would greatly affect the practice of Christianity. It gave full dogmatic sanction to the controversial doctrine of **transubstantiation**, according to which the bread and wine of the Lord's Supper become the true body and blood of Christ when consecrated by a priest in the sacrament of the Eucharist. It reflected the influence of the Cluniac monks and those of a newer order, the Cistercians. During the twelfth century, these orders made the adoration of the Virgin Mary, the patron saint of the Cistercians, and the worship of Christ in the Eucharist the centerpieces of a reformed, Christocentric piety. The doctrine of transubstantiation was an expression of the popularity of this piety. It also enhanced the power and authority of the clergy because it specified that only they could perform the miracle of the Eucharist.

In addition, the council made annual confession and Easter communion mandatory for every adult Christian. This legislation formalized the sacrament of penance as the church's key instrument of religious education and discipline in the later Middle Ages.

7.2.4.4 FRANCISCANS AND DOMINICANS
During his reign, Pope Innocent gave official sanction to two new monastic orders: the **Franciscans** and the **Dominicans**. No other action of the pope had more of an effect on spiritual life. Unlike other regular clergy, the members of these mendicant orders, known as *friars*, did not confine themselves to the cloister. They went out into the world to preach the church's mission and to combat heresy, begging or working to support themselves (hence the term *mendicant*).

Lay interest in spiritual devotion, especially among urban women, was particularly intense at the turn of the twelfth century. In addition to the heretical Albigensians, there were movements of Waldensians, Beguines, and Beghards, each of which stressed biblical simplicity in religion and a life of poverty in imitation of Christ. Such movements were especially active in Italy and France. Their heterodox teachings—teachings that, although not necessarily heretical, nonetheless challenged church orthodoxy—and the critical frame of mind they promoted caused the pope deep concern. Innocent feared they would inspire lay piety to turn militantly against the church. The Franciscan and Dominican orders, however, emerged from the same background of intense religiosity. By sanctioning them and thus keeping their followers within the confines of church organization, the pope provided a response to heterodox piety as well as an answer to lay criticism of the worldliness of the papal monarchy.

The Franciscan order was founded by Saint Francis of Assisi (1182–1226), the son of a rich Italian cloth merchant, who became disaffected with wealth and urged his followers to live a life of extreme poverty. Pope Innocent recognized the order in 1210, and its official rule was approved in 1223. The Dominican order, the Order of Preachers, was founded by Saint Dominic (1170–1221), a well-educated Spanish cleric, and was sanctioned in 1216. Both orders received special privileges from the pope and were solely under his jurisdiction. Their special relationship with Rome gave the friars an independence from local clerical authority that bred resentment among some secular clergy.

Pope Gregory IX (r. 1227–1241) canonized Saint Francis only two years after Francis's death—a fitting honor for Francis and a stroke of genius by the pope. Gregory managed to enhance papal authority by bringing within the confines of the church the most popular religious figure of the age, one who had miraculously received the *stigmata* (bleeding wounds like those of the crucified Jesus).

Two years after the canonization, however, Gregory canceled Saint Francis's own *Testament* as an authoritative rule for the Franciscan order. He did this because he found the *Testament* to be an impractical guide and because the unconventional nomadic life of strict poverty it advocated conflicted with his plans to enlist the order as an arm of church policy. Most Franciscans themselves, under the leadership of moderates like Saint Bonaventure, general of the order between 1257 and 1274, also came to doubt the wisdom of extreme asceticism. During the thirteenth century, the main branch of the order progressively complied with papal wishes. In the fourteenth century, the pope condemned a radical branch, the Spiritual Franciscans, extreme followers of Saint Francis who considered him almost a new Messiah. In his condemnation, the pope declared absolute poverty a fictitious ideal that not even Christ endorsed.

The Dominicans, a less factious order, combated doctrinal error through visitations and preaching. They adapted new convents of **Beguines**—lay religious sisterhoods of single lay women in the Netherlands and Belgium—to the church's teaching, led the church's campaign against heretics in southern France, and staffed the offices of the Inquisition after Pope Gregory centralized it in 1223. The great Dominican theologian Thomas Aquinas (d. 1274) was canonized in 1322 for his efforts to synthesize faith and reason in an enduring definitive statement of Catholic belief.

The Dominicans and the Franciscans strengthened the church among the laity. Through the institution of so-called Third Orders, they provided ordinary men and women the opportunity to affiliate with the monastic life and pursue the high religious ideals of poverty, obedience, and chastity while remaining laypeople. Laity who joined such orders were known as **Tertiaries**. Such organizations helped keep lay piety orthodox and within the church during a period of heightened religiosity.

7.3 England and France: Hastings to Bouvines

How did England and France develop strong monarchies?

In 1066, the death of the childless Anglo-Saxon ruler Edward the Confessor (so named because of his reputation for piety) brought about the most important change in English political life. Edward's mother was a Norman, giving the duke of Normandy a competitive, if not the best, hereditary claim to the English throne. Before his death, Edward, who was not a strong ruler, acknowledged that claim and even directed that his throne be given to the reigning duke of Normandy, William, known as **William the Conqueror** (r. 1066–1087) after his accession to the throne of England. Yet the Anglo-Saxon assembly, which customarily bestowed royal power, had a mind of its own and vetoed Edward's last wishes, choosing instead Harold Godwinson. This action triggered the swift conquest of England by the powerful Normans. William's forces defeated Harold's army at the **Battle of Hastings** on October 14, 1066. Within weeks of the invasion, William was crowned king of England in Westminster Abbey, by both right of heredity and right of conquest.

7.3.1 William the Conqueror

Thereafter, William embarked on a twenty-year conquest that eventually made all of England his domain. Every landholder, whether large or small, was to be his vassal, holding land legally as a fief from the king. William organized his new English nation shrewdly. He established a strong monarchy whose power was not fragmented by independent territorial princes. He kept the Anglo-Saxon tax system and the practice of court writs, or legal warnings, as a flexible form of central control over localities. And he took care not to destroy the Anglo-Saxon quasi-democratic tradition of frequent "parleying"—that is, the holding of conferences between the king and lesser powers who had vested interests in royal decisions.

The practice of parleying had been initially nurtured by Alfred the Great (r. 871–899). A strong and willful king

BATTLE OF HASTINGS Detail of the Battle of Hastings, from the *Bayeux Tapestry*, ca. 1073–1083. In this battle on October 14, 1066, William of Normandy defeated Harold II of England and thereby established the Normans as the rulers of England.
SOURCE: Erich Lessing/Art Resource, NY

who had forcibly unified England, Alfred cherished the advice of his councilors in the making of laws. His example was respected and emulated by Canute (r. 1016–1035), the Dane who restored order and brought unity to England after the civil wars that had engulfed the land during the reign of the incompetent Ethelred II (r. 978–1016). Although he thoroughly subjugated his noble vassals to the crown, William consulted with them regularly about decisions of state, continuing to maintain the tradition of parleying. The result was a unique blending of the "one" and the "many," a balance between monarchical and parliamentary elements that has ever since been a feature of English government—although the English Parliament as we know it today did not formally develop as an institution until the late thirteenth century.

For administration and taxation purposes William commissioned a county-by-county survey of his new realm, a detailed accounting known as the *Domesday Book* (1080–1086). The title of the book may reflect the thoroughness and finality of the survey: as none could escape the doomsday judgment of God, no property was overlooked by William's assessors.

7.3.2 Henry II

William's son, Henry I (r. 1100–1135), died without a male heir, throwing England into virtual anarchy until the accession of Henry II (r. 1154–1189). Son of the count of Anjou and Matilda, daughter of Henry I, Henry ascended the throne as head of the new Plantagenet dynasty, the family name of the Angevin, or Anjouan, line of kings who ruled England until the death of Richard III in 1485. Henry tried to recapture the efficiency and stability of his grandfather's regime, but in the process he steered the English monarchy rapidly toward oppressive rule. Thanks to his inheritance from his father Anjou and his marriage to **Eleanor of Aquitaine** (ca. 1122–1204), Henry won virtually the entire west coast of France.

The union with Eleanor created the Angevin, or English–French, Empire. Eleanor married Henry while he was still the count of Anjou and not yet king of England. The marriage occurred eight weeks after the annulment of Eleanor's fifteen-year marriage to the ascetic French king Louis VII in March 1152. Although the annulment was granted on grounds of consanguinity—blood relationship—the true reason for the dissolution of the marriage was Louis's suspicion of her infidelity. According to rumor, Eleanor had been intimate with a cousin. The annulment was costly to Louis, who lost Aquitaine along with his wife. Eleanor and Henry had eight children, five of them sons, among them the future kings Richard the Lion-Hearted and John.

In addition to gaining control of most of the coast of France, Henry also conquered part of Ireland and made the king of Scotland his vassal. Louis VII recognized a mortal threat to France in this English expansion. He responded by adopting what came to be a permanent French policy of containment and expulsion of the English from their continental holdings in France. This policy succeeded in the mid-fifteenth century, when English power on the Continent collapsed after the Hundred Years' War.

7.3.3 Eleanor of Aquitaine and Court Culture

Eleanor of Aquitaine was a powerful influence on both politics and culture in twelfth-century France and England. She accompanied her first husband, King Louis VII, on the Second Crusade, setting an example for women of lesser stature, who were also then venturing in increasing numbers into war and business and other areas previously considered men's domain. After marrying Henry, she settled in Angers, the chief town of Anjou, where she sponsored troubadours and poets at her lively court. There the troubadour Bernart de Ventadorn composed in Eleanor's honor many of the most popular love songs of high medieval aristocratic society. Eleanor spent the years 1154 to 1170 as Henry's queen in England. She separated from Henry in 1170, partly because of his public philandering and cruel treatment, and took revenge on him by joining ex-husband Louis VII in provoking Henry's three

surviving sons, who were unhappy with their inheritance, into an unsuccessful rebellion against their father in 1173. From 1179 until his death in 1189, Henry kept Eleanor under mild house arrest to prevent any further mischief from her.

After her separation from Henry in 1170 and until her confinement in England, Eleanor lived in Poitiers with her daughter Marie, the countess of Champagne, and the two made the court of Poitiers a famous center for the literature of courtly love. This genre, with its thinly veiled eroticism, has been viewed as an attack on medieval ascetic values. Be that as it may, it was certainly a commentary on contemporary domestic life within the aristocracy. The troubadours hardly promoted promiscuity at court: the code of chivalry that guided relations between lords and their vassals condemned the seduction of the wife of one's lord as the most heinous offense, punishable in some places by castration, execution, or both. In a frank and entertaining way, the troubadours, rather, satirized carnal love or depicted it with tragic irony, while praising the ennobling power of friendly, or "courteous," love. The most famous courtly literature was that of Chrétien de Troyes, whose stories of King Arthur and the Knights of the Round Table recounted the tragic story of Sir Lancelot's secret and illicit love for Arthur's wife, Guinevere.

7.3.4 Baronial Revolt and Magna Carta

As Henry II acquired new lands abroad, he became more autocratic at home. In 1164, he forced his will on the clergy in the Constitutions of Clarendon. These measures limited judicial appeals to Rome, subjected the clergy to the civil courts, and gave the king control over the election of bishops. The result was a strong baronial revolt from the nobility and the clergy. The archbishop of Canterbury, Thomas à Becket (1118?–1170), once Henry's compliant chancellor, broke openly with the king and fled to Louis VII in France. Becket's subsequent assassination in 1170 and his canonization by Pope Alexander III in 1172 helped focus resentment against the king's heavy-handed tactics.

Under Henry's successors—the brothers Richard I the Lion-Hearted (r. 1189–1199) and John (r. 1199–1216)—new burdensome taxation in support of unnecessary foreign Crusades and a failing war with France turned resistance into outright rebellion. In 1209, Pope Innocent III, in a dispute with King John over the pope's choice for archbishop of Canterbury, excommunicated the king and placed England under interdict. To extricate himself and keep his throne, John had to make humiliating concessions, even declaring England a fief of the pope. The last straw for the English, however, was the defeat of the king's forces by the French at **Bouvines** in 1214. With the full support of the clergy and the townspeople, English barons revolted

THE MURDER OF ST. THOMAS À BECKET Illustration of the murder of Thomas à Becket in Canterbury Cathedral, from a devotional book of hours (or prayer book).
SOURCE: V&A Images, London/Art Resource, NY

The Magna Carta had more to do with political accident than with political genius. Nevertheless, the English did manage to avoid both dissolution of the monarchy by the nobility and abridgment of the rights of the nobility by the monarchy. Although King John continued to resist the Magna Carta in every way, and succeeding kings ignored it, the Magna Carta nonetheless became a cornerstone of modern English law.

7.3.5 Philip II Augustus

The English struggle in the High Middle Ages had been to secure the rights of the privileged many, not the authority of the king. (The Plantagenets had unbroken rule in the male line from 1154 to 1485.) The French, by contrast, faced the opposite problem. In 987, noblemen chose Hugh Capet to succeed the last Carolingian ruler, replacing the Carolingian dynasty with the Capetian, a third Frankish dynasty that ruled France for twelve generations, until 1328. For two centuries thereafter, until the reign of **Philip II Augustus** (r. 1180–1223), powerful feudal princes contested Capetian rule, burying the principle of election.

During this period, after a rash attempt to challenge the more powerful French nobility before they had enough strength to do so, the Capetian kings concentrated their limited resources on securing the royal domain, their uncontested territory around Paris and the Ile-de-France to the northeast. Aggressively exercising their feudal rights, French kings, especially after 1100, gained near absolute obedience from the noblemen in

against John. The Baronial Revolt ended with the king's grudging recognition of **Magna Carta**, or "Great Charter," in 1215.

The Magna Carta put limits on autocratic behavior of the kind exhibited by the Norman kings and Plantagenet kings. It also secured the rights of the privileged against the monarchy. In the Magna Carta, the privileged preserved their right to be represented at the highest levels of government in important matters like taxation. The monarchy, however, was also preserved and kept strong. This balancing act, which gave power to both sides, had always been the ideal of feudal government.

this area and established a solid base of power. By the reign of Philip II Augustus, Paris had become the center of French government and culture, and the Capetian dynasty a secure hereditary monarchy. Thereafter, the kings of France could impose their will on the French nobles, who were always in law, if not in political fact, the king's sworn vassals.

The Norman conquest of England, in an indirect way, helped stir France to unity, making it possible for the Capetian kings to establish a truly national monarchy. The duke of Normandy, who after 1066 was master of all of England, was also among the vassals of the French king in Paris. Capetian kings understandably watched with alarm as the power of their Norman vassal grew. Other powerful vassals of the king also watched with alarm. King Louis VI, the Fat (r. 1108–1137), formed an alliance with Flanders, traditionally a Norman enemy. King Louis VII (r. 1137–1180), assisted by a brilliant minister, Suger, abbot of St. Denis and famous for his patronage of Gothic architecture, found allies in the great northern French cities and used their wealth to build a royal army.

When he succeeded Louis VII as king, Philip II Augustus inherited financial resources and a skilled bureaucracy that put him in a strong position. Able to resist the competition of the French nobility and the clergy, he focused on the contest with the English king. Confronted at the same time with an internal and an international struggle, Philip proved successful at both. His armies occupied all

the English king's territories on the French coast except for Aquitaine. As a showdown with the English neared on the continent, however, Holy Roman Emperor Otto IV (r. 1198–1215) entered the fray on the side of the English, and the French were assailed from both east and west. But when the international armies finally clashed at Bouvines in Flanders on July 27, 1214, in what history records as the first great European battle, the French won handily over the opposing Anglo–Flemish–German army. This victory unified France politically around the monarchy, laying the foundation for French ascendancy in the later Middle Ages. The defeat so weakened Otto IV that he fell from power in Germany. (It also, as we have seen, sparked the rebellion in England that forced King John to accept Magna Carta.)

Encountering the Past

Pilgrimages

A MEDIEVAL PILGRIMAGE WAS both a spiritual and a social event, and everyone, from king to peasant, might join it. For penitent Christians, a priest might impose a pilgrimage as a temporal "satisfaction" for their sins, a pious act that canceled the

ON PILGRIMAGE TO CANTERBURY This thirteenth-century stained glass window depicts pilgrims traveling to Canterbury Cathedral.
SOURCE: DEA/G. DAGLI ORTI/Getty Images

punishment that God meted out to sinners. Because travel to faraway shrines required self-sacrifice and posed dangers, the church considered pilgrimages especially pleasing to God. The pilgrims' destination was always the shrine, and often the tomb, of a saint, before whose remains and relics pilgrims gained both forgiveness for sins and the saint's friendship and protection. Saints' "bones" and the waters from springs, wells, and streams at the site were believed to cure the ills of body and mind, so pilgrims also came in search of miracles. Infertile women believed a pilgrimage could "open their womb," and parents took ill or crippled children on pilgrimage to beg for a cure. Some parents even carried dead infants, desperately hoping the saint would move God to restore their children's lives.* The three great pilgrimage tombs were those of St. Peter in Rome, St. James in Santiago de Compostela in northern Spain, and Jesus in Jerusalem. Businesses sprang up along the pilgrim trails and at the shrines, providing transportation, shelter, and emergency services. Manuscript "guidebooks" described the routes to the shrines. For example, a mid-twelfth-century guide told pilgrims headed for Santiago de Compostela what to expect in southwestern France:

This is a desolate region. . . . there is no bread, wine, meat, fish, water, or springs; villages are rare here. The sandy and flat land abounds none the less in honey, millet, panic-grass (fodder), and wild boars. If you . . . cross in summertime, guard your face diligently from the enormous flies [wasps and horseflies] that abound there. And if you do not watch your feet . . . you will rapidly sink up to the knees in the sea-sand.**

Pilgrimages were also often group "outings" that medieval people must have found diverting as well as edifying. Most pilgrims traveled with bands of friends, relatives, or neighbors. In the fourteenth century, English poet Geoffrey Chaucer (ca. 1345–1400) wrote his famous work *The Canterbury Tales*, about a group of pilgrims traveling to the shrine of St. Thomas à Becket (1118–1170), the martyred archbishop of Canterbury, who passed the time telling each other amusing stories.

Because the shrines were usually in or near great churches, pilgrimages also gave the best history and architecture lessons available in the Middle Ages. Thus, in Canterbury Cathedral, pilgrims could venerate Becket's relics, which were housed in a glittering jewel-encrusted shrine, and learn about the conflict that had led to the archbishop's murder in that same cathedral by the knights of King Henry II (r. 1154–1189).

Questions

1. List three reasons why people went on pilgrimages in medieval times.
2. Name the three great tombs to which pilgrims journeyed in the Middle Ages.

SOURCES: Klaus Arnold, *Kind und Gesellschaft in Mittelalter und Renaissance* (Munich: Paderborn, 1980), pp. 30–31; Georges Duby, *The Age of the Cathedrals*, trans. by E. Levieux and B. Thompson (Chicago: University of Chicago Press, 1981), pp. 50–51; H. W. Janson and A. F. Janson, *History of Art* (New York: Prentice Hall, 1997), pp. 386–387; Compton Reeves, *Pleasures and Pastimes in Medieval England* (Oxford, UK: Oxford University Press, 1998), pp. 174–175, 180.

NOTES: (*) Klaus Arnold, *Kind und Gesellschaft in Mittelalter und Renaissance* (Munich: Paderborn, 1980), pp. 30–31. (**) H. W. Janson and A. F. Janson, *History of Art* (New York: Prentice Hall, 1997), pp. 386–387.

7.4 France in the Thirteenth Century: The Reign of Louis IX

In what ways was Louis IX of France the ideal medieval monarch?

If Innocent III realized the fondest ambitions of medieval popes, **Louis IX** (r. 1226–1270), the grandson of Philip Augustus, embodied the medieval view of the perfect ruler. Coming to power after the French victory at Bouvines in 1214, Louis inherited a unified and secure kingdom. Not beset by the problems of sheer survival, and a reformer at heart, Louis found himself free to concentrate on what medieval people believed to be the business of civilization.

7.4.1 Generosity Abroad

Magnanimity in politics is not always a sign of strength, and Louis could be very magnanimous. Although in a strong position during negotiations for the Treaty of Paris in 1259, which temporarily settled the dispute between France and England, Louis refused to take advantage of it to drive the English from their French possessions. Had he done so and ruthlessly confiscated English territories on the French coast, he might have lessened, if not averted altogether, the conflict underlying the Hundred Years' War, which began in the fourteenth century. Instead, Louis surrendered disputed territory on the borders of Gascony to the English king, Henry III, and confirmed Henry's possession of the duchy of Aquitaine.

Although he occasionally chastised popes for their crude political ambitions, Louis remained neutral during the long struggle between the German Hohenstaufen emperor Frederick II and the papacy, and his neutrality worked to the pope's advantage. Louis also remained neutral when his brother, Charles of Anjou, intervened in Italy and Sicily against the Hohenstaufens, again to the pope's advantage. Urged on by the pope and his noble supporters, Charles was crowned king of Sicily in Rome, and his subsequent defeat of the son and grandson of Frederick II ended the Hohenstaufen dynasty. For such service to the church, by both action and inaction, the Capetian kings of the thirteenth century received many papal favors.

7.4.2 Order and Excellence at Home

Louis's greatest achievements lay at home. The efficient French bureaucracy, which his predecessors had used to exploit their subjects, became under Louis an instrument of order and fair play in local government. He sent royal commissioners, or *enquêteurs*, reminiscent of Charlemagne's far less successful *missi dominici*, to monitor the royal officials responsible for local governmental administration and to ensure that justice would truly be meted out to all. These royal ambassadors were received as genuine tribunes of the people. Louis further abolished private wars and serfdom within his royal domain. He gave his subjects the judicial right of appeal from local to higher courts and made the tax system, by medieval standards, more equitable. The French people came to associate their king with justice; consequently, national feeling, the glue of nationhood, grew strong during his reign.

Respected by the kings of Europe and possessing far greater moral authority than the pope, Louis became an arbiter among the world's powers. During his reign, French society and culture became an example to all of Europe, a pattern that would continue into the modern period. Northern France became the showcase of monastic reform, chivalry, and Gothic art and architecture. Louis's reign also coincided with the golden age of Scholasticism, which saw the convergence of Europe's greatest thinkers on Paris, among them Saint Thomas Aquinas and Saint Bonaventure.

Louis's perfection remained, however, that of a medieval king. He sponsored the French Inquisition. He led two French Crusades against the Muslims, which, although inspired by the purest religious motives, proved to be personal disasters. During the first Crusade (1248–1254), Louis was captured and had to be ransomed out of Egypt. He died of a fever during the second in 1270. It was especially for this selfless, but also useless, service on behalf of the church that Louis later received the rare honor of sainthood.

7.5 The Hohenstaufen Empire

Map 7–2 GERMANY AND ITALY IN THE MIDDLE AGES

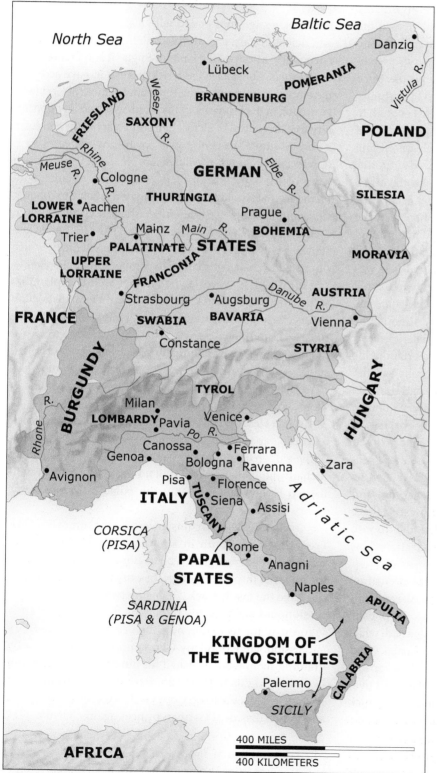

How did the policies of the Hohenstaufens lead to the fragmentation of Germany?

During the twelfth and thirteenth centuries, stable governments developed in both England and France. In England, Magna Carta balanced the rights of the nobility against the authority of the kings, and in France the reign of Philip II Augustus secured the authority of the king over the competitive claims of the nobility. During the reign of Louis IX, the French exercised international influence over politics and culture. But the story within the Holy Roman Empire, which embraced Germany, Burgundy, and northern Italy by the mid-thirteenth century, was different. (See Map 7–2.) There, primarily because of the efforts of the Hohenstaufen dynasty (1152–1272) to extend imperial power into southern Italy, disunity and blood feuding remained the order of the day for two centuries. It left as a legacy the fragmentation of Germany until the nineteenth century.

As shown in this map, medieval Germany and Italy were divided lands. The Holy Roman Empire (Germany) encompassed hundreds of independent territories that the emperor ruled only in name. The papacy controlled the Rome area and tried to enforce its will on Romagna. Under the Hohenstaufens (mid-twelfth to mid-thirteenth centuries), internal German divisions and papal conflict reached new heights; German rulers sought to extend their power to southern Italy and Sicily.

7.5.1 Frederick I Barbarossa

The investiture struggle had earlier weakened imperial authority. After the Concordat of Worms, the German princes were the supreme lay powers within the rich ecclesiastical territories and greatly influenced the appointment of the church's bishops.

The power of the emperor promised to return, however, with the accession to the throne of Frederick I Barbarossa (r. 1152–1190) of the Hohenstaufen dynasty, the strongest line of emperors yet to succeed the Ottonians. This new dynasty not only reestablished imperial authority but also began a new, deadlier phase in the contest between popes and emperors. Never have kings and popes despised and persecuted one another more than during the Hohenstaufen dynasty.

Frederick I confronted powerful feudal princes in Germany and Lombardy and a pope in Rome who still viewed the emperor as his creature. However, the incessant strife among the princes and the turmoil caused by the papacy's pretensions to great political power alienated many people. Such popular sentiment presented Frederick with an opportunity to recover imperial authority, and he was shrewd enough to take advantage of it. Frederick especially took advantage of the contemporary revival of Roman law, which served him on two fronts. On one hand, it praised centralized authority, that of king or emperor, against the nobility; on the other, it stressed the secular origins of imperial power against the tradition of Roman election and papal coronation of the emperor, thus reducing papal involvement to a minimum.

From his base in Switzerland, Frederick attempted to hold his empire together by invoking feudal lands. He was relatively successful in Germany, thanks largely to the fall from power and exile in 1180 of his strongest German rival, Henry the Lion (d. 1195), the duke of Saxony. Although he could not defeat the many German duchies, Frederick never missed an opportunity to remind each German ruler of his prescribed duties as one who held his land legally as a fief of the emperor. The Capetian kings of France had used the same tactic when they faced superior forces of the nobility.

Italian popes proved to be the greatest obstacle to Frederick's plans to revive his empire. In 1155, he restored Pope Adrian IV (r. 1154–1159) to power in Rome after a religious revolutionary had taken control of the city. For his efforts, Frederick won a coveted papal coronation—and strictly on his terms, not on those of the pope. Despite fierce resistance to Frederick in Italy, led by Milan, the door to Italy had opened, and an imperial assembly sanctioned his claims to Italian lands.

As this challenge to royal authority was occurring, Cardinal Roland, a skilled lawyer, became Pope Alexander III (r. 1159–1181). In a clever effort to strengthen the papacy against growing imperial influence, the new pope had, while still a cardinal, negotiated an alliance between the papacy and the Norman kingdom of Sicily. Knowing him to be a capable foe, Frederick opposed his election as pope and backed a rival candidate after the election in a futile effort to undo it. Frederick now found himself at war with the pope, Milan, and Sicily.

By 1167, the combined forces of the northern Italian communes had driven Frederick back into Germany, and, a decade later, in 1176, Italian forces soundly defeated his armies at Legnano. In the Peace of Constance in 1183, which ended the hostilities, Frederick recognized the claims of the Lombard cities to full rights of self-rule, a great blow to his imperial plans.

7.5.2 Henry VI and the Sicilian Connection

Frederick's reign thus ended with a stalemate in Germany and defeat in Italy, and at his death in 1190, he was a ruler not equal in stature to the kings of England and France. After the Peace of Constance, Frederick seemed to have accepted the empire's division among the feudal princes of Germany. However, in the last years of his reign he seized an opportunity to gain control of Sicily, then still a papal ally, and form a new territorial base of power for future emperors. This opportunity arose when William II (r. 1166–1189), the Norman ruler of the kingdom of Sicily, sought an alliance with Frederick that would free him to pursue a scheme to conquer Constantinople. In 1186, a fateful marriage occurred between Frederick's son, the future Henry VI (r. 1190–1197), and Constance, the eventual heiress to the kingdom of Sicily, which promised to change the balance of imperial-papal power.

It proved, however, to be another well-laid plan that went awry. The Sicilian kingdom became a fatal distraction for succeeding Hohenstaufen kings, tempting them to sacrifice their traditional territorial base in northern Europe for dreams of imperialism. Equally disastrous for the Hohenstaufens, the union of the empire with Sicily left Rome encircled, ensuring even greater enmity from a papacy already thoroughly distrustful of the emperor.

When Henry VI became emperor in 1190, he thus faced a hostile papacy; German princes more defiant than ever of the emperor; and an England whose adventurous king, Richard the Lion-Hearted, plotted against Henry VI with the old Hohenstaufen enemy, the exiled duke of Saxony, Henry the Lion.

It was into these circumstances that the future Emperor Frederick II was born in 1194. Previously, the German princes had not recognized birth alone as qualification for the imperial throne, although the offspring of the emperor did have the inside track. To ensure baby Frederick's succession and stabilize his monarchy, Henry campaigned vigorously for recognition of the principle of hereditary succession. He won many German princes to his side by granting them what he asked for himself and his son: full hereditary rights to their own fiefs. Not surprisingly, the encircled papacy strongly opposed hereditary succession and joined dissident German princes against Henry.

7.5.3 Otto IV and the Welf Interregnum

Henry died in September 1197, leaving his son Frederick a ward of the pope. Henry's brother succeeded him as German king, but the Welf family, who were German rivals of the Hohenstaufens, put forth their own candidate, whom the English supported. The French, beginning a series of interventions in German affairs, remained with the Hohenstaufens. The papacy supported first one side and then the other, depending on which seemed most to threaten it. The struggle for power threw Germany into anarchy and civil war.

The Welf candidate, Otto of Brunswick, outlasted his rival and was crowned Otto IV by his followers in Aachen in 1198, thereafter winning general recognition in Germany. In October 1209, Pope Innocent III (r. 1198–1216) boldly meddled in German politics by crowning Otto emperor in Rome. Playing one German dynasty against the other in an evident attempt to curb imperial power in Italy, while fully restoring papal power there, Innocent had badly underestimated the ambition of the new German emperor. After his papal coronation, Otto proceeded to attack Sicily, an old imperial policy that was threatening to Rome. Four months after crowning Otto emperor, Pope Innocent excommunicated him.

7.5.4 Frederick II

As he searched for a counterweight to the treacherous Otto, the pope joined with the French, who had remained loyal to the Hohenstaufens. His new ally, French king Philip Augustus, impressed on Innocent that a solution to their mutual problem with Otto IV lay was near at hand in the person of Innocent's ward: Frederick of Sicily, son of the late Hohenstaufen emperor Henry VI, who had now come of age. Unlike Otto, the young Frederick had an immediate hereditary claim to the imperial throne. In December 1212, with papal, French, and German support, Frederick was crowned king of the Romans in the German city of Mainz. Within a year and a half, Philip Augustus ended the reign of Otto IV on the battlefield of Bouvines, and three years later in 1215, Frederick II was crowned emperor again, this time in the sacred imperial city of Aachen.

During his reign, Frederick effectively turned dreams of a unified Germany into a nightmare of disunity, assuring German fragmentation into modern times. Raised Sicilian and dreading travel beyond the Alps, Frederick spent only nine of his thirty-eight years as emperor in Germany, and six of those were before 1218. Although he pursued his royal interests in Germany, Frederick did so mostly through representatives, seeming to desire only the imperial title for himself and his sons, and willing to give the German princes whatever they wanted to secure it. It was this eager compliance with the princes' demands that laid the foundation for six centuries of German division. In 1220, Frederick recognized the jurisdictional claims of the ecclesiastical princes of Germany, and twelve years later in 1232, he extended the same recognition to the secular princes.

Frederick's concessions amounted to an abdication of imperial power in Germany, and some viewed them as a kind of German Magna Carta that secured the rights of the German nobility for the foreseeable future. But unlike the king of England within his realm, Frederick did little to secure the rights of the emperor in Germany. Whereas Magna Carta had the long-term consequence of promoting a balance of power between king and parliament, Frederick made the German princes little emperors within their respective realms. Centuries of petty absolutism, not parliamentary government, were the result.

Frederick's relations with the pope were equally disastrous, leading to his excommunication on four different occasions—the first in 1227 for refusing to finish a crusade he had begun at the pope's request. Frederick was also determined to control Lombardy and Sicily, a policy that was anathema to the pope. The papacy came to view Frederick as the Antichrist, the biblical beast of the Apocalypse, whose persecution of the faithful signaled the end of the world.

The papacy won the long struggle that ensued, although its victory was arguably a Pyrrhic one. During this bitter contest, Pope Innocent IV (r. 1243–1254) launched the church into European politics on a massive scale, a policy that left the church vulnerable to criticism from both religious reformers and royal apologists. Pope Innocent organized the German princes against Frederick, who—thanks to Frederick's grand concessions—were the superior force and gained full control of Germany by the 1240s.

When Frederick died in 1250, the German monarchy died with him. The princes established their own informal electoral college in 1257, which thereafter controlled the succession. Through this institution, which the emperor recognized in 1356, the "king of the Romans" became a puppet of the princes, and one with firmly attached strings. The princes elected him directly, and his offspring had no hereditary right to succeed him. The last male Hohenstaufen was executed in 1268.

Independent princes henceforth controlled Germany, while the imperial kingdom in Italy fell to local Italian magnates. The connection between Germany and Sicily ended forever, and the papal monarchy emerged as one of Europe's most formidable powers, soon to enter its most costly conflict of the Middle Ages with the new French and

English monarchies. Internal division and the absence of a representative system of government persisted in Germany for six centuries. Even after Chancellor Bismarck created a new German empire in 1871, the legacy of the Hohenstaufen dynasty's defeat was still evident until the end of World War I.

Romanesque and Gothic Architecture

THE HIGH MIDDLE AGES WITNESSED the peak of **Romanesque** art and the transition to the **Gothic**. Romanesque literally means "like Rome," and the art and architecture of the High Middle Ages embraced the classical style of ancient Rome. Romanesque churches were fortress-like, and rounded arches, thick stone walls, and heavy columns supported their vaults or ceilings. In the early Middle Ages, this architecture expressed the church's role as a refuge for the faithful and a new world power. Developed under the Carolingians and Ottonians, the Romanesque attained its perfection and predominated between 1050 and 1200.

EKKEHARD AND UTA, CA. 1240–1250 This famous noble pair founded Naumburg Cathedral in Germany in the middle of the thirteenth century. The sculptures hint at the distinct personalities of Ekkehard and Uta and represent German Gothic artistry at its best.
SOURCE: VPC Travel Photo/Alamy Stock Photo

The Gothic style of art and architecture, appearing first in mid-twelfth-century France, was mainly adopted in Northern Europe. Its distinctive features were ribbed, crisscrossed ceiling, with pointed arches in place of rounded ones, a clever construction technique that allowed Gothic churches to soar far above their Romanesque predecessors. The greater weight on the walls was off-loaded by exterior "flying" buttresses built directly into them. With the walls thus shored up, they could be filled with wide expanses of stained glass windows that flooded the churches with colored light.

Beginning in the mid-twelfth century, the Gothic style evolved from Romanesque architecture. The term Gothic was at first pejorative; it meant "barbaric" and was applied to the new style by its critics. Gothic style was also often known in the Middle Ages as the "French style" because of its unusual popularity in France. Its most distinctive visible features are its ribbed, crisscrossing vaulting, its pointed arches rather than rounded ones, and its frequent exterior buttresses, essentially giving an impression of vertical lines. The vaulting allowed more height than the Romanesque style had achieved, and the "flying" buttresses made even greater height possible. Walls therefore did not have to carry all of a structure's weight, making wide expanses of stained glass windows possible, which reflected the colored light characteristic of Gothic cathedrals. These windows were used to depict stories of saints' lives and of local events, as well as Biblical tales. A similar effect had been achieved by mosaics of earlier times.

ROMANESQUE CATHEDRAL ARCHITECTURE The Romanesque style of architecture derives from the majestic Doric style of classical Greece, and, in Christian Europe, it was meant to inspire detachment and transcendence as well as a sense of awe for God's omnipotence. The Tower of Pisa appears in the background on the far right in photograph on the left of the cathedral complex at Pisa, in Tuscany. At right, the Romanesque interior of the nave of San Clemente in Rome.

SOURCES: Andre Jenny Stock Connection Worldwide/Newscom (left). Erich Lessing/Art Resource, NY (right).

GOTHIC CATHEDRAL ARCHITECTURE: INTERIORS The distinctive features of Gothic architecture, seen in these photographs of the interiors of Salisbury Cathedral (left) and Amiens Cathedral (right), are a ribbed, crisscrossed ceiling, with pointed arches in place of rounded ones, a clever construction technique that allowed Gothic churches to soar far above their Romanesque predecessors.

SOURCES: Silbilbernicus/Alamy Stock Photo (left). Prisma by Dukas Presseagentur GmbH/Alamy Stock Photo (right).

GOTHIC CATHEDRAL ARCHITECTURE: EXTERIORS Located in the city of Reims, France, northeast of Paris, the Cathedral de Notre-Dame de Reims was the coronation site for the kings of France. Its elaborate Gothic façade at its west entrance is seen on the left. Flying buttresses, when viewed from the south, are visible at right.
SOURCES: Carl & Ann Purcell/Corbis/Getty Images (left), Heritage Image Partnership Ltd/Alamy Stock Photo (right)

The Chapter in Perspective

With its borders finally secured, Western Europe was free to develop its political institutions and cultural forms during the High Middle Ages. The map of Europe as we know it today began to take shape. England and France were formed into modern nation-states, but within Germany and the Holy Roman Empire the story was different. There, imperial rule first revived under the Ottonians and then collapsed totally under the Hohenstaufens. The consequences for Germany were ominous, and it became Europe's most fractured land. On a local level, however, an effective organization of society from noble to serf emerged throughout Western Europe.

The major disruption of the period was an unprecedented conflict between former allies, church and state. During the investiture struggle and the period of the Crusades, the church became a powerful monarchy in its own right. For the first time, it competed with secular states on its own terms, dethroning emperors, kings, and princes by excommunication and interdict. In doing so, it inadvertently laid the foundation for the Western doctrine of the separation of church and state.

Having succeeded so brilliantly in defending its spiritual authority against rulers, popes ventured boldly into the realm of secular politics as well, especially during the pontificates of Innocent III and Innocent IV. As the sad story of the Hohenstaufen dynasty attests, the popes had remarkable, if short-lived, success there also. But the church was to pay dearly for its successes, both spiritually and politically.

Secularization of the papacy during the High Middle Ages left it vulnerable to the attacks of a new breed of unforgiving religious reformers, and the powerful monarchs of the later Middle Ages would subject it to bold and vengeful bullying.

KEY POLITICAL EVENTS OF THE HIGH MIDDLE AGES

955	Otto I defeats Hungarians at Lechfeld, securing Europe's eastern border
1066	Normans win the Battle of Hastings and assume English rule
1152	Frederick I Barbarossa becomes first Hohenstaufen emperor; reestablishes imperial authority
1154	Henry II assumes the English throne as the first Plantagenet or Angevin king
1164	Henry II forces the Constitutions of Clarendon on the English clergy
1170	Henry II's defiant archbishop, Thomas à Becket, is assassinated
1176	Papal and other Italian armies defeat Frederick I at Legnano
1194	Future Hohenstaufen ruler Frederick II is born, who becomes a ward of the pope
1198	Welf interregnum in the empire begins under Otto IV
1212	Frederick II crowned emperor in Mainz with papal, French, and German support
1214	French armies under Philip II Augustus defeat combined English and German forces at Bouvines in the first major European battle
1215	English barons revolt against King John and force the king's recognition of Magna Carta
1227	Frederick II excommunicated for the first of four times by the pope; conflict between Hohenstaufen dynasty and papacy begins
1250	Frederick II dies, having been defeated by the German princes with papal support
1257	German princes establish their own electoral college to elect future emperors

The Chapter in Review

Review Questions

1. How was the Saxon king Otto I able to consolidate political rule over the various German duchies and use the church to his advantage? Does he deserve the title "the Great"?

2. What were the main reasons for the Cluny reform movement? Why did it succeed? How did this reform movement influence the subsequent history of the medieval church?

3. Why did Pope Gregory VII and King Henry IV conflict over the issue of lay investiture? What was the outcome of their struggle? What did each side have at stake, and how did the struggle affect the emperor's power in Germany?

4. The eighteenth-century French intellectual Voltaire said the Holy Roman Empire was neither holy, nor Roman, nor an empire. What did he mean? Do you agree with him?

5. What major development in western and eastern Europe encouraged the emergence of the Crusades? Why did the Crusaders fail to establish lasting political and religious control over the Holy Land?

6. What were some of the factors preventing German consolidation under the Hohenstaufens? Why did Germany remain in feudal chaos while France and England eventually coalesced into reasonably strong states?

Key Terms

Albigensians (Al-bi-GEN-see-uns) Thirteenth-century advocates of a dualist religion, who took their name from the city of Albi in southern France. Also called *Cathars*.

Battle of Hastings Battle in 1066 in which William, the reigning duke of Normandy, defeated Harold's army to become king of England.

Beguines (bi-GEENS) Lay sisterhoods not bound by the rules of a religious order.

Bouvines Site of decisive French victory over opposing Anglo-Flemish-German army on July 27, 1214, in what is known as the first great European battle.

Cluny reform movement Monastic reform movement of the tenth century based in Cluny monastery in east-central France; established the Western separation of church and state and the strict rule of celibacy for the clergy.

Crusades Religious wars directed by the church against infidels and heretics.

Dominicans A mendicant Order of Preachers founded by Saint Dominic and sanctioned by the pope in 1216.

Eleanor of Aquitaine After divorcing her first husband, King Louis VII, became Henry II's queen in England from 1154 to 1170; a powerful influence on both politics and culture in twelfth-century France and England.

Fourth Lateran Council (1215) Under the direction of Innocent III, sanctioned the doctrine of transubstantiation, and made annual confession and Easter communion mandatory for every adult Christian.

Franciscans A religious order founded by Saint Francis of Assisi, who urged his followers to live a life of extreme poverty; recognized by Pope Innocent in 1210.

Gothic Style of art and architecture that appeared first in mid-twelfth-century France, which evolved from the Romanesque, and includes distinctive features such as ribbed, crisscrossed ceilings, with pointed arches in place of rounded ones, and frequent exterior buttresses.

Inquisition A tribunal created by the Catholic Church in the mid-twelfth century to detect and punish heresy.

investiture controversy The medieval conflict between the church and lay rulers over who would control bishops and abbots, symbolized by the ceremony of "investing" them with the symbols of their authority.

Louis IX King of France (r. 1226–1270), whose reign saw French society and culture become an example for all of Europe.

Magna Carta (MAG-nuh CAR-tuh) The "Great Charter" limiting royal power that the English nobility forced King John to sign in 1215.

Otto I Holy Roman Emperor (r. 962–973) who defeated the Hungarians at Lechfeld to secure German borders and unify the German duchies.

Philip II Augustus King of France (r. 1180–1223) who succeeded Louis VII; unified France around the monarchy after his victory at Bouvines in 1214.

Romanesque Style of art and architecture of the High Middle Ages characterized by rounded arches, thick stone walls, and heavy columns that support their vaults or ceilings.

Tertiaries (TER-she-air-ees) Laypeople affiliated with the monastic life who took vows of poverty, chastity, and obedience but remained in the world.

Transubstantiation The doctrine that the entire substances of the bread and wine are changed in the Eucharist into the body and blood of Christ.

William the Conqueror (r. 1066–1087) The duke of Normandy who defeated the English at the Battle of Hastings, in 1066, to become the first Norman king of England.

Note

1. Joseph Strayer, *Western History in the Middle Ages—A Short History* (New York: Appleton-Century-Crofts, 1955).

Chapter 8
Medieval Society: Hierarchies, Towns, Universities, and Families (1000–1300)

THE HARVEST The livelihood of towns and castles in medieval society depended on the labor of peasants in surrounding villages. Here a peasant family collects the September grape harvest from a vineyard outside a fortified castle in France in preparation for making wine.
SOURCE: PRISMA ARCHIVO/Alamy Stock Photo

 ## Contents and Focus Questions

The Chapter in Brief

BETWEEN THE TENTH and twelfth centuries, European agricultural production steadily improved, due to a warming climate and improved technology. With steadily increasing food supplies came a population explosion by the eleventh century. The recovery of the countryside in turn stimulated new migrations into, and trade with, long-dormant towns. Old towns revived and new ones arose. A rich and complex fabric of life developed, integrating town and countryside, allowing civilization to flourish in the twelfth and thirteenth centuries as it had not done in the West since the Roman Empire. Beginning with the Crusades, trade with distant towns and foreign lands also revived. With the rise of towns, a new merchant class, the ancestors of modern capitalists, appeared. Large numbers of skilled artisans and day workers, especially in the cloth-making industries, laid the foundations of the new urban wealth.

Urban culture and education also flourished. The revival of trade with the East and contacts with Muslim intellectuals, particularly in Spain, made possible the recovery of ancient scholarship and science. Beyond the comparative dabbling in antiquity during Carolingian times, the twelfth century enjoyed a true renaissance of classical learning. Schools and curricula broadened to educate laymen and some laywomen, thereby increasing literacy and the laity's role in government and society.

8.1 The Traditional Order of Life

What was the relationship among the three basic groups in medieval society?

In the art and literature of the Middle Ages, three social groups were represented: those who fought as knights (the landed nobility), those who prayed (the clergy), and those who labored in fields and shops (rural peasants and village artisans). After the revival of towns in the eleventh century, a fourth social group emerged: the long-distance traders and merchants. Like the peasantry, they also labored, but in ways strange to the traditional groups. They were freemen who often possessed great wealth, but unlike the nobility and the clergy, they owned no land, and unlike the peasantry, they did not toil in fields or shops. Their rise to power put a large crack in the old social order, leading to the growth of urban artisan groups and an accompanying revival of trade.

8.1.1 Nobles

As a distinctive social group, not all noblemen were originally great men with large hereditary lands. Many rose from

MEDIEVAL KNIGHT Knights were armored cavalry who constituted the core of medieval armies. Metal plate and meshes of interlinking "mail armor" were the dominant forms of protection. Most of the early knights came from humble origins. But, by the late twelfth century, knights came to be regarded as nobles and identified with chivalry.
SOURCE: Panther Media GmbH/Alamy Stock Photo

the ranks of feudal vassals, or warrior knights. The successful vassal attained a special social and legal status based on his landed wealth, or accumulated fiefs, his exercise of authority over others, and his distinctive social customs—all of which set him apart from others in medieval society. By the late Middle Ages, a distinguishable higher and lower nobility living both in town and country evolved. The higher nobility included the great landowners and territorial magnates, who had long been the dominant powers in their regions, while the lower nobility were comprised of petty landlords, descendants of minor knights, newly rich merchants looking to buy country estates, and wealthy farmers patiently risen from their ancestral serfdom.

A special characteristic of the nobility was that they lived off the labor of others. Basically lords of manors, the nobility of the early and High Middle Ages neither tilled the soil like the peasantry nor engaged in the commerce of merchants—activities considered beneath their dignity. The nobleman resided in a country mansion or, if he was particularly wealthy, a castle. Although his fiefs were usually rural manors, personal preference drew him to the countryside.

8.1.1.1 WARRIORS Arms were the nobleman's profession; to wage war was his sole occupation and reason for living.

In the eighth century, the adoption of stirrups made the mounted warriors, or cavalry, indispensable to a successful army, as they permitted the rider to strike a blow without falling off the horse. Good horses and the accompanying armor and weaponry of horse warfare were expensive; only those with means could pursue the life of a cavalryman. The nobleman's fief gave him the means to acquire the expensive military equipment that his rank required. He maintained that enviable position in the same way he had gained it, by fighting for his chief.

The nobility celebrated the physical strength, courage, and constant activity of warfare. Warring gave them new riches and an opportunity to gain honor and glory. In war, everything became fair game. Knights were given a share in the plunder of victory, and they had special war wagons, designed to collect and transport booty. Periods of peace were greeted with sadness, as they brought economic stagnation and boredom. Whereas the peasants and the townspeople required peace for their occupational success, the nobility despised it as an unnatural state.

The superior nobility looked down on the peasantry as cowards who ran and hid during war. And they also held urban merchants, who amassed wealth by methods foreign to feudal society, in equal contempt, which only increased as the affluence and political power of townspeople grew. The nobility possessed as strong a sense of superiority toward "unwarlike" people as the clergy did toward the general run of the laity. (See the "Encountering the Past" sidebar on children's games, which follows below.)

8.1.1.2 KNIGHTHOOD The nobleman acquired status within medieval society through the accolade, a ceremony to confer knighthood, also known as dubbing or *adoubement* (Lat., *benedictio militis*, benediction of the soldier). This chivalric ritual marking the entrance into the nobility became almost a religious sacrament. It was preceded by a bath of purification, confession, communion and a prayer vigil. Thereafter, a priest blessed the knight's standard, lance and sword. As prayers were chanted, the priest girded the knight with his sword and presented him with his shield, enlisting him as much into the defense of the church as into the service of his lord. Dubbing of the nobleman to a state sacred in his sphere was equal to the priest's clerical ordination. The comparison is legitimate: the clergy and the nobility were medieval society's privileged estates. The appointment of noblemen to high ecclesiastical office and their eager participation in the church's Crusades had strong ideological and social underpinnings as well as economic and political motives.

In the twelfth century, knighthood was legally restricted to men of high birth. This circumscription of noble ranks was a reaction to the growing wealth, political power, and successful social climbing of newly rich townspeople (mostly merchants), who formed a new urban patriciate that was increasingly competitive with the lower nobility. However, kings remained free to confer knighthoods at will and were eager to increase royal revenues by selling noble titles to wealthy merchants. But the law was building fences—fortunately, with gates—between town and countryside in the High Middle Ages.

8.1.1.3 SPORTSMEN In peacetime, the nobility had two favorite amusements: hunting and tournaments. Where they could, noblemen monopolized the rights to game, forbidding commoners from hunting in the lord's forests. Such denials caused the common man to revolt, and free game, fishing, and access to wood were the basic demands in petitions of grievance.

Tournaments also sowed seeds of social disruption, but more within the ranks of the nobility. The popular jousts were designed not only to keep men fit for war but also to provide the excitement of war without maiming and killing prized vassals. But as regions competed fiercely with each another for victory and glory, even mock battles with blunted weapons proved to be deadly, and often, tournaments got out of hand, ending in bloodshed and animosity. The intense emotion that accompanies interregional soccer in Europe today may be viewed as a relic of such rivalry.

The church opposed tournaments as occasions for pagan revelry and senseless violence. Kings and princes also turned against them as sources of division within their realms. King Henry II of England condemned tournaments in the twelfth century. Jousting did not end in France until the mid-sixteenth century, only after Henry II of France was mortally wounded by a shaft thrust through his visor during a tournament celebrating his daughter's marriage. (For more about the joys and pains of jousting, see the "Closer Look" sidebar, which follows below.)

8.1.1.4 COURTLY LOVE From the repeated assemblies in the courts of barons and kings, codes of social conduct, or "courtesy," developed in noble circles. With the French leading the way, mannered behavior and court etiquette became almost as important as expertise on the battlefield. Knights learned to be literate gentlemen, and lyric poets sang and moralized at court. The cultivation of this code of behavior and a special literature to eulogize it was not unrelated to problems within the social life of the nobility. Noblemen were notorious philanderers; their illegitimate children mingled openly with their legitimate offspring. The advent of courtesy was, in part, an effort to reform such behavior.

Although the poetry of **courtly love** was sprinkled with eroticism and the beloved in the epics were married women pursuing married men, the poet recommended love at a distance, unconsummated by sexual intercourse. The ideal was love without touching. As the court poets reminded, those who succumbed to illicit carnal love reaped as much suffering as joy.

Encountering the Past

Children's Games, Warrior Games

IN THE MIDDLE Ages, the nobility—the warrior class—dominated society, and their favorite games grew out of their work, which was lethal fighting. Boys of the warrior class learned to ride early. Some received horses and daggers at age two! At fourteen, they were given a man's sword and thereafter engaged in sports that prepared them for battle.

Peasants, townspeople, and clergy also engaged in war games and sports. Peasants and townspeople attended tournaments and imitated what they saw there. Among children's toys were homemade lances, shields, and pikes. Favored games were mock combats and "sheriffs and outlaws."

Although there were famous clerical sportsmen and warriors, the clergy's "penchant for violence" was largely vicarious. One of the great achievements of Norman Romanesque art, the *Bayeux Tapestry* (1077), was commissioned by bishop Odo of Bayeux (d. 1097), half-brother of William the Conqueror (r. 1066–1087). It is very well preserved and, although incomplete, it measures nearly 230 feet (70 meters) in length. Its rich embroidery depicts about fifty scenes of the Norman conquest of

CHILDREN AT PLAY Pieter Brueghel's painting of *Children's Games* (1560) depicts boys and girls engaged in seventy-eight different games. Some of them, like jousting and wrestling, are adapted from the war preparation activities of the European nobility.
SOURCE: Erich Lessing/Art Resource, NY

England, culminating in the Battle of Hastings (1066). The aristocratic women who wove such tapestries might ride to the hunt, enjoying the tournaments while remaining spectators, not participants, in the violent pastimes of the nobility.

More reflective of the contemplative life of the religious and of pious noblewomen were the indoor board games played in the manor houses and the cloisters. Two of these games were "Tick, Tack, Toe" and "Fox and the Geese." The object of the second game was to capture the most geese, or spaces in the board, by covering them with pebbles or fruit pits. Men and women of leisure, both clerical and lay, also played chess and backgammon.

By the late fifteenth century, changes in warfare reduced the role of mounted knights in battle and, tournaments were mostly held as pastimes. At the fairs, horse races and mock combats were spread among ball games (rugby, soccer, and football), animal acts, puppet shows, juggling, and the like. Games that prepared the citizenry for real war, like wrestling and jousting, were matched by others invented to overcome boredom and idleness: hoops, leapfrog, blind man's bluff, marbles, golf, stilts, masquerades, tug-of-war, and jacks.

Questions

1. Why did the medieval nobility play warlike games?
2. How did medieval women and children participate in these pastimes?

SOURCE: John Marshall Carter, *Medieval Games: Sports and Recreations in Feudal Society* (New York: Greenwood Press, 1992), pp. 25, 30–33, 34, 69; John Marshall Carter, "The Ludic Life of the Medieval Peasant: A Pictorial Essay," *Arete* III (1986): 169–187; J. T. Micklethwaite, "On the Indoor Games of School Boys in the Middle Ages," *Archeological Journal* (1892), pp. 319–328; Carter, "Ludic Life," p. 177; Steven Ozment, *Ancestors: The Loving Family in Old Europe* (Cambridge, MA: Harvard University Press, 2001), pp. 71–72.

A Closer Look

The Joys and Pains of the Medieval Joust

THIS SCENE FROM a manuscript (ca. 1300–1340) idealizes noblemen and the medieval joust. Revived in the late Middle Ages, jousts were frequently held in peacetime. They kept the warring skills of noblemen sharp and were popular entertainment. Only the nobility was legally allowed to joust, but with time, uncommon wealth enabled a persistent commoner to qualify. The goal of the joust was to knock the crests, or helmet ornamentation, off an opponent's head.

Not depicted are the nonparticipant knights who rode about on their chargers with noblewomen sitting sidesaddle at their backs with one hand firmly around the rider's waist.

Musicians and trumpeters provided the hoopla that accompanied a joust.

The goal of jousting was to knock the crests off helmets. These crests, like body armor, shields and flags, displayed coats of arms to distinguish men of noble birth from their opponents during chivalric competitions as well as on the battlefield.

The helmet was designed to protect the face, while providing a thin window for visibility.

Although jousts often led to mayhem and death, the jouster's intent was not to inflict bodily harm on his opponent; for that reason, lances had blunt ends.

MEDIEVAL JOUST
SOURCE: Bettmann/Getty Images

Questions

1. Although jousts sometimes led to death, were they meant to inflict bodily harm on one's opponent? What do the blunt lances and sturdy helmet in the illustration tell us?
2. Why were jousts frequently held in peacetime?
3. Why were jousts limited to the nobility? What did the nobility gain by keeping their warring skills sharp?
4. What are the attitudes of the observing noblewomen shown in the picture?

8.1.1.5 SOCIAL DIVISIONS No medieval group—not the nobility, the clergy, the townspeople, or the peasantry—was absolutely uniform. Noblemen encompassed a broad spectrum—from minor vassals without subordinate vassals, to mighty barons who were the principal vassals of a king or prince, who in turn had many vassals of their own. Dignity and status within the nobility were directly related to the exercise of authority over others. A chief with many vassals dwarfed the small country nobleman who served a higher nobleman and was lord only over himself.

Even among the domestic servants of the nobility, a social hierarchy developed according to manorial duties. Although they were peasants in the eyes of the law, the chief stewards were charged with the oversight of the manor and the care and education of the lord's children. They became powerful "lords" within their "domains." Some freemen found the status of the steward enviable enough to surrender their own freedom and become domestic servants hoping to attain a still greater freedom.

AN EXPRESSION OF COURTLY LOVE Lovers playing chess on an
ivory mirror back, ca. 1300.
SOURCE: Louvre, Paris, France/Bridgeman Art Library

In the late Middle Ages, the landed nobility suffered a
steep economic and political decline. Climatic changes and
agricultural failures created large famines, and the great
plague brought unprecedented population loss. The cavalry
of knights was made almost obsolete by new military tactics, such as infantry and heavy artillery, employed during
the Hundred Years' War. Also, the alliance of wealthy towns
with kings posed a challenge to the nobility within their
own domains. A waning of the landed nobility occurred
after the fourteenth century when the effective possession of
land and wealth counted more than lineage for membership
in the highest social class. However, a shrinking nobility
continued to dominate society until the nineteenth century.

8.1.2 Clergy

Unlike the nobility and the peasantry, the clergy was an
open estate. Although the clerical hierarchy reflected the
social classes from which the clergy came, one was still a
cleric by religious training and ordination, not through by
any circumstances of birth or military prowess.

8.1.2.1 REGULAR AND SECULAR CLERICS   There were
two basic types of clerical vocation: the **regular clergy** and
the **secular clergy**. The first was comprised of the orders
of monks who lived under a special ascetic rule, or *regula*,
in cloisters separated from the world. They were the spiritual elite among the clergy, and theirs was not a way of
life one entered lightly. Canon law required that a man
be at least twenty-one years old before taking the monastic vows of poverty, chastity, and obedience. The monks'

personal sacrifices and high religious ideals made them
much respected in high medieval society. This popularity was a major factor in the success of the Cluny reform
movement and of the Christian Crusades of the eleventh
and twelfth centuries. By joining the Crusades and holy
pilgrimages, laypeople were introduced to the ascetic life
of prayer wherein they, following the monks, imitated the
suffering and death of Jesus in retreat from the world and
severe self-denial.

Many monks, and also nuns, increasingly embraced the
vows of poverty, obedience, and chastity without a clerical rank and secluded themselves completely. The regular
clergy, for the most part, was never completely cut off
from the secular world. They maintained frequent contact
with the laity through charitable activities such as feeding
the destitute and tending the sick, providing liberal arts
instruction in monastic schools, and acting as supplemen-
tal preachers and confessors in parish churches during Lent
and other peak religious seasons. This dual ability to live a
common life according to a special rule and still be active in
a worldly ministry defined the lives of the Dominican and
Franciscan friars. Some monks, because of their learning
and rhetorical skills, even rose to prominence as secretaries
and private confessors to kings and queens.

The secular clergy, who lived and worked among the
laity in the world, formed a vast hierarchy. At the top were
the high prelates—the wealthy cardinals, archbishops, and
bishops, who were drawn almost exclusively from the
nobility—and below them were the urban priests, the cathedral canons, and the court clerks. Finally, there was the great
mass of poor parish priests, who were neither financially
nor intellectually far above the common people they served.
Their basic educational requirement was an ability to say
the mass. Before the Gregorian church reform in the eleventh century, parish priests lived with women in relationships similar to marriage, and the communities they served
accepted their concubines and children. Because of their
relative poverty, priests often took second jobs as teachers,
artisans, or farmers, and their parishioners accepted and
admired this practice.

8.1.2.2 NEW ORDERS   One of the results of the Gregorian
reform was the creation of new religious orders aspiring
to lives of poverty and self-sacrifice in imitation of Christ
and the first apostles. The more important were the **Canons
Regular** (fd. 1050–1100), the **Carthusians** (fd. 1084), the
Cistercians (fd. 1098), and the **Praemonstratensians**
(fd. 1121). Carthusians, Cistercians, and Praemonstratensians practiced extreme austerity in their quest to recapture
the pure religious life of the early church.

Strictest of them all were the Carthusians. Members
lived in isolation and fasted three days a week. They also
devoted themselves to long periods of silence and even self-
flagellation to achieve the perfect self-denial and conform
to Christ.

The Cistercians, from Cîteaux in Burgundy, were a reform wing of the Benedictine order and were known as the "white monks," a reference to their all-white attire symbolic of apostolic purity. (The Praemonstratensians also wore white.) They hoped to avoid the materialistic influences of urban society and maintain uncorrupted the original *Rule of Saint Benedict*, which their leaders believed Cluny was compromising. The Cistercians accordingly stressed anew the inner life and spiritual goals of monasticism. They located their houses in remote areas and denied themselves worldly comforts and distractions. Remarkably successful, the order could count 300 chapter houses within a century of its founding, and many others imitated its more austere spirituality.

The Canons Regular were independent groups of secular clergy (and also earnest laity) who in addition to serving laity in the world, adopted the *Rule of Saint Augustine*, a monastic guide dating from around the year 500, and practiced the ascetic virtues of regular clerics. By merging the life of the cloister with traditional clerical duties, the Canons Regular foreshadowed the mendicant friars of the thirteenth century: the Dominicans and the Franciscans, who combined the ascetic ideals of the cloister with an active ministry in the world.

The monasteries and nunneries of the established orders recruited candidates from among wealthy social groups. Crowding in these convents and the absence of patronage gave rise in the thirteenth century to lay satellite convents known as Beguine houses. These convents housed religiously earnest single women from the upper and middle social strata. In the German city of Cologne, one hundred such houses were established between 1250 and 1350, each with eight to twelve "sisters." Several of these convents fell prey to heresy. The church made the new religious orders of Dominicans and Franciscans responsible for "regularizing" such convents.

8.1.2.3 PROMINENCE OF THE CLERGY The medieval clergy comprised a greater proportion of medieval society than they do in modern society. Estimates suggest that 1.5 percent of fourteenth-century Europe was in clerical garb. The clergy was concentrated in urban areas, especially in towns with universities and cathedrals, where in addition to studying, they found work in a wide variety of religious services.[1] In large university towns, the clergy might exceed 10 percent of the population.

Despite the moonlighting of poorer parish priests, the clergy, like the nobility, lived off the labor of others. Their income came from the regular collection of tithes and church taxes according to an elaborate system that evolved in the High and later Middle Ages. The church was, of course, a major landowner and regularly collected rents and fees. Monastic communities and high prelates amassed great fortunes; as one popular saying had it: "monastery granaries were always full." The immense secular power attached to high clerical posts can be seen in the intensity of the investiture struggle.

For most of the Middle Ages, the clergy was the "first estate," and theology the queen of the sciences. Much of the clergy's prominence was self-proclaimed, but there were also popular respect and reverence for the clergy's role as a mediator between God and man. The priest brought the very Son of God down to earth when he celebrated the sacrament of the Eucharist; his absolution released penitents from punishment for mortal sin. It was improper for mere laypeople to sit in judgment of such a priest.

Theologians elaborated the distinction between the clergy and the laity to the clergy's benefit. Secular rulers were not supposed to tax the clergy, without special permission from the ecclesiastical authorities. Clerical crimes were under the jurisdiction of special ecclesiastical courts, not the secular courts. Because churches and monasteries were deemed holy places, they too were free from secular taxation and legal jurisdiction. Hunted criminals, lay and clerical, regularly sought asylum within them, disrupting the normal processes of law and order. When city officials violated this privilege, ecclesiastical authorities threatened excommunication and interdict. People feared this suspension of the church's sacraments, including Christian burial, almost as much as they feared the criminals to whom the church gave asylum.

By the late Middle Ages, townspeople increasingly resented the special immunities of the clergy. They complained that the clergy had greater privileges, yet fewer responsibilities, than others who lived within the town walls. An early-sixteenth-century lampoon reflected what had by then become a widespread sentiment:

> Priests, monks, and nuns
> Are but a burden to the earth.
> They have decided
> That they will not become citizens.
> That's why they're so greedy—
> They stand firm against our city
> And will swear no allegiance to it.
> And we hear their fine excuses:
> "It would cause us much toil and trouble
> Should we pledge our troth as burghers."[2]

The separation of church and state and the distinction between the clergy and the laity have persisted into modern times. After the fifteenth century, however, the clergy ceased to be the superior class they had been for much of the Middle Ages. In both Protestant and Catholic lands, governments progressively subjected the clergy to the basic responsibilities of citizenship.

8.1.3 Peasants

The largest and lowest social group in medieval society was the one on whose labor all others depended: the agrarian peasantry. Many peasants lived on and worked the manors

IMAGES OF RUSTIC LABORS In these images, peasants clear ground, mow fields, plant seed, harvest grain, shear sheep, stomp grapes, and slaughter hogs, among other chores, while the lord of the manor hunts with his falcon in the fields.
SOURCE: Réunion des Musées Nationaux/Art Resource, NY

of the nobility, the primitive cells of rural social life. All were to one degree or another dependent on their lords and considered to be their property. The manor in Frankish times was a plot of land within a village, ranging from twelve to seventy-five acres in size, assigned to a certain member by a settled tribe or clan. This member and his family became lords of the land, and those who came to dwell there formed a smaller, self-sufficient community within a larger village. In the early Middle Ages, such manors consisted of the dwellings of the lord and his family, the huts of the peasants, agricultural sheds, and fields.

8.1.3.1 THE DUTIES OF TENANCY The landowner or lord of the manor required a certain amount of produce (grain, eggs, and the like) and a certain number of services from the peasant families that dwelled on and farmed his land. The tenants were free to divide the labor as they wished and could keep goods that remained after the lord's levies were met. A powerful lord might own many such manors, and kings later based their military and tax assessments on the number of manors a vassal landlord owned. No set rules governed the size of manors. There were manors of a hundred acres or fewer and some of several thousand or more.

There were both servile and free manors. The tenants of the latter had originally been freemen known as *coloni*. Original inhabitants of the territory and petty landowners, they swapped their small possessions for a guarantee of security from a more powerful lord, who in this way came to possess their land. Unlike the pure serfdom of the servile manors, whose tenants had no original claim to a part of the land, the tenancy obligations on free manors tended to be limited, and the tenants' rights more carefully defined. It was a milder serfdom. Tenants of servile manors were, by comparison, far more vulnerable to the whims of their landlords. These two types of manors tended, however, to merge. There were manors on which tenants of greater and lesser degrees of servitude lived together, their services to the lord defined by their personal status and local custom. In many regions free, self-governing peasant communities existed without any overlords and tenancy obligations.

The lord held both judicial and police powers and owned and operated the machines that processed crops into food and drink. The lord also had the right to subject his tenants to exactions known as **banalities**. He could, for example, force tenants to breed their cows with his bull and to pay for the privilege, also to grind their bread grains in his mill, to bake their bread in his oven, to make their wine in his wine press, to buy their beer from his brewery, and even to surrender to him the tongues or other choice parts of all animals slaughtered on his lands. The lord also collected a serf's best animal as an inheritance tax. Without the lord's permission, serfs could neither travel nor marry outside the manor in which they served.

Exploited as the serfs may have been, their status was far from chattel slavery. It was to the lord's advantage to keep his serfs healthy and happy, because the welfare of both lord and serf depended on a successful harvest. Serfs had their own dwellings and modest strips of land and lived by the produce of their own labor and organization. They could market for their own profit the surpluses that remained after the harvest. They were free to choose their spouses within the local village, although they needed the lord's permission to marry a wife or husband from another village. Serfs could also pass their property (dwellings and field strips) and worldly goods on to their children.

Peasants lived in timber-framed huts. Except for the higher domestic servants, they seldom ventured far beyond their villages. Sunday masses and church festivals were their major communal entertainment. Rarely was there an abundance of bread and ale, the peasants' staple foods. The two important American crops, potatoes and corn (maize), were unknown in Europe until the sixteenth century. Pork was the major source of protein, and every peasant household had its pigs. Everyone depended on the grain crops, and when they failed, peasants went hungry unless their lord had surplus stores to share.

8.1.3.2 CHANGES IN THE MANOR Two basic changes occurred in the evolution of the manor. The first was its fragmentation, along with the rise to dominance of the single-family holding. Such technological advances as the collar harness (ca. 800), the horseshoe (ca. 900), and the three-field system of crop rotation facilitated this development by making it easier for small family units to support themselves apart from the manor. As the lords parceled out their land to new tenants, their own plots became progressively smaller. This increase in tenants and decrease in the lord's fields led to a corresponding reduction in the labor services exacted from the tenants. Bringing new fields into production increased individual holdings and modified labor services. During the reign of Louis IX (r. 1226–1270), only a few days of labor a year were required. Five hundred years earlier in the time of Charlemagne (r. 768–814), peasants worked the lords' fields several days a week.

As the single-family unit replaced the clan as the basic nuclear group, assessments of goods and services fell on individual fields and households and not on manors as a whole. Individual family farms replaced the manorial units. The peasants' carefully nurtured communal life made possible a family's retention of its land and dwelling after the death of the head of the household. In this way, land and property remained in the possession of a single family from generation to generation.

The second change in the evolution of the manor was the conversion of the serf's just dues, or earnings, into money payments, a change brought about by the revival of trade and the rise of the towns. This development, completed by the thirteenth century, permitted serfs to hold their lands as rent-paying tenants and thereby overcome their servile status. But while the tenants gained more freedom, they were not necessarily better off materially. Whereas servile workers could count on the benevolence of their landlords in hard times, rent-paying workers were left, by and large, to their own devices.

Lands and properties occupied by generations of peasants were always under the threat of the lord's claim to a prior right of inheritance and outright usurpation. As their *demesnes*, or landed property, declined, the lords were increasingly tempted to encroach on such common lands. Instinctively clinging to the little they had, the peasantry fiercely resisted such efforts.

By the mid-fourteenth century, a declining nobility in England and France, faced with the ravages of the great plague and the Hundred Years' War, tried to turn back the historical clock by increasing taxes on the agrarian peasantry and restricting their migration into the cities. The peasantry responded with armed revolts, the rural equivalent of the organization of medieval cities into communes, to protect their self-interests against the powerful territorial rulers. The peasant revolts, like those of the urban proletariats, were brutally crushed. They are a violent testimony to the breakup of medieval society. Growing national sentiment had broken society's political unity, and heretical movements ended its religious unity.

8.2 Towns and Townspeople

What processes led to the rise of towns and a merchant class?

In the eleventh and twelfth centuries, towns represented only about 5 percent of Western Europe's population. By comparison with modern towns, they were small. Of Germany's 3,000 towns, for example, 2,800 had populations under 1,000, and only fifteen German towns exceeded 10,000. The largest, Cologne, had 30,000. In England, only London had a population greater than 10,000. Paris was larger than London, but not by much.

The largest European towns were in Italy. Florence approached a population of 100,000, and Milan was not far behind. Italian towns were not feudally chartered, giving them greater political independence. In the Middle Ages, cities and towns were where the action was. The towns encompassed all of medieval society, including the most creative segments.

8.2.1 The Chartering of Towns

Feudal lords, both lay and clerical, originally dominated towns. The lords created the towns by granting charters to those who agreed to live and work within them. The charters guaranteed their inhabitants' safety and granted them a degree of independence unknown to the peasants on the land. The purpose was originally to concentrate skilled laborers who could manufacture the finished goods lords and bishops wanted. By the eleventh century, skilled serfs began to pay their manorial dues in manufactured goods, rather than in field labor, eggs, chickens, and beans, as they had earlier done. In return for a fixed rent and proper subservience, serfs were also encouraged to move to the towns. There they gained special rights and privileges from the charters.

As towns grew and beckoned, serfs fled the countryside with their valuable skills to settle in new urban centers. There they found the freedom and profits that might lift an industrious craftsperson to higher social ranks and wealth. As the migration of serfs to the towns accelerated, the lords in the countryside offered them favorable terms of tenure to keep them on the land. But after they had discovered the opportunities of town life, serfs could not easily be kept down on the farms. In this way, the growth of towns improved the lives of serfs generally.

8.2.2 The Rise of Merchants

Rural society gave the towns their skilled craftsmen and day laborers, but the first merchants may also have been enterprising serfs. These long-distance traders were men who had nothing to lose and everything to gain through the enormous risks of foreign trade. They traveled together in armed caravans and convoys, buying goods and products as cheaply as possible at the source, and selling them for all they could get in Western ports. (See Map 8–1.)

At first, the traditional social groups—nobility, clergy, and peasantry—considered the merchants an oddity. As late as the fifteenth century, the landed nobility was still snubbing the urban patriciate. Such snobbery never died out among the older landed nobility, who looked down on the traders as men of poor breeding and character possessed of money they did not properly earn or deserve. In time, the powerful townsmen came to respect the merchants, and the weak to imitate them. There was a good reason for this: wherever the merchants went, they left a trail of wealth behind.

Map 8–1 MEDIEVAL TRADE ROUTES AND REGIONAL PRODUCTS

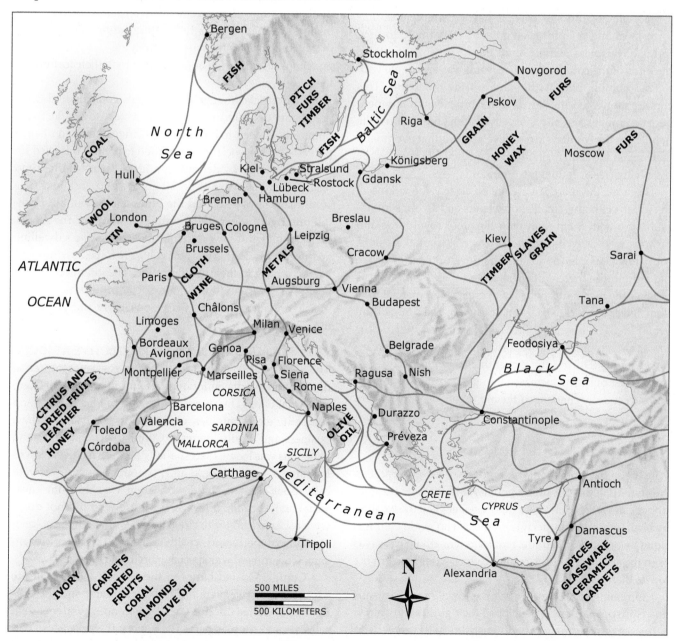

The map shows some of the medieval trade routes used in interregional commerce, as well as the products traded in particular regions.

8.2.3 Challenging the Old Lords

As they grew in wealth and numbers, merchants formed their own protective associations and were soon challenging traditional seigneurial authority. They especially wanted to end the tolls and tariffs imposed by regional authorities on the surrounding countryside. Such regulations disrupted the flow of commerce on which both merchant and craftsperson depended in the growing urban export industries. Wherever merchants settled in large numbers, they opposed tolls, tariffs, and other restrictions on trade. Merchant guilds, which were protective associations, also sprang up in the eleventh century to be followed in the twelfth by craft guilds (drapers, haberdashers, furriers, hosiers, and goldsmiths). Both guilds quickly found themselves in conflict with the norms of the comparatively static agricultural society.

Merchants and craftspeople needed simple and uniform laws and a fluid government sympathetic to new forms of business activity—not the fortress mentality of the lords of the countryside. The result was a struggle with the old nobility both within and outside the towns. This conflict motivated the towns to form their own independent communes and ally themselves with kings against the nobility in the countryside, a development that eventually rearranged the centers of power in medieval Europe, while dissolving classic feudal government.

Because the merchants were so clearly the engine of the urban economy, small shopkeepers and artisans identified more with them than with the aloof royal lords and bishops who were the chartered town's original masters. Most townspeople found that the development of urban life around the merchants best served their own interests because the merchants' way led to greater commercial freedom, fewer barriers to trade and business, and a more fluid urban life. The lesser nobility (small knights) outside the towns also embraced the opportunities of the new mercantile economy. During the eleventh and twelfth centuries, upper-class burghers increased the cities' economic strength and successfully challenged the old urban lords for control of the towns.

8.2.4 New Models of Government

With urban autonomy came new models of self-government. Around 1100, the old urban nobility and the new burgher upper class merged. It was a marriage between the wealthy by birth (inherited property) and those who made their fortunes in long-distance trade. From this new ruling class was born the aristocratic town council, which would govern the towns thereafter.

Enriching and complicating the towns, small artisans and craftspeople slowly developed their **guilds** and gained a voice in government. The towns' ability to protect and provide opportunities for the "little person" created the slogan: "Town air brings freedom." In the countryside, the air one breathed still belonged to the ruler of the land. But within town walls, the air belonged to every citizen who was endowed with basic rights. Economic hardship, however, did not disappear from the lower urban groups, and social mobility also remained a possibility in the towns.

8.2.4.1 KEEPING PEOPLE IN THEIR PLACES Traditional measures of success had great appeal within the towns. Despite their economic independence, the wealthiest urban groups admired and imitated the lifestyle of the old landed nobility. Although the latter treated the urban patriciate with disdain, successful merchants longed to live the noble, knightly life. They wanted coats of arms, castles, country estates, and the life of a gentleman or a lady in a great manor. This became particularly true in the later Middle Ages, when reliable bills of exchange and international regulation of trade allowed merchant firms to conduct their business by mail. Then only the young apprentices did a lot of traveling to learn the business from the ground up. When merchants became rich enough, they took their fortunes to the countryside.

Such social climbing disturbed city councils, and when merchants departed for the countryside, towns lost economically. A need to be socially distinguished and distinct pervaded urban society. Towns tried to control this need for fame and success by defining grades of luxury in dress and residence for the various social groups and vocations. The sumptuary laws restricted the types and amount of clothing one might wear (the length and width of fur pieces, for example) and how one might decorate one's dwelling architecturally. In this way, people were forced to dress and live according to their station in life. The intention of such laws was positive: to maintain social order and dampen social conflict by keeping everyone clearly and peacefully in their place.

8.2.4.2 SOCIAL CONFLICT AND PROTECTIVE ASSOCIATIONS (GUILDS) Despite their unified resistance to external domination, medieval towns were not internally harmonious social units. They were a collection of many selfish and competitive communities, each seeking to advance its own business and family interests. Conflict between haves and have-nots was inevitable, especially because medieval towns had little concept of social and economic equality. Theoretically, poor artisans could work their way up from lower social and vocational levels. Yet those who did not do so were excluded from the city council. Only families of long-standing property and wealth gained full rights of citizenship. Government was special, inbred, and aristocratic.

Conflict existed between the poorest workers in the export trades (weavers and wool combers) and the economically better off and socially ascending independent workers and shopkeepers. The better-off workers also had their differences with the wealthy merchants, whose export trade often brought competitive foreign goods into the city. Independent workers and small shopkeepers organized to restrict foreign trade to a minimum and corner the local market in certain items.

Over time, the formation of artisan guilds gave workers in the trades a direct voice in government. Ironically, the long-term effect of the guilds limited the social mobility of the poorest artisans. The guilds gained representation on city councils, where, to discourage imports, they used their power to enforce quality standards and fair prices on local businesses. These actions tightly restricted guild membership, squeezing out poorer artisans and tradesmen. As a result, lesser merchants and artisans found their opportunities progressively limited. So rigid and exclusive did the dominant guilds become that they often stifled their own work and inflamed the journeymen whom they excluded from their ranks. Unrepresented artisans and craftspeople constituted a true urban proletariat prevented by law from forming their own guilds or joining existing ones. The efforts by guild-dominated governments to protect local craftspeople and industries tended to narrow trade and depress the economy for all.

8.2.5 Towns and Kings

By providing kings with the resources they needed to curb factious noblemen, towns became a major factor in the transition from feudal societies to national governments. In many places kings and towns formally allied against the traditional lords of the land. A notable exception to this general development is England, where the towns joined with the barons against the oppressive monarchy of King John (r. 1199–1216), becoming part of the parliamentary opposition to the crown. But by the fifteenth century, kings and towns had also joined forces in England, so much so that Henry VII's (r. 1485–1509) support of towns brought him the title, the "burgher king."

Towns attracted kings and emperors for obvious reasons. They were a ready source of educated bureaucrats and lawyers who knew Roman law, the ultimate tool for running kingdoms and empires. Kings also found money in great quantity in towns, enabling them to hire their own armies instead of relying on the nobility. Towns had the human, financial, and technological resources to empower kings. Through such alliances, towns won royal political recognition and guarantees for their constitutions. In France, towns were integrated early into royal government.

In Germany, they fell under ever tighter control by the princes. In Italy uniquely, towns dominated the surrounding countryside, becoming genuine city-states during the Renaissance.

It was also in the towns' interest to have a strong monarch as protector against despotic local lords and princes, who were always eager to integrate or engulf the towns within their expanding territories. Unlike a local magnate, a king tended to remain at a distance, allowing towns to exercise their precious autonomy. A king was thus the more desirable overlord. It was also an advantage for a town to conduct its long-distance trade in the name of a powerful monarch. This gave predators pause and improved official cooperation along the way. Such alliances profited both sides—kings and towns.

Between the eleventh and fourteenth centuries, towns had considerable freedom and autonomy. As in Roman times, they again became the flourishing centers of Western civilization. But after the fourteenth century, and even earlier in France and England, the towns, like the church before them, were steadily bent to the political will of kings and princes. By the seventeenth century, few towns were truly autonomous, and most had by then been integrated thoroughly into the larger purposes of the "state."

8.2.6 Jews in Christian Society

The major urban centers, particularly in France and Germany, attracted many Jews during the late twelfth and

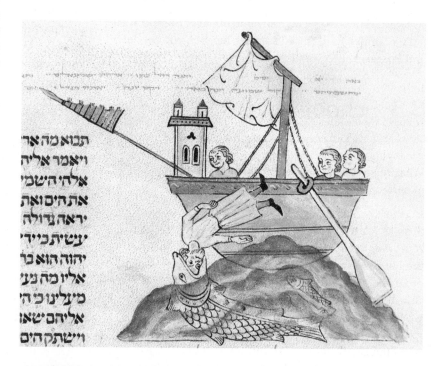

BOOK OF JONAH Jonah is swallowed by a great fish in this scene from a thirteenth-century illustrated Hebrew Torah from Portugal, an example of the rich Jewish heritage of medieval Iberia.
SOURCE: Instituto da Biblioteca Nacional, Lisbon, Portugal/Bridgeman Images

thirteenth centuries. Jews gathered there both by choice and for safety in the increasingly hostile Christian world. Mutually wary of one another, Christians and Jews limited their direct contact to exchanges between their merchants and scholars. The church expressly forbade Jews from hiring Christians in their businesses and from holding any public authority over them. Jews freely conducted their own small businesses, catering to private clients, both Christian and Jewish. The wealthier Jews became bankers to kings and popes.

Jewish intellectual and religious culture, always elaborate and sophisticated, both dazzled and threatened Christians who viewed it from outside. The separateness of Jews, their exceptional economic power, and their rich cultural strength created envy, suspicion, and distrust among many Christians, whose religious teaching taught that Jews were responsible for the death of Christ.

Between the late twelfth and fourteenth centuries, Jews were exiled from France and persecuted elsewhere on an order of expulsion issued by Phillip II Augustus. Two factors lay behind this unprecedented surge in anti-Jewish sentiment. The first was a desire by kings to confiscate Jewish wealth and property and to eliminate the Jews as economic competitors with the monarchy. The church's increasing political vulnerability to the new dynastic monarchies also contributed to the surge in anti-Jewish sentiment. Faced with the loss of its political power, the church became more determined than ever to maintain its spiritual hegemony over Christendom. Beginning with the Crusades and the creation of new mendicant orders, the church reasserted its claims to spiritual sovereignty over Europe, instigating campaigns against dissenters, heretics, witches, Jews, and infidels at home and abroad.

8.3 Schools and Universities

What intellectual trends accompanied the rise of universities?

In the twelfth century, Byzantine and Spanish Islamic scholars made the works of Aristotle, Euclid, and Ptolemy available to the Latin West, along with the basic works of Greek physicians and Arab mathematicians. The translation and study of these works created an intellectual ferment that gave rise to a renaissance of ancient knowledge and the birth of Western universities. The study of the liberal arts in medieval Europe took place in the Church's cathedral and monastery schools from which arose the first universities. The liberal arts provided

the foundation for advanced study in the higher sciences of medicine, theology, and law. Whereas the earlier schools trained clergy, the universities satisfied the needs of secular society for bureaucrats and civil servants.

8.3.1 University of Bologna

The first important Western university was established by Emperor Frederick I Barbarossa in 1158 in Bologna. At the **University of Bologna** were the first formal organizations of students and masters and degree programs—the institutional foundations of the modern university. Originally, the term *university* meant a corporation of individuals (students and masters) who joined together for their mutual protection from episcopal authority and local townspeople who were often at odds with the student body. Because townspeople then looked on students as foreigners without civil rights, protective unions were deemed necessary. In creating these unions, students followed the model of the urban trade guild, which put them in a stronger position to bargain for fair rents and other prices demanded by their often-reluctant hosts in both church and town. Students also demanded regular, high-quality teaching from their masters. In Italy, they hired their own teachers, set their own pay scales, and drew up desired lecture topics. Masters who did not keep their promises or meet student expectations were boycotted. Students could threaten to move a university to another town, possible because the university was not at this time tied to a fixed physical plant. Students and masters moved freely from town to town as they chose, a mobility that gave them both safety and independence from their surroundings.

Like Bologna, the model for southern European universities and the study of law, Paris was the model for northern European universities and the study of theology.

A MEDIEVAL SCHOOL SCENE Education and religion were inseparable in medieval times. This illustration shows a teacher and a student in a Jewish community.
SOURCE: PRISMA ARCHIVO/Alamy Stock Photo

Oxford and Cambridge in England, and later Heidelberg in Germany, were among its imitators. These universities required a foundation in the liberal arts for advanced study in the higher sciences of medicine, theology, and law. The **liberal arts** program consisted of the *trivium* (grammar, rhetoric, and logic) and the *quadrivium* (arithmetic, geometry, astronomy, and music), both the language arts and the mathematical arts.

8.3.2 Cathedral Schools

Before the emergence of universities, the liberal arts were taught in the Church's cathedral and monastery schools that trained beginning clergy. By the eleventh and twelfth centuries, these schools provided lectures for nonclerical students, while broadening their curriculum to include training of students for purely secular vocations. In 1179, the pope obliged the cathedrals to provide teachers for laity who wanted to learn.

After 1200, increasing numbers of aspiring notaries and merchants who had no interest in becoming priests, but needed Latin and related intellectual disciplines to gain their secular positions, studied side by side with aspiring priests in the cathedral and monastery schools. By the thirteenth century, demand for secretaries and notaries in expanding urban and territorial governments was great. With the appearance of these schools and their immediate success, the church began to lose its monopoly on higher education.

8.3.3 University of Paris

The **University of Paris** grew institutionally out of the cathedral school of Notre Dame, among others. At Paris the college, or house system, was born. At first, a college was just a hospice providing room and board for poor students who could not rent rooms in town. But the educational life of the university quickly expanded into fixed structures and began to thrive on sure endowments.

The most famous college in Paris was the Sorbonne, founded for theological students (ca. 1257) by the king's chaplain and the college's namesake, Robert de Sorbon. In Oxford and Cambridge, the colleges became the basic unit of student life and were indistinguishable from the university proper. By the end of the Middle Ages, the colleges were tied to the physical plants and fixed foundations of the universities. (See the "Compare and Connect" sidebar, which follows below, on royal charters for medieval universities.)

8.3.4 The Curriculum

Before the "renaissance" of the twelfth century, the education available in cathedral and monastery schools was limited. However, with the recovery of antiquity, growing numbers of students learned grammar, rhetoric, and elementary geometry and astronomy. By the mid-thirteenth century, almost

ENGRAVING OF THE UNIVERSITY OF PARIS In this engraving of the University of Paris, a teacher leads fellow scholars in a discussion. As shown here, all the students wore the scholar's cap and gown.
SOURCE: DEA/G. DAGLI ORTI/Getty Images

all of Aristotle's works circulated in translation, a boon to education in the colleges and universities in the West.

At this time, the learning process was still basic. The guiding assumption was that truth already existed and that one did not have to go search for it. It was there to behold, and one knew it when one saw it. Students had only to memorize, organize, elucidate, and defend it as the scholars of antiquity presented it. Such conviction made logic and **dialectic** the focus of education. Students wrote commentaries on the authoritative texts, especially those of Aristotle and the Church Fathers. Built on logic and dialectic, this method of study, known as **Scholasticism**, reigned supreme in all the faculties—in law and medicine as well as in philosophy and theology. In the classrooms, students read the traditional authorities in their fields of study, wrote summaries of what they were taught, disputed them with their peers, and drew the obvious conclusions.

Logic and dialectic dominated education because they were the tools that disciplined knowledge and thought. *Dialectic* is negative, logical inquiry, the art of discovering a truth by finding the contradictions in arguments against it. Contrary to being abstract and boring, the reading and harmonizing of learned authorities in direct debate and disputation exhilarated students.

Compare and Connect

What Do Kings Have to Do with Universities?

MEDIEVAL UNIVERSITIES OFTEN ENJOYED the protection and patronage of secular rulers. While earlier cathedral and monastery schools were under the authority of the church, universities attracted the support of kings and princes. This support was a reflection of more than simple royal generosity. As medieval governments expanded, so too did demand for educated clerks, officials, and advisors. Universities supplied such men. Moreover, the relationship between rulers and universities contributed to the status and legitimacy of each. Rulers gained reputations as patrons of learning and the arts, while universities benefited from the prestige that came from association with the crown. The excerpts included below provide a window into the relationship between professors and princes. In the first, Holy Roman Emperor Frederick I offers his protection to university scholars. In the second, Rupert I, Count Palatine of the Rhine, founds a new university in Heidelberg.

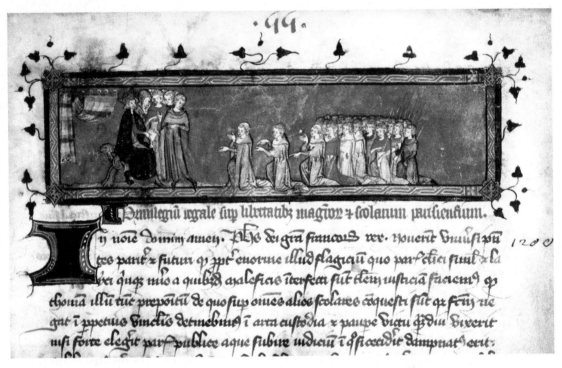

CHARTERING THE UNIVERSITY OF PARIS In this fourteenth-century illustration, the masters and students of the University of Paris kneel before the king as he grants them a charter.
SOURCE: Photo 12/Alamy Stock Photo

Before Reading

- Consider the motives of each ruler for supporting scholars and institutions of higher learning.
- Ask yourself why universities might have needed support and protection.
- Think about the larger context of developments in medieval government and society.

Questions

1. How did Frederick I explain his decision to offer protection to scholars?
2. What does the charter for the University of Heidelberg tell us about university organization?
3. What do the two documents reveal about the development of universities between the twelfth and fourteenth centuries?

I. EDICT OF EMPEROR FREDERICK I (1158)

After a careful consideration of this subject by the bishops, abbots, dukes, counts, judges, and other nobles of our sacred palace, we, from our piety, have granted this privilege to all scholars who travel for the sake of study, and especially to the professors of divine and sacred laws, namely, that they may go in safety to the places in which the studies are carried on, both them themselves and their messengers, and may dwell there in security. For we think it fitting that, during good behavior, those should enjoy our praise and protection, by whose learning the world is enlightened to the obedience of God and of us, his ministers, and the life of the subject is molded; and by a special consideration we defend them from all injuries.

For who does not pity those who exile themselves through love for learning, who wear themselves out in poverty in place of riches, who expose their lives to all perils and often suffer bodily injury from the vilest men? This must be endured with vexation. Therefore, we declare by this general and perpetual law, that in the future no one shall be so rash as to venture to inflict any injury on scholars, or to occasion any loss to them on account of a debt owed by an inhabitant of their province—a thing which we have learned is sometimes done by an evil custom. And let it be known to the violators of this constitution, and also to those who shall at the time be the rulers of the places, that a fourfold restitution of property shall be exacted from all and that, the mark of infamy being affixed to them by the law itself, they shall lose their office forever.

II. CHARTER OF THE UNIVERSITY OF HEIDELBERG (1386)

We, Rupert the elder, by the grace of God count palatine the Rhine, elector of the Holy Empire, and duke of Bavaria . . . do decree, with provident counsel (which decree is to be observed unto all time), that the University of Heidelberg shall be ruled, disposed, and regulated according to the modes and manners accustomed to be observed in the University of Paris. Also that, as a handmaid of Paris—a worthy one let us hope—the latter's steps shall be imitated in every way possible; so that, namely, there shall be four faculties in it: the first, of sacred theology and divinity; the second, of canon and civil law, which, by reason of their similarity, we think best to comprise under one faculty; the third, of medicine; the fourth, of liberal arts of the three-fold philosophy, namely, primal, natural, and moral, three mutually subservient daughters. We wish this institution to be divided and marked out into four nations, as it is at Paris; and that all these faculties shall make one university, and that to it the individual students, in whatever of the said faculties they are, shall unitedly belong like lawful sons to one mother.

SOURCES: (I) Frederick Austen, ed., *A Source Book of Medieval History* (New York: American Book Company, 1908), pp. 341–342. (II) Frederick Austen, ed., *A Source Book of Medieval History* (New York: American Book Company, 1908), pp. 345–346.

Few books existed for students, and those available were expensive works hand-copied on animal skins. Students could not master a subject leisurely, and quietly, in a library as they do today. They had to learn through give-and-take debate, which required memorization and the ability to think on one's feet. Rhetoric, or persuasive argument, was the student's ultimate goal, an ability to eloquently defend the knowledge one had gained by logic and dialectic. The best students became virtual encyclopedias.

8.3.5 Philosophy and Theology

Great academic debates sprang from the perceived conflict between philosophy and theology. Hard-core Christian minds viewed Aristotle's writings as heresy. Aristotle, for example, taught the eternality of the world, calling into question the Judeo-Christian teaching that God created the world in time. Aristotle also taught that intellect, or mind, was ultimately one—a seeming threat to individuality and to the Christian belief of individual responsibility and personal immortality after death. Islamic commentators on Aristotle increased the conflict by embracing such heresies as scientifically true. But Church authorities wanted the works of Aristotle and all other ancient authorities to be "submissive handmaidens" to Christian scripture.

8.3.5.1 ABELARD Few philosophers and theologians gained greater notoriety for wrongful interpretation of Jewish and Christian Scripture than **Peter Abelard** (1079–1142). Possibly the brightest logician and dialectician of the High Middle Ages, he was the first European scholar to gain a large student audience. No scholar promoted the new Aristotelian learning more boldly than he, nor did any other pay more dearly for doing so. Abelard ended his life not as the academic superstar he was but as a humble monk in a monastery, lucky to be alive. His bold subjection of church teaching to Aristotelian logic and dialectic made him powerful enemies at a time when there was no tenure to protect genius and free speech in schools and universities. Accused of multiple transgressions of church doctrine, Abelard recounted in an autobiography the "calamities" that befell him over a lifetime.

Abelard's critics condemned him for his subjective interpretations of Holy Scripture. For example, he compared the Trinitarian bonds among God the Father, the Son, and the Holy Spirit to sworn human documents and covenants. Rather than a God-begotten cosmic ransom of humankind from the Devil, as the church had taught, he argued that Christ's crucifixion redeemed Christians by its impact on their hearts and minds, when they heard the story of Christ. Stomping still again on sacred ground, Abelard's ethical teaching stressed "intent" over deed: the subjective motives of the doer, he declared, made an act good or evil, not the act itself. Feelings were thus more important for receiving divine forgiveness than were the church's sacrament of penance administered by a priest.

Abelard's native genius and youthful disrespect for seniority and tradition now brought him grief. If his heresies were not condemnation enough, he gave his enemies

ADAM AND EVE Adam and Eve were cast out of the Garden of Eden not because of their lust for each other but because of their disobedience to God in eating the forbidden fruit from the Tree of Knowledge of Good and Evil. St. Augustine who, like Abelard, was known to exhibit a certain weakness for the charms of the opposite sex, taught that before their Fall, Adam and Eve had complete control over their libidos. Abelard and Héloïse's lust and shame are a commentary on fallen humankind, tracing back to Adam and Eve.
SOURCE: Library of Congress

a golden opportunity to strike him down. While in Paris, Abelard held the position of Master of Students at Notre Dame. There he met and seduced Héloïse, the bright, seventeen-year-old niece of a powerful old canon, who hired him to be her tutor in his home. Their passionate affair ended in public scandal, with Héloïse pregnant. Unable to marry officially because university teachers then had to be single and celibate, they wed secretly and placed their illegitimate offspring with Abelard's sister to raise.

Intent on punishing Abelard and ending his career, Héloïse's enraged uncle exposed their secret marriage and hired strongmen to track down and castrate Abelard. In the aftermath of that terrible event, the lovers entered cloisters nearby Paris: Héloïse at Argenteuil, Abelard at St. Denis. She continued to love Abelard, constantly reliving their passion

in her mind, while Abelard became a self-condemning recluse, assuring Héloïse in his letters that his "love had only been wretched desire."

The famous philosopher ended his life as a platitudinous monk. In 1121, a church synod ordered all his writings to be burned. Another synod in 1140 condemned nineteen propositions from his philosophical and theological works as heresy. Retracting his teaching, Abelard lived out the remaining two years of his life in an obscure priory near Chalons. Héloïse lived another twenty years and became renowned for her positive efforts to improve the life of cloistered women.

8.4 Women in Medieval Society

How was life for women during the Middle Ages?

The image and the reality of medieval women's lives were very different. Male Christian clergy, who lived celibate lives of chastity, poverty, and obedience, strongly influenced the image of women. Drawing on biblical and classical antiquity, and sources both Christian and pagan, Christian thinkers depicted women as physically, mentally, and morally weaker than men. Based on such assumptions, the religious life was considered superior to marriage, and virgins and celibate widows were praised over wives. A wife was expected to be subservient and obedient to her husband who, as the stronger of the two, had the duty to protect and discipline her. Based on this image, medieval women seemed to have two choices: to become either a subjugated housewife or a confined nun. In reality, most medieval women became neither.

8.4.1 Image and Status

Both within and outside Christianity, the image of women is contradictory. In the chivalric romances and courtly love literature of the twelfth and thirteenth centuries, for example, as in the contemporaneous cult of the Virgin Mary, women were placed on pedestals and considered superior to men in purity. And although the church harbored misogynist sentiments, it also condemned them, as in the case of the late-thirteenth-century *Romance of the Rose* and other popular bawdy literature.

The learned churchman **Peter Lombard** (1100–1169), whose *Four Books of the Sentences* was read and annotated by

MEDIEVAL WOMEN AT WORK These illustrations from a fourteenth-century English manuscript show women at their daily tasks: carrying jugs of milk from the sheep pen, feeding the chickens, and carding and spinning wool.
SOURCE: British Library, London, UK / © British Library Board. All Rights Reserved / Bridgeman Images(top),British Library, London, UK© British Library Board. All Rights Reserved/Bridgeman Art Library(center),World History Archive/Alamy Stock Photo(bottom)

every theological student, asked why Eve had been created from Adam's rib rather than from his head or his feet. The answer was that God took Eve from Adam's side because she was meant neither to rule over man nor to be man's slave, but rather to stand squarely at his side as his companion and partner in mutual aid and trust. By insisting that men and women were spiritually equal and shared responsibility in marriage, the church also helped protect the dignity of women.

Germanic law arguably treated women better than Roman law had done, recognizing their basic rights that forbade their treatment as chattel. Unlike Roman women, who as teens married men much older than themselves, German women married husbands of similar age. A German groom gave a portion, or dowry (*dos*), to his bride, which became hers in the event of his death. All major Germanic law codes recognized the economic freedom of women: their right to inherit, administer, dispose of, and confer property and wealth on their children. They could also press charges in court against men for bodily injury and rape, whose punishment, depending on the circumstances, ranged from fines, flogging, and banishment to blinding, castration, and death.

8.4.2 Life Choices

The nunnery was an option for single women from the higher social classes. Entrance required a dowry and could be almost as expensive as a wedding, although usually cheaper. Within the nunnery, a woman could rise to a position of leadership as an abbess or a mother superior, exercising authority denied her in much of secular life. The nunneries of the established religious orders remained under male supervision, however, so that even abbesses had to answer to higher male authority.

In the ninth century, under the influence of Christianity, the Carolingians made monogamous marriage official policy. Previously, they had practiced polygamy and concubinage and permitted divorce. The result was both a boon and a burden to women. On one hand, wives gained greater dignity and legal security. On the other hand, as household manager and bearer of children, a wife's labor greatly increased. And the Carolingian wife was now also the sole object of her husband's wrath and pleasure. Such demands clearly took their toll: The mortality rates of Frankish women increased and their longevity decreased after the ninth century. Under such conditions, the cloister became an appealing refuge for women. However, the number of women in cloisters was never large. In late medieval England, only 3,500 women entered the cloister.

8.4.3 Working Women

Most medieval women were neither housewives nor nuns, but workers like their husbands. The evidence suggests that their husbands respected and loved them, perhaps because they worked shoulder to shoulder with them in running the household and home-based businesses. Between the ages of ten and fifteen, girls were apprenticed and learned trade skills as boys did. If they married, they often continued their trade, operating their bake or dress shops next to their husbands' businesses, or becoming assistants and partners in their husbands' shops. Women worked in virtually every "blue-collar" trade, from butcher to goldsmith, but mostly worked in the food and clothing industries. Women belonged to guilds, just like men, and they became craft masters. By the fifteenth century, townswomen increasingly had the opportunity to go to school and gain at least vernacular literacy.

Although women did not have as wide a range of vocations as men, women's vocational destinies were also fixed. Gender excluded women from the learned professions of scholarship, medicine, and law. A woman's freedom of movement within a profession was more often regulated than a man's, and women's wages were also not as great. Still, women remained a prominent and creative part of working medieval society as men. A medieval woman rarely considered herself merely a wife.

8.5 The Lives of Children

What were the characteristics of childhood in the Middle Ages?

The image of medieval children and their historical reality are also contradictory. Until recently, historians believed that medieval parents were emotionally distant from their offspring, citing evidence of low parental esteem for children. On the one hand, medieval writers and artists tend to represent children in a manner that supports this view. On the other hand, considering a broader range of evidence, scholars have begun to develop a fuller and more nuanced understanding of the role and status of children during the Middle Ages.

8.5.1 Children as "Little Adults"

Based on the images and activities of children shown in medieval art, sculpture, and literature, some historians have concluded that children in the distant past were "little adults," barely different from grownups in appearance and in their activities. Perhaps medieval adults were unaware that childhood was a separate period of life requiring special care and treatment. Other historians, drawing on the high infant and child mortality rates in the Middle Ages, theorize that medieval parents were discouraged with childrearing, and invested very little in their children both emotionally and financially. A medieval parent might not want to become deeply attached to a child

when children had a 30–50 percent chance of dying before the age of five.

During the Middle Ages children assumed adult responsibilities very early in life. The children of peasants labored in the fields alongside their parents as soon as they could physically manage the work. Urban artisans and burghers sent their children between the ages of eight and twelve out of the household into apprenticeships in various crafts and trades. Could truly loving parents remove their children from the home at so tender an age? The medieval canonical age for marriage—twelve for girls and fourteen for boys—is evidence that children were expected to grow up fast, although very few (mostly royalty) married at such young ages.

The practice of infanticide also suggests low esteem for children in ancient and early medieval times. According to the Roman historian Tacitus (ca. 55–120), the Romans exposed unwanted children, especially girls, at birth to regulate family size. Yet, the surviving children appear to have been given plenty of attention and affection.

The Germanic tribes of medieval Europe, by contrast, had large families but tended to neglect the children in comparison to the Romans. Infanticide, particularly of girls, continued to be practiced by the Germanic tribes in the early Middle Ages, most likely confirmed by the condemnation of

A SCENE OF CHILDREN AT PLAY This illustration of popular medieval childhood pastimes, toys, and games—spinning tops, catching butterflies, toddling in a walker—exemplifies the recognition of a child's world in the Middle Ages.
SOURCE: British Library, London, UK© British Library Board. All Rights Reserved/Bridgeman Art Library

it in contemporary church penance books and the decrees of church synods.

Among the German tribes, a much lower compensatory fine, a *wergild*, was paid for injury to a child than to an adult—one-fifth of what was paid for injury to an adult. The payment for injury to a female child under fifteen was one-half of that of a male child of the same age. Mothers appear also to have nursed boys longer than they did girls, which favored the boys' health and survival. A woman's wergild, however, increased eightfold between infancy and her childbearing years.[3]

8.5.2 Childhood as a Special Stage

Despite evidence of parental distance and neglect, love and indifference, there is another side to the story that rings truer. From the early Middle Ages, physicians and theologians had understood childhood to be a distinct and special stage of life. Isidore (560–636), bishop of Seville and a leading intellectual authority throughout the Middle Ages, distinguished six stages of life, the first four of which were infancy, childhood, adolescence, and youth.

According to ancient and medieval physicians, infancy extended roughly from six months to two years, a period of speechlessness and suckling. The years from two to seven were a second, higher level of infancy, the beginning of the child's weaning and ability to converse. At seven, a child could think, act decisively, and speak clearly. Adolescence began at his time. An adolescent child could be reasoned with, profit from discipline, do household chores, and began to learn vocational skills. After seven, a youth was also ready for schooling, private tutoring, or apprenticeship in a chosen craft or trade. Until physical growth was complete, the youth remained legally under the guardianship of parents, or a surrogate authority.

Rather than distancing parents from their children, evidence suggests that high infant and child mortality made children even more precious to them. The respected medical authorities of the Middle Ages—Hippocrates, Galen, and Soranus of Ephesus—dealt at length with postnatal care and childhood diseases. Both the physician's medicine and the layman's medicine were quickly applied when the leading killers of children (diarrhea, worms, pneumonia, and fever) struck. When infants and children died, medieval parents grieved as pitiably as modern parents do. In the art and literature of the Middle Ages, we find mothers baptizing dead infants and children, even carrying their dead bodies to pilgrim shrines in the hope of a miraculous revival of their children. There are numerous stories of parental mental illness and suicide brought on by the death of a beloved child.[4]

Clear evidence of special attention being paid to children can be seen in the array of their toys, games, and special aids (e.g., walkers and potty chairs). While not withholding the rod, medieval authorities emphatically condemned child abuse and urged moderation in all discipline and punishment of minor children. In church art and drama, parents were urged to love their children as Mary loved Jesus. Early apprenticeships were believed to be a true expression of parental love and concern for a child. In the Middle Ages, no parental responsibility was greater than equipping a child for useful and gainful work. Certainly, by the High Middle Ages, if not earlier, children were widely viewed as "special," having their own needs and rights.

The Chapter in Perspective

During the High Middle Ages, the growth of Mediterranean trade revived old cities and created new ones. The Crusades aided and abetted this development. Italian cities especially flourished during the late eleventh and twelfth centuries. Venice dominated Mediterranean trade and extended its political and economic influence throughout the Near East. It had its own safe ports as far away as Syria. As cities grew in population and became rich from successful trade, a new social group, the long-distance traders, rose to prominence. Through marriage and political organization, these merchant families organized themselves into an unstoppable force. They successfully challenged the old nobility in and around the cities.

This new elite of merchants gained control of city governments almost everywhere. They brought with them a policy of open trade and the blessings and problems of nascent capitalism. Artisans and small shopkeepers at the lower end of the economic spectrum aspired to follow their example, as new opportunities opened for all. The seeds of social conflict and of urban class struggle had been sown.

One positive result of the new wealth of towns was the patronage of education and culture, emphasized in a way never experienced since Roman times. Western Europe's first universities appeared in the eleventh century and steadily expanded over the next four centuries. There were twenty universities by 1300. Not only did Scholasticism flourish but literature, art, and architecture reflected both a new human vitality and the reshaping of society and politics. For all of these changes, Western Europeans had to thank the new class of merchants, whose greed, daring, and ambition made it all possible.

The Chapter in Review

Review Questions

1. How did the responsibilities of the nobility differ from those of the clergy and the peasantry in the High Middle Ages? What did each social class contribute to the stability of society?

2. What led to the revival of trade and the growth of towns in the twelfth century? How did towns change medieval society?

3. What were the strengths and weaknesses of higher education during the Middle Ages? Describe the university curriculum.

4. What was Scholasticism, and how did it change education? Who were its main critics, and what were their complaints?

5. Assess the position of women living under Germanic law and Roman law. Which gave women a better position in life?

6. Were children viewed as small adults in the High Middle Ages? What are the best sources for the study of parent–child relations in the High Middle Ages?

Key Terms

Peter Abelard (1079–1142). Brilliant logician and dialectician of the High Middle Ages, who promoted the new Aristotelian learning.

banalities Exactions that the lord of a manor could make on his tenants.

Canons Regular Independent groups of secular clergy (fd. 1050–1100) that adopted the *Rule of Saint Augustine* and practiced the ascetic virtues of regular clerics.

Carthusians The strictest of the new religious orders (fd. 1084) that resulted from the Gregorian reform, whose members lived in isolation and fasted three days a week.

Cistercians A reform wing of the Benedictine order (fd. 1098), known as the "white monks," a reference to their all-white attire, symbolic of apostolic purity.

courtly love A literary conception of love that involved married women pursuing married men. The poet recommended unconsummated love at a distance.

demesnes The landed property attached to a manor and retained for the owner's use.

dialectic A negative, logical inquiry that seeks truth by finding the contradictions in the arguments against it.

guilds Associations of merchants or craftsmen that offered protection to their members and set rules for their work and products.

liberal arts The medieval university program that consisted of the *trivium* (TRI-vee-um): grammar, rhetoric, and logic, and the *quadrivium* (qua-DRI-vee-um): arithmetic, geometry, astronomy, and music.

Peter Lombard (1100–1169). The learned churchman who wrote the *Four Books of the Sentences*, which every student of theology read and annotated.

Praemonstratensians A Roman Catholic religious order of canons regular founded in 1120 by Saint Norbert that practiced extreme austerity to recapture the life of the early church.

quadrivium (qua-DRI-vee-um) The liberal arts program made up of arithmetic, geometry, astronomy, and music.

regular clergy Monks and nuns who belong to religious orders.

Rule of Saint Augustine A monastic guide dating from around the year 500.

Scholasticism Method of study based on logic and dialectic that dominated the medieval schools. Assumed that truth already existed and that students had only to organize, elucidate, and defend knowledge learned from authoritative texts, especially those of Aristotle and the Church Fathers.

secular clergy Parish clergy who did not belong to a religious order.

trivium (TRI-vee-um) The liberal arts program consisting of grammar, rhetoric, and logic.

University of Bologna The first important Western university; became the model for southern European universities and the study of law.

University of Paris Grew out of the cathedral school of Notre Dame and received its charter in 1200. The most famous college in Paris, the Sorbonne, was founded for students of theology.

Notes

1. Denys Hay, *Europe in the Fourteenth and Fifteenth Centuries*, 2nd ed. (New York: Holt, Rinehart, 1966), pp. 58–59.
2. Cited by S. Ozment, *The Reformation in the Cities* (New Haven, CT: Yale University Press, 1975), p. 36.
3. David Herlihy, "Medieval Children," in *Essays on Medieval Civilization*, ed. by B. K. Lackner and K. R. Phelp (Austin: University of Texas Press, 1978), pp. 109–131.
4. Klaus Arnold, *Kind und Gesellschaft in Mittelater und Renaissance* (Munich: Paderborn, 1980), pp. 31–37.

The West and the World

The Invention of Printing in China and Europe

THE ABILITY TO put information and ideas on paper and to circulate them widely in multiple identical copies has been credited in the West with the rise of humanism, the Protestant Reformation, the modern state, and the scientific revolution. In truth, the message preceded the machinery: It was a preexisting desire to rule more effectively and to shape and control the course of events that brought the printing press into existence in both China and Europe. Before there was printing, rulers, religious leaders, and merchants hoped to disperse their laws, scriptures, and wares more widely and efficiently among their subjects, followers, and customers.

To create the skilled agents and bureaucrats, leaders of state, church, and business cooperated in the sponsorship of schools and education, which spurred the growth of reading and writing among the middle and upper urban classes. Literacy, in turn, fueled the desire for easily accessible and reliable information. Literacy came more slowly to the lower social classes, because authorities feared too much knowledge in the hands of the uneducated or poorly educated would only fan the fires of discontent. To the many who remained illiterate after the invention of printing, information was conveyed carefully in oral and pictorial form. Printed official statements were designed to be read to, as well as read by, people; and religious leaders put images and pictures in the hands of simple folk, hoping to content them with saints and charms.

Resources and Technology: Paper and Ink

Among the indispensable materials of the print revolution were sizable supplies of durable, inexpensive paper and a reliable ink. As early as the Shang period (1766–1122 B.C.E.), a water-based soot and gum ink was used across Asia. (Europe would not have such an ink until the early Middle Ages.) Also in the Shang period, official seals and stamps used to authenticate documents were made by carving bronze, jade, ivory, gold, and stone in a reverse direction (that is, in a mirror form, to prevent the print from appearing backward).

Similar seals appeared in ancient Mesopotamia and Egypt, but only for religious use—not for the affairs of daily secular life. Later, more easily carved clay or wax seals reproduced characters on silk or bamboo surfaces.

Silk in the East and parchment in the West had been early, but very expensive, print media. Bamboo and wood were cheaper, but neither was suited to large-scale printing.

A step forward occurred in the second century B.C.E. when the Chinese invented a crude paper from hemp fibers, which was previously used only for wrappings. Three centuries later in 105 C.E., an imperial eunuch named Ts'ia Lun combined tree bark, hemp, rags, and old fishnets into a superior and reliable paper. A better blend of mulberry bark, fishnets, and natural fibers became the standard paper mixture. By the Tang period (618–907 C.E.), high-quality paper manufacturing had become a major industry.

In the eighth century C.E., the improved Chinese recipe began to make its way west, after Chinese prisoners taught their Arab captors how to make paper. By the ninth century C.E., Samarkand in Russian Turkestan had become the leading supplier of paper in the East. A century later, Baghdad and Damascus shipped fine paper to Egypt and Europe. Italy became a major Western manufacturer in the thirteenth century C.E. followed by Nuremberg, Germany, in the late fourteenth century C.E.

Early Printing Techniques

By the seventh century C.E., multiple copies of the *Confucian Scriptures* were made by taking paper rubbings from stone and metal engravings, a direct prelude to block printing. At this time in the West, the arts of engraving, and particularly of coin casting (by hammering hot alloy on an anvil that bore a carved design), enabled the first steps toward printing with movable type.

The invention of printing occurred much earlier in the East than in the West. The Chinese invented *block printing* (that is, printing with carved wooden blocks) in the eighth century C.E., almost 600 years before the technique appeared in Europe (1395). The Chinese also far outpaced the West in printing with *movable type* (that is, with individual characters or letters that could be arranged by hand to make a page)—a technique invented by Pi Scheng in the 1040s C.E.,

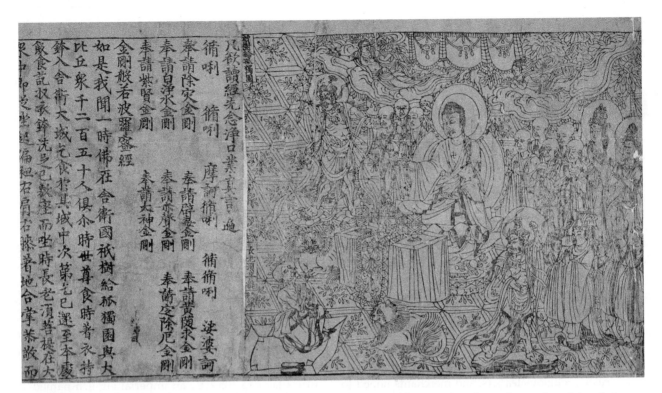

THE DIAMOND SUTRA The Chinese translation of the Buddhist text *The Diamond Sutra* consists of a scroll more than sixteen feet long, made up of a long series of printed pages. Printed in China in 868 C.E., it was found in the Dunhuang Caves in 1907, in the northwestern province of Gansu.
SOURCE: PBL Collection/Alamy Stock Photo

400 years before Johann Gutenberg set up the first Western press in Mainz, Germany (around 1450 C.E.).

Block printing used hard wood (preferably from pear or jujube trees), whose surface was glazed with a filler (glue, wax, or clay). A paper copy of what one wanted to duplicate (be it a drawn image, a written sentence, or both) was placed face down on a wet glaze covering the block and the characters cut into it. The process accommodated any artistic style while allowing text and illustration to coexist harmoniously on a page. Once carved, the block was inked and mild pressure applied, allowing a great many copies to be made before it wore out.

The first movable type was ceramic. The printer set each character or piece in an iron form and arranged them on an iron baking plate filled with heated resin and wax, which when cooled, created a tight page. After the print run was finished, the plate was heated again to melt the wax and free the type for new settings. Ceramic and later metal type was fragile and left uneven impressions, and metal type was expensive as well and did not hold water-based Chinese inks.

Carved wooden type did not have these problems and therefore became the preferred tool. Set in a wooden frame and tightened with wooden wedges, the readied page was inked up and an impression made, just as in printing with carved wooden blocks. Cutting a complete set of type or font required much time and effort because of the complexity and enormity of Chinese script. To do the latter justice, a busy press required 10,000 individual characters, and that number could increase several-fold, depending on the project.

Printing Comes of Age

In 952 C.E., after a quarter-century of preparation, a standardized Chinese text, unblemished by any scribal errors, was printed for the first time on a large scale. That text, the *Confucian Classics*, was an epochal event in the history of printing. The main reading of the elite, these famous scrolls became the basis of the entry exam for a government office. In awakening people to the power of printing, the *Confucian Classics* may be compared to the publication of Gutenberg's Latin Bible.

The Sung period (960–1278 C.E.) saw the first sustained flowering of block printing. Even today among the Chinese, the phrase "Sung style" connotes high quality. Three monumental publications stand out: the *Standard Histories* of previous Chinese dynasties, appearing serially between 994 and 1063 C.E.; the *Buddhist Scriptures* in scrolls up to sixty feet and longer, requiring 130,000 carved wooden blocks (971–983 C.E.); and the *Daoist Scriptures* (early eleventh century C.E.). For the literate, but not necessarily highly educated, numerous how-to books on medical, botanical, and agricultural topics became available. Printed paper money also appeared for the first time in copper-poor Szechwan during the Sung.

There is no certain evidence that printing was a complete gift of the Far East to the West. Although some scholars believe Chinese block printing accompanied playing cards through the Islamic world and into Europe, connecting links have not yet been demonstrated. Although there was a definite paper trail from East to West, Europe appears to have developed its own inks and invented its own block and movable type printing presses independently.[1]

Indeed, in the East and the West, different writing systems would favor distinct forms of printing. In China, carved wooden blocks suited an ideographic script that required a seemingly boundless number of characters. Each ideograph, or character, expressed a complete concept. In contrast, European writing was based on a very small phonetic alphabet. Each letter could express meaning only when connected to other letters, forming words. For such a system, movable metal type worked far better than carved wooden blocks. Although China mastered movable type printing earlier than the West, the enormous number of characters required by the Chinese language made movable type impractical.

Ironically, the simpler machinery of block printing did greater justice to China's more intricate and complex script, whereas Europe's far simpler script required the more complex machinery of movable type. Today the Chinese still face the problem of storing and retrieving their rich language in digitized form, "the space-age equivalent of movable type." In telecommunications, they prefer faxes, "the modern-day equivalent of the block print."[2]

Society and Printing

In neither the East nor the West do the availability of essential material resources (wood, ink, and paper) and the development of new technologies sufficiently explain the advent of printing. Cultural and emotional factors played an equally large role. In China,

the religious and moral demands of Buddhists, Taoists, and Confucians lay behind the invention of block printing. For Buddhists, copying and disseminating their sacred writings had always been a traditional path of salvation. Taoists, who wanted to hang protective charms or seals around their necks, printed sacred messages blessed by their priests that were up to four inches wide. These were apparently the first block prints. Confucianists, too, lobbied

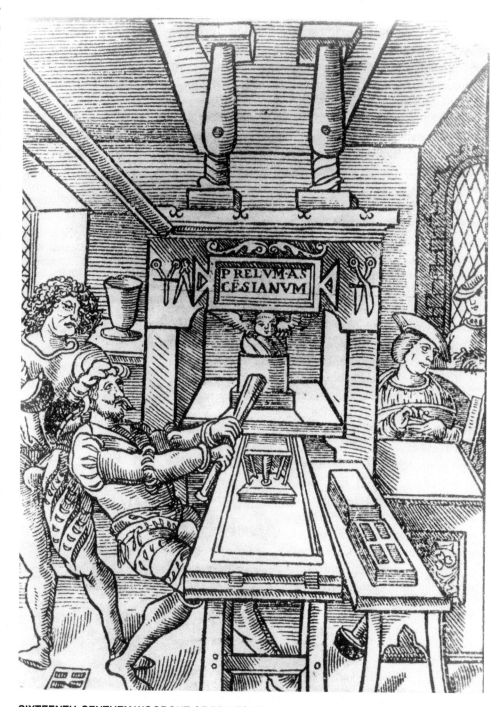

SIXTEENTH-CENTURY WOODCUT OF PRINTSHOP This woodcut shows typesetting and printing underway in an early printshop. Printing made it possible to reproduce exactly and in quantity both text and illustrations, leading to the distribution of scientific and technical information on a scale unimaginable in the preprint world.
SOURCE: Library of Congress

for standardized printed copies of their texts, which they had for centuries duplicated by crude rubbings from stone-carved originals.

In Europe, the major religious orders (Augustinians, Dominicans, and Franciscans) and popular lay religious movements (Waldensians, Lollards, and Hussites) joined with humanists to promote the printing of standardized, orthodox editions of the Bible and other religious writings. As the numbers of literate laity steadily grew, the demand for cheap, practical reading material (calendars, newssheets, and how-to pamphlets) also rapidly increased. By 1500, fifty years after Gutenberg's invention, 200 printing presses operated throughout Europe, sixty of them in German cities. Just as in China, the large print runs of the new presses tended to be religious or moral subjects in the early years: Latin Bibles and religious books, indulgences and Protestant pamphlets, along with decorated playing cards often bearing moral messages.

With the printing press came the first copyright laws. Knowledge had previously been considered "free." The great majority of medieval scholars and writers were clergy, who lived by the church or other patronage and whose knowledge was deemed a gift of God to be shared freely with all. After the printing press, however, a new sense of intellectual property emerged. In Europe, primitive protective laws took the form of a ruler's "privilege," by which a ruler pledged to punish the pirating of a particular work within his or her realm over a limited period of time. Such measures had clear limits: More than half of the books published during the first century of print in the West were pirated editions, a situation that would not change significantly until the eighteenth century.

Government censorship laws also ran apace with the growth of printing. The clergy of Cologne, Germany, issued the first prohibition of heretical books in 1479. In 1485, the church banned the works of the heretics John Wycliffe and John Huss throughout Europe, and two years later the pope promulgated the first bull against any books "harmful to the faith." In 1521, Emperor Charles V banned Martin Luther's works throughout the Holy Roman Empire, along with their author. In 1527, the first publisher was hanged for printing a banned book of Luther's. And in 1559, the pope established the *Index of Forbidden Books*, which still exists.

Printing stimulated numerous new ancillary trades. In addition to the proliferation of bookstores and the rise of traveling booksellers, who carried flyers from town to town promoting particular works, there were new specialized stationery shops, ink and inkstone stores, bookshelf and reading-table makers, and businesses manufacturing brushes and other printing tools. The new print industry also brought social and economic upheaval to city and countryside when, like modern corporations relocating factories to underdeveloped countries, it searched for cheaper labor by moving presses out of guild-dominated cities and into the freer marketplace of the countryside.

For society's authorities, the new numbers of literate citizens and subjects made changes and reforms both easier and more difficult. As a tool of propaganda, the printing press remained a two-edged sword. On the one hand, it gave authorities the means to propagandize more effectively than ever. On the other hand, the new literate public found itself in an unprecedented position to recognize deceit, challenge tradition, and expose injustice.

SOURCES: Thomas F. Carter, *The Invention of Printing in China and Its Spread Westward* (1928); Elisabeth L. Eisensrein, *The Printing Press as an Agent of Change*, I–II (1979); Rudolf Hirsch, *Printing, Selling and Reading 1450–1550* (Wiesbaden: Harrassowitz, 1967); Constance R. Miller, *Technical and Cultural Prerequisites for the Invention of Printing in China and the West* (Chinese Materials Center, 1983); Denis Twitchett, *Printing and Publishing in Medieval China* (New York: Frederic C. Beil, 1983).

Questions

1. Why did the invention of printing occur earlier in the East than in the West? Did the West inherit all of its knowledge of printing from the East?

2. What are the differences between the Chinese and European writing systems? What problems do these systems create for printing?

3. Why might one Chinese scholar prefer to send another Chinese scholar a fax rather than an e-mail?

4. What was the impact of printing on Chinese and European societies?

Notes

1. Carter, *Invention of Printing in China*, pp. 143, 150, 182.
2. Twitchett, *Printing and Publishing in Medieval China*, p. 86.

Chapter 9
The Late Middle Ages: Social and Political Breakdown (1300–1453)

A PROCESSION OF FLAGELLANTS AT TOURNAI In Flanders in 1349, the flagellants march with the crucified Christ and scourge themselves in imitation of his suffering.
SOURCE: ARPL/HIP/The Image Works

 Contents and Focus Questions

The Chapter in Brief

DURING THE LATE Middle Ages epidemic plagues contributed to almost unprecedented political, social, and ecclesiastical calamity. Sweeping over almost all of Europe, the great pandemic that struck between 1346 and 1353 left two-fifths of the population dead. No one then, however, called it the **Black Death**, a term invented in the sixteenth century. In these same years, France and England grappled with each other in a prolonged conflict known as the **Hundred Years' War** (1337–1453). In the war's later stages, mutual, willful self-destruction was made even more horrible by the introduction of gunpowder and the invention of heavy artillery. If those two events were not calamity enough, a great Schism erupted in the church (1378–1417), creating the spectacle of three elected competing popes and colleges of cardinals.

In 1453, the Turks marched invincibly through Constantinople into the West. As political and religious institutions buckled, disease, bandits, wolves, and Islamic armies gathered on the borders. Confronting overwhelming calamities, Europeans beheld what seemed to be the imminent collapse of their civilization. These centuries saw rulers resist wisdom, nature strain mercy, and the clergy turn its back on its flock.

9.1 The Black Death

What were the social and economic consequences of the Black Death?

The Black Death not only devastated the population of Europe in the fourteenth century; it also caused upheavals in the class relations that had come to define medieval society over the previous two centuries. Numerous factors came together to intensify the effects of the plague in major urban areas. This resulted in extreme social change, including religious persecution and the breakdown of traditional social customs. At the same time, certain elements

of society, such as kings and the guilds, saw their economic and political power increase. (For more information about the many ways the Black Death affected medieval society, see "Encountering the Past" sidebar, which follows below.)

9.1.1 Preconditions and Causes of the Plague

The virulent plagues struck Europe at a time of overpopulation and malnutrition. Nine-tenths of the population lived and worked in the countryside. Over time, the three-field system of crop production increased the amount of arable land and with it the food supply. As the food supply increased again, so did the population, now estimated to have doubled over the two centuries between 1000 and 1300. Once again, there were more people than there was food to feed them and jobs to employ them.

The average European could then face the probability of extreme hunger at least once in an expected thirty-five-year life span. Between 1315 and 1317, crop failures produced the greatest famine of the Middle Ages. Densely populated urban areas, such as the industrial towns of the Netherlands, suffered the most. Decades of overpopulation, economic depression, famine, and bad health weakened Europe's population, leaving it highly vulnerable to a bubonic plague that struck with full force in 1348. The description of the plague as the Black Death referred to the discoloration of its victims. Riding the backs of rats, plague-infested fleas from the Black Sea area boarded the sailing ships on the trade routes from Asia to Europe, thereby planting the plague in Western Europe. Appearing in Constantinople in 1346 and in Sicily a year later, it entered Europe through the ports of Venice, Genoa, and Pisa by 1347, sweeping rapidly through Spain and southern France into northern Europe. (See Map 9–1.)

9.1.2 Popular Remedies

The source of the plague was most often a victim's lungs. Sneezing and wheezing spread the plague by direct contact from person to person. Despite the plague's power, physicians, academics, and educated laypeople found effective ways to cope with and defend themselves against the plague. The advice literature described the plague as punishment for sin and recommended penance as the best resolution. Physicians had numerous guidelines to promote health. They applied natural, herbal medications in good conscience and often to good effect. There were also "green" measures, such as fumigating rooms and aerating city spaces with herbs and smoke, a remedy that lowered the

THE TRIUMPH OF DEATH This fresco, entitled *The Triumph of Death*, highlights themes of death and destruction common to allegorical compositions of the time. At the center is Death personified, a skeletal figure astride an emaciated horse. On the periphery, people representing different social groups, await their common fate.
SOURCE: Francesco Palermo/Alamy Stock Photo

Encountering the Past

Dealing with Death

DEATH WAS ALL too familiar in the late Middle Ages, and not just in the time of the plague, when both princes and the simple folk buried their children in the same communal pits. In popular art and literature, the living and the dead embraced in the "Dance of Death," reminding rich and poor, young and old, of their mortality. In the fourteenth century, death divided the Middle Ages from the Renaissance: On one side of the divide was an overpopulated medieval society devastated by the four horsemen of the Apocalypse. On the other side, a newly disciplined Renaissance society learned to forestall famine, plague, war, and conquest by abstinence, late marriage, birth control, and diplomacy.

Yet death rates in the past were three times those of the modern West and life expectancy only half as long. Life was a progressive dying, and death a promise of everlasting life. In sixteenth-century Florence, one-third of newborns died in infancy. In seventeenth-century England, infant mortality was 2 percent on the day of birth, 4 percent at the first week, 9 percent by the first month, and 13 percent at the end of the first year. By their teens and adulthood almost everyone had suffered from some chronic illness (tuberculosis), debilitating condition (arthritis, gout), and/or life-threatening infection (streptococci).

In Renaissance Italy, Lorenzo de' Medici, duke of Urbino (d. 1519), was plagued with leg ulcers and syphilis in his early twenties. At twenty-five, he received a head wound that was treated by trephination (i.e., the boring of holes in his skull). The poor man also developed an abscessed foot that never healed. At twenty-six, he fell prey to chills, fever, diarrhea, vomiting, joint pains, and anorexia, and was dead at twenty-seven. His physicians identified the cause of death as a catarrhal phlegm, or "suffocation of the heart."

Looking ahead, in Reformation Germany, at the age of sixty-two Saxon Elector Frederick the Wise of Saxony (d. 1525), who was Martin Luther's protector, spent the last year of his life enclosed in his favorite residence. When his strength permitted, he rolled about the castle on a specially made stool with wheels. Cursed with kidney stones, he died from septic infection and kidney failure when the stones became too many and too large to pass through his urethra. An autopsy discovered stones "almost two finger joints long and spiked."

La Mort jouant des timbales. —D'après Holbein

DEATH AND THE PHYSICIAN Sixteenth-century woodcuts of the Dance of Death designed by Hans Holbein the Younger and cut by Hans Lützelburger took many forms. This woodcut, called "Bones of All Men," depicts skeletons playing various musical instruments. Spectators, also portrayed as skeletal figures, look on.

SOURCE: Mid-Manhattan Picture Collection

Those who suffered from such afflictions found themselves, in the words of a sixteenth-century merchant, "between God and the physicians," a precarious position for the chronically ill in any age. The clergy and the physicians profited greatly from the age's great mortality. People feared both dying and dying out of God's grace. Together, the physician and the priest prepared the way to a good temporal death, while the priest guided the dead through purgatory and into heaven, assisted by the laity's purchase of **indulgences** and commemorative masses. Like the physicians' bleedings and herbal potions, the church's sacraments and commemorations exploited and eased the passage into eternity that every Christian soul had to make.

Questions

1. How do illness and death shape history and culture?
2. How well prepared were the physicians and the clergy to address and heal the stricken? Were the afflicted only wasting their time with herbal remedies and prayers?
3. Name some contemporary medicines and procedures that might have given the afflicted at least some relief, comfort, and hope.

SOURCES: Bruce Gordon and Peter Marshall, eds. *The Place of the Dead: Death and Remembrance in Late Medieval and Early Modern Europe* (Cambridge, UK: Cambridge University Press, 2008), chaps. 2, 14; Ann C. Carmichael, "The Health Status of Florentines in the Fifteenth Century," in M. Tetel et al., eds. *Life and Death in Fifteenth-Century Florence* (Durham, NC: Duke University Press, 1989), chap. 3.

Map 9–1 SPREAD OF THE BLACK DEATH

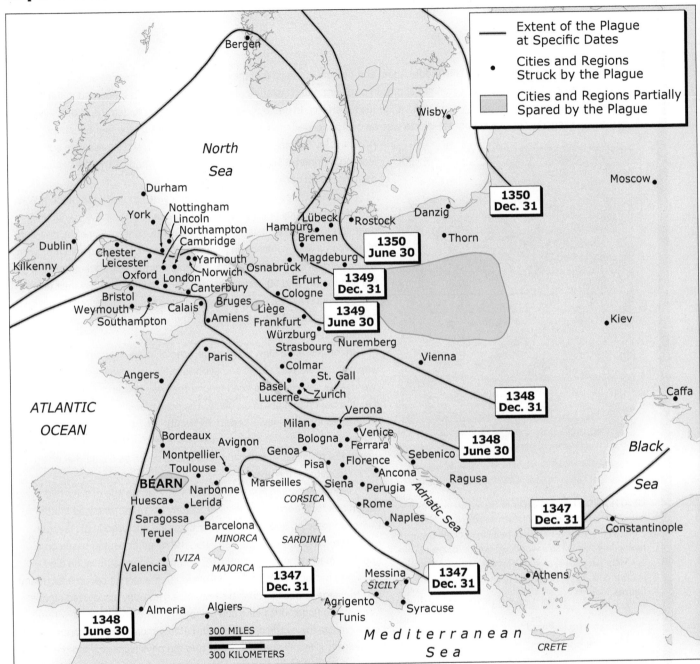

Apparently introduced by seaborne rats from Black Sea areas where plague-infested rodents had long been known, the Black Death had huge human, social, and economic consequences. One of the lower estimates of European deaths is 25 million. This map charts the plague's spread in the mid-fourteenth century. Generally following trade routes, the plague reached Scandinavia by 1350; some believe it then went on to Iceland and even Greenland. Areas off the main trade routes were largely spared.

number of fleas. Other measures were washing and cleansing with scented waters.

Popular speculation held that corruptions in the atmosphere caused the plague. Some blamed poisonous fumes released by earthquakes, which moved many to seek protection in aromatic amulets. Famous Italian writer **Giovanni Boccaccio** was an eyewitness to the 1348 plague, and he

recorded different reactions to it in his collection of tales titled the *Decameron*. Some of the afflicted sought escape in moderation and a temperate life, while more fatalistic minds gave themselves over entirely to their passions. In the stricken areas, sexual promiscuity ran high. "The best remedy perhaps," wrote Boccaccio, "was flight and seclusion, migration to non-infected lands, and keeping faith."

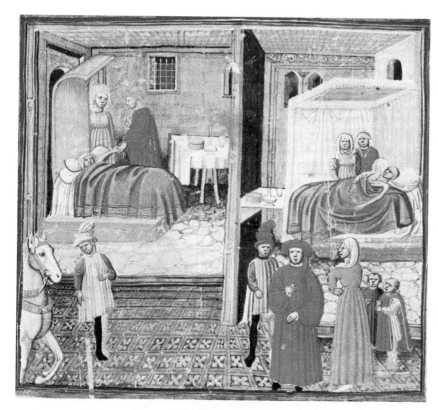

CANON OF MEDICINE This illustration from the *Canon of Medicine* by the Persian physician and philosopher Avicenna (980–1037), whose Arabic name was Ibn Sina, shows him visiting the homes of rich patients. In the High Middle Ages, the *Canon of Medicine* was the standard medical textbook in the Middle East and Europe.
SOURCE: Scala/Art Resource, NY

One extreme reaction to the plague was the procession of flagellants, religious fanatics who beat themselves in ritual penance, believing it would bring divine help. More likely, their dirty, bleeding bodies both increased the terror and spread the disease. So socially disruptive and threatening did they become that the church outlawed all such processions. In some places Jews were cast as scapegoats, the result of centuries of Christian propaganda that bred hatred toward Jews, as their role as society's moneylenders also did. Pogroms occurred in several cities, sometimes incited by the flagellants.

Modern DNA studies of plagues past are shedding new light on the medieval epidemics. The exploration of ancient burial pits across Europe confirm the bacterium *Yersinia pestis* to have caused the plague, while researchers continue to study unknown strains of the bacterium. (See the "Closer Look," which follows below, on the burying of plague victims.) The debate today continues over whether bubonic plague was the sole lethal agent. Perhaps there were more disease agents in the mix, such as anthrax, typhus, smallpox, dysentery, or an ebola-like virus, Still to be resolved is the question of how the bacillus, fleas, rats, and humans interacted at various temperatures, humidity, and geographical locations to spread the epidemic across Europe.

9.1.3 Social and Economic Consequences

Whole villages vanished in the wake of the plague. Among the social and economic consequences of such high depopulation were a shrunken labor supply and a decline in the value of the estates of the nobility. The enormous loss of workers increased both the demand for labor and the level of wages. Forced to pay higher wages and confronted with a decrease in rents, the nobility was hit hard by the effects of the plague. The attempts by landowners to reverse their fortunes gave rise to peasant revolts. In addition, kings used the newfound vulnerability of the nobles and clergy to centralize their states.

9.1.3.1 FARMS DECLINE As the number of farm laborers decreased, wages increased and those of skilled artisans soared. Many serfs chose to commute their labor services into money payments and pursue more interesting and rewarding jobs in skilled craft industries in the cities. Agricultural prices fell because of waning demand, and the price of luxury and manufactured goods—the work of skilled artisans—rose. The noble landholders suffered the greatest decline in power. They were forced to pay more for finished products and for farm labor, while receiving a smaller return on their agricultural produce. Everywhere rents declined after the plague.

9.1.3.2 PEASANTS REVOLT To recoup their losses, some landowners converted arable land to sheep pasture, substituting more profitable wool production for labor-intensive grains. Others abandoned the farms, leasing them to the highest bidder. Landowners also sought to reverse their misfortune by new repressive legislation. In 1351, the English Parliament passed a Statute of Laborers, which limited wages to pre-plague levels and restricted the ability of peasants to leave their masters' land. Opposition to such legislation sparked the English peasants' revolt in 1381. In France the direct tax on the peasantry, the *taille*, was increased, and opposition to it helped ignite the French peasant uprising known as the Jacquerie. (See the "Compare and Connect sidebar, which follows below, on peasant uprisings in England and France.)

9.1.3.3 CITIES REBOUND Although the plague hit urban populations hard, the cities and their skilled industries came in time to prosper from its effects. Cities had always protected their own interests, passing legislation as they

A Closer Look

The Burying of Plague Victims in Tournai

ORIGINATING IN ASIA, the Black Death reached Europe around 1347. Raging for close to four years in some areas, the disease affected every class in European society and destroyed between one-quarter to one-third of the population. This illustration, *The Burying of Plague Victims in Tournai*, is from a 1349 manuscript titled *Annals of Gilles de Muisis*. Tournai was a thriving trading center in Belgium at the time of the plague. The entire image is filled with those burying the dead and the many that wait to be buried. Approximately 7,500 people died from the disease every day.

Children were especially vulnerable to the plague. Jean de Venette, a Carmelite friar in Paris, noted that many men "left many inheritances and temporal goods to churches and monastic orders, for in many cases they had seen their close heirs and children die before them."

There was often a shortage of coffins, and it was impractical to wait until they could be built before burying the deceased. As a result, large, makeshift graves were common.

The necessity of a quick burial created disorderliness and chaos. Bodies needed to be disposed of as quickly as possible to prevent the spread of disease. In the rush to bury the dead, graves were dug with little attention to detail or ritual.

THE BURYING OF PLAGUE VICTIMS, AN ILLUSTRATION
SOURCE: Snark/Art Resource, NY

Questions

1. How does this illustration depict the enormous consequences of the plague?
2. How did the plague impact towns such as Tournai?
3. What might be deduced from this picture about the spiritual and emotional toll the pandemic took on the population of Europe?

---

grew to regulate competition from outside rural areas and to control immigration. After the plague, the reach of such laws extended beyond the cities to include the surrounding lands of nobles and landlords, many of whom now peacefully integrated into urban life.

The omnipresence of death also whetted the appetite for goods that only skilled industries could produce.

Expensive clothes and jewelry, furs from the north, and silks from the south were in great demand in the decades after the plague. Initially this new demand could not be met. The basic unit of urban industry, the master and his apprentices (usually one or two), purposely kept its numbers low, jealously guarding its privileges. The first wave of plague turned this already restricted supply of skilled artisans into

Compare and Connect

Peasant Revolts in England and France

THE LATE MIDDLE AGES SAW LARGE-SCALE PEASANT UPRISINGS in both England and France. In both countries, the efforts of landowners to control wages and to tie agricultural laborers to the land led to violent revolts. And, in each case, the rebels enjoyed initial success, only to suffer terrible defeats once the crown and aristocracy organized their forces and had recovered from the initial shock of rebellion.

The two excerpts offer contemporary descriptions of the peasant revolts. In the first, Jean Froissart describes the initial outbreak of violence in France. In the second, a chronicler describes a meeting between King Richard II of England and Wat Tyler, the leader of the English peasants, in which the king told Tyler that he would acquiesce to the peasants' demands, a promise Richard had no intention of keeping.

MEETING OF RICHARD II AND WAT TYLER Shortly after the meeting between Tyler and Richard II, the king went back on his word and crushed the peasants' revolt.
SOURCE: Photo 12/Alamy Stock Photo

Before Reading

- Think about the similarities between conditions in France and England.
- Consider the social and economic background of the authors.
- Ask yourself how a medieval peasant might have described the revolts.

Questions

1. How did Froissart characterize the French rebels?
2. What were Wat Tyler's demands? What do they tell you about how English peasants saw their world?
3. Was the defeat of these two uprisings inevitable? Why or why not?

I. A FRENCH HISTORAN DISCUSSES THE JACQUERIE

Anon after the deliverance of the king of Navarre there began a marvellous tribulation in the realm of France, as in Beauvoisin, in Brie, on the river of Marne, in Laonnois, and about Soissons. For certain people of the common villages, without any head or ruler, assembled together in Beauvoisin. In the beginning they passed not a hundred in number. They said how the noblemen of the realm of France, knights and squires, shamed the realm, and that it should be a great wealth to destroy them all: and each of them said it was true, and said all with one voice: "Shame have he that cloth not his power to destroy all the gentlemen of the realm!"

Thus they gathered together without any other counsel, and without any armour saving with staves and knives, and so went to the house of a knight dwelling thereby, and brake up his house and slew the knight and the lady and all his children great and small and rent his house. And they then went to another castle, and took the knight thereof and bound him fast to a stake, and then violated his wife and his daughter before his face and then slew the lady and his daughter and all his other children, and then slew the knight by great torment and burnt and beat down the castle. And so they did to divers other castles and good houses; and they multiplied so that they were a six thousand, and ever as they went forward they increased, for such like as they were fell ever to them, so that every gentleman fled from them and took their wives and children with them, and fled ten or twenty leagues off to be in surety, and left their house void and their goods therein. These mischievous people thus assembled without captain or armour robbed, rent and slew all gentlemen that they could lay hands on, and forced and ravished ladies and damsels, and did such shameful deeds that no human creature ought to think on any such, and he that did most mischief was most praised with them and greatest master. I dare not write the horrible deeds that they did to ladies and damsels; among other they slew a knight and after did put him on a broach and roasted him at the fire in the sight of the lady his wife and his children; and after the lady had been enforced and ravished with a ten or twelve, they made her perforce to eat of her husband and after made her to die an evil death and all her children. They made among them a king, one of Clermont in Beauvoisin: they chose him that was the most ungracious of all other and they called him king Jaques Goodman, and so thereby they were called companions of the Jaquery.

II. AN ENGLISH CHRONICLER DESCRIBES THE MEETING BETWEEN RICHARD II AND WAT TYLER

Then the King caused a proclamation to be made that all the commons of the country who were still in London should come to Smithfield, to meet him there; and so they did.

And when the King and his train had arrived there they turned into the Eastern meadow in front of St. Bartholomew's, which is a house of canons: and the commons arrayed themselves on the west side in great battles. At this moment the Mayor of London, William Walworth, came up, and the King bade him go to the commons, and make their chieftain come to him. And when he was summoned by the Mayor, by the name of Wat Tyler of Maidstone, he came to the King with great confidence, mounted on a little horse, that the commons might see him. And he dismounted, holding in his hand a dagger which he had taken from another man, and when he had dismounted he half bent his knee, and then took the King by the hand, and shook his arm forcibly and roughly, saying to him, "Brother, be of good comfort and joyful, for you shall have, in the fortnight that is to come, praise from the commons even more than you have yet had, and we shall be good companions." And the King said to Walter, "Why will you not go back to your own country?" But the other answered, with a great oath, that neither he nor his fellows would depart until they had got their charter such as they wished to have it, and had certain points rehearsed and added to their charter which they wished to demand. And he said in a threatening fashion that the lords of the realm would rue it bitterly if these points were not settled to their pleasure. Then the King asked him what were the points which he wished to have revised, and he should have them freely, without contradiction, written out and sealed. Thereupon the said Walter rehearsed the points which were to be demanded; and he asked that there should be no law within the realm save the law of Winchester, and that from henceforth there should be no outlawry in any process of law, and that no lord should have lordship save civilly, and that there should be equality among all people save only the King, and that the goods of Holy Church should not remain in the hands of the religious, nor of parsons and vicars, and other churchmen; but that clergy already in possession should have a sufficient sustenance from the endowments, and the rest of the goods should be divided among the people of the parish. And he demanded that there should be only one bishop in England and only one prelate, and all the lands and tenements now held by them should be confiscated, and divided among the commons, only reserving for them a reasonable sustenance. And he demanded that there should be no more villeins in England, and no serfdom or villeinage, but that all men should be free and of one condition. To this the King gave an easy answer, and said that he should have all that he could fairly grant, reserving only for himself the regality of his crown. And then he bade him go back to his home, without making further delay.

SOURCES: (I) From G. C. Macauly, ed., *The Chronicles of Froissart* (London: Macmillan and Co., 1904), pp. 136–137. (II) From Charles Oman, *The Great Revolt of 1381* (Oxford: Clarendon Press, 1906), pp. 200–202.

a shortage almost overnight. As a result, the prices of manufactured and luxury items rose to new heights, which, in turn, encouraged workers to migrate from the countryside to the city and learn the skills of artisans. Townspeople profited coming and going. As wealth poured into the cities and per capita income rose, the prices of agricultural products from the countryside, now less in demand, declined.

9.1.4 New Conflicts and Opportunities

The economic and political power of local artisans and trade guilds grew steadily in the late Middle Ages, along with the demand for goods and services. The strong merchant and patrician classes found it increasingly difficult to

maintain their traditional dominance and only grudgingly gave guild masters a voice in city government. As the guilds won political power, they lobbied for restrictive legislation to protect local industries. The restrictions, in turn, caused conflict among master artisans, who wanted to keep their numbers low and expand their industries at a snail's pace, thereby denying many journeymen a chance to rise to the rank of master.

After 1350, the results of the plague put the two traditional "containers" of monarchy—the landed nobility and the church—on the defensive. Kings now exploited growing national sentiment in an effort to centralize their governments and economies. At this same time, the battles of the Hundred Years' War demonstrated the superiority of paid professional armies over the old noble cavalry, bringing the latter's future role into question. The plague also killed around one-third of the German clergy who fell victim as they dutifully attended to the sick and the dying. This reduction in clerical ranks occurred in the same century in which the pope moved from Rome to Avignon in southeastern France (1309–1377) and the Great Schism (1378–1417) divided the church into new warring factions.

9.2 The Hundred Years' War and the Rise of National Sentiment

How did the Hundred Years' War contribute to a growing sense of national identity in France and England?

Medieval governments were by no means all-powerful and secure. The rivalry of petty lords kept lands in constant turmoil, allowing dynastic rivalries to plunge entire lands into war, especially when power was being transferred to a new ruler. This doubled the woes of the ruling dynasty that failed to produce a male heir.

To field the armies and collect the revenues that made their existence possible, late medieval rulers depended on carefully negotiated alliances among a wide range of lesser powers. To maintain the order they required, the Norman kings of England and the Capetian kings of France fine-tuned traditional feudal relationships by stressing the sacred duties of lesser powers to higher ones, and the unquestioning loyalty noble vassals owed their king. The result was a

degree of centralized royal power unseen before in these lands, accompanied by a growing national consciousness that prepared both France and England for a prolonged, international war.

KEY EVENTS IN THE HUNDRED YEARS' WAR (1337–1453)	
1340	English victory at Battle of Sluys
1346	English victory at Crécy and seizure of Calais
1347	Black Death strikes
1356	English victory at Poitiers
1358	Jacquerie disrupts France
1360	Peace of Brétigny-Calais recognizes English holdings in France
1381	English peasants revolt
1415	English victory at Agincourt
1420	Treaty of Troyes recognizes the English king as heir to the French throne
1422	Henry VI proclaimed king of both England and France
1429	Joan of Arc leads French to victory at Orléans
1431	Joan of Arc executed as a heretic
1453	War ends; English retain only Calais

9.2.1 The Causes of the War

The great conflict came to be known as the Hundred Years' War because it began in May 1337 and extended off and on to October 1453. English king **Edward III** (r. 1327–1377), the grandson of Philip the Fair of France (r. 1285–1314), may have started the war by asserting his claim to the French throne after the French king Charles IV (r. 1322–1328), the last of Philip the Fair's surviving sons, died without a male heir. The French barons had no intention of placing the then fifteen-year-old Edward on the French throne. They chose instead the first cousin of Charles IV, Philip VI of Valois (r. 1328–1350), the first of a new French dynasty that would rule into the sixteenth century.

There was of course more to the war than just English king Edward's claim to the French throne. England and France were then two emerging territorial powers in close proximity to one another. Edward, a vassal of Philip VI, controlled several sizable French territories as fiefs from the king of France, a relationship dating back to the days of the Norman conquest. English possession of any French land was repugnant to the French because it threatened the royal policy of centralization. The two lands also quarreled over control of

EDWARD III PAYS HOMAGE TO HIS FEUDAL LORD PHILIP VI OF FRANCE English king Edward III may have started the war by asserting his claim to the French throne, which was ultimately given to Philip VI of Valois. Legally, Edward was a vassal of Philip VI.
SOURCE: Snark/Art Resource, NY

Flanders: Although it was a French fief, it was subject to England's political influence because its principal industry, the manufacture of cloth, was dependent on supplies of imported English wool. Compounding these frictions was a long history of animosity between the French and English people, who continually confronted one another on the high seas and in ports. Taken together, these factors made the Hundred Years' War a struggle for national identity as well as for control of territory.

9.2.1.1 FRENCH WEAKNESS France had three times the population of England, was far the wealthier of the two lands, and fought on its own soil. Yet for most of the conflict before 1415, the major battles ended in often stunning English victories. (See Map 9–2.) The primary reason for these French failures was the internal disunity brought on by endemic social conflict. Unlike England, fourteenth-century France was still struggling to make the transition from a splintered feudal society to a centralized "modern" state.

Desperate to raise money for the war, French kings resorted to such financial policies as depreciating the currency and borrowing heavily from Italian bankers, which aggravated internal conflicts. In 1355, in a bid to secure funds, the king turned to the **Estates General**, a representative council of townspeople, clergy, and nobles. Although it levied taxes at the king's request, the council's independent members exploited the king's plight to broaden their own regional sovereignty, thereby deepening territorial divisions.

9.2.1.2 ENGLISH STRENGTH France's defeats also reflected English military superiority. The English infantry was more disciplined than the French, and English archers mastered a formidable weapon, the longbow, capable of firing six arrows a minute with enough force to pierce an inch of wood or the armor of a knight at 200 yards. French weakness during the long war was also due in no small degree to the mediocrity

Map 9–2   THE HUNDRED YEARS' WAR

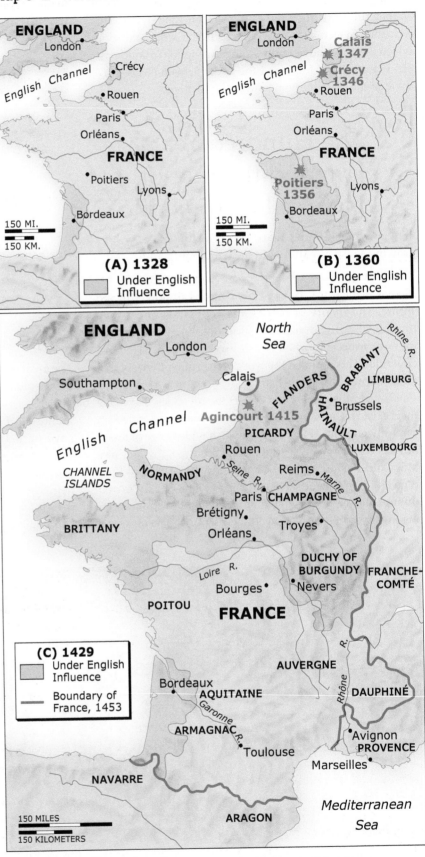

The Hundred Years' War went on intermittently from the late 1330s until 1453. These maps show the remarkable English territorial gains up to the sudden and decisive turning of battle in favor of the French by the forces of Joan of Arc in 1429.

of its rulers. The English kings were far shrewder in state building.

9.2.2 Progress of the War

The war had three major stages of development, each ending with seemingly decisive victory by one side or the other. England dominated the conflict and was victorious in several battles until the entry of Joan of Arc and the war's conclusion.

9.2.2.1 THE CONFLICT DURING THE REIGN OF EDWARD III

In the first stage of the war, Edward embargoed English wool to Flanders, sparking urban rebellions by merchants and the trade guilds. Inspired by a rich merchant, Jacob van Artevelde, the Flemish cities, led by Ghent, revolted against the French and in 1340 signed an alliance with England acknowledging Edward as king of France. On June 23 of the same year, in the first great battle of the war, Edward defeated the French fleet in the Battle of Sluys, but his subsequent effort to invade France by way of Flanders failed.

In 1346, Edward attacked Normandy and after a series of easy victories culminating in the **Battle of Crécy**, he seized the port of Calais. Exhaustion on both sides and the onset of the Black Death forced a truce in late 1347, as the war stopped for a brief lull. In 1356, the English won their greatest victory, routing the French cavalry and taking the French king captive back to England after a complete breakdown of the political order in France.

Power in France now lay with the Estates General. Led by the powerful merchants of Paris, that governing body took advantage of royal weakness, demanding and receiving rights similar to those Magna Carta had granted to the English privileged classes. Yet, unlike the English Parliament, which represented the interests of a comparatively unified English nobility, the French Estates General was too divided to be an instrument for effective government.

To secure their rights, the French privileged classes forced the peasantry to pay ever-increasing taxes and to repair their war-damaged properties without compensation. This bullying was more than the simple folk could bear, and they rose up in several regions in a series of bloody rebellions known as the **Jacquerie** of 1358. The name was taken from the peasant revolutionary known popularly as Jacques Bonhomme, or "simple Jack." The nobility quickly put his revolt down, matching the rebels atrocity for atrocity.

On May 9, 1360, another milestone of the war occurred when England forced the Peace of Brétigny-Calais on the French. This agreement declared an end to Edward's vassalage to the king of France and affirmed his sovereignty over English territories in France. Such a partition was unrealistic, and sober observers on both sides knew it could not

last. France struck back in the late 1360s and, by the time of Edward's death in 1377, had beaten the English back into their coastal enclaves.

9.2.2.2 FRENCH DEFEAT AND THE TREATY OF TROYES

During the reign of Richard II (r. 1377–1399), England had its own version of the Jacquerie. In June 1381, long-oppressed peasants and artisans joined in a great revolt of the underprivileged classes led by John Ball, a secular priest, and Wat Tyler, a journeyman. As in France, the revolt was brutally crushed within the year, and the country divided for decades.

England recommenced the war under Henry V (r. 1413–1422), whose army routed the French at Agincourt on October 25, 1415. In the years thereafter, the Burgundians closed ranks with French royal forces, another coalition promising to bring victory over the English, only to see the dream shattered in September 1419, when the duke of Burgundy was assassinated.

France was now Henry V's for the taking, at least in the short run. The Treaty of Troyes in 1420 disinherited the legitimate heir to the French throne and proclaimed Henry V successor to the French king, Charles VI. When Henry and Charles died within months of one another in 1422, the infant king Henry VI of England was proclaimed king of both France and England in Paris. Edward III's dream that had set the great war in motion, of making the ruler of England also the ruler of France, had come true.

The story did not end here. The son of Charles VI now became, upon the death of his father, King Charles VII to most French people, who ignored the Treaty of Troyes. Displaying unprecedented national feeling inspired by the remarkable Joan of Arc, Charles VII now rallied to his cause and gathered a victorious coalition.

9.2.2.3 JOAN OF ARC AND THE WAR'S CONCLUSION

Joan of Arc (1412–1431), a peasant from Domrémy in Lorraine in eastern France, presented herself to Charles VII in March 1429, declaring that the King of Heaven had called her to deliver the besieged city of Orléans from the English. Charles was skeptical, but in retreat from what seemed to be a hopeless war, he was willing to roll the dice to reverse French fortunes. The deliverance of Orléans, a key city that controlled the territory south of the Loire River, would indeed be a godsend for him. King Charles's desperation overcame his skepticism, and he gave Joan his leave.

Circumstances worked perfectly to her advantage. The English force was exhausted by a six-month siege at the point of withdrawal when Joan arrived with fresh French troops. After driving the English from Orléans, the French enjoyed a succession of victories popularly attributed to Joan. She did indeed deserve much credit, but not because she was a military genius. She gave the French soldiers something military experts could not: a proud, enraged sense of national identity and destiny. Within a few months

JOAN OF ARC (1412–1431) A peasant from Domrémy in Lorraine in eastern France, Joan of Arc claimed that the King of Heaven had called her to deliver the besieged city of Orléans from the English.
SOURCE: Bridgeman-Giraudon/Art Resource, NY

of the liberation of Orléans, Charles VII was crowned in Rheims, ending the nine-year "disinheritance" prescribed by the Treaty of Troyes.

The new king forgot his liberator Joan as quickly as he had embraced her. When the Burgundians took her captive in May 1430, he could have secured her release, but chose not to help her. The Burgundians and the English wanted her publicly discredited, believing this would also discredit King Charles VII and demoralize French resistance.

In the end, Joan was turned over to the Inquisition in English-held Rouen. The inquisitors broke the courageous "Maid of Orléans" after ten weeks of interrogation. She was executed as a relapsed heretic on May 30, 1431. In 1435, the duke of Burgundy made peace with Charles, allowing France to force the English back. By 1453, the war ended, and the English held only their coastal enclave of Calais.

In 1456, Charles reopened Joan of Arc's trial, as the French state and church hoped to get on history's side.

She was then declared innocent of all the charges against her. In 1920, the Roman Catholic Church declared her a saint.

The Hundred Years' War comprised sixty-eight years of nominal peace and forty-four of hot war, and left lasting political and social consequences. It devastated France, but it also awakened French nationalism, which in turn hastened the transition of France from a feudal monarchy to a centralized state. The war also made Burgundy a major European political power.

9.3 Ecclesiastical Breakdown and Revival: The Late Medieval Church

How did secular rulers challenge papal authority in the fourteenth and fifteenth centuries?

At first glance, the popes may appear to have been in a favorable position in the latter thirteenth century. Frederick II had been vanquished and imperial pressure on Rome had been removed. The French king, Louis IX, was an enthusiastic supporter of the church, as evidenced by his two disastrous Crusades, which won him sainthood. Although it would last for only seven years, a reunion of the Eastern and Roman churches was proclaimed by the **Council of Lyons** in 1274, after the Western church took advantage of Byzantine Emperor Michael VII Palaeologus's (r. 1261–1282) request for aid against the Turks. Despite these positive events, Rome's position would turn out to be less favorable than it appeared.

9.3.1 The Thirteenth-Century Papacy

As early as the reign of Pope Innocent III (r. 1198–1216), when papal power had reached its height, there were ominous developments. Innocent's transformation of the papacy into a great secular power weakened the church spiritually even as it strengthened it politically. Thereafter, the church as a papal monarchy increasingly parted company with the church as the "body of the faithful."

What Innocent began, his successors perfected. Under Urban IV (r. 1261–1264), the papacy established its own court, the *Rota Romana*, which tightened and centralized the church's legal proceedings. In the last half of the thirteenth century there was also a new elaboration of the system of clerical taxation. During the same period, papal power determined all appointments to major and minor church offices—the so-called "reservation of benefices" was greatly broadened. By the thirteenth century, the papal office had become a powerful, political institution governed by its own laws and courts and serviced by an efficient international bureaucracy, thoroughly preoccupied with secular tasks and goals.

9.3.1.1 INTERNAL STRIFE Papal centralization of the church undermined both diocesan authority and popular support. Rome's interests—not local need—controlled church appointments, policies, and discipline. Discontented lower clergy turned to Rome to address the lax discipline of local bishops, and in the second half of the thirteenth century, bishops and abbots protested the undercutting of their powers. To its critics, the church in Rome was hardly more than a legalized, fiscalized, bureaucratic institution. As early as the late twelfth century, heretical movements of Cathars and Waldensians had appealed to the biblical ideal of simplicity and separation from the world. Other reformers who had been unquestionably loyal to the church, such as Saint Francis of Assisi, also protested perceived materialism cloaked in official religious garb.

9.3.1.2 POLITICAL FRAGMENTATION More disturbing than internal religious quarreling was the spiritual undermining of the thirteenth-century church. The demise of imperial power meant the papacy in Rome was no longer the leader of anti-imperial (Guelf, or pro-papal) sentiment in Italy. Instead of being the conduit for Italian resistance to the emperor, popes were now on the defensive against their old allies. That was the ironic price the papacy paid to conquer the Hohenstaufen rulers. With a large stake in Italian politics, rulers now directed intrigue formerly intended for the emperor toward the College of Cardinals.

9.3.2 Boniface VIII and Philip the Fair

Pope Boniface VIII (r. 1294–1303) came to rule when England and France were maturing as nation-states. In England, a long tradition of consultation between the king and powerful members of English society evolved into formal parliaments during the reigns of Henry III (r. 1216–1272) and Edward I (r. 1272–1307), and these meetings helped create a unified kingdom. The reign of the French king Philip IV the Fair (r. 1285–1314) saw France become an efficient, centralized monarchy. Philip was no St. Louis, but a ruthless politician. He was determined to end England's continental holdings, control wealthy Flanders, and establish French hegemony within the Holy Roman Empire.

Boniface had the misfortune of reminding the papal throne of how earlier popes had brought kings and emperors to their knees. Painfully, he discovered that the papal monarchy of the early thirteenth century was no match for the new political juggernauts of the late thirteenth century.

9.3.2.1 THE ROYAL CHALLENGE TO PAPAL AUTHORITY France and England were on the brink of all-out war when Boniface became pope in 1294. Only Edward I's preoccupation with rebellion in Scotland, which the French

POPE BONIFACE VIII (r. 1294–1303) Pope Boniface VIII opposed the taxation of the clergy by the kings of France and England and issued the bull *Unam Sanctam*, one of the strongest declarations of papal authority over temporal rulers. This statue of Boniface is in the Museo Civico, Bologna, Italy.
SOURCE: Scala/Art Resource, NY

encouraged, prevented him from invading France and start-ing the Hundred Years' War a half-century earlier. As both countries mobilized for war, they used the pretext of prepar-ing for a Crusade to tax the clergy heavily. Viewing English and French taxation of the clergy as an assault on traditional clerical rights, Boniface took a strong stand against it. On February 5, 1296, he issued a bull, *Clericis laicos*, which for-bade lay taxation of the clergy without papal approval and revoked all previous papal dispensations in this regard.

In England, Edward I retaliated by denying the clergy the right to be heard in royal court, in effect denying them the protection of the king. Philip the Fair struck back with a vengeance: In August 1296, he forbade the exportation of money from France to Rome, thereby denying the papacy the revenues it needed to operate. Boniface had no choice but to come to terms quickly with Philip.

Boniface was also under siege by powerful Italian ene-mies, whom Philip did not fail to patronize. A noble fam-ily (the Colonnas), rivals of Boniface's family (the Gaetani) and radical followers of Saint Francis of Assisi (the **Spiritual Franciscans**), hoped to invalidate Boniface's election as pope on the grounds that Celestine V had been forced to resign the office. Charges of heresy, simony, and even the murder of Celestine were now hurled against Boniface.

Boniface's fortunes appeared to revive in 1300, a so-called "Jubilee year." In such a year, all Catholics who visited Rome and fulfilled certain conditions had the penalties for their unexpiated sins remitted. Tens of thousands of pilgrims flocked to Rome, and Boniface, heady with this display of popular religiosity, reinserted himself into international politics. He championed Scottish resistance to England, for which he received a firm rebuke from an outraged Edward I and the English Parliament.

But again, a confrontation with the king of France proved too costly. Seemingly eager for another fight with the pope, Philip arrested Boniface's Parisian legate, Bernard Saisset, whose independence Philip had opposed. Accused of heresy and treason, Saisset was tried and convicted in the king's court. Thereafter, Philip demanded that Boniface rec-ognize the royal process against Saisset. Boniface could only do this if he was prepared to surrender his jurisdiction over the French episcopate. Unable to sidestep this challenge, Boniface acted swiftly to champion Saisset as a defender of clerical, political independence within France. Demanding Saisset's unconditional release, Boniface revoked all previ-ous agreements with Philip regarding clerical taxation and ordered the French bishops to convene in Rome within a year. A bull, titled *Ausculta fili*, or "Listen, My Son," was sent to Philip in December 1301, pointedly informing the French king that "God has set popes over kings and kingdoms."

9.3.2.2 *UNAM SANCTAM* Philip now unleashed a ruthless antipapal campaign. Two royal apologists, Pierre Dubois and John of Paris, rebutted papal claims to the right to

intervene in secular matters. Increasingly placed on the defensive, Boniface made a last-ditch stand against state control of national churches. On November 18, 1302, he issued the bull **Unam Sanctam**. This famous statement of papal power declared royal, temporal authority to be "sub-ject" to the spiritual power of the church. On its face a bold assertion, *Unam Sanctam* was, in truth, a desperate act of a besieged papacy.

After *Unam Sanctam*, the French and their allies moved against Boniface with force. Philip's chief minister, Guillaume de Nogaret, denounced Boniface to the French clergy as a heretic and common criminal. In mid-August 1303, his army surprised the pope at his retreat in Anagni, beat him up, and almost executed him before an aroused populace returned him safely to Rome. The ordeal, however, proved to be too much, and Boniface died in October 1303.

Boniface's immediate successor, Pope Benedict XI (r. 1303–1304), excommunicated Nogaret for his deed, but there was to be no lasting papal retaliation. Benedict's suc-cessor, Clement V (r. 1305–1314), was forced into French subservience. A former archbishop of Bordeaux, Pope Clement had declared that *Unam Sanctam* should not be interpreted as a way of diminishing French royal authority. He released Nogaret from excommunication and pliantly condemned the Knights Templars, whose treasure Philip thereafter seized.

In 1309, Clement moved the papal court to Avignon, an imperial city on the southeastern border of France. Situated on land that belonged to the pope, the city maintained its independence from the French king. In 1311, Clement made it his permanent residence to escape a strife-ridden Rome and further pressure from Philip. There the papacy would remain until 1377.

After Boniface's humiliation, popes never again seri-ously threatened kings and emperors, despite continuing papal excommunications and political intrigue. The rela-tionship between church and state now tilted in favor of the state, and the control of religion fell into the hands of powerful monarchies. Ecclesiastical authority now became subordinate to larger secular political policies.

9.3.3 The Avignon Papacy (1309–1377)

The **Avignon papacy** was in appearance, although not always in fact, under strong French influence. Under Pope Clement V, the French dominated the College of Cardinals, testing the papacy's agility politically and eco-nomically. Finding itself cut off from its Roman estates, the papacy had to innovate to get needed funds. Clement expanded papal taxes, especially *annates*, the first year's revenue of a church office, or benefice, bestowed by the pope. Clement VI (r. 1342–1352) began the practice of sell-ing indulgences. To make the purchase of indulgences more compelling, church doctrine on purgatory—the place where souls would atone for venial sins—developed enterprisingly during this period. By the fifteenth century, the church had extended indulgences to cover the souls of people already dead, allowing the living to buy a reduced sentence in purgatory for deceased loved ones. Such practices contributed to the Avignon papacy's reputation for materialism and political scheming, giving reformers new ammunition against the church.

9.3.3.1 POPE JOHN XXII

Pope John XXII (r. 1316–1334), the most powerful Avignon pope, tried to restore papal independence and its return to Italy. This goal led him to war with the Visconti, the powerful ruling family of Milan, and a costly contest with Emperor Louis IV (r. 1314–1347). John challenged Louis's election as emperor in 1314 in favor of the rival Habsburg candidate. When John obstinately and without legal justification refused to recognize Louis's election, the emperor deposed him and put in his place an antipope. As Philip the Fair had also done, Louis enlisted the support of the Spiritual Franciscans, whose views on absolute poverty John condemned as heretical. Two outstanding pamphleteers wrote lasting tracts for the royal cause: William of Ockham, whom John excommunicated in 1328, and Marsilius of Padua (ca. 1290–1342), whose teaching John declared heretical in 1327.

In his *Defender of Peace* (1324), Marsilius stressed the independent origins and autonomy of secular government. Clergy were to be subjected to the strictest apostolic ideals and confined to purely spiritual functions, and the pope was denied all power of coercive judgment. In the clerical judgment of kings, so wrote Marsilius, spiritual crimes must await eternal punishment. Transgressions of divine law, where the pope held jurisdiction, were to be punished in the next life, not in the present one, unless the secular ruler should declare a divine law also a secular law. This assertion directly challenged the power of the pope to excommunicate rulers and place countries under interdict. The *Defender of Peace* depicted the pope as a subordinate member of a society, where the emperor ruled supreme and where temporal peace was the highest good.

Pope John XXII made the papacy a sophisticated international agency and adroitly adjusted it to the growing European money economy. The more the **Curia**, or papal court, mastered the latter, the more vulnerable it became to secular criticism. Under John's successor, Benedict XII (r. 1334–1342), the papacy became entrenched in the city of Avignon. Seemingly forgetting Rome altogether, Benedict began to build the great Palace of the Popes from which he attempted to reform both papal government and the religious life. His high-living French successor, Pope Clement VI (r. 1342–1352), placed papal policy in lockstep with the French. In this period, the cardinals became barely more than lobbyists for policies their secular patrons favored.

9.3.3.2 NATIONAL OPPOSITION TO THE AVIGNON PAPACY

As Avignon's fiscal tentacles probed new areas, monarchies took strong action to protect their interests. The latter half of the fourteenth century saw new legislation restricting papal jurisdiction and taxation in France, England, and Germany. In England, Parliament several times passed statutes that restricted payments and appeals to Rome along with the pope's power to make high ecclesiastical appointments.

In France, the so-called Gallican, or "French liberties," regulated ecclesiastical appointments and taxation. These national rights over religion had long been exercised, and the church legally acknowledged them in the *Pragmatic Sanction of Bourges* in 1438. This agreement recognized the right of the French church to elect its own clergy without papal interference, prohibited the payment of annates to Rome, and limited the right of appeals from French courts to the Curia in Rome. In Germany and Switzerland local city governments also limited and overturned traditional clerical privileges and immunities.

9.3.4 John Wycliffe and John Huss

The popular lay religious movements that attacked the late medieval church most successfully were the **Lollards** in England and the **Hussites** in Bohemia. The Lollards looked

JOHN HUSS (CA. 1370–1415) LED TO THE STAKE AT CONSTANCE This pen-and-ink drawing of John Huss being led to the stake is from Ulrich von Richenthal's *Chronicle of the Council of Constance* (ca. 1450). After his execution, Huss's bones and ashes were scattered in the Rhine River to prevent his followers from claiming them as relics.
SOURCE: ullstein bild Dtl./Getty Images

to the writings of John Wycliffe (d. 1384) to justify their demands, while moderate and extreme Hussites turned to those of John Huss (d. 1415), although both men would have disclaimed the extremists who revolted in their names.

Wycliffe was an Oxford theologian and a philosopher of high standing. His work initially served the anticlerical policies of the English government. He became for England what William of Ockham and Marsilius of Padua had been for Emperor Louis IV: a major intellectual spokesman for the rights of royalty against the secular pretensions of popes. After 1350, English kings greatly reduced the power of the Avignon papacy to make ecclesiastical appointments and to collect taxes within England, a position Wycliffe strongly supported. His views on clerical poverty followed original Franciscan ideals and more by accident than by design, gave justification to government restriction and even confiscation of church properties within England. Wycliffe also argued that the clergy "ought to be content with food and clothing."

For Wycliffe, personal merit and morality, not rank and office, were the true basis of religious authority. The allegedly good people rightly deserved the money and power of the allegedly immoral people. This was a dangerous teaching for all governments because it placed allegedly pious laypeople above allegedly corrupt ecclesiastics regardless of their official stature. It directly threatened civic-secular dominion and governance, as well as that of the church. At his posthumous condemnation by the pope, Wycliffe was accused of the ancient heresy of **Donatism**—the teaching that the efficacy of the church's sacraments not only lies in their true performance but also depends on the moral character of the clergy who administered them. Wycliffe also anticipated Protestant criticisms of the medieval church by challenging papal infallibility, the sale of indulgences, the authority of Scripture, and the dogma of transubstantiation.

The Lollards were the English advocates of Wycliffe's teaching. They preached in the vernacular, disseminated translations of Holy Scripture, and championed clerical poverty. They also joined with the nobility and the gentry in confiscating clerical properties. After the English peasants' revolt of 1381, an uprising based on egalitarian notions, Lollardy was officially viewed as subversive. Opposed by an alliance of church and crown, the heresy became a capital offense in England in 1401.

Heresy was less easily brought to heel in Bohemia, where it coalesced with a strong national movement. The University of Prague, founded in 1348, became the center for both Bohemian nationalism and a new religious reform movement. The latter began within the bounds of orthodoxy. It was led by local intellectuals and preachers, the most famous of whom was John Huss, the rector of the university after 1403.

The Czech reformers supported vernacular translations of the Bible and were critical of traditional ceremonies and alleged superstitious practices, particularly

JUSTICE IN THE LATE MIDDLE AGES This illustration exhibits common forms of corporal and capital punishment in Europe in the late Middle Ages and the Renaissance. At top: burning, hanging, drowning. At center: blinding, quartering, the wheel, cutting of hair (a mark of great shame for a freeman). At bottom: thrashing, decapitation, amputation of hand (for thieves).
SOURCE: DEA PICTURE LIBRARY/Getty Images

those accompanying the sacrament of the Eucharist. They advocated lay communion with cup as well as bread, which had traditionally been reserved for the clergy as a sign of their spiritual superiority over the laity. The Hussites taught that bread and wine remained bread and wine after priestly consecration, and they questioned the validity of sacraments performed by priests in mortal sin.

Wycliffe's teaching appears to have influenced the movement early. Regular traffic between England and Bohemia had existed since the marriage of Anne of Bohemia to King Richard II in 1318. Bohemian students studied at Oxford and returned home with Wycliffe's writings.

John Huss became the leader of the pro-Wycliffe faction at the University of Prague. In 1410, his activities brought about his excommunication, and Prague was placed under papal interdict. In 1414, Huss won an audience with the newly assembled Council of Constance. He journeyed to the council eagerly under a safe-conduct pass from Emperor Sigismund (r. 1410–1437), naïvely believing he would convince his strongest critics of the truth of his teaching. Within weeks of his arrival in early November 1414, he was accused of heresy and imprisoned. He died at the stake on July 6, 1415, and was followed there less than a year later by his colleague Jerome of Prague.

The reaction in Bohemia to the execution of these national heroes was a fierce revolt. Militant Hussites and Taborites set out to transform Bohemia by force into a religious and social paradise under the military leadership of John Ziska. After a decade of belligerent protest, the Hussites won significant religious reforms and control over the Bohemian church from the Council of Basel.

9.3.5 The Great Schism (1378–1417) and the Conciliar Movement in the Church to 1449

Pope Gregory XI (r. 1370–1378) reestablished the papacy in Rome in January 1377, ending what had come to be known as the "Babylonian Captivity" of the church in Avignon, a reference to the biblical bondage of the Israelites. The return to Rome proved to be short lived, however. The struggle to resolve the subsequent Great Schism would have profound results for the laity and the ability of the secular world to exert control over the church.

9.3.5.1 URBAN VI AND CLEMENT VII On Gregory's death, the cardinals, in Rome, elected an Italian archbishop as Pope Urban VI (r. 1378–1389), who immediately announced his intention to reform the Curia. The cardinals, most of whom were French, responded by calling for the return of the papacy to Avignon. The French king, Charles V (r. 1364–1380), wanting to keep the papacy within the sphere of French influence, lent his support to what came to be known as the **Great Schism**.

On September 20, 1378, five months after Urban's election, thirteen cardinals, all but one of them French, formed their own conclave and elected Pope Clement VII (r. 1378–1397), a cousin of the French king. They insisted they had voted for Urban in fear of their lives, surrounded by a Roman mob demanding the election of an Italian pope. Be that as it may, the papacy had now become a "two-headed thing" and a scandal to Christendom. Allegiance to the two papal courts divided along political lines. England and its allies acknowledged Urban VI, while France and its orbit supported Clement VII. Subsequent church history has recognized the Roman line of popes as legitimate.

Two approaches were initially taken to end the Great Schism. The first attempted to win the mutual cession of both popes, thereby clearing the way for the election of a new one. The other sought to secure the resignation of the one in favor of the other. Both approaches failed. Each pope considered himself fully legitimate, and too much was at stake for either to make a magnanimous concession. Only one approach remained: a special church council empowered to depose them both. Legally, only a pope could convene and dissolve a church council, and the competing popes were not about to summon a council they knew would depose them both. Also, the removal of a legitimate pope against his will by a council of the church was as serious as deposing a monarch by a representative assembly.

The correct way to conduct a conciliar deposition of a pope was debated for thirty years before any action was taken. Advocates of the **conciliar theory** hoped to create a church in which a representative council could effectively regulate the actions of the pope. To that end the conciliarists defined the church as the whole body of the faithful, of which the elected head, the pope, was only one part. The sole purpose was to maintain the unity and well-being of the church—something the schismatic popes were far from doing. The conciliarists argued that a council of the church acted with greater authority than the pope alone. In the eyes of the pope(s), such a concept of the church threatened both its political and religious unity.

Based on the arguments of the conciliarists, cardinals representing both popes convened another council on their own authority in Pisa in 1409. There they deposed both the Roman and the Avignon popes, and elected a single pope, Alexander V. To the council's consternation, neither pope accepted its action, and Christendom suddenly faced the spectacle of three contending popes. Although most of Latin Christendom accepted Alexander and his Pisan successor John XXIII (r. 1410–1415), the popes of Rome and Avignon refused to step down.

This intolerable situation ended when Emperor Sigismund prevailed on John XXIII to summon a new council in Constance in 1414, which the Roman pope Gregory XII also recognized. In a famous declaration entitled

Sacrosancta, the council asserted its supremacy and elected a new pope, Martin V (r. 1417–1431), after the three contending popes had either resigned or were deposed. The council then made provisions for regular meetings of church councils, within five, then seven, and thereafter every ten years.

9.3.5.2 THE COUNCIL OF BASEL Conciliar government of the church peaked at the Council of Basel (1431–1449), when the council directly negotiated church doctrine with heretics. In 1432, the Hussites of Bohemia presented the *Four Articles of Prague* to the council as a basis for negotiations. This document contained requests for (1) giving the laity the Eucharist with cup as well as bread; (2) free, itinerant preaching; (3) the exclusion of the clergy from holding secular offices and owning property; and (4) just punishment of clergy who commit mortal sins.

In November 1433, an agreement among the emperor, the council, and the Hussites gave the Bohemians jurisdiction over their church. Three of the four Prague articles were conceded: communion with cup, free preaching by ordained clergy, and similar punishment of clergy and laity for mortal sins.

The exercise of such powers by a council did not please the pope, and in 1438, he upstaged the Council of Basel by negotiating a reunion with the Eastern church. Although the agreement, signed in Florence in 1439, was short lived, it restored papal prestige and signaled the demise of the conciliar movement. Having overreached itself, the Council of Basel collapsed in 1449. A decade later, Pope Pius II (r. 1458–1464) issued the papal bull *Execrabilis* (1460) condemning appeals to councils as "erroneous and abominable" and "completely null and void."

A major consequence of the short-lived conciliar movement was the greater religious responsibility given to the laity and secular governments. Without effective papal authority and leadership, secular control of national or territorial churches increased. Kings asserted their power over the church in England and France, while in German, Swiss, and Italian cities, magistrates and city councils reformed and regulated religious life. The High Renaissance did not reverse this development. On the contrary, as the papacy became a limited, Italian territorial regime, national control of the church ran apace. Perceived as just one among several Italian states, the Papal States could now be opposed as much on grounds of "national" policy as for religious reasons.

9.4 Medieval Russia

How did Mongol rule shape Russia's development?

In the late tenth century, Prince Vladimir of Kiev (r. 980–1015), then Russia's dominant city, received delegations of Muslims, Roman Catholics, Jews, and Greek Orthodox Christians, each of which hoped to persuade the Russians to embrace their religion. Vladimir chose Greek Orthodoxy, which became the religion of Russia, adding strong cultural bonds to the close commercial ties that had long linked Russia to the Byzantine Empire. The Byzantine Empire, now only a shadow of its magnificent self, was still a significant force among the cultures of the world after the passage of almost a century.

9.4.1 Politics and Society

Vladimir's successor, Yaroslav the Wise (r. 1016–1054), developed Kiev into a magnificent political and cultural

GENGHIS KHAN HOLDING AUDIENCE This Persian miniature shows the great conqueror and founder of the Mongol empire with members of his army and entourage as well as an apparent supplicant (lower right).
SOURCE: Sonia Halliday Photo Library/Alamy Stock Photo.

center, with architecture rivaling that of Constantinople. He also pursued contacts with the West in an unsuccessful effort to counter the political influence of the Byzantine emperors. After his death, rivalry among their princes slowly divided Russians into three cultural groups: the Great Russians, the White Russians, and the Little Russians (Ukrainians). Autonomous principalities also challenged Kiev's dominance, and it became just one of several national centers. Government in the principalities combined monarchy (the prince), aristocracy (the prince's council of noblemen), and democracy (a popular assembly of all free adult males). The broadest social division was between freemen and slaves. Freemen included the clergy, army officers, **boyars** (wealthy landowners), townspeople, and peasants. Slaves were mostly prisoners of war. Debtors working off their debts made up a large, semifree, group.

9.4.2 Mongol Rule (1243–1480)

In the thirteenth century, Mongol, or Tatar, armies swept through China, much of the Islamic world, and Russia. Genghis Khan (1155–1227) invaded Russia in 1223, and Kiev fell to his grandson Batu Khan in 1240. Russian cities became dependent, tribute-paying principalities of the segment of the Mongol Empire known as the *Golden Horde* (the Tatar words for the color of Batu Khan's tent). Geographically, the Golden Horde included the steppe region of what is today southern Russia and its capital at Sarai on the lower Volga. The conquerors stationed their officials in all the principal Russian towns to oversee taxation and the conscription of Russians into Tatar armies. The Mongols filled their harems with Russian women and sold Russians who resisted into slavery in foreign lands. Russian women—under the influence of Islam, which became the religion of the Golden Horde—began to wear veils and lead more secluded lives. This forced integration of Mongols and Russians created further cultural divisions between Russia and the West.

The Mongols, however, left Russian political and religious institutions largely intact and, thanks to their far-flung trade, brought most Russians greater prosperity. Princes of Moscow collected tribute for their overlords and grew wealthy under Mongol rule. As that rule weakened, the Moscow princes took control of the territory surrounding the city in what was called "the gathering of the Russian Land." Gradually the principality of Moscow expanded through land purchases, colonization, and conquest. In 1380, Grand Duke Dimitri of Moscow (r. 1350–1389) defeated Tatar forces at Kulikov Meadow, a victory that marked the beginning of the decline of the Mongol hegemony. Another century would pass, however, before Ivan III, the Great (d. 1505), would bring all northern Russia under Moscow's control and end Mongol rule (1480). Moscow replaced Kiev as the political and religious center of Russia. After Constantinople fell to the Turks in 1453, the city became, in Russian eyes, the "third Rome."

The Chapter in Perspective

Plague, war, and schism convulsed much of late medieval Europe throughout the fourteenth and into the fifteenth centuries. Two-fifths of the population, particularly along the major trade routes, died from plague in the fourteenth century. War and famine continued to take untold numbers after the plague had passed. Revolts erupted in town and countryside as ordinary people attempted to defend their traditional communal rights and privileges against the new autocratic territorial regimes. Even God's house seemed to be in shambles in 1409, when three popes came to rule simultaneously.

There is, however, another side to the late Middle Ages. By the end of the fifteenth century, the population losses were rapidly being made up. Between 1300 and 1500, education had become far more accessible, especially to laypeople. The number of universities increased from twenty to seventy, and the rise in the number of residential colleges was even more impressive, especially in France, where sixty-three were built. The fourteenth century saw the birth of humanism, and the fifteenth century gave us the printing press. Most impressive were the artistic and cultural achievements of the Italian Renaissance during the fifteenth century. The later Middle Ages were thus a period of growth and creativity, as well as one of waning and decline.

The Chapter in Review

Review Questions

1. What were the underlying and precipitating causes of the Hundred Years' War? What advantages did each side have? Why were the French finally able to drive the English almost entirely out of France?

2. What were the causes of the Black Death, and why did it spread so quickly throughout Western Europe? Where was it most virulent? How did it affect European society?

3. Why did Pope Boniface VIII quarrel with King Philip the Fair? Why was Boniface so impotent in the conflict? How had political conditions changed since the reign of Pope Innocent III in the late twelfth century, and what did that mean for the papacy?

4. How did the church change from 1200 to 1450? What was its response to the growing power of monarchs? How great an influence did the church have on secular events?

5. What was the Avignon papacy, and why did it occur? How did it affect the papacy? What relationship did it have to the Great Schism? How did the church become divided, and how was it reunited? Why was the conciliar movement a setback for the papacy?

6. Why were kings in the late thirteenth and early fourteenth centuries able to control the church more than the church could control the kings? How did kings attack the church during this period?

Key Terms

Avignon papacy (1309–1377) Known as the "Babylonian Captivity" of the church, refers to the time when Clement V moved the papal court to Avignon, an imperial city on the southeastern border of France.

Battle of Crécy (1346) The culmination of a series of victories for Edward III against Normandy, ending with his seizing the port of Calais.

Black Death The bubonic plague that killed millions of Europeans in the fourteenth century.

boyars The Russian nobility.

conciliar theory The argument that general councils were superior in authority to the pope and represented the whole body of the faithful.

Council of Lyons (1274) Church council that proclaimed a reunion of the Eastern and Roman churches, which lasted for only seven years.

Curia (CURE-ee-a) The papal government.

Donatism The heresy that taught the efficacy of the sacraments depended on the moral character of the clergy who administered them.

Edward III (r. 1327–1377) English king, the grandson of Philip the Fair of France, who may have started the Hundred Years' War by asserting his claim to the French throne.

Estates General The medieval French parliament that consisted of three separate groups, or "estates": clergy, nobility, and commoners. Last met in 1789 at the outbreak of the French Revolution.

Giovanni Boccaccio An Italian who wrote a famous collection of tales of the plague, the *Decameron* (1358).

Great Schism A split within the Catholic Church that lasted from 1378 to 1417. Three men simultaneously claimed to be the true pope. Driven by politics rather than any theological disagreement, the split ended with the Council of Constance (1414–1418).

Hundred Years' War (May 1337–October 1453) A great off-and-on conflict fought between England and France for control of territory and national identity.

Hussites (HUS-Its) Followers of John Huss (d. 1415) who questioned Catholic teachings about the Eucharist.

indulgence Remission of the temporal penalty of punishment in purgatory that remained after sins had been forgiven. The practice of selling pardons for unexpiated sins began under Clement VI (r. 1342–1352).

Jacquerie (jah-KREE) Revolt of the French peasantry.

Lollards (LALL-erds) Followers of John Wycliffe (d. 1384) who questioned the supremacy and privileges of the pope and the church hierarchy.

Spiritual Franciscans A group of radical followers of Saint Francis of Assisi, who devoted themselves to extreme poverty.

taille **(TIE)** The direct tax on the French peasantry.

Unam Sanctam (1302) The bull issued by Pope Boniface VIII, which declared royal, temporal authority to be "subject" to the spiritual power of the church.

Chapter 10
Renaissance and Discovery

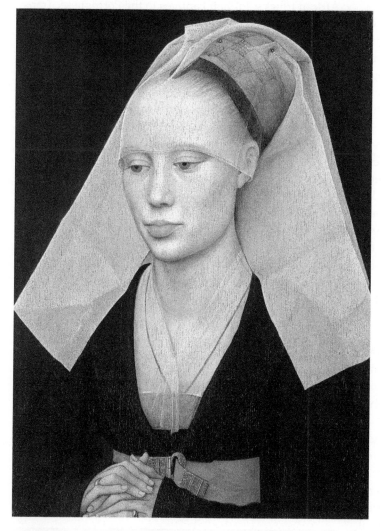

PORTRAIT OF A LADY The Renaissance celebrated human beauty and dignity. *Portrait of a Lady* by Flemish painter Rogier van der Weyden (1400–1464) portrayed an ordinary woman more perfectly on canvas than she could ever have appeared in real life.

SOURCE: SuperStock/Getty Images

 ## Contents and Focus Questions

The Chapter in Brief

IF THE LATE Middle Ages saw unprecedented chaos, it also witnessed a recovery that continued into the seventeenth century. There was both a waning and a harvest; much was dying away, while new fruit was being gathered and seed grain sown. The late Middle Ages were a time of creative fragmentation and new synthesis.

By the late fifteenth century, Europe was recovering from two of the three crises of the times: the demographic and the political. The great losses in population were being replenished, and able monarchs and rulers were imposing a new political order. A solution to the growing religious crisis would have to wait until the Reformation and Counter-Reformation of the sixteenth century.

The city-states of Italy survived a century and a half (1300–1450) better than the territorial states of northern Europe. This was due to Italy's strategic location between East and West and its lucrative Eurasian trade. Great wealth gave the rulers and merchants the ability to impose their will on both society and culture. They were now the grand patrons of government, education, and the arts both by self-aggrandizement and benevolence. Whether the patron was a family, firm, government, or the church, their endowments enhanced their reputation and power. The result of such patronage was a cultural Renaissance in the Italian cities unmatched elsewhere.

With the fall of Constantinople to the Turks in 1453, Italy's once unlimited trading empire began to shrink. City-state now turned against city-state, warring that opened the door to French armies in the 1490s. Within a quarter-century, Italy's great Renaissance had peaked.

The fifteenth century also saw an unprecedented scholarly renaissance. Italian and northern humanists recovered classical knowledge and languages that set educational reforms and cultural changes in motion that spread throughout Europe in the fifteenth and sixteenth centuries. In the process Italian humanists invented, for all practical purposes, what we today call critical historical scholarship, which was widely disseminated by a new fifteenth-century invention, the art of printing with movable type.

In this period, the vernacular—the local language—began to take its place alongside Latin, the international language, as the widely used literary and political means of communication. European states also progressively superseded the church as the community of highest allegiance, as patriotism and incipient nationalism captured hearts and minds as strongly as did religion. States and nations henceforth "transcended" themselves not only by journeys to Rome, but also by competitive voyages to the Far East and the Americas, opening the age of lucrative, global exploration.

For Europe, the late fifteenth and sixteenth centuries were a period of unprecedented expansion and experimentation. Permanent colonies were established within the Americas, and the exploitation of the New World's human and mineral resources never stopped after it began. Imported American gold and silver spurred scientific invention and a new weapons industry. The new bullion helped create the international traffic in African slaves, as rival African tribes sold their captives to the Portuguese. Transported in ever-increasing numbers, these slaves worked the mines and plantations of the New World, taking the place of American natives whose population declined precipitously following the conquest.

The period also saw social engineering and political planning on a large scale, as newly centralized governments began putting long-range economic policies into practice, a development that came to be called *mercantilism*.

10.1 The Renaissance in Italy (1375–1527)

How did humanism affect culture and the arts in fourteenth- and fifteenth-century Italy?

Medieval Europe before the twelfth century was a fragmented feudal society with an agricultural economy, whose ideas and culture were largely dominated by the church. By contrast, Renaissance Europe after the fourteenth century displayed a growing national consciousness and political centralization. The new urban economy, based on organized commerce and capitalism, brought about lay control of thought and culture independent from the clergy and religious authorities.

This creative expansion was threatened around 1527, when Spanish-imperial soldiers looted and torched Renaissance Rome, recalling the sacking of ancient Rome by the

KEY POLITICAL EVENTS OF THE ITALIAN RENAISSANCE (1375–1527)	
1378–1382	The Ciompi Revolt in Florence
1434	Medici rule in Florence established by Cosimo de' Medici
1454–1455	Treaty of Lodi allies Milan, Naples, and Florence (in effect until 1494)
1494	Charles VIII of France invades Italy
1494–1498	Savonarola controls Florence
1495	League of Venice unites Venice, Milan, the Papal States, the Holy Roman Empire, and Spain against France
1499	Louis XII invades Milan (the second French invasion of Italy)
1500	The Borgias conquer Romagna
1512–1513	The Holy League (Pope Julius II, Ferdinand of Aragon, Emperor Maximilian, and Venice) defeats the French
1513	Machiavelli writes the *Prince*
1515	Francis I leads the third French invasion of Italy
1516	Concordat of Bologna between France and the papacy
1527	Sack of Rome by imperial soldiers

Visigoths and Vandals. At this time, the French king, Francis I, joined with the Holy Roman Emperor, Charles V, making Italy the battleground for their mutual dynastic claims on Burgundy and parts of Italy. According to many scholars, that was the beginning of the end of the cultured Italian Renaissance.

10.1.1 The Italian City-States

Renaissance society first took shape within the merchant cities of late medieval Italy. Italy had always had a cultural advantage over the rest of Europe because its geography made it the natural gateway between East and West. Venice, Genoa, and Pisa traded with the Near East throughout the

Map 10–1 RENAISSANCE ITALY

The city-states of Renaissance Italy shown here were self-contained principalities whose internal strife was monitored by their despots and whose external aggression was long successfully controlled by treaty.

Middle Ages, growing vibrant, urban societies. When in the eleventh century commerce revived on a grand scale, Italian merchants quickly mastered the business skills of organizing, bookkeeping, developing new markets, and securing monopolies. The trade-rich cities became powerful city-states, dominating the political and economic life of their surrounding countryside. By the fifteenth century, those cities were the bankers for much of Europe.

10.1.1.1 GROWTH OF CITY-STATES The endemic warfare between the pope and the emperor, both the Guelf (pro-papal) and Ghibelline (pro-imperial) factions, assisted the expansion of Italian cities and urban culture. Either one of these warring factions might have subdued the cities, if only they had permitted one another to do so. Instead, they weakened one another, thereby strengthening the merchant oligarchies. Unlike the great cities of northern Europe, where kings and regional princes utterly dominated, the large Italian cities remained free to expand on their own. Becoming independent states, they absorbed the surrounding countryside and assimilated the local nobility in an urban meld of old and new rich. Five major competitive states evolved at this time: the duchy of Milan, the republics of Florence and Venice, the Papal States, and the kingdom of Naples. (See Map 10–1.)

Social strife and competition for political power were so intense within the cities that most evolved into despotisms to survive. A notable exception was Venice, which was ruled by a merchant oligarchy. The Venetian government controlled a patrician senate of 300 members and a ruthless judicial body, known as the Council of Ten, who were quick to suppress rival groups.

10.1.1.2 SOCIAL CLASS AND CONFLICT Florence was the most striking example of social division and anarchy. Four distinguishable social groups existed within the great city: (1) the old rich, or *grandi*, the noblemen and merchants who ruled the city; (2) the newly rich merchant class, the capitalists and bankers known as the *popolo grosso*, "the fat people," who in the late thirteenth and early fourteenth centuries, challenged the old rich for political power; (3) the middling burgher ranks of the guild masters, shop owners, and professionals, the small business people who in Florence, as elsewhere, sided with the new rich against the conservative policies of the old; and (4) the *popolo minuto*, or the "little people," the bottom of society, the lower socioeconomic classes. In 1457, one-third of the population of Florence—about 30,000—were officially listed as paupers, having no wealth at all. (For a description of Renaissance gardens, which reflected the various social groups and divisions of Renaissance society, see the "Encountering the Past" sidebar, which follows below.)

These social divisions produced conflict at every level of society. In 1378, a great uprising of the poor, known as the **Ciompi Revolt**, occurred. It resulted from a combination of three factors that made life unbearable for the unfortunate: the feuding between the old rich and the new rich; the social anarchy created when the Black Death cut the city's population almost in half; and, last but not least, the collapse of the great banking houses of Bardi and Peruzzi, which left the poor more vulnerable than ever. The Ciompi Revolt established a chaotic four-year reign of power by the lower Florentine classes. After the Ciompi Revolt, real stability did not return to Florence until the ascent to power of the fabled Florentine banker and statesman **Cosimo de' Medici** (1389–1464) in 1434.

FLORENTINE WOMEN Needlework, spinning, and weaving took up much of a Florentine woman's time and contributed to the elegance of dress for which Florentine men and women were famed.
SOURCE: Alinari/Art Resource, NY

10.1.1.3 DESPOTISM AND DIPLOMACY Cosimo de' Medici was the wealthiest Florentine and a natural statesman. He controlled the city internally from behind the scenes, manipulating the constitution and influencing elections. A council, first of six and later of eight members, known as the *Signoria*, governed the city. These men were chosen from the most powerful guilds, those representing the major clothing industries (cloth, wool, fur, and silk), and other strong groups such as bankers, judges, and doctors. Through informal, cordial relations with the electors, Cosimo kept councilors in the Signoria loyal to him. From his position as the head of the Office of Public Debt, he favored congenial factions.

Cosimo's grandson, **Lorenzo the Magnificent** (1449–1492; r. 1478–1492), ruled Florence in almost totalitarian fashion during the last, chaotic quarter of the fifteenth century. The assassination of his brother in 1478 by a rival family, the Pazzi, who had long plotted with the pope against the Medicis, made Lorenzo a cautious and determined ruler.

Despotism elsewhere was even less subtle. To prevent internal social conflict and foreign intrigue from paralyzing their cities, the dominant groups cooperated to install hired strongmen, or despots. Known as a *podestà*, the despot's sole

purpose was to maintain law and order. He held executive, military, and judicial authority, and his mandate was direct and simple: to permit, by whatever means required, the normal flow of business activity without which the old rich, the new rich, or the poor of a city, could long survive, much less prosper. Because despots could not count on the loyalty of the divided populace, they operated through mercenary armies obtained through military brokers known as *condottieri*.

It was a hazardous job. Not only was a despot subject to dismissal by the oligarchies that hired him, he was also a popular object of assassination attempts. The spoils of success, however, were great. In Milan, it was as despots that the Visconti family came to power in 1278 and the Sforza family in 1450, both ruling without constitutional restraints or serious political competition.

Mercifully, the political turbulence and warfare of the times also gave birth to the art of diplomacy. Through skilled diplomats, the city-states stayed abreast of foreign military developments and when shrewd, gained power and advantage over their enemies without going to war. Most city-states established resident embassies in the fifteenth century for that very purpose. Their ambassadors not only represented them in ceremonies and at

Encountering the Past

The Renaissance Garden

IN THE MIDDLE Ages and early Renaissance, few possessions were as prized, or as vital, as a garden. Within that enclosed space grew both ornamental and medicinal flowers and herbs. The more common kitchen garden existed in every manor, castle, monastery, guildhall, and small household. In addition to their large, elaborate gardens, the rich also had orchards and vineyards to grow the fruit from which they made sweet drinks and wine. Behind their shops and guildhalls, apothecaries and barber-surgeons cultivated the curative flowers and herbs from which they concocted the medicines of their trades. Beyond manor and guildhall walls, small householders and cottagers hoed the small, narrow plots behind their houses in which they grew the basic herbs and vegetables of their diet. Although the grandeur and variety of a garden reflected the prestige of its owner, every garden's main purpose was to serve the immediate needs of the household.

Versatility and pungency distinguished the most popular flowers and herbs. The violet was admired for its beauty, fragrance, and utility. Medieval people put violets in baths, oils, and syrups, prizing its soft scent and healing power as well as its ability to color, flavor, and garnish dishes. Nonetheless, subtlety and delicacy were not as important to the medieval palate as they are to ours. An herb or flower was only as good as its impact on the senses. Potent scents and flavors were loved for their ability to bring an otherwise starchy and lackluster meal to life. Fruit, although it was the main ingredient for sweet drinks, rarely appeared on a medieval plate, and vegetables were only slightly more common. Cabbage, lentils, peas, beans, onions, leeks, beets, and parsnips were the most often served vegetables at the medieval table, made palatable by heavy application of the sharpest and bitterest spices.

MEDIEVAL GARDEN A wealthy man oversees apple picking at harvest time in a fifteenth-century French orchard. In the town below, individual house gardens can be seen. Protective fences, made of woven sticks, keep out predatory animals. In the right foreground, a boar can be seen overturning an apple barrel.
SOURCE: The British Library Board

Beyond its practical function as a source of food and medicine, the medieval garden was a space of social and religious significance. In Christian history, gardens represented sacred places on earth. During the Middle Ages and early Renaissance, it was not the sprawling paradise of the Garden of Eden that captured the imagination, but rather the closed garden of the Bible's Song of Songs (4:12): "A garden enclosed is my sister, my spouse; a spring shut up, a fountain sealed." Such sensuous imagery symbolized the soul's union with God, Christ's union with the Catholic Church, and the bond of love between a man and a woman.

Although enclosed behind walls, fences, or hedges to protect them as vital food sources, gardens were also the private places of dreamers and lovers. Pleasure gardens bloomed around the homes of the wealthy. There, amid grottoes and fountains, lovers breathed the warm scents of roses and lilies and pursued the romantic trysts popularized in court poetry. The stories of courtly love were cautionary as well as titillating, for as the catechism reminded every medieval Christian, the garden was also a place of temptation and lost innocence.

Questions

1. What kinds of gardens existed in the Middle Ages and the early Renaissance?
2. How did religion give meaning to gardens?
3. How were gardens maintained, and what kinds of fruits and vegetables did they contain?

SOURCES: Teresa McClean, *Medieval English Gardens* (New York: Viking Press, 1980), pp. 64, 133; Marilyn Stokstad and Jerry Stannard, *Gardens of the Middle Ages* (Lawrence, KS: Spencer Museum, 1983), pp. 19–21, 61.

negotiations but also became their watchful eyes and ears at rival courts.

Whether in the comparatively tranquil republic of Venice, the strong-arm democracy of Florence, or the undisguised despotism of Milan, the disciplined Italian city proved a congenial climate for an unprecedented flowering of thought and culture. Italian Renaissance culture was promoted vigorously by both despots and republicans, and as enthusiastically by secularized popes as by spiritually minded ones. Such widespread support occurred because the main requirement for patronage of the arts and letters was the one thing Italian cities of the High Renaissance had in abundance: very great wealth.

10.1.2 Humanism

Scholars still debate the meaning of the term *humanism*. Some see the Italian Renaissance as the birth of modernity, a cultural and educational movement driven by a philosophy that stressed the dignity of humankind, individualism, and secular values. Others argue that the humanists were the champions of Catholic Christianity, opposing the pagan teaching of the ancient Greek philosopher Aristotle and the Scholasticism his writings nurtured. For still others, humanism was a neutral form of empirical-minded historical scholarship adopted to promote political liberty and a sense of civic responsibility.

Through the scholarly study of the Latin and Greek classics and the works of the ancient church fathers, the humanists advocated the ***studia humanitatis***, a liberal arts program of study that embraced grammar, rhetoric, poetry, history, politics, and moral philosophy. The Florentine humanist Leonardo Bruni (ca. 1370–1444) was the first to give the name humanitas, or "humanity," to the learning that resulted from such studies. Bruni was a star student of Manuel Chrysoloras (ca. 1355–1415), the great Byzantine scholar who opened the world of Greek scholarship to Italian humanists when he taught in Florence between 1397 and 1403.

The first humanists were orators and poets who wrote original literature in both classical and vernacular languages inspired by the ancients. They also taught rhetoric in the universities, and when they were not teaching, royal and papal courts hired them as secretaries, speechwriters, and diplomats.

10.1.2.1 PETRARCH, DANTE, AND BOCCACCIO Francesco Petrarch (1304–1374) was the "father of humanism." Petrarch celebrated ancient Rome in his *Letters to the Ancient Dead*, imagined personal letters to Cicero, Livy, Vergil, and Horace. He also wrote the Latin epic poem *Africa*, a poetic historical tribute to the Roman general Scipio Africanus, and *Lives of Illustrious Men*, biographies of famous Roman men. His most famous contemporary work was a collection of highly introspective love sonnets to a certain Laura, a married woman he admired romantically from a safe distance.

Petrarch's critical textual studies, elitism, and contempt for the learning of the Scholastics were features many later humanists also shared. As with many later humanists, classical and Christian values coexist uneasily in his work. Medieval Christian values can be seen in his imagined dialogues with Saint Augustine and in tracts he wrote to defend the personal immortality of the soul against the Aristotelians.

Petrarch was, however, far more secular in orientation than his famous near-contemporary Dante Alighieri (1265–1321), whose *Vita Nuova* and *Divine Comedy* are, with Petrarch's sonnets, the cornerstones of Italian vernacular literature. Petrarch's student and friend Giovanni Boccaccio (1313–1375) was also a pioneer of humanist studies. His *Decameron*—one hundred often bawdy tales told by three men and seven women in a safe country retreat away from the plague that ravaged Florence in 1348—is both a stinging social commentary (it exposes sexual and economic misconduct) and a sympathetic look at human behavior.

10.1.2.2 EDUCATIONAL REFORMS AND GOALS Humanists took their mastery of ancient languages directly from the past, refusing to be slaves to their own times. Such an attitude not only made them innovative educators, but also kept them in search of new sources of information that addressed the ills of contemporary society. In their searches, they assembled magnificent manuscript collections brimming with the history of the past, potent remedies for contemporaries, and sound advice for politicians and rulers everywhere.

The goal of humanist studies was wisdom eloquently spoken, both knowledge of the good and the ability to inspire others to desire it. Learning was not meant to remain abstract and unpracticed. "It is better to will the good than to know the truth," Petrarch taught. That became a motto of many later humanists, who like Petrarch, believed learning always ennobled people. Pietro Paolo Vergerio (1349–1420), the author of *On the Morals That Befit a Free Man*, the most influential Renaissance tract on education, left a classic summary of the humanist concept of a liberal education:

> We call those studies liberal which are worthy of a free man; those studies by which we attain and practice virtue and wisdom; that education which calls forth, trains, and develops those highest gifts of body and mind, which ennoble men and which are rightly judged to rank next in dignity to virtue only. For a vulgar temper, gain and pleasure are the one aim of existence, but to a lofty nature, moral worth and fame.[1]

The ideal of a useful education and well-rounded people inspired far-reaching reforms in traditional education. The Roman orator Quintilian's (ca. 35–100) *Education of the Orator*, the complete text of which was discovered in 1416, became the basic classical guide for the humanist curriculum. Vittorino da Feltre (d. 1446) exemplified those ideals. Not only did he have his students read the difficult works of Pliny, Ptolemy, Terence, Plautus, Livy, and Plutarch, he also subjected them to vigorous physical exercise and games.

Despite the grinding process of acquiring ancient knowledge, humanistic studies were not confined to the classroom. As Baldassare Castiglione's (1478–1529) *Book of the Courtier* illustrates, the rediscovered knowledge of the past was both a model and a challenge for the present day. Written as a practical guide for the nobility at the court of Urbino, a small duchy in central Italy, the book embodies the highest ideals of Italian humanism. Castiglione describes the successful courtier as one who knows how to integrate knowledge of ancient languages and history with athletic, military, and musical skills, while at the same time practicing good manners and exhibiting a high moral character.

Privileged, educated noblewomen also promoted the new education and culture at royal courts. Among them was **Christine de Pisan** (ca.1363–1434), the Italian-born daughter of the physician and astrologer of French king Charles V. She became an expert in classical, French, and Italian languages and literature. Married at fifteen and the widowed mother of three at twenty-seven, she wrote lyric poetry to support herself and was much read throughout the courts of Europe. Her most famous work, *The Treasure of the City of Ladies*, is a chronicle of the accomplishments of the great women of history.

10.1.2.3 THE FLORENTINE "ACADEMY" AND THE REVIVAL OF PLATONISM

Of all the important recoveries of the past made during the Italian Renaissance, none stands out more than the revival of Greek studies—especially the works of Plato—in fifteenth-century Florence. Many factors combined to bring this revival about. The foundation, mentioned above, was laid in 1397 when the city invited Manuel Chrysoloras to come from Constantinople to promote Greek learning. A half-century later in 1439, the ecumenical Council of Ferrara-Florence convened to negotiate the reunion of the Eastern and Western churches, opening the door for many Greek scholars and manuscripts to pour into the West. After the fall of Constantinople to the Turks in 1453, many Greek scholars fled to Florence for refuge. It was against this historical backdrop that the Florentine Platonic Academy evolved under the patronage of Cosimo de' Medici and the supervision of Marsilio Ficino (1433–1499) and **Pico della Mirandola** (1463–1494).

Renaissance thinkers were especially attracted to the Platonic tradition and to those church fathers who tried to synthesize Platonic philosophy with Christian teaching. The **Florentine Academy** was actually not a formal school, but an informal gathering of influential Florentine humanists devoted to the revival of the works of Plato and the Neoplatonists: Plotinus, Proclus, Porphyry, and Dionysius the Areopagite. To this end, Ficino edited and published the complete works of Plato.

The appeal of **Platonism** lay in its flattering view of human nature. It distinguished between an eternal sphere of being and a perishable world in which humans actually live. Human reason was believed to have preexisted in the pristine world and to still commune with it, a theory supported by human knowledge of eternal mathematical and moral truths.

Strong Platonic influence is evident in Pico's *Oration on the Dignity of Man*, perhaps the most famous Renaissance statement on the nature of humankind. (See the "Compare and Connect" sidebar, which follows below.) The *Oration* drew on Platonic teaching to depict humans as the only creatures in the world who possess the freedom to do and to be whatever they choose, to fly with angels or wallow with pigs.

CHRISTINE DE PISAN Christine de Pisan is considered the first European feminist. Here she presents her internationally famous book the *Treasure of the City of Ladies*, also known as the *Book of Three Virtues*, to Isabella of Bavaria amid her ladies in waiting.

SOURCE: Historical Picture Archive/Getty Images

Compare and Connect

Is the "Renaissance Man" a Myth?

DÜRER'S SELF-PORTRAIT AT AGE 28 WITH FUR COAT, 1500
Oil on wood, 67 × 49 cm. Alte Pinakothek, Munich, Germany.
SOURCE: Bildarchiv Preussischer Kulturbesitz/Art Resource, NY

DÜRER'S MELENCOLIA I, 1514
Engraving. 23.8 × 18.9 cm.
SOURCE: Library of Congress Prints and Photographs Division [LC-USZ62-32058]

AS SEVERAL ILLUSTRATIONS in this chapter attest, the great artists of the Renaissance (Raphael, Leonardo da Vinci, Albrecht Dürer) romanticized their human subjects and portrayed them as larger than life. Not only was the iconic "Renaissance man" perfectly proportioned physically, he also was effective in everything he undertook, endowed with the divine freedom and power to be and to do whatever he chose.

Before Reading

- Determine the choices Pico della Mirandola asserts are open to man according to his human nature and freedom.
- Compare the two works of Albrecht Dürer, and explain how the self-portrait embodies Renaissance ideals while the *Melencolia* engraving seems to negate them.
- Contrast Martin Luther's understanding of human limits with the great confidence of Pico in man's free will.

Questions

1. Who or what are Pico and Dürer's glorified humans? Is the vaunted Renaissance man real or fictional?
2. Why were Renaissance artists so fixated on the perfect body and mind?
3. Is Martin Luther's rejoinder (the bondage of the human will) truer to life, or is it religious misanthropy?

I. PICO DELLA MIRANDOLA, *ORATION ON THE DIGNITY OF MAN* (ca. 1486)

One of the most eloquent descriptions of the Renaissance image of human beings comes from Italian humanist Pico della Mirandola (1463–1494). In his famed Oration on the Dignity of Man *(ca. 1486), Pico describes humans as free to become whatever they choose.*

Pico's Renaissance man stands in stark contrast to the devout Christian pilgrim of the Middle Ages, who was always at the crossroads of heaven and hell; in constant fear of sin, death, and the devil; and regularly confessing his sins and receiving forgiveness in an unending penitential cycle. Had the Middle Ages misjudged human nature, or was there a great transformation in human nature between the Middle Ages and the Renaissance?

The best of artisans [God] ordained that that creature (man) to whom He had been able to give nothing proper to himself should have joint possession of whatever had been peculiar to each of the different kinds of being. He therefore took man as a creature of indeterminate nature and, assigning him a place in the middle of the world, addressed him thus: "Neither a fixed abode nor a form that is thine alone nor any function peculiar to thyself have we given thee, Adam, to the end that according to thy longing and according to thy judgment thou mayest have and possess what abode, what form, and what functions thou thyself shalt desire. The nature of all other beings is limited and constrained within the bounds of laws prescribed by Us. Thou, constrained by no limits, in accordance with thine own free will, in whose hand We have placed thee, shalt ordain for thyself the limits of thy nature. We have set thee at the world's center that thou mayest from thence more easily observe whatever is in the world. We have made thee neither of heaven nor of earth, neither mortal nor immortal, so that with freedom of choice and with honor, as though the maker and molder of thyself, thou mayest fashion thyself in whatever shape thou shalt prefer. Thou shalt have the power to degenerate into the lower forms of life, which are brutish. Thou shalt have the power, out of thy soul's judgment, to be reborn into the higher forms, which are divine." O supreme generosity of God the Father, O highest and most marvelous felicity of man! To him it is granted to have whatever he chooses, to be whatever he wills.

II. ALBRECHT DÜRER

In 1500, Albrecht Dürer, then twenty-eight years old, painted the most famous self-portrait of the European Renaissance and Reformation. Dürer celebrated his own beauty and genius by imposing his face on a portrayal of Christ, a work of art that has been called "the birth of the modern artist."

Fourteen years later (1514), on the occasion of his mother's death, Dürer engraved another famous image of himself, now as a man in deep depression or melancholy, his mind darkened and his creativity throttled. In this self-portrait, he is neither effective nor handsome, much less heroic and divine—certainly not a self-portrait of a Renaissance man.

III. MARTIN LUTHER, *THE BONDAGE OF THE WILL* (1525)

The greater challenge to the Renaissance man came from Martin Luther, who met his "Pico" in northern humanist Desiderius Erasmus. Like Pico, Erasmus, flying in the face of Reformation theology, conceived free will to be "a power of the human will by which a man may apply himself to those things that lead to eternal salvation, or turn away from the same." Of such thinking, Luther made short shrift.

It is in the highest degree wholesome and necessary for a Christian to know whether or not his will has anything to do in matters pertaining to salvation. . . . We need to have in mind a clear-cut distinction between God's power and ours and God's work and ours, if we would live a godly life. . . . The will, be it God's or man's, does what it does, good or bad, under no compulsion, but just as it wants or pleases, as if totally free. . . . Wise men know what experience of life proves, that no man's purposes ever go forward as planned, but events overtake all men contrary to their expectation. . . . Who among us always lives and behaves as he should? But duty and doctrine are not therefore condemned, rather they condemn us.

God has promised His grace to the humbled, that is, to those who mourn over and despair of themselves. But a man cannot be thoroughly humbled till he realizes that his salvation is utterly beyond his own powers, counsels, efforts, will and works, and depends absolutely on the will, counsel, pleasure, and work of Another: GOD ALONE. As long as he is persuaded that he can make even the smallest contribution to his salvation, he . . . does not utterly despair of himself, and so is not humbled before God, but plans for himself a position, an occasion, a work, which shall bring him final salvation. But he who [no longer] doubts that his destiny depends entirely only on the will of God. . . . waits for God to work in him, and such a man is very near to grace for his salvation. So if we want to drop this term ("free will") altogether, which would be the safest and most Christian thing to do, we may, still in good faith, teach people to use it to credit man with "free will" in respect not of what is above him, but of what is below him. . . . However, with regard to God and in all that bears on salvation or damnation, he has no "free will" but is a captive, prisoner and bond-slave, either to the will of God, or to the will of Satan.

SOURCES: (I) From Giovanni Pico della Mirandola, *Oration on the Dignity of Man*, in *The Renaissance Philosophy of Man*, ed. by E. Cassirer et al. (Chicago: Phoenix Books, 1961), pp. 224–225. (III) From Martin Luther, *On the Bondage of the Will*, ed. by J. I. Packer and O. R. Johnston (Westwood, NJ: Fleming H. Fevell Co., 1957), pp. 79, 81, 83, 87, 100, 104, 107, 137.

10.1.2.4 CRITICAL WORK OF THE HUMANISTS: LORENZO VALLA

Because they were guided by scholarly ideals of philological accuracy and historical truth, learned humanists could become critics of tradition. Their dispassionate critical scholarship shook long-standing foundations, not the least of which were those of the medieval church. The works of Lorenzo Valla (1406–1457), author of the standard Renaissance text on Latin philology, the *Elegances of the Latin Language* (1444), reveal the explosive character of this new learning. Although a good Catholic, Valla became a hero to later Protestant reformers. His popularity among them stemmed from his brilliant exposé of the *Donation of Constantine* and his defense of predestination against the advocates of free will.

The fraudulent *Donation*, written in the eighth century, purported to be a good-faith grant of vast territories to the pope and the church by the Roman emperor Constantine (r. 307–337). Using textual analysis and historical logic, Valla demonstrated that the document was filled with anachronistic terms, such as fief, and was fraudulent because it contained information that could not have existed in a fourth-century document. In the same dispassionate way, he also pointed out errors in the Latin Vulgate, then the authorized version of the Bible for Western Christendom.

Such discoveries did not make Valla any less loyal to the church, nor did they prevent his faithful fulfillment of the office of apostolic secretary in Rome under Pope Nicholas V (r. 1447–1455). Nonetheless, historical humanistic criticism of this type also served those far less loyal to the medieval church. Young humanists formed the first identifiable group of Martin Luther's supporters.

10.1.2.5 CIVIC HUMANISM

Humanists criticized Scholastic education, declaring much of its purpose useless. They believed that education should promote individual virtue and self-sacrificing public service: hence the designation, civic humanism. The most striking examples of civic humanism were found in Florence, where three humanists served as chancellors of the city: Coluccio Salutati (1331–1406), Leonardo Bruni (ca. 1370–1444), and Poggio Bracciolini (1380–1459). Each used his rhetorical skills to rally the Florentines against their aggressors. However, many modern scholars doubt these famous chancellors of Florence demonstrated civic humanism and view them as men who simply wanted to exercise great power.

Toward the end of the Renaissance, many humanists became cliquish and snobby intellectual elites more concerned with narrow Latin scholarly interests than with revitalizing civic and social life. In reaction to this elitist trend, the humanist historians Niccolò Machiavelli (1469–1527) and Francesco Guicciardini (1483–1540) wrote in Italian and made contemporary history their primary source and subject matter. Here, arguably, we can see the two sides of humanism: deep historical scholarship and practical transparent politics.

10.1.3 High Renaissance Art

In Renaissance Italy, as in Reformation Europe, the values and interests of the laity were no longer subordinated to those of the clergy. In education, culture, and religion, the laity now assumed a leading role and established models for the clergy to emulate. This development was due in part to the church's loss of international power during the great crises of the late Middle Ages. The rise of national sentiment and the emergence of national bureaucracies staffed by laymen, rather than clerics, encouraged the rapid growth of lay education during the fourteenth and fifteenth centuries. And medieval Christians adjusted to a more secular spirit and mission.

This new perspective on life is prominent in the painting and sculpture of the High Renaissance (1450–1527), when art and sculpture reached their full maturity. Whereas medieval art had tended to be abstract and formulaic, Renaissance art emphatically embraced the natural world and human emotions. Renaissance artists gave their works a rational, even mathematical, order—perfect symmetry and proportion reflecting a belief in the harmony of the universe. (See the "Closer Look" sidebar, which follows below, on Leonardo's application of science and mathematics to the rendering of the perfect human being.)

High Renaissance artists were helped by the development of new technical skills during the fifteenth century. In addition to the availability of oil paints, two special techniques gave them an edge: *chiaroscuro*, the use of shading to enhance naturalness, and *linear perspective*, the adjustment of the size of figures to give the viewer a feeling of continuity with the painting. These techniques enabled the artist to portray space realistically and to paint a more natural world. The result, compared to their flat Byzantine and Gothic counterparts, was a three-dimensional canvas filled with energy and life.

Giotto (1266–1336), the father of Renaissance painting, signaled the new direction. An admirer of Saint Francis of Assisi, whose love of nature he shared, he painted a more natural world. Though still filled with religious seriousness, his work was no longer an abstract and unnatural depiction of the world. The painter Masaccio (1401–1428) and the sculptor Donatello (1386–1466) also portrayed the world around them literally and naturally. The great masters of the High Renaissance, Leonardo da Vinci (1452–1519), Raphael (1483–1520), and Michelangelo Buonarroti (1475–1564), reached the pinnacle of such painting.

10.1.3.1 LEONARDO DA VINCI

A man of many talents, Leonardo exhibited the Renaissance ideal of the universal person. One of the greatest painters of all time, he also advised Italian princes and the French king Francis I (r. 1515–1547) on military engineering. He approached his work empirically as a modern scientist, dissecting corpses to learn anatomy, and was a self-taught botanist. His inventive mind imagined such modern machines as airplanes and

A Closer Look

Leonardo da Vinci Plots the Perfect Man

IN THE DRAWING *VITRUVIAN MAN*, ca. 1490, Leonardo attempts to represent the ideal human proportions by means of a scientific portrayal and a set of descriptive notes that read counterclockwise. The name *Vitruvian* comes from a first-century C.E. Roman architect and engineer, Marcus Pollio Vitruvius, who used squares and circles to demonstrate the symmetry and proportionality of the human body.

Leonardo, like most artists of his time, shared the classical ideal of human perfection even in his gloomiest etchings and paintings. With few exceptions, the great painters of the age wanted to portray men and women in a more-than-human beauty and glory.

The fingers and toes of the figure's hands and feet touch the circumference of a circle whose center is located at the figure's navel.

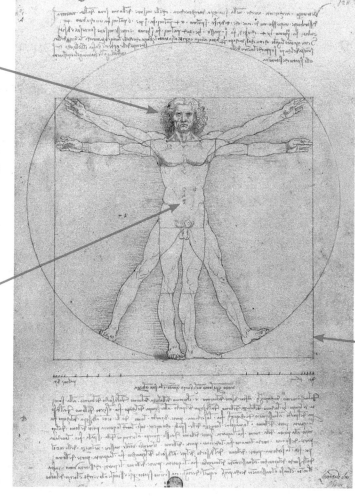

Leonardo's figure study of human proportions renders the figure's height and width (of arms outstretched) as equal, like the sides of a square.

VITRUVIAN MAN
SOURCE: PAINTING/Alamy Stock Photo

Questions

1. Compare Leonardo's study of the human form with that of Adam and Eve by northern Renaissance painter Lucas Cranach the Elder (which appears later in this chapter). Which of these images is truer to real life?

2. Is Leonardo's *Vitruvian Man* a true representation of human perfection or a representation of man as a perfect machine?

SOURCE: From Marilyn Stokstad and David Cateforis, *Art History* (New York: Pearson, 2005), p. 651.

THE VIRGIN AND CHILD WITH THE INFANT JOHN THE BAPTIST Combining the artistic qualities of all the Renaissance masters, Raphael created scenes of tender beauty and subjects sublime in both flesh and spirit.
SOURCE: Bridgeman Art Library/SuperStock

DÜRER'S MOORISH WOMAN The portrait by Albrecht Dürer provides evidence of African slavery in Europe during the sixteenth century. Katharina was in the service of one João Brandão, a Portuguese economic minister living in Antwerp, then the financial center of Europe. Dürer became friends with Brandão during his stay in the Low Countries in the winter of 1520–1521.
SOURCE: Print Collector/Getty Images

submarines. In fact, the variety of his interests was enormous, and biographer Giorgio Vasari believed it may have detracted from his paintings. Leonardo's ability to convey inner moods through complex facial expression is apparent in his most famous painting, the *Mona Lisa.*

10.1.3.2 RAPHAEL A man of great kindness and a painter of great sensitivity, Raphael was loved by his contemporaries as much for his person as for his work. He is most famous for his tender madonnas and the great fresco in the Vatican, the *School of Athens*, a virtually perfect example of Renaissance technique. It depicts Plato and Aristotle surrounded by other great philosophers and scientists of antiquity who bear the features of Raphael's famous contemporaries.

10.1.3.3 MICHELANGELO The melancholy genius Michelangelo also excelled in a variety of arts and crafts. His eighteen-foot sculpture of David, which long stood majestically in the great square of Florence, is a perfect example of Renaissance devotion to harmony, symmetry, and proportion, all glorifying the human form. Four different popes commissioned works by Michelangelo. The frescoes in the Vatican's Sistine Chapel are the most famous, painted during the pontificate of Pope Julius II (r. 1503–1513), who also had Michelangelo work on his own magnificent tomb. The Sistine frescoes originally covered 10,000 square feet and involved 343 figures, more than half of which exceeded ten feet in height, but their

originality and perfection as works of art are most impressive. This labor of love and piety took four years to complete.

Michelangelo's later works mark, artistically and philosophically, the end of High Renaissance painting and the advent of a new style known as **mannerism**. Mannerism was a reaction to the simplicity and symmetry of High Renaissance art that also had parallels in contemporary music and literature. It made room for the strange and the abnormal, emphasizing the individual perceptions of the artist, who now felt free to paint, compose, or write in a "mannered" or "affected" way. Tintoretto (d. 1594) and El Greco (d. 1614) are mannerism's supreme masters.

10.1.4 Slavery in the Renaissance

Throughout Renaissance Italy, slavery flourished as extravagantly as art and culture. A thriving western slave market existed as early as the twelfth century, when the Spanish sold Muslim slaves captured in raids and war to wealthy Italians and other buyers. Contemporaries looked on such slavery as a merciful act, because slaves would have otherwise been killed by their captors. In addition to widespread household or domestic slavery, collective plantation slavery, following East Asian models, also developed in the eastern Mediterranean during the High Middle Ages. In the savannas of Sudan and the Venetian estates on the islands of Cyprus and Crete, gangs of slaves cut sugarcane, setting the model for later slave plantations in the Mediterranean and the New World.

After the Black Death (1348–1350) reduced the supply of laborers everywhere in Western Europe, the demand for slaves soared. Slaves were imported from Africa, the Balkans, Constantinople, Cyprus, Crete, and the lands surrounding the Black Sea. Taken randomly from conquered people, they consisted of many races: Tatars, Circassians, Greeks, Russians, Georgians, and Iranians as well as Asians and Africans. According to one source, "By the end of the fourteenth century, there was hardly a well-to-do household in Tuscany without at least one slave: brides brought them [to their marriages] as part of their dowry, doctors accepted them from their patients in lieu of fees—and it was not unusual to find them even in the service of a priest."[2]

Owners had complete dominion over their slaves; in Italian law, this meant the "[power] to have, hold, sell, alienate, exchange, enjoy, rent or unrent, dispose of in [their] will[s], judge soul and body, and do with in perpetuity whatsoever may please [them] and [their] heirs and no man may gainsay [them]."[3] A strong, young, healthy slave cost the equivalent of the wages paid a free servant over several years. Considering the life span of free service thereafter, slaves were well worth the price.

Tatars and Africans appear to have been the worst treated, but as in ancient Greece and Rome, slaves at this time were generally accepted as family members and integrated into households. Not a few women slaves became mothers of their masters' children. Fathers often adopted children of such unions and raised them as their legitimate heirs. It was also in the interest of owners to keep their slaves healthy and happy; otherwise they would be of little use and possibly become a threat. Slaves nonetheless remained a foreign and suspected presence in Italian society.

10.2 Italy's Political Decline: The French Invasions (1494–1527)

What were the causes of Italy's political decline?

As a land of autonomous city-states, Italy had always relied on internal cooperation for its peace and safety from foreign invasion—especially by the Turks. Such cooperation was maintained during the second half of the fifteenth century, thanks to a political alliance known as the **Treaty of Lodi** (1454–1455). Its terms brought Milan and Naples, long traditional enemies, into the alliance with Florence. These three

stood together for decades against Venice, which frequently joined the Papal States to maintain an internal balance of power. However, when a foreign enemy threatened Italy, the five states could also present a united front.

Around 1490, after the rise to power of the Milanese despot Ludovico il Moro, hostilities between Milan and Naples resumed. The peace made possible by the Treaty of Lodi ended in 1494 when Naples threatened Milan. Ludovico made a fatal move in response to these new political alignments: He appealed to the French for aid. French kings had ruled Naples from 1266 to 1442 before being driven out by Duke Alfonso of Sicily. Breaking a wise Italian rule, Ludovico invited the French to reenter Italy and revive their dynastic claim to Naples. In his haste to check rival Naples, Ludovico did not recognize that France also had dynastic claims to Milan. Nor did he foresee how insatiable the French appetite for new territory would become once French armies had crossed the Alps and encamped in Italy.

10.2.1 Charles VIII's March Through Italy

The French king Louis XI had resisted the temptation to invade Italy while nonetheless keeping French dynastic claims in Italy alive. His successor, Charles VIII (r. 1483–1498), an eager youth in his twenties, responded to the call with lightning speed. Within five months, in August 1494, he had crossed the Alps and raced through Florence and the Papal States into Naples. As Charles approached Florence, its Florentine ruler, Piero de' Medici, tried to placate the French king by handing over Pisa and other Florentine possessions. But Florence was under the influence of a radical Dominican preacher named Girolamo Savonarola (1452–1498). Savonarola convinced the fearful Florentines that Charles's arrival was a long-delayed and fully justified divine vengeance on their immorality. This led to Piero's exile by a citizenry, who resisted his attempt to appease Charles.

That enabled Charles to enter Florence without resistance. Savonarola's fatal flattery and the payment of a large ransom allowed the city to escaped destruction. After Charles's departure, Savonarola exercised virtual rule over Florence for four years, but in the end, the Florentines were not the stuff theocracies are made of. Savonarola's moral rigor and antipapal policies made it impossible for him to survive indefinitely in Italy. After the Italian cities reunited and ousted the French invader, Savonarola's days were numbered. In May 1498, he was imprisoned and executed.

Charles's lightning march through Italy also struck terror in non-Italian hearts. Ferdinand of Aragon (r. 1479–1516), who had hoped to expand his own possessions in Italy from his base in Sicily, was now vulnerable to a French–Italian axis. In response, he created a new counteralliance—the **League of Venice**. Formed in March 1495, it brought Venice, the Papal States, and Emperor Maximilian I (r. 1493–1519) together with Ferdinand against the French. The stage was now set for a conflict between France and Spain that would not end until 1559.

Meanwhile, the Milanese despot, Ludovico il Moro, recognized that he had helped bring about the French invasion. Having desired an invasion only if it weakened his enemies, Moro now understood how the events he had himself created threatened Milan. In reaction, he joined the League of Venice, which was now strong enough to send Charles into retreat and to end the menace he posed to Italy.

10.2.2 Pope Alexander VI and the Borgia Family

The French returned to Italy under Charles's successor, Louis XII (r. 1498–1515). This time a new Italian ally, the Borgia pope, **Alexander VI**, assisted them. Probably the most corrupt pope who ever sat on the papal throne, he openly promoted the political careers of Cesare and Lucrezia Borgia, the children he had had before he became pope. He used papal policy in tandem with the efforts of his powerful family to secure a political base in Romagna in north central Italy.

In Romagna, several principalities had fallen away from the church during the Avignon papacy. Venice, the pope's ally within the League of Venice, continued to contest the Papal States for their loyalty. Seeing that a French alliance would allow him to reestablish control over the region, Alexander took steps to secure French favor. He annulled Louis XII's marriage to Charles VIII's sister so Louis could marry Charles's widow, Anne of Brittany—a popular political move designed to keep Brittany French. The pope also bestowed a cardinal's hat on the archbishop of Rouen, Louis's favorite cleric. Most important, Alexander agreed to abandon the League of Venice, a withdrawal of support that made the league too weak to resist a French reconquest of Milan.

It was a scandalous trade-off, but one that made it possible for both the French king and the pope to realize their ambitions within Italy. Louis invaded Milan in August 1499. Ludovico il Moro, who had originally opened the Pandora's box of French invasion, spent his last years languishing in a French prison. In 1500, Louis and Ferdinand of Aragon divided Naples between them, and the pope and Cesare Borgia conquered the cities of Romagna without opposition. Alexander's victorious son was given the title "duke of Romagna."

10.2.3 Pope Julius II

Cardinal Giuliano della Rovere, a strong opponent of the Borgia family, succeeded Alexander VI as Pope Julius II (r. 1503–1513). He suppressed the Borgias and placed their newly conquered lands in Romagna under papal jurisdiction. Julius raised the Renaissance papacy to its peak of military prowess and diplomatic intrigue, gaining him the title of "warrior pope." Shocked, as were other contemporaries, by this thoroughly secular papacy, the humanist **Desiderius Erasmus** (1466–1536), who had witnessed in disbelief a bullfight in the papal palace during a visit to Rome, wrote a popular anonymous satire titled *Julius Excluded from Heaven*. This humorous account purported to describe the pope's unsuccessful efforts to convince Saint Peter that he was worthy of admission to heaven.

Assisted by his powerful allies, Pope Julius drove the Venetians out of Romagna in 1509 and fully secured the Papal States. Having realized this long-sought papal goal, Julius turned to the second major undertaking of his pontificate: ridding Italy of his former ally, the French invader. Julius, Ferdinand of Aragon, and Venice formed a second Holy League in October 1511 and were joined by Emperor Maximilian I and the Swiss. In 1512, the league had the French in full retreat, and the Swiss defeated them in 1513 at Novara.

The French were nothing if not persistent. They invaded Italy a third time under Louis's successor, Francis I (r. 1515–1547). This time French armies massacred Swiss soldiers of the Holy League at Marignano in September 1515, avenging the earlier defeat at Novara. The victory won the Concordat of Bologna from the pope in August 1516; this agreement gave the French king control over the French clergy in exchange for French recognition of the pope's superiority over church councils and his right to collect annates in France. This concordat helped keep France Catholic after the outbreak of the Protestant Reformation, but the new French entry into Italy set the stage for the first of four major wars with Spain in the first half of the sixteenth century: the Habsburg-Valois wars, none of which France won.

10.2.4 Niccolò Machiavelli

The foreign invasions destroyed Italy. The period of Italy's cultural peak, with the work of Leonardo, Raphael, and Michelangelo, was also one of political tragedy. Niccolò Machiavelli (1469–1527) watched as French, Spanish, and German armies wreaked havoc on Italy. The more he saw, the more convinced he became that Italian political unity and independence were ends that justified any means.

A humanist and a careful student of ancient Rome, Machiavelli was impressed by the way Roman rulers and citizens had then defended their homeland. They possessed *virtù*, the ability to act decisively and heroically for the good of their country. Stories of ancient Roman patriotism and self-sacrifice were Machiavelli's favorites, and he lamented the absence of such traits among his compatriots.

Machiavelli also had republican ideals, which he did not want to see vanish from Italy. He believed that a strong and determined people could struggle successfully with fortune. He scolded the Italian people for the self-destruction their own internal feuding was causing. He especially wanted an end to that behavior, so a reunited Italy could drive all foreign armies out.

His fellow citizens were not up to such a challenge. The juxtaposition of what Machiavelli believed the ancient Romans had been, with the failure of his contemporaries to attain such high ideals, made him the famous cynic whose name—in the epithet "Machiavellian"—has become synonymous with ruthless political expediency. Only a strong-man, Machiavelli concluded, could impose order on so divided and selfish a people; the salvation of Italy required, for the present, cunning dictators.

It has been argued that Machiavelli wrote the *Prince* in 1513 as a cynical satire on the way rulers truly behaved and not as a serious recommendation of unprincipled despotic rule. But Machiavelli seems earnest when he advises rulers to discover the advantages of fraud and brutality, at least as a temporary means to the higher end of a unified Italy. He apparently hoped to see a strong ruler emerge from the Medici family, which had captured the papacy in 1513 with the pontificate of Leo X (r. 1513–1521). At the same time, the Medici family retained control over the powerful territorial state of Florence. *The Prince* was pointedly dedicated to Lorenzo de' Medici, duke of Urbino and grandson of Lorenzo the Magnificent.

Whatever Machiavelli's hopes may have been, the Medicis proved not to be Italy's deliverers. The second Medici pope, Clement VII (r. 1523–1534), watched helplessly as the army of Emperor Charles V sacked Rome in 1527, also the year of Machiavelli's death.

10.3 Revival of Monarchy in Northern Europe

How were the powerful monarchies of northern Europe different from their predecessors?

After 1450, sovereign rulers set in motion a shift from divided feudal monarchy to unified national monarchies. Dynastic and chivalric ideals of feudal monarchy did not, however, vanish. Territorial princes remained on the scene, and representative bodies persisted and even grew in influence.

The feudal monarchy of the High Middle Ages was characterized by the division of the basic powers of government between the king and his semiautonomous vassals. The nobility and the towns then acted with varying degrees of unity and success through evolving representative assemblies, such as the English Parliament, the French Estates General, and the Spanish *Cortés*, to thwart the centralization of royal power into a united nation. But after the Hundred Years' War and the Great Schism in the church, the

nobility and the clergy were in decline and less able to block growing national monarchies.

The increasingly important towns now began to ally with the king. Loyal, business-wise townspeople, not the nobility and the clergy, increasingly staffed royal offices and became the king's lawyers, bookkeepers, military tacticians, and foreign diplomats. This new alliance between king and town broke the bonds of feudal society and made possible the rise of sovereign states.

In a sovereign state, the powers of taxation, war-making, and law enforcement no longer belong to semiautonomous vassals but were controlled by the monarch and exercised by his or her chosen agents. Taxes, wars, and laws became national, rather than merely regional, matters. Only as monarchs became able to act independently of the nobility and representative assemblies could they overcome the decentralization that impeded nation-building. Ferdinand and Isabella of Spain rarely called the Cortés into session. The French Estates General met irregularly, mostly in time of crisis, but was never essential to royal governance. Henry VII (r. 1485–1509) of England managed to raise revenues without going begging to Parliament, which had voted him customs revenues for life in 1485. Brilliant theorists, from Marsilius of Padua in the fourteenth century to Machiavelli in the fifteenth to Jean Bodin (1530–1596) in the sixteenth, emphatically defended the sovereign rights of monarchy.

The many were, of course, never totally subjugated to the one. But in the last half of the fifteenth century, rulers demonstrated that the law was their creature. They appointed civil servants whose vision was no longer merely local or regional. In Castile, they were the *corregidores*, in England the justices of the peace, and in France bailiffs operating through well-drilled lieutenants. These royal ministers and agents became closely attached to the localities they administered in the ruler's name. Throughout England, for example, local magnates represented the Tudor dynasty that seized the throne in 1485. These new executives remained royal bureaucrats whose outlook was "national" and loyal to the "state."

Monarchies also created standing national armies in the fifteenth century. The noble cavalry receded as the infantry and the artillery became the backbone of royal armies. Mercenary soldiers from Switzerland and Germany became the major part of the "king's army." Professional soldiers who fought for pay and booty were far more efficient than feudal vassals. However, monarchs who failed to meet their payrolls now faced a new danger of mutiny and banditry by foreign troops.

The growing cost of warfare in the fifteenth and sixteenth centuries increased the monarch's need for new national sources of income. The great obstacle was the stubborn belief of the highest social classes that they were immune from government taxation. The nobility guarded their properties and traditional rights and despised taxation as an insult and a humiliation. Royal revenues accordingly had to grow at the expense of those least able to resist and least able to pay.

The monarchs had several options when it came to raising money. As feudal lords, they could collect rents from their royal domains. They could also levy national taxes on basic food and clothing, such as the salt tax, or *gabelle*, in France and the 10 percent sales tax, or *alcabala*, on commercial transactions in Spain. The rulers could also levy direct taxes on the peasantry, which they did through agreeable representative assemblies of the privileged classes in which the peasantry did not sit. The taille, which the French kings determined independently each year after the Estates General was suspended in 1484, was such a tax. Innovative fund-raising devices in the fifteenth century included the sale of public offices and the issuance of high-interest government bonds. Rulers still did not levy taxes on the powerful nobility, but instead, they borrowed from rich nobles and the great bankers of Italy and Germany. In money matters, the privileged classes remained as much the kings' creditors and competitors as their subjects.

10.3.1 France

Charles VII (r. 1422–1461) was a king made great by those who served him. His ministers created a permanent professional army, which—thanks initially to the inspiration of Joan of Arc—drove the English out of France. In addition, an enterprising independent merchant banker named Jacques Coeur helped develop a strong economy, diplomatic corps, and national administration throughout Charles's reign. These sturdy tools in turn enabled Charles's son and successor, the ruthless Louis XI (1461–1483), to make France a great power.

French nation-building had two political cornerstones in the fifteenth century. The first was the collapse of the English Empire in France following the Hundred Years' War. The second was the defeat of Charles the Bold (r. 1467–1477) and his duchy of Burgundy. Louis XI and Habsburg emperor Maximilian I divided the conquered Burgundian lands between them, with the treaty-wise Habsburgs getting the better part. The dissolution of Burgundy ended its constant intrigue against the French king and left Louis XI free to secure the monarchy. Between the newly acquired Burgundian lands and his own inheritance, the king was able to end his reign with a kingdom almost twice the size he had inherited. Louis successfully harnessed the nobility, expanded the trade and industry that Jacques Coeur so carefully had nurtured, created a national postal system, and even established a lucrative silk industry.

A strong nation is a two-edged sword. Because Louis's successors inherited a secure and efficient government, they felt free to pursue what proved ultimately to be bad foreign policy. Conquests in Italy in the 1490s and a long series of losing wars with the Habsburgs in the first half of the sixteenth century left France, by the mid-sixteenth century, once again a defeated nation almost as divided as it had been during the Hundred Years' War.

10.3.2 Spain

Both Castile and Aragon had been poorly ruled and divided kingdoms in the mid-fifteenth century, but the union of Isabella of Castile (r. 1474–1504) and Ferdinand of Aragon (r. 1479–1516) changed that situation. The two future sovereigns married in 1469, despite strong protests from neighboring Portugal and France, both of which envisioned the formidable European power the marriage would create. Castile was by far the richer and more populous of the two, having an estimated five million inhabitants to Aragon's population of less than one million. Castile was also distinguished by its lucrative sheep-farming industry, run by a government-backed organization called the *Mesta*, another example of developing centralized economic planning. Although the marriage of Ferdinand and Isabella dynastically united the two kingdoms, they remained constitutionally separated. Each retained its respective government agencies—separate laws, armies, coinage, and taxation—and cultural traditions.

Ferdinand and Isabella could do together what neither was able to accomplish alone: subdue their realms, secure their borders, venture abroad militarily, and Christianize the whole of Spain. Between 1482 and 1492 they conquered the Moors in Granada. Naples became a Spanish possession in 1504. By 1512, Ferdinand had secured his northern borders by conquering the kingdom of Navarre. Internally, the Spanish king and queen won the allegiance of the *Hermandad*, a powerful league of cities and towns that served them against stubborn noble landowners.

Spain had long been remarkable among European lands as a place where three religions—Islam, Judaism, and Christianity—coexisted with a certain degree of toleration. That toleration was to end dramatically under Ferdinand and Isabella, who made Spain the prime example of state-controlled religion.

Ferdinand and Isabella exercised almost total control over the Spanish church. They appointed the higher clergy and the officers of the Inquisition. The latter, run by Tomás de Torquemada (d. 1498), Isabella's confessor, was a key national agency established in 1479 to monitor the activity of converted Jews, or conversos, and Muslims, or Moriscos, in Spain. In 1492, the Jews were exiled and their properties confiscated. In 1502, nonconverting Moors in Granada were driven into exile by Cardinal Francisco Jiménez de Cisneros (1437–1517), under whom Spanish spiritual life was successfully affirmed. This was a major reason why Spain remained a loyal Catholic country throughout the sixteenth century and provided a secure base of operation for the European Counter-Reformation.

Ferdinand and Isabella were rulers with wide horizons. They contracted anti-French marriage alliances that came to determine a large part of European history in the sixteenth century. In 1496, their eldest daughter, Joanna, later known as "the Mad," married Archduke Philip, the son of Emperor Maximilian I. The fruit of this union, Charles I, was the first to rule over a united Spain; because of his inheritance and election as emperor in 1519, his empire almost equaled in size that of Charlemagne. A second daughter, Catherine of Aragon, wed Arthur, the son of the English king Henry VII. After Arthur's premature death, Catherine was betrothed to his brother, the future King Henry VIII (r. 1509–1547), whom she married eight years later, in 1509. The failure of this marriage became the key factor in the emergence of the Anglican church and the English Reformation.

Spain's new power was also exhibited in Ferdinand and Isabella's promotion of overseas exploration. They sponsored the Genoese adventurer Christopher Columbus (1451–1506), who arrived at the islands of the Caribbean while sailing west in search of a shorter route to the spice markets of the Far East. This patronage led to the creation of the Spanish Empire in Mexico and Peru, whose gold and silver mines helped make Spain Europe's dominant power in the sixteenth century.

10.3.3 England

The latter half of the fifteenth century was a period of especially difficult political trial for the English. Following the Hundred Years' War, civil warfare broke out between two rival branches of the royal family: the House of York and the House of Lancaster. The roots of the war lay in succession irregularities after the forced deposition of the erratic king Richard II (r. 1377–1399). This conflict, known to us today as the Wars of the Roses (because York's symbol, according to legend, was a white rose and Lancaster's a red rose), kept England in turmoil from 1455 to 1485.

The duke of York and his supporters in the prosperous southern towns challenged the Lancastrian monarchy of Henry VI (r. 1422–1461). In 1461, Edward IV (r. 1461–1483), son of the duke of York, seized power and instituted a strong-arm rule that lasted more than twenty years; it was only briefly interrupted, in 1470–1471, by Henry VI's short-lived restoration. Assisted by able ministers, Edward effectively increased the power and finances of the monarchy.

His brother, Richard III (r. 1483–1485), usurped the throne from Edward's son, and after Richard's death, the new Tudor dynasty portrayed him as an unprincipled villain who had also murdered Edward's sons in the Tower of London to secure his hold on the throne. Shakespeare's *Richard III* is the best-known version of this characterization—unjust according to some. Regardless, Richard's reign saw the growth

of support for the exiled Lancastrian Henry Tudor, who returned to England to defeat Richard on Bosworth Field in August 1485.

Henry Tudor ruled as Henry VII (r. 1485–1509), the first of the new Tudor dynasty that would dominate England throughout the sixteenth century. To bring the rival royal families together and to make the hereditary claim of his offspring to the throne uncontestable, Henry married Edward IV's daughter, Elizabeth of York. He succeeded in disciplining the English nobility through a special instrument of the royal will known as the Court of Star Chamber. Created with the sanction of Parliament in 1487, the court was intended to end the perversion of English justice by "over-mighty subjects," that is, powerful nobles who used intimidation and bribery to win favorable verdicts in court cases. In the Court of Star Chamber, the king's councilors sat as judges, and the nobles' tactics did not sway them. The result was a more equitable court system.

It was also a court more amenable to the royal will. Henry shrewdly used English law to further the ends of the monarchy. He confiscated lands and fortunes of nobles with such success that he managed to govern without dependence on Parliament for royal funds, always a cornerstone of a strong monarchy. In these ways, Henry began to shape a monarchy that would develop into one of early modern Europe's most exemplary governments during the reign of his granddaughter, Elizabeth I (r. 1558–1603).

10.3.4 The Holy Roman Empire

Germany and Italy were the striking exceptions to the steady development of politically centralized lands in the last half of the fifteenth century. Unlike England, France, and Spain, the Holy Roman Empire saw the many thoroughly repulse the one. In Germany, territorial rulers and cities resisted every effort at national consolidation and unity. As in Carolingian times, rulers continued to partition their kingdoms, however small, among their sons. By the late fifteenth century, Germany was hopelessly divided into some 300 autonomous political entities.

The princes and the cities did work together to create the machinery of law and order, if not of union, within the divided empire. Emperor Charles IV (r. 1346–1378) and the major German territorial rulers reached an agreement in 1356 known as the **Golden Bull**. It established a seven-member electoral college consisting of the archbishops of Mainz, Trier, and Cologne; the duke of Saxony; the margrave of Brandenburg; the count Palatine; and the king of Bohemia. This group also functioned as an administrative body. They elected the emperor and, in cooperation with him, provided what transregional unity and administration existed.

The figure of the emperor gave the empire a single ruler in law if not in fact. The conditions of his rule and the extent of his powers over his subjects, especially the seven electors, were renegotiated with every imperial election. Therefore, the rights of the many—the princes—were always balanced against the power of the one—the emperor.

In the fifteenth century, an effort was made to control incessant feuding by the creation of an imperial diet known as the *Reichstag*. This was a national assembly of the seven electors, the nonelectoral princes, and representatives from the sixty-five imperial free cities. The cities were the weakest of the three bodies represented in the diet. During such an assembly in Worms in 1495, the members won from Emperor Maximilian I an imperial ban on private warfare, the creation of a Supreme Court of Justice to enforce internal peace, and an imperial Council of Regency to coordinate imperial and internal German policy. The emperor grudgingly conceded the latter, unhappy because it gave the princes a share in executive power.

These reforms were still a poor substitute for true national unity. In the sixteenth and seventeenth centuries, the territorial princes became virtually sovereign rulers in their various domains. Such disunity aided religious dissent and conflict. It was in the cities and territories of still feudal, fractionalized, backward Germany that the Protestant Reformation broke out in the sixteenth century.

ADAM AND EVE The bodies of Adam and Eve in Lucas Cranach the Elder's painting present an interesting counterpoint to the body of the "perfect man" depicted in Leonardo's *Vitruvian Man* (reproduced earlier in this chapter).
SOURCE: INTERFOTO/Alamy Stock Photo

10.4 The Northern Renaissance

How did the northern Renaissance affect culture in Germany, England, France, and Spain?

The scholarly works of northern humanists created a climate favorable to religious and educational reforms on the eve of the Reformation. Northern humanism was initially stimulated by the importation of Italian learning through such varied intermediaries as students who had studied in Italy, merchants who traded there, and the Brothers of the Common Life. This last was an influential lay religious movement that began in the Netherlands and permitted men and women to live a shared religious life without making formal vows of poverty, chastity, and obedience.

The northern humanists, however, developed their own distinctive culture. They tended to come from more diverse social backgrounds and to be more devoted to religious reforms than their Italian counterparts. They were also more willing to write for lay audiences as well as for a narrow intelligentsia. Thanks to the invention of printing with movable type, it became possible for humanists to convey their educational ideals to laypeople and clerics alike. Printing gave new power and influence to elites of both church and state, who could now popularize their viewpoints freely and widely.

10.4.1 The Printing Press

A variety of forces converged in the fourteenth and fifteenth centuries to give rise to the invention of the printing press. Since the days of Charlemagne, kings and princes had encouraged schools and literacy to help educated bureaucrats staff the offices of their kingdoms. Without people who could read, think critically, and write reliable reports, no kingdom, large or small, could be properly governed. By the fifteenth century, a new literate lay public had been created, thanks to the expansion of schools and universities during the late Middle Ages.

The invention of a cheap way to manufacture paper also helped make books economical as well as broaden their content. Manuscript books had been inscribed on vellum, a cumbersome and expensive medium (170 calfskins or 300 sheepskins were required to make a single vellum Bible). Single-sheet woodcuts had long been printed, a process involving carving words and pictures on a block of wood, inking it, and then stamping out as many copies as possible before the wood deteriorated. The end product was much like a cheap modern poster.

In response to the demand for books created by the expansion of lay education and literacy, Johann Gutenberg

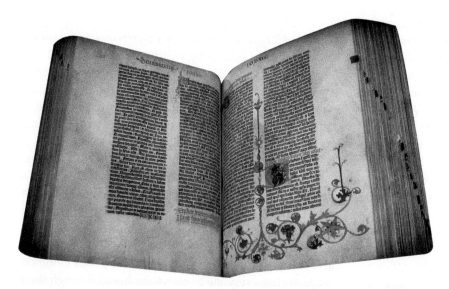

GUTENBERG BIBLE The printing press made possible the diffusion of Renaissance learning, but no book stimulated thought more at this time than did the Bible. With Gutenberg's publication of a printed Bible in 1455, shown above, scholars gained access to a dependable, standardized text, and Scripture could be discussed and debated as never before.

SOURCE: Peter Horree/Alamy Stock Photo

(d. 1468) invented printing with movable type in the mid-fifteenth century in the German city of Mainz, the center of printing for all Western Europe. Thereafter, books were rapidly and handsomely produced, on topics both profound and practical, and were intended for ordinary lay readers, scholars, and clerics alike. Especially popular in the early decades of print were books of piety and religion, calendars and almanacs, and how-to books (for example, on childrearing, making brandies and liquors, curing animals, and farming).

The new technology proved enormously profitable to printers, whose numbers exploded. By 1500, within just fifty years of Gutenberg's press, printing presses operated in at least sixty German cities and in more than 200 cities throughout Europe. The printing press was a boon to the careers of humanists, who now gained international audiences.

Literacy deeply affected people everywhere, nurturing self-esteem and a critical frame of mind. By standardizing texts, the print revolution made anyone who could read an instant authority. Rulers in church and state now had to deal with a less credulous and less docile laity. Print was also a powerful tool for political and religious propaganda. Kings could now indoctrinate people as never before, and clergymen were able to mass-produce both indulgences and pamphlets.

10.4.2 Desiderius Erasmus

The far-reaching influence of Desiderius Erasmus (1466–1536), the most famous northern humanist, illustrates the

impact of the printing press. Through his printed works, Erasmus gained fame both as an educational and as a religious reformer. A lifelong Catholic, Erasmus, through his life and work, made clear that many loyal Catholics wanted major reforms in the church long before the Reformation made them a reality.

When patronage was scarce (authors received no royalties and had to rely on private patrons for their livelihood), Erasmus earned his living by tutoring well-to-do youths. He prepared short Latin dialogues for his students, intended to teach them how to speak and live well, and how to internalize good manners and language based on what they read.

These dialogues were entitled *Colloquies*. In consecutive editions, they grew in number and length, including anticlerical dialogues and satires on religious dogmatism and superstition. Erasmus also collected ancient and contemporary proverbs, which appeared under the title *Adages*. Early *Adages* contained 800 examples, and the final edition included more than 5,000. Among the locutions the *Adages* popularized are such common expressions as "Leave no stone unturned" and "Where there is smoke, there is fire."

Erasmus aspired to unite classical ideals of humanity and civic virtue with the Christian ideals of love and piety. He believed disciplined study of the classics and the Bible, if begun early enough, was the best way to reform individuals and society. Erasmus summarized his own beliefs with the phrase *philosophia Christi*, a simple, ethical piety in imitation of Christ. He upheld this ideal in stark contrast to what he believed to be the dogmatic, ceremonial, and bullying religious practices of the later Middle Ages. What most offended him about the Scholastics, both the old authorities of the Middle Ages and the new Protestant ones, was how they let dogma and argument overshadow Christian piety and practice.

Erasmus was a true idealist, who expected more from people than the age's theologians believed them capable of doing. To promote what he deemed to be the essence of Christianity, he made ancient Christian sources available in their original versions, believing that by imbibing the pure sources of the faith, people would recover the moral and religious health the New Testament promises. To accomplish this, Erasmus edited the works of the church fathers and produced a Greek edition of the New Testament in 1516, later adding a new Latin translation of the latter in 1519. Martin Luther used both of these works when he translated the New Testament into German in 1522.

These various enterprises did not please the church authorities. They remained unhappy with Erasmus's "improvements" on the Vulgate, Christendom's Bible for over a thousand years, and his popular anticlerical writings. At one point in the mid-sixteenth century, all of Erasmus's works were on the church's *Index of Forbidden Books*. Luther also condemned Erasmus for his views on the freedom of human will. Still, Erasmus's works put strong tools of reform in the hands of both Protestant and Catholic reformers. In the 1520s, there was already a popular saying: "Erasmus laid the egg that Luther hatched."

10.4.3 Humanism and Reform

In Germany, England, France, and Spain, humanism stirred both educational and religious reform. In each case Italian learning and scholarship played a key role in the work of northern humanists to combine the classics with Christian faith.

10.4.3.1 GERMANY Rudolf Agricola (1443–1485), the "father of German humanism," spent ten years in Italy and introduced Italian learning to Germany when he returned. Conrad Celtis (d. 1508), the first German poet laureate, and Ulrich von Hutten (1488–1523), a fiery knight, gave German humanism a nationalist coloring hostile to non-German cultures, particularly Roman culture. Von Hutten especially illustrated the union of humanism, German nationalism, and Luther's religious reform. A poet who admired Erasmus, he attacked indulgences and published an edition of Valla's exposé of the *Donation of Constantine*. He died in 1523, the victim of a hopeless knights' revolt against the princes.

The controversy that brought von Hutten onto the historical stage and unified reform-minded German humanists was the Reuchlin affair. Johann Reuchlin (1455–1522) was Europe's foremost Christian authority on Hebrew and Jewish learning. He wrote the first reliable Hebrew grammar by a Christian scholar and was attracted to Jewish mysticism. Around 1506, supported by the Dominican order in Cologne, a Christian who had converted from , whose name was Pfefferkorn, began a movement to suppress Jewish writings. When he attacked Reuchlin, many German humanists, in the name of academic freedom and good scholarship—not for any pro-Jewish sentiment—came to Reuchlin's defense. The controversy lasted for years and produced one of the great satires of the period, the *Letters of Obscure Men* (1515), a merciless satire of monks and Scholastics to which von Hutten contributed. When Martin Luther came under attack in 1517 for his famous ninety-five theses against indulgences, many German humanists saw it as a repetition of the Scholastic attack on Reuchlin and rushed to his side.

10.4.3.2 ENGLAND Italian learning came to England by way of English scholars and merchants and visiting Italian prelates. Lectures by William Grocyn (d. 1519) and Thomas Linacre (d. 1524) at Oxford and those of Erasmus at Cambridge marked the scholarly maturation of English humanism. John Colet (1467–1519), dean of Saint Paul's Cathedral, patronized humanist studies for the young and promoted religious reform.

Thomas More (1478–1535), a close friend of Erasmus, is the best-known English humanist. His *Utopia* (1516), a conservative criticism of contemporary society, rivals the plays of Shakespeare as the most read sixteenth-century English work. *Utopia* depicted an imaginary society based on reason and tolerance that overcame social and political injustice by making all property and goods common and requiring everyone to earn their bread through their own work.

More became one of Henry VIII's most trusted diplomats. His repudiation of the Act of Supremacy (1534), which made the king of England head of the English church in place of the pope, and his refusal to recognize the king's marriage to Anne Boleyn, however, led to his execution in July 1535. Although More remained Catholic, humanism in England, as also in Germany, helped prepare the way for the English Reformation.

10.4.3.3 FRANCE The French invasions of Italy made it possible for Italian learning to penetrate France, stirring both educational and religious reform. Guillaume Budé (1468–1540), an accomplished Greek scholar, and Jacques Lefèvre d'Etaples (1454–1536), a biblical authority, were the leaders of French humanism. Lefèvre's scholarly works exemplified the new critical scholarship and influenced Martin Luther. Guillaume Briçonnet (1470–1533), the bishop of Meaux, and Marguerite d'Angoulême (1492–1549), sister of King Francis I, the future queen of Navarre, and a successful spiritual writer in her own right, cultivated a generation of young reform-minded humanists. The future Protestant reformer John Calvin was a product of this native reform circle.

10.4.3.4 SPAIN Whereas in England, France, and Germany humanism prepared the way for Protestant reforms, in Spain humanism served the Catholic Church. The key figure was Francisco Jiménez de Cisneros (1437–1517), a confessor to Queen Isabella and after 1508, the "Grand Inquisitor"—a position that allowed him to enforce the strictest religious orthodoxy. His great achievement, which took fifteen years to complete, was the *Complutensian Polyglot Bible*, a six-volume work that placed the Hebrew, Greek, and Latin versions of the Bible in parallel columns. Such scholarly projects and internal church reforms combined with the repressive measures of Ferdinand and Isabella to keep Spain strictly Catholic throughout the Age of Reformation.

10.5 Voyages of Discovery and the New Empires in the West and East

What were the motives for European voyages of discovery, and what were the consequences?

The discovery of the Americas dramatically expanded the horizons of Europeans, both geographically and intellectually. Knowledge of the New World's inhabitants and the exploitation of its mineral and human wealth set new cultural and economic forces in motion throughout Western Europe.

Beginning with the voyages of the Portuguese and Spanish in the fifteenth century, commercial supremacy progressively shifted from the Mediterranean and Baltic Seas to the Atlantic seaboard, setting the stage for global expansion. (See Map 10–2.)

10.5.1 The Portuguese Chart the Course

Seventy-seven years before Columbus, who sailed under the flag of Spain, set foot in the Americas, Prince Henry "the Navigator" (1394–1460), brother of the king of Portugal, captured the North African Muslim city of Ceuta. His motives were mercenary and religious, both a quest for gold and spices and the pious work of saving the souls of Muslims and pagans who had no knowledge of Christ. Thus began the Portuguese exploration of the African coast, first in search of gold and slaves, and by century's end, of a sea route around Africa to Asia's spice markets. Pepper and cloves topped the list of spices, as they both preserved and enhanced the dull diet of most Europeans. Initially the catch of raiders, African slaves were soon taken by Portuguese traders in direct commerce with tribal chiefs, who readily swapped captives for horses, grain, and finished goods (cloth and brassware). Over the second half of the fifteenth century, Portuguese ships delivered 150,000 slaves to Europe.

Before there was a sea route to the East, Europeans could only get spices through the Venetians, who bought or bartered them from Muslim merchants in Egypt and the Ottoman Empire. The Portuguese resolved to beat this powerful Venetian–Muslim monopoly by sailing directly to the source. Overland routes to India and China had long existed, but their transit had become too difficult and unprofitable by the fifteenth century. The route by sea posed a different obstacle and risk—fear of the unknown—making the first voyages of exploration slow and tentative. Venturing down the African coast, the Portuguese ships were turned out into the deep ocean by every protruding cape, and the farther out they sailed to round them, the more the sailors feared the winds would not return them to land. Each cape rounded became a victory and a lesson, giving the crews the skills they needed to cross the oceans to the Americas and East Asia.

In addition to new spice markets, the voyagers also gained new allies against Western Europe's archenemies, the Muslims. In 1455, a self-interested pope granted the Portuguese explorers all the spoils of war—land, goods, and slaves—from the coast of Guinea in West Africa to the Indies in East Asia. The church expected exploration to lead to mass conversions—a Christian coup as well as a mercantile advantage. The explorers also kept an eye out for a legendary Eastern Christian ruler known as Prester John.

Bartholomeu Dias (ca. 1450–1500) pioneered the eastern Portuguese Empire after safely rounding the Cape of Good Hope at the tip of Africa in 1487. A decade later, in 1498, Vasco da Gama (1469–1525) stood on the shores of India. When he returned to Portugal, he carried a cargo of spices worth sixty times the cost of the voyage. Later, the Portuguese established colonies in Goa and Calcutta on the coast of India, whence they challenged the Arabs and the Venetians for control of the spice trade.

The Portuguese had concentrated their explorations on the Indian Ocean. The Spanish turned west, believing they could find a shorter route to the East Indies by sailing across the Atlantic. Instead, Christopher Columbus (1451–1506) discovered the Americas.

10.5.2 The Spanish Voyages of Columbus

Thirty-three days after departing the Canary Islands, on October 12, 1492, Columbus landed in San Salvador (Watlings Island) in the eastern Bahamas. Thinking he was in the East Indies, he mistook his first landfall as an outer island of Japan. The error was understandable given the information Columbus relied on, namely Marco Polo's thirteenth-century account of his years in China and geographer Martin Behaim's spherical map of the presumed world. That map showed only ocean and Cipangu, or Japan, between the west coast of Europe and the east coast of Asia. Not until his third voyage to the Caribbean in 1498 did Columbus realize that Cuba was not Japan and South America was not China.

Naked, friendly natives met Columbus and his crew on the beaches of the New World. They were Taino Indians, who spoke a variant of a language known as Arawak. Believing the island on which he landed to be the East Indies, Columbus called these people Indians, a name that stuck with Europeans even after they realized he had actually discovered a new continent. The natives' generosity amazed Columbus, as they freely gave his men all the corn, yams, and sexual favors they desired. "They never say no," Columbus marveled. He also observed how easily the Spanish could enslave them.

Map 10–2 EUROPEAN VOYAGES OF DISCOVERY AND THE COLONIAL CLAIMS OF SPAIN AND PORTUGAL IN THE FIFTEENTH AND SIXTEENTH CENTURIES

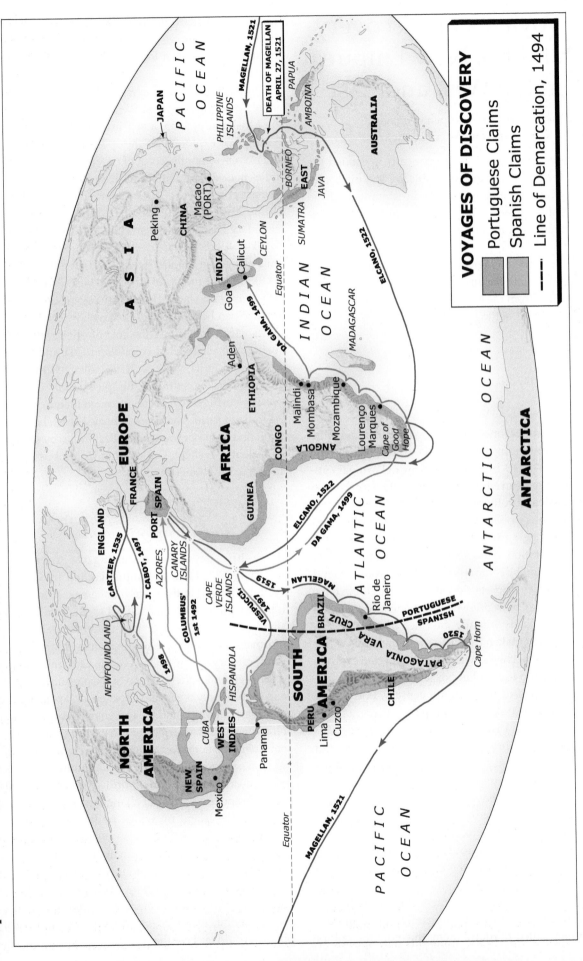

This map dramatizes Europe's global expansion in the fifteenth and sixteenth centuries.

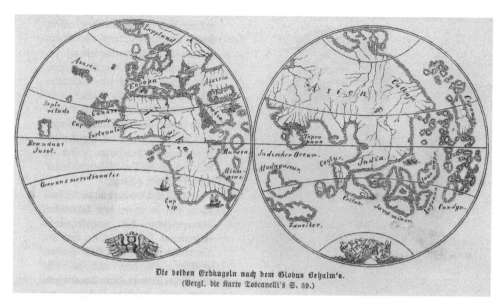

Die beiden Erdkugeln nach dem Globus Behaim's.
(Vergl. die Karte Toscanelli's S. 39.)

BEHAIM WORLD MAP Everything Columbus knew of the world in was contained in this map by Nuremberg geographer Martin Behaim, creator of the first spherical globe of the earth. Departing the Canary Islands, Columbus expected his first major landfall to be Japan, and upon landing in Cuba, he assumed he was in Japan.
SOURCE: Chronicle/Alamy Stock Photo

fruits, vegetables, and animals into the Americas and brought American species back to Europe. European expansion also spread European diseases. Vast numbers of Native Americans died from measles and smallpox epidemics, while Europeans died from a virulent form of syphilis that may have originated in the Americas.

For the Native Americans, the voyages of discovery were the beginning of a long history of conquest, disease, and slave labor they could neither evade nor survive. In both South and North America, Spanish rule left a lasting imprint of Roman Catholicism, economic dependency, and hierarchical social structure, all still visible today.

10.5.2.1 ON THE HEELS OF COLUMBUS On the heels of Columbus, Amerigo Vespucci (1451–1512), after whom America is named, and Ferdinand Magellan (1480–1521) explored the coastline of South America. Their travels proved that the new lands Columbus had discovered were an entirely unknown continent that opened on the still greater Pacific Ocean. Magellan, who continued the search for a westward route to the Indies, made it all the way around South America and across the Pacific to the Philippines, where he was killed in a skirmish with the inhabitants. The remnants of his squadron eventually sailed on to Spain, making them the first sailors to circumnavigate the globe.

10.5.2.2 INTENDED AND UNINTENDED CONSEQUENCES OF COLUMBUS'S VOYAGES Columbus's first voyage marked the beginning of more than three centuries of a vast Spanish empire in the Americas. What began as voyages of discovery became expeditions of conquest, not unlike the warfare Christian Aragon and Castile waged against Islamic Moors. Those wars had just ended in 1492, and their conclusion imbued the early Spanish explorers with a zeal for conquering and converting non-Christian peoples.

Much to the benefit of Spain, the voyages of discovery created Europe's largest and longest surviving trading bloc and spurred other European countries to undertake their own colonial ventures. The wealth extracted from its American possessions financed Spain's commanding role in the religious and political wars of the sixteenth and seventeenth centuries, while fueling a Europe-wide economic expansion.

European expansion also had a profound biological impact. Europeans introduced numerous new species of

10.5.3 The Spanish Empire in the New World

When the first Spanish explorers arrived, the Aztec Empire dominated Mesoamerica, which stretches from Central Mexico to Guatemala, and the Inca Empire dominated Andean South America. Both were rich, and their conquest promised the Spanish the possibility of acquiring large quantities of gold.

10.5.3.1 THE AZTECS IN MEXICO The forebears of the Aztecs had arrived in the Valley of Mexico early in the twelfth century, where they lived as a subservient people. In 1428, however, they began a period of imperial expansion. By the time of Spanish conquest, the Aztecs ruled almost all central Mexico from their capital Tenochtitlán (modern-day Mexico City). The Aztecs demanded heavy tribute in goods and labor from their subjects and, believing the gods must literally be fed with human blood to guarantee sunshine and fertility, they also took thousands of captives each year for human sacrifice. These policies bred resentment and fear among the subject peoples.

In 1519, Hernán Cortés (1485–1547) landed in Mexico with about 500 men and a few horses. He opened communication with Moctezuma II (1466–1520), the Aztec emperor. Moctezuma may initially have believed Cortés to be the god Quetzalcoatl, who according to legend, had been driven away centuries earlier but had promised to return. Whatever the reason, Moctezuma hesitated to confront Cortés, attempting at first to appease him with gold, which only whetted Spanish appetites. Cortés forged alliances with the Aztecs' subject peoples, most importantly,

PEDRO DE ALVARADO BESEIGED In this image by sixteenth-century Spanish artist Diego Duran, armored Spanish soldiers, under the command of Pedro de Alvarado (d. 1541) and bearing crossbows, engage unprotected and crudely armed Aztecs, who nonetheless are portrayed as larger than life.

SOURCE: Biblioteca Nacional, Madrid, Spain/Bridgeman Art Library

The conquests of Mexico and Peru are among the most dramatic and brutal events in modern history. Small military forces armed with advanced weapons subdued, in a remarkably brief time, two powerful peoples. The spread of European diseases, especially smallpox, among the Native Americans also aided the conquest. But beyond the drama and bloodshed, these conquests, as well as those of other Native American peoples, marked a fundamental turning point. Whole civilizations with long histories and enormous social, architectural, and technological achievements were destroyed. Native American cultures endured, accommodating themselves to European dominance, but the Spanish conquests of the early sixteenth century marked the beginning of the transformation of South America into Latin America.

with Tlaxcala, an independent state and traditional enemy of the Aztecs. His forces then marched on Tenochtitlán, where Moctezuma welcomed him. Cortés soon seized Moctezuma, who died in unexplained circumstances. The Aztecs' wary acceptance of the Spaniards turned to open hostility. The Spaniards were driven from Tenochtitlán and were nearly wiped out, but they returned and laid siege to the city. The Aztecs, under their last ruler, Cuauhtémoc (ca. 1495–1525), resisted fiercely but were finally defeated in 1521. Cortés razed Tenochtitlán, building his own capital over its ruins, and proclaimed the Aztec Empire to be New Spain.

10.5.3.2 THE INCAS IN PERU The second great Native American civilization conquered by the Spanish was that of the Incas in the highlands of Peru. Like the Aztecs, the Incas also began to expand rapidly in the fifteenth century and by the time of the Spanish conquest, controlled an enormous empire. Unlike the Aztecs, who extracted tribute from their subject peoples, the Incas compelled their subjects to work for the state on a regular basis.

In 1532, largely inspired by Cortés's example in Mexico, Francisco Pizarro (c. 1478–1541) landed on the western coast of South America with about 200 men to take on the Inca Empire. Pizarro lured Atahualpa (ca. 1500–1533), the Inca ruler, into a conference and then seized him, killing hundreds of Atahualpa's followers in the process. The imprisoned Atahualpa tried to ransom himself with a hoard of gold, but instead of releasing him, Pizarro executed him in 1533. The Spaniards then captured Cuzco, the Inca capital, but Incan resistance did not end until the 1570s.

10.5.4 The Church in Spanish America

Roman Catholic priests had accompanied the earliest explorers and the conquerors of the Native Americans. Steeped in the social and religious ideals of Christian humanism, these first clergy members believed they could foster Erasmus's concept of the "philosophy of Christ" in the New World. They were filled with zeal not only to convert the inhabitants to Christianity but also to bring to them European learning and civilization.

Tension, however, existed between the early Spanish conquerors and the mendicant friars who sought to minister to the Native Americans. Without conquest, the church could not convert the Native Americans, but the priests often deplored the harsh conditions imposed on the native peoples. By far the most effective and outspoken clerical critic of the Spanish conquerors was Bartolomé de Las Casas (1474–1566), a Dominican, who contended that conquest was not necessary for conversion. One result of his campaign was new royal regulations to protect the Indians after 1550.

Another result of Las Casas's criticism was the emergence of the "Black Legend," according to which all Spanish treatment of the Native Americans was unprincipled and inhumane. Those who created this legend of Spanish behavior drew heavily on Las Casas's writings. Although substantially true, the "Black Legend" exaggerated the case against Spain. Certainly, the rulers of the native empires—as the Aztec demands for sacrificial victims attest—had often themselves been exceedingly cruel to their subjects.

By the end of the sixteenth century, the church in Spanish America had become largely an institution upholding the colonial status quo. Although individual priests defended the communal rights of Indian peoples, the colonial church prospered as the Spanish elite prospered by exploiting the resources and peoples of the New World. The church became a great landowner through crown grants and bequests from Catholics who died in the New World. The monasteries took on an economic as well as a spiritual life of their own. Whatever its concern for the spiritual welfare of the Native Americans, the church remained one of the indications that Spanish America was a conquered world. Those who spoke for the church did not challenge Spanish domination or any but the most extreme modes of Spanish economic exploitation. By the end of the colonial era in the late eighteenth century, the Roman Catholic Church had become one of the most conservative forces in Latin America.

10.5.5 The Economy of Exploitation

From the beginning, both the Native Americans and their lands were part of the Atlantic economy and the world of competitive European commercialism. For the Indians of Latin America and, somewhat later, the black peoples of Africa, that world meant forced labor.

The colonial economy of Latin America had three major components: mining, agriculture, and shipping. Each involved labor servitude and the intertwining of the New World economy with that of Spain.

10.5.5.1 MINING The early *conquistadores*, or "conquerors," were primarily interested in gold, but by the mid-sixteenth century, silver mining provided the chief source of metallic wealth. The great mining centers were Potosí in Peru and somewhat smaller sites in northern Mexico. Exploring for silver continued throughout the colonial era. Its production by forced labor for the benefit of Spaniards and the Spanish crown epitomized the wholly extractive economy that stood at the foundation of colonial life.

10.5.5.2 AGRICULTURE The major rural and agricultural institution of the Spanish colonies was the *hacienda*, a large landed estate owned by persons originally born in Spain (*peninsulares*) or persons of Spanish descent born in America (*creoles*). Laborers on the hacienda were usually subject in some legal way to the owner and were rarely free to move from working for one landowner to another.

The hacienda economy produced two major products: foodstuffs for mining areas and urban centers and leather goods used in mining machinery. Both farming and ranching were subordinate to the mining economy.

In the West Indies, the basic agricultural unit was the plantation. In Cuba, Hispaniola, Puerto Rico, and other islands, the labor of black slaves from Africa produced sugar to supply an almost insatiable demand for the product in Europe.

10.5.5.3 SHIPPING A final major area of economic activity in the Spanish colonies was urban service occupations, including government offices, the legal profession, and shipping. Those who worked in these occupations were either peninsulares or creoles, with the former dominating most often.

10.5.6 Labor Servitude

All this extractive and exploitive economic activity required labor, and the Spanish in the New World decided early that the native population would supply it. A series of social devices was used to exploit them in the new economic life the Spanish imposed.

The first of these was the *encomienda*, a formal grant of the right to the labor of a specific number of Indians, usually a few hundred, but sometimes thousands, for a particular period of time. The encomienda was in decline by the mid-sixteenth century because the Spanish monarchs feared its holders might become too powerful. There were also humanitarian objections to this kind of exploitation of the Indians.

The passing of the encomienda led to a new arrangement of labor servitude: the *repartimiento*. This device required adult male Indians to devote a certain number of days of labor annually to Spanish economic enterprises. Repartimiento service was often harsh, and some Indians did not survive their stint. The limitation on labor time led some Spanish managers to abuse their workers on the assumption that new workers would soon replace them.

The eventual shortage of workers and the crown's pressure against extreme versions of forced labor led to the use of free labor. The freedom, however, was more in appearance than reality. Free Indian laborers were required to purchase goods from the landowner or mine owner, to whom they became forever indebted. This form of exploitation, known as *debt peonage*, continued in Latin America long after the nineteenth-century wars of liberation.

Black slavery was the final mode of forced or subservient labor in the New World. Both the Spanish and the Portuguese had earlier used African slaves in Europe. The sugar plantations of the West Indies and Brazil now became the major center of black slavery.

The conquest, the forced labor of the economy of exploitation, and the introduction of European diseases had devastating demographic consequences for the Native Americans. For centuries, Europeans had lived in a far more complex human and animal environment than Native Americans did. They had frequent contact with different ethnic and racial groups and with a variety of domestic animals. Such interaction helped them develop strong immune systems that enabled them to survive measles, smallpox, and typhoid. Native Americans, by contrast, grew up in a simpler and more sterile environment and were defenseless against these diseases. Within a generation, the native population of New Spain (Mexico) was reduced to an estimated 8 percent of its numbers, from twenty-five million to two million.

10.5.7 The Impact on Europe

Among contemporary European intellectuals, Columbus's discovery increased skepticism about the wisdom of the ancients. If traditional knowledge about the world had been so incorrect geographically, they wondered how trustworthy it could be on other matters. For many, Columbus's discovery demonstrated the folly of relying on any presumed authoritative knowledge. Both in Europe and in the New World, there were those who condemned the explorers' treatment of American natives, as more was learned about their cruelty. Three centuries later, however, on the third centenary of Columbus's discovery (1792), the great thinkers of the age lionized Columbus for having opened new possibilities for civilization and morality. By establishing new commercial contacts among different peoples of the world, Columbus was said to have made cooperation, civility, and peace among them indispensable. Enlightenment thinkers drew parallels between the discovery of America and the invention of the printing press—both were portrayed as historical world events opening new eras in communication and globalization, an early multicultural experiment.[4]

On the material side, the influx of spices and precious metals into Europe from the new Portuguese and Spanish Empires was a mixed blessing. It contributed to a steady rise in prices during the sixteenth century that created an inflation rate estimated at 2 percent a year. The new supply of bullion from the Americas combined with greater European production to increase the amount of coinage in circulation, and this increase, in turn, fed inflation. Fortunately, the rise in prices was mostly spread over a long period and was not sudden. Prices doubled in Spain by 1550, quadrupled by 1600. In Wittenberg, in Luther's Germany, the cost of basic food and clothing increased almost 100 percent between 1519 and 1540. Generally, wages and rents remained well behind the rise in prices.

The new wealth enabled governments and private entrepreneurs to sponsor basic research and expansion in the printing, shipping, mining, textile, and weapons industries. There is also evidence of large-scale government planning in such ventures as the French silk industry and the Habsburg-Fugger development of mines in Austria and Hungary.

In the thirteenth and fourteenth centuries, capitalist institutions and practices had already begun to develop in the rich Italian cities (for example, the Florentine banking houses of Bardi and Peruzzi). Those who owned the means of production, either privately or corporately, were clearly distinguished from the workers who operated them. Wherever possible, entrepreneurs created monopolies in basic goods. High interest was charged on loans—actual, if not legal, usury. The "capitalist" virtues of thrift, industry, and orderly planning were evident everywhere all intended to permit the free and efficient accumulation of wealth.

The late fifteenth and the sixteenth centuries reflected the maturation of this type of capitalism together with its attendant social problems. The Medicis of Florence grew rich as bankers of the pope, as did the Fuggers of Augsburg, who bankrolled Habsburg rulers. The Fuggers lent Charles I of Spain more than 500,000 florins to buy his election as the Holy Roman Emperor in 1519 and boasted they had created the emperor. The new wealth and industrial expansion also raised the expectations of the poor and the ambitious and heightened the reactionary tendencies of the wealthy. This effect, in turn, aggravated the traditional social divisions between the clergy and the laity, the urban patriciate and the guilds, and the landed nobility and the agrarian peasantry.

These divisions indirectly prepared the way for the Reformation as well, causing many people to be critical of traditional institutions and open to new ideas—especially those that seemed to promise greater freedom and a chance at a better life.

The Chapter in Perspective

As it recovered from national wars during the late Middle Ages, Europe saw the establishment of permanent centralized states and regional governments. The foundations of modern France, Spain, England, Germany, and Italy were laid at this time. As rulers imposed their will on regions outside their immediate domains, the "one" progressively took control of the "many," and previously divided lands came together as nations.

Thanks to the work of Byzantine and Islamic scholars, ancient Greek science and scholarship found its way into the West in these centuries. Europeans had been separated from their classical cultural heritage for almost eight centuries. No other world civilization had experienced such a disjunction from its cultural past. The discovery of classical civilization occasioned a rebirth of intellectual and artistic activity in both southern and northern Europe. One result

was the splendor of the Italian Renaissance, whose scholarship, painting, and sculpture remain among Western Europe's most impressive achievements.

Ancient learning was not the only discovery of the era. New political unity spurred both royal greed and national ambition. By the late fifteenth century, Europeans were in a position to venture far away to the shores of Africa, the southern and eastern coasts of Asia, and the New World of the Americas. European discovery was not the only outcome of these voyages: The exploitation of the peoples and lands of the New World revealed a dark side of Western civilization. Some penalties were paid even then. The influx of New World gold and silver created new human and economic problems on the European mainland. Some Europeans even began to question their civilization's traditional values.

The Chapter in Review

Review Questions

1. What did the term *Renaissance* mean in the context of fifteenth- and sixteenth-century Italy? What criticisms have been leveled against it?

2. How would you define Renaissance humanism? In what ways was the Renaissance a break with the Middle Ages, and in what ways did it owe its existence to medieval civilization?

3. Who were some of the famous literary and artistic figures of the Italian Renaissance? What did they have in common that might be described as "the spirit of the Renaissance"?

4. Why did the French invade Italy in 1494? How did this event trigger Italy's political decline? How did the actions of Pope Julius II and the ideas of Niccolò Machiavelli signify a new era in Italian civilization?

5. How did the Renaissance in the north differ from the Italian Renaissance? In what ways was Erasmus the embodiment of the northern Renaissance?

6. What factors led to the voyages of discovery? Why were the Portuguese interested in finding a route to the East? Why did Columbus sail west across the Atlantic in 1492?

Key Terms

Alexander VI (1431–1503) Known as the Borgia pope, who openly promoted the political careers of Cesare and Lucrezia Borgia, the children he had had before he became pope.

chiaroscuro (kyar-eh-SKEW-row) The use of shading to enhance naturalness in painting and drawing.

Christine de Pisan (1363–1434) Italian-born noblewoman and writer whose most famous work, *The Treasure of the City of Ladies*, chronicles the great women of history.

Ciompi Revolt A great uprising in 1378 of the poor in Florence, which established a chaotic four-year reign of power by the lower Florentine classes.

condottieri (con-da-TEE-AIR-ee) Military brokers who furnished mercenary forces to the Italian states during the Renaissance.

conquistadores (kahn-KWIS-teh-door-hez) Meaning "conquerors." The Spanish conquerors of the New World.

Cosimo de' Medici (1389–1464) Florentine banker and statesman, the first of the Medici political dynasty, who used his great wealth as a patron of learning, the arts, and architecture.

Desiderius Erasmus (1466–1536) Most famous northern humanist who looked to combine the classical ideals of humanity and civic virtue with Christian love and piety.

encomienda (en-co-mee-EN-da) The grant by the Spanish crown to a colonist of the labor of a specific number of Indians for a set period of time.

Florentine Academy An informal gathering of Florentine humanists devoted to reviving the works of Plato and the Neoplatonists.

Francesco Petrarch (1304–1374) The "father of humanism," who celebrated Rome in his *Letters to the Ancient Dead*, imaginary personal letters to Cicero, Livy, Vergil, and Horace.

Golden Bull The agreement in 1356 to establish a seven-member electoral college of German princes to choose the Holy Roman Emperor.

hacienda (ha-SEE-hen-da) A large landed estate in Spanish America.

League of Venice An alliance founded by Ferdinand of Aragon in 1495 to counter the French in Italy.

Lorenzo the Magnificent (1442–1492; r. 1478–1492) The grandson of Cosimo de' Medici and one of the most powerful patrons of the Renaissance; brought great splendor to the city of Florence and was the model for Machiavelli's *Prince*.

Mannerism A style of art in the mid- to late sixteenth century that permitted artists to express their own "manner" or feelings in contrast to the symmetry and simplicity of the art of the High Renaissance.

Pico della Mirandola (1463–1494) Author of *Oration on the Dignity of Man*, which gives perhaps the most famous Renaissance statement on the nature of humankind.

Platonism Philosophy of Plato that posits preexistent Ideal Forms of which all earthly things are imperfect models.

studia humanitatis (STEW-dee-a hew-MAHN-ee-tah-tis) During the Renaissance, a liberal arts program of study that embraced grammar, rhetoric, poetry, history, philosophy, and politics.

Treaty of Lodi (1454–1455) A political alliance that brought Milan and Naples, traditional enemies, into a union with Florence.

Notes

1. Cited by De Lamar Jensen, *Renaissance Europe: Age of Recovery and Reconciliation* (Lexington, MA: D. C. Heath, 1981), p. 111.

2. Iris Origo, *The Merchant of Prato: Francesco di Marco Datini, 1335–1410* (New York: David Godine, 1986), pp. 90–91.

3. Origo, *The Merchant of Prato*, p. 209.

4. Cf. Anthony Pagden, "The Impact of the New World on the Old: The History of an Idea," *Renaissance and Modern Studies* 30 (1986): pp. 1–11.

Chapter 11
The Age of Reformation

SCENES OF THE CRUCIFIXION
Painted on the eve of the Reformation, Matthias Grunewald's (ca. 1480–1528) *Crucifixion* shows a Christ who takes all the sins of the world into his own body, as the Blessed Virgin Mary, John the Baptist, and Mary Magdalene share the pain of his afflictions.
SOURCE: Art Archive/SuperStock

Contents and Focus Questions

The Chapter in Brief

IN THE SECOND decade of the sixteenth century, a long-building, powerful religious movement began in Saxony in Germany and spread rapidly throughout northern Europe, deeply affecting society and politics, as well as the spiritual lives of men and women. Attacking what they believed to be burdensome superstitions that robbed people of both their money and their peace of mind, Protestant reformers led a broad revolt against the medieval church. In a short time, hundreds of thousands of people from all social classes set aside the beliefs of centuries and adopted a more simplified religious practice.

The Protestant Reformation also challenged aspects of the Renaissance, especially its tendency to glorify human nature and its loyalty to Rome. Protestants were more impressed by the human potential for evil than by the inclination to do good. They encouraged parents, teachers, and magistrates to be firm disciplinarians, but they also embraced much of the Renaissance, especially its educational reforms and the training of students in ancient history and languages. Like the Italian humanists, the Protestant reformers prized the tools that allowed them to go directly to original sources, both biblical and classical. It was especially the study of the Hebrew and Greek scriptures that enabled them to root their challenge to Rome in the authority of biblical antiquity.

11.1 Society and Religion

What was the social and religious background of the Reformation?

The Protestant **Reformation** occurred at a time of sharp conflict between the emerging nation-states of Europe bent on conformity and centralization within their realms and the self-governing towns and villages long accustomed to running their own affairs. Since the late fourteenth century, the territorial ruler's law and custom had progressively overridden local law and custom almost everywhere. The towns remained keenly sensitive to the loss of traditional rights and freedoms. Many townspeople and village folk perceived in the Protestant revolt an ally in their struggle to remain politically free and independent.

11.1.1 Social and Political Conflict

The Reformation broke out first in the free imperial cities of Germany and Switzerland, and the basic tenets of Lutheran and Zwinglian Protestantism remained visible in subsequent Protestant movements. There were sixty-five free imperial cities, each a small kingdom unto itself. Most had Protestant movements but with mixed success and duration: Some quickly became Protestant and remained so, some were Protestant only for a short time, and still others developed mixed confessions. Frowning on sectarianism and aggressive proselytizing, they made it possible for Catholics and Protestants to live side by side with appropriate barriers between them.

A seeming life-and-death struggle with higher princely or royal authority was not the only conflict late medieval cities were experiencing. They also coped with deep social and political divisions. Certain groups favored the Reformation more than others. In many places, the guilds, whose members were socially rising and economically prospering, were in the forefront of the Reformation. Evidence also suggests that people who felt pushed around and bullied by either local or distant authority—a guild by an autocratic local government, or a city or region by a powerful prince or king—could find an ally in the Protestant movement.

Social and political experience also influenced religious change in town and countryside. A Protestant sermon or pamphlet praising religious freedom seemed directly relevant, for example, to the townspeople of German and Swiss cities facing incorporation into the territory of a powerful local prince, who viewed them as his subjects rather than as free citizens. When Martin Luther and his followers wrote, preached, and sang about a priesthood of all believers, while ridiculing papal laws as arbitrary human inventions, they touched both political and religious nerves. This was also true in the villages and in the towns. Like city dwellers, the peasants on the land heard in Protestant sermons and read in Protestant pamphlets promises of political liberation, even a degree of social betterment. More than the townspeople, the peasants found their traditional liberties—from fishing and hunting rights to representation in local diets—progressively being chipped away by the secular and ecclesiastical landlords of the age.

11.1.2 Popular Religious Movements and Criticism of the Church

The Protestant Reformation could not have occurred without the challenges to the medieval church during its "exile" in Avignon, the Great Schism, the Conciliar period, and the Renaissance papacy. For too many, the medieval church had ceased to provide a viable foundation for religious piety. Many intellectuals and laypeople felt a sense of spiritual crisis. At the Diet of Worms in 1521, the German nobility presented the emperor with a list of 102 "oppressive [church] burdens and abuses" said to be corrupting the care of German souls. Between the secular pretensions of the papacy and the dry teaching of Scholastic theologians, laity and clerics both sought a more heartfelt religious piety.

A variety of factors contributed to the growing lay criticism of the church. Urban laypeople were increasingly knowledgeable about the world around them and the rulers who controlled their lives. They had traveled widely—as soldiers, pilgrims, explorers, and traders. New postal systems and the printing press increased the information at their disposal, and a new age of books and libraries raised literacy and heightened curiosity. Laypeople were free to shape the cultural and religious life of their communities.

From the Albigensians, Waldensians, Beguines, and Beghards in the thirteenth century to the Lollards and Hussites in the fifteenth, lay religious movements shared a common goal of religious simplicity in the imitation of Jesus. (For an example of faith as serenity and inner peace in the face of evil, see the "Closer Look" sidebar, which follows below.) The laity were inspired by a simple religion of love and self-sacrifice like that of Jesus and the disciples, and they looked to a more egalitarian church—one that gave its members a voice.

11.1.2.1 LAY CONTROL OVER RELIGIOUS LIFE   On the eve of the Reformation, Rome's international network of church offices, which had unified Europe religiously during the Middle Ages, was falling apart in many areas. The collapse was hurried along by a growing sense of regional identity, an increasingly competent local secular administration, and a newly emerging nationalism. The long-entrenched system of *benefices* of the medieval church had permitted ecclesiastical posts to be sold to the highest bidders and had often failed to require that priests and bishops live in their parishes and dioceses. Such a system threatened a vibrant, lay spiritual life. The substitutes hired by nonresident, clerical holders of benefices frequently lived elsewhere, many in Rome. They milked the revenues of their offices, performed their clerical chores mechanically, and had neither firsthand knowledge of, nor much sympathy for, local spiritual needs and problems. Rare was the late medieval German town that did not have complaints about the maladministration, concubinage, and financial greed of its clergy—especially the higher clergy—the bishops, abbots, and prelates.

Communities loudly protested the financial and spiritual abuses of the medieval church long before Luther published his summary of economic grievances in a treatise titled *Address to the Christian Nobility of the German Nation* in 1520. The sale of **indulgences**, in particular, had been repeatedly attacked before Luther came on the scene. On the eve of the Reformation, this practice had expanded to permit people to buy release from time in purgatory for both themselves and their deceased loved ones!

Rulers and magistrates had little objection to the sale of indulgences as long as a portion of the income from the sales remained in the local coffers. Yet when an indulgence was offered primarily for the benefit of distant interests, as with the sale of indulgences to raise money for a new Saint Peter's basilica in Rome, resistance arose for strictly financial reasons: their sale drained away local revenues.

City governments also acted to improve local religious life on the eve of the Reformation by endowing preacherships. These positions, supported by benefices, made possible the hiring of well-trained priests who provided regular preaching and pastoral care beyond the performance of the Mass. These preacherships often became platforms for Protestants.

Magistrates carefully restricted the growth of ecclesiastical properties and clerical privileges. During the Middle Ages, canon and civil law had recognized special clerical rights in both property and person. Because they were holy places of "sacral peace" and asylum, churches and monasteries were exempted from the taxes and laws that affected others. Church law also deemed it inappropriate for the clergy to burden themselves with such "dirty jobs" as military service, compulsory labor, standing watch at city gates, and other ordinary civic obligations. Nor was it thought right that the laity should sit in judgment on those who were their shepherds and intermediaries with God. The clergy, accordingly, came to enjoy an immunity from the jurisdiction of civil courts.

Already on the eve of the Reformation, the medieval church passed measures to restrict these clerical privileges and to end their abuses. Governments also grew tired of church interference in what they considered strictly secular political spheres of competence and authority. Secular authorities accordingly began to scrutinize the church's acquisition of new properties; they found ways to get around the church's right of asylum when it interrupted the secular administration of justice, placing the clergy under local tax codes.

11.2 Martin Luther and German Reformation to 1525

Why did Martin Luther challenge the church?

The conditions in Germany at the start of the sixteenth century aided the spread of Martin Luther's protest against church abuses. On the one hand, Luther experienced a profound crisis of faith that led him to question the basis of Catholic theology. Yet it was the timing of Luther's attack that made him far more successful than earlier humanists at manipulating popular anger against the clergy.

Unlike England and France, late medieval Germany lacked the political unity to enforce "national" reforms during the late Middle Ages. There were no lasting Statutes of Provisors and Praemunire, as in England, nor a Pragmatic Sanction of Bourges, as in France, limiting papal jurisdiction

A Closer Look

A Saint at Peace in the Grasp of Temptation

Unlike the saint, the demons look perplexed and disbelieving, as their every thrust fails to injure.

Although the demons are all over him, Anthony remains untouched. The artist's remarkably distinct lines keep saint and demons apart, reinforcing the saint's inner peace and serenity.

THE TRIBULATIONS OF SAINT ANTHONY
SOURCE: Martin Schongauer/National Gallery of Art, Washington D.C.

MARTIN SCHONGAUER (c. 1430–1491) was the best engraver in the Upper Rhine. In the *Tribulations of Saint Anthony*, he portrayed the devil's temptation of St. Anthony in the wilderness as a robust physical attack by demons rather than the traditional melancholic introspection. This rendering of faith as serenity amid the most brutal assault anticipated Martin Luther's great hymn of the Reformation: "A Mighty Fortress Is Our God," in which "one little word," or belief in Christ, is said to slay the devil and his minions.

Questions

1. What in this image might sway late medieval Christians to the Protestant gospel?
2. Is the caricature more humorous than frightening?
3. How effective was art in winning hearts and minds to the Reformation?
4. Asked what the Christian should do when facing the devil and his entourage, Martin Luther replied: "Spit in his Face!" Does this image reinforce Luther's stance?
5. How is faith personified in this rendering?

AETHERNA IPSE SVAE MENTIS SIMVLACHRA LVTHERVS
EXPRIMIT·AT VVLTVS CERA LVCAE OCCIDVOS·
·M·D·XX·

EARLIEST KNOWN PORTRAIT OF MARTIN LUTHER This portrait
of Martin Luther, dated 1520, depicted him as a tough, steely-eyed
monk. Afraid that this portrayal might convey defiance rather than
reform to Emperor Charles V, Elector Frederick the Wise of Saxony,
Luther's protector, ordered court painter Lucas Cranach to soften
the image. The result was an image of Luther in a traditional monk's
niche reading an open Bible—a reformer, unlike the one shown here,
who was prepared to listen as well as to instruct.
SOURCE: Foto Marburg/Art Resource, NY

and taxation on a national scale. What took place on a unified national level in England and France occurred only
locally and in piecemeal fashion within German territories
and towns. As popular resentment of clerical immunities
and ecclesiastical abuses spread among German cities and
towns, an unorganized "national" opposition to Rome
formed. German humanists had long given voice to such
criticism, and by 1517 resentment was pervasive enough
to provide a solid foundation for Luther's protest of indulgences and the theology that legitimated them.

11.2.1 "Justification by Faith Alone"

The son of a successful Thüringian miner, Martin Luther
(1483–1546) was educated in Mansfeld, Magdeburg, where
the Brothers of the Common Life had been his teachers,
and in Eisenach. Between 1501 and 1505, he attended the
University of Erfurt, where the nominalist teachings of William of Ockham and Gabriel Biel (d. 1495) prevailed. After
receiving his Master of Arts degree in 1505, Luther registered with the law faculty in accordance with his parents'

wishes, but he never studied law. To the disappointment
of his family, he instead joined the Order of the Hermits of
Saint Augustine in Erfurt on July 17, 1505.

Ordained in 1507, Luther pursued a traditional course
of study. In 1510, he journeyed to Rome on the business
of his order, finding there justification for the many criticisms of the church he had heard in Germany. In 1511, he
moved to the Augustinian monastery in Wittenberg, where
he earned his doctorate in theology in 1512; then he became
a leader within the monastery, the new university, and the
spiritual life of the city.

Luther was especially plagued by the disproportion
between his own sense of sinfulness and the perfect righteousness God required for salvation, according to traditional
church teaching. He came to despise the phrase "righteousness of God" because it demanded of him a perfection neither
he nor any other human being could attain. His insight into the
meaning of *sola fide*, "justification by faith alone," was a gradual process that took place from 1513 to 1518. The righteousness that God demands, he concluded, did not result from
charitable acts and religious ceremonies but from belief and
trust in Jesus Christ as perfect righteousness satisfying God.

The medieval church had always taught that salvation
was a joint venture, a combination of divine mercy and
human good works, what God alone could do and what
man was expected to do in return. Luther also taught that
faith without charitable service to one's neighbor was dead.
According to Luther, it was not whether good works should
be done, but how those works should be regarded. It was
unbiblical, Luther argued, to treat good works as contributing to one's eternal salvation, something only an almighty
God could bestow. He also believed that the Roman church's
conditioning of salvation on good works left many Christians counting their merits and demerits, unable to act selflessly and struggling to maintain inner peace of mind.

Good works were expected over a lifetime, Luther
taught, but not because they earned salvation. The believer
who is bound to Christ by faith already possesses God's perfect righteousness. It is this faith that sets narcissistic souls
free to serve their neighbors selflessly. Such service is ethical,
not soteriological—a good work, not a saving work. God is
pleased when those who believe in him do good works, and
he expects his people always to do them. But he does not take
those works into account when he is merciful and bestows
eternal life, which would make God a puppet of man.

11.2.2 The Attack on Indulgences

An indulgence was a remission of the temporal penalty
imposed on penitents by priests as a "work of satisfaction"
for their confessed mortal sins. According to medieval theology, after the priest absolved a penitent of guilt for sin, the
penitent remained under an eternal penalty, a punishment
God justly imposed. Priestly absolution, however, was said
to transform this eternal penalty into a temporal penalty, a

Johannes Tezelius Dominicaner Müuch/mit sei-
nen Römischen Ablaßkram/welchen er im Jahr Christi 1517. in Deutschen
landen zu marckt gebracht/wie er in der Kirchen zu Pirn in seinem
Vaterland abgemahlet ist.

JOHN TETZEL, SELLER OF INDULGENCES A contemporary caricature depicts John Tetzel, the famous indulgence preacher. The last lines of the jingle read, "As soon as gold in the basin rings, right then the soul to Heaven springs." It was Tetzel's preaching that inspired Luther to publish his ninety-five theses.
SOURCE: akg-images

In 1517, Pope Leo X (r. 1513–1521) revived a plenary Jubilee Indulgence that had first been issued by Pope Julius II (r. 1503–1513), the proceeds of which were to rebuild St. Peter's Basilica in Rome. Such an indulgence promised forgiveness of all outstanding unexpiated sins upon the completion of certain acts. That indulgence was subsequently preached on the borders of Saxony in the territories of the future Archbishop Albrecht of Mainz, who was much in need of revenues because of the large debts he had incurred to gain a papal dispensation to hold three ecclesiastical appointments at the same time.

The selling of the indulgence became a joint venture of Albrecht, the Augsburg banking house of Fugger, and Pope Leo X, with half the proceeds going to the pope and half to Albrecht and his creditors. The famous indulgence preacher John Tetzel (d. 1519) was enlisted to preach the indulgence in Albrecht's territories. A seasoned professional, he knew how to stir ordinary people to action:

Don't you hear the voices of your dead parents and other relatives crying out, "Have mercy on us, for we suffer great punishment and pain. From this you could release us with a few alms. . . . We have created you, fed you, cared for you, and left you our temporal goods. Why do you treat us so cruelly and leave us to suffer in the flames, when it takes only a little to save us?"[1]

When Luther posted his ninety-five theses against indulgences on the door of Castle Church in Wittenberg on October 31, 1517, he protested especially Tetzel's claim that indulgences remitted sins and released unrepentant sinners from punishment in purgatory. Luther believed that these claims went far beyond the traditional practice and implied that salvation could be bought and sold.

11.2.3 Election of Charles V

The ninety-five theses were embraced by Nuremberg humanists, who translated and widely circulated them. This made Luther a central figure in an already organized national German cultural movement against foreign influence and competition, particularly on the part of the Italians. In October, he was summoned before the general of the Dominican order in Augsburg to answer for his criticism of the church. Yet as sanctions were being prepared against him, Emperor Maximilian I died on January 12, 1519—a fortunate event for the budding Reformation as it turned attention away from heresy in Saxony to the contest for a new Holy Roman Emperor. In that contest, the pope backed the French king, Francis I. However, Charles I of Spain, only nineteen years old, successfully succeeded his grandfather as Emperor **Charles V.** (See Map 11–1.)

manageable "work of satisfaction" a penitent might perform here and now through prayer, fasting, almsgiving, retreats, or pilgrimages. Penitents who defaulted on such prescribed works of satisfaction could expect to suffer for them in purgatory for an indefinite time before entering heaven.

Indulgences had originally been given to Crusaders who could not complete their penances because they had fallen in battle. By the late Middle Ages, indulgences had become an aid to laypeople anxious over future suffering in purgatory for neglected penances or unexpiated sins. In 1343, Pope Clement VI (r. 1342–1352) proclaimed the existence of a "treasury of merit," an infinite reservoir of good works in the church's possession that could be dispensed at the pope's discretion. Based on this treasury, Rome sold "letters of indulgence," which made good on the works of satisfaction owed by penitents. In 1476, Pope Sixtus IV (r. 1471–1484) extended indulgences to the unrepented sins of all Christians in purgatory.

By Luther's time, indulgences were regularly dispensed for small cash payments, modest sums that were regarded as a good work of almsgiving. Indulgence preachers presented them to the laity as remitting not only their own future punishments, but also those of dead relatives presumed still to be suffering in purgatory.

Map 11–1 THE EMPIRE OF CHARLES V

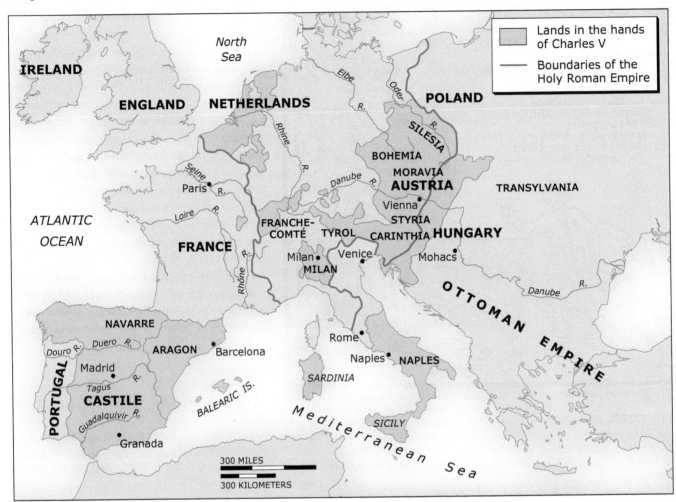

Dynastic marriages and simple chance placed into Charles's hands power over the lands shown here, plus Spain's overseas possessions. Crowns and titles rained down on him; his election in 1519 as emperor gave him new distractions and responsibilities.

Charles was blessed by both the long tradition of the Habsburg imperial rule and a massive Fugger campaign chest that secured the votes of the seven imperial **electors**. The most prominent among the seven was Frederick the Wise, Luther's lord and protector. Frederick took great pride in his new University of Wittenberg, and he was not about to let any harm come to his famous court preacher.

11.2.4 Luther's Excommunication and the Diet of Worms

In the same month in which Charles was elected emperor, Luther debated Ingolstadt professor **John Eck** in Leipzig on June 27, 1519. During this contest, Luther challenged the infallibility of the pope and the inerrancy of church councils, appealing for the first time to the sovereign authority of Scripture alone. He cut all ties to the old church when he further defended certain teachings of John Huss, who had been condemned to death for heresy at the Council of Constance.

In 1520, Luther signaled his new direction with three famous pamphlets. The *Address to the Christian Nobility of the German Nation* urged the German princes to force reforms on the Roman church, especially to curtail its political and economic power in Germany. The *Babylonian Captivity of the Church* attacked the traditional seven sacraments, arguing that only two—baptism and the Eucharist—were unquestionably biblical, and it exalted the authority of Scripture, church councils, and secular princes over that of the pope. The eloquent *Freedom of a Christian* summarized the new teaching of salvation by faith alone.

On June 15, 1520, Leo's papal bull *Exsurge Domine* or "Arise, O Lord," condemned Luther for heresy and gave him sixty days to retract. The final bull of excommunication was issued on January 3, 1521.

In April 1521, Luther presented his views before the **Diet of Worms**, over which the newly elected Emperor Charles V presided. Ordered to recant, Luther declared that to do so would be to act against Scripture, reason, and his conscience. On May 26, 1521, he was placed under the

Compare and Connect

Can Anyone Understand the Word of God?

BOTH LUTHER AND ERASMUS WERE FIERCE CRITICS of papal excesses and priestly malfeasance. This did not mean, however, that they agreed on fundamental issues of Christian theology and doctrine. For all his complaints, Erasmus was a Catholic and believed that the Church could be reformed from within. Luther, in contrast, believed that a return to authentic Christianity required a complete rethinking of Christian institutions. In 1524, Erasmus laid out his objections to Luther's teachings in a pamphlet entitled *On the Freedom of the Will*. The following year, Luther responded with *The Bondage of the Will*. In the excerpts included below, Luther and Erasmus debated a crucial point of contention between Catholics and Protestants. Can anyone understand the Bible, or is it necessary for the Church and its priests to interpret the Bible for ordinary believers?

Before Reading

- Take note of the tone of the exchange. Is it respectful, contentious, angry?
- Think about what was at stake and why Luther and Erasmus would think this issue was so important.
- Consider the larger audience and who the two men may have been seeking to influence.

Questions

1. Why did Erasmus believe that authoritative interpretations of the Bible were necessary? Why did Luther believe that they were not?
2. How did each man support his argument? What kinds of evidence did they rely on?
3. What were the larger implications of Luther's position? Why did Erasmus believe that Luther's ideas were so dangerous?

I. ERASMUS OF ROTTERDAM, *ON THE FREEDOM OF THE WILL* (1524)

I hear the objection, What need is there of an interpreter when the Scripture itself is crystal clear? But if it is so clear, why have so many outstanding men in so many centuries been blind, and in a matter of such importance, as these would appear? If there is no obscurity in Scripture, what was the need of the work of prophecy in the days of the apostles? . . . If to those who have succeeded to the place of the apostles, they will object that for many centuries many have succeeded to the office of the apostles who have nothing of the apostolic Spirit. And yet of these men, other things being equal, it may be concluded as more probable that God has infused his Spirit into those whom he has ordained, just as we may more probably believe grace to be given to the baptized than to the unbaptized. . . . You say, "What has a miter to do with the understanding of Holy Scripture?" I reply, "What has a sack-cloth or a cowl?" You say, "What has the knowledge of philosophy to do with the knowledge of sacred letters?" I reply, "What has ignorance?" You say, "What has an assembled synod to do with the understanding of Scripture, in which it may be that there is nobody who has the Spirit?" I reply, "What, then, of private conventicles of the few, of whom it is much more likely that none has the Spirit?" Paul cries, "Do you wish for proof of Christ who dwells in me?" (II Cor. 13:3). The apostles were not believed unless miracles created belief in their doctrine. Now every Tom, Dick and Harry claims credence who testifies that he has the Spirit of the gospel. Seeing that the apostles shook off vipers, healed the sick, raised the dead, and by laying on of hands bestowed the gift of tongues, they were at length believed, but they were scarcely believed for teaching paradoxes! But now these people bring forth what common opinion accounts as more than paradoxes, yet not one of them has so far appeared who can cure even a lame horse! And miracles apart, would that they could equal the sincerity and simplicity of the apostolic character which for us slow of heart would suffice instead of miracles.

II. MARTIN LUTHER, *THE BONDAGE OF THE WILL* (1525)

I admit, of course, that there are many texts in the Scriptures that are obscure and abstruse, not because of the majesty of their subject matter, but because of our ignorance of their vocabulary and grammar; but these texts in no way hinder a knowledge of all the subject matter of Scripture. For what still sublimer thing can remain hidden in the Scriptures, now that the seals have been broken, the stone rolled from the door of the sepulcher (Matt. 27:66; 28:2), and the supreme mystery brought to light, namely that Christ the Son of God has been made man, that God is three and one, that Christ has suffered for us and is to reign eternally? . . . It is true that for many people much remains abstruse; but this is not due to the obscurity of Scripture, but to the blindness or indolence of those who will not take the trouble to look at the very clearest truth. It is as Paul says of the Jews in II. Cor. (3:15): A veil lies over their minds"; and again: "If our gospel is veiled, it is veiled only to those who are perishing, whose minds the god of this world has blinded" (II Cor. 4:3 f.). With similar temerity a man might veil his own eyes or go out of the light into the darkness and hide himself and then blame the sun and the day for being obscure. Let miserable men, therefore, stop imputing with blasphemous perversity the darkness and obscurity of their own hearts to the wholly clear Scriptures of God. . . . To put it briefly, there are two kinds of clarity in Scripture, just as there are also two kinds of obscurity: one external and pertaining to the ministry of the Word, the other located in the understanding of the heart. If you speak of the internal clarity, no man perceives one iota of what is in the Scriptures unless he has the Spirit of God. All men have a darkened heart, so that even if they can recite everything in Scripture, and know how to quote it, yet they apprehend and truly understand nothing of it. They neither believe in God, nor that they themselves are creatures of God nor anything else, as Ps. 13(14:1) says: "The fool has said in his heart, 'There is no god.'" For the Spirit is required for the understanding of Scripture, both as a whole and in any part of it. If, on the other hand, you speak of the external clarity, nothing at all is left obscure or ambiguous, but everything there is in the Scriptures has been brought out by the Word into the most definite light, and published to all the world.

SOURCES: (I) From E. Gordon Rupp and Philip S. Watson, eds., *Luther and Erasmus: Free Will and Salvation* (Louisville, Kentucky: Westminster John Knox Press, 1969), pp. 44–46. (II) From E. Gordon Rupp and Philip S. Watson, eds., *Luther and Erasmus: Free Will and Salvation* (Louisville, Kentucky: Westminster John Knox Press, 1969), pp. 109–112.

imperial ban, which made him an "outlaw" to secular as well as religious authority. For his own protection, friends disguised and hid him in Wartburg Castle at the instruction of Elector Frederick. There, he spent almost a year, from April 1521 to March 1522. During his stay, he translated the New Testament into German using Erasmus's new Greek text and Latin translation, while directing by correspondence the first steps of the Reformation in Wittenberg.

11.2.5 Imperial Distractions: War with France and the Turks

The Reformation was greatly helped in these early years by the emperor's war with France and the advance of the Ottoman Turks into eastern Europe. Against both adversaries Charles V, who remained a Spanish king with dynastic responsibilities in Spain and Austria, needed loyal German troops, to which end he sought friendly relations with the German princes. From 1521 to 1559, the Habsburg dynasty in Spain and the Valois dynasty in France fought four major wars over disputed territories within Italy and along their respective borders.

Thus preoccupied, the emperor agreed through his representatives at the German Diet of Speyer in1526 that each German territory was free to enforce the Edict of Worms of 1521 against Luther "so as to be able to answer in good conscience to God and the emperor." That concession in effect gave the German princes, who five years earlier had refused to publish the emperor's condemnation of Luther, territorial sovereignty in their religious matters. It also bought the Reformation some time to put down deep roots in Germany and Switzerland. Speyer proved to be a true precedent for the final settlement of religious conflict in the empire. Later, the Peace of Augsburg in 1555 would enshrine regional princely control over religion in imperial law.

11.2.6 How the Reformation Spread

In the late 1520s and 1530s, the Reformation passed from the free hands of the theologians and pamphleteers into the firmer ones of the magistrates and princes. In many cities, the latter quickly mandated new religious reforms. Many rulers had themselves worked for decades to bring about basic church reforms, and they welcomed Lutheran preachers as new allies. Reform now ceased to be merely slogans and was transformed into laws all townspeople had to obey.

The elector of Saxony and the prince of Hesse, the two most powerful German Protestant rulers, led the politicization of religious reform within their territories. Like the urban magistrates, the German princes recognized the political and economic opportunities offered them by the demise of the Roman Catholic Church in their lands. Soon they were pushing Protestant faith and politics onto their neighbors. In the 1530s, German Protestant lands formed a powerful defensive alliance, the Schmalkaldic League, and prepared for war with the Catholic emperor. (See "Encountering the Past" sidebar on the diffusion of Protestant ideas, which follows below.)

11.2.7 The Peasants' Revolt

In its first decade, the Reformation suffered more from internal division than from imperial interference. By 1525, Luther had become almost as much an object of protest within Germany as was the pope. Original allies, sympathizers, and fellow travelers increasingly declared their independence from Wittenberg.

Like the German humanists, the German peasantry also had at first believed Luther to be an ally. Since the late fifteenth century, the peasantry had opposed the efforts of their secular and ecclesiastical lords to override their traditional laws and customs and to subject them to new territorial regulations and taxes. Peasant leaders, several of whom had been Lutherans, saw in Luther's teaching about Christian freedom and his criticism of monastic landowners a point of view close to their own. They openly solicited Luther's support of their alleged "Christian" political and economic rights, including a revolutionary demand of release from serfdom.

Luther had initially sympathized with the peasants, condemning the tyranny of the princes and urging them to meet the just demands of the peasants. Lutheran pamphleteers made Karsthans ("Hans with a hoe"), the burly, hardworking peasant who earned his bread by the sweat of his brow, a model of the honest life God wanted all people to live.

The Lutherans, however, were not social revolutionaries, and they saw no hope for their movement if it became intertwined with a peasant revolution. When the peasants revolted

Encountering the Past

Pictures, Preachers, and Songs

THERE IS NO QUESTION THAT PRINTING played an important role in the spread of Protestant ideas. Historians have long noted the explosion of pamphlet literature that accompanied the Reformation, and pointed out that earlier, less-successful reform efforts lacked this powerful tool. To fully understand how Protestant ideas spread and developed, however, we must go beyond

ARMED ONLY WITH THE BIBLE In this woodcut, the Jesuits try to prop up Pope Leo X in a debate with Martin Luther. Although the pope has an army of clergy behind him, Luther is armed with nothing but the Bible. Note the contrast between the simplicity of Luther's dress and that of Leo X.
SOURCE: INTERFOTO/Alamy Stock Photo

the invention of the printing press. After all, the vast majority of early modern Europeans were illiterate. We know that many ordinary people were deeply engaged in the religious upheavals of the sixteenth and seventeenth centuries. So how did the Reformation reach them? How did they learn about the ideas of Luther, Calvin, and others?

We can start by recognizing that the print revolution went beyond the printed word. It also allowed for printed woodcuts and engravings. Protestant reformers used images to illustrate their points and to attack the Catholic Church. Sometimes these images were meant to inspire and uplift, and to show Protestant leaders as truly righteous men. In other cases, images were used to denigrate the opponents of Protestantism in the crudest possible ways. One widely circulated woodcut was titled, "The Origins of Monks," and showed demons and devils defecating Catholic clergymen into a large vat.

More important than images, however, was the preaching revival that accompanied the Reformation. Protestant sermons played a crucial role in spreading new religious ideas. In the decade following Luther's break with Rome, Protestant preachers often lacked formal churches. So they preached outdoors or in public buildings to large crowds. The relative informality of such settings contributed to a more interactive relationship between speaker and audience. Protestant preachers expected their listeners to respond to their sermons, to voice their approval, to register the importance of what they were hearing.

Finally, the active participation of lay people in Protestant sermons and services was taken to another level with religious songs and hymns. Singing came to hold a central place in Protestant services, and Protestants used songs to communicate their message both inside and out of churches. Many Protestant groups used songs to record the history of their movement, writing new hymns to celebrate the faith and courage of those who were persecuted for their Protestant beliefs. These songs were shared between congregations, and spread as believers taught them to each other.

Questions

1. How did the Reformation spread among illiterate people?
2. How might the *way* the Reformation spread have affected the development of Protestant ideas?

SOURCE: Robert Scribner, *Popular Culture and Popular Movements in Reformation Germany* (London: The Hambledon Press, 1987).

PEASANT LEADER JACOB RORBACH AT THE STAKE After the defeat of rebellious peasants in and around the city of Heilbronn, Jacob Rorbach, a well-to-do peasant leader from a nearby village, was tied to a stake and slowly roasted to death.

SOURCE: Library of Congress Prints and Photographs Division

against their landlords from 1524 to1525, invoking Luther's name, Luther predictably condemned them as "un-Christian" and urged the princes to crush the revolt mercilessly. Tens of thousands of peasants (estimates run between 70,000 and 100,000) died by the time the revolt was suppressed.

For Luther, the freedom of the Christian lay in inner spiritual release from guilt and anxiety, not in revolutionary politics. Had he and the reformers joined the **peasants' revolt**, Luther would have contradicted his own teaching, likely sharing the fate of former Lutherans who died as leaders of such revolts. In that scenario, the German Reformation would not have survived beyond the 1520s. Still, many critics believe that Luther's decision ended the promise of the Reformation as a social and moral force in history.

11.3 The Reformation Elsewhere

Where did other reform movements develop, and how were they different from Luther's?

Although the German Reformation was the first, Switzerland and France had their own independent church reform movements almost simultaneously with Germany's. From them developed new churches as prominent and lasting as the Lutheran. As in Germany, the reform movement

in Zurich relied on a compelling leader with both personal inspiration and strong popular support, but discontent with the modest results of Martin Luther and Ulrich Zwingli gave rise to the formation of more radical splinter groups. In Geneva, however, John Calvin would take advantage of political revolt to create a new church.

11.3.1 Ulrich Zwingli and the Swiss Reformation

Switzerland was a loose confederacy of thirteen autonomous *cantons*, or states, and their allied areas. (See Map 11–2.) Some cantons became Protestant, some remained Catholic, and a few others managed to find a compromise. There were two conditions that inspired the Swiss Reformation. First was the growth of national sentiment stemming from popular opposition to foreign mercenary service. (Providing mercenaries for Europe's warring nations was a major source of Switzerland's livelihood.) Second was a desire for church reform that had persisted in Switzerland since the councils of Constance (1414–1417) and Basel (1431–1449).

11.3.1.1 THE REFORMATION IN ZURICH Ulrich Zwingli (1484–1531), the leader of the Swiss Reformation, had been humanistically educated. He credited Erasmus over Luther with having set him on the path to reform. He served as a chaplain with Swiss mercenaries who were on the losing side in the disastrous Battle of Marignano in Italy in 1515. Thereafter he became an eloquent critic of Swiss mercenary service, believing it threatened both the political sovereignty and the moral fiber of the Swiss confederacy. By 1518, Zwingli was also widely known for his opposition to the sale of indulgences and to religious superstition.

In 1519, Zwingli competed for the post of people's priest in the main church of Zurich. His candidacy was initially questioned after he acknowledged fornicating with a barber's daughter, who had since delivered a child. Zwingli successfully minimized the affair, claiming the woman in question had been a skilled seducer, and denying any paternity as she had had affairs with other men as well. Zwingli's conduct was not so scandalous to contemporaries, who sympathized with the plight of a celibate clergy. In fact, one of Zwingli's first acts as a reformer was to petition for an end to clerical celibacy and for the right of clergy legally to marry, a practice accepted in all Protestant lands.

From his new position as people's priest in Zurich, Zwingli engineered the Swiss Reformation. In March 1522, he was party to the breaking of the Lenten fast—then an act of protest analogous to burning one's national flag today. Zwingli's reform guideline was simple and effective: Teachings that lacked literal support in Scripture were neither to be believed nor to be practiced. As had also happened with Luther, that Zwingli's instruction soon raised questions about such honored traditional teachings and practices as fasting, transubstantiation, the worship of

Map 11–2 THE SWISS CONFEDERACY

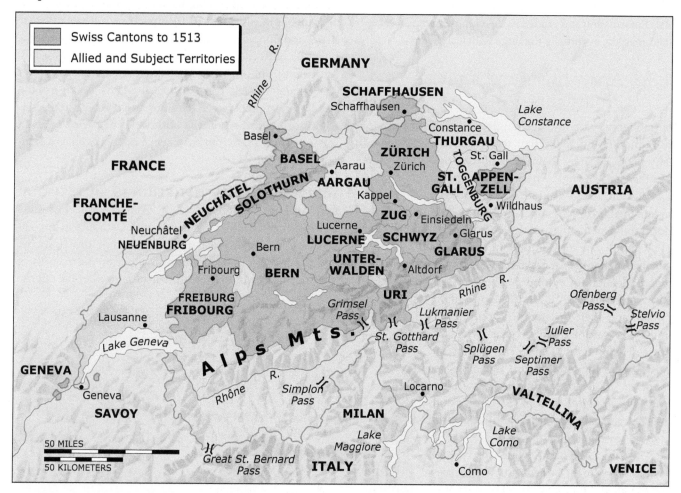

Although nominally still a part of the Holy Roman Empire, Switzerland grew from a loose defensive union of the central forest cantons in the thirteenth century into a fiercely independent association of regions with different languages, histories, and finally, religions.

saints, pilgrimages, purgatory, clerical celibacy, and certain sacraments. A disputation held on January 29, 1523, concluded with the city government's sanction of Zwingli's Scripture test. Thereafter Zurich became the center of the Swiss Reformation. The new regime imposed a harsh discipline that made the city one of the first examples of puritanical Protestantism.

11.3.1.2 THE MARBURG COLLOQUY Landgrave Philip of Hesse (1504–1567) sought to unite Swiss and German Protestants in a mutual defense pact. However, Luther and Zwingli's bitter theological differences, especially over the nature of Christ's presence in the Eucharist, spoiled his efforts. Zwingli favored a symbolic interpretation of Christ's words, "This is my body." Christ, he argued, was spiritually, not bodily, present in the bread and wine of the Eucharist. Luther, on the contrary, insisted that Christ's human nature shared the properties of his divine nature. Hence, where Christ was spiritually present, he could also be bodily present, because of his special human nature. Luther wanted no part of an abstract, spiritualized Christ, while Zwingli feared Luther was still mired in medieval sacramental theology.

Philip of Hesse brought the two Protestant leaders together in his castle in Marburg in early October 1529 to work out their differences, but the effort proved to be in vain. Although cooperation between the two Protestant sides did not cease altogether, the disagreement splintered the Protestant movement theologically and politically. Separate defense leagues formed, and semi-Zwinglian theological views came to be embodied in the non-Lutheran *Tetrapolitan Confession* prepared by the Strasbourg reformers Martin Bucer and Caspar Hedio in 1530.

11.3.1.3 SWISS CIVIL WARS As the Swiss cantons divided between Protestantism and Catholicism, civil wars erupted. There were two major battles, both at Kappel, one in June 1529 and a second in October 1531. The first ended in a Protestant victory, which forced the Catholic cantons to break their foreign alliances and to recognize the rights of Swiss Protestants. After the second battle, Zwingli lay wounded on the battlefield; when discovered, he was unceremoniously executed, his remains then hacked into pieces and scattered so his followers would have no relics to console and inspire them. The subsequent treaty confirmed the right of each canton to determine its own religion. Heinrich Bullinger (1504–1575), Zwingli's protégé and later son-in-law, became the new leader of the Swiss Reformation and guided its development into an established religion, eventually to merge with Calvinism.

11.3.2 Anabaptists and Radical Protestants

The moderate pace and seemingly low ethical results of the Lutheran and Zwinglian reformations discontented many people, among them some of the original followers of Luther and Zwingli. These were devout fundamentalist Protestants who desired a more rapid and thorough implementation of Apostolic Christianity. They accused the reform movements that went before them of having gone only halfway. The most important of these radical groups were the **Anabaptists**, the sixteenth-century ancestors of the modern Mennonites and Amish. The Anabaptists were especially distinguished by their rejection of infant baptism and their insistence on only adult baptism, as was the case with Jesus, who was baptized as an adult. (The term *Anabaptism* derives from the Greek word meaning "to rebaptize.") Only a thoughtful consenting adult, able to understand the Scriptures and what the biblical way of life required, could enter the covenant of faith.

Although Luther and Zwingli also taught that believers must believe for themselves (Luther called it the "priesthood of all believers"), they retained the historical practice of infant baptism, despite the absence of any clear biblical mandate. They argued that the congregation "believed for the infant," stood in his or her place, and pledged to raise the baptized infant in the faith. According to Luther and Zwingli, the communal nature and responsibility of the church were more significant to Christianity than the radical individualism the Anabaptists asserted.

11.3.2.1 CONRAD GREBEL AND THE SWISS BRETHREN Conrad Grebel (1498–1526), with whom Anabaptism originated, performed the first adult rebaptism in Zurich in January 1525. Initially a coworker of Zwingli's and an even greater biblical literalist, Grebel broke openly with him. In a religious disputation in October 1523, Zwingli supported the city government's plea for a peaceful, gradual removal of resented traditional religious practices—not the rush to perfection the Anabaptists demanded.

The alternative of the Swiss Brethren, as Grebel's group came to be called, was embodied in the *Schleitheim Confession* of 1527. This document distinguished Anabaptists not only by their practice of adult baptism but also by their pacifism, refusal to swear oaths, and nonparticipation in the offices of secular government. By both choice and coercion, Anabaptists physically separated from established society to form a more perfect communion modeled on the first Christians. Because of the close connection between religious and civic life in the sixteenth century, the political authorities also viewed such separatism as a threat to basic social bonds, even as a form of sedition.

11.3.2.2 THE ANABAPTIST REIGN IN MÜNSTER At first, Anabaptism drew adherents from all social classes. As Lutherans and Zwinglians joined with Catholics in opposition and persecuted Anabaptists within the cities, however, a more rural, agrarian class came to make up the majority of the Anabaptists. In 1529, rebaptism became a capital offense

ANABAPTISTS BURNED AT THE STAKE IN MÜNSTER
SOURCE: Foto Marburg/Art Resource, NY

within the Holy Roman Empire. At least 1,000 and perhaps as many as 5,000 men and women were executed for rebaptizing themselves as adults between 1525 and 1618.

Brutal measures were universally applied against nonconformists after Anabaptist extremists came to power in the German city of Münster in 1534 to1535. Led by two Dutch emigrants—a baker, Jan Matthys of Haarlem, and a tailor, Jan Beukelsz of Leiden—the Anabaptists in Münster forced Lutherans and Catholics in the city either to convert or to emigrate. After their departure, the city was blockaded by besieging armies. Under such pressures, Münster was transformed into an Old Testament theocracy, replete with charismatic leaders and the practice of polygamy. The latter was implemented as a measure of social control to deal with the many recently widowed and deserted women left behind in the city. Women opposed to the practice were allowed to leave polygamous marriages.

These developments shocked the outside world, and Protestant and Catholic armies united to crush the radicals. The skeletons of the Anabaptist leaders long hung in public view as a warning to all who would offend traditional Christian sensitivities. After this episode, moderate, pacifistic Anabaptism became the norm among most nonconformists. Menno Simons (1496–1561), the founder of the Mennonites, set an example of nonprovocative separatist Anabaptism, which became the historical model for Anabaptist sects to this day.

11.3.2.3 SPIRITUALISTS Another diverse and highly individualistic group of Protestant dissenters was the **Spiritualists**. These were mostly isolated individuals distinguished by their disdain for external, institutional religion. They believed that the only religious authority was the Spirit of God, which spoke not in some past revelation, but here and now in the heart and mind of every listening individual.

11.3.2.4 ANTITRINITARIANS A final group of persecuted radical Protestants also destined for prominence in the modern world was the **Antitrinitarians**. These thinkers were exponents of a commonsense, rational, and ethical religion. They were the strongest opponents of Calvinism, especially its belief in original sin and **predestination**, and have a well-deserved reputation as defenders of religious toleration.

11.3.3 John Calvin and the Genevan Reformation

In the second half of the sixteenth century, Calvinism replaced Lutheranism as the dominant Protestant force in Europe. Calvinism was the religious ideology that inspired or accompanied massive political resistance in France, the Netherlands, and Scotland. During the reign of Elector Frederick III (r. 1559–1576), Calvinism established

PORTRAIT OF THE YOUNG JOHN CALVIN The namesake of Calvinism and its perfect embodiment, John Calvin (1509–1564), was born into a well-to-do French family, the son of the secretary to the bishop of Noyon.
SOURCE: Erich Lessing/Art Resource, NY

itself within the geographical region of the Palatinate, the German state in the Rhineland in which the Thirty Years' War, the worst of the wars of religion, would break out in 1618. Calvinists believed strongly in both divine predestination and the individual's responsibility to reorder society according to God's plan. They were determined to transform society so men and women lived their lives externally as they professed to believe internally and were presumably destined to live eternally.

The namesake of Calvinism and its perfect embodiment, **John Calvin** (1509–1564), was born into a well-to-do French family, the son of the secretary to the bishop of Noyon. At age twelve, he received church benefices that financed the best possible education at Parisian colleges and a law degree. In the 1520s, Calvin identified with the French reform party. Although he would finally reject this group as ineffectual compromisers, its members contributed much to his intellectual preparation as a religious reformer.

It was probably in the spring of 1534 that Calvin experienced that conversion to Protestantism by which he said his "long stubborn heart" was "made teachable" by God. His own experience became a personal model of reform by which he would measure the recalcitrant citizenry of

Geneva. His mature theology stressed the sovereignty of God's will over all creation and the necessity of humankind's conformity to it. In May 1534, he dramatically surrendered the benefices that had educated him and joined the budding Reformation in Geneva.

11.3.3.1 POLITICAL REVOLT AND RELIGIOUS REFORM IN GENEVA
Whereas in Saxony religious reform paved the way for a political revolution against the emperor, in Geneva a political revolution against the local prince-bishop laid the foundation for the religious change. Genevans revolted against their resident prince-bishop in the late 1520s, and the city council assumed his legal and political powers in 1527.

In late 1533, the Protestant city of Bern dispatched two reformers to Geneva: Guillaume Farel (1489–1565) and Antoine Froment (1508–1581). In the summer of 1535, after much internal turmoil, the Protestants triumphed, and the traditional Mass and other religious practices were removed. On May 21, 1536, Geneva voted officially to adopt the Reformation: "by living according to the Gospel and the Word of God … without any more Masses, statues, idols, or other papal abuses." Calvin arrived in Geneva in July 1536 after these events. He was actually en route to a scholarly refuge in Strasbourg, in flight from the persecution of French Protestants, but warring between France and Spain forced him to turn sharply south to Geneva. The Protestant leader there persuaded him to stay in the city and assist the expansion of the Reformation, threatening him with divine vengeance if he turned away from the task.

Calvin seized the opportunity and drew up the articles for the governance of the new church, as well as a catechism to guide and discipline the citizens. Both were presented for approval before the city councils in early 1537. Because of the strong measures the reformers proposed to govern Geneva's moral life, many suspected they were intent on creating a "new papacy." Opponents soon feared that Calvin and Farel were going too far too fast. Geneva's powerful Protestant ally, Bern, which had adopted a more moderate Protestant reform, pressured Geneva's magistrates to restore traditional religious ceremonies and holidays that Calvin and Farel had abolished. When Calvin and Farel opposed the magistrates' actions, they were exiled from the city.

Calvin went to Strasbourg, a model Protestant city, where he became pastor to French exiles and wrote biblical commentaries. He also produced a second edition of his masterful *Institutes of the Christian Religion*, which many consider to be the definitive theological statement of the Protestant faith. Most importantly for Calvin he had learned from the Strasbourg reformer Martin Bucer how to achieve his goals.

11.3.3.2 CALVIN'S GENEVA
In 1540, Geneva elected officials both favorable to Calvin and determined to establish full Genevan political and religious independence from Bern. They knew Calvin would be a valuable ally in that undertaking and invited him to return. He returned in September 1540, never to leave the city again. Within months of his return, the city implemented new ecclesiastical ordinances that enabled cooperation between the magistrates and the clergy in matters of internal discipline.

The controversial doctrine of predestination was at the center of Calvin's theology as justification by faith was at Luther's. Both doctrines have been criticized, Luther's for seeming to deny the believer's need to do good works and Calvin's for seeming to deny the existence of human free will. Luther believed that works were a mark of a true Christian, even though they did not make him such or save him. Calvin did not discuss predestination until the end of his great theological work, the *Institutes of the Christian Religion*. Explaining why he delayed its discussion, he described predestination as a doctrine only for mature Christians. For true believers, Calvin argued, predestination recognized that the world and all who dwell in it are in God's hands from eternity to eternity, regardless of all else. According to Calvin, when the world seems utterly godless and the devil to be its only lord, the true Christian takes consolation from the knowledge that his present life and future destiny are determined irrevocably by a loving and everlasting God. By believing that, and living as the Bible instructed them to do, Calvinists found consoling, presumptive evidence that they were among God's elect.

Possessed of such assurance, Calvinists turned their energies to transforming society spiritually and morally. Faith, Calvin taught, did not sit idly in the mind but conformed one's every action to God's law. The "elect" should at least live in a manifestly God-pleasing way if they are truly God's "elect." In the attempted realization of that goal, Calvin spared no effort. The consistory, or Geneva's regulatory court, became his instrument of power. Comprised of the elders and the pastors and presided over by one of the city's chief magistrates, this body implemented the strictest moral discipline.

After 1555, Geneva soon became home to thousands of exiled Protestants who had been driven out of France, England, and Scotland. Refugees numbering more than 5,000, most of them utterly loyal to Calvin, made up more than one-third of Geneva's population. All of Geneva's magistrates were now devout Calvinists, greatly strengthening Calvin's position in the city.

To the thousands of persecuted Protestants who flocked to Geneva in mid-century, the city was a beacon and a refuge, Europe's only free city. During Calvin's lifetime, Geneva also gained the reputation of being a "woman's paradise" because its laws severely punished men who beat their wives, behavior deemed unbefitting a true Calvinist Christian.

11.4 Political Consolidation of the Lutheran Reformation

What were the political ramifications of the Reformation?

By 1530, the Reformation was in Europe to stay. It would, however, take several decades and major attempts to eradicate it, before all would recognize this fact. With the political triumph of Lutheranism in the empire by the 1550s, Protestant movements elsewhere gained a new lease on life. The Diet of Augsburg became essential for the Lutherans to attain official status.

11.4.1 The Diet of Augsburg

Emperor Charles V devoted most of his first decade to the pursuit of politics and military campaigns outside the empire, particularly in Spain and Italy. In 1530, he returned to the empire to direct the Diet of Augsburg. This assembly of Protestant and Catholic representatives had been called to address the growing religious division within the empire in the wake of the Reformation's success. With its terms dictated by the Catholic emperor, the diet adjourned with a blunt and unrealistic order to all Lutherans to revert to Catholicism.

The Reformation was by this time too firmly established for that to occur. In February 1531, the Lutherans responded with the formation of their own defensive alliance, the Schmalkaldic League. The league took as its banner the **Augsburg Confession**, a moderate statement of Protestant beliefs that had been rejected by the emperor at the Diet of Augsburg. Under the leadership of Landgrave Philip of Hesse and Elector John Frederick of Saxony, the league achieved a stalemate with the emperor, who was again distracted by renewed war with France and the ever-resilient Turks.

11.4.2 The Expansion of the Reformation

In the 1530s, German Lutherans formed regional consistories, judicial bodies made up of theologians and lawyers, which oversaw and administered the new Protestant churches and replaced the old Catholic episcopates. Educational reforms provided for compulsory primary education, schools for girls, a humanist revision of the traditional curriculum, and instruction of the laity in the new religion.

The Reformation also entrenched itself elsewhere. Introduced into Denmark by King Christian II (r. 1513–1523), Lutheranism thrived there under Frederick I (r. 1523–1533), who joined the Schmalkaldic League. Under Christian III (r. 1536–1559), Lutheranism became the official state religion.

In Sweden, King Gustavus Vasa (r. 1523–1560), supported by a Swedish nobility greedy for church lands, embraced Lutheranism, confiscated church property, and subjected the clergy to royal authority at the Diet of Vasteras (1527).

In politically splintered Poland, Lutherans, Anabaptists, Calvinists, and even Antitrinitarians found room to practice their beliefs. Primarily because of the absence of a central political authority, Poland became a model of religious pluralism and toleration in the second half of the sixteenth century.

11.4.3 Reaction Against Protestants

Charles V made abortive efforts from 1540 to 1541 to enforce a compromise between Protestants and Catholics. As these and other conciliar efforts failed, he turned to a military solution. In 1547, imperial armies crushed the Protestant Schmalkaldic League, defeating and capturing John Frederick of Saxony and Philip of Hesse.

The emperor established puppet rulers in Saxony and Hesse and issued an imperial law

EMPEROR CHARLES V AT THE DIET OF AUGSBURG The Augsburg Confession, also known by its Latin name Confessio Augustana, summarized the key positions of the Lutheran Reformation. It was presented to the Holy Roman emperor Charles V at the Diet of Augsburg on June 25, 1530.
SOURCE: Falkenstein Heinz-Dieter/Alamy Stock Photo

mandating that Protestants everywhere readopt old Catholic beliefs and practices. Protestants were granted a few cosmetic concessions, for example, clerical marriage, with papal approval of individual cases, and communion in both bread and wine. Many Protestant leaders went into exile. In Germany, the city of Magdeburg became a refuge for persecuted Protestants and the center of Lutheran resistance.

11.4.4 The Peace of Augsburg

The Reformation was too entrenched by 1547 to be ended even by brute force. Maurice of Saxony, handpicked by Charles V to rule Saxony, had recognized the inevitable and shifted his allegiance to the Lutherans. Confronted by fierce resistance and weary from three decades of war, Charles was forced to relent. After a defeat by Protestant armies in 1552, Charles reinstated the Protestant leaders and guaranteed Lutherans religious freedoms in the Peace of Passau in August 1552. With this declaration, Charles effectively surrendered his lifelong quest for European religious unity.

The Peace of Augsburg in September 1555 made the division of Christendom permanent. This agreement recognized in law what had already been well established in practice: *Cuius regio, eius religio*, meaning the ruler of a land would determine its religion. Those discontented with the religion of their region were permitted to migrate to another.

The Peace of Augsburg did not extend official recognition to Calvinism and Anabaptism as legal forms of Christian belief and practice. Anabaptists had long adjusted to such exclusion by forming their own separatist communities. Calvinists, however, were not separatists. They remained determined to secure the right to worship publicly as they pleased and to shape society according to their own religious convictions. While Anabaptists retreated and Lutherans enjoyed the security of an established religion, Calvinists organized to lead national revolutions throughout northern Europe in the second half of the sixteenth century.

11.5 The English Reformation to 1553

How did royal dynastic concerns shape the Reformation in England?

Late medieval England had a well-earned reputation for maintaining the rights of the crown against the pope. Edward I (r. 1272–1307) had rejected efforts by Pope Boniface VIII to prevent secular taxation of the clergy. Statutes of Provisors and Praemunire passed in the mid-fourteenth century laid a foundation for curtailing payments and judicial appeals to Rome and rejecting papal appointments in England. Lollardy, a derisive description of the lower and middle working classes, aligned with humanism and

widespread anticlerical sentiment, preparing the way for Protestant ideas, which appeared in England in the early sixteenth century.

KEY EVENTS OF THE ENGLISH REFORMATION	
1529	Reformation Parliament convenes
1532	Parliament passes the Submission of the Clergy
1533	Henry VIII weds Anne Boleyn; Convocation invalidates marriage to Catherine of Aragon
1534	Act of Succession makes Anne Boleyn's children legitimate heirs to the English throne
1534	Act of Supremacy declares Henry VIII "the only supreme head of the Church of England"
1535	Thomas More executed for opposition to Acts of Succession and Supremacy
1535	Publication of Coverdale Bible
1539	Henry VIII imposes the Six Articles
1547	Edward VI succeeds the throne under protectorships of Somerset and Northumberland
1549	First Act of Uniformity imposes *Book of Common Prayer* on English churches
1553–1558	Mary Tudor restores Catholic doctrine
1558–1603	Elizabeth I fashions an Anglican religious settlement

11.5.1 The Preconditions of Reform

In the early 1520s, future English reformers met in Cambridge to discuss Lutheran writings smuggled into England by merchants and scholars. One of these future reformers was William Tyndale (ca. 1492–1536), who translated the New Testament into English from 1524 to 1525 while in Germany. Printed in Cologne and Worms, Tyndale's New Testament began to circulate in England in 1526.

Cardinal Thomas Wolsey (ca. 1475–1530), the chief minister of King Henry VIII (r. 1509–1547), and Sir Thomas More (1478–1535), Wolsey's successor, guided royal opposition to incipient English Protestantism. King Henry himself defended the seven sacraments against Luther, receiving as a reward the title "Defender of the Faith" from Pope Leo X.

11.5.2 The King's Affair

Lollardy and humanism may have provided some native seeds for religious reform, but it was Henry's unhappy marriage to Catherine of Aragon (d. 1536) and obsession to produce a male heir that broke the soil and allowed the seeds to take root. In 1509, Henry had married Catherine, the daughter of Ferdinand and Isabella of Spain and the aunt of Emperor Charles V. By 1527, the union had produced only one surviving child, a daughter, Mary. Although women could inherit the throne, Henry fretted over the political consequences of leaving only a female heir.

Henry came even to believe that God had cursed his union with Catherine, who had many miscarriages and stillbirths. The reason lay in Catherine's previous marriage to Henry's brother Arthur. After Arthur's premature death,

A SEEMINGLY ALMIGHTY HENRY VIII Hans Holbein the Younger (1497–1543) was the most famous portrait painter of the Reformation.
SOURCE: Scala/Art Resource, NY

1518, Wolsey had long been Henry's "heavy" and the object of much popular resentment. When he failed to secure the annulment through no fault of his own, he was dismissed in disgrace in 1529. Thomas Cranmer (1489–1556) and Thomas Cromwell (1485–1540), both of whom harbored Lutheran sympathies, thereafter became the king's closest advisers. Finding the path to a papal annulment unnavigable, Henry's new advisers struck a different course: why not simply declare the king supreme in English spiritual affairs as he was in English temporal affairs? Then the king could settle the king's affair himself.

11.5.3 The "Reformation Parliament"

In 1529, Parliament convened for what would be a seven-year session that earned it the title of the **"Reformation Parliament**." During this period, it passed a flood of legislation that harassed, and finally placed royal reins on, the clergy. In so doing, Parliament established a precedent that would remain a feature of English government: whenever fundamental changes are made in religion, the monarch consult with and work through Parliament. In January 1531, the Convocation (a legislative assembly representing the English clergy) publicly recognized Henry as head of the church in England "as far as the law of Christ allows." In 1532, Parliament published official grievances against the church, ranging from alleged indifference to the needs of the laity to an excessive number of religious holidays. In the same year, Parliament passed the Submission of the Clergy, which effectively placed canon law under royal control and thereby the clergy under royal jurisdiction.

In January 1533, Henry wed the pregnant Anne Boleyn, with Thomas Cranmer officiating. In February 1533, Parliament made the king the highest court of appeal for all English subjects. In March 1533, Cranmer became archbishop of Canterbury and led the Convocation in invalidating the king's marriage to Catherine. In 1534, Parliament ended all payments by the English clergy and laity to Rome and gave Henry sole jurisdiction over high ecclesiastical appointments. The Act of Succession in the same year made Anne Boleyn's children legitimate heirs to the throne, and the **Act of Supremacy** declared Henry "the only supreme head in earth of the Church of England."

When Thomas More and John Fisher, bishop of Rochester, refused to recognize the Act of Succession and the Act of Supremacy, Henry had them executed, making clear his determination to have his way regardless of the cost. In 1536 and 1538, Parliament dissolved England's monasteries and nunneries.

Henry's father, Henry VII, betrothed her to Henry to keep the English alliance with Spain intact. The two were wed in 1509, a few days before Henry VIII received his crown. Because marriage to the wife of one's brother was prohibited by both canon and biblical law (see Leviticus 18:16, 20:21), the marriage had required a special dispensation from Pope Julius II.

By 1527, Henry was also thoroughly enamored of Anne Boleyn, one of Catherine's ladies-in-waiting. He determined to put Catherine aside and take Anne as his wife. In Catholic England, however, this required a papal annulment of the marriage to Catherine. Therein lay a special problem. Pope Clement VII was then a prisoner of Emperor Charles V, who also happened to be Catherine's nephew, and he was not about to encourage the pope to annul the royal marriage. Even without Charles's coercion, it would have been virtually impossible for the pope to annul a marriage that not only had survived for eighteen years but also had been made possible by a special papal dispensation.

Cardinal Wolsey, who aspired to become pope, was placed in charge of securing the royal annulment. Lord Chancellor since 1515 and papal legate at large since

11.5.4 Wives of Henry VIII

Henry's domestic life lacked the consistency of his political life. In 1536, Anne Boleyn was executed for alleged treason and adultery, and her daughter Elizabeth, like Elizabeth's half-sister Mary before her, was declared illegitimate by her father. Henry had four more marriages. His third wife, Jane Seymour, died in 1537 shortly after giving birth to the future Edward VI. Henry wed Anne of Cleves sight unseen on the advice of Thomas Cromwell, in order to create by the marriage an alliance with the Protestant princes of Germany. Neither the alliance nor the marriage proved worth the trouble; the marriage was annulled by Parliament, and Cromwell was dismissed and executed. Catherine Howard, Henry's fifth wife, was beheaded for adultery in 1542. His last wife, Catherine Parr, a patron of humanists and reformers, for whom Henry was the third husband, survived him to marry still a fourth time—obviously she was a match for the English king.

11.5.5 The King's Religious Conservatism

Henry's boldness in politics and domestic affairs did not extend to religion. Because of Henry's actions, the pope had ceased to be head of the English church and English Bibles were placed in English churches; but despite the break with Rome, Henry remained decidedly conservative in his religious beliefs. With the Ten Articles of 1536, he made only mild concessions to Protestant tenets. Otherwise Catholic doctrine was maintained in a country filled with Protestant sentiment. Despite his many wives and amorous adventures, Henry forbade the English clergy to marry and threatened to execute clergy who were caught twice in concubinage.

Angered by the growing popularity of Protestant views, even among his chief advisers, Henry attacked them directly in the Six Articles of 1539. These reaffirmed transubstantiation, denied the Eucharistic cup to the laity, declared celibate vows inviolable, provided for private Masses, and ordered the continuation of oral confession. Protestants referred to the articles as the "whip with six stings," a clear warning from the king that religious reform would not race ahead in England during his reign. Although William Tyndale's English New Testament grew into the Coverdale Bible in 1535 and the Great Bible in 1539, and the latter was mandated for every English parish, England had to await Henry's death before it could become a genuinely Protestant country.

11.5.6 The Protestant Reformation Under Edward VI

When Henry died in 1547, his son and successor, Edward VI (d. 1553), was only ten years old. Edward reigned under the successive regencies of Edward Seymour, who became the duke of Somerset (1547–1550), and the earl of Warwick, who became known as the duke of Northumberland (1550–1553). During this time, England enacted Protestant Reformation. The new king and Somerset corresponded directly with John Calvin. During Somerset's regency, Henry's Six Articles and laws against Protestant heresy were repealed, and clerical marriage and communion with cup were sanctioned.

In 1547, the chantries, places where endowed Masses had traditionally been said for the dead, were dissolved. In 1549, the **Act of Uniformity** imposed Thomas Cranmer's *Book of Common Prayer* on all English churches. Images and altars were removed from the churches in 1550. After Charles V's victory over the German princes in 1547, German Protestant leaders had fled to England for refuge. Several of these refugees, with Martin Bucer prominent among them, now directly assisted the completion of the English Reformation.

The Second Act of Uniformity, passed in 1552, imposed a revised *Book of Common Prayer* on all English churches. A forty-two-article confession of faith, also written by Thomas Cranmer, proposed a moderate Protestant doctrine. It taught justification by faith and the supremacy of Holy Scripture, denied transubstantiation (although not the real presence), and recognized only two sacraments.

These changes were short-lived, however. In 1553, Catherine of Aragon's daughter succeeded Edward, who had died in his teens, to the throne as Mary I (d. 1558) and restored Catholic doctrine and practice with a single-mindedness rivaling that of her father. It was not until the reign of Anne Boleyn's daughter, Elizabeth I (r. 1558–1603), that England worked out a lasting religious settlement.

11.6 Catholic Reform and Counter-Reformation

What was the Counter-Reformation, and how successful was it?

The Protestant Reformation did not take the medieval church completely by surprise. There were many internal criticisms of the church and efforts at reform before there was a **Counter-Reformation** in reaction to Protestant successes. In order to sustain an adequate reform effort, the church needed to recognize a number of new orders within its ranks. With a revived ability to inspire obedience, the papacy was able to reassert church doctrine.

11.6.1 Sources of Catholic Reform

Before the Reformation began, ambitious proposals had been made for church reform. But sixteenth-century popes, ever mindful of how the councils of Constance and Basel had stripped the pope of his traditional powers, squelched such efforts to change the laws and institutions of the church.

Despite such papal foot-dragging, the old church was not without its reformers. Many new religious orders also sprang up in the sixteenth century to lead a broad revival of piety within the church. The first of these orders was the Theatines, founded in 1524 to groom devout and reform-minded leaders at the higher levels of the church hierarchy. Another new order, whose mission pointed in the opposite direction, was the Capuchins. Recognized by the pope in 1528, they hoped to return to the original ideals of Saint Francis and became popular among the ordinary people to whom they directed their ministry. The Somaschi, who became active in the mid-1520s, and the Barnabites, founded in 1530, worked to repair the moral, spiritual, and physical damage done to people in war-torn Italy.

For women, there was the influential new order of Ursulines. Founded in 1535, it established convents in Italy and France for the religious education of girls from all social classes. Another new order, the Oratorians, officially recognized in 1575, was an elite group of clerics devoted to the promotion of religious literature and church music. Among their members was the great hymnist and musician Giovanni Pierluigi da Palestrina (1526–1594).

In addition to these lay and clerical movements, the mystical piety of medieval monasticism was revived and popularized by two Spanish mystics, Saint Teresa of Avila (1515–1582) and Saint John of the Cross (1542–1591).

11.6.2 Ignatius of Loyola and the Jesuits

Of the various reform groups, none was more instrumental in the success of the Counter-Reformation than the Society of Jesus, the new order of Jesuits. Organized by **St. Ignatius of Loyola** in the 1530s, the church recognized the society in 1540. The society grew within a century from its original ten members to more than 15,000 members scattered throughout the world, with thriving missions in India, Japan, and the Americas.

Ignatius of Loyola (1491–1556) was a heroic figure. A dashing courtier and *soldiero* in his youth, he began his spiritual pilgrimage in 1521 after he had been seriously wounded during a battle with the French. During a lengthy and painful convalescence, he passed the time by reading Christian classics. So impressed was he with the heroic self-sacrifice of the church's saints and their methods of overcoming mental anguish and pain that he underwent a profound religious conversion. Henceforth, he too would serve the church as a soldier of Christ.

After recuperating, Ignatius applied the lessons he had learned during his convalescence to a program of religious and moral self-discipline that came to be embodied in the *Spiritual Exercises*. This psychologically perceptive devotional guide contained mental and emotional exercises designed to teach absolute spiritual self-mastery over one's feelings. It taught that a person could shape his or her own behavior—even create a new religious self—through disciplined study and regular practice.

Whereas in Jesuit eyes Protestants had distinguished themselves by disobedience and religious innovation, the exercises of Ignatius were intended to teach good Catholics to deny themselves and submit without question to higher church authority and spiritual direction. Perfect discipline and self-control were the essential conditions of such obedience, along with the enthusiasm of traditional spirituality and mysticism and uncompromising loyalty to the church's cause. This potent combination helped counter the Reformation and win many Protestants back to the Catholic fold, especially in Austria and parts of Germany. (See Map 11–3.)

11.6.3 The Council of Trent (1545–1563)

The broad success of the Reformation and the insistence of the Emperor Charles V forced Pope Paul III (r. 1534–1549) to call a general council of the church to reassert church doctrine. In anticipation, the pope appointed a reform commission, chaired by Caspar Contarini (1483–1542), a leading liberal theologian. Contarini's report, presented to the pope in February 1537, was so critical of the fiscal practices and simony of the papal Curia that Paul attempted unsuccessfully to suppress its publication, while Protestants circulated it as justification of their criticism.

The long-delayed council of the church, the **Council of Trent**, met in 1545 in the imperial city of Trent in northern Italy. There were three sessions, spread over eighteen years, with long interruptions due to war, plague, and imperial and papal politics. The council met from 1545 to 1547, from 1551 to 1552, and from 1562 to 1563, a period that spanned the reigns of four different popes.

Unlike the general councils of the fifteenth century, Trent was strictly under the pope's control, with high Italian prelates prominent in the proceedings. At its final session in 1562, more than three-quarters of the council fathers were Italians. Voting was limited to the high levels of the clergy; university theologians, the lower clergy, and the laity did not share in the council's decisions.

The council's most important reforms concerned internal church discipline. Steps were taken to curtail the selling of church offices and other religious goods. Many bishops who resided in Rome were forced to move to their dioceses. Trent strengthened the authority of local bishops so they could effectively discipline popular religious practices. The bishops were also subjected to new rules that required

Map 11–3 THE RELIGIOUS SITUATION, ca. 1560

By 1560, Luther, Zwingli, and Loyola were dead, Calvin was near the end of his life, the English break from Rome was complete, and the last session of the Council of Trent was about to assemble. This map shows "religious geography" of Western Europe at the time.

them to preach regularly and conduct annual visitations of their diocesan parishes, making them highly visible. Parish priests were required to be neatly dressed, better educated, strictly celibate, and active among their parishioners. To train priests, Trent also called for a seminary in every diocese.

Not a single doctrinal concession was made to the Protestants, however. Instead, the Council of Trent reaffirmed the traditional Scholastic education of the clergy; the role of good works in salvation; the authority of tradition; the seven sacraments; transubstantiation; the withholding of the Eucharistic cup from the laity; clerical celibacy; purgatory; the veneration of saints, relics, and sacred images;

and indulgences. The council resolved medieval Scholastic quarrels in favor of the theology of Saint Thomas Aquinas, further enhancing his authority within the church. Thereafter, the church most resisted groups like the Jansenists, who endorsed the medieval Augustinian tradition, a source of alternative Catholic, as well as many Protestant, doctrines.

Rulers initially resisted Trent's reform decrees, fearing a revival of papal political power and new confessional conflicts within their lands. Over time, however, and with the pope's assurances that religious reforms were his sole intent, the new legislation took hold, and parish life revived under a devout and better-trained clergy.

11.7 The Social Significance of the Reformation in Western Europe

What was the social significance of the Reformation, and how did it affect family life?

The Lutheran, Zwinglian, and Calvinist reformers all sought to work within the framework of reigning political power. Luther, Zwingli, and Calvin viewed themselves and their followers as subject to definite civic responsibilities and obligations. They wanted reform to take shape within reigning laws and institutions and remained highly sensitive to what was politically and socially possible in their age. Some scholars believe the reformers were too cautious, changed late medieval society very little, and actually encouraged acceptance of the sociopolitical status quo.

11.7.1 The Revolution in Religious Practices and Institutions

The Reformation may have been politically conservative, but by the end of the sixteenth century, it had brought about radical changes in traditional religious practices and institutions in those lands where it succeeded.

11.7.1.1 RELIGION IN FIFTEENTH-CENTURY LIFE   In the fifteenth century, on the streets of the great cities of Europe that later turned Protestant (for example, Zurich, Strasbourg, Nuremberg, and Geneva), the clergy and the religious were everywhere. They made up 6 to 8 percent of the urban population, and they exercised considerable political as well as spiritual power. They legislated and taxed, they tried cases in special church courts, and they enforced their laws with threats of excommunication.

KEY EVENTS IN THE PROTESTANT REFORMATION AND CATHOLIC REFORM ON THE CONTINENT	
1517	Luther posts ninety-five theses against indulgences
1519	Charles I of Spain elected Holy Roman Emperor (as Charles V)
1519	Luther challenges authority of pope and inerrancy of church councils at Leipzig Debate
1521	Papal bull excommunicates Luther for heresy
1521	Diet of Worms condemns Luther
1521–1522	Luther translates the New Testament into German
1524–1525	Peasants' revolt in Germany
1527	The *Schleitheim Confession* of the Anabaptists
1529	Marburg Colloquy between Luther and Zwingli
1530	Diet of Augsburg fails to settle religious differences
1531	Protestant Schmalkaldic League is formed
1534–1535	Anabaptists assume political power in Münster
1536	Calvin arrives in Geneva
1540	Jesuits, founded by Ignatius of Loyola, recognized as order by pope
1546	Luther dies
1547	Armies of Charles V crush Schmalkaldic League
1555	Peace of Augsburg recognizes rights of Lutherans to worship as they please
1545–1563	Council of Trent institutes reforms and responds to the Reformation

The church calendar regulated daily life. About one-third of the year was reserved for religious observance or celebration. There were frequent periods of fasting. On almost a hundred days of each year, a pious Christian could not, without special dispensation, eat eggs, butter, animal fat, or meat.

Monasteries, and especially nunneries, were prominent and influential institutions. The children of society's most powerful citizens resided there. Local aristocrats identified with particular churches and chapels, whose walls recorded their lineage and proclaimed their generosity. On the streets, friars begged alms from passersby. In the churches, the Mass and liturgy were read entirely in Latin. Images of saints were regularly displayed, and on certain holidays their relics were paraded about and venerated.

VIEW OF NUREMBERG   Nuremberg is a German city in Bavaria. During the Reformation, Nuremberg became a predominantly Lutheran city.
SOURCE: FALKENSTEINFOTO/Alamy Stock Photo

Local religious shrines enjoyed a booming business. Pilgrims gathered there by the hundreds—even thousands—many sick and dying, all in search of a cure or a miracle, but also for diversion and entertainment. Several times during the year, special preachers arrived in the city to sell letters of indulgence.

Many clergy walked the streets with concubines and children, although they were sworn to celibacy and forbidden to marry. The church tolerated such relationships upon payment of penitential fines.

People everywhere complained about the clergy's exemption from taxation and often from the civil criminal code. People also grumbled about having to support church offices whose occupants lived and worked elsewhere, turning the cure of souls over to poorly trained and paid substitutes. Townspeople expressed concern that the church had too much influence over education and culture.

11.7.1.2 RELIGION IN SIXTEENTH-CENTURY LIFE In these same cities, after the Reformation had firmly established itself, few changes in politics and society were evident. The same aristocratic families governed as before, and the rich generally got richer and the poor poorer. Overall numbers of clergy fell by two-thirds, and religious holidays shrank by one-third. Cloisters were nearly gone, and many that remained were transformed into hospices for the sick and poor or into educational institutions, their endowments turned over for these new purposes. A few cloisters remained for devout old monks and nuns who could not be pensioned off or lacked families and friends to care for them. These remaining cloisters died with their present inhabitants, since no new religious were allowed to enter.

The churches were reduced in number by at least one-third, and worship was conducted almost completely in the vernacular. In some, particularly those in Zwinglian cities, the walls were stripped bare and whitewashed to make sure the congregation meditated only on God's word. The laity observed no obligatory fasts. Indulgence preachers no longer appeared. Local shrines were closed, and anyone found openly venerating saints, relics, and images was subject to fine and punishment.

Copies of Luther's translation of the New Testament (1522) or, more often, excerpts from it could be found in private homes, and the new clergy encouraged meditation on the Bible. The clergy could marry, and most did. They paid taxes and were punished for their crimes in civil courts. Committees comprised of roughly equal numbers of laity and clergy, whose decisions were monitored by secular magistrates, regulated domestic moral life.

Not all Protestant clergy remained enthusiastic about this new lay authority in religion, and the laity was also ambivalent about aspects of the Reformation. More than one-half of the original converts returned to the Catholic fold before the end of the sixteenth century. Whereas one-half of Europe could be counted in the Protestant camp in the mid-sixteenth century, only one-fifth would be left by the mid-seventeenth century.[2]

11.7.2 The Reformation and Education

Another major cultural achievement of the Reformation was its implementation of many humanist educational reforms in new Protestant schools and universities. Many Protestant reformers in Germany, France, and England were humanists. And even when the reformers' views on church doctrine and human nature separated them from the humanist movement, they continued to share a common opposition to Scholasticism and a belief in the unity of wisdom, eloquence, and action. The humanist program of studies, which provided the language skills to deal authoritatively with original sources, proved to be a more appropriate tool for Protestant doctrine than it did for Scholastic dialectic, which remained dominant in the Counter-Reformation.

The Catholic counter-reformers recognized the close connections between humanism and the Reformation. Ignatius of Loyola observed how the new learning had been embraced by and served the Protestant cause. In his *Spiritual Exercises*, he insisted that when read directly, the Bible and the Church Fathers should be read under the guidance of the authoritative Scholastic theologians: Peter Lombard, Bonaventure, and Saint Thomas Aquinas. Aquinas especially, Ignatius argued, being "of more recent date," had the clearest understanding of what Scripture and the Fathers meant and therefore should guide the study of the past.

In August 1518, when Philip Melanchthon (1497–1560), "the praeceptor of Germany," a young humanist and professor of Greek, arrived at the University of Wittenberg, his first act was to reform the curriculum based on the humanist model. In his inaugural address, entitled *On Improving the Studies of the Young*, Melanchthon presented himself as a defender of good letters and classical studies against "barbarians who practice barbarous arts." By the latter, he meant the Scholastic theologians of the later Middle Ages, whose methods of reconciling the views of conflicting authorities by disputation had, he believed, undermined both good letters and sound biblical doctrine. Melanchthon saw Scholastic dominance breeding contempt for the Greek language and classical learning, and so urged the careful study of history, poetry, and other humanist disciplines.

Together, Luther and Melanchthon restructured Wittenberg's curriculum. Commentaries on Lombard's *Sentences* were dropped, as was canon law. Straightforward historical study replaced Scholastic lectures on Aristotle. Students read primary sources directly, rather than with accepted Scholastic commentary. Candidates for theological degrees defended the new doctrine based on their own study of the Bible. New chairs of Greek and Hebrew were created.

In Geneva, John Calvin and his successor, Theodore Beza, founded the Genevan Academy, which later evolved into the University of Geneva. Calvinist refugees who studied there later carried Protestant educational reforms to France, Scotland, England, and the New World.

Some famous contemporaries decried what they saw as a Protestant narrowing of the original humanist program. Erasmus, for example, came to fear the Reformation as a threat to the liberal arts and good learning. Sebastian Franck drew parallels between Luther's and Zwingli's debates over Christ's presence in the Eucharist and the old Scholastic disputation over the Immaculate Conception of the Virgin.

Humanist culture and learning nonetheless remained indebted to the Reformation. The Protestant endorsement of the humanist program of studies remained as significant for the humanist movement as the latter had been for the Reformation. Protestant schools and universities consolidated and preserved for the modern world many of the basic pedagogical achievements of humanism. There, the studia humanitatis, although often as little more than a handmaiden to theological doctrine, found a permanent home, one that remained hospitable even in the heyday of conservative Protestantism.

11.7.3 The Reformation and the Changing Role of Women

Protestant reformers favored clerical marriage and opposed monasticism and the celibate life. From this position, they challenged the medieval tendency alternately to degrade women as temptresses (following the model of Eve) and to exalt them as virgins (following the model of Mary). Protestants opposed the popular antiwoman and antimarriage literature of the Middle Ages. They praised woman in her own right, but especially in her biblical vocation as mother and housewife. Although wives remained subject to their husbands, new laws gave them greater security and protection.

Relief of sexual frustration and a remedy for fornication were prominent in Protestant arguments for universal marriage. But the reformers also viewed their wives as indispensable companions in their work, and this not solely because they took domestic cares off their husbands' minds. Luther, who married in 1525 at the age of forty-two, wrote the following of women:

> Imagine what it would be like without women. The home, cities, economic life, and government would virtually disappear. Men cannot do without women. Even if it were possible for men to beget and bear children, they still could not do without women.[3]

John Calvin wrote this upon the death of his wife:

> I have been bereaved of the best companion of my life, of one who, had it been so ordered, would not only have been the willing sharer of my indigence, but even of my death. During her life she was the faithful helper of my ministry.[4]

Such tributes were intended to counter Catholic criticism of clerical marriage as a distraction of the clergy from their ministry. They were an expression of the high value Protestants placed on marriage and family life. In opposition to the celibate ideal of the Middle Ages, Protestants stressed, as no religious movement before them had ever done, the sacredness of home and family.

The ideal of the companionate marriage—that is, of husband and wife as coworkers in a special God-ordained community of the family, sharing authority equally within the household—led to an expansion of the grounds for divorce in Protestant lands as early as the 1520s. Women gained an equal right with men to divorce and remarry in good conscience—unlike in Catholicism, where only a separation from bed and table, not divorce and remarriage, was permitted a couple in a failed marriage. The reformers were more willing to permit divorce and remarriage on grounds of adultery and abandonment than were secular magistrates, who feared liberal divorce laws would lead to social upheaval.

Typical of reforms and revolutions in their early stages, Protestant doctrines emboldened women as well as men. Renegade nuns wrote exposés of the nunnery in the name of Christian freedom and justification by faith; they declared the nunnery to be no special woman's place and that supervisory male clergy, who alone could hear the nuns' confessions and administer sacraments to them, made their lives as unpleasant and burdensome as any abusive husband. Women in the higher classes, who enjoyed new social and political freedoms during the Renaissance, found in Protestant theology a religious complement to their greater independence in other walks of life. Some cloistered noblewomen, however, protested the closing of nunneries, arguing that the cloister provided a more interesting and independent way of life than they would have known in the secular world.

Because Protestants wanted women to become pious housewives, they encouraged the education of girls to literacy in the vernacular, with the expectation that they would thereafter model their lives on the Bible. However, women also found biblical passages stressing their equality to men in the presence of God. Education also gave some women roles as independent authors on behalf of the Reformation. Although small advances from a modern perspective, these were also steps toward the emancipation of women.

11.8 Family Life in Early Modern Europe

What was family life like in early modern Europe?

Changes in the timing and duration of marriage, family size, and infant and child care suggest that family life was under a variety of social and economic pressures in the sixteenth and seventeenth centuries. These pressures manifested themselves in new marital customs as well as changes in the nature of family life.

11.8.1 Later Marriages

Between 1500 and 1800, men and women in Western Europe married at later ages than they had in previous centuries: men in their mid- to late twenties, and women in their early to mid-twenties. The canonical, or church-sanctioned, age for marriage remained fourteen for men and twelve for women. The church also recognized as valid free, private exchanges of vows between a man and a woman for whom no impediment to marriage existed. After the Reformation, which condemned such clandestine unions, both Protestants and Catholics required parental consent and public vows in church before a marriage could be deemed fully licit.

Late marriage in the West reflected the difficulty couples had supporting themselves independently. It simply took the average couple a longer time than before to prepare themselves materially for marriage. In the sixteenth century, one in five women never married, and these, combined with the estimated 15 percent who were unmarried widows, constituted a large unmarried female population. A later marriage was also a shorter marriage; in an age when few people lived into their sixties, couples who married in their thirties spent less time together than couples who married in their twenties. Also, because women who bore children for the first time at advanced ages had higher mortality rates, late marriage meant more frequent remarriage for men. As the rapid growth of orphanages and foundling homes from 1600 to 1800 makes clear, delayed marriage increased premarital sex and the number of illegitimate children.

11.8.2 Arranged Marriages

Marriage tended to be "arranged" in the sense that the parents met and discussed the terms of the marriage before the prospective bride and bridegroom became directly party to the preparations. The wealth and social standing of the bride and the bridegroom, however, were not the only things considered when youth married. By the fifteenth century, it was usual for the future bride and bridegroom to have known each other and to have had some prior relationship. Also, parents respected the couple's emotional feeling for one another. Parents did not force total strangers to live together, and children had a legal right to resist a coerced marriage, which was by definition invalid. The best marriage was one desired by both the bride and groom and their families.

11.8.3 Family Size

The Western European family was conjugal, or nuclear, consisting of a father and a mother and two to four children who survived into adulthood. This nuclear family lived within a larger household, including in-laws, servants, laborers, and boarders. The average husband and wife had six to seven children, a new birth about every two years. Of these, an estimated one-third died by age five, and one-half by their teens. Rare was the family, at any social level, that did not experience child death.

11.8.4 Birth Control

Artificial birth control, such as sponges and acidic ointments, has existed since antiquity. The church's condemnation of *coitus interruptus*, or male withdrawal before ejaculation, during the thirteenth and fourteenth centuries suggests the existence of a contraceptive mentality, that is, a conscious, regular effort at birth control. Early birth control measures, when applied, were not very effective, and for both historical and moral reasons, the church opposed them. According to Saint Thomas Aquinas, a moral act must aid and abet, never frustrate, nature's goal, and the natural end of sex was the birth of children and their godly rearing within the bounds of holy matrimony and the community of the church.

11.8.5 Wet Nursing

The church allied with the physicians of early modern Europe on another intimate family matter: Both condemned women who hired wet nurses to suckle their newborn children. Wet nursing, it appears, increased the risk of infant mortality by exposing infants to milk from women often not as healthy as the infants' own mothers and who lived under less sanitary conditions. But wet nursing was popular among upper-class women and reflected their social standing. Nursing was distasteful to some upper-class women and their husbands. Among women, vanity and convenience appear to have been motives for hiring a wet nurse, while for husbands, even more was at stake. Because the church forbade lactating women from indulging in sexual intercourse, a nursing wife could become a reluctant lover. Nursing also had a contraceptive effect (about 75 percent effective). Some women prolonged nursing their children to delay a new pregnancy, and some husbands cooperated in this form of family planning. For other husbands, however, especially noblemen and royalty who desired an abundance of male heirs, nursing could rob them of offspring and jeopardize their patrimony—hence their support of hired wet nurses.

11.8.6 Loving Families?

The traditional Western European family seemed cold and distant. Children between the ages of eight and thirteen had to leave their homes for apprenticeships, school, or employment in the homes and businesses of relatives, friends, and occasionally strangers. The emotional ties between spouses also seem to have been as tenuous as those between parents and children. Widowers and widows often married again within a few months of their spouses' deaths, and marriages with extreme difference in age between partners suggest limited affection.

In response to modern-day criticism, an early modern parent might have asked: "What greater love can parents have for their children than to equip them well for a worldly vocation?" A well-apprenticed child was a self-supporting child—a child with a future. In light of the comparatively primitive living conditions in early modern Europe, the purely utilitarian and humane side of marriage was appreciated, and it was understood when widowers and widows quickly remarried. Marriages with extreme disparity in age, however, were no more the norm in early modern Europe than the practice of wet nursing, and they received just as much criticism and ridicule.

DON QIXOTE IN ENGLISH Cover of the 1620 English translation of *The History of Don-Quichote, The First Parte.*
SOURCE: Fotosearch/Stringer/Getty Images

11.9 Literary Imagination in Transition

How was the transition from medieval to modern reflected in the works of the great literary figures of the era?

Alongside the political and cultural changes brought about by the new religious systems of the Reformation (Lutheranism, Calvinism, and Puritanism) and Catholic Reform, medieval outlooks and religious values continued to be debated, embraced, and rejected into the seventeenth century. Major literary figures of the post-Reformation period included elements of both the old and the new in their own new transitional works. Two great writers of the post-Reformation are Miguel de Cervantes Saavedra (1547–1616), writing in still deeply Catholic Spain, and William Shakespeare (1564–1616), who wrote in newly Anglican England.

11.9.1 Miguel de Cervantes Saavedra: Rejection of Idealism

Spanish literature of the sixteenth and seventeenth centuries reflects the peculiar religious and political history of Spain in this period. Traditional Catholic teaching was a major influence on Spanish life. Since the joint reign of Ferdinand and Isabella (1479–1504), the church had received the unqualified support of the reigning political power. Although there was religious reform in Spain, and genuine Protestant groups were persecuted for "Lutheranism," a Protestant Reformation never occurred there, thanks largely to the entrenched power of the church and the Inquisition. Spanish literature was greatly influenced by the lack of major Protestant movements in Spain.

A second influence on Spanish literature was the aggressive piety of Spanish rulers. Their intertwining of Catholic devotion and political power led to a preoccupation with medieval chivalric virtues, especially questions of honor and loyalty. These medieval values were a third influence on Spanish literature; the novels and plays of the period almost always focused on a test of character, bordering on the heroic, that threatened honor and reputation. In this regard, Spanish literature remained more Catholic and medieval in nature than that of England and France, where major Protestant movements had occurred. Cervantes, the writer generally acknowledged to be Spain's greatest, focused his writing on the strengths and weaknesses of traditional religious idealism.

Cervantes (1547–1616) had only a smattering of formal education. He educated himself through wide reading in popular literature and immersion in the "school of life." As a young man, he worked in Rome for a Spanish cardinal. As a soldier, he was decorated for gallantry in the Battle of Lepanto against the Turks in 1571. He also spent five years as a slave in Algiers after his ship was pirated in 1575. Later, while working as a tax collector, he was imprisoned several times for padding his accounts, and it was in prison that he began, in 1603, to write his most famous work, *Don Quixote*.

The first part of *Don Quixote* appeared in 1605. The original intent of this work was to satirize the chivalric romances then popular in Spain. But Cervantes could not conceal his deep affection for Don Quixote, the character he created as an object of ridicule: The book is satiric only on the surface and appeals as much to philosophers and theologians as to students of Spanish literature. Cervantes presented Don Quixote as a none-too-stable middle-aged man. Driven mad by reading too many chivalric romances, Quixote came to believe he was an aspiring knight obliged to prove his worthiness through brave deeds. To this end, he donned a rusty suit of armor and chose for his inspiration an unworthy peasant girl, Dulcinea, a noble lady to whom he fancied he could, with honor, dedicate his life.

Don Quixote's foil, Sancho Panza—a clever, worldly, wise peasant who served as Quixote's squire—watched with bemused skepticism as his lord battled a windmill, which he had mistaken for a dragon, and repeatedly made a fool of himself galloping across the countryside. The story ends tragically with Don Quixote's humiliating defeat at the hand of a well-meaning friend: Disguised as a knight, he defeats Quixote, forcing him to renounce his quest for knighthood. Don Quixote did not, however, come to his senses but rather returned to his village to die a brokenhearted old man.

Throughout the novel, Cervantes juxtaposes the down-to-earth realism of Sancho Panza with the old-fashioned religious idealism of Don Quixote. Readers can easily discern that Cervantes admired both characters equally and meant to portray both men as representing attitudes necessary for a happy life.

11.9.2 William Shakespeare: Dramatist of the Age

There is much less factual knowledge about Shakespeare (1564–1616) than we would expect of the greatest playwright in the English language. He married at the early age of eighteen, in 1582, and he and his wife, Anne Hathaway, were the parents of three children (including twins) by 1585. He apparently worked as a schoolteacher for a time and in this capacity gained his broad knowledge of Renaissance literature. His own reading and enthusiasm for the learning of his day are manifest in the many literary allusions that appear in his plays.

Shakespeare lived the life of a country gentleman. There is no Puritan distress over worldliness in his work. He took the new commercialism and the bawdy pleasures of the Elizabethan Age in stride and with amusement. He was a radical neither in politics nor religion. The few allusions in his works to the Puritans seem more critical than complimentary.

That Shakespeare was interested in politics is apparent from his historical plays and the references to contemporary political events that fill his work. In terms of government, he believed in the character of the individual ruler, whether Richard III or Elizabeth Tudor, rather than ideal systems or social goals. By modern standards, he was a political conservative, accepting the social rankings and the power structure of his day and demonstrating unquestioned patriotism.

Shakespeare participated in every phase of the theater's life—as a playwright, an actor, and part owner of a theater. He was a member and principal writer of a famous company of actors known as the King's Men. Between 1590 and 1610, many of his plays were performed at court, where he moved with comfort and received enthusiastic royal patronage.

Elizabethan drama was already a distinctive form when Shakespeare began writing. Unlike French drama of the seventeenth century, which was dominated by classical models, English drama developed in the sixteenth and seventeenth centuries as a blending of many forms: classical comedies and tragedies, medieval morality plays, and contemporary Italian short stories.

Two contemporaries, Thomas Kyd and Christopher Marlowe, influenced Shakespeare's tragedies. Kyd (1558–1594) wrote the first dramatic version of *Hamlet*. The tragedies of Marlowe (1564–1593) were a model for character, poetry, and style that only Shakespeare among the English playwrights of the period surpassed. Shakespeare synthesized the best past and current achievements. A keen student of human motivation and passion, he had a unique talent for getting into people's minds.

Shakespeare wrote histories, comedies, and tragedies. *Richard III* (1593), an early play, stands out among the histories, although some scholars view its portrayal of Richard as an unprincipled villain as "Tudor propaganda." Shakespeare's comedies did not reach the heights of his tragedies, but they surpass his history plays in originality.

Shakespeare's tragedies are considered his unique achievement. Four of these were written within a three-year period: *Hamlet* (1603), *Othello* (1604), *King Lear* (1605), and *Macbeth* (1606). The most original of the tragedies, *Romeo and Juliet* (1597), transformed an old popular story into a moving drama of "star-cross'd lovers."

Shakespeare's works struck universal human themes, many of which were deeply rooted in contemporary religious traditions. His plays were immensely popular with both the playgoers and the play readers of Elizabethan England. Still today, the works of no other dramatist from his age are performed in theaters or on film more regularly than his.

The Chapter in Perspective

During the early Middle Ages, Christendom had been divided into Western and Eastern churches with irreconcilable theological differences. When, in 1517, Martin Luther posted ninety-five theses questioning the selling of indulgences and the traditional sacrament of penance that lay behind them, he created a division within Western Christendom itself—an internal division between Protestants and Catholics.

The Lutheran protest came at a time of political and social discontent with the church. Not only princes and magistrates but many ordinary people as well resented traditional clerical rights and privileges. The clergy were exempted from many secular laws and taxes while remaining powerful landowners whose personal lifestyles were not that different from those of the laity. Spiritual and secular protest combined to make the Protestant Reformation a successful assault on the old church. In town after town and region after region within Protestant lands, the major institutions and practices of traditional piety were transformed.

It soon became clear, however, that the division would not stop with the Lutherans. Making Scripture the only arbiter in religion had opened a Pandora's box. People proved to have different ideas about what Scripture taught. Indeed, there seemed to be as many points of view as there were readers. Rapidly, the Reformation created Lutheran, Zwinglian, Anabaptist, Spiritualist, Calvinist, and Anglican versions of biblical religion—a splintering of Protestantism that has endured and increased until today.

Catholics had been pursuing reform before the Reformation broke out in Germany, although without papal enthusiasm and certainly not along clear Protestant lines. When major reforms finally came to the Catholic Church around the mid-sixteenth century, they were doctrinally reactionary, but administratively and spiritually flexible. The church enforced strict obedience and conformity to its teaching, but it also provided the laity with a better-educated and disciplined clergy. For laity who wanted a deeper and more individual piety, experimentation with proven spiritual practices was now permitted. By century's end, such measures had countered, and in some areas even spectacularly reversed, Protestant gains.

After the Reformation, pluralism steadily became a fact of Western religious life. It did so at first only by sheer force, since no one religious body was then prepared to concede the validity of alternative Christian beliefs and practices. During the sixteenth and seventeenth centuries, only those groups that fought doggedly for their faith gained the right to practice it freely. Despite these struggles, religious pluralism endured. Never again would there be only a Catholic Christian Church in Europe.

The Chapter in Review

Review Questions

1. What problems in the church contributed to the Protestant Reformation? Why was the church unable to suppress dissent as it had earlier?
2. What were the basic similarities and differences between the ideas of Luther and Zwingli? Between Luther and Calvin? How did the differences tend to affect the success of the Protestant movement?
3. Why did the Reformation begin in Germany? What political factors contributed to its success there as opposed to in France, Spain, or Italy?
4. What was the Catholic Counter-Reformation? What reforms did the Council of Trent introduce? Was the Protestant Reformation healthy for the Catholic Church?
5. Why did Henry VIII break with Rome? Was the "new" church he established really Protestant? How did the English church change under his successors?
6. How did relations between men and women, family size, and child care change during the Age of Reformation?

Key Terms

Act of Supremacy The declaration by Parliament in 1534 that Henry VIII, not the pope, was the head of the church in England.

Act of Uniformity Imposed Thomas Cranmer's *Book of Common Prayer* on all English churches in 1549.

Anabaptists Protestants who insisted that only adult baptism conformed to Scripture.

Antitrinitarians A group of Protestants who were the strongest opponents of Calvin's belief in original sin and predestination.

Augsburg Confession (AWGS-berg) The definitive statement of Lutheran belief made in 1530.

benefices Ecclesiastical offices for which holders receive incomes from endowments in return for services performed.

Charles V (1500–1558) The ruler of the Holy Roman Empire from 1519 until stepping down from the throne in 1556.

Council of Trent (1545–1563) A general council of the church called by Pope Paul III to reassert church doctrine in response to the Protestant Reformation.

Counter-Reformation The movement within the Catholic Church to reform in reaction to the success of the Protestants.

Diet of Worms (1521) An imperial diet of the Holy Roman Empire over which Charles V presided, in which Luther expressed his views and refused to recant.

electors Seven German princes who had the right to elect the Holy Roman Emperor.

indulgence Remission of the temporal penalty of punishment in purgatory that remained after sins had been forgiven. The practice of selling pardons for unexpiated sins began under Clement VI (r. 1342–1352).

John Calvin (1509–1564) The namesake of Calvinism who stressed the sovereignty of God's will over all creation and the necessity for humanity to conform to it.

John Eck A German Scholastic theologian and a defender of Catholicism during the Reformation; debated Luther in 1519.

peasants' revolt (1524–1525) A rebellion of the German peasantry against their landlords, which Luther condemned.

predestination The doctrine that God had foreordained all souls to salvation (the "elect") or damnation; especially associated with Calvinism.

Reformation The sixteenth-century religious movement that sought to reform the Roman Catholic Church and led to the establishment of Protestantism.

Reformation Parliament (1519) Established that the English monarch must consult with and work through parliament whenever fundamental religious changes are made.

Spiritualists A group of Protestant dissenters who believed that the Spirit of God was the only religious authority.

St. Ignatius of Loyola Organized the Society of Jesus in the 1530s to counter the Reformation and win many Protestants back to the Catholic Church.

Ulrich Zwingli (1484–1531) The leading figure of the Swiss Reformation; he opposed any belief that lacked literal support in Scripture.

Notes

1. *Die Reformation in Augenzeugenberichten*, ed. by Helmar Junghans (Düsseldorf: Karl Rauch Verlag, 1967), p. 44.

2. Geoffrey Parker, *Europe in Crisis, 1598–1648* (Ithaca, NY: Cornell University Press, 1979), p. 50.

3. *Luther's Works*, Vol. 54: *Table Talk*, ed. and trans. by Theodore G. Tappert (Philadelphia: Fortress Press, 1967), p. 161.

4. *Letters of John Calvin*, Vol. 2, trans. by J. Bonnet (Edinburgh, UK: T. Constable, 1858), p. 216; E. G. Schwiebert, *Luther and His Times* (St. Louis, MO: Concordia, 1950), pp. 226–227, 266–268, 581–602; Steven Ozment, *Protestants: The Birth of a Revolution* (New York: Doubleday, 1992), pp. 17, 154, 159–162.

Chapter 12
The Age of Religious Wars

MASSACRE OF WORSHIPPING PROTESTANTS AT VASSY, FRANCE On March 1, 1562, French troops acting on the order of the Duke of Guise attacked Protestants. The event came to be known as the Massacre of Vassy and is considered the opening act of the French wars of religion.
SOURCE: PRISMA ARCHIVO/Alamy Stock Photo

Contents and Focus Questions

The Chapter in Brief

THE LATE SIXTEENTH and seventeenth centuries saw combined religious and political conflicts fired by religion and state-building across Europe. New confessional and dynastic rivalries born of the Reformation continued to fuel bloody wars for much of the century, giving it the accursed name "The Age of Religious Wars." In France, the Netherlands, England, and Scotland, Calvinists fought Catholic rulers for the right to govern and maintain their own territories, while practicing their religious confession openly without fear. In the first half of the seventeenth century, Lutherans, Calvinists, and Catholics marched against each other in central and northern Europe in what is today remembered as The Thirty Years' War. By the mid-seventeenth century, English Puritans successfully revolted against both the Stuart monarchy and the Anglican Church.

12.1 Renewed Religious Struggle

How did religious conflict in Europe evolve over the course of the second half of the sixteenth century?

In the sixteenth century—a century prior to the **Treaty of Westphalia**—religious strife engulfed Western Europe as non-Lutheran Protestant groups fought for legal status. At the same time, the Jesuits launched a counterattack that pitted the hierarchy and central authority of the Roman Catholic Church against the decentralized rule of the Calvinists. These struggles took on both political and social significance. They also gave rise to new artistic and intellectual styles.

12.1.1 Conflict in Western Europe

In the first half of the sixteenth century, religious conflict had been confined to central Europe and was primarily a struggle by Lutherans and Zwinglians to secure rights and freedoms. In the second half of the century, the focus shifted to Western Europe—to France, the Netherlands, England, and Scotland—and became a struggle by Calvinists for recognition. After the Peace of Augsburg in 1555 and acceptance of the principle that the ruler of a region determined its religion (cuius regio, eius religio), Lutheranism became a fully legal confession in the Holy Roman Empire. The Peace of Augsburg did not, however, extend recognition to non-Lutheran Protestants. Anabaptists and other sectarian separatists continued to be labeled as heretics and anarchists, while Calvinists were not strong enough to attain legal status.

12.1.2 Conflict Outside the Empire

Outside the empire, the struggle for political and religious freedom had intensified in most lands. After the Council of Trent adjourned in 1563, Catholics organized a Jesuit-led international counteroffensive against Protestants. At the time of John Calvin's death in 1564, Geneva had become both a refuge for Europe's persecuted Protestants and an international school for Protestant resistance, producing leaders equal to the new Catholic challenge.

12.1.3 Religious Struggles: Political and Social Effects

Genevan Calvinism and Roman Catholicism, as revived by the Council of Trent, were two equally dogmatic, aggressive, and irreconcilable forces. To their critics, Calvinists may have looked like "new papists" when they dominated cities like Geneva. But when, as minorities, they found their civil and religious rights denied, Calvinists became firebrands and revolutionaries. Calvinists successfully adopted

a political organization that magnified regional and local authority. Boards of **presbyters**, or elders, represented and instructed the individual congregations that were directly shaping policies both sacred and secular.

By contrast, the **Counter-Reformation** sponsored a centralized episcopal church system hierarchically arranged from pope to parish priest, stressing obedience without question to the person at the top. The high clergy—the pope and his bishops—not the synods of local churches, were supreme. Calvinism was attractive to proponents of political decentralization who opposed hierarchical rule, whereas the Roman Catholic Church, an institution also devoted to one head and one law, found absolute monarchy congenial.

This clash between the two religions is evident in their respective art and architecture. The Catholic Counter-Reformation enjoyed the baroque style. A successor to mannerism, **baroque** art presented life in a grandiose, three-dimensional display of raw energy. The great baroque artists Peter Paul Rubens (1571–1640) and Gian Lorenzo Bernini (1598–1680) were Catholics. By contrast, the works of prominent Protestant artists were restrained, as can be seen in the gentle, searching portraits of the Dutch Mennonite, Rembrandt van Rijn (1606–1669). (See the juxtaposition of Bavarian Catholic and Palatine Calvinist churches in the "Closer Look sidebar, which follows below.)

As the religious wars engulfed Europe, the intellectuals understood the wisdom of religious pluralism and toleration more quickly than did the politicians. A new skepticism, relativism, and individualism became respectable in the sixteenth and seventeenth centuries. Bold humanist Sebastian Castellio (1515–1563) coined this pithy censure for John Calvin after his role in the execution of Anti-Trinitarian physician Michael Servetus: "To kill a man is not to defend a doctrine, but to kill a man."[1] French essayist Michel de Montaigne (1533–1592) also scornfully asked about the dogmatic mind, "What do I know?" Lutheran Valentin Weigel (1533–1588), surveying a half-century of religious strife in Germany, advised people to look within themselves for religious truth, and no longer to the hardened churches and their creeds.

Such skeptical views gained popularity in larger political circles, but at great sacrifice. Religious strife and civil war were best held in check where rulers acted to subordinate theological doctrine to political unity, urging tolerance, moderation, and compromise—even indifference—in religious matters. Rulers of this kind came to be known as *politiques*, and the most successful among them was Elizabeth I of England. By contrast, Mary I of England, Philip II of Spain, and Oliver Cromwell—all of whom took their religion with the utmost seriousness and refused any compromise—did not, in the end, achieve their political goals.

The wars of religion were both internal national conflicts and truly international wars. Catholic and Protestant subjects struggled against one another for control of

A Closer Look

Baroque and Plain Church: Architectural Reflections of Belief

Decorated altars dominate the interior of the Catholic church and make the sacrifice of the Eucharist in the Mass the center of worship.

CATHOLIC BAROQUE CHURCH, OTTOBEUREN, BAVARIA
SOURCE: Vanni/Art Resource, NY

The open Bible and raised pulpit dominate the Protestant church.

CALVINIST CHURCH, THE PALATINATE, SOUTHWESTERN GERMANY
SOURCE: PHAS/Getty Images

THE EIGHTEENTH-CENTURY CATHOLIC BAROQUE CHURCH in Ottobeuren, Bavaria, and the plain seventeenth-century Calvinist church in the Palatinate express different architectural styles and great differences in theology and worship. The Catholic church, with the intent to inspire transcendence, displays sculptures, paintings, and ornamentation, while the Calvinist church has been stripped of every possible decoration, with the intent to keep worshippers' focus on the word of God and on their own mortal souls.

Questions

1. Based on these images, what were the prominent features of a Catholic church? Of a Calvinist church?

2. What might explain or account for the differences in the two churches?

the crown of France, the Netherlands, and England. The Catholic governments of France and Spain conspired and finally sent armies against Protestant regimes in England and the Netherlands. The outbreak of the Thirty Years' War in 1618 made the international dimension of the religious conflict especially clear: Before it ended in 1648, the war drew every major European nation directly or indirectly into its deadly net.

12.2 The French Wars of Religion (1562–1598)

What caused the civil war between the Huguenots and the Catholics in France, and what was the outcome?

KEY EVENTS OF THE FRENCH WARS OF RELIGION	
1559	Treaty of Cateau-Cambrésis ends Habsburg-Valois wars
1559	Francis II succeeds to French throne under regency of his mother, Catherine de Médicis
1560	Conspiracy of Amboise fails
1562	Protestant worshippers are massacred at Vassy in Champagne by the duke of Guise
1572	The Saint Bartholomew's Day Massacre leaves thousands of Protestants dead
1589	Assassination of Henry III brings the Huguenot Henry of Navarre to the throne as Henry IV
1593	Henry IV embraces Catholicism
1598	Henry IV grants Huguenots religious and civil freedoms in the Edict of Nantes
1610	Henry IV is assassinated

French Protestants known as **Huguenots** were already under surveillance in France in the early 1520s when Lutheran writings and doctrines began to circulate in Paris. The capture of French king Francis I by the forces of Emperor Charles V at the Battle of Pavia in 1525 motivated the first wave of Protestant persecution in France. The French government hoped thereby to pacify the Habsburg victor, a fierce opponent of German Protestants, and to win their king's swift release.

A second major crackdown came a decade later. When Protestants plastered Paris and other cities with anti-Catholic placards on October 18, 1534, mass arrests of suspected Protestants followed. The government retaliation drove John Calvin and other members of the French reform party into exile. In 1540, the Edict of Fontainebleau subjected French Protestants to the Inquisition. Henry II (r. 1547–1559)

established new measures against Protestants in the Edict of Chateaubriand in 1551. Save for a few brief interludes, the French monarchy remained a staunch foe of the Protestants until the ascension to the throne of Henry IV of Navarre in 1589.

The Habsburg-Valois wars had ended with the Treaty of Cateau-Cambrésis in 1559, after which Europe experienced a moment of peace. The same year, however, marked the beginning of internal French conflict and a shift of the European balance of power away from France to Spain. This unforeseen event brought to the throne Henry II's sickly fifteen-year-old son, Francis II, who died after reigning only a year (r. 1559–1560). With the monarchy weakened, three powerful families saw their chance to control France and competed for the young king's ear: the Bourbons, whose power lay in the south and west; the Montmorency-Chatillons, who controlled the center of France; and the strongest among them, the Guises, who were dominant in eastern France.

The Guises had little trouble establishing firm control over the young king. Francis, duke of Guise, had been Henry II's general, and his brothers, Charles and Louis, were cardinals of the church. Mary Stuart, Queen of Scots, the eighteen-year-old widow of Francis II, was their niece. Throughout the latter half of the sixteenth century, the name "Guise" was interchangeable with militant, reactionary Catholicism.

The Bourbon and Montmorency-Chatillon families, in contrast, developed strong Huguenot sympathies, largely for political reasons. The Bourbon Louis I, prince of Condé (d. 1569), and the Montmorency-Chatillon admiral Gaspard de Coligny (1519–1572) became the political leaders of the French Protestant resistance.

12.2.1 Appeal of Calvinism

Often for different reasons, ambitious aristocrats and discontented townspeople joined the Calvinist churches in opposing the Guise-dominated French monarchy. Although they made up only about one-fifteenth of the population, Huguenots held important geographic areas and were heavily represented among the more powerful segments of French society. A good two-fifths of the French aristocracy became Huguenots. Many apparently hoped to establish within France a principle of territorial sovereignty similar to what the Peace of Augsburg had secured within the Holy Roman Empire. Calvinism thus served the forces of political decentralization.

John Calvin and Theodore Beza hoped to advance their cause by currying favor with powerful aristocrats.

Beza converted Jeanne d'Albert, the mother of the future Henry IV. The prince of Condé was apparently converted in 1558 under the influence of his Calvinist wife. For many aristocrats—Condé probably among them—Calvinist religious convictions were useful politically.

The military organization of Condé and Coligny progressively merged with the religious organization of the French Huguenot churches, creating a potent combination that benefited both political and religious dissidents. Calvinism justified and inspired political resistance, while the resistance made Calvinism a viable religion in Catholic France, and each side had much to gain from the other. The confluence of secular and religious motives, however, made Calvinism a less appealing religion to some. Clearly, religious conviction was neither the only nor the main reason for becoming a Calvinist in France in the second half of the sixteenth century.

12.2.2 Catherine de Médicis and the Guises

Following Francis II's death in 1560, the queen mother, Catherine de Médicis (1519–1589) became regent for her minor son, Charles IX (r. 1560–1574). At a meeting in Poissy, she tried unsuccessfully to reconcile the Protestant and Catholic factions. Fearing the power and guile of the Guises, Catherine, whose first concern was always to preserve the monarchy, sought allies among the Protestants. In 1562, after conversations with Beza and Coligny, she issued the January Edict, which granted Protestants freedom to worship publicly outside towns—although only privately within them—and to hold synods. In March 1562, this royal toleration ended abruptly when the duke of Guise surprised a Protestant congregation at Vassy in Champagne and massacred many worshippers. That event marked the beginning of the French wars of religion.

Had Condé and the Huguenot armies rushed immediately to the queen's side after this attack, Protestants might have secured an alliance with the crown. But the queen mother's fear of Guise power was great. Condé's hesitation, however, placed the young king and the queen mother, against their deepest wishes, under firm Guise control. Cooperation with the Guises became the only alternative to capitulation to the Protestants.

12.2.2.1 THE PEACE OF SAINT-GERMAIN-EN-LAYE
During the first French war of religion, fought between April 1562 and March 1563, the duke of Guise was assassinated. A brief resumption of hostilities from 1567 to 1568 was followed by the bloodiest of all the conflicts, from September 1568 to August 1570. Condé was killed, and Huguenot leadership passed to Coligny. In the peace of Saint-Germain-en-Laye in 1570, which ended the third war, the crown, acknowledging the power of the Protestant nobility, granted the Huguenots religious freedoms within their territories and the right to fortify their cities.

CATHERINE DE MÉDICIS (1519–1589) Catherine de Médicis exercised power in France during the reigns of her three sons, Francis II (r. 1559–1560), Charles IX (r. 1560–1574), and Henry III (r. 1574–1589).
SOURCE: North Wind Picture Archives/Alamy Stock Photo

Perpetually caught between fanatical Huguenot and Guise extremes, Queen Catherine always sought to balance one side against the other. Like the Guises, she wanted a Catholic France, but feared a Guise-dominated monarchy. After the Peace of Saint-Germain-en-Laye, the crown tilted manifestly toward the Bourbon faction and the Huguenots, and Coligny became Charles IX's most trusted adviser. Unknown to the king, Catherine began to plot with the Guises against the ascendant Protestants. As she had earlier sought Protestant support when Guise power threatened to subdue the monarchy, she now sought Guise support as Protestant influence grew.

Catherine had reason to fear Coligny's hold on the king. Louis of Nassau, the leader of Protestant resistance in the Netherlands, had gained Coligny's ear. Coligny used his influence to persuade the king of France to invade the Netherlands in support of the Dutch Protestants. Catherine recognized far better than her son that France stood little chance in such a contest, and that it would be set on a collision course with mighty Spain. News of the stunning

Spanish victory over the Turks at the **Battle of Lepanto** in October 1571 had sobered Catherine and her advisors.

12.2.2.2 THE SAINT BARTHOLOMEW'S DAY MASSACRE

When Catherine lent her support to the infamous **Saint Bartholomew's Day Massacre** of Protestants, it was with far less reasoned judgment. Her decision appears to have been made in near panic. On August 22, 1572, Coligny was struck down, although not killed, by an assassin's bullet. Catherine had apparently been party to the Guise plot to eliminate Coligny. After its failure, she feared both the king's reaction to her complicity with the Guises and Coligny's response. Catherine convinced Charles that a Huguenot coup was near, inspired by Coligny, and that only the swift execution of Protestant leaders could save the crown from a Protestant attack on Paris.

On Saint Bartholomew's Day, August 24, 1572, a date that has lived in infamy for Protestants, Coligny and 3,000 fellow Huguenots were butchered in Paris. Within three days, coordinated attacks across France killed an estimated 20,000 Huguenots.

Pope Gregory XIII and Philip II of Spain reportedly greeted the news of the Protestant massacre with special religious celebrations. Philip had good reason to rejoice. By throwing France into civil war, the massacre ended any planned French opposition to Philip's efforts to subdue his rebellious subjects in the Netherlands. But the massacre of thousands of Protestants also gave the discerning Catholic world cause for new alarm. The event changed the nature of the struggle between Protestants and Catholics both within and beyond the borders of France. The contest was no longer an internal struggle between Guise and Bourbon factions for French political influence, nor was it simply a Huguenot campaign to win basic religious freedoms. In Protestant eyes, it became an international struggle for sheer survival against an adversary whose cruelty justified any means of resistance.

12.2.2.3 PROTESTANT RESISTANCE THEORY

Only as Protestants faced suppression and sure defeat did they begin to sanction active political resistance. At first, they tried to practice the biblical precept of obedient subjection to worldly authority (Romans 13:1). Luther had only grudgingly approved resistance to the emperor after the Diet of Augsburg in 1530. In 1550, however, Lutherans in Magdeburg published an influential defense of the right of lower authorities to oppose the emperor's order that all Lutherans return to the Catholic fold.

Calvin, who never faced a total political defeat after his return to Geneva in September 1540, had always condemned willful disobedience and rebellion against lawfully constituted governments as un-Christian. Yet he also taught that lower magistrates, as part of the lawfully constituted government, had the right and duty to oppose tyrannical higher authority.

The exiled Scots reformer John Knox (1513–1572), who had seen Mary of Guise, the Regent of Scotland, and Mary I

of England crush his cause, laid the groundwork for later Calvinist resistance. In 1558, in his *First Blast of the Trumpet against the Terrible Regiment of Women* he declared that the removal of a heathen tyrant was not only permissible, but also a Christian duty. He had the Catholic queen of England in mind.

After the great massacre of French Protestants on Saint Bartholomew's Day in 1572, Calvinists everywhere came to appreciate the need for an active defense of their religious rights. Classical Huguenot theories of resistance appeared in three major works of the 1570s. The first was the *Franco-Gallia* of François Hotman (1573), a humanist argument that the representative Estates General of France historically held higher authority than the French king. The second was Theodore Beza's *On the Right of Magistrates over Their Subjects* (1574), which justified the correction and even the overthrowing of tyrannical rulers by lower authorities. Finally, Philippe du Plessis Mornay's *Defense of Liberty against Tyrants* (1579) admonished princes, nobles, and magistrates beneath the king, as guardians of the rights of the body politic, to take up arms against tyranny in other lands.

12.2.3 The Rise to Power of Henry of Navarre

Henry III (r. 1574–1589) was the last of Henry II's sons to wear the French crown. He found the monarchy wedged between a radical **Catholic League**, formed in 1576 by Henry of Guise, and vengeful Huguenots. Like the queen mother, Henry sought to steer a middle course. In this effort, he received support from a growing body of neutral Catholics and Huguenots, who put the political survival of France above its religious unity. Such politiques were prepared to compromise religious creeds to save the nation.

The **Peace of Beaulieu** in May 1576 granted the Huguenots almost complete religious and civil freedom. France, however, was not ready then for such sweeping toleration. Within seven months of the Peace, the Catholic League forced Henry to return to the illusory quest for absolute religious unity in France. In October 1577, the king truncated the Peace of Beaulieu and once again limited areas of permitted Huguenot worship. Thereafter, Huguenot and Catholic factions returned to their accustomed anarchical military solutions. The Protestants were led by Henry of Navarre, a legal heir to the French throne by virtue of his descent in a direct male line from St. Louis IX (d. 1270).

In the mid-1580s, the Catholic League, with Spanish support, became dominant in Paris. In what came to be known as the Day of the Barricades, Henry III attempted to rout the league with a surprise attack in 1588. The effort failed, and the king had to flee Paris. Forced by his weakened position into "un-kingly" guerrilla tactics, and emboldened by news of the English victory over the Spanish Armada in 1588, Henry had both the duke and the cardinal of Guise assassinated. Led by still another Guise brother, the Catholic League reacted with a fury that matched the earlier Huguenot response to the Saint Bartholomew's Day Massacre. The king was now forced to strike an alliance with the Protestant Henry of Navarre in April 1589.

As the two Henrys prepared to attack the Guise stronghold of Paris, however, an enraged Dominican friar killed Henry III. The Bourbon Huguenot Henry of Navarre succeeded the childless Valois king to the French throne as Henry IV (r. 1589–1610). Pope Sixtus V and King Philip II were aghast at the sudden prospect of a Protestant France. Spain had always wanted to keep France religiously Catholic and politically weak, and they rushed troops to support the besieged Catholic League.

Direct Spanish intervention in the affairs of France seemed only to strengthen Henry IV's grasp on the crown. The French people viewed his right to hereditary succession more seriously than his Protestantism. Henry was also widely liked. Notoriously informal in dress and manner—which

made him especially popular with the soldiers—Henry also had the wit and charm to neutralize the strongest enemy in a face-to-face confrontation. He came to the throne as a politique, long weary with religious strife and fully prepared to place political peace above absolute religious unity. He believed that a royal policy of tolerant Catholicism would be the best way to achieve such peace. On July 25, 1593, he publicly abandoned the Protestant faith and embraced the traditional and majority religion of his country. "Paris is worth a Mass," he is reported to have said.

Henry made that decision only after a long period of personal agonizing. The Huguenots were horrified, and Pope Clement VIII was skeptical of Henry's sincerity, but most of the French church and people, having known internal strife too long, rallied to his side. By 1596, the Catholic League was dispersed, its ties with Spain were broken, and the wars of religion in France, to all intents, had ground to a close.

HENRY IV OF FRANCE ON HORSEBACK Equestrian portrait of Henry IV of France (R. 1589–1610), painted in 1594. When the Huguenot Henry of Navarre ascended to the French throne, Pope Sixtus V and King Philip II of Spain were aghast at the sudden prospect of a Protestant France.

SOURCE: Réunion des Musées Nationaux/Art Resource, NY

12.2.4 The Edict of Nantes

On April 13, 1598, Henry IV's Edict of Nantes proclaimed a formal religious settlement. The following month, the Treaty of Vervins ended hostilities between France and Spain.

In 1591, Henry IV had already assured the Huguenots of qualified religious freedoms. The Edict of Nantes made good that promise. It recognized minority religious rights within what was to remain an officially Catholic country. This religious truce—and it was never more than that—granted the Huguenots, who by this time numbered more than a million, freedom of public worship, right of assembly, admission to public offices and universities, and permission to maintain fortified towns. Huguenots were to exercise most new freedoms, however, within their own towns and territories. Concession of the right to fortify their towns revealed the continuing distrust between Protestants and Catholics. Significant tho it was, the edict only transformed a long hot war between irreconcilable enemies into a long cold one. To its critics, the edict had created a state within a state.

In May 1610, a Catholic fanatic assassinated Henry IV. Although he is best remembered for the Edict of Nantes, Henry IV's political and economic policies were equally important. They laid the foundations for the transformation of France into the absolute state it would become under Cardinal Richelieu and Louis XIV.

12.3 Imperial Spain and Philip II (r. 1556–1598)

How was Philip II able to dominate international politics for much of the latter half of the sixteenth century?

The second half of the sixteenth century saw Spanish power, financed by wealth acquired in the New World colonies, rule the Mediterranean. But the new wealth and population growth that fueled Spain's military in southern Europe did not lead to equal success in the Netherlands. Philip II's preoccupation with the affairs of France and England strained Spanish resources.

12.3.1 Pillars of Spanish Power

Until the English defeated the mighty Spanish Armada in 1588, no person stood larger in the second half of the sixteenth century than Philip II of Spain. Philip was heir to the intensely Catholic and militarily supreme western Habsburg kingdom. His father, Charles V, had given the eastern Habsburg lands of Austria, Bohemia, and Hungary to Philip's uncle, the emperor Ferdinand I (r. 1558–1564). These lands, together with the imperial title, remained in the possession of the Austrian branch of the family until 1918.

12.3.1.1 A RECLUSIVE RULER A reclusive man, Philip managed his kingdom by pen and paper rather than by personal presence. He was also a learned and pious Catholic, although some popes suspected he used religion as much for political as for devotional purposes. A generous patron of the arts and culture, Philip's love of the arts can be seen in his unique retreat outside Madrid, the Escorial, a combination palace, church, tomb, and monastery.

12.3.1.2 NEW WORLD RICHES Populous and wealthy Castile gave Philip a solid home base. The regular arrival in Seville of bullion from the Spanish colonies in the New World provided additional wealth. In the 1540s, great silver mines had been opened in Potosí in present-day Bolivia and in Zacatecas in Mexico. These provided the great sums needed to pay Philips's bankers and mercenaries. He nonetheless never managed to erase the debts his father left or to finance his own foreign adventures fully.

12.3.1.3 INCREASED POPULATION The new American wealth brought dramatic social change to the peoples of Europe during the second half of the sixteenth century. As Europe became richer, it was also becoming more populous. In the economically and politically active towns of France, England, and the Netherlands, populations had tripled and quadrupled by the early seventeenth century. Europe's population exceeded seventy million by 1600.

The combination of increased wealth and population triggered inflation. A steady 2-percent-a-year rise in prices in much of Europe had serious cumulative effects by the mid-sixteenth century. There were more people and more coinage in circulation than before, but less food and fewer jobs; wages stagnated while prices doubled and tripled in much of Europe.

This was especially the case in Spain. Because the new wealth was concentrated in the hands of a few, the traditional gap between the haves—the propertied, privileged, and educated classes—and the have-nots widened. Nowhere did the unprivileged suffer more than in Spain, where the Castilian peasantry, the backbone of Philip II's great empire, became the most heavily taxed people of Europe.

But a subjugated peasantry and wealth from the New World were not the only pillars of Spanish strength. Philip II shrewdly organized the lesser nobility into a loyal and efficient national bureaucracy.

12.3.1.4 SUPREMACY IN THE MEDITERRANEAN During the first half of Philip's reign, attention focused almost exclusively on the Mediterranean and the Turkish threat. By history, geography, and choice, Spain had traditionally been Catholic Europe's champion against Islam. During the 1560s, the Turks advanced deep into Austria, and their fleets dominated the Mediterranean. Between 1568 and 1570, armies under Philip's half-brother, Don John of Austria (1547–1578), the illegitimate son of Charles V, suppressed and dispersed the Moors in Granada.

In May 1571, a Holy League of Spain, Venice, Genoa, and the pope, again under Don John's command, formed to check Turkish belligerence in the Mediterranean. In the largest naval battle of the sixteenth century, Don John's fleet engaged the Ottoman navy under Ali Pasha off Lepanto in the Gulf of Corinth on October 7, 1571. Before the engagement ended, over one-third of the Turkish fleet had been sunk or captured, and 30,000 Turks had died. However, the resilient Ottomans still maintained their base in Cyprus and would soon rebuild their fleet and regain control of the eastern Mediterranean. For the moment, however, the Mediterranean belonged to Spain, and the Europeans were left to fight each other. Philip's armies also suppressed resistance in neighboring Portugal, when Philip inherited that kingdom in 1580. The union with Portugal not only enhanced Spanish sea power but also brought Portugal's overseas empire in Africa, India, and Brazil into the Spanish orbit.

12.3.2 The Revolt in the Netherlands

The spectacular Spanish military success in southern Europe was not repeated in northern Europe. When Philip attempted to impose his will within the Netherlands and on England and France, he learned the lessons of defeat. The Netherlands' resistance especially undid Spanish dreams of world empire. (See Map 12–1.)

12.3.2.1 CARDINAL GRANVELLE
The Netherlands was the richest area not only of Philip's Habsburg kingdom, but of Europe as well. In 1559, Philip departed the Netherlands for Spain and never returned. His half-sister, Margaret of Parma, assisted by a special council of state, became regent in his place. The council was headed by the extremely able Antoine Perrenot (1517–1586), known after 1561 as **Cardinal Granvelle**, who hoped to check Protestant gains by internal church reforms. He planned to break down the traditional local autonomy of the seventeen Netherlands provinces by stages and establish in its place a centralized royal government directed from Madrid. A politically docile and religiously uniform country was the goal.

The merchant towns of the Netherlands were, however, Europe's most independent; many, like magnificent Antwerp, were also Calvinist strongholds. By tradition and habit, the people of the Netherlands were far more disposed to variety and toleration than to obedient conformity and hierarchical order. Two members of the council of state led a stubborn opposition to the Spanish overlords, who now attempted to reimpose their traditional rule with a vengeance. They were the Count of Egmont (1522–1568) and William of Nassau, the Prince of Orange (1533–1584), known as "the Silent" because of his small circle of confidants.

In 1561, Cardinal Granvelle proceeded with his planned ecclesiastical reorganization of the Netherlands. It was intended to tighten the control of the Catholic hierarchy over the country and to accelerate its consolidation as a Spanish ward. Organizing the Dutch nobility in opposition, Orange and Egmont succeeded in removing Granvelle's office in 1564. Aristocratic control of the country after Granvelle's departure, however, proved woefully inefficient. Popular unrest grew, especially among urban artisans, who joined the congregations of radical Calvinist preachers in large numbers.

12.3.2.2 THE COMPROMISE
The year 1564 also saw the first fusion of political and religious opposition to Regent Margaret's government. This opposition resulted from Philip II's unwise insistence on enforcing the decrees of the Council of Trent throughout the Netherlands. William of Orange's younger brother, Louis of Nassau, who had been raised a Lutheran, led the opposition with support from the Calvinist-inclined lesser nobility and townspeople. A national covenant called the *Compromise* was drawn up, a solemn pledge to resist the decrees of Trent and the Inquisition. Grievances were loudly and persistently voiced. When Regent Margaret's government spurned the protesters as "beggars" in 1566, Calvinists rioted throughout the country. Louis called for aid from French Huguenots and German Lutherans, and a full-scale rebellion against the Spanish regency appeared imminent.

12.3.2.3 THE DUKE OF ALBA
The rebellion failed to materialize, however, because the higher nobility of the Netherlands would not support it. Their shock at Calvinist iconoclasm and anarchy was as great as their resentment of Granvelle's more subtle repression. Philip, determined to make an example of the Protestant rebels, dispatched the **Duke of Alba** to suppress the revolt. His army of 10,000 journeyed northward from Milan in 1567 in a show of combined Spanish and papal might. A special tribunal, known to the Spanish as the Council of Troubles and among the Netherlanders as the Council of Blood, reigned over the land. Before Alba's reign of terror ended, the counts of Egmont and Horn and several thousand suspected heretics were publicly executed.

The Spanish levied new taxes, forcing the Netherlands to pay for the suppression of its own revolt. One, the "tenth penny," a 10 percent sales tax, met such resistance from merchants and artisans that it could not be collected in some areas even after reduction to 3 percent. Combined persecution and taxation sent tens of thousands fleeing from the Netherlands during Alba's six-year rule, from a man more hated than Granvelle or the radical Calvinists had ever seen.

12.3.2.4 RESISTANCE AND UNIFICATION
William of Orange was an exile in Germany during these turbulent years. He now emerged as the leader of a broad movement for the independence of the Netherlands from Spain. The northern, Calvinist-inclined provinces of Holland, Zeeland, and Utrecht, of which Orange was the *Stadholder*,

Map 12–1   THE NETHERLANDS DURING THE REFORMATION

Shown here are the northern and southern provinces of the Netherlands. The former, the United Provinces, were mostly Protestant in the second half of the sixteenth century; the southern Spanish Netherlands made peace with Spain and remained largely Catholic.

or governor, became his base. As in France, political resistance in the Netherlands gained both organization and inspiration by merging with Calvinism.

The early victories of the resistance attest to the popular character of the revolt. A case in point is the capture of the port city of Brill by the "Sea Beggars," an international group of anti-Spanish exiles and criminals, among them many Englishmen. In 1572, the Beggars captured Brill and other seaports in Zeeland and Holland. Mixing with the native population, they quickly sparked rebellions against

Alba in town after town and spread the resistance southward. In 1574, the people of Leiden heroically resisted a long Spanish siege. The Dutch opened the dikes and flooded their country to repulse the hated Spanish. The faltering Alba had by that time ceded power to Don Luis de Requesens, who replaced him as commander of the Spanish forces in the Netherlands in November 1573.

12.3.2.5 THE PACIFICATION OF GHENT   The greatest atrocity of the war came after Requesens's death in 1576.

Spanish mercenaries, leaderless and unpaid, ran amok in Antwerp on November 4, 1576, leaving 7,000 people dead in the streets. The event came to be known as the Spanish Fury.

These atrocities accomplished in just four days what neither religion nor patriotism had previously been able to do. The ten largely Catholic southern provinces (what is roughly modern Belgium) now came together with the seven largely Protestant northern provinces (what is roughly the modern Netherlands) in unified opposition to Spain. This union, known as the **Pacification of Ghent**, was accomplished on November 8, 1576. It declared internal regional sovereignty in matters of religion, a key clause that permitted political cooperation among the signatories, who did not agree over religion. It was a Netherlands version of the territorial settlement of religious differences brought about in the Holy Roman Empire in 1555 by the Peace of Augsburg. Four provinces initially held out, but they soon made the resistance unanimous by joining the all-embracing Union of Brussels in January 1577. For the next two years, the Spanish faced a unified and determined Netherlands.

Don John, the victor over the Turks at Lepanto in 1571, had taken command of Spanish land forces in November 1576. He now experienced his first defeat. Confronted by unified Netherlands' resistance, he signed the humiliating Perpetual Edict in February 1577, which would remove all Spanish troops from the Netherlands within twenty days. The withdrawal gave the country to William of Orange and effectively ended, for the time being, whatever plans Philip may have had for using the Netherlands as a staging area for an invasion of England.

12.3.2.6 THE UNION OF ARRAS AND THE UNION OF UTRECHT The Spanish, however, were nothing if not persistent. Don John and Alexander Farnese of Parma, Regent Margaret's son, revived Spanish power in the southern provinces, where fear of Calvinist extremism had moved the leaders to break the Union of Brussels. In January 1579, the southern provinces formed the Union of Arras and soon made peace with Spain. The northern provinces responded by forming the Union of Utrecht.

THE MILCH COW *The Milch Cow,* a sixteenth-century satirical painting depicting the Netherlands as a cow in whom all the great powers of Europe have an interest. Elizabeth of England is feeding her (England had long-standing commercial ties with Flanders); Philip II of Spain is attempting to ride her (Spain was trying to reassert its control over the entire area); William of Orange is trying to milk her (he was the leader of the anti-Spanish rebellion); and the king of France holds her tail (France hoped to profit from the rebellion at Spain's expense).
SOURCE: Artokoloro Quint Lox Limited/Alamy Stock Photo

12.3.2.7 NETHERLANDS' INDEPENDENCE Seizing what now appeared to be a last opportunity to break the back of Netherlands' resistance, Philip II declared William of Orange an outlaw and placed a bounty of 25,000 crowns on his head. The act predictably stiffened the resistance of the northern provinces. In a defiant speech to the Estates General of Holland in December 1580 known as "the Apology," Orange publicly denounced Philip as a heathen tyrant whom the Netherlands need no longer obey.

Spanish efforts to reconquer the Netherlands continued into the 1580s. William of Orange, assassinated in July 1584, was succeeded by his seventeen-year-old son, Maurice (1567–1625), who, with the assistance of England and France, continued the Dutch resistance. Fortunately for the Netherlands, Philip II began now to meddle directly in French and English affairs. In December 1584, he signed a secret treaty with the Guises the Treaty of Joinville, and sent armies under Alexander Farnese into France in 1590. Hostilities with the English also increased. Gradually, they built to a climax in 1588, when Philip's great Armada was defeated in the English Channel.

These new fronts overextended Spain's resources, thus strengthening the Netherlands. Spanish preoccupation with France and England now permitted the northern provinces to drive out all Spanish soldiers by 1593. In 1596, France and England formally recognized their independence. Peace was not, however, concluded with Spain until 1609, when the Twelve Years' Truce gave the northern provinces virtual independence. Full recognition came with the Peace of Westphalia in 1648.

MARY I, QUEEN OF ENGLAND During Mary's reign, the great Protestant leaders of the Edwardian Age—John Hooper, Hugh Latimer, and Thomas Cranmer—were executed for heresy.
SOURCE: Prado, Madrid, Spain/Bridgeman Art Library

12.4 England and Spain (1553–1603)

What role did Catholic and Protestant extremism play in the struggle for supremacy between England and Spain?

Before Edward VI died in 1553, he agreed to a plan to make Lady Jane Grey his successor in place of the Catholic Mary Tudor (r. 1553–1558). Jane was the teenage daughter of a powerful Protestant nobleman and the granddaughter of Henry VIII's younger sister Mary. Unfortunately for poor Jane, popular support for the principle of hereditary monarchy was too strong to deprive Mary of her rightful rule. Uprisings in London and elsewhere led to Jane Grey's removal from the throne within days of her crowning, and she was eventually beheaded.

12.4.1 Mary I (r. 1553–1558)

Once enthroned, Mary's actions were even beyond the worst fears of the Protestants. In 1554, she entered a highly unpopular political marriage with Philip (later Philip II) of Spain, a symbol of militant Catholicism to English Protestants. At his direction, Mary pursued a foreign policy that in 1558 cost England its last enclave on the Continent, Calais.

Mary's domestic measures were equally shocking to the English people and even more divisive. During her reign, Parliament repealed the Protestant statutes of Edward and reverted to the Catholic religious practice of her father, Henry VIII. The great Protestant leaders of the Edwardian Age—John Hooper, Hugh Latimer, and Thomas Cranmer—were executed for heresy. Hundreds of Protestants either joined them in martyrdom (287 were burned at the stake during Mary's reign) or fled to the Continent. These "Marian exiles" settled in Germany and Switzerland. John Knox, the future leader of the Reformation in Scotland, was prominent among them. There, they waited for the time when a Protestant counteroffensive could be launched in their homelands. Many of these exiles later held positions in the Church of England under Elizabeth I's reign. (To learn more about the religious persecutions of the time, see the "Compare and Connect" sidebar on the debate over religious tolerance, which follows below.)

Compare and Connect

The Great Debate over Religious Tolerance

ON OCTOBER 27, 1553, Spanish physician and amateur theologian Michael Servetus died at the stake in Geneva for alleged "blasphemies against the Holy Trinity." A bold and confident man, he had also incurred the wrath of Rome before battling John Calvin in Geneva on theological issues. In the wake of Servetus's execution, Calvin was much criticized for fighting heresy with capital punishment. In 1544, he came to his own defense in a tract entitled *Defense of the Orthodox Faith in the Holy Trinity Against the Monstrous Errors of Michael Servetus of Spain*. Thereafter, Sebastian Castellio, an accomplished humanist and former rector of the college in Geneva, whom Calvin had driven out of the city years earlier, began a series of writings against Calvin. One of his titles, *Whether Heretics Should Be Punished by the Sword of the Magistrates*, was an anonymous anthology on religious toleration that included a supporting excerpt from John Calvin himself! Writing through the years under several pseudonyms, Castellio excerpted statements from Calvin's works and used them in a sustained "debate" with his own liberal point of view.

ELIZABETH I OF ENGLAND (r. 1558–1603) Queen Elizabeth I of England was as an example of religious tolerance during her reign. Despite her Protestant sympathies, she steered clear of both Catholic and Protestant extremism.
SOURCE: Library of Congress Prints and Photographs Division

Before Reading

- Consider the arguments John Calvin makes on behalf of capital punishment for heresy.
- Notice how Sebastian Castellio attempts to refute Calvin's main points.

Questions

1. Why does Calvin believe that heresy deserves capital punishment?
2. What are Castellio's best rebuttal arguments?
3. Why does Castellio write under pseudonyms?

CALVIN VERSUS CASTELLIO ON RELIGIOUS TOLERANCE

Calvin: Kings are duty bound to defend the doctrine of piety.

Castellio: [Yes, but] to kill a man is not to defend doctrine, but rather to kill a man. . . .

Calvin: What of today? The majority of people have lost all sense of shame and openly mock God. They burst as boldly into God's awesome mysteries as pigs poke their snouts into costly storehouses.

Castellio: Calvin appears to be criticizing himself. For truly the awesome mysteries of God are the Trinity, predestination, and election. But this man [Calvin] speaks so assuredly about these matters that one would think he was in Paradise. So thorny is his own teaching about the Trinity . . . that by his own curiosity he weakens and makes doubtful the consciences of the simple. He has taught so crudely about predestination that innumerable men have been seduced into a security as great as that which existed before the Flood. . . .

Tell me, in brief, what you think about predestination.

Calvin:	I have been taught the following about predestination: All men are not created in an equal state. Rather in eternity, God, by inevitable decree, determined in advance those whom he would save and those whom he would damn to destruction. Those whom he has deemed worthy of salvation have been chosen by his mercy without consideration of their worthiness. And those given damnation, he shuts off from life by a just and irreprehensible, albeit incomprehensible, judgment.
Castellio:	So you maintain that certain men are created by God already marked for damnation so that they cannot be saved?
Calvin:	Precisely.
Castellio:	But what if they *should* obey God? Would they not then be saved?
Calvin:	They would then be saved. However, they are not able to obey God, because God excludes them from the knowledge of his name and the spirit of his justification so that they can and will do only evil and are inclined only to every kind of sin.
Castellio:	Hence, they have that inclination [to sin] from God's creation and predestination?
Calvin:	They have it so, just as surely as God has created the wolf with the inclination to eat sheep!
Castellio:	Therefore they have been damned and rejected by God even before they existed?
Calvin:	Exactly.
Castellio:	But are they not damned for their sins?
Calvin:	Indeed so. Those who were destined to that [damned] lot are completely worthy of it.
Castellio:	When were they worthy of it?
Calvin:	When they were destined to it?
Castellio:	Then they have *been* before they *are*. Do you see what you are saying?!
Calvin:	I don't understand.
Castellio:	If they were worthy, then they *were*. For to be worthy is to be. And if you concede that they have been damned before they are, then they have *been* before they were.
Calvin:	God elects the foolish things of the world to confound the wise.
Castellio:	Calvin and his kind reject the foolish things of the world so that they may exalt the wise [themselves]. Hence, they admit hardly anyone into . . . their circle who is not accomplished in sciences and languages . . . If Christ himself came to them, he would certainly be turned away if he spoke no Latin. . . . [But] Christ wishes to be judged by common sense and refers the matters of the gospel to human judgment. . . . He would never have employed such analogies had he wished to deprive us of our common sense. And who would have believed him had he taught things repugnant to nature and contradictory to human experience . . .? What kind of master would he have been, had he said to the woman who cried out to him and washed his feet with her hair: *O woman, whatever your sin, it was done by God's decree!*

SOURCE: From Steven Ozment, *Mysticism and Dissent: Religious Ideology and Social Protest in the Sixteenth Century* (New Haven, CT: Yale University Press, 1973), pp. 171–179.

12.4.2 Elizabeth I (r. 1558–1603)

Mary's successor was her half-sister, Elizabeth I, the daughter of Henry VIII and Anne Boleyn. Elizabeth had remarkable and enduring successes in both domestic and foreign policy. Assisted by a shrewd adviser, Sir William Cecil (1520–1598), she built a true kingdom on the ruins of Mary's reign. Between 1559 and 1603, she and Cecil guided a religious settlement through Parliament that prevented religious differences from tearing England apart in the sixteenth century. A ruler who subordinated religious to political unity, Elizabeth merged a centralized episcopal system that she firmly controlled with broadly defined Protestant doctrine and traditional Catholic ritual. The resulting Anglican Church harbored inflexible religious extremes for decades.

In 1559, the Act of Supremacy passed Parliament. It repealed all the anti-Protestant legislation of Mary Tudor's reign and asserted Elizabeth's right as "supreme governor" over both spiritual and temporal affairs. In the same year, the Act of Uniformity mandated a revised version of the second *Book of Common Prayer* of 1552 for every English parish. A decade later, the **Thirty-Nine Articles**, a revision of Thomas Cranmer's original forty-two, made a moderate Protestantism the official religion within the Church of England.

12.4.2.1 CATHOLIC AND PROTESTANT EXTREMISTS Elizabeth hoped to avoid both Catholic and Protestant extremism by finding a middle path. Her first archbishop of Canterbury, Matthew Parker (d. 1575), represented this ideal. Elizabeth could not prevent the actions of subversive Catholic and Protestant zealots, however. When she ascended the throne, Catholics were the majority in England. The extremists among them, encouraged by the Jesuits, plotted against her. The Spanish, piqued both by Elizabeth's Protestant sympathies and by her refusal to take Philip II's hand in marriage, encouraged and later directly assisted Catholic radicals. Elizabeth deliberately remained unmarried throughout her reign, using the possibility of a royal marriage to her diplomatic advantage.

ELIZABETH TUDOR (ca. 1551), LATER ELIZABETH I An idealized likeness of Elizabeth Tudor when she was a princess, attributed to Flemish court painter L. B. Teerling, ca. 1551. The painting shows her blazing red hair and alludes to her learning by the addition of books.
SOURCE: The Artchives/Alamy Stock Photo

Catholic extremists hoped eventually to replace Elizabeth with Mary Stuart, Queen of Scots. Elizabeth acted swiftly against Catholic assassination plots, rarely letting her emotions override her political instincts. Despite proven cases of Catholic treason and even attempted regicide, she executed fewer Catholics during her forty-five years on the throne than Mary Tudor had executed Protestants during her brief five-year reign.

Elizabeth showed little mercy, however, to any who threatened the unity of her rule. She was cautious with the Puritans, who were Protestants working within the national church to "purify" it of every vestige of "popery" and to make its Protestant doctrine more precise. The Puritans had two special grievances against her reign: (1) the retention of Catholic ceremony and vestments within the Church of England, which made it seem that no Reformation had occurred; and (2) the continuation of the episcopal system of church governance, which conceived the English church as the true successor to Rome, while placing it politically in the firm hands of the queen and her compliant archbishop.

Sixteenth-century Puritans were not true separatists. They enjoyed popular support and were led by widely respected men like Thomas Cartwright (d. 1603). They worked through Parliament to create an alternative national church of semiautonomous congregations governed by representative presbyteries, or **Presbyterians**, following the model of Calvin and Geneva. Elizabeth dealt firmly, but subtly, with them, conceding nothing that lessened the hierarchical unity of the Church of England and her control over it.

The more extreme Puritans wanted every congregation to be autonomous, a law unto itself, with neither higher episcopal nor presbyterian control. They came to be known as **Congregationalists**. Elizabeth and her second archbishop of Canterbury, John Whitgift (d. 1604), refused to tolerate this group, whose views on independence they found patently subversive. The Conventicle Act of 1593 gave such separatists the option to either conform to the practices of the Church of England or face exile or death.

12.4.2.2 DETERIORATION OF RELATIONS WITH SPAIN
A series of events led inexorably to war between England and Spain, despite the sincere desires of both Philip II and Elizabeth to avoid a confrontation. In 1567, the Spanish Duke of Alba marched his mighty army into the Netherlands, which was, from the English point of view, simply a convenient staging area for a Spanish invasion of England. Pope Pius V (r. 1566–1572), who favored a military conquest of Protestant England, "excommunicated" Elizabeth for heresy in 1570. This mischievous act encouraged both internal resistance and international intrigue against the queen. Two years later, the piratical sea beggars, many of whom were Englishmen, occupied the port of Brill in the Netherlands and aroused the surrounding countryside against the Spanish.

Following Don John's demonstration of Spain's awesome sea power at Lepanto in 1571, England signed a mutual defense pact with France. Also in the 1570s, Elizabeth's famous seamen John Hawkins (1532–1595) and Sir Francis Drake (ca. 1545–1596) began to prey regularly on Spanish shipping in the Americas. Drake's circumnavigation of the globe between 1577 and 1580 was one in a series of dramatic demonstrations of English ascendancy on the high seas.

After the Saint Bartholomew's Day Massacre, Elizabeth was the only protector of Protestants in France and the Netherlands. In 1585, she signed the Treaty of Nonsuch, which provided English soldiers and cavalry to the Netherlands. Funds that had previously been funneled covertly to support Henry of Navarre's army in France now flowed openly.

12.4.2.3 MARY, QUEEN OF SCOTS
These events made a tinderbox of English–Spanish relations. The spark that finally touched it off was Elizabeth's execution of Mary, Queen of Scots (1542–1587).

Mary Stuart was the daughter of King James V of Scotland and Mary of Guise and had resided in France from the time she was six years old. This thoroughly French and Catholic queen had returned to Scotland after the death of her husband, the French king Francis II, in 1561. There she found a successful, fervent Protestant Reformation legally sanctioned the year before by the Treaty of Edinburgh in 1560. As hereditary heir to the throne of Scotland, Mary remained queen by divine and human right, and the Protestants who controlled her realm did not intimidate her. She established an international French court culture, with gaiety and sophistication that impressed many Protestant nobles whose religion often made their lives exceedingly dour.

In 1568, a public scandal forced Mary's abdication and flight to her cousin Elizabeth in England. Mary's reputed lover, the Earl of Bothwell, was, with cause, suspected of having killed her legal husband, Lord Darnley. When a packed court acquitted Bothwell, he subsequently married Mary. The outraged reaction of Protestant nobles forced Mary to surrender the throne to her one-year-old son, the future James VI of Scotland, and later, Elizabeth's successor as King James I of England. Because of Mary's clear claim to the English throne, she was an international symbol of a future Catholic England and consumed by the desire to be England's queen. For this reason, her presence in England, where she resided under house arrest for nineteen years, was a constant discomfort to Elizabeth.

In 1583, Elizabeth's vigilant secretary, Sir Francis Walsingham, uncovered a plot against Elizabeth involving the Spanish ambassador Bernardino de Mendoza. After Mendoza's deportation in January 1584, popular antipathy toward Spain and support for Protestant resistance in France and the Netherlands were rampant throughout England.

In 1586, Walsingham uncovered still another plot against Elizabeth, the so-called Babington plot, after Anthony Babington, who was caught seeking Spanish support for an attempt on the queen's life. This time he had uncontestable proof of Mary's complicity. Elizabeth believed the execution of a sovereign, even a dethroned sovereign, weakened royalty everywhere. She was also aware of the outcry that Mary's execution would create throughout the Catholic world, and she sincerely wanted peace with English Catholics. Believing she had no choice in the matter, Elizabeth consented to Mary's execution, which took place on February 18, 1587. This event dashed all Catholic hopes for a bloodless reconversion of Protestant England. After the execution of the Catholic queen of Scotland, Pope Sixtus V (r. 1585–1590), who feared Spanish domination almost as much as he abhorred English Protestantism, could no longer withhold public support for a Spanish invasion of England. Philip II ordered his Armada to make ready.

12.4.2.4 THE ARMADA In the spring of 1587, Sir Francis Drake shelled the port of Cádiz, inflicting heavy damages

DESTRUCTION OF THE SPANISH ARMADA Engraving of the destruction of the Spanish Armada by Captain Morgan. Ut enim ad minim veniam, quis nostrud exercitation ullamco laboris nisi ut aliquip ex ea commodo consequat.
SOURCE: Culture Club/Getty Images

on Spanish ships and stores and interrupting Spain's war preparations. After "singeing the beard of Spain's king," as he put it, Drake raided the coast of Portugal, further incapacitating the Spanish. These strikes forced the Spanish to postpone their invasion of England until 1588.

On May 30 of that year, 130 ships bearing 25,000 sailors and soldiers under the command of the Duke of Medina-Sidonia set sail for England. In the end, however, the English won a stunning victory. The invasion barges that were to transport Spanish soldiers from the galleons onto English shores were prevented from leaving Calais and Dunkirk. The swifter English and Netherlands' ships, helped by what came to be known as an "English wind," dispersed the waiting Spanish fleet, more than one-third of which never returned to Spain.

The news of the Armada's defeat gave heart to Protestant resistance everywhere. Although Spain continued to win impressive victories in the 1590s, it never fully recovered. Spanish soldiers faced unified and inspired French, English, and Dutch armies. By the time of Philip's death on September 13, 1598, his forces had been rebuffed on all fronts. His seventeenth-century successors were inferior leaders who never had responsibilities equal to his, and Spain never again knew such imperial grandeur. The French soon dominated the Continent, and in the New World the Dutch and the English whittled away at Spain's overseas empire.

Elizabeth died on March 23, 1603, leaving behind her a strong nation poised to expand into a global empire. William Shakespeare, who wrote the history of the age for an Elizabethan audience, left behind another kind of legacy. (To learn more about the history of English theater in Elizabeth's time, see the "Encountering the Past" sidebar, which follows below.)

12.5 The Thirty Years' War (1618–1648)

What toll did the Thirty Years' War take on Germany?

The **Thirty Years' War** in the Holy Roman Empire was the last and most destructive of the wars of religion. The Thirty Years' War was so devastating because of the entrenched hatred of the various sides and their determination to sacrifice all for their religious beliefs. When the hostilities ended in 1648, the peace terms shaped the map of northern Europe much as we know it today.

12.5.1 Preconditions for War

There were a variety of circumstances that contributed to the outbreak of the Thirty Years' War. First, the fragmented nature of German politics and its complex internal divisions

were matched by the rival legal and commercial claims of Europe's rulers and German princes. Second, the religious conflict in the Holy Roman Empire between Catholics and Protestants, as well as Lutherans and Calvinists, was bitter and deep-rooted by the start of the war.

12.5.1.1 FRAGMENTED GERMANY In the second half of the sixteenth century, Germany was an almost ungovernable land of about 360 autonomous political entities. (See Map 12–2.) There were independent secular principalities— duchies, landgraviates, and marches; ecclesiastical principalities—archbishoprics, bishoprics, and abbeys; and numerous free cities; and knights ruling small areas from castles. The Peace of Augsburg in 1555 had given each of them significant sovereignty within its own borders. Each levied its own tolls and tariffs and coined its own money, which made land travel and trade among the various regions difficult to impossible. Many of these little lands also had great power pretensions. As the seventeenth century opened, Germany was decentralized and divided; it was not a unified nation like Spain, England, or even strife-filled France.

Because of its central location, Germany had always been Europe's highway for merchants and traders going north, south, east, and west. Europe's rulers pressed in on Germany both because of trade and because some held lands or legal privileges within certain German principalities. German princes, in turn, looked to import and export markets beyond German borders and opposed efforts to consolidate the Holy Roman Empire, fearing their territorial rights, confirmed by the Peace of Augsburg, might be overturned. German princes were not loath to turn to Catholic France or to the kings of Denmark and Sweden for allies against the Habsburg emperor.

After the Council of Trent, Protestants in the empire suspected the existence of an imperial and papal conspiracy to re-create the Catholic Europe of pre-Reformation times. The imperial diet, which the German princes controlled, demanded strict observance of the constitutional rights of Germans as set forth in agreements with the emperor since the mid-fourteenth century. In the late sixteenth century, the emperor ruled only to the degree to which he was prepared to use force of arms against his subjects.

12.5.1.2 RELIGIOUS DIVISION Religious conflict accentuated the international and internal political divisions. (See Map 12–3.) During this period, the population within the Holy Roman Empire was about equally divided between Catholics and Protestants, the latter having perhaps a slight numerical edge by 1600. The terms of the Peace of Augsburg had attempted to freeze the territorial holdings of the Lutherans and the Catholics, with the so-called *ecclesiastical reservation*. In the intervening years, however, the Lutherans had gained and kept political control in some Catholic areas, as had the Catholics in a few previously

Encountering the Past

Going to the Theater

THE MODERN ENGLISH stage play originated in the religious dramas that educated and entertained medieval Europeans for centuries before Shakespeare's birth in 1564. Teaching a lesson as well as telling a suspenseful story, these dramas were known as *morality plays* and typically were presented in the countryside by roving bands of players under church supervision. The medieval theater usually consisted of a small circular field for the actors, ringed by earthen mounds for the spectators. The circular stage was divided into four quadrants, each with its own tent at the four points of the compass: heaven at the east, evil at the north, worldly rulers at the west, and good characters at the south.

Each player emerged from his tent in turn to speak his lines, then went back in to await his next appearance. This format was a way of shifting scenes, much like the custom of ending a scene by lowering a curtain in modern theaters.

In England in the fifteenth century, as the urban population grew, ambitious promoters moved their productions into the courtyards of inns. London, the seat of the royal court, became the center of English theatrical life.

This sheltered, urban setting gave theater companies several advantages. Audiences were larger, and the inns could be easily renovated to provide permanent stages and more complex sets. The enclosed courtyards also helped keep out nonpaying crashers, the greatest enemies of the new showmen—capitalists who produced and often wrote the plays and had to make a living from them.

Several of London's more scrupulous clergymen decried another advantage of the combined inn and theater—the opportunity it gave for sexual license. By the sixteenth century, the allegorical moralizing of the medieval country theater had evolved into the ribald, worldly entertainment of the London stage. Going to the theater was now more like being part of a festival than listening to a sermon. The workmen and young women who comprised much of the audience found it convenient to hire rooms in which they might romance one another during or after the performance.

London's theater world reached full maturity in the late sixteenth and early seventeenth centuries. The Rose and the Globe theaters, where many of Shakespeare's plays were presented, were built in the 1590s on the south bank of the River Thames, reachable only by water taxis. During Shakespeare's heyday, some 40,000 waterboys were said to ferry customers to these theaters. Performances by troupes of adult males or boys (women were banned from the stage) were often rowdy affairs, the crowds egged on by both the witty repartee on stage and the food and beer sold in the pit.

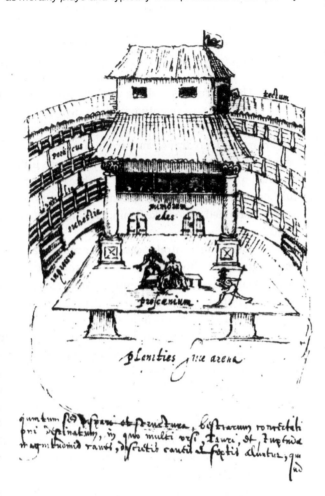

THE ELIZABETHAN SWAN THEATER A seventeenth-century sketch of the Swan Theater, which stood near Shakespeare's Globe Theater on the south bank of the Thames.
SOURCE: Private Collection/Bridgeman Art Library

Questions

1. What were the basic elements and purpose of the medieval stage?
2. What features were carried over from it to the Elizabethan theater?

SOURCES: E. K. Chambers, *The Elizabethan Stage*, Vols. I–IV (Oxford, UK: Oxford University Press, 1923); Lawrence M. Clopper, *Drama, Play, and Game: English Festive Culture in the Medieval and Early Modern Period* (Chicago: University of Chicago Press, 2001); F. E. Halliday, *Shakespeare in His Age* (New York: Duckworth, 1956).

Map 12–2 GERMANY IN 1547

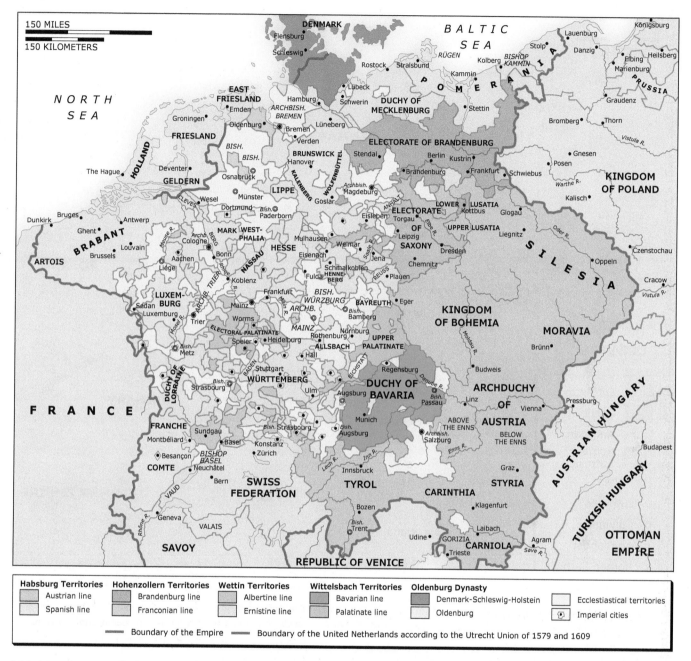

150 MILES

150 KILOMETERS

Habsburg Territories	Hohenzollern Territories	Wettin Territories	Wittelsbach Territories	Oldenburg Dynasty	
Austrian line	Brandenburg line	Albertine line	Bavarian line	Denmark-Schleswig-Holstein	Ecclesiastical territories
Spanish line	Franconian line	Ernistine line	Palatinate line	Oldenburg	Imperial cities

Boundary of the Empire — Boundary of the United Netherlands according to the Utrecht Union of 1579 and 1609

Mid-sixteenth-century Germany was a decentralized divided land with about 360 autonomous political entities.

SOURCE: Based on Hajo Holborn, *A History of Modern Germany: The Reformation* (New York, A. A. Knopf, 1959), pp. 202–203.

Lutheran areas. Such territorial reversals, or the threat of them, only increased the suspicion and antipathy between the two sides.

The Lutherans had been far more successful in securing their rights to worship in Catholic lands than the Catholics had been in securing such rights in Lutheran lands. The Catholic rulers, who were in a weakened position after the Reformation, had made, but resented, concessions to Protestant communities within their territories. As time passed, they demanded that ecclesiastical princes, electors, archbishops, bishops, and abbots who had deserted Catholicism be immediately deprived of their religious offices and

their ecclesiastical holdings be promptly returned to Catholic control in accordance with the ecclesiastical reservation. However, the Lutherans and, even more so, the Calvinists in the Palatinate ignored this stipulation at every opportunity.

There was also religious strife in the empire between liberal and conservative Lutherans and between Lutherans and the growing numbers of Calvinists. The last half of the sixteenth century was a time of warring Protestant factions within German universities. And in addition to the heightened religious strife, a new scientific and material culture was becoming prominent in intellectual and political circles, increasing the anxiety of religious people of all persuasions.

Map 12–3 RELIGIOUS DIVISIONS ABOUT 1600

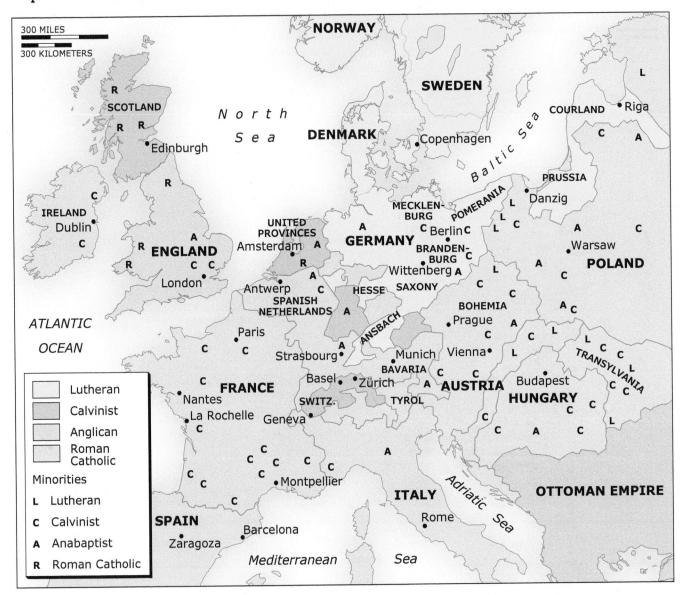

By 1600, few could seriously expect Christians to return to a uniform religious allegiance. In Spain and southern Italy, as shown here, Catholicism remained relatively unchallenged, but large religious minorities, both Catholic and Protestant, elsewhere, demonstrate internal divisions.

12.5.1.3 CALVINISM AND THE PALATINATE As elsewhere in Europe, Calvinism was the political and religious leaven within the Holy Roman Empire on the eve of the Thirty Years' War. Unrecognized as a legal religion by the Peace of Augsburg, Calvinism had a strong presence within the empire when Frederick III (r. 1559–1576), a devout convert to Calvinism, became Elector Palatine, or ruler within the Palatinate. Heidelberg became a German Geneva in the 1560s: both a great intellectual center of Calvinism and a staging area for Calvinist penetration into the empire. By 1609, Palatine Calvinists headed a Protestant defensive alliance that received support from Spain's sixteenth-century enemies: England, France, and the Netherlands.

The Lutherans came to fear the Calvinists almost as much as they did the Catholics. By their bold missionary

forays into the empire, Palatine Calvinists threatened the Peace of Augsburg—and the legal foundation of the Lutheran states. Also, outspoken Calvinist criticism of the doctrine of Christ's real presence in the Eucharist shocked the more religiously conservative Lutherans. The Elector Palatine once expressed his disbelief in transubstantiation by publicly shredding the host and mocking it as a "fine God." To Lutherans, such religious disrespect disgraced the Reformation as well as the elector.

12.5.1.4 MAXIMILIAN OF BAVARIA AND THE CATHOLIC LEAGUE If the Calvinists were active within the Holy Roman Empire, then so were their Catholic counterparts, the Jesuits. Bavaria, staunchly Catholic and supported by Spain, became militarily and ideologically for the Counter-Reformation what the Palatinate was for Protestantism. From Bavaria, the Jesuits launched successful missions throughout the empire, winning such major cities as Strasbourg and Osnabrück back to the Catholic fold by 1600. In 1609, Maximilian I, Duke of Bavaria (r. 1597–1651), organized a Catholic league to counter a new Protestant alliance that had been formed in the same year under the leadership of Calvinist Elector Palatine, Frederick IV (r. 1583–1610). When the league fielded a great army under the command of Count Johann von Tilly, the stage was set, both internally and internationally, for the worst of the religious wars, the Thirty Years' War. (See Map 12–4.)

Map 12–4 THE HOLY ROMAN EMPIRE ABOUT 1618

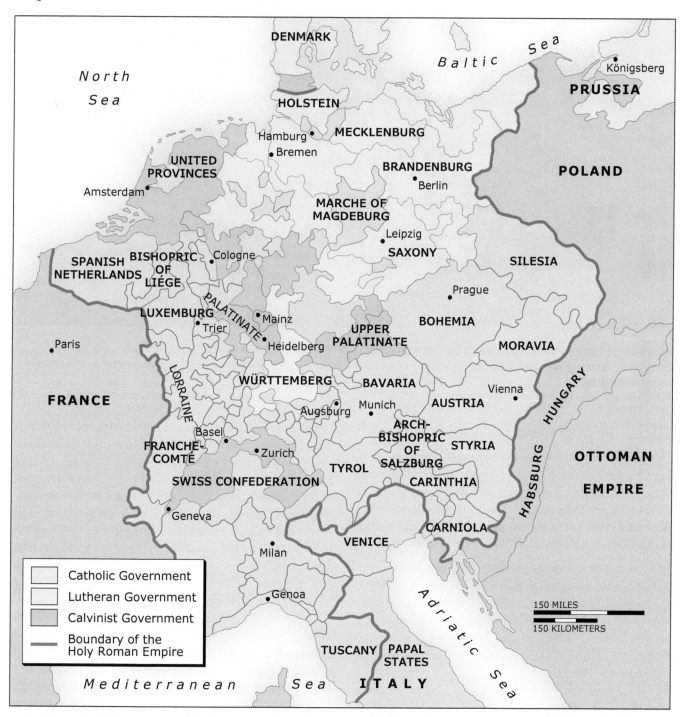

On the eve of the Thirty Years' War, the Holy Roman Empire was politically and religiously fragmented, as shown in this somewhat simplified map. Lutherans dominated the north and Catholics the south; Calvinists controlled the United Provinces and the Palatinate and were important in Switzerland and Brandenburg.

RESPONSE OF BOHEMIAN PROTESTANTS TO THE REVOCATION OF THEIR RELIGIOUS FREEDOMS In the "defenestration of Prague," Bohemian Protestants throw three of Emperor Ferdinand II's agents out of windows at Hradschin Castle in Prague to protest his revocation of Protestant freedoms.
SOURCE: Bildarchiv Preussischer Kulturbesitz/Art Resource, NY

12.5.2 Four Periods of War

The war went through four distinguishable periods. During its course, it drew in every major Western European nation—at least diplomatically and financially if not by direct military intervention. The four periods were the Bohemian (1618–1625), the Danish (1625–1629), the Swedish (1630–1635), and the Swedish-French (1635–1648).

12.5.2.1 THE BOHEMIAN PERIOD The war broke out in Bohemia after the ascent to the Bohemian throne in 1618 of the Habsburg Ferdinand, Archduke of Styria, who was also heir to the imperial throne. Educated by the Jesuits and a fervent Catholic, Ferdinand was determined to restore the traditional faith to the eastern Habsburg lands—Austria, Bohemia, and Hungary.

No sooner had Ferdinand become king of Bohemia than he revoked the religious freedoms of Bohemian Protestants. Enforced in 1575, these freedoms had even been recently broadened by Emperor Rudolf II (r. 1576–1612) in his Letter of Majesty in 1609. The Protestant nobility in

Prague responded to Ferdinand's act in May 1618 by throwing his regents out the window of the royal palace. The event has ever since been known as the "defenestration of Prague," when three officials fell fifty feet into a dry moat that fortunately, was padded with manure, which cushioned their fall and spared their lives. In the following year, Ferdinand became Holy Roman Emperor as Ferdinand II (r. 1619–1637) by the unanimous vote of the seven electors. The Bohemians, however, defiantly deposed him in Prague and declared the Calvinist elector Palatine, Frederick V (r. 1616–1623), their king.

A revolt of the Protestant nobility against an unpopular king of Bohemia now escalated into an international war. Spain sent troops to Ferdinand, who found more motivated allies in Maximilian of Bavaria and the Lutheran elector John George I of Saxony (r. 1611–1656). But the latter had their own agendas. Maximilian hoped to wrest the electoral title from his distant Palatine cousin, while John George saw a sure route to territorial gain by joining in an easy victory over the weaker elector Palatine. This was not the only time politics and greed would overshadow religion during the long conflict, although Lutheran-Calvinist religious animosity also overrode a common Protestantism.

Ferdinand's army under Tilly routed Frederick V's troops at the Battle of White Mountain in 1620. By 1622, Ferdinand had not only subdued and re-Catholicized Bohemia but also conquered the Palatinate as well. Meanwhile, Maximilian of Bavaria pressed the conflict into northwestern Germany, laying claim to land as he went.

12.5.2.2 THE DANISH PERIOD These events raised new fears of a reconquest and re-Catholicization of the empire, which was precisely Ferdinand II's design. The Lutheran king Christian IV (r. 1588–1648) of Denmark, who already held territory within the empire as the Duke of Holstein, was eager to extend Danish influence to the coastal towns of the North Sea. With English, French, and Dutch encouragement, he picked up the Protestant banner of resistance, opening the Danish period of the conflict (1625–1629). Entering Germany with his army in 1626, he was, however, quickly humiliated by Maximilian and forced to retreat into Denmark.

As military success made Maximilian stronger and an untrustworthy ally, Emperor Ferdinand found a more pliant tool for his policies in Albrecht of Wallenstein (1583–1634), a powerful mercenary. A brilliant and ruthless military strategist, Wallenstein carried Ferdinand's campaign into Denmark. By 1628, he commanded a crack army of more than 100,000 men and also became a law unto himself, completely outside of the emperor's control.

Wallenstein, however, had so broken Protestant resistance that Ferdinand could issue the **Edict of Restitution** in 1629, reasserting the Catholic safeguards of the Peace of Augsburg of 1555. It reaffirmed the illegality of Calvinism—a completely unrealistic move by 1629—and it ordered the return of all church lands the Lutherans had acquired since 1552, an equally unrealistic goal despite its legal basis. Compliance would have involved the return of no fewer than sixteen bishoprics and twenty-eight cities and towns to Catholic allegiance. The new edict struck panic in the hearts of Protestants and Habsburg opponents everywhere.

12.5.2.3 THE SWEDISH PERIOD Gustavus Adolphus II of Sweden (r. 1611–1632), a deeply pious king of a unified Lutheran nation, became the new leader of Protestant forces within the empire, opening the Swedish period of the war (1630–1635). He was controlled by two interested bystanders: (1) the French minister Cardinal Richelieu (1585–1642), whose foreign policy was to protect French interests by keeping the Habsburg armies tied down in Germany, and (2) the Dutch, who had not forgotten Spanish Habsburg rule in the sixteenth century. In alliance with the electors of Brandenburg and Saxony, Gustavus won a smashing victory at Breitenfeld in 1630—one that reversed the course

of the war so dramatically that it has been regarded as the most decisive engagement of the long conflict.

One of the reasons for the overwhelming Swedish victory at Breitenfeld was the military genius of Gustavus Adolphus. The Swedish king brought a new mobility to warfare by having both his infantry and his cavalry employ fire-and-charge tactics. At six deep, his infantry squares were smaller than the traditional ones, yet he filled them with equal numbers of musketeers and pikemen. His cavalry also alternated pistol shots with charges with the sword, and his artillery was lighter and more mobile in battle. Each unit of his army—infantry, cavalry, and artillery—had both defensive and offensive capability and could quickly change from one to the other.

Gustavus Adolphus died at the hands of Wallenstein's forces during the Battle of Lützen in November 1632—a costly engagement for both sides that created a brief standstill. Ferdinand had long resented Wallenstein's independence, although he was the major factor in imperial success. In 1634, Ferdinand had Wallenstein assassinated. The episode is a telling commentary on this war without honor: Despite deep religious motivations, greed and political gain were the real forces at work in the Thirty Years' War. Even allies that owed one another their success were not above treating the other as mortal enemies.

In the Peace of Prague in 1635, the German Protestant states, led by Saxony, reached a compromise with Ferdinand. France and the Netherlands, however, continued to support Sweden. Hoping to maximize their investment in the war, they refused to join the agreement. Their resistance to settlement plunged the war into its fourth and most devastating phase.

12.5.2.4 THE SWEDISH–FRENCH PERIOD The French openly entered the war in 1635, sending men and munitions as well as financial subsidies. Thereafter, the war dragged on for thirteen years. Germany was looted by French, Swedish, and Spanish soldiers—warring, it seemed, simply for the sake of warfare itself—while the Germans, long weary of devastation, were too disunited to repulse the foreign armies. By the time peace talks began at Münster and Osnabrück in Westphalia in 1644, the war had killed an estimated one-third of the German population. It has been called the worst European catastrophe since the Black Death of the fourteenth century.

12.5.3 The Treaty of Westphalia

The Treaty of Westphalia in 1648 ended all hostilities within the Holy Roman Empire. It was the first general peace in Europe after a war unprecedented for its number of warring parties. (See Map 12–5.) Written not in Latin, but in French—now to become the international diplomatic language—the treaty rescinded Ferdinand's Edict of Restitution and reasserted the major feature of the religious

Map 12–5 EUROPE IN 1648

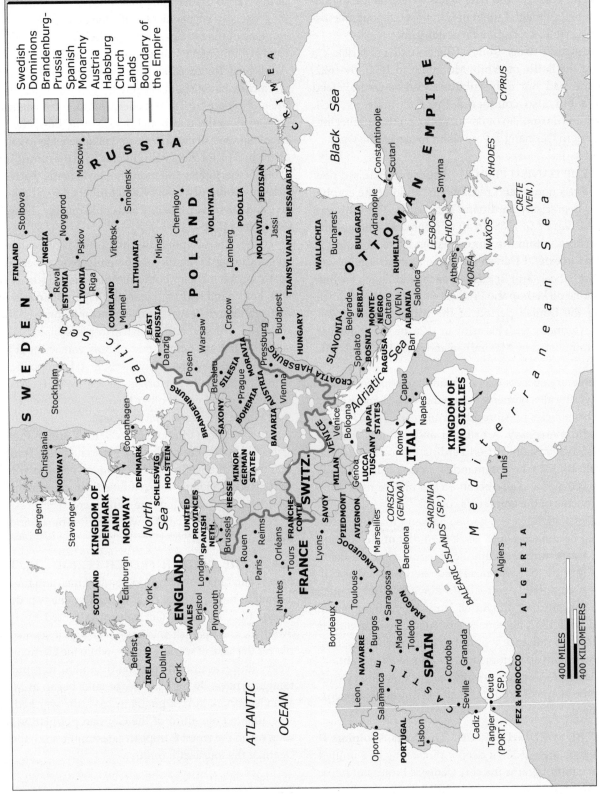

Legend:
- Swedish Dominions
- Brandenburg-Prussia
- Spanish Monarchy
- Austria Habsburg
- Church Lands
- Boundary of the Empire

At the end of the Thirty Years' War, Spain still had extensive possessions. Austria and Brandenburg-Prussia were rising powers, the independence of the United Provinces and Switzerland was recognized, and Sweden had footholds in northern Germany.

TREATY OF WESTPHALIA The Dutch celebrate the Treaty of Westphalia, ending the Thirty Years' War.
SOURCE: North Wind Picture Archives/Alamy Stock Photo

settlement of the Peace of Augsburg ninety-three years earlier: The ruler of a land determines the official religion of that land. The treaty also gave the Calvinists their long-sought legal recognition. The independence of the Swiss Confederacy and the United Provinces of the Netherlands, long recognized in fact, was now proclaimed in law. Bavaria became an elector state, Brandenburg-Prussia emerged as the most powerful northern German state, and the other German princes became supreme over their principalities. Yet, as guarantors of the treaty, Sweden and France found many opportunities to meddle in German affairs until the century's end—France for reasons of considerable territorial gain. Because the treaty broadened the legal status of

Protestantism, the pope opposed it altogether, but he had no power to prevent it.

By confirming the territorial sovereignty of Germany's many political entities, the Treaty of Westphalia perpetuated German division and political weakness into the modern period. Only two German states attained international significance during the seventeenth century: Austria and Brandenburg-Prussia. The petty regionalism within the empire also reflected on a small scale the future of larger European politics. In the seventeenth century, distinctive nation-states, each with their own political, cultural, and religious identity, reached maturity, firmly establishing the competitive nationalism of the modern world.

The Chapter in Perspective

Religion and politics played major roles in each of the great conflicts of the Age of Religious Wars—the internal struggle in France, Spain's unsuccessful effort to subdue the Netherlands, England's successful resistance to Spain, and the intervention of every major European power in the hapless Holy Roman Empire during the first half of the seventeenth century. Each conflict involved parties and armies of different religious persuasions in a life-or-death political struggle.

The wars ended with the recognition of minority religious rights and a guarantee of the traditional boundaries of political sovereignty. In France, the **Edict of Nantes** of 1598 brought peace by granting Huguenots basic religious and civil freedoms and by recognizing their towns and

territories. With the departure of the Spanish, peace and sovereignty also came to the Netherlands, guaranteed initially by the Twelve Years' Truce of 1609 and secured fully by the Peace of Westphalia of 1648. The conflict between England and Spain ended with the removal of the Spanish threat to English sovereignty in politics and religion, which had resulted from the execution of Mary, Queen of Scots in 1587 and the English victory over the Armada in 1588. In the Holy Roman Empire, the political principle of the Peace of Augsburg of 1555 was reaffirmed, as the Peace of Westphalia brought the Thirty Years' War to an end by again recognizing the sovereignty of rulers within their lands and their right to determine the religious beliefs of their subjects. Europe at mid-century had real, if brief, peace.

The Chapter in Review

Review Questions

1. How did politics shape the religious positions of the French leaders? What led to the Saint Bartholomew's Day Massacre, and what did it achieve?
2. What were Philip II's successes and failures?
3. Henry of Navarre (Henry IV of France), Elizabeth I, and William of Orange were all politiques. What does that term mean, and why does it apply to these three rulers?
4. What led to the establishment of the Anglican Church in England? Why did Mary I fail? What was Elizabeth I's settlement, and why was it difficult to impose on England? Who were Elizabeth I's detractors, and what were their criticisms?
5. Why was the Thirty Years' War fought? Was politics or religion more important in determining the outcome of the war? What were the main terms of the Treaty of Westphalia in 1648?
6. Why has the Thirty Years' War been called the outstanding example in European history of meaningless conflict? Is this true? Were the results worth the cost of the war?

Key Terms

baroque (bah-ROWK) A style of art marked by heavy and dramatic ornamentation and curved rather than straight lines that flourished between 1550 and 1750; especially associated with the Catholic Counter-Reformation.

Battle of Lepanto (October 7, 1571) A Holy League of Spain, Venice, Genoa, and the pope that defeated the Ottoman navy in the largest naval battle of the sixteenth century.

Cardinal Granvelle In 1561, tried to reorganize the Netherlands to tighten the control of the Spanish monarchy over the country.

Catholic League The league formed by Henry of Guise in 1576 to enforce absolute religious unity in France.

Congregationalists Put a group or assembly above any one individual and preferred an ecclesiastical polity that allowed each congregation to be autonomous, or self-governing.

Counter-Reformation The sixteenth-century reform movement in the Roman Catholic Church in reaction to the Protestant Reformation.

Duke of Alba Spanish general and governor sent by Philip II into the Netherlands to suppress the revolt in 1567 and root out heretics.

Edict of Nantes (April 13, 1598) A formal settlement announced by Henry IV to recognize minority religious rights in France.

Edict of Restitution (1629) An attempt by Ferdinand II, the Holy Roman Emperor, to reassert the Catholic safeguards of the Peace of Augsburg.

Gustavus Adolphus II The Swedish king who led the Protestant forces to a decisive victory at Breitenfeld in 1630.

Huguenots (HYOU-gu-nots) French Calvinists.

Pacification of Ghent (November 8, 1576) The union against Spain of the ten largely Catholic southern provinces with the seven largely Protestant northern provinces of the Netherlands.

Peace of Beaulieu (May 1576) Peace in which Henry III of France granted religious and civil freedom to the Huguenots.

politiques Rulers or people in positions of power who put the success and well-being of their states above all else.

Presbyterians Scottish Calvinists and English Protestants who advocated a national church composed of semiautonomous congregations governed by "presbyteries."

presbyters (PRESS-bi-ters) Meaning "elder." People who directed the affairs of early Christian congregations.

Saint Bartholomew's Day Massacre (August 24, 1572) The slaughter of thousands of Huguenots carried out during three days of coordinated attacks across France.

Thirty-Nine Articles (1563) The official statement of the beliefs of the Church of England that established a moderate form of Protestantism.

Thirty Years' War (1618–1648) The culmination and the most destructive of the European wars of religion, which took place in the Holy Roman Empire.

Treaty of Westphalia (1648) Peace that ended all hostilities within the Holy Roman Empire, whose terms shaped the map of northern Europe and established the concept of sovereign states.

William of Orange The leader of a movement for the independence of the Netherlands from Spain.

Note

1. *Contra libellum Calvini* (N.P., 1562), p. E2a.

Chapter 13
European State Consolidation in the Seventeenth and Eighteenth Centuries

PETER THE GREAT Peter the Great, hoping to make Russia a military power modeled after Western Europe, reorganized the country's political, social, and economic structures. He also radically changed the relationship of the Russian Church to the Russian state. During his reign, Russia entered fully into European power politics.

SOURCE: bpk, Bildagentur/Art Resource, NY

 Contents and Focus Questions

The Chapter in Brief

BETWEEN THE EARLY seventeenth and the mid-twentieth centuries, no region had dominated other parts of the world politically, militarily, and economically as Europe had. This was not the case before and would not be the case after World War II. However, for approximately three and a half centuries, Europe became the chief driving force in one world historical development after another. This era of European dominance, which appears quite temporary in the larger scope of history, also coincided with a shift in power within Europe itself from the Mediterranean, where Spain and Portugal had taken the lead in the conquest and early exploitation of the Americas, to the states of northwest and later north-central Europe.

During the seventeenth and early eighteenth centuries, certain northern Europe states organized politically to dominate Europe and later to influence and even govern other large areas of the world through military and economic strength. Even within northern Europe, there was a division of influence among political states, with some successfully establishing long-term dominance and others passing from the scene after relatively brief periods of either military or economic strength.

By the mid-eighteenth century, five major states had come to dominate European politics and would continue to do so until at least World War I. They were Great Britain, France, Austria, Prussia, and Russia. Through their military strength, economic development, and, in some cases, colonial empires, they would affect virtually every other world civilization. Within Europe, these states established their dominance at the expense of Spain, Portugal, the United Provinces of the Netherlands, Poland, Sweden, and the Ottoman Empire. Equally essential to their rise was the weakness of the Holy Roman Empire after the Peace of Westphalia in 1648.

In Western Europe, Britain and France emerged as the dominant powers. This development represented a shift of influence away from Spain and the United Netherlands. Both of these countries had been powerful during the sixteenth and seventeenth centuries, but they became politically and militarily marginal during the eighteenth century. Neither, however, disappeared from the map, and both retained considerable economic vitality and influence. Spanish power declined after the War of the Spanish Succession, but the case of the Netherlands was more complicated.

13.1 The Netherlands: Golden Age to Decline

What was the Dutch Golden Age, and what led to its decline?

The seven provinces that became the United Provinces of the Netherlands emerged as a nation after revolting against Spain in 1572. During the seventeenth century, the Dutch engaged in a series of naval wars with England. Then, in 1672, the armies of Louis XIV invaded the Netherlands. Prince William III of Orange (1650–1702), the grandson of William the Silent (1533–1584) and the hereditary chief executive, or stadtholder, of Holland, the most important of the provinces, rallied the Dutch and eventually led the entire European coalition against France. As a part of that strategy, he accepted the invitation of Protestant English aristocrats in 1688 to assume, along with his wife Mary, the English throne.

During both the seventeenth and eighteenth centuries, the political and economic life of the Netherlands differed from that of the rest of Europe. The other major nations established strong central governments generally under monarchies, as with France, or in the case of England, under a strong parliamentary system. By contrast, the Netherlands was formally a republic. Each of the provinces retained considerable authority, and the central government, embodied in the States General that met in The Hague, exercised its authority through a kind of ongoing negotiation with the provinces. Prosperous and populous Holland dominated the States General.

The Dutch deeply distrusted monarchy and the ambitions of the House of Orange. Nonetheless, when confronted with major military challenges, the Dutch would permit the House of Orange and, most notably, William III to assume dominant leadership. These political arrangements proved highly resilient and allowed the republic to establish itself permanently in the European state system during the seventeenth century. When William died in 1702 and the wars with France ended in 1714, the Dutch reverted to their republican structures.

Although the provinces making up the Netherlands were traditionally identified with the Protestant cause in Europe, toleration marked Dutch religious life. The Calvinist Reformed Church was the official church of the nation, but it was not an established church. There was always a significant number of Roman Catholics and Protestants who did not belong to the Reformed Church. The country also became a haven for Jews. Consequently, while governments in other European states attempted to impose a single religion on their people or tore themselves apart in religious conflict, in the Netherlands people of differing religious faiths lived together peacefully.

13.1.1 Urban Prosperity

Beyond the climate of religious toleration, what most amazed seventeenth-century contemporaries about the Dutch Republic was its economic prosperity. Its remarkable economic achievement was built on the foundations of high urban consolidation, transformed agriculture, extensive trade and finance, and an overseas commercial empire.

In the Netherlands, more people lived in cities than in any other area of Europe. Key changes in Dutch farming were a model for the rest of Europe and made this urban transformation possible. During the seventeenth century, the Dutch drained and reclaimed land from the sea, which they used for highly profitable farming. Because Dutch shipping provided a steady supply of cheap grain, Dutch farmers themselves could produce more profitable dairy products and beef and cultivate cash products such as tulip bulbs.

Dutch fishermen dominated the market for herring and supplied much of the Continent's dried fish. The Dutch also supplied textiles to many parts of Europe. Dutch ships appeared in harbors all over the Continent, with their captains purchasing goods that they then transported and resold at a profit to other nations. The overseas trades also supported a vast shipbuilding and ship supply industry. The most advanced financial system of the day supported this trade, commerce, and manufacturing.

The final source of Dutch prosperity was a seaborne empire. Dutch traders established a major presence in East Asia, particularly in spice-producing areas of Java, the Moluccas, and Sri Lanka. The **Dutch East India Company**, chartered in 1602, made this possible. The company eventually displaced Portuguese dominance in the spice trade of East Asia and for many years prevented English traders from establishing a major presence there. Initially, the Dutch had only wanted commercial dominance of the spice trade, but in time, they produced the spices themselves, which required them to control many of the islands that now constitute Indonesia. The Netherlands remained the colonial master of this region until after World War II.

13.1.2 Economic Decline

The decline in political influence of the United Provinces of the Netherlands occurred in the eighteenth century. After the death of William III of Britain in 1702, the provinces prevented the emergence of another strong stadtholder. Unified political leadership therefore vanished. Naval supremacy slowly but steadily passed to the British. The fishing industry declined, and the Dutch lost their technological superiority in shipbuilding. Countries between which Dutch ships had once carried goods now traded directly with each other.

Similar stagnation overtook the Dutch domestic industries. The disunity of the provinces hastened this economic decline and prevented action that might have halted it.

The continued financial dominance of the United Provinces saved them from becoming completely insignificant in European affairs. Well past the middle of the eighteenth century, Dutch banks continued to finance European trade, and the Amsterdam stock exchange remained an important financial institution.

13.2 Two Models of European Political Development

What factors led to the different political paths taken by England and France in the seventeenth century?

The United Netherlands, like Venice and the Swiss cantons, was a republic governed without a monarch. Elsewhere in Europe, monarchy of two fundamentally different patterns

THE SEABORNE DUTCH EMPIRE The technologically advanced fleet of the Dutch East India Company, shown here at anchor in Amsterdam, linked the Netherlands' economy with that of Southeast Asia.
SOURCE: Johnny van Haeften Gallery, London, UK/Bridgeman Art Library

predominated in response to the military challenges of international conflict. The two models became known as **parliamentary monarchy** and **political absolutism**. England embodied the first, and France, the second.

The political forces that led to the creation of these two models had arisen from military concerns. During the second half of the sixteenth century, changes in military organization, weapons, and tactics sharply increased the cost of warfare. Because their traditional sources of income could not finance these growing expenses, in addition to the other costs of government, monarchs sought new revenues. Only monarchies that succeeded in building a secure financial base that was not deeply dependent on the support of noble estates, diets, or assemblies achieved absolute rule. The French monarchy succeeded in this effort, whereas the English monarchy failed. That success and failure led to the two models of government—political absolutism in France and parliamentary monarchy in England—that shaped subsequent political development in Europe.

13.3 Constitutional Crisis and Settlement in Stuart England

How did conflicts over taxation and religion lead to civil war in Stuart England?

It was not inevitable that the English monarchy would have to govern through parliament. The Stuart kings of England aspired to the autocracy Louis XIV achieved, and some English political philosophers eloquently defended the **divine right of kings** and absolute rule. At the beginning of the seventeenth century, the English monarchy was strong. Queen Elizabeth, after a reign of almost forty-five years (1558–1603), was much revered. Parliament met only when the monarch summoned it to provide financial support. These conditions would change dramatically by the late seventeenth century.

THE STUARTS	
1603	James VI of Scotland becomes James I of England
1604	James rebuffs the Puritans at the Hampton Court conference
1611	Authorized, or King James, version of the English Bible is published
1625	Charles I becomes English monarch
1628	Charles I recognizes Petition of Right
1629	Charles I dissolves Parliament and embarks on eleven years of personal rule
1640	April–May, Short Parliament convenes; November, Long Parliament convenes
1642–1646	Outbreak of the Civil War

THE STUARTS	
1645	Charles I defeated at Naseby
1648	Pride's Purge
1649	Charles I executed
1649–1660	Various attempts at a Puritan Commonwealth
1660	Charles II restored to the English throne
1670	France and England ally against the Dutch in the Secret Treaty of Dover
1672	Parliament passes the Test Act
1678	Unsuccessful attempts made to exclude James from succession to the throne in the Popish Plot
1685	James II becomes king of England
1688	King James overthrown by the union of Parliament and William of Orange in the "Glorious Revolution"
1689	William and Mary proclaimed English monarchs
1701	Acts of Settlement provide for Hanoverian succession
1702–1714	Reign of Queen Anne, the last of the Stuarts
1707	Act of Union combines England and Scotland
1713	Treaty of Utrecht ends the War of the Spanish Succession
1714	George I becomes king of Great Britain and establishes the Hanoverian dynasty

13.3.1 James I

In 1603 James VI, the son of Mary Stuart, Queen of Scots, who had been King of Scotland since 1567, succeeded without opposition or incident the childless Elizabeth I as James I of England. He also inherited a large royal debt and a fiercely divided church. A strong believer in the divine right of kings, he expected to rule with minimum consultation beyond his own royal court.

Parliament met only when the monarch summoned it, which James hoped to do rarely. In place of parliamentarily approved revenues, James developed other sources of income, largely by levying new custom duties known as *impositions*. Members of Parliament regarded this as an affront to their authority over the royal purse, but they did not seek a serious confrontation. Rather, throughout James's reign they wrangled and negotiated.

The religious problem also festered under James. Since the days of Elizabeth, **Puritans** within the Church of England hoped to eliminate elaborate religious ceremonies and replace the hierarchical episcopal system of church governance under bishops appointed by the king with a more representative Presbyterian form like that of Calvinist churches in Scotland and on the Continent. At the Hampton Court Conference of January 1604, James rebuffed the Puritans and firmly declared his intention to maintain and even enhance the Anglican episcopacy.

Religious dissenters began to leave England. In 1620, Puritan separatists founded Plymouth Colony on Cape Cod Bay in North America, preferring flight from England to Anglican conformity. Later in the 1620s, a larger, better-financed group of Puritans left England to found the Massachusetts Bay Colony. In each case, the colonists believed that

JAMES I OF ENGLAND One of the most well-educated English monarchs, James I was well-read in theology and political theory and wrote on various topics. The English translation of the Bible, called aptly the King James Bible, was issued during his reign.
SOURCE: Ellyn Juritz/Alamy Stock Photo

reformation would not be fully realized in England and that only in America could they worship freely and organize a truly reformed church.

James's court became a center of scandal and corruption. He governed by favorites, of whom the most influential was the Duke of Buckingham, who was rumored to be the king's homosexual lover. Buckingham controlled royal patronage and openly sold peerages and titles to the highest bidders—a practice that angered the nobility because it cheapened their rank. (The court of King James was known for one rather puritanical prohibition: James absolutely detested smoking. James felt nothing but repugnance for smokers, as this chapter's "Encountering the Past" sidebar, makes clear.)

James's foreign policy roused further opposition and doubt about his Protestant loyalty. In 1604, he concluded a much-needed peace with Spain, England's longtime adversary. The war had been ruinously expensive, but his subjects considered the peace a sign of pro-Catholic sentiment. James's unsuccessful attempt to relax penal laws against

Catholics further increased suspicions, as did his wise hesitancy in 1618 to rush English troops to the aid of German Protestants at the outbreak of the Thirty Years' War. In 1624, shortly before James's death, England again went to war against Spain, largely in response to parliamentary pressures.

13.3.2 Charles I

Parliament had favored the war with Spain but would not adequately finance it because its members distrusted the monarchy. Unable to gain adequate funds from Parliament, Charles I (r. 1625–1649), like his father, resorted to extra-parliamentary measures. These included levying new tariffs and duties, attempting to collect discontinued taxes, and subjecting English property owners to a so-called forced loan—a tax theoretically to be repaid—and then imprisoning those who refused to pay. These actions, as well as quartering troops in private homes, challenged local political influence of nobles and landowners.

When Parliament met in 1628, its members would grant new funds only if Charles recognized the **Petition of Right**. This document required that there should be no more forced loans or taxation without the consent of Parliament, that no freeman should be imprisoned without due cause, and that troops should not be billeted in private homes. Charles agreed to the petition, but whether he would keep his word was doubtful. The next year after further disputes, Charles dissolved Parliament and did not recall it until 1640.

13.3.2.1 YEARS OF PERSONAL RULE　To conserve his limited resources, Charles made peace with France in 1629 and Spain in 1630, again rousing fears that he was too friendly with Roman Catholic powers. To allow Charles to rule without renegotiating financial arrangements with Parliament, his chief adviser, Thomas Wentworth (1593–1641; after 1640, Earl of Strafford), implemented strict efficiency and administrative centralization in the government and exploited every legal fundraising device, enforcing previously neglected laws and extending existing taxes into new areas.

Charles might have ruled indefinitely without Parliament had not his religious policies provoked war with Scotland. James I had allowed a wide variety of religious observances in England, Scotland, and Ireland; by contrast, Charles hoped to impose religious conformity at least within England and Scotland. In 1637, Charles and his high-church archbishop William Laud (1573–1645), against the opposition of both the English Puritans and the Presbyterian Scots, tried to impose on Scotland the English episcopal system and a prayer book almost identical to the Anglican Book of Common Prayer.

The Scots rebelled, and Charles, with insufficient resources for war, was forced in 1640 to call Parliament. It refused even to consider funds for war until the king agreed to redress a long list of political and religious grievances. The

Encountering the Past

Early Controversy over Tobacco and Smoking

SMOKING TODAY IS widely condemned throughout the West, but the controversy over tobacco goes back to the earliest European encounter with the plant, which was native to the Americas.

On his first voyage in 1492, Christopher Columbus saw Native Americans smoking tobacco. Later, the first Spanish missionaries associated smoking with pagan religious practices and tried to stop Native Americans from using tobacco. Once tobacco reached Europe in the late sixteenth century, more opposition to smoking arose (although—ironically—some physicians thought it might cure diseases of the lungs and internal organs). As early as 1610, Sir Francis Bacon (1561–1626) noted that smokers found it difficult to stop smoking. The Christian clergy throughout Europe denounced smoking as immoral, and Muslim clerics condemned the practice as contrary to Islam when it spread to the Ottoman Empire. Nonetheless, smoking tobacco in pipes became popular.

TOBACCO-SMOKING GENTLEMEN Introduced from the Americas, tobacco spread quickly throughout Europe. In the seventeenth century, it became the target of regulation as states sought to tax its trade or curb its consumption or both. Some people believed tobacco had medicinal effects, but its main usage was recreational, as suggested by this illustration.
SOURCE: gameover/Alamy Stock Photo

The chief British critic of the new practice was none other than King James I (r. 1603–1625). While he defended Sunday sports against Puritan critics who believed any amusements on the Sabbath were sinful, he detested smoking. In 1604, he published his *Counterblaste to Tobacco* in which he declared, "Have you not reason then to be ashamed, and to forbear this filthy novelt . . . ? In your abuse thereof sinning against God, harming yourselves in person . . . and taking thereby the marks . . . of vanity upon you . . . A custom loathsome to the eye, hateful to the nose, harmful to the brain, dangerous to the lungs, and the black stinking fume thereof, nearest resembling the horrible Stygian smoke of the pit that is bottomless."*

To discourage smoking, James's government placed a high tax on tobacco. Yet when a brisk trade in smuggled tobacco developed, the government lowered the tax to a level where people would not evade it. In 1614, James created a royal monopoly to import tobacco into England, which created a steady government revenue that the increasingly unpopular king badly needed. James, like governments to the present day, may also have regarded this policy as a tax on sin. By 1619, James approved the incorporation of a company of clay pipe makers in London, and 40,000 pounds of tobacco arrived from Virginia the next year. Other European governments would also find tobacco a significant source of tax revenue. They would often tax tobacco and at the same time attempt to regulate its use, especially among the young.

Questions

1. Which groups in Europe in the sixteenth and seventeenth centuries opposed the habit of smoking tobacco?
2. Why did the English government under King James I modify its opposition to tobacco?

K. James I (England) A Counterblaste to Tobacco. Rodale Press, London 1954.

king, in response, immediately dissolved that Parliament—hence its name, the Short Parliament (April–May 1640). When the Scots defeated an English army at the Battle of Newburn in the summer of 1640, Charles reconvened Parliament—this time on its terms—for a long and fateful duration.

13.3.3 The Long Parliament and Civil War

The landowners and the merchant classes represented in Parliament had long resented the king's financial measures and paternalistic rule. The Puritans in Parliament resented his religious policies and distrusted the influence of his Roman Catholic wife. What became known as the Long Parliament (1640–1660) thus acted with widespread support and general unanimity when it convened in November 1640.

The House of Commons impeached both Strafford and Laud. Both were executed—Strafford in 1641, Laud in 1645. Parliament abolished the courts that had enforced royal policy and prohibited the levying of new taxes without its consent. Finally, Parliament resolved that no more than three years should elapse between its meetings and that the king could not dissolve it without its own consent.

Parliament, however, was sharply divided over religion. Both moderate Puritans (the Presbyterians) and more extreme Puritans (the Independents) wanted to abolish bishops and the Book of Common Prayer. Yet religious conservatives in both houses of Parliament were determined to preserve the Church of England in its current form.

These divisions intensified in October 1641, when Parliament was asked to raise funds for an army to suppress the rebellion in Scotland. Charles's opponents argued that he could not be trusted with an army and that Parliament should become the commander in chief of English armed forces. In January 1642, Charles invaded Parliament, intending to arrest certain of his opponents, but they escaped. The king then left London and began to raise an army. Shocked, a majority of the House of Commons passed the **Militia Ordinance**, which gave Parliament authority to raise an army of its own. The die was now cast. For the next four years (1642–1646), civil war engulfed England with the king's supporters known as Cavaliers and the parliamentary opposition as Roundheads.

13.3.4 Oliver Cromwell and the Puritan Republic

Two factors led finally to Parliament's victory. The first was an alliance with Scotland in 1643 that committed Parliament to a Presbyterian system of church government. The second was the reorganization of the parliamentary army under **Oliver Cromwell** (1599–1658), a country squire of iron discipline and strong, independent religious sentiment. Cromwell and his "godly men" were willing to tolerate an established majority church, but only if it permitted Protestant dissenters to worship outside it.

Defeated militarily by June 1645, for the next several years Charles tried to take advantage of divisions within Parliament, but Cromwell and his army foiled him. Members who might have been sympathetic to the monarch were expelled from Parliament in December 1648. After a trial by a special court, Charles was executed on January 30, 1649, as a public criminal. Parliament then abolished the monarchy, the House of Lords, and the Anglican Church.

From 1649 to 1660, England became officially a Puritan republic, although Cromwell dominated it. His army brutally conquered Scotland and Ireland, where his radically Protestant army carried out numerous atrocities against Irish Catholics. As a national leader, however, Cromwell proved to be no politician. When in 1653 the House of Commons wanted to disband his expensive army of 50,000 men, Cromwell instead disbanded Parliament. He ruled thereafter as Lord Protector. (See the "Compare and Connect" sidebar, which follows below, on the publication of radical

"INVASION" OF PARLIAMENT A key moment in the conflict between Charles I and Parliament, captured in this illustration, occurred in January 1642 when Charles personally arrived at the House of Commons to arrest five members responsible for opposing him only to learn that they had already fled. Thereafter Charles departed London to raise his army.
SOURCE: Print Collector/Getty Images

OLIVER CROMWELL Oliver Cromwell's New Model Army defeated the royalists in the English Civil War. After the execution of Charles I in 1649, Cromwell dominated the short-lived English republic, conquered Ireland and Scotland, and ruled as Lord Protector from 1653 until his death in 1658.
SOURCE: Beryl Peters Collection/Alamy Stock Photo

views being expressed during the "distracted times" of the 1640s.)

Cromwell's military dictatorship, however, proved no more effective than Charles's rule and became just as harsh and hated. People deeply resented his Puritan prohibitions of drunkenness, theatergoing, and dancing. Political liberty vanished in the name of religious conformity. When Cromwell died in 1658, the English were ready by 1660 to restore both the Anglican Church and the monarchy.

13.3.5 Charles II and the Restoration of the Monarchy

After negotiations with the army, Charles II (r. 1660–1685) returned to England amid great rejoicing. A man of considerable charm and political skill, Charles set a refreshing new tone after eleven years of somber Puritanism. England returned to the status quo of 1642, with a hereditary monarch, a Parliament of Lords and Commons that met only when the king summoned it, and the Anglican Church, with its bishops and prayer book, supreme in religion.

The king, however, had secret Catholic sympathies and favored religious toleration. He wanted to allow loyal Catholics and Puritans to worship freely. Yet ultra-royalists in

Parliament between 1661 and 1665, through a series of laws known as the Clarendon Code, excluded Roman Catholics, Presbyterians, and Independents from the official religious and political life of the nation.

In 1670 by the Treaty of Dover, England and France formally allied against the Dutch, their chief commercial competitor. In a secret portion of this treaty, Charles pledged to announce his conversion to Catholicism as soon as conditions in England permitted this to happen. In return for this announcement, which Charles never made, Louis XIV promised to pay Charles a substantial subsidy. In an attempt to persuade the English people to back the war with Holland, and as a sign of good faith to Louis XIV, Charles issued a **Declaration of Indulgence** in 1672, suspending all laws against Roman Catholics and non-Anglican Protestants. Parliament refused to fund the war, however, until Charles rescinded the measure. After he did so, Parliament passed the **Test Act** requiring all civil and military officials of the crown to swear an oath against the doctrine of transubstantiation—which no loyal Roman Catholic could honestly do. Parliament had directed the Test Act largely at the king's brother, James, duke of York, heir to the throne and a recent, devout convert to Catholicism.

In 1678, a notorious liar named Titus Oates swore before a magistrate that Charles's Catholic wife, through her physician, was plotting with Jesuits and Irishmen to kill the king so James could assume the throne. Parliament believed Oates. In the ensuing hysteria, known as the Popish Plot, several innocent people were tried and executed. Riding the crest of anti-Catholic sentiment and led by the Earl of Shaftesbury (1621–1683), opposition members of Parliament, called Whigs, made an unsuccessful effort to exclude James from succession to the throne.

More suspicious than ever of Parliament, Charles II again increased customs duties and requested the assistance of Louis XIV for extra income. By these means, he was able to rule from 1681 to 1685 without recalling Parliament. In those years, Charles drove Shaftesbury into exile, executed several Whig leaders for treason, and bullied local corporations into electing members of Parliament submissive to the royal will. When Charles died in 1685, after a deathbed conversion to Catholicism, he left James the prospect of a Parliament filled with royal friends.

13.3.6 The "Glorious Revolution"

When James II (r. 1685–1688) became king, he immediately demanded the repeal of the Test Act. When Parliament balked, he dissolved it and proceeded to appoint Catholics to high positions in both his court and the army. In 1687, he issued another Declaration of Indulgence suspending all religious tests and permitting free worship. In June 1688, James imprisoned seven Anglican bishops who had refused

Compare and Connect

The World Turned Upside Down

THE CHAOS CREATED BY THE ENGLISH CIVIL WAR loosened governmental controls on political and religious expression. For a few years, English men and women were free to publish views that would have been censored in the decades proceeding the war and would be censored again in the decades to follow. The excerpts included below provide two examples of radical publications. In the first, a group known as the Levellers called for communal ownership of all land in England, starting with George Hill, a plot of land the Levellers had claimed for themselves. In the second, an unnamed pamphleteer, W. P., known only by his initials, denounced war itself, arguing that neither king nor Parliament was fighting for a just cause.

THE WORLD TURNED UPSIDE DOWN This illustration from a 1647 pamphlet conveys the sense of many English observers that the English Civil War had overturned all norms and conventions.

SOURCE: Pictorial Press Ltd / Alamy Stock Photo

Before Reading

- Think about the impact of the English Civil War on the functioning of secular and religious institutions.
- Ask yourself how widespread radical views might have been at the time.
- Consider the larger religious and ideological context in which these views were expressed.

Questions:

1. What did the Levellers want?
2. How did the Levellers' views of the rights of English citizens differ from those of most supporters of Parliament?
3. What did W. P. see as the real cause of the English Civil War?
4. On what might W. P. and the Levellers have agreed?

I. THE TRUE LEVELLERS STANDARD (1649)

Take notice, That *England* is not a Free People, till the Poor that have no Land, have a free allowance to dig and labour the Commons, and so live as Comfortably as the Landlords that live in their Inclosures. For the People have not laid out their

Monies, and shed their Bloud, that their Landlords, the *Norman* power, should still have its liberty and freedom to rule in Tyranny in his Lords, landlords, Judges, Justices, Bayliffs, and State Servants; but that the Oppressed might be set Free, Prison doors opened, and the Poor peoples hearts comforted by an universal Consent of making the Earth a Common Treasury, that they may live together as one House of Israel, united in brotherly love into one Spirit; and having a comfortable livelihood in the Community of one Earth their Mother.

If you look through the Earth, you shall see, That the landlords, Teachers and Rulers, are Oppressors, Murtherers, and Theeves in this manner; But it was not thus from the Beginning. And this is one Reason of our digging and labouring the Earth one with another; That we might work in righteousness, and lift up the Creation from bondage: For so long as we own Landlords in this Corrupt Settlement, we cannot work in righteousness; for we should still lift up the Curse, and tread down the Creation, dishonour the Spirit of universal Liberty, and hinder the work of Restauration.

Secondly, in that we begin to Digge upon *George-Hill,* to eate our Bread together by righteous labour, and sweat of our browes, It was shewed us by Vision in Dreams, and out of Dreams, That that should be the Place we should begin upon; And though that Earth in view of Flesh, be very barren, yet we should trust the Spirit for a blessing. And that not only this Common, or Heath should be taken in and Manured by the People, but all the Commons and waste Ground in *England,* and in the whole World, shall be taken in by the People in righteousness, not owning any Propriety; but taking the Earth to be a Common Treasury, as it was first made for all.

II. W. P. (gent.), THE BLOODY PROJECT (1648)

To be short, all the quarrel we have at this day in the Kingdom, is no other than a quarrel of Interests, and Parties, a pulling down of one Tyrant, to set up another, and instead of Liberty, heaping upon ourselves a greater slavery than that we fought against: certainly this is the Liberty that is so much strove for, and for which there are such fresh endeavors to engage men; but if you have not killed and destroyed men enough for this, go on and destroy, kill and slay, till your consciences are swollen so full with the blood of the People, that they burst again, and upon your death-beds may you see yourselves the most horrid Murderers that ever lived, since the time that Cain killed his brother without a just Cause; for where, or what is your cause? Believe it you have a heavy reckoning to make, and must undergo a sad repentance, or it will go ill with you at the great day, when all the sophistry of your great Reformers will serve you to little purpose, every man for himself being to give an account for the things which he hath done in the body, whether they be good or evil: Then it will serve you to little purpose to say, the King, Parliament, Army, Independents, Presbyterians, such an Officer, Magistrate, or Minister deluded me; no more than it did Adam, to say the woman whom thou gavest, etc. It being thus decreed in heaven, the soul which sinneth shall surely die.

For shame therefore, Royalists, Presbyterians, Independents, before you murder another man hold forth your Cause plainly and expressly; and if any Adversaries appear either within or without the Land, reason it out with them if it be possible, deal as becomes Christians, argue, persuade, and use all possible means to prevent another War, and greater bloodshed; your great ones, whether the King, Lords, Parliament men, rich Citizens, etc. feel not the miserable effects thereof, and so cannot be sensible; but you and your poor friends that depend on Farms, Trades, and small pay, have many an aching heart when these live in all pleasure and deliciousness: The accursed thing is accepted by them, wealth and honor, and both comes by the bleeding miserable distractions of the Commonwealth, and they fear an end of trouble would put an end to their glory and greatness.

Oh therefore all you Soldiers and People, that have your Consciences alive about you, put to your strength of Judgment, and all the might you have to prevent a further effusion of blood; let not the covetous, the proud, the blood-thirsty man bear sway amongst you; fear not their high looks, give no ear to their charms, their promises or tears; they have no strength without you, forsake them and ye will be strong for good, adhere to them, and they will be strong to evil; for which you must answer and give an account at the last day.

SOURCES: (I) From Jerrard Winstanley, William Everard, Richard Goodgroome et al., *The True Levellers Standard Advanced: The State of Community Opened, and Presented to the Sons of Men* (London: 1649). (II). From W. P., Gent., *The Bloody Project: Or a Discovery of the New Designe, in the Present War* (London: 1648).

to publicize his suspension of laws against the Catholics. Each of these actions represented a direct royal attack on the local authority of nobles, landowners, the church, and other corporate bodies whose members believed they possessed special legal privileges. James desired not only to aid his fellow Roman Catholics but also to pursue absolutist policies similar to those of Louis XIV, whom he deeply admired.

The English had hoped that James would be succeeded by Mary (r. 1689–1694), his Protestant eldest daughter. She was the wife of William III of Orange, the leader of European opposition to Louis XIV. But on June 20, James II's

Catholic second wife gave birth to a son. There was now a Catholic male heir to the throne. The Parliamentary opposition invited William to invade England to preserve its "traditional liberties," that is, the Anglican Church and parliamentary government.

William of Orange arrived with his army in November 1688 and was received with considerable popular support. James fled to France, and Parliament, in 1689, proclaimed William III and Mary II the new monarchs, thus completing the "**Glorious Revolution**." William and Mary, in turn, recognized a Bill of Rights that limited the powers of the monarchy and guaranteed the civil liberties of the English privileged classes. Henceforth, England's monarchs would be subject to law and would rule by the consent of Parliament, which would be called into session every three years. The Bill of Rights also prohibited Roman Catholics from occupying the English throne. The Toleration Act of 1689 permitted worship by all Protestants and outlawed only Roman Catholics and those who denied the Christian doctrine of the Trinity. It did not, however, extend full political rights to persons outside the Church of England.

The parliamentary measure closing this century of strife was the Act of Settlement in 1701. It allowed the English crown to go to the Protestant House of Hanover in Germany if Queen Anne (r. 1702–1714), the second daughter of James II and the heir to the childless William III, died without issue. Thus, at Anne's death in 1714, the Elector of Hanover became King George I of Great Britain (r. 1714–1727) since England and Scotland had been combined in an Act of Union in 1707.

13.3.7 The Age of Walpole

George I almost immediately confronted a challenge to his title. James Edward Stuart (1688–1766), the Catholic son of James II, landed in Scotland in December 1715, but met defeat less than two months later.

SIR ROBERT WALPOLE Sir Robert Walpole (1676–1745), far left, is shown talking with the Speaker of the House of Commons. Walpole, who dominated British political life from 1721 to 1742, was considered the first prime minister of Britain.
SOURCE: Mansell/Getty Images

Despite the victory over the Stuart pretender, the political situation after 1715 remained in flux until **Sir Robert Walpole** (1676–1745) took over government. Walpole's ascendancy from 1721 to 1742 was based on royal support, his ability to handle the House of Commons, and his control of government patronage. Walpole maintained peace abroad and promoted the status quo at home. Britain's foreign trade spread from New England to India. Because the central government refrained from interfering with the local political influence of nobles and other landowners, they were willing to serve as local government administrators, judges, and military commanders, and to collect and pay the taxes to support a powerful military force, particularly a strong navy. As a result, Great Britain became not only a European power of the first order but eventually a world power as well.

The power of the British monarchs and their ministers had real limits. Parliament could not wholly ignore popular pressure. Newspapers and public debate flourished, and free speech could be exercised, as could freedom of association. There was no large standing army, and there was significant religious toleration. Walpole's enemies could and did openly oppose his policies, which would not have been possible on the Continent. Consequently, the English state combined considerable military power with both religious and political liberty. British political life became the model for all progressive Europeans who questioned the absolutist political developments of the Continent. Furthermore, many of the political values that had emerged in the British Isles during the seventeenth century also took deep root among their North American colonies.

13.4 Rise of Absolute Monarchy in France: The World of Louis XIV

Why were efforts to establish absolute monarchy successful in France but unsuccessful in England?

Historians once portrayed Louis XIV's reign (r. 1643–1715) as a time when the French monarchy had far-reaching, direct control of the nation at all levels. A somewhat different picture has now emerged.

The French monarchy, which had faced numerous challenges from strong, well-armed nobles and discontented Protestants during the first half of the seventeenth century, only gradually achieved the firm authority for which it became renowned later in the century. The groundwork for Louis XIV's absolutism had been laid by two powerful

LOUIS XIV OF FRANCE Louis XIV of France came to symbolize absolute monarchy, though his government was not truly absolute. This state portrait was intended to convey the grandeur of the king and of his authority. The portrait was brought into royal council meetings when the king was absent.
SOURCE: Gift of J. Paul Getty

local social and political institutions, Louis largely worked through them. Nevertheless, the king was clearly the senior partner in the relationship.

KEY EVENTS IN FRANCE: FROM LOUIS XIV TO CARDINAL FLEURY	
1643	Louis ascends the French throne at the age of five
1643–1661	Cardinal Mazarin directs the French government
1648	Peace of Westphalia
1649–1652	The *Fronde* revolt, a series of rebellions among French nobles, begins
1653	The pope declares Jansenism a heresy
1660	Papal ban on Jansenists enforced in France
1661	Louis commences personal rule
1667–1668	Louis supports the alleged right of his first wife, Marie Thérèse, to inherit the Spanish Netherlands in the War of Devolution
1670	France and Great Britain ally against Dutch in Secret Treaty of Dover
1672–1679	French war against the Netherlands
1685	Louis revokes the Edict of Nantes
1688–1697	War of the League of Augsburg
1701	Outbreak of the War of the Spanish Succession
1713	Treaty of Utrecht between France and Great Britain
1714	Treaty of Rastatt between France and the empire and Holland allows the Habsburgs to further extend their domains
1715	Louis XIV dies
1715–1720	Regency of the Duke of Orléans in France
1720	Mississippi Bubble bursts in France
1726–1743	Cardinal Fleury serves as Louis XV's chief minister

13.4.1 Years of Personal Rule

On the death of Mazarin in 1661, Louis XIV assumed personal control of the government at the age of twenty-three. He appointed no single chief minister. Rebellious nobles would now be challenging the king directly; they could not claim to be resisting only a bad minister.

Louis devoted enormous personal energy to his political tasks. He ruled through councils that controlled foreign affairs, the army, domestic administration, and economic regulations. Each day he spent hours with the ministers of these councils, whom he chose from families long in royal service or from among people just beginning to rise in the social structure. Unlike the more ancient noble families, the latter had no real or potential power bases in the provinces and depended solely on the king for their standing in both government and society.

Louis made sure, however, that the nobility and other major social groups would benefit from the growth of his authority. Although he controlled foreign affairs and limited the influence of noble institutions on the monarchy, Louis never tried to abolish those institutions or limit their local authority. For example, the crown usually met informally with regional judicial bodies, called *parlements*, before making rulings that would affect them. Likewise, the crown

chief ministers, Cardinal Richelieu (1585–1642), under Louis XIII (r. 1610–1643), and Cardinal Mazarin (1602–1661). Both Richelieu and Mazarin attempted to implement direct royal administration in France. Richelieu had also circumscribed many of the political privileges Henry IV had extended to French Protestants in the Edict of Nantes in 1598. The centralizing policies of Richelieu and then of Mazarin, however, finally provoked a series of widespread rebellions among French nobles between 1649 and 1652 known as the *Fronde*, after the slingshots used by street boys.

Though unsuccessful, these rebellions convinced Louis XIV and his advisers that heavy-handed policies could endanger the throne. Thereafter Louis would concentrate unprecedented authority in the monarchy, but he would be more subtle than his predecessors. His genius was to make the monarchy the most important and powerful political institution in France while also assuring the nobles and other wealthy groups of their social standing and influence on the local level. Rather than destroying existing would rarely enact economic regulations without consulting local opinion.

13.4.2 Versailles

Louis and his advisers became masters of propaganda and political image creation. Louis never missed an opportunity to impress the French people, especially the French nobility, with the grandeur of his crown. He did so by the manipulation of symbols. For example, when the *dauphin*, the heir to the French throne, was born in 1662, Louis appeared for the celebration dressed as a Roman emperor. He also dominated the nobility by demonstrating that he could outspend them and create a greater social display than the strongest nobles in the land.

The greatest symbol of the monarchy was the palace of Versailles, which, when completed, was the largest secular structure in Europe. (See the "Closer Look" sidebar, which follows below, to learn more about Versailles.) More than any other monarch of the day, Louis XIV used the physical setting of his court to exert political control. Versailles, built between 1676 and 1708 on the outskirts of Paris, became Louis's permanent residence after 1682. It was a temple to royalty, designed and decorated to proclaim the glory of the Sun King, as Louis was known. A spectacular estate with magnificent fountains and gardens, it housed thousands of the more important nobles, royal officials, and servants. The stables alone could hold 12,000 horses. Some nobles paid for their own residence at the palace, thus depleting their resources; others required royal patronage to remain in residence. In either case, they became dependent on the monarch. Although it consumed over half of Louis's annual revenues, Versailles paid significant political dividends.

Because Louis ruled personally, he was himself the chief source of favors and patronage in France. To emphasize his prominence, he organized life at court around every aspect of his own daily routine. Elaborate etiquette governed every detail of life at Versailles. Moments near the king were important to most court nobles because they were effectively excluded from the real business of government. The king's rising and dressing were times of rare intimacy, when nobles could whisper their special requests in his ear. Fortunate nobles held his night candle when he went to his bed.

Some nobles, of course, avoided Versailles. They managed their estates and cultivated their local influence. Many others were simply too poor to cut a figure at court. The nobility understood, however, that Louis, unlike Richelieu and Mazarin, would not threaten their local social standing, because Louis supported France's traditional social structure and the social privileges of the nobility. Yet even the most powerful nobles knew they could strike only a modest figure when compared to the Sun King.

13.4.3 King by Divine Right

An important source for Louis's concept of royal authority was his devout tutor, political theorist Bishop Jacques-Bénigne Bossuet (1627–1704). Bossuet defended what he called the "divine right of kings" and cited examples of Old Testament rulers divinely appointed by and answerable only to God. Medieval popes had insisted that only God could judge a pope, so Bossuet argued that only God could judge the king. Although kings might be duty bound to reflect God's will in their rule, as God's regents on earth they could not be bound to the dictates of mere nobles and parliaments. Such assumptions lay behind Louis XIV's alleged declaration: *"L'état, c'est moi"* or "I am the state."

Despite these claims, Louis's rule did not exert the oppressive control over the daily lives of his subjects that police states would in the nineteenth and twentieth centuries. His absolutism focused primarily on the classic areas of European state action—the making of war and peace, the regulation of religion, and the oversight of economic activity. Even at the height of his power, local institutions, some controlled by townspeople and others by nobles, retained their administrative authority. The king and his ministers supported the social and financial privileges of these local elites. In contrast to the Stuart kings of England, however, Louis firmly prevented them from interfering with his authority on the national level. This system would endure until a financial crisis demoralized the French monarchy in the 1780s.

13.4.4 Louis's Early Wars

By the late 1660s, France was superior to any other European nation in population, administrative bureaucracy, army, and national unity. Because of the economic policies of Jean-Baptiste Colbert (1619–1683), his most brilliant minister, Louis could afford to raise and maintain a large and powerful army. His enemies and some later historians claimed that Louis wished to dominate all of Europe, but it appears that his chief military and foreign policy goal was to achieve secure international boundaries for France. He was particularly concerned about securing its northern borders along the Spanish Netherlands, the Franche-Comté, Alsace, and Lorraine from which foreign armies had invaded France and could easily do so again. Louis was also determined to frustrate Habsburg ambitions that endangered France and, as part of that goal, wanted to secure his southern borders toward Spain. Whether reacting to external events or pursuing his own ambitions, Louis's pursuit of French interests threatened and terrified neighboring states and led them to form coalitions against France.

The early wars of Louis XIV included conflicts with Spain and the United Netherlands. The first was the War of the Devolution in which Louis supported the alleged right of his first wife, Marie Thérèse, to inherit the Spanish

A Closer Look

Versailles

LOUIS XIV CONSTRUCTED his great palace at Versailles, as painted here in 1668 by Pierre Patel the Elder (1605–1676), to demonstrate the new centralized power he hoped to imbue in the French monarchy. Its interiors, particularly, were decorated with themes from mythology, presenting Louis XIV as the "Sun King" around whom his kingdom revolved. Given the extravagant scale of the palace and gardens, it took armies of servants with shears to keep the green forest lawn and vegetation (*tapis vert*) "royal."

The outer wings, extending from the front of the central structure, housed governmental offices.

The central building is the hunting lodge his father Louis XIII built earlier in the century.

The gardens and ponds behind the main structure were sites of elaborative entertainment, concerts, and fireworks.

PERSPECTIVE VIEW OF VERSAILLES
SOURCE: DEA/G. DAGLI ORTI/Getty Images

Questions

1. How might the size of Versailles, as experienced by visitors and by viewers of paintings and prints of the structure, have overwhelmed Louis's subjects? How might French nobility in particular have reacted to the setting? What other buildings of the day approached Versailles in size?

2. Do you think people who viewed Versailles or images of it wondered how this extraordinary royal community was financed? What conclusions might have been made about the structure of French taxes?

3. By the end of his life, Louis rarely ventured outside Versailles, and neither did his eighteenth-century royal successors. Do you think the limitation of royal experience to Versailles distorted the monarchs' view of their kingdom?

4. Did the the use of mythology in portraying Louis create a sense that he and his power were vaster than those of ordinary mortals? Explain.

Netherlands. He contended that through complex legal arrangements they should have "devolved" upon her, hence the name of the war. In 1667, Louis's armies invaded Flanders and the Franche-Comté. Louis was repulsed by the Triple Alliance of England, Sweden, and the United Provinces. Through the Treaty of Aix-la-Chapelle of 1668, he gained control of certain towns bordering the Spanish Netherlands. (See Map 13–1.)

In 1670, with the secret Treaty of Dover, England and France became allies against the Dutch. Louis invaded the Netherlands again in 1672. The Prince of Orange, the future William III of England, forged an alliance with the Holy Roman Emperor, Spain, Lorraine, and Brandenburg against Louis, now regarded as a menace to the whole of Western Europe, Catholic and Protestant alike. The war ended inconclusively with the Peace of Nijmwegen, signed with different parties in successive years (1678, 1679). France gained more territory, including the Franche-Comté.

Map 13–1   THE FIRST THREE WARS OF LOUIS XIV

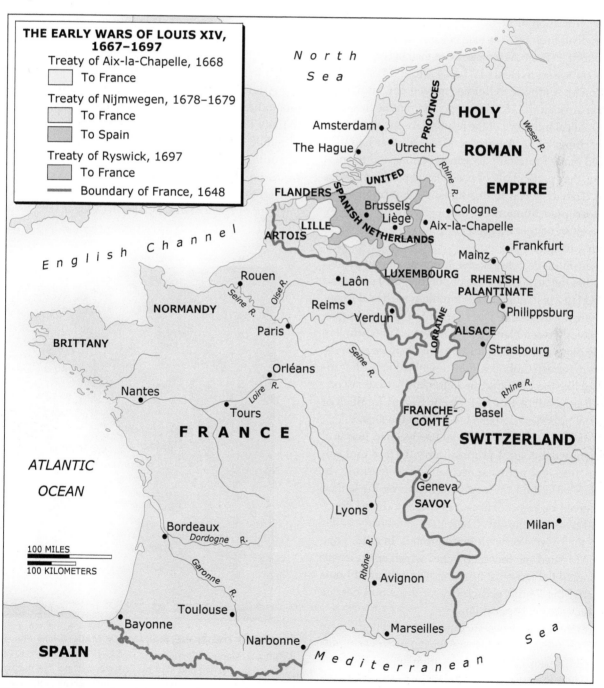

This map shows the territorial changes resulting from Louis XIV's first three major wars that took place from 1667 to 1697.

13.4.5 Louis's Repressive Religious Policies

Like Richelieu before him, Louis believed that political unity and stability required religious conformity. To that end he carried out repressive actions against both Roman Catholics and Protestants.

13.4.5.1 SUPPRESSION OF THE JANSENISTS

The French crown and the French Roman Catholic Church had long jealously guarded their ecclesiastical independence or **Gallican Liberties** from papal authority in Rome. However, after the conversion to Roman Catholicism of Henry IV in 1593, the Jesuits, fiercely loyal to the authority of the Pope, had monopolized the education of French upper-class men, and their devout students promoted the religious reforms and doctrines of the Council of Trent. As a measure of their success, Jesuits served as confessors to Henry IV, Louis XIII, and Louis XIV.

A Roman Catholic religious movement known as *Jansenism* arose in the 1630s in opposition to the theology and the political influence of the Jesuits. Jansenists adhered to the teachings of St. Augustine (354–430) that had also influenced many Protestant doctrines. Serious and uncompromising, they particularly opposed Jesuit teachings about free will. They believed with Augustine that original sin had so corrupted humankind that individuals could by their own effort neither do good nor contribute anything to their own salvation.

Jansenism made considerable progress among prominent families in Paris. They were opposed to the Jesuits and supported Jansenist religious communities such as the convent at Port-Royal outside Paris. Jansenists, whose Augustinian theology resembled Calvinism, were known to live extremely pious and morally austere lives. In these respects, though firm Roman Catholics, they resembled English Puritans. Also, like the Puritans, the Jansenists became associated with opposition to royal authority, and families of Jansenist sympathies had been involved in the *Fronde*.

On May 31, 1653, Pope Innocent X declared heretical five Jansenist theological propositions on grace and salvation. In 1656, the pope banned Jansen's *Augustinus*. In 1660, Louis permitted the papal bull banning Jansenism to be enforced in France. He also eventually closed down the Port-Royal community. Thereafter, Jansenists either retracted their views or went underground. In 1713, Pope Clement XI issued the bull *Unigenitus*, which again extensively condemned Jansenist teaching. The now aged Louis XIV ordered the French church to accept the bull despite internal ecclesiastical opposition.

The theological issues surrounding Jansenism were complex. By persecuting the Jansenists, however, Louis XIV turned his back on the long tradition of protecting the Gallican Liberties of the French Church and fostered within the French Church a core of opposition to royal authority. This had long-term political significance. During the eighteenth century after the death of Louis XIV, the Parlement of Paris and other French judicial bodies would reassert their authority in opposition to the monarchy. These courts were sympathetic to the Jansenists because of their common resistance to royal authority. Jansenism, because of its austere morality, came to embody religious and moral values that contrasted with what eighteenth-century public opinion believed was the corruption of the mid-eighteenth century French royal court.

13.4.5.2 REVOCATION OF THE EDICT OF NANTES

After the Edict of Nantes in 1598, relations between the Catholic majority (nine-tenths of the French population) and the Protestant minority had remained hostile. There were about 1.75 million Huguenots in France in the 1660s (out of an overall population of around 18 million), but their numbers were declining. The French Catholic Church had long supported their persecution as both pious and patriotic.

After the Peace of Nijmwegen, Louis launched a methodical campaign against the Huguenots in an effort to unify France religiously. Louis hounded Huguenots out of public life, banning them from government office and excluding them from such professions as printing and medicine. He used financial incentives to encourage them to convert to Catholicism. In 1681, he bullied them by quartering troops in their towns. Finally, in October 1685, believing

FRANÇOISE D'AUBIGNE, MADAME DE MAINTENON Françoise d'Aubigne, Madame de Maintenon (1635–1719), a mistress to Louis XIV, secretly married him after his first wife's death. The deeply pious Maintenon influenced Louis's methodical campaign against the Huguenots to make Roman Catholicism France's only religion.
SOURCE: RMN-Grand Palais/Art Resource, NY

a country could not be governed by one king and one law unless it also had one religious system, Louis XIV stunned much of Europe in October 1685 by revoking the Edict of Nantes, which had protected the religious freedoms and civil rights of French Protestants since 1598. Extensive religious repression followed. Protestant churches and schools were closed, Protestant ministers exiled, nonconverting laity were condemned to be galley slaves, and Protestant children were baptized by Catholic priests.

The revocation was a major blunder. Henceforth, Protestants across Europe considered Louis a fanatic who must be resisted at all costs. More than a quarter million people, many of whom were highly skilled, left France. They formed new communities abroad and joined the resistance to Louis in England, Germany, Holland, and the New World. As a result of the revocation of the Edict of Nantes and the ongoing persecution of Jansenists, France became a symbol of religious repression in contrast to England's reputation for moderate, if not complete, religious toleration.

13.4.6 Louis's Later Wars

Having succeeded in his initial set of wars to secure his nation's borders, Louis met resistance as he appeared to threaten the balance of power in Europe. In Germany, he encountered the League of Augsburg. Then the Grand Alliance frustrated his designs on the Spanish crown as Louis's shortfalls in the latest military technology and tactics surfaced.

13.4.6.1 THE LEAGUE OF AUGSBURG AND THE NINE YEARS' WAR After the Treaty of Nijmwegen in 1678–1679, Louis maintained his army at full strength and restlessly probed beyond his borders. In 1681 his forces occupied the free city of Strasbourg on the Rhine River, prompting new defensive coalitions to form against him. One of these, the League of Augsburg, grew to include England, Spain, Sweden, the United Provinces, and the major German states. It also had the support of the Habsburg emperor Leopold I (r. 1658–1705). Between 1689 and 1697, the League and France battled each other in the Nine Years' War, while England and France struggled to control North America.

The Peace of Ryswick, signed in September 1697, which ended the war, secured Holland's borders and thwarted Louis's expansion into Germany.

13.4.6.2 WAR OF THE SPANISH SUCCESSION On November 1, 1700, the last Habsburg king of Spain, Charles II (r. 1665–1700), died without direct heirs. Before his death, negotiations had begun among the nations involved to partition his inheritance in a way that would preserve the existing balance of power. Charles II, however, left his entire inheritance to Louis's grandson Philip of Anjou, who became Philip V of Spain (r. 1700–1746).

Spain and the vast trade with its American empire appeared to have fallen to France. In September 1701, England, Holland, and the Holy Roman Empire formed the Grand Alliance. It preserved the balance of power by once and for all securing Flanders as a neutral barrier between Holland and France and by giving the emperor, who was also a Habsburg, his fair share of the Spanish inheritance. Louis soon increased the political stakes by recognizing the Stuart claim to the English throne.

In 1701 the War of the Spanish Succession (1701–1714) began, and it soon enveloped Western Europe. For the first time in Louis's reign France went to war with inadequate finances, a poorly equipped army, and mediocre generals. The English, in contrast, had advanced weaponry—flintlock rifles, paper cartridges, and ring bayonets—and superior tactics—thin, maneuverable troop columns rather than the traditional deep ones. John Churchill, the Duke of Marlborough (1650–1722), bested Louis's soldiers in every major engagement, although French arms triumphed in Spain. After 1709 the war became a bloody stalemate.

France finally made peace with England at Utrecht in July 1713, and with Holland and the emperor at Rastatt in March 1714. Philip V remained king of Spain, but England got Gibraltar and the island of Minorca, making it a Mediterranean power. (See Map 13–2.) Louis also recognized the right of the House of Hanover to the English throne.

13.4.7 France After Louis XIV

Despite its military reverses in the War of the Spanish Succession, France remained a great power. It was less strong in 1715 than in 1680, but it still possessed the largest European population; an advanced, if troubled, economy; and the administrative structure created by Louis XIV. Moreover, even if France and its resources had been drained by the last of Louis's wars, the other major states of Europe were similarly debilitated.

Louis XIV was succeeded by his five-year-old great-grandson Louis XV (r. 1715–1774). The young boy's uncle, the Duke of Orléans, became regent and remained so until his death in 1720. The regency, marked by financial and moral scandals, further undermined the faltering prestige of the monarchy.

13.4.7.1 JOHN LAW AND THE MISSISSIPPI BUBBLE The Duke of Orléans was a gambler, and for a time he turned over the financial management of the kingdom to John Law (1671–1729), a Scottish mathematician and fellow gambler. Law believed an increase in the paper-money supply would stimulate France's economic recovery. With the permission of the regent, he established a bank in Paris that issued paper money. Law then organized a monopoly, called the Mississippi Company, on trading privileges with the French colony of Louisiana in North America.

The Mississippi Company also took over the management of the French national debt. The company issued shares of its own stock in exchange for government bonds, which had fallen sharply in value. To redeem large quantities of bonds, Law encouraged speculation in the

Map 13–2   EUROPE IN 1714

The War of the Spanish Succession ended a year before the death of Louis XIV. The Bourbons had secured the Spanish throne, but Spain had forfeited its possessions in Flanders and Italy.

Mississippi Company stock. In 1719, the price of the stock rose handsomely. Smart investors, however, sold their stock in exchange for paper money from Law's bank, which they then hoped to exchange for gold. The bank, however, lacked enough gold to redeem all the paper money brought to it.

In February 1720, all gold payments were halted in France. Soon thereafter, Law himself fled the country. The Mississippi Bubble, as the affair was called, had burst, and the fiasco brought disgrace on the government that had sponsored Law. The Mississippi Company was later reorganized and functioned profitably, but fear of paper money and speculation marked French economic life for decades.

13.4.7.2 RENEWED AUTHORITY OF THE PARLE-MENTS   The Duke of Orléans made a second decision that also lessened the power of the monarchy. He attempted to draw the French nobility once again into the decision-making processes of the government. He set up a system of councils on which nobles were to serve along with bureaucrats. The most effective instrument in this process was the previously mentioned parlements, or courts dominated by the nobility.

The Duke of Orléans reversed the previously noted policy of Louis XIV and formally approved the reinstitution of the full power of the Parlement of Paris to allow or disallow laws. Moreover, throughout the eighteenth century that and other local parlements also succeeded in identifying their authority and resistance to the monarchy with wider public opinion. This situation meant that until the revolution in 1789, the parlements became natural centers not only for aristocratic but also for popular resistance to royal authority. In a vast transformation from the days of Louis XIV, the

LOUIS XV OF FRANCE Under Louis XV (r. 1715–1774) France suffered major defeats in Europe and around the world and lost most of its North American empire. Louis himself was an ineffective ruler, and during his reign, the monarchy encountered numerous challenges from the French aristocracy.
SOURCE: Bettmann/Getty Images

La Rue Quincampoix.

FINANCIAL PANIC ON LA RUE QUINCAMPOIX The impending collapse of John Law's bank triggered a financial panic throughout France. Desperate investors sought to exchange their paper currency for gold and silver before the banks' supply of precious metals was exhausted.
SOURCE: Musee de la Ville de Paris, Musee Carnavalet, Paris, France/Archives Charmet/Bridgeman Art Library

parlements rather than the monarchy would soon be seen as more closely representing the nation.

By 1726, the general political direction of the nation had come under the authority of Cardinal Fleury (1653–1743). He worked to maintain the authority of the monarchy, including ongoing repression of the Jansenists, while continuing to preserve the local interests of the French nobility. Like Walpole in Britain, he pursued economic prosperity at home and peace abroad. Again like Walpole, after 1740, Fleury could not prevent France from entering a worldwide colonial conflict.

13.5 Central and Eastern Europe

What were the main characteristics that defined the Polish, Austrian, and Prussian states in the seventeenth and eighteenth centuries?

Central and eastern Europe were economically much less advanced than Western Europe. Except for the Baltic ports, the economy was agrarian. There were fewer cities and many more large estates worked by serfs. The states in this region did not possess overseas empires, nor did they engage in extensive overseas trade of any kind, except for supplying grain to Western Europe—grain, more often than not, carried on Western European ships.

During the sixteenth and early seventeenth centuries, the political authorities in this region, which lay largely east

of the Elbe River, were weak. The almost constant warfare of the seventeenth century had led to a habit of temporarily shifting political loyalties with princes and aristocracies of small states refusing to subordinate themselves to central monarchical authorities.

During the last half of the seventeenth century, however, three strong dynasties, whose rulers aspired to the absolutism of France, emerged in central and eastern Europe. After the Peace of Westphalia in 1648, the Austrian Habsburgs recognized the basic weakness of the position of the Holy Roman Emperor and began consolidating their power outside Germany. At the same time, Prussia under the Hohenzollern dynasty emerged as a factor in north German politics and as a major challenger to the Habsburg domination of Germany. Most important, Russia under the Romanov dynasty at the opening of the eighteenth century became a military and naval power of the first order. These three monarchies would dominate central and eastern Europe until the close of World War I in 1918. By contrast, during the eighteenth century, Poland became the single most conspicuous example in Europe of a land that failed to establish a viable centralized government.

13.5.1 Poland: Absence of Strong Central Authority

The Polish monarchy was elective, but the deep distrust and divisions among the nobility usually prevented their electing a king from among themselves. Most of the Polish monarchs were foreigners and the tools of foreign powers. The Polish nobles did have a central legislative body called the *Sejm*, or diet. The diet, however, had a practice known as the *liberum veto*, whereby the staunch opposition of any single member, who might have been bribed by a foreign power, could require the body to disband. Such opposition, termed "exploding the diet," was most often the work of a group of dissatisfied nobles rather than of one person. Nonetheless, the requirement of unanimity was a major stumbling block to effective government. The price of this noble liberty would eventually be the disappearance of Poland from the map of Europe in the late eighteenth century. In no other part of Europe was the failure to maintain a competitive political position as complete as in Poland.

13.5.2 The Habsburg Empire and the Pragmatic Sanction

The close of the Thirty Years' War marked a fundamental turning point in the history of the Austrian Habsburgs. Previously, in alliance with their Spanish cousins, they had hoped to bring all of Germany under their control and back to the Catholic fold. In this they had failed, and the decline of Spanish power meant that the Austrian Habsburgs were on their own. (See Map 13–3.)

After 1648, the Habsburg family retained a firm hold on the title of Holy Roman Emperor, but the power of the emperor depended less on the force of arms than on the cooperation he could elicit from the various political bodies in the empire. These included large German units (such as Saxony, Hanover, Bavaria, and Brandenburg) and scores of small German cities, bishoprics, principalities, and territories of independent knights. While establishing their new dominance among the German states, the Habsburgs also began to consolidate their power and influence within their hereditary possessions outside the Holy Roman Empire: the Crown of Saint Wenceslas, encompassing the kingdom of Bohemia (in the modern Czech Republic) and the duchies of Moravia and Silesia; and the Crown of Saint Stephen, which ruled Hungary, Croatia, and Transylvania.

Through the Treaty of Rastatt in 1714, the Habsburgs further extended their domains, receiving the former Spanish (thereafter Austrian) Netherlands and Lombardy in northern Italy. Thereafter, the Habsburgs' power and influence would be based primarily on their territories outside of Germany.

Map 13–3   AUSTRIAN HABSBURG EMPIRE, 1521–1772

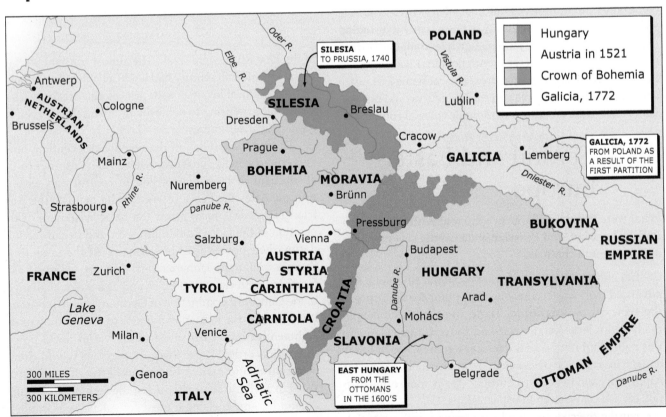

The Habsburg Empire had three main units—Austria, Bohemia, and Hungary. Expansion was mainly eastward: eastern Hungary from the Ottomans (seventeenth century) and Galicia from Poland (1772). Meantime, Silesia was lost after 1740, but the Habsburgs remained Holy Roman Emperors.

In each of their many territories the Habsburgs ruled with a different title—king, archduke, and duke—and they needed the cooperation of the local nobility, which was not always forthcoming. They repeatedly had to bargain with nobles in one part of Europe to maintain their position in another. Their domains were so geographically diverse and the people who lived in them of so many different languages and customs that there was almost no way to unify them politically. Even Roman Catholicism proved ineffective as a common bond, particularly in Hungary, where many Magyar nobles were Calvinist and seemed ever ready to rebel.

Despite these internal difficulties, Leopold I (r. 1658–1705) managed to resist the advances of the Ottoman Empire into central Europe, which included a siege of Vienna in 1683 and thwarting the aggression of Louis XIV. He achieved Ottoman recognition of his sovereignty over Hungary in 1699 and extended his territorial holdings over much of the Balkan Peninsula and western Romania. With these conquests, the Habsburgs hoped to develop Mediterranean trade through the port of Trieste on the northern coast of the Adriatic Sea and compensate for their loss of effective power over the Holy Roman Empire. Strength in the East gave them greater political leverage in Germany. Joseph I (r. 1705–1711) continued Leopold's policies.

When Charles VI (r. 1711–1740) succeeded Joseph, a new problem was added to the chronic one of territorial diversity. He had no male heir, and there was only the weakest of precedents for a female ruler of the Habsburg domains. Charles feared that on his death the Austrian Habsburg lands might fall prey to the surrounding powers, as had those of the Spanish Habsburgs in 1700. He was determined to prevent that disaster and to provide his domains with the semblance of legal unity. To those ends, he devoted most of his reign to seeking the approval of his family, the estates of his realms, and the major foreign powers for a document called the **Pragmatic Sanction**.

This document provided the legal basis for a single line of inheritance within the Habsburg dynasty through Charles VI's daughter Maria Theresa (r. 1740–1780). When Charles VI died in October 1740, he believed he had secured legal unity for the Habsburg Empire and a safe succession for his daughter. Despite the Pragmatic Sanction, however, his failure to provide his daughter with a strong army or a full treasury left her inheritance open to foreign aggression. In December 1740, Frederick II of Prussia invaded the Habsburg province of Silesia in eastern Germany, and Maria Theresa had to fight for her inheritance.

13.5.3 Prussia and the Hohenzollerns

The rise of Prussia occurred within the German power vacuum created by the Peace of Westphalia. The extraordinary Hohenzollern family, which had ruled Brandenburg since 1417, was responsible for the new Prussian power. Through inheritance the family had acquired the duchy of Cleves and the counties of Mark and Ravensburg in 1614, East Prussia in 1618, and Pomerania in 1648. (See Map 13–4.) Except for Pomerania, none of these lands shared a border with Brandenburg. Still, by the late seventeenth century, the geographically scattered Hohenzollern holdings represented a block of territory within the Holy Roman Empire, second in size only to that of the Habsburgs.

Frederick William (r. 1640–1688), who became known as the Great Elector, forged these areas into a modern state. He established himself and his successors as the central uniting power by breaking the local noble estates, organizing a royal bureaucracy, and building a strong army. (He also issued a proclamation, granting refuge to French Huguenots, whose productive skills, he hoped, would contribute to the economic development of his domains.)

Between 1655 and 1660, Sweden and Poland fought each other across the Great Elector's holdings in Pomerania and East Prussia. Frederick William had neither an adequate army nor the tax revenues to confront this threat. In 1655, the Brandenburg estates refused to grant him new taxes; however, he proceeded to collect them by military force. In 1659, a different grant of taxes, originally made in 1653, elapsed; Frederick William continued to collect them as well as those he had imposed by his own authority. He used the money to build an army, which allowed him to continue to enforce his will without the approval of the nobility. Similar coercion took place against the nobles in his other territories.

THE SIEGE OF VIENNA In 1683, the Ottomans laid siege to Vienna. Only the arrival of Polish forces under King John III Sobieski (r. 1674–1696) saved the Habsburg capital.
SOURCE: Erich Lessing/Art Resource, NY

Map 13–4   EXPANSION OF BRANDENBURG-PRUSSIA

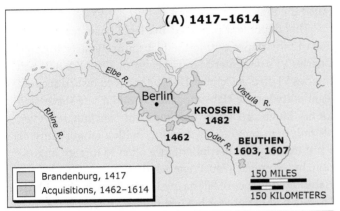

(A) 1417–1614

KROSSEN 1482

1462

BEUTHEN 1603, 1607

Berlin

Elbe R. — Vistula R. — Oder R. — Rhine R.

150 MILES
150 KILOMETERS

- ☐ Brandenburg, 1417
- ☐ Acquisitions, 1462–1614

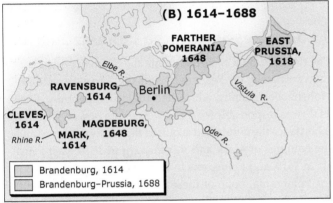

(B) 1614–1688

FARTHER POMERANIA, 1648

EAST PRUSSIA, 1618

RAVENSBURG, 1614

CLEVES, 1614

MAGDEBURG, 1648

MARK, 1614

Berlin

Elbe R. — Vistula R. — Oder R. — Rhine R.

- ☐ Brandenburg, 1614
- ☐ Brandenburg–Prussia, 1688

(C) 1688–1748

EAST FRIESLAND, 1744

SILESIA FROM AUSTRIA, 1740

Berlin

Elbe R. — Vistula R. — Oder R. — Rhine R.

- ☐ Prussia, 1688
- ☐ Acquisitions, 1715–1748

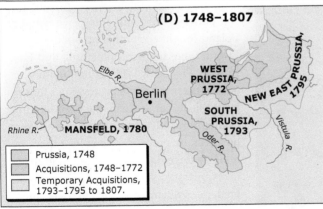

(D) 1748–1807

WEST PRUSSIA, 1772

NEW EAST PRUSSIA, 1795

SOUTH PRUSSIA, 1793

MANSFELD, 1780

Berlin

Elbe R. — Vistula R. — Oder R. — Rhine R.

- ☐ Prussia, 1748
- ☐ Acquisitions, 1748–1772
- ☐ Temporary Acquisitions, 1793–1795 to 1807.

In the seventeenth century, Brandenburg-Prussia expanded mainly by acquiring dynastic titles in geographically separated lands. In the eighteenth century, it expanded through aggression to the east, seizing Silesia in 1740 and various parts of Poland in 1772, 1793, and 1795.

There was, however, a political and social trade-off between the Elector and his various nobles. In exchange for their obedience to the Hohenzollerns, the **Junkers**, or German noble landlords, received the right to demand obedience from their serfs. Frederick William also chose as the local administrators of the tax structure men who would normally have been members of the noble branch of the old parliament. As the years passed, Junkers increasingly dominated the army officer corps, and this situation became even more pronounced during the eighteenth century. All officials and army officers took an oath of loyalty directly to the Elector. The army and the Elector thus came to embody the otherwise absent unity of the state. The army made Prussia a valuable potential ally.

Yet even with the considerable accomplishments of the Great Elector, the house of Hohenzollern did not possess a crown. The achievement of a royal title was one of the few state-building accomplishments of Frederick I (r. 1688–1713). This son of the Great Elector was the least "Prussian" of his family during these crucial years. He built palaces, founded Halle University (1694), patronized the arts, and lived luxuriously. In the War of the Spanish Succession, he put his army at the disposal of the Habsburg Holy Roman Emperor Leopold I. In exchange, the emperor permitted Frederick to assume the title of "King in Prussia" in 1701.

His successor, Frederick William I (r. 1713–1740), was both the most eccentric monarch to rule the Hohenzollern domains and one of the most effective. He organized the bureaucracy along military lines, and the discipline that he applied to the army was fanatical. The Prussian military grew from about 39,000 in 1713 to more than 80,000 in 1740, making it the third or fourth largest army in Europe. Prussia's population, in contrast, ranked thirteenth in size. Separate laws applied to the army and to civilians. Laws, customs, and royal attention made the officer corps the highest social class of the state, and military service thus attracted the sons of Junkers. In this fashion the army, the Junker nobility, and the monarchy were forged into a single political entity. Military priorities and values dominated Prussian government, society, and daily life as in no other state in Europe. It has often been said that whereas other states possessed armies, the Prussian army possessed its state.

Although Frederick William I built the best army in Europe, he avoided conflict. His army was a symbol of Prussian power and unity, not an instrument for foreign adventures or aggression. At his death in 1740, he passed to his son Frederick II, later known as Frederick the Great (r. 1740–1786), this superb military machine, but not the wisdom to refrain from using it. Almost immediately on coming to the throne, Frederick II upset the Pragmatic Sanction and invaded Silesia, crystallizing the Austrian–Prussian rivalry for control of Germany that would dominate central European affairs for more than a century.

13.6 Russia Enters the European Political Arena

How did Peter the Great transform Russia into a powerful, centralized nation?

The emergence of Russia in the late seventeenth century as an active European power was a new factor in European politics. Previously, Russia had been considered part of Europe only by courtesy. Before 1673, it did not send permanent ambassadors to Western Europe, though it had sent various diplomatic missions since the fifteenth century. Geographically and politically, it lay on the periphery. Hemmed in by Sweden on the Baltic and by the Ottoman Empire on the Black Sea, Russia had no warm water ports. Its chief outlet for trade to the West was Archangel on the White Sea, which was ice free for only part of the year.

13.6.1 The Romanov Dynasty

The reign of Ivan IV (r. 1533–1584), later known as Ivan the Terrible, had commenced well but ended badly. About midway in his reign he underwent a personality change that caused him to move from a program of sensible reform of law, government, and the army toward violent personal tyranny. A period known as the "Time of Troubles" followed upon his death. In 1613, hoping to end the uncertainty, an assembly of nobles elected as tsar a seventeen-year-old boy named Michael Romanov (r. 1613–1645). Thus began the dynasty that ruled Russia until 1917.

Michael Romanov and his two successors, Aleksei (r. 1654–1676) and Theodore II (r. 1676–1682), brought stability and modest bureaucratic centralization to Russia. The country remained, however, weak and impoverished. After years of turmoil, the *boyars*, the old nobility, still largely controlled the bureaucracy. Furthermore, the government and the tsars faced the danger of mutiny from the *streltsy*, or guards of the Moscow garrison.

13.6.2 Peter the Great

In 1682, another boy—ten years old at the time—ascended the fragile Russian throne as co-ruler with his half-brother. His name was Peter (r. 1682–1725), and Russia would never be the same after him. He and the sickly Ivan V had come to power on the shoulders of the streltsy, who expected to be rewarded for their support. Violence and bloodshed had surrounded the disputed succession. Matters became even more confused when the boys' sister, Sophia, was named regent. Peter's followers overthrew her in 1689. From that date on, Peter ruled personally, although in theory he shared the crown until Ivan died in 1696. The dangers and turmoil of his youth convinced Peter of two things: First, the power of the tsar must be secured from the jealousy of the boyars and the greed of the streltsy; second, Russian military power must be increased. In both respects, Peter self-consciously resembled Louis XIV of France, who had experienced the turmoil of the Fronde during his youth and resolved to establish a strong monarchy safe from the nobility and defended by a powerful army.

Northwestern Europe, particularly the military resources of the maritime powers, fascinated Peter I, who eventually became known as Peter the Great. In 1697, he made a famous visit in transparent disguise to Western Europe. There he dined and talked with the great and the powerful, who considered this almost seven-foot-tall ruler crude. He spent his happiest moments on the trip inspecting shipyards, docks, and the manufacture of military hardware in England and the Netherlands. An imitator of the first order, Peter returned to Moscow determined to copy what he had seen abroad, knowing warfare would be necessary to make Russia a great power. Yet he understood his goal would mean confronting the long-standing power and traditions of the Russian nobles.

13.6.2.1 TAMING THE STRELTSY AND BOYARS

In 1698, while Peter was abroad, the streltsy had rebelled. Upon his return, Peter brutally suppressed the revolt. Approximately a thousand rebels were put to death, and their corpses remained on public display to discourage disloyalty.

The new military establishment that Peter built would serve the tsar and not itself. He introduced effective and ruthless policies of conscription, drafting an unprecedented 130,000 soldiers during the first decade of the eighteenth century and almost 300,000 troops by the end of his reign. He had adopted policies for the officer corps and general military discipline patterned on those of West European armies.

Peter also made a sustained attack on the boyars and their attachment to traditional Russian culture. After his European journey, he personally shaved the long beards of the court boyars and sheared off the customary long hand-covering sleeves of their shirts and coats, which had made them the butt of jokes among other European courts. Peter became highly skilled at pitting one group against another, never completely excluding any as he organized Russian government and military forces along the lines of the more powerful European states.

13.6.2.2 DEVELOPING A NAVY

In the mid-1690s, Peter oversaw the construction of ships to protect his interests in the Black Sea against the Ottoman Empire. In 1695, he began a war with the Ottomans and captured Azov on the Black Sea in 1696.[1] One purpose of Peter's trip to Western Europe in 1697 was to learn how to build still better warships, this time for combat on the Baltic. The construction of a Baltic fleet was essential to Peter's struggles with Sweden that over the years accounted for many of his major steps toward westernizing his realm.

13.6.3 Russian Expansion in the Baltic: The Great Northern War

Following the end of the Thirty Years' War in 1648, Sweden had consolidated its control of the Baltic, preventing Russian possession of a port on that sea and permitting Polish and German access to the sea only on Swedish terms. The Swedes also had one of the better armies in Europe. Sweden's economy, however, based primarily on the export of iron, was not strong enough to ensure continued political success.

In 1697, Charles XII (r. 1697–1718) came to the Swedish throne. He was headstrong, to say the least, and perhaps insane. In 1700, Peter the Great began a drive to the west against Swedish territory to gain a foothold on the Baltic. In the resulting Great Northern War (1700–1721), Charles XII led a vigorous and often brilliant campaign, defeating the Russians at the Battle of Narva (1700). As the conflict dragged on, however, Peter strengthened his forces, and by 1709 he decisively defeated the Swedes at the Battle of Poltava in Ukraine. Thereafter, the Swedes could maintain only a holding action against their enemies. When the Great

Northern War ended in 1721, the Peace of Nystad confirmed the Russian conquest of Estonia, Livonia, and part of Finland. Henceforth, Russia had ice-free ports and a permanent influence on European affairs.

13.6.3.1 FOUNDING ST. PETERSBURG

At one point, the domestic and foreign policies of Peter the Great intersected. On the Gulf of Finland Peter founded his new capital city of St. Petersburg in 1703. There he built government structures and compelled the boyars to construct town houses, imitating European monarchs who had copied Louis XIV by constructing smaller versions of Versailles. However, St. Petersburg was more than a central imperial court; it symbolized both the new Western orientation of Russia and Peter's determination to maintain his position on the Baltic coast.

13.6.3.2 THE CASE OF PETER'S SON ALEKSEI

Peter's son Aleksei, with whom he had a hostile relationship, had been born to his first wife whom he had divorced in 1698. By 1716, Peter was becoming convinced that his opponents wanted Aleksei to join their possible sedition while Russia remained at war with Sweden. There was some truth to Peter's concerns because the next year, on a trip to Vienna, Aleksei attempted to join a vague conspiracy with the Habsburg emperor Charles VI.

Peter, who was investigating official corruption, realized his son might become a rallying point for those he accused. Early in 1718, when Aleksei reappeared in St. Petersburg, the tsar began investigating his son's relationships with Charles VI. During this six-month investigation, Peter personally interrogated Aleksei, who was eventually condemned to death and died under mysterious circumstances on June 26, 1718.

13.6.3.3 REFORMS OF PETER THE GREAT'S FINAL YEARS

The interrogations surrounding Aleksei had revealed greater degrees of court opposition than Peter had

ST. PETERSBURG Peter the Great built St. Petersburg on the Gulf of Finland to facilitate contact between Russia and Western Europe. He moved Russia's capital there from Moscow in 1712. This eighteenth-century view of the city depicts a location on the Neva River between the Winter Palace and the Academy of Sciences.
SOURCE: PRISMA ARCHIVO/Alamy Stock Photo

suspected. Recognizing he could not eliminate his opponents the way he had attacked the streltsy in 1698, Peter undertook radical administrative reforms designed to bring the nobility and the Russian Orthodox Church more closely under the authority of persons loyal to the tsar.

13.6.3.4 ADMINISTRATIVE COLLEGES

In December 1717, Peter reorganized his domestic administration to sustain his own personal authority and to fight rampant corruption. To achieve this goal, Peter looked to Swedish institutions called *colleges*—bureaus of several persons operating according to written instructions rather than departments headed by a single minister. He created eight of these colleges to oversee matters such as the collection of taxes, foreign relations, war, and economic affairs. Each college was to receive advice from a foreigner. Peter divided the members of these colleges among nobles and persons he was certain would be personally loyal to himself.

13.6.3.5 TABLE OF RANKS

Peter made another major administrative reform with important consequences when in 1722 he published a **Table of Ranks**, which was intended to draw the nobility into state service. That table equated a person's social position and privileges with his rank in the bureaucracy or the military, rather than with

his lineage among the traditional landed nobility, many of whom continued to resent the changes Peter had introduced into Russia. Peter thus made the social standing of individual boyars a function of their willingness to serve the central state.

13.6.3.6 ACHIEVING SECULAR CONTROL OF THE CHURCH

Peter also moved to suppress the independence of the Russian Orthodox Church in which some bishops and clergy had displayed sympathy for the tsar's son. In 1721, Peter simply abolished the position of *patriarch*, the bishop who had been head of the church. In its place he established a government department called the *Holy Synod*, which consisted of several bishops headed by a layman called the *procurator general*. This body would govern the church in accordance with the tsar's secular requirements. This ecclesiastical reorganization was the most radical transformation of a traditional institution in Peter's reign.

For all the numerous decisive actions Peter had taken since 1718, he still had not settled on a successor. Consequently, when he died in 1725, there was no clear line of succession to the throne. For more than thirty years, soldiers and nobles again determined who ruled Russia. Peter had laid the foundations of a modern Russia, but not the foundations of a stable state.

The Chapter in Perspective

By the second quarter of the eighteenth century, the major European powers were not yet nation-states in which the citizens felt themselves united by a shared sense of community, culture, language, and history. Rather, they were monarchies in which the personality of the ruler and the personal relationships of the great noble families continued to exercise considerable influence over public affairs. The monarchs, except in Great Britain, had generally succeeded in making their power greater than that of the nobility. The power of the aristocracy and its capacity to resist or obstruct the policies of the monarch were not destroyed, however.

In Britain, of course, the nobility had tamed the monarchy, but even there tension between nobles and monarchs would continue throughout the rest of the century.

In foreign affairs, the new arrangement of military and diplomatic power established early in the century prepared the way for two long conflicts. The first was a commercial

rivalry for trade and the overseas empire between France and Great Britain. During the reign of Louis XIV, these two nations had collided over the French bid for dominance in Europe. During the eighteenth century, they would duel for control of commerce on other continents. The second arena of warfare would arise in central Europe, where Austria and Prussia fought for the leadership of the German states.

During these times of international conflicts and domestic rivalry of monarchs and nobles, however, the society of eighteenth-century Europe began to change. The character and the structures of the societies over which the monarchs ruled were beginning to take on some features associated with the modern age. These economic and social developments would eventually transform the life of Europe to a degree beside which the state-building of the early eighteenth-century monarchs paled. With these economic advances, Europeans developed new knowledge and an understanding of nature.

The Chapter in Review

Review Questions

1. What were the sources of Dutch prosperity, and why did the Netherlands decline in the eighteenth century?

Why did England and France develop different systems of government and religious policies?

2. Why did the English king and Parliament quarrel in the 1640s? What were the most important issues in the war between them, and who bears more responsibility for it? What was the Glorious Revolution, and why did it take place?

3. Why did France become an absolute monarchy? How did Louis XIV consolidate his monarchy, and what limits were there on his authority? What was Louis's religious policy? What were the goals of his foreign policy? How did Louis use ceremony and his royal court to strengthen his authority? What features of French government might Europeans outside of France have feared?

4. How were the Hohenzollerns able to forge their diverse landholdings in the state of Prussia? Who were the major figures involved in this process, and what were their individual contributions? Why was the military so important in Prussia? What major problems did the Habsburgs face, and how did they seek to resolve them? Which family—the Hohenzollerns or the Habsburgs—was more successful and why?

5. How and why did Russia emerge as a great power but Poland did not? How were Peter the Great's domestic reforms related to his military ambitions? What were his methods of reform? How did family conflict influence his later policies? Was Peter a successful ruler? In what respects might one regard Peter as an imitator of Louis XIV?

Key Terms

Declaration of Indulgence   Issued by Charles II in 1672 to suspend all laws against Roman Catholics and non-Anglican Protestants.

divine right of kings   A form of absolute rule that asserts that the monarch derives his right to rule directly from the will of God and is not subject to earthly authority.

Dutch East India Company   Founded by the Dutch to compete with the Portuguese in the spice trade of East Asia and chartered in 1602, it was the first company in history to issue bonds and shares of stock to the general public.

Frederick William   (r. 1640–1688) Became known as the Great Elector and established himself and his successors as the central uniting power in Prussia.

Fronde   Refers to the series of rebellions among French nobles between 1649 and 1652.

Gallican Liberties   The ecclesiastical independence of the French crown and of the French Roman Catholic church from papal authority in Rome.

Glorious Revolution   The overthrow of King James II in 1688 by the union of Parliament and William of Orange.

Jansenism   A Roman Catholic religious movement that arose in the 1630s, which opposed the Jesuits and adhered to the teachings of St. Augustine.

Junkers   Members of the class of German noble landlords.

Militia Ordinance   A piece of legislation passed by the House of Commons in 1642 to give Parliament the authority to raise an army of its own.

Oliver Cromwell   (1599–1658) The dominant military and political figure in England from 1649 to 1660.

parlements   A set of regional judicial bodies in France with which the crown usually conferred before making rulings that would affect them.

parliamentary monarchy   A form of monarchy in which the sovereign has to govern according to a constitution.

Petition of Right   A document recognized by Charles I in 1628 requiring that there should be no forced loans or taxation without the consent of Parliament, that no freeman should be imprisoned without due cause, and that troops should not be billeted in private homes.

political absolutism   A form of monarchy in which one person rules with absolute sovereignty and whose authority is not restricted by any laws or customs.

Pragmatic Sanction   A document sought by Charles VI (r. 1711–1740) to provide the legal basis for a single line of inheritance within the Habsburg dynasty through his daughter Maria Theresa.

Puritans   A group of English Reformed Protestants who sought to "purify" the Church of England from the practices characteristic of the Roman Catholic Church.

Sejm   A central legislative body of the Polish nobles, which excluded representatives from corporate bodies, such as the towns.

Sir Robert Walpole   (1676–1745) The British statesman regarded as the first prime minister of Great Britain.

Table of Ranks   Published by Peter the Great to draw the nobility into state service, it equated a person's social position and privileges with his rank in the bureaucracy or the military.

Test Act   An act of the English Parliament that required all civil and military officials of the crown to swear an oath against the doctrine of transubstantiation.

Note

1. Although Peter had to return Azov to the Ottomans in 1711, its recapture became a goal of Russian foreign policy. See Chapter 18 for more on the subject.

Chapter 14
New Directions in Thought and Culture in the Sixteenth and Seventeenth Centuries

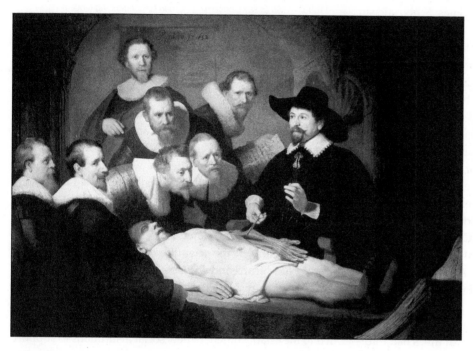

THE ANATOMY LESSON OF DR. TULP
The great Dutch artist Rembrandt van Rijn (1606–1669) recorded the contemporary life of the United Provinces of the Netherlands during its golden age. The new sciences, including medicine, made much progress in the Netherlands, which was a center for publishing and instrument making and known for its religious toleration. *The Anatomy Lesson of Dr. Tulp* (1632) portrays the dissection of a cadaver of an executed criminal by noted Dutch physician Dr. Nicolaes Tulp, who stands at the right surrounded by other members of the Amsterdam guild of surgeons. Such dissections were a controversial part of new emerging medical education, with only one a year permitted in Amsterdam. The use of light and darkness is characteristic of the baroque style of painting.
SOURCE: Scala/Art Resource, NY

 Contents and Focus Questions

The Chapter in Brief

THE SIXTEENTH and seventeenth centuries witnessed a sweeping change in the scientific view of the universe. An earth-centered picture gave way to one in which the earth was only another planet orbiting about the sun. The sun itself became one of millions of stars. This transformation of humankind's perception of its place in the larger scheme of things led to a profound rethinking of moral and religious matters, as well as of scientific theory. Faith and reason needed new modes of reconciliation, as did faith and science. The new scientific ideas and methods, usually termed *natural philosophy* at the time, challenged those modes of thought associated with late medieval times: Scholasticism and Aristotelian philosophy.

The impact of the new science that explored the realm of the stars through the newly invented telescope and the world of microorganisms through the newly invented microscope must be viewed in the context of two other factors that simultaneously challenged traditional modes of European thought and culture in the sixteenth and seventeenth centuries. The first of these was the Reformation, which permanently divided the religious unity of central and Western Europe and fostered decades of warfare and theological dispute. Although by no means a complete break with medieval thought, the theology of the Reformation did question many ideas associated with medieval Christianity and society. The second factor was the cultural impact of Europe's encounter with the New World of the Americas. The interaction with the Americas meant that Europeans directly or indirectly acquired knowledge of new peoples, plants, and animals wholly different from their own and about which Europeans in neither ancient nor medieval times had information. Consequently, new uncertainties and unfamiliar vistas confronted many Europeans as they considered their souls, geographical knowledge, and physical nature.

With this new knowledge and science, however, came a new wave of superstition and persecution. The changing world of religion, politics, and knowledge also created profound fear and anxiety among both the simple and the learned, resulting in the worst witch hunts in European history.

14.1 The Scientific Revolution

What was the scientific revolution?

The process that established the new view of the universe is normally termed the **scientific revolution**. The revolution-in-science metaphor must be used carefully, however. Not everything associated with the "new" science was necessarily new. Sixteenth- and seventeenth-century natural philosophers were often reexamining and rethinking

KEY WORKS OF THE SCIENTIFIC REVOLUTION	
1543	*On the Revolutions of the Heavenly Spheres* (Copernicus)
1605	*The Advancement of Learning* (Bacon)
1609	*The New Astronomy* (Kepler)
1610	*The Starry Messenger* (Galileo)
1613	*Letters on Sunspots* (Galileo)
1620	*Novum Organum* (Bacon)
1632	*Dialogue on the Two Chief World Systems* (Galileo)
1637	*Discourse on Method* (Descartes)
1651	*Leviathan* (Hobbes)
1687	*Principia Mathematica* (Newton)
1689	*Letter Concerning Toleration* (Locke)
1690	*An Essay Concerning Human Understanding* (Locke)
1690	*Treatises of Government* (Locke)

theories and data from the ancient world and the late Middle Ages. Moreover, the word *revolution* normally denotes rapid, collective political change involving many people. The scientific revolution was not rapid. It was a complex movement with many false starts and brilliant people suggesting wrong as well as useful ideas. Nor did it involve more than a few hundred people who labored in widely separated studies and crude laboratories located in Poland, Italy, Denmark, Bohemia, France, and Great Britain. Furthermore, the achievements of the new science were not simply the work of isolated brilliant scientific minds. The leading figures of the scientific revolution often relied on the aid of artisans and craftspeople to help them construct new instruments for experimentation and to carry out those experiments. Additionally, because the practice of science involved social activity as well as knowledge, the revolution led to the establishment of new social institutions to support the emerging scientific enterprise.

Natural knowledge was only in the process of becoming science as we know it today during the era of the scientific revolution. In fact, the word *scientist*, which was first coined in the 1830s, did not yet exist in the seventeenth century, nor did anything resembling the modern scientific career. Individuals devoted to natural philosophy might work in universities or in the court of a prince or even in their own homes and workshops. Only in the second half of the seventeenth century did formal societies and academies devoted to the pursuit of natural philosophy emerge. Even then, the process of the pursuit of natural knowledge was a largely informal one.

Yet by the close of the seventeenth century, the new scientific concepts and methods were so impressive that they set the standard for assessing the validity of knowledge in the Western world. From the early seventeenth century through the end of the twentieth century, science achieved greater cultural authority in the Western world than any other form of intellectual activity, and the authority and application of scientific knowledge became one of the defining characteristics of modern Western civilization.

Although new knowledge emerged in many areas during the sixteenth and seventeenth centuries, including medicine, chemistry, and natural history, the scientific achievements that most captured the learned imagination and persuaded people of the cultural power of natural knowledge were those that occurred in astronomy.

14.1.1 Nicolaus Copernicus Rejects an Earth-Centered Universe

Nicolaus Copernicus (1473–1543) was a Polish priest and an astronomer who enjoyed a high reputation during his life, but was not known for strikingly original or unorthodox thought. In 1543, the year of his death, Copernicus published *On the Revolutions of the Heavenly Spheres*, which has been described as "a revolution-making rather than a revolutionary text."[1] Copernicus provided an intellectual springboard for a complete criticism of the then-dominant view of the position of the earth in the universe. He had undertaken this task to help the papacy reform the calendar, so that it could correctly calculate the date for Easter based on a more accurate understanding of astronomy.

14.1.1.1 THE PTOLEMAIC SYSTEM
In Copernicus's time, the standard explanation of the place of the earth in the heavens combined the mathematical astronomy of Ptolemy, contained in his work entitled the *Almagest* (150 C.E.), with the physical cosmology of Aristotle. Over the centuries, commentators on Ptolemy's work had developed several alternative **Ptolemaic systems**, from which they made mathematical calculations relating to astronomy. Most of these writers assumed the earth was the center of the universe, an outlook known as *geocentrism*. Drawing on Aristotle, they assumed that above the earth lay a series of concentric spheres, probably fluid in character, one of which contained the moon, another the sun, and still others the planets and the stars. At the outer regions of these spheres lay the realm of God and the angels. The earth had to be the center because of its heaviness. The stars and the other heavenly bodies had to be enclosed in the spheres so they could move, since nothing could move unless something was moving it. The state of rest was presumed to be natural; motion required explanation. This was the astronomy found in such works as Italian poet Dante Alighieri's *Divine Comedy*.

The Ptolemaic model had many problems, which had long been recognized. The most important was the observed motions of the planets. At certain times the planets appeared to be going backward. Other intellectual, but nonobservational, difficulties related to the immense speed at which the spheres had to move around the earth. To say the least, the Ptolemaic systems were cluttered. They were effective, however, if one assumed Aristotelian physics to be correct.

14.1.1.2 COPERNICUS'S UNIVERSE
Copernicus's *On the Revolutions of the Heavenly Spheres* challenged the Ptolemaic picture in the most conservative manner possible. He adapted many elements of the Ptolemaic model to a *heliocentric* (sun-centered) model, which assumed the earth moved about the sun in a circle.

The repositioning of the earth had not been Copernicus's goal. Rather, he hoped to achieve new intelligibility and mathematical elegance in astronomy by rejecting Aristotle's cosmology and by removing the earth from the center of the universe. But his system was no more accurate than existing ones for predicting the location of the planets. He had used no new evidence. The major impact of his work was to provide another way of confronting some of the difficulties inherent in Ptolemaic astronomy. The Copernican system did not immediately replace the old astronomy, but it allowed those who were also discontented with the Ptolemaic view to consider new possibilities. Indeed, for at least a century, only a minority of natural philosophers and astronomers embraced the Copernican system.

14.1.2 Tycho Brahe and Johannes Kepler Make New Scientific Observations

Danish astronomer **Tycho Brahe** (1546–1601) took the next major step toward the conception of a sun-centered system. He did not embrace Copernicus's view of the universe and actually spent most of his life advocating an earth-centered system. Brahe constructed scientific instruments with which he made more extensive naked-eye observations of the planets than anyone else had ever done. He produced a vast body of astronomical data from which his successors could work.

When Brahe died, his assistant, **Johannes Kepler** (1571–1630), a German astronomer, took possession of this data. Kepler was a convinced Copernican and a more consistently rigorous advocate of a heliocentric model than Copernicus himself had been. Like Copernicus, Kepler was deeply influenced by Renaissance Neoplatonism, which held the sun in special honor. In keeping with this outlook, Kepler was determined to find in Brahe's numbers mathematical harmonies that would support a sun-centered universe. Based on the mathematical relationships emerging from his study of Brahe's observations, Kepler presented the first astronomical model to show that the orbits of the planets were not circular but elliptical. He had combined Copernicus's concept of a sun-centered universe and Brahe's empirical data to solve the problem of planetary motion. Kepler published his findings in his 1609 book titled *The New Astronomy*.

Kepler had also defined a new problem. None of the available theories could explain why the planetary orbits

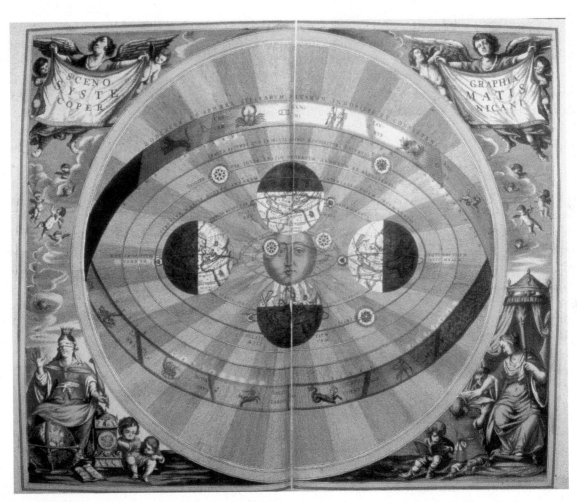

COPERNICAN MAP OF THE HEAVENS This 1543 map of the heavens based on the writings of Nicolaus Copernicus shows the earth and the other planets moving around the sun. Until well into the 1600s, however, astronomers continued to debate whether the sun revolved around the earth.
SOURCE: British Library, London, UK© British Library Board. All Rights Reserved/Owner/Bridgeman Art Library

were elliptical or, for that matter, why planetary motion was orbital rather than simply moving along a tangent. That solution awaited the work of Sir Isaac Newton.

14.1.3 Galileo Galilei Argues for a Universe of Mathematical Laws

From Copernicus to Brahe to Kepler, little had been learned about the heavens that might not have been considered by Ptolemy. In 1609, however, the same year that Kepler published *The New Astronomy*, **Galileo Galilei** (1564–1642), an Italian mathematician and natural philosopher, first turned a telescope on the heavens. Using this recently invented Dutch instrument, he saw stars where none had been known to exist, mountains on the moon, spots moving across the sun, and moons orbiting Jupiter. He proved that the heavens were far more complex than anyone had suspected.

Galileo's discoveries, with some work, could have been adapted to the Ptolemaic model but would, however, have required a highly technical understanding of Ptolemaic astronomy. Galileo knew that few possessed such complex

knowledge. Consequently, in the *Starry Messenger* (1610) and *Letters on Sunspots* (1613), he used his considerable rhetorical skills to argue that his newly observed physical evidence, particularly the phases of Venus, required a Copernican interpretation of the heavens.

Galileo's career illustrates that scientific discovery involved more than just presenting arguments and evidence. In 1610, he had left the University of Padua for Florence, where he became the philosopher and mathematician to the Grand Duke of Tuscany, a Medici. Galileo, now pursuing natural philosophy in a princely court, had become dependent on princely patronage. To win continued support for both his work and his theories, Galileo named the moons of Jupiter after the Medicis. Through the empirical data gathered with the implementation of the telescope, and by virtue of his political skills and excellent rhetoric, Galileo became the most prominent advocate for Copernicanism. But in so doing, he provoked the ire of envious academicians accusing him of creating "optical illusions" and of church dogmatists, unwilling to reconsider the Aristotelian-Ptolemaic model that had been dogmatized by Thomas Aquinas and Scholasticism.

GALILEO GALILEI Galileo achieved a European-wide reputation as a leading mathematician, astronomer, and instrument maker. His telescope revealed objects in the heavens never viewed by human beings, but his writings in defense of the Copernican system clashed with church dogma and led to his condemnation by church authorities. It was only in 1992, under Pope John Paul II, that the church cancelled the condemnation against Galileo and his scientific observations.
SOURCE: Nimatallah/Art Resource, NY

Galileo not only popularized the Copernican system but also articulated the concept of a universe subject to mathematical laws. More than any other writer of the century, he argued that nature displayed mathematical regularity in its most minute details:

> Philosophy is written in that great book which ever lies before our eyes—I mean the universe—but we cannot understand it if we do not first learn the language and grasp the symbols in which it is written. This book is written in the mathematical language, and the symbols are triangles, circles, and other geometrical figures, without whose help it is impossible to comprehend a single word of it; without which one wanders through a dark labyrinth.[2]

The universe was rational; however, its rationality lay not in medieval Scholastic logic but in mathematics. Copernicus had thought the heavens conformed to mathematical regularity; Galileo saw this regularity throughout physical nature.

A world of quantities was replacing one of qualities. The new natural philosophy portrayed nature as cold, rational, mathematical, and mechanistic. What was real and lasting

was what was mathematically measurable. For many, these irrefutable mathematical arguments were more persuasive than the physical observations that were so controversial. Few intellectual shifts have led to such momentous changes for Western civilization.

14.1.4 Isaac Newton Discovers the Laws of Gravitation

The question that continued to perplex seventeenth-century scientists who accepted the theories of Copernicus, Kepler, and Galileo was how the planets and other heavenly bodies moved in an orderly fashion. The Ptolemaic and Aristotelian answer had been the spheres and a universe arranged in the order of the heaviness of its parts. It was this issue of planetary motion that Englishman **Isaac Newton** (1642–1727) addressed and, in doing so, established a basis for physics that endured for more than two centuries.

SIR ISAAC NEWTON Sir Isaac Newton (1642–1727) synthesized the ideas of the thinkers who had come before him and postulated theories that continue to influence science today. His experiments dealing with light passing through a prism exemplified the experimental scientific method. This sculpture of Newton, at the Oxford University Museum of Natural History in England, captures Newton in a moment of thoughtful reflection.
SOURCE: Ian Bottle/Alamy Stock Photo

In 1687, Newton published *The Mathematical Principles of Natural Philosophy*, better known by its Latin title of *Principia Mathematica*. Galileo's mathematical bias permeated Newton's thought, as did his view that inertia applied to bodies both at rest and in motion. Newton reasoned that the planets and all other physical objects in the universe moved through mutual attraction, or gravity. Every object in the universe affected every other object through gravity, and the attraction of gravity explained why the planets moved in an orderly, rather than a chaotic, manner.[3] Newton demonstrated this relationship mathematically; he made no attempt to explain the nature of gravity itself.

Newton was a mathematical genius, but he also believed in the importance of empirical data and observation. The final test of any theory or hypothesis for Newton was whether it described what was actually observed. Newton was a great opponent of the rationalism of French philosopher René Descartes, which he believed included insufficient guards against error. Like Francis Bacon, he believed in **empiricism**—the idea that one must observe phenomena before attempting to explain them. Consequently, as Newton's theory of universal gravitation was increasingly accepted, so, too, was Baconian empiricism.

14.2 Philosophy Responds to Changing Science

What impact did the new science have on philosophy?

The revolution in scientific thought contributed directly to a major reexamination of Western philosophy. Several of the most important figures in the scientific revolution, such as Francis Bacon and René Descartes, were also philosophers discontented with the Scholastic heritage. Bacon stressed the importance of empirical research. Descartes attempted to find certainty through the exploration of his own thinking processes. Newton's interests likewise extended to philosophy; he wrote broadly on many topics, including scientific method and theology.

14.2.1 Nature as Mechanism

If a single idea informed these philosophers, though in different ways, it was the idea of *mechanism*. The proponents of the new science explained the world in terms of mechanical metaphors, or the language of machinery. The image to which many of them turned was that of the clock. Johannes Kepler once wrote, "I am much occupied with the investigation of the physical causes. My aim in this is to show that the machine of the universe is not similar to a divine animated being, but similar to a clock."[4] Nature conceived as machinery removed much of the mystery of the world and the previous assumption of a divine purpose in nature. The

qualities that seemed to inhere in matter were now discerned as the result of mechanical arrangement. Some writers came to understand God as a kind of divine watchmaker or mechanic who had arranged the world as a machine that would function automatically. A mechanical understanding of nature also meant that the language of science and of natural philosophy would become largely that of mathematics.

This new mode of thinking transformed physical nature from a realm in which Europeans looked for symbolic or sacramental meaning related to the divine into a realm where they looked for utility or usefulness. Natural knowledge led to the physical improvement of human beings through their ability to command and manipulate the processes of nature. Many proponents of the new science also believed such knowledge would strengthen the power of their monarchs.

14.2.2 Francis Bacon: The Empirical Method

Francis Bacon (1561–1626) was an Englishman of almost universal accomplishment. He was a lawyer, a high royal official, and the author of histories, moral essays, and philosophical discourses. Traditionally, he has been regarded as the father of empiricism and of experimentation in science. Much of this reputation was actually not earned. Bacon was not a natural philosopher, except in the most amateur fashion. His real accomplishment was setting an intellectual tone and helping create a climate conducive to scientific work.

In books such as *The Advancement of Learning* (1605), the *Novum Organum* (1620), and *The New Atlantis* (1627), Bacon attacked the Scholastic belief that most truth had already been discovered and only required explanation, as well as the Scholastic reverence for authority in intellectual life. He believed Scholastic thinkers focused too much on the tradition and the knowledge of the ancients, and he urged contemporaries to search for a new understanding of nature. He believed seventeenth-century Europeans should have confidence in themselves and their own abilities rather than in the people and methods of the past. Bacon was one of the first major European writers to champion innovation and change.

Bacon believed that human knowledge should produce useful results—deeds rather than words. In particular, Bacon thought, knowledge of nature should be used to improve the human condition. These goals required modifying or abandoning Scholastic modes of learning and thinking. Bacon contended, "The [scholastic] logic now in use serves more to fix and give stability to the errors which have their foundation in commonly received notions than to help the search after truth."[5] Scholastic philosophers were trapped by their syllogisms, which they used to examine the foundations of their thought and intellectual presuppositions.

NOVUM ORGANUM Published in 1620, *Novum Organum* ("new organ or instrument") by Francis Bacon is one of the most important works of the scientific revolution. In this and other works, Bacon attacked the long-held belief that most truth had already been discovered. This allegorical image, from the frontispiece of *Novum Organum*, shows a ship striking out for unknown territories, seeking, as did Bacon, a new understanding of the natural world. The ship is flanked by the mythical pillars of Hercules that stand at the point where the Mediterranean meets the Atlantic—the realm of the unknown and unexplored. **SOURCE:** Library of Congress

be created and with it new capabilities for humankind.

Bacon boldly compared himself with Columbus, plotting a new route to intellectual discovery. This comparison displays the consciousness of a changing world that appeared so often in writings of the late sixteenth and early seventeenth centuries. These writers rejected the past not from simple contempt or arrogance, but rather from a firm understanding that the world was much more complicated than their medieval forebearers had thought. Neither Europe nor European thought could remain self-contained. Like the new worlds on the globe, new worlds of the mind were also emerging.

Most of the people of Bacon's day, including the intellectuals influenced by humanism, thought the best era of human history lay in antiquity. Bacon dissented vigorously from that view. He looked to a future of material improvement achieved through the empirical examination of nature. His own theory of induction from empirical evidence was unsystematic, but his insistence on appealing to experience influenced others whose methods were more productive. Bacon and others of his outlook received almost daily support from the reports not only of European explorers but also of ordinary seamen who now sailed all over the world and could describe wondrous cultures, as well as plants and animals, unknown to the European ancients.

Bacon believed that expanding natural knowledge had a practical purpose and its goal was human improvement. Some scientific investigation does have this character. Much pure research does not. Bacon, however, linked science and material progress in the public mind. This was a powerful idea that still influences Western civilization. It has made science and those who can appeal to the authority of science major forces for change and innovation. Thus, although Bacon did not make a major scientific contribution himself, he pointed investigators of nature toward a new method and a new purpose. As a person actively associated with politics, Bacon also believed the pursuit of new knowledge would increase the power of governments and monarchies. Again, his contribution in this area helped create strong links between governments and the scientific enterprise.

Bacon urged philosophers and investigators of nature to examine the evidence of their senses before constructing logical speculations. In a famous passage, he divided all philosophers into "men of experiment and men of dogmas."[6] By directing natural philosophy toward an examination of empirical evidence, Bacon hoped new knowledge would

14.2.3 René Descartes: The Method of Rational Deduction

René Descartes (1596–1650) was a gifted mathematician who invented analytic geometry. His most important contribution, however, was developing a scientific method that relied more on deduction—reasoning from general principle to arrive at specific facts—than empirical observation and induction.

In 1637, Descartes published his *Discourse on Method*, in which he rejected Scholastic philosophy and education and advocated for thought based on a mathematical model. (To assess a debate between Descartes and the satirist **Jonathan Swift** on the scientific enterprise, see the "Compare and Connect" sidebar, which follows below.) He began the *Discourse* by saying he would doubt everything except those propositions that led to clear and distinct ideas. This approach rejected all forms of intellectual authority, except the conviction of his own reason. Descartes concluded that he could not doubt his own act of thinking and his own existence. On this basis, he deduced the existence of God. The presence of God was important to Descartes's theory because God guaranteed the correctness of clear and distinct ideas. Since God was not a deceiver, the ideas of God-given reason could not be false.

Compare and Connect

René Descartes and Jonathan Swift Debate the Scientific Enterprise

THROUGHOUT THE SEVENTEENTH and eighteenth centuries various writers asserted that the growth of scientific knowledge promised to improve the human situation. Others, who did not dispute the truth or correctness of the new natural knowledge, nonetheless questioned whether it could improve the human situation. In the first document, French philosopher René Descartes defends scientific enterprise while many decades later, in the second document, English satirist Jonathan Swift questions the usefulness of the new scientific knowledge pursued by the Royal Society of London and by other European scientific academies.

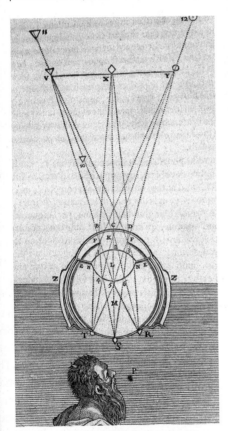

VISUAL PERCEPTION À LA DESCARTES
This illustration taken from *Discourse on Method* (1637) by René Descartes examines the focal properties of the eye.
SOURCE: Library of Congress

Before Reading

- Point out the advantages that René Descartes believed science had over previous ways of thinking.
- Describe the limitations that Jonathan Swift found in the promise of science.

Questions

1. How does Descartes compare the usefulness of science with previous speculative philosophy?

2. What, if any, limits does Descartes place on the extension of scientific knowledge?

3. Why might Swift have emphasized so strongly what he considered the impracticality of science?

4. Can Swift's presentation be seen as an expression of jealousy of the growing influence of science?

5. How does Swift's passage refute the promise of science championed by Bacon and Descartes?

I. RENÉ DESCARTES EXPLORES THE PROMISE OF EXPANDING NATURAL KNOWLEDGE

In 1637, René Descartes published his Discourse on Method. *He argued against what he believed to be the useless speculations of Scholastic philosophy. He championed the careful investigation of physical nature on the grounds that it would expand human knowledge beyond anything previously achieved and make human beings the masters of nature. The following passage exemplifies this broad intellectual and cultural argument that led to the ever-growing influence and authority of science from the seventeenth century onward.*

Although my speculations greatly pleased myself, I believed that others had theirs, which perhaps pleased them still more. But as soon as I had acquired some general notions respecting physics, and beginning to make trial of them in various particular difficulties, had observed how far they can carry us, and how much they differ from the principles that have been employed up to the present time, I believed that I could not keep them concealed without sinning grievously against the law by which we are bound to promote, as far as in us lies, the general good of mankind. For by them I perceived it to be possible to arrive at knowledge highly useful in life; and [instead] of the speculative philosophy usually taught in the schools, to discover a practical [philosophy], by means of which, knowing the force and action of fire, water, air, the stars, the heavens, and all the other bodies that surround us, as distinctly as we know the various crafts of our artisans, we might also apply them in the same way to all the uses to which they are adapted, and thus render ourselves the lords and possessors of nature. And this is a result to be desired, not only [my desire for] an infinity of arts by which we might be enabled to enjoy without any trouble the fruits of the earth, and all its comforts, but also and especially the preservation of health, which is without doubt, of all the blessings of this life, the first and fundamental one; for the mind is so intimately dependent upon the condition and relation of the organs of the body, that if any means can ever be found to render men wiser and more ingenious than hitherto, I believe that it is in medicine they must be sought for . . . without any wish to depreciate it, I am confident that there is no one, even among those whose profession it is, who does not admit that all at present known in it is almost nothing in comparison of what remains to be discovered; and that we could free ourselves from an infinity of maladies of body as well as of mind, and perhaps also even from the debility of age, if we had sufficiently ample knowledge of their causes, and of all the remedies provided for us by nature.

II. JONATHAN SWIFT SATIRIZES SCIENTIFIC SOCIETIES

Jonathan Swift, the greatest English satirist of the eighteenth century, was a deeply pessimistic person who thought the promise of scientific enterprise would never be realized. In the Third Voyage of Gulliver's Travels, *published in 1726, Swift portrays Gulliver visiting the land of Lagado, where he encounters a learned academy of scholars pursuing outlandish projects. Swift tells the stories of a series of Projectors, each of which is more impractical than the next. The following passage in which Swift pillories the scientists hoping to receive patronage for projects from the Royal Society of London remains one of the most famous satires of science in the English language. It is a testimony to the cultural authority that science had achieved by the early eighteenth century.*

Gulliver reports a conversation he encountered while visiting Lagado:

"The Sum of his Discourse was to this Effect. That about Forty Years ago, certain Persons went up to *Laputa*, either upon Business or Diversion; and after five Months Continuance, came back with a very little Smattering in Mathematics, but full of Volatile Spirits acquired in that Airy Region. That these Persons upon their Return, began to dislike the Management of every Thing below; and fell into Schemes of putting all Arts, Sciences, Languages, and Mechanics upon a new Foot. To this End they procured a Royal Patent for erecting an Academy of *Projectors* in *Lagado*; And the Humour prevailed so strongly among the People, that there is not a Town of any Consequence in the Kingdom without such an Academy. In these Colleges, the Professors contrive new Rules and Methods of Agriculture and Building, and new Instruments and Tools for all Trades and Manufactures, whereby, as they undertake, one Man shall do the Work of Ten; a Palace may be built in a Week, of Materials so durable as to last for ever without repairing. All the Fruits of the Earth shall come to Maturity at whatever Season we think fit to chuse; and increase an Hundred Fold more than they do at present; with innumerable other happy Proposals. The only Inconvenience is, that none of these Projects are yet brought to Perfection; and in the mean time, the whole Country lies miserably waste, the Houses in Ruins, and the People without Food or Cloaths. By all which, instead of being discouraged they are Fifty Times more violently bent upon prosecuting their Schemes, driven equally on by Hope and Despair. . . ."

Gulliver then reports what he found occurring in the rooms of an academy in Lagado:

"The first Man I saw . . . had been Eight Years upon a Project for extracting Sun-Beams out of Cucumbers, which were to be put into Vials hermetically sealed, and let out to warm the Air in raw inclement Summers. . . .

I saw another at work to calcine ice into Gun-powder. . . .

There was another most ingenius Architect who had contrived a new Method for building Houses, by beginning at the Roof, and working downwards to the Foundation. . . .

In another Apartment I was highly pleased with a Projector, who had found a Device of plowing the Ground with Hogs, to save the Charges of Plows, Cattle, and Labour. The Method is this: In an Acre of Ground you bury at six Inches Distance, and eight deep, a quantity of Acorns, Dates, Chesnuts, and other Masts or Vegetables whereof these Animals are fondest; then you drive six Hundred or more of them into the Field, where in a few Days they will root up the whole Ground in search of their Food, and make it fit for sowing, at the same time manuring it with their Dung. It is true, upon Experiment they found the Charge and Trouble very great, and they had little or no Crop. However, it is not doubted that this Invention may be capable of great Improvement."

SOURCES: (I) From René Descartes, *Discourse on Method*, in John Veitch, trans., *The Methods, Meditations and Philosophies of Descartes* (New York: E. P. Dutton and Co., 1912), pp. 49–50. (II) From Jonathan Swift, *Gulliver's Travels*, Part III, chaps. iv and v (New York: The Heritage Press, 1960), pp. 193–194, 197–199.

Based on this analysis, Descartes concluded that human reason could fully comprehend the world. He divided things into two basic categories: thinking things and things occupying space—mind and body, respectively. Thinking was the defining quality of the mind, and extension (the property by which things occupy space) was the defining quality of material bodies. Human reason, Descartes concluded, could grasp and understand the world of extension, which became the realm of the natural philosopher. That world had no place for spirits, divinity, or anything nonmaterial. Descartes separated mind from body to disconnect nonmaterial matters from the realm of scientific speculation and analysis. Reason was to be applied only to the mechanical realm of matter or to the exploration of itself.

Descartes's emphasis on deduction, rational speculation, and internal reflection, all of which he explored more fully in his *Meditations* of 1641, has influenced philosophers from his time to the present. His deductive methodology, however, eventually lost favor to **scientific induction**, whereby scientists make generalizations derived from, and test hypotheses against, empirical observations.

14.2.4 Thomas Hobbes: Apologist for Absolute Government

The impact of the new scientific methods deeply affected the political thought of **Thomas Hobbes** (1588–1679), the most original political philosopher of the seventeenth century.

An urbane and much-traveled man, Hobbes enthusiastically supported the new scientific movement. During the 1630s, he visited Paris, where he came to know Descartes, and Italy, where he spent time with Galileo. He took special interest in the works of William Harvey (1578–1657), famous for his discovery of the circulation of blood through the body. Hobbes was also a superb classicist. His earliest published work was the first English translation of

Thucydides's *History of the Peloponnesian War*, which is still being reprinted today. Part of Hobbes's dark view of human nature appears to derive from Thucydides's historical analysis.

Hobbes had written works of political philosophy before the English Civil War, but the turmoil of that struggle led him in 1651 to publish his influential work *Leviathan*. His goal was to provide a rigorous philosophical justification for a strong central political authority. Hobbes portrayed human beings and society in a thoroughly materialistic and mechanical way. He described human psychology as solely based on sensory needs and all human motivations as egoistical, intended to increase pleasure and minimize pain. According to his analysis, human reasoning achieved no deeper reality or wisdom than those physical sensations. Consequently, for Hobbes, unlike both previous Christian and ancient philosophers, human beings existed only to meet the needs of daily life, not for higher spiritual ends or for any larger moral purpose. Only a sovereign commonwealth established by a contract between the ruler and the ruled could enable human beings to attain such spirituality by limiting the free exercise of the natural human pursuit of self-interest, with its potential for great conflict.

According to Hobbes, human beings in their natural state are inclined to a "perpetual and restless desire" for power. Because all people want and, in their natural state, possess a natural right to everything, their equality breeds enmity, competition, diffidence, and perpetual quarreling—"a war of every man against every man," as Hobbes put it in a famous summary:

In such condition there is no place for industry, because the fruit thereof is uncertain; and consequently no culture of the Earth; no navigation nor use of the commodities that may be imported by sea; no commodious building; no instruments of moving and removing such things as require much force; no knowledge of the face of the Earth;

no account of time; no arts; no letters; no society; and, which is worst of all, continual fear and danger of violent death; and the life of man solitary, poor, nasty, brutish, and short.[7]

As seen in this passage, Hobbes, contrary to Aristotle and Christian thinkers like Thomas Aquinas (1225–1274), rejected the view that human beings were naturally sociable, claiming they were self-centered creatures who lack a master. Thus, whereas earlier and later philosophers saw the original human state as a paradise from which humankind had fallen, Hobbes saw it as a state of natural, inevitable conflict in which safety, security, and final authority did not exist. Human beings in this state of nature were constantly haunted by fear of destruction and death.

Human beings escaped this terrible state of nature, according to Hobbes, only by entering into a political contract according to which they agreed to live in a commonwealth tightly ruled by a recognized sovereign. This contract obliged every person, for the sake of peace and self-defense, to set aside personal rights and to be content with as much liberty for others as he or she would allow for him- or herself. Living according to this contract meant agreeing to live according to a secularized version of the golden rule, "Do not that to another which you would not have done to yourself."[8]

Because, however, words and promises are insufficient to guarantee this agreement, the contract also established the coercive use of force by the sovereign to ensure compliance. Believing the dangers of anarchy to be always greater than those of tyranny, Hobbes thought that rulers should be absolute and unlimited in their power, once established as authority. Hobbes's political philosophy had no room for individual conscience or for individual appeal to some other legitimate authority beyond the sovereign.

The specific structure of this absolute government was not of enormous concern to Hobbes. He believed absolute authority might be expressed in either a monarch or a legislative body, but once that person or body had been granted authority, there existed no argument for appeal. For all practical purposes, obedience to the Hobbesian sovereign was absolute.

Hobbes's argument for an absolute political authority that could ensure order aroused sharp opposition. Monarchists objected to his willingness to assign sovereign authority to a legislature. Republicans rejected his willingness to accept a monarchical authority. Many Christian writers, including those who supported the divine right of kings, furiously criticized his materialist arguments for an absolute political authority. Other Christian writers attacked his refusal to recognize the authority of either God or the church as standing beside or above his secular sovereign. The religious critique of Hobbes's arguments did not allow his ideas to have immediate practical impact, but his ideas influenced philosophical literature from the late seventeenth century onward.

14.2.5 John Locke: Defender of Moderate Liberty and Toleration

John Locke (1632–1704) proved to be the most influential philosophical and political thinker of the seventeenth century. Although he was less original than Hobbes, his political writings were a major source of criticism of absolutism and provided a foundation for later liberal political philosophy in both Europe and America. His philosophical works dealing with human knowledge became the most important work of psychology for the eighteenth century.

Locke wrote two treatises on government that were eventually published in 1690. In the *First Treatise of Government*, he rejected arguments for absolute government that based political authority on the patriarchal model of fathers ruling over a family. After the publication of this treatise, no major political philosopher again appealed to the patriarchal model. Though not widely read today, Locke's *First Treatise* was enormously important by clearing the philosophical decks, so to speak, of a long-standing traditional argument that could not stand up to rigorous analysis.

In his *Second Treatise of Government*, Locke presented an extended argument for a government that must necessarily

JOHN LOCKE John Locke (1632–1704) defended the rights of the people against rulers who believed their power to be absolute.
SOURCE: IanDagnall Awaiting Deletion/Alamy Stock Photo

be both responsible for and responsive to the concerns of the governed. Locke portrayed the natural human state as one of perfect freedom and equality in which everyone enjoyed, in an unregulated fashion, the natural rights of life, liberty, and property. Contrary to Hobbes, Locke regarded human beings in their natural state as creatures of reason and basic goodwill rather than of uncontrolled passion and selfishness. For Locke, human beings possessed a strong capacity for dwelling more or less peacefully in society before they entered a political contract. What they experienced in their natural state was not war, but a condition of competition and modest conflict that required a political authority to sort out problems rather than to impose sovereign authority. They entered into the contract to form a political society to secure and preserve the rights, liberty, and property that they already possessed prior to the existence of political authority. In this respect, government existed to protect the best achievements and liberty of the state of nature, not to overcome them. Thus, by its very foundation, Locke's government was one of limited authority.

The conflict that Hobbes believed characterized the state of nature existed for Locke only when rulers failed to preserve people's natural freedom and attempted to enslave them through absolute rule. The relationship between rulers and the governed was one of trust, and if the rulers betrayed that trust, the governed had the right to replace them.

In his *Letter Concerning Toleration* (1689), Locke used the premises of the yet unpublished *Second Treatise* to defend extensive religious toleration among Christians, which he believed was the answer to the destructive religious conflict of the previous two centuries. To make his case for toleration, Locke claimed that each individual was responsible for his or her own religious salvation and that these efforts might lead people to join different religious groups. Government existed, according to Locke, by its very nature to preserve property, not to make religious decisions for its citizens. Consequently, Locke encouraged a wide degree of religious toleration among differing voluntary Christian groups. He did not, however, extend toleration to Roman Catholics, whom he believed had given allegiance to a foreign prince (i.e., the pope), to non-Christians, or to atheists, and could not be trusted to keep their word. Despite these limitations, Locke's *Letter Concerning Toleration* established a powerful foundation for future toleration, religious liberty, and separation of church and state. His vision of such expansive toleration was partially realized in England after 1688 and most fully in the United States after the American Revolution.

Finally, just as Newton had clarified laws of astronomy and gravitation, Locke hoped to elucidate the basic structures of human thought. He did so in the most immediately influential of his books, his *Essay Concerning Human Understanding* (1690), which became the major work of European psychology during the eighteenth century. In it, Locke described a person's mind at birth as a blank tablet whose content would be determined by sensory experience. It was a reformer's psychology, based on the idea that the human condition could be improved by changing the environment.

Locke's view of psychology rejected the Christian understanding of original sin, yet he believed his psychology had preserved religious knowledge. Religious knowledge, he thought, came through divine revelation in Scripture and also from the conclusions that human reason could draw from observing nature. Locke hoped his interpretation of religious knowledge would prevent fanaticism stemming from alleged private revelations, and irrationality arising from superstition. For Locke, reason and revelation were compatible and together could sustain a moderate religious faith that would avoid religious conflict.

14.3 The New Institutions of Expanding Natural Knowledge

What were the social and political contexts for scientific inquiry in the seventeenth century?

One of the most fundamental features of the expansion of science was the emerging idea that *genuinely new knowledge* about nature and humankind could be discovered. In the late Middle Ages, the recovery of Aristotle and the rise of humanistic learning rediscovered ancient knowledge that later Europeans needed. Luther and other Reformers had seen themselves as incorporating a better understanding of the original Christian message. By contrast, the proponents of the new natural knowledge and the new philosophy pursued what Bacon called the advancement of learning. New knowledge would be continuously created. This outlook required new institutions.

14.3.1 The New Knowledge and Its Consequences

The expansion of natural knowledge had powerful social implications. Proponents of both the new science and the philosophical outlook associated with it opposed Scholasticism and Aristotelianism. However, most scholars in the universities of the day still believed in these older outlooks for approaching the world of knowledge. Not surprisingly, the advanced thinkers of the seventeenth century often criticized the universities. For example, in his *Discourse on Method*, Descartes was highly critical of the education he had received. Hobbes's *Leviathan* was filled with caustic remarks about the kind of learning then dominating schools and universities, and Locke advocated educational reform.

Some of the criticism of universities was exaggerated. Medical faculties, on the whole, welcomed the advancement of learning. Most of the natural philosophers had themselves received their education at universities. Moreover, however slowly new ideas might be accepted in universities, the world of natural knowledge would eventually open up to future generations. With the incorporation of science into the universities came new supporters of scientific knowledge beyond the small group of natural philosophers. Universities also provided much of the physical and financial support for teaching and investigating natural philosophy and employed many scientists, most important of whom was Newton himself.

14.3.2 The New Scientific Institutions and Societies

Because of the reluctance of universities to rapidly assimilate the new science, its pioneers quickly understood that they required a network for cooperating and sharing information that went beyond existing intellectual institutions. Consequently, they and their supporters established what have been termed "institutions of sharing" that allowed information and ideas associated with the new science to be gathered, exchanged, and debated.[9] The most famous of these institutions was the Royal Society of London, founded in 1660, whose members consciously saw themselves as following the path laid out by Bacon almost a half-century earlier. In addition to these major institutions, the new science was discussed and experiments were carried out in many local societies and academies.

These societies met regularly to hear papers and observe experiments. These groups also published information relating to natural philosophy and often organized libraries for their members. Perhaps most important, they attempted to separate the discussion and exploration of natural philosophy from the religious and political conflicts of the day. The believed science was to be an arena for the polite exchange of ideas and for civil disagreement and debate.

The societies were a kind of crossroads with their own members always drawn from the literate classes, as well as people outside the elite classes, whose skills and practical knowledge might be important for advancing the new science. The latter included craftspeople who could manufacture scientific instruments, sailors who had traveled to foreign lands who might report on the plants and animals they had seen, and workers with practical knowledge of problems in the countryside. In this respect, the expansion of the European economy and empires contributed to the growth of scientific endeavor by bringing back to Europe experiences and knowledge that required classification, analysis, and observation.

The work, publications, and interaction of the scientific societies with both the government and private business established a distinct role and presence for scientific knowledge in European social life. By 1700, that presence was relatively modest, but it would grow steadily during the coming decades. The groups associated with the new science believed they were championing modern practical achievements of applied knowledge and encouraging religious toleration, mutual forbearance, and political liberty. Such groups would form the social base for the eighteenth-century movement known as the **Enlightenment**.

14.4 Women in the World of the Scientific Revolution

What role did women play in the scientific revolution?

The same factors that had long excluded women from participating in most intellectual life continued to exclude them from pursuing the emerging natural philosophy.

RENÉ DESCARTES AT THE COURT OF CHRISTINA OF SWEDEN Queen Christina of Sweden (r. 1632–1654), shown here with French philosopher and scientist René Descartes, was one of many women from the elite classes interested in the new science. In 1649 she invited Descartes to live at her court in Stockholm, but he died a few months after moving to Sweden.
SOURCE: Chateau de Versailles, France/Bridgeman Art Library

Traditionally, the institutions of European intellectual life had all but excluded women. Women did exercise influence over princely courts where natural philosophers, such as Galileo, sought patronage, but they usually did not determine those patronage decisions or benefit from them. Queen Christina of Sweden (r. 1632–1654), who brought René Descartes to Stockholm to provide the regulations for a new science academy, was an exception. When various scientific societies were founded, women were not admitted as members. There were virtually no social spaces that might have permitted women to pursue science easily. (For a view of how women were excluded from scientific societies, see the "Closer Look" sidebar, which follows below.) Yet a few isolated women from two different social settings did manage to engage in the new scientific activity: noblewomen and women from the artisan class. In both cases, they could do so only through their husbands or male relatives.

A Closer Look

The Sciences and the Arts

PAINTERS DURING the seventeenth century were keenly aware that they lived in an age of expanding knowledge of nature and of the world. Adriaen van Stalbemt (1580–1662) portrayed this close relationship between natural knowledge and artistic expression in *The Sciences and the Arts*. Across Europe, societies were founded to study the expanding realm of natural knowledge. As evident from this painting, women were only rarely, if ever, admitted to the meetings of these societies or to the rooms where modern knowledge was pursued or discussed.

Paintings on themes from the Bible and from ancient mythology contrast with the symbols of modern knowledge displayed elsewhere in the room.

A globe and volumes of maps allowed observers to trace explorations of the Americas and other parts of the non-European world.

Astronomical instruments (an armillary sphere, possibly, shown here) were used by natural philosophers to illustrate the theories of Copernicus, Kepler, and Galileo.

ADRIAEN VAN STALBEMT, THE SCIENCES AND THE ARTS, CA. 1650
SOURCE: Erich Lessing/Art Resource, NY

Notice that the paintings include works produced by the great masters of the day, some of whom drew on ancient mythological themes, biblical scenes, and contemporary landscapes. Sophisticated viewers would have been able to identify each painting and its artist.

Questions

1. What does van Stalbemt's painting communicate about mid-seventeenth-century Europe?
2. What are some of the political, religious, and cultural themes exhibited in this painting?
3. What commentary might van Stalbemt be making about the state of art and science at the time?

14.4.1 Noblewomen: Margaret Cavendish

The social standing of certain noblewomen allowed them to command the attention of ambitious natural philosophers who were part of their husbands' social circles. **Margaret Cavendish** (1623–1673) made significant contributions to the scientific literature of the day. As a girl she had been privately tutored and become widely read. Her marriage to the Duke of Newcastle introduced her to a circle of natural philosophers. She understood the new science, quarreled with the ideas of Descartes and Hobbes, and criticized the **Royal Society of London** for being more interested in novel scientific instruments than in solving practical problems. Her most important works were *Observations Upon Experimental Philosophy* (1666) and *Grounds of Natural Philosophy* (1668). She was the only woman in the seventeenth century to be allowed to visit a meeting of the Royal Society of London.

14.4.2 Women Artisans

Women associated with artisan crafts achieved greater freedom to pursue the new sciences than did noblewomen. Traditionally, women had worked in artisan workshops, often with their husbands, and might take over the business when their spouses died. In Germany, the study of astronomy occurred in these workshops, with women assisting their fathers or husbands. One German female astronomer, Maria Cunitz, published a book on astronomy that many thought her husband had written until he added a preface supporting her sole authorship. Elisabetha and Johannes Hevelius were a wife-and-husband astronomical team, as were Maria Winkelmann and her husband Gottfried Kirch. Winkelmann had worked jointly with her husband, who was the official astronomer of the Berlin Academy of Sciences and responsible for an official calendar the academy published. When her husband died in 1710, Winkelmann applied for permission to continue his work, basing her application on the guild's tradition of allowing women to continue their husbands' work, in this case the completion of observations required to create an accurate calendar. After much debate, the academy formally rejected her application on the grounds of her gender, although its members knew of her ability and previous accomplishments. Years later, she returned to the Berlin Academy as an assistant to her son, who had been appointed astronomer. Again, the academy insisted that she leave, forcing her to abandon astronomy.

14.4.3 Women's Contributions to Science

Such policies of exclusion, however, did not altogether prevent women from acquiring knowledge about scientific endeavors. Margaret Cavendish had composed a *Description of a New World, Called the Blazing World* (1666) to introduce women to the new science. Other examples of scientific writings for a female audience were Bernard de Fontenelle's *Conversations on the Plurality of Worlds* (1686) and Francesco Algarotti's *Newtonianism for Ladies* (1737). During the 1730s, Emilie du Châtelet (1706–1749) aided French writer Voltaire in his composition of an important French popularization of Newton's science. Her knowledge of mathematics was more extensive than his, and crucial to his completing his book. She also translated Newton's *Principia* into French, an accomplishment made possible only by her exceptional understanding of advanced mathematics.

By the early eighteenth century, despite isolated precedents of women pursuing natural knowledge, reading scientific literature, and engaging socially with natural philosophers, it had become a fundamental assumption of European intellectual life that the pursuit of scientific knowledge was a male vocation. With, few exceptions, women were barred from science and medicine until the late nineteenth century, and not until the twentieth century did they enter these fields in significant numbers.

14.5 The New Science and Religious Faith

What efforts were made to reconcile the new science and religion?

For many contemporaries, the new science posed a potential challenge to religion. Three major issues were at stake. First, certain theories and discoveries did not agree with biblical statements about the heavens. Second, who would decide conflicts between religion and science—church authorities or the natural philosophers? Finally, for many religious thinkers, the new science replaced a universe of spiritual meaning and significance with a purely materialistic one. Yet most of the natural philosophers genuinely saw their work as supporting religious belief by contributing to a deeper knowledge of the divine. Their efforts and those of their supporters to reconcile faith and the new science constituted a fundamental factor in the widespread acceptance of science in educated European circles.

14.5.1 The Case of Galileo

The condemnation of Galileo by Roman Catholic authorities in 1633 is the single most famous conflict between modern science and religious institutions. For centuries it was thought of as the forces of religion smothering scientific knowledge. More recent research has modified that picture.

The condemnation of Copernicanism and of Galileo occurred at a particularly difficult moment in the history of the Roman Catholic Church. In response to Protestant emphasis on private interpretation of Scripture, the Council of Trent (1545–1563) had stated that only the church itself had the authority to interpret the Bible. Furthermore, after the Council, the Roman Catholic Church had adopted a more literalist mode of reading the Bible in response to the Protestant emphasis on the authority of Scripture. The Roman Catholic Church, on the one hand, could not surrender interpretation of the Bible to the laity and, on the other, could not move beyond a literal reading of the Bible, for fear that the Protestants would accuse it of abandoning Scripture. Galileo's championing of Copernicanism took place in this climate of opinion and practice.

In 1615, in a letter to the Grand Duchess Christina, Galileo, as a layman, had published his own views about how Scripture should be interpreted to accommodate the new science. To certain Roman Catholic authorities, Galileo's actions resembled those of a Protestant opting for a personal rather than the church's interpretation of the Bible. In 1615 and 1616, Galileo visited Rome and discussed his views openly and aggressively. In early 1616, however, the Roman Catholic Inquisition formally censured Copernicus's views, placing *On the Revolutions of the Heavenly Spheres* in the Index of Prohibited Books. The grounds for the condemnation was Copernicus's disagreement with the literal word of the Bible and the biblical interpretations of the church fathers. At the time, satisfactory empirical evidence to support Copernicus's views did not yet exist, even in Galileo's mind.

Galileo, who was not on trial in 1616, was formally informed of the condemnation of Copernicanism. The agreement he and the Roman Catholic authorities reached as to what he would be permitted to write about Copernicanism remains unclear. It appears that he agreed not to advocate Copernican astronomy, but only to suggest that it could be true in theory.

In 1623, however, a Florentine acquaintance of Galileo's was elected as Pope Urban VIII. He gave Galileo permission to resume discussing the Copernican system, which he did in *Dialogue on the Two Chief World Systems* (1632). The book clearly was designed to defend the physical truthfulness of Copernicanism. Moreover, the voices in the dialogue favoring the older system appeared slow-witted—and those voices presented the views of Pope Urban. Feeling humiliated and betrayed, the pope ordered an investigation of Galileo's book. At issue in Galileo's trial of 1633 was whether he had disobeyed the mandate of 1616, and he was judged to have done so even though the exact nature of that mandate was not certain. Galileo was condemned, ordered to renounce his views, and placed under the equivalent of house arrest in his home near Florence for the last nine years of his life.

14.5.2 Blaise Pascal: Reason and Faith

Blaise Pascal (1623–1662), a French mathematician and a physical scientist who surrendered his wealth to pursue an austere, self-disciplined life, was influential in his efforts to reconcile faith and the new science. He aspired to write a work that would refute both dogmatism, which he saw epitomized by the Jesuits, and skepticism. Pascal considered the Jesuits' casuistry—arguments designed to minimize and excuse sinful acts—a distortion of Christian teaching. He rejected the skeptics of his age because they were either atheists who denied religion altogether or deists who accepted it only as it conformed to reason. He never produced a definitive refutation of the two sides. Rather, he formulated his views on these matters in piecemeal fashion in a provocative collection of reflections on humankind and religion published posthumously under the title *Pensées* (*Thoughts*).

Pascal believed that in religious matters, only the reasons of the heart and a "leap of faith" could prevail because religion was not the domain of reason and science. He saw two essential truths in the Christian religion: A loving God exists, and human beings, because they are corrupt by nature, are utterly unworthy of God. He believed the atheists and the deists of his age had overestimated reason and that reason was too weak to resolve the problems of human nature and destiny. Ultimately, reason should lead those who truly heeded it to faith in God and reliance on divine grace.

Pascal made a famous wager with the skeptics. It is a better bet, he argued, to believe God exists and to stake everything on his promised mercy than not to do so. If God does exist, Pascal claimed, the believer will gain everything, whereas, should God prove not to exist, comparatively little will have been lost by having believed in him.

Convinced that belief in God improved life psychologically and disciplined it morally (regardless of whether God proved in the end to exist), Pascal worked to strengthen traditional religious belief. He urged his contemporaries to seek self-understanding by "learned ignorance" and to discover humankind's greatness by recognizing its misery. He hoped thereby to counter what he believed to be the false optimism of the new rationalism and science.

14.5.3 The English Approach to Science and Religion

Francis Bacon established a key framework for reconciling science and religion that long influenced the English-speaking world. He argued there were two books of divine revelation: the Bible and nature. In studying nature, the natural philosopher could achieve a deeper knowledge of things divine, just as could the theologian studying the Bible. Because both books of revelation shared the same author, they must be compatible, and any discord that might first appear between science and religion must eventually be reconciled. Natural theology based on a scientific understanding of the natural order would thus support theology derived from Scripture.

Later in the seventeenth century, with the work of Newton, the natural universe became a realm of law and regularity. Most natural philosophers were devout people who saw in the new picture of physical nature a new picture of God. The Creator of this rational, lawful nature must also be rational, and studying nature led to a better understanding of that Creator. Science and religious faith were not only compatible, but also mutually supportive. As Newton wrote, "The main Business of Natural Philosophy is to argue from Phaenomena without feigning Hypothesis, and to deduce Causes from Effects, till we come to the very first Cause, which certainly is not mechanical."[10]

The religious thought associated with deducing of religious conclusions from nature became known as *physico-theology*. This reconciliation of faith and science allowed the new physics and astronomy to spread rapidly. At a time when Europeans were finally tiring of the wars of religion, the new science inspired a view of God that might lead away from irrational disputes and wars over religious doctrine. Faith in a rational God encouraged faith in the rationality of human beings and in their capacity to improve their lives once liberated from the traditions of the past. The scientific revolution was a great model for the desire for change and of criticism of inherited views.

Finally, the new science and the technological and economic innovations associated with its culture were again, especially among English thinkers, interpreted as part of a divine plan. By the late seventeenth century, natural philosophy and its practical achievements had become associated in the public mind with consumption and the market economy. Scientific advance and economic enterprise came to be understood in the public mind as the fulfillment of God's plan: human beings were meant to improve the world. This outlook provided a religious justification for the economic improvement that would characterize much of eighteenth-century Western Europe.

14.6 Continuing Superstition

What explains the witch hunts and panics of the sixteenth and seventeenth centuries?

Despite great optimism of European thinkers associated with the new ideas in science and philosophy, traditional beliefs and fears retained their hold on Western popular culture. During the sixteenth and seventeenth centuries, Europeans remained preoccupied with sin, death, and the devil. Religious people, many who were learned and many who were sympathetic to emerging scientific ideas, continued to believe in the power of magic and the occult. Until the end of the seventeenth century, almost all Europeans in one way or another believed in the devil and the power of demons.

14.6.1 Witch Hunts and Panic

Nowhere is the dark side of early modern thought and culture more strikingly visible than in the witch hunts and panics that erupted in almost every Western land. Between 1400 and 1700, courts sentenced an estimated 70,000 to 100,000 people to death for *maleficium*, or harmful magic, and diabolical witchcraft. In addition to inflicting harm on their neighbors, witches were said to attend mass meetings known as *sabbats*, to which they were also believed to fly. They were also said to indulge in sexual orgies with the devil, who appeared in animal form, most often as a he-goat. Other imagined charges against

EXECUTIONS AT SCHONGAU This engraving shows three women and a child being burned at the stake during the great witch trial of Schongau, 1589–1592.
SOURCE: Interfoto/Alamy Stock Photo

them were cannibalism—particularly the devouring of small Christian children—and a variety of ritual acts and practices, often sexual in nature, that denied or perverted Christian beliefs.

Why did witch panics occur in the sixteenth and early seventeenth centuries? The disruptions created by religious division and warfare were major factors. The peak years of the religious wars were also those of the witch hunts. Some blamed the Reformation for taking away the traditional defenses against the devil and demons, compelling gullible believers to protect themselves by searching for and executing witches.

14.6.2   Village Origins

The roots of belief in witches are found in both popular and elite culture. In village societies, respected "cunning folk" helped the simple folk cope with natural disasters and disabilities incurred by magical powers. Those who were most in need of security and influence, particularly old, impoverished single or widowed women, often made claims to possessing such authority. Occult, village beliefs may also have been a way to defy urban Christian society's attempts to impose its orthodox beliefs, laws, and institutions on the countryside. Under church persecution local fertility cults, whose semipagan practices were intended to ensure good harvests, acquired the features of diabolical witchcraft.

14.6.3   Influence of the Clergy

Popular belief in magical power was the essential foundation of the witch hunts. Had ordinary people not believed that "gifted persons" could help or harm by magical means, and had they not been willing to accuse them, the hunts would never have occurred. However, the contribution of Christian theologians was equally great. When the church expanded into areas where its power and influence were small, it encountered semi-pagan cultures rich in folkloric beliefs and practices that predated Christianity. There, it clashed with so-called cunning men and women, who were respected spiritual authorities in local communities, the folk equivalents of Christian priests. In the eyes of the simple folk, Christian clergy also practiced a kind of high magic. They could transform bread and wine into the body and blood of Christ in the sacrament of the Eucharist and eternal penalties for sin into temporal ones in the sacrament of Penance or Confession. They also claimed the power to cast out demons who possessed the faithful.

In the late thirteenth century, the church declared its so-called magic to be not that of the occult, but the true powers invested in them by the Christian God. Since occult powers were not innate to humans, the theologians reasoned, they must come either from God or from the devil.

Those from God were properly exercised within and by the church. Those who practiced magic outside and against the church did so on behalf of the devil. From such reasoning grew allegations of "pacts" between nonpriestly magicians and Satan.

In working its will, the church had an important ally in the princes of the age, who were attempting to extend and consolidate their authority over villages and towns within their lands. As the church sought to supplant folk magic with the true power of church ritual, the princes sought to supplant customary laws with Roman law. Here the stage was set for a one-sided conflict. Witch trials became one of the ways church and state realized their overlapping goals. To identify, try, and execute witches became a demonstration of absolute spiritual and political authority over a village or a town.

14.6.4   Who Were the Witches?

Roughly 80 percent of the victims of witch hunts were women, most single and aged over forty. Three groups of women appear especially to have drawn the clerical witch-hunters' attention. The first was widows who, living alone in the world after the deaths of their husbands, were now often dependent on others, unhappy, and known to strike out. A second group was midwives, whose work made them unpopular when mothers and/or newborns died in childbirth. Surviving family members remembered those deaths. Finally, there were women healers and herbalists, targeted because their work gave them a moral and spiritual authority over people that the church wished to reserve for its priests.

14.6.5   End of the Witch Hunts

Several factors helped end the witch hunts. One was the emergence of a more scientific point of view. In the seventeenth century, mind and matter came to be viewed as two independent realities, making it harder to believe that thoughts in the mind or words on the lips could alter the physical world. A witch's curse was mere words. With advances in medicine, the rise of insurance companies, and the availability of lawyers, people gained greater physical security against the physical afflictions and natural calamities that drove the witch panics.

The witch hunts also began to get too far out of hand. Tortured witches, when asked whom they saw at witches' sabbats, sometimes alleged having seen leading townspeople and even the judges there. At this point the witch trials simply could no longer serve the interests of those conducting them. In the minds of skeptical lawyers, politicians, and clergy, the witch hunts had become dysfunctional and only threatened anarchy in villages and towns.

Encountering the Past

The Science of Healthy Eating

SIXTEENTH AND SEVENTEENTH-CENTURY PHYSICIANS were convinced that diet played an important role both in maintaining good health and in curing illness. They did not, however, divide foods into healthy and unhealthy categories, as many doctors and dieticians do today. Instead, they sought to match foods to patients, identifying the specific foods that they believed would promote good health in a given individual.

Their starting point for dietary advice was the theory of bodily humors advanced by the Greek physician Galen. Writing in the second century C.E., Galen argued that illness was the result of an imbalance in the body's four fluids, or humors. Thus, all Galenic medical treatments aimed at the same goal, the restoration of humoral balance. What constituted balance, however, varied from individual to individual. According to Galen, one or more humors predominated in each

THE FRUIT SELLER In this late sixteenth-century painting by Vincenzo Campi, a host of fresh fruits and vegetables are spread out before the viewer.
SOURCE: Art Collection 2/Alamy Stock Photo

person, and that specific mix was reflected in their personality. Illness resulted from disturbances in an individual's innate natural balance of humors.

Early modern physicians believed that all organic matter was made up of a mix of four elements that paralleled the human body's four humors. Thus, feeding a patient foods rich in an element in which they were deficient was thought to restore balance and, therefore, health. Traditionally, physicians would carry out a detailed analysis of a patient's humoral makeup and then offer specific, customized dietary recommendations. In the early modern period, however, physicians began to produce and publish advice on diet aimed at the growing reading public. Instead of tailoring their recommendations to individuals, they began to formulate general dietary guidelines for specific groups. Each profession was thought to have its own signature humoral qualities, so physicians recommended one diet to students and scholars and another to soldiers and sailors. Men and women, believed to have different humoral tendencies, were prescribed different foods. Likewise, different age groups required different foods. Finally, many physicians believed that the humoral balance was affected by the weather and recommended different foods for each season as a consequence.

Questions:

1. What connection did early modern physicians make between food and diet?
2. How did they determine what foods were healthy and which were unhealthy?

SOURCE: David Gentilcore, *Food and Health in Early Modern Europe: Diet, Medicine, and Society, 1450-1800* (London: Bloomsbury Academic, 2016).

14.7 Baroque Art

How did baroque art serve both religious and secular ends?

Art historians use the term **baroque** for the style associated with seventeenth-century painting, sculpture, and architecture. As with other terms used in art history, the word *baroque* covers a variety of related styles that developed during the century and moved in various directions in different countries.

14.7.1 Style and Treatment

Baroque painters depicted their subjects in a thoroughly naturalistic, rather than an idealized, manner. This faithfulness to nature paralleled the interest in natural knowledge associated with the rise of the new science and the deeper understanding of human anatomy that was achieved during this period. These painters, the most famous of whom was Michelangelo Caravaggio (1573–1610), also are known for creating dramatic scenes with sharp contrasts between light and darkness. Consequently, both baroque painting and sculpture have a theatrical quality that engages the observer emotionally with the subject that is being portrayed.

14.7.2 Religious and Secular Subjects

The work of baroque artists served both religious and secular ends. Baroque painters, especially in Roman Catholic countries, often portrayed scenes from the Bible and from the lives of saints intended to instruct the observer in religious truths. Artists used the same style of painting, however, to present objects and scenes of everyday life in new realistic detail. Dutch painters of still lifes portrayed all manner of elaborate foodstuffs, and artists such as Louis Le Nain (1593–1648) painted scenes of French peasant life.

Baroque art became associated, rightly or wrongly, with both Roman Catholicism and absolutist politics. Baroque art first emerged in papal Rome. Gian Lorenzo Bernini's work (1598–1680) in St. Peter's Basilica was the most famous example of baroque decoration. At the direction of Pope Urban VIII (r. 1623–1644), during whose reign Galileo was condemned, Bernini designed and oversaw the construction of the great tabernacle that stands beneath the church's towering dome and directly over the space where St. Peter is said to be buried. Behind the tabernacle, Bernini also designed a monument to papal authority with the chair of St. Peter resting on the shoulders of four of the church fathers. In front of the cathedral, he designed the two vast colonnades that he said symbolized the arms of the church reaching out to the world. In the church of Santa Maria della Vittoria in Rome, Bernini created the dramatic sculpture of the Spanish mystic St. Teresa of Avila (1515–1582), depicting her in religious ecstasy.

The association of baroque art with Roman Catholicism had its counterpart in the secular world. Charles I (r. 1625–1649) of England, employed Roman Catholic Flemish artist **Peter Paul Rubens** (1577–1640) to decorate the ceiling of the Banqueting Hall at his palace in London with paintings commemorating his father James I (r. 1603–1625). Rubens was the leading religious painter of the Catholic Reformation, feeding puritan suspicions that the king harbored Roman Catholic sympathies. It was not by coincidence that Charles I was led in 1649 through the

ALTAR AND BALDACHIN, ST. PETER'S BASILICA, VATICAN
Bernini designed an elaborate baldachin, or canopy, that stands under the dome of St. Peter's Basilica. It is one of the major examples of baroque interior design.
SOURCE: Scala/Art Resource, NY

HALL OF MIRRORS, VERSAILLES
The decorative brilliance of the Hall of Mirrors is decidedly baroque in its grandiosity and intense emphasis on light.
SOURCE: Russell Kord/Alamy Stock Photo

Rubens-decorated Banqueting Hall to his execution on the scaffold erected outside.

The most elaborate baroque monument to political absolutism was Louis XIV's palace at Versailles. The exterior of the palace was classical in its restrained design. Room after room in the interior, however, was decorated with vast, dramatic paintings and murals presenting Louis as the Sun King. The Hall of Mirrors, which ran across the entire rear of the palace, allowed for a glittering and elaborate play of light meant to reflect the power of the monarch. In the gardens of Versailles, fountains depicted mythical gods as if they had come to pay court or to amuse the Sun King. Across Europe, monarchs, Protestant as well as Catholic, who hoped to achieve Louis's absolutism in their own domains, erected similar, if smaller, elaborately decorated palaces. Baroque architecture dominated the capitals of the rulers of the smaller German states as well as the imperial court of the Habsburgs in Vienna.

The Chapter in Perspective

The scientific revolution and the thought of writers whose work was contemporaneous with it mark a major turning point in the history of Western culture and eventually had a worldwide impact. The scientific and political ideas of the late sixteenth and seventeenth centuries gradually overturned many of the most fundamental premises of the medieval worldview. The sun replaced the earth as the center of the solar system. The solar system itself came to be viewed as one of many possible systems in the universe. Mathematics began to replace theology and metaphysics as the tool for understanding nature.

This new knowledge of the physical universe led to changes in the authority of the church and Scripture. Parallel to scientific developments and sometimes related to them, political thought became much less concerned with religious issues. Hobbes's theory of political obligation made virtually no reference to God. Locke's political theories recognized God, but paid little attention to Scripture, and championed greater freedom of religious and political expression. His ideas about psychology emphasized the influence of environment on human character and action. These new ideas gradually displaced or reshaped theological and religious modes of thought and placed humankind and life on earth at the center of Western thinking. Intellectuals in the West consequently developed greater self-confidence in their own capacity to shape the world and their own lives.

None of these changes came easily, however. The new science and enlightenment were accompanied by new anxieties that were reflected in a growing preoccupation with sin, death, and the devil. The worst expression of this preoccupation was a succession of witch hunts and trials that took the lives of as many as 100,000 people between 1400 and 1700.

The Chapter in Review

Review Questions

1. What did Copernicus, Brahe, Kepler, Galileo, and Newton each contribute to the scientific revolution? Which do you think made the most important contributions and why? What did Francis Bacon contribute to the foundation of scientific thought?
2. How would you define the term *scientific revolution*? In what ways was it truly revolutionary?
3. What were the differences between the political philosophies of Thomas Hobbes and John Locke? How did each view human nature? Would you rather live under a government designed by Hobbes or by Locke? Why?
4. Why were women unable to participate fully in the new science? How did family relationships help some women become involved in the advance of natural philosophy?
5. Why did the Catholic Church condemn Galileo? How did Pascal seek to reconcile faith and reason? How did English natural theology support economic expansion?
6. How do you explain the phenomena of witchcraft and witch hunts in an age of scientific enlightenment? Why did the witch panics occur in the late sixteenth and early seventeenth centuries? How might the Reformation have contributed to them?

Key Terms

baroque (bah-ROWK)   A style of art marked by heavy and dramatic ornamentation and curved rather than straight lines that flourished between 1550 and 1750, especially associated with the Catholic Counter-Reformation.

Blaise Pascal   (1623–1662) French mathematician and a physical scientist who sought to refute both dogmatism and skepticism.

empiricism (em-PEER-ih-cism)   The use of experiment and observation derived from sensory evidence to construct scientific theory or philosophy of knowledge.

Enlightenment   The eighteenth-century movement led by the *philosophes* who believed that change and reform were both desirable through the application of reason and science.

Francis Bacon   (1561–1626) Englishman known as the father of empiricism and of experimentation in science.

Galileo Galilei   (1564–1642) Italian mathematician and natural philosopher who used his observations of the heavens to argue in favor of the Copernican system.

Isaac Newton   (1642–1727) Englishman whose work on planetary motion established a basis for physics that endured for more than two centuries.

Johannes Kepler   (1571–1630) German astronomer who argued that the orbits of the planets were elliptical in a sun-centered universe.

John Locke   (1632–1704) The greatest English philosopher of the seventeenth century, whose political writings provide the basis for later liberal thought in both Europe and America.

Jonathan Swift   (1667–1745) The author of *Gulliver's Travels*, considered the greatest prose satirist in the English language.

Margaret Cavendish   (1623–1673) English noblewoman renowned for her extensive writing on scientific subjects.

Nicolaus Copernicus   (1473–1543) Polish astronomer who challenged the Ptolemaic system by positing a heliocentric model of the universe.

Peter Paul Rubens   (1577–1640) Flemish baroque artist and the leading religious painter of the Catholic Reformation.

Ptolemaic system (tow-LEM-a-ick)   The pre-Copernican explanation of the universe, with the earth at the center of the universe, which originated in the ancient world.

René Descartes   (1596–1650) French philosopher who invented analytic geometry and developed a deductive scientific method.

Royal Society of London   Founded in 1660, the most famous of the institutions set up in the seventeenth century to allow information and ideas associated with the new science to be gathered, exchanged, and debated.

scientific induction   Method of inquiry whereby scientists make generalizations derived from, and test hypotheses against, empirical observations.

scientific revolution   The sweeping change in the scientific view of the universe that occurred in the sixteenth and seventeenth centuries, including new scientific concepts and the method of their construction that became the standard for assessing the validity of knowledge in the West.

Thomas Hobbes   (1588–1679) The most original political philosopher of the seventeenth century, who argued that human society requires strong central political authority to overcome the perils of the state of nature.

Tycho Brahe   (1546–1601) Danish astronomer whose observations helped advance the concept of a sun-centered system.

Notes

1. Thomas S. Kuhn, *The Copernican Revolution: Planetary Astronomy in the Development of Western Thought* (New York: Vintage, 1959), p. 135.
2. Quoted in E. A. Burtt, *The Metaphysical Foundations of Modern Physical Science* (Garden City, NY: Anchor-Doubleday, 1954), p. 75.
3. Quoted in A. Rupert Hall, *From Galileo to Newton, 1630–1720* (London: Fontana, 1970), p. 300.
4. Quoted in Steven Shapin, *The Scientific Revolution* (Chicago: University of Chicago Press, 1996), p. 33.
5. Quoted in Franklin Baumer, *Main Currents of Western Thought*, 4th ed. (New Haven, CT: Yale University Press, 1978), p. 281.
6. Quoted in Baumer, *Main Currents of Western Thought*, p. 288.
7. Thomas Hobbes, *Leviathan*, Parts I and II, ed. by H. W. Schneider (Indianapolis, IN: Bobbs-Merrill, 1958), pp. 86, 106–107.
8. Hobbes, *Leviathan*, Parts I and II, p. 130.
9. Lewis Pyenson and Susan Sheets-Pyenson, *Servants of Nature: A History of Scientific Institutions, Enterprises, and Sensibilities* (New York: W. W. Norton, 1999), p. 75.
10. Quoted in Baumer, *Main Currents of Western Thought*, p. 323.

Chapter 15
Society and Economy Under the Old Regime in the Eighteenth Century

THE RURAL DOMESTICITY OF PREREVOLUTIONARY EUROPE During the eighteenth century, farm women normally worked in the home and performed such tasks as churning butter as well as caring for children. As time passed tasks such as making butter were mechanized and women were displaced from such work.

SOURCE: Yale Center for British Art, Paul Mellon Collection, USA/Bridgeman Art Library

 ## Contents and Focus Questions

The Chapter in Brief

DURING THE FRENCH REVOLUTION and the turmoil that upheaval spawned, it became customary to refer to the patterns of social, political, and economic relationships that had existed in France before 1789 as the *ancien régime*, or the **Old Regime**. The term has come to be applied generally to the life and institutions of prerevolutionary Europe. Politically, on the Continent, though not in Great Britain, the Old Regime meant the rule of theoretically absolute monarchies with growing bureaucracies and aristocratically led armies. Economically, a scarcity of food, the predominance of agriculture, slow transport, a low level of iron production, comparatively unsophisticated financial institutions, and in some cases, competitive commercial overseas empires characterized the Old Regime. Socially, men and women living during the period saw themselves less as individuals than as members of distinct corporate bodies that possessed certain privileges or rights as a group.

Tradition, hierarchy, a corporate feeling, and privilege were the chief social characteristics of the Old Regime. Yet it was by no means a static society. Change and innovation were fermenting in its midst. Farming became more commercialized, and both food production and the size of the population increased. The early stages of the Industrial Revolution made more consumer goods available, and domestic consumption expanded throughout the century. The colonies in the Americas created strong demand for European goods and manufactures. Merchants in seaports and other cities were expanding their businesses. By preparing their states for war, European governments put new demands on the resources and the economic organizations of their nations. The spirit of rationality that had been so important to the scientific revolution of the seventeenth century continued to manifest itself in the economic life of the eighteenth century. The Old Regime itself fostered the changes that eventually transformed it into a different kind of society.

PREREVOLUTIONARY FRENCH COAT OF ARMS Coats of arms date back to early medieval times, when they were used in battle to identify sides and combatants. Over time, coats of arms came to be associated with non-military forms of community, such as family lines, alliances, and professions. By the eighteenth century, the coat of arms symbolized inherited privilege and became more elaborate, as seen in this French example.
SOURCE: Yui/Shutterstock

15.1 Major Features of Life in the Old Regime

How did tradition, hierarchy, and privilege shape life in the Old Regime?

Socially, prerevolutionary Europe was based on (1) aristocratic elites possessing a wide variety of inherited legal privileges; (2) established churches intimately related to the state and the aristocracy; (3) an urban labor force usually organized into guilds; and (4) a rural peasantry subject to high taxes and feudal dues. Of course, the men and women living during this period did not know it was the Old Regime. Most of them earned their livelihoods and lived their lives as their forebearers had done for generations before them and as they expected their children to do after them.

15.1.1 Maintenance of Tradition

During the eighteenth century, few persons outside the government bureaucracies, the expanding merchant groups, and the movement for reform called the Enlightenment considered change or innovation desirable. This was especially true of social relationships. Both nobles and peasants, for different reasons, repeatedly called for the restoration of traditional, or customary, rights. The nobles asserted what they considered their ancient rights against the intrusion of the expanding monarchical bureaucracies. The peasants, through petitions and revolts, called for the revival or the maintenance of the customary manorial rights that allowed them access to particular lands, courts, or grievance procedures.

Except for the early industrial development in Britain and the accompanying expansion of personal consumption, the eighteenth-century economy was also predominantly traditional. The quality and quantity of the grain harvest remained the most important fact of life for most of the population and the gravest concern for governments.

15.1.2 Hierarchy and Privilege

Closely related to this traditional social and economic outlook was the hierarchical structure of the society. The medieval sense of rank and degree not only persisted but also became more rigid during the century.

Each state or society was considered a community comprised of numerous smaller communities. Eighteenth-century Europeans did not enjoy what Americans regard as "individual rights." Instead, they enjoyed the rights and privileges that were guaranteed to the particular communities or groups of which they were a part. The "community" might include the village, the municipality, the nobility, the church, the guild, a university, or the parish. In turn, each of these members of the community enjoyed certain privileges, some great and some small. These privileges might involve exemption from taxation or from some especially humiliating punishment, the right to practice a trade or craft, the right of one's children to pursue a particular occupation, or for the church, the right to collect the tithe.

15.2 The Aristocracy

What was the foundation of wealth and power for the eighteenth-century aristocracy?

The eighteenth century was the great age of the aristocracy. The nobility constituted approximately 1–5 percent of the population of any given country. Yet in every country, it was the single wealthiest sector of the population; had the widest degree of social, political, and economic power; and set the tone of polite society.

15.2.1 Varieties of Aristocratic Privilege

To be an aristocrat was a matter of birth and legal privilege. The aristocracy had this much in common across the Continent. In almost every other respect, they differed markedly from country to country.

15.2.1.1 BRITISH NOBILITY The smallest, wealthiest, best defined, and most socially responsible aristocracy resided in Great Britain. It consisted of about 400 families, and the eldest male members of each family sat in the House of Lords. Through the corruption of the electoral system, these families also controlled many seats in the House of Commons. The estates of the British nobility ranged from a few thousand to 50,000 acres, from which they received rents. The nobles owned about one-fourth of all the arable land in the country. Increasingly, the British aristocracy invested its wealth in commerce, canals, urban real estate, mines, and even industrial ventures. Because only the eldest son inherited the title (called a **peerage**), the right to sit in

the House of Lords, and the land, younger sons moved into commerce, the army, the professions, and the church. British landowners in both houses of Parliament levied taxes and also paid them. They had few significant legal privileges, but their direct or indirect control of local government gave them immense political power and social influence. The aristocracy dominated the society and politics of the English counties. Their country houses, many of which were built in the eighteenth century, were the centers of local society. (For a telling visual portrait of an aristocratic couple and their estate, see the "Closer Look" sidebar, which follows below.)

15.2.1.2 FRENCH NOBILITY The situation of the continental nobilities was less clear-cut. In France, the approximately 400,000 nobles were divided between nobles "of the sword," or those whose nobility was derived from military service, and those "of the robe," who had acquired their titles either by serving in the bureaucracy or by having purchased them. The two groups had quarreled in the past but often cooperated during the eighteenth century to defend their common privileges.

The French nobles were also divided between those who held office or favor with the royal court at Versailles and those who did not. The court nobility reaped the immense wealth that could be gained from holding high office. The nobles' control of such offices intensified during the century. By the late 1780s, appointments to the church, the army, and the bureaucracy, as well as other profitable positions, tended to go to the nobles already established in court circles. Whereas these well-connected aristocrats were rich, the provincial nobility, called *hobereaux*, were often little better off than wealthy peasants.

Despite differences in rank, origin, and wealth, certain hereditary privileges set all French aristocrats apart from the rest of society. They were exempt from many taxes. For example, most French nobles did not pay the taille, or land tax, the basic tax of the Old Regime. The nobles were technically liable for payment of the *vingtième*, or the "twentieth," which resembled an income tax, but they rarely had to pay it in full. They were not liable for the royal *corvées*, or forced labor on public works, which fell on the peasants. In addition to these exemptions, French nobles could collect feudal dues from their tenants and enjoyed exclusive hunting and fishing privileges.

15.2.1.3 EASTERN EUROPEAN NOBILITIES East of the Elbe River, the character of the nobility became even more complicated and repressive. Throughout the area, the military traditions of the aristocracy remained important. In Poland, there were thousands of nobles, or *szlachta*, who were entirely exempt from taxes after 1741. Until 1768, these Polish aristocrats controlled the life and death of their serfs. Most of the Polish nobility were relatively poor. Only a few rich nobles who had immense estates exercised political power in the fragile Polish state.

A Closer Look

An English Aristocratic Couple of the Eighteenth Century

THIS LARGE OIL on canvas by Thomas Gainsborough dates to around 1750. A few years before, ca. 1747–1748, Gainsborough had also painted a smaller and similar portrait of the wealthy parents of the bride. In the painting shown here, Robert Andrews and his wife, Frances Mary, are depicted against the background of the large estate that was bequeathed to her as part of her dowry. The body language of the newlyweds symbolizes their respective worth and authority, as well as their ability to support each other by means of their different but complementary skills.

The husband leans against a wrought-iron bench in a relaxed and natural pose. He holds a hunting rifle, which may symbolize his ability to protect his family and provide for them.

The bride sits in a position of authority against the trunk of a large tree, symbol of the genealogical tree of their families and their future progeny (indeed, she gave birth to nine children). Her high status is indicated by her sitting position as well as by the sheer amount of space occupied by her elegant dress.

The painting was left incomplete and probably meant to include the couple's first child on her lap. Other possibilities: a letter or a book, a small pet. some embroidery/ knit work; or a pheasant, being the hunting season.

A hunting dog is a traditional symbol of fidelity.

THE ANDREWS AND THEIR ESTATE
SOURCE: National Gallery / Art Resource, NY

Questions

1. What cares and fears would couple of the Andrewses' high standing have?
2. What may the darkening clouds in the background suggest?

In Austria and Hungary, the nobility continued to exercise broad judicial powers over the peasantry through their manorial courts. They also enjoyed various degrees of exemption from taxation.

In Prussia, after the accession of Frederick the Great in 1740, the position of the Junker nobles became much stronger. Frederick's various wars required their full support, and he drew his officers almost wholly from the Junker class. Nobles also increasingly made up the bureaucracy. As in other parts of eastern Europe, the Prussian nobles had extensive judicial authority over the serfs.

In Russia, the eighteenth century marked the beginning of the creation of the nobility. Through the Table of Ranks (1792), Peter the Great (r. 1682–1725) linked state service and noble social status, which established among Russian nobles a self-conscious class identity that had not previously existed. In 1785, in the Charter of the Nobility, Catherine the Great (r. 1762–1796) legally defined the rights and privileges of noble men and women in exchange for the assurance that the nobility would serve the state voluntarily. Noble privileges included the right of transmitting noble status to a nobleman's wife and children, the judicial protection of noble rights and property, considerable power over the serfs, and exemption from personal taxes.

15.2.2 Aristocratic Resurgence

The Russian Charter of the Nobility constituted one aspect of the broader European-wide development termed the **aristocratic resurgence**. This was the nobility's reaction to the threat to their social position and privileges that they felt from the expanding power of the monarchies. This resurgence took several forms in the eighteenth century.

First, all nobilities tried to preserve their exclusiveness by making it more difficult to become a noble. Second, they pushed to reserve appointments to the officer corps of the armies, the senior posts in the bureaucracies and government ministries, and the upper ranks of the church exclusively for nobles.

Third, the nobles attempted to use the authority of existing aristocratically controlled institutions against the power of the monarchies. These institutions included the British Parliament; the French courts, or parlements; and the local aristocratic estates and provincial diets in Germany and the Habsburg Empire.

Fourth, the nobility sought to improve its financial position by gaining further exemptions from taxation or by collecting higher rents or long-forgotten feudal dues from the peasantry. The nobility tried to shore up its position by various appeals to traditional and often ancient privileges that had lapsed over time. This aristocratic challenge to the monarchies was a fundamental political fact of the day and a potentially disruptive one.

15.3.1 Peasants and Serfs

Rural social dependency related directly to the land. The nature of the dependency differed sharply for free peasants, such as English tenants and most French cultivators, and for the serfs of Germany, Austria, and Russia, who were legally bound to a particular plot of land and a particular lord. Yet everywhere, the class that owned most of the land also controlled the local government and the courts.

15.3.2 Obligations of Peasants

The power of the landlord increased as one moved across Europe from west to east. Most French peasants owned some land, but there were a few serfs in eastern France. Nearly all French peasants were subject to certain feudal dues, called ***banalités***. These included the required use-for-payment of the lord's, or *seigneur's*, mill to grind grain and his oven to bake bread. The seigneur also required a certain number of days each year of the peasant's labor. This practice of forced labor was termed the *corvée*. Because French peasants rarely possessed enough land to support their families, they had to rent more land from the seigneur and were also subject to feudal dues attached to those plots.

In Prussia and Austria, despite attempts by the monarchies late in the century to improve the lot of the serfs, the landlords continued to exercise almost complete control over them. In many of the Habsburg lands, law and custom required the serfs to provide service, or *robot*, to the lords.

15.3 The Land and Its Tillers

How were peasants and serfs tied to the land in eighteenth-century Europe?

Land was the economic basis of eighteenth-century life and the foundation of the status and power of the nobility. Well over three-fourths of all Europeans lived in the country, and few of them ever traveled more than a few miles from their birthplace. Except for the nobility and the wealthier nonaristocratic landowners, most people who dwelled on the land were poor and in many regions, desperately poor. They lived in various states of economic and social dependency, exploitation, and vulnerability.

THE *CORVÉE* Eighteenth-century France had some of the best roads in the world, but they were often built with forced labor. French peasants were required to work part of each year on such projects. This system, called the *corvée*, was not abolished until the French Revolution in 1789. **SOURCE:** Erich Lessing/Art Resource, NY

15.3.3 Treatment of Peasants and Serfs

Serfs were worst off in Russia. Russian landlords, in effect, regarded serfs merely as economic commodities. They could demand as many as six days a week of labor, known as *barshchina*, from the serfs. Like Prussian and Austrian landlords, they enjoyed the right to punish their serfs. On their own authority, Russian landlords could even exile a serf to Siberia. Serfs had no legal recourse against the orders and whims of their lords. There was little difference between Russian serfdom and slavery.

In southeastern Europe, where the Ottoman Empire ruled, peasants were free, though landlords tried to exert authority in every way. The domain of the landlords was termed a *çift*. The landlord was often an absentee who managed the estate through an overseer. During the seventeenth and eighteenth centuries, disorder originating in Constantinople (now Istanbul), the capital, spilled over into the Balkan Peninsula. In this climate, landlords increased their authority by offering their peasants protection from bandits or rebels who might destroy peasant villages. As in medieval times, the manor house or armed enclosure of a local landlord became the peasants' refuge. These landlords owned all the housing and tools the peasants needed to work the land and also furnished their seed grain. Consequently, despite legal independence, Balkan peasants under the Ottoman Empire became largely dependent on the landlords, though never to the extent of serfs in eastern Europe or Russia.

15.3.4 Peasant Rebellions

The Russian monarchy itself contributed to the further degradation of the serfs. Peter the Great gave whole villages to favored nobles. Later in the century, **Catherine the Great** confirmed the authority of the nobles over their serfs in exchange for the landowners' political cooperation. Russia experienced vast peasant unrest, with well over fifty peasant revolts between 1762 and 1769. These culminated in Pugachev's Rebellion between 1773 and 1775, when **Emelyan Pugachev** (1726–1775) promised the serfs land of their own and freedom from their lords. All of southern Russia was in turmoil until the government brutally suppressed the rebellion.

Pugachev's was the largest peasant uprising of the eighteenth century, but smaller peasant revolts or disturbances took place in Bohemia in 1775, in Transylvania in 1784, in Moravia in 1786, and in Austria in 1789. There were almost no revolts in Western Europe, but England experienced many rural riots. Rural rebellions were violent, but the peasants and serfs normally directed their wrath against property rather than persons. The rebels usually hoped to reassert traditional or customary rights against practices that they perceived as innovations. Their targets were carefully chosen and included unfair pricing, onerous new or increased feudal dues, changes in methods of payment or land use, unjust officials, or extraordinarily brutal overseers and landlords. Peasant revolts were thus conservative in nature.

15.4 Family Structures and the Family Economy

What role did the family play in the economy of preindustrial Europe?

In preindustrial Europe, the household was the basic unit of production and consumption. Few productive establishments employed more than a handful of people not belonging to the family of the owner, and those rare exceptions

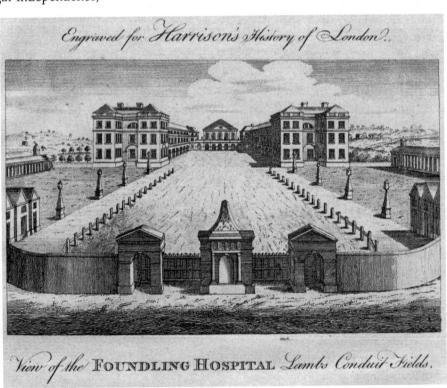

FOUNDLING HOSPITAL, LONDON (SINCE DEMOLISHED) The philanthropist Thomas Coram opened this Foundling Hospital in London in 1741. The name hospital implied a place of hospitality more than a center of medical care. Destitute mothers could bring their babies, most of them illegitimate, to the hospital, which provided child care and schooling.
SOURCE: Antiqua Print Gallery/Alamy Stock Photo

were in cities. Most Europeans, however, lived in rural areas. There, as well as in small towns and cities, the household mode of organization predominated on farms, in artisans' workshops, and in small merchants' shops. With that mode of economic organization, the **family economy** developed. Its structure, as described here, had prevailed throughout most of Europe for centuries.

15.4.1 Households

What was a household in the preindustrial Europe of the Old Regime? There were two basic models: one characterizing northwestern Europe and the other eastern Europe.

15.4.1.1 NORTHWESTERN EUROPE

In northwestern Europe, the household almost invariably consisted of a married couple, their children through their early teenage years, and their servants. Except for the few wealthy people, households usually consisted of no more than five or six members. Furthermore, in these households, more than two generations of a family rarely lived under the same roof. High mortality and late marriage prevented the formation of families of three generations or more. In other words, grandparents rarely lived in the same household as their grandchildren, and families consisted of parents and children. The family structure of northwestern Europe was thus nuclear rather than extended.

Historians assumed that before industrialization Europeans lived in extended familial settings, with several generations living together in a household. Demographic investigation has now sharply transformed this picture. Children lived with their parents only until their early teens. Then they normally left home, usually to enter the workforce of young servants who lived and worked in another household. A child of a skilled artisan might remain with his or her parents to learn a valuable skill; but it was rare for more than one child do so, because children earned more working outside the home.

Those young men and women who had left home would eventually marry and form their own independent households. This practice of moving away from home is known as **neolocalism**. These young people married relatively late. Men were usually over twenty-six, and women over twenty-three. The new couple usually had children as soon after marriage as possible. Frequently, the woman was already pregnant at marriage, and family and community pressure often compelled the man to marry her. In any case, premarital sexual relations were common. The new couple would soon employ a servant who, together with their growing children, would become part of the household livelihood.

The word *servant* in this context does not refer to someone looking after the needs of wealthy people. Rather, in preindustrial Europe, a servant was a person—either male or female—who was hired, often under a clear contract, to work for the head of the household in exchange for room, board, and wages. The servant was usually young and by no means always socially inferior to his or her employer. Normally, the servant was an integral part of the household and ate with the family.

Young men and women became servants when their labor was no longer needed in their parents' household or when they could earn more money for their family outside the parental household. Being a servant for several years—often as many as eight or ten—allowed young people to acquire the productive skills and the monetary savings necessary to begin their own household. These years spent as servants largely account for the late age of marriage in northwestern Europe.

15.4.1.2 EASTERN EUROPE

As one moved eastward across the Continent, the structure of the household and the pattern of marriage changed. In eastern Europe, both men and women usually married before the age of twenty. Consequently, children were born to much younger parents. Often—especially among Russian serfs—wives were older than their husbands. Eastern European households were generally larger than those in the West. Frequently a rural Russian household consisted of more than nine, and possibly more than twenty, members, with three or perhaps even four generations of the same family living together. Early marriage made this situation more likely. In Russia, marrying involved not starting a new household but remaining in and expanding one already established.

The landholding structure in eastern Europe accounts, at least in part, for these patterns of marriage and the family. The lords of the manor who owned land wanted to ensure that it would be cultivated, so they could receive their rents. Thus, in Poland, for example, landlords might forbid marriage between their own serfs and those from another estate. They might also require widows and widowers to remarry to ensure adequate labor for a particular plot of land. Polish landlords also frowned on the hiring of free laborers—the equivalent of servants in the West—to help cultivate land. The landlords preferred to use other serfs. This practice inhibited the formation of independent households. In Russia, landlords ordered the families of young people in their villages to arrange marriages within a short set time. These lords discouraged single-generation family households because the death or serious illness of one person in such a household might mean the land assigned to it would go out of cultivation.

15.4.2 The Family Economy

Throughout Europe, most people worked within the family economy, with the household the basic unit of production and consumption. Almost everyone lived within a household of some kind because it was virtually impossible for ordinary people to support themselves independently. Indeed, except for members of religious orders, people living outside a household were viewed with great suspicion. They were considered potentially criminal, disruptive, or at least dependent on the charity of others. Everywhere beggars met deep hostility.

Depending on their ages and skills, everyone in the household worked. The need to survive poor harvests or economic slumps meant that no one could be idle. Within this family economy, all goods and income produced went to the benefit of the household rather than to the individual family member. On a farm, much of the effort went directly into raising food or producing other agricultural goods that could be exchanged for food. Few Western Europeans, however, had enough land to support their household from farming alone. Thus, one or more family members might work elsewhere and send wages home; for example, the father and older children might work as harvesters, fishermen, or engage in other labor either in the neighborhood or farther from home. If the father was such a migrant worker, his wife and their younger children would have to work the family farm. This was not an uncommon pattern.

The family economy also dominated the life of skilled urban artisans. The father was usually the chief artisan. He normally employed one or more servants but would expect his children to also work in the enterprise. He usually trained his eldest child in the trade. His wife often sold his wares or opened a small shop of her own. Wives of merchants also frequently ran their husbands' businesses, especially when the husband traveled to purchase new goods. In any case, everyone in the family was involved. If business was poor, family members would look for employment elsewhere—not to support themselves as individuals, but to ensure the survival of the family unit.

In Western Europe, the death of a father often brought disaster to the household. The continuing economic life of the family usually depended on his land or skills. The widow might take on the farm or the business, or his children might do so. The widow usually sought to remarry quickly to restore the labor and skills of a male to the household and to prevent herself from becoming dependent on relatives or charity.

The high mortality rate of the time meant that many households were reconstituted second-family groups that included stepchildren. Because of the advanced age of the widow or economic hard times, however, some households might simply dissolve. The widow became dependent on charity or relatives. The children became similarly dependent or entered the workforce as servants earlier than they would have otherwise. In other cases, the situation could be so desperate that they would resort to crime or to begging. The personal, emotional, and economic vulnerability of the family cannot be overemphasized.

In eastern Europe, the family economy functioned in the context of serfdom and landlord domination. Peasants clearly thought in terms of their families and expanding the land available for cultivation. The village structure may have mitigated the pressures of the family economy, as did the multigenerational family. Dependence on the available land was the chief fact of life. There were many fewer artisan and merchant households, and there was far less geographical mobility than in Western Europe.

15.4.3 Women and the Family Economy

The family economy was the source of many constraints on the lives and personal experiences of women in preindustrial society. Most of the historical research that has been undertaken on this subject relates to Western Europe. There, a woman's life experience was largely the function of her capacity to establish and maintain a household. For women, marriage was an economic necessity, as well as an institution that fulfilled sexual and psychological needs. Outside a household, a woman's life was vulnerable and precarious. Some women became economically independent, but they were the exception. Normally, unless she were an aristocrat or a member of a religious order, a woman probably could not support herself solely by her own efforts. Consequently, a woman devoted much of her life first to maintaining her parents' household and then to devising some means of getting her own household to live in as an adult. Bearing and rearing children were usually subordinate to these goals.

By the age of seven, a girl would have begun to help with the household work. On a farm, this might mean looking after chickens, watering the animals, or carrying food to the adults working the land. In an urban artisan's household, she would do light work, perhaps cleaning or carrying, and later sewing or weaving. The girl would remain in her parents' home as long as she made a contribution to the family enterprise or as long as her labor elsewhere was not more remunerative to the family.

An artisan's daughter might not leave home until marriage, because at home she could learn increasingly valuable skills associated with the trade. The situation was different for the much larger number of girls growing up on farms. Their parents and brothers could often do all the necessary farm work, and a girl's labor at home quickly became of little value to her family. She would then leave home, usually between the ages of twelve and fourteen. She might take up residence on another farm, but more likely she would migrate to a nearby town or city. She would rarely travel more than thirty miles from her parents' household. She would then normally become a servant, once again living in a household, but this time in the household of an employer. Having left home, the young woman's chief goal was to accumulate enough capital for a dowry. Her savings would make her eligible for marriage because she could make the necessary contribution to form a household with her husband. Marriage within the family economy was a joint economic undertaking, and the wife was expected to make an immediate contribution of capital to establish the household. A young woman might well work for ten years or more to accumulate a dowry. This practice meant that marriage was usually postponed until her mid- to late twenties.

Within marriage, earning enough money or producing enough farm goods to ensure an adequate food supply dominated women's concerns. Domestic duties, childbearing, and childrearing were subordinate to economic pressures. Consequently, couples tried to limit the number of children they had, usually through the practice of *coitus interruptus*, the withdrawal of the male before ejaculation.

The work of married women differed markedly between city and country and was in many ways a function of their husbands' occupations. If the peasant household had enough land to support itself, the wife spent much of her time literally carrying things for her husband—water, food, seed, harvested grain, and the like. Such landholdings, however, were few. If the husband had to do work besides farming, such as fishing or migrant labor, the wife might actually be in charge of the farm and do the plowing, planting, and harvesting. In the city, the wife of an artisan or a merchant might be in charge of the household finances and help manage the business. When her husband died, she might take over the business and perhaps hire an artisan. Finally, if economic disaster struck the family, it was usually the wife who organized what Olwen Hufton has called the "economy of expedients,"[1] within which family members might be sent off to find work elsewhere or even to beg in the streets.

Despite this economic activity, women found many occupations were closed to them because of prejudice. Women at all levels of society consistently found fewer opportunities for education, and for the same work often received lower wages than men.

15.4.4 Children and the Family Economy

For women of all social ranks, childbirth meant fear and vulnerability. Contagious diseases endangered both mother and child. Puerperal fever was frequent, as were other infections from unsterilized medical instruments. Not all midwives were skillful practitioners. Furthermore, most mothers gave birth in conditions of immense poverty and wretched housing. Assuming both mother and child survived, the mother might nurse the infant, but often the child would be sent to a wet nurse. The wealthy may have done this for convenience, but economic necessity dictated it for the poor. The structures and customs of the family economy did not permit a woman to devote herself entirely to rearing a child. The wet-nursing industry was well organized, with urban children being frequently transported to wet nurses in the country, where they would remain for months or even years.

The birth of a child was not always welcome. The child might represent another economic burden on an already hard-pressed household, or it might be illegitimate. The number of illegitimate births seems to have increased during the eighteenth century, possibly because increased migration of the population led to fleeting romances.

Through at least the end of the seventeenth century, unwanted or illegitimate births could lead to infanticide, especially among the poor. The parents might smother the infant or expose it to the elements. These practices were one result of both the ignorance and the prejudice surrounding contraception.

The late seventeenth and the early eighteenth centuries brought a new interest in preserving the lives of abandoned children. Sadness and tragedy surrounded abandoned children. Most of them were illegitimate infants from across the social spectrum. Many, however, were left with the foundling hospitals because their parents could not support them. Parents would sometimes leave personal tokens or saints' medals on the abandoned baby in the vain hope they might one day be able to reclaim the child. Few children were reclaimed. Leaving a child at a foundling hospital did not guarantee its survival. In Paris, only about 10 percent of all abandoned children lived to the age of ten. Although foundling hospitals established to care for abandoned children had existed before, their size and number expanded during these years. Such hospitals cared for thousands of children, and the demand for their services increased during the eighteenth century.

Despite these perils of early childhood, children did grow up and come of age across Europe. The child may not have received the kind of attention it does today, but during the eighteenth century, the seeds of that modern sensibility were sown. Particularly among the upper classes, new interest arose in educating children. In most areas, education remained firmly in the hands of the churches. As economic skills became more demanding, literacy became more valuable, and literacy rates rose during the century. Yet most Europeans remained illiterate. Not until the late nineteenth century was childhood inextricably linked to the process of education. Then children would be reared to become members of a national citizenry. In the Old Regime, they were reared to contribute to the economy of their parents' family and then to set up their own households.

15.5 The Revolution in Agriculture

What led to the agricultural revolution of the eighteenth century?

The main goal of traditional peasant society was a stable local food supply. Despite differences in rural customs across Europe, tillers resisted changes that might endanger the supply of food, which they generally believed traditional methods of cultivation would ensure. But food supply was never certain, and the farther east one traveled, the more uncertain it became. Failure of the harvest meant not only hardship but also death from either outright starvation or malnutrition. People living in the countryside often had more difficulty finding food than did city dwellers, whose local government usually stored reserve supplies of grain.

Poor harvests also wreaked havoc with prices. Smaller supplies or larger demand raised grain prices. Even small increases in the cost of food could put pressure on peasant or artisan families. If prices increased sharply, many of those families fell back on poor relief from their local government or the church.

Historians now believe that during the eighteenth century bread prices slowly but steadily rose, spurred largely by population growth. Since bread was their main food, inflation put pressure on the poor. Prices rose faster than urban wages and brought no appreciable advantage to the small peasant producer. However, the rise in grain prices benefited landowners and those wealthier peasants who had surplus grain to sell.

The rising grain prices gave landlords an opportunity to improve their incomes and lifestyle. To achieve those ends, landlords in Western Europe began a series of innovations in farm production known as the **Agricultural Revolution**. Landlords commercialized agriculture, challenging the traditional peasant ways of production. Peasant revolts and disturbances often resulted. The governments of Europe, hungry for new taxes and dependent on the goodwill of the nobility, used their armies and militias to crush peasants who defended traditional practices.

15.5.1 New Crops and New Methods

The drive to improve agricultural production began during the sixteenth and seventeenth centuries in the Low Countries, where the pressures of the growing population and the shortage of land required changes in cultivation. Dutch landlords and farmers devised better ways to build dikes and to drain land so they could farm more land. They also experimented with new crops, such as clover and turnips, that would increase the supply of animal fodder and restore the soil.

English landlords provided the most striking examples of eighteenth-century agricultural improvement. They originated almost no new farming methods, but they popularized ideas developed in the previous century either in the Low Countries or in England. Some of these landlords and agricultural innovators became famous. For example, **Jethro Tull** (1674–1741) was willing to conduct experiments himself and to finance the experiments of others. Many of his ideas, such as the rejection of manure as fertilizer, were wrong. Others, however, such as using iron plows to turn the earth more deeply and planting wheat with a seed drill rather than by just casting seeds, were excellent. His methods permitted land to be cultivated for longer periods without having to leave it fallow.

SEED DRILL The English agricultural improver Jethro Tull devised this seed drill, which increased wheat crops by planting seed deep in the soil rather than just casting it randomly on the surface.
SOURCE: Mary Evans Picture Library / The Image Works

Charles "Turnip" Townsend (1674–1738) encouraged other important innovations. He learned from the Dutch how to cultivate sandy soil with fertilizers. He also instituted crop rotation, using wheat, turnips, barley, and clover. This new system of rotation replaced the fallow field with a cultivated one that both restored nutrients to the soil and supplied animal fodder. The additional fodder meant that more livestock could be raised. These fodders allowed animals to be fed during the winter and assured a year-round supply of meat. The larger number of animals increased the quantity of manure available as fertilizer for the grain crops. Consequently, in the long run, both animals and human beings had more food.

A third British agricultural improver was Robert Bakewell (1725–1795), who pioneered new methods of animal breeding that produced more and better animals and more milk and meat.

15.5.1.1 ENCLOSURE REPLACES OPEN-FIELD METHOD
Many of the agricultural innovations, which were adopted only slowly, were incompatible with the existing organization of land in England. Small cultivators who lived in village communities still farmed most of the soil. Each farmer tilled an assortment of unconnected strips. The two- or three-field systems of rotation left large portions of land fallow and unproductive each year. Animals grazed on the common land in the summer and on the stubble of the harvest in the winter. Until at least the mid-eighteenth century, the entire community decided what crops to plant. This village system discouraged improvement and favored the poorer farmers, who needed the common land and stubble fields for their animals. The existing method precluded expanding pastureland to raise more animals that would, in turn, produce

more manure for fertilizer. Thus, the methods of traditional production led to a steady, but not a growing, supply of food.

In 1700, approximately half the arable land in England was farmed by this open-field method. By the second half of the century, the rising price of wheat encouraged landlords to consolidate or enclose their lands to increase production. The **enclosures** were intended to use land more sensibly and to achieve greater commercial profits. The process involved the fencing of common lands, the reclamation of previously untilled waste, and the transformation of strips into block fields. These procedures brought turmoil to the economic and social life of the countryside. Riots often ensued.

Because many English farmers either owned their strips or rented them in a manner similar to ownership, the larger landlords usually resorted to parliamentary acts to legalize the enclosure of the land, which they owned but rented to the farmers. Because the large landowners controlled Parliament, such measures passed easily. Between 1761 and 1792, almost 500,000 acres were enclosed through acts of Parliament, compared with 75,000 acres between 1727 and 1760. In 1801, a general enclosure act streamlined the process.

The enclosures permitted the extension of both farming and innovation and thus increased food production on larger agricultural units. They also disrupted small traditional communities; they forced off the land independent farmers, who had needed the common pasturage, and poor cottage dwellers, who had lived on the reclaimed wasteland. The enclosures, however, did not depopulate the countryside. In some counties where lands were enclosed, the population increased. New soil had come into production, and services that supported farming also expanded.

The enclosures did not create the labor force for the British Industrial Revolution. Mostly, they introduced the entrepreneurial or capitalistic attitude of the urban merchant into the countryside. This commercialization of agriculture, which spread from Britain slowly across the Continent during the next century, strained the paternal relationship between the governing and governed classes. Previously, landlords had often looked after the welfare of the lower orders through price controls or waivers of rent during hard times. As the landlords became increasingly concerned about profits, they began to leave the peasants to the mercy of the marketplace.

15.5.1.2 LIMITED IMPROVEMENTS IN EASTERN EUROPE Improving agriculture tended to characterize farm production west of the Elbe River. Dutch farming was efficient. In France, despite the efforts of the government to improve agriculture, enclosures were restricted.

In Prussia, Austria, Poland, and Russia, agricultural improvement was limited. The relationships of the serfs to their lords did not encourage innovation. In eastern Europe, the chief method of increasing production was to plow previously untilled lands. The landlords or their agents, and not the villages, normally directed farm management. By extending tillage, the great landlords hoped to squeeze more labor from their serfs, rather than greater productivity from the soil. Eastern European landlords, like their Western counterparts, sought to increase their profits, but they were less ambitious and successful. The only significant nutritional gain they achieved was the introduction of maize and the potato. Livestock production did not increase significantly.

15.5.2 Expansion of the Population

The population explosion with which the entire world must contend today had its origins in the eighteenth century. Before that time, Europe's population had experienced dramatic increases, but plagues, wars, or famine had redressed the balance. Beginning in the second quarter of the eighteenth century, the population began to increase steadily. The need to feed this population caused food prices to rise, which spurred agricultural innovation. The need to provide everyday consumer goods for the expanding numbers of people fueled the demand side of the Industrial Revolution.

In 1700, Europe's population, excluding the European provinces of the Ottoman Empire, was probably between 100 million and 120 million people. By 1800, the figures had risen to almost 190 million and by 1850, to 260 million. The population of England and Wales rose from 6 million in 1750 to more than 10 million in 1800. France grew from 18 million in 1715 to about 26 million in 1789. Russia's population increased from 19 million in 1722 to 29 million in 1766. Such extraordinary sustained growth placed new demands on all resources and considerable pressure on the existing social organization.

The population expansion occurred across the Continent in both the country and the cities. Only a limited consensus exists among scholars about the causes of this growth. The death rate clearly declined. There were fewer wars and epidemics in the eighteenth century. Hygiene and sanitation also improved. Better medical knowledge and techniques, however, did not contribute much to the decline in deaths. The more important medical advances came after the initial population explosion and did not affect it directly.

Instead, changes in the food supply itself may have allowed population growth to be sustained. Improved and expanding grain production made one contribution. Another and even more important change was the cultivation of the potato. This tuber was a product of the New World and was widely produced in Europe during the eighteenth century. (See "The West & The World," page 509.) On a single acre, a peasant family could grow enough potatoes to feed itself for an entire year. This more certain food supply enabled more children to survive to adulthood and rear children of their own.

The impact of the population explosion can hardly be overestimated. It created new demands for food, goods, jobs, and services. It provided a new pool of labor. Traditional modes of production and living had to be revised. More people lived in the countryside than could find employment there, and migration increased. There were also more people who might become socially and politically discontented. Because the population growth fed on itself, these pressures and demands continued to increase. The society and the social practices of the Old Regime literally outgrew their traditional bounds.

15.6 The Industrial Revolution of the Eighteenth Century

Why did the Industrial Revolution begin in Britain?

The second half of the eighteenth century witnessed the beginning of the industrialization of the European economy. That achievement of sustained economic growth is termed the **Industrial Revolution**. Previously, the economy of a province or a country might grow, but growth soon reached a plateau. Since the late eighteenth century, however, Europe has managed to expand economically at an almost uninterrupted pace. Depressions and recessions have been temporary, and even during such economic downturns, the Western economy has continued to grow.

At considerable social cost, industrialization made possible the production of more goods and services than ever before in human history. Industrialization in Europe eventually overcame the economy of scarcity. The new means of production demanded new kinds of skills, new discipline in work, and a large labor force. The goods produced met immediate consumer demand and also created new demands. In the long run, industrialization raised the standard of living and overcame the poverty that most Europeans who lived during the eighteenth century and earlier had taken for granted. It gave human beings greater control over nature than they had ever known before; yet by the mid-nineteenth century, industrialism

would also cause new and unanticipated problems with the environment.

During the eighteenth century, people did not call these economic developments a *revolution*. That term came to be applied to the British economic phenomena only after the French Revolution. Then Continental writers observed that what had taken place in Britain was the economic equivalent of the political events in France, hence an Industrial Revolution. It was revolutionary less in its speed, which was rather slow, than in its implications for the future of European society.

15.6.1 A Revolution in Consumption

The most familiar side of the Industrial Revolution was the invention of new machinery, the establishment of factories, and the creation of a new kind of workforce. Recent studies, however, have emphasized the demand side of the process and the vast increase in both the desire and the possibility of consuming goods and services that arose in the early eighteenth century.

The inventions of the Industrial Revolution increased the supply of consumer goods as never before in history. The supply of goods was only one side of the economic equation, however. An unprecedented demand for the humble goods of everyday life created the supply. Those goods included clothing, buttons, toys, china, furniture, rugs, kitchen utensils, candlesticks, brassware, silverware,

FEATHER ADORNMENT WORKSHOP (an illustration from Diderot's *Encyclopédie*)
The purchase of consumer goods increased greatly in the eighteenth century. This engraving illustrates a shop, probably in Paris. Here women, working apparently for a woman manager, are adorning dresses and hats with feathers to meet the demands of the fashion trade.
SOURCE: Bpk, Berlin/Art Resource, NY

pewterware, glassware, watches, jewelry, soap, beer, wines, and foodstuffs. It was the ever-increasing demand for these goods that sparked the ingenuity of designers and inventors. Furthermore, consumer demand seemed unlimited. (In this chapter's "Compare and Connect" sidebar, which follows below, two intellectuals of the time, one French and one English, consider the economic structures of society.)

Many social factors helped establish the markets for these consumer goods. During the seventeenth century, the Dutch had enjoyed enormous prosperity and had led the way in new forms of consumption. For reasons that are still not clear, during the eighteenth century, first the English and then the people on the Continent came to have more disposable income. This wealth may have resulted from improvements in agriculture. Those incomes allowed people to buy consumer goods that previous generations had inherited or did not possess. This change in consumption depended primarily on expanding the various domestic markets in Europe, and it was not an automatic process.

Often, entrepreneurs caused a desire for consumer goods by developing new methods of marketing, so people would become persuaded that they wanted or needed them. For example, English porcelain manufacturer Josiah Wedgwood (1730–1795) first found customers among the royal family and the aristocracy. After gaining their business with luxury goods, he then produced a less expensive version of the chinaware for middle-class customers. He also used advertising, opened showrooms in London, and sent salespeople all over Britain with samples and catalogs of his wares. On the Continent, his salespeople used bilingual catalogs. There seemed to be no limit to the consumer goods market that social emulation on the one hand and advertising on the other could stimulate.

This expansion of consumption quietly, but steadily, challenged the social assumptions of the day. Fashion publications made all levels of society aware of new styles. Clothing fashions could be copied, and servants could begin to dress well, if not luxuriously. Changes in the consumption of food and drink demanded new kinds of dishware for the home. Tea and coffee became staples, and the brewing industry became fully commercialized. Those developments required new kinds of cups and mugs and many more of them.

Compare and Connect

Turgot and Hume: Two Eighteenth-Century Writers Contemplate the Effects of Different Economic Structures

AMONG EIGHTEENTH-CENTURY public officials and commentators there existed a broad agreement that European economic life needed to be reorganized and stimulated to achieve greater productivity and wealth. These writers also understood that different modes of productive activity resulted in very different kinds of societies. In these two documents a French writer, Robert Jacques Turgot, bemoans the problems of French agriculture and landholding while a Scottish writer, David Hume, praises the wealth and good society that flow from growing commerce and refinement of both mechanical and liberal arts.

AERIAL VIEW OF PARIS, 1739 This detail of a 1739 map by Louis Bretez, a member of the Academy of Painting and Sculpture, shows an aerial view of the city of Paris. The primary function of the map was to reestablish Paris as the universal model of a capital city.
SOURCE: Library of Congress

Before Reading

- Make a list of the factors that make farmers productive and nonproductive.
- Think about how industry and the arts complement one another in the economic life of a nation.

Questions

1. Why does Turgot favor those farmers who can make investments in the land they rent from proprietors?
2. What is the structure of the *métayer* system? Why did it lead to poor investments and unproductive harvests?
3. Why does Hume link industry and the arts? How does he see a commercial, improving economy producing important intellectual outlooks and social skills?
4. What benefits to agriculture might Hume have attributed to prosperous cities, and in what ways might Turgot have seen agriculture contributing to urban life?

I. ROBERT JACQUES TURGOT DECRIES FRENCH LANDHOLDING

During the eighteenth century, many became keenly aware that various systems of landholding led to different attitudes toward work and to different levels of production and wealth. Robert Jacques Turgot (1727–1781), who later became finance minister of France, analyzed these differences in an attempt to reform French agriculture. He especially favored those arrangements that encouraged long-term investment. In the following passage, he targets the métayer *system—an arrangement whereby land-holders owned land farmed by peasants who received part of the harvest as payment for their work, but the peasants had no long-term interest in the land. The system was widely regarded as inefficient.*

The real and fundamental distinction between the areas of large-scale cultivation and those where farming is done only on a small scale is that in the former, the landowners make deals with *fermiers* or tenant farmers who promise them a fixed payment for their land in exchange for the right to cultivate it during a certain number of years. These tenant farmers are responsible for all the expenses of cultivation, ploughing, seeds, and for stocking the farm with cattle, other animals, and tools. These tenant farmers are true agricultural entrepreneurs; like all other entrepreneurs, they have their own capital, which they use to make a profit by cultivating land. . . .

[The demand for land that makes it valuable is a result of] this indispensable kind of men who have not only their own labor, but capital to consecrate to agriculture, and who have no other occupation except to work the land, not to earn their living by the sweat of their brow as workers do, but to use their capital in a profitable way, like the shipowners of Nantes and Bordeaux who use theirs in overseas commerce. . . .

[The sharecropping system]: The regions of small-scale agriculture, which is to say at least four-sevenths of the land in the kingdom, are areas where there are no agricultural entrepreneurs, where a landowner who wants to profit from his land can only find unfortunate peasants who have no resources except their own labor, where he has to use his own money for all the expenses of growing crops, livestock, tools, seeds, and even to lend his *métayer* (sharecropper) enough to feed himself until the first harvest. In this situation, a landowner who has no resources other than his land, would have to leave it unplanted. . . .

After having deducted the cost of seed and of any interest payments due on the land, the landowner and the sharecropper divide what is left of the profits, according to the agreement they have made. The landowner, who has advanced all the money, runs all the risks of loss due to harvest failures and the loss of animals; he is the only real agricultural entrepreneur. The sharecropper is just a workman, a farmhand whom he pays with a share of the profits instead of wages. But this kind of landowner doesn't have the same advantages as the entrepreneurial farmer, who directs everything himself with attention and intelligence. The landowner has to trust all the money he advances to a man who may be negligent or dishonest, and who can't be held responsible for anything.

This kind of sharecropper, accustomed to most meager existence and without any hope or even any desire of improving his condition, farms badly and doesn't even try to use the land for products that can be sold for the best profit. He prefers to grow things that take less work and that he can consume himself, such as buckwheat and especially chestnuts, which only have to be collected. He doesn't even worry about not having enough to eat; he knows that, if the harvest fails, his master will have to feed him to avoid having to abandon his land.

II. DAVID HUME PRAISES LUXURY AND THE REFINEMENT OF THE ARTS

David Hume (1711–1776) was a Scottish philosopher, historian, and economic commentator. He was deeply committed to the modernization of the Scottish and wider European economy through the growth of commerce and improved means of mechanical production. In this essay published in 1752, Hume outlines the beneficial social consequences resulting from commercial wealth and new mechanical inventions. He believed such economic activity not only increased riches but also produced a population capable of providing a national defense. In this passage, Hume demonstrates that luxury and the economy that fostered it would not result in moral decay.

In times when industry and the arts flourish, men are kept in perpetual occupation, and enjoy, as their reward, the occupation itself, as well as those pleasures which are the fruit of their labour. The mind acquires new vigour; enlarges its powers and faculties; and by an assiduity in honest industry, both satisfies its natural appetites, and prevents the growth of unnatural ones, which commonly spring up, when nourished by ease and idleness. . . .

Another advantage of industry and of refinements in the mechanical arts, is, that they commonly produce some refinements in the liberal; nor can one be carried to perfection, without being accompanied, in some degree, with the other. . . .

The more these refined arts advance, the more sociable men become. . . . They flock into cities; love to receive and communicate knowledge; to show their wit or their breeding; their taste in conversation or living, in clothes or furniture. Curiosity allures the wise; vanity the foolish, and pleasure both. Particular clubs and societies are everywhere formed: Both sexes meet in an easy and sociable manner: and the tempers of men, as well as their behaviour, refine apace. So that, beside the improvements which they receive from knowledge and the liberal arts, it is impossible but they must feel an encrease of humanity, from the very habit of conversing together, and contributing to each other's pleasure and entertainment. Thus *industry, knowledge,* and *humanity,* are linked together by an indissoluble chain, and are found, from experience as well as reason, to be peculiar to the more polished, and, what are commonly denominated, the more luxurious ages. . . .

But industry, knowledge, and humanity are not advantageous in private life alone: They diffuse their beneficial influence on the *public,* and render the government as great and flourishing as they make individuals happy and prosperous. The encrease and consumption of all the commodities . . . are advantageous to society; because . . . they are a kind of *storehouse* of labour, which, in the exigencies of state, may be turned to the public service. In a nation, where there is no demand for such superfluities, men sink into indolence, lose all enjoyment of life, and are useless to the public, which cannot maintain or support its fleets and armies, from the industry of such slothful members.

SOURCES: (I) From *Œuvres, et documents les concernant,* by Robert Jacques Turgot, ed. by F. Schelle, 5 vols. (Paris, 1914), Vol. II, pp. 448–450. Translated by Jeremy D. Popkin. (II) From David Hume, "Of Refinement in the Arts (1752)," in *Essays: Moral, Political and Literary* (Indianapolis, IN: Liberty Classics, 1985), pp. 270–272.

There would always be critics of this consumer economy. The vision of luxury and comfort it offered contrasted with the asceticism of ancient Sparta and contemporary Christian ethics. Yet, the ever-increasing consumption and production of everyday goods became hallmarks of modern Western society from the eighteenth century to our day. It is difficult to overestimate the importance of consumer goods and the higher standard of living that they made possible in Western history after the eighteenth century. The presence and accessibility of such goods became the symbol of a nation's prosperity. It was the absence of such consumer goods, as well as of civil liberties, that during the 1980s led to such deep discontent with the communist regimes in eastern Europe and the former Soviet Union.

15.6.2 Industrial Leadership of Great Britain

Great Britain was the home of the Industrial Revolution and, until the middle of the nineteenth century, remained the industrial leader of Europe. Several factors contributed to the early start in Britain.

Great Britain took the lead in the **consumer revolution** that increased the demand for goods that could be efficiently supplied. London was the largest city in Europe. It was the center of a world of fashion and taste to which hundreds of thousands, if not millions, of British citizens were exposed each year. That world of fashion enticed people to accumulate goods. The social structure of Britain also encouraged people to buy goods to imitate the expensive lifestyles of their social superiors. In London, people became accustomed to wanting the consumer goods they saw on trips for business and pleasure. Newspapers thrived in Britain during the eighteenth century, and their printed advertisements increased consumer wants. In addition to

the domestic consumer demand, the British economy benefited from demand from the colonies in North America.

Britain was also the single largest free-trade area in Europe. The British had good roads and waterways without internal tolls or other trade barriers. The country had rich deposits of coal and iron ore. Its political structure was stable, and property was secure. Their sound systems of banking and public credit established a stable climate for investment. Taxation in Britain was heavy, but it was efficiently and fairly collected, largely from indirect taxes. Furthermore, British taxes received legal approval through Parliament, with all social classes and all regions of the nation paying the same taxes. In contrast to the Continent, there was no pattern of privileged tax exemptions.

Finally, British society was mobile by the standards of the time. Persons who had money or could earn it could rise socially. The British aristocracy would receive into its ranks people who had amassed large fortunes. Wealthy people who did not join the aristocracy could still enjoy their riches, receive social recognition, and exert political influence.

No one of these factors preordained the British trend toward industrialism. Together, however, along with the progressive state of British agriculture, they gave the nation the marginal advantage to create a new mode of economic production.

15.6.3 New Methods of Textile Production

Textile production pioneered the Industrial Revolution and is the key example of industrialism emerging to supply the demands of an ever-growing market for everyday goods. Furthermore, it illustrates surprisingly that much of the earliest industrial change took place not in cities, but in the countryside.

KEY INVENTIONS IN THE TEXTILE-MANUFACTURING REVOLUTION	
1733	John Kay's flying shuttle
1765	James Hargreaves's spinning jenny (patented 1770)
1769	James Watt's steam engine patent
1769	Richard Arkwright's water frame patent
1787	Edmund Cartwright's power loom

Although the eighteenth-century economy was primarily agricultural, textile manufacturing also permeated rural areas. The basic production unit was not the factory, but rather the peasant family living in a one- or two-room cottage. The same peasants who tilled the land in spring and summer often spun thread or wove textiles in the winter.

Under what is termed the **domestic system of textile production**, or putting-out system of textile production, agents of urban textile merchants brought wool or other unfinished fibers to the homes of peasants, who spun it into thread. The agent then transported the thread to other peasants, who wove it into the finished product. The merchant sold the wares. In thousands of peasant cottages from Ireland to Austria, there stood a spinning wheel or a hand loom. Sometimes the spinners or weavers owned their own equipment, but more often by the middle of the century, the merchant capitalist owned the machinery as well as the raw material.

The domestic system of textile production was a basic feature of the family economy and would continue to be so in Britain and on the Continent well into the nineteenth century. By the mid-eighteenth century, however, production bottlenecks had developed within the domestic system. The demand for cotton textiles was growing more rapidly than production, especially in Britain, which had a large domestic and North American market for these goods. In response, inventors created some of the most famous machines of the early Industrial Revolution to meet consumer demand for cotton textiles.

15.6.3.1 THE SPINNING JENNY Cotton textile weavers had the technical capacity to produce the quantity of fabric demanded. The spinners, however, did not have the equipment to produce as much thread as the weavers needed. John Kay's invention of the flying shuttle, which increased the productivity of the weavers, had created this imbalance during the 1730s. Thereafter, manufacturers and merchants offered prizes for the invention of a machine to eliminate this bottleneck.

About 1765, James Hargreaves (d. 1778) invented the **spinning jenny**. Initially, this machine allowed sixteen spindles of thread to be spun, but by the close of the century, it could operate 120 spindles.

15.6.3.2 THE WATER FRAME The spinning jenny eliminated the bottleneck between the productive capacity

SPINNING JENNY James Hargreaves's spinning jenny permitted the spinning of numerous spindles of thread on a single machine. **SOURCE:** PHAS/Getty Images

of the spinners and the weavers, but it was still a machine used in the cottage. The invention that took cotton textile manufacture out of the home and into the factory was Richard Arkwright's (1732–1792) **water frame**, patented in 1769. This was a water-powered device that allowed the production of a purely cotton fabric, rather than a cotton fabric containing linen fiber for durability. Eventually Arkwright lost his patent rights, and other manufacturers used his invention freely. As a result, many factories sprang up in the countryside near streams that provided the necessary water power. From the 1780s onward, the cotton industry could meet an ever-expanding demand. Cotton output increased by 800 percent between 1780 and 1800. By 1815, cotton made up 40 percent of the value of British domestic exports and by 1830, just more than 50 percent.

The Industrial Revolution had commenced in earnest by the 1780s, but the full economic and social ramifications of this unleashing of human productive capacity were not felt until the early nineteenth century. The expansion of industry and the incorporation of new inventions often occurred slowly. For example, Edmund Cartwright (1743–1822) invented the power loom for machine weaving in the late 1780s, but it wasn't until the 1830s that there more power-loom weavers than hand-loom weavers in Britain. The social effects of industrialism also did not appear immediately. The first cotton mills used water power, were located in the country, and rarely employed more than two dozen workers. Not until the late-century application of the steam engine, perfected by **James Watt** (1736–1819) in 1769, to run textile machinery could factories easily be located in or near urban centers. The steam engine not only vastly increased and regularized the available energy but also made possible the combination of urbanization and industrialization.

15.6.4 The Steam Engine

More than any other invention, the steam engine permitted industrialization to continually move from one area of production to another. This machine provided for the first time in human history a steady and essentially unlimited source of inanimate power. Unlike engines powered by water or wind, the steam engine, driven by burning coal, provided a portable source of industrial power that remained constant as the seasons of the year changed. Unlike human or animal power, the steam engine depended on mineral energy that never tired. Finally, the steam engine could be applied to many industrial and, eventually, transportation uses.

Thomas Newcomen (1663–1729) in the early eighteenth century had invented the first practical engine to use steam power. When the steam was induced into the cylinder condensed, it caused the piston of this device to fall. The Newcomen machine was large and inefficient in its use of energy because both the condenser and the cylinder were heated, and practically untransportable. Despite these problems, English mine operators used the Newcomen machines to pump water out of coal and tin mines.

During the 1760s, James Watt, a Scottish engineer and machine maker, experimented with a model of a Newcomen machine at the University of Glasgow. He gradually understood that separating the condenser from the piston and the cylinder would achieve much greater efficiency. In 1769, he patented his new invention, but transforming his idea into a practical application presented difficulties. His design required precise metalwork. Watt soon partnered with Matthew Boulton (1728–1809), a successful toy and button manufacturer in Birmingham, the city with the most skilled metalworkers in Britain. Watt and Boulton, in turn, consulted with John Wilkinson (1728–1808), a cannon manufacturer, to drill the precise metal cylinders Watt's design required. In 1776, the Watt steam engine found its first commercial application pumping water from mines in Cornwall.

The use of the steam engine spread slowly because until 1800 Watt retained the exclusive patent rights.

He was also reluctant to make further changes to permit the engine to operate more rapidly. Boulton eventually persuaded him to make modifications and improvements that allowed the engines to be used not only for pumping but also for running cotton mills. By the early nineteenth century, the steam engine had become the main catalyst for all industry. With its application to ships and then to wagons on iron rails, the steam engine also revolutionized transportation.

15.6.5 Iron Production

The manufacture of high-quality iron has been significant to modern industrial development. Iron is the chief element of all heavy industry and of land or sea transport. Most productive machinery itself is also manufactured from iron. During the early eighteenth century, British ironmakers produced somewhat less than 25,000 tons of iron annually. Three factors held back the production. First, charcoal rather than coke was used to smelt the ore. Charcoal, derived from wood, was becoming scarce as forests in Britain diminished, and it does not burn at as high a temperature as coke, derived from coal. Second, until the perfection of the steam engine, furnaces could not

BLACKSMITH'S SHOP–A FAMILY OPERATION During the eighteenth century, most goods were produced in small workshops, such as this iron forge painted by Joseph Wright of Derby (1734–1797), or in the homes of artisans. A few factories appeared only very late into the century, with the early stages of industrialization. In the small early workshops, it would not have been uncommon for the family of the owner to visit, as portrayed in this painting.
SOURCE: Broadlands Trust, Hampshire, UK/Bridgeman Art Library

achieve high enough blasts. Finally, the demand for iron was limited. The elimination of the first two problems also eliminated the third.

Eventually, British ironmakers began to use coke, and the steam engine provided new power for the blast furnaces. Coke was an abundant fuel because of Britain's large coal deposits. The newly powered steam engine both improved iron production and increased the demand for iron.

In 1784, Henry Cort (1740–1800) introduced a new puddling process, that is, a new method for melting and stirring molten ore. Cort's process allowed the removal of more slag—the impurities that bubbled to the top of the molten metal—and thus the production of purer iron. Cort also developed a rolling mill that continuously shaped the still-molten metal into bars, rails, or other forms. Previously, the metal had to be pounded into these forms.

These innovations achieved a better, more versatile, cheaper product. The demand for iron consequently grew. By the early nineteenth century, the British produced more than a million tons annually. The lower cost of iron, in turn, lowered the cost of steam engines and allowed them to be used more widely.

15.6.6 The Impact of the Agricultural and Industrial Revolutions on Working Women

The transformation of agriculture and industry led to a series of seemingly modest changes that, taken collectively, diminished the importance and the role of those women already in the workforce.

Women had been an important part of traditional European agriculture. They worked in farms and often were permitted to glean the grain left over after the general harvest. Women also managed industries like milking and cheese production. However, primarily in Western Europe, increasing commercialization and mechanization eroded these traditional roles. Machinery operated by men displaced the women's work in the field and their skills in dairying and home industry, particularly in Britain. Even non-mechanized labor came to favor men. For example, during the late eighteenth century, heavy scythes wielded by men replaced the lighter sickles that women had used to harvest grain. Moreover, the drive to maximize profits led landlords to enclose lands and curtail customary rights like gleaning.

This transformation of farming constricted women's ability to earn their living from the land. Women were viewed as opponents of agricultural improvement because these changes hurt them economically. As a result, proponents of the new agriculture often demeaned the role of women in farming 1and their related work. Indeed, the vast literature on agricultural improvement specifically advocated removing women from the agricultural workforce.

A similar transformation took place in textile manufacturing, where mechanization deprived many women of one of their most traditional sources of income. Before mechanization, thousands of women worked at spinning wheels to produce thread that hand-loom weavers, who were often their husbands, then wove. The earlier, small spinning jennies did not immediately disrupt their work because women could use them in the lofts of their homes, but the larger ones required a factory setting where men often ran the machinery. As a result, most women spinners were put out of work, and those women who moved into the factories performed less skilled work than men. Ultimately, the mechanization of spinning left many women deprived of one of their most traditional means of earning income.

Many working women, displaced from spinning thread or from farming, slowly turned to cottage industries—such as knitting, button making, straw plaiting, bonnet making, or glove stitching—that invariably paid them less than their former occupations had. In later generations, women who earlier would have been spinners or farm workers moved directly into cottage industries. The work and skills these occupations involved were considered inferior; and because it paid so poorly, women in the cottage industries might become prostitutes or engage in other criminal activity. Consequently, the reputation and social standing of many working women suffered.

Among women who did not work in the cottage industries, thousands became domestic servants in the homes of landed or commercial families. During the nineteenth century, such domestic service became the largest area of female employment. It was far more respectable than the cottage industries, but it was isolated from the technologically advanced world of factory manufacture or transport.

By the end of the eighteenth century, the work and workplaces of men and women were becoming increasingly separate and distinct.

This shift in female employment,[2] produced several long-term results. First, women's work, whether in cottage industries or domestic service, became associated with the home rather than with places where men worked. Second, women's work was detached from the new technologies in farming, transportation, and manufacturing. Woman's work appeared traditional, and it was assumed women could do only such work. Third, during the nineteenth and early twentieth centuries, Europeans assumed most women worked only to supplement their husbands' income. Finally, because women's work was considered marginal and supplementary to males' income, men were paid much more than women. While many associate the Industrial Revolution with factories, for working women, the revolution led to a life more centered on the home than ever before. (See the "Encountering the Past" sidebar on gender and the brewing industry, which follows below.)

Encountering the Past

Brewing Becomes a Man's Profession

FOR MUCH OF THE MEDIEVAL AND EARLY MODERN periods, women played a central role in the production of beer and ale. Women brewed beer and ale at home and then sold it to local customers. The degree of female participation in brewing varied by region, but in some areas women were the primary brewers for their communities. Many of these "alewives" were widows for whom brewing was a crucial supplement to their income. Alewives would place an ale wand outside their doors to let customers know when brewing was complete and ready for sale.

The formation of brewing guilds in the early modern period began a slow process of forcing women out of the profession. Over time, the number of female brewers decreased, and the number of larger-scale breweries owned and operated by men increased. Women continued to be involved in the brewing business, but in diminished roles as servers in pubs and taverns. The association of such places with immoral activities contributed to a further decline in the reputation and status of women associated with the brewing trade.

In England, the eighteenth century saw an acceleration of the trends that began in the sixteenth and seventeenth centuries. This time, the driving force behind the changes in the brewing business was new technology. Thermometers and hydrometers gave brewers much greater control over the brewing process, allowing them to produce a more consistent product. The construction of larger vats permitted production of larger quantities of beer and ale for local and regional markets. However, it was the invention of

THE ALE-HOUSE DOOR This 1790 painting by Henry Singleton illustrates the place of women in the late-eighteenth century beer and ale business. Where once the woman depicted in the scene might well have made ale, now she only serves it.
SOURCE: ART Collection/Alamy Stock Photo

James Watt's steam engine that made the biggest difference. London's large breweries had abundant capital, and they quickly seized on the opportunities steam engines provided. Steam engines powered mechanical rakes that stirred mixes of malt, grain, and water. Mechanized conveyor belts carried heavy bags of ingredients from place to place inside breweries, and steam-powered pumps moved beer from vat to vat and from vat to barrel. By the end of the eighteenth century, large-scale brewing in London was a mechanized, and decidedly masculine, industry.

SOURCE: Frank Clark, *A Most Wholesome Liquor: A Study of Beer and Brewing in 18th-Century England and Her Colonies* (Williamsburg, Virginia: Colonial Williamsburg Foundation Library Research Report Series, 1999).

Questions

1. What role did women play in medieval and early modern brewing?
2. What explains the changes in the brewing business between the sixteenth and eighteenth centuries?

15.7 The Growth of Cities

What problems arose as a result of the growth of cities?

Remarkable changes occurred in the pattern of city growth between 1500 and 1800. In 1500, within Europe (excluding Hungary and Russia) 156 cities had a population greater than 10,000. Only four of those cities—Paris, Milan, Venice, and Naples—had populations larger than 100,000. By 1800, 363 cities had 10,000 or more inhabitants, and 17 of them had populations larger than 100,000. The percentage of the European population living in urban areas had risen from just over 5 percent to just over 9 percent. A major shift in urban concentration from southern, Mediterranean Europe to the north had also occurred.

15.7.1 Patterns of Preindustrial Urbanization

The eighteenth century witnessed a considerable growth of towns, closely related to the tumult of the day and the revolutions with which the century closed. London grew from about 700,000 inhabitants in 1700 to almost 1 million in 1800. By the time of the French Revolution, Paris had more than 500,000 inhabitants. Berlin's population tripled during the century, reaching 170,000 in 1800. Warsaw had 30,000 inhabitants in 1730, but almost 120,000 in 1794. St. Petersburg, founded in 1703, numbered more than 250,000 inhabitants a century later. The number of smaller cities with 20,000 to 50,000 people also increased considerably. This urban growth must, however, be kept in perspective. Even in France and Great Britain, less than 20 percent of the population lived in cities. And the town of 10,000 inhabitants was much more common than the giant urban center.

These raw figures conceal significant changes in how cities grew and how the population redistributed itself. The major urban development of the sixteenth century had been followed by a leveling off, and even a decline, in the seventeenth. New growth began in the early eighteenth century and accelerated during the late eighteenth and the early nineteenth centuries.

Between 1500 and 1750, major urban expansion took place within already established and generally already large cities. After 1750, the pattern changed with the birth of new cities and the rapid growth of older, smaller cities.

15.7.1.1 GROWTH OF CAPITALS AND PORTS Between 1600 and 1750, the cities that grew most vigorously were capitals and ports. This growth reflected the success of monarchical state-building during those years and the consequent burgeoning of bureaucracies, armies, courts, and other groups who lived in the capitals. The growth of port cities, in turn, reflected the expansion of European overseas trade—especially that of the Atlantic routes. Except for

Manchester in England and Lyons in France, the new urban conglomerates were nonindustrial cities.

Furthermore, between 1600 and 1750, cities with populations of fewer than 40,000 inhabitants declined. These included older landlocked trading centers, medieval industrial cities, and ecclesiastical centers. These cities contributed less to the new political regimes, and the expansion of the putting-out system transferred production from medieval cities to the countryside because rural labor was cheaper than urban labor.

15.7.1.2 THE EMERGENCE OF NEW CITIES AND THE GROWTH OF SMALL TOWNS In the mid-eighteenth century, a new pattern emerged. The rate of growth of existing large cities declined, new cities emerged, and existing smaller cities grew. Several factors contributed to this process, which Jan De Vries has termed "an urban growth from below."[3] First was the general overall population increase. Second, the early stages of the Industrial Revolution, particularly in Britain, occurred in the countryside and fostered the growth of smaller towns and cities located near factories. Factory organization itself led to new concentrations of population.

Cities also grew as a result of the new prosperity of European agriculture, even where there was little industrialization. Improved agricultural production promoted the growth of nearby market towns and other urban centers that served agriculture and allowed more prosperous farmers access to consumer goods and recreation. This new pattern of urban growth—new cities and the expansion of smaller existing ones—would continue into the nineteenth century.

15.7.2 Urban Classes

Social divisions were as marked in eighteenth-century cities as they were in nineteenth-century industrial centers. The urban rich were often visibly segregated from the urban poor. Aristocrats and the upper middle class lived in fashionable town houses, often constructed around newly laid-out green squares. The poorest town dwellers usually congregated along the rivers, while small merchants and artisans lived above their shops. Whole families might live in a single room. Modern sanitary facilities were unknown, and pure water was rare. Cattle, pigs, goats, and other animals roamed the streets. Reports on the cities of Europe during this period emphasize on the one hand the striking beauty and grace of the dwellings of the wealthy; and on the other, the dirt, filth, and stench that filled the streets.

Poverty was not just an urban problem; it was usually worse in the countryside. In the city, however, poverty took the more visible forms of crime, prostitution, vagrancy, begging, and alcoholism. Many young men and women from the countryside migrated to the nearest cities to seek better lives—only to discover poor housing, little food, disease, degradation, and finally death. But it was not only the Industrial Revolution and the urban factories that transformed the cities into hellholes for the poor and the dispossessed. The consumption of liquor in the midcentury "gin age" blinded and killed many poor people, contributing to the overall dinginess of London life.

Also contrasting with the serenity of the aristocratic and upper-commercial-class lifestyle were the public executions that took place throughout Europe, the breaking of men and women on instruments of torture in Paris, and the public floggings in Russia. Brutality condoned and carried out by the ruling classes was a fact of everyday life.

15.7.2.1 THE UPPER CLASSES

At the top of the urban social structure stood a generally small group of nobles, large merchants, bankers, financiers, clergy, and government officials. These upper-class men controlled the political and economic affairs of the town. Normally, they constituted a self-appointed and self-electing oligarchy that governed the city through its corporation or city council. Some form of royal charter usually gave the city corporation its authority and the power to select its own members. In a few cities on the Continent, artisan guilds controlled the corporations, but generally, the local nobility and the wealthiest commercial people dominated the councils.

15.7.2.2 THE MIDDLE CLASS

Another group in the city was the prosperous, but not always immensely wealthy, merchants, trades people, bankers, and professional people. They were the most dynamic element of the urban population and made up the middle class, or bourgeoisie. The concept of the middle class was much less clear-cut than that of the nobility. The middle class was and would remain diverse and divided, with profession people often resentful of those in commerce. Less wealthy members of the middle class of various occupations resented wealthier members who might be connected to the nobility through social or business relationships.

The middle class had less wealth than most nobles, but more than urban artisans. They lived in the cities and towns, and their sources of income had little or nothing to do with the land. In one way or another, members of the middle class all benefited from expanding trade and commerce, whether as merchants, lawyers, or small-factory owners. Their world of earning and saving money enabled rapid social mobility and change in lifestyle. They viewed themselves as willing to put their capital and energy to work, whereas they considered the nobility idle. The members of the middle class tended to be economically aggressive and socially ambitious, and they were often made fun of because of these characteristics. The middle class normally supported reform, change, and economic growth, and they also wanted more rational regulations for trade and commerce, as did some progressive aristocrats.

The middle class was comprised of people whose lives fostered the revolution in consumption. On one hand, as owners of factories and of wholesale and retail businesses, they produced and sold goods for the expanding consumer market; on the other hand, members of the middle class were among the chief consumers. It was to their homes that the vast array of new consumer goods made their way. Their social values also most fully embraced the commercial spirit. Although they might not enjoy the titles or privileges of the nobility, they could enjoy material comfort and prosperity. It was this lifestyle that less well-off people could emulate as they acquired consumer goods for themselves.

During the eighteenth century, the relationship between the middle class and the aristocracy was complicated. On one hand, the nobles, especially in England and France, increasingly embraced the commercial spirit associated with the middle class by improving their estates and investing in cities. On the other hand, wealthy members of the middle class often tried to imitate the lifestyle of the nobility by purchasing landed estates. The aspirations of the middle class for social mobility, however, conflicted with the nobles' determination to maintain and reassert their privileges and to protect their wealth. Middle-class commercial figures—traders, bankers, manufacturers, and lawyers—often found their pursuit of profit and prestige blocked by the privileges of the nobility and its social exclusiveness, by the inefficiency of monarchical bureaucracies dominated by the nobility, or by aristocrats who controlled patronage and government contracts.

The bourgeoisie did not rise to challenge the nobility; rather, both were seeking to increase their existing political power and social prestige. The tensions between the nobles and the middle class during the eighteenth century normally involved issues of power-sharing or access to political influence, rather than clashes over values or goals associated with class.

The middle class in the cities feared the lower urban classes as much as they envied the nobility. The lower orders were a potentially violent element in society, a threat to property, and, an impoverished drain on national resources. The lower classes, however, were much more varied than either the city aristocracy or the middle class cared to admit.

15.7.2.3 ARTISANS

Shopkeepers, artisans, and wage earners were the single largest group in any city. They were grocers, butchers, fishmongers, carpenters, cabinetmakers, smiths, printers, hand-loom weavers, and tailors, to give a few examples. They had their own culture, values, and institutions. Like the peasants, they were, in many respects, conservative. Their economic position was vulnerable. If a poor harvest raised the price of food, their own businesses suffered. These urban classes, however, also contributed to the revolution in consumption. They could buy more goods than ever before, and to the extent their incomes permitted, many of them hoped to copy the domestic consumption of the middle class.

The lives of these artisans and shopkeepers centered on their work and their neighborhoods. They usually lived near or at their place of employment. Most of them worked in shops with fewer than a half dozen other artisans. Their primary institution had historically been the guild, but by the eighteenth century, the guilds rarely exercised the influence their predecessors had in medieval or early modern Europe.

Nevertheless, the guilds were not to be ignored. They played a conservative role. Rather than seeking economic growth or innovation, they tried to preserve the jobs and skills of their members. In many countries, the guilds still determined who could pursue a craft. To lessen competition, they attempted to prevent too many people from learning a particular skill.

The guilds also provided a framework for social and economic advancement. At an early age, a boy might become an apprentice to learn a craft or trade. After several years, he would be made a journeyman. Still later, if successful and competent, he might become a master. The artisan could also receive social benefits from the guilds, including aid for his family during illness or the promise of admission for his son. The guilds were the chief providers of protection for artisans against the commercial market. They were particularly strong in central Europe.

15.7.3 The Urban Riot

The artisan class, with its generally conservative outlook, maintained a rather fine sense of social and economic justice based largely on traditional practices. If they felt an economically "just" practice had been offended, artisans frequently manifested their displeasure by rioting. The most sensitive area was the price of bread, the staple food of the poor. If a baker or a grain merchant set a price that was considered unjustly high, a riot might well ensue. Artisan leaders would confiscate the bread or grain and sell it for what the urban crowd considered a "**just price**." They would then give the money paid for the grain or bread to the baker or merchant.

The danger of bread riots restrained the greed of merchants. Such disturbances represented a collective method of imposing the just price in place of the price set by the commercial marketplace. These bread and food riots, which occurred throughout Europe, were not irrational protests of screaming, hungry people, but highly ritualized social phenomena of the Old Regime and its economy of scarcity.

Other kinds of riots also characterized eighteenth-century society and politics. The riot was a way in which people who were excluded in every way from the political processes could make their will known. Sometimes religious bigotry led to urban riots. For example, in 1753, London Protestant mobs compelled the government to withdraw an act to legalize Jewish naturalization.

In these riots and in food riots, violence was normally directed against property rather than people. The rioters themselves were not disreputable people but usually small shopkeepers, freeholders, artisans, and wage earners, who wanted only to restore a traditional right or practice that seemed endangered. Nevertheless, their actions could cause considerable turmoil and destruction.

During the last half of the century, urban riots increasingly involved political ends. Though often simultaneous with economic disturbances, the political riot always had nonartisan leadership or instigators. In fact, an eighteenth-century "crowd" was often the tool of the upper classes. In Paris, the aristocratic parlement often urged crowd action in its disputes with the monarchy. In Geneva, middle-class citizens supported artisan riots against the local oligarchy. In Great Britain in 1792, the government incited mobs to attack English sympathizers of the French Revolution. Such outbursts indicate that the crowd or mob had entered the European political and social arena well before the revolution in France.

15.8 The Jewish Population: The Age of the Ghetto

How did the suppression of Jews in European cities lead to the formation of ghettos?

Although the small Jewish communities of Amsterdam and other Western European cities became famous for their intellectual life and financial institutions, most European Jews lived in eastern Europe. In the eighteenth century and thereafter, the Jewish population of Europe was concentrated in Poland, Lithuania, and Ukraine, where no fewer than 3 million Jews dwelled. Perhaps 150,000 Jews lived in the Habsburg lands, primarily Bohemia, around 1760. Fewer than 100,000 Jews lived in Germany. France had approximately 40,000 Jews. England and Holland each had a Jewish population of fewer than 10,000. There were even smaller groups of Jews elsewhere.

15.8.1 Life in the Jewish Ghetto

Jews dwelled in most nations without enjoying the rights and privileges that other subjects had unless specifically granted to them by the monarchs. Jews were regarded as a kind of resident alien whose residence might well be temporary or changed at the whim of rulers.

No matter where they dwelled, Old Regime Jews lived apart in separate communities from non-Jewish Europeans.

During the Old Regime, European Jews were separated from non-Jews, typically in districts known as ghettos. Most of them lived in poverty, relegated to the least desirable section of a city or rural village. This watercolor painting depicts a street in Kazimierz, the Jewish quarter of Kraków, Poland.
SOURCE: Erich Lessing / Art Resource, NY

These communities might be distinct districts of cities, known as **ghettos**, or in primarily Jewish villages in the countryside. Jews were also treated as a distinct people religiously and legally. In Poland for much of the century, they were virtually self-governing. In other areas, they lived under the burden of discriminatory legislation. Except in England, Jews could not and did not mix with the mainstream of the societies in which they dwelled. This period, which may have begun with the expulsion of the Jews from Spain at the end of the fifteenth century, is known as the age of the ghetto, or separate community.

15.8.2 Jews in Society

During the seventeenth century, a few Jews had helped finance the wars of major rulers. These financiers often became close to the rulers and were known as "court Jews." Perhaps the most famous was Samuel Oppenheimer (1630–1703), who helped the Habsburgs finance their struggle against the Turks and the defense of Vienna. However, these loans were often not repaid. The court Jews and their financial abilities became famous. They tended to marry among themselves.

Most European Jews, however, lived in poverty. They occupied the most undesirable sections of cities or poor villages. Some were small-time moneylenders, but most worked at the lowest occupations. Their religious beliefs, rituals, and community set them apart. All laws and social institutions kept them socially inferior to and apart from their Christian neighbors.

Under the Old Regime, this discrimination was based on religious separateness. Jews who converted to Christianity were welcomed, even if not always warmly, to join the major political and social institutions of Gentile European society. Until the last two decades of the eighteenth century, in every part of Europe, however, those Jews who remained loyal to their faith were subject to various religious, civil, and social disabilities. They could not pursue the professions freely, they often could not change residence without official permission, and they were excluded from the political structures of the nations in which they lived. Jews could be expelled from their homes, and their property could be confiscated. They could be required to listen to sermons that insulted their religion. Their children could be taken away from them and given Christian instruction. They knew their non-Jewish neighbors might suddenly turn against them and kill them.

The end of the Old Regime would bring major changes in the lives of European Jews and in their relationship to the larger culture.

The Chapter in Perspective

Near the close of the eighteenth century, European society was on the brink of a new era. That society had remained traditional and corporate largely because of an economy of scarcity. Beginning in the eighteenth century, however, the commercial spirit and the values of the marketplace, although not new, were permitted fuller play than ever before in European history. The newly unleashed commercial spirit led increasingly to a conception of human beings as individuals rather than as members of communities. In particular, that spirit manifested itself in the Agricultural and Industrial Revolutions, as well as in the drive toward greater consumption. Together, those two vast changes in production overcame most of the scarcity that had haunted Europe and the West generally. The accompanying changes in landholding and production would transform the European social structure.

The expansion of the population further stimulated change. More people meant more labor, more energy, and more minds contributing to the creation and solution of social difficulties. Cities had to accommodate expanding populations. Corporate groups, such as the guilds, had to confront the existence of a larger labor force. New wealth meant that birth would eventually become less and less a determining factor in social relationships, except for the social roles assigned to the two sexes. Class structure and social hierarchy remained, but the boundaries became more blurred.

Finally, the conflicting ambitions of monarchs, the nobility, and the middle class generated innovation. In the pursuit of new revenues, the monarchs interfered with the privileges of the nobles. In the name of ancient rights, the nobles attempted to secure and expand their existing social privileges. The middle class, with its diversity, was growing wealthier from trade, commerce, and the practice of the professions. Its members wanted social prestige and influence equal to their wealth. They resented privileges, frowned on hierarchy, and rejected tradition.

Together, these factors signified that eighteenth-century society stood at the close of one era in European history and at the opening of another.

The Chapter in Review

Review Questions

1. What kinds of privileges separated European aristocrats from other social groups? How did their privileges and influence affect other people living in the countryside? What was the condition of serfs in central and eastern Europe?

2. How would you define the term *family economy?* How did the family economy constrain the lives of women in preindustrial Europe?

3. What caused the Agricultural Revolution? How did the English aristocracy contribute to the Agricultural Revolution? Why did peasants revolt in the eighteenth century?

4. Why did Europe's population increase in the eighteenth century? How did population growth affect consumption?

5. What was the Industrial Revolution, and what caused it? Why did Great Britain take the lead in the Industrial Revolution? How did consumers contribute to the Industrial Revolution?

6. How did the distribution of population in cities and towns change? How did the lifestyle of the upper class compare to that of the middle and lower classes? What were some of the causes of urban riots?

7. Where were the largest Jewish populations in eighteenth-century Europe? What was their social and legal position? What were the sources of prejudices against Jews?

Key Terms

Agricultural Revolution The innovations in farm production that began in the eighteenth century and led to a scientific and mechanized agriculture.

aristocratic resurgence Term applied to the eighteenth-century aristocratic efforts to resist the expanding power of European monarchies.

banalités The feudal dues to which nearly all French peasants were subject, such as payment to grind grain at the lord's mill or to bake bread in his oven.

Catherine the Great (r. 1762–1796) The Empress of Russia, the longest-ruling and one of the most renowned women leaders in Russian history.

consumer revolution   The vast increase in both the desire and the possibility of consuming goods and services that began in the early eighteenth century and created the demand for sustaining the Industrial Revolution.

domestic system of textile production   Method of producing textiles in which agents furnished raw materials to households whose members spun them into thread and then wove cloth, which the agents then sold as finished products.

Emelyan Pugachev   (1726–1775) The leader of the largest peasant revolt in Russian history, having promised the serfs land of their own and freedom from their lords.

enclosures   The consolidation or fencing in of common lands by British landlords to increase production and achieve greater commercial profits, which also involved the reclamation of wasteland and the consolidation of strips into block fields.

family economy   The basic structure of production and consumption in preindustrial Europe.

ghettos   Separate communities in which Jews were required by law to live.

Industrial Revolution   Mechanization of the European economy that began in Britain in the second half of the eighteenth century.

James Watt   (1736–1819) Scottish inventor best known for the improvements he made to the Newcomen steam engine that was crucial to the Industrial Revolution.

Jethro Tull   (1674–1741) The Englishman whose ideas, such as using iron plows to turn the earth and planting wheat by a drill, helped bring about the Agricultural Revolution.

just price   Imposed in place of the price set in the commercial marketplace when the urban crowd considered the market price unjustly high.

neolocalism   The practice of young men and women leaving home to eventually marry and form their own independent households.

Old Regime   Term applied to the pattern of social, political, and economic relationships and institutions that existed in Europe before the French Revolution.

peerage   A practice of the British aristocracy whereby the eldest son inherited the title of the father.

spinning jenny   A machine invented in England by James Hargreaves around 1765 to mass-produce thread.

water frame   A water-powered device invented by Richard Arkwright to produce a more durable cotton fabric that led to the shift in the production of cotton textiles from households to factories.

Notes

1. Olwen Hufton, "Women and the Family Economy in Eighteenth-Century France," *French Historical Studies* 9 (1976), p. 19.

2. Deborah Valenze, *The First Industrial Woman* (New York: Oxford University Press, 1995), p. 183.

3. Jan De Vries, "Patterns of Urbanization in Pre-Industrial Europe, 1500–1800," in H. Schmal, ed., *Patterns of Urbanization since 1500* (London: Croom Helm, 1981), p. 103.

Chapter 16
The Transatlantic Economy, Trade Wars, and Colonial Rebellion

THE DEATH OF WOLFE General James Wolfe was mortally wounded during his victory over the French at Quebec in 1759. This painting by American artist Benjamin West (1738–1820) became famous for portraying the dying Wolfe and the officers around him in poses modeled after classical statues.

SOURCE: National Trust Photo Library / Art Resource, NY

 Contents and Focus Questions

The Chapter in Brief

THE MID-EIGHTEENTH century witnessed a renewal of European warfare on a worldwide scale. The conflict involved two separate, but interrelated, rivalries. Austria and Prussia fought for dominance in central Europe while Great Britain and France dueled for commercial and colonial supremacy in Europe, North America, and Asia. The wars were long, extensive, and costly in both effort and money. They resulted in a new balance of power on the Continent and on the high seas. Prussia emerged as a great power, and Great Britain gained a world empire.

The expense of these wars led every major European government to reconstruct its policies of taxation and finance after the Peace of Paris of 1763. Among the results of these policies were the American Revolution, state-led reform in central Europe, a continuing financial crisis for the French monarchy, and a reform of the Spanish Empire in South America.

SHIPS MOORED AT LONDON QUAYS During the seventeenth and eighteenth centuries, European maritime nations established overseas empires and set up trading monopolies within them to magnify their economic strength. As this painting of the Old Custom House Quay in London suggests, trade from these empires and the tariffs imposed on it were expected to generate revenue for the home country. But many of the goods carried in these great sailing ships in the harbor and on these docks were the result of the labor of African slaves working on the plantations of North and South America.
SOURCE: Historical Picture Archive/Getty Images

16.1 Periods of European Overseas Empires

How did European contact with the rest of the world evolve in the centuries since the Renaissance?

Since the Renaissance, European contacts with the rest of the world have gone through four distinct stages. The first was that of the European discovery, exploration, initial conquest, and settlement of the New World. This phase also witnessed the penetration of Southeast Asian markets by Portugal and the Netherlands, which established major imperial outposts and influence in the region. This period closed by the end of the seventeenth century.

The second era—that of the mercantile empires, which are largely the concern of this chapter—was one of colonial trade rivalry among Spain, France, and Great Britain. As a result, the various imperial ventures led to the creation of large navies and a series of major naval wars at mid-century—wars that in turn became linked to warfare on the European continent.

A fundamental element in these first two periods of European imperial ventures in the Americas was slavery. By the eighteenth century, the slaves of the New World consisted almost entirely of a black population that had either recently been forcibly imported from Africa or born to slaves whose forebears had been forcibly imported from Africa. Both the forced migration of so many people from one continent to another, and the mid-Atlantic plantation economies that such slave labor supported, were unprecedented. The creation in the Americas of this slave-based plantation economy led directly to more than three centuries of extensive involvement by Europeans and white Americans in the slave trade with Africa—particularly with the societies of West Africa. In turn, on the American continent the slave trade created extensive communities of Africans from the Chesapeake region of Maryland and Virginia south to Brazil. The Africans brought to the American experience not only their labor but also their languages, customs, and ethnic associations. The Atlantic economy and the societies that arose in the Americas were, consequently, created by both Europeans and Africans while, as a result of European incursions into their territory, Native Americans were pressed toward the margins of those societies. In this respect, from the sixteenth century onward, Africans became a significant factor in the forging of European prosperity and industrialization. Africans were not just "commodities" in the slave trade, but actual contributors to distinctive American cultures. The slave trade itself enriched the daily life of peoples in Europe as well as European settlers and their descendants in the Americas.

Finally, during the second period, both the British colonies of the North American seaboard and the Spanish colonies of Mexico and Central and South America emancipated themselves from European control. This era of independence may be said to have closed during the 1820s. This same revolutionary era included the beginning of the antislavery movement that extended through the third quarter of the nineteenth century.

The third stage of European contact with the non-European world occurred in the nineteenth century. During that period, European governments largely turned from the Americas to carve out new formal empires involving the direct European administration of indigenous peoples in Africa and Asia. Those nineteenth-century empires also included new areas of European settlement, such as Australia, New Zealand, South Africa, and Algeria. The bases of these empires were trade, national honor, Christian missionary enterprise, and military strategy. Unlike the previous two eras, the nineteenth-century empires were based on formally free labor forces, although they still involved much harsh treatment of nonwhite indigenous populations.

The last period of European empire began in the mid-twentieth century, with the decolonization of peoples who had previously lived under European colonial rule.

During the four-and-one-half centuries before decolonization, Europeans exerted political, military, and economic dominance over much of the rest of the world that was far disproportional to the geographic size or population of Europe. What allowed the Europeans to influence and dominate so much of the world for such a long period of time was not any innate cultural superiority, but a combination of epidemiological advantage and technological supremacy related to naval power and gunpowder. European diseases weakened indigenous populations in the New World; ships and guns allowed the Europeans to exercise their will almost wherever they chose.

16.2 Mercantile Empires

What were the characteristics of European mercantile empires?

Navies and merchant shipping were the keystones of the mercantile empires that were meant to bring profit to a nation rather than to provide areas for settlement. The **Treaty of Utrecht** of 1713 established the boundaries of empire during the first half of the eighteenth century.

Except for Brazil, which Portugal governed, and Dutch Guiana, Spain controlled all of mainland South America. In North America, Spain ruled vast territories including Florida, Mexico, California, and the southwest. The Spanish also governed Central America and the islands of Cuba, Puerto Rico, Trinidad, and the eastern part of Hispaniola that is today the Dominican Republic.

The British Empire was comprised of the colonies along the North Atlantic seaboard, Nova Scotia, Newfoundland, Bermuda, Jamaica, and Barbados. Britain also possessed a few trading stations on the Indian subcontinent.

The French domains covered the Saint Lawrence River valley and the Ohio and Mississippi River valleys. They included the West Indian islands of Guadeloupe and Martinique as well as the western half of Hispaniola, then called Saint Domingue and today known as Haiti. France also maintained stations in India and on the west coast of Africa. To the French and British merchant communities, India appeared as a vast potential market for European goods, as well as the source of calico cloth and spices that were in great demand in Europe.

The Dutch controlled Surinam, or Dutch Guiana, in South America; Cape Colony in what is today South Africa; and trading stations in West Africa, Sri Lanka, and Bengal in India. Most importantly, they also controlled the trade with Java in what is now Indonesia. The Dutch had opened these markets largely in the seventeenth century and had created a trading empire far vaster in extent, wealth, and importance than the geographical size of the United Netherlands would have led one to expect. The Dutch had been daring sailors and they made important technological innovations in sailing.

These powers, as well as Denmark, also possessed numerous smaller islands in the Caribbean. In the eighteenth century, the major rivalries were among the Spanish, the French, and the British. Together, they prevented other European powers, such as Austria, from securing substantial colonies outside of Europe.

16.2.1 Mercantilist Goals

If any formal economic theory lay behind the conduct of eighteenth-century empires, it was **mercantilism**, whereby governments heavily regulated trade and commerce in hope of increasing national wealth. The terms *mercantilism* and *mercantile system* were invented by later opponents and critics of the system, but its defenders believed mercantilism was the best way for a nation to gain a favorable trade balance of gold and silver bullion. They regarded bullion as the measure of a country's wealth, and believed a nation was truly wealthy only if it amassed more bullion than its rivals.

The mercantilist statesmen and traders regarded the world as an arena of scarce resources and economic limitations. They assumed that only modest levels of economic growth were possible. Such thinking predated the expansion of agricultural and later industrial productivity. Before such sustained economic growth began, the wealth of one nation was assumed to grow or increase largely at the direct expense of another. The wealth of one state might expand only if its armies or navies conquered the domestic or colonial territory of another state and thus gained the productive capacity of that area; if a state expanded its trading monopoly over new territory; or if, by smuggling, a state could intrude on the trading monopoly of another state.

From beginning to end, the economic well-being of the home country was the primary concern of mercantilist writers. Colonies existed to provide markets and natural resources for the industries of the home country, as well as an outlet for surplus capital. In turn, the home country was to protect and administer the colonies. Both sides assumed the colonies were subordinate in the relationship. To encourage the home country and its colonies to trade exclusively with each other, governments used navigation laws, tariffs, bounties to encourage production, and prohibitions against trading with the subjects of other monarchs. National monopoly was the ruling principle.

Although they made sense on paper, by the early eighteenth century, mercantilist assumptions were far removed from the economic realities of the colonies. The colonial and home markets simply did not mesh. Spain could not produce enough goods for South America. Economic production in the British North American colonies challenged English manufacturing and led to British attempts to limit certain colonial industries, such as iron and hat making.

Colonists of different countries wished to trade with each other. English colonists could buy sugar more cheaply from the French West Indies than from English suppliers. The traders and merchants of one nation always hoped to break the monopoly of another. For these reasons, the eighteenth century became what one historian many years ago termed the "golden age of smugglers."[1] Governments could not effectively control their subjects' activities. Clashes among colonists and, in North America, between settlers and indigenous peoples, led to conflicts between European governments.

16.2.2 French–British Rivalry

Major flash points existed between France and Britain in North America. Their colonists quarreled endlessly with each other over the coveted regions of the lower Saint Lawrence River valley, upper New England, and later, the Ohio River valley. Other rivalries arose over fishing rights, the fur trade, and alliances with Native Americans. Native Americans, in turn, used imperial rivalries to serve their own purposes.

The heart of the eighteenth-century colonial rivalry in the Americas, however, lay in the West Indies. The West Indies plantations raised tobacco, cotton, indigo, coffee, and, most importantly, sugar. European demand for these commodities rose tremendously as they increasingly became part of daily life. Sugar in particular had become a staple rather than a luxury. It was used in coffee, tea, and cocoa; for making candy and preserving fruits; and in the brewing industry. There seemed no limit to its uses, no limit to consumer demand for it and, for a time, almost no limit to the riches it might bring to plantation owners. The profitable

cultivation of these products during the seventeenth and eighteenth centuries relied upon the exploitation of African slave labor. (See this chapter's "Encountering the Past" sidebar, a consideration of the connection between slavery and the trade in sugar, which follows below.)

India was another area of French–British rivalry. In India, both France and Britain granted legal monopolies on trade to privileged chartered companies like the *Compagnie des Indes* and the East India Company. Although Indian and Asian trade figured only marginally in the economics of early eighteenth-century empire, some Europeans hoped to develop profitable commerce with India. Others regarded India as a springboard into the even larger potential market of China. The original European footholds in India were trading posts called *factories*. They existed through privileges granted by various Indian governments that in theory were themselves subject to the decaying Mughal Empire, which exercised little authority.

Two circumstances in the mid-eighteenth century changed this situation in India. First, the administration and government of several Indian states had weakened. Second, Joseph Dupleix (1697–1763) for the French and Robert Clive (1725–1774) for the British saw the developing power vacuum as an opportunity to increase control of their respective companies. To maintain their security and to expand their privileges, each of the two companies began in effect to take over the government of some of the regions. Each group of Europeans hoped to checkmate the other.

The Dutch maintained their extensive commercial empire further to the east in what today is Indonesia. By the eighteenth century, the other European powers had acknowledged Dutch predominance in that region.

16.3 The Spanish Colonial System

How did Spanish colonial organization reflect its imperial goals?

Spanish control of its American Empire involved two aspects: government and monopolistic trade regulation. Both were more rigid in appearance than in practice. Actual government was often informal, and the trade monopoly was frequently breached. Until the mid-eighteenth century, the primary purpose of the Spanish Empire was to supply Spain with the precious metals mined in the New World.

16.3.1 Colonial Government

Because **Queen Isabella of Castile** (r. 1474–1504) had commissioned Columbus, the technical legal link between the New World and Spain was the crown of Castile.

Encountering the Past

Sugar Enters the Western Diet

BEFORE THE EUROPEAN discovery of the Americas, sugar was a luxury product that only the wealthy could afford. Because it required subtropical temperatures and heavy rainfall, sugarcane could not be grown in Europe. Sugar had to be imported, at great expense, from the Arab world or from the Spanish and Portuguese islands off the coast of Africa, which were too arid for the plant to flourish.

THE PRODUCTION OF SUGAR Sugar was both raised and processed on plantations such as this one in Brazil. Raw sugarcane from the nearby fields was placed between vertical crushers to extract juice to be distilled into sugar crystals elsewhere on the plantation in cauldrons over fires. Animal power was used to move the crushers until the late eighteenth century when wealthy plantation owners replaced horses or mules with steam engines.
SOURCE: Library of Congress

The Caribbean, however, was ideal for sugarcane. Columbus carried it to the New World in 1493, and within about a decade sugar was being cultivated—by slaves—on Santo Domingo.

Yet, sugar production did not begin to soar until Britain and France established themselves in the Caribbean in the seventeenth century and the demand for sugar began to grow in Europe, first slowly and then insatiably. By the eighteenth century, the small British and French islands in the Caribbean where sugar was produced by African slave labor had become some of the most valuable real estate on earth.

Whereas the North American colonies imported Caribbean molasses to make rum, Europeans desired sugar to sweeten other foods. Sugar, the largest colonial import into Britain, represented the mercantile policy of a closed economic system. It was raised in British colonies, paid for by British exports, shipped on British ships, insured by British firms, refined in British cities, and consumed on British tables.

The voracious demand for sugar as a sweetener was tied up with three other tropical products—coffee, tea, and chocolate—that European consumers began to drink in enormous quantities in the seventeenth and eighteenth centuries. Each of these beverages is a stimulant, which helps explain their popularity, but by themselves they taste bitter. Sugar made them palatable to European consumers. The demand for sugar and these drinks became mutually reinforcing: English markets for coffee, tea, chocolate, and sugar grew together.

As the production of sugar rose, its price fell. The cheaper sugar became, the more of it Europeans consumed. By the end of the eighteenth century, tea with sugar was cheaper than beer or milk, and it had become the most popular drink among the British poor (while remaining an elegant drink for the wealthy). Workers in English factories could feel energized by a short break and a cup of sweetened tea, even though the tea provided less nutrition than the food and beverages it replaced. Tea was easier to prepare than warm porridge, and more stimulating than nutrient-rich beer.

During the nineteenth century, sugar consumption continued to grow, and sugar became even cheaper when free-trade policies reduced protective import duties and when the French began to manufacture it from sugar beets, which could easily be grown in Europe. Nineteenth-century Westerners developed the custom of ending a meal with dessert, food usually sweetened with sugar.

Questions

1. How did the colonization of the Americas affect the European demand for sugar?
2. Why did sugar consumption increase so rapidly in Europe during the eighteenth and nineteenth centuries?

SOURCE: From Sidney Mintz, *Sweetness and Power: The Place of Sugar in Modern History* (New York: Penguin Books, 1985).

RETURN OF COLUMBUS FROM THE NEW WORLD Spain had financed Christopher Columbus's voyage across the Atlantic. This illustration shows what Columbus presented to his sponsors upon his return. In addition to the gold, Columbus brought back with him a few indigenous people from the Americas.
SOURCE: Library of Congress Prints and Photographs Division

Its powers both at home and in America were subject to few limitations. The Castilian monarch assigned the government of America to the Council of the Indies, which, with the monarch, nominated the viceroys of New Spain (Mexico) and Peru. These viceroys served as the chief executives in the New World and carried out the laws issued by the Council of the Indies.

Virtually all power flowed from the top of this political structure downward; in effect, local initiative or self-government scarcely existed.

16.3.2 Trade Regulation

The colonial political structures largely functioned to support Spanish commercial self-interests. The *Casa de Contratación* (House of Trade) in Seville regulated all trade with the New World. The *Casa* was the most influential institution of the Spanish Empire. Its members worked closely with the *Consulado* (Merchant Guild) of Seville and other groups involved with American commerce in Cádiz, the only port authorized for American trade.

A complicated system of trade and bullion fleets administered from Seville maintained Spain's trade monopoly. Each year, the *flota*, a fleet of commercial vessels controlled by Seville merchants and escorted by warships, carried merchandise from Spain to a few specified ports in America. After selling their wares, the ships were loaded with silver and gold bullion; they usually spent the winter in heavily fortified Caribbean ports and then sailed back to Spain. The flota system always worked

imperfectly, but trade outside it was illegal. Regulations prohibited the Spanish colonists within the American Empire from establishing direct trade with each other and from building their own shipping and commercial industry. Foreign merchants were also forbidden to breach the Spanish monopoly. Spanish ships continued to transport precious metals and coins from the Americas to Spain through the early nineteenth century. Modern-day treasure hunters still occasionally discover troves of precious metal from shipwrecked vessels of the colonial Spanish Empire.

16.3.3 Colonial Reform Under the Spanish Bourbon Monarchs

In the early eighteenth century, the War of the Spanish Succession (1701–1714) and the Treaty of Utrecht in 1713 led to a change in the dynasty holding the Spanish throne: the Spanish Habsburgs were replaced by the Bourbons of France. The Bourbon king **Philip V** (r. 1700–1746) and his successors tried to use French administrative skills to reinvigorate the imperial trade monopoly, which had lapsed under the last Spanish Habsburgs, and thus to improve Spain's economic and political power in Europe.

Under Philip V, Spanish coastal patrol vessels tried to suppress smuggling in American waters. This policy led to war with England in 1739, the year in which Philip established the viceroyalty of New Granada in the area that today includes Venezuela, Colombia, and Ecuador. His goal was to strengthen the royal government there, but the ensuing wars exposed the vulnerability of the Spanish empire to naval attack and economic penetration. Government circles then became convinced that the colonial system had to be reformed.

Charles III (r. 1759–1788), the most important of the imperial reformers, attempted to reassert Spain's control of the empire. Like his Bourbon predecessors, Charles emphasized royal ministers rather than councils. Thus, the roles of both the Council of the Indies and the *Casa de Contratación* diminished. After 1765, Charles abolished the monopolies of Seville and Cádiz and permitted other Spanish cities to trade with America. He also opened more South American and Caribbean ports to trade and authorized commerce between Spanish ports in America. In 1776, he organized a fourth viceroyalty in the region of Río de la Plata, which included much of present-day Argentina, Uruguay, Paraguay, and Bolivia. (See Map 16–1.)

Map 16–1 VICEROYALTIES IN LATIN AMERICA IN 1780

The late eighteenth-century viceroyalties in Latin America were the result of the Spanish Bourbon monarchy's efforts to directly control colonies through the introduction of more royal officials and more governmental districts.

To increase the efficiency of tax collection and end bureaucratic corruption, Charles III introduced the institution of the *intendant* to the Spanish Empire. These royal bureaucrats were patterned on the famously effective agents of French royal administration during the absolutist reign of Louis XIV.

The late-eighteenth-century Bourbon reforms stimulated the imperial Spanish economy. Trade expanded and became more varied. These reforms, however, also brought the empire more fully under direct Spanish control. Many *peninsulares*, or persons born in Spain, entered the New World to fill new posts, which were often the most profitable jobs in the region. Expanding trade brought more Spanish merchants to Latin America. The economy remained export oriented, and the colonies' economic life was still organized to benefit Spain. As a result of these policies, the **creoles**, or persons of European descent born in the Spanish colonies, came to feel they were second-class subjects. In time, their resentment would be a major source of the discontent leading to the wars of independence in the early nineteenth century. The imperial reforms of Charles III were the Spanish equivalent of the new colonial measures the British government undertook after 1763, which led to the American Revolution.

16.4 Black African Slavery, the Plantation System, and the Atlantic Economy

What were the origins of slavery in the Americas?

Slavery had existed in various parts of Europe since ancient times. Before the eighteenth century, little or no moral or religious stigma was attached to slave owning or slave trading. It continued to exist in the Mediterranean world, where the sources of slaves changed over the centuries. After the conquest of Constantinople in 1453, the Ottoman Empire forbade the exportation of white slaves from regions under its control, but continued to enslave young Christian boys from southeastern Europe and convert them to Islam under the *devşirme* system. The Portuguese imported African slaves into the Iberian Peninsula from the Canary Islands and West Africa. Black slaves from Africa were also not uncommon in other parts of the Mediterranean, and a few found their way into northern Europe. There they were

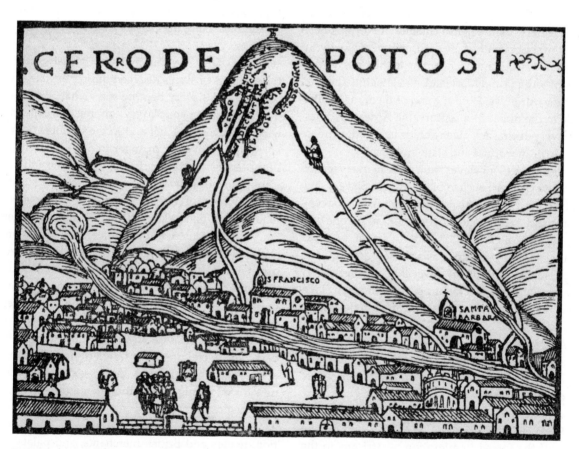

THE SILVER MINES OF POTOSÍ The Spanish had discovered precious metals in their South American Empire early in the sixteenth century; the mines provided Spain with a vast treasure in silver until the eighteenth century. The silver mines of Potosí were worked by conscripted Indian laborers under extremely harsh conditions (note the head impaled on a stake in the foreground).
SOURCE: INTERFOTO/Alamy Stock Photo

favored as personal servants in royal courts or in wealthy homes because of the novelty of their color.

Yet, from the sixteenth century on, first within the West Indies and the Spanish and Portuguese settlements in South America and then in the British colonies on the South Atlantic seaboard of North America, slave labor became a fundamental social and economic factor. The development of plantation economies based on slave labor led to unprecedented interaction between the peoples of Europe and Africa and between the European settlers in the Americas and Africa. From that point on, Africa and Africans were drawn into the Western experience as never before in history.

16.4.1 The African Presence in the Americas

Once they had encountered and begun to settle the New World, the Spanish and Portuguese faced a severe shortage of labor. They and most of the French and English settlers who came later had no intention of undertaking manual work themselves. At first, they used Native Americans as laborers, but during the sixteenth century as well as afterward, disease killed hundreds of thousands of indigenous people. As a result, labor soon became scarce. The Spanish and Portuguese then turned to the labor of imported African slaves. Settlers in the English colonies of North America during the seventeenth century turned more slowly to slavery, with the largest number coming to the Chesapeake Bay region of Virginia and Maryland, and later into the low country of the Carolinas. Until the end of the transatlantic slave trade in the nineteenth century, the African peoples sold into slavery during any given decade largely depended on internal African warfare and state-building.

The major sources for slaves were slave markets on the West African coast from Senegambia to Angola. Slavery and an extensive slave trade had existed in West Africa for centuries. Just as social and economic conditions in Europe had led to the voyages of exploration and settlement, political and military conditions in Africa and warfare among African nations created a supply of slaves that certain African societies were willing to sell to Europeans. European slave traders did not face passive West African societies easily controlled by force and commerce. Rather, they encountered dynamic African societies with their own internal historic power relationships and rivalries that led to Africans being sold and acquired from different regions and nations as slaves by other Africans.

16.4.1.1 THE WEST INDIES AND BRAZIL To grasp the full impact of the forced immigration of Africans to the Americas, we must understand the entire picture of the transatlantic economy. Far more slaves were imported into the West Indies and Brazil than into North America. Although most U.S. citizens mark the beginning of slavery in 1619 with the arrival of African slaves on a Dutch ship in Jamestown, Virginia, more than a century of slave trading in the West Indies and South America had preceded that event. Indeed, by the late sixteenth century, Africans had become a major social presence in the West Indies and in the major cities of both Spanish and Portuguese South America. Their influence in these regions would grow over the centuries. The sugar plantations on which many Caribbean economies depended were so deadly and slave mortality rates were so high that plantation owners had to import enslaved Africans continually; the constant influx of new African slaves sustained the African cultural presence in the West Indies. African labor and African immigrant slave communities were the most prominent social features of these regions, making the development of their economies and cultures what one historian has described as "a Euro-African phenomenon."[2] In these places, African slaves equaled or more generally surpassed the numbers of white European settlers in what soon constituted multiracial societies. Passing through the marketplace of these towns and cities, one would have heard a great number of African, as well as European, languages. Although Native American labor continued to be exploited on the South American continent, it was increasingly a marginal presence in the ever-expanding African slave-based plantation economy of the Atlantic seaboard, the Caribbean, and offshore islands.

16.4.1.2 SUGAR Within much of Spanish South America, the numbers of slaves declined during the late seventeenth century, and slavery became somewhat less fundamental there than elsewhere. Slavery continued to expand its influence, however, in Brazil and in the Caribbean through the spreading cultivation of sugar to meet the demand of the European market. By the close of the seventeenth century, the Caribbean islands were the world center for sugar production. New areas of cultivation and other economic enterprises required additional slaves during the eighteenth century.

A great increase in the number of Africans brought as slaves to the Americas occurred during the eighteenth century, with most arriving in the Caribbean or Brazil. Early in the century, as many as 20,000 new Africans a year arrived in the West Indies as slaves. By 1725, it has been estimated that almost 90 percent of the population of Jamaica consisted of black slaves. After the mid-century, the numbers were even larger. The influx of new Africans in most areas—even in the British colonies—meant the numbers of new forced immigrants outnumbered the slaves of African descent already present.

Sugar was extremely profitable for European plantation owners and British merchants, and palatable among European consumers, but it was catastrophic for the slaves who grew it in the West Indies and Brazil. One historian has recently called it a "murderous commodity."[3] (See the Closer Look" sidebar, which follows below, for a diagram of

A Closer Look

A Sugar Plantation in the West Indies

WEST INDIES SUGAR plantations, owned by Europeans who often stayed only long enough to make their fortunes, were located on the fertile islands of the Caribbean. The sugar plantations employed slave laborers imported from Africa, and they combined the agricultural production of sugar cane with its industrial processing for export to Europe. In particular, the industrial processing of sugar cane could be quite dangerous, as it involved unsafe machinery and people working near fires and hot metal equipment.

Plantation owners generally lived in a "Great House" on high windswept areas of their estates.

Slaves dwelled in humble housing close to the areas where sugarcane was cultivated and where animals, which were used for food and for sugar production, grazed.

Wind-powered mills crushed the sugarcane to extract the juice.

RAISING CANE
SOURCE: DEA/G. DAGLI ORTI/Getty Images

Questions

1. What do the locations of buildings in this image of a plantation indicate about the expected roles of people in maintaining sugar plantation life?
2. What impression of sugar plantation work do these images attempt to create?
3. From the perspective of a sugar plantation owner, what made a plantation successful?

a sugar plantation that gives clues to the slaves' conditions.) Consequently, one of the elements in the social life of many of the areas of American slavery during the eighteenth century was the arrival of new persons from Africa, carrying with them African languages, religion, culture, and local African ethnic identities that would be absorbed into the existing slave communities. Thus, the eighteenth century witnessed an enormous new African presence throughout the Americas.

16.4.2 Slavery and the Transatlantic Economy

Different nations dominated the slave trade in different periods. During the sixteenth century, the Portuguese and the Spanish were most involved. The Dutch supplanted them during most of the seventeenth century. Thereafter, during the late seventeenth and eighteenth centuries, the English were the chief slave traders. French traders also participated in the trade.

Slavery touched most of the economy of the transatlantic world. (See Map 16–2.) Colonial trade followed roughly a geographic triangle, but not all ships covered all three legs of the journey. European goods, including guns, were carried to Africa to be exchanged for slaves. Slaves were then taken to the West Indies, where they were traded for sugar and other tropical goods, and these products were finally shipped to Europe. Another major trade pattern existed between New England and the

Map 16–2 THE SLAVE TRADE, 1400–1860

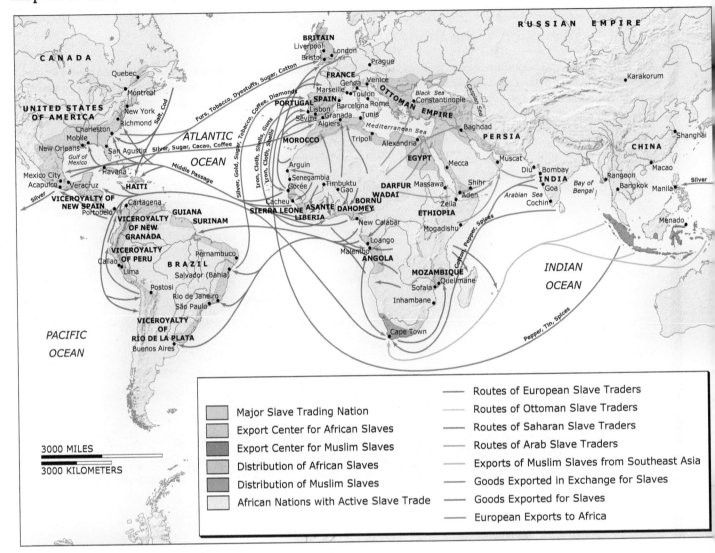

Complex slave-trading routes existed in Africa, the Middle East, and Asia for centuries, but it was the need to supply labor to the plantations of the Americas that led to the greatest movement of peoples across the face of the earth.

West Indies with New England fish, rum, or lumber being traded for sugar. At various times, the prosperity of such cities as Amsterdam (Netherlands), Liverpool (England), and Nantes (France) depended largely on the slave trade. Cities in the British North American colonies, such as Newport, Rhode Island, profited from slavery sometimes by trading in slaves, but more often by supplying other goods to the West Indian market. The manufacturers who produced finished products for the consumer market depended on slavery, even though probably they were not in direct contact with slaves. On the other hand, the shippers who handled cotton, tobacco and sugar, as well as the ship builders who constructed the vessels, used to carry people and goods across the Atlantic and were more intimately connected with the slave trade.

As had been the case during previous centuries, eighteenth-century political turmoil in Africa, such as the civil wars in the Kingdom of Kongo (modern Angola and Republic of Congo), increased the supply of slaves during that period. Similar political unrest and turmoil in the Gold Coast area (modern Ghana) during the eighteenth century increased the supply of African captives to be sold into American slavery. Consequently, warfare in West Africa, often far into the interior, and the economic development of the American Atlantic seaboard were closely related.

16.4.3 The Experience of Slavery

The Portuguese, Spanish, Dutch, French, and English slave traders transported nearly 12 million Africans (perhaps more, the exact number is disputed), which was the largest forced intercontinental migration in human history. During the first four centuries of settlement, far more black slaves came involuntarily to the New World than did free

European settlers or European indentured servants. The conditions of slaves' passage across the Atlantic were wretched. Many Africans died in the "First Passage" that took them from their native villages to the African coast; many more perished during the crossing, or "**Middle Passage**." (See this chapter's "Compare and Connect" sidebar to sample two primary source artifacts of the transatlantic passage from Africa.) There were always more African men than women transported, so it was difficult to preserve traditional African extended family structures. During the passage and later, many Africans attempted to recreate such structures among themselves, even if they were not related by direct family ties.

In the Americas, the slave population was divided among new Africans recently arrived, old Africans who had lived there for some years, and creoles who were the descendants of earlier generations of African slaves. Plantation owners preferred the two latter groups, who were already accustomed to the life of slavery. They sold for higher prices. The newly arrived Africans were subjected to a process known as *seasoning*, during which they were prepared for the laborious discipline of slavery and made to understand that they were no longer free. This forcible reeducation might involve receiving new names, acquiring new work skills, and learning, to some extent, the local European language. Generally, North American plantation

Compare and Connect

The Atlantic Passage

SLAVERY LAY AT the core of the eighteenth-century transatlantic economy. At the heart of slavery lay the forced transportation of millions of Africans in slave ships across the Atlantic to the Americas. The frightening and horrific character of the Atlantic, or Middle, Passage, became widely known through the memoirs of sailors and slave trade captains. Groups who, beginning in the mid-eighteenth century, sought the abolition of slavery described the inhumanity of the passage in published attacks on the slave trade. They also widely distributed illustrations of slave ships, such as the *Brookes*.

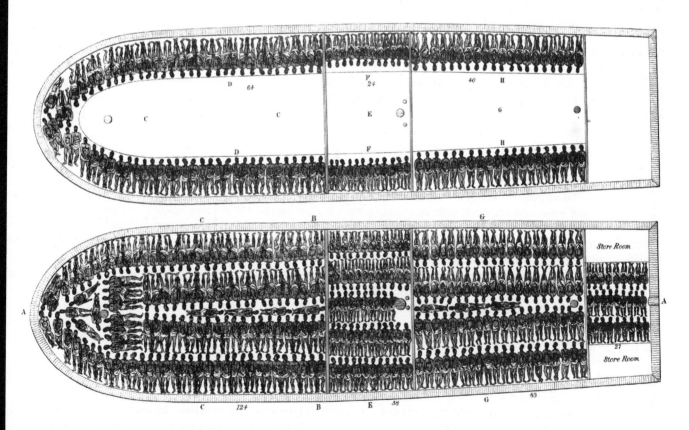

INTERIOR OF THE SLAVE SHIP *BROOKES* The *Brookes* measured 25 feet wide and 100 feet long. Men and women were separated by barriers that sectioned them off from one another. Through the most inhumane commercial use of space, between 609 and 740 slaves were crammed on board for the nightmarish passage to America. A parliamentary inquiry in 1788 found that the ship had been designed to carry no more than approximately 450 persons.
SOURCE: Library of Congress

The average space for each African destined for slavery in the Americas was 78 inches by 16 inches, smaller than an adult coffin. The Africans were normally shackled to ensure discipline, to prevent rebellions that might injure the crew or lead to the slaves' escape, and to break down normal social relations among the captives. Iron shackles also prevented Africans from committing suicide on the voyage.

Before Reading

- Look closely at the diagram of the slave ship provided.

Questions

1. Which people described in this document by Captain Thomas Phillips were involved in or profited from the slave trade?
2. What dangers did the Africans face on the voyage?
3. What contemporary attitudes could have led Phillips to treat his human cargo as goods to be transported?
4. How might the publication of the diagrams of the slave ship *Brookes* have helped the cause of antislavery? Would this illustration of a slave ship have been more or less persuasive in rousing antislavery sentiment than a prose description?
5. How would these diagrams and the description of the Atlantic Passage have contrasted with contemporary illustrations and memoirs of victorious naval battles on the high seas?

I. A SLAVE TRADER DESCRIBES THE ATLANTIC PASSAGE

During 1693 and 1694, Captain Thomas Phillips sailed on the ship Hannibal *to the west coast of Africa, where he purchased Africans who had been sold into slavery by an African king. He then transported the slaves from Africa to Barbados. The financial backer of the voyage was the Royal African Company of London, which held an English crown monopoly on slave trading. In the following excerpt, Phillips describes his experiences with and impressions of slaves aboard the* Hannibal.

Having bought my complement of 700 slaves, 480 men and 220 women, and finish'd all my business at Whidaw [on the Gold Coast of Africa], I took my leave of the old king and his *cappasheirs* [attendants], and parted, with many affectionate expressions on both sides, being forced to promise him that I would return again the next year, with several things he desired me to bring from England. . . . I set sail the 27th of July in the morning, accompany'd with the East-India Merchant, who had bought 650 slaves, for the Island of St. Thomas. . . . from which we took our departure on August 25th and set sail for Barbadoes.

We spent in our passage from St. Thomas to Barbadoes two months eleven days, from the 25th of August to the 4th of November following: in which time there happened such sickness and mortality among my poor men and Negroes. Of the first we buried 14, and of the last 320, which was a great detriment to our voyage, the Royal African Company losing ten pounds by every slave that died, and the owners of the ship ten pounds ten shillings, being the freight agreed on to be paid by the charter-party for every Negro delivered alive ashore to the African Company's agents at Barbadoes. . . . The loss in all amounted to near 6500 pounds sterling.

The distemper which my men as well as the blacks mostly died of was the white flux, which was so violent and inveterate that no medicine would in the least check it, so that when any of our men were seized with it, we esteemed him a dead man, as he generally proved. . . .

The Negroes are so incident to [subject to] the small-pox that few ships that carry them escape without it, and sometimes it makes vast havoc and destruction among them. But tho' we had 100 at a time sick of it, and that it went thro' the ship, yet we lost not above a dozen by it. All the assistance we gave the diseased was only as much water as they desir'd to drink, and some palm-oil to annoint their sores, and they would generally recover without any other helps but what kind nature gave them. . . .

But what the smallpox spar'd, the flux swept off, to our great regret, after all our pains and care to give them their messes in due order and season, keeping their lodgings as clean and sweet as possible, and enduring so much misery and stench so long among a parcel of creatures nastier than swine, and after all our expectations to be defeated by their mortality. . . .

No gold-finders can endure so much noisome slavery as they do who carry Negroes; for those have some respite and satisfaction, but we endure twice the misery; and yet by their mortality our voyages are ruin'd, and we pine and fret ourselves to death, and take so much pains to so little purpose.

II. THE SLAVE SHIP *BROOKES*

These diagrams record the main decks of the 320-ton slave ship *Brookes*. They were first published in 1789 by abolitionists hoping to influence new regulation of the slave trade. The original diagrams contained seven different views, including the two reproduced here. The popularization of these diagrams is considered to be one of the breakthroughs in the nineteenth-century movement against slavery.

SOURCES: (I) From Thomas Phillips, "Journal," *A Collection of Voyages and Travels*, Vol. 6, ed. by Awnsham and John Churchill (London, 1746), as quoted in Thomas Howard, ed., *Black Voyage: Eyewitness Accounts of the Atlantic Slave Trade* (Boston: Little, Brown & Company, 1971), pp. 85–87.

owners were willing to purchase only recently arrived Africans who had already been seasoned in the West Indies.

16.4.3.1 LANGUAGE AND CULTURE
The plantation to which the slaves eventually arrived always lay in a more or less isolated rural setting, but its inhabitants could sometimes visit their counterparts on other plantations or in nearby towns on market days. Within the sharply restricted confines of slavery, the recently arrived Africans were able, at least for a time, to sustain elements of their own culture and social structures. From the West Indies southward throughout the eighteenth century, there were more people whose first language was African rather than European. For example, Coromantee was the predominant language on Jamaica. In South Carolina and on St. Domingue, most African slaves spoke Kikongo. It would take more

FOLK ART WATERCOLOR OF PLANTATION SLAVES, CA. 1785 Slaves on the plantations of the American South were the chattel property of their masters, and their lives were grim. Some artists disguised this harsh reality by depicting the lighter moments of slave society as in this scene of slaves dancing.
SOURCE: MPI/Stringer/Getty Images

than two generations for the colonial language to dominate, and even then, the result was often a dialect combining an African and a European language.

Through these languages, Africans on plantation estates could organize themselves into nations with similar, though not necessarily identical, ethnic ties to regions of West Africa. The loyalty achieved through a shared African language in the American setting created a solidarity among African slaves stronger than what in Africa had probably been a primary loyalty to a village. These nations organized and sustained by the plantation experience also became the basis for a variety of religious communities among African slaves that had roots in their African experience. In this manner, some Africans remained loyal to the Islamic faith of their homeland. Nevertheless, as reminders of the pain of the Middle Passage, some newly arrived Africans were ostracized by established slave communities in the Americas.

Many of the African nations on plantations, such as those of Brazil, organized lay religious brotherhoods that did various kinds of charitable work within the slave communities. In the Americas, the African nations would elect their own kings and queens, who might preside over gatherings of the members of the nation drawn from various plantations.

The shared language of a particular African nation in the Americas enabled the slaves to communicate among themselves during revolts such as that in South Carolina in 1739, in Jamaica in the early 1760s, and most successfully, during the Haitian Revolution of the 1790s. In the South Carolina revolt, slave owners believed their slaves had communicated among themselves by playing African

drums. In the aftermath of the revolt, the owners attempted to suppress such drum playing in the slave community.

16.4.3.2 DAILY LIFE
The living conditions of plantation slaves differed from colony to colony. Black slaves living in Portuguese areas had the fewest legal protections. In the Spanish colonies, the church attempted to provide some protection for black slaves, but devoted more effort toward the welfare of Native Americans. Spanish law, however, allowed for self-purchase and manumission, leading to substantial communities of free blacks. Slave codes were developed in the British and the French colonies during the seventeenth century, but they provided only the most limited protection to slaves while ensuring the dominance of their owners.

Slave owners always feared a revolt, and legislation and other regulations were intended to prevent one. Furthermore, to prevent a revolt, slaves were often forbidden to gather in large groups. Slave masters were permitted to whip slaves and inflict other harsh corporal punishment. In most of these slave societies, the law did not recognize slave marriages. Legally, the children of slaves were slaves, and the owner of their parents owned them too.

The daily life of most slaves during these centuries involved hard agricultural labor, poor diet, and inadequate housing. Owners could separate slave families, or their members could be sold separately after owners died. The slaves' welfare and their lives were sacrificed to the continuing expansion of the sugar, rice, and tobacco plantations that made their owners wealthy and that produced goods for European consumers. While climate, occupation, labor regime, possibility of emancipation, and the character of their masters could lead to variations in the quality of life of slaves, all slaves lived at another human being's mercy and were dependent on his or her whim or fortune. The commonality of their exposed and difficult lives makes it impossible to call any form of slavery "mild."

16.4.3.3 CONVERSION TO CHRISTIANITY Most African slaves transported to the Americas were, like the Native Americans, eventually converted to Christianity. In the Spanish, French, and Portuguese domains, they became Roman Catholics. In the English colonies, most became Protestants of one denomination or another. Both forms of Christianity preached to slaves to accept both their slavery and a natural social hierarchy with their masters at the top. The abolitionists' later insistence that Christianity and slavery were incompatible was not a widespread belief before the mid-seventeenth century.

Although organized African religion eventually disappeared in the Americas, especially in the British colonies, some African religious practices survived in muted forms, gradually separated from African religious belief. These included an African understanding of nature and the cosmos, and the belief in people with special spiritual powers, such as conjurers and healers. Although many slaves found tremendous comfort in their new religion, the conversion of Africans to Christianity was nonetheless another example, like that of the Native Americans, of the forcible replacement of non-European cultural values in the context of New World economies and social structures.

16.4.3.4 EUROPEAN RACIAL ATTITUDES Slavery had not always been racial: Christians and Muslims had enslaved one another for centuries in the Mediterranean before Atlantic plantation slavery was established. While scholars disagree about whether slavery or racism came first, the slave trade was key in transforming religious understandings of difference into racial ones. In the Atlantic system of slavery, that slaves were black and masters were white was as fundamental as that slaves were chattel property. The European settlers in the Americas and the slave traders carried with them prejudices against black Africans. Many Europeans considered Africans to be uncivilized savages. Still others looked down on them simply because they were slaves. In virtually all these plantation societies, race was an important element in keeping black slaves subservient. Racial thinking about slavery became especially important in the nineteenth century.

The plantations that stretched from the Middle Atlantic colonies of North America through the West Indies and into Brazil constituted a vast corridor of slave societies in which social and economic subordination was based on both involuntary servitude and race. These societies had not existed before the European discovery and exploitation of the Americas. In its complete dependence on slave labor and racial differences, this kind of society was unique in both European and world history. Its social and economic influence

transformed not only the plantation societies themselves but West Africa, Western Europe, and New England as well. This society existed from the sixteenth century through the late nineteenth century, when the emancipation of slaves had been completed through the slave revolt of Saint Domingue, which became Haiti (1794); the British outlawing of the slave trade (1807); the United States outlawing of the slave trade (1808); the Latin American wars of independence; the Emancipation Proclamation of 1863 and the Civil War in the United States; and the Brazilian emancipation of 1888. To the present day, every society in which plantation slavery once existed still contends with the long-term effects of that institution.

16.5 Mid-Eighteenth-Century Wars

Why did mid-eighteenth-century European wars often involve both continental and global conflicts?

The chattel slavery that characterized the plantation economies of the New World conflicts with early-twentieth-century European views about human rights, but before the Enlightenment and the abolitionist movement of the late eighteenth century, such views were irrelevant to the way people thought about labor. Similarly, in the mid-eighteenth century, statesmen had no principled commitment to peace. The statesmen of the period generally assumed that warfare could further national interests. There were no forces or powers that found it in their interest to prevent war or maintain peace. In fact, European nations often viewed periods of peace following a war as opportunities to recoup their strength and start fighting again to seize another nation's territory or disrupt another empire's trading monopoly.

The two fundamental areas of great power rivalry were the overseas empires and central and eastern Europe. Conflict in one of these regions repeatedly overlapped with conflict in the other, and this interaction influenced strategy and the pattern of alliances among the great powers.

CONFLICTS OF THE MID-EIGHTEENTH CENTURY	
1713	Treaty of Utrecht
1739	Outbreak of War of Jenkins's Ear between England and Spain
1740	Outbreak of War of the Austrian Succession
1748	Treaty of Aix-la-Chapelle ends War of Austrian Succession
1756	Convention of Westminster between England and Prussia
1756	Outbreak of Seven Years' War
1757	Battle of Plassey
1759	British forces capture Quebec
1763	Treaty of Hubertusburg
1763	Treaty of Paris ends Seven Years' War

16.5.1 The War of Jenkins's Ear

By the mid-eighteenth century, the West Indies had become a hotbed of trade rivalry and illegal smuggling. Much to British chagrin, the Spanish government took its alleged trading monopoly seriously and maintained coastal patrols, which boarded and searched English vessels to look for contraband.

In 1731, during one such boarding operation, there was a fight, and the Spaniards cut off the ear of an English captain named Robert Jenkins. Thereafter he carried about his severed ear preserved in a jar of brandy. This incident was of little importance until 1738, when Jenkins appeared before the British Parliament, reportedly brandishing his ear as an example of Spanish atrocities to British merchants in the West Indies. British merchants and West Indian planters lobbied Parliament to prevent Spanish intervention in their trade. Sir Robert Walpole (1676–1745), the British prime minister, could not resist these pressures. In late 1739, Britain went to war with Spain. This war, the **War of Jenkins's Ear** (1739–1748), might have been a relatively minor event, but because of developments in continental European politics, it became the first encounter in a series of European wars fought across the world until 1815.

MARIA THERESA OF AUSTRIA AND FAMILY Maria Theresa of Austria's leadership saved the Habsburg Empire from possible disintegration after the Prussian invasion of Silesia in 1740.
SOURCE: Imagno/Getty Images

16.5.2 The War of the Austrian Succession (1740–1748)

In December 1740, only seven months after becoming king of Prussia, Frederick II (r. 1740–1786) opportunistically seized the Austrian province of Silesia in eastern Germany. The new Habsburg ruler, **Maria Theresa** (r. 1740–1780), had only occupied the throne herself for two months, was only twenty-three, and whose control of the dynasty's holdings had yet to be established. The invasion shattered the provisions of the Pragmatic Sanction and upset the continental balance of power. The young king of Prussia had treated the House of Habsburg simply as another German state rather than as the leading power in the region. Silesia was a valuable possession, and Frederick was determined to keep his ill-gotten prize.

16.5.2.1 MARIA THERESA PRESERVES THE HABSBURG EMPIRE The Prussian seizure of Silesia could have marked the opening of a general hunting season on Habsburg holdings and the beginning of revolts by Habsburg subjects.

Instead, it led to new political allegiances. Although Maria Theresa was unable to regain Silesia, her preservation of the Habsburg Empire as a major political power was itself a great achievement.

Maria Theresa won loyalty and support from her various subjects by granting new privileges to the nobility. Most significantly, the empress recognized Hungary as the most important of her crowns and promised the Hungarian nobility local autonomy. Following in her father's footsteps, Maria preserved the Habsburg state, but at considerable cost to the power of the central monarchy. Hungary would continue to be, as it had been in the past, a particularly troublesome area in the Habsburg Empire. When the monarchy was strong and secure, it could ignore guarantees made to Hungary. But when the monarchy was threatened, or when the Hungarians could stir up enough opposition, the Habsburgs promised new concessions.

16.5.2.2 FRANCE DRAWS GREAT BRITAIN INTO THE WAR The War of the Austrian Succession and the British–Spanish commercial conflict could have remained separate disputes. What united them was the role of France. Just as British

merchant interests had pushed Sir Robert Walpole into war, aggressive court aristocrats compelled the elderly Cardinal Fleury (1653–1743), first minister of Louis XV (r. 1715–1774), to abandon France's planned naval attack on British trade and instead to support Prussian aggression against Austria, the traditional enemy of France. This was among the more fateful decisions in French history.

First, aid to Prussia consolidated a new and powerful state in central Europe. That new power could, and indeed later did, endanger France. Second, the French move against Austria brought Great Britain into the continental war, as Britain sought to make sure the Low Countries remained in the friendly hands of Austria, not France. In 1744, the British–French conflict expanded into the New World where France supported Spain against Britain. As a result, French military and economic resources were badly divided, and France could not bring sufficient strength to the colonial struggle. Having chosen to continue the old continental struggle with Austria, France lost the colonial struggle for the future against Great Britain. The war ended in a stalemate in 1748 with the Treaty of Aix-la-Chapelle. Prussia retained Silesia, and in 1713, Spain renewed the privilege granted Britain in the Treaty of Utrecht to import slaves into the Spanish colonies.

16.5.3 The "Diplomatic Revolution" of 1756

Although the Treaty of Aix-la-Chapelle had brought peace in Europe, France and Great Britain continued to struggle unofficially in the Ohio River valley and in upper New England. These clashes were the prelude to what is known in American history as the French and Indian War, which formally erupted in the summer of 1755.

Before war commenced again in Europe, however, a dramatic shift of alliances took place, in part the result of events in North America. The British king, George II (r. 1727–1760), who was also the Elector of Hanover, was concerned that the French might attack Hanover in response to the conflict in America. Frederick II of Prussia feared an alliance between Russia and Austria. In January 1756, Britain and Prussia signed the Convention of Westminster, a defensive alliance that prevented the entry of foreign troops into the German states. The convention meant that Great Britain, the ally of Austria since the wars of Louis XIV, had now joined forces with Austria's major eighteenth-century enemy.

The new alliance deeply troubled Maria Theresa, but it delighted her foreign minister, Prince Wenzel Anton Kaunitz (1711–1794). He had long thought an alliance with France was Austria's best chance of defeating Prussia. In May 1756, France and Austria signed a defensive alliance. Kaunitz had succeeded in completely reversing the direction of French foreign policy since the sixteenth century. France would now fight to restore Austrian supremacy in central Europe.

16.5.4 The Seven Years' War (1756–1763)

Britain and France had already been engaged in protracted conflict in North America. Now Frederick II precipitated a European war that extended that colonial rivalry.

16.5.4.1 FREDERICK THE GREAT OPENS HOSTILITIES In August 1756, Frederick II began what would become the **Seven Years' War** by invading the neighboring German state of Saxony. Frederick considered this to be a preemptive strike against a conspiracy by Saxony, Austria, and France to destroy Prussian power. The invasion itself, however, created the very destructive alliance that Frederick feared. In the spring of 1757, France and Austria formed a new alliance dedicated to the destruction of Prussia. Sweden, Russia, and many of the smaller German states joined them.

Two factors in addition to Frederick's skilled leadership saved Prussia. First, Britain furnished considerable financial aid. Second, in 1762, Empress Elizabeth of Russia (r. 1741–1762) died. Her successor, Tsar Peter III, greatly admired Frederick. Although Peter III was murdered the same year, he reigned long enough to make immediate peace with Prussia, thus relieving Frederick of one enemy and allowing him to hold off Austria and France. The Treaty of Hubertusburg of 1763 ended the continental conflict with no significant changes in prewar borders. The postwar balance of power, however, continued to tilt in Prussia's favor. After this war, Frederick II was called **Frederick the Great**. Prussia, formerly a small German state overshadowed by the Habsburgs, now firmly stood among the ranks of the great powers.

16.5.4.2 WILLIAM PITT'S STRATEGY FOR WINNING NORTH AMERICA The survival of Prussia was less impressive to the rest of Europe than were the victories of Great Britain in every theater of conflict. The architect of these victories was **William Pitt the Elder** (1708–1778), a person of colossal ego and administrative genius. Although he had previously criticized British involvement in Continental disputes, once he became secretary of state in charge of the war in 1757, he pumped huge sums into the coffers of Frederick the Great. He regarded the German conflict as a way to divert French resources and attention from the colonial struggle. He later boasted of having won America on the plains of Germany.

North America was the center of Pitt's real concern. Put simply, he wanted all of North America east of the Mississippi for Great Britain, and he came very close to getting it all. He sent more than 40,000 regular English and colonial troops against the French in Canada. Never had so many soldiers been devoted to colonial warfare. He achieved unprecedented cooperation with the American colonies, whose leaders realized they might finally defeat their French neighbors.

The French government was unwilling and unable to direct similar resources against the English in America. Their military administration was corrupt, the military and political commands in Canada were divided, and France could not adequately supply its North American forces. In September 1759, on the Plains of Abraham, overlooking the valley of the Saint Lawrence River at Quebec City, the British army under James Wolfe defeated the French under Louis Joseph de Montcalm. The French Empire in Canada was ending.

Pitt's colonial vision, however, extended beyond the Saint Lawrence valley and the Great Lakes basin. The major islands of the French West Indies fell to British fleets. Income from the sale of captured sugar helped finance the British war effort. British slave interests secured the bulk of the French slave trade for themselves. Between 1755 and 1760, the value of the French colonial trade fell by more than 80 percent. In India, the British forces under the command of Robert Clive defeated France's Indian allies in 1757 at the Battle of Plassey. This victory opened the way for the eventual conquest of Bengal in northeast India and later of the entire subcontinent by the British East India Company. Never had Great Britain or any other European power experienced such a complete worldwide military victory.

THE BEGINNING OF THE BRITISH EMPIRE IN INDIA This scene, painted by artist Edward Penny, shows Robert Clive receiving a sum of money from Siraj-ud-daulah, the Mughal Nawab of Bengal, for injured officers and soldiers at Plassey. Clive's victory in 1757 at the Battle of Plassey led to English domination of the Indian subcontinent for almost two centuries. Clive had won the battle largely through bribing many of the Nawab's troops and potential allies.
SOURCE: Erich Lessing/Art Resource, NY

16.5.4.3 THE TREATY OF PARIS OF 1763 The **Treaty of Paris** in 1763 reflected somewhat less of a victory than Britain had won on the battlefield. Pitt was no longer in office. The new king, George III (r. 1760–1820), and Pitt had quarreled over policy, and the minister had resigned. His replacement was the Earl of Bute (1713–1792), a favorite of the young monarch. Bute was responsible for the peace settlement. Britain received all of Canada, the Ohio River valley, and the eastern half of the Mississippi River valley. To Pitt's consternation, Britain returned Pondicherry and Chandernagore in India and the West Indian sugar islands of Guadeloupe and Martinique to the French. Nevertheless, with the British East India Company imposing its authority on weakened indigenous governments in India and large territorial holdings in North America, from this time until World War II, Great Britain was a world power, not just a European one.

The Seven Years' War had been a vast worldwide conflict. Tens of thousands of soldiers and sailors had been killed or wounded around the globe. At great internal sacrifice, Prussia had permanently wrested Silesia from Austria and had fundamentally undermined the integrity of the Holy Roman Empire. Habsburg power now depended largely on the dynasty's own domains—especially Hungary. France found its colonial dominions and influence substantially reduced. The Spanish Empire remained largely intact, but the British were more confident than ever that they could penetrate its markets.

The quarter century of warfare also caused a long series of domestic crises among the European powers. Defeat convinced many in France of the necessity for political and administrative reform. The financial burdens of the wars had astounded all participants. Every power had to increase its revenues to pay its war debt and finance its preparation for the next conflict. This search for revenue lead to far-ranging consequences in the British colonies in North America.

16.6 The American Revolution and Europe

What were the causes of the American Revolution?

The revolt of the British colonies in North America was an event in both transatlantic and European history. It marked the beginning of the end of European colonial domination of the American continents. This revolt that led eventually to revolution erupted from problems of revenue collection common to all the major powers after the Seven Years' War. The American Revolution also continued the conflict between France and Great Britain. French support of the colonists deepened the existing financial and administrative difficulties of the French monarchy.

SIGNING THE DECLARATION In this painting by John Trumbull, Thomas Jefferson (standing on the left) presents a draft of the Declaration of Independence to the head of the Second Continental Congress, John Hancock (seated on the right). Behind Jefferson stand the other members of the committee charged with writing the Declaration. The painting was completed in 1818 and installed in the Rotunda of the U.S. Capitol in 1826.
SOURCE: Library of Congress Prints and Photographs Division

KEY EVENTS IN BRITAIN AND AMERICA AT THE TIME OF THE AMERICAN REVOLUTION	
1760	George III becomes king
1763	Treaty of Paris concludes the Seven Years' War
1763	John Wilkes publishes issue number 45 of *The North Briton*
1764	Sugar Act
1765	Stamp Act
1766	Stamp Act repealed and Declaratory Act passed
1767	Townshend Acts
1768	Parliament refuses to seat John Wilkes after his election
1770	Lord North becomes George III's chief minister
1770	Boston Massacre
1773	Boston Tea Party
1774	Intolerable Acts
1774	First Continental Congress
1775	Second Continental Congress
1776	Declaration of Independence
1778	France enters the war on the side of America
1778	Yorkshire Association Movement founded
1781	British forces surrender at Yorktown
1783	Treaty of Paris concludes the American Revolution

16.6.1 Resistance to the Imperial Search for Revenue

After the Treaty of Paris of 1763, the British government faced two imperial problems. The first was the sheer cost of maintaining their empire, which the British believed they could no longer carry alone. The national debt had risen considerably, as had domestic taxation. Since the American colonies had been the chief beneficiaries of the conflict, the British felt it was rational for the colonies to now bear part of the cost of their protection and administration. The second problem was the vast expanse of new territory in North America that the British had to organize. This included all the land from the mouth of the Saint Lawrence River to the Mississippi River, with its French settlers and more importantly, its Native Americans. (See Map 16–3.)

The British drive for revenue began in 1764 with the passage of the Sugar Act, which attempted to produce more revenue from imports into the colonies by the collection of what was actually a lower tax. Smugglers who violated the law were to be tried in admiralty courts without

Map 16–3 NORTH AMERICA IN 1763

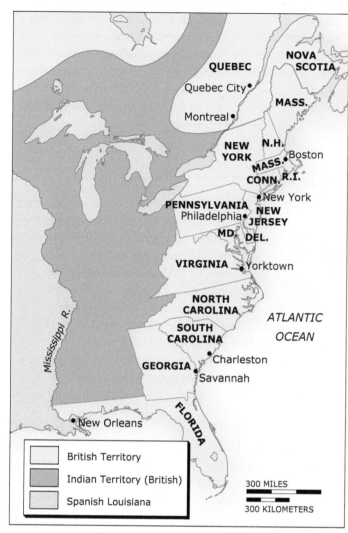

In 1763, the year of British victory over France, English colonies lay, as shown here, along the Atlantic seaboard. British difficulties in organizing the previous French territory in Canada and west of the Appalachian Mountains would contribute to the start of the American Revolution.

In 1766, Parliament repealed the Stamp Act, but through the Declaratory Act insisted it had the power to legislate for the colonies.

The Stamp Act crisis set the pattern for the next ten years. Parliament, under the leadership of a royal minister, would approve revenue or legislation for the colonies. The Americans would then resist by reasoned argument, economic pressure, and violence. Then the British would repeal the legislation, and the process would begin again. Each time, tempers on both sides became more frayed and positions more irreconcilable. With each clash, the colonists more fully developed their own thinking about political liberty.

16.6.2 The Crisis and Independence

In 1767, Charles Townshend (1725–1767), as Chancellor of the Exchequer, the British finance minister, led Parliament to pass a series of revenue acts relating to colonial imports. The colonists again resisted. The ministry sent over its own customs agents to administer the laws. To protect these new officers, the British sent troops to Boston in 1768. Predictable tensions resulted. In March 1770, British troops killed five citizens in an incident that came to be known in the colonies as the Boston Massacre. That same year, Parliament repealed all of the Townshend duties except the one on tea.

In May 1773, Parliament passed a new law relating to the sale of tea by the East India Company. The measure permitted the direct importation of tea into the American colonies. It actually lowered the price of tea while retaining the tax imposed without the colonists' consent. In some cities, the colonists refused to permit the unloading of the tea; in Boston, a shipload of tea was thrown into the harbor.

The British ministry of Lord North (1732–1792) was determined to assert the authority of Parliament over the colonies. During 1774, Parliament passed a series of laws known in American history as the **Intolerable Acts**. These measures closed the port of Boston, reorganized the government of Massachusetts, allowed troops to be quartered in private homes, and removed the trials of royal customs officials to England. The same year, the Quebec Act extended the boundaries of Quebec to include the Ohio River valley. The Americans regarded the Quebec Act as preventing their mode of self-government from spreading beyond the Appalachian Mountains.

During these years, citizens critical of British policy had established committees of correspondence throughout the colonies. They made the various sections of the eastern seaboard aware of common problems and encouraged united action. In September 1774, these committees organized the First Continental Congress in Philadelphia. This body hoped to persuade Parliament

juries. The next year, Parliament passed the **Stamp Act**, which taxed legal documents and other items such as newspapers. The British considered these taxes legal, because Parliament had approved the decision to collect them, and fair, because the money was to be spent in the colonies.

The Americans responded that they alone, through their colonial assemblies, had the right to tax themselves and that they were not represented in Parliament. They feared that if their colonial government was financed from outside, they would lose control over it. In October 1765, the Stamp Act Congress met in America and drew up a protest to the crown. Groups known as the Sons of Liberty roused disorder in the colonies, particularly in Massachusetts. The colonists agreed to refuse to import British goods.

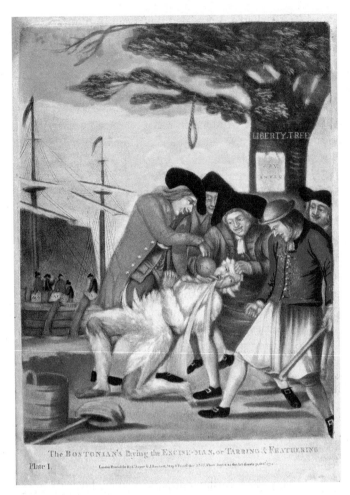

VICTIMIZATION OF THE KING'S TAX COLLECTOR WITH TAR AND FEATHERS Many Americans fiercely objected to the British Parliament's attempts to tax the colonies. This print of a British tax collector being tarred and feathered warned officials of what could happen to them if they tried to collect these taxes.
SOURCE: Art Resource, NY

to restore self-government in the colonies and abandon its direct supervision of colonial affairs. Conciliation, however, was not forthcoming. In April and June 1775, colonists and British regular troops clashed in the Battles of Lexington and Concord and the Battle of Bunker Hill. The colonial assemblies began to meet under their own authority rather than under that of the king.

The Second Continental Congress gathered in May 1775. While it still sought conciliation with Britain, it also began to conduct the government of the colonies. By August 1775, George III had declared the colonies in rebellion. During the winter, **Thomas Paine** (1737–1809) published *Common Sense*, a pamphlet that galvanized public opinion in favor of separation from Great Britain. A colonial army and navy were organized. In April 1776, the Continental Congress opened American ports to the trade of all nations. On July 4, 1776, the Continental Congress adopted the

Declaration of Independence. Early in 1778, Benjamin Franklin (1706–1790) persuaded the French government to support the rebellion, which widened the struggle into a European conflict. In 1779, the Spanish also joined the war against Britain. The American Revolution continued until 1781, when the forces of George Washington defeated those of Lord Cornwallis at Yorktown. The 1783 Treaty of Paris concluded the conflict, and the thirteen American colonies established their independence.

16.6.3 American Political Ideas

The political ideas of the American colonists had stemmed from the struggle of the seventeenth-century English aristocrats and gentry against the absolutism of the Stuart monarchs. The American colonists looked to the English Revolution of 1688 as the source of many of their own fundamental political liberties. The colonists claimed that, through the measures imposed from 1763 to 1776, George III and the British Parliament were attacking those liberties and dissolving the moral and political allegiance that had formerly united the two peoples. Consequently, the colonists believed that what had justified an aristocratic rebellion also supported their own popular revolution.

These Whig political ideas, largely derived from the writings of John Locke, were, however, only a part of the English ideological heritage that affected the Americans. Throughout the eighteenth century, they had become familiar with a series of British political writers called the **Commonwealthmen**, whose republican political ideas had their intellectual roots in the most radical thought of the puritan revolution. During the early eighteenth century, these writers, the most influential of whom were John Trenchard (1662–1723) and Thomas Gordon (d. 1750) in *Cato's Letters* (1720–1723), had relentlessly criticized the government patronage and parliamentary management of Sir Robert Walpole and his successors. They argued that such government was corrupt and undermined liberty, that parliamentary taxation was simply a means of financing political corruption, and that standing armies were instruments of tyranny. In Great Britain, this republican political tradition had only a marginal impact because most British subjects regarded themselves as the freest people in the world. Colonists, however, often accepted the radical books and pamphlets at face value. The policy of Great Britain toward America following the Treaty of Paris of 1763 had made many colonists believe the worst fears of the Commonwealthmen were coming true. Political events coinciding with the accession of George III to the throne appeared to confirm these fears.

16.6.4 Events in Great Britain

George III also believed the king should choose his own ministers and that Parliament should function under royal, rather than aristocratic, management. When William Pitt resigned in 1761, George ignored the great Whig families that had run the country since 1715 and appointed the Earl of Bute as his first minister.

Between 1761 and 1770, George tried one minister after another, but each, in turn, failed to gain enough support from the various factions in the House of Commons. Finally, in 1770, he turned to Lord North, who remained the king's first minister until 1782. Powerful Whig families and other political spokespersons claimed that George III was attempting to impose a tyranny, and was seeking to curb the power of a particular group of the aristocracy. George III certainly was seeking to restore more royal influence to the government of Great Britain, but he was not trying to make himself a tyrant.

16.6.4.1 THE CHALLENGE OF JOHN WILKES
John Wilkes (1725–1797), a London political radical and member of Parliament, published a newspaper called *The North Briton*. In issue number 45 (April 1763), Wilkes strongly criticized Earl Bute's handling of peace negotiations with France. Wilkes was arrested under a general warrant issued by the secretary of state. He pleaded the privileges of a member of Parliament and was released. Despite widespread popular support of Wilkes, and although they concluded that the general warrant had been illegal, the House of Commons ruled that issue number 45 of *The North Briton* constituted seditious libel, and it expelled Wilkes. He soon fled the country and was outlawed.

In 1768, Wilkes returned to England and was reelected to Parliament, but the House of Commons, under the influence of George III's friends, refused to seat him even after he was elected three more times. Large, unruly demonstrations of shopkeepers, artisans, and small-property owners supported Wilkes as did aristocratic politicians who wished to humiliate George III. "Wilkes and Liberty" became the slogan of political radicals and many noble opponents of the monarch. Wilkes was finally seated in 1774, after having become the lord mayor of London.

The American colonists followed these developments closely. Events in Britain confirmed their fears about a monarchical and parliamentary conspiracy against liberty. The Wilkes affair displayed the arbitrary power of the monarch, the corruption of the House of Commons, and the contempt of both for popular electors. That same monarch and Parliament were attempting to overturn the traditional relationship of Great Britain to its colonies by imposing parliamentary taxes. The same government had then landed troops in Boston, changed the government of Massachusetts, and undermined the traditional right of jury trial. All these events confirmed the image of political tyranny that had developed over the years in the minds of politically engaged colonists.

16.6.4.2 MOVEMENT FOR PARLIAMENTARY REFORM
The political influences between America and Britain operated both ways. The colonial demand for no taxation without representation and the criticism of the British system of representation struck at the core of the eighteenth-century British political structure. British subjects at home who were no more directly represented in the House of Commons than were the American colonists could adopt the colonial arguments. The colonial questioning of the tax-levying authority of the House of Commons was related to the protest of John Wilkes. Both the colonists and Wilkes challenged the power of the monarch and the authority of Parliament, appealed to popular opinion and popular demonstrations, and protested the power of a largely self-selected aristocratic political body.

The American colonists also demonstrated to Europe how a politically restive people in the Old Regime could fight tyranny and protect political liberty. They established revolutionary, but orderly, political bodies that could function outside the existing political framework: the congress and the convention. These began with the Stamp Act Congress of 1765 and culminated in the Constitutional Convention of 1787. The legitimacy of these congresses and conventions lay not in existing law, but in the alleged consent of the governed. This approach represented a new way to found a government.

16.6.4.3 THE YORKSHIRE ASSOCIATION MOVEMENT
By the close of the 1770s, many in Britain resented the mismanagement of the American war, the high taxes, and Lord North's ministry. In northern England in 1778, Christopher Wyvil (1740–1822), a landowner and retired clergyman, organized the **Yorkshire Association Movement**. Property owners, or freeholders, of Yorkshire met in a mass meeting to demand moderate changes in the corrupt system of parliamentary elections. They organized corresponding societies elsewhere. The Association Movement was a popular attempt to establish an extralegal institution to reform the government.

Parliament was not insensitive to the demands of the Association Movement. In April 1780, the Commons passed a resolution that called for lessening the power of the crown. In 1782, Parliament adopted a measure that abolished some patronage. In 1783, shifts in Parliament obliged Lord North to form a ministry with Charles James Fox (1749–1806), a longtime critic of George III, to the king's distress.

In 1783, the king approached William Pitt the Younger (1759–1806), son of the victorious war minister, to manage the House of Commons. During the election of 1784, Pitt received immense patronage support from the crown and constructed a House of Commons favorable to the monarch. Thereafter, Pitt sought to formulate trade policies that would give his ministry broad popularity. In 1785, he attempted one measure of modest parliamentary reform. When it failed, the young prime minister, only twenty-four at the time of his appointment, abandoned the cause of reform.

By the mid-1780s, George III had achieved part of what he had sought since 1761. Economically, British trade with America after independence had actually increased. Domestically, George III had reasserted the influence of the monarchy in political affairs. The cost of his years of dominance had been high, however. His own mental illness, which would eventually require a regency, weakened royal power. On both sides of the Atlantic, the issue of popular sovereignty had been widely discussed. The American colonies had been lost.

16.6.5 Broader Impact of the American Revolution

The Americans—through their state constitutions, the Articles of Confederation, and the federal Constitution adopted in 1788—had demonstrated to Europe the possibility of government without kings and hereditary nobilities. They had established the example of a nation where the highest political authority was held by written documents based on popular consent and popular sovereignty rather than on divine law, natural law, tradition, or the will of kings. The political novelty of these assertions should not be ignored.

As the crisis with Britain unfolded during the 1760s and 1770s, the American colonists had come to see themselves first as preserving traditional English liberties against the tyrannical crown and corrupt Parliament and then as developing a new sense of liberty. By the mid-1770s, the colonists had rejected monarchical government and embraced republican political ideals. Once a constitution was adopted, they would insist on a Bill of Rights specifically protecting a series of civil liberties. The Americans would reject the aristocratic social hierarchy that had existed in the colonies and embrace democratic ideals—even if the franchise remained limited. They would assert the equality of white male citizens not only before the law but also in ordinary social relations. For white men, they would also reject social status based on birth and inheritance and demand liberty for all citizens to improve their social standing and economic lot by engaging in free commercial activity. They did not free their slaves, nor did they address issues of the rights of women or of Native Americans. Yet in their revolution, the American colonists of the eighteenth century produced a society that would eventually expand the circle of political and social liberty. In all these respects, the American Revolution was a genuinely radical movement, whose influence would widen as Americans moved across the Continent and as other peoples began to question traditional modes of European government.

The Chapter in Perspective

During the sixteenth and seventeenth centuries, the West European maritime powers established extensive commercial, mercantile empires in North and South America. The point of these empires was to extract wealth and to establish commercial advantage for the colonial power. Spain had the largest of these empires, but by the end of the seventeenth century, Britain and France had also each established a major American presence. As a vast plantation economy emerged, significant portions of these American empires became economically dependent on slave labor, drawn from the forced importation of Africans. Through this large slave labor force, African linguistic, social, and religious influences became major cultural factors in these regions.

During the eighteenth century, the great European powers engaged in warfare over their American empires and over their power in India. These colonial wars became entangled in dynastic wars in central and eastern Europe and resulted in worldwide mid-century European conflict.

In the New World, Britain, France, and Spain battled for commercial dominance. France and Britain also clashed in India. By the third quarter of the century, Britain had ousted France from its major holdings in North America and from any significant presence in India. Spain, though no longer a military power of the first order, had managed to maintain its vast colonial empire in Latin America and much of its monopoly over the region's trade.

On the Continent, France, Austria, and Prussia collided over conflicting territorial and dynastic ambitions. Britain used the continental wars to divert France from the colonial arena. With British aid, Prussia had emerged in 1763 as a major continental power. Austria had lost territory to Prussia, while France had accumulated great debt.

The mid-century conflicts, in turn, caused major changes in all the European states. Each of the monarchies needed more money and tried to govern itself more efficiently. This problem led Britain to attempt to tax the North American colonies, which resulted in a revolution and the colonies' independence. Already deeply in debt, the French monarchy aided the Americans, fell into a deeper financial crisis, and soon clashed sharply with the nobility as royal ministers tried to find new revenues. That clash eventually unleashed the French Revolution. Spain moved to administer its Latin American empire more efficiently, which increased revolutionary discontent in the early nineteenth century. In preparation for future wars, the rulers of Prussia, Austria, and Russia pursued a mode of activist government known as Enlightened Absolutism. In that regard, the mid-eighteenth-century wars set in motion most of the major political developments of the next half-century.

The Chapter in Review

Review Questions

1. What were the fundamental ideas associated with mercantile theory? Did they work? Which European country was most successful in establishing a mercantile empire? Least successful? Why?
2. What were the main points of conflict between Britain and France in North America, the West Indies, and India? How did the triangles of trade function among the Americas, Europe, and Africa?
3. How was the Spanish colonial empire in the Americas organized and managed? What changes did the Bourbon monarchs institute in the Spanish Empire?
4. What was the nature of slavery in the Americas? How was it linked to the economies of the Americas, Europe, and Africa? Why was the plantation system unprecedented? How did the plantation system contribute to the inhumane treatment of slaves?
5. What were the results of the Seven Years' War?
6. How did European ideas and political developments influence the American colonists? How did their actions, in turn, influence Europe? What was the relationship between American colonial radicals and contemporary political radicals in Great Britain?

Key Terms

Commonwealthmen British political writers whose radical republican ideas influenced the American revolutionaries.

creoles (KRAY-ol-ez) Persons of Spanish descent born in the Spanish colonies.

Frederick the Great (r. 1740–1786) Frederick II, king of Prussia; reorganized the Prussian army, initiated the Seven Years' War, and made Prussia one of the great powers.

Intolerable Acts Measures passed by the British Parliament in 1774 to punish the colony of Massachusetts and strengthen Britain's authority in the colonies, which provoked colonial opposition and led immediately to the American Revolution.

Maria Theresa (r. 1740–1780) Habsburg ruler who preserved the Habsburg Empire despite the Prussian seizure of Silesia.

mercantilism Close government control of the economy that maximizes exports and accumulates as many precious metals as possible in order to enable the state to defend its economic and political interests.

"Middle Passage" The stage of the Atlantic slave trade where millions of Africans were transported across the ocean to the New World.

peninsulares (pen-in-SUE-la-rez) Persons born in Spain who settled in the Spanish colonies.

Philip V (r. 1700–1746) The first member of the Bourbon monarchs to rule as the king of Spain.

Queen Isabella of Castile (r. 1474–1504) The monarch who commissioned Columbus's 1492 voyage to the New World.

Seven Years' War (1756–1763) A global conflict fought between the kingdom of Great Britain and the kingdom of France, and involving all the great powers in Europe.

Stamp Act (1765) An act of the Parliament of Great Britain that imposed a direct tax on the American colonies.

Thomas Paine (1737–1809) One of the Founding Fathers of the United States, who wrote *Common Sense*, one of the most influential pamphlets at the start of the American Revolution.

Treaty of Paris The peace agreement in 1763 that was signed at the close of the Seven Years' War between France and Great Britain, which recognized Great Britain as a world power.

Treaty of Utrecht The series of individual treaties in 1713 that established the Peace of Utrecht at the close of the War of the Spanish Succession.

War of Jenkins's Ear (1739–1748) The conflict waged by Britain against Spain to prevent Spanish intervention in their trade.

William Pitt the Elder (1708–1778) The British statesman best known as the leader in charge of Britain during the Seven Years' War.

Yorkshire Association Movement A popular attempt by property owners, or freeholders, to reform the government in Britain.

Notes

1. Walter Dorn, *Competition for Empire, 1740–1763* (New York: Harper, 1940), p. 266.
2. John Thornton, *Africa and the Africans in the Making of the Atlantic World, 1400–1800*, 2nd ed. (Cambridge, UK: Cambridge University Press, 1998), p. 140.
3. Vincent Brown, "Eating the Dead: Consumption and Regeneration in the History of Sugar," *Food and Foodways* 16 (2008), 117.

The Columbian Exchange: Disease, Animals, and Agriculture

THE EUROPEAN ENCOUNTER with the Americas produced remarkable ecological transformations that have shaped the world to the present moment. The same ships that carried Europeans and Africans to the New World also transported animals, plants, and germs that had never appeared in the Americas. There was a similar transport back to Europe and Africa. Alfred Crosby, the leading historian of this process, has named this cross-continental flow "the Columbian exchange." Many tragedies arose from the encounter between the people of the Americas and those of Europe, as well as from the forging of new nations and civilizations in the Americas.

Diseases Enter the Americas

With the exception of a few ships that had gone astray or, in the case of the Vikings, that had gone in search of new lands, the American continents had been biologically separated from Europe, Africa, and Asia for tens of thousands of years. In the Americas no native animals could serve as major beasts of burden, except for the llama, which could not transport more than about a hundred pounds. Nor did animals constitute a major source of protein for Native Americans, whose diets consisted largely of maize, beans, peppers, yams, and potatoes. Moreover, it also appears that native peoples had lived on the long-isolated American continents without experiencing major epidemics.

By the second voyage of Columbus in 1493, that picture began to change in remarkable ways. On his return voyage to Hispaniola and other islands of the Caribbean, Columbus brought a number of animals and plants that were previously unknown to the New World. The men on all his voyages and those on subsequent European voyages also carried diseases novel to the Americas.

Diseases transported by Europeans ultimately accounted for the conquest of the people of the Americas as much as advanced European weaponry. Much controversy surrounds the question of the actual size of the populations of Native Americans in the Caribbean islands, Mexico, Peru, and the North Atlantic coast. All accounts present those populations as quite significant, with those of Mexico numbering many millions. Yet in the first two centuries after the encounter, wherever Europeans went either as settlers or as conquerors, extremely large numbers of Native Americans

died from diseases they had never before encountered. The most deadly disease was smallpox, which killed millions of people. Beyond the devastation wrought by that disease, bubonic plague, typhoid, typhus, influenza, measles, chicken pox, whooping cough, malaria, and diphtheria produced deadly results in more localized epidemics. For example, an unknown disease, but quite possibly typhus, caused major losses among the Native Americans of New England between approximately 1616 and 1619.

FIRST IMPRESSIONS Within one year of Columbus's encounter with the Americas, the event had been captured in this woodcut (c. 1493). Columbus's several voyages, and those of later Europeans as well, not only introduced European warfare but also began a vast ecological exchange of diseases, animals, and agriculture between the Old and New Worlds.
SOURCE: Library of Congress

Native Americans appear to have been highly susceptible to these diseases because, with no earlier exposure, they lacked immunity. Wherever such outbreaks are recorded, Europeans either contracted or died from them at a much lower rate than the Native Americans. These diseases would continue to victimize Native Americans at a higher rate than Americans of European descent through the end of the nineteenth century, when smallpox and measles still killed large numbers of the Plains Indian peoples of North America.

Although many historical and medical questions still surround the subject, it appears likely that syphilis, which became a rampant venereal disease in Europe at the close of the fifteenth century and eventually spread around the globe, was first transmitted to Europe by the returning crew on Columbus's ships. It seems to have been an entirely new disease, spawned by a mutation when the causal agent for yaws migrated from the Americas to new climatic settings in Europe. Until the discovery of penicillin in the 1940s, syphilis remained a major concern of public health throughout the world.

Animals and Agriculture

The introduction of European livestock to the Americas quite simply revolutionized the agriculture of two continents. The most important new animals were pigs, cattle, horses, goats, and sheep. Once transported to the New World, these animals multiplied at unprecedented rates. The place where this first occurred was in the islands of the Caribbean, during the first forty years of Spanish settlement and exploitation. This occurrence led to the later Spanish conquest of both Mexico and Peru by providing the Spanish with strong breeds of animals, especially horses, acclimated to the Americas when they set out to conquer the mainland of South America.

The horse became first the animal of conquest and then the animal of colonial Latin American culture. Native Americans had no experience with such large animals that would obey the will of a human rider. Mounted Spanish horsemen struck fear into these people, and for good reason. After the conquest, however, the Americas from Mexico southward became the largest horse-breeding region of the world, with ranches raising thousands of animals. Horses became relatively cheap, and even Native Americans could acquire them. By the nineteenth century, the possession of horses would allow the Plains Indians of North America to resist the advance of their white attackers.

The flourishing of pigs, cattle, and sheep allowed a vast economic exploitation of the Americas. These animals produced enormous quantities of hides and wool. Their presence in such large numbers also meant the Americas from the sixteenth century through the present would support a diet more plentiful in animal protein than anywhere else in the world.

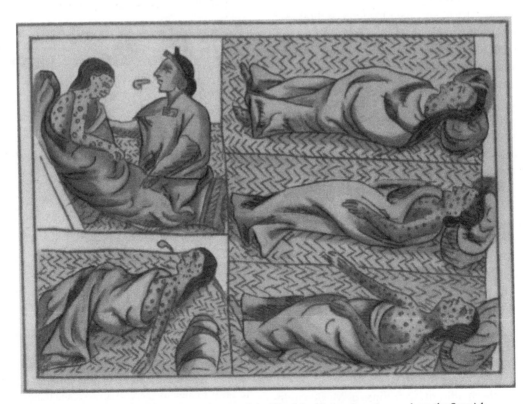

A BIOLOGICAL HOLOCAUST Nothing destroyed the life of the Native Americans whom the Spanish encountered as the introduction of smallpox. With no immunity to this new disease, millions of Native Americans died of smallpox during the sixteenth and seventeenth centuries.
SOURCE: Everett Historical/Shutterstock

Europeans also brought their own plants to the New World, including peaches, oranges, grapes, melons, bananas, rice, onions, radishes, and various green vegetables. Socially, for three centuries the most significant of these was sugarcane, whose cultivation created the major demand for slavery throughout the transatlantic plantation economy. Nutritionally, European wheat would, over the course of time, allow the Americas not only to feed themselves, but also to export large amounts of grain throughout the world. This American production of wheat on the great plains of the two continents contrasted sharply with the difficulty Europeans faced raising grain in the northern and northeastern parts of the Continent, particularly in Russia.

No significant animals from the Americas, except the turkey, actually came to be raised in Europe. The Americas did send to Europe, however, a series of plants that eventually changed the European diet: maize, potatoes, sweet potatoes, peppers, beans, manioc (tapioca), peanuts, squash, pumpkin, pineapple, cocoa, and tomatoes. All of these, to a greater or lesser degree, eventually entered the diet of Europeans and of European settlers and their descendants in the Americas. Maize and the potato, however, had the most transforming impact. Each of these two crops became a major staple in European farming, as well as in the European diet. Both crops grow rapidly, supplying food quickly and steadily if not attacked by disease. Tobacco, we should note, originated in the Americas, too.

Maize was established as a crop in Spain within thirty years of the country's encounter with the New World. A century and a half later it was commonplace in the Spanish diet, and its cultivation had spread to Italy and France. Maize produced more grain for the seed and farming effort than wheat did. Throughout Europe, maize was associated primarily with fodder for animals. As early as the eighteenth century, travelers noted the presence of polenta in the peasant diet, and other forms of maize dishes spread.

The Spanish encountered the potato only when Pizarro conquered Peru, where it was a major part of the Native American food supply. It was adopted slowly by Europeans because it needed to be raised in climates more temperate than those of Spain and the Mediterranean. It appears to have become a major peasant food in Scotland, Ireland, and parts of Germany during the eighteenth century. It became more widely cultivated elsewhere in Europe only after new strains of the plant were imported from Chile in the late nineteenth century. In the middle of the seventeenth century, Irish peasants were urged to cultivate the potato as a major source of cheap nutrition that could grow in quantity on a small plot. The food shortages arising from the wars of Louis XIV and then during the eighteenth century led farmers in northern Europe to adopt the potato for similar reasons. It was nutrient insurance against failure of the grain harvest. There is good reason to believe the cultivation of the potato was one of the major causes of the population increase in eighteenth- and nineteenth-century Europe. It was the quintessential food of the poor. By the mid-nineteenth century, Irish peasants had become almost wholly dependent on the potato as a source of food. In the middle of the 1840s, an American parasite infected the Irish potato crop. The result of the failure of the crop and misguided policymaking was the death of hundreds of thousands of Irish peasants and the migration of still more hundreds of thousands to the Americas and elsewhere in the world.

Questions

1. Define the Columbian exchange.
2. What was the impact of European diseases on the Americas? Why was the impact so profound?
3. Why could so many European crops grow well in the Americas?
4. What was the cultural impact of animals taken from Europe to the Americas?
5. How did food from the Americas change the diet of Europe and then later, as Europeans immigrated, the diet of the entire world?

Chapter 17
The Age of Enlightenment: Eighteenth-Century Thought

AN ENLIGHTENMENT SALON The salon of Madame Marie Thérèse Geoffrin (1699–1777) was one of the most important Parisian gathering spots for Enlightenment writers during the mid-eighteenth century. Well-connected women such as Madame Geoffrin were instrumental in helping the *philosophes* they patronized bring their ideas to the attention of influential people in French society and politics.
SOURCE: RMN-Grand Palais/Art Resource, NY

Contents and Focus Questions

The Chapter in Brief

OVER THE COURSE of the eighteenth century, the expanding literate sectors of European society became increasingly convinced that the human condition could be improved through science, education, philosophy, economic growth, and political reform. This attitude is now commonplace, but it came into its own only after 1700. It represents one of the primary continuing intellectual inheritances from the age of Enlightenment.

The Enlightenment was inspired by the scientific revolution, but it was a self-conscious movement in its own right. Unlike the scientific revolution, which came to be called by that name only in the twentieth century, the Enlightenment was named by its participants, who discussed vigorously what sorts of improvement were most enlightening. While it had its roots in the seventeenth century, the Enlightenment did not reach its height until the mid-eighteenth century. By 1784, when the German philosopher Immanuel Kant defined Enlightenment as "man's emergence from his self-imposed immaturity," the term was well known across the Continent. From 1740 to the French Revolution, enlightened thinkers and writers challenged traditional intellectual and ecclesiastical authority in the name of reason. They believed that human beings could comprehend physical nature and use it to achieve material and moral improvement, economic growth, and administrative reform. They advocated agricultural improvement, increased commerce and consumption, and the application of innovative rational methods to traditional social and economic practices. The rationality of the physical universe became a standard against which they measured and criticized the customs and traditions of society. In religious matters, they generally opposed the claims of religious privilege made by state-supported established churches, whether Roman Catholic or Protestant, and advocated a policy of toleration. As the criticisms of Enlightenment writers penetrated every corner of contemporary society, politics, and religious opinion, the spirit of innovation and improvement came to characterize modern European society.

Although many participants in the Enlightenment looked to France and Britain as models, the movement found adherents in cities and towns across the Continent. Their common interest in reason and reform transcended national boundaries as well as the divide between republican and monarchist political systems. Some of the ideas and outlooks of the Enlightenment had a direct impact on rulers in central and eastern Europe. These rulers, whose policies came to be called **enlightened absolutism**, sought to centralize their authority to reform their countries. They often attempted to restructure religious institutions and to sponsor economic growth. The confidence with which enlightened thinkers, or *philosophes*, believed they could describe the entire universe made it possible for one German writer to publish a book in 1719 with the typically ambitious title *Rational Thoughts on God, the World, the Human Soul and All Things in General*.

The Enlightenment had its limits. Enlightened absolutists pursued some military and foreign policies in direct opposition to Enlightenment ideals. Enlightened thinkers throughout Europe continued to believe strongly in social hierarchies that left little room for the equality of women or people from outside of Europe. Nonetheless, both the Enlightenment writers and the absolutist monarchs inspired by them were forces of modernization in European life.

17.1 Formative Influences on the Enlightenment

What was the intellectual and social background of the Enlightenment?

The chief factors that fostered the ideas of the Enlightenment and the call for reform throughout Europe were, among others: the Newtonian worldview; the political stability and commercial prosperity of Great Britain after 1688; the need for administrative and economic reform in France after the wars of Louis XIV; the consolidation of what is known as *print culture* and the increased opportunities for interaction with peoples from other continents.

17.1.1 Newton and Locke

Isaac Newton (1642–1727) and **John Locke** (1632–1704) were the major intellectual forerunners of the Enlightenment. Newton's formulation of the law of universal gravitation exemplified the newly perceived power of the human mind. Newtonian physics had portrayed a pattern of mechanical and mathematical rationality in the physical world. During the eighteenth century, thinkers from a variety of backgrounds applied Newton's insight to society. If nature was rational, they reasoned, society, too, should be organized rationally. Furthermore, Newton had encouraged natural philosophers to approach the study of nature directly and to avoid metaphysics and supernaturalism. He had insisted on the use of empirical experience to check rational speculation. This emphasis on concrete experience became a key feature of Enlightenment thought.

VOLTAIRE'S INSPIRATION The frontispiece to Voltaire's *Elements of the Philosophy of Newton* (1738) shows Voltaire writing by a light deflected from a celestial Newton by a woman, his muse and lover, Émilie Du Châtelet. Du Châtelet helped Voltaire work through and come to understand Newton's *Principia Mathematica* while working on her own translation of it.
SOURCE: Culture Club/Getty Images

Newton's physics and Locke's psychology provided the theoretical basis for a reformist approach to society. The domestic stability of Great Britain after the revolution of 1688 was a living example of a society in which, to many contemporaries, enlightened reforms appeared to benefit everyone. England permitted religious toleration to all except Unitarians and Roman Catholics, and even they were not actively persecuted. Relative freedom of the press and free speech prevailed. The authority of the monarchy was limited, and political sovereignty resided in Parliament. The courts protected citizens from arbitrary government action. The army was small. Furthermore, the domestic economic life of Great Britain displayed far less regulation than that of France or other continental nations, and English commerce flourished. As reformist observers on the Continent noted, these liberal policies had produced neither disorder nor instability, but instead economic prosperity, political stability, and a loyal citizenry.

This view may have been idealized, but England was nonetheless significantly freer than any other European monarchy at the time. Many writers of the continental Enlightenment contrasted what they regarded as the wise, progressive features of English life with the absence of religious toleration, the extensive literary censorship, the possibility of arbitrary arrest, the overregulation of the economy, and the influence of aristocratic military values in their own nations and most particularly in France.

17.1.2 The Emergence of a Print Culture

The Enlightenment flourished in a **print culture**, that is, a culture in which books, journals, newspapers, and pamphlets had achieved a status of their own. During the eighteenth century, the volume of printed material—books, journals, magazines, and daily newspapers—increased sharply throughout Europe. Prose came to be valued as highly as poetry, and the novel emerged as a distinct literary genre.

KEY WORKS OF THE ENLIGHTENMENT	
1687	Newton's *Principia Mathematica*
1690	Locke's *Essay Concerning Human Understanding*
1696	Toland's *Christianity Not Mysterious*
1719	Wolff's *Rational Thoughts on God, the World, the Human Soul and All Things in General*
1721	Montesquieu's *Persian Letters*
1733	Voltaire's *Letters on the English*
1738	Voltaire's *Elements of the Philosophy of Newton*
1748	Montesquieu's *Spirit of the Laws*
1748	Hume's *Inquiry into Human Nature*, with the chapter "Of Miracles"
1750	Rousseau's *Discourse on the Moral Effects of the Arts and Sciences*
1751	First volume of the *Encyclopedia*, edited by Diderot
1755	Rousseau's *Discourse on the Origin of Inequality*
1759	Voltaire's *Candide*
1762	Rousseau's *Social Contract* and *Émile*
1763	Voltaire's *Treatise on Tolerance*
1764	Voltaire's *Philosophical Dictionary*
1764	Beccaria's *On Crimes and Punishments*
1776	Gibbon's *Decline and Fall of the Roman Empire*
1776	Smith's *Wealth of Nations*
1779	Lessing's *Nathan the Wise*
1783	Mendelssohn's *Jerusalem; or, On Ecclesiastical Power and Judaism*
1784	Kant's *"What Is Enlightenment?"*
1792	Wollstonecraft's *Vindication of the Rights of Woman*
1793	Kant's *Religion within the Limits of Reason Alone*

One of the driving forces behind this expansion of printed materials was the increase in literacy that occurred across Europe. Significantly more people, especially in the urban centers of Western and central Europe, could read. As a result, the printed word became the chief vehicle for communicating information and ideas and would remain so until the electronic revolution of today.

A growing concern with everyday life and material concerns—with secular as opposed to religious issues—accompanied this increase of printed forms. Toward the end of the seventeenth century, half the books published in Paris were religious; by the 1780s, only about 10 percent were. An English journal observed unhappily in 1790: "Novels spring into existence like insects on the banks of the Nile; and, if we may be indulged in another comparison, cover the shelves of circulating libraries, as locusts crowd the fields of Asia. Their great and growing number is a serious evil; for, in general, they exhibit delusive views of human life; and while they amuse, frequently they poison the mind."[1] While people criticized the moral influence of the novel, they did not deny its influence.

Books were not inexpensive in the eighteenth century, but they, and the ideas they conveyed, circulated in a variety of ways to reach a broad public. Private and public libraries grew in number, allowing single copies to reach many readers. Authors might also publish the same material in different formats—first in serial form in newspapers or journals, and later collected together in a book.

Within both aristocratic and middle-class society, people were increasingly expected to be familiar with books and secular ideas. Popular publications fostered the value of polite conversation and the reading of books. Coffeehouses became centers for discussing writing and ideas. (See the "Encountering the Past" sidebar on coffeehouses, which follows below.) The lodges of Freemasons were also sites for discussing secular ideas and secular books.

The expanding market for printed matter allowed writers to earn a living from their work for the first time, making authorship an occupation. Parisian ladies who hosted fashionable salons sought out popular writers. Some writers, notably Alexander Pope (1688–1744) in England and Voltaire in France, grew wealthy, providing an example for their young colleagues. Challenging older aristocratic values, the new print culture and status of authors were based on merit and commercial competition, not heredity and patronage.

A division, however, soon emerged between high and low literary culture. Successful authors of the Enlightenment addressed monarchs, nobles, the upper middle classes, and professional groups, and they were read and accepted in these upper levels of society. Other aspiring authors found social and economic disappointment. They lived marginally, writing professionally for whatever newspaper or journal would pay for their work. Many of these lesser writers grew resentful, blaming a corrupt society for their lack of success. They often espoused radical ideas or took moderate Enlightenment ideas to radical extremes, bitterly transmitting them in this form to their audience.

Robespierre wrote a number of unsuccessful essays on political theory; while in 1789, on the eve of the Revolution, Sainte-Just anonymously published *Organt, Poem in Twenty Cantos,* a would-be epic poem against "monarchs, nobles and the upper classes." Before being beheaded themselves,

Robespierre and Sainte-Just managed to execute tens of thousands of people, including the king of France, Louis XVI, and other members of the royal family. Even more people were dispossessed and condemned to jail without a fair trial. According to present-day research and statistics, more than 40,000 people were summarily executed in those years, while many more died in jail due to illness and abuse.

An expanding, literate public and the growing influence of secular printed materials created a new and increasingly influential social force called *public opinion.* This force—the collective effect on political and social life of views circulated in print and discussed in the home, the workplace, and centers of leisure—seems not to have existed before the middle of the eighteenth century. Books and newspapers could have thousands of readers, who in effect supported the writers whose works they bought by discussing their ideas and circulating them widely. The writers, in turn, had to answer only to their readers. The result changed the cultural and political climate in Europe. In 1775, a new member of the French Academy declared:

> A tribunal has arisen independent of all powers and that all powers respect, that appreciates all talents, that pronounces on all people of merit. And in an enlightened century, in a century in which each citizen can speak to the entire nation by way of print, those who have a talent for instructing men and a gift for moving them—in a word, men of letters—are, amid the public dispersed, what the orators of Rome and Athens were in the middle of the public assembled.[2]

Governments could no longer operate wholly in secret or with disregard to the larger public sphere. They, as well as their critics, had to explain and discuss their views and policies openly.

Continental European governments sensed the political power of the new print culture. They initially regulated the book trade, censored books and newspapers, confiscated offending titles, and imprisoned offending authors. But the eventual expansion of freedom of the press represented also an expansion of print culture—with its independent readers, authors, and publishers—along with the challenges it posed to traditional intellectual, social, and political authorities.

17.2 The *Philosophes*

Who were the *philosophes*?

The writers and critics who flourished in the expanding print culture and who championed reform and toleration were known as the *philosophes.* Not usually philosophers in a formal sense, but more frequently literary figures, economists, or historians, the *philosophes* sought to apply the rules of reason, criticism, and common sense to nearly all the major institutions, economic practices, and exclusivist religious policies of the day. The most famous *philosophes*

Encountering the Past

Coffeehouses and Enlightenment

THE IDEAS OF the Enlightenment spread through not only books and journals but also public conversation. These ideas took on a life of their own in public discussions in a new popular institution of European social life—the coffeehouse. Coffee, originally imported to Europe from the Ottoman Empire, is the chief Turkish contribution to the Western diet. Coffeehouses had long existed in the Muslim world, encouraged by the Islamic prohibition on alcoholic drink. The first European coffeehouse appeared in Venice in the 1640s, and the first coffeehouse in Vienna opened its doors in 1683 with coffee left behind when the Turks abandoned their siege of the city.

By the mid-eighteenth century, thousands of coffeehouses dotted European cities and towns. They varied tremendously in atmosphere and clientele, from coffeehouses like Tom and Moll King's that offered "late-night rakish carousing and prostitution" to others more like libraries with "twenty or thirty men sitting around in deep silence, reading newspapers, and drinking port."*

Throughout Europe, the coffeehouses were a social arena for the open, spontaneous discussion of events, politics, literature, and ideas—but only for men (respectable women did not enter coffeehouses). By furnishing copies of newspapers and other journals, the proprietors of coffeehouses linked their customers to the growing print culture. In London coffeehouses, members of the Royal Society and other men associated with the new science mixed with merchants and bankers. Some London coffeehouse proprietors invited learned persons to lecture, usually for a fee, on Newtonian physics, the mechanical philosophy, ethics, and the relationship of science and religion.

Lloyd's of London, which would become one of the most important insurance markets in the world in the nineteenth century, flourished in the eighteenth century as a coffeehouse where ship captains and insurers exchanged news and conducted business.

COFFEEHOUSE "PATRIOTS" Satirical attacks on coffeehouse patrons, such as W. Dickinson's *The Coffeehouse Patriots; or News, from St. Eustatia* (London, 15 October 1781), were common by the late eighteenth century. In this cartoon, the patrons are accused of putting their own business interests ahead of patriotic allegiance to the crown. The men gather in the center of the coffeehouse, sharing a newspaper, upset by the news that St. Eustatius, a Dutch Caribbean port used by British merchants for illegal trade with the American colonies, had been captured by the British. The furnishings and animals shown were typical of the London coffeehouse of the late eighteenth century.
SOURCE: Library of Congress

In France the *philosophes*, such as Voltaire, Jean-Jacques Rousseau, and Denis Diderot, used the café as a place to meet other writers. By 1743, a German commented, "A coffeehouse is like a political stock exchange, where the most gallant and wittiest heads of every estate come together. They engage in wide-ranging and edifying talk, issue well-founded judgments on matters concerning the political and the scholarly world, converse sagaciously about the most secret news from all courts and states, and unveil the most hidden truths."**

One irony, however, should be noted about the eighteenth-century European coffeehouses. Although they were one of the chief locations for the public discussion of Enlightenment ideas, which fostered greater liberty of thought in Europe, the coffee and sugar consumed in these establishments were cultivated by slave labor on plantations in the Caribbean and Brazil. The coffeehouse was one of many institutions of European life intimately connected to the transatlantic plantation slave economy.

Question

1. How did coffeehouses help spread Enlightenment ideas?

*Brian Cowan, *The Social Life of Coffee: The Emergence of the British Coffeehouse* (New Haven, CT: Yale University Press, 2005), pp. 166 and 86.
**Quoted in James Van Horn Melton, *The Rise of the Public in Enlightenment Europe* (Cambridge, UK: Cambridge University Press, 2001), p. 243.

included Voltaire, Montesquieu, Diderot, d'Alembert, Rousseau, Hume, Gibbon, Smith, Lessing, and Kant.

A few of these *philosophes*, particularly those in Germany, were university professors. Most, however, were free agents who might be found in London coffeehouses, Edinburgh drinking spots, the salons of fashionable Parisian ladies, the country houses of reform-minded nobles, or the courts of the most powerful monarchs on the Continent. In eastern Europe, they were often royal bureaucrats. The successful *philosophe* required not only bold ideas and a sharp wit but also the patronage of wealthy and powerful supporters. While rulers and aristocrats were often eager to promote and profit from *philosophes* and their reformist ideas, on more than one occasion, Enlightenment writers and thinkers were limited by what their patrons would support.

Philosophes were not an organized group; they disagreed on many issues and did not necessarily like or respect each other. Their relationship to one another and to lesser figures of the same turn of mind has been compared with that of a family, which, despite quarrels and tensions, preserves a basic unity. Another historian has portrayed the participants in the Enlightenment across many different local cultures as "members of a wider intellectual movement, dedicated to understanding and publicizing the cause of human betterment on this earth."[3]

The *philosophes*' readers were mostly from the prosperous commercial and professional urban classes who had enough income to buy and the leisure to read the *philosophes*' works. Along with forward-looking aristocrats, these readers discussed the reformers' writings and ideas in local philosophical societies, Freemason lodges, and clubs. Enlightenment writers created an intellectual ferment and were a source of ideas that could be used to undermine existing social practices and political structures based on aristocratic privilege. They taught their contemporaries, including reform-minded aristocrats, how to pose pointed, critical questions. Moreover, the *philosophes* generally supported the expansion of trade, the improvement of agriculture and transport, and the invention of new manufacturing machinery that were transforming the society and the economy of the eighteenth century and enlarging the business and commercial classes.

The chief bond among the *philosophes* was their common desire to advocate reason and reform religion, political thought, society, government, and the economy for the sake of human liberty. As historian Peter Gay once suggested, this goal included "freedom from arbitrary power, freedom of speech, freedom of trade, freedom to realize one's talents, freedom of aesthetic response, freedom, in a word, of moral man to make his way in the world."[4] In order to bring meaningful improvement to the lives of more than men in Europe's chattering classes, these ideas had to be pushed further than enlightened thinkers would allow. They have also been challenged over the last three centuries. Nevertheless, no other single set of ideas has done so much to shape and define the modern Western world.

17.2.1 Voltaire and Kant

By far the most influential of the *philosophes* was François-Marie Arouet, known to posterity by his pen name Voltaire (1694–1778). Voltaire's career was full of disruptions caused by his offenses against the rulers of France. During the 1720s, Voltaire had offended first the French monarch and then certain nobles by his politically and socially irreverent poetry and plays. He was arrested and twice briefly imprisoned, in comfortable conditions, in the Bastille, the royal prison-fortress in Paris. In 1726, to escape the wrath of a powerful aristocrat whom he had offended, Voltaire went into exile in England. There he visited its best literary circles, observed its tolerant intellectual and religious climate, relished the freedom he felt in its moderate political atmosphere, and admired its science and economic prosperity. He returned to France in 1728, and in 1733 he published *Letters on the English*. The book praised the virtues of the English, especially their religious liberty, and implicitly criticized the abuses of French society. The Parlement of Paris condemned the book, and the authorities harassed Voltaire. He moved to Cirey from which, if necessary, he could easily escape France into what was then the nearby independent duchy of Lorraine. There he lived with Countess Émilie Du Châtelet (1706–1749), a brilliant mathematician, who became his mistress and muse. In 1738, with her considerable help, he published *Elements of the Philosophy of Newton*, which more than any other single book popularized the thought of Isaac Newton across the Continent. In 1749, Du Châtelet died.

Shortly thereafter, Voltaire took up residence for three years in Berlin at the court of Frederick the Great of Prussia with whom he had corresponded for several years. The residency ended unhappily. Voltaire briefly settled in Switzerland near Geneva but clashed with local conservative Calvinist clergy. Thereafter he acquired the estate of Ferney, just across the French border but close enough to flee to Geneva should the French authorities bother him. Voltaire's most popular plays, essays, histories, and stories along with his far-flung correspondence made him the literary dictator of Europe. For the rest of his long life, he turned his venomous satire and sarcasm against one evil after another in French and European life.

In 1755 a huge earthquake struck Lisbon, Portugal, killing at least 60,000 people. Voltaire wrote a deeply pessimistic poem commemorating the event. Other contemporary writers questioned his pessimism, arguing for a more optimistic view of life and nature. In 1759, Voltaire replied in the novel *Candide*, his still widely read satire attacking war, religious persecution, and what he considered unwarranted optimism about the human condition. Like most of the *philosophes*, Voltaire believed human society could and should be improved, but he was never certain that reform, if achieved, would be permanent. In that respect his thought reflected the broader pessimistic undercurrent of the Enlightenment. As his fellow *philosophe* Jean d'Alembert wrote, "Barbarism lasts for centuries; it seems that it is our natural element; reason and good taste are only passing."[5]

Voltaire died in 1778 in Paris after a triumphal return to that city, which he had not seen for decades.

Like Voltaire, **Immanuel Kant** (1724–1804) admired Frederick the Great. Unlike Voltaire, Kant's relationship with authority did not require years of restless travel. Born in the capital of Prussia, Königsberg, Kant spent his entire life in the city. In 1784, he published an essay answering the question "What is Enlightenment?" in which he defined Enlightenment as "man's emergence from his self-incurred immaturity." Through the application of reason, Kant claimed, men could earn the right to be fully autonomous adults, no longer dependent on the guidance of church or state authorities to determine what is right. According to Kant, this condition of full autonomy had not yet been achieved, and his age was therefore "an age of Enlightenment" but not "an enlightened age." At the same time, Kant credited Frederick the Great for recognizing his subjects' right to freedom of thought, and most especially freedom of religious ideas. When Kant's views on religious freedom were criticized by one of Frederick the Great's successors, Kant chose loyalty to his monarch and ceased publishing on the topic, but only until the accession of the next king: "Repudiation and denial of one's inner conviction are evil, but silence in a case like the present one is the duty of a subject; and while all that one says must be true, this does not mean that it is one's duty to speak out the whole truth in public."[6]

17.3 The Enlightenment and Religion

How did the *philosophes* challenge traditional religious ideas and institutions?

For many, but not all, *philosophes* of the eighteenth century, ecclesiastical institutions, especially with their frequently privileged position as official parts of the state, were the chief impediment to human improvement and happiness. Voltaire's cry, "Crush the Infamous Thing," summed up the attitude of a number of *philosophes* toward the intolerance that they believed characterized parts of organized Christianity. Almost all varieties of Christianity, especially Roman Catholicism, as well as Judaism and Islam, were the targets of their criticism.

The *philosophes* complained that Christian churches hindered the pursuit of a rational life and the scientific study of humanity and nature by turning attention away from this world to the world to come. Both Roman Catholic and Protestant clergy taught that humans were basically depraved and worthy only through divine grace. According to the doctrine of original sin, improvement

in human nature on earth was impossible. The *philosophes* argued, for example, that the Calvinist doctrine of predestination denied that virtuous behavior in this life could affect a person's soul after death. Mired in conflicts over obscure doctrines, the churches promoted intolerance and bigotry, inciting torture, war, and other forms of human suffering.

With their attack on religious intolerance, the *philosophes* challenged not only a set of ideas but also some of Europe's most powerful institutions. The churches were deeply enmeshed in the power structure of the Old Regime. They owned large amounts of land and collected tithes from peasants before any secular authority collected its taxes. Most clergy were legally exempt from taxes and made only annual voluntary grants to the government. The upper clergy in most countries were relatives or clients of aristocrats. High clerics were actively involved in politics. Bishops served in the British House of Lords, and on the Continent, cardinals and bishops advised rulers or were sovereign princes themselves. In Protestant countries, the leading local landowner usually appointed the parish clergyman. Membership in the state church conferred political and social advantages, and those who did not belong to it were often excluded from political life, the universities, and the professions. Clergy frequently provided intellectual justification for the social and political status quo, and they were active agents of religious and literary censorship.

17.3.1 Deism

The *philosophes*, although critical of many religious institutions and frequently anticlerical, did not oppose all religion. What the *philosophes* sought, however, was religion without fanaticism and intolerance, a religious life that would largely substitute human reason for the authority of churches. The Newtonian worldview had convinced many writers that nature was rational. Therefore, according to the *philosophes*, the God who had created nature must also be rational, and the religion through which that God was worshipped should be rational. Most of them believed the life of religion and of reason could be combined, giving rise to a broad set of ideas known as **deism**. Deists regarded God as a kind of divine watchmaker who had created the mechanism of nature, set it in motion, and then departed.

The deists' informal creed had two major points. The first was belief in the existence of God, which they thought the contemplation of nature could empirically justify, and in this respect many Protestant and Roman Catholic writers fully agreed with them. Because nature provided evidence of a rational God, that deity must also favor rational morality. The second point in the deists' creed was a belief in life after death, when rewards and punishments would be meted out according to the virtue of the lives people led on this earth.

Deism, Enlightenment writers urged, was empirical, tolerant, reasonable, and capable of encouraging virtuous living. Voltaire once wrote,

> The only gospel one ought to read is the great book of Nature, written by the hand of God and sealed with his seal. The only religion that ought to be professed is the religion of worshiping God and being a good man.[7]

Deists hoped that wide acceptance of their faith would end rivalry among the various Christian sects and with it religious fanaticism, conflict, and persecution. They also believed deism would remove the need for priests and ministers who, in their view, were often responsible for fomenting religious differences and denominational hatred. Deistic thought led some contemporaries to believe God had revealed himself in various ways and that many different religions might embody divine truth.

There was never a formal or extensive deist movement, but deist ideas spread informally throughout the culture and provided for some people a framework for a non-dogmatic religious outlook. Deism was relatively successful in America but not so much in France, where it became the official "religion" of the Terror.

17.3.2 Toleration

The *philosophes* presented religious toleration as a primary social condition for the virtuous life. Again, Voltaire took the polemical lead in championing this cause.

In 1762, the Roman Catholic political authorities in the city of Toulouse ordered the execution of a Huguenot named Jean Calas, who had been accused of murdering his son to prevent him from converting to Roman Catholicism.

Voltaire learned of the case only after Calas's death. In 1763, he published his *Treatise on Tolerance* and hounded the authorities for a new investigation. Finally, in 1765, the judicial decision against the unfortunate man was reversed. For Voltaire, the case illustrated the fruits of religious fanaticism and the need for rational reform of judicial processes.

In 1779, German playwright and critic Gotthold Lessing (1729–1781) wrote *Nathan the Wise*, a plea for toleration not only of different Christian groups, but also of religious faiths other than Christianity. The premise behind all of these calls for toleration was, in effect, that life on earth and human relationships should not be subordinated to religious zeal that permitted one group of people to persecute, harm, or repress other groups.

17.3.3 Radical Enlightenment Criticism of Christianity

Some *philosophes* went beyond the formulating a rational religious alternative to Christianity and advocating toleration to attack the churches and the clergy with vehemence. Scottish philosopher **David Hume** (1711–1776) argued in "Of Miracles," a chapter in his *Inquiry into Human Nature* (1748), that no empirical evidence supported the belief in divine miracles central to much of Christianity. Voltaire repeatedly questioned the truthfulness of priests and the morality of the Bible. In his *Philosophical Dictionary* (1764), he humorously pointed out inconsistencies in biblical narratives and immoral acts of biblical heroes. Many of these ideas had existed before the Enlightenment in the anti–Roman Catholic polemics of Protestant writers and were brought back into circulation by the *philosophes*.

A few—actually very few—*philosophes* went further than criticism. Most of the *philosophes* sought not the abolition of religion but its transformation into a humane force that would encourage virtuous living. In the words of the title of a work by Kant, they sought to pursue *Religion within the Limits of Reason Alone* (1793).

17.3.4 The Limits of Toleration

Despite their emphasis on toleration, the *philosophes*' criticisms of traditional religion often reflected an implicit contempt not only for Christianity but also, and sometimes more vehemently, for Judaism and, as we see later, for Islam as well. Their attack on the veracity of biblical miracles and biblical history undermined the authority of the Hebrew scriptures as well as the Christian. Some *philosophes* characterized Judaism as a more primitive faith than Christianity and one from which philosophical rationalism provided an escape. The Enlightenment view of religion thus in some ways further stigmatized Jews and Judaism in the eyes of non-Jewish Europeans.

Unlike Judaism, Islam had few adherents in eighteenth-century Europe, with the notable exception of the Balkan Peninsula. Although European merchants traded with the Ottoman Empire or with parts of South Asia where Islam prevailed, most Europeans learned the little they knew about Islam as a religion through books—the religious commentaries of Christian missionaries, histories, and reports of travelers—that, with rare exceptions, were hostile to Islam and deeply misleading.

Enlightenment *philosophes* spoke with two voices regarding Islam. Voltaire expressed his opinion along with that of many of his contemporaries in the title of his 1742 tragedy *Fanaticism, or Mohammed the Prophet*. Although he sometimes spoke well of the *Qur'an*, Voltaire declared in a later historical work, "We must suppose that Muhammed, like all enthusiasts, violently impressed by his own ideas, retailed them in good faith, fortified them with fancies, deceived himself in deceiving others, and finally sustained with deceit a doctrine he believed to be good."[8] Thus, for Voltaire, Muhammad and Islam in general represented simply one more example of the religious fanaticism he had so often criticized among Christians.

VIEW OF CONSTANTINOPLE Few Europeans visited the Ottoman Empire. The little they knew about it came from reports of travelers and from illustrations such as this early eighteenth-century view of a bustling street in Constantinople, the empire's capital. A mosque stands prominently in the foreground.

SOURCE: GRI Digital Collections/Getty Museum

Some *philosophes* criticized Islam on cultural and political grounds. In *The Persian Letters* (1721), supposedly written by two Muslim Persians visiting Europe, the young *philosophe* Charles de Montesquieu used Islamic culture as a foil to criticize European society. Yet, by the time he wrote his more influential *Spirit of the Laws* (1748), discussed more fully later in this chapter, Montesquieu associated Islamic society with a passive people subject to political despotism. Like other Europeans, Montesquieu believed the excessive influence of Islamic religious leaders prevented the Ottoman Empire from adapting to new advances in technology.

European voices demanding fairness and expressing empathy for Islam were rare throughout the eighteenth century. As one historian has commented, "The basic Christian attitude was still what it had been for a millennium: a rejection of the claim of Muslims that Muhammad was a prophet and the Qur'an the word of God, mingled with a memory of periods of fear and conflict, and also, a few thinkers and scholars apart, with legends, usually hostile and often contemptuous."[9]

MOSES MENDELSSOHN, "JEWISH SOCRATES" Moses Mendelssohn, the leading philosopher of the Jewish Enlightenment, was often called the "Jewish Socrates."
SOURCE: bpk Bildagentur/Art Resource, NY

17.3.5 The Jewish Enlightenment

Like Catholics and Protestants engaged in the Enlightenment, Jewish thinkers of the eighteenth century embraced the new emphasis on reason as well as new discoveries in science and philosophy as a way of reinvigorating their faith. According to one historian, "the Enlightenment posed a set of questions to which all of the religions in [Europe] found it necessary to provide answers," and Jews were no exception.[10]

The Jewish Enlightenment, sometimes known by the Hebrew word *Haskalah*, involved both an engagement with the secular world and a vibrant study of Jewish religious books. Two major Jewish writers—one a few decades before the opening of the Enlightenment and one toward the close—entered the larger debate over religion and the place of Jews in European life. These were Baruch Spinoza (1632–1677), who lived in the Netherlands, and the German Moses Mendelssohn (1729–1786), who lived in Berlin, the center of the Jewish Enlightenment. Spinoza set the example for a secularized version of Judaism, and Mendelssohn established the main outlines of an assimilationist position.

The new science of the mid-seventeenth century deeply influenced Spinoza, the son of a Jewish merchant in Amsterdam. Like his contemporaries, Hobbes and Descartes, he looked to the power of human reason to reconceptualize traditional thought. In that regard his thinking reflected the age of scientific revolution and looked toward the later Enlightenment.

Mendelssohn, the leading Jewish philosopher of the eighteenth century, was known as the "Jewish Socrates." Writing almost a century after Spinoza, he also advocated the assimilation of Jews into modern European life. In contrast to Spinoza, however, Mendelssohn argued that Jews could combine loyalty to Judaism with adherence to rational, Enlightenment values.

Mendelssohn's most influential work was *Jerusalem; or, On Ecclesiastical Power and Judaism* (1783), in which he argued both for extensive religious toleration and for maintaining the religious distinction of Jewish communities. Mendelssohn urged that religious diversity did not impede loyalty to government; therefore, governments should be religiously neutral and Jews should enjoy the same civil rights as other subjects. Then, in the spirit of the deists, he presented Judaism as one of many religious paths revealed by God. Jewish law and practice, Mendelssohn claimed, were intended for the moral benefit of Jewish communities; other religions similarly served other people. Consequently, various communities should be permitted to practice their religious faith alongside other religious groups.

Unlike Spinoza, Mendelssohn advocated religious toleration while genuinely sustaining the traditional religious practices and faith of Judaism. Nevertheless, Mendelssohn believed Jewish communities should not have the right to excommunicate their members because of differences in theological opinions or if their members embraced modern secular ideas. He thus sought both toleration of Jews within European society and toleration by Jews of a wider spectrum of opinion within their own communities. He hoped that the rationalism of the Enlightenment would make both types of toleration possible.

17.4 The Enlightenment and Society

How did the *philosophes* apply Enlightenment ideas to social and economic problems?

The rationalism of Enlightenment writers, closely connected to the spirit of improvement that influenced so much of eighteenth century, also sought to achieve a science of society that would uncover how to maximize human productivity and material happiness.

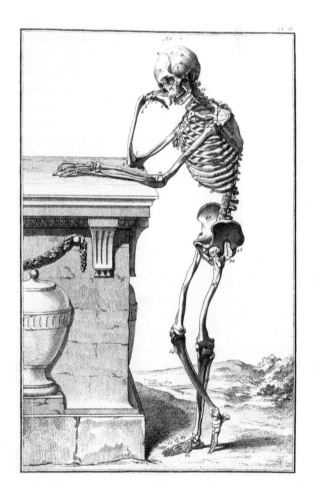

ILLUSTRATION FROM DIDEROT'S *ENCYCLOPEDIA*
"Anatomy," one of the many illustrations included in Denis Diderot's *Encyclopedia*, included labels for each of the bones in an articulated skeleton that were then identified and named in the text.
SOURCE: bpk Bildagentur/Art Resource, NY

17.4.1 The *Encyclopedia:* Freedom and Economic Improvement

The midcentury witnessed the publication of the **Encyclopedia,** one of the greatest achievements of the Enlightenment and its most monumental undertaking in the realm of print culture. Under the guidance of **Denis Diderot** (1713–1784) and Jean Le Rond d'Alembert (1717–1783), the first volume appeared in 1751. Eventually, numbering seventeen volumes of text and eleven of plates (illustrations), the project was completed in 1772. No other work of the Enlightenment illustrated the movement's determination to probe life on earth rather than in the religious realm. As one writer in the *Encyclopedia* observed, "Man is the unique point to which we must refer everything, if we wish to interest and please amongst considerations the most arid and details the most dry."[11] The use of the word *man* in this passage was not simply an accident of language. Most *philosophes* were thinking primarily of men, not women, when they framed their reformist ideas.

The *Encyclopedia*, in part a collective plea for freedom of expression, reached fruition only after many attempts to censor it and halt its publication. It was the product of the collective effort of more than a hundred authors, and its editors had at one time or another solicited articles from all the major French *philosophes*. It included the most advanced critical ideas of the time on religion, government, and philosophy. To avoid official censure, these ideas often had to be buried in obscure articles or steeped in irony. The *Encyclopedia* also included numerous important articles and illustrations on manufacturing, canal-building, ship construction, and improved agriculture, making it an important source of knowledge about eighteenth-century social and economic life.

The project had been designed to secularize learning and to undermine intellectual assumptions that lingered from the Middle Ages and the Reformation. The articles on politics, ethics, and society ignored divine law and concentrated on humanity and its immediate well-being. The Encyclopedists looked to antiquity rather than to the Christian centuries for their intellectual and ethical models. For them, the future welfare of humankind lay not in pleasing God or following divine commandments but in harnessing the power and resources of the earth and in living at peace with one's fellow human beings. The publication of the *Encyclopedia* was greeted by Enlightenment enthusiasts throughout the Continent, and was read in German and Russian intellectual and political circles.

17.4.2 Beccaria and Reform of Criminal Law

Although the term did not appear until later, the idea of *social science* originated with the Enlightenment. *Philosophes*

hoped to end human cruelty by discovering social laws and making people aware of them. These concerns are most evident in the *philosophes'* work on law and prisons.

In 1764, Marquis Cesare Beccaria (1738–1794), an Italian aristocrat and *philosophe*, published *On Crimes and Punishments*, in which he applied critical analysis to the problem of making punishments both effective and just. He wanted the laws of monarchs and legislatures—that is, positive law—to conform to the rational laws of nature, and he rigorously and eloquently attacked both torture and capital punishment. He thought the criminal justice system should ensure speedy trials and certain punishment, with the intent to deter further crime. The purpose of laws, Beccaria claimed, was not to impose the will of God or some other ideal of perfection, but to secure the greatest good or happiness for the greatest number of human beings. This utilitarian philosophy based on happiness in this life permeated most Enlightenment writing on practical reforms and profoundly influenced rulers in central and eastern Europe.

17.4.3 The Physiocrats and Economic Freedom

Economic policy was another area in which the *philosophes* saw existing legislation and administration preventing the operation of natural social laws. They believed mercantilist legislation, designed to protect a country's trade from external competition, and the regulation of labor by governments and guilds actually hampered the expansion of trade, manufacture, and agriculture. In France, these economic reformers were called the **physiocrats**.

The physiocrats believed the primary role of government was to protect property and to permit its owners to use it freely. They argued that agriculture was the basis on which all economic production depended. They favored the consolidation of small peasant holdings into larger, more efficient farms. Here, as elsewhere, the rationalism of the Enlightenment was closely connected to the spirit of improvement that influenced so much of eighteenth-century European economic life.

17.4.4 Adam Smith on Economic Growth and Social Progress

The most important economic work of the Enlightenment, *Inquiry into the Nature and Causes of the Wealth of Nations* (1776), was written by **Adam Smith** (1723–1790). Smith, who was for a time a professor at Glasgow University in Scotland, believed economic liberty was the foundation of a natural economic system. As a result, he urged that the mercantile system of England—including the navigation acts governing colonial trade, the bounties the government gave to favored merchants and industries, most tariffs, trading monopolies, and the domestic regulation of labor and manufacture—be abolished. These regulations were intended to preserve the wealth of the nation, to capture wealth from other nations, and to maximize the work available for the nation's laborers. Smith argued, however, that they hindered the expansion of wealth and production. The best way to encourage economic growth, he maintained, was to allow individuals to pursue their own selfish economic interests. As self-interested individuals enriched themselves by meeting the needs of others in the marketplace, the economy would grow. Consumers would find their wants met as manufacturers and merchants competed for their business.

Mercantilism assumed that the earth's resources were limited and scarce, so one nation could acquire wealth only at the expense of others. Smith's book challenged this assumption. He saw the resources of nature—water, air, soil, and minerals—as boundless. To him, they demanded exploitation for the enrichment and comfort of humankind.

Smith is usually regarded as the founder of *laissez-faire* economic thought and policy, which favors a limited role for the government in economic life. *The Wealth of Nations* was, however, a complex book and Smith was no simple dogmatist. For example, he did not oppose all government activity in the economy. The government, he argued, should provide schools, armies, navies, and roads. It should also undertake certain commercial ventures, such as opening dangerous new trade routes that were economically desirable but too expensive or risky for private enterprise. The public should in particular support education of those people who occupied the humbler occupations of life.

In *The Wealth of Nations*, Smith, like other Scottish thinkers of the day, embraced an important theory of human social and economic development known as the *four-stage theory*. According to this theory, human societies can be classified as hunting and gathering, pastoral or herding, agricultural, or commercial. The hunters and gatherers have little or no settled life. Pastoral societies are nomadic like the herds they tend, but develop some private property. Agricultural or farming societies are settled and have clear-cut property arrangements. Finally, the commercial state includes advanced cities, the manufacture of numerous items for wide consumption, extensive trade between cities and the countryside, and elaborate forms of property and financial arrangements. Smith and other writers described the passage of human society through these four stages as a movement from barbarism to civilization.

The four-stage theory implicitly evaluated the later stages of economic development, and the people who had achieved them, as higher, more progressive, and more civilized than earlier ones. A social theorist could use this theory to quickly look at a society and, based on its economic development and organizations, rank it by the stage it had achieved. The commercial stage described society as it appeared in northwestern Europe. Smith's theory consequently allowed Europeans to always place themselves at the highest level of human achievement in the world. This outlook helped Europeans justify their economic and imperial domination of the world during the following century. They repeatedly portrayed themselves as bringing a higher level of civilization to people who, according to the four-stage theory, occupied lower stages of human social and economic development. Europeans thus imbued with the spirit of the Enlightenment believed they were carrying out a civilizing mission to the rest of the world.

17.5 Political Thought of the *Philosophes*

How did the *philosophes* apply Enlightenment ideas to political issues?

The *philosophes*' reformist agenda, as well as their internal tensions, was extremely apparent in their political thought. Most *philosophes* were discontented with political features of their countries, but French *philosophes* were especially discontented. There, the corruption around the royal court, the blundering of the bureaucracy, the less-than-glorious mid-century wars, and the power of the church seemed to make problems worse. Consequently, the most important political thought of the Enlightenment occurred in France. The French *philosophes*, however, were divided over how to solve their country's problems. Their proposed solutions spanned a wide political spectrum, from aristocratic reform to democracy to absolute monarchy.

17.5.1 Montesquieu and *Spirit of the Laws*

Charles Louis de Secondat, baron de Montesquieu (1689–1755), was a French lawyer, a noble of the robe, and a member of a provincial parlement. He also belonged to the Bordeaux Academy of Science, before which he presented papers on scientific topics.

Although living comfortably in the bosom of French society, Montesquieu saw the need for reform. In 1721, as already noted, he published *The Persian Letters* to satirize contemporary institutions. Behind the humor lay an exposition of the cruelty and irrationality of European life.

Montesquieu held up the example of the British constitution as the wisest model for regulating the power of government. His *Spirit of the Laws* (1748), one of the most influential books of the century, exhibits the internal tensions of the Enlightenment. In it, Montesquieu pursued an empirical method, taking illustrative examples from the political experience of both ancient and modern polities. From these, he concluded that no single set of political laws

ALL MORTALS ARE EQUAL Like many of his fellow *philosophes* in France, Voltaire was fascinated by people and cultures outside of Europe. The title character in his play *Mahomet* is Mohammad, the founder of Islam. The caption in this illustration of the play reads "All mortals are equal; it is not birth but virtue that makes the difference."
SOURCE: Bridgeman-Giraudon/Art Resource, NY

could apply to all peoples at all times and in all places, and that a good political life depended rather on the relationship among many variables. Whether the best form of government for a country was a monarchy or a republic, for example, depended on that country's size, population, social and religious customs, economic structure, traditions, and climate. Only a careful examination and evaluation of these elements could reveal what mode of government would most benefit a particular people.

For France, Montesquieu favored a monarchical government tempered and limited by various intermediary institutions, including the aristocracy, the towns, and the other corporate bodies that enjoyed liberties the monarch had to respect. These corporate bodies might be said to represent segments of the general population and thus of public opinion. In France, he regarded the aristocratic courts, or parlements, as a major example of an intermediary association. Their role was to limit the power of the monarchy and thus to preserve the liberty of its subjects.

In championing these aristocratic bodies and the general oppositional role of the aristocracy, Montesquieu was a political conservative. He adopted this conservatism in the hope of achieving reform, however, for he believed the oppressive and inefficient absolutism of the monarchy accounted for the degradation of French life.

One of Montesquieu's most influential ideas was that of the division of power in government. In Great Britain, he believed, executive power resided in the king, legislative power in the Parliament, and judicial power in the courts. He thought any two branches could check and balance the power of the other.

Montesquieu's analysis illustrated his strong belief that monarchs should be subject to constitutional limits on their power and that a separate legislature, not the monarch, should formulate laws. Although he had set out to defend the political privileges of the French aristocracy, Montesquieu's ideas have had a profound effect on the constitutional form of liberal democracies for more than two centuries.

17.5.2 Rousseau: A Radical Critique of Modern Society

Jean-Jacques Rousseau (1712–1778) hated the world and the society in which he lived. It seemed to him impossible for human beings living according to the commercial values of his time to achieve moral, virtuous, or sincere lives. He argued that human beings in a primeval state of nature had been good, but as they eventually formed social relations and then social institutions, they had lost that goodness. Society itself was the source of human evil for Rousseau, and one manifestation of that unnatural evil was unequal distribution of property.

Rousseau questioned material and intellectual progress and the morality of a society in which commerce, industry, and the preservation of property rights were regarded as among the most important human activities. The other *philosophes* generally believed life would improve if people could enjoy more of the fruits of the earth or could produce more goods. Rousseau raised the more fundamental questions of what constitutes the good life and how human society can be reshaped to achieve that life. This question has haunted European social thought ever since the eighteenth century.

These same concerns were reflected in Rousseau's political thought. In the tradition of John Locke, most eighteenth-century political thinkers regarded human beings as individuals and society as a collection of individuals pursuing personal, selfish goals. These writers wished to liberate individuals from the undue bonds of government. In Rousseau's most extensive discussion of politics, *The Social Contract* (1762), Rousseau picked up the stick from the other end. His book opens with the declaration, "All men are born free, but everywhere they are in chains."[12] The rest of the volume is a defense of the chains of a properly organized society over its members.

Rousseau suggested that society is more important than its individual members because they exist only through their relationship to the larger community. Independent human beings living alone can achieve little, he claimed, but through their relationship to the larger political community, they become moral creatures capable of significant action. The question then becomes: What kind of community allows people to behave morally? In his two previous discourses, Rousseau had explained that the contemporaneous European society was not such a community; it was merely an aggregate of competing individuals whose chief social goal was to preserve selfish independence despite all potential social bonds and obligations.

Rousseau envisioned a society in which each person could maintain personal freedom while behaving as a loyal member of the larger community. Drawing on the traditions of Plato and Calvin, he defined freedom as obedience to law.

In his case, the law to be obeyed was that created by the general will. In a society with virtuous customs and morals in which citizens are adequately informed about important issues, the concept of the general will is normally equivalent to the will of a majority of voting citizens. Democratic participation in decision making would bind the individual citizen to the community. Rousseau believed the general will, thus understood, must always be right and that to obey the general will is to be free. This argument led him to the notorious conclusion that under certain circumstances some people must be forced to be free. Rousseau's politics thus constituted a justification for radical direct democracy and for collective action against individual citizens.

Rousseau had, in effect, attacked the eighteenth-century cult of the individual and the fruits of selfishness. He stood at odds with the commercial spirit that was transforming the society in which he lived. Rousseau would have disapproved of the main thrust of Adam Smith's *Wealth of Nations*, which he may or may not have read, and would no doubt have preferred a study on the virtue of nations. Smith wanted people to be prosperous; Rousseau wanted them to be good even if being good meant they might remain poor. He saw human beings not as independent individuals but as creatures enmeshed in necessary social relationships. He believed loyalty to the community should be encouraged. To achieve that loyalty, he suggested that properly governed societies should decree a civic religion based on the creed of deism. Such a shared religion could, he argued, help unify a society even if it had to be enforced by repressive legislation.

Rousseau had only a marginal impact on his own time. The other *philosophes* questioned his critique of material improvement. Aristocrats and royal ministers could hardly be expected to welcome his proposal for radical democracy. Too many people were either making or hoping to make money to appreciate his criticism of commercial values.

17.5.3 Enlightened Critics of European Empires

Most European thinkers associated with the Enlightenment favored the extension of European empires across the world. Like the Scottish writers who embraced the four-stage theory, they believed that the extension of the political structures and economies of northwestern Europe amounted to the spread of progress and civilization. The Scottish commentators and their followers were not without their criticisms of European civilization and of excessive economic regulation in contemporary empires, but they largely believed European civilization to be superior to that of other cultures.

A few Enlightenment voices, however, did criticize the European empires on moral grounds, especially the European conquest of the Americas, the treatment of Native Americans, and the enslavement of Africans on the two American continents. The most important of these critics were Denis Diderot; Nicolas de Condorcet; and two German philosophers, Immanuel Kant and Johann Gottfried Herder (1744–1803).

What ideas allowed these Enlightenment thinkers to criticize their empires? As Sankar Muthu has recently written, "The first and most basic idea is that human beings deserve some modicum of moral and political respect simply because of the fact that they are human."[13]

In other words, the Enlightenment critics of their empires argued for a form of shared humanity that the sixteenth-century European conquerors and their successors in the Americas and in other areas of imperial conquest had ignored. Immanuel Kant wrote, "When America, the Negro countries, the Spice Islands, the Cape, and so forth were discovered, they were to them [the Europeans] countries belonging to no one since they counted the inhabitants as *nothing*."[14]

Kant, Diderot, and Herder rejected this dismissive outlook and the harsh policies that had come from it. They believed no single definition of human nature could be made the standard throughout the world and then used to dehumanize people whose appearance or culture differed from it.

A second critical idea was that the people whom Europeans had encountered in the Americas possessed cultures that should have been respected and understood rather than destroyed. Some Europeans in the early encounters with America had argued that while the native peoples were human, their way of life was too degraded to treat them as the human equals of Europeans. In the late eighteenth century, Herder rejected such a view: "'European culture' is a mere abstraction, an empty concept. Where does or did it actually exist in its entirety? In which nation? In which period? … Only a misanthrope could regard European culture as the universal condition of our species. The culture of *man* is not the culture of the *European;* it manifests itself according to time and place in every people."[15] For Herder, human beings living in different societies possessed the capacity to develop in culturally different fashions. He thus embraced an outlook later known as *cultural relativism*.

A third idea, closely related to the second, was that human beings may develop distinct cultures with intrinsic values that cannot be compared, one to the detriment of another, because each culture possesses deep inner social and linguistic complexities that make any simple comparison impossible. Indeed, Diderot, Kant, and Herder argued that being a human includes the ability to develop a variety of distinctly different cultures.

17.6 Women in the Thought and Practice of the Enlightenment

What role did women play in the Enlightenment?

Women, especially in France, helped significantly to promote the careers of the *philosophes*. In Paris, the salons of women such as Marie Thérèse Geoffrin (1699–1777), Julie de Lespinasse (1733–1776), and Claudine de Tencin (1689–1749) gave the *philosophes* access to useful social and political contacts and a receptive environment in which to circulate their ideas. The women who organized the salons were well connected to political figures who could help protect the *philosophes* and secure royal pensions for them.

17.6.1 Traditional View of Women

Despite this help and support from the learned women of Paris and other urban centers, most *philosophes* did not advocate equality for women. Many urged better and broader education for women. They criticized the education women did receive as overly religious, and they tended to reject ascetic views of sexual relations. In general, however, they

MARY WOLLSTONECRAFT Mary Wollstonecraft (1759–1797) is regarded as a pioneer in modern feminism. In her most famous work, *A Vindication of the Rights of Woman,* she defends the equality of women and men on the grounds that they share the human capacity to reason.
SOURCE: New York Public Library

displayed traditional views toward women and advocated no radical changes in their social condition.

Montesquieu, for example, maintained that women's status in a society was the result of climate, the political regime, culture, and women's physiology. He believed women were not naturally inferior to men and should have a wider role in society. Yet Montesquieu's willingness to consider social change for women in European life had limits. Although in the *Spirit of the Laws* he indicated a belief in the equality of the sexes, he still retained a traditional view of marriage and family and expected men to dominate those institutions. Furthermore, although he supported the right of women to divorce and opposed laws that oppressed them, he upheld the ideal of female chastity.

The views about women expressed in the *Encyclopedia* were even less generous than those of Montesquieu. The *Encyclopedia* suggested ways to improve women's lives, but it did not emphasize that the condition of women needed reform. Almost all the contributors were men, and the editors, Diderot and d'Alembert, saw no need to include many articles by women. The Encyclopedists discussed women primarily within a family context—as daughters, wives, and mothers—and presented motherhood as a woman's most important occupation. On sexual behavior, the Encyclopedists upheld an unquestioned double standard.

17.6.2 Different Roles for Women

In contrast to the articles, however, illustrations in the *Encyclopedia* showed women deeply involved in the economic activities of the day. The illustrations also portrayed the activities of lower-class and working-class women, about whom the articles had little to say.

One of the most influential analyses of the position of women came from Jean-Jacques Rousseau. This most radical of all Enlightenment political theorists when defining relations between men urged a traditional and conservative role for women. In his novel *Émile* (1762), he presented a radical version of the view that men and women occupy separate spheres. He declared that women should be educated for positions subordinate to men's, emphasizing especially women's function in bearing and rearing children. In Rousseau's view, there was little else for women to do but make themselves pleasing to men. He portrayed them as weaker and inferior to men in almost all respects, except perhaps for their capacity for feeling and giving love. He excluded them from political life, as only men were to occupy the world of citizenship, political action, and civic virtue. Women were relegated to the domestic sphere.

Many of these attitudes were not new—some have roots as ancient as Roman law—but Rousseau's powerful presentation and the influence of his other writings gave them new life in the late eighteenth century. Rousseau

deeply influenced many leaders of the French Revolution, who often incorporated his view on gender roles in their policies.

Despite these views and despite his own ill treatment of the women who bore his many children, Rousseau achieved a vast following among women in the eighteenth century. One explanation is that his writings, although they did not advocate liberating women or expanding their social or economic roles, did stress the importance of their emotions. He portrayed the domestic role of wife and mother as a noble and fulfilling vocation, giving middle- and upper-class women a sense that their daily roles had a purpose. Women were assigned a degree of influence in the domestic sphere that they could not achieve competing with men outside it.

In 1792, in *A Vindication of the Rights of Woman*, **Mary Wollstonecraft** (1759–1797) brought Rousseau before the judgment of the rational Enlightenment ideal of progressive knowledge. The immediate incentive for this essay was her opposition to certain policies of the French Revolution, unfavorable to women, that Rousseau had inspired. Wollstonecraft accused Rousseau and others after him who upheld traditional roles for women of attempting to narrow women's vision and limit their experience. She argued that to relegate women to the separate domestic sphere because of supposed limitations of their physiology was to make them the sensual slaves of men. Confined in this separate sphere, women were the victims of male tyranny, their obedience was blind, and they could never achieve their own moral or intellectual identity. Denying good education to women would impede the progress of all humanity. Wollstonecraft demanded for women the kind of liberty that male writers of the Enlightenment had been championing for men for more than a century. In doing so, she earned a place among the *philosophes* and broadened the agenda of the Enlightenment to include the rights of women as well as those of men.

17.7 Rococo and Neoclassical Styles in Eighteenth-Century Art

How did rococo and neoclassical styles reflect and contribute to the prevailing trends of the age?

Two contrasting styles dominated eighteenth-century European art and architecture. The **rococo** style embraced lavish, often lighthearted decoration with an emphasis on pastel colors and the play of light. **Neoclassicism** embodied a

ROCOCO STYLE The color, light, and elaborate decorative details associated with rococo style are splendidly exemplified in the Imperial Hall (Kaisarsaal) built in Würzburg, Bavaria, according to the design of Balthasar Neumann (1687–1753). Shown here: a detail of a ceiling fresco. **SOURCE:** Erich Lessing/Art Resource, Inc.

return to figurative and architectural models drawn from the Renaissance and the ancient world. The rococo became associated with the aristocracies of the Old Regime, while neoclassicism recalled ancient republican values that implicitly criticized the Old Regime. Toward the end of the century, neoclassicism was embraced by the French Revolution and Napoleon.

17.7.1 Rococo Style

Rococo architecture and decoration originated in early eighteenth-century France. After Louis XIV's death in 1715, the Regent Philippe d'Orleans (1674–1723) and the French aristocracy spent less time at Versailles and began to enjoy the diversions of Paris. There, wealthy French aristocrats built houses known as *hôtels*. Their designers compensated for the relatively small scale and nondescript exteriors of these mansions with interiors that were elaborately decorated and painted in light colors to make the rooms seem brighter and more spacious. It was in such aristocratic urban settings that fashionable Parisian hostesses held the salons the *philosophes* attended. Louis XV also liked rococo art, and he had both **Madame de Pompadour (Jeanne**

Antoinette Poisson) and other mistresses painted, sometimes in compromising poses, by rococo artists, especially Francois Boucher (1700–1770). Consequently, rococo also became to be known as the style of Louis XV, suggesting a social and political world more accommodating to the French aristocracy and less religiously austere than that of Louis XIV.

Beyond such domestic and personally intimate settings in France, rococo style spread across Europe and was adapted to many public buildings and churches. One of the most spectacular rococo spaces was the Imperial Hall (*Kaisarsaal*) built in Würzburg, Bavaria, to the design of Balthasar Neumann (1687–1753), with ceilings painted with scenes from Greek mythology by the Venetian Gianbattista Tiepolo (1696–1770).

The paintings associated with rococo art often portrayed the aristocracy, and particularly the French aristocracy, at play. Artists depicted what were known as *fêtes galantes* or scenes of elegant parties in lush gardens. The paintings showed not reality but an idealized landscape with carefree men and women pursuing a life of leisure, romance, and seduction. Among the most prominent of such artists was Jean-Antoine Watteau (1684–1721) in whose *Pilgrimage to Isle of Cithera* young lovers embark to pay homage to the goddess Venus.

As the eighteenth century wore on, the way of life illustrated in rococo paintings and in more popular prints produced from them convinced many people in France that the monarchy, the court, and the aristocracy were frivolous and decadent. In reality, many French and European aristocrats were hardworking and disciplined, and Louis XVI, who succeeded Louis XV in 1774, was a well-intentioned, pious, and highly moral monarch. Nonetheless, the lighthearted carelessness of rococo art increased hostility toward the political and social elites of the Old Regime.

17.7.2 Neoclassicism

Contemporaries, moreover, did not have to wait for the tumult of the French Revolution to view art that directly criticized the society rococo art portrayed. The mid-eighteenth century witnessed a new admiration for the art of the ancient world. In 1755, **Johann Joachim Winckelmann** (1717–1768), a German archaeologist, published *Thoughts on the Imitation of Greek Works in Painting and Sculpture*, followed in 1764 by *The History of Ancient Art*. In both works he either directly or indirectly contrasted the superficiality of the rococo with the seriousness of ancient art and architecture. His books and the simultaneous rediscovery and partial excavation of the ancient Roman cities of Pompeii and Herculaneum in southern Italy ushered in neoclassicism in art and architecture. This movement constituted a return to themes, topics, and styles drawn from antiquity itself and from the Renaissance appeal to antiquity.

NEOCLASSICAL PALACE, WARSAW The passion for neoclassical architecture stretched from France to the eastern reaches of Europe. This palace in Warsaw was designed in 1764 to 1795 by Domenico Merlini for the King of Poland, Stanisław August Poniatowski (1732–1798).

SOURCE: Look Die Bildagentur der Fotografen GmbH/Alamy Stock Photo

The popularity of the city of Rome as a destination for artists and aristocratic tourists contributed to the rise of neoclassicism. European aristocrats who came to Italy in the mid-eighteenth century on what was called the "Grand Tour" increasingly admired both the ancient and Renaissance art on view there and the neoclassical works that contemporary artists were producing there. These wealthy and influential travelers not only purchased paintings and statues to bring home with them but also commissioned architects to rebuild their own houses and public buildings in neoclassical style.

Figures in neoclassical paintings rarely seemed to move; they seemed to stand still in a kind of tableau illustrating a moral theme. These paintings were didactic rather than emotional or playful. Their subject matter was usually concerned with public life or public morals, rather than the depiction of intimate family life, daily routine, or the leisure activity favored by rococo painters.

Many neoclassical painters used scenes of heroism and self-sacrifice from ancient history to impart contemporary moral and political lessons (as shown in the "Closer Look" sidebar, which follows below). Such scenes provided a sharp moral contrast to the works of Watteau or Boucher in which lovers seek only pleasure and escape from care. Other neoclassical artists intended their paintings to convey direct political criticism. Jacques-Louis David (1748–1825), the foremost French neoclassical painter, used ancient republican themes in the 1780s to emphasize the corruption of French monarchical government.

The *philosophes* themselves became the subjects of neoclassical artists. French sculptor Jean-Antoine Houdon (1741–1828) produced numerous portraits in stone of leading *philosophes*, including Voltaire and Rousseau as well as American representatives of the Enlightenment such as Benjamin Franklin (1706–1790) and Thomas Jefferson (1743–1826).

Even religious structures built in the neoclassical style were, by the end of the century, transformed to monuments to the Enlightenment and revolution. Modeled on its ancient pagan namesake in Rome, the Pantheon in Paris was begun in 1758 as a Jesuit church. During the French revolution, the new government transformed it into a national monument where the remains of French heroes could be interred. Voltaire's remains were placed there in 1791 and Rousseau's in 1794.

A Closer Look

An Eighteenth-Century Artist Ennobles the Civic Virtue of Ancient Rome

JACQUES-LOUIS DAVID completed *The Oath of the Horatii* in 1784. Like many of his other works, it used themes from the supposedly morally austere ancient Roman Republic to criticize the politics of his day. David intended the painting to contrast ancient civic virtue with the luxurious aristocratic culture of contemporary France.

The Horatii take an oath administered by their father to protect the Roman Republic against enemies even if it means sacrificing their own lives.

The sharp division of the painting into a male world on the left and a female world on the right illustrates how eighteenth-century republican thinkers, such as Rousseau, excluded women from civic and political life.

The sisters and mother of the Horatii weep on the outskirts of the scene. Political divisions can, and often do, cause tragic divisions in families and across society.

THE OATH OF THE HORATII
SOURCE: RMN-Grand Palais/Art Resource, NY

Questions

1. What social role did Enlightenment thinkers expect women to fulfill?
2. What kind of values are exhibited in this painting?
3. What kind of education would be required for a viewer to understand the symbolism of this painting fully?

17.8 Enlightened Absolutism

What was enlightened absolutism?

Most of the *philosophes* favored neither Montesquieu's reformed and revived aristocracy nor Rousseau's democracy as a solution to contemporary political problems. Like other thoughtful people of the day in other stations and occupations, they looked to the existing monarchies. Because of his personal clash with aristocrats as a young writer and his general distrust of democratic ideas, Voltaire was a strong monarchist. In 1759, he published a *History of the Russian Empire under Peter the Great*, which declared, "Peter was born, and Russia was formed."[16] Voltaire and other *philosophes*, such as Diderot, who visited Catherine II of Russia,

CATHERINE THE GREAT Catherine the Great (1729–1796) ascended to the Russian throne after the murder of her husband. This painting shows Catherine in her coronation robe. Considered an enlightened monarch, she tried initially to enact major reforms but never intended to abandon absolutism. She strengthened the status and privileges of the nobility and by the end of her reign had imposed press censorship.

SOURCE: Photo Josse/Leemage / Corbis via Getty Images

of Austria (r. 1765–1790), and Catherine II (r. 1762–1796) of Russia, known as Catherine the Great.

Frederick II corresponded with the *philosophes*; gave Voltaire and others places at his court; and even wrote history, political tracts, literary criticism, and music. Catherine II, adept at what would later be called public relations, consciously created the image of an enlightened ruler. She read and cited the works of the *philosophes*; subsidized Diderot; and corresponded with Voltaire, lavishing compliments on him, in the hope of receiving favorable comments from them, as she indeed did. Joseph II continued numerous initiatives begun by his mother, Maria Theresa (r. 1740–1780). He imposed a series of religious, legal, and social reforms that contemporaries believed he had derived from the *philosophes*' suggestions.

The relationship between these rulers and these Enlightenment writers was, however, more complicated than suggested. The humanitarian and liberating zeal of the Enlightenment writers was only part of what motivated the policies of the rulers. Frederick II, Joseph II, and Catherine II were also determined to play major diplomatic and military roles in Europe. In no small measure, they adopted Enlightenment policies favoring the rational economic and social integration of their realms because these policies also increased their military strength and political power. The major European states had emerged from the Seven Years' War knowing they would need stronger armies for future wars and increased revenues to finance these armies. The search for new revenues and internal political support was one of the incentives prompting the enlightened reforms of the monarchs of Russia, Prussia, and Austria. Consequently, they and their advisers used rationality to pursue goals most *philosophes* admired and also to further what some *philosophes* considered irrational militarism.

The flattery of monarchs could bend the opinions of a *philosophe*. For example, Voltaire, who had written against war, could praise the military expansion of Catherine's Russia because it appeared to bring civilization to peoples he regarded as uncivilized and because he enjoyed being known as a literary confidant of the empress.

17.8.1 Frederick the Great of Prussia

More than any other ruler of the age, Frederick the Great of Prussia embodied enlightened absolutism. Drawing upon the accomplishments of his Hohenzollern forebears, he forged a state that commanded the loyalty of the military, the Junker nobility, the Lutheran clergy, a growing bureaucracy recruited from an educated middle class, and university professors. Because the Prussian monarchy and military were so strong and because the nobles, bureaucracy, clergy, and professors were so loyal, Frederick was able to permit open discussion of Enlightenment ideas and to put into effect more Enlightenment values, such as extensive religious toleration,

and the physiocrats, some of whom were ministers to Louis XV and Louis XVI, did not wish to limit the power of monarchs. Rather, they hoped to use their power to rationalize economic and political structures and liberate intellectual life. Most *philosophes* were not opposed to monarchy if they could use it for their own purposes or if they could profit from their personal relationships with strong monarchs. For this reason, it is important to see Enlightenment political thought not only as a source of modern liberal outlooks.

During the last third of the century, some believed that several European rulers had embraced many of the reforms the *philosophes* advocated. Historians use the term *enlightened absolutism* for this form of monarchical government in which the central absolutist administration was strengthened and rationalized at the cost of other, lesser centers of political power, such as the aristocracy, the church, and the parliaments or diets that had survived the Middle Ages. The monarchs most closely associated with the Enlightenment were Frederick II (r. 1740–1786) of Prussia, Joseph II than any other continental ruler. Consequently, in marked contrast to France, Prussians sympathetic to the Enlightenment tended to support the state rather than criticize it.

17.8.1.1 PROMOTION THROUGH MERIT Reflecting an important change in the European view of the ruler, Frederick frequently described himself as "the first servant of the State," contending that his own personal and dynastic interests should always be subordinate to the good of his subjects. Like earlier Hohenzollern rulers, he protected the local social and political interests of the Prussian nobility as well as their role in the army, but he also required nobles who sought positions in his well-paid bureaucracy to qualify for those jobs by merit. By 1770, a Prussian Civil Service Commission oversaw the education and examinations required for all major government appointments. Frederick thus made it clear that merit rather than privilege of birth would determine who served the Prussian state.

During his reign Frederick created few new nobles, and those persons whom he did ennoble earned their titles by merit for having served the king and the state well. Frederick's policy of ennobling only for merit and of protecting the nobility's local social interests and leadership of the army meant that Prussia did not experience the conflicts between the aristocracy and the monarchy that troubled other eighteenth-century European states.

Frederick felt comfortable in the intellectual life of his day and personally participated in the culture of the Enlightenment. He favored the Prussian universities and allowed professors wide latitude to discuss new ideas. In turn, Prussian professors were virtually unanimous in their praise and support of Frederick.

Because the Prussian state required academic training for appointment to positions of authority, nobles attended the universities. There they studied with middle-class Prussians who were training to serve the state either as Protestant clergy or bureaucrats. Consequently, nobles, clergy, and bureaucrats in Prussia shared a similar educational background that combined a moderate exposure to Enlightenment ideas with broadly shared religious values and loyalty to the state.

17.8.1.2 RELIGIOUS TOLERATION No single policy so associated Frederick with the Enlightenment as full religious toleration. Continuing the Hohenzollern policy of toleration for foreign workers who brought important skills into Prussia, Frederick allowed Catholics and Jews to settle in his predominantly Lutheran country, and he protected the Catholics living in Silesia after he conquered that province from the Habsburgs in the 1740s. He even stated that he would be willing to build mosques for Turks should they move into his country. His religious toleration won the strong support of philosophers, such as Immanuel Kant and Moses Mendelssohn. Frederick nonetheless tended to appoint Protestants to most key positions in the bureaucracy and army.

17.8.1.3 ADMINISTRATIVE AND ECONOMIC REFORMS Frederick also ordered a new codification of Prussian law, which was completed after his death. His objective was to rationalize the existing legal system and make it more efficient, eliminating regional peculiarities, reducing aristocratic influence, abolishing torture, and limiting the number of capital crimes.

The mid-century wars had inflicted considerable economic damage on Prussia. Thereafter, Frederick used the power of the state to foster economic growth. He continued the long-standing Hohenzollern policy of importing workers from outside Prussia. He sought to develop Prussian agriculture, and under state supervision, swamps were drained, new crops introduced, and peasants encouraged and sometimes compelled to migrate where they were needed. For the first time in Prussia, potatoes and turnips became important crops. Frederick also established a land-mortgage credit association to help landowners raise money for agricultural improvements. Despite these efforts, however, most Prussians did not prosper under Frederick's reign, and the burden of taxation, reflecting his protection of the interests of the nobles, fell disproportionately on peasants and townspeople.

17.8.2 Joseph II of Austria

No eighteenth-century ruler so embodied rational, impersonal force as did the emperor Joseph II of Austria. He was the son of Maria Theresa and co-ruler with her from 1765 to 1780. Thereafter, he ruled alone until his death in 1790. Joseph II sincerely wished to improve the lot of his people. He was much less a political opportunist and cynic than either Frederick the Great of Prussia or **Catherine the Great** of Russia. Nonetheless, the ultimate result of his well-intentioned efforts was a series of aristocratic and peasant rebellions extending from Hungary to the Austrian Netherlands.

17.8.2.1 CENTRALIZATION OF AUTHORITY Of all the rising states of the eighteenth century, Austria was the most diverse in its people and problems. To preserve the monarchy during the War of the Austrian Succession (1740–1748), Maria Theresa had guaranteed the aristocracy considerable independence, especially in Hungary.

During and after the conflict, however, she took steps to strengthen the power of the crown outside of Hungary, building more of a bureaucracy than had previous Habsburg rulers. In the Habsburgs' so-called core lands (corresponding roughly to today's Austria and Bohemia), the empress imposed a much more efficient system of tax collection that extracted funds even from the clergy and the nobles. She also established central councils to deal with governmental problems. To ensure her government had a supply of educated officials, she sought to bring all educational institutions into the service of the crown and expanded primary education on the local level.

Maria Theresa was concerned about the welfare of the peasants and serfs. She brought them some relief by expanding the authority of the royal bureaucracy over the local power of the nobility and limiting the amount of labor, or robot, landowners could demand from peasants. Her motives were less humanitarian than to ensure a good pool from which to draw military recruits. In these policies and in her desire to stimulate prosperity and military strength by royal initiative, Maria Theresa anticipated the policies of her son.

Joseph II was more determined than his mother, and his projected reforms were more wide ranging. He aimed to extend his territories at the expense of Poland, Bavaria, and the Ottoman Empire. His greatest ambition, however, was to increase the authority of the Habsburg emperor over his various realms. He sought to overcome the pluralism of the Habsburg holdings by imposing central authority on areas of political and social life in which Maria Theresa had judiciously chosen not to interfere.

In particular, Joseph sought to reduce Hungarian autonomy. To avoid having to guarantee Hungary's existing privileges or extend new ones at the time of his coronation, he refused to be crowned king of Hungary and even had the Crown of Saint Stephen, symbol of the Hungarian state, sent to the Imperial Treasury in Vienna. He reorganized local government in Hungary to increase the authority of his own officials. He also required the use of German in all governmental matters.

17.8.2.2 ECCLESIASTICAL POLICIES Another target of Joseph's royal absolutism was the church. Since the reign of Charles V (r. 1510–1558), the Habsburgs had been the most important dynastic champions of Roman Catholicism. Maria Theresa was devout, but she had not allowed the church to limit her authority. Although she had attempted to discourage certain of the more extreme modes of Roman Catholic popular religious piety, such as public flagellation, she was adamantly opposed to religious toleration. (See the "Compare and Connect" sidebar, which follows below, for a debate between Maria Theresa and Joseph on the issue of religious tolerance.)

Joseph II was also a practicing Catholic, but based on both Enlightenment values and pragmatic politics, he favored a policy of toleration. In October 1781, Joseph extended freedom of worship to Lutherans, Calvinists, and the Greek Orthodox. They were permitted to have their own places of worship, to sponsor schools, to enter skilled trades, and to hold academic appointments and positions in the public service. Joseph also granted the right of private worship to Jews and relaxed the financial and social burdens imposed on them, though he did not give Jews full equality with other Habsburg subjects.

Above all, Joseph sought to bring the Roman Catholic Church directly under royal control. He forbade the bishops of his realms to communicate directly with the pope. Since he considered religious orders that did not run schools or hospitals to be unproductive, he dissolved more than 600 monasteries, confiscated their lands, and used some of their revenue to found new parishes in areas where there was a shortage of priests. He also reorganized the training of priests. The emperor believed the traditional Roman Catholic seminaries, which were run by various dioceses, instilled in priests too great a loyalty to the papacy and too little concern for their future parishioners. They were therefore replaced by eight general seminaries under government supervision whose training emphasized parish duties. In effect, Joseph's policies made Roman Catholic priests the employees of the state, ending the influence of the Roman Catholic Church as an independent institution in Habsburg lands. In many respects, his ecclesiastical policies, known as *Josephinism*, prefigured those of the French Revolution.

17.8.2.3 ECONOMIC AND AGRARIAN REFORM Like Frederick of Prussia, Joseph sought to improve the economic life of his domains. He abolished many internal tariffs, encouraged road-building, and improved river transport. He personally inspected arms and manufacturing districts. Joseph also reconstructed the judicial system to make laws more uniform and rational and to lessen the influence of local landlords. All of these improvements were expected to bring new unity to the state and more taxes into the imperial coffers in Vienna.

Joseph's policies toward serfdom and the land were a far-reaching extension of those Maria Theresa had initiated. During his reign, he introduced reforms that touched the very heart of the rural social structure. He did not abolish the authority of landlords over their peasants, but he did seek to make that authority more moderate and subject to the oversight of royal officials. He abolished serfdom as a legally sanctioned state of servitude. He granted peasants a wide array of personal freedoms, including the right to marry, to engage in skilled work, and to have their children learn a skill without having to secure the landlord's permission.

Joseph reformed the procedures of the manorial courts and opened avenues of appeal to royal officials. He also encouraged landlords to change land leases so that peasants could more easily inherit land or transfer it to other peasants. His goal in all of these efforts to reduce traditional burdens on peasants was to make them more productive and industrious farmers.

Near the end of his reign, Joseph proposed a new and daring system of land taxation. He decreed in 1789 that all proprietors of the land were to be taxed regardless of social status. No longer were the peasants alone to bear the burden of taxation. He commuted *robot* into a monetary tax, only part of which was to go to the landlord, the rest reverting to the state. Angry nobles blocked the implementation of this decree, and it died with Joseph in 1790. This and other of Joseph's earlier measures, however, brought turmoil

Compare and Connect

Maria Theresa and Joseph II of Austria Debate Toleration

THE ISSUE OF religious toleration was widely debated throughout the age of Enlightenment. Many rulers feared that their domains would be overcome by religious turmoil and potential political unrest if their subjects could pursue religious freedom. The issue divided the Empress Maria Theresa and her son, Joseph II, who became her co-regent in 1765. In 1777 they exchanged important letters setting forth their sharply differing views of the subject.

Joseph believed some religious toleration should be introduced into the Habsburg realms. Maria Theresa refused to consider toleration. The toleration of Protestants that is in dispute in these letters related only to Lutherans and Calvinists. Maria Theresa died in 1780; the next year Joseph issued an edict of toleration.

TOMB OF JOSEPH II, HOLY ROMAN EMPEROR (R. 1765–1790)

Joseph's coffin was placed in the Capuchin Crypt directly in front of his parents' monument. Joseph had ordered that his sarcophagus be simple in design and constructed of copper, with no embellishment but a cross. The contrast with the elaborate sarcophagus of his parents, Maria Theresa and Francis Stephen, could not be more stark.

SOURCE: Deposit Photo/Glow Images

Before Reading

- Consider the differences in how Joseph II and Maria Theresa define toleration.
- Describe what Joseph wants to achieve through religious toleration.
- Detail the reasons why Maria Theresa objects to Joseph's views.

Questions

1. How does Joseph define religious toleration, and why does Maria Theresa believe it is the same as religious indifference?
2. What, according to Joseph, are the advantages of toleration to Protestants? To Catholics? To the state?
3. Why does Maria Theresa fear that toleration will bring about political as well as religious turmoil?

I. JOSEPH TO MARIA THERESA, JULY 20, 1777

Dear Mother,

. . .The definition of the word "toleration" is to blame for our entire misunderstanding. You have taken it in an entirely different sense. God preserve me from thinking it is a matter of no consequence if your subjects become Protestant or remain Catholic, still less, if they do not believe in or at least observe the religion which they have been given by their fathers. I would give all I possess if all the Protestants of your lands would become Catholics!

As I use it, "tolerance" means only that, when it comes to purely temporal affairs, I would employ, allow to own property, pursue trades, be citizens, without regard to religion, all those who are capable and can bring advantage or industry to our lands. Those who unfortunately hold a false faith are even further from conversion if they remain in their own country than if they move to one in which they will see and hear the striking truths of the Catholic faith. At the same time, the undisturbed practice of their religion makes them far better subjects and causes them to avoid atheism, which is much more dangerous to our Catholics than the observation of other religions.

II. MARIA THERESA TO JOSEPH, LATE JULY 1777

Without a dominant religion? Toleration and indifference are precisely the true means of undermining everything so that nothing remains. . . . It is no "friend of humanity," a phrase frequently used, who abandons each to his own ideas. I speak only politically, not as a Christian: nothing is as necessary and beneficial as religion. Would you have each create a religion according to his own imagination? No fixed religion, no submission to the church; what would become of us? Tranquility, contentment will not follow from that; the rule of force and more unfortunate times like those we have already seen. Such talk from you could cause the greatest misfortune and make you responsible for thousands of souls. But think of what I would suffer on account of your erroneous principles. Not only the welfare of the state is at stake, not only the preservation of a son who has been the sole object of my actions since his birth—but also your very salvation. . . . In combining your simultaneous desire to vex and to create, you lose yourself, but at the same time you carry away the entire monarchy. . . . No spirit of persecution, but still less one of indifference or "tolerantism," is the path I hope to follow as long as I live, and I do not wish to live unless I can descend in the company of my ancestors with the consolation that my son will be just as great, just as religious as his predecessors, and will turn away from his false thinking and from evil books and from those who let their wit sparkle at the expense of everything that is most holy and most respectable and who wish to introduce an imaginary liberty that can never exist and that will result in license and total upheaval.

SOURCE: From Alfred Arneth, ed., *Maria Theresia und Joseph II, Ihre Correspondenz* vol. II (Vienna: Carl Gerold's Sohn, 1867), 151–152, 157–158. [Translation by Alison Frank]

throughout the Habsburg realms. Peasants revolted over disagreements with landlords about their newly granted rights. The nobles of the various Habsburg realms protested the taxation scheme. The Magyars resisted Joseph's centralization measures in Hungary and forced him to rescind them.

Joseph was succeeded by his brother Leopold II (r. 1790–1792). Although sympathetic to Joseph's goals, Leopold was forced to repeal many of the most controversial decrees, such as that on taxation. In other areas, Leopold considered his brother's policies simply wrong. For example, he returned political and administrative power to local nobles because he thought it expedient for them to have a voice in government. Still, he did not repudiate his brother's program wholesale. He retained, in particular, Joseph's religious policies and maintained as much political centralization as he thought possible.

17.8.3 Catherine the Great of Russia

Joseph II never grasped the practical necessity of forging political constituencies to support his policies. Catherine II, who had been born a German princess, but who became empress of Russia, understood only too well the fragility of the Romanov dynasty's base of power.

After the death of Peter the Great in 1725, the court nobles and the army repeatedly determined the Russian succession. As a result, the crown fell primarily into the hands of people with little talent. Peter's wife, Catherine I, ruled for two years (1725–1727) and was succeeded for three years by Peter's grandson, Peter II. In 1730, the crown devolved on Anna, a niece of Peter the Great. During 1740

and 1741, a child named Ivan VI, who was less than a year old, was the nominal ruler. Finally, in 1741, Peter the Great's daughter Elizabeth came to the throne. She held the title of empress until 1762, but her reign was not notable for new political departures or sound administration. Her court was a shambles of political and romantic intrigue. Much of the power the tsar possessed at the opening of the century had vanished.

At her death in 1762, Elizabeth was succeeded by her nephew Peter III. He was a weak ruler whom many contemporaries considered mad. He immediately exempted the nobles from compulsory military service and then rapidly made peace with Frederick the Great, whom he greatly admired. That decision probably saved Prussia from military defeat in the Seven Years' War. The most significant event in Peter's life was his marriage in 1745 to a young German princess born in the Prussian city of Stettin, in Pomerania, to a member of the ruling dynasty of Anhalt-Zerbst. This was the future Catherine the Great.

For almost twenty years, Catherine lived in misery and frequent danger at the court of Elizabeth. During that time, she befriended important nobles and read widely the books of the *philosophes*. She was a shrewd person whose experience in a court crawling with rumors, intrigue, and conspiracy had taught her how to survive. She exhibited neither love nor fidelity toward her demented husband. A few months after his accession as tsar, Peter was deposed and murdered with Catherine's approval, although not her direct intervention, and she was immediately proclaimed empress.

Catherine's familiarity with the Enlightenment and the general culture of Western Europe convinced her Russia was backward and that it needed major reforms to remain a great power. She understood that any significant reform must have a wide base of political and social support, especially since she had assumed the throne through a palace coup. In 1767, she summoned a legislative commission to advise her on revising the law and government of Russia. There were more than 500 delegates drawn from all sectors of Russian life.

Russian law, however, was not revised for more than a half-century. In 1768, Catherine dismissed the commission before several of its key committees had reported. Yet the meeting had not been useless, for it had gathered a vast amount of information about the conditions of local administration and economic life throughout Russia. The inconclusive debates and the absence of programs from the delegates themselves suggested that most Russians saw no alternative to an autocratic monarchy, and Catherine had no intention of departing from absolutism.

KEY MILESTONES IN RUSSIA FROM PETER THE GREAT THROUGH CATHERINE THE GREAT	
1725	Death of Peter the Great
1725–1727	Catherine I
1727–1730	Peter II
1730–1741	Anna
1740–1741	Ivan VI
1741–1762	Elizabeth
1762	Peter III
1762	Catherine II (the Great) becomes empress
1767	Legislative commission summoned
1769	War with Turkey begins
1773–1775	Pugachev's Rebellion
1772	First Partition of Poland
1774	Treaty of Kuchuk-Kainardji ends war with Turkey
1775	Reorganization of local government
1783	Russia annexes Crimea
1785	Catherine issues the Charter of the Nobility
1793	Second Partition of Poland
1795	Third Partition of Poland
1796	Death of Catherine the Great

17.8.3.1 LIMITED ADMINISTRATIVE REFORM Catherine carried out limited reforms on her own authority. In 1775, she reorganized local government to solve problems the legislative commission had brought to light. She placed most local offices in the hands of nobles rather than creating a royal bureaucracy. In 1785, Catherine issued the Charter of the Nobility, which guaranteed nobles many rights and privileges. In part, the empress had to favor the nobles because they could topple her from the throne. Moreover, Russia's educated class was too small to provide an independent bureaucracy, and the treasury could not afford an

army strictly loyal to the crown. Catherine wisely made a virtue of necessity: She strengthened her crown by making friends of her nobles.

17.8.3.2 ECONOMIC GROWTH Part of Catherine's program was to continue the economic development begun under Peter the Great. She attempted to suppress internal barriers to trade. Exports of grain, flax, furs, and naval stores grew dramatically. She also favored the expansion of the small Russian urban middle class that was so vital to trade. Through these actions, Catherine tried to maintain ties of friendship and correspondence with the *philosophes*. She knew that if she treated them kindly, they would be sufficiently flattered to spread her reputation as a progressive throughout Europe. At the same time, Catherine had a more realistic understanding of how to balance reform with maintaining the loyalty of the nobility than did Joseph II of Austria. While she considered emancipating serfs, she knew doing so would infuriate her noble supporters, and left serfdom intact.

17.8.3.3 TERRITORIAL EXPANSION Catherine's limited administrative reforms and her policy of economic growth had a counterpart in the diplomatic sphere. The Russian drive for warm-water ports continued. (See Map 17–1.) This goal required warfare with the Turks. In 1769, in response to a minor Russian incursion, the Ottoman Empire declared war on Russia. Russia responded with a series of successful military strikes.

During 1769 and 1770, the Russian fleet sailed all the way from the Baltic Sea into the eastern Mediterranean. The Russian army won several major victories that by 1771 gave Russia control of Ottoman provinces on the Danube River and the Crimean coast of the Black Sea. The conflict dragged on until 1774, when the Treaty of Kuchuk-Kainardji gave Russia a direct outlet on the Black Sea, free navigation rights in its waters, and free access through the Bosporus. Crimea became an independent state, which Catherine painlessly annexed in 1783. Finally, under this treaty, Catherine, as empress of Russia, was made the protector of the Orthodox Christians living in the Ottoman Empire. In the future this would cause conflict with France, whose monarch had previously been recognized as the protector of Roman Catholic Christians in the empire.

17.8.4 The Partitions of Poland

The Russian military successes increased Catherine's domestic political support, but they made her neighbors, Prussia and Austria, uneasy. These anxieties were overcome by an extraordinary division of Polish territory known as the First Partition of Poland.

The Russian victories along the Danube River were most unwelcome to Austria, which also harbored ambitions

Map 17–1   EXPANSION OF RUSSIA, 1689–1796

The overriding territorial aim of the two most powerful Russian monarchs of the eighteenth century, Peter the Great (in the first quarter of the century) and Catherine the Great (in the last half of the century), was to secure navigable outlets to the sea in both the north and the south for Russia's vast empire; hence Peter's push to the Baltic Sea and Catherine's to the Black Sea. Russia also expanded into Central Asia and Siberia during this time.

Map 17–2   PARTITIONS OF POLAND, 1772, 1793, AND 1795

The callous eradication of Poland from the map displayed eighteenth-century power politics at its most extreme. Poland, without a strong central government, fell victim to the strong absolute monarchies of central and eastern Europe.

of territorial expansion in that direction. At the same time, the Ottoman Empire was pressing Prussia for aid against Russia. Frederick the Great made a proposal to Russia and Austria that would give each something it wanted, prevent conflict among the powers, and save appearances. After long, complicated, secret negotiations, Russia agreed to abandon the conquered Danubian provinces. In compensation, it received a large portion of Polish territory with almost 2 million inhabitants. As a reward for remaining neutral, Prussia annexed most of the territory between East Prussia and Prussia proper. This land allowed Frederick to unite two previously separate sections of his realm. Finally, Austria took southern Poland, with its important salt mines, and other Polish territory with more than 2.5 million inhabitants. (See Map 17–2.)

In September 1772, the helpless Polish aristocracy, paying the price for maintaining internal liberties at the expense of developing a strong central government, ratified this seizure of nearly one-third of Polish territory. The loss was not immediately fatal to Poland's continued existence, and it inspired a revival of national feeling. Attempts were made to strengthen the Polish state and reform its feeble central government, but they proved to be too little and too late. Poland was no match for its stronger, more ambitious neighbors. The partition of Poland clearly demonstrated that any nation without a strong monarchy, bureaucracy, and army could no longer compete within the European state system. It also demonstrated that the major powers in eastern Europe were prepared to settle their own rivalries at the expense of such a weak state. If Polish territory had not been available to ease tensions, international rivalries might have led to warfare among Russia, Austria, and Prussia.

17.8.5 The End of the Eighteenth Century in Central and Eastern Europe

During the last two decades of the eighteenth century, all three regimes based on enlightened absolutism became more conservative and politically repressive. In Prussia and Austria, rulers' innovations stirred resistance among the nobility. In Russia, fear of peasant unrest was the chief factor.

Frederick the Great of Prussia grew remote during his old age, leaving the aristocracy to fill important military and administrative posts. A reaction to Enlightenment ideas also set in among Prussian Lutheran writers.

In Austria, Joseph II's plans to restructure society and administration in his realms provoked growing frustration and political unrest, with the nobility calling for an end to innovation. In response, Joseph turned increasingly to censorship, which he had initially lessened, and his secret police.

Russia faced a peasant uprising, Pugachev's Rebellion, between 1773 and 1775, and Catherine the Great never fully recovered from the fears of social and political upheaval that it evoked. Once the French Revolution broke out in 1789, the Russian empress censored books based on Enlightenment thought and sent offensive authors into Siberian exile.

By the close of the century, fear of, and hostility to, change permeated the ruling classes of central and eastern Europe. This reaction had begun before 1789, but the events in France bolstered and sustained it for almost a half-century.

The Chapter in Perspective

The writers of the Enlightenment, known as *philosophes*, charted a major new path in modern European and Western thought. The print culture made public opinion into a distinct, cultural force. Admiring Newton and the achievements of physical science, they applied reason and the principles of science to the cause of social reform. They also believed that passions and feelings were essential parts of human nature. Throughout their writings they championed reasonable moderation in social life. More than any other previous group of Western thinkers, they opposed the authority of the established churches. Most of them championed some form of religious toleration. They also sought to achieve a science of society that could maximize human productivity and material happiness. The great dissenter among them was Rousseau, who also wished to reform society, but in the name of virtue rather than material happiness.

The political influence of these writers was diverse and far-reaching. The founding fathers of the American republic looked to them for political guidance, as did moderate liberal reformers throughout Europe, especially within royal bureaucracies. The autocratic rulers of eastern Europe consulted the *philosophes*, hoping Enlightenment ideas might allow them to rule more efficiently. The revolutionaries in France would honor them. These varied followers illustrate the diverse character of the *philosophes* themselves. They show that Enlightenment thought could not be reduced to a single formula. Rather, it was an outlook that championed change and reform, emphasizing humans and their welfare on earth rather than God and the hereafter.

The Chapter in Review

Review Questions

1. How did the Enlightenment change basic Western attitudes toward reform, faith, and reason? What were the major formative influences on the *philosophes*? How important were Voltaire and the *Encyclopedia* in the success of the Enlightenment?

2. Why did some *philosophes* consider organized religion to be their greatest enemy? What were the basic tenets of deism? How did Jewish writers contribute to Enlightenment thinking about religion? What are the similarities and differences between the Enlightenment evaluation of Islam and its evaluations of Christianity and Judaism?

3. What were the attitudes of the *philosophes* toward women? What was Rousseau's view of women? What were the separate spheres he imagined men and women occupying? What were Mary Wollstonecraft's criticisms of Rousseau's view?

4. How did the views of the mercantilists about the earth's resources differ from those of Adam Smith in his book *The Wealth of Nations*? Why might Smith be regarded as an advocate of the consumer? How did his theory of history work to the detriment of less economically advanced non-European peoples?

How did some Enlightenment writers criticize European empires?

5. How did the political views of Montesquieu differ from those of Rousseau? Was Montesquieu's view of England accurate? Was Rousseau a child of the Enlightenment or its enemy? Which did Rousseau value more, the individual or society?

6. What does the partition of Poland indicate about the spirit of enlightened absolutism?

Key Terms

Adam Smith (1723–1790) A Scottish economist and moral philosopher and the author of *The Wealth of Nations*, a pioneering work of political economy.

Catherine the Great (1729–1796) Empress of Russia from 1762 to 1796; under her rule Russia became one of the great powers of Europe; she supported the local power of her nobles while promoting Enlightenment ideals and continuing the economic development begun under Peter the Great.

Charles Louis de Secondat, baron de Montesquieu (1689–1755) French political philosopher who argued that no single set of laws can apply to all peoples, at all times, in all places; his *Spirit of the Laws* is one of the most influential books of the eighteenth century.

David Hume (1711–1776) Scottish philosopher best known for his empiricism, skepticism, and naturalism; in his *Inquiry into Human Nature*, he argues that no empirical evidence supports the belief in divine miracles.

deism A belief in rewards and punishment for human actions after death; a belief in a rational God who creates the universe and allows it to function independently according to the mechanism of nature.

Denis Diderot (1713–1784) A French philosopher and a leading figure of the Enlightenment who served as the chief editor of the *Encyclopedia*.

Encyclopedia (1751–1772) One of the greatest monuments of the Enlightenment, a seventeen-volume work that included the most advanced critical ideas of the time on religion, government, and philosophy.

enlightened absolutism A form of monarchy in which the rulers in central and eastern Europe took inspiration from the ideas and outlooks of the Enlightenment to centralize their authority and to reform their countries.

Immanuel Kant (1724–1804) German philosopher who argued that reason is the source of morality and criticized the European empires on moral grounds.

Jean-Jacques Rousseau (1712–1778) A Genevan philosopher, whose political thought, claiming that society itself, not human beings, were the source of human evil, influenced the Enlightenment in France and across Europe.

Johann Joachim Winckelmann (1717–1768) A German archaeologist, whose books, *Thoughts on the Imitation of Greek Works in Painting and Sculpture* and *The History of Art*, fostered the rise of neoclassicism in art and architecture.

John Locke (1632–1704) An English empirical philosopher whose contributions to social contract theory made him one of the most influential Enlightenment thinkers.

laissez-faire (lay-ZAY-faire) Meaning "allow to do." In economics, the doctrine of minimal government interference in the working of the economy.

Madame de Pompadour (Jeanne Antoinette Poisson) (1721–1764) The mistress of Louis XV and a patron of the *philosophes* of the Enlightenment.

Mary Wollstonecraft (1759–1797) English author and feminist who wrote *A Vindication of the Rights of Woman* to oppose certain policies of the French Revolution that Rousseau had inspired, such as keeping the spheres for men and women distinct and separate.

neoclassicism An artistic movement that began in the 1760s and reached its peak in the 1780s and 1790s and was a reaction against the frivolously decorative rococo style that had dominated European art from the 1720s and on.

philosophes (fee-lou-SOPHS) The eighteenth-century writers and critics who forged the new attitudes favorable to change and who applied reason and common sense to the institutions and societies of their day.

physiocrats Eighteenth-century French thinkers who attacked the mercantilist regulation of the economy, advocated a limited economic role for government, and believed that all economic production depended on sound agriculture.

print culture A culture in which books, journals, newspapers, and pamphlets had achieved a status of their own.

rococo An artistic style that embraced lavish, often light-hearted decoration with an emphasis on pastel colors and the play of light.

Notes

1. T. C. W. Blanning, *The Culture of Power and the Power of Culture: Old Regime Europe 1660–1789* (Oxford, UK: Oxford University Press, 2002), p. 151.

2. Chrétien-Guillaume, as quoted in Roger Chartier, *The Cultural Origins of the French Revolution*, trans. by Lydia G. Cochran (Durham, NC: Duke University Press, 1991), pp. 30–31.

3. John Robertson, *The Case for the Enlightenment: Scotland and Napes 1680–1760* (Cambridge: 2005), p. 377.

4. Gay, *The Enlightenment*, p. 3.

5. Jean Le Rond d'Alembert, *Preliminary Discourse to the Encyclopedia of Diderot*, trans. by Richard N. Schwab (Indianapolis, IN: Bobbs-Merrill, 1985), p. 103.

6. Immanuel Kant, *Political Writings*, ed. by H. Reiss (Cambridge, UK: Cambridge University Press, 1991), p. 2.

7. J. H. Randall, *The Making of the Modern Mind*, rev. ed. (New York: Houghton Mifflin, 1940), p. 292.

8. Theodore Besterman, *Voltaire* (New York: Harcourt, Brace, & World, 1969), p. 409.

9. A. Hourani, *Islam in European Thought* (Cambridge, UK: Cambridge University Press, 1991), p. 136.

10. David Sorkin, *The Berlin Haskalah and German Religious Thought: Orphans of Knowledge* (London: Vallentine Mitchell, 2000), p. 4.

11. F. L. Baumer, *Main Currents of Western Thought*, 4th ed. (New Haven, CT: Yale University Press, 1978), p. 374.

12. Jean-Jacques Rousseau, *The Social Contract and Discourses*, trans. by G. D. H. Cole (New York: Dutton, 1950), p. 3.

13. Sankar Muthu, *Enlightenment Against Empire* (Princeton, NJ: Princeton University Press, 2003), p. 268. This section draws primarily from this excellent recent book.

14. Muthu, *Enlightenment Against Empire*, p. 267.

15. F. M. Barnard, *Self-Direction and Political Legitimacy: Rousseau and Herder* (Oxford, UK: Clarendon Press, 1988), p. 227.

16. Larry Wolff, *Inventing Eastern Europe: The Map of Civilization on the Mind of the Enlightenment* (Palo Alto, CA: Stanford University Press, 1994), p. 200.

Chapter 18
The French Revolution

STORMING THE BASTILLE On July 14, 1789, crowds stormed the Bastille, a prison in Paris. This event, whose only practical effect was to free a few prisoners, marked the first time the populace of Paris redirected the course of the revolution.

SOURCE: Scala/Art Resource, NY

 ## Contents and Focus Questions

The Chapter in Brief

IN THE SPRING of 1789 political turmoil erupted in France. By the summer it had led to a revolution that marked the beginning of a new political order in France and eventually throughout the west. The French Revolution brought to the foreground the principles of civic equality and popular sovereignty that challenged the major political and social institutions of Europe and that in evolving forms have continued to shape and reshape Western political and social life to the present day. During the 1790s the forces the revolution unleashed would cause small-town provincial lawyers and Parisian street orators to exercise more influence over the fate of the Continent than aristocrats, royal ministers, or monarchs. Citizen armies commanded by people of modest origin and filled by conscripted village youths would defeat armies comprised of professional soldiers led by officers from the nobility. The king and queen of France, as well as thousands of French peasants and shopkeepers, would be executed. The existence of the Roman Catholic faith in France and indeed of Christianity itself would be challenged. Finally, Europe would embark on almost a quarter century of war that would eventually extend across the continent and result in millions of casualties.

18.1 The Crisis of the French Monarchy

How did the financial weakness of the French monarchy lay the foundations of revolution in 1789?

Although the French Revolution would shatter many of the political, social, and ecclesiastical structures of Europe, its origins lay in a much more mundane problem. By the late 1780s, thanks in large part to the expenditures associated with supporting the American revolution, the French royal government could not command sufficient taxes to finance itself. The monarchy's unsuccessful search for adequate revenues led to ongoing conflicts with aristocratic and ecclesiastical institutions. The resulting deadlock was so complete that Louis XVI and his ministers were required to summon the French Estates General, which had not met since 1614. Once the deputies to that body gathered, a new set of problems quickly emerged that led to the revolution itself. Yet, none of this would have occurred if the monarchy had not reached a financial crisis so great that it could no longer function within the limits and practices of existing political institutions.

18.1.1 The Monarchy Seeks New Taxes

The French monarchy emerged from the Seven Years' War (1756–1763) defeated, deeply in debt, and unable thereafter to put its finances on a sound basis. French support of the American revolt against Great Britain further deepened the financial difficulties of the government. Given the economic vitality of France, its debt was neither overly large nor disproportionate to the debts of other European powers. The problem lay with the royal government's inability to tap the nation's wealth through taxes to repay the debt. Paradoxically, France was a rich nation in which the inability to collect sufficient taxes led to an impoverished government. Peasants, who had the least to spare, bore the heaviest tax burden. They paid taxes not only to the king but also to the church and their local lords. A bad harvest in

1788 meant that peasants were not only impoverished but also in danger of starvation as bread prices soared. Without increased taxation on the aristocracy and the church, there was no way that taxation of peasants alone could resolve France's financial crisis.

The debt was symptomatic of the failure of the late-eighteenth-century French monarchy to come to terms with the political power of aristocratic institutions, in particular the parlements. French absolutism had always involved ongoing negotiation between the monarchy and local aristocratic interests. This process had become more difficult after the death of Louis XIV (r. 1643–1715) when the aristocracy had sought to reclaim influence it had lost. Nonetheless, for the first half-century, the monarchy had retained most of its authority.

For twenty-five years after the Seven Years' War, however, a standoff occurred between the monarchy and the aristocracy, as one royal minister after another attempted to devise new tax schemes that would tap the wealth of the nobility, only to be confronted by opposition from both the Parlement of Paris and provincial parlements. Both Louis XV (r. 1715–1774) and Louis XVI (r. 1774–1792) lacked the character, resolution, and political skills to resolve the dispute. In place of a consistent policy for dealing with the growing debt and aristocratic resistance to change, the monarchy hesitated, retreated, and even lied.

In 1770, Louis XV appointed René Maupeou (1714–1792) as chancellor. The new minister was determined to increase taxes on the nobility. He abolished the parlements and exiled their members to different parts of the country. He then

LOUIS XVI OF FRANCE Well-meaning, but weak and vacillating, Louis XVI (r. 1774–1792) stumbled from concession to concession until he finally lost all power to save his throne.
SOURCE: Bridgeman—Giraudon/Art Resource, NY

began an ambitious program to make the administration more efficient. However, when Louis XV died of smallpox in 1774, his successor, Louis XVI, attempted to regain popular support by dismissing Maupeou, restoring all the parlements, and confirming their old powers.

Although the parlements spoke for aristocratic interests, they appear to have enjoyed public support. By the second half of the eighteenth century, many French nobles shared with the wealthy professional and commercial classes similar goals for administrative reforms that would support economic growth. Moreover, throughout these initial and later disputes with the monarchy, the parlements, though completely dominated by the aristocracy, used the language of liberty and reform to defend their cause. They portrayed the monarchy as despotic—that is, as acting arbitrarily in defiance of the law. They drew on the ideas and arguments of many Enlightenment writers, such as Montesquieu and the physiocrats.

The monarchy was unable to rally public opinion to its side because it had lost much of its moral authority. Louis XVI was considered detached and ineffective. His wife, Marie Antoinette (1755–1793), was always suspect because of her Austrian background. She was viciously accused of sexual misconduct and personal extravagance in an underground pamphlet campaign that became increasingly prurient, misogynist, and xenophobic. Furthermore, Louis XVI and his family continued to live at Versailles, rarely leaving its grounds to mix with his subjects and with the aristocracy, who, unlike in the days of Louis XIV, often dwelled in Paris or on their estates. Hence, the French monarch stood at a distinct popular disadvantage in his clashes first with the parlements and later with other groups of the aristocracy.

In these respects, the public image and daily reality of the French monarchy were much more problematical than those of other contemporary monarchs. Frederick II of Prussia and Joseph II of Austria genuinely saw themselves, and were seen by their subjects, as patriotic servants of the state. In central Europe, rulers were often the generators of reform, which meant even criticism of current policy was generally combined with confidence in the monarchy's ability to correct any errors. George III of Great Britain, despite his political difficulties, was regarded by most Britons as having a model character and as seeking the economic improvement of his nation. Frederick II, Joseph II, and George III all had reputations for personal frugality, and they moved frequently among the people they governed.

18.1.2 Necker's Report

France's successful intervention on behalf of the American colonists against the British only worsened the financial problems of Louis XVI's government. By 1781, as a result of the aid to America, its debt was larger and its sources of revenues were unchanged. The new royal director-general of finances, **Jacques Necker** (1732–1804), did not want to admit that the situation was as bad as feared. Necker, a Swiss banker, produced a public report in 1781 that used a financial sleight of hand to downplay France's financial difficulties. He argued that if the expenditures for the American war were removed, the budget was in surplus. Necker's report also revealed that a large portion of royal expenditures went to funding the pensions of aristocrats and other royal court favorites. Necker was pressured to leave office not because of his dubious accounting but because court aristocratic circles were embarrassed by his revelations. But the damage had already been done: Necker's misleading assessment of French finances made it more difficult for government officials to present a real need to raise new taxes.

18.1.3 Calonne's Reform Plan and the Assembly of Notables

The monarchy hobbled along without a plan for financial improvement until 1786. By this time, Charles Alexandre de Calonne (1734–1802) was the minister of finance. Calonne proposed to encourage internal trade; to lower some taxes, such as the *gabelle* on salt; and to transform the corvée, peasants' labor services on public works, into money payments. He also sought to remove internal barriers to trade and reduce government regulation of the grain trade. More important, Calonne wanted to introduce a new land tax that all landowners would have to pay regardless of their social status. Calonne also intended to establish new local assemblies made up of landowners to approve land taxes; in these assemblies the voting power would depend on the amount of land a person owned rather than on his social status. These proposals would have undermined both the political and the social power of the French aristocracy. Some of Calonne's other proposals touched the economic privileges of the French Church. These policies reflected much advanced economic and administrative thinking.

The monarchy, however, had little room to maneuver. The creditors were at the door, and the treasury was nearly empty. Calonne needed public support for such bold new undertakings. In February 1787, he met with an Assembly of Notables, nominated by the royal ministry from the upper ranks of the aristocracy and the church, to seek support for his plan. The assembly adamantly refused to give it. There was some agreement that reform and greater fairness in taxation were necessary, but the assembly did not trust the information they had received from Calonne. In his place they called for the reappointment of Necker, who they believed had left the country in sound fiscal condition. Finally, they claimed that only the Estates General of France, a medieval institution that had not met since 1614, could consent to new taxes. The notables believed that calling the

Estates General, which had been traditionally organized to allow aristocratic and church dominance, would actually allow the nobility to have a direct role in governing the country alongside the monarchy.

18.1.4 Deadlock and the Calling of the Estates General

Again, Louis XVI backed off. He replaced Calonne with Étienne Charles Loménie de Brienne (1727–1794), archbishop of Toulouse and the chief opponent of Calonne at the Assembly of Notables. Once in office, Brienne found, to his astonishment, that the financial situation was as bad as his predecessor had asserted. Brienne himself now sought to reform the land tax. The Parlement of Paris, however, in its self-appointed role as the embodiment of public opinion, took the new position that it lacked authority to authorize the tax and that only the Estates General could do so. Shortly thereafter, Brienne appealed to the Assembly of the Clergy to approve a large subsidy to fund that part of the debt then coming due for payment. The clergy, like the Parlement dominated by aristocrats, not only refused the subsidy but also reduced the voluntary contribution, or *don gratuit*, that it paid to the government in lieu of taxes.

As these unfruitful negotiations were taking place at the center of political life, local aristocratic parlements and estates in the provinces were making their own demands. They wanted to restore the privileges they had enjoyed during the early seventeenth century, before Richelieu and Louis XIV had crushed their independence. Making the financial crisis even more urgent, in the summer of 1788 bankers refused to extend necessary short-term credit to the government. Consequently, in July 1788, the king, through Brienne, agreed to convoke the Estates General the next year. Brienne resigned, and Necker replaced him. Political reform was coming, but the form it would take and how it would happen would be largely determined by the conflicts that emerged from summoning the Estates General.

18.2 The Revolution of 1789

How did the calling of the Estates General lead to revolution?

By the time the Estates General convened, agreement had become impossible for the three groups. The difficulty arose over the limits the aristocracy wanted to impose on the Third Estate. The differences centered on the voting rules and the representation each group should receive in the Estates General. But the ensuing struggle unleased radical forces that required much more than the denial of certain aristocratic privileges.

18.2.1 The Estates General Becomes the National Assembly

The Estates General had been called because of the political deadlock between the French monarchy and the vested interests of aristocratic institutions and the church. Almost immediately after it was summoned, however, the three groups, or estates, represented within it clashed with each other. The First Estate was the clergy, the Second Estate the nobility, and the **Third Estate** was, theoretically, all other adult men in the kingdom, although its representatives were drawn primarily from wealthy members of the commercial and professional middle classes. All the representatives in the Estates General were men. During the widespread public discussions preceding the meeting of the Estates General, representatives of the Third Estate made it clear they would not permit the monarchy and the aristocracy to decide the future of the nation.

A comment by a priest, the Abbé Siéyès (1748–1836), in a pamphlet published in 1789, captures the spirit of the Third Estate's representatives: "What is the Third Estate? Everything. What has it been in the political order up to the present? Nothing. What does it ask? To become something."[1] The spokesmen for the Third Estate became more determined to assert their role less from any preexisting conflicts with the nobility than from the conflicts that emerged during the debates and electioneering for the Estates General in late 1788 and early 1789.

18.2.1.1 DEBATE OVER ORGANIZATION AND VOTING Before the Estates General gathered, a public debate over its proper organization drew the lines of basic disagreement. The aristocracy made two important attempts to limit the influence of the Third Estate. First, a reconvened Assembly of Notables demanded that each estate have an equal number of representatives. Second, in September 1788, the Parlement of Paris ruled that voting in the Estates General should be conducted by order, or estate, rather than by head—that is, each estate in the Estates General, rather than each individual member, should have one vote. This procedure would in all likelihood have ensured the aristocratically dominated First and Second Estates could always outvote the Third by a vote of two estates to one estate.

In many respects, the interests of the aristocracy and the most prosperous and well-educated members of the Third Estate had converged during the eighteenth century, and many nobles had spouses from wealthy families of the Third Estate. Yet a fundamental social distance separated the members of the two orders. Many aristocrats were much richer than members of the Third Estate, and noblemen had all but monopolized the high command in the army and navy. The Third Estate had also experienced various forms of political and social discrimination from the nobility. The resistance of the nobility to voting by head confirmed the suspicions and resentments of the members of the Third Estate.

18.2.1.2 DOUBLING THE THIRD In the face of widespread public uproar over the aristocratic effort to dominate composition and procedures of the Estates General, the royal council decided that strengthening the Third Estate would best serve the interests of the monarchy and the cause of fiscal reform. In December 1788, the council announced the Third Estate would elect twice as many representatives as either the nobles or the clergy. This so-called doubling of the Third Estate meant it could easily dominate the Estates General if voting proceeded by head rather than by order. The method of voting had not yet been decided when the Estates General gathered at Versailles in May 1789.

18.2.1.3 THE *CAHIERS DE DOLÉANCES* When the representatives came to the royal palace, they brought with them *cahiers de doléances*, or lists of grievances, registered by the local electors, to be presented to the king. Many of these lists have survived and provide considerable information about the state of France on the eve of the revolution. The documents criticized government waste, indirect taxes, church taxes and corruption, and the hunting rights of the aristocracy. They included calls for periodic meetings of the Estates General, more equitable taxes, more local control of administration, unified weights and measures to facilitate trade and commerce, and a free press. The overwhelming demand of the *cahiers* was for equality of rights among the king's subjects. Yet the *cahiers* that originated among the nobility were

not radically different from those of the Third Estate. There was broad agreement that the French government needed major reform, that greater equality in taxation and other matters was desirable, and that many aristocratic privileges must be abandoned. But it became clear almost from the moment the Estates General opened that conflict among the estates, rather than cooperation, was to be the rule.

18.2.1.4 THE THIRD ESTATE CREATES THE NATIONAL ASSEMBLY The complaints, demands, and hopes for reform expressed in the *cahiers* could not, however, be discussed until the questions of the organization and voting in the Estates General had been decided. From the beginning, the Third Estate, whose members consisted largely of local officials, professionals, and other persons of property, refused to sit as a separate order as the king desired. For several weeks there was a standoff. Then, on June 1, the Third Estate invited the clergy and the nobles to join them in organizing a new legislative body. A few priests did so. On June 17, that body declared itself the **National Assembly**, and on June 19 by a narrow margin, the Second Estate voted to join the assembly.

18.2.1.5 THE TENNIS COURT OATH At this point, Louis XVI hoped to reassert a role in the proceedings. He intended to call a "Royal Session" of the Estates General for June 23 and closed the room where the National Assembly

THE TENNIS COURT OATH In the center foreground of this painting of the Tennis Court Oath by Jacques-Louis David (1748–1825), members of different estates join hands in cooperation as equals. The presiding officer, Jean-Sylvain Bailly, would soon become mayor of Paris.
SOURCE: RMN-Grand Palais/Art Resource, NY

had been gathering. On June 20, finding themselves unexpectedly locked out of their usual meeting place, the National Assembly moved to a nearby indoor tennis court. There, its members took an oath to continue to sit until they had given France a constitution. This was the famous **Tennis Court Oath**. Louis XVI ordered the National Assembly to desist, but many clergy and nobles joined the assembly in defiance of the royal command.

On June 27, the king, now having completely lost control of the events around him, capitulated and formally requested the First and Second Estates to meet with the National Assembly, where voting would occur by head rather than by order. Because of the doubling of its membership, the Third Estate had twice as many members as either of the other estates that joined them. Had nothing further occurred, the government of France would already have been transformed. The monarchy could now govern only in cooperation with the National Assembly, and the National Assembly would not be a legislative body organized according to privileged orders. The National Assembly, which renamed itself the National Constituent Assembly because of its intention to write a new constitution, was comprised of a majority of members drawn from all three orders, who shared liberal goals for the administrative, constitutional, and economic reform of the country. The revolution in France against government by privileged hereditary orders, however, rapidly extended beyond events occurring at Versailles.

18.2.2 Fall of the Bastille

Two new factors soon influenced the events at Versailles. First, Louis XVI again attempted to regain the political initiative by mustering royal troops near Versailles and Paris. On the advice of Queen Marie Antoinette, his brothers, and the most conservative aristocrats at court, he seemed to be contemplating the use of force against the National Constituent Assembly. On July 11, without consulting assembly leaders, Louis abruptly dismissed Necker, his minister of finance. Louis's gathering troops and dismissal of Necker marked the beginning of a steady, but consistently poorly executed, royal attempt to undermine the assembly and halt the revolution. Most of the National Constituent Assembly wished to establish some form of constitutional monarchy, but from the start, Louis's refusal to cooperate thwarted that effort. The king fatally threw in his lot with the conservative aristocracy against the emerging forces of reform drawn from across the social and political spectrum.

The second new factor that influenced the events at Versailles was the populace of Paris, which numbered more than 600,000 people. The mustering of royal troops created anxiety in the city, where throughout the winter and spring of 1789 high prices for bread, which was the staple food

of the poor, had produced riots. Those Parisians who had elected representatives to the Third Estate had continued to meet after the elections. By June they were organizing a citizen militia and collecting arms. They regarded the dismissal of Necker as the opening of a royal offensive against the National Constituent Assembly and the city. They intended to protect the assembly, and the revolution had begun.

On July 14, large crowds of Parisians, most of them small shopkeepers, tradespeople, artisans, and wage earners, marched to the **Bastille** to get weapons for the militia. This great fortress, with ten-foot-thick walls, had once held political prisoners. Through miscalculations and ineptitude by the governor of the fortress, the troops in the Bastille fired into the crowd, killing ninety-eight people and wounding many others. Thereafter, the crowd stormed the fortress. They released the seven prisoners inside, none of whom was a political prisoner, and killed several troops and the governor.

On July 15, the militia of Paris, by then called the National Guard, offered its command to a young liberal aristocrat, the Marquis de Lafayette (1757–1834). This hero of the American Revolution gave the guard a new insignia: the red and blue stripes from the colors of the coat of arms of Paris, separated by the white stripe of the royal flag. The emblem became the revolutionary *cockade* (badge) and eventually the tricolor flag of revolutionary France.

The attack on the Bastille marked the first of many crucial *journées*, days on which the populace of Paris redirected the course of the revolution. The fall of the fortress signaled that the National Constituent Assembly alone would not decide the political future of the nation. As the news of the taking of the Bastille spread, similar disturbances took place in provincial cities. A few days later, Louis XVI again bowed to the force of events and personally visited Paris, where he wore the revolutionary cockade and recognized the organized electors as the legitimate government of the city. The king also recognized the National Guard.

18.2.3 The "Great Fear" and the Night of August 4

Simultaneous with the popular urban disturbances, a movement known as the **"Great Fear"** swept across much of the French countryside. Rumors that royal troops would be sent into the rural districts intensified the peasant disturbances that had begun during the spring. The Great Fear saw the burning of *châteaux*, the destruction of legal records and documents, and the refusal to pay feudal dues. The peasants were determined to take possession of food supplies and land that they considered rightfully theirs. They vented their anger against the injustices of rural life and reclaimed rights and property they had lost through administrative tightening of the collection of feudal dues during the past century. Their targets were both aristocratic and ecclesiastical landlords. (For a satiric depiction of the relationships among royalty, aristocracy, clergy, and peasantry, see the "Closer Look" sidebar, which follows below.)

A Closer Look

Challenging the French Political Order

THIS LATE-EIGHTEENTH-CENTURY cartoon satirizes French society and politics as the events and tensions leading up to the outbreak of the French Revolution unfolded. The image represents a highly radical critique of the refusal, in 1787, of the French nobility and church to aid the monarchy during a period of financial crisis. It is one of a series of similar cartoons, most of which, unlike this example, depict men. The caption reads "Long Live the King, Long Live the Nation. I always knew we would have our turn!" Only after the calling of the Estates General was Louis XVI seen as siding with the church and nobility against the people.

Her hat is adorned with a cockade in revolutionary colors.

A woman holding a distaff (a tool used in spinning) and simultaneously nurshing a baby rides on the back of an aristocrat. Her shoes are wooden, indicating her peasant back-ground.

The noblewoman clutches onto a nun for support, suggesting the collusion of aristocracy and church.

LONG LIVE THE KING, LONG LIVE THE NATION
SOURCE: Library of Congress

Questions

1. Is this image meant to celebrate the peasantry's newfound power or lament it? What hints does the artist provide as to his or her sympathy?

2. Similar images depicting men were very common. What does this image suggest about the role of women in the Old Regime and in the revolution?

3. What is the symbolic significance of the suckling infant?

On the night of August 4, 1789, aristocrats in the National Constituent Assembly attempted to halt the spreading disorder in the countryside. By prearrangement, several liberal nobles and clerics rose in the assembly and renounced their feudal rights, dues, and tithes. In a scene of great emotion, they surrendered hunting and fishing rights, judicial authority, and legal exemptions. These nobles and clerics gave up what they had already lost and what they could not have regained without civil war in the rural areas. Many of them later received financial compensation for their losses. Nonetheless, after the night of August 4, all French citizens were subject to the same and equal laws. Since the sale of government offices was also abolished, the events of that night opened political and military positions, careers, and advancement to talent rather than basing them exclusively on birth or wealth. This dramatic session of the assembly effectively abolished the major social institutions of the Old Regime and created an unforeseen situation that required a vast legal and social reconstruction of the nation.

Both the attack on the Bastille and the Great Fear displayed characteristics of the urban and rural riots that had occurred often in eighteenth-century France. Louis XVI first thought the attack on Bastille was simply another bread riot. But the popular disturbances were only partly related to the events at Versailles. A deep economic downturn had struck France in 1787 and continued into 1788. The harvests for both years had been poor, and the food prices in 1789 were higher than at any time since 1703. Wages had not kept up with the rise in prices. Throughout the winter of 1788 to 1789, an unusually cold one, many people suffered from hunger. Wage and food riots had erupted in several cities. These economic problems fanned the fires of revolution.

18.2.4 The Declaration of the Rights of Man and Citizen

In late August 1789, the National Constituent Assembly decided that before writing a new constitution, it should publish a statement of broad political principles. On August 27, the assembly issued the **Declaration of the Rights of Man and Citizen**. This declaration drew on the political language of the Enlightenment and the Declaration of Rights that the state of Virginia had adopted in June 1776.

The French declaration proclaimed that all men were "born and remain free and equal in rights." The natural rights so proclaimed were "liberty, property, security, and resistance to oppression." Governments existed to protect those rights. All political sovereignty resided in the nation and its representatives. All citizens were to be equal before the law and were to be "equally admissible to all public dignities, offices, and employments, according to their capacity, and with no other distinction than that of their virtues and talents." There were to be due process of law and presumption of innocence until proof of guilt. Freedom of religion

was affirmed. Taxation was to be apportioned equally according to the capacity to pay. Property constituted "an inviolable and sacred right."[2]

The Declaration of the Rights of Man and Citizen was directed in large measure against specific abuses of the old French monarchical and aristocratic regime, but it was framed in abstract universalistic language applicable to other European nations. In this respect, the ideas expressed in the declaration like those of the Protestant reformers three centuries earlier could cross national borders and find adherents outside France. The two most powerful, universal political ideas of the declaration were civic equality and popular sovereignty. The first would challenge the legal and social inequities of European life, and the second would assert that governments must be responsible to the governed. These two principles, in turn, could find themselves in tension with the declaration's principle of the protection of property.

It was not accidental that the Declaration of the Rights of Man and Citizen specifically applied to men and not to women. Much of the political language of the Enlightenment, and especially that associated with Rousseau, separated men and women into distinct gender spheres. According to this view, which influenced legislation during the revolution, men were suited for citizenship, women for motherhood and the domestic life. Nonetheless, in the charged atmosphere of the summer of 1789, many politically active and informed Frenchwomen hoped the guarantees of the declaration would be extended to them. They were particularly concerned with property, inheritance, family, and divorce. Some saw in the declaration a framework within which women might eventually enjoy the rights and protection of citizenship. Those hopes would be disappointed during the years of the revolution and for many decades thereafter.

Still, over the succeeding two centuries the universalist language of the Declaration of the Rights of Man and Citizen would provide an intellectual framework for bringing into the realm of active civic life many groups who were excluded in the late eighteenth century.

18.2.5 The Parisian Women's March on Versailles

Louis XVI stalled before ratifying both the Declaration of the Rights of Man and Citizen and the aristocratic renunciation of feudalism. His hesitations fueled suspicions that he might again try to resort to force. Moreover, bread remained scarce and expensive. On October 5, 1789, some 7,000 Parisian women armed with pikes, guns, swords, and knives marched to Versailles demanding more bread. Deeply suspicious of the monarch and believing that he must be kept under the watchful eye of the people, the Parisians demanded that Louis and his family return to Paris with them. The monarch

THE WOMEN OF PARIS ON THE MARCH TO VERSAILLES As shown in this image, the women of Paris marched to Versailles on October 5, 1789. Although they did not make any demands specific to women's rights, the mere sight of so many women expressing political demands alarmed the king and his supporters. The following day the royal family was forced to return to Paris with them. Henceforth, the French government would function under the constant threat of mob violence.

SOURCE: Bridgeman—Giraudon/Art Resource, NY

had no real choice. On October 6, 1789, his carriage followed the crowd into the city, where he and his family settled in the old palace of the Tuileries in the heart of Paris.

The National Constituent Assembly also soon moved to Paris. Thereafter, both Paris and France remained relatively stable and peaceful until the summer of 1792. A decline in the price of bread in late 1789 helped to calm the atmosphere.

18.3 The Reconstruction of France

How did the National Constituent Assembly reorganize France?

In Paris, the National Constituent Assembly set about reorganizing France. In government, it pursued a policy of constitutional monarchy; in administration, rationalism; in economics, unregulated freedom; and in religion, anticlericalism. Throughout its proceedings and following the principles of the Declaration of the Rights of Man and Citizen, the assembly was determined to protect property in all its forms and to limit the impact on the national life of those French people who had no property or only small

amounts of it. Although championing civic equality before the law, the assembly, with the aristocrats and middle-class elite united, spurned social equality and extensive democracy. It thus charted a general course that, to a greater or lesser degree, nineteenth-century liberals across Europe would follow.

18.3.1 Political Reorganization

In the Constitution of 1791, the National Constituent Assembly established a constitutional monarchy. The major political authority of the nation would be a unicameral legislative assembly, in which all laws would originate. The monarch was allowed a suspensive veto that could delay, but not halt, legislation. The assembly also had the power to make war and peace.

18.3.1.1 ACTIVE AND PASSIVE CITIZENS The constitution provided for an elaborate system of indirect elections to thwart direct popular pressure on the government. The citizens of France were divided into active and passive categories. Only active citizens could vote, that is, men paying annual taxes equal to three days of local labor wages. They chose electors, who then in turn, voted for members of the legislature. Further property qualifications were required to serve as an elector or member of the legislature. Only about

50,000 citizens of a population of about 25 million could qualify as electors or members of the legislative assembly. Women could neither vote nor hold office.

These constitutional arrangements effectively transferred political power from aristocratic wealth to all forms of propertied wealth in the nation. The accumulation of wealth from land and commercial property, not hereditary privilege or the purchase of titles or offices, would open the path to political authority. These new political arrangements based on property rather than birth reflected the changes in French society over the past century and allowed more social and economic interests to have a voice in governing the nation.

18.3.1.2 OLYMPE DE GOUGES'S DECLARATION OF THE RIGHTS OF WOMAN

The laws that excluded women from voting and holding office did not pass unnoticed. In 1791, Olympe de Gouges (d. 1793), a butcher's daughter from Montauban in northwest France who became a major revolutionary radical in Paris, composed a Declaration of the Rights of Woman, which she ironically addressed to Queen Marie Antoinette. Much of the document reprinted the Declaration of the Rights of Man and Citizen, adding the word *woman* to the various original clauses. That strategy demanded that women be regarded as citizens and not merely as daughters,

sisters, wives, and mothers of citizens. Olympe de Gouges further outlined rights that would permit women to own property and require men to recognize the paternity of their children. She called for equality of the sexes in marriage and improved education for women. She declared, "Women, wake up; the *tocsin* of reason is being heard throughout the whole universe; discover your rights."[3] Her declaration illustrated how the list of rights in the Declaration of the Rights of Man and Citizen created a structure of universal civic expectations even for those it did not cover.

18.3.1.3 DEPARTMENTS REPLACE PROVINCES

In reconstructing the local and judicial administration, the National Constituent Assembly applied the rational spirit of the Enlightenment. It abolished the ancient French provinces, such as Burgundy and Brittany, and established in their place eighty-three administrative units called *départements* of generally equal size named after rivers, mountains, and other geographical features. The departments in turn were subdivided into districts, cantons, and communes. Elections for departmental and local assemblies were also indirect. This administrative reconstruction proved to be permanent. The departments still exist in twenty-first-century France. (See Map 18–1.)

Map 18–1 FRENCH PROVINCES AND THE REPUBLIC

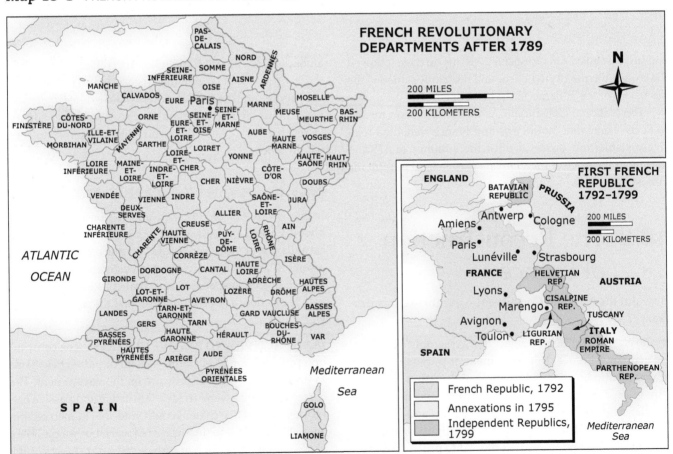

In 1789, the National Constituent Assembly redrew the map of France. The ancient provinces were replaced with a larger number of new, smaller departments. This redrawing of the map was part of the assembly's effort to impose greater administrative rationality in France.

All the ancient judicial courts, including the seigneurial courts and the parlements, were also abolished and replaced by uniform courts with elected judges and prosecutors. Procedures were simplified, and the most degrading punishments, such as branding, torture, and public flogging, were outlawed.

18.3.2 Economic Policy

In economic matters, the National Constituent Assembly continued the policies Louis XVI's reformist ministers had formerly advocated. It suppressed the guilds and liberated the grain trade. A metric system was established to provide the nation with uniform weights and measures.

18.3.2.1 WORKERS' ORGANIZATIONS FORBIDDEN The new policies of economic freedom and uniformity disappointed both peasants and urban workers. In 1789, the assembly placed the burden of proof on the peasants to rid themselves of the residual feudal dues for which compensation was to be paid. On June 14, 1791, the assembly crushed the attempts of urban workers to protect their wages by enacting the Chapelier Law, which forbade workers' associations. The assembly interpreted the workers' efforts to organize as a recreation of the abolished guilds of the Old Regime in order to oppose the new values of political and social individualism that the revolution championed. Peasants and workers were henceforth to be left to the freedom and mercy of the marketplace, without the protection of association.

18.3.2.2 CONFISCATION OF CHURCH LANDS While these various reforms were being put into effect, the financial crisis that had occasioned the calling of the Estates General persisted. The assembly did not repudiate the royal debt because it was owed to the bankers, the merchants, and the commercial traders of the Third Estate. The National Constituent Assembly had suppressed many of the old, hated indirect taxes (such as taxes on staples like salt, bread, and wine) and had substituted new land taxes, but these proved insufficient. Moreover, there were not enough officials to collect the new taxes, and many people simply evaded them in the general confusion of the day. The continuing financial problem led the assembly to take what may well have been its most decisive action for the future of French life and society. The assembly decided to finance the debt by confiscating and then selling the land and property of the Roman Catholic Church in France. The results were further inflation, religious schism, and civil war. In effect, the National Constituent Assembly had opened a new chapter in the relations of church and state in Europe.

ASSIGNAT OF 10,000 FRANCS *Assignats* were government bonds that were backed by confiscated church lands. They circulated as money. When the government printed too many of them, inflation resulted and their value fell.
SOURCE: bpk Bildagentur/Art Resource, NY

18.3.2.3 THE *ASSIGNATS* Having chosen to plunder the church, the assembly authorized the issuance of *assignats*, or government bonds, in December 1789. Their value was guaranteed by the revenue to be generated from the sale of church property. Initially, a limit was set on the quantity of assignats to be issued. The bonds, however, proved so acceptable to the public that they began to circulate as currency. The assembly issued an ever-larger number of them to liquidate the national debt and to create a large body of new property owners with a direct stake in the revolution. Within a few months, however, the value of the assignats began to fall and inflation increased, putting new stress on the urban poor. Fluctuation in the worth of this currency would plague the revolutionary government throughout the 1790s.

18.3.3 The Civil Constitution of the Clergy

The confiscation of church lands required an ecclesiastical reconstruction. In July 1790, the National Constituent Assembly issued the Civil Constitution of the Clergy, which transformed the Roman Catholic Church in France into a branch of the secular state. This legislation reduced the number of bishoprics from 135 to 83, making one diocese for each of the new departments. It also provided for the election of pastors and bishops, who henceforth became salaried employees of the state. The assembly, which also dissolved all religious orders in France except those that cared for the sick or ran schools, consulted neither Pope Pius VI (r. 1775–1799) nor the French clergy about these sweeping changes. The king approved the measure only with the greatest reluctance.

The Civil Constitution of the Clergy was the major blunder of the National Constituent Assembly. It embittered relations between the French church and the state, a problem that has persisted to the present day. The measure immediately created immense opposition within the French church, even from bishops who had long championed Gallican liberties over papal domination. In the face of this resistance, the assembly unwisely ruled that all clergy must take an oath to support the Civil Constitution. Only seven bishops and a little less than half the lower clergy did so. In reprisal, the assembly designated those clergy who had not taken the oath as "refractory" and removed them from their clerical functions. Angry reactions were swift. Refractory priests celebrated Mass in defiance of the assembly. In February 1791, Pope Pius VI condemned not only the Civil Constitution of the Clergy but also the Declaration of the Rights of Man and Citizen. That condemnation marked the opening of a Roman Catholic offensive against the revolution and liberalism more broadly that continued throughout the nineteenth century. Within France itself, the pope's action created a crisis of conscience and political loyalty for all sincere Catholics. Religious devotion and revolutionary loyalty became incompatible for many. French citizens were divided between those who supported the constitutional priests and those who, like the royal family, followed the refractory clergy. (See the "Compare and Connect" sidebar, which follows below, on differing views of the National Assembly.)

18.3.4 Counterrevolutionary Activity

The revolution had other enemies besides the pope and devout Catholics. As it became clear that the old political and social order was undergoing fundamental and probably permanent change, many aristocrats, eventually more than 16,000, left France. Known as the *émigrés*, they settled in countries near the French border, where they sought to foment counterrevolution. Among the most important of them was the king's younger brother, the count of Artois (1757–1836). In the summer of 1791, his agents and the queen persuaded Louis XVI to attempt to flee the country.

18.3.4.1 FLIGHT TO VARENNES On the night of June 20, 1791, Louis and his immediate family, disguised as servants, left Paris. They traveled as far as Varennes on their way to Metz in eastern France where a royalist military force was waiting for them. At Varennes the king was recognized, and his flight was halted. On June 24, a company of soldiers escorted the royal family back to Paris. Eventually the leaders of the National Constituent Assembly, determined to save the constitutional monarchy, announced the king had

been abducted from the capital. This convenient public fiction could not cloak the reality that the king was now the chief counterrevolutionary in France and that the constitutional monarchy might not last long. Profound distrust now dominated the political scene.

18.3.4.2 DECLARATION OF PILLNITZ Two months later, on August 27, 1791, under pressure from the *émigrés*, Emperor Leopold II (r. 1790–1792) of Austria, who was the brother of Marie Antoinette, and King Frederick William II (r. 1786–1797) of Prussia issued the Declaration of Pillnitz. The two monarchs promised to intervene in France to protect the royal family and to preserve the monarchy if the other major European powers agreed. This provision rendered the declaration practically meaningless because, at the time, Great Britain would not have given its consent. The declaration was, however, taken seriously in France, where the revolutionaries saw the nation surrounded by aristocratic and monarchical foes seeking to undo all that had been accomplished since 1789.

18.4 The End of the Monarchy: A Second Revolution

What led to the radicalization of the French Revolution?

The National Constituent Assembly drew to a close in September 1791, having completed its task of reconstructing the government and the administration of France. The assembly had passed a measure that forbade any of its own members to sit in the legislative assembly established by the new constitution. That new assembly, filled with entirely new members, met on October 1 and immediately had to confront the challenges stemming from the resistance to the Civil Constitution of the Clergy, the king's flight, and the Declaration of Pillnitz.

18.4.1 Emergence of the Jacobins

Ever since the original gathering of the Estates General, deputies from the Third Estate had organized themselves into clubs composed of politically like-minded persons. The most famous and best organized of these clubs were the **Jacobins**, named because the group met in a former Dominican priory dedicated to St. Jacques (James) in Paris. The Jacobins had also established a network of local clubs throughout the provinces. They had been the most advanced political group in the National Constituent Assembly and had pressed for a republic rather than

Compare and Connect

What Did the National Assembly Accomplish?

IN THE HEADY DAYS OF LATE 1789 and 1790, the National Assembly swept aside much of the institutional basis of the Old Regime. It seemed to many that France was being remade anew. But not all French people were pleased with the changes. Even some who were highly critical of the monarchy found fault with the National Assembly, arguing that the reforms were too radical, too rapid, and insufficiently thought through. In the first of the two excerpts presented here, members of the National Assembly address the nation, responding to their critics and claiming credit for the dawning of a new and glorious age. In the second, Mallet du Pan, the editor of a popular journal, calls the National Assembly to task for its failures and points out that despotism and revolution were not the only two options available to France.

Before Reading

- Think about the forces supporting and undermining the National Assembly.
- Consider the makeup of the National Assembly and the goals of its members.
- Ask yourself how ordinary French people might have responded to the dramatic changes instituted by the National Assembly.

Questions

1. What did the National Assembly claim to have accomplished?
2. What might explain the defensive tone of the National Assembly's address to the French people?
3. What was Mallet du Pan's central criticism of the National Assembly?

I. ADDRESS OF THE NATIONAL ASSEMBLY TO THE FRENCH PEOPLE (1790)

They pretend to be unaware of the good that the National Assembly has accomplished; this we propose to recall to your mind. Objections have been raised against what has been done; these we propose to meet. Doubts and anxiety have been disseminated as to what we propose to do in the future; this we will explain to you. What has the Assembly accomplished? In the midst of storms, it has, with a firm hand, traced the principles of a constitution which will assure your liberty forever. The rights of man had been misconceived and insulted for centuries; they have been reestablished for all humanity in that declaration, which shall serve as an everlasting war cry against oppressors and as a law for the legislators themselves. The nation had lost the right to decree both the laws and the taxes; this right has been restored to it, while at the same time the true principles of monarchy have been solemnly established, as well as the inviolability of the august head of the nation and the heredity of the throne in a family so dear to all Frenchmen.

Formerly you had only the Estates General; now you have a National Assembly of which you can never be again deprived. In the Estates General the several orders, which were necessarily at odds and under the domination of ancient pretensions, dictated the decrees and could check the free action of the national will. These orders no longer exist; all have disappeared before the honorable title of citizen. All being citizens alike, you demanded citizen-defenders and, at the first summons, the National Guard arose, which, called together by patriotism and commanded by honor, has everywhere maintained or established order and watches with untiring zeal over the safety of each for the benefit of all.

II. MALLET DU PAN, WRITING IN *LE MECURE DE FRANCE* (1791)

The Constitutional Assembly cannot fail, without denying positive and accepted facts, to recognize that, as a result of its doctrines and action, it leaves every religious principle destroyed, morals in the last stage of degradation, free sway to every vice, the rights of property violated and undermined, our forces, both land and naval, in a worse state than at the opening of its reign; that it has shaken, if not destroyed, the foundation of all military organization; that it leaves our finances in chaos, the public debt considerably augmented, the annual deficit, according to the most favorable calculators, increased by half, the taxes in arrears, their payment suspended, having struck at their very roots by the recklessness of an absolutely new system of which the immediate effects have been to make the people regard themselves as freed from taxation. It cannot disguise from itself that our influence and reputation in Europe are eclipsed; that our commerce is less flourishing, our industry less productive, our population less numerous; that our labor has decreased as well as the national wealth; that it has caused the disappearance of the specie and dissipated an enormous amount of the public capital; that, finally, our internal police, in spite of numerous guards, is more oppressive and less effective than it was before the Revolution. . . .

In order justly to appreciate the conduct of our first lawmakers, we must avoid the sophism by which they have constantly fascinated the common people—that of comparing the present situation of France with the disastrous results of the most horrible despotism. That is a false standpoint to which knaves and fools are always careful to revert. A vast number of citizens do not desire the old any more than the new regime, and the reproaches heaped upon the latter have no bearing on the reform of the older system.

SOURCES: (I) James Harvey Robinson, ed., *Readings in European History,* vol. II (Boston: Ginn and Company, 1906), p. 418. (II) From James Harvey Robinson, ed. *Readings in European History*, vol. II (Boston: Ginn and Company, 1906), pp. 433–435.

a constitutional monarchy. They drew their political language from the most radical thought of the Enlightenment, particularly Rousseau's emphasis on equality, popular sovereignty, and civic virtue. Such thought and language became even more effective because the events of 1789 to 1791 had destroyed the old political framework, and the old monarchical political vocabulary was less and less relevant. The rhetoric of republicanism filled that vacuum and for a time set the political values of the day. The flight of Louis XVI in the summer of 1791 and the Declaration of Pillnitz led to renewed demands for a republic.

Factionalism plagued the legislative assembly throughout its short life from 1791 to 1792. A group of Jacobins known as the *Girondists* (because many of them came from the department of the Gironde in southwest France) assumed leadership of the assembly. They were determined to oppose the forces of counterrevolution. They passed one measure ordering the *émigrés* to return or suffer the loss of their property and another requiring the refractory clergy to support the Civil Constitution or lose their state pensions. The king vetoed both acts.

Furthermore, on April 20, 1792, the Girondists led the legislative assembly to declare war on Austria, by this time governed by Leopold II's son, Francis II (r. 1792–1835), and allied with Prussia. This decision launched a period of armed conflict across Western Europe that with only brief intervals of peace lasted until the final defeat of France at Waterloo in June 1815.

The Girondists believed the war would preserve the revolution from domestic enemies and bring the most advanced revolutionaries to power. Paradoxically, Louis XVI and other monarchists also favored the war. They thought the conflict would strengthen the executive power of the monarchy. The king also hoped that foreign armies might defeat French forces and restore the Old Regime. Both sides were playing a dangerous, deluded political game. The war radicalized French politics and within months led to what is usually called the second revolution, which overthrew the constitutional monarchy and established a republic.

Initially, the war effort went poorly. In July 1792, the duke of Brunswick, commander of the Prussian forces, issued a manifesto threatening to destroy Paris if the French royal family were harmed. This statement stiffened support for the war and increased distrust of the king.

Late in July, under radical working-class pressure, the government of Paris passed from the elected council to a committee, or *commune*, of representatives from the sections (municipal wards) of the city. Thereafter the Paris commune became an independent political force, casting itself in the role of the protector of the revolution against both internal and external enemies. Its activities and forceful modes of intimidation largely accounted for the dominance of Paris

in many of the future decisions of the revolutionary government for the next three years.

On August 10, 1792, a large crowd invaded the Tuileries palace and forced Louis XVI and Marie Antoinette to take refuge in the legislative assembly. The crowd fought with the royal Swiss guards. When Louis was finally able to call off the troops, several hundred of them and many Parisian citizens lay dead in the most extensive violence since the fall of the Bastille. Thereafter the royal family was imprisoned. Their quarters were comfortable, but the king was allowed to perform none of his political functions.

18.4.2 The Convention and the Role of the *Sans-culottes*

Having removed the reigning monarch, the more extreme elements of the Jacobins and the people of Paris extended the causes of the revolution. Economic hardship helped convince the **sans-culottes** that the original demands of the movement's leaders would not remedy their situation.

18.4.2.1 THE SEPTEMBER MASSACRES Early in September, the Parisian crowd again made its will felt. During the first week of the month, in what are known as the **September Massacres**, the Paris commune summarily executed or murdered about 1,200 people who were in the city jails. Some of these people were aristocrats or priests, but most were simply common criminals. The crowd had mistakenly assumed the prisoners were all counterrevolutionaries. News of this event, the August massacre of the Swiss guards, and the imprisonment of the royal family spread rapidly across Europe, rousing new hostility toward the revolutionary government.

The Paris commune then compelled the legislative assembly to call for the election by universal male suffrage of still another new assembly to write a democratic constitution. That body, called the **Convention** after the American Constitutional Convention of 1787, met on September 21, 1792. The previous day, the French army, filled with patriotic recruits willing to die for the revolution, had halted the Prussian advance at the Battle of Valmy in eastern France. Victory on the battlefield had confirmed the victory of democratic forces at home. As its first act, the Convention declared France a republic—that is, a nation governed by an elected assembly without a monarch.

18.4.2.2 GOALS OF THE *SANS-CULOTTES* The second revolution had been the work of Jacobins more radical than the Girondists and of the people of Paris known as the *sans-culottes*. The name of this group means "without breeches" and derived from the long trousers that,

CLOTHING OF THE *SANS-CULOTTES* French Revolution–era clothing worn by the *sans-culottes* or members of the poorer classes and their leaders was comprised of the *pantalon* (long trousers), *carmagnole* (short-skirted coat), and red cap of liberty.
SOURCE: Mark Hamilton/DK Images

as working people, they wore instead of aristocratic knee breeches. The *sans-culottes* were shopkeepers, artisans, wage earners, and, in a few cases, factory workers. The politics of the Old Regime had ignored them, and the policies of the National Constituent Assembly had left them victims of unregulated economic liberty. The government, however, required their labor and their lives if the war was to succeed. From the summer of 1792 until

the summer of 1794, their attitudes, desires, and ideals were the primary factors in the internal development of the revolution.

The *sans-culottes* generally knew what they wanted. The Parisian tradespeople and artisans sought immediate relief from food shortages and rising prices through price controls. The economic hardship of their lives made them impatient to see their demands met. They believed all people had a right to subsistence, and they resented most forms of social inequality. This attitude made them intensely hostile to the aristocracy and the original leaders of the revolution of 1789 from the Third Estate who, they believed, wanted to share political power, social prestige, and economic security with the aristocracy. The *sans-culottes'* hatred of inequality did not take them so far as to demand the abolition of property. Rather, they advocated a community of small property owners who would also participate in the political nation.

In politics they were antimonarchical, strongly republican, and suspicious even of representative government. They believed the people should make the decisions of government to an extent as great as possible. In Paris, where their influence was most important, the *sans-culottes* had gained their political experience in meetings of the Paris sections. The Paris commune organized the previous summer was their chief political vehicle and the crowd their chief instrument of action.

18.4.2.3 THE POLICIES OF THE JACOBINS The goals of the *sans-culottes* were not wholly compatible with those of the Jacobins, republicans who sought representative government. Jacobin hatred of the aristocracy and hereditary privilege did not extend to a general suspicion of wealth. Basically, the Jacobins favored an unregulated economy. From the time of Louis XVI's flight to Varennes onward, however, the more extreme Jacobins began to cooperate with leaders of the Parisian *sans-culottes* and the Paris commune to overthrow the monarchy. Once the Convention began to deliberate, these Jacobins, known as the *Mountain* because their seats were high up in the assembly hall, worked with the *sans-culottes* to carry the revolution forward and to win the war. This willingness to cooperate with the forces of the popular revolution separated the Mountain from the Girondists, who were also members of the Jacobins.

18.4.2.4 EXECUTION OF LOUIS XVI By the spring of 1793, several issues had brought the Mountain and its sans-culottes allies to dominate the Convention and the revolution. In December 1792, Louis XVI was put on trial as "Citizen Capet," the original medieval name of the royal family. An overwhelming majority convicted Louis of conspiring against the liberty of the people and the security of the state. Condemned to death by a smaller majority, he was beheaded on January 21, 1793. Marie Antoinette was

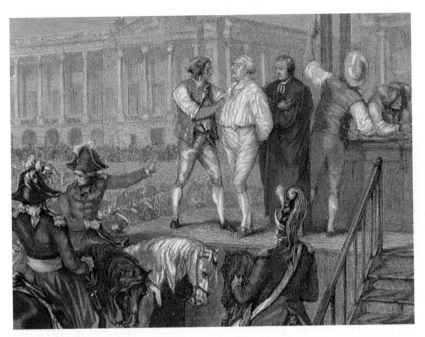

LOUIS XVI GUILLOTINED Condemned to death for conspiring against the liberty of the people and the security of the state, Louis XVI was beheaded on January 21, 1793.
SOURCE: Album/Art Resource, NY

subsequently tried and executed in October of the same year; their son died in 1795 in prison of disease exacerbated by neglect.

In February 1793, the Convention declared war on Great Britain and Holland, and a month later on Spain. Soon thereafter, the Prussians renewed their offensive and drove the French out of Belgium. To make matters worse, General Dumouriez (1739–1823), the Girondist victor of Valmy, deserted to the enemy. Finally, in March 1793, a royalist revolt led by aristocratic officers and priests erupted in the Vendée in western France and roused much popular support. Thus, the revolution was now at war with most of Europe and much of the French nation. The Girondists had led the country into the war but had been unable either to win it or to suppress the enemies of the revolution at home. The Mountain stood ready to take up the task.

18.5 Europe at War with the Revolution

How did Europe respond to the French Revolution?

Initially, the rest of Europe had been ambivalent toward the revolutionary events in France. Those who favored political reform regarded the revolution as wisely and rationally reorganizing a corrupt and inefficient government. The major foreign governments thought that the revolution

meant France would cease to be an important factor in European affairs for years.

18.5.1 Edmund Burke Attacks the Revolution

In 1790, however, Irish-born writer and British statesman Edmund Burke (1729–1799) argued a different position in *Reflections on the Revolution in France*. Burke condemned the reconstruction of the French administration as the application of a blind rationalism that ignored the historical realities of political development and the concrete complexities of social relations. He also forecast further turmoil as people without political experience tried to govern France; predicted the deaths of Louis XVI and Marie Antoinette at the hands of the revolutionaries; and anticipated that the revolution would end in military despotism. As the revolutionaries proceeded to attack the church, the monarchy, and finally the rest of Europe, Burke's ideas came to have many admirers.

By the outbreak of the war with Austria in April 1792, the other European monarchies recognized, along with Burke, the danger of both the ideas and the aggression of revolutionary France. In the United States, no amount of gratitude for France's assistance during the revolutionary war could move Washington to offer support to France; throughout his presidency, Washington insisted that the new republic must resist foreign entanglements. The increasing radicalism of the French Revolution alienated even those foreign statesmen initially sympathetic to its early reformist impulses. Instead of seeing France as a positive model, one European government after another turned to repressive domestic policies to forestall revolutionary activity at home.

18.5.2 Suppression of Reform in Britain

In Great Britain, William Pitt the Younger (1759–1806), the prime minister, who had unsuccessfully supported moderate reform of Parliament during the 1780s, turned against both reform and popular movements. The government suppressed the London Corresponding Society, founded in 1792 as a working-class reform group. In Birmingham, the government sponsored mob action to drive Joseph Priestley (1733–1804), a famous chemist and a radical political thinker, out of the country. In early 1793, Pitt secured parliamentary approval for acts suspending *habeas corpus* and making the writing of certain ideas treasonable. With less success, Pitt also attempted to curb freedom of the press. All political groups who dared oppose the government faced being associated with sedition.

18.5.3 The Second and Third Partitions of Poland: 1793 and 1795

The final two partitions of Poland occurred as a direct result of fears by the central and east European powers that French Revolution principles were establishing themselves in Poland. After the first partition in 1772, Polish leaders had commenced reforms to provide for a stronger state.

The Polish government also adopted equality before the law and religious toleration. Frederick William II of Prussia (r. 1786–1797) promised to defend the new Polish constitutional order because he believed that a stronger Poland was in Prussia's interest against the growing Russian power. Catherine the Great of Russia also understood that a reformed Polish state would diminish Russian influence in Poland and eastern Europe.

In April 1792, conservative Polish nobles who opposed the reforms invited Russia to restore the old order. The Russian army quickly defeated the reformist Polish forces led by Tadeusz Kosciuszko (1746–1817), a veteran of the American Revolution. In response to the Russian invasion, Frederick William II moved his troops from the west where they were confronting the French revolutionary army to his eastern frontier with Poland. That transfer of Prussian troops proved crucial to the important later French victories in the autumn of 1792. However, rather than protecting Poland as he had promised, Frederick William reached an agreement with Catherine early in 1793 to carry out a second partition of Poland. The reformed constitution was abolished, and the new Polish government remained under the influence of Russia.

In the spring of 1794, Polish officers mutinied against efforts to unite their forces with the Russian army. As the rebellion expanded, the language and symbols of the French Revolution appeared in Polish cities. Before long, Prussia, Austria, and Russia sent troops into Poland. On November 4, 1794, in the single bloodiest day of combat in the decade, Russian troops killed more than 10,000 Poles outside Warsaw. Polish officers and troops who escaped Poland after the last partition later fought with the armies of the French Revolution and Napoleon against the forces of the partitioning powers.

18.6 The Reign of Terror

How did war and ideology combine to create the Reign of Terror?

The leaders of the French Revolution used various methods to promote their ideals and to protect the republic against its real and perceived enemies. The resulting reign of terror touched almost every aspect of national life to safeguard the movement.

18.6.1 War with Europe

The French invasion of the Austrian Netherlands (Belgium) and the revolutionary reorganization of that territory in 1792 roused the rest of Europe to active hostility. In November 1792, the Convention declared it would aid all peoples who wished to cast off aristocratic and monarchical oppression. The Convention had also proclaimed the Scheldt River in the Netherlands open to the commerce of all nations and thus had violated a treaty that Great Britain had made with Austria and Holland. The British were on the point of declaring war on France because of this issue when the Convention issued its own declaration of hostilities against Britain in February 1793.

By April 1793, when the Jacobins began to direct the French government, the nation was at war with Austria, Prussia, Great Britain, Spain, Sardinia, and Holland. The governments of these nations, allied in what is known as the First Coalition, endeavored to protect their social structures, political systems, and economic interests against the aggression of the revolution.

This widening of the war in the winter and spring of 1792 to 1793 provoked new, radical political actions within France as the revolutionary government mobilized itself and the nation for the conflict. Throughout France, there was the sense that a new kind of war had erupted. In this war the major issue was not protection of national borders but rather the defense of the bold new republican political and social order that had emerged since 1789. The immediate need to defend the revolution against enemies, real or imagined, from across the spectrum of French political and social life was considered more important than the security of property or even of life. These actions to protect the revolution and silence dissent came to be known as the **Reign of Terror**.

18.6.2 The Republic Defended

To mobilize for war, the revolutionary government organized a collective executive in the form of powerful committees. These, in turn, sought to organize all French national life on a wartime footing. The result was an immense military effort dedicated both to protecting and promoting revolutionary ideals. (See "Encountering the Past" sidebar on "La Marseillaise," the French national anthem, which follows below.)

18.6.2.1 THE COMMITTEE OF PUBLIC SAFETY In April 1793, the Convention established a Committee of General Security and a **Committee of Public Safety** to carry out the executive duties of the government. The latter committee eventually enjoyed almost dictatorial power. All of the revolutionary leaders who served on the Committee of Public

Encountering the Past

"La Marseillaise"

IN A FAMOUS SCENE in the movie *Casablanca*, French nightclub patrons drown out the militaristic songs of German officers by singing "La Marseillaise," the French national anthem. The scene reflects the place the song had come to hold in popular culture.

COMMEMORATIVE STAMP OF "LA MARSEILLAISE" COMPOSER Images of Rouget de Lisle singing "La Marseillaise" for the first time have become iconic in France. Over the years, De Lisle has been featured on numerous French postage stamps, most recently in 2006.
SOURCE: Hipix/Alamy Stock Photo

By the early 1940s, "La Marseillaise" was associated with revolutionaries everywhere, and with the fight for freedom against the forces of tyranny. But just as the U.S. national anthem was inspired by a specific event—a battle during the War of 1812—so too was "La Marseillaise" a product of particular historical circumstances. It was written in the context of the War of the First Coalition, when Austria, Prussia, Great Britain, Spain, Sardinia, and Holland allied themselves against revolutionary France.

On April 25, 1792, with coalition armies advancing across France's borders, and the French army in disarray, Rouget de Lisle composed "War Song for the Army of the Rhine" to help rally French forces. A young soldier and physician named François Mireur sung it at a gathering of French patriots in Marseille, and it became the marching song of the city's National Guard. On July 30, the National Guard of Marseille sang the song as they entered Paris to join the forces mustered to turn back the foreign invasion. From then on, the song was known as "La Marseillaise." On July 14, 1795, the National Convention adopted it as France's first national anthem.

The lyrics reflect the fact that the War of the First Coalition was a different kind of conflict. In the century preceding the French Revolution, European wars had centered on territorial acquisitions, dynastic ambitions, and imperial rivalries. They were fought, for the most part, by professional armies, by men who saw war as their occupation. This new war would be fought by the French people as a nation, and it would be fought against an enemy that was seen, not as a threat to France's territorial ambitions, but to French freedom. "La Marseillaise" is addressed to the "children of the fatherland" who must rise up against "tyranny's bloody banner." There is nothing subtle or abstract about the danger. The invading army was coming to "cut the throats of your sons" and "your women." The enemy brought with it "long-prepared irons" with which to shackle the people of France and return them to "the old slavery."

Despite its power and popularity, "La Marseillaise" did not remain France's national anthem for long. Under Napoleon, it was replaced with a song celebrating Napoleon's imperial achievements, and after the French monarchy was restored in 1814, "La Marseillaise" was banned. However, the efforts to suppress the song failed. Over the course of the nineteenth century it became an international anthem of revolution, helping to inspire resistance to authoritarian rule in 1830, 1848, and 1871. In 1879, France readopted "La Marseillaise" as the national anthem. And when the Germans invaded France in 1940, it once again became an anthem of resistance.

Question

1. What inspired "La Marseillaise"?

Safety were convinced republicans who had long opposed the more vacillating policies of the Girondists. They saw their task as saving the revolution from mortal enemies at home and abroad. They enjoyed a working political relationship with the *sans-culottes* of Paris, but this was an alliance of expediency for the committee.

18.6.2.2 THE *LEVÉE EN MASSE* The major problem for the Convention was to wage the war and at the same time to secure domestic support for the war effort. In early June 1793, the Parisian *sans-culottes* invaded the Convention and successfully demanded the expulsion of the Girondist members. That action further radicalized the Convention and gave the Mountain complete control. On June 22, the Convention approved a fully democratic constitution but delayed its implementation until the conclusion of the war. In fact, it was never implemented. On August 23, Lazare Carnot (1753–1823), the member of the Committee of Public Safety in charge of the military, began a mobilization for victory by issuing a *levée en masse*, a military requisition on the entire population, conscripting males into the army and directing economic production to military purposes.

Following the *levée en masse*, the Convention on September 29, 1793, established a ceiling on prices in accord with *sans-culotte* demands. During these same months, the armies of the revolution also successfully crushed many of the counterrevolutionary disturbances in the provinces. Europe never before had seen a nation organized in this way nor one defended by a citizen army, which by late 1794, with somewhere around a million men, had become larger than any ever organized in European history.

Other events within France astounded Europeans even more. The Reign of Terror had begun. Those months of quasi-judicial executions and murders stretching from the autumn of 1793 to the midsummer of 1794 are probably the most famous or infamous period of the revolution. They can be understood only in the context of the war on one hand and the revolutionary expectations of the Convention and the *sans-culottes* on the other.

18.6.3 The "Republic of Virtue" and Robespierre's Justification of Terror

The presence of armies closing in on the nation made it easy to dispense with legal due process. The people who sat in the Convention and those sitting on the Committee of Public Safety, however, did not see their actions simply in terms of expediency made necessary by war. They also believed they had created something new in world history, a "republic of virtue." In this republic, civic virtue largely understood in terms of Rousseau's *Social Contract*, the sacrifice of one's self and one's interest for the good of the republic, would replace selfish aristocratic and monarchical corruption.

The republic of virtue manifested itself in many ways: in the renaming of streets from the egalitarian vocabulary of the revolution; in republican dress copied from that of the *sans-culottes* or the Roman Republic; in the absence of powdered wigs; in the suppression of plays and other literature that were insufficiently republican; and in a general attack against crimes, such as prostitution, that were supposedly characteristic of aristocratic society. Yet the core value of the republic of virtue in line with Rousseau's thought was the upholding of the public over the private good or the championing of the general will over individual interests. It was in the name of the public good that the Committee of Public Safety carried out the policies of the terror.

The person who embodied this republic of virtue defended by terror was **Maximilien de Robespierre** (1758–1794), who by late 1793, had emerged as the dominant figure on the Committee of Public Safety. This revolutionary figure has remained controversial from his day to the present. From the beginning of the revolution, he had favored a republic. The Jacobin Club provided his primary forum and base of power. A shrewd and sensitive politician, Robespierre had opposed the war in 1792 because he feared it might aid the monarchy. He depended largely on the support of the *sans-culottes* of Paris, but he continued to dress as he had before the revolution in powdered wig and knee breeches. For him, the republic of virtue meant wholehearted support of the republican government, the renunciation of selfish gains from political life, and the assault on foreign and domestic enemies of the revolution. Portraying revolutionary France as endangered on all sides, he told the Convention early in 1794,

> Without, all the tyrants encircle you; within, all the friends of tyranny conspire—they will conspire until crime has been robbed of hope. We must smother the internal and external enemies of the Republic or perish with them. Now, in this situation, the first maxim of your policy ought to be to lead the people by reason and the people's enemies by terror. If the mainspring of popular government in peacetime is virtue, amid revolution it is at the same time [both] virtue and *terror:* virtue, without which terror is fatal; terror, without which virtue is impotent. Terror is nothing but prompt, severe, inflexible justice; it is therefore an emanation of virtue. It is less a special principle than a consequence of the general principle of democracy applied to our country's most pressing needs.[4]

Robespierre and those who supported his policies were among the first of a succession of secular ideologues of the left and the right who, in the name of humanity, would bring so much suffering to Europe in the following two centuries. The policies associated with terror in the name of republican virtue included the exclusion of women from active political life, the de-Christianization of France, and the use of revolutionary tribunals to dispense justice to alleged enemies of the republic.

18.6.4 Repression of the Society of Revolutionary Republican Women

Revolutionary women established their own distinct institutions during these months. In May 1793, Pauline Léon and Claire Lacombe founded the Society of Revolutionary Republican Women. Its purpose was to fight the internal enemies of the revolution. Its members saw themselves as militant citizens. Initially, the Jacobin leaders welcomed the organization. Members of the society and other women filled the galleries of the Convention to hear the debates and cheer their favorite speakers. The society became increasingly radical, however. Its members sought stricter controls on the price of food and other commodities, worked to ferret out food hoarders, and brawled with working market women whom they thought to be insufficiently revolutionary. The women of the society also demanded the right to wear the revolutionary cockade that male citizens usually wore in their hats. By October 1793, the Jacobins in the Convention had begun to fear the turmoil the society was causing and banned all women's clubs and societies. The debates over these decrees show that the Jacobins believed the society opposed many of their economic policies, but the deputies used Rousseau's language of separate spheres for men and women to justify their exclusion of women from active political life.

There were other examples of repression of women in 1793. Olympe de Gouges, author of the Declaration of the Rights of Woman, opposed the Terror and accused Jacobins of corruption. She was guillotined in November 1793. The same year, women were formally excluded from serving in the French army and from the galleries of the Convention. The exclusion of women from public political life was part of the Jacobin republic of virtue: in such a republic, men would be active citizens in the military and political sphere, and women would be active only in the domestic sphere.

18.6.5 De-Christianization

The most dramatic step taken by the republic of virtue, and one that illustrates its imposition of political values to justify the Terror, was the Convention's attempt to de-Christianize France. In November 1793, the Convention proclaimed a new calendar dating from the first day of the French Republic. There were twelve months of thirty days each, with names associated with the seasons and climate. Every tenth day, rather than every seventh, was a holiday. In November 1793, the Convention decreed the Cathedral of Notre Dame in Paris to be a "Temple of Reason."

The legislature then sent trusted members, known as deputies on mission, into the provinces to enforce de-Christianization by closing churches; persecuting clergy and believers, both Roman Catholic and Protestant; occasionally forcing priests to marry; and sometimes by killing priests and nuns. Churches were desecrated, torn down, or used as barns or warehouses. This radical religious policy attacking both clergy and religious property roused enormous popular opposition and alienated parts of the French provinces from the revolutionary government in Paris. Robespierre personally opposed de-Christianization because he was convinced it would prove a political blunder that would erode loyalty to the republic.

18.6.6 Revolutionary Tribunals

The Reign of Terror manifested itself in revolutionary tribunals that the Convention established during the summer of 1793. The mandate of these tribunals, the most prominent of which was in Paris, was to try the enemies of the republic, but the definition of who was an "enemy" shifted as the months passed. Those whom the tribunal condemned in Paris were beheaded on the guillotine, a recently invented instrument of efficient and supposedly humane execution. (The drop of the blade of the guillotine was certain to sever the head of the condemned at once, whereas beheading by axe or sword could, and often did, require multiple blows and cause unnecessary pain.) Other modes of execution, such as mass shootings and drowning, were used in the provinces.

The first victims of the Terror were Marie Antoinette, other members of the royal family, and aristocrats, who were executed in October 1793. Girondist politicians who

THE DISGRACED MARIE ANTOINETTE On the way to her execution in 1793, Marie Antoinette was sketched from life by Jacques-Louis David as she passed his window. Note her cropped hair, which had recently been shorn as a symbol of her degradation.
SOURCE: Bridgeman—Giraudon/Art Resource, NY

had been prominent in the legislative assembly followed them. These executions took place in the same weeks that the Convention had moved against the Society of Revolutionary Republican Women, whom it had also seen as endangering Jacobin control.

In early 1794, the Terror moved to the provinces, where the deputies on mission presided over the summary execution of thousands of people, most of whom were peasants, who had allegedly supported internal opposition to the revolution. One of the most infamous incidents occurred in Nantes on the west coast of France, where several hundred people, including many priests, were tied to rafts and drowned in the river Loire. The victims of the Terror now came from every social class, including the *sans-culottes*.

18.6.7 The End of the Terror

The most extreme actions of the Terror culminated in the ruin of perhaps the most controversial figure of the revolution.

18.6.7.1 REVOLUTIONARIES TURN AGAINST THEMSELVES In Paris during the late winter of 1794, Robespierre began to orchestrate the Terror against republican political figures of the left and right. On March 24, he secured the execution of certain extreme *sans-culottes* leaders known as the *enrages*, who had wanted further measures to regulate prices, secure social equality, and press de-Christianization. Robespierre then turned against other republicans in the Convention. Most prominent among them was Jacques Danton (1759–1794), who had provided heroic national leadership in the dark days of September 1792 and had later served briefly on the Committee of Public Safety before Robespierre joined the group. Danton and others were accused of being insufficiently militant on the war, profiting monetarily from the revolution, and rejecting the link between politics and moral virtue. Danton was executed in April 1794. Robespierre thus exterminated the leadership of both groups that might have threatened his position. Finally, on June 10, he secured passage of the Law of 22 Prairial, which permitted the revolutionary tribunal to convict suspects without hearing substantial evidence against them. The number of executions grew steadily.

18.6.7.2 FALL OF ROBESPIERRE In May 1794, at the height of his power, Robespierre, considering the worship of "Reason" too abstract for most citizens, replaced it with the "Cult of the Supreme Being." This deistic cult reflected Rousseau's vision of a civic religion that would induce morality among citizens. Robespierre, however, did not long preside over his new religion.

On July 26, Robespierre made an ill-tempered speech in the Convention, declaring that other leaders of the government were conspiring against him and the revolution. Similar accusations against unnamed persons had preceded

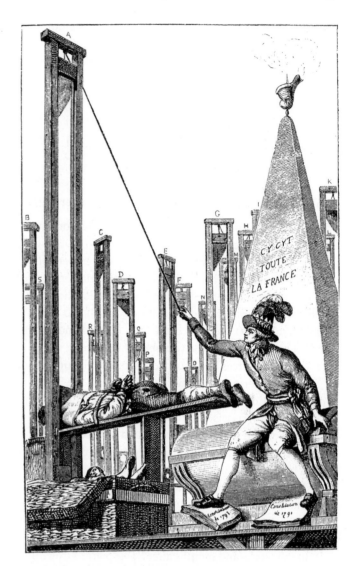

EXECUTION OF THE EXECUTIONER Maximilien Robespierre (1758–1794) emerged as the most powerful revolutionary figure in 1793 and 1794, dominating the Committee of Public Safety. He considered the Terror essential for the success of the revolution. In this caricature, having already guillotined all the people in France, Robespierre must himself execute the executioner.
SOURCE: INTERFOTO/Alamy Stock Photo

his earlier attacks. No member of the Convention could now feel safe. On July 27—the Ninth of Thermidor on the revolutionary calendar—members of the Convention, by prearrangement, shouted Robespierre down when he rose to make another speech. That night Robespierre was arrested, and the next day he and approximately eighty of his supporters were executed without trial. The revolutionary *sans-culottes* of Paris did not try to save him because he had deprived them of their chief leaders. He had also recently supported a measure to cap workers' wages. Other Jacobins turned against him because, after Danton's death, they feared they would be his next victims. Robespierre had destroyed rivals for leadership without creating supporters for himself. He had also for months tried to persuade the Paris populace that the Convention itself was harboring enemies of the revolution. Assured by the Convention that Robespierre was seeking dictatorial powers, Parisians saw him as one more of those internal enemies. Robespierre was the unwitting creator of his own destruction.

18.7 The Thermidorian Reaction

What course did the French Revolution take after 1794?

The fall of Robespierre might simply have been one more shift in the turbulent politics of the revolution, but instead it proved to be a major turning point. The members of the Convention used the event to reassert their authority over the executive power of the Committee of Public Safety. Within a short time, the Reign of Terror, which had claimed more than 25,000 victims, came to a close. It no longer seemed necessary since the war abroad was going well and the republican forces had crushed the provincial uprisings.

This tempering of the revolution, called the **Thermidorian Reaction** because of its association with the events of 9 Thermidor, consisted of the destruction of the machinery of terror and the establishment of a new constitutional regime. It resulted from a widespread feeling that the revolution had become too radical. In particular, it displayed a weariness of the Terror and a fear that the *sans-culottes* had become too powerful. The influence of generally wealthy middle-class and professional people soon replaced that of the *sans-culottes*.

In the weeks and months after Robespierre's execution, the Convention allowed the Girondists who had been in prison or hiding to return to their seats. A general amnesty freed political prisoners. The Convention restructured the Committee of Public Safety and diminished its power while repealing the notorious Law of 22 Prairial. Some, though by no means all, of the people responsible for the Terror were removed from public life. The Paris commune was outlawed, and its leaders and deputies on mission were executed. The Paris Jacobin Club was closed, and Jacobin clubs in the provinces were forbidden to correspond with each other.

The end of the Reign of Terror did not mean the end of violence in France. Executions of former terrorists marked the beginning of "the white terror." Throughout the country, people who had been involved in the Reign of Terror were attacked and often murdered. Jacobins were executed with little more due process than they had extended to their victims a few months earlier. The Convention itself approved some of these trials. In other cases, gangs of youths who had aristocratic connections or who had avoided serving in the army roamed the streets, beating known Jacobins. In Lyons, Toulon, and Marseilles, these so-called "bands of Jesus" dragged suspected terrorists from prisons and murdered

them much as alleged royalists had been murdered during the September Massacres of 1792.

The republic of virtue gave way, if not to one of vice, at least to one of frivolous pleasures. The dress of the sans-culottes and the Roman Republic disappeared among the middle class and the aristocracy. New plays appeared in the theaters, and prostitutes again roamed the streets of Paris. Families of victims of the Reign of Terror gave parties in which they appeared with shaved necks, like the victims of the guillotine, and with red ribbons tied about them. Although the Convention continued to favor the Cult of the Supreme Being, it allowed Catholic services to be held. Many refractory priests returned to the country. One of the unanticipated results of the Thermidorian Reaction was a genuine revival of Catholic worship.

The Thermidorian Reaction also saw the repeal of legislation that had been passed in 1792 making divorce more equitable for women. As the passage of that measure suggests, the reaction did not extend women's rights nor improve their education. The Thermidorians and their successors had seen enough attempts at political and social change. They sought to return family life to its status before the outbreak of the revolution. Political authorities and the church were determined to reestablish separate spheres for men and women and to reinforce traditional gender roles. As a result, in at least some respects, Frenchwomen had less freedom after 1795 than before 1789.

18.7.1 Establishment of the Directory

The Thermidorian Reaction led to still another new constitution. The democratic constitution of 1793, which had never gone into effect, was abandoned. In its place, the Convention issued the Constitution of the Year III, which reflected the Thermidorian determination to reject *both* constitutional monarchy and democracy. In recognition of the danger of a legislature with only one chamber and unlimited authority, this new document provided for a legislature of two houses. Members of the upper body, or Council of Elders, were to be men over forty years of age who were either husbands or widowers. The lower Council of Five Hundred was to consist of men of at least thirty who could be either married or single. The executive body was to be a five-person **Directory** whom the Elders would choose from a list the Council of Five Hundred submitted. Property qualifications limited the franchise, except for soldiers, who were permitted to vote whether they had property or not.

Historically, the term *Thermidor* has come to be associated with political reaction. That association requires considerable qualification. By 1795, the political structure and society of the Old Regime in France based on rank and birth had given way permanently to a political system based on civic equality and social status based on property ownership. People who had never been allowed direct, formal access to political power had, to different degrees, been granted it. Their entrance into political life had given rise to questions of property distribution and economic regulations that could not again be ignored. Representation was an established principle of politics. Henceforth, the question for France and eventually for all of Europe would be which new groups would be permitted representation. In the *levée en masse*, the French had demonstrated to Europe the power of the secular ideal of nationhood and of the willingness of citizen soldiers to embrace self-sacrifice.

The post-Thermidorian course of the French Revolution did not undo these stunning changes in the political and social contours of Europe. The triumph in the Constitution of the Year III was the revolution of property holders. For this reason, the French Revolution has often been considered a victory of the bourgeoisie, or middle class. The property that won the day, however, was not industrial wealth, but the wealth stemming from commerce, the professions, and land. The largest new propertied class to emerge from the revolutionary turmoil was the peasantry, who, as a result of the destruction of aristocratic privileges, now owned their own land. Unlike peasants liberated from traditional landholding in other parts of Europe during the next century, French peasants had to pay no monetary compensation either to their former landlords or to the state.

18.7.2 Removal of the *Sans-culottes* from Political Life

The most decisively reactionary element in the Thermidorian Reaction and the new constitution was the removal of the *sans-culottes* from political life. With the war effort succeeding, the Convention severed its ties with the sans-culottes. True to their belief in an unregulated economy, the Thermidorians repealed the ceiling on prices. As a result, the winter of 1794 to 1795 brought the worst food shortages of the period. There were many food riots, which the Convention suppressed to prove that the days of the *sans-culottes* had come to a close.

Royalist agents, who aimed to restore the monarchy, tried to take advantage of the *sans-culottes'* discontent. On October 5, 1795—13 Vendémiaire—the sections of Paris led by the royalists rose up against the Convention. The government turned the artillery against the royalist rebels. A general named Napoleon Bonaparte (1769–1821) commanded the cannon, and with a "whiff of grapeshot," he dispersed the crowd.

By the Treaties of Basel in March and June 1795, the Convention concluded peace with Prussia and Spain. The legislators, however, feared a resurgence of both radical democrats and royalists in the upcoming elections for the Council of Five Hundred. Consequently, the Convention ruled that at least two-thirds of the new legislature must have served in the Convention itself. The Two-Thirds Law, which hoped to foster continuity but also clearly favored politicians already in office, quickly undermined public faith in the new constitutional order.

The Directory faced almost immediate social unrest. During the spring of 1796 in Paris, Gracchus Babeuf (1760–1797) led the Conspiracy of Equals. He and his followers called for more radical democracy and more equality of property. They declared at one point, "The aim of the French Revolution is to destroy inequality and to re-establish the general welfare [. . .] The Revolution is not complete, because the rich monopolize all the property and govern exclusively, while the poor toil like slaves, languish in misery, and count for nothing in the state."[5] In a sense, they were correct. The Directory intended to resist any further social changes in France that might endanger property or political stability. Babeuf was arrested, tried, and executed. This minor plot became famous decades later, when European socialists attempted to find their historical roots in the French Revolution.

The suppression of the *sans-culottes*, the narrow franchise of the constitution, the Two-Thirds Law, and the Catholic royalist revival presented the Directory with challenges that it was never able to overcome. Because France remained at war with Austria and Great Britain, it needed a broader-based active loyalty than it was able to command. Instead, the Directory came to depend on the power of the army to govern France. All soldiers could vote. Moreover, within the army that the revolution had created and sustained were ambitious officers who were eager for power. The instability of the Directory, the growing role of the army, and the ambitions of its leaders had profound consequences not only for France but for the entire Western world.

The Chapter in Perspective

The French Revolution is the central political event of modern European history. It unleashed political and social forces that shaped Europe and much of the rest of the world for the next two centuries.

The revolution began with a clash between the monarchy and the nobility. Once the Estates General gathered, however, the traditional boundaries of eighteenth-century political life could not contain the discontent. The Third Estate, in all of its diversity, demanded real influence in government. Initially that meant the participation of middle-class members of the Estates General, but soon the people of Paris and the peasants made their own demands. Thereafter, popular nationalism exerted itself on French political life and the destiny of Europe.

Revolutionary legislation and popular uprisings in Paris, the countryside, and other cities transformed the social as well as the political life of the nation. Nobles surrendered traditional social privileges. The church saw its property confiscated and its operations brought under state control. For a time, there was an attempt to de-Christianize France. Vast amounts of landed property changed hands, and France became a nation of peasant landowners. Urban workers lost the protection they had enjoyed under the guilds and became more subject to the forces of the marketplace.

Violence accompanied many of the revolutionary changes. Thousands died during the Reign of Terror. France also found itself at war with virtually the rest of Europe. Resentment, fear, and a new desire for stability eventually brought the Terror to an end. That desire for stability, combined with a determination to defeat the foreign enemies of the revolution and to carry it abroad, would in turn, work to the advantage of the army. Eventually, Napoleon Bonaparte would claim leadership in the name of stability and national glory.

KEY EVENTS OF THE FRENCH REVOLUTION	
February–May 1787	Unsuccessful negotiations with the Assembly of Notables
August 8, 1788	Louis XVI summons the Estates General
May 5, 1789	The Estates General opens at Versailles
June 17, 1789	The Third Estate declares itself the National Assembly
June 20, 1789	The National Assembly takes the Tennis Court Oath
July 14, 1789	Fall of the Bastille in the city of Paris
Late July, 1789	The Great Fear spreads in the countryside
August 27, 1789	Declaration of the Rights of Man and Citizen
July 12, 1790	Civil Constitution of the Clergy adopted
June 14, 1791	Chapelier Law
August 27, 1791	The Declaration of Pillnitz
April 20, 1792	France declares war on Austria
September 2–7, 1792	The September Massacres
September 20, 1792	France wins the Battle of Valmy
January 21, 1793	King Louis XVI is executed
February 1, 1793	France declares war on Great Britain
April 1793	The Committee of Public Safety is formed
June 22, 1793	The Constitution of 1793 is adopted but not implemented
August 23, 1793	*Levée en masse* proclaimed
October 16, 1793	Queen Marie Antoinette is executed
November 10, 1793	The Cult of Reason is proclaimed; the revolutionary calendar, beginning on September 22, 1792, is adopted
March 24, 1794	Execution of the leaders of the *sans-culottes* known as the *enrages*
May 7, 1794	Cult of the Supreme Being proclaimed
July 28, 1794	Robespierre is executed
November 12, 1794	Closing of Jacobin Club in Paris
May 31, 1795	Abolition of revolutionary tribunal
August 22, 1795	The Constitution of the Year III establishes the Directory
September 23, 1795	Two-Thirds Law adopted
May 10, 1796	Babeuf's Conspiracy of Equals
November 9, 1799	Napoleon's (18 Brumaire) *coup d'état* overthrows the Directory

The Chapter in Review

Review Questions

1. Why has France been called a rich nation with an impoverished government? How did the financial weaknesses of the French monarchy lay the foundations of the revolution of 1789?

2. What were Louis XVI's most serious mistakes during the French Revolution? Had he been a more able ruler, could the French Revolution have been avoided or a constitutional monarchy have succeeded? How much did the revolution have to do with the competence of the monarch?

3. How was the Estates General transformed into the National Assembly? How were France and its government reorganized in the early years of the revolution? Why has the Civil Constitution of the Clergy been called the greatest blunder of the National Assembly?

4. Why were some political factions dissatisfied with the constitutional settlement of 1791? What was the revolution of 1792, and why did it occur? Who were the *sans-culottes*, and how did they become a factor in the politics of the period? How influential were they during the Terror in particular? Why did the *sans-culottes* and the Jacobins cooperate at first? Why did that cooperation end?

5. Why did France go to war with Austria in 1792? What were the benefits and drawbacks for France of fighting an external war in the midst of a domestic political revolution?

6. What were the causes of the Terror? How did the rest of Europe react to the French Revolution and the Terror? How did events in France influence the last two partitions of Poland?

7. A motto of the French Revolution was "equality, liberty, and fraternity." How did the revolution both support and violate this motto? Did Frenchwomen benefit from the revolution? Did French peasants benefit from it?

Key Terms

Bastille   A great fortress in Paris once used to hold political prisoners.

cahiers de doléances   The list of grievances drawn up in 1789 by each of the three estates in France to be presented to the king.

Committee of Public Safety   A committee set up by the Convention in April 1789 to carry out the executive duties of the government.

Convention   French radical legislative body from 1792 to 1794.

Declaration of the Rights of Man and Citizen   The statement in August 1789 of broad political principles issued by the National Constituent Assembly before they wrote a new constitution.

départements   The eighty-three administrative units that the National Constituent Assembly set up to replace the ancient French provinces.

Directory   The five-person executive body in the Constitution of Year III, which governed France from November 1795 to November 1799.

émigrés (em-ee-GRAYS)   French aristocrats who fled France during the revolution.

"Great Fear"   A wave of peasant riots and violence that swept through France in July and August 1789.

Jacobins (JACK-uh-bins)   The radical republican party during the French Revolution that displaced the Girondins.

Jacques Necker   (1732–1804) The royal director-general of finances who issued a misleading report in 1781 to downplay France's financial problems.

levée en masse (le-VAY en MASS)   The French revolutionary conscription in 1792 of all males into the army and the harnessing of the economy for war production.

Maximilien de Robespierre   (1758–1794) A French lawyer and one of the most influential figures associated with the French Revolution and the Reign of Terror.

National Assembly   The new legislative body created by the Third Estate during the French Revolution.

Reign of Terror   The period between the summer of 1793 and the end of July 1794 when the French revolutionary state used extensive executions and violence to defend the revolution and suppress its alleged internal enemies.

sans-culottes (SAHN coo-LOTS)   Meaning "without knee breeches." The lower-middle classes and artisans of Paris during the French Revolution.

September Massacres   The executions or murders of about 1,200 people who were in the Paris city jails (mostly common criminals) by the Parisian mob in the first week of September 1792 during the French Revolution.

Tennis Court Oath   The oath members of the National Assembly of France took at an indoor tennis court on June 20, 1789 after the king locked them out of their usual meeting place.

Thermidorian Reaction   The reaction against the radicalism of the French Revolution that began in July 1794. Associated with the end of the Reign of Terror and establishment of the Directory.

Third Estate   The branch of the French Estates General representing all of the kingdom outside the nobility and the clergy.

Notes

1. Leo Gershoy, *The French Revolution and Napoleon* (New York: Appleton-Century-Crofts, 1964), p. 102.

2. Georges Lefebvre, *The Coming of the French Revolution*, trans. by R. R. Palmer (Princeton, NJ: Princeton University Press, 1967), pp. 221–223.

3. Sara E. Melzer and Leslie W. Rabine, eds., *Rebel Daughters: Women and the French Revolution* (New York: Oxford University Press, 1992), p. 88.

4. Richard T. Bienvenu, *The Ninth of Thermidor: The Fall of Robespierre* (New York: Oxford University Press, 1968), p. 38.

5. John Hall Stewart, *A Documentary Survey of the French Revolution* (New York: Macmillan, 1966), pp. 656–657.

Chapter 19
The Age of Napoleon and the Triumph of Romanticism

NAPOLEON ENTHRONED This portrait of Napoleon on his throne by Jean Ingres (1780–1867) shows the splendor of an imperial monarch who embodies the total power of the state.
SOURCE: Erich Lessing/Art Resource

 ## Contents and Focus Questions

The Chapter in Brief

BY THE LATE 1790s, the French people, especially property owners, who now included the peasants, longed for stability. The Directory was not providing it. Only the army was able to take charge of the nation as a symbol of both order and the popular values of the revolution. The most politically astute general was Napoleon Bonaparte, who had been a radical during the early revolution, a victorious commander in Italy, and a supporter of the repression of revolutionary disturbances after Thermidor.

Once in power, Napoleon consolidated many of the achievements of the revolution. He also repudiated much of it by establishing an empire. Thereafter, his ambitions drew France into wars of conquest and liberation across the Continent. For more than a decade, Europe was at war, with only brief periods of armed truce. Through his conquests, Napoleon spread many of the ideas and institutions of the revolution and overturned much of the old political and social order. He also provoked popular nationalism outside of France in opposition to French domination. This new force and the great alliances that opposed France eventually defeated Napoleon.

Throughout these Napoleonic years, new ideas and sensibilities, known as **romanticism**, grew across Europe. Many of the ideas had originated in the eighteenth century, but they flourished in the turmoil of the French Revolution and the Napoleonic Wars. The revolution spurred the imagination of poets, painters, and philosophers. Some romantic ideas, such as nationalism, supported the revolution; others, such as the emphasis on history and religion, opposed its values.

19.1 The Rise of Napoleon Bonaparte

How did Napoleon come to power in France?

The chief threat to the Directory came from royalists, who hoped to restore the Bourbon monarchy by legal means. Many of the *émigrés* had returned to France. Their plans for a restoration drew support from devout Catholics and from those citizens horrified by the excesses of the revolution. Monarchy, they thought, promised a return to stability. The spring elections of 1797 replaced most incumbents with constitutional monarchists and their sympathizers, who now commanded a majority in the national legislature.

To preserve the republic and prevent a peaceful restoration of the Bourbons, the antimonarchist Directory staged a coup d'état on 18 Fructidor (September 4, 1797). They filled the legislative seats their opponents had won with their own supporters. They then imposed censorship and exiled some of their enemies. At the request of the Directors, Napoleon Bonaparte, the general in charge of the French invasion of Italy, had sent a subordinate to Paris to guarantee the success of the coup. In 1797, as in 1795, the army and Bonaparte had saved the day for the government installed in the wake of the Thermidorian Reaction.

Napoleon Bonaparte was born in 1769 to a poor family of lesser nobles at Ajaccio, on the Mediterranean island of Corsica. Because France had annexed Corsica in 1768, he went to French schools and, in 1785, obtained a commission as a French artillery officer. He favored the revolution and was a fiery Jacobin. In 1793, he played a leading role in recovering the port of Toulon from the British. As a reward for his service, he was appointed to brigadier general. During the Thermidorian Reaction, his defense of the new regime on 13 Vendémiaire won him a command in Italy.

19.1.1 Early Military Victories

By 1795, French arms and diplomacy had shattered the enemy coalition, but France's annexation of Belgium guaranteed continued fighting with Britain and Austria. The invasion of the Italian peninsula aimed to deprive Austria of its rich northern Italian province of Lombardy. In a series of lightning victories, Bonaparte crushed the Austrian and Sardinian armies. On his own initiative, and against the wishes of the government in Paris, he concluded the Treaty of Campo Formio in October 1797. The treaty took Austria out of the war and crowned Napoleon's campaign with success. Before long, France dominated all the Italian peninsula and Switzerland.

In November 1797, the triumphant Bonaparte returned to Paris as a hero and to confront France's only remaining enemy, Britain. He judged it impossible to cross the Channel and invade England at that time. Instead, he chose to attack British interests through the eastern Mediterranean by capturing Egypt from the Ottoman Empire. By this strategy, he hoped to drive the British fleet from the Mediterranean, cut off British communications with India, damage British trade, and threaten the British Empire.

Napoleon easily overran Egypt, but the invasion was a failure. Admiral **Horatio Nelson** (1758–1805) destroyed the French fleet at Abukir on August 1, 1798. The French army was cut off from France. To make matters worse, the situation in Europe was deteriorating. The invasion of Egypt had alarmed Russia, which had its own ambitions in the Near East. Russia, Austria, and the Ottomans joined Britain to form the Second Coalition against France. In 1799, the Russian and Austrian armies defeated the French in Italy and Switzerland and threatened to invade France.

19.1.2 The Constitution of the Year VIII

Economic troubles and the dangerous international situation eroded the Directory's fragile support. One of the Directors, the Abbé Sièyes (1748–1836), proposed a new constitution. The author of the pamphlet *What Is the Third Estate?* (1789), Sièyes now wanted an executive body independent of the whims of electoral politics, a government based on the principle of "confidence from below, power from above." The change would require another coup d'état with military support. News of France's domestic troubles had reached Napoleon in Egypt. Without orders and leaving his army behind, he returned to France in October 1799 to popular acclaim. Soon he joined Sièyes. On 19 Brumaire (November 10, 1799), his troops ensured the success of the coup (and Napoleon issued a proclamation to legitimate his seizure of power).

Sièyes appears to have thought that Napoleon could be used and then dismissed, but he misjudged his man. The proposed constitution divided executive authority among three consuls. Bonaparte quickly pushed Sièyes aside, and in December 1799, he issued the Constitution of the Year VIII. Behind a screen of universal male suffrage that suggested democratic principles, a complicated system of checks and balances that appealed to republican theory, and a Council of State that evoked memories of Louis XIV, the new constitution established the rule of one man—the First Consul, Bonaparte. In an age of widespread interest in classical analogies, Napoleon's takeover was reminiscent of Caesar and Augustus in ancient Rome, and to the Greek tyrants of the sixth century B.C.E. From the perspective of the twenty-first century, however, Bonaparte's career points forward to the dictators of the twentieth century. He was the first modern political figure to use the rhetoric of revolution and nationalism, to back it with military force, and to combine these elements into a mighty weapon of imperial expansion in the service of his own power.

19.2 The Consulate in France (1799–1804)

How did the Consulate end the revolution in France?

The **Consulate** in effect ended the revolution in France. The leading elements of the Third Estate—that is, officials, landowners, doctors, lawyers, and financiers—had achieved most of their goals by 1799. They had abolished hereditary privilege, and their talent allowed them to achieve wealth, status, and security for their property. The peasants were also satisfied. They had gained the land they had always wanted and had destroyed oppressive feudal privileges. The newly established dominant classes had little or no desire to share their new privileges with the lower social orders. Bonaparte seemed just the person to give them security. When he submitted his constitution to the voters in a plebiscite, they overwhelmingly approved it.

19.2.1 Suppressing Foreign Enemies and Domestic Opposition

Throughout much of the 1790s, the pressures of warfare, particularly conscription, had accounted for much of France's internal instability. Bonaparte justified the public's confidence in himself by making peace with France's enemies. Russia had already left the Second Coalition. The Treaty of Luneville early in 1801 took Austria out of the war. In 1802, Britain, now alone, concluded the Treaty of Amiens, which brought peace to Europe.

Bonaparte also restored peace and order at home. He used generosity, flattery, and bribery to win over enemies. He issued a general amnesty and employed men from all political factions, requiring only that they be loyal to him. Men who had been radicals during the Reign of Terror, who had fled the Terror and favored constitutional monarchy, or who had been high officials under Louis XVI occupied some of the highest offices.

Bonaparte, however, ruthlessly suppressed opposition. He established a highly centralized administration in which prefects responsible to the government in Paris managed all departments. He employed secret police. He stamped out the royalist rebellion in the west and made the rule of Paris effective in Brittany and the Vendée for the first time in years.

Napoleon also invented and used opportunities to destroy his enemies. A plot on his life in 1804 provided an excuse to attack the Jacobins, though it was the work of the royalists. Also in 1804, he violated the sovereignty of the German state of Baden to seize and execute the Bourbon duke of Enghien (1772–1804).

19.2.2 Concordat with the Roman Catholic Church

No single set of revolutionary policies had aroused as much domestic opposition as those regarding the French Catholic Church; nor were there any other policies to which fierce supporters of the revolution seemed so attached. When the French armies had invaded Italy, they had driven Pope Pius VI (r. 1775–1799) from Rome, and he eventually died in exile in France. In 1801, to the shock and dismay of his anticlerical supporters, Napoleon concluded a concordat with Pope Pius VII (r. 1800–1823). The agreement was possible because Pius VII, before becoming pope, had written that Christianity was compatible with the ideals of equality and democracy. The concordat gave Napoleon what he most wanted. The agreement required both the refractory clergy and those who had accepted the revolution to resign. Their replacements received their spiritual investiture from the pope, but the state named the bishops and paid their salaries and the salary of one priest in each parish. In return, the church gave up its claims to its confiscated property.

The concordat declared, "Catholicism is the religion of the great majority of French citizens." This mere statement of fact fell far short of what the pope had wanted: religious dominance for the Roman Catholic Church. The clergy were required to swear an oath of loyalty to the state. The Organic Articles of 1802, which the government issued on its own authority without consulting the pope, established the supremacy of state over church. Similar laws were applied to the Protestant and Jewish communities, reducing still further the privileged position of the Catholic Church.

19.2.3 The Napoleonic Code

In 1802, a plebiscite ratified Napoleon as consul for life, and he soon produced another constitution that granted him what amounted to full power. He thereafter set about reforming and codifying French law. The result was the Civil Code of 1804, usually known as the **Napoleonic Code**. The Napoleonic Code safeguarded all forms of property and tried to secure French society against internal challenges. All the privileges based on birth that the revolution had overthrown remained abolished.

The conservative attitudes toward labor and women that had emerged during the revolution continued to receive full support. Workers' organizations remained forbidden, and workers had fewer rights than their employers. Fathers were granted extensive control over their children and husbands over their wives. However, primogeniture—the right of an eldest son to inherit most or all of his parents' property—remained abolished, and property was distributed among all children, males and females. Married women needed their husbands' consent to dispose of their own property, and divorce remained more difficult for women than for men. Before this code, French law had differed from region to region. That confused set of laws had given women opportunities to protect their interests. The universality of the Napoleonic Code ended that.

19.2.4 Establishing a Dynasty

In 1804, Bonaparte seized on a bomb attack on his life to make himself emperor. He argued that establishing a dynasty would make the new regime secure and make further attempts on his life useless. Another new constitution declared Napoleon Bonaparte Emperor of the French, instead of First Consul of the Republic. A plebiscite also overwhelmingly ratified this constitution.

To conclude the drama, Napoleon invited Pope Pius VII to Notre Dame to take part in his coronation. At the last minute, however, Napoleon would not allow anyone to think his power and authority depended on the church. Henceforth, he was called Napoleon I. (For an artist's portrayal of Napoleon's elaborate ceremonious coronation, see the "Closer Look" sidebar, which follows below.)

A Closer Look

The Coronation of Napoleon

JACQUES-LOUIS DAVID recorded the elaborate coronation of Napoleon in this monumental painting that revealed the enormous political and religious tensions of that event, which involved the kind of ritual and ceremony associated with the monarchy of the Old Regime.

Napoleon's mother sits in a balcony-like setting, presiding over her son's coronation. The beginning of Napoleon's new reigning dynasty in France and across Europe is symbolized by the placement of his relatives on various thrones.

Napoleon places a crown on the head of his wife, Josephine, whom he will later divorce because of her inability to conceive an heir.

NAPOLEON, THE EMPEROR OF FRANCE
SOURCE: Scala/Art Resource, NY

Pope Pius VII observes the event but is not a real participant. He had signed a concordat with Napoleon that had restored some but by no means all Rome's prerevolutionary authority in France. Pius is aware, obviously, that his authority is now largely subject to the wishes of the French emperor.

Questions

1. What tools does Jacques-Louis David use to make Napoleon's singular significance apparent?
2. Napoleon's mother did not actually attend the coronation. Why was it important to include her in the image?

19.3 Napoleon's Empire (1804–1814)

How did Napoleon build an empire?

From the time of his coronation as emperor until his final defeat at Waterloo in 1815, Napoleon conquered most of Europe. France's victories changed the map of the Continent. The wars put an end to the Old Regime and its feudal trappings throughout Western Europe and forced those European states that remained independent to reorganize themselves to resist Napoleon's armies.

Everywhere, Napoleon's advance unleashed the powerful force of nationalism. His weapon was the militarily mobilized French nation, one of the achievements of the revolution. Napoleon could put 700,000 men under arms at one time, risk 100,000 troops in a single battle, endure heavy losses, and fight again. He could conscript citizen soldiers in unprecedented numbers, thanks to their loyalty to the nation and to him. No single enemy could match such resources. Even coalitions were unsuccessful, until Napoleon's own mistakes led to his defeat.

KEY EVENTS IN NAPOLEONIC EUROPE	
1797	Napoleon concludes the Treaty of Campo Formio
1799	Consulate established in France
1802	Treaty of Amiens
1803	War renewed between France and Britain
1804	Napoleonic Civil Code issued
1804	Napoleon crowned as emperor
1805 (October 21)	Nelson defeats French and Spanish fleet at Trafalgar
1805 (December 2)	Battle of Austerlitz
1806	Battle of Jena
1807	Battle of Friedland
1807	Treaty of Tilsit; Russia becomes an ally of Napoleon
1809	Battle of Wagram
1812	Invasion of Russia and French defeat at Borodino
1813	Leipzig (Battle of the Nations)
1814 (March)	Treaty of Chaumont establishes Quadruple Alliance
1814 (September)	Congress of Vienna convenes
1815 (March 1)	Napoleon returns from Elba
1815 (June 18)	Battle of Waterloo
1815 (September 26)	Holy Alliance formed at Congress of Vienna
1815 (November 20)	Quadruple Alliance renewed at Congress of Vienna
1821	Napoleon dies on Saint Helena

19.3.1 Conquering an Empire

The Peace of Amiens in 1802 between France and Great Britain was merely a truce. Napoleon's unlimited ambitions shattered any hope that it might last. He sent an army to restore the rebellious colony of Haiti to French rule. This move aroused British fears that Napoleon was planning a new French empire in America because Spain had restored Louisiana to France in 1801. More serious were his interventions in the Dutch Republic, the Italian peninsula, and Switzerland and his reorganization of the German states. The Treaty of Campo Formio had required a redistribution of territories along the Rhine River, and the petty princes of the region scrambled to enlarge their holdings. Among the results were the reduction of Austrian influence and the emergence of fewer, but larger, German states in the West, all dependent on Napoleon.

19.3.1.1 BRITISH NAVAL SUPREMACY Alarmed by these developments, the British issued an ultimatum. When Napoleon ignored it, Britain declared war in May 1803. William Pitt the Younger returned to office as prime minister in 1804 and began constructing the Third Coalition. By August 1805, he had persuaded Russia and Austria to move once more against France. A great naval victory soon raised the fortunes of the allies. On October 21, 1805, the British admiral Lord Nelson destroyed the combined French and Spanish fleets at the **Battle of Trafalgar** off the Spanish coast. Trafalgar ended all French hope of invading Britain and ensured Britain would maintain its opposition to France for the duration of the war. Britain had hoped to establish supremacy on the high seas for centuries; now the navy dominated global commercial shipping and seemed undefeatable in military confrontation as well. The Battle of Trafalgar foreshadowed Napoleon's ultimate defeat by exposing French vulnerability to English strength. Furthermore, it seems to validate a longstanding British belief that, in the words of one historian, "concentrating resources upon the navy would render Britain 'the guardian of liberty' throughout Europe."[1] Britain's dominance of the seas would not be seriously challenged until World War I. (For an interesting narrative about the French navy and the canning process, see the "Encountering the Past" sidebar, which follows below.)

19.3.1.2 NAPOLEONIC VICTORIES IN CENTRAL EUROPE On land the story was different. Even before Trafalgar, Napoleon had marched to the Danube River to attack his continental enemies. In mid-October he forced an Austrian army to surrender at Ulm and occupied Vienna. On December 2, 1805, in perhaps his greatest victory, Napoleon defeated the combined Austrian and Russian forces at Austerlitz. The **Treaty of Pressburg** that followed won major concessions from Austria. The Austrians withdrew from Italy and left Napoleon in control of everything north of Rome. He was recognized as king of Italy.

Napoleon also made extensive political changes in the German states. In July 1806, he organized the Confederation of the Rhine, which included most of the western German princes. Their withdrawal from the Holy Roman Empire led the current Holy Roman emperor, the Habsburg Francis

NELSON ON HIS DEATHBED DURING THE BATTLE OF TRAFALGAR By the time this painting was completed in 1807, Horatio Nelson (1758–1805) was already a hero in Britain. Here he is depicted on his deathbed aboard his ship the *Victory* during the British defeat of French and Spanish fleets at the Battle of Trafalgar in 1805. The light illuminating Nelson's suffering face imparts religious meaning, suggesting martyrdom.
SOURCE Ian G Dagnall/Alamy Stock Photo

II, to dissolve that ancient political body and thereafter call himself Emperor Francis I of Austria.

Prussia, which had remained neutral up to this point, now foolishly went to war against France. Napoleon's forces quickly crushed the famous Prussian army at Jena and Auerstädt on October 14, 1806. Two weeks later, Napoleon was in Berlin. There, on November 21, recognizing the connection between Britain's commercial and military strength, Napoleon issued the Berlin Decrees, forbidding his allies from importing British goods. On June 13, 1807, Napoleon defeated the Russians at Friedland and occupied East Prussia. Having occupied or co-opted the west German states, humbled and humiliated Austria, and defeated Prussia, the French emperor was master of all Germany.

19.3.1.3 TREATY OF TILSIT Unable to fight another battle or to retreat into Russia, Tsar Alexander I (r. 1801–1825) was ready to make peace. He and Napoleon met on a raft in the Niemen River while the two armies and the nervous king of Prussia watched from the bank. On July 7, 1807, they signed the **Treaty of Tilsit**, which confirmed France's gains. Prussia lost half its territory. Only the support of Alexander saved it from extinction. Prussia openly, and Russia secretly, became allies of Napoleon.

NAPOLEON, THE "BAKER" OF KINGS In this 1806 caricature by the famous English artist James Gillray, Napoleon is shown as a baker who creates new kings as easily as gingerbread cookies. His new allies in the Rhine Confederation, including the rulers of Württemberg, Bavaria, and Saxony, are placed in the "New French Oven for Imperial Gingerbread."
SOURCE: Leeds Museums and Galleries (Leeds Art Gallery) U.K./Bridgeman Imagesl

Napoleon established his family as the collective sovereigns of Europe. The great French Empire was ruled directly by the head of the clan, Napoleon. On its borders lay satellite states ruled by members of his family. His stepson ruled Italy for him, and three of his brothers and his brother-in-law were made kings of other conquered states. The French emperor expected his relatives to take orders without question, and when they failed to do so, he rebuked and even punished them. The imposition of Napoleonic rule provoked political opposition that needed only encouragement and assistance to flare up into serious resistance.

19.3.2 The Continental System

After the Treaty of Tilsit, such assistance could come only from Britain, and Napoleon knew he must defeat the British before he could feel safe. Unable to compete with the British navy, he continued the economic warfare the Berlin Decrees had begun. He planned to cut off all British trade with the European continent, crippling British commercial and financial power. He hoped to cause domestic unrest and drive Britain from the war. The Milan Decree of 1807 went further and attempted to stop neutral nations from trading with Britain. (See Map 19–1.) Britain responded with its own set of decrees, the Orders of Council, which in turn forbade British subjects, allies, or even neutral countries from trading with France.

Despite initial drops in exports, domestic unrest, and tension between Britain and neutral countries that resented the ban, the British economy survived. British control of the seas ensured access to the growing markets of North and South America and of the eastern Mediterranean. At the same time, the Continental System badly hurt the European economies. Napoleon rejected advice to turn his empire into a free-trade area. Such a policy would have been both popular and helpful. Instead, his tariff policies favored France, increased the resentment of foreign merchants, and made them less willing to enforce the system and more ready to engage in smuggling. It was, in part, to prevent smuggling that Napoleon invaded Spain in 1808. The resulting peninsular campaign in Spain and Portugal helped bring on his ruin.

Map 19–1 THE CONTINENTAL SYSTEM, 1806–1810

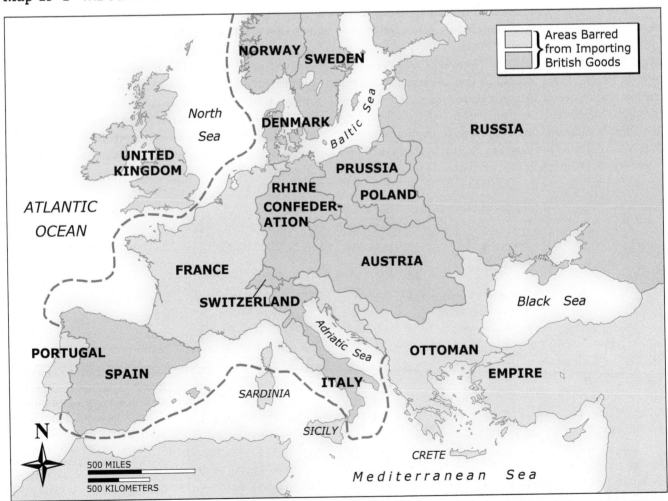

With the Continental System, Napoleon hoped to cut off all British trade with the European continent and thereby drive the British from the war.

Encountering the Past

Sailors and Canned Food

IN 1803, DURING the Napoleonic wars, the French navy undertook a secret experiment—provisioning a few of its naval vessels involved in long overseas voyages or blockades with food preserved by the then novel process of canning. The results were excellent: the crews thrived, and the French government ordered more canned goods.

Until the discovery of canning, the chief methods for preserving food were drying, salting, pickling, smoking, fermenting, and condensing. Most of these techniques are still used, but they strongly alter the taste of food and remove some of its nutritive value. Although vitamins were unknown in the eighteenth century, military authorities knew that something in fresh fruit and vegetables kept their men healthy. In the 1790s, the French government offered a reward to anyone who could invent a method of preserving food that would match the taste and texture of fresh products while nourishing sailors and soldiers, who suffered from scurvy and malnutrition from their rations of dried bread and salted meat. Preserved food would allow armies to campaign without having to live off the land, and it would allow ships to stay at sea longer without having to put into port for fresh food.

Nicholas Appert, a French chef, was determined to produce preserved food that would be both tasty and healthful. In 1795, he established a small food preservation laboratory on the outskirts of Paris. He discovered that if he filled glass jars with fresh vegetables, fruit, soups, or meat; added water or a sauce; sealed the jars with tight stoppers; and then cooked them in a hot water bath, the result was a tasty preserved food that lasted indefinitely as long as the jars remained sealed. Although Appert did not know it, one reason the food remained unspoiled was that his process killed any microbes in it.

Although many fine French foods are still canned in jars, the process quickly took a new turn in Great Britain where the navy as well as food producers were interested in it. Appert published a book on his method in 1810, and by 1813 an English company began canning in tins, which were less expensive and more durable than glass jars. Soon other canning companies appeared in Europe, including those that produced canned sardines. By mid-century, millions of people, particularly in Western Europe and North America, were eating canned food. By 1900, canned goods had become what they are today—part of everyday life around the world. The basic process used in canning today is still the one Appert devised in the 1790s.

Questions

1. What advantages did canning have over other methods of preserving food?
2. How did canning become a part of everyday life?

SOURCE: From Sue Shephard, *Pickled, Potted, and Canned: How the Art and Science of Food Processing Changed the World* (New York: Simon & Schuster, 2000).

19.4 European Response to the Empire

Why did Napoleonic rule breed resentment in Europe?

Wherever Napoleon ruled, he imposed the Napoleonic Code and abolished hereditary social distinctions. Feudal privileges disappeared, and the peasants were freed from serfdom and manorial dues. In the towns, the guilds and the local oligarchies that had been dominant for centuries were dissolved or deprived of their power. The established churches lost their traditional independence and were made subordinate to the state. Toleration replaced monopoly of religion by an established church. Despite these reforms, however, it was always clear that Napoleon's policies were intended first for his own glory and that of France. The Continental System demonstrated that Napoleon's rule was intended to enrich France, rather than Europe generally. Consequently, before long, the conquered states and peoples grew restive.

19.4.1 German Nationalism and Prussian Reform

The German response to Napoleon's success was particularly interesting and important. There had never been a unified German state. The great German writers of the Enlightenment, such as Immanuel Kant and Gotthold Lessing, were neither deeply politically engaged nor nationalistic.

At the beginning of the nineteenth century, the romantic movement had begun to take hold. One of its basic features in Germany was the emergence of nationalism, which went through two distinct stages there. Initially, nationalistic writers emphasized the unique and admirable qualities of German culture, which, they argued, arose from the history of the German people. Such cultural nationalism prevailed until Napoleon's humiliation of Prussia at Jena in 1806.

At that point many German intellectuals began to resist Napoleon on the basis of German nationalism. The French conquest endangered the independence and achievements of all German-speaking people. Many nationalists also criticized the German princes, who ruled selfishly and inefficiently and who seemed ever ready to lick Napoleon's boots. Only a people united through its language and culture could resist the French onslaught. France itself, which had attained greatness by enlisting the active support of its entire people in the patriotic cause, was a model that helped forge a German national sentiment. Henceforth, many Germans sought to solve their internal political problems by attempting to establish a unified German state, reformed to harness the energies of the entire people.

After Tilsit, only Prussia could arouse such patriotic feelings. Elsewhere, German rulers were either under Napoleon's thumb or collaborating with him. Defeated, humiliated, and diminished, Prussia continued to resist, however feebly. German nationalists from other states fled to Prussia. Once there, they called for reforms and unification that King Frederick William III (r. 1797–1840) and the Junker nobility feared and hated. These reforms came about despite such opposition because the defeat at Jena had shown that the Prussian state needed to change to survive.

The Prussian administrative and social reforms were the work of Baron vom Stein (1757–1831) and Prince von Hardenberg (1750–1822). Neither of these reformers intended to reduce the autocratic power of the Prussian monarch or to end the dominance of the Junkers, who formed the bulwark of the state and of the officer corps. Rather, they wanted to fight French power with their own version of France's weapons. As Hardenberg declared,

> Our objective, our guiding principle, must be a revolution in the better sense, a revolution leading directly to the great goal, the elevation of humanity through the wisdom of those in authority. . . . Democratic rules of conduct in a monarchical administration, such is the formula . . . which will conform most comfortably with the spirit of the age.[2]

Although the reforms came from the top, they brought important changes in Prussian society.

Stein's reforms broke the Junker monopoly of landholding. Serfdom was abolished. However, unlike in the western German states where all remnants of serfdom disappeared, in Prussia the Junkers ensured that vestiges of the system survived. Former Prussian serfs were free to leave the land if they chose, but those who stayed had to continue to perform manorial labor. They could obtain the ownership of the land they worked only if they forfeited one-third of it to the lord. The result was that Junker holdings grew larger. Some peasants went to the cities to find work, others became agricultural laborers, and some did actually become small freeholding farmers. In Prussia and elsewhere, serfdom had ended, but the rise in the numbers of landless laborers created new social problems.

Military reforms sought to increase the supply of soldiers and to improve their quality. Jena had shown that an army of free patriots commanded by officers chosen on merit rather than by birth could defeat an army of serfs and mercenaries commanded by incompetent nobles. To remedy the situation, the Prussian reformers abolished inhumane military punishments, sought to inspire patriotic feelings in the soldiers, opened the officer corps to commoners, gave promotions on the basis of merit, and organized war colleges that developed new theories of strategy and tactics.

These reforms soon enabled Prussia to regain its former power.

19.4.2 The Wars of Liberation

Unlike Germany, Spain had been a unified state for centuries, so once Napoleon threatened the Bourbons and the church, resistance became fierce. The difficulties the French encountered in Spain inspired the Austrians to avenge themselves.

19.4.2.1 SPAIN In Spain more than elsewhere in Europe, national resistance to France had deep social roots. Spain had achieved political unity as early as the sixteenth century. The Spanish peasants were devoted to the ruling dynasty and especially to the Roman Catholic Church. France and Spain had been allies since 1796. In 1807, however, a French army entered the Iberian Peninsula to force Portugal to abandon its traditional alliance with Britain. The army stayed in Spain to protect lines of supply and communication. When a revolt broke out in Madrid in 1808, Napoleon used it as a pretext to depose the Spanish Bourbons and to place his brother Joseph (1768–1844) on the Spanish throne. Attacks on the privileges of the church were interpreted as attacks on Catholicism itself and increased public outrage. Although many members of the upper classes were prepared to collaborate with Napoleon, the peasants, urged on by the lower clergy and the monks, rebelled.

In Spain, Napoleon faced a new kind of warfare. Guerrilla bands cut lines of communication, killed stragglers, destroyed isolated units, and then disappeared into the mountains. The British landed an army under Sir Arthur Wellesley (1769–1852), later the Duke of Wellington, to support the Spanish insurgents. That was the beginning of the long peninsular campaign which would drain French strength from elsewhere in Europe and hasten Napoleon's eventual defeat. (See the "Compare and Connect" sidebar, which follows below, for three viewpoints on the experience of war in the time of Napoleon.)

19.4.2.2 AUSTRIA France's troubles in Spain encouraged Austria to renew the war in 1809. Since their defeat at Austerlitz, they had longed for revenge. The Austrians counted on Napoleon's distraction in Spain, French war weariness, and aid from other German princes. Napoleon was fully in command in France, however, and the German princes did not move. The French army marched swiftly into Austria and won the Battle of Wagram. The resulting Peace of Schönbrunn deprived Austria of substantial territory and 3.5 million subjects.

Compare and Connect

The Experience of War in the Napoleonic Age

THE NAPOLEONIC WARS spread violence across Europe. Different participants, writers, and artists portrayed the experience of war differently. Heinrich von Brandt reported his own heroism in a quite matter-of-fact manner. The German poet and historian Ernest Moritz Arndt recalled moments of intense nationalistic patriotism. The Spanish painter Francisco Goya portrayed a terribly brutal event experienced by the Spanish at the hands of French troops.

EXECUTION OF SPANISH GUERRILLAS ON THE THIRD OF MAY, 1808 In Goya's *The Third of May, 1808,* one group of humble Spaniards has already been shot, another is being executed, and a third group, some of whom are hiding their eyes, will be the next victims.
SOURCE: Imagno/Getty Images

Before Reading

- Notice how the tactics of "guerrilla" warfare differ from the classic battles of the eighteenth century.
- Compare the points of view of Brandt, Arndt, and Goya regarding the violence of modern warfare and its effects on the people involved.

Questions

1. How did the warfare in Spain differ from the classic battles of the eighteenth century? What distinguished the new guerrilla warfare?
2. According to Arndt, why would each of the various groups he lists want war? How does he suggest the possibility of a united nation that did not yet exist?
3. How does Goya portray Spaniards as victims of harsh, unmerciful military violence?
4. How do Brandt's memoir, Arndt's call to arms, and Goya's painting illustrate different ways of interpreting the violence of modern warfare?

I. A POLISH LEGIONNAIRE RECALLS GUERRILLA WARFARE IN SPAIN

Heinrich von Brandt (1789–1868), was a German-speaking Prussian who lived in territory that became part of the Duchy of Warsaw in 1807. Like many Germans his age, he was a great admirer of Napoleon's accomplishments, even if he resented his violation of Prussian sovereignty. Having first trained as a member of the Prussian military (in preparation to fight against Napoleon), he was subsequently enlisted to fight in the newly constituted Polish army, allied with Napoleon. As a member of the Vistula legion, he was sent to Spain in 1808. This excerpt from his memoirs refers to the siege of Saragossa in January and February 1809.

The more we advanced the more dogged resistance became. We knew that in order not to be killed, or to diminish that risk, we would have to take each and every one of these houses converted into redoubts and where death lurked in the cellars, behind doors and shutters—in fact, everywhere. When we broke into a house we had to make an immediate and thorough inspection from the cellar to the rooftop. Experience taught us that sudden and determined resistance could well be a trick. Often as we were securing one floor we would be shot at from point blank range from the floor above through loopholes in the floorboards. All the nooks and crannies of these old-fashioned houses aided such deadly ambushes. We also had to maintain a good watch on the rooftops. With their light sandals, the Aragonese could move with the ease of and as silently as a cat and were thus able to make surprise incursions well behind the front line. It was indeed aerial combat. We would be sitting peacefully around a fire, in a house occupied for some days, when suddenly shots would come through some window just as though they had come from the sky itself. . . .

The Spanish stopped at nothing to slow our advance down. Even when they were at last forced to abandon a building, they would scatter resin soaked faggots everywhere and set them alight. The ensuing fires would not destroy the stone buildings but served to give the besieged time to prepare their defences in neighboring houses. . . .

It was all over by the evening of 20 February. . . . [The next day] the vanguard of the famous defenders of Saragossa began to appear. A certain number of young men, aged between sixteen and eighteen, without uniforms and wearing grey cloaks and red cockades, lined up in front of us, nonchalantly smoking their cigarettes. Not long after we witnessed the arrival of the rest of the army: a strange collection composed of humanity of all shades and conditions. A few were in uniform but most were dressed like peasants. . . . Most of them were of such non-military bearing that our men were saying aloud that we should never have had so much trouble in beating such a rabble.

II. A GERMAN WRITER DESCRIBES THE WAR OF LIBERATION

Although many Germans, including historian Ernst Moritz Arndt (1769–1860), initially greeted the French Revolution with enthusiasm, the French army's invasion of German territory was met with a wave of nationalist resistance. As Napoleon's army retreated from Moscow in 1813, people from German-speaking lands overcame internal rivalry to join forces against a common enemy. Arndt described the excitement of that moment in this passage subsequently reprinted in German history textbooks for more than a century.

Fired with enthusiasm, the people rose, "with God for King and Fatherland." Among the Prussians there was only one voice, one feeling, one anger and one love, to save the Fatherland and to free Germany. . . . War, war, sounded the cry from the Carpathians to the Baltic, from the Niemen to the Elbe. War! cried the nobleman and landed proprietor who had become impoverished. War! that peasant who was driving his last horse to death. . . . War! the citizen who was growing exhausted from quartering soldiers and paying taxes. War! the widow who was sending her only son to the front. War! the young girl who, with tears of pride and pain, was leaving her betrothed. . . . Even young women, under all sorts of disguises, rushed to arms; all wanted to drill, arm themselves and fight and die for the Fatherland. . . .

The most beautiful thing about all this holy zeal and happy confusion was . . . that the one great feeling for the Fatherland, its freedom and honor, swallowed all other feelings, caused all other considerations and relationships to be forgotten.

III. FRANCISCO GOYA, *THE THIRD OF MAY, 1808* (PAINTED 1814–1815)

Napoleon sent troops into Spain in 1807 after the king of Spain had agreed to aid France against Britain's ally, Portugal. By early 1808, Spain had essentially become an occupied nation. The French troops included Islamic soldiers whom Napoleon had recruited in Egypt. Many Spaniards associated French soldiers with a threat to the Catholic faith. On May 2, riots took place in Madrid between French troops and Spanish civilians. In response, the French general Murat ordered the execution of numerous citizens of Madrid, which occurred on the nights of May 2 and 3. The events of these two days marked the beginning of the Spanish effort to rid their peninsula of French rule.

*After the restoration of the Spanish monarchy, **Francisco Goya** (1745–1828) depicted the savagery of those executions in the most memorable war painting of the Napoleonic era,* The Third of May, 1808.

The painting illustrates two very different kinds of warfare of the Napoleonic age: the professional solider and the guerrilla, a term coined during the Spanish resistance of this era. The Spanish guerrilla fights with the few resources and few advanced weapons he has. By contrast, the well-disciplined French soldiers, equipped with modern rifles, carry out the execution by the light of technologically advanced lanterns fueled by either gas or oil with which Napoleon equipped his troops. Goya succeeds in portraying ordinary people and the poor clergy as not only victims but also symbolic heroes of the national war of liberation.

SOURCES: (I) From Heinrich von Brandt, *In the Legions of Napoleon: The Memoirs of a Polish Officer in Spain and Russia, 1808–1813*, trans. and ed. Jonathan North (London: Greenhill Books, 1999), pp. 58–63. (II) From Louis L., Snyder, trans., *Documents of German History*. Copyright © 1958 by Rutgers, the State University. Reprinted by permission of Rutgers University Press.

Another spoil of victory was the Austrian archduchess Marie Louise (1791–1847), daughter of Emperor Francis I. Napoleon's first wife, Josephine de Beauharnais (1763–1814), was forty-six and had borne him no children. His dynastic ambitions, as well as the desire for a royal marriage, led him to divorce Josephine and marry the eighteen-year-old Marie Louise.

19.4.3 The Invasion of Russia

The failure of Napoleon's marriage negotiations with Russia emphasized the shakiness of the Franco–Russian alliance concluded at Tilsit. Russian nobles disliked the alliance because of the liberal politics of France and because the Continental System prohibited timber sales to Britain. Only French aid in gaining Constantinople could

justify the alliance in their eyes, but Napoleon gave them no help against the Ottoman Empire. The organization of the Polish Duchy of Warsaw as a Napoleonic satellite on the Russian doorstep and its enlargement with Austrian territory in 1809 after the Battle of Wagram angered Tsar Alexander I. The tsar was furthermore disturbed by (or annoyed at) Napoleon's annexation of Holland in violation of the Treaty of Tilsit; by his recognition of the French Marshal Bernadotte (1763–1844) as the future King Charles XIV of Sweden; and by his marriage to Marie Louise. At the end of 1810, Russia withdrew from the Continental System and began to prepare for war. (See Map 19–2.)

Napoleon was determined to end the Russian military threat. He amassed an army of more than 600,000 men, including a core of Frenchmen and more than 400,000 other

Map 19–2 NAPOLEONIC EUROPE IN LATE 1812

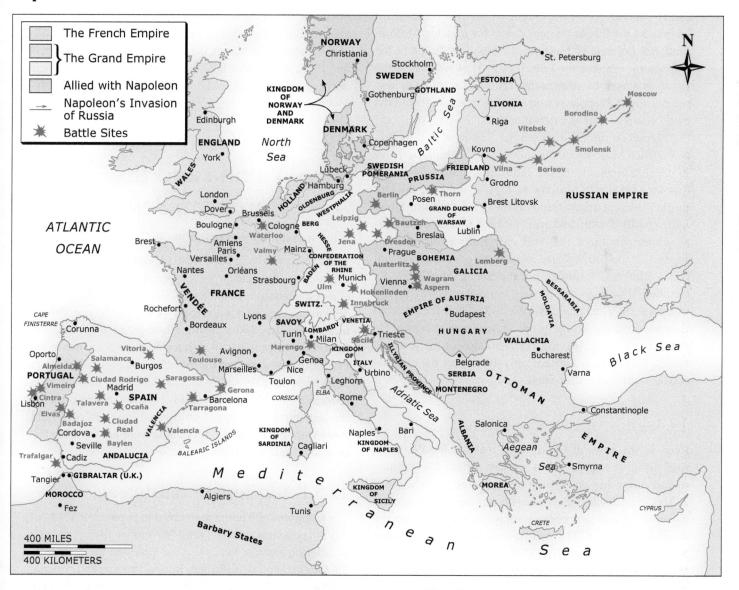

By mid-1812 the areas shown in peach were incorporated into France, and most of the rest of Europe was directly controlled by or allied with Napoleon. But Russia had withdrawn from the failing Continental System, and the decline of Napoleon was about to begin.

soldiers drawn from the rest of his empire. He intended the usual short campaign crowned by a decisive battle, but the Russians retreated before his advance. His vast superiority in numbers—the Russians had only about 160,000 troops—made it foolish for them to risk a battle. Instead, they followed a "scorched-earth" policy, destroying all food and supplies as they retreated. The so-called Grand Army of Napoleon could not live off the country, and the expanse of Russia made supply lines too long to maintain. Terrible rains, fierce heat, shortages of food and water, and the courage of the Russian rear guard eroded the morale of Napoleon's army. Napoleon's advisers urged him to abandon the venture, but he feared an unsuccessful campaign would undermine his position in the empire and in France. He pinned his faith on the Russians' unwillingness to abandon Moscow without a fight.

In September 1812, Russian public opinion forced the army to give Napoleon the battle he wanted despite the canny Russian general Mikhail Kutuzov's (1745–1813) wish to let the Russian winter defeat the invader. At Borodino, not far west of Moscow, the bloodiest battle of the Napoleonic era cost the French 30,000 casualties and the Russians almost twice as many. Yet the Russian army was not destroyed. Napoleon won nothing substantial, and the battle was regarded as a defeat for him.

Napoleon underestimated the Russians' willingness to sacrifice Moscow in the interests of victory. In order to deprive French troops of food, fuel, and housing, the Russians set fire to Moscow as they abandoned the city to the invading army. Napoleon was left far from home with a badly diminished army lacking adequate supplies as winter came to a vast and unfriendly country. After capturing the burned city, Napoleon proposed several peace offers to Alexander, but the tsar ignored them. By October, what was left of the Grand Army was forced to retreat. By December, Napoleon realized the Russian fiasco would encourage plots against him at home. He returned to Paris, leaving the remnants of his army to struggle westward. Perhaps only 100,000 of the original 600,000 survived their ordeal.

19.4.4 European Coalition

Even as the news of the disaster reached the West, the final defeat of Napoleon was far from certain. He was able to put down his opponents in Paris and raise another 350,000 men. Neither the Prussians nor the Austrians were eager to risk another contest with Napoleon, and even the Russians hesitated. The Austrian foreign minister, Prince **Klemens von Metternich** (1773–1859), would have preferred a negotiated peace that would leave Napoleon on the throne of a shrunken and chastened France rather than see Russia dominate Europe. Napoleon might have negotiated a reasonable settlement had he been willing to make concessions that would have split his jealous opponents. He would not consider that solution, however. As he explained to Metternich,

> Your sovereigns born on the throne can let themselves be beaten twenty times and return to their capitals. I cannot do this because I am an upstart soldier. My domination will not survive the day when I cease to be strong, and therefore feared.[3]

In 1813, patriotic pressure and national ambition brought together the last and most powerful coalition against Napoleon. The Russians drove westward, and Prussia and then Austria joined them. The British sent vast amounts of money to assist them. From Spain, Wellington marched his army into France. Napoleon's new army was inexperienced and poorly equipped. His generals had lost confidence in him and were tired, and the emperor himself was worn out and sick. Still, he waged a skillful campaign in central Europe and defeated the allies at Dresden. In October, however, the combined armies of the enemy decisively defeated him at Leipzig in what the Germans called the Battle of the Nations. In March 1814, the allied armies marched into Paris. A few days later, Napoleon abdicated and went into exile on the island of Elba, off the coast of central Italy.

19.5 The Congress of Vienna and the European Settlement

What were the consequences of the Congress of Vienna?

Fear of Napoleon and hostility to his ambitions had held the victorious coalition together. As soon as he was removed, the allies pursued their separate ambitions. Nevertheless, Robert Stewart, Viscount Castlereagh (1769–1822), the British foreign secretary, brought about the signing of the Treaty of Chaumont on March 9, 1814. It restored the Bourbons to the French throne and kept the French frontiers of 1792. Even more important, Britain, Austria, Russia, and Prussia agreed to form a Quadruple Alliance for twenty years to preserve the settlement they agreed on. Remaining problems—and there were many—and final details were left for a conference to be held at Vienna.

19.5.1 Territorial Adjustments

The **Congress of Vienna** assembled in September 1814 but did not conclude its work until November 1815. Although a glittering array of heads of state attended the gathering, the four great powers (Britain, Russia, Prussia, and Austria) conducted the important work of the conference. The only full session of the congress met to ratify the arrangements the big four made. The easiest problem the great powers faced was France. All the victors agreed that no single state should be allowed to dominate Europe, and all were determined to prevent France from doing so again. The restoration of the French Bourbon monarchy, which was temporarily popular, and a nonvindictive boundary settlement were designed to keep France calm and satisfied.

The powers also strengthened the states around France's borders as barriers to renewed French expansion. In the north, they established the kingdom of the Netherlands, which included Belgium and Luxembourg, and they added the important port of Genoa to strengthen Piedmont in the south. Prussia was given important new territories along the Rhine River to deter French aggression in the West. Austria gained full control of northern Italy to prevent a repetition of Napoleon's conquests there. As for the rest of the German states, most of Napoleon's territorial arrangements were left untouched. The venerable Holy Roman Empire, which had been dissolved in 1806, was not revived. (See Map 19–3.) In all these areas, the congress established the rule of legitimate monarchs and rejected any hint of the republican and democratic policies that had flowed from the French Revolution.

On these matters agreement was not difficult, but the settlement of eastern Europe sharply divided the victors. Alexander I of Russia wanted all of Poland under his rule. Prussia was willing to give it to him in return for all of Saxony, which had been allied with Napoleon. Austria, however, was unwilling to surrender its share of Poland or to see either Prussian or Russian power in central Europe grow. The Polish–Saxon question almost caused a new war

Map 19–3 THE GERMAN STATES AFTER 1815

The German states continued to cooperate in a loose confederation but maintained their independence. Independence was not restored to the small principalities that had been eliminated during the Napoleonic era.

LE CONGRÈS.

THE CONGRESS OF VIENNA, LAMPOONED In this political cartoon of the Congress of Vienna, Talleyrand simply watches which way the wind is blowing, Castlereagh hesitates, while the monarchs of Russia, Prussia, and Austria form the dance of the Holy Alliance. The king of Saxony holds on to his crown, and the republic of Geneva pays homage to the kingdom of Sardinia.
SOURCE: bpk Bildagentur/Art Resource, NY

among the victors, but defeated France provided a way out. The wily Talleyrand, now representing France at Vienna, suggested the weight of France added to that of Britain and Austria might bring Alexander to his senses. When news of a secret treaty among the three leaked out, the tsar agreed to become ruler of a smaller Poland, and Prussia settled for only part of Saxony. Thereafter, France was included as a fifth great power in all deliberations.

19.5.2 The Hundred Days and the Quadruple Alliance

Napoleon's return from Elba on March 1, 1815, further united the victors. The French army was still loyal to the former emperor, and many of the French people preferred his rule to that of the restored Bourbons. Napoleon escaped to France, and soon regained power. He promised a liberal constitution and a peaceful foreign policy. The allies were not convinced. They declared Napoleon an outlaw (a new device under international law) and sent their armies to crush him. Wellington, with the crucial help of the Prussians under Field Marshal von Blücher (1742–1819), defeated Napoleon at Waterloo in Belgium on June 18, 1815. Napoleon again abdicated and was exiled on Saint Helena, a tiny Atlantic island off the coast of Africa, where he died in 1821.

The Hundred Days, as the period of Napoleon's return is called, frightened the great powers and made the peace settlement harsher for France. In addition to some minor territorial adjustments, the victors imposed a war indemnity and an army of occupation on France. Tsar Alexander proposed a Holy Alliance, whereby the monarchs promised to act together in accordance with Christian principles. Austria and Prussia signed, but Castlereagh thought it absurd, and Britain abstained. The tsar, who was then embracing mysticism, believed his proposal a valuable tool for international relations. The Holy Alliance soon became a symbol of extreme political reaction.

Britain, Austria, Prussia, and Russia renewed the Quadruple Alliance on November 20, 1815. Henceforth, it was as much a coalition for maintaining peace as for pursuing victory over France. A coalition with such a purpose had never existed in European diplomacy before. It represented an important new departure in European affairs. Unlike eighteenth-century diplomacy, certain powers were determined to prevent war. The statesmen at Vienna had seen the armies of the French Revolution and Napoleon overturning the political and social order of much of the Continent. Their nations had experienced unprecedented destruction and had had to raise enormous military forces. They knew war affected not just professional armies and navies but entire civilian populations as well. They were determined to prevent any more such upheaval and destruction.

The leaders of Europe had learned that a treaty should secure not victory but peace. The diplomats aimed to establish a framework for stability, rather than to punish France. The great powers sought to ensure that each would respect the Vienna settlement and not use force to change it.

Though chastened by Prussia's power and its defeat by France, Austria continued to be a powerful player in European diplomacy. Much of the credit for this goes to Metternich, who emerged as the leading statesman of Europe at the Congress of Vienna. Metternich's commitment to preventing international war by preventing domestic revolution enabled him to take the lead in a new system of cooperative conservatism that would become known as the Concert of Europe.

The Congress of Vienna achieved its goals. France accepted the new situation without undue resentment, in part, because the new international order recognized it as a great power. The victorious powers settled difficult problems reasonably. They established a new legal framework whereby treaties were made between states rather than between monarchs. The treaties remained in place when a monarch died. Furthermore, during the quarter century of warfare, European leaders had come to calculate the nature of political and economic power in ways that went beyond the simple vision of gaining a favorable balance of trade that had caused so many eighteenth-century wars. They took into account nations' natural resources and economies; their systems of education; and the possibility that general growth in agriculture, commerce, and industry would benefit all states and not one at the expense of others.

The Congress has been criticized for failing to recognize and provide for the great forces that would stir the nineteenth century—nationalism and democracy. Such criticism is inappropriate. At the time, nationalist pressures were relatively rare; the general desire was for peace. The settlement, like all such agreements, was meant to solve past ills and in that it succeeded. The success of the Vienna settlement was that it remained essentially intact for almost a half-century and prevented general war for a hundred years. (See Map 19–4.)

19.6 The Romantic Movement

Why did the romantic movement emerge in the eighteenth century?

Reflecting on the social, political, and cultural changes within Europe from the mid-eighteenth century to the Congress of Vienna, one German writer asserted in 1818, "In the

Map 19–4   EUROPE, 1815, AFTER THE CONGRESS OF VIENNA

The Congress of Vienna resulted in the post-Napoleonic territorial adjustments shown on this map. These changes affected areas along France's borders (the Netherlands, Prussia, Switzerland, and Piedmont) and in Poland and northern Italy.

three generations alive today, our own age has combined what cannot be combined. No sense of continuity informs the tremendous contrast inherent in the years 1750, 1789 and 1815."[4] The years of the French Revolution and the conquests of Napoleon saw the emergence of a new and important intellectual movement throughout Europe that has come to be called **romanticism**. The romantic movement was a reaction against much of Enlightenment thought and the social transformation of the Industrial Revolution. Not surprisingly, given its emphasis on the individual, scholars have never been able to agree on a general definition of romanticism. There was, however, a consensus that romanticism represented a turn toward "absolute inwardness,"

in the words of Hegel: an emphasis on the artist over his or her work, on the subjective experience and potential heroism of the individual, and the inability to understand the external world through reason. Romantic writers and artists thought the imagination was superior to reason as a means of perceiving the world. Instead of controlling nature, they believed, people should be awestruck by it. Many of them urged a revival of Christianity so that it would once again permeate Europe. Unlike the philosophes, the romantics liked the art, literature, and architecture of medieval times. They were also deeply interested in folklore, folk songs, and fairy-tales. Dreams, hallucinations, sleepwalking, and other phenomena that suggested the existence of a world beyond that of empirical observation, sensory data, and discursive reasoning fascinated the romantics. Although their specific interests, tools of expression, and priorities varied, romantics shared an alienation from what they considered to be the cold rationalism that characterized the industrial economy and Enlightenment thought.

19.7   Romantic Questioning of the Supremacy of Reason

How did Rousseau and Kant contribute to the development of romanticism?

The romantic movement had roots in the individualism of the Renaissance, Protestant devotion and personal piety, sentimental novels of the eighteenth century, and dramatic German poetry of the *Sturm und Drang* (literally, "storm and stress") movement, which rejected the influence of French rationalism on German literature. However, two writers who were also closely related to the Enlightenment provided the immediate intellectual foundations for

romanticism: Jean-Jacques Rousseau and Immanuel Kant questioned whether the rationalism of the philosophes was sufficient to explain human nature and to be the bedrock for organizing human society.

19.7.1   Rousseau and Education

Jean-Jacques Rousseau, though sharing in the reformist spirit of the Enlightenment, opposed many of its other facets. Romantic writers were profoundly influenced by Rousseau's conviction that society and material prosperity had corrupted human nature.

Rousseau presented his view on how the individual could lead a good and happy life uncorrupted by society in his novel *Émile* (1762). In *Émile*, Rousseau stressed the difference between children and adults. He distinguished among the stages of human maturation and urged that children be raised with maximum individual freedom. Each child, he claimed, should be allowed by trial and error to understand reality and how best to deal with it. Beyond providing the necessities of life and warding off harm, parents and teachers should stay completely out of the way.

To romantic writers, this concept of human development vindicated the rights of nature over those of artificial society. They believed this form of open education would eventually lead to a natural society. In its fully developed form, this view of life led the romantics to value the uniqueness of each individual and to explore childhood in detail. The romantics saw humankind, nature, and society as organically interrelated.

19.7.2   Kant and Reason

Immanuel Kant (1724–1804) wrote the two greatest philosophical works of the late eighteenth century: *The Critique of Pure Reason* (1781) and *The Critique of Practical Reason* (1788). He sought to accept the rationalism of the Enlightenment and to still preserve a belief in human freedom, immortality, and the existence of God. For Kant, the human mind did not passively reflect the world around it like a mirror. Rather, the mind actively generated the "categories of understanding" and "forms of sensibility," and imposed them on the world of sensory experience. This meant that human perceptions were the product of both sensory experience and the mind's own activity.

According to Kant, "pure reason" could comprehend the phenomenal world of sensory experience. But beyond this world of sensory experience, there existed what he called the "noumenal" world, to which pure reason had only limited access. The noumenal world was a sphere of moral and aesthetic reality known through "practical reason" and conscience. Kant thought all human beings possessed an innate sense of moral duty or an awareness of what he called a **categorical imperative**. This

GOETHE, AGE 38 The quintessential polymath Johann Wolfgang von Goethe (1749–1832) authored works in the late eighteenth and early nineteenth centuries that have since become synonymous with German culture. His writing is indicative of the major cultural trends of the time: *Sturm und Drang*, romanticism, and classicism. His best-known work, *Faust*, is widely regarded as a masterpiece of German literature.
SOURCE: Fine Art Images/Glow Images

term refers to an inner command to act in every situation as one would have all other people always act in that situation. Based on humankind's moral sense, Kant postulated the existence of God, eternal life, and future rewards and punishments. He believed that reason alone could not prove these transcendental truths. Still, he was convinced they were realities to which every reasonable person could attest.

To many romantic writers, Kantian philosophy refuted the Enlightenment's narrow idea of rationality. The romantics believed that the human mind possessed other powers or faculties—whether they called them "practical reason," "fancy," "imagination," "intuition," or simply "feeling"—with which it was possible to grasp the complexity of reality deeper than with reason alone.

19.8 Romantic Literature

How were the ideals of romanticism reflected in English and German literature?

The term *romantic* appeared in English and French literature as early as the seventeenth century. Neoclassical writers then used the word to describe literature they considered unreal, sentimental, or excessively fanciful. Later, in both England and Germany, the term came to be applied to all literature that did not observe classical forms and rules and gave free play to the imagination. The romantic movement had peaked in Germany and England before it became a major force in France under the leadership of Madame de Staël (1766–1817) and Victor Hugo (1802–1885). The first French writer to declare himself a romantic was Henri Beyle (1783–1842), who wrote under the pseudonym Stendhal.

KEY EIGHTEENTH- AND NINETEENTH-CENTURY ROMANTIC WORKS	
1762	Rousseau's *Émile*
1774	Goethe's *Sorrows of Young Werther*
1781	Kant's *Critique of Pure Reason**
1788	Kant's *Critique of Practical Reason**
1798	Wordsworth and Coleridge's *Lyrical Ballads*
1799	Schlegel's *Lucinde*
1799	Schleiermacher's *Speeches on Religion to Its Cultured Despisers*
1802	Chateaubriand's *Genius of Christianity*
1806	Hegel's *Phenomenology of Mind*
1808	Goethe's *Faust*, Part I
1812	Byron's *Childe Harold's Pilgrimage*
1819	Byron's *Don Juan*
1825	Scott's *Tales of the Crusaders*
1841	Carlyle's *On Heroes and Hero-Worship*

*Kant's books were not themselves part of the romantic movement, but they were fundamental to later romantic writers.

19.8.1 English Romantic Writers

The English romantics believed poetry was enhanced by freely following the creative impulses of the mind. For Samuel Taylor Coleridge (1772–1834), for example, the artist's imagination was God at work in the mind. Poetry thus could not be considered idle play. Rather, it was the highest of human acts, humankind's self-fulfillment in a transcendental world.

19.8.1.1 WORDSWORTH William Wordsworth (1770–1850) was Coleridge's closest friend. Together they published *Lyrical Ballads* in 1798 as a manifesto of a new poetry that rejected the rules of eighteenth-century criticism. Among Wordsworth's most important later poems is his "Ode on Intimations of Immortality" (1803). Its subject is the loss of poetic vision, something Wordsworth felt then in himself. Nature, which he had worshipped, no longer spoke freely to him, and he feared it might never speak to him again. He mourned the loss of his childlike vision and closeness to spiritual reality—a loss he believed was part of the necessary process of maturation. For Wordsworth and Coleridge, childhood was the bright period of creative imagination. Aging and urban living corrupted and deadened the imagination, making inner feelings and the beauty of nature less important.

GEORGE GORDON, LORD BYRON A central figure in the romantic movement, the English poet Lord Byron (1788–1824) boasted that he could embody multiple personalities and embraced different cultural traditions. He chose Albanian attire for this portrait. Byron supported Greek independence, a cause that would cost him his life.
SOURCE: Classic Image/Alamy Stock Photo

19.8.1.2 LORD BYRON A true rebel among the romantic poets was **Lord Byron** (1788–1824). In Britain, even most of the other romantic writers distrusted and disliked him. Outside England, however, Byron was regarded as the embodiment of the new person the French Revolution had created. He rejected old traditions, was divorced and famous for his many love affairs, and championed the cause of personal liberty. Byron was outrageously skeptical and mocking, even of his own beliefs. In *Childe Harold's Pilgrimage* (1812), he created a brooding, melancholy romantic hero. In *Don Juan* (1819), he wrote with ribald humor, acknowledged nature's cruelty as well as its beauty, and even expressed admiration for urban life.

19.8.1.3 MARY GODWIN SHELLEY **Mary Godwin Shelley** (1797–1851) was the daughter of Mary Wollstonecraft, author of *A Vindication of the Rights of Woman*. Wollstonecraft died of puerperal fever shortly after Godwin's birth. At the age of sixteen, Godwin fell in love with romantic poet Percy Bysshe Shelley, who was already married. Fleeing ostracism and scandal in England, they traveled through Europe and married after the suicide of Shelley's first wife. While spending the summer of 1816 on Lake Geneva with their mutual friend, Lord Byron, Godwin conceived of the idea for *Frankenstein*, which she published in 1818. Often considered the first science fiction novel, it tells the story of a Swiss doctor, Frankenstein, who deliberately creates a living being out of components of dead bodies. Frankenstein finds he has created not a beautiful creature but instead an abhorrent "monster." When Godwin, by then Mary Shelley, was revealed as the author, contemporary critics complained that the gruesome subject matter was inappropriate for a young female mind.

19.8.2 The German Romantic Writers

Almost all major German romantics wrote at least one novel. Romantic novels often were highly sentimental and borrowed material from medieval romances. The characters in romantic novels were treated as symbols of the truths of real life. Purely realistic description was avoided. Friedrich Schlegel (1767–1845) wrote the progressive early romantic novel *Lucinde* (1799), which attacked prejudices against women as being little more than lovers and domestics. Schlegel's novel revealed the ability of the romantics to also write about the social issues of their day. He depicted Lucinde as the perfect friend and companion, as well as the unsurpassed lover, of the hero. The work shocked contemporary morals with its frank discussion of sexuality and its description of Lucinde as equal to the male hero.

19.8.2.1 GOETHE Perhaps the greatest German writer of modern times, **Johann Wolfgang von Goethe** (1749–1832) defies easy classification. Much of his literary work fits the romantic mold, and much of it was a condemnation of romantic excesses. The book that made his early reputation was *The Sorrows of Young Werther*, published in 1774. This novel, like many in the eighteenth century, is a series of letters. The hero falls in love with Lotte, who is married to another man. Eventually Werther and Lotte part, but in his grief, Werther takes his own life. This novel became popular throughout Europe. Romantic authors admired its emphasis on feeling and on living outside the bounds of polite society.

Goethe's masterpiece was *Faust*, a long dramatic poem. Part I, published in 1808, tells the story of Faust, who makes a pact with the devil: he will exchange his soul for greater knowledge than other human beings possess. As the story progresses, Faust seduces a young woman named Gretchen. She dies but is received into heaven as the grief-stricken Faust realizes he must continue to live. At the conclusion of Part II, completed in 1832, Faust dedicates what remains of his life to the improvement of humankind. This dedication, Faust believes, will allow him to overcome the restless striving that induced him to make the pact with the devil. That new knowledge breaks the pact. Faust dies and is received by angels.

19.9 Romantic Art

How were the ideals of romanticism reflected in English and German art?

The art of the romantic era, like its poetry and philosophy, was largely a reaction to that of the eighteenth century. Whereas the rococo artists had looked to Renaissance models and neoclassical painters to the art of the ancient world, romantic painters often portrayed scenes from medieval life. For them, the Middle Ages represented the social stability and religious reverence that was slowly disappearing.

19.9.1 The Cult of the Middle Ages and neo-Gothicism

Like many early romantic artists, English landscape painter John Constable (1776–1837) was politically conservative. In *Salisbury Cathedral from the Meadows*, he portrayed a stable world in which neither political turmoil nor industrial development challenged the traditional dominance of the church and the landed classes. Although the clouds and sky in the painting depict a severe storm, both nature (the trees) and humankind (the cathedral) present a powerful sense of enduring order. Constable saw the church and the British constitution as intimately related. Like many English conservatives of his day, he expected religious institutions to deter political radicalism.

Constable and other romantics tended to idealize rural life because they believed it opposed the increasingly urban, industrializing, commercial society that was developing around them. In fact, the rural landscape and rustic society that Constable depicted in his paintings had already largely disappeared from England.

THE IDEALS OF ROMANTICISM The English painter John Constable (1776–1837), who painted outdoors in all kinds of weather, was famous for his masterful landscapes of the English countryside. In this idyllic scene, the daily activities of farm life and the sublime power of nature are celebrated in a typically romantic manner.
SOURCE: Ian Dagnall / Alamy Stock Photo

The neo-Gothic revival in architecture dotted the European landscape with modern imitations of medieval structures. Many medieval cathedrals were restored during this era, and new churches were designed to resemble their medieval forerunners. The British Houses of Parliament built from 1836 to 1837 were the most famous public buildings in the neo-Gothic style, but town halls, schools, and even railroad stations were designed to look like medieval buildings, while aristocratic country houses were rebuilt to resemble medieval castles.

19.9.2 Nature and the Sublime

Beyond their attraction to history, romantic artists also portrayed nature in all of its majestic power as no previous generation of European artists had ever done. Like romantic poets, the artists of the era were drawn toward the mysterious and unruly side of nature rather than toward the rational Newtonian order that had prevailed during the Enlightenment. Their works often portrayed what they and others termed *the sublime*—that is, subjects from nature that aroused strong emotions, such as fear, dread, and awe, and raised questions about whether and how much we control our lives. Painters often traveled to remote areas such as the Scottish Highlands or the Swiss Alps to illustrate scenes

from nature that were dangerous and would immediately engage viewers' emotions.

Romantics saw nature as a set of infinite forces that overwhelmed the smallness of humankind. For example, in 1824,

THE POLAR SEA Caspar David Friedrich's *The Polar Sea* illustrates the power of nature to destroy the creations of humankind, as seen in the wrecked ship on the right of the painting.
SOURCE: akg-images/SuperStock

NATURE V. INDUSTRIALISM
Joseph Mallord William Turner's *Rain, Steam, and Speed—The Great Western Railway* captured the
tensions many Europeans felt between their natural environment and the new technology of the industrial age.
SOURCE: Peter Willi/Getty Images

the German artist Caspar David Friedrich (1774–1840) in *The Polar Sea* painted the plight of a ship trapped and crushed by a vast polar ice field. In direct contrast to eighteenth-century artists' portrayal of sunny Enlightenment, Friedrich also painted scenes in which human beings stand shrouded in the mysterious darkness of night where moonlight and torches cast only fitful illumination.

An artist who similarly understood the power of nature but also the forces of the new industrialism that was challenging them was **Joseph Mallord William Turner** (1775–1851) whose painting *Rain, Steam and Speed—The Great Western Railway* of 1844 illustrated the recently invented railway engine barreling through an enveloping storm. In this scene the new technology is both part of the natural world and strong enough to dominate it.

Friedrich's and Turner's paintings taken together symbolize the contradictory forces affecting romantic artists—the sense of the power, awe, and mastery of nature coupled with the sense that the advance of industry represented a new kind of awesome human power that could challenge or even surpass the forces of nature itself.

19.10 Religion in the Romantic Period

How did romantic religious thinkers view the religious experience?

During the Middle Ages, the foundation of religion had been the authority of the church. The Reformation leaders had appealed to the authority of the Bible. Then, many Enlightenment writers attempted to derive religion from the rational nature revealed by Newtonian physics, while others attacked it altogether. Romantic religious thinkers, in contrast, sought the foundations of religion in the inner emotions of humankind. Reacting to the anticlericalism of both the Enlightenment and the French Revolution, these thinkers also saw religious faith and institutions as central to human life. One of the first great examples of a religion characterized by romantic impulses—Methodism—arose in mid-eighteenth-century England during the Enlightenment itself and became one of the most powerful forces in transatlantic religion during the nineteenth century.

19.10.1 Methodism

Methodism originated in the middle of the eighteenth century as a revolt against the deism and rationalism of the Church of England. The Methodist revival formed an important part of the background of English romanticism. The leader of the Methodist movement was John Wesley (1703–1791). His mother, Susannah Wesley, who bore eighteen children, had carefully supervised his education and religious development.

After studying at Oxford University to be an Anglican priest, Wesley left England for missionary work in the new colony of Georgia in America, where he arrived in 1735. While he was crossing the Atlantic, a group of German Moravians on the ship deeply impressed him with their unshakable faith and confidence during a storm. When he returned to England, Wesley began to worship with Moravians in London. There, in 1739, he underwent a conversion experience that he described in the words, "My heart felt strangely warmed."

Wesley began to preach in the open fields near the cities and towns of western England. Thousands of humble people responded to his message of repentance and good works. Soon he and his brother Charles (1707–1788), who became famous for his hymns, began to organize Methodist societies. By the late eighteenth century, the Methodists had become a separate church. They ordained their own clergy and sent missionaries to America.

Methodism stressed inward, heartfelt religion and the possibility of Christian perfection in this life. Methodist preachers emphasized the role of enthusiastic, emotional experience as part of Christian conversion. After Wesley, religious revivals became highly emotional in style and content.

19.10.2 New Directions in Continental Religion

Similar religious developments based on feeling appeared on the Continent. After the Thermidorian Reaction, a strong Roman Catholic revival took place in France. Its followers disapproved of both the religious policy of the revolution and the anticlericalism of the Enlightenment. The most important book to express these sentiments was *The Genius of Christianity* (1802) by Viscount François René de Chateaubriand (1768–1848). In this work, which became known as the "bible of romanticism," Chateaubriand argued that the essence of religion is "passion" and that the foundation of faith in the church was the emotion that its teachings and sacraments inspired in the heart of the Christian.

Unlike the Newtonian view of the world and of a rational God, the romantics found God immanent in nature. No one stated the romantic religious ideal more eloquently or with greater impact on the modern world than Friedrich Schleiermacher (1768–1834). In 1799, he published a response to both Lutheran orthodoxy and Enlightenment rationalism, *Speeches on Religion to Its Cultured Despisers*. According to Schleiermacher, religion was an intuition or feeling of absolute dependence on an infinite reality.

19.11 Romantic Views of Nationalism and History

What were the romantic views of history and national identity?

A distinctive feature of romanticism, especially in Germany, was its glorification of both the individual person and individual cultures. Behind these views lay the philosophy of German idealism, which understood the world as the creation of subjective egos. J. G. Fichte (1762–1814), an important German philosopher and nationalist, identified the individual ego with the Absolute that underlies all existing things. According to Fichte, the world is as it is because especially strong persons conceived of it in a particular way and imposed their wills on the world and other people. Napoleon was the contemporary example of such a great person. This philosophy has ever since justified the glorification of great persons and their actions in overriding all opposition to their will.

19.11.1 Herder and Culture

New historical studies also contributed to the German glorification of individual cultures. German romantic writers went in search of their own past in reaction to the copying of French manners in eighteenth-century Germany, the impact of the French Revolution, and the imperialism of Napoleon. An early leader in this effort was **Johann Gottfried Herder** (1744–1803). He saw human beings and societies as developing organically, like plants, over time.

Herder revived German folk culture by urging the collection and preservation of distinctive German songs and sayings. His most important followers in this work were the Grimm brothers, Jakob (1785–1863) and Wilhelm (1786–1859), famous for their collection of fairy-tales. Believing each language and culture were the unique expression of a people, Herder opposed both the concept and the use of a "common" language, such as French, and "universal" institutions,

FRENCH VICTORY AT ABOUKIR When Napoleon invaded Egypt in 1799, he met stiff resistance. On July 25, however, the French won a decisive victory at the Battle of Aboukir. This painting of that battle by Baron Antoine Gros (1771–1835) emphasizes French heroism and Ottoman defeat in a manner that was typical of European views of Arabs and of the Islamic world at the time.
SOURCE: Niday Picture Library/Alamy Stock Photo

such as those Napoleon had imposed on Europe. These, he believed, were forms of tyranny over the individuality of a people. Herder's writings led to a broad revival of interest in history and philosophy. Although initially directed toward identifying German origins, such work soon expanded to embrace other world cultures. Eventually, the ability of the romantic imagination to find a home in any age or culture spurred the study of comparative religion, comparative literature, and philology.

19.11.2 Hegel and History

The most important philosopher of history in the romantic period was the German **Georg Wilhelm Friedrich Hegel** (1770–1831). He is one of the most complicated and significant philosophers in the history of Western civilization.

Hegel believed ideas develop in an evolutionary fashion that involves conflict. At any given time, a predominant set of ideas, which he termed the *thesis*, holds sway. Conflicting ideas, which Hegel termed the *antithesis*, challenge the thesis. As these patterns of thought clash, a *synthesis* emerges that eventually becomes the new thesis. Then the process begins all over again. Periods of world history were also characterized by the patterns of thought

that predominated during them. Several important philosophical conclusions followed from this analysis. One of the most significant was the belief that all periods of history have been of almost equal value because each was, by definition, necessary to the achievements of those that came later. Also, all cultures are valuable because each contributes to the necessary clash of values and ideas that allows humankind to develop. Hegel discussed these concepts in *The Phenomenology of Mind* (1806), *Lectures on the Philosophy of History* (1822–1831), and other works, many of which were published only after his death. During his lifetime, his ideas became widely known through his university lectures at Berlin.

19.11.3 Islam, the Middle East, and Romanticism

The new religious, literary, and historical sensibilities of the romantic period altered the European understanding of both Islam and the Arab world while at the same time preserving long-standing attitudes.

The energized Christianity associated with Methodist-like forms of Protestantism on the one hand and Chateaubriand's emotional Roman Catholicism on the other renewed the traditional sense of necessary conflict between Christianity and Islam. Chateaubriand wrote a travelogue of his journey from Paris to Jerusalem in 1811. A decade later, when he was a member of the French parliament, he invoked the concept of a crusade against the Muslim world in a speech on the danger posed by the Barbary pirates of North Africa.

The medieval Crusades against Islam fired the romantic imagination. Nostalgic European artists painted from a Western standpoint the great moments of the Crusades including the bloody capture of Jerusalem. Stories from those conflicts filled historical novels such as *Tales of the Crusaders* (1825) by Sir Walter Scott (1771–1832). But although they presented heroic images of Muslim warriors, these paintings and novels ignored the havoc that the Crusaders had visited on the peoples of the Middle East.

The general nineteenth-century association of nationalistic aspirations with romanticism also cast the Ottoman Empire and Islam in an unfavorable political light. Romantic poets and intellectuals championed the cause of the Greek Revolution and revived older charges of Ottoman despotism.

By contrast, other romantic sensibilities induced Europeans to see the Muslim world in a more positive fashion. The romantic emphasis on the value of literature drawn from different cultures and ages allowed many nineteenth-century European readers to enjoy the stories from *The Thousand and One Nights*, which first appeared in English in 1778 from a French translation. In 1859, Edward FitzGerald (1809–1883) published his highly popular translation of the *Rubáiyát of Omar Khayyám* of Nishapur, a Persian poet of the twelfth century.

Herder's and Hegel's concepts of history gave both the Arab peoples and Islam distinct roles in history. For Herder, Arab culture was one of the numerous communities of the human race that manifested the human spirit. The Prophet Muhammad, while giving voice to the ancient spirit of the Arab people, had transformed them from a polytheistic faith to a great monotheistic vision. For Hegel, Islam represented an important stage of the development of the world spirit. However, Hegel believed Islam had fulfilled its role in history and no longer had any significant part to play. These outlooks, which characterized much of nineteenth-century intellectual life, made it easy for Europeans to believe that Islam could, for all practical purposes, be ignored or reduced to a spent historical force.

British historian and social commentator Thomas Carlyle (1795–1881) attributed new, positive qualities to Muhammad himself. Carlyle disliked the Enlightenment's disparagement of religion and spiritual values and was drawn to German theories of history. In his book *On Heroes and Hero-Worship* (1841), Carlyle presented Muhammad as the embodiment of the hero as prophet. He repudiated the traditional Christian and general Enlightenment view of Muhammad as an impostor. To Carlyle, Muhammad was a person who had experienced God subjectively and had communicated a sense of the divine to others. Although friendly to Muhammad from a historical standpoint, Carlyle nonetheless saw him as one of many great religious figures but not, as Muslims believed, as the last of the prophets through whom God had spoken.

The person who perhaps did the most to reshape the ideas of Islam and the Middle East in the European imagination was Napoleon himself. With his Egyptian expedition of 1798, the first European military invasion of the Near East since the Crusades, the study of the Arab world became an important part of French intellectual life. For his invasion of Egypt to succeed, Napoleon had to make it clear that he had no intention of destroying Islam but rather to liberate Egypt from the military clique that governed the country in the name of the Ottoman Empire. To that end, he took with him scholars of Arabic and Islamic culture whom he urged to converse with the most educated people they could meet. Napoleon personally met with the local Islamic leaders and had all his speeches and proclamations translated into classical Arabic. Such cultural sensitivity and the serious efforts of the French scholars to learn Arabic and study the *Qur'an* impressed Egyptian scholars. (When the French sought to levy new taxes, however, the Egyptians' enthusiasm waned.)

It was on this expedition that the famous Rosetta Stone was discovered. Now housed in the British Museum, it eventually led to the decipherment of ancient Egypt's hieroglyphic writing. Napoleon's scholars also published a twenty-three volume *Description of Egypt* (1809–1828), which concentrated largely on ancient Egypt. Their approach suggested the history of the Ottoman Empire needed to be related first to the larger context of Egyptian history and that Islam, although enormously important, was only part of a larger cultural story. The implication was that if Egypt and Islam were to be understood, it would be through European—if not necessarily Christian—categories of thought.

Two cultural effects in the West of Napoleon's invasion were an increase in the number of European visitors to the Middle East and a demand for architecture based on ancient Egyptian models. Perhaps the most famous example of this trend is the Washington Monument in Washington, D.C., which is modeled after ancient Egyptian obelisks.

The Chapter in Perspective

Romantic ideas made a major contribution to the emergence of nationalism, which proved to be one of the strongest motivating forces of the nineteenth and twentieth centuries. The writers of the Enlightenment had generally championed a cosmopolitan outlook on the world. By contrast, the romantic thinkers emphasized the individuality and worth of each separate people and culture. A people or a nation was defined by a common language, history, and customs and by the possession of a historical homeland. This cultural nationalism gradually became transformed into a political creed. It came to be widely believed that every people, ethnic group, or nation should constitute a separate political entity and only then could the nation be secure in its own character.

France under the revolutionary government and Napoleon had demonstrated the power of nationhood. Other peoples came to desire similar strength and confidence. Napoleon's toppling of ancient political structures, such as the Holy Roman Empire, proved the need for new political organization in Europe. By 1815, only a few Europeans aspired to this, but as time passed, peoples from Ireland to Ukraine came to share these yearnings. The Congress of Vienna could ignore such feelings, but for the rest of the nineteenth century, as shall be seen in subsequent chapters, statesmen had to confront the growing power these feelings had unleashed.

The Chapter in Review

Review Questions

1. How did Napoleon rise to power? What groups supported him? What were his major domestic achievements? Did his rule fulfill or betray the French Revolution?
2. What regions made up Napoleon's realm, and what was the status of each region within it? Did his administration show foresight, or was the empire a burden he could not afford?
3. Why did Napoleon decide to invade Russia? Why did the operation fail?
4. What were the results of the Congress of Vienna? Was the Vienna settlement a success?
5. Why did romantic writers champion feelings over reason? What questions did Rousseau and Kant raise about reason?
6. Why was poetry important to romantic writers? How did the romantic concept of religion differ from Reformation Protestantism and Enlightenment deism?

Key Terms

Battle of Trafalgar   A naval conflict on October 21, 1805, that marked a great victory for the British against the combined fleets of the French and Spanish fleets.

categorical imperative   According to Emmanuel Kant (1724–1804), the internal sense of moral duty or awareness possessed by all human beings.

Congress of Vienna   A meeting of ambassadors from European states that took place from November 1814 to June 1815 and sought to prevent the recurrence of the Napoleonic Wars and arrange a lasting peace.

Consulate   French government dominated by Napoleon from 1799 to 1804.

Émile   The novel of Rousseau that presents his view on how the individual could lead a good and happy life uncorrupted by society.

Francisco Goya   (1745–1828) Romantic painter and the most important Spanish artist of the late eighteenth and early nineteenth century.

Georg Wilhelm Friedrich Hegel   (1770–1831) German philosopher. The most important philosopher of history in the romantic period and one of the most important thinkers in the history of Western civilization.

Horatio Nelson   (1758–1805) The great British admiral responsible for the victory at Trafalgar against the French and Spanish, who also destroyed the French fleet at Abukir in 1798.

Johann Gottfried Herder   (1744–1803) German romantic writer and critic of European colonialism, who revived German folk culture by encouraging the collection and preservation of distinctive German songs and sayings.

Johann Wolfgang von Goethe   (1749–1832) Perhaps the greatest German writer of modern times, whose masterpiece, *Faust*, describes the pact with the devil.

Joseph Mallord William Turner   (1775–1851) English romantic artist who depicted the power of nature and the forces of the new industrialism.

Klemens von Metternich   (1773–1859) German diplomat who served as the Austrian empire's foreign minister and who took the lead role in a new system of cooperative conservatism that would become known as the Concert of Europe.

Lord Byron   (1788–1824) British romantic writer who rejected old traditions and championed the cause of personal liberty.

Mary Godwin Shelly   (1797–1851) English writer and author of *Frankenstein*, considered the first scientific fiction novel.

Methodism   An English religious movement begun by John Wesley (1703–1791) that stressed inward, heartfelt religion and the possibility of attaining Christian perfection in this life.

Napoleonic Code   The Civil Code of 1804 through which Napoleon reformed and codified French law; confirmed the abolishment of all forms of property and privileges based on birth.

romanticism   A reaction in early-nineteenth-century literature, philosophy, and religion against what many considered the excessive rationality and scientific narrowness of the Enlightenment.

Sturm and Drang **(SHTURM und DRAHNG)**   Meaning "storm and stress." A movement in German romantic literature and philosophy that emphasized feeling and emotion.

Treaty of Pressburg   The peace of December 2, 1805, that followed Napoleon's great victory over the combined forces of Austria and Russia at Austerlitz, in which Napoleon became recognized as king of Italy.

Treaty of Tilsit   Peace of July 7, 1807, concluded by Russian tsar Alexander I and Napoleon I that confirmed France's gains and allied it with Russia.

Notes

1. David Armitage, *The Ideological Origins of the British Empire* (Cambridge, UK: Cambridge University Press, 2000), p. 185. I.

2. Geoffrey Brunn, *Europe and the French Imperium* (New York: Harper & Row, 1938), p. 174.

3. Felix Markham, *Napoleon and the Awakening of Europe* (New York: Macmillan, 1965), pp. 115–116.

4. Tim Blanning, *The Romantic Revolution: A History* (New York: Modern Library, 2010), p. ix.

Chapter 20
The Conservative Order and the Challenges of Reform (1815–1832)

LIBERTY LEADING THE PEOPLE In 1830, revolution again erupted in France as well as elsewhere on the Continent. Eugène Delacroix's *Liberty Leading the People* was the most famous image recalling that event. In this portrait, persons from different social classes and occupations join the revolution led by the figure of Liberty.
SOURCE: Scala/Art Resource, NY

 ## Contents and Focus Questions

The Chapter in Brief

THE CONGRESS OF Vienna was followed by a decade in which conservative political forces controlled virtually all of Europe. In the international arena, these forces attempted to maintain peace and to prevent the outbreak of war that would unleash destruction and disorder. They did so through unprecedented forms of cooperation and mutual consultation. Domestically, they sought to maintain the authority of monarchies and aristocracies after the turmoil the French Revolution and Napoleon had provoked. This conservative order faced new and powerful challenges. Nationalists wished to redraw the map of Europe according to the boundaries of nationalities or ethnic groups. Liberals sought moderate political reform and freer economic markets. The goals of nationalists and liberals threatened the dominance of landed aristocracies and the rule of monarchs who governed by dynastic inheritance rather than nationality. In some cases, nationalists advocated a political shift from rule in the name of God to rule in the name of the nation. In others, they advocated the independence of colonies from European states, or dependent regions on the peripheries of empires.

For the first fifteen years after the Congress of Vienna, the forces of conservatism were successful within Europe, although Spain and Portugal failed to retain control of Latin America. In the late 1820s, however, the conservatives faced stronger challenges. Thereafter, certain major liberal goals were achieved when a revolution occurred in France in 1830 and a sweeping reform bill passed through the British Parliament in 1832. During the same period, Russia, Austria, Prussia, and the other German states continued to resist political and social change.

20.1 The Conservative Order

How did early-nineteenth-century nationalists define the nation?

At the Congress of Vienna, the major powers—Russia, Austria, Prussia, and Great Britain—had agreed to consult with each other from time to time on matters affecting Europe. Such consultation was one of the new departures in international relations the Congress achieved. The vehicle for this consultation was a series of postwar congresses, or conferences. Later, as differences arose among the powers, the consultations became more informal. This new arrangement for resolving mutual foreign policy issues was known as the **Concert of Europe**. It prevented one nation from taking a major action in international affairs without working in concert with and obtaining the assent of the others. Its goal—a novel one in European affairs—was to maintain the peace. Initially, this meant maintaining the balance of power against new French aggression and against the military might of Russia. The Concert of Europe continued to function, however, on large and small issues until the third quarter of the century. In that respect, although the great powers sought to maintain conservative domestic governments, they were taking genuinely new steps to regulate their international relations.

LORD CASTLEREAGH, BY SIR THOMAS LAWRENCE

ROBERT STEWART, VISCOUNT CASTLEREAGH, MARQUESS OF LONDONDERRY Robert Stewart (1769–1822) served as the British foreign secretary from 1812 to 1822. He supported the Grand Alliance against France, represented Britain at the Congress of Vienna, and was instrumental in creating the Concert of Europe, which shaped international relations after the Napoleonic Wars.
SOURCE: New York Public Library

20.1.1 The Congress System

In the years immediately after the Congress of Vienna, the new **congress system** of cooperation and consultation functioned well. The first congress took place in 1818 at Aix-la-Chapelle in Germany near the border of Belgium. As a result of this gathering, the four major powers removed their troops from France, which had paid its war reparations, and readmitted France to good standing among the European nations. Despite unanimity on these decisions, the conference was not without friction. Tsar Alexander I (r. 1801–1825) suggested that the Quadruple Alliance agree to uphold the borders and the existing governments of all European countries. Castlereagh (1769–1822), representing Britain, flatly rejected the proposal. He insisted the Quadruple Alliance was intended only to prevent future French aggression. These disagreements appeared somewhat academic until revolutions broke out in southern Europe.

20.1.2 The Domestic Political Order

Despite Castlereagh's resistance to the intervention of one power in the domestic affairs of another, other European

PRINCE KLEMENS VON METTERNICH Prince Klemens von Metternich (1773–1859) epitomized nineteenth-century conservatism.
SOURCE: World History Archive/Alamy Stock Photo

statesmen believed that preventing domestic unrest was the key to maintaining international peace. The principle proponent of this view was the chancellor of Austria, Prince Metternich (1773–1859). This devoted servant of the Habsburg emperor had been, along with Britain's Viscount Castlereagh, the chief architect of the Vienna settlement. It was Metternich who seemed to exercise chief control over the forces of European reaction and who, more than any other early-nineteenth-century statesman, epitomized conservatism.

20.1.3 Conservative Outlooks

The major pillars of nineteenth-century **conservatism** were legitimate monarchies, landed aristocracies, and established churches. The institutions themselves were ancient, but the self-conscious alliance of throne, land, and altar was new. In the eighteenth century, these groups had often quarreled. Only the upheavals of the French Revolution and the Napoleonic era transformed them into natural, if sometimes reluctant, allies. In that sense, conservatism as an articulated

outlook and set of cooperating institutions was as new a feature on the political landscape as **nationalism** and **liberalism**.

The more theoretical political and religious ideas of the conservative classes were associated with thinkers such as Edmund Burke and Friedrich Hegel. Conservatives shared other, less formal attitudes forged by the revolutionary experience. The execution of Louis XVI at the hands of radical democrats convinced most monarchs they could trust only aristocratic governments or governments of aristocrats in alliance with the wealthiest middle-class and professional people. The European aristocracies believed that no form of genuinely representative government would protect their property and influence. All conservatives spurned the idea of a written constitution unless they were permitted to write the document themselves. Even then, some rejected the concept.

The churches equally distrusted popular movements, except their own revivals. Ecclesiastical leaders throughout the Continent regarded themselves as entrusted with the educational task of supporting the social and political status quo. They also feared and hated most ideas associated with the Enlightenment because those rational concepts and reformist writings enshrined the critical spirit and undermined revealed religion.

Conservative aristocrats retained their former arrogance, but not their former privileges or their old confidence. They saw themselves as surrounded by enemies and permanently on the defensive against the forces of liberalism, nationalism, and popular sovereignty. They knew that political groups that hated them could topple them. They also understood that revolution in one country could spill over into another.

All the nations of Europe in the years immediately after 1815 confronted problems arising directly from the new era of peace after a quarter century of armed conflict. The war effort, with its loss of life and property and its need to organize people and resources, had distracted attention from other problems. The wartime footing had allowed all the belligerent governments to exercise firm control over their populations. War had fueled economies and had furnished vast areas of employment in armies, navies, military industries, and agriculture. The onset of peace meant citizens could raise new political issues and that economies were no longer geared to supplying military needs. Soldiers and sailors came home and looked for jobs as civilians as the vast demands of the military effort on industries subsided and caused unemployment. The young were no longer growing up in a climate of war and could think about other issues. For these reasons, the conservative statesmen who led every major government in 1815 confronted new pressures that would cause domestic unrest and would lead them to resort to differing degrees of repression.

20.2 The Emergence of Nationalism and Liberalism

What explains the strength of conservatism in the early nineteenth century?

The greatest of the new pressures challenging conservative regimes in the first half of the nineteenth century were the related, but distinct, ideologies of nationalism and liberalism. On the one hand, nationalism fostered the creation of nations through the founding of a common language, a common culture, and history of a people. The ideals of liberalism, on the other hand, were legal equality, religious toleration, freedom of the press, and securing the person and property of citizens against arbitrary power. These viewpoints might often oppose one another but just as often could be compatible.

ITALIAN STATESMAN GIUSEPPE MAZZINI Giuseppe Mazzini (1805–1872) was a leader of the *Risorgimento*, the nineteenth-century political movement formed to unify Italy. He interpreted Italy's natural borders—its mountains, rivers, and oceans—as indications of how God intended to subdivide humanity into distinct nations. Mazzini's nationalist vision inspired many on the Italian peninsula to work toward political unification.
SOURCE: Bpk Bildagentur/Art Resource, NY

20.2.1 Nationalism

Nationalism proved to be the single most powerful European political ideology of the nineteenth and early twentieth centuries. It has reasserted itself in present-day Europe following the collapse of Communist governments in eastern Europe and in the former Soviet Union, and in connection with anxiety about immigration in western Europe. As a political outlook, nationalism was and is based on the relatively modern concept that a nation is composed of people joined together by the bonds of a common language, as well as common customs, culture, and history, and who, because of these bonds, should be administered by the same government. That is to say, nationalists in the past and the present contend that political and ethnic boundaries should coincide. This was a radical, new idea; political units had not been defined or governed according to the presumptive nationality of their populations previously in European history. The idea came into its own during the late eighteenth and the early nineteenth centuries.

20.2.1.1 OPPOSITION TO THE VIENNA SETTLEMENT

Early nineteenth-century nationalism directly opposed the principle upheld at the Congress of Vienna that legitimate monarchies or dynasties, rather than nationality, provide the basis for political unity. Nationalists objected to multinational states such as the Austrian and Russian empires. They also insisted that peoples who belonged to one nation, such as Germans and Italians, should all dwell in the same political units instead of being divided among smaller states. Consequently, nationalists challenged both the domestic and the international order of the Vienna settlement.

Behind the concept of nationalism usually, though not always, lay the idea of popular sovereignty since the qualities of peoples, rather than their rulers, determined a national character. This aspect of nationalism, however, frequently led to confusion or conflict because Europe was not organized into groups of people sharing both one recognized nationality and one contiguous territory. Although nationalists liked to think of nations as homogeneous with easily defined boundaries, this was rarely the case. Most states included people speaking different languages and dialects, practicing different religions, and defining themselves in relation to various groups. Nationalists claimed that they were insisting on new political rights for nations that were themselves very old. When confronted with people who did not share their aspirations, nationalists argued that those people were slumbering members of a nation that had to be awakened. In reality, it was the nationalists who created nations in the nineteenth century.

20.2.1.2 CREATING NATIONS During the first half-century, small groups of nationalist writers or other intellectual elites used the printed word to express their concept of the nation. First they recruited historians who could chronicle, and in some cases create, a people's past, as well as literary scholars who could establish a national literature by collecting and publishing earlier writings in the people's language. They were joined by ethnographers who collected evidence of a distinctive folk culture, including myths, fairy tales, poetry, and song, and linguists who could define what constituted their nation's formal literary language and codify grammars and dictionaries. Together, these nationalists gave people a sense of their past and a literature of their own. As time passed, schoolteachers spread nationalistic ideas by imparting a nation's official language and history. These small groups of early nationalists established the cultural beliefs and political expectations on which the later mass-supported nationalism of the second half-century would grow.

Which language to use in the schools and in government offices was always a point of contention for nationalists. In France and Italy, official versions of the national language were imposed in the schools and replaced local dialects. In parts of Scandinavia and eastern Europe, nationalists attempted to resurrect from earlier times what they regarded as purer versions of the national language. Often, modern scholars or linguists virtually invented these resurrected languages, although they always argued for their antiquity. Establishing national languages led to far more linguistic uniformity in European nations than had existed before the nineteenth century. Yet even in 1850, perhaps fewer than half the inhabitants of France spoke the official French language.

Language could become an effective cornerstone in the foundation of nationalism thanks largely to the emergence of a print culture. The presence of a great many printed books, journals, magazines, and newspapers "fixed" language more permanently than did the spoken word. This uniform language found in printed works overcame regional spoken dialects, establishing its dominance. In most countries, spoken and written proficiency in the official, printed language became a path to social and political advancement. The growth of a uniform language helped persuade people that they constituted a nation.

20.2.1.3 MEANING OF NATIONHOOD Nationalists used a variety of arguments and metaphors to express what they meant by *nationhood*. Some argued that gathering, for example, Italians into a unified Italy or Germans into a unified Germany, thus eliminating or at least federating the petty dynastic states that governed those regions, would promote economic and administrative efficiency. Adopting a tenet from political liberalism, some nationalist writers suggested that nations determining their own destinies resembled individuals exploiting personal talents to determine their careers. Some nationalists claimed that nations, like biological species in the natural world, were distinct creations of God. Other nationalists claimed a place for their nations in the divine order of things. Throughout the nineteenth century, for example, Polish nationalists portrayed Poland as the suffering Christ among nations, thus implicitly suggesting that Poland, like Christ, would experience resurrection and a new life.

A significant difficulty for nationalism was, and is, determining which ethnic groups could be considered nations, with claims to territory and political autonomy. In theory, any of them could. But in reality, nationhood came to be associated with groups who were large enough to support a viable economy; who successfully claimed a significant cultural history; who had a cultural elite that could nourish and spread the national language; and who had the military capacity to establish and protect their independence. Throughout the century, many smaller ethnic groups claimed to fulfill these criteria but could not effectively achieve either independence or recognition. They could and did, however, create domestic unrest within the political units they inhabited. (See the "Compare and Connect" sidebar, which follows, for a debate on the principles of nationalism.)

20.2.1.4 REGIONS OF NATIONALIST PRESSURE During the nineteenth century, nationalists challenged the political status quo throughout Europe. England had brought Ireland under direct rule in 1800, abolishing the separate Irish Parliament and allowing the Irish to elect members to the British Parliament in Westminster. Irish nationalists, however, wanted independence or at least larger measures of self-government. The so-called **"Irish problem"** would haunt British politics for the next two centuries. German nationalists sought political unity for all German-speaking peoples, challenging the legitimacy of the Prussian and Austrian monarchies, which both contained large non-German-speaking populations. Italian nationalists wanted to unify Italian-speaking peoples on the Italian peninsula and to drive out their Austrian and Bourbon rulers. Polish nationalists, targeting primarily their Russian rulers, struggled to restore Poland as an independent nation. In eastern Europe, a host of national groups, including Hungarians, Czechs, Slovenes, and others, desired either independence or, more frequently, some form of autonomy and recognition within the Austrian Empire. Finally, in southeastern Europe on the Balkan peninsula and eastward, national groups, including Serbs, Greeks, Albanians, Romanians, and Bulgarians, sought independence from Ottoman and Russian control.

Compare and Connect

The Political Principles of Nationalism

NO POLITICAL FORCE in the nineteenth and twentieth centuries was stronger than nationalism. It eventually replaced loyalty to a dynasty with loyalty based on ethnic considerations and gained new strength after World War I when the self-determination of nations became a cornerstone of the Paris Peace treaties. Still later, former European colonies embraced this powerful idea. Yet from the earliest beginnings of nationalism, there were major critics who understood its potential destructiveness. In these two documents, Giuseppe Mazzini, the great Italian nationalist, expresses his understanding of nationalism, and Lord Acton, the distinguished nineteenth-century English historian, points to the dangers of the ideas and realities of politics based on nationalism.

CELEBRATION OF [HUNGARIAN] NATIONALISM The celebration of nationalism included attempts to classify different groups of people according to language, religion, and culture. Sketches of regional folk costumes both celebrated diversity and institutionalized difference. This mid-nineteenth-century lithograph exhibits the peasant attire of the different national groups in Hungary. Depicted from left to right are the Walachians (Romanians), Hungarians, Slavs (Slovaks), and Germans.
SOURCE: Veber/H. (fl.1855)/The Bridgeman Art Library

Before Reading

- Note the main points Giuseppe Mazzini makes in favor of nationalism.
- Note the dangers that, according to Lord Acton, the idea of nationalism poses to liberty.
- Examine the threats minority groups face because of nationalism.

Questions

1. What qualities of people does Mazzini associate with nationalism?
2. How and why does Mazzini relate nationalism to divine purposes?
3. Why does Acton see the principle of nationalism as dangerous to liberty?
4. Why does Acton see nationalism as a threat to minority groups and to democracy?
5. How might the connection that Mazzini draws between nationalism and divine will justify the repression of minority rights that Acton feared?

I. GIUSEPPE MAZZINI DEFINES NATIONALITY

In 1835 Italian nationalist Giuseppe Mazzini (1805–1872) explained his understanding of nationalism. He combined a generally democratic view of politics with a religious concept of the divine destiny of nations. Once in power, however, nationalist states in Europe and the rest of the world were often not democratic states.

The essential characteristics of a nationality are common ideas, common principles and a common purpose. A nation is an association of those who are brought together by language, by given geographical conditions or by the role assigned them by history, who acknowledge the same principles and who march together to the conquest of a single definite goal under the rule of a uniform body of law.

The life of a nation consists in harmonious activity (that is, the employment of all individual abilities and energies comprised within the association) towards this single goal. . . .

But nationality means even more than this. Nationality also consists in the share of mankind's labors which God assigns to a people. This mission is the task which a people must perform to the end that the Divine Idea shall be realized in this world; it is the work which gives a people its rights as a member of Mankind; it is the baptismal rite which endows a people with its own character and its rank in the brotherhood of nations. . . .

Nationality depends for its very existence upon its sacredness within and beyond its borders.

If nationality is to be inviolable for all, friends and foes alike, it must be regarded inside a country as holy, like a religion, and outside a country as a grave mission. It is necessary too that the ideas arising within a country grow steadily, as part of the general law of Humanity which is the source of all nationality. It is necessary that these ideas be shown to other lands in their beauty and purity, free from any alien mixture, from any slavish fears, from any skeptical hesitancy, strong and active, embracing in their evolution every aspect and manifestation of the life of the nation. These ideas, a necessary component in the order of universal destiny, must retain their originality even as they enter harmoniously into mankind's general progress.

The people must be the basis of nationality; its logically derived and vigorously applied principles its means; the strength of all its strength; the improvement of the life of all and the happiness of the greatest possible number its results; and the accomplishment of the task assigned to it by God its goal. This is what we mean by nationality.

II. LORD ACTON CONDEMNS NATIONALISM

As well as being a historian, Lord Acton (1834–1902) was an important nineteenth-century commentator on contemporary religious and political events. He was deeply concerned with the character and preservation of liberty. In his 1862 essay "Nationality," Lord Acton was one of the earliest to warn that nationalism or what he here termed "the modern theory of nationality" could endanger liberty of individuals who were part of a national minority within a state dominated by a different national majority. Acton's words would prove prophetic regarding the fate of minorities within Europe for the next century. Acton also pointed out that the pursuit of nationalist goals might encourage a government to ignore the economic well-being of its peoples.

The greatest adversary of the rights of nationality is the modern theory of nationality. By making the State and the nation commensurate with each other in theory, it reduces practically to a subject condition all other nationalities that may be within the boundary. It cannot admit them to an equality with the ruling nation which constitutes the State, because the State would then cease to be national, which would be a contradiction of the principle of its existence. According, therefore, to the degree of humanity and civilization in that dominant body which claims all the rights of the community, the inferior races are exterminated, or reduced to servitude, or outlawed, or put in a condition of dependence.

If we take the establishment of liberty for the realization of moral duties to be the end of civil society, we must conclude that those states are substantially the most perfect which, like the British and Austrian Empires, include various distinct nationalities without oppressing them. Those in which no mixture of races has occurred are imperfect; and those in which its effects have disappeared are decrepit. A State which is incompetent to satisfy different races condemns itself; a State which labors to neutralize, to absorb, or to expel them, destroys its own vitality; a State which does not include them is destitute of the chief basis of self-government. The theory of nationality, therefore, is a retrograde step in history. . . .

[N]ationality does not aim either at liberty or prosperity, both of which it sacrifices to the imperative necessity of making the nation the mold and measure of the State. Its course will be marked with material as well as moral ruin, in order that a new invention may prevail over the works of God and the interests of mankind. There is no principle of change, no phrase of political speculation conceivable, more comprehensive, more subversive, or more arbitrary than this. It is a confutation of democracy, because it sets limits to the exercise of the popular will, and substitutes for it a higher principle.

SOURCES: (I) From Herbert H. Rowen, ed., *From Absolutism to Revolution, 1648–1848*, 2nd ed. (Upper Saddle River, NJ: Prentice Hall, 1969), pp. 277–280. © 1969. Reprinted by permission of Prentice Hall, Inc., Upper Saddle River, NJ. (II) From John Emerich Edward Dalbert-Acton, First Baron Acton, *Essays in the History of Liberty*, ed. by J. Rufus Fears (Indianapolis, IN: Liberty Classics, 1985), pp. 431–433.

20.2.2 Early-Nineteenth-Century Political Liberalism

The word *liberal*, as applied to political activity, entered the European and American vocabulary during the nineteenth century. Its meaning has varied over time. Nineteenth-century European conservatives often regarded as liberal almost anyone or anything that challenged their own political, social, or religious values. European conservatives of the last century saw liberals as more radical than they were. For twenty-first-century Americans, the word liberal carries with it meanings and connotations that have little or nothing to do with its significance to nineteenth-century Europeans. It is therefore critical to understand nineteenth-century liberalism in its own context.

20.2.2.1 POLITICAL GOALS Nineteenth-century liberals derived their political ideas from the writers of the Enlightenment, the example of English liberties, and the so-called principles of 1789 embodied in the French Declaration of the Rights of Man and Citizen. They wished to establish a political framework of legal equality, religious toleration, and freedom of the press. Their general goal was a political structure that would limit the arbitrary power of government against the persons and property of individual citizens, and they generally believed the legitimacy of government emanated from the freely given consent of the governed. The popular basis of such government was to be expressed through elected representative, or parliamentary, bodies. Most importantly, free government required government ministers to be responsible to the representatives rather than to the monarch. Liberals sought to achieve these political arrangements through written constitutions. They wanted to see constitutionalism and constitutional governments installed across the Continent.

Those who espoused liberal political structures often were educated, relatively wealthy people—academics, members of the learned professions, and people involved in the rapidly expanding commercial and manufacturing segments of the economy—who were excluded in one manner or another from the existing political processes. Because of their wealth and education, they felt their exclusion was unjustified. They believed in, and were products of, a career open to talent. The monarchical and aristocratic regimes, as restored after the Congress of Vienna, often failed both to recognize their new status sufficiently and to provide for their economic and professional interests.

Although liberals wanted broader political participation, they did not advocate democracy. What they wanted was to extend representation to the propertied classes. Second only to their hostility to the privileged aristocracies was their contempt for the lower, unpropertied classes. They imagined an active citizenry of educated men, inspired by reason and by their own investment, through their private property, in peace and stability. Liberals transformed the eighteenth-century concept of aristocratic liberty into a new concept of privilege based on wealth and property rather than on birth. As French liberal theorist Benjamin Constant (1767–1830) wrote in 1814,

> Those whom poverty keeps in eternal dependence are no more enlightened on public affairs than children, nor are they more interested than foreigners in national prosperity, of which they do not understand the basis and of which they enjoy the advantages only indirectly. Property alone, by giving sufficient leisure, renders a man capable of exercising his political rights.[1]

By the middle of the century, this widely shared attitude meant that throughout Europe liberals had separated themselves from both the rural peasantry and the urban working class, a division that was to have important consequences.

Because the social and political circumstances of various countries differed, the specific programs of liberals also differed from one country to another. In Great Britain, the monarchy was already limited, and most individual liberties had been secured. With reform, Parliament could provide more nearly representative government. Links between land, commerce, and industry were in place. France also already had many structures liberals favored. The Napoleonic Code gave France a modern legal system. French liberals could justify calls for greater rights by appealing to the widely accepted "principles of 1789." As in England, representatives of the different economic interests in France had worked together. The problem for liberals in both countries was to protect civil liberties, define the respective powers of the monarch and the elected legislature, and expand the electorate moderately while avoiding democracy.

Liberals were divided on the subject of women's role in society. While some, like Harriet Taylor and her husband, **John Stuart Mill**, argued in favor of women's enfranchisement, most liberals were suspicious of women's education and inclination to rely on the counsel of others, including conservative priests. Women's suffrage played no role in liberal politics in the first two-thirds of the nineteenth century.

The complex political situation in German-speaking Europe was different from that in France or Britain, and German liberalism differed accordingly from its French and British counterparts. In the German states and Austria, monarchs and aristocrats offered stiffer resistance to liberal ideas, leaving German liberals with less access to direct political influence. A sharp social divide separated the aristocratic landowning classes, which filled the bureaucracies and officer corps, from the small middle-class commercial and industrial interests. Little or no precedent existed for middle-class participation in the government or the military, and there was no strong tradition of civil or individual liberty. There was also a greater tradition of reform from above than existed in France, which German rulers used to argue that they were more trustworthy and constitutions were less necessary.

Most German liberals favored a united Germany and looked either to Austria or to Prussia as the instrument of unification. As a result, they were more tolerant of a strong state and monarchical power than other liberals were. They believed that unification would lead to a freer social and political order. The monarchies in Austria and Prussia refused to cooperate with these dreams of unification, frustrating German liberals and forcing them to settle for more modest achievements, such as lowering internal trade barriers.

20.2.3 Classical Economics

The economic goals of nineteenth-century liberals also divided them from working people. Economists whose thought derived largely from Adam Smith's *The Wealth of Nations* (1776) dominated private and public discussions of industrial and commercial policy. Their ideas are often associated with the phrase *laissez-faire* (a French phrase that means roughly "let people do as they please"). Although they thought the government should perform many important functions, the classical economists favored economic growth through competitive free enterprise. They conceived of society as consisting of atomistic individuals whose competitive efforts met consumers' demands in the marketplace and believed that the mechanism of the marketplace should govern most economic decisions. They believed most government action to be mischievous and corrupt and that the government should maintain a sound currency, enforce contracts, protect property, impose low tariffs and taxes, and leave the remainder of economic life to private initiative. The economists naturally assumed the state would maintain enough armed forces and naval power to protect the nation's economic structure and foreign trade. With emphasis on thrift, competition, and personal industriousness, the political economists' voice appealed to the middle classes.

The manufacturers of Great Britain, the landed and manufacturing middle class of France, and the commercial interests of Germany and Italy were deeply influenced by Smith's classical economics. They sought to abolish the economic restraints associated with mercantilism or the regulated economies of enlightened absolutists and to manufacture and sell goods freely. To that end, they favored the removal of international tariffs and internal barriers to trade. Economic liberals opposed the old paternalistic legislation that established wages and labor practices by government regulation or by guild privileges. They saw labor as simply one more commodity to be bought and sold freely.

Liberals wanted an economic structure in which people were at liberty to use whatever talents and property they possessed to enrich themselves. Such a structure, they contended, would produce more goods and services for everyone at lower prices and provide the basis for material progress. Liberals' commitment to the principles of classical economics placed them at odds with the working class and impeded cooperation toward social and economic reform.

20.2.3.1 MALTHUS ON POPULATION
The classical economists had complicated and pessimistic ideas about the working class. **Thomas Malthus** (1766–1834) and **David Ricardo** (1772–1823), probably the most influential of all these writers, suggested, in effect, that nothing could improve the condition of the working class. In 1798, Malthus published the first edition of his *Essay on the Principle of Population*. His ideas have haunted the world ever since. He contended that population must eventually outstrip the food supply because human population grows geometrically, while food supply can expand only arithmetically. There was little hope of averting the disaster, in Malthus's opinion, except through late marriage, chastity, and contraception, the last of which he considered a vice. It took three-quarters of a century for contraception to become a socially acceptable method of containing the population explosion.

Malthus contended that the immediate plight of the working class could only become worse. If wages were raised, the workers would simply produce more children, who would, in turn, consume both the extra wages and more food. Later in his life, Malthus suggested, in a more optimistic vein, that if the working class could be persuaded to adopt a higher standard of living, their increased wages might be spent on consumer goods rather than on begetting more children.

20.2.3.2 RICARDO ON WAGES
In his *Principles of Political Economy* (1817), David Ricardo transformed the concepts of Malthus into the "iron law of wages." If wages were raised, he contended, parents would have more children. They, in turn, would enter the labor market, thus expanding the number of workers and lowering wages. As wages fell, working people would produce fewer children. Wages would then rise, and the process would start all over again. Consequently, in the long run, wages would always tend toward a minimum level. These arguments supported employers in their natural reluctance to raise wages and also provided strong theoretical support for opposing labor unions.

20.2.4 Relationship of Liberalism to Nationalism

Nationalism was not necessarily or even logically linked to liberalism. Indeed, nationalism could be, and often was, directly opposed to liberal political values. Conservative nationalists might seek political autonomy for their own group but have no intention of establishing liberal political institutions thereafter. Some nationalists wanted their own group to dominate minority groups within a particular region, denying them political rights based on nationality instead of wealth or property. Nationalists also often defined their own national group in opposition to other national groups whom they might regard as cultural inferiors or historical enemies.

Nonetheless, although liberalism and nationalism were not identical, they were often compatible. By espousing representative government, civil liberties, and economic freedom, nationalist groups in one country could gain the support of liberals elsewhere in Europe who might not otherwise share their nationalist interests. Many nationalists in central Europe and the Italian peninsula adopted this tactic. Some nationalists took other symbolic steps to arouse sympathy. Nationalists in Greece, for example, made Athens their capital because they believed it would associate their struggle for independence with ancient Athenian democracy, which English and French liberals revered.

20.3 Conservative Restoration in Europe

What were the goals of the Concert of Europe?

Despite the challenges of liberalism and nationalism, the domestic political order that the restored conservative institutions of Europe established showed remarkable resilience. Not until World War I did their power come to an end. In Britain, rapid social and economic change brought new challenges to the conservative order that were met with determined resistance. In France and Spain, the Bourbon monarchies tried to avoid binding themselves to constitutions. For the first few years after the Congress of Vienna, all these reactionary measures appeared successful.

ROBERT BANKS JENKINSON, EARL OF LIVERPOOL Robert Banks Jenkinson, Earl of Liverpool (1770–1828), served as prime minister of Britain from 1812 to 1827. On the international front, he steered Britain through the War of 1812 and through the last stages of the Napoleonic Wars. On the domestic front, he supported repressive measures to maintain order and stability in the face of political radicalism and social unrest.
SOURCE: National Trust Photo Library/Art Resource, NY

20.3.1 Liberalism and Nationalism Resisted in Austria and the Germanies

Nowhere did nationalism threaten the existing order as much as in German-speaking Europe, where the creation of one single German nation-state would unseat dozens of ruling princes and destroy as many historically independent countries.

20.3.1.1 DYNASTIC INTEGRITY OF THE HABSBURG EMPIRE The Austrian government was fundamentally threatened by the programs of liberalism and nationalism, and while it could accommodate the former to some degree, the latter threatened to undermine the basic integrity of the state. Most Austrians did not think of themselves in national terms. Their sense of belonging was determined by their religion or by regional and local communities, combined with loyalty to the dynasty. Those Austrians who did identify with a nation could consider themselves German, Hungarian, Polish, Czech, Slovak, Slovene, Italian, Croat, Ruthenian (Ukrainian), Romanian, or Serb. Through client governments, Austria also dominated other parts of the Italian peninsula that it did not rule directly.

For Metternich and other Austrian officials, the recognition of the political rights and aspirations of any of the various national groups would mean the probable dissolution of the empire. If Austria permitted representative government, Metternich feared the national groups would fight their battles internally at the cost of Austria's international influence.

20.3.1.2 DEFEAT OF PRUSSIAN REFORM An important victory for this conservative policy came in Prussia in the years immediately after the Congress of Vienna. In 1815, Frederick William III (r. 1797–1840), caught up in the exhilaration that followed the War of Liberation, as Germans called the last part of their conflict with Napoleon, had promised some form of constitutional government. After stalling, he formally reneged on his pledge in 1817. Instead, he created a new Council of State, which, although it improved administrative efficiency, was responsible to him alone.

In 1819, the king moved further from reform. After a major disagreement over the organization of the army, he replaced his reform-minded ministers with hardened conservatives. On their advice, in 1823, Frederick William III established eight provincial estates, or diets. These bodies were dominated by the Junkers and exercised only an advisory function. The old bonds linking monarchy, army, and landholders in Prussia had been reestablished. The members of this alliance would oppose the threats that German nationalists posed to the conservative social and political order.

KARL SAND, NATIONALIST MARTYR In May 1820, Karl Sand, a German student and a member of a *Burschenschaft*, was executed for his murder of the conservative playwright August von Kotzebue the previous year. In the eyes of many young German nationalists, Sand was a political martyr.
SOURCE: Bpk Bildagentur/Art Resource, NY

20.3.1.3 STUDENT NATIONALISM AND THE CARLSBAD DECREES To widen their bases of political support, the monarchs of three southern German states—Baden, Bavaria, and Württemberg—had granted constitutions after 1815. None of these constitutions, however, recognized popular sovereignty, and all defined political rights as the gift of the monarch. Yet in the aftermath of the defeat of Napoleon, many young Germans continued to cherish nationalist and liberal expectations.

University students who had grown up during the days of the reforms of Stein and Hardenberg and had read the writings of early German nationalists made up the most important of these groups. At university, they continued to dream of a united Germany, and they formed *Burschenschaften*, or student associations. Like student groups today, these clubs served numerous social functions, one of which was to replace old provincial attachments with loyalty to the concept of a united German state. Later in the nineteenth century, these clubs became increasingly anti-Semitic. (See the "Encountering the Past" sidebar on the connection between physical culture and German nationalism, which follows below.)

In 1817, in Jena, one such student club organized a large celebration for the fourth anniversary of the Battle of Leipzig and the tercentenary of Luther's Ninety-five Theses. There were bonfires, songs, and processions as more than 500 people gathered for the festivities. The event made German rulers uneasy because the student clubs included a few republicans.

Two years later, in March 1819, a student named Karl Sand, a *Burschenschaft* member, assassinated conservative dramatist August von Kotzebue, who had ridiculed the *Burschenschaft* movement. Sand, who was tried and publicly executed, became a nationalist martyr. Although Sand had acted alone, Metternich used the incident to suppress institutions associated with liberalism.

In July 1819, Metternich persuaded the major German states to issue the **Carlsbad Decrees**, which dissolved the *Burschenschaften*. The Carlsbad Decrees also allowed for university inspectors and press censors. The next year the German Confederation issued the Final Act, which limited the subjects that the constitutional chambers of Bavaria, Württemberg, and Baden could discuss. The measure also asserted the right of the monarchs to resist demands of constitutionalists. For many years thereafter, the secret police of the various German states harassed potential dissidents. In the opinion of the princes, these included almost anyone who advocated even moderate social or political change.

Encountering the Past

Gymnastics and German Nationalism

TODAY CITIZENS TAKE great pride in the performance of their nations' athletes in the Olympics. This modern link between athletics and nationalism originated in early nineteenth-century Germany with the *Turnvereine*, or gymnastic unions.

Friedrich Ludwig Jahn (1778–1852) was the father of the movement, which he described as "Love of the Fatherland through Gymnastics." He was also an innovator in gymnastic equipment, credited with inventing the parallel bars and improving the pommel vault.

Jahn became a fervent patriot when he saw the German states and particularly Prussia humiliated by Napoleon. He attacked what he regarded as foreign influence on German life, including that of German Jews. Jahn was convinced that Germans must cultivate their bodily strength to overcome external enemies. In 1811, he established an open-air gymnasium in a meadow near Berlin. The young men who attended this gymnasium and others that he soon founded throughout the German states saw themselves as an advanced nationalist guard.

ON THE POMMEL HORSE Friedrich Ludwig Jahn (1778–1852) is credited as the "father" of German gymnastics. As an educator in Germany, he believed that physical exercise was just as important as intellectual activity. He encouraged his students to use athletic equipment to increase strength and agility. Pictured here: an open-air gymnasium typical of the ones that Jahn instituted.

SOURCE: INTERFOTO/Alamy Stock Photo

After the defeat of Napoleon in 1815, gymnastic clubs spread across Germany, fostered nationalist sentiment, and challenged the social and political status quo. The clubs embodied social equality. All members wore plain gray exercise uniforms that Jahn had designed and addressed each other with the familiar *Du*. Conservatives were suspicious and saw these early gymnastic clubs as a state within the various disunited German states. For a time, Prussia banned gymnastics and sent Jahn to prison.

During the 1840s, however, the gymnastic movement revived. Germany soon had tens of thousands of adult gymnasts, and the clubs became increasingly nationalist, often excluding Jews. After German unification in 1870, national festivals often featured gymnastic performances, and national monuments had areas for gymnastic display. Political figures from Bismarck to Hitler cultivated their links to the gymnastic societies. The connection between gymnastics and German nationalism was so strong that even liberal Germans who immigrated to the United States founded *Turnvereine* in their new homes.

Questions

1. What factors attracted Friedrich Ludwig Jahn to nationalism?
2. Why did *Turnvereine*, or gymnastic unions, spread easily in the Germanies?

SOURCES: Liah Greenfeld, *Nationalism: Five Roads to Modernity* (Cambridge, MA: Harvard University Press, 1992), pp. 367–370; Matthew Levinger, *Enlightened Nationalism: The Transformation of Prussian Political Culture, 1806–1848* (New York: Oxford University Press, 2000); George L. Mosse, *The Nationalization of the Masses: Political Symbolism and Mass Movements in Germany from the Napoleonic Wars through the Third Reich* (New York: New American Library, 1975), p. 128.

20.3.2 Postwar Repression in Great Britain

The years 1819 and 1820 marked a high tide for conservative influence and repression in western as well as eastern Europe. After 1815, Great Britain experienced two years of poor harvests. At the same time, discharged sailors and soldiers and out-of-work industrial workers swelled the ranks of the unemployed.

20.3.2.1 LORD LIVERPOOL'S MINISTRY AND POPULAR UNREST
The Tory ministry of Lord Liverpool (1770–1828) was unprepared to deal with these problems of postwar dislocation. Instead, it sought to protect the interests of the landed and wealthy classes. In 1815, Parliament passed a **Corn Law** to maintain high prices for domestically produced grain (called "corn" in Britain) by levying import duties on foreign grain. The next year, Parliament replaced the income tax that only the wealthy paid with excise or sales taxes on consumer goods that both the wealthy and the poor paid. These laws continued a legislative trend that marked the abandonment by the British ruling class of its traditional role of paternalistic protector of the poor. In 1799, the Combination Acts had outlawed workers' organizations or unions. During the war, wage protection had been removed. Many in the taxpaying classes wanted to abolish the Poor Law that provided public relief for the destitute and unemployed.

In light of these policies and the postwar economic downturn, it is hardly surprising that the lower social orders began to doubt the wisdom of their rulers and to demand political changes. Mass meetings called for the reform of Parliament. Reform clubs were organized, and radical newspapers demanded change.

The government's answer to the discontent was repression. In December 1816, an unruly mass meeting took place at Spa Fields near London. This disturbance gave Parliament an excuse to pass the Coercion Acts of March 1817, which temporarily suspended *habeas corpus* and extended existing laws against seditious gatherings.

20.3.2.2 "PETERLOO" AND THE SIX ACTS
This initial repression, in combination with improved harvests, calmed the political landscape for a time. By 1819, however, the people were restive again. In the industrial north, well-organized mass meetings demanded the reform of Parliament. The radical reform campaign culminated on August 16, 1819, with a meeting in the industrial city of Manchester at Saint Peter's Fields. Royal troops and the local militia were on hand to ensure order. As the speeches were about to begin, a local magistrate ordered the militia to move into the audience. The result was panic and death. At least eleven people in the crowd were killed; scores were injured. The event became known as the **Peterloo Massacre**, a phrase that drew a contemptuous comparison with Wellington's victory at Waterloo.

Peterloo had been the act of local officials, whom the Liverpool ministry felt it must support. The cabinet also decided to act once and for all to end these troubles. Most of the radical leaders were arrested and imprisoned. In December 1819, a few months after the German Carlsbad Decrees, Parliament passed a series of laws called the Six Acts, which (1) forbade large unauthorized, public meetings; (2) raised the fines for seditious libel; (3) speeded up the trials of political agitators; (4) increased newspaper taxes; (5) prohibited the training of armed groups; and (6) allowed local officials to search homes in certain disturbed counties. In effect, the Six Acts prevented radical leaders from agitating and gave the authorities new powers.

RESTORATION OF THE BOURBONS
The French Bourbons were restored to the throne in 1815 but would rule only until 1830. This picture shows Louis XVIII, seated, second from left, and his brother, the Count of Artois, who would become Charles X, standing at left. The bust of Henry IV in the background was placed there to associate the restored rulers with their popular late sixteenth-century forebear.
SOURCE: Bpk Bildagentur / Art Resource, NY

20.3.3 Bourbon Restoration in France

The abdication of Napoleon in 1814 paved the way for a restoration of Bourbon rule in the homeland of the great revolution. The new king was Louis XVIII (r. 1814–1824), the former Count of Provence and a brother of Louis XVI. The son of the executed monarch Louis XVI had died in prison. Royalists had regarded the dead son as Louis XVII and so his uncle became Louis XVIII (r. 1814–1824). During his more than twenty years of exile, Louis XVIII had become a political realist and understood that he could not turn back the clock to 1789. France had undergone too many irreversible changes, hence he agreed to become a constitutional monarch—but under a constitution of his own making called the Charter.

20.3.3.1 THE CHARTER The Charter provided for a hereditary monarchy and a bicameral legislature. The monarch appointed the upper house, the Chamber of Peers, modeled on the British House of Lords; a narrow franchise with a high property qualification elected the lower house, the Chamber of Deputies. The Charter guaranteed most of the rights the Declaration of the Rights of Man and Citizen had enumerated. There was to be religious toleration, but Roman Catholicism was designated the official religion of the nation. Most importantly for thousands of French people at all social levels, the Charter promised not to challenge the property rights of current owners of land that had been confiscated from aristocrats and the church. With this provision, Louis XVIII hoped to reconcile beneficiaries of the revolution to his regime.

20.3.3.2 ULTRAROYALISM This moderate spirit did not penetrate deeply into the ranks of royalist supporters whose families had suffered during the revolution. Rallying around Louis's brother and heir, the count of Artois (1757–1836), those people who were more royalist than the monarch now demanded their revenge. The ultraroyalist majority elected in 1816 proved so dangerously reactionary that the king soon dissolved the chamber. The second election returned a more moderate majority. Several years of political give-and-take followed, with the king making mild accommodations to liberals.

In February 1820, however, the Duke of Berry, son of the Count of Artois and second in line to the throne after his father, was murdered by a lone assassin. The ultraroyalists persuaded Louis XVIII that the murder was the result of his ministers' cooperation with liberal politicians, and the king responded with repressive measures. New electoral laws gave wealthy electors two votes. Press censorship was imposed, and people suspected of dangerous political activity were subject to easy arrest. By 1821, the government placed secondary education under the control of the Roman Catholic bishops.

These actions revealed the contradiction of the French restoration. By the early 1820s, the veneer of constitutionalism had worn away. Liberals were being driven out of politics and into a near illegal status.

20.3.4 The Spanish Revolution of 1820

When the Bourbon Ferdinand VII of Spain (r. 1814–1833) was placed on his throne after Napoleon's downfall, he had promised to govern according to a written constitution. Once in power, however, he ignored his pledge, dissolved the *Cortés* (the parliament), and ruled alone. In 1820, army officers about to be sent to suppress revolution in Spain's Latin American colonies rebelled. In March, Ferdinand once again announced he would abide by the provisions of the constitution. For the time being, the revolution had succeeded.

Almost at the same time, in July 1820, revolution erupted in Naples, where the king of the Two Sicilies quickly accepted a constitution. There were other, lesser revolts in Italy, but none of them succeeded.

These events frightened the ever-nervous Metternich. Italian disturbances were especially troubling to him. Austria hoped to dominate the peninsula as a buffer against the spread of revolution on its own southern flank. Britain, however, opposed joint intervention in either Italy or Spain. Metternich turned to Prussia and Russia, the other members of the Holy Alliance formed in 1815, for support. The three eastern powers, along with unofficial delegations from Britain and France, met at the Congress of Troppau in late October 1820. Led by Tsar Alexander, the members of the Holy Alliance issued the Protocol of Troppau. This declaration asserted that stable governments might intervene to restore order in countries experiencing revolution. Yet even Russia hesitated to authorize Austrian intervention in Italian affairs. That decision was finally reached in January 1821 at the Congress of Laibach. Shortly thereafter, Austrian troops marched into Naples and restored the absolutist rule of the king of the Two Sicilies. The final postwar congress took place in October 1822 at Verona. Its primary purpose was to resolve the situation in Spain. Once again, Britain balked at joint action. At Verona, Britain, in effect, withdrew from continental affairs. Austria, Prussia, and Russia agreed to support French intervention in Spain. In April 1823, a French army crossed the Pyrenees and within a few months suppressed the Spanish revolution. French troops remained in Spain to prop up King Ferdinand until 1827.

What did not happen in Spain, however, was as important for the new international order as what did happen. France did not use intervention as an excuse to aggrandize its power or increase its territory. The same had been true of all such interventions under the congress system, which the great powers had authorized to preserve or restore conservative regimes, not to conquer territory. Their goal was to maintain the international order established at Vienna. This attempt to preserve international order sharply contrasted with the alliances created by the European powers to invade or confiscate territory during the eighteenth century and the wars of the French Revolution and Napoleon. This new mode of international restraint through formal and informal consultation prevented war among the great powers until the middle of the century and averted a general European conflict until 1914. As one historian has commented, "The statesmen of the Vienna generation . . . did not so much fear war because they thought it would bring revolution as because they had learned from bitter experience that war was revolution."[2]

The Congress of Verona and the Spanish intervention had a second diplomatic result. The new British foreign minister, George Canning, was much more interested in British commerce and trade than Castlereagh had been. Canning sought to curtail European reaction to Spain's colonies in Latin America, which were then in revolt. He intended to exploit these South American revolutions to break Spain's old trading monopoly with its colonies and gain British access to Latin American trade. To that end, he supported the American Monroe Doctrine in 1823, prohibiting further colonization and intervention by European powers in the Americas. Britain soon recognized the Spanish colonies as independent states. For the rest of the century, British commercial interests dominated Latin America.

20.4 The Conservative Order Shaken in Europe

How did Russia, France, and Britain respond to challenges to the conservative order?

In the first years following the Congress of Vienna, the restored conservative order had, in general, successfully resisted the forces of liberalism. Beginning in the mid-1820s, however, challenges to conservative governments intensified. The Ottoman Empire was unable to prevent successful nationalist uprisings in Greece and Serbia. Conservative regimes in Russia, France, and Great Britain faced new political discontent. (See Map 20–1.) In Russia the result was suppression; in France, revolution; and in Britain, accommodation. Belgium emerged as a newly independent state.

Map 20–1 CENTERS OF REVOLUTION, 1820–1831

The conservative order imposed by the great powers in post-Napoleonic Europe was challenged by various uprisings and revolutions, beginning in 1820 to 1821 in Spain, Naples, and Greece and spreading to Russia, Poland, France, and Belgium later in the decade.

20.4.1 Revolt Against Ottoman Rule in the Balkans

The reaction to Ottoman rule in the Balkans took shape in the Greek revolution and the movement toward independence in Serbia. The nation's link with classical antiquity gave special meaning to the struggle in Greece. An inconsistent set of goals in the region on the part of the great powers complicated their response.

20.4.1.1 THE GREEK REVOLUTION OF 1821 While the powers were plotting conservative interventions in Italy and Spain, a third Mediterranean revolt erupted—in Greece. The Greek revolution became one of the most famous of the century because it attracted the support and participation of many illustrious writers. Liberals throughout Europe, who were seeing their own hopes crushed at home, imagined that the ancient Greek democracy was being reborn. Lord Byron went to fight in Greece and died there in 1824 (of cholera). Philhellenic ("pro-Greek") societies were founded in nearly every major country. The struggle was posed in the eighteenth-century Enlightenment terms of Western liberal Greek freedom against the Asian oriental despotism of the Ottoman Empire.

Ottoman weakness and instability troubled European diplomacy throughout the nineteenth century, raising what was known as "the Eastern Question": What should the European powers do about the Ottoman inability to ensure political and administrative stability in its possessions in and around the eastern Mediterranean? Most of the major powers had a keen interest in those territories. Russia and Austria coveted land in the Balkans. France and Britain were concerned with the empire's commerce and with control of key naval positions in the eastern Mediterranean. Also at issue was the treatment of the Christian inhabitants of the empire and access to the Christian shrines in the Holy Land. The goals of the great powers often conflicted with the desire for independence of the many national groups in the Ottoman Empire. Yet, because the powers had little desire to strengthen the empire, they were often more sympathetic to nationalistic aspirations there than elsewhere in Europe.

These conflicting interests, as well as mutual distrust, prevented any direct intervention in Greek affairs for several years. Eventually, however, Britain, France, and Russia concluded that an independent Greece would benefit their strategic interests and would not threaten their domestic security. In 1827, they signed the Treaty of London, demanding Turkish recognition of Greek independence, and sent a joint fleet to support the Greek revolt. In 1828, Russia sent troops into the Ottoman holdings in what is today Romania, ultimately gaining control of that territory in 1829 with the Treaty of Adrianople. The treaty also stipulated the Turks would allow Britain, France, and Russia to decide the future of Greece. In 1830, a second Treaty of London declared Greece an independent kingdom.

20.4.1.2 SERBIAN INDEPENDENCE The year 1830 also saw the establishment of a second independent state on the Balkan peninsula. Since the late eighteenth century, some Serbians had sought independence from the Ottoman Empire. During the Napoleonic wars, Serbia's fate had been linked to Russian policy and Russian relations with the Ottoman Empire. Between 1804 and 1813, a remarkable Serbian leader, Kara George (1762–1817), had led a guerrilla war against the Ottomans. This ultimately unsuccessful revolution developed a greater sense of national belonging among some Serbs and attracted the interest of the great powers.

In 1815 and 1816, a new leader, Miloš Obrenović (1780–1860), succeeded in negotiating greater administrative autonomy for some Serbian territory, but most Serbs lived outside the borders of this new entity. In 1830, the Ottoman sultan formally granted independence to Serbia, and by the late 1830s, the major powers granted it diplomatic recognition. Serbia's political structure, however, remained in doubt for many years.

In 1833, Obrenović, now a hereditary prince, pressured the Ottoman authorities to extend the borders of Serbia, which they did. These new boundaries persisted until 1878. Serbian leaders continued to seek additional territory, however, creating tensions with Austria. The status of minorities, particularly Muslims, within Serbian territory was also a problem.

In the mid-1820s, Russia, which like Serbia was a Slav state and Eastern Orthodox in religion, became Serbia's formal protector. In 1856, Serbia came under the collective protection of the great powers, but the special relationship between Russia and Serbia would continue until World War I and would play a decisive role in the outbreak of that conflict.

20.4.2 Russia: The Decembrist Revolt of 1825

Tsar Alexander I had come to the throne in 1801 after a palace coup against his father, Tsar Paul (r. 1796–1801). After flirting with Enlightenment ideas, Alexander turned permanently away from reform. Both at home and abroad, he took the lead in suppressing liberalism and nationalism. There would be no significant challenge to tsarist autocracy until his death.

20.4.2.1 UNREST IN THE ARMY As Russian forces drove Napoleon's army across Europe and then occupied defeated France, many Russian officers were exposed to the ideas of the French Revolution and the Enlightenment. Some of them, realizing how economically backward and politically stifled their own nation remained, developed reformist sympathies. Unable to express themselves openly because of Alexander's repressive policies, they formed secret societies. One of these, the Southern Society, led by an officer named Pavel Ivanovich Pestel, advocated representative government and the abolition of serfdom. Pestel himself even favored limited independence for Poland and democracy. Another secret society, the Northern Society, was more moderate. It favored constitutional monarchy and the abolition of serfdom but wanted to protect the interests of the aristocracy. Both societies were small and often in conflict with one another. They agreed only that Russia's government must change. Sometime during 1825, they apparently decided to carry out a *coup d'état* in 1826.

20.4.2.2 DYNASTIC CRISIS In late November 1825, Tsar Alexander I died unexpectedly. His death created two crises. The first was dynastic. Alexander had no direct heir. His brother Constantine (1779–1831), the next in line to the throne and at the time the commander of Russian forces in occupied Poland, had married a Roman Catholic Polish woman who refused to convert to Orthodoxy. He had thus excluded himself from the throne and was more than willing to renounce any claim to it. Through a series of secret instructions made public only after his death, Alexander had named his younger brother, Nicholas (r. 1825–1855), as the new tsar.

Once Alexander was dead, the legality of these instructions became uncertain. Constantine acknowledged Nicholas as tsar, and Nicholas acknowledged Constantine. This family muddle continued for about three weeks, during which, to the astonishment of all Europe, Russia had no ruler. Then, in early December, the army command informed Nicholas of a conspiracy among some officers. Unable to wait any longer, Nicholas had himself declared tsar, much to the delight of the by-now-exasperated Constantine.

The second crisis then unfolded. Junior officers had indeed plotted to rally the troops under their command to the cause of reform. On December 26, 1825, the army was to take the oath of allegiance to Nicholas, who was less popular than Constantine and regarded as more conservative. Most regiments took the oath, but the Moscow regiment, whose chief officers surprisingly were not secret society members, marched into Senate Square in Saint Petersburg and refused to swear allegiance. Instead, they called for a constitution and Constantine as tsar. Attempts to settle the situation peacefully failed. Late in the afternoon, Nicholas ordered the cavalry and the artillery to attack the insurgents. More than sixty people were killed. Early in 1826, Nicholas himself presided over the commission that investigated the **Decembrist Revolt** and the secret army societies. Five of the plotters were executed, and more than a hundred others were exiled to Siberia. (See "A Closer Look," which follows below, for an artistic view of the insurrection of the Decembrists.)

A Closer Look

An Unsuccessful Military Coup in Russia

ALTHOUGH A TOTAL FAILURE, the Decembrist Revolt demonstrated the desire of all Russian liberals in the nineteenth century for a constitutional government. Nonetheless, the plans of the insurrectionists remained secret, their aims little understood, and involvement in the uprising limited to only a few hundred participants.

Although a large crowd of civilians witnessed the uprising, the rebels failed to reach out to the broader public.

The tsar attempted to defeat the rebels using a cavalry attack, but credit for ending the rebellion went to the less "romantic" artillery.

The insurrection took place beneth an equestrian statue of Peter the Great that had been erected by Catherine II in 1782.

Like the supporters of the new tsar, Nicholas I, who suppressed the uprising, the insurrectionists were members of the military.

THE INSURRECTION OF THE DECEMBRISTS
SOURCE: Private Collection/The Bridgeman Images

The famous Russian poet, Alexander Pushkin, who was sympathetic to the Decembrists, wrote a poem about the rebellion called "The Bronze Horseman." In it, he considered the ambiguity of the tsar as both protector of, and threat to, the Russian people: "Whither do you gallop, haughty steed, And where will you plant your hooves?"

Questions

1. What is the role of the civilian population in this image? In what ways does the presence of civilians make the uprising seem less harmful?
2. What is the significance of the location of the insurrection?
3. Is it easy to tell what is happening in this painting? Why or why not?

Although the Decembrist Revolt failed completely, it was the first rebellion in modern Russian history whose instigators had had specific political goals. They wanted a constitutional government and the abolition of serfdom. As the century passed, the political martyrdom of the Decembrists came to symbolize the yearnings of the never numerous Russian liberals.

20.4.2.3 THE AUTOCRACY OF NICHOLAS I Although Nicholas I (r. 1825–1855) was neither an ignorant nor a bigoted reactionary, he came to symbolize the most extreme form of nineteenth-century autocracy. He knew economic growth and social improvement in Russia required reform, but he was afraid of change. In 1842, he told his State Council, "There is no doubt that serfdom, in its present form, is a flagrant evil which everyone realizes, yet to attempt to remedy it now would be, of course, an evil more disastrous."[3] To remove serfdom would necessarily, in his view, have undermined the nobles' support of the tsar so Nicholas turned his back on this and practically all other reforms. Literary and political censorship and a widespread system of surveillance by secret police flourished throughout his reign. Nicholas hoped that strict censorship would prevent liberal west European ideas from penetrating Russia. There was little attempt to forge even an efficient and honest administration. Nicholas's only significant reform was a codification of Russian law, published in 1833.

20.4.2.4 OFFICIAL NATIONALITY In place of reform, Nicholas and his closest advisers embraced a program called Official Nationality. Presiding over this program was Count S. S. Uvarov, minister of education from 1833 to 1849. Its slogan, published repeatedly in government documents, newspapers, journals, and schoolbooks, was "Orthodoxy, Autocracy, and Nationalism." The Russian Orthodox church was to provide the basis for morality, education, and intellectual life. The church, which, since the days of Peter the Great, had been an arm of the secular government controlled the schools and universities. Young Russians were taught to accept their place in life and to spurn social mobility.

Autocracy meant the unrestrained power of the tsar as the only authority that could hold the vast expanse of Russia and its peoples together. Political writers stressed that only under the autocracy of Peter the Great, Catherine the Great, and Alexander I had Russia prospered and exerted a major influence on world affairs.

Through the glorification of Russian nationality, Russians were urged to see their religion, language, and customs as a source of perennial wisdom that separated them from the moral corruption and political turmoil of the West. This program alienated serious Russian intellectuals from the tsarist government.

20.4.2.5 REVOLT AND REPRESSION IN POLAND Nicholas I was also extremely conservative in foreign affairs, as became apparent in Poland in the 1830s. A large part of former Poland had been partitioned in the late eighteenth century and ceased to exist as an independent state. It remained under Russian domination after the Congress of Vienna but was granted a constitutional government with a parliament, called the diet, that had limited powers. Under this arrangement, the tsar also reigned as king of Poland. Both Alexander and Nicholas delegated their brother, the Grand Duke Constantine, to run Poland's government. Although both tsars frequently infringed on the constitution and quarreled with the Polish diet, this arrangement lasted through the 1820s. Nevertheless, Polish nationalists continued to agitate for change.

In late November 1830, after news of the French and Belgian revolutions of that summer had reached Poland, a small insurrection of soldiers and students broke out in Warsaw. Disturbances soon spread throughout the country. On December 18, the Polish diet declared the revolution a nationalist movement. Early the next month, the diet deposed Nicholas as king of Poland. The tsar sent troops into the country and suppressed the revolt. In February 1832, Nicholas issued the Organic Statute, declaring Poland to be an integral part of the Russian Empire. Although this statute guaranteed certain Polish liberties, in practice, the Russian government systematically ignored them. The Polish uprising had confirmed the tsar's worst fears. Henceforth Russia and Nicholas became the gendarme of Europe, ever ready to provide troops to suppress liberal and nationalist movements.

20.4.3 Revolution in France (1830)

The Polish revolt was the most distant of several disturbances that erupted from the overthrow of the Bourbon dynasty in France during July 1830. When Louis XVIII had died in 1824, his brother, the count of Artois, the leader of the ultraroyalist faction, succeeded him as Charles X (r. 1824–1830). The new king was a firm believer in rule by divine right.

20.4.3.1 THE REACTIONARY POLICIES OF CHARLES X Charles X's first action was to have the Chamber of Deputies in 1824 and 1825 indemnify aristocrats who had lost their lands in the revolution. He did this by lowering the interest rates on government bonds to create a fund to pay an annual sum to the survivors of the émigrés who had forfeited land. Middle-class bondholders, who had also lost income, resented this measure. Charles also restored the rule of primogeniture, whereby only the eldest son of an aristocrat inherited the family domains. To support the Roman Catholic Church, he enacted a law that punished sacrilege with imprisonment or death. Liberals disapproved of all these measures.

In the elections of 1827, the liberals gained enough seats in the Chamber of Deputies to compel the king to compromise. He appointed a less conservative ministry. Laws against the press were eased as was government dominance

On July 5, 1830, French forces captured Algiers, which France would continue to rule until 1962. The drawing contrasts the power and modernity of the French conquerors with the almost medieval appearance of the Algerian defenses.
SOURCE: Snark/Art Resource, NY

of education. Liberals, however, wanted a genuinely constitutional regime and remained unsatisfied. In 1829, the king replaced his moderate ministry with an ultraroyalist cabinet headed by Prince de Polignac (1780–1847). The opposition, in desperation, opened negotiations with the liberal Orléans branch of the royal family.

20.4.3.2 THE JULY REVOLUTION In 1830, Charles X called for new elections, in which the liberals scored a stunning victory. Instead of accepting the new Chamber of Deputies, the king and his ministers attempted a royalist seizure of power. In June and July 1830, Polignac sent a naval expedition against Algiers, which was nominally under Ottoman rule but had in fact become a pirate state whose ships preyed on the merchant vessels of all nations. News of the capture of Algiers and the founding of a French Empire in North Africa reached Paris on July 9. Taking advantage of the euphoria this victory created, Charles issued the Four Ordinances on July 25, 1830, staging what amounted to a royal coup d'état. These ordinances restricted freedom of the press, dissolved the recently elected Chamber of Deputies, limited the franchise to the wealthiest people in the country, and called for new elections.

The Four Ordinances provoked swift and decisive popular reaction. Liberal newspapers called on the nation to reject the monarch's actions. The workers of Paris, burdened since 1827 by an economic downturn, erected barricades in the streets. The king called out troops, and although more than 1,800 people died during the ensuing battles, the army was not able to gain control of Paris.

On August 2, Charles X abdicated and went into exile in England. The Chamber of Deputies named a new ministry comprised of constitutional monarchists. In an act that finally ended the rule of the Bourbon dynasty, it also proclaimed Louis Philippe (r. 1830–1848), the Duke d'Orléans, the new king instead of the Count de Chambord, the infant grandson of Charles X in whose favor Charles had abdicated.

In the Revolution of 1830, also known as the **July Revolution**, the liberals of the Chamber of Deputies had filled a power vacuum the Paris uprising and the failure of effective royal action had created. Had Charles X provided himself with sufficient troops in Paris, the outcome could have been different. Moreover, had the liberals, who favored a constitutional monarchy, not acted quickly, the workers and shopkeepers of Paris might have attempted to form a republic. By seizing the moment, the middle class, the bureaucrats, and the moderate aristocratic liberals overthrew the restoration monarchy and still avoided a republic. These liberals feared a new popular revolution such as the one that had swept France in 1792. They had no desire for another sans-culotte republic. A fundamental political and social tension thus underlay the new monarchy. The revolution had succeeded thanks to a temporary alliance between hard-pressed laborers and the prosperous middle class, but these two groups soon realized that their basic goals were different.

20.4.3.3 MONARCHY UNDER LOUIS PHILIPPE

Politically, the **July Monarchy**, as the new regime was called, was more liberal than the restoration government. Louis Philippe was called the "king of the French" rather than "king of France." The tricolor flag of the revolution replaced the white flag of the Bourbons. The new constitution was regarded as a right of the people rather than as a concession of the monarch. Catholicism became the religion of a majority of the people rather than "the official religion." The new government was strongly anticlerical. Censorship was abolished. The franchise became wider but remained restricted. The king had to cooperate with the Chamber of Deputies; he could not dispense with laws on his own authority.

Socially, however, the Revolution of 1830 proved conservative. The hereditary peerage was abolished in 1831, but the everyday economic, political, and social influence of the landed oligarchy continued. Money was the path to power and influence in the government, and there was much corruption.

Most importantly, the liberal monarchy displayed little or no sympathy for the lower and working classes. In 1830, the workers of Paris had called for the protection of jobs, better wages, and the preservation of the traditional crafts, rather than for the usual goals of political liberalism. The government of Louis Philippe ignored their demands and their plight. The laboring classes of Paris and the provincial cities seemed just one more possible source of disorder. In late 1831, troops suppressed a workers' revolt in Lyons. In July 1832, an uprising occurred in Paris during the funeral of a popular Napoleonic general. Again the government called out troops, and more than 800 people were killed or wounded. In 1834, a large strike by silk workers in Lyons was crushed. Such discontent might be smothered for a time, but unless the government addressed the social and economic conditions that created it, new turmoil would eventually erupt.

The new French government of 1830 was only too happy to retain the control of the city of Algiers that Charles X had achieved less than a month before his overthrow. The occupation of Algeria gave French merchants in Marseilles new economic ties to North Africa. Moreover, the French quickly dismantled the structures of the Ottoman government that had survived in Algeria in order to conquer and administer the interior of the country, which was larger than France itself and where Ottoman rule had never penetrated. By the 1850s, the French had extended their rule, after constant warfare against Muslim tribesmen, as far as the northern Sahara desert. France now had a vast new empire, and French citizens and other Europeans also began to settle in Algeria in large numbers, especially in the cities. In the second half of the nineteenth century, the French government came to regard Algeria, despite its overwhelmingly Muslim population, as not a colony but an integral part of France itself. This was to have serious repercussions after World War II when a pro-independence movement developed among Muslim Algerians.

20.4.4 Belgium Becomes Independent (1830)

The July Revolution in Paris sent sparks to other political tinder on the Continent. The revolutionary fires first flared in neighboring Belgium. The former Austrian Netherlands, Belgium, had been merged with the kingdom of Holland in 1815. The two countries differed in language, religion, and economy, however, and the Belgian upper classes never reconciled themselves to Dutch rule.

On August 25, 1830, disturbances broke out in Brussels after the performance of an opera about a rebellion in Naples against Spanish rule. To end the rioting, the municipal authorities and people from the propertied classes formed a provisional national government. When compromise between the Belgians and the Dutch failed, King William I of Holland (r. 1815–1840) sent troops and ships against Belgium. By November 10, 1830, the Dutch had been defeated. A national congress then wrote a liberal Belgian constitution, which was issued in 1831.

Although the major powers saw the revolution in Belgium as upsetting the boundaries the Congress of Vienna had established, they were not inclined to intervene to reverse it. Russia was preoccupied with the Polish revolt. Prussia and the other German states were suppressing small uprisings in their own domains. The Austrians were busy putting down disturbances in Italy. Under Louis Philippe, France hoped to dominate an independent Belgium. Britain could tolerate a liberal Belgium if it was free of foreign domination.

In December 1830, Lord Palmerston (1784–1865), the British foreign minister, persuaded representatives of the powers in London to recognize Belgium as an independent and neutral state. In July 1831, Prince Leopold of Saxe-Coburg (r. 1831–1865), who had connections to the British royal family and had married the daughter of Louis Philippe, became king of the Belgians. The Convention of 1839 guaranteed Belgian neutrality, which remained an article of faith in European international relations for almost a century.

Both Belgium and Serbia gained independence in 1830, and ironically, diplomatic crises involving both nations led to World War I. The assassination of an Austrian archduke by a Serbian nationalist in Sarajevo in 1914 triggered the war, and Germany's violation of Belgian neutrality brought Britain into it.

20.4.5 The Great Reform Bill in Britain (1832)

In Great Britain, the revolutionary year of 1830 saw the election of a House of Commons that debated the first major bill to reform Parliament. The death of George IV (r. 1820–1830) and the accession of William IV (r. 1830–1837) required the calling of a parliamentary election, held in the summer of 1830. Historians once believed the July Revolution in France influenced voting in Britain, but close analysis of the time and character of individual county and borough elections has shown otherwise. The passage of the **Great Reform Bill**, which became law in 1832, was the result of a series of events different from those that occurred on the Continent. In Britain, the forces of conservatism and reform accommodated each other.

20.4.5.1 POLITICAL AND ECONOMIC REFORM
Several factors contributed to this spirit of compromise. First, the commercial and industrial class was larger in Britain than in other countries. No government could ignore their economic interests without damaging British prosperity. Second, Britain's liberal Whig aristocrats, who regarded themselves as the protectors of constitutional liberty, had a long tradition of favoring moderate reforms that would make revolutionary changes unnecessary. Early Whig sympathy for the French Revolution had reduced their influence. After 1815, however, they reentered the political arena. Finally, British law, tradition, and public opinion all showed a strong respect for civil liberties.

In 1820, the year after the passage of the notorious Six Acts, Lord Liverpool shrewdly reshaped his cabinet. Although they were conservatives, the new members of the government believed it had to accommodate to the changing social and economic life of the nation. They favored greater economic freedom and repealed the Combination Acts that had prohibited labor organizations.

20.4.5.2 THE CATHOLIC EMANCIPATION ACT
English determination to maintain its union with Ireland brought about another key reform. England's relationship to Ireland was similar to that of Russia to Poland or Austria to its several national groups. In 1800, fearful that Irish nationalists might rebel as they had in 1798 and perhaps turn Ireland into a base for a French invasion, William Pitt the Younger had persuaded Parliament to pass the Act of Union between Ireland and England. Ireland now sent hundred members to the House of Commons. Only Protestant Irishmen, however, could be elected to represent their overwhelmingly Roman Catholic nation.

During the 1820s, under the leadership of Daniel O'Connell (1775–1847), Irish nationalists organized the Catholic Association to agitate for Catholic emancipation. In 1828, O'Connell secured his own election to Parliament, where he could not legally take his seat. The Duke of Wellington, who was now prime minister, realized that Ireland

DANIEL O'CONNELL, THE IRISH LIBERATOR Beginning in the 1820s Daniel O'Connell revolutionized Irish politics. He created a grassroots organization and collected funds to finance Irish nationalist activities. He was also known as one of the great public speakers of his generation.
SOURCE: Holmes Garden Photos/Alamy Stock Photo

might elect an overwhelmingly Catholic delegation. If they were not seated, civil war might erupt across the Irish Sea. Consequently, in 1829, Wellington and Robert Peel steered the **Catholic Emancipation Act** through Parliament. Roman Catholics could now become members of Parliament. This measure, together with the repeal in 1828 of restrictions against Protestant nonconformists, ended the Anglican monopoly on British political life.

Catholic emancipation was a liberal measure passed for the conservative purpose of preserving order in Ireland. It included a provision raising the property qualification to vote in Ireland so that only the wealthier Irish could vote. Nonetheless, this measure alienated many of Wellington's Anglican Tory supporters in the House of Commons. The election of 1830 restored many supporters of parliamentary reform to Parliament. Even some Tories supported reform because they believed only a corrupt House of Commons could have passed Catholic emancipation. The Tories consequently were badly divided, and the Wellington ministry soon fell. King William IV then turned to the leader of the Whigs, Earl Grey (1764–1845), to form a government.

20.4.5.3 LEGISLATING CHANGE
The Whig ministry presented the House of Commons with a major reform bill that had two broad goals. The first was to replace "rotten

boroughs," or boroughs that had few voters, with representatives for the previously unrepresented manufacturing districts and cities. Second, the number of voters in England and Wales was to be increased by about 50 percent through a series of new franchises. In 1831, the House of Commons narrowly defeated the bill. Earl Grey called for a new election and won a majority in favor of the bill. The House of Commons passed the reform bill, but the House of Lords rejected it. Mass meetings were held throughout the country, and riots broke out in several cities. Finally, William IV agreed to create enough new peers to give a third reform bill a majority in the House of Lords. Under this pressure, the measure became law in 1832.

The **Great Reform Bill** expanded the size of the English electorate, but it was not a democratic measure. It increased the number of voters by more than 200,000, or almost 50 percent, but it kept a property qualification for the franchise. (Gender was also a qualification. No thought was given to enfranchising women.) Some members of the working class actually lost the right to vote because certain old franchise rights were abolished. New urban boroughs were created to allow the growing cities to have a voice in the House of Commons. Yet the passage of the reform act did not, as was once thought, constitute the triumph of middle-class interests in England: for every new urban electoral district, a new rural district was also drawn, and the aristocracy was expected to dominate rural elections. What the bill permitted was a wider variety of property to be represented in the House of Commons.

The success of the reform bill reconciled previously unrepresented property owners and economic interests with the political institutions of the country. The act laid the groundwork for further orderly reforms of the church, municipal government, and commercial policy. By admitting into the political forum people who desired change and giving them access to the legislative process, the bill made revolution in Britain unnecessary. Great Britain thus maintained its traditional institutions of government while allowing an increasingly diverse group of people to influence them.

20.5 The Wars of Independence in Latin America

What sparked the wars of independence in Latin America?

The wars of the French Revolution and, more particularly, those of Napoleon sparked movements for independence from European domination throughout Latin America. In less than two decades, between 1804 and 1824, France was driven from Haiti, Portugal lost control of Brazil, and Spain was forced to withdraw from all its American Empire except Cuba and Puerto Rico. Three centuries of

Iberian colonial government over the South American continent ended. These wars ended the era of European political domination and economic exploitation of the American continents that had begun with the encounter between the peoples of the New World and Spain at the end of the fifteenth century. The period of transatlantic history beginning with the American Revolution and ending with the Latin American Wars of Independence thus constituted the first era of decolonization from European rule. (See Map 20–2.)

20.5.1 Wars of Independence on the South American Continent

Haiti's revolution involved the popular uprising of a repressed social group. It was the great exception in the Latin American struggle for liberty from European masters. In general, on the South American continent, the Creole elite—merchants, landowners, and professional people of Spanish descent but who were born in the colonies—led the movements against Spain and Portugal. Few Native Americans, Africans or their descendants, or people of mixed race, whether enslaved or free, became involved in or benefited from the end of Iberian rule. Indeed, the example of the Haitian slave revolt haunted the Creoles, as did the revolts of Indians in the Andes in 1780 and 1781. The Creoles were determined that any drive for political independence from Spain and Portugal should not cause social disruption or the loss of their privileges. In this respect, the Creole revolutionaries were not unlike American revolutionaries in the southern colonies, who rejected British rule but wanted to keep their slaves, or French revolutionaries, who wanted to depose the king without extending liberty to the French working class.

20.5.1.1 CREOLE DISCONTENT Creole discontent with Spanish colonial government had many sources. Latin American merchants wanted to trade more freely within the region and with North American and European markets. They wanted commercial regulations that would benefit them rather than Spain. They had also resented increases in taxation by the Spanish crown. Creoles resented Spanish policies that favored peninsulares—white people born in Spain—for political patronage, including appointments to the colonial government, church, and army.

Creole leaders had read the Enlightenment philosophes and regarded their reforms as potentially beneficial to the region. They were also aware of the events and the political philosophy of the American Revolution. But transforming Creole discontent into revolt against the Spanish government required more, however, than reform programs and revolutionary examples. That transforming event occurred in Europe when Napoleon invaded Portugal in 1807 and made his brother king of Spain in 1808.

Map 20–2 LATIN AMERICA IN 1830

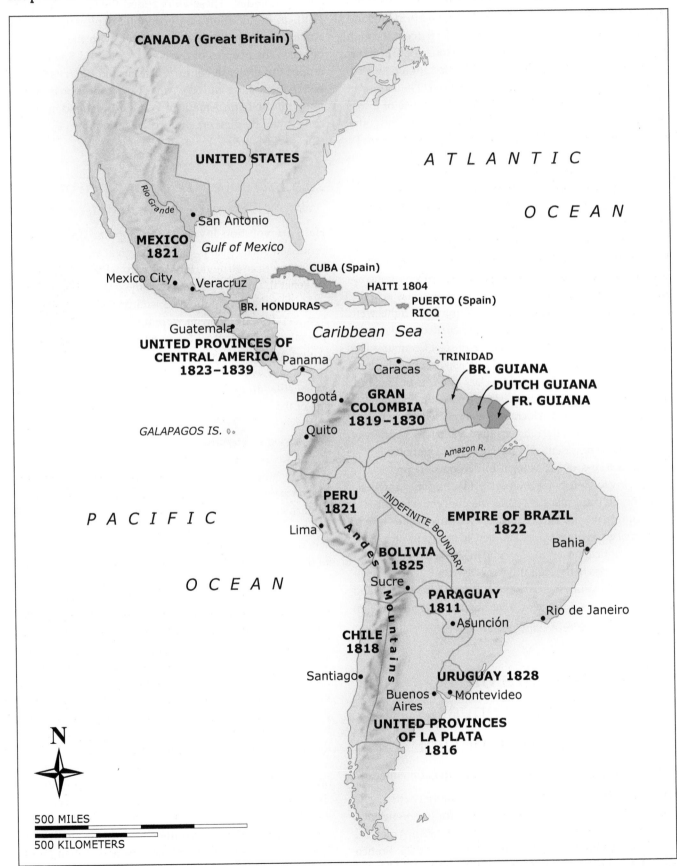

By 1830 most of Latin America had been liberated from Europe. Shown here are the initial borders of the states of the region with the dates of their independence. The United Provinces of La Plata formed the nucleus of what later became Argentina.

Napoleon's overthrow of the Spanish Bourbon monarchy created an imperial political vacuum throughout Spanish Latin America that encouraged Creole leaders to act.

The Creole elite feared a liberal Napoleonic monarchy in Spain would impose reforms in Latin America that would harm their economic and social interests. They also feared a French-controlled Spain would drain the region of the wealth and resources Napoleon needed for his wars. To protect their interests and seize the opportunity to control their political destiny, between 1808 and 1810 Creole *juntas*, or political committees, claimed the right to govern different regions of Latin America. After the establishment of these local juntas, Spain never effectively reestablished its authority in South America, The establishment of the juntas also ended the privileges of the peninsulares, whose welfare had always depended on the favors of the Spanish crown. Creoles now took over positions in the government and army.

20.5.1.2 SAN MARTÍN IN RÍO DE LA PLATA The vast size of Latin America, its geographical barriers, its distinct regional differences, and the absence of an even marginally integrated economy meant there would be several different paths to independence. The first region to assert itself was the Río de la Plata, or modern Argentina. The center of revolt was the city of Buenos Aires, whose citizens, as early as 1806, had fought off a British invasion and thus had learned they could protect themselves without Spanish assistance. In 1810, the junta in Buenos Aires not only thrust off Spanish authority but also sent forces into Paraguay and Uruguay to liberate them from Spain. These armies were defeated, but Spain nevertheless lost control of both areas. Paraguay asserted its own independence, and Brazil took over Uruguay.

These early defeats did not discourage the Buenos Aires government, which determined to liberate Peru, the stronghold of royalist power and loyalty on the Continent. By 1817, José de San Martín (1778–1850), the leading general of the Río de la Plata forces, led an army in a daring march over the Andes Mountains and occupied Santiago in Chile, where Chilean independence leader Bernardo O'Higgins (1778–1842) was established as the supreme dictator. From Santiago, San Martín organized a fleet that in 1820 carried his army by sea to Peru. The next year, San Martín drove royalist forces from Lima and became Protector of Peru.

20.5.1.3 SIMÓN BOLÍVAR'S LIBERATION OF VENEZUELA
While the army of San Martín had been liberating the southern portion of the Continent, **Simón Bolívar** (1783–1830) had been pursuing a similar task in the north. Bolívar had been involved in the organization of a liberating junta in Caracas, Venezuela, in 1810. He was a firm advocate of both independence and a republic. Between 1811 and 1814, civil war broke out throughout Venezuela as both royalists, on the one hand, and slaves and *llaneros* (Venezuelan cowboys), on the other, challenged the authority of the republican government. Bolívar had to go into exile first in Colombia and then

SIMÓN BOLÍVAR, THE LATIN AMERICAN LIBERATOR Simón Bolívar was the liberator of much of Latin America. He favored a policy of political liberalism.
SOURCE: Pictorial Press Ltd/Alamy Stock Photo

in Jamaica. In 1816, with help from Haiti, he returned to the Continent. By the summer of 1821, Bolívar's forces captured Caracas, and he was named president.

A year later, in July 1822, the armies of Bolívar and San Martín joined as they moved to liberate Quito, the capital of what is today Ecuador. At a famous meeting in Guayaquil, the two liberators sharply disagreed about the future political structure of Latin America. San Martín believed the peoples of the region required monarchies; Bolívar maintained his republicanism. Not long after the meeting, San Martín quietly retired from public life and went into exile in Europe. Meanwhile, Bolívar deliberately allowed the political situation in Peru to disintegrate, and in 1823, he sent in troops to establish his control. On December 9, 1824, at the Battle of Ayacucho, the liberating army crushed the main Spanish royalist forces. This battle marked the end of Spain's effort to retain its South American empire.

20.5.2 Independence in New Spain

The drive for independence in New Spain, which included present-day Mexico as well as Texas, California, and the rest of the southwest United States, illustrates better than in any other region the socially conservative outcome of the Latin American colonial revolutions. As elsewhere, a local governing junta was organized in 1808. Before it had undertaken any significant measures, however, a Creole priest, Miguel Hidalgo y Costilla (1753–1811), in 1810 called the Indians in his parish to rebellion. Father Hidalgo presented a program of social reform, including hints of changes in landholding. Soon he stood at the head of a loosely organized group of 80,000 followers, who captured several major cities and then marched on to Mexico City. In July 1811, the revolutionary priest was captured and executed. Leadership of his movement then fell to José María Morelos y Pavón (1765–1815), a mestizo priest. Far more radical than Hidalgo, he called for an end to forced labor and for substantial land reforms. He was executed in 1815, ending five years of popular uprising.

The uprising and its demand for fundamental social reforms united all conservative political groups in Mexico, both Creole and Spanish. These groups opposed any kind of reform that might diminish their privileges. In 1820, however, their recently achieved security was unexpectedly challenged. As already discussed, the revolution in Spain had forced Ferdinand VII to accept a liberal constitution. Conservative Mexicans feared the new liberal monarchy would impose liberal reforms on Mexico. Therefore, for the most conservative of reasons, they rallied behind a former royalist general, Augustín de Iturbide (1783–1824), who declared Mexico independent of Spain in 1821. Shortly thereafter, Iturbide was declared emperor. His regime did not last long, but he had created an independent Mexico, governed by groups determined to resist significant social reform.

20.5.3 Brazilian Independence

Brazilian independence, in contrast to that of Spanish Latin America, came relatively simply and peacefully. As already noted, the Portuguese royal family, along with several thousand government officials and members of the court, fled to Brazil in 1807. Their arrival immediately transformed Rio de Janeiro into a royal city. The prince regent João addressed many of the local complaints, equivalent to those of the Spanish Creoles, by for example, taking measures that expanded trade. In 1815, he made Brazil a kingdom, meaning it was no longer to be regarded merely as a colony of Portugal. This change was in many respects long overdue since Brazil was far larger and more prosperous than Portugal itself. Then, in 1820, a revolution occurred in Portugal, and its leaders demanded João's return to Lisbon. They also demanded the return of Brazil to colonial status. João, who had become King João VI in 1816 (r. 1816–1826), returned to Portugal but left his son Dom Pedro as regent in Brazil and encouraged him to support the political aspirations of the Brazilians. In September 1822, Dom Pedro embraced the cause of Brazilian independence against the recolonizing efforts of Portugal. By the end of the year, he had become emperor of an independent Brazil, Thus, in contrast to virtually all other Latin American nations, Brazil achieved independence in a way that left no dispute over where the center of political authority lay.

Two other factors aided the peaceful transition to independence in Brazil. First, the political and social elite of Brazil wished to avoid the destruction that the wars of independence had unleashed in the Spanish American Empire. Second, these leaders had every intention of preserving slavery. The wars of independence elsewhere had generally led to the abolition of slavery or moved the new states closer to abolishing it. Warfare in Brazil might have caused social turmoil with similar consequences.

The Chapter in Perspective

The French Revolution and Napoleonic wars brought tremendous political and social instability to Europe. The congress system, spearheaded by Metternich, set up a process for mediating conflicts among European powers without going to war. Immediately after the Congress of Vienna, most countries in Europe experienced territorial and political stability. Although the great powers were able to negotiate their conflicts with each other peacefully, they faced increasing domestic pressure for reform. Nationalists demanded a realignment of political boundaries to reflect what they thought were meaningful cultural communities. Liberals demanded an end to the arbitrary rule of monarchs and the political dominance of the landed aristocracy through the introduction of constitutions. Many of the revolutionary disturbances in Europe were suppressed without substantial concessions.

Nonetheless, during the 1820s, liberal political ideas and some liberal political figures began to make inroads into the otherwise conservative domestic order. Although the Decembrist Revolt of 1825 in Russia only lasted a few hours, the Greek revolt that broke out in 1821 was successful. In 1830, revolution and reform again began to move across Europe. The French replaced the Bourbons with a more liberal monarchy. Belgium also achieved independence under a liberal government. Britain moved slowly toward a more liberal position. Popular pressures at home led the British aristocratic leadership to enact a moderate reform bill in 1832. Thereafter, Britain would be viewed as the leading liberal state in Europe and one that would support nationalistic causes.

As conservative regimes weathered these challenges within Europe, Spain and Portugal were pushed out of their colonies in the New World. Unlike the Haitian Revolution, however, the revolutions in Latin America were fundamentally socially conservative.

The Chapter in Review

Review Questions

1. What is nationalism? What were the goals of nationalists? What difficulties did nationalists confront in realizing those goals? Why was nationalism a special threat to the Austrian Empire? What areas saw significant nationalist movements between 1815 and 1830? Which were successful and which unsuccessful?

2. What were the tenets of liberalism? Who were the liberals, and how did liberalism affect the political developments of the early nineteenth century? What is the relationship of liberalism to nationalism?

3. What difficulties did the conservatives in Austria, Prussia, and Russia face after the Napoleonic wars? How did they attempt to solve those difficulties at home and in international affairs? What were the aims of the Concert of Europe? How did the Congress of Vienna change international relations?

4. What were the main reasons for Creole discontent with Spanish rule, and to what extent did Enlightenment political philosophy influence the Creole leaders? Who were some of the primary leaders of Latin American independence? Why was Brazil's path to independence different from that of Spanish America?

5. What were the main provisions of the constitution of the restored monarchy in France? What did Charles X hope to accomplish? Why did revolution break out in France in 1830? What did this revolution achieve, and what problems did it fail to resolve?

6. What was the purpose of the Great Reform Bill? What did it achieve? Would you call it a "revolutionary" document?

7. By approximately 1830, how had European political ambitions and the ideas of liberalism and nationalism begun to undermine the Ottoman Empire? Which Ottoman territories were lost by that date?

Key Terms

Carlsbad Decrees Decrees issued by the major German states in 1819 to dissolve the student associations.

Catholic Emancipation Act Act in 1829 that allowed Roman Catholics to become members of the English Parliament.

Concert of Europe Term applied to the European great powers acting together (in "concert") to resolve international disputes from 1815 to the 1850s.

congress system A series of international meetings among the European great powers to promote mutual cooperation from 1818 to 1822.

conservatism Support for the established order in church and state that, in the nineteenth century, implied support for legitimate monarchies, landed aristocracies, and established churches; favored only gradual, or "organic," change.

Corn Law Passed by the British Parliament in 1815 to maintain high prices for domestically produced grain by levying import duties on foreign grain; it was the first in a series of Corn Laws enacted in the United Kingdom from 1815 to 1846.

David Ricardo (1772–1823) British political economist who in his most famous work, *Principles of Political Economy*, argued for the "iron law of wages." Claimed that as wages increase, parents have more children, who in turn, enter the labor force and thus depress wages by increasing the number of workers.

Decembrist Revolt Crisis that took place on December 14, 1825, when Nicholas I ordered his cavalry and artillery to attack the Moscow regiment of the Russian army, which had refused to take the oath of allegiance to the new tsar.

Great Reform Bill A limited reform of the British House of Commons and an expansion of the electorate to include a wider variety of the propertied classes and that laid the groundwork for further orderly reforms within the British constitutional system.

"Irish problem" Under English rule in 1800, Irish nationalists who wanted independence or at least some measure of autonomy.

John Stuart Mill (1806–1873) English philosopher and political economist and one of the most important thinkers in the history of liberalism, whose idea of liberty endorsed the freedom of the individual as opposed to the unlimited control of the state.

July Monarchy Following the abdication of Charles X, the proclamation in 1830 of the Chamber of Deputies that Louis Philippe was the "king of the French," thus ending the rule of the Bourbon Dynasty.

July Revolution The king and his ministers' attempt at a royalist seizure of power in 1830 in the wake of the stunning liberal victory in the French elections.

liberalism Support for the protection and enhancement of individual rights; in the nineteenth century, shared the ideas of the Enlightenment as stated in the Declaration of the Rights of Man and Citizen.

nationalism The belief that people are part of a nation, defined as a community with its own language, traditions, customs, and history that distinguish it from other nations and make it the primary focus of people's loyalty and sense of identity.

nationhood In the eyes of nineteenth-century nationalists, a concept of that would promote economic and administrative efficiency; enable nations to pursue their own destinies; distinguish nations as distinct creations of God; and allow nations to take their place in the divine order of things.

Nicholas I (1796–1855) Emperor of Russia (r. 1825–1855); represented autocracy, with the use of censorship and surveillance by secret police throughout his reign.

Peterloo Massacre Response on August 16, 1819 to a mass meeting in the industrial city of Manchester, which demanded the reform of Parliament, in which royal troops and local militia fired on the crowd on the orders of local officials.

Simón Bolívar (1783–1830) Venezuelan military and political leader and an advocate of both independence and a republic; crushed the main Spanish royalist forces at the Battle of Ayacucho.

Thomas Malthus (1766–1834) English cleric and scholar who argued in his book, *Essay on the Principle of Population*, that the human population grows at a geometric rate, thus outstripping the food supply, which expands at an arithmetic rate.

Notes

1. Frederick B. Artz, *Reaction and Revolution, 1814–1832* (New York: Harper, 1934), p. 94.
2. Paul W. Schroeder, *The Transformation of European Politics, 1763–1848* (Oxford, UK: Clarendon Press, 1994), p. 802.
3. Michael T. Florinsky, *Russia: A History and an Interpretation*, Vol. 2 (New York: Macmillan, 1953), p. 755.

Chapter 21
Economic Advance and Social Unrest (1830–1850)

ROMANIAN PEASANT REVOLUTIONARIES RALLY AT BLAJ IN TRANSYLVANIA Romanian peasants rally at Blaj in Transylvania on May 15, 1848. In 1848 Ana Ipatescu helped lead Transylvanian revolutionaries against Russian rule. Transylvania is part of present-day Romania. The revolutions of 1848 in eastern Europe were primarily uprisings of nationalist groups. Although generally repressed in the revolutions of that year, subject nationalities were a source of political upheaval and unrest in the region throughout the rest of the century, ultimately providing the spark for the outbreak of World War I.

SOURCE: Private Collection/Archives Charmet/Bridgeman Images

 ## Contents and Focus Questions

The Chapter in Brief

BY 1830, EUROPE was headed toward an industrial society. Only Great Britain had already attained that status, but the pounding of new machinery and the grinding of railway engines soon began to echo across much of the Continent. Yet what characterized the second quartercentury was not the triumph of industrialism but the final protests of those economic groups who opposed it. Intellectually, the period saw the formulation of the major creeds supporting and criticizing the newly emerging society.

These were years of uncertainty for almost everyone. Even the most confident entrepreneurs knew the trade cycle could bankrupt them within weeks. For the industrial workers and the artisans, unemployment became a haunting and recurring problem. For peasants and agricultural workers, the question was sufficiency of food. It was a period of self-conscious transition that culminated in 1848 with a continent-wide outbreak of revolution. People knew one mode of life was passing, but no one knew what would replace it.

21.1 Toward an Industrial Society

How did industrialization spread across Europe?

The Industrial Revolution had begun in eighteenth-century Great Britain with advances in textile production. Natural resources, adequate capital, native technological skills, a growing food supply, a social structure that allowed considerable mobility, the tremendously profitable slave trade, and strong foreign and domestic demand for goods had given Britain an edge in achieving a vast new capacity for production in manufacturing. British factories and recently invented machines allowed producers to furnish customers with a greater number of consumer products of a higher quality and for lower prices than those of any competitors. Also, the French Revolution and the wars of Napoleon had finally destroyed the French Atlantic trade and thus disrupted continental economic life for two decades. The Latin American wars of independence opened the markets of South America to British goods. In North America, both the United States and Canada demanded British products. Through its control of India, Britain commanded the markets of southern Asia. British banks similarly dominated the international financial markets.

The British textile industry was a worldwide economic network. For much of its supply of raw cotton, this industry depended on the labor of American slaves, although abolitionists had succeeded in outlawing direct British participation in the slave trade in 1807. In turn, the finished textiles were shipped all over the world along sea-lanes the British navy protected. The wealth that Britain gained through textile production and its other industries of iron making, shipbuilding, china production, and the manufacture of other finished goods was invested all over the world, but especially in the United States and Latin America. This enormous activity established the economic foundation for British dominance of the world throughout the nineteenth century. (To examine Britain's leadership in the Industrial Revolution and its worldwide economic power, see the "Closer Look" sidebar, which follows below.)

Despite their economic lag, the continental nations were beginning to make material progress. By the 1830s, in Belgium, France, and the German states, the number of steam engines in use was growing steadily. Exploitation of the coalfields of the Ruhr and the Saar basins had begun.

Although there were pockets of production—such as Lyons, Rouen, and Lille in France and Liege in Belgium—in Western Europe, most continental manufacturing still took place in the countryside. New machines were integrated into the existing domestic system. The slow pace of continental imitation of the British example meant that, at mid-century, peasants and urban artisans remained more important politically than industrial factory workers.

THE "ROCKET" George Stephenson (1781–1848) invented the locomotive in 1814, but the "Rocket," his improved design shown here, did not win out over other competitors until 1829. In the following two decades the spread of railways transformed the economy of Western Europe.

SOURCE: Mary Evans Picture Library/The Image Works.

A Closer Look

The Great Exhibition in London

THE GREAT EXHIBITION of 1851 was held in London to celebrate progress in industry and commerce achieved through the new industrial order. Its organizers invited governments and businesses from around the globe to display the products they manufactured. The organizers generally supported free trade and believed the displays would demonstrate the value of peaceful commerce.

An architectural innovation: the structural iron in the barrel vault and framing.

The crowds at the Great Exhibition demonstrate a welcome return to peaceful public gatherings, after a quarter-century of social turmoil and political discontent.

Flags labeled "India" and "silk" represent the industry of Britain's most important colony.

Classical statues indicate that the new industrialism produced wealth, which could be used to acquire luxury goods and social status.

Glass, once a scarce luxury good used only for small greenhouses, not for vast exhibition halls, is now being industrially produced in large amounts for everyday consumption.

LONDON'S CRYSTAL PALACE DURING THE GREAT EXHIBITION OF 1851
SOURCE: V&A Images, London/Art Resource, NY.

Questions

1. How does this image promote the British Empire?
2. What role does this image suggest that women play in Britain's commercial society?
3. What tools does the artist use to depict British prosperity?

21.1.1 Population and Migration

While the process of industrialization spread, the population of Europe continued to grow based on the eighteenth-century population explosion. The number of people in France rose from 32.5 million in 1831 to 35.8 million in 1851. During approximately the same period, the population of the German states rose from 26.5 million to 33.5 million and that of Britain from 16.3 million to 20.8 million. More and more of the people of Europe lived in cities. By mid-century, one-half of the population of England and Wales and

one-quarter of the population of France and the German states had become town dwellers. Further to the east and south, by contrast, Europeans continued to live overwhelmingly in rural settings, with little industrial manufacturing.

The sheer numbers of human beings put considerable pressure on the physical resources of the cities. Migration from the countryside meant that existing housing, water, sewers, food supplies, and lighting were completely inadequate. Slums with indescribable filth grew, and disease, especially cholera, ravaged the population. Crime increased and became a way of life for those who could make a living in no other manner. Human misery and degradation in many early-nineteenth-century cities seemed to have no bounds.

The situation in the countryside was scarcely better. During the first half-century, the productive use of the land remained the basic fact of life for most Europeans. The enclosures of the late eighteenth century, the land redistribution of the French Revolution, and the emancipation of serfs in Prussia and later throughout Austria in 1848 and Russia in 1861 commercialized landholding. Liberal reformers had hoped the legal revolution in ownership would transform peasants into progressive, industrious farmers. Instead, most peasants became conservative landholders without enough land to make agricultural innovations or, oftentimes, even to support themselves.

It is important to note the differing dates of rural emancipation across Europe. In England, France, and the Low Countries, persons living in the countryside could move freely between country and town. In many of the German states, Austria, and Russia, such migration was difficult until the serfs were emancipated. Even when emancipation did occur, as throughout the German states early in the century, it did not make migration simple. Where there was no fluid market for free labor moving to the cities, the pace of industrialization was slower.

The specter of poor harvests still haunted Europe. The worst such experience of the century was the Irish famine of 1845 to 1847. Perhaps as many as half a million Irish peasants with no land or small plots simply starved when disease blighted the potato crop. Hundreds of thousands emigrated.

By mid-century, the revolution in landholding led to greater agricultural production. It also resulted in a vast uprooting of people from the countryside into cities and from Europe into the rest of the world. The countryside was the source of many of the workers for the new factories, as well as people with few economic skills who slowly emigrated to cities in hope of finding work.

21.1.2 Railways

Industrial advance itself had also contributed to this migration. The 1830s and 1840s ushered in the first great age of railway building. At mid-century, Britain had 9,797 kilometers of railway, France 2,915, and the German states 5,856. (See Map 21-1.)

Map 21-1   EUROPEAN RAILROADS IN 1850

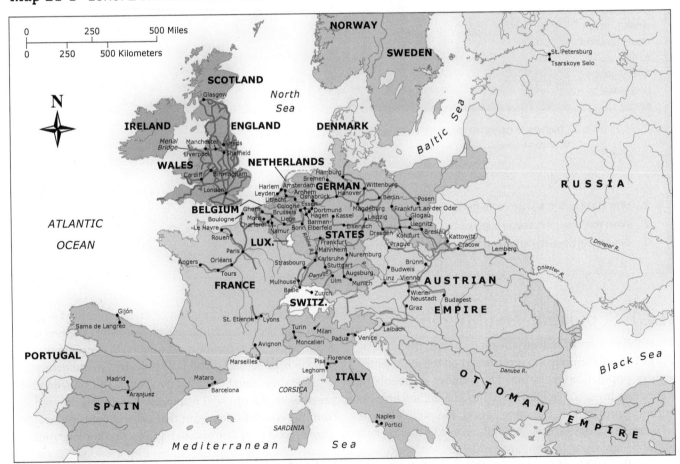

At mid-century Britain had the most extensive rail network and the most industrialized economy in Europe, but rail lines were expanding rapidly in France, the German states, and Austria. Southern and eastern Europe had few railways, and the Ottoman Empire had none.

The railroads, plus canals and improved regular roads, meant people could leave the place of their birth more easily than ever before. The improvement in transportation also allowed cheaper and more rapid passage of raw materials and finished products.

Railways epitomized the character of the industrial economy during the second quarter of the century. They represented investment in capital goods rather than in consumer goods. Consequently, there was a shortage of consumer goods at cheap prices. This favoring of capital over consumer production was one reason the working class was often unable to purchase much for its wages. The railways, which embodied the most dramatic application of the steam engine, in and of themselves also brought about still more industrialization. Rails and railway cars sharply increased demand for iron and steel, fabrics, glass, and wood. Preparing the ground for tracks, laying the tracks, and constructing railroad stations were major projects that created jobs and required skilled labor. The new iron and steel capacity soon permitted the construction of ironclad ships and iron machinery rather than ships and machinery made of wood. These new capital industries led

to the formation of vast industrial fortunes that would be invested in still newer enterprises. Industrialism had begun to grow on itself.

21.2 The Labor Force

How did industrialization change the European labor force?

The composition and experiences of the early nineteenth-century labor force was varied. Some of the workforce was reasonably well off and enjoyed steady employment and decent wages. Other workers were the "laboring poor," who held jobs, but earned little more than subsistence wages. Then there were those, such as the women and children who worked nearly naked in the mines of Wales, whose conditions of life shocked Europe when a parliamentary report in the 1840s publicized them. Furthermore, the conditions of workers varied from decade to decade and from industry to industry within any particular decade.

Although historians have traditionally emphasized the role and experience of industrial factory workers, only the

CHARTIST MEETING AT KENNINGTON COMMON, 1848 Estimates of the number people who attended at Chartist gather in Kennington Common vary from 20,000 to 50,000. Out of an overabundance of caution, the government called in law enforcement and the military to maintain order.
SOURCE: The Artchives/Alamy Stock Photo

textile-manufacturing industry became thoroughly mechanized and moved into the factory setting during the first half of the century. Far more of the nonrural, nonagricultural workforce consisted of skilled artisans living in cities or small towns. They were attempting to maintain the value of their skills and control over their trades in the face of changing features of production. All these working people faced possible unemployment, with little or no provision for their security, and they confronted the dissolution of many of the traditional social ties of custom and community.

21.2.1 The Emergence of a Wage-Labor Force

During the nineteenth century, artisans as well as factory workers eventually came to participate in a wage-labor force in which their labor became a commodity of the labor marketplace. This process has often been termed **proletarianization**. In the process of becoming wage laborers, artisans gradually lost both significant ownership of the means of production, such as tools and equipment, and control over their trades. The process occurred most rapidly wherever the factory system arose, displacing previous skilled labor. The factory owner provided the financial capital to construct the factory, to purchase the machinery, and to secure the raw materials. The factory workers contributed their labor for a wage. The process could also occur outside the factory setting if a new invention, such as a mechanical printing press, could do the work of several artisans within an urban or rural workshop setting.

Factory workers also had to submit to various kinds of discipline that were always unpopular and difficult to impose. This discipline meant the demands for a smooth operation of machinery largely determined working conditions. Closing of factory gates to late workers, fines for such lateness, dismissal for drunkenness, and public scolding of faulty laborers were attempts to match human discipline with the mechanical regularity of the cables, wheels, and pistons. The factory worker had no direct say about the quality of a product or its price.

For all the difficulties of workers in factory conditions, however, their economic situation was often better than that of textile workers, who resisted the factory mode of production. In particular, English hand-loom weavers, who continued to work in their homes, experienced decades of declining trade and growing poverty in their failing attempt to compete with power looms.

POWER LOOMS Power looms, such as the ones pictured here, mechanized weaving and enabled the mass production of textiles. Because these looms were powered by steam, textile factories were usually located along rivers or seacoasts.
SOURCE: North Wind Picture Archives/Alamy Stock Photo

Urban artisans in the nineteenth century entered the wage-labor force more slowly than factory workers, and machinery had little to do with the process. The emergence of factories in and of itself did not harm urban artisans. Many even prospered from the development. For example, the construction and maintenance of the new machines generated major demand for metalworkers, who consequently did well. The erection of factories and the expansion of cities benefited all craftspeople in the building trades, such as carpenters, roofers, joiners, and masons. The lower prices for machine-made textiles aided artisans involved in making clothing, such as tailors and hatters, by reducing the costs of their raw materials. Where the urban artisans encountered difficulty and where they found their skills and livelihood threatened was in the organization of production.

In the eighteenth century, a European town or city workplace had usually consisted of a few artisans laboring for a master. They labored first as apprentices and then as journeymen, according to established guild regulations and practices. The master owned the workshop and the larger equipment, and the apprentices and journeymen owned their tools. The journeyman could expect eventually to become a master. This guild system had allowed workers to exercise a considerable degree of control over labor recruitment and training, the pace of production, the quality of the product, and its price. The guild functioned to protect the integrity of the craft and the prosperity of the craftsmen.

In the nineteenth century, it became increasingly difficult for artisans to exercise corporate or guild direction and control over their trades. The legislation of the French Revolution had outlawed such organizations in France. Across Europe, political and economic liberals disapproved of labor and guild organizations and attempted to ban them. These thinkers believed guilds raised the price of both labor and products to the disadvantage of owners of capital and consumers.

Other destructive forces were also at work. The masters were under increased competitive pressure from larger, more heavily capitalized establishments, or from the introduction of machine production into a previously craft-dominated industry. In many workshops masters began to follow a practice, known in France as *confection*, whereby goods, such as shoes, clothing, and furniture, were produced in standard sizes and styles rather than by special orders for individual customers.

This practice increased the division of labor in the workshop. Each artisan produced a smaller part of the more-or-less uniform final product. Thus, less skill was required of each artisan, and the particular skills a worker possessed became less valuable. To increase production and reduce costs, masters also tried to lower the wages they paid for piecework. Those attempts often led to work stoppages or strikes. Migrants from the countryside or small towns into the cities created, in some cases, a surplus of relatively unskilled workers. They were willing to work for lower wages or under less favorable and protected conditions than traditional artisans. This situation made it much more difficult for urban journeymen to hope to become masters of their own workshops. Increasingly, these artisans became lifetime wage laborers whose skills were simply bought and sold in the marketplace.

21.2.2 Working-Class Political Action: The Example of British Chartism

By mid-century, such artisans, proud of their skills and frustrated in their social and economic expectations, became the most radical political element in the European working class. From at least the 1830s onward, these artisans took the lead in one country after another in attempting to formulate new ways to protect their social and economic interests.

By the late 1830s, many British workers linked the solution of their economic plight to a program of political reform known as **Chartism**. In 1836, William Lovett (1800–1877) and other London radical artisans formed the London Working Men's Association. In 1838, the group issued the Charter, demanding six specific reforms. The Six Points of the Charter included universal male suffrage, annual election of the House of Commons, the secret ballot, equal electoral districts, and the abolition of property qualifications for and the payment of salaries to members of the House of Commons.

For more than ten years, the Chartists, who were never tightly organized, agitated for their reforms. On three occasions the Charter was presented to Parliament, which refused to pass it. Petitions with millions of signatures were presented to the House of Commons. Strikes were called. The Chartists published a newspaper, the *Northern Star*. Feargus O'Connor (1794–1855), the most important Chartist leader, made speeches across Britain. Despite this vast activity, **Chartism** as a national movement failed. Its ranks were split between those who advocated violence and those who wanted to use peaceful tactics. On the local level, however, the Chartists scored several successes and controlled the city councils in Leeds and Sheffield.

As prosperity returned after the depression of the late 1830s and early 1840s, many working people abandoned the movement. Chartists' demonstrations in 1848 fizzled. Nevertheless, Chartism was the first large-scale European working-class political movement. It had specific goals and largely working-class leadership. Eventually, several of the Six Points became law (for example, the secret ballot was enacted in 1872). Continental working-class observers believed Chartism was the kind of mass movement that workers must eventually adopt if they were to improve their situation.

21.3 Family Structures and the Industrial Revolution

How did industrialization affect European families?

It is more difficult to generalize about the European working-class family structure in the age of early industrialism than under the Old Regime. Industrialism developed at different rates across the Continent, and the impact of industrialism cannot be separated from that of migration and urbanization. Furthermore, industrialism did not touch all families directly; the structures and customs of many peasant families changed little for much of the nineteenth century.

Much more is known about the relationships of the new industry to family in Great Britain than elsewhere. Many of the British developments foreshadowed those in other countries as the factory system spread.

21.3.1 The Family in the Early Factory System

Contrary to what historians and other observers once believed, the adoption of new machinery and factory production did not destroy the working-class family. Before the late-eighteenth-century revolution in textile production in England, the individual family involved in textiles was the chief unit of production. The earliest textile-related inventions, such as the spinning jenny, did not change that situation. The new machine was initially simply brought into the home to spin the thread. It was the mechanization of weaving that led to major changes. Fathers who became machine weavers were then employed in factories, and their work was separated from their homes. Although the departure of fathers for the factory led to changes in family life, the structure of early English factories enabled fathers to preserve certain traditional family roles that had existed before the factory system.

In the domestic system of the family economy, fathers and mothers had worked with their children in textile production as a family unit. They had trained and disciplined the children within the home setting, and their home life and economic life were largely the same. Moreover, in the home setting, wives who worked as spinners might have earned as much or even more than their husbands. Early factory owners and supervisors permitted fathers to employ their wives and children as their assistants. Thus, parental training and discipline could be transferred from the home to the early factory. In some cases, in both Britain and France, entire families would move near a new factory so they could work there as a unit. Despite those accommodations to family life, family members still had to face the new work discipline of the factory setting. Moreover, women assisting their husbands in the factory often did less skilled work than they had in their homes.

A major shift in this family and factory structure began in the mid-1820s in England and had been more or less completed by the mid-1830s. As spinning and weaving were put under one roof, the size of factories and of the machinery grew. These newer machines required fewer skilled operators, but many relatively unskilled attendants. This unskilled labor became the work of unmarried women and children. Factory owners knew these workers would accept lower wages and were less likely than adult men to form worker organizations or unions.

Factory wages for the more skilled adult males, however, were sufficiently high to allow some fathers to remove their children from the factory and send them to school. The children left working in the factories as assistants were often the children of the economically depressed handloom weavers. Most wives of the skilled operatives no longer worked in the factories, so the family connections within the British textile factory that had existed for more than a quarter-century largely disappeared. Men were supervising women and children who did not belong to their families.

21.3.1.1 CONCERN FOR CHILD LABOR At this point in the 1830s, workers became concerned about the plight of child laborers because parents were no longer exercising discipline over their children in the factories. The English Factory Act of 1833 forbade the employment of children under age nine, limited the workday of children aged nine to thirteen to nine hours a day, and required factory owners to pay for two hours of education a day for these children. The effect further divided work and home life. The workday for adults and older teenagers remained twelve hours, while younger children often worked in relays of four or six hours. Consequently, the parental link was thoroughly broken. The education requirement removed nurturing and training from the home and family to schools, where teachers rather than the parents were in charge of education.

By the mid-1840s, the roles of men as breadwinners and as fathers and husbands had become distinct in the British textile industry. Furthermore, reformers' concerns about the working conditions of women in factories and in mines developed in part from the relatively new view that women's place was in the home rather than in an industrial or even agrarian workplace.

21.3.1.2 CHANGING ECONOMIC ROLE FOR THE FAMILY

What occurred in Britain predicted what would happen elsewhere with the spread of industrial capitalism and public education. The European family moved from being the chief unit of both production and consumption to becoming the chief unit of consumption alone. This development did not mean the end of the family as an economic unit. Parents and children, however, came to depend on sharing wages often derived from several sources, rather than on sharing work in the home or factory.

Ultimately, the wage economy meant that families were less closely bound together than in the past. Because wages could be sent over long distances to parents, children might now move farther away from home. Once they moved, the economic link was, in time, often broken. In contrast, when a family settled in an industrial city, the wage economy might, in that or the next generation, discourage children from leaving home as early as they had in the past. Children could find wage employment in the same city and then live at home until they had accumulated enough savings to marry and begin their own household.

WOMEN'S WORK As textile production became increasingly automated in the nineteenth century, textile factories required fewer skilled workers and more unskilled attendants. To fill these unskilled positions, factory owners turned increasingly to unmarried women and widows, who worked for lower wages than men and were less likely to form labor organizations.
SOURCE: Library of Congress

21.4 Women in the Early Industrial Revolution

What role did women play in the Industrial Revolution?

The industrial economy ultimately produced an immense impact on the home and family life of women. First, it eventually took most productive work out of the home and allowed families to live on the wages of the male spouse. That transformation hardened gender-determined roles in the home and in domestic life generally. Women came to be associated with domestic duties, such as housekeeping, food preparation, childrearing and nurturing, and household management, or with poorly paid, largely unskilled cottage industries. Men came to be associated almost exclusively with financial support of the family. Children were raised to conform to these expected gender patterns.

21.4.1 Opportunities and Exploitation in Employment

Because the early Industrial Revolution had begun in textile production, women and their labor were deeply involved from the start. Although both spinning and weaving were still domestic industries, women usually worked in all stages of production. Hand spinning was virtually always a woman's task. At first, when spinning moved into factories and involved large machines, men often displaced women. Furthermore, the higher wages male cotton-factory workers commanded allowed many married women not to work or to work only to supplement their husbands' wages.

21.4.1.1 WOMEN IN FACTORIES

With the next generation of machines in the 1820s, however, unmarried women rapidly became employed in the factories, where they often constituted the majority of workers. Their new jobs often demanded fewer skills than those they had previously exercised in the home production of textiles. Women's factory work also required fewer skills than most work men did. Tending a machine required less skill than spinning or weaving or acting as forewoman. The impact of the factory on women's work was both positive and negative: it opened many new jobs to them but lowered the level of skills they needed to have. The supervisors of women were almost invariably men.

Moreover, almost always, the women in factories were young, single women or widows. Upon marriage or perhaps after the birth of their first child, their husbands earned enough money for them to leave the factory. Sometimes the factory owners, who disliked employing married women because of the likelihood of pregnancy, the influence of their husbands, and the duties of childrearing, no longer wanted them. Widows might return to factory work because they lacked their husbands' former income.

21.4.1.2 WORK ON THE LAND AND IN THE HOME   In Britain and elsewhere by mid-century, industrial factory work still accounted for less than half of all employment for women. The largest group of employed women in France continued to work on the land. In England, they were domestic servants. Throughout Western Europe, domestic cottage industries, such as lace making, glove making, garment making, and other kinds of needlework, employed many women. In almost all cases, their conditions of labor were harsh, whether they worked in their homes or in sweatshops. It cannot be overemphasized that all work by women commanded low wages and involved low skills, and they had no effective modes to protect themselves from exploitation. The charwoman, hired by the day to do rough house cleaning or washing, was a common sight across the Continent and symbolized the plight of working women.

The low wages of female workers in all areas of employment sometimes led them to become prostitutes to supplement their wage income. This situation prevailed across Europe throughout the century. Such sexual exploitation of women was hardly new to European society, but the transformation of the economy from one of skilled artisans to that of unskilled factory workers made many women especially vulnerable.

21.4.2 Changing Expectations in the Working-Class Marriage

Moving to cities and entering the wage economy gave women wider opportunities for marriage. Cohabitation before marriage was not uncommon. Parents had less to do with arranging marriages than in the past. Marriage now usually meant a woman would leave the workforce to live on her husband's earnings. If all went well, that arrangement might improve her situation. If the husband

became ill or died, however, or if he deserted his wife, she would have to reenter the market for unskilled labor at an advanced age.

Despite these changes, many of the traditional practices associated with the family economy survived into the industrial era. As a young woman came of age, both family needs and her desire to marry still directed what she would do with her life. The most likely early occupation for a young woman was domestic service. A girl born in the country normally migrated to a nearby town or city for such employment, often living initially with a relative. As in the past, she would try to earn enough in wages for a dowry, so she might marry and set up her own household. If she became a factory worker, she would probably live in a supervised dormitory. These dormitories helped attract young women to factory work by convincing parents their daughters would be safe.

Marriage in the wage industrial economy was also different in certain respects from marriage in earlier times. It still involved starting a separate household, but the structure of gender relationships within the household was different. Marriage was less an economic partnership, and the husband's wages might well be able to support the entire family. The wage economy and the industrialization separating workplace from home made it difficult for women to combine domestic duties with work. When married women worked, it was usually in the nonindustrial sector of the economy. More often than not, the children rather than the wife were sent to work. This may help explain the increase in the number of births within marriages, as children in the wage economy usually were an economic asset. Married women worked outside the home only when family needs, illness, or widowhood forced them to.

In the home, working-class women were by no means idle. Wives were concerned primarily with food and cooking, but they were also often in charge of the family's finances. The role of the mother expanded when the children still living at home became wage earners. She now provided home support for her entire wage-earning family and created the environment to which the family members returned after work. The longer period of home life of working children may also have increased and strengthened familial bonds of affection between those children and their hardworking homebound mothers. In all these respects, the culture of the working-class marriage and family mirrored the family patterns of the middle and upper classes, whose members had often accepted the view of separate gender spheres proposed by Rousseau and popularized in hundreds of novels, journals, and newspapers.

21.5 Problems of Crime, Order, and Poverty

How did the establishment of police forces and the reform of prisons change society?

Throughout the nineteenth century, the political and economic elite in Europe was profoundly concerned about social order. The revolutions of the late eighteenth and early nineteenth centuries made them fearful of future disorder and threats to life and property. Industrialization and urbanization also contributed to this problem of order. Thousands of Europeans migrated from the countryside to the towns and cities. There, they often encountered poverty or unemployment and general social frustration and disappointment. Cities became associated with criminal activity, especially crimes against property, such as theft and arson. Throughout the first sixty years of the nineteenth century, crime appears to have increased slowly but steadily before reaching a plateau.

Historians and social scientists are divided about the reasons for this rise in the crime rate. So little is known about crime in rural settings that comparisons with the cities are difficult. Moreover, crime statistics in the nineteenth century are problematic. No two nations kept them in the same manner. Different legal codes and systems of judicial administration were in effect in various areas of the Continent, with somewhat different legal definitions of what constituted criminal activity. The result has been confusion, difficult research, and tentative conclusions.

LONDON POLICE OFFICER Professional police forces did not exist before the early nineteenth century. The London police force was created in 1829.
SOURCE: Private CollectionPeter Newark Pictures/Bridgeman Images

21.5.1 New Police Forces

From the propertied, elite classes, two major views about containing crime and criminals emerged during the nineteenth century: better systems of police and prison reform. The result was the triumph in Europe of the idea of a policed society in which a paid, professionally trained group of law-enforcement officers kept order, protected property and lives, investigated crime, and apprehended offenders. These officers were distinct from the army and charged specifically with domestic security. It was to them that the civilian population normally turned for law enforcement. According to the theory of a policed society, the visible presence of law-enforcement officers may prevent crime. These police forces, again at least in theory, did not perform a political role, although many countries ignored that distinction. Police forces also became one of the largest groups of municipal government employees.

Professional police forces did not exist until the early nineteenth century. They differed from one country to another in both authority and organization, but their

creation proved crucial to the emergence of an orderly European society.[1] Professional police forces appeared in Paris in 1828. The next year, the British Parliament passed legislation sponsored by **Sir Robert Peel** (1788–1850) that placed police on London streets. Berlin deployed similar police departments after the Revolution of 1848. All these forces were distinguished by an easily recognizable uniform. Police on the Continent carried guns; those in Britain did not.

Although citizens sometimes viewed police with suspicion, especially in Britain where many opposed the creation of a professional police force as a threat to traditional British liberties, by the end of the century, most Europeans regarded the police as their protectors. Persons from the upper and middle classes felt police made their property more secure. Persons from the working class also frequently turned to the police to protect their lives and property and to aid them in emergencies. Of course, most people hated and feared political or secret police wherever governments, especially in Russia, created them.

21.5.2 Prison Reform

Before the nineteenth century, European prisons were local jails or state prisons, such as the Bastille. Governments also sent criminals to prison ships, called *hulks*. Some Mediterranean nations sentenced prisoners to naval galleys, where, chained to their benches, they rowed until they died or were eventually released. In prisons, inmates lived under wretched conditions. Men, women, and children were housed together. Persons guilty of minor offenses were left in the same room with those guilty of the most serious offenses.

Beginning in the late eighteenth century, the British government sentenced persons convicted of the most serious offenses to transportation. Transportation to the colony of New South Wales in Australia was regarded as an alternative to capital punishment, and the British used it until the mid-nineteenth century, when the colonies began to object. Thereafter, the British government housed long-term prisoners in public works prisons in Britain.

By the close of the eighteenth century and in the early nineteenth century, reformers, such as John Howard (1726–1790) and Elizabeth Fry (1780–1845) in England and Charles Lucas (1803–1889) in France, exposed the horrendous conditions in prisons and demanded change. Reform came slowly because of the expense of constructing new prisons and lack of sympathy for criminals.

In the 1840s, however, both the French and the English undertook several bold efforts at prison reform. These efforts indicated a shift in opinion whereby crime was seen not as an assault on order or on authority but as a mark of a character fault in the criminal. Thereafter, part of the goal of imprisonment was to rehabilitate or transform the prisoner. The result of this change was the creation of exceedingly repressive prison systems designed according to the most advanced scientific modes of understanding criminals and criminal reform.

Europeans used various prison models originally established in the United States. These experiments were based on separating prisoners from each other, with individual cells for each prisoner and long periods of separation and silence among prisoners. The point of the system was to induce self-reflection in which the prisoners would think about their crimes and eventually decide to repudiate their criminal tendencies. As time passed, the prison system became more relaxed because the intense isolation of prisoners often led to their mental collapse.

These attempts to create a police force and to reform prisons illustrate the concern of European political and

PRISON TREADMILLS In many English prisons, treadmills like these were the only source of exercise available to prisoners.
SOURCE: Bpk Bildagentur / Art Resource, NY

social elites about order and stability that developed after the French Revolution. Overall, these efforts succeeded. By the end of the century, an orderly society had been established, and the new police force and prisons had no small role in that development.

21.5.3 Government Policies Based on Classical Economics

The principles of classical economics contributed to cooperation between the middle classes and governments, both of whom were threatened by the demands of the working class for more fundamental change. Louis Philippe (1773–1850) and his minister François Guizot (1787–1874) told the French to go forth and enrich themselves. People who simply displayed sufficient energy need not be poor. A number of the French middle class did just that. The July Monarchy (1830–1848) saw the construction of major capital-intensive projects, such as roads, canals, and railways. Little, however, was done about the poverty in the cities and the countryside.

In the German states, the middle classes also made headway. After the Napoleonic wars, the Prussian reformers had learned that abolishing internal tariffs impeded economic growth. In 1834, all the major German states, except Austria, formed the *Zollverein*, or free trading union. Classical economics was moderated in the German states by the tradition dating from the enlightened absolutism of state direction of economic development.

Britain was the home of the major classical economists, and their policies were widely accepted. The utilitarian thought of **Jeremy Bentham** (1748–1832) increased their influence. Although **utilitarianism** did not originate with him, Bentham sought to create codes of scientific law that were founded on the principle of utility, that is, the greatest happiness for the greatest number. In his *Fragment on Government* (1776) and *The Principles of Morals and Legislation* (1789), Bentham explained the application of the principle of utility would overcome the special interests of privileged groups who prevented rational government. He regarded the existing legal and judicial systems as burdened by traditional practices that harmed the very people the law should serve. The application of reason and utility would remove the legal clutter that prevented justice from being realized. He believed the principle of utility could be applied to other areas of government administration.

Bentham gathered around him political disciples who combined his ideas with those of classical economics. In 1834, the reformed House of Commons passed a new Poor Law that followers of Bentham had prepared. This measure established a Poor Law Commission that set out to make poverty the most undesirable of all social situations.

Government poor relief was to be disbursed only in workhouses. Life in the workhouse was consciously designed to be more unpleasant than life outside. Husbands and wives were separated, the food was bad, and the enforced work was distasteful. The social stigma of the workhouse was even worse. The law and its administration presupposed that people would not work because they were lazy. The laboring class, not unjustly, regarded the workhouses as new "bastilles."

The second British monument to applied classical economics was the repeal of the **Corn Laws** in 1846. The Anti–Corn Law League, organized by manufacturers, had sought this goal for more than six years. The League wanted to abolish the tariffs protecting the domestic price of grain. That change would lead to lower food prices, which would then allow lower wages at no real cost to the workers. In turn, the prices on British manufactured goods could also be lowered to strengthen their competitive position in the world market.

The actual reason for Sir Robert Peel's repeal of the Corn Laws in 1846 was the Irish famine. Peel had to open British ports to foreign grain to feed the starving Irish. He realized the Corn Laws could not be reimposed. Peel accompanied the abolition measure with a program for government aid to modernize British agriculture and to make it more efficient. The repeal of the Corn Laws was the culmination of the lowering of British tariffs that had begun during the 1820s. It marked the beginning of an era of free trade that continued until the twentieth century.

21.6 Early Socialism

How did socialism challenge classical economics?

During the twentieth century, the Socialist movement, in the form of either Communist or Social Democratic political parties, constituted one of the major political forces in Europe. Less than 150 years ago, the advocates of socialism lacked any meaningful political following, and their doctrines confused most of their contemporaries. These early ideas, which for many years appeared on the margins of European political life, assumed great importance in the late nineteenth century and beyond.

The early Socialists generally applauded the new productive capacity of industrialism. They denied, however, that the free market could adequately produce and distribute goods the way the classical economists claimed. In the capitalist order, the Socialists saw primarily mismanagement, low wages, misdistribution of goods, and suffering arising from the unregulated industrial system. Moreover, the Socialists thought human society should be organized as a community, rather than merely as a conglomerate of atomistic, selfish individuals.

21.6.1 Utopian Socialism

Among the earliest people to define the social question was a group of writers whom their critics called the **utopian Socialists**. They were considered utopian because their ideas were often visionary and because they frequently advocated the creation of ideal communities. They were called Socialists because they questioned the structures and values of the existing capitalistic framework. In some cases, they deserved neither description. A significant factor in the experience of almost all these groups was the discussion, and sometimes the practice, of radical ideas about sexuality and the family. People who might have been sympathetic to their economic concerns were profoundly unsympathetic to their views on free love and open family relationships.

21.6.1.1 SAINT-SIMONIANISM Count Claude Henri de Saint-Simon (1760–1825) was the earliest of the Socialist pioneers. Above all else, Saint-Simon believed modern society would require rational management. Private wealth, property, and enterprise, he claimed, should be subject to an administration other than that of its owners. His ideal government would have consisted of a large board of directors organizing and coordinating the activity of individuals and groups to achieve social harmony. Not the *redistribution* of wealth but its *management* by experts would alleviate the poverty and social dislocation of the age.

When Saint-Simon died in 1825, he had persuaded only a handful of people that his ideas were correct. Nonetheless, Saint-Simonian societies were always centers for lively discussion of advanced social ideals. Some of the earliest debates in France over feminism took place within these societies. During the late 1820s and 1830s, the Saint-Simonians became well known for advocating sexuality outside marriage.

21.6.1.2 OWENISM The major British contributor to the early Socialist tradition was **Robert Owen** (1771–1858), a self-made cotton manufacturer. In his early twenties, Owen became a partner in one of the largest cotton factories in Britain at New Lanark, Scotland. Owen was a firm believer in the environmentalist psychology of the Enlightenment inspired by the thought of John Locke. If human beings were placed in the correct surroundings, Owen believed, their character could be improved. Moreover, Owen saw no incompatibility between creating a humane industrial environment and making a good profit.

At New Lanark, Owen put his ideas into practice. Workers were provided with good quarters. Recreational possibilities abounded, and children received an education. There were several churches, although Owen himself was a notorious freethinker on matters of religion and sex. In the factory itself, rewards were given for good work. His plant made a fine profit. Visitors flocked from all over

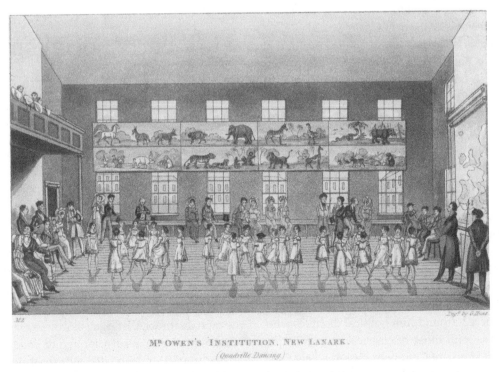

Mᴿ OWEN'S INSTITUTION, NEW LANARK.
(Quadrille Dancing)

NEW LANARK Robert Owen, a Scottish industrialist and early Socialist, created an ideal industrial community at New Lanark, Scotland. He believed deeply in the power of education and ensured that children of workmen were properly educated.
SOURCE: Chronicle/Alamy Stock Photo

Europe to see what Owen had created through enlightened management.

In numerous articles and pamphlets, as well as in letters to influential people, Owen pleaded for a reorganization of industry based on his own successful model. He envisioned a series of communities shaped like parallelograms in which factory workers and farm workers might live together and produce their goods in cooperation. During the 1820s, Owen sold his New Lanark factory and then went to the United States, where he established the community of New Harmony, Indiana. When quarrels among the members led to the community's failure, he refused to give up his reformist causes. He returned to Britain, where he became the moving force behind the organization of the Grand National Union, an attempt to draw all British trade unions into a single body. It collapsed along with other labor organizations during the early 1830s.

21.6.1.3 FOURIERISM Charles Fourier (1772–1837) was Owen's French intellectual counterpart. He was a commercial salesperson who never succeeded in attracting the same kind of public attention as Owen. He wrote his books and articles and waited at home each day at noon, hoping to meet a patron who would undertake his program. No one ever arrived to meet him. Fourier believed the industrial order ignored the passionate side of human nature and that social discipline ignored the pleasures that human beings naturally seek.

Fourier advocated the construction of communities, called *phalanxes*, in which liberated living would replace the boredom and dullness of industrial existence. According to Fourier, agrarian rather than industrial production would predominate in these communities. Sexual activity would be relatively free, and marriage was to be reserved only for later life. Fourier also believed no person should be required to perform the same kind of work for the entire day and that people would be both happier and more productive if they moved from one task to another. Through his emphasis on the problem of boredom, Fourier isolated one of the key difficulties of modern economic life.

Saint-Simon, Owen, and Fourier expected some existing government to carry out their ideas. They failed to confront the political difficulties their envisioned social transformations would arouse. Other figures paid more attention to the politics of the situation. In 1839, Louis Blanc (1811–1882) published *The Organization of Labor*. Like other Socialist writers, this Frenchman demanded an end to competition, but he did not seek a wholly new society. He called for political reform that would give the vote to the working class. Once so empowered, workers could use the vote to turn the political processes to their own economic advantage. A state controlled by a working-class electorate, Blanc claimed, would finance workshops to employ the poor. In time, such workshops might replace private

enterprise, and industry would be organized to ensure jobs. Blanc recognized the power of the state to improve life and the conditions of labor. The state itself could become the great employer of labor.

21.6.2 Anarchism

Other writers and activists of the 1840s, however, rejected both industry and the dominance of government. These were the **anarchists**. Usually included in the Socialist tradition, they do not exactly fit there. Some favored programs of violence and terrorism; others were peaceful. Auguste Blanqui (1805–1881) was a major spokesperson for terror. He spent most of his adult life in jail. Seeking to abolish both capitalism and the state, Blanqui advocated the development of a professional revolutionary vanguard to attack capitalist society. His ideas for the new society were vague, but in his call for professional revolutionaries, he foreshadowed Lenin.

Pierre-Joseph Proudhon (1809–1865) represented the other strain of anarchism. In his most famous work *What Is Property?* (1840), Proudhon attacked the banking system, which rarely extended credit to small-property owners or the poor. He wanted credit expanded to allow such people to engage in economic enterprise that would not involve unfair or unearned profits. Society should be organized, Proudhon believed, on the basis of mutualism, a system of small businesses and other cooperative enterprises with peaceful exchange of goods based on mutual recognition of the labor each area of production required. With such a social system, the state as the protector of property would be unnecessary. Later in the century, anarchists would support a wide variety of cooperative businesses that favored the community good over that of the individual and ensured fair exchange. Proudhon's ideas later influenced the French labor movement, which was less directly political in its activities than the labor movements in Britain and the German states.

21.6.3 Marxism

The mode of Socialist thought that eventually exerted more influence over modern European history than any other was **Marxism**. During the late nineteenth century, its ideas permeated the major continental Socialist parties. With the Bolshevik Revolution of November 1917, Vladimir Lenin's interpretation of Marxist thought came to dominate the Soviet Union and, after World War II, Eastern Europe and revolutionary movements in the colonial and postcolonial world. After the collapse of the Soviet Union and of the Communist governments in Eastern Europe in the last twenty years of the twentieth century, it is difficult for many people to recapture the power that Marx's political and social vision exerted over Europe and other parts of the world for more than a hundred years.

KARL MARX Karl Marx's Communist philosophy became the most widespread of the many varieties of socialism, but his *Manifesto* was subject to varying interpretations, criticisms, and revisions that continue to this day.
SOURCE: Library of Congress

Too often, the history of European socialism has been regarded as a linear development leading naturally or necessarily to the late-nineteenth-century triumph of Marxism within the major Socialist political parties. Nothing could be further from the truth. Marxist ideas came to define what "Socialism" meant to many people but only through competition with other Socialist formulas and largely as a result of the political situation in Germany during the last quarter of the nineteenth century. At mid-century, the ideas of Karl Marx were simply one more contribution to a heady mixture of concepts and programs criticizing the emerging industrial capitalist society. Marxism differed from its competitors in its claims to scientific accuracy, its rejection of liberal reform, its harsh criticism of other contemporary Socialist platforms, and its call for revolution, though the character of that revolution was not well defined. Furthermore, Marx placed the industrial workforce in the context of a world historical development from which he drew sweeping political conclusions.

Karl Marx (1818–1883) was born in the Prussian Rhineland. Marx's middle-class parents sent him to the University of Berlin, where he became deeply involved in Hegelian philosophy and radical politics. Soon the Prussian authorities drove him into exile. He lived in poverty, first in Paris, then in Brussels, and finally, after 1849, in London.

21.6.3.1 PARTNERSHIP WITH ENGELS In 1844, Marx met **Friedrich Engels** (1820–1895), another young middle-class German, whose father owned a textile factory in Manchester, England. The next year Engels published *The Condition of the Working Class in England*, which presented a devastating picture of industrial life. The two men became fast friends. Late in 1847, they were asked to write a pamphlet for a newly organized and ultimately short-lived secret Communist League. *The Communist Manifesto*, published in German, appeared early in 1848. Marx, Engels, and the League had adopted the name *Communist* because it was much more self-consciously radical than Socialist. Communism implied the outright abolition of private property, rather than a less extensive rearrangement of society. Neither Marx nor his thought had any effect on the revolutionary events of 1848, which is discussed more fully later in this chapter. Only later would the *Manifesto*, a work of fewer than fifty pages, earn its status as one of the most influential political tracts in modern European history.

21.6.3.2 SOURCES OF MARX'S IDEAS Marx derived the major ideas of the *Manifesto* and of his later work, including *Capital* (Vol. 1, 1867), from German Hegelianism, French utopian socialism, and British classical economics. Marx applied to concrete historical, social, and economic developments Hegel's abstract philosophical concept that thought develops from the clash of thesis and antithesis into a new intellectual synthesis. For Marx, the conflict between dominant and subordinate social groups led to the emergence of a new dominant social group. These new social relationships, in turn, generated new discontent, conflict, and development. The French **utopian Socialists** had depicted the problems of capitalist society and had raised the issue of property redistribution. Both Hegel and Saint-Simon led Marx to see society and economic conditions as developing through historical stages. The classical economists had provided the analytical tools for an empirical, scientific examination of the industrial capitalist society.

Using the intellectual tools that Hegel, the French utopian Socialists, and the British classical economists provided, Marx developed a philosophy that gave a special role or function to the new industrial workforce as the single most important driving force of contemporary history. Marx later explained to a friend:

What I did that was new was to prove: (1) that the existence of classes is bound up with particular historical phases in the development of production; (2) that the class struggle necessarily leads to the dictatorship of the proletariat; (3) that this dictatorship itself only constitutes the transition to the abolition of all classes and to a classless society.[2]

In *The Communist Manifesto* and his numerous other writings, Marx equated the fate of the proletariat—that is, the new industrial labor force—with the fate of humanity itself. According to Marx, as the proletariat came to liberate itself from its bondage to the capitalist mode of industrial production, it would eventually lead to the liberation of all humanity. It was this utopian vision of human emancipation, no matter how much the later development of the European and world economy failed to conform to Marx's predictions, that drew people from Europe and elsewhere to embrace Marx's thought and to base their political actions on their understanding of his philosophy. Besides this wider vision, however, the details of Marx's argument were also important for later nineteenth-century and twentieth-century European political life.

21.6.3.3 REVOLUTION THROUGH CLASS CONFLICT In
The Communist Manifesto, Marx and Engels contended that human history must be understood rationally and as a whole. History, they believed, is the record of humankind's coming to grips with physical nature to produce the goods necessary for survival. That basic productive process determines the structures, values, and ideas of a society. Historically, the organization of the means of production has always involved conflict between the classes that owned and controlled the means of production and the classes that worked for them. That necessary conflict has provided the engine for historical development; it is not an accidental by-product of mismanagement or bad intentions. Thus, piecemeal reforms cannot eliminate the social and economic evils inherent in the very structures of production. To achieve that, a radical social transformation is required. The development of capitalism will make such a revolution inevitable.

In Marx's and Engels's eyes, the class conflict that had characterized previous Western history had become simplified during the early nineteenth century into a struggle between the bourgeoisie and the proletariat, or between the middle class associated with industry and commerce, on the one hand, and the workers, on the other. The character of capitalism itself ensured the sharpening of the struggle. Capitalist production and competition would steadily increase the size of the unpropertied proletariat. As this ever-expanding body of workers suffered increasingly from the competition among the ever-enlarging firms, Marx contended, they would eventually begin to foment revolution. Finally, they would overthrow the few remaining owners of the means of production. For a time, the workers would organize the means of production through a dictatorship of the proletariat. This would eventually give way to a propertyless and classless Communist society.

This proletarian revolution was inevitable, according to Marx and Engels. The structure of capitalism required

competition and consolidation of enterprise. Although the class conflict involved in the contemporary process resembled that of the past, it differed in one major respect: The struggle between the capitalistic bourgeoisie and the industrial proletariat would culminate in a wholly new society that would be free of class conflict. The victorious proletariat, by its very nature, could not be a new oppressor class: "The proletarian movement is the self-conscious, independent movement of the immense majority, in the interest of the immense majority."[3] The result of the proletarian victory would be "an association in which the free development of each is the condition for the free development of all."[4] The victory of the proletariat over the bourgeoisie would represent the culmination of human history. For the first time in human history, one group of people would not be oppressing another.

The economic environment of the 1840s had conditioned Marx's analysis. The decade had seen much unemployment and deprivation. During the later part of the century, however, European and American capitalism did not collapse as he had predicted, nor did the middle class become proletarianized. Rather, the industrial system benefited more and more people. Nonetheless, within a generation of the publication of *The Communist Manifesto*, Marxism had captured the imagination of many Socialists, especially in German-speaking Europe, and large segments of the working class. Marxist doctrines appeared to be based on the empirical evidence of hard economic fact. Marxism's scientific claim helped spread the ideology as science became more influential during the second half of the century. At its core, however, the ideology's attraction was its utopian vision of ultimate human liberation, no matter how illiberal or authoritarian the governments embracing the Marxist vision in the twentieth century were.

21.7 1848: Year of Revolutions

Why did a series of revolutions erupt across Europe in 1848?

In 1848, a series of liberal and nationalist revolutions erupted across the Continent. (See Map 21-2.) No single factor caused this general revolutionary groundswell; rather, similar conditions existed in several countries. Severe food shortages had prevailed since 1846, and grain and potato harvests had been poor. The famine in Ireland was simply the worst example of a more widespread situation. The commercial and industrial economy was also depressed. Unemployment was widespread, and systems of poor relief were overburdened. These difficulties, added to the wretched living conditions in the cities and

Map 21-2 CENTERS OF REVOLUTION, 1848–1849

The revolution that toppled the July Monarchy in Paris in 1848 soon spread to Austria and many of the other German and Italian states. Yet by the end of 1849, most of these uprisings had been suppressed.

liberals, who were generally drawn from the middle classes. Throughout the Continent, liberals were pushing for their program of a more representative government, civil liberty, and unregulated economic life. The repeal of the English Corn Laws and the example of peaceful agitation by the Anti–Corn Law League encouraged them. The liberals on the Continent wanted to pursue similar peaceful tactics. To put additional pressure on their governments, however, they appealed for the support of the urban working classes. The latter, however, wanted improved working and economic conditions, rather than a more liberal government. Moreover, their tactics were frequently violent rather than peaceful. The temporary alliance of liberals and workers in several states overthrew or severely shook the old order; then the allies began to fight each other.

Finally, outside France, nationalism was an important common factor in the uprisings. Germans, Hungarians, Italians, Czechs, and smaller national groups in Eastern Europe sought to either create independent national states that would reorganize or replace existing political entities or, in some cases, achieve substantial national autonomy within larger empires. This brought them into conflict not only with existing states but also with other nationalist movements. The Austrian Empire, as usual, was the state most profoundly endangered by nationalism.

The immediate results of the 1848 revolutions were stunning. Never in a single year had Europe known so many major uprisings. The French monarchy fell, and other thrones were shaken. Yet the revolutions proved to be a false spring for progressive Europeans. Without exception, the revolutions failed to establish genuinely liberal or national states. The conservative order proved stronger and more resilient than anyone had expected. The liberals refused to follow political revolution with social reform and thus isolated themselves from the working classes. Once separated from potential mass support, the liberal revolutions became easy prey for the armies of the reactionary classes.

increasing doubts about the capabilities of various rulers, heightened the frustration and discontent of the urban artisan and laboring classes. People expected their governments to intervene to alleviate the economic crisis. Government inaction, because of a principled opposition to intervention or confusion about what policies would help, fueled popular anger and a loss of faith in the wisdom and legitimacy of rule.

The dynamic force for change in 1848 originated, however, not with the working classes, but with the political

21.7.1 France: The Second Republic and Louis Napoleon

As had happened twice before, the revolutionary tinder first blazed in Paris. The liberal political opponents of the corrupt regime of Louis Philippe and his minister François Guizot organized a series of political banquets. They used these occasions to criticize the government and demand a further role for them and their middle-class supporters in the political process. The poor harvests of 1846 and 1847 and the resulting high food prices and unemployment brought working-class support to the liberal campaign. On February 21, 1848, the government forbade further banquets. On February 22, disgruntled Parisian workers paraded through the streets demanding reform and Guizot's ouster. The next morning the crowds grew, and by afternoon, Guizot had resigned. The crowds erected barricades, and numerous clashes occurred between the citizenry and the municipal guard. On February 24, 1848, Louis Philippe abdicated and fled to England.

21.7.1.1 THE NATIONAL ASSEMBLY AND PARIS WORKERS
The liberal opposition, led by the poet Alphonse de Lamartine (1790–1869), organized a provisional government. The liberals intended to call an election for an assembly that would write a republican constitution. The various working-class groups in Paris, however, had other ideas: They wanted a social as well as a political revolution. Led by Louis Blanc, they demanded representation in the cabinet. Blanc and two other radical leaders became ministers. Under their pressure, the provisional government organized national workshops to provide work and relief for thousands of unemployed workers.

On Sunday, April 23, an election based on universal male suffrage chose the new National Assembly. The result was a legislature dominated by moderates and conservatives. In the French provinces, many people resented the Paris radicals and were frightened by their ideas. The church and the local notables still exercised considerable influence. Peasants feared that Parisian Socialists would confiscate their small farms. The new conservative National Assembly showed little support for the expensive national workshops, which they incorrectly perceived to be Socialistic.

Throughout May, government troops and the unemployed workers and artisans of Paris clashed. As a result, the assembly closed the workshops to new entrants and planned to eject many enrolled workers. By late June, barricades again appeared in Paris. On June 24, under orders from the government, General Louis Cavaignac (1802–1857), with troops drawn largely from the conservative countryside, moved to destroy the barricades and quell disturbances. During the next two days, more than 400 people were killed. Thereafter, troops hunted down another 3,000 persons in street fighting. The drive for social revolution had ended.

21.7.1.2 EMERGENCE OF LOUIS NAPOLEON
The so-called June Days confirmed the political predominance of conservative property holders in French life. They wanted a state that was safe for small property. Late in 1848, the election for president confirmed this search for social order. The new president was **Louis Napoleon Bonaparte** (1808–1873), a nephew of the great emperor. After the corruption of Louis Philippe and the turmoil of the early months of the Second Republic, the voters turned to the name of Bonaparte as a source of stability and greatness.

THE FRENCH REVOLUTION OF 1848 During the February days of the French Revolution of 1848, crowds in Paris burned the throne of Louis Philippe.
SOURCE: Bpk Bildagentur/Art Resource, NY

(See the "Compare and Connect" sidebar, which follows below, and consider the rise of Louis Napoleon along with the hopes that many in France had had for an enduring democratic regime.)

The election of the "Little Napoleon" doomed the Second Republic. Louis Napoleon was dedicated to his own fame rather than to republican institutions. He was the first of the modern dictators who, by playing on unstable politics and social insecurity, changed European life. He quarreled with the National Assembly and claimed that he, rather than they, represented the will of the nation. In 1851, the assembly refused to amend the constitution to allow the president to run for reelection. Consequently, on December 2, 1851, the anniversary of the great Napoleon's victory at Austerlitz, Louis Napoleon seized power. Troops dispersed the assembly, and the president called for new elections. More than 200 people died resisting the coup, and more than 26,000 persons were arrested throughout the country. Almost 10,000 persons who opposed the coup were transported to Algeria.

Yet, in the plebiscite of December 21, 1851, more than 7.5 million voters supported the actions of Louis Napoleon and approved a new constitution that consolidated his power. Only about 600,000 citizens dared to vote against him. A year later, in December 1852, an empire was proclaimed, and Louis Napoleon became Emperor Napoleon III. Again a plebiscite approved the action. For the second time in just over fifty years, France had turned from republicanism to Caesarism.

21.7.1.3 FRENCHWOMEN IN 1848

The years between the February Revolution of 1848 and the Napoleonic coup of 1851 saw major feminist activity by Frenchwomen. Especially in Paris, women used the collapse of the July Monarchy as an opportunity to voice demands for reform of their social conditions. They joined the wide variety of political clubs that emerged in the wake of the revolution. Some of these clubs emphasized women's rights. Some women even tried unsuccessfully to vote in the elections of 1848. Both middle-class and working-class women were involved in these activities. The most radical group of women called themselves the Vesuvians, after the volcano in Italy, and claimed the demands of women would erupt like pent-up lava. They demanded full domestic household equality between men and women, the right of women to serve in the military, and similarity in dress for both sexes. They also conducted street demonstrations. The radical character of their demands and actions lost them the support of more moderate women.

Certain Parisian women quickly attempted to use for their own cause the liberal freedoms that suddenly had become available. They organized the *Voix des femmes* (*The Women's Voice*), a daily newspaper that addressed issues of concern to women. The newspaper insisted that improving the lot of men would not necessarily improve the condition of women. They soon organized a society with the same name as the newspaper. Members of the *Voix des femmes* group were relatively

Compare and Connect

From Republic to Empire, Again

THE SWIFT FALL OF THE CORRUPT government of Louis Philippe convinced many reformers that the time had come to complete the work begun during the French Revolution. They would bring about a new order in France but would avoid the mistakes of their illustrious predecessors. This time, France would not descend into terror and dictatorship. But just eight months after the founding of the Second Republic, Louis Napoleon would win the presidency, and three years after that, France would once again be ruled by a single man. The excerpts included below reflect the optimism that initially surrounded the founding of the Second Republic and the ease with which Louis Napoleon convinced French voters to support the nephew of an emperor.

LOUIS NAPOLEON AFTER THE END OF THE SECOND REPUBLIC In the presidential election of December 1848, Louis Napoleon would emerge victorious. Later, to retain power, he staged a coup and became emperor.
SOURCE: De Agostini/G. Dagli Orti/Getty Images

Before Reading

- Consider the ways that memories of the French Revolution shaped the events of 1848.
- Think about the place of Napoleon Bonaparte in French historical memory.
- Think about the role of Paris in the revolutions of 1789 and 1848.

Questions

1. What claims are made by the authors of the proclamation of the Second Republic?
2. What connections do the authors of the proclamation make between their actions and those of earlier generations of revolutionaries?
3. How did Louis Napoleon try to assuage the concerns of French republicans?

I. PROCLAMATION OF THE SECOND FRENCH REPUBLIC (February 1848)

In the name of the French people:
Citizens: royalty, under whatever form, is abolished; no more legitimism [political legitimacy based on a claim to the throne by direct descent], no more Bonapartism, no regency.

The provisional government has taken all the measures necessary to render impossible the return of the former dynasty or the advent of a new dynasty.

The republic is proclaimed.

The people are united.

All the forts which surround the capital are ours.

The brave garrison of Vincennes is a garrison of brothers.

Let us retain that old republican flag whose three colors made with our fathers the circuit of the globe.

Let us show that this symbol of equality, of liberty, and of fraternity is at the same time the symbol of order—of order the more real, the more durable, since justice is its foundation and the whole people its instrument.

The people have already realized that the provisioning of Paris requires a freer circulation in the streets, and those who have erected the barricades have already in several places made openings large enough for the passage of wagons and carts. Let this example be imitated everywhere. Let Paris reassume its accustomed appearance and trade its activity and confidence. . . .

II. LOUIS NAPOLEON TO HIS FELLOW CITIZENS (November 1848)

In order to recall me from exile, you have elected me a representative of the people; on the eve of choosing a chief magistrate for the republic my name presents itself to you as a symbol of order and security.

Those proofs of so honorable a confidence are, I am well aware, addressed to my name rather than to myself, who, as yet, have done nothing for my country; but the more the memory of the Emperor protects me and inspires your suffrages, the more I feel compelled to acquaint you with my sentiments and principles. There must be no equivocation between us.

I am moved by no ambition which dreams one day of empire and war, the next of the application of subversive theories. Brought up in free countries, disciplined in the school of misfortune, I shall ever remain faithful to the duties which your suffrages and the will of the Assembly impose upon me.

If elected president, I shall shrink from no danger, from no sacrifice, in the defense of society, which has been so outrageously assailed. I shall devote myself wholly and without reservation to the consolidation of the republic, so that it may be wise in its laws, honest in its aims, great and strong in its deeds. My greatest honor would be to hand on to my successor, after four years of office, the public power consolidated, its liberties intact, and a genuine progress assured. . . .

SOURCES: (I) James Harvey Robinson, ed.. *Readings in European History*, vol. II (Boston: Ginn and Company, 1906), p. 561. (II) James Harvey Robinson, ed., *Readings in European History*, vol. II (Boston: Ginn and Company, 1906), p. 562.

---

conservative feminists. They cooperated with male political groups, and they urged the integrity of the family and fidelity in marriage. They furthermore warmly embraced the maternal role of women but tried to use it to raise the importance of women in society. Because motherhood and childrearing are so important to a society, they argued, women must receive better education, economic security, equal civil rights, property rights, and the rights to work and vote. The provisional government made no move to enact these rights, although some members of the assembly supported the women's groups. The emphasis on family and motherhood represented, in part, a defensive strategy to prevent conservatives from accusing advocates of women's rights of seeking to destroy the family and traditional marriage.

The fate of French feminists in 1848 was similar to that of the radical workers. They were thoroughly defeated and their efforts wholly frustrated. Once the elections were held that spring, the new government expressed no sympathy for their causes. The closing of the national workshops adversely affected women workers as well as men and blocked one outlet that women had used to make their needs known. The conservative crackdown on political clubs closed another arena in which women had participated. Women were soon specifically forbidden to participate in political clubs either by themselves or with men. These repressive actions repeated what had happened to politically active French-women and their organizations in 1793.

At this point, women associated with the *Voix des femmes* attempted to organize workers' groups to improve the economic situation for working-class women. Two leaders of this effort, Jeanne Deroin (d. 1894) and Pauline Roland (1805–1852), were arrested, tried, and imprisoned for these activities. The former eventually left France; the latter was sent off to Algeria during the repression after the coup of Louis Napoleon. By 1852, the entire feminist movement that had sprung up in 1848 had been eradicated.

21.7.2 The Habsburg Empire: Nationalism Resisted

The events of February 1848 in Paris immediately reverberated throughout the Habsburg domains. The empire was susceptible to revolutionary challenge on every score. Its government rejected liberal institutions. Its borders cut across national lines that more people found meaningful than ever before. Its society perpetuated serfdom. In 1848, the regime confronted rebellions in Vienna, Prague, Hungary, and its Italian holdings. The disturbances that broke out in many German cities also threatened Habsburg predominance. In the initial months, rebels appeared to work together in their demands for reform. By the fall, however, fundamental differences in their priorities became apparent. While some demands focused on national autonomy, others concerned liberal political priorities, like a constitution. Workers' interest in radical social and economic change was not shared by liberal revolutionaries.

21.7.2.1 THE VIENNA UPRISING

The Habsburg troubles began on March 3, 1848, when **Louis Kossuth** (1802–1894), a Hungarian nationalist and member of the Hungarian diet, attacked Austrian domination, called for the independence of Hungary, and demanded a responsible ministry under the Habsburg dynasty. Ten days later, inspired by Kossuth's speeches, students led a series of disturbances in Vienna. The army failed to restore order. Metternich resigned and fled the country. The feeble-minded Emperor Ferdinand (r. 1835–1848) promised a moderately liberal constitution. Unsatisfied, the radical students then formed democratic clubs to press the revolution further. On May 17, the emperor and the imperial court fled to Innsbruck. The government of Vienna at this point lay in the hands of a committee of more than 200 persons concerned primarily with alleviating the economic plight of the city's workers.

What the Habsburg government most feared was not the urban rebellions but an uprising of the serfs in the countryside. Already a few serfs had invaded manor houses and burned property records. Consequently, almost immediately after the Vienna uprising, the imperial government emancipated the serfs in much of Austria. The Hungarian diet also abolished serfdom in March 1848. These actions smothered the most serious potential threat to order in the empire. The emancipated serfs now had little reason to support the revolutionary movement in the cities. These emancipations were one of the most important permanent results of the revolutions of 1848.

21.7.2.2 THE HUNGARIAN REVOLT

The Vienna revolt had emboldened the Hungarians. The Hungarian leaders of the March Revolution were primarily liberals supported by nobles who wanted their aristocratic liberties guaranteed against the central government in Vienna. The Hungarian diet passed the March Laws, which mandated equality of religion, jury trials, the election of the lower chamber of the diet, a relatively free press, and payment of taxes by the nobility. Emperor Ferdinand approved these measures because in the spring of 1848 he could do little else.

Hungarian nationalists also hoped to establish a separate Hungarian state within the Habsburg domains. They would exercise local autonomy while Ferdinand remained their emperor. As part of this scheme for a partially independent state, the Hungarians attempted to annex Transylvania, Croatia, and other eastern territories of the Habsburg Empire. That annexation would have brought Romanians, Croatians, and Serbs under Hungarian government. These national groups resisted the drive toward Magyarization (based on the Hungarian word for Hungarian, *Magyar*), especially the imposition on them, for the purposes of the government and administration, of the Hungarian language. The national groups whom the Hungarians were now repressing believed the Habsburgs offered them a better chance to preserve their national or ethnic identity, their languages, and their economic self-interest. In late March, the Vienna government sent Count Josip Jelačić (1801–1859) to aid the national groups who were rebelling against the rebellious Hungarians. By early September 1848, he invaded Hungary with the support of the national groups who were resisting Magyarization. These events in Hungary represented a prime example of the clash between liberalism and

A CALL FOR HUNGARIAN INDEPENDENCE FROM AUSTRIA In this image, Louis Kossuth, a Hungarian nationalist, calls for troops to fight for Hungarian independence during the revolutionary disturbances of 1848.
SOURCE: Bpk Bildagentur/Art Resource, NY

nationalism. The Hungarian March Laws would have created a state that was liberal in political structure but would not have allowed autonomy to non-Hungarian-speaking peoples within Hungary's borders.

21.7.2.3 CZECH NATIONALISM In mid-March 1848, with Vienna and Budapest in revolt, Czech nationalists demanded that the Czech provinces of Bohemia and Moravia be permitted to constitute an autonomous Slavic state within the empire similar to that just enacted in Hungary. Conflict immediately developed, however, between the Czechs and the Germans living in these regions. The Czechs summoned a congress of Slavs, including Poles, Ruthenians, Czechs, Slovaks, Croats, Slovenes, and Serbs, which met in Prague in early June. Under the leadership of František (Francis) Palacky (1798–1876), this first Pan-Slavic Congress called for the national equality of Slavs within the Habsburg Empire. The manifesto also protested the repression of all Slavic peoples under Habsburg, Hungarian, German, and Ottoman domination. It did not, however, call for the full political independence of the Slavic nations. **František Palacky** was convinced that the Czechs, Poles, and other Slavs were too small and weak to defend themselves against an aggressive Russia. But if **Pan-Slavism** were allowed to develop enough to create a vast east European Slavic nation or federation of Slavic states that would extend from Poland south and eastward through Ukraine, it was clear that Russian interests would surely dominate it. Although such a state never came into being, the prospect of a unified Slavic people freed from Ottoman, Habsburg, and German control was an important political factor in later European history. Despite the fear many non-Russian Slavs had of Russia, Russia would use Pan-Slavism as a tool to attempt to gain the support of nationalist minorities in Eastern Europe and the Balkans and to bring pressure against both the Habsburg Empire and Germany.

On June 12, the day the Pan-Slavic Congress closed, a radical insurrection broke out in Prague. General Prince Alfred Windischgraetz (1787–1862), whose wife had been killed by a stray bullet, moved his troops against the uprising. The Prague middle class was happy to see the radicals suppressed, which was finalized by June 17. The Germans in the area approved the smothering of Czech nationalism. The policy of "divide and conquer" had succeeded.

21.7.2.4 REBELLION IN NORTHERN ITALY While repelling the Hungarian and Czech bids for autonomy, the Habsburg government also faced war in northern Italy. A revolt against Habsburg domination began in Milan on March 18. Five days later, Austrian commander General Count Joseph Wenzel Radetzky (1766–1858) retreated from the city. King Charles Albert of Piedmont (r. 1831–1849), who wanted to annex Lombardy (the province of which Milan is the capital), aided the rebels. The Austrian forces fared badly until July, when Radetzky, reinforced by new

troops, defeated Piedmont and suppressed the revolt. For the time being, Austria held its position in northern Italy.

Vienna and Hungary remained to be recaptured. In midsummer, the emperor returned to the capital. A newly elected assembly was trying to write a constitution, and within the city, the radicals continued to press for concessions. The imperial government decided to reassert its control. When a new insurrection occurred in October, the imperial army bombarded Vienna and crushed the revolt. On December 2, Emperor Ferdinand, clearly too feeble to govern, abdicated in favor of his young nephew Francis Joseph (r. 1848–1916). Real power now lay with Prince Felix Schwarzenberg (1800–1852), who intended to use the army with full force.

On January 5, 1849, troops occupied Budapest. By March the triumphant Austrian forces had imposed military rule over Hungary, and the new emperor repudiated the recent constitution. The Hungarian nobles attempted one last revolt. In August, Austrian troops, reinforced by 200,000 soldiers that Tsar Nicholas I of Russia (r. 1825–1855) happily furnished, finally crushed the Hungarians. Croatians and other nationalities that had resisted Magyarization welcomed the collapse of the revolt. The imperial Habsburg government survived its gravest internal challenge because of the divisions among its enemies and its willingness to use military force with a vengeance.

21.7.3 Italy: Republicanism Defeated

The brief war between Piedmont and Austria in 1848 marked only the first stage of the Italian revolution. Many Italians hoped King Charles Albert of Piedmont would drive Austria from the peninsula and thus prepare the way for Italian unification. The defeat of Piedmont was a sharp disappointment to them. Liberal and nationalist hopes then shifted to the pope. Pius IX (r. 1846–1878) had a liberal reputation. He had reformed the administration of the Papal States. Nationalists believed a united Italian state might emerge under his leadership.

In Rome, however, as in other cities, political radicalism was on the rise. On November 15, 1848, a democratic radical assassinated Count Pelligrino Rossi (r. 1787–1848), the liberal minister of the Papal States. The next day, popular demonstrations forced the pope to appoint a radical ministry. Shortly thereafter, Pius IX fled to Naples for refuge. In February 1849, the radicals proclaimed the Roman Republic. Republican nationalists from all over Italy, including Giuseppe Mazzini (1805–1872) and Giuseppe Garibaldi (1807–1882), two of the most prominent, flocked to Rome. They hoped to use the new republic as a base of operations to unite the rest of Italy under a republican government.

In March 1849, radicals in Piedmont forced Charles Albert to renew the patriotic war against Austria. After the almost immediate defeat of Piedmont at the Battle of Novara, the king abdicated in favor of his son, Victor Emmanuel II

(r. 1849–1878). The defeat meant the Roman Republic must defend itself alone. The troops that attacked Rome and restored the pope came from France. The French wanted to prevent the rise of a strong, unified state on their southern border. Moreover, protection of the pope was good domestic politics for the French Republic and its president, Louis Napoleon. In early June 1849, 10,000 French soldiers laid siege to Rome. By the end of the month, the Roman Republic had dissolved.

Garibaldi attempted to lead an army north against Austria, but he was defeated. On July 3, Rome fell to the French forces, which stayed there to protect the pope until 1870.

Pius IX renounced his liberalism. He became one of the arch conservatives of the next quarter-century. Leadership for Italian unification would have to come from another direction. (See the "Encountering the Past" sidebar on the role of opera in the drive for Italian unification, which follows below.)

Encountering the Past

Opera and Italian Nationalism

THE NINETEENTH CENTURY SAW a surge in the popularity of opera. As audiences expanded to include the fast-growing middle classes, singers and composers competed for public acclaim and for the financial rewards and career opportunities such fame could produce. This dynamic led to a shift in the subject matter of European opera. Composers whose artistic and political sensibilities meshed with those of the public tended to have the most success. It was in this context that opera became intertwined with nineteenth-century nationalism.

VIVA VERDI In 1859, the year this print was produced, the slogan "Viva Verdi" was used to show support for unification of Italy under the rule of Victor Emmanuel, then king of Sardinia. The slogan was an acronym for *Viva Victor Emmanuel, Re D'Italia* ("Long Live Victor Emmanuel, King of Italy").
SOURCE: Music-Images/Alamy Stock Photo

Composers whose artistic and political sensibilities were the most attuned to those of the public tended to have the greatest success. Giuseppe Verdi's career provides an example. He was born in 1813 in the duchy of Parma. At the time, Parma was controlled by Napoleon's army, but after Napoleon's defeat, Italy faced more decades of Austrian rule. It was against this historical background that Verdi began composing operas in the 1830s.

Verdi enjoyed little initial success. His first opera, *Oberto*, was performed only thirteen times before it closed. His second was staged but once. In 1841, however, Verdi began working on a new opera that would catapult him to international fame and make him a symbol of Italian national ambitions. *Nabucco*, which premiered in 1842, told the story of the suffering of the Hebrews living in exile under the Babylonian king Nebuchadrezzar. In the opera's most famous chorus, the "Chorus of the Hebrew Slaves," the Hebrews express their anguish over the loss of their homeland. For Italian audiences, the true meaning of the story was clear. They were the ancient Hebrews and the Austrian emperor was Nebuchadrezzar. The chorus would become an anthem for Italian patriots throughout the 1840s and 1850s.

While Verdi's direct involvement in nationalist politics was limited, over the course of his career he became a symbol of Italian independence and a source of great pride for Italian nationalists. When Verdi died in 1901 in Milan, the Italian parliament mourned him as an Italian hero and the embodiment of Italy's culture and spirit. Shops and theaters in Milan were closed for three days. As Verdi's funeral procession made its way through the streets of the city, the crowds broke into the "Chorus of the Hebrew Slaves."

Questions

1. How was opera affected by larger social and political developments in the nineteenth century?

21.7.4 The German Confederation: Liberalism Frustrated

The revolutionary contagion had also spread rapidly through the German states. Insurrections calling for liberal government and greater German unity erupted in Wurtemburg, Saxony, Hanover, and Bavaria where King Ludwig I (r. 1825–1848) was forced to abdicate in favor of his son. The major revolution, however, occurred in Prussia. Prussia's king, Frederick William IV (r. 1840–1861), had long opposed the introduction of any constitution.

21.7.4.1 REVOLUTION IN PRUSSIA By March 15, 1848, large popular disturbances had erupted in Berlin. **Frederick William IV**, believing the trouble stemmed from foreign conspirators, refused to turn his troops on the Berliners. He even announced limited reforms. Nevertheless, on March 18, several citizens were killed when troops cleared a square near the palace.

The monarch was still hesitant to use his troops forcefully, and the government was divided and confused. The king called for a Prussian constituent assembly to write a constitution. The next day, as angry Berliners crowded around the palace, Frederick William IV appeared on the balcony to salute the corpses of his slain subjects. He made further concessions and implied that henceforth Prussia would help unify Germany. For all practical purposes, the Prussian monarchy had capitulated.

Frederick William IV appointed a cabinet headed by David Hansemann (1790–1864), a widely respected moderate liberal. The Prussian constituent assembly, however, proved to be radical and democratic. As time passed, the king and his conservative supporters decided to ignore the assembly. The liberal ministry resigned, and a conservative one replaced it. In April 1849, the assembly was dissolved, and the monarch proclaimed his own constitution. One of its key elements was a system of three-class voting.

21.7.4.2 THE FRANKFURT PARLIAMENT While Prussia was moving from revolution to reaction, other events were unfolding in the German Confederation. On May 18, 1848, representatives from all the German states gathered in Saint Paul's Church in Frankfurt to revise the organization of the German Confederation. The Frankfurt Parliament intended to write a moderately liberal constitution for a united Germany. The liberal character of the Frankfurt Parliament alienated both German conservatives and the German working class. The very existence of the parliament, representing a challenge to the existing political order, offended the conservatives. The Frankfurt Parliament's refusal to restore the protection of the guilds cost it the support of the industrial workers and artisans. The liberals were too attached to the concept of a free labor market to offer meaningful legislation to workers. This failure marked the beginning of a profound split between German liberals and the German working class. For the rest of the century, German conservatives would be able to exploit that division.

The Frankfurt Parliament also floundered on the issue of unification. Members differed over whether to include Austria in a united Germany. The "large German [*grossdeutsch*] solution" favored Austria's inclusion, whereas the "small German [*kleindeutsch*] solution" advocated its exclusion. Although it was an uncle of the Austrian emperor, Archduke John, who was asked to be regent of the German nation, the rest of the Habsburg dynasty rejected the notion of German unification, which raised too many other nationality problems within the Habsburg domains. Consequently, the Frankfurt Parliament looked to Prussian, rather than Austrian, leadership.

On March 27, 1849, the parliament produced its constitution. Shortly thereafter, its delegates offered the crown of a united Germany to Frederick William IV of Prussia. He rejected the offer, referring to the crown as a "dog collar" and asserting that kings ruled by the grace of God rather than by the permission of man-made constitutions. Upon his refusal, the Frankfurt Parliament began to dissolve. Not long afterward, troops drove off the remaining members.

German liberals never fully recovered from this defeat. The Frankfurt Parliament had alienated the artisans and the working class without gaining any compensating support from the conservatives. The liberals had proved to be awkward, hesitant, unrealistic, and ultimately dependent on the armies of the monarchies. They had failed to unite Germany or to confront effectively the realities of political power in the German states. The various revolutions did manage to extend the franchise in some of the German states and to establish conservative constitutions. These gains were not negligible, but they were a far cry from the hopes of March 1848.

The Chapter in Perspective

The first half of the nineteenth century brought unprecedented social change to Europe. The foundations of the industrial economy were laid. That emerging economy changed virtually every existing institution. Railways crossed the Continent. New consumer goods became available. Family patterns changed, as did the social and economic expectations of women. The crowding of cities presented new social and political problems. The new concern about crime and the establishment of police forces brought issues of social order to the foreground. An urban working class became one of the chief facts of both political and social life. The ebb and flow of the business cycle increased economic anxiety for workers and property owners alike.

While all these fundamental social changes took place, Europe was also experiencing continuing political strife. The turmoil of 1848 through 1850 ended the era of liberal revolution that had begun in 1789. Liberals and nationalists discovered that rational argument and small, local insurrections would not achieve their goals. The political initiative passed for a time to the conservative political groups. Henceforth, nationalists were less romantic and more hardheaded. Railways, commerce, guns, soldiers, and devious diplomacy, rather than language and cultural heritage, became the future weapons of national unification. The working class also adopted new tactics and a new organization. The era of the riot and urban insurrection was ending; in the future, workers would turn to trade unions and political parties to achieve their political and social goals.

Perhaps most importantly after 1848, the European middle class ceased to be revolutionary. It became increasingly concerned about protecting its property against radical political and social movements associated with socialism and, as the century passed, with Marxism. The middle class remained politically liberal only as long as liberalism seemed to promise economic stability and social security for its own style of life.

Finally, the revolutions of 1848 also changed European conservatism. Metternich's conservative policies had not prevented the upheavals of 1848. In the following decades, European conservatives would find new ways to adapt some of the new forces of European politics to their ends. They would embrace their own forms of nationalism and even democratic structures to ensure that they remained dominant over much of Europe.

The Chapter in Review

Review Questions

1. What inventions were particularly important in the development of industrialism? How did industrialism change society? Why was industrialism so difficult for artisans? How was the European labor force transformed into a wage-labor workforce?

2. How did the industrial economy change the working-class family? What roles and duties did various family members assume? How did the role of women change in the new industrial era?

3. What were the goals of the working class in the new industrial society, and how did they differ from middle-class goals? Why did the working class and the middle class pursue different goals?

4. Why did European states create police forces in the nineteenth century? How and why did prisons change during this era?

5. How would you define Socialism? What were the chief ideas of the early Socialists? How did the ideas of Karl Marx differ from those of the Socialists? What historical role did Marx assign to the proletariat?

6. What factors, old and new, led to the widespread outbreak of the revolutions in 1848? Were the causes in the various countries essentially the same, or did each have its own particular set of circumstances?

Key Terms

anarchists Believed that government and social institutions were oppressive and unnecessary and that society should be based on voluntary cooperation among individuals.

Charles Fourier (1772–1837) French Socialist thinker who hoped to set up communities, called phalanxes, in which agrarian rather than industrial production would prevail.

Chartism The first large-scale European working-class political movement that fought for political reforms that would favor the interests of skilled British workers in the 1830s and 1840s.

The Communist Manifesto (1848) The document in which Karl Marx and Friedrich Engels portrayed human history as developing from ancient times to the present through a series of economic class struggles.

Corn Laws British tariffs on imported grain that protected the price of grain grown within the British Isles.

Count Claude Henri de Saint-Simon (1760–1825) French Socialist pioneer who believed that the management of wealth by experts would ease poverty and dislocation.

František Palacky (1798–1876) Czech historian and linguist who argued that the Czech people were not members of the German nation.

Frederick William IV (r. 1840–1861) Prussian king who declared his own constitution with a system of three-tier voting.

Friedrich Engels (FREE-drick ENG-ulz) (1820–1895) German philosopher who founded Marxist theory together with Karl Marx, with whom he co-authored *The Communist Manifesto*.

Jeremy Bentham (1748–1832) English philosopher and social reformer who created codes of scientific law founded on the principle of utility, namely the greatest happiness for the greatest number.

Louis Kossuth (1802–1894) Hungarian nationalist who called for the independence of Hungary from Austrian rule.

Louis Napoleon (1808–1873) The President of the French Second Republic (1848–1852) and the emperor of the Second French Empire (1852–1870).

Marxism The theory of Karl Marx (1818–1883) and Friedrich Engels (1820–1895) that history is the result of class conflict, which will end in the inevitable triumph of the industrial proletariat over the bourgeoisie and the abolition of private property and social class.

Pan-Slavism The movement to create a nation or federation that would embrace all the Slavic peoples of Eastern Europe.

Pierre-Joseph Proudhon (1809–1865) French politician and philosopher who thought society should be organized based on mutualism, with peaceful exchange of goods and mutual recognition of the labor each area of production required.

proletarianization The process in the nineteenth century whereby artisans as well as factory workers became wage laborers and lost both ownership of the means of production and control over the conduct of their trades.

Robert Owen (1771–1858) A Welsh social reformer and a founder of utopian socialism and the cooperative movement who believed that if human beings were placed in the correct surroundings, their character could be improved.

Sir Robert Peel (1788–1850) A British statesman and a member of the conservative party who sponsored legislation that placed police on London streets.

utilitarianism The theory associated with Jeremy Bentham (1748–1832) that the principle of utility, defined as the greatest good for the greatest number of people, should be applied to government, the economy, and the judicial system.

utopian Socialists Early-nineteenth-century writers who wished to replace the existing capitalist structure and values with visionary solutions or ideal communities.

Notes

1. Clive Emsley, *Policing and Its Context, 1750–1870* (London: Macmillan, 1983), p. 58.
2. Albert Fried and Ronald Sanders, eds., *Socialist Thought: A Documentary History* (Garden City, NY: Anchor Doubleday, 1964), p. 295.
3. Robert C. Tucker, ed., *The Marx-Engels Reader* (New York: W. W. Norton, 1972), p. 353.
4. Tucker, *The Marx-Engels Reader*, p. 353.

The West and the World

The Abolition of Slavery in the Transatlantic Economy

RESCUED SLAVES ABOARD THE HMS *DAPHNE* After 1833, the British Royal Navy patrolled the African coasts, attempting to intercept slave-trading ships. In 1868, the British ship HMS *Daphne* captured a slaving ship and freed the slaves. A British lieutenant, John Armstrong Challice, included photographs of the freed slaves in his report to the foreign office to apply pressure to end the slave trade out of Zanzibar.
SOURCE: National Archives

ONE OF THE most important developments during the age of Enlightenment and revolution was the opening of a crusade to abolish chattel slavery in the transatlantic economy. The antislavery movement constituted the greatest and most extensive achievement of liberal reformers during the eighteenth and nineteenth centuries. Indeed, it marked the first time in the history of the world that a society actually tried to abolish slavery. This achievement came as the result of the impact of Christian ethics, Enlightenment ideals,

slave revolts, revolutionary wars in America and Europe, civil war in the United States, and economic dislocation in the slave economies themselves. In 1750, almost no one seriously questioned the existence of slavery, but, by 1888, the institution no longer existed in the transatlantic economy.

Chattel slavery—the ownership of one human being by another—had existed in the West as well as elsewhere in the world since ancient times and had received intellectual and religious justification throughout the history of the West. Both Plato and Aristotle provided arguments for slavery based on the assertion that persons in bondage were intended by nature to be slaves. Christian writers similarly accommodated themselves to the institution. They contended that the most harmful form of slavery was the enslavement of the soul to sin rather than the enslavement of the physical body. They also argued that genuine freedom was realized through one's relationship to God and that problems relating to the injustices of inequality would be solved in the hereafter. Christian scholastic thinkers in the Middle Ages portrayed slavery as part of the natural and necessary hierarchy of the universe.

Slavery Spreads to the Americas

A vast slave trade existed throughout the Mediterranean world through the end of the Middle Ages, but—to the extent that serfdom can be distinguished from slavery—slavery was no longer a dominant institution on the European continent or within the European economy. The European encounter with America at the end of the fifteenth century radically transformed this situation. The American continent and the West Indies presented opportunities for achieving great wealth, but a major labor shortage existed in these regions. Eventually slavery provided the means to resolve this labor shortage.

The establishment and maintenance of slavery in the transatlantic economy drew Europeans and Americans into various relationships with Africa. About the same time as the encounter with America, Europeans made contact with areas of West Africa where slavery already existed. This region became the chief source of slaves imported into the Americas. Four centuries later, during the antislavery movement, Europeans used their commitment to ending the African economy's dependence on the slave trade to justify imperialist intervention in the Continent. Those efforts led to the penetration of Africa by European traders, missionaries, and finally colonial forces and administrators.

Although at one time or another slaves labored throughout the Americas, the system of slavery became primarily identified with the plantation economy stretching from Maryland south to Brazil, where tropical products, primarily sugar, were produced by slave labor. This plantation economy existed from approximately the late sixteenth through the late nineteenth centuries. The slaves on whose labor this economy was based included Native Americans enslaved within both the Spanish Empire and North America, and Africans forcibly imported into the Americas. Slaves were virtually always defined by their masters as belonging to a different race, even if one of their parents was a slaveholder. Race itself soon became part of the justification for the social hierarchy of the plantation world. In and of itself, the fact of slavery in the Americas was not unusual to the Western experience or to that of other societies in Africa or

Asia. Slavery had existed at most times and places in human history. Far more unusual in the history of the West, and for that matter in the experience of all other societies that had held and continued to hold slaves, was the emergence after 1760 of an international movement to abolish chattel slavery in the transatlantic economy.

The Crusade Against Slavery

The eighteenth-century crusade against slavery originated in a profound change in the religious and intellectual outlooks on slavery among small but influential groups in both America and Europe. The entire thrust of Enlightenment reasoning to the extent that it challenged or questioned the wisdom of existing institutions gnawed away at the older defenses of slavery, most particularly the concept of an unchanging social hierarchy. Although some writers associated with the Enlightenment, including John Locke, were reluctant to question slavery and even defended it, the general Enlightenment rhetoric of equality stood in sharp contrast to the radical inequality of slavery. Montesquieu sharply satirized slavery in *The Spirit of the Laws* (1748). Similarly, the emphasis of Adam Smith in *The Wealth of Nations* (1776) on free labor and efficiency of free markets undermined defenses of slavery.

Within much eighteenth-century literature, there emerged a tendency to idealize primitive peoples living in cultures very different from those of Europe. Previously such peoples had been regarded as backward and rebellious. Now numerous writers portrayed them as embodying a lost human virtue. This expanding body of literature transformed the way many people thought about slavery and allowed some Europeans to look on African slaves in the Americas as having been betrayed and robbed of an original innocence. Additionally, much eighteenth-century European ethical thinking, as well as later romantic poetry, emphasized empathy and feeling. In such a climate, attitudes toward slavery were transformed. Once considered to be the natural and deserved result of some deficiency in slaves themselves, slavery now grew to be regarded as undeserved and unacceptable. The same kind of ethical thinking led reformers to believe that by working against slavery, for virtually the first time defined as an unmitigated evil, they would realize their own highest ethical character.

Religious movements became the single most important cultural force to foster the antislavery crusade. The evangelical religious revival associated with Methodism and with other forms of Protestant preaching emphasized the conversion experience and the change of heart as a sign of having received salvation. In 1774, John Wesley, the founder of Methodism, attacked slaveholding in *Thoughts on Slavery*. Turning against slaveholding and slave trading by plantation owners and slave traders illustrated one clear example of such a change of heart. Some slaveholders and slave traders feared they might be endangering their own salvation by their association with the institution. John Newton, a former slave trader who underwent an evangelical conversion, wrote the hymn "Amazing Grace."

The initial religious protest against slavery originated among English Quakers, a radical Protestant religious group founded by George Fox in the seventeenth century. By the early eighteenth century, it had solidified itself into a small but relatively wealthy sect in England. Members of Quaker congregations at that time actually owned slaves in the West Indies and participated in the transatlantic slave trade. During the Seven Years' War (1756–1763), however, many Quakers experienced economic hardship. Furthermore, the war created other difficulties for the English population as a whole. Certain Quakers decided the presence of the evil of slavery in the world explained these troubles. They then sought to remove this evil from their own lives and that of their congregations and took action against the whole system of slavery that characterized the transatlantic economy.

Just as the slave system was a transatlantic affair so was the crusade against it. Quakers in both Philadelphia and England soon moved against the institution. The most influential of the early antislavery writers was Anthony Benezet, a Philadelphia Quaker, whose most important publications were *Some Considerations on the Keeping of Negroes* (1754) and *A Short Account of That Part of Africa Inhabited by the Negroes* (1762). The latter work emphasized the manner in which the slave trade degraded African society itself. Benezet also drew heavily on Montesquieu. This may not be surprising because Enlightenment writers often admired the English Quakers as exemplifying a religion of tolerance and reason.

By the earliest stages of the American Revolution a small group of reformers, normally spearheaded by Quakers, had established an antislavery network. They published pamphlets, sermons, and books on the subject. The Society for the Relief of Free Negroes Illegally Held in Bondage, the first antislavery society in the world, was founded in Philadelphia in 1775 and, when reorganized in 1784 as the Pennsylvania Abolition Society, Benjamin Franklin became its president. In 1787, the Committee for the Abolition of the Slave Trade was organized in England. In France, the Société des Amis des Noirs was founded in 1778.

The turmoil of the American Revolution and the founding of the American republic gave these groups the occasion for some of their earliest successes. Emancipation gradually, but nonetheless steadily, spread among the northern states. In 1787, the Continental Congress forbade the presence of slavery in the newly organized Northwest Territory north of the Ohio River. The crusade against slavery led to the disappearance of slavery in approximately half of the new nation and the commitment not to extend it to an important new territory. Despite these American developments, Great Britain became and remained the center for the antislavery movement. In 1772, a decision by the chief justice affirmed that slaves brought into Great Britain could not forcibly be removed. The decision, though of less immediate importance than some thought at the time, gave further impetus to the small but growing group of antislavery reformers.

During the early 1780s, the antislavery reformers in Great Britain decided to work toward ending the slave trade rather than the institution of slavery. The horrors of the slave trade caught the public's attention in 1783 when the captain of the slave ship *Zong* threw more than 130 slaves overboard to collect insurance. For the reformers, attacking the trade rather than the institution appeared a less radical and a more achievable reform. To many, the slave trade appeared to be a more obvious crime than the holding of slaves, which seemed a more nearly passive act. Furthermore, attacking slavery itself involved serious issues of property rights that might alienate potential supporters of the abolition of the slave trade. The antislavery groups also believed that if the trade was ended, planters would have to treat their remaining slaves more humanely.

By the end of the 1780s, the English Quakers were joined by evangelical Christians from the Church of England to form the Society for the Abolition of the Slave Trade. The most famous of the new leaders was William Wilberforce who, for the rest of his life, fought the slave trade. Year after year, he introduced a bill to abolish the slave trade. Finally, in 1807, he saw it passed.

Slave Revolts

While the British reformers worked for the abolition of the slave trade, slaves themselves in certain areas took matters into their own hands. The largest emancipation of slaves to occur in the eighteenth century took place on the island of Saint Domingue, Haiti, France's wealthiest colony, as a result of the slave revolt of 1794 led by Toussaint L'Ouverture and Jean-Jacques Dessalines. The revolt in Haiti and Haiti's eventual independence in 1804 was a warning to slave owners throughout the West Indies. There would be other slave revolts such as those in Virginia led by Gabriel Prosser in 1800 and by Nat Turner in 1831, in South Carolina led by Denmark Vesey in 1822, in British-controlled Demarra in 1823 and 1824, and in Jamaica in 1831. Each of these was brutally suppressed.

Economic Pressures

Through the conclusion of the Seven Years' War, the West Indies interest group had been one of the most powerful in the British Parliament. During the second half of the eighteenth century and beyond, new and different economic interest groups began to displace the influence of that group. Within the West Indies themselves the planters were

SLAVE REVOLT ON HAITI The slave revolt on the French island of St. Domingue in 1794 led to the largest emancipation of slaves in the eighteenth century. In this print, Toussaint L'Ouverture leads the revolt against the French.
SOURCE: Mary Evans Picture Library Ltd/AGE Fotostock

experiencing soil exhaustion and competition from newly tilled islands controlled by France and other new islands opened for sugar cultivation. Some older plantations were being abandoned, while others operated with low profitability. Now with the new islands under cultivation, there was a glut of sugar on the market, and as a consequence the price was falling.

Under these conditions some British West Indies planters, for reasons that had nothing to do with religion or humanitarianism, began to favor curtailing the slave trade. Without new slaves, French planters would lack the labor they needed to exploit their islands. During the Napoleonic Wars, the British captured several valuable French islands. To protect the planters on the older British West Indies islands, in 1805, the British cabinet issued Orders in Council, which forbade the importation of slaves into the newly acquired French islands. By 1807, the abolition sentiment was strong enough for Parliament to pass Wilberforce's measure prohibiting slave trading from any British port.

The suppression of this trade through the navy became one of the fundamental pillars of nineteenth-century British foreign policy. Throughout the rest of the Napoleonic era the

British attempted to draw allies into a policy of forbidding the slave trade. They also attempted unsuccessfully to incorporate the abolition of the slave trade into the settlement of the Congress of Vienna. In addition, the British navy maintained squadrons of ships around the coast of West Africa to halt slave traders. Although the French and Americans also patrolled the West African coast, neither was deeply committed to ending the slave trade. Nonetheless, in 1824, the American Congress made slave trading a capital offense.

The French invasion of Spain in 1808 provided the spark for the Latin American wars of independence. The leaders of these movements had been influenced by the liberal ideas of the Enlightenment and were thus generally predisposed to disapprove of slavery. The political groups seeking independence from Spain also sought the support of slaves by promises of emancipation. Furthermore, the newly independent nations depended on good relations with Britain to support their economies, and consequently, most of them very quickly freed their slaves. The actual freeing of slaves was gradual and often came some years after the emancipation legislation. In Brazil, slavery continued into the 1880s. Except for Brazil, slavery would gradually disappear by approximately the middle of the nineteenth century from all of the newly independent nations of Latin America.

Abolishing Slavery in the New World

British reformers gradually recognized that the abolition of the slave trade had not actually improved the lot of slaves. In 1823, they adopted as a new goal the gradual emancipation of slaves. The chief voices calling for this change were those of William Wilberforce and Thomas Clarkson, who were active in founding the Abolition Society. The savagery with which West Indian planters put down slave revolts in 1823 and 1824 and again in 1831 strengthened the resolve of the antislavery reformers. By 1830, the reformers had abandoned the goal of gradual abolition and demanded the complete abolition of slavery. In 1833, after the passage of the Reform Bill in Great Britain, they achieved that goal when Parliament abolished the right of British subjects to hold slaves. In the British West Indies, 750,000 slaves were freed within a few years.

The other old colonial powers in the New World tended to be much slower in their abolition of slavery. Portugal did little or nothing about slavery in Brazil, and when that nation became independent of Portugal, its new government continued slavery. Portugal ended slavery elsewhere in its American possessions in 1836; the Swedes, in 1847; the Danes, in 1848; but the Dutch not until 1863. France had witnessed a significant antislavery movement throughout the first half-century, but slavery was not abolished in its West Indian possessions until the revolution of 1848.

During the first thirty years of the nineteenth century, the institution of slavery revived and achieved strong new footholds in the transatlantic world. These areas were the lower south of the United States for the cultivation of cotton, Brazil for the cultivation of coffee, and Cuba for the cultivation of sugar. World demand for these products made the slave system economically viable in these regions. Consequently, despite the drive for emancipation, which had succeeded in the northern states of the United States, slavery persisted in much of the Caribbean and in most of Latin America.

An antislavery movement had existed in the United States since the end of the eighteenth century, but it took on a new life in the early 1830s. The British abolition of slavery in the West Indies served as an inspiration to a new generation of American antislavery leaders, the most famous of whom was William Lloyd Garrison. He and other American abolitionists raised the question of slavery throughout the 1830s and 1840s. It was, however, the disposition of lands the United States had acquired in the Mexican War of 1847 that placed slavery at the heart of the American political debate. For more than a decade the question of

slavery sharply divided Americans. The election of Lincoln in 1860 brought those sectional tensions to a head, and the American Civil War erupted in the spring of 1861. In 1863, Lincoln issued the Emancipation Proclamation, which ended slavery in the combatant states. The passage of the Thirteenth Amendment to the American Constitution in 1865 abolished slavery in the United States.

The end of slavery in the United Sates left both Cuba, the most important remaining possession of the Spanish Empire in the Americas, and Brazil with slave economies. In 1868, an insurgency against Spanish colonial policy broke out in Cuba and lasted for ten years. This war disrupted much of the Cuban economy, and some planters moved toward using free labor. The Spanish forces attacked other planters by freeing their slaves. In 1870, the Spanish government passed a measure for gradual emancipation of slaves in both Cuba and Puerto Rico. In subsequent years, the sugar economy collapsed, making slavery unprofitable. Abolitionist agitation grew in Spain, and slavery was abolished in its New World colonies in 1886.

Brazil, under British pressure, had effectively ended the slave trade in 1850, but the question of the abolition of slavery was postponed for many years. In 1871, as a result of abolitionist agitation and because the Emperor Pedro II opposed slavery, a law providing for an extremely gradual abolition of slavery was passed. During the next two decades, abolitionist sentiment grew, and public figures from across the political spectrum voiced opposition to slavery. In 1888, Isabel Christiana, then regent while her father Pedro II was in Europe for medical treatment, signed a law abolishing slavery in Brazil without any form of compensation to the slave owners.

The abolition of slavery in Brazil ended a system of forced labor that had characterized the transatlantic economy for almost 400 years. Wherever slavery had existed, however, its presence left and would continue to leave long-term consequences for the realization of equality and social justice. The end of slavery, consequently, did not end the problems that slavery created in the transatlantic world.

Africa and the End of Slavery

The transatlantic slave trade itself had adversely affected African life with the vast loss of population over the centuries as well as the undermining of African society through the internal slave trade. Similarly, the crusade against transatlantic slavery had drawn Europeans much more deeply into the affairs of the African continent. The various efforts by antislavery groups began to impact Africa in the first half of the nineteenth century. Their goal was to transform the African economy by substituting new peaceful trade in tropical goods for the slave trade. The reformers hoped to spread both free trade and Christianity into Africa. "Christianity and civilization" and "Christianity and commerce" were popular slogans of the day. Missionaries and traders saw themselves as natural allies in the cause.

The first effort in this direction was the resettlement of black slaves or children of black slaves into Africa. In 1787, the British established a colony of poor free blacks from Britain in Sierra Leone. The effort went badly, but a few years later former slaves once owned by British loyalists in America were settled there. Then former slaves from the Caribbean were brought to Sierra Leone. The colony became relatively successful only after 1807, when the British navy landed slaves rescued from captured slave trading ships. Sierra Leone, though quite small, became a place on the coast of West Africa where Christianity and commerce rather than the slave trade flourished. The French established a smaller experiment at Libreville in Gabon. The most famous and lasting attempt to resettle former black slaves in Africa was the establishment of Liberia by the efforts of the American Colonization Society after 1817. Liberia became an independent republic in 1847. All these efforts to move former slaves back to Africa had only modest success, but they did affect the life of West Africa.

Other antislavery reformers were less interested in establishing outposts for the settlement of former slaves than in transforming the African economy itself. In 1841, the African Civilization Society under the leadership of Thomas Fowell Buxton sent a group of paddle steamers up the Niger River in the hope of creating the basis for new trade with Africa. The goal was to establish free trade between Britain and Africa in which the manufactured goods of the former, most particularly textiles, would be exchanged for tropical agricultural goods produced by Africans. The expedition failed because most of its members died of disease. Yet the impulse to penetrate Africa for purposes of spreading trade and Christianity would continue for the rest of the century.

The antislavery movement marked the first of the intrusions of the European powers well beyond the coast of West Africa into the heart of the Continent. After the American Civil War finally halted any large-scale demand for slaves from Africa, the antislavery reformers began to focus on ending the slave trade in East Africa and the Indian Ocean. This drive against slavery and the slave trade in Africa itself became one of the rationales for European interference in Africa during the second half of the nineteenth century and was one of the foundations for the establishment of the late-century colonial empires.

The crusade against slavery in the transatlantic economy eventually touched most of the world. It radically transformed the economies and societies of both North and South America. It led to a transformation of the African economy and eventually to a significant European presence in the life of African societies. Efforts to eradicate slavery, particularly the efforts by British reformers, caused the spread of the reform movement into Asia. Slavery has not been abolished throughout the world, and antislavery societies still exist, though they receive little publicity. Yet the abolition of slavery in the transatlantic world remains one of the most permanent achievements of the forces of eighteenth-century Enlightenment and revolution.

Questions

1. What were the justifications of slavery prior to the eighteenth century?

2. What religious and intellectual developments led some Europeans and some Americans to question and criticize the institution of slavery?

3. Why did antislavery reformers first concentrate on the abolition of the slave trade?

4. How did both slavery and antislavery lead Americans and Europeans to become involved with Africa? How did that involvement change between approximately 1600 and 1870?

Chapter 22
The Age of Nation-States

UNIFICATION OF GERMANY AS A CONSTITUTIONAL MONARCHY In 1884, William I, the new emperor of Germany, laid the cornerstone for the Reichstag, or German parliament, in Berlin. Behind him the German chancellor Otto von Bismarck stands out, as usual, in his white uniform. Although William I was the titular head of the German empire, it was Bismarck who held the reins of power.
SOURCE: ullstein bild Dtl./Getty Images

 ## Contents and Focus Questions

The Chapter in Brief

THE REVOLUTIONS OF 1848 collapsed in defeat for both liberalism and nationalism. In the 1850s, conservative regimes were entrenched across the Continent. Yet only a quarter-century later, many of the major goals of early-nineteenth-century liberals and nationalists appeared to have been reached. Italy and Germany were each united under constitutional monarchies, albeit conservative ones. The Habsburg emperor accepted constitutional government and granted wide-ranging autonomy to Hungary. In Russia, the tsar emancipated the serfs. France had become a republic. Liberalism and even democracy flourished in Great Britain. The Ottoman Empire also undertook major reforms.

Paradoxically, most of these developments occurred under conservative political leadership. War and competition with other states compelled some governments to pursue new policies at home as well as abroad. They had to find novel methods to maintain the loyalty of their subjects. Some conservative leaders preferred to carry out popular policies on their own terms so that they, rather than the liberals, would receive credit. Other leaders acted as they did because they had no choice. Across Europe, the franchise was extended to an ever larger number of men, irrespective of their income. Political rights became increasingly linked to adulthood and manhood, rather than status, inherited privilege, or wealth.

22.1 The Crimean War (1853–1856)

Why was the Crimean War fought?

As has so often been true in modern European history, the impetus for change originated in war. The **Crimean War** (1853–1856) was rooted in the long-standing desire of Russia to extend its influence over the Ottoman Empire. (See Map 22–1.) Two disputes led to the conflict. First, the Russians had, since the time of Catherine the Great (r. 1762–1796), been given protective oversight of Orthodox Christians in the Empire, and France had similar oversight of Roman Catholics. In 1851, yielding to French pressure, the Ottoman sultan had given protection of certain holy places in Palestine to Roman Catholics. This decision angered the Russians and damaged Russian prestige. Second, Russia wanted to extend its control over the Ottoman provinces of Moldavia and Walachia (now in Romania). In the summer of 1853, the Russians used their right to protect Orthodox Christians in the Ottoman Empire as the pretext to occupy the two provinces. Shortly thereafter, the Ottoman Empire declared war on Russia.

Of far more significance to the great powers than the protection of Christian sites in Palestine was the fate of the weak Ottoman Empire. The Russian government envisioned the eventual breakup of the empire and hoped to extend its

Map 22–1 THE CRIMEAN WAR

Although named after the Crimean Peninsula, the Crimean War was fought across the entire northern and eastern coasts of the Black Sea.

CALLING THE ROLL In *Calling the Roll After an Engagement, Crimea*, completed two decades after the war, Elizabeth Thompson, Lady Butler, emphasizes the suffering of ordinary troops as well as their comradeship.
SOURCE: Her Majesty Queen Elizabeth II, 2017/Bridgeman Images

influence at Ottoman expense. France, Britain, and Austria, who used the difficulties of the Ottoman government to their own advantage when the opportunity presented itself, opposed Russian expansion in the eastern Mediterranean, where they had extensive naval and commercial interests. The French emperor Napoleon III (r. 1852–1870) also thought an activist foreign policy would shore up domestic support for his regime.

On March 28, 1854, France and Britain declared war on Russia in alliance with the Ottomans. Much to the disappointment of Tsar Nicholas I, Austria and Prussia remained neutral. Prussia proceeded cautiously until its own foreign policy interest in the matter became clearer. Austria, concerned about its own interests in the Balkans, mobilized troops as a symbol of support of Britain and France's move but did not declare war.

Both sides conducted the conflict ineptly, a fact that became widely known in Western Europe because the Crimean War was the first to be covered by war correspondents and photographers. The ill-equipped and poorly commanded armies became bogged down along the Crimean coast of the Black Sea. In September 1855, after a long siege, the Russian fortress of Sevastopol fell to the French and British. Thereafter, both sides moved to end the war.

22.1.1 Peace Settlement and Long-Term Results

In March 1856, a conference in Paris concluded the Treaty of Paris. This treaty required Russia to surrender territory near the mouth of the Danube River, to recognize the neutrality of the Black Sea, and to renounce its claims to protect Orthodox Christians in the Ottoman Empire. Even before the conference, Austria had forced Russia to withdraw from Moldavia and Walachia. The image of an invincible Russia that had prevailed across Europe since the close of the Napoleonic Wars was shattered. The new Russian tsar, Alexander II, undertook far-reaching reforms intended to address the fundamental weakness he believed the Crimean War had revealed.

Also shattered was the Concert of Europe (see Chapter 20) as a means of dealing with international relations on the Continent. Following the successful repression of the 1848 uprisings, the great powers feared revolution less than they had earlier in the century, and, consequently, they were less reverent of the Vienna settlement. As historian Gordon Craig put it, "After 1856, there were more powers willing to fight to overthrow the existing order than there were to take up arms to defend it."[1] As a result, for about twenty-five years after the Crimean War, European affairs were unstable, leading to a period of adventurism in foreign policy.

Although Russia was the formal loser of the Crimean War, in some ways it was Austria's position that was most fatefully weakened. Russia felt betrayed by Austria's lack of support following Russia's assistance in suppressing the Hungarian revolt of 1848–1849. The Western powers were not satisfied with Austria's half-hearted and noncommittal expressions of sympathy. Austria thus became isolated diplomatically, making it seem vulnerable to domestic political pressure.

22.2 Reforms in the Ottoman Empire

How did the Ottoman Empire attempt to reform itself?

The short-lived Napoleonic invasion of the Ottoman province of Egypt from 1798 to 1799 sparked a drive for change in the Ottoman Empire. The Ottomans never gained true control over Egypt, and the viceroy of Egypt's embrace of reform threatened to make Egypt an alternative source of power in the eastern Mediterranean. (See the "Closer Look" sidebar, which follows below, to learn about Egypt's bold move to improve international commerce throughout the world.)

A Closer Look

The Suez Canal

UNTIL THE third quarter of the nineteenth century, ships sailing between the Indian Ocean and the Mediterranean Sea or Atlantic Ocean had to navigate all the way around Africa, or to portage their goods overland across the Suez Isthmus, which separated the Red Sea from the Mediterranean Sea. In the mid-1850s, the viceroy of Egypt agreed to a bold plan: the Frenchman Ferdinand de Lesseps, using plans drawn up by Tyrolian engineer Alois Negrelli, proposed to dig a canal across the isthmus and open it to traffic from all nations. The canal's construction began in 1859 and was completed ten years later. The construction of the canal came to symbolize European technological superiority, although British critics condemned Egypt's use of slave labor.

From the start, the project was characterized by great optimism and faith in inevitable progress, despite financial difficulties that plagued its backers and the opposition of Great Britain to the undertaking. In promoting the canal, De Lesseps said that anyone "preoccupied with questions of civilization and progress cannot look at a map and not be seized with a powerful desire to make disappear the only obstacle interfering with the flow of the commerce of the world."*

The canal, although not yet completed in 1864, is portrayed as if already busy with traffic.

Port Said, to the left, was a new city constructed to manage exports out of the canal.

The artist ignores classic rules of perspective in order to depict something of the canal's full grandeur.

The travelers on camels suggest the slow progress of overland transportation. The rocks in the foreground emphasize the obstacles to transit.

A VIEW OF THE SUEZ CANAL
SOURCE: DEA PICTURE LIBRARY/Getty Images

Questions

1. This painting was commissioned by a financial backer of the Suez Canal. How does the image promote the canal?
2. What image of Egypt does this painting evoke? How is it consistent or inconsistent with reforms sweeping across the Ottoman Empire at this time?

*Zachary Karabell, *Parting the Desert: The Creation of the Suez Canal* (New York: Knopf, 2003), p. 78.

22.2.1 Reorganization of the Ottoman Empire

In 1839, under pressure from imperial bureaucrats who had studied in Europe, the Ottoman sultan issued a decree, called the *Hatt-i Sharif of Gülhane*, that attempted to reorganize the empire's administration and military along European lines. This decree opened what became known as the *Tanzimat* ("reorganization") era of the Ottoman Empire, lasting from 1839 to 1876. The reforms, which were drawn up by administrative councils and not issued arbitrarily by the sultan, liberalized the economy, ended the practice of tax farming, and sought to eliminate corruption. The *Hatt-i Sharif* was particularly remarkable for extending civic equality to Ottoman subjects regardless of their religion. Muslims, Christians, and Jews were now equal before the law. The empire also made it much easier for Muslims to enter into commercial agreements with non-Muslims, both within the empire and from abroad.

Another reform decree, called the *Hatti-i Hümayun*, was promulgated in 1856 at the close of the Crimean War. Under the influence of Britain and France, it spelled out the rights of non-Muslims more explicitly, giving them equal obligations with Muslims for military service and equal opportunity for state employment and admission to state schools. The decree also abolished torture and allowed foreigners to acquire some forms of property. In time, printing presses and Western-oriented schools appeared in the empire mainly via Christian missionaries, many of whom were Americans. For the first time in its long history, the Ottoman Empire actually sought to copy European legal and military institutions and the secular values flowing from liberalism.

The imperial government took these steps to gain the loyalty of its Christian subjects at a time when nationalism was making increasing inroads among them. In effect, during this reform era the Ottoman government broke down the millet system and sought to define all its citizens as Ottoman subjects rather than as members of particular religious communities.

However, putting these reforms into practice proved difficult. In some regions of the empire, especially in Egypt and Tunis, local rulers were virtually independent of Istanbul. They carried out their own modernizing reforms, often working closely with European powers.

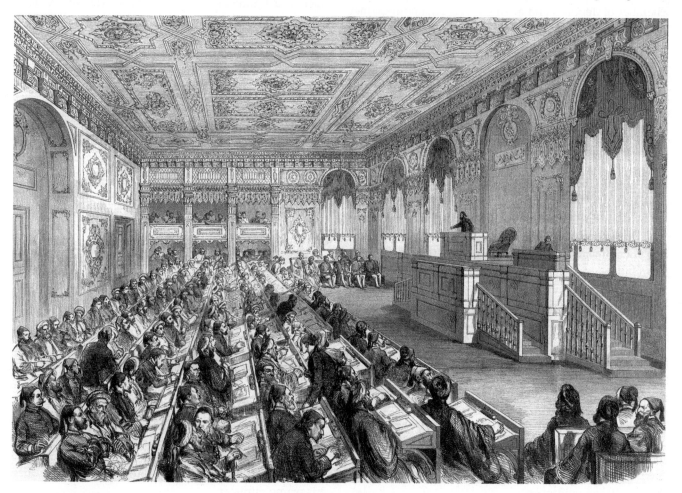

FIRST OTTOMAN PARLIAMENT Ottoman reformers established a parliament in 1877. The new parliament had limited power, however, as the sultan retained most political authority. Illustrated here, from a popular London-based news journal of the time, the opening of the first Ottoman parliament in Istanbul.

SOURCE: Illustrated London/Mary Evans Picture Library Ltd/AGE Fotostock

In the capital itself, power struggles developed among courtiers; European-oriented administrators and army officers; merchants who prospered from the changes; and the *ulama*, which sought to maintain the rule of Islamic law. Because of these tensions, as well as growing nationalism in various regions, the Ottoman Empire failed to achieve genuine political strength and stability. Many Ottomans—including local leaders in parts of "European Turkey" like Bosnia—questioned the wisdom of Tanzimat and warned that replacing long-standing Islamic institutions with European ones would lead to disaster.

The Balkan wars of the late 1870s, which resulted in either the independence of, or Russian or Austrian dominance over, most of the empire's European holdings, demonstrated the inability of the Ottoman Empire to control its destiny. The response to these foreign defeats resulted in greater efforts to modernize the army and the economy and to build railways and telegraphs. In 1876, reformers persuaded the sultan to proclaim an Ottoman constitution on the grounds that European political arrangements as well as technology accounted for European strength. The constitution called for a parliament consisting of an elected chamber of deputies and an appointed senate (these met for the first time in 1877) but left the sultan's power mostly intact. Nonetheless, a new sultan soon rejected even these limited steps toward constitutionalism and dismissed the parliament. In 1908, military officers carried out a revolution against the authority, though not the person, of the sultan. Another group of reformist officers, known as the **Young Turks**, came to the fore with another program to modernize the empire. They were still in charge when World War I broke out, and their decision to enter the war on the side of the Central Powers in November 1914 led to the empire's defeat and collapse.

Underlying these attempts at reform and modernization from 1839 to 1914 was the increasing secularization of the government, which sought less to question the Islamic foundations of society than to reduce the influence of the Muslim religious authorities on the state.

22.3 Italian Unification

How did Italy achieve unification?

In the mid-nineteenth century, the Italian peninsula consisted of nearly a dozen independent states, many of them under the direct or indirect rule of the Habsburgs. Nationalists had long wanted to unite the small, mostly absolutist principalities of the Italian peninsula into a single state. During the first half-century, however, opinion differed about how to achieve Italian unification.

22.3.1 Romantic Republicans

One approach to the issue was **romantic republicanism**. After the Congress of Vienna, secret republican societies were founded throughout Italy, the most famous of which was the Carbonari or "charcoal burners." They were widely feared but ineffective.

After the failure of nationalist uprisings in Italy in 1831, the leadership of romantic republican nationalism passed to **Giuseppe Mazzini** (1805–1872). He became the most important nationalist leader in Europe and brought new fervor to the cause. He once declared, "Nationality is the role assigned by God to a people in the work of humanity. It is its mission, its task on earth," to the end that God's thought may be realized in the world."[2] In 1831, he founded the Young Italy Society to drive Austria from the peninsula and establish an Italian republic.

During the 1830s and 1840s, Mazzini and his fellow republican **Giuseppe Garibaldi** (1807–1882) led insurrections. Both were involved in the ill-fated Roman Republic of 1849. Throughout the 1850s, they continued to conduct what amounted to guerrilla warfare. Because both men spent much time in exile, they became well known across the Continent and in the United States.

Republican nationalism frightened moderate Italians, who wanted to rid themselves of Austrian domination but not to establish a republic. For a time, these people had hoped the papacy would sponsor unification. That solution became impossible after the experience of Pius IX with the Roman Republic in 1849. Consequently, at mid-century, "Italy" remained, in the words of the Austrian foreign minister, Prince Metternich, "a geographical expression" rather than a political entity.

Yet by 1860, the Italian peninsula was transformed into a nation-state under a constitutional monarchy. **Count Camillo Cavour** (1810–1861), the prime minister of Piedmont—not romantic republicans—made this possible. His method was to combine force of arms with secret diplomacy.

22.3.2 Cavour's Policy

Piedmont (officially styled the Kingdom of Sardinia), in northwestern Italy, was the most independent state on the peninsula. The Congress of Vienna had restored the kingdom as a buffer between French and Austrian ambitions. During 1848 and 1849, King Charles Albert of Piedmont, after having promulgated a conservative constitution, twice fought Austria unsuccessfully. After the second defeat, he abdicated in favor of his son, Vittorio Emanuele (r. 1849–1878). In 1852, the new monarch chose Cavour as his prime minister.

A cunning statesman, Cavour had begun political life as a conservative but had gradually moved toward a moderately liberal position. He was deeply imbued with the ideas of the Enlightenment, classical economics, and utilitarianism. Cavour was a nationalist of a new breed who had no respect for Mazzini's ideals. A strong monarchist, Cavour rejected republicanism. He favored a unified state on the Italian peninsula because he believed it was necessary for economic and material progress, not romantic ideals.

Cavour believed that the first step toward independence was proving to the great powers that Italians were efficient and economically progressive. As premier of Piedmont, he promoted free trade, railway construction, expansion of credit, and agricultural improvement. He believed that such material and economic bonds, rather than fuzzy romantic yearnings, must unite the Italians. Cavour also recognized the need to capture the loyalties of those Italians who believed in other varieties of nationalism. He thus

COUNT CAMILLO CAVOUR Count Camillo Cavour (1810–1861), using an opportunistic alliance with France against Austria and military interventions in the Papal States and in southern Italy, secured Italian unification under Vittorio Emanuele II. Later he became the first prime minister of a unified Italy.
SOURCE: Realy Easy Star/Toni Spagone/Alamy Stock Photo

fostered the Nationalist Society, which established chapters in other Italian states to press for unification under the leadership of Piedmont. Finally, Cavour believed the Habsburgs would never agree to Italian unification and that consequently an alliance with France was necessary to defeat Austria. The accession of Napoleon III in France seemed to open the way for such aid.

22.3.2.1 FRENCH SYMPATHIES Cavour used the Crimean War to bring the Italian question to the attention of the great powers. In 1855, Piedmont sent 10,000 troops to help France and Britain capture Sebastopol. At the same time that Piedmont had assisted France and Great Britain, Austria had remained neutral. Piedmont's small but significant participation in the war allowed Cavour to raise the question of unification at the Paris conference. He left Paris with no immediate reward, but his intelligence and political capacity had impressed everyone, especially Napoleon III. During the rest of the decade, he achieved further international respectability for Piedmont by opposing Mazzini, who was still attempting to lead nationalist uprisings. By 1858, Cavour represented a moderate, monarchist alternative to both republicanism and reactionary absolutism in Italy.

Cavour bided his time. Then, in January 1858, an Italian named Felice Orsini attempted to assassinate Napoleon III. The incident heightened the emperor's interest in the Italian issue. He saw himself continuing his more famous uncle's liberation of the peninsula. He also saw Piedmont as a potential ally against Austria. In July 1858, Cavour and Napoleon III met at Plombières in southern France. The two men plotted to provoke a war in Italy that would permit them to defeat Austria. A formal treaty in December 1858 confirmed the agreement.

22.3.2.2 WAR WITH AUSTRIA In early 1859, tension grew between Austria and Piedmont as Piedmont mobilized its army. Austria played right into Cavour's hands. On April 22, Austria demanded that Piedmont demobilize. That allowed Piedmont to claim that Austria was provoking a war. France intervened to aid its ally. On June 4, the Austrians were defeated at Magenta and on June 24 at Solferino. Meanwhile, revolutions had broken out in Tuscany, Modena, Parma, and the Romagna provinces of the Papal States.

With the Austrians in retreat and the new revolutionary regimes calling for union with Piedmont, Napoleon III feared too extensive a Piedmontese victory. On July 11, he concluded peace with Austria at Villafranca. Piedmont received Lombardy, but Venetia remained under Austrian control. Cavour felt betrayed by France, but the war had driven Austria from most of northern Italy. Later that summer, Parma, Modena, Tuscany, and the Romagna voted to unite with Piedmont. (See Map 22–2.)

Map 22–2   THE UNIFICATION OF ITALY

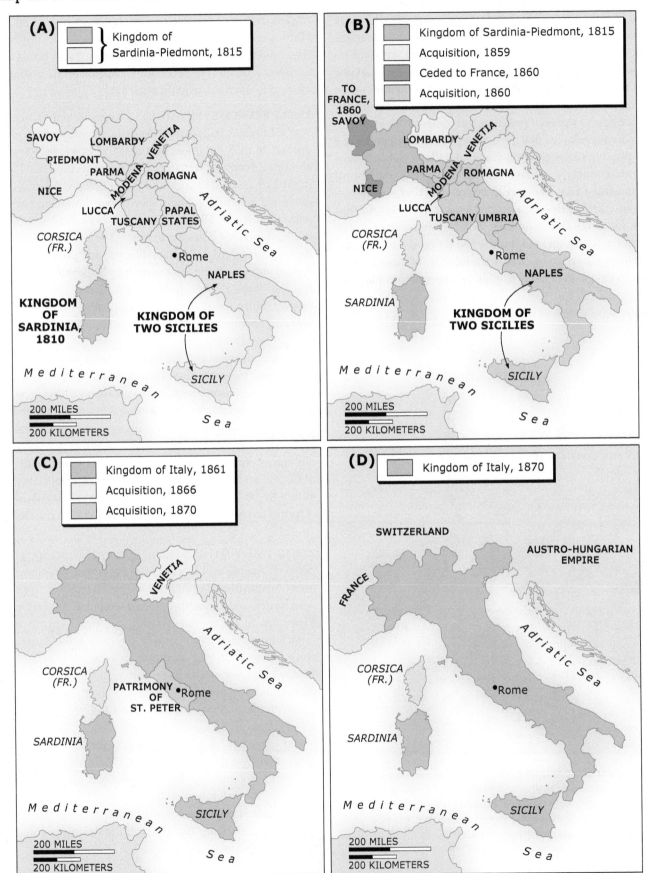

Beginning with the association of Sardinia and Piedmont by the Congress of Vienna in 1815, unification was achieved through the expansion of Piedmont between 1859 and 1870. Both Cavour's statesmanship and the campaigns of ardent nationalists played large roles.

22.3.2.3 GARIBALDI'S CAMPAIGN At this point, the forces of romantic republican nationalism compelled Cavour to pursue the complete unification of northern and southern Italy. In May 1860, Garibaldi landed in Sicily with more than 1,000 troops, who had been outfitted in the north. He captured Palermo and prepared to attack the mainland. By September he controlled the city and kingdom of Naples, probably the most corrupt example of Italian absolutism. For more than two decades Garibaldi had hoped to form a republican Italy but Cavour forestalled him. He rushed Piedmontese troops south to confront Garibaldi. On the way, they conquered the rest of the Papal States except the area around Rome, which French troops saved for the pope. Recognizing that to persist would guarantee further bloodshed and a protracted civil war, Garibaldi's nationalism won out over his republicanism, and he accepted Piedmontese domination and a monarchical, rather than republican, Italy. In late 1860, Naples and Sicily voted to join the Italian kingdom. (See the "Compare and Connect" sidebar, for two sides of the nationalism argument.)

22.3.3 The New Italian State

In March 1861, **Vittorio Emanuele II** was proclaimed king of Italy. Three months later Cavour died. The new state more than ever needed his skills because Piedmont had, in effect, not so much united Italy as conquered it. The republicans resented the treatment of Garibaldi. The clericals were appalled at the conquest of the Papal States. In the south, armed resistance against the imposition of Piedmontese-style administration continued until 1866. The economies and societies of north and south Italy were incompatible. The south was rural, poor, and backward. The north was industrializing, and its economy was increasingly linked to that of the rest of Europe. The social structures of the two regions reflected these differences, with large landholders and peasants dominant in the south and an urban working class emerging in the north.

The political framework of the united Italy could not overcome these problems. The constitution, which was that promulgated for Piedmont in 1848, provided for a conservative constitutional monarchy. Parliament consisted of two houses: a senate appointed by the king and a chamber of deputies elected on a narrow franchise. Ministers were responsible to the monarch, not to parliament. These arrangements did not foster vigorous parliamentary life. Political leaders often simply avoided major problems. In place of efficient, progressive government, such as Cavour had brought to Piedmont, a system called *transformismo* developed. Bribery, favors, or a seat in the cabinet

RIGHT LEG IN THE BOOT AT LAST.

Garibaldi. "IF IT WON'T GO ON, SIRE, TRY A LITTLE MORE POWDER."

A MONARCHICAL, RATHER THAN REPUBLICAN, ITALY In this *Punch* cartoon from November 1860, Garibaldi's acceptance of Vittorio Emanuele as king of Italy is portrayed as submissive. Garibaldi ultimately decided that Italian unification—and avoiding Civil War—was more important than pursuing his radical social and political goals. **SOURCE:** UniversalImagesGroup/Getty Images

"transformed" political opponents into government supporters. Italian politics became a byword for corruption.

The unification was not complete. Many Italians believed other territories should be added to their nation. The most important of these were Venetia and Rome. The former was gained in 1866 in return for Italy's alliance with Prussia in the **Austro-Prussian War**. French troops continued to guard Rome and the papacy until the troops were withdrawn during the **Franco-Prussian War** of 1870. The Italian state then annexed Rome and made it the capital. The papacy confined itself to the Vatican and remained hostile to the Italian state until the Lateran Accord of 1929.

By 1870, the only areas with large Italian-speaking populations that remained outside Italy were the province of Trent, or Southern Tyrol, and the city of Trieste. Both were ruled by Austria, and neither was inhabited solely by people who considered themselves Italian or even spoke Italian. Conflicts in these areas among Italians, Germans, Slovenes, and people who had no national affiliation fueled the continued hostility of Italian nationalists toward Austria. The desire to liberate *Italia irredenta*, or "unredeemed Italy," was one reason for the Italian support of the Allies against Austria and Germany during World War I.

Compare and Connect

Nineteenth-Century Nationalism: Two Sides

THE SECOND QUARTER of the nineteenth century witnessed the unification first of Italy and then of Germany. Both processes involved warfare. The Kingdom of Sardinia conquered and united northern Italy, and then Garibaldi led his "Red Shirts" to conquer the south. Prussia united Germany in a series of wars against Denmark, Austria, and France. The following two documents illustrate different justifications for unifying each nation using military action. Garibaldi presents his forces as liberators against tyranny. Historian Heinrich von Treitschke argues for the German annexation of Alsace and Lorraine on the grounds of national security and history.

GENERAL GIUSEPPE GARIBALDI Giuseppe Garibaldi (1807–1882) was the most charismatic figure in the drive for Italian unification.
SOURCE: Universal Images Group/Getty Images

Before Reading

- Notice the main arguments Giuseppe Garibaldi makes in favor of unifying southern Italy.
- Consider the grounds on which Heinrich von Treitschke bases the German claim to Alsace and Lorraine.

Questions

1. How does Garibaldi's manifesto transform the war for unification in southern Italy into a popular campaign?
2. How does Garibaldi portray the struggle for unification as a battle against tyranny?
3. Why does Treitschke believe it acceptable to ignore the wishes of the people of Alsace?
4. How could Garibaldi, whose goal was popular liberation, and Treitschke, whose goal was reclaiming lost regions of a national homeland, both be nationalists? Are these two views compatible or distinctly different?

I. GUISEPPE GARIBALDI CALLS ITALIANS TO ACT TO UNIFY THEIR NATION

Giuseppe Garibaldi was the most charismatic figure in the drive for Italian unification. He was the leader of guerrilla military forces known as the Red Shirts. In May 1860 after northern Italy had been united under the Kingdom of Sardinia whose monarch was Vittorio Emanuele, Garibaldi landed his force of about a thousand men in Sicily and then crossed into southern Italy to conquer the kingdom of Naples and make it part of a united Italian state. Garibaldi was a republican, but he reconciled himself to supporting Vittorio Emanuele. Before leaving Sicily for the mainland, Garibaldi called the Italians of southern Italy to arms against the kingdom of Naples. The various geographical areas Garibaldi mentions below were located from the south northward to Rome. Garibaldi's reference to the Tincino River in northern Italy recalls the participation of his troops in the war that unified the north.

Italians! The Sicilians are fighting against the enemies of Italy and for Italy. To help them with money, arms, and especially men, is the duty of every Italian.

Let the Marches, Umbria, Sabine, the Roman Campagna, and the Neapolitan territory rise, so as to divide the enemy's forces.

If the cities do not offer a sufficient basis for insurrection, let the more resolute throw themselves into the open country. A brave man can always find a weapon. In the name of Heaven, hearken not to the voice of those who cram themselves at well-served tables. Let us arm. Let us fight for our brothers; tomorrow we can fight for ourselves.

A handful of brave men, who have followed me in battles for our country, are advancing with me to the rescue. Italy knows them; they always appear at the hour of danger. Brave and generous companions, they have devoted their lives to their country; they will shed their last drop of blood for it, seeking no other reward than that of a pure conscience.

"Italy and Vittorio Emanuele!"—that was our battle-cry when we crossed the Tincino; it will resound into the very depths of Aetna [the volcanic mountain]. As this prophetic battle-cry re-echoes from the hills of Italy to the Tarpeian Mount, the tottering thrones of tyranny will fall to pieces, and the whole country will rise like one man.

II. HEINRICH VON TREITSCHKE DEMANDS THE ANNEXATION OF ALSACE AND LORRAINE

The Franco-Prussian War witnessed outbursts of extreme nationalist rhetoric on both sides. One voice was that of German historian Heinrich von Treitschke (1834–1896). In a newspaper article excerpted below, he demanded German annexation of Alsace and Lorraine from France, even though the population of Alsace wished to remain part of France and German was not the dominant language in the region. He appealed to an earlier time when the region had been German in language and culture, and he asserted that might makes right to ensure German domination.

The sense of justice to Germany demands the lessening of France. . . .
What is demanded by justice is, at the same time, absolutely necessary for our security. . . .
Every State must seek the guarantees of its own security in itself alone. . . .

In view of our obligation to secure the peace of the world, who will venture to object that the people of Alsace and Lorraine do not want to belong to us? The doctrine of the right of all the branches of the German race to decide on their own destinies, the plausible solution of demagogues without a fatherland, shiver to pieces in presence of the sacred necessity of these great days. These territories are ours by the right of the sword, and we shall dispose of them in virtue of a higher right—the right of the German nation, which will not permit its lost children to remain strangers to the German Empire. We Germans, who know Germany and France, know better than these unfortunates themselves what is good for the people of Alsace. . . . . Against their will we shall restore them to their true selves. We have seen with joyful wonder the undying power of the moral forces of history, manifested far too frequently in the immense changes of these days, to place much confidence in the value of a mere popular disinclination. The spirit of a nation lays hold, not only of the generation which lives beside it, but of those who are before and behind it. We appeal from the mistaken wishes of the men who are there today to the wishes of those who were there before them. We appeal to all those strong German men who once stamped the seal of our German nature on the language and manners, the art and the social life of the Upper Rhine. Before the nineteenth century closes, the world will recognize that . . . we were only obeying the dictates of national honor when we made little account of the preferences of the people who live in Alsace today. . . .

At all times the subjection of a German race to France has been an unhealthy thing; today it is an offence against the reason of History—a vassalship of free men to half-educated barbarians. . . .

There is no perfect identity between the political and national frontier of any European country. Not one of the great Powers, and Germany no more than the rest of them, can ever subscribe to the principle that "language alone decides the formation of States." It would be impossible to carry that principle into effect. . . .

The German territory which we demand is ours by nature and by history. . . . In the tempests of the great Revolution the people of Alsace, like all the citizens of France, learned to forget their past. . . .

Most assuredly, the task of reuniting there the broken links between the ages is one of the heaviest that has ever been imposed upon the political forces of our nation. . . .

The people of Alsace are already beginning to doubt the invincibility of their nation, and at all events to divine the mighty growth of the German Empire. Perverse obstinacy, and a thousand French intrigues creeping in the dark, will make every step on the newly conquered soil difficult for us: but our ultimate success is certain, for on our side fights what is stronger than the lying artifices of the stranger—nature herself and the voice of common blood.

SOURCES: (I) From "History," *The Annual Register . . . 1860* (London, 1861), p. 221, as quoted in Raymond Phineas Stearns, *Pageant of Europe: Sources and Selections from the Renaissance to the Present Day* (New York: Harcourt, Brace & Company, 1948), pp. 583–584. (II) From Heinrich von Treitschke, "What We Demand from France" (1870), in Heinrich von Treitschke, *Germany, France, Russia and Islam* (New York: G. P. Putnam's Sons, 1915), pp. 100, 102, 106, 109, 120, 122, 134–135, 153, 158.

Map 22–3 THE UNIFICATION OF GERMANY

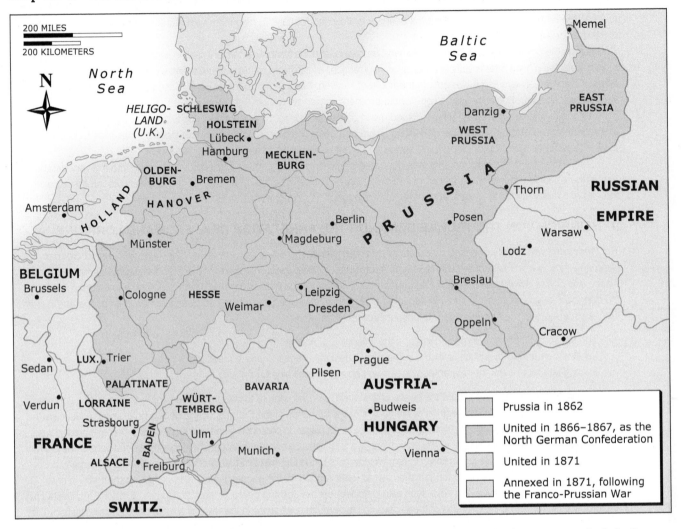

Under Bismarck's leadership, and with the strong support of its royal house, Prussia used diplomatic and military means, on both the German and international stages, to unify the German states into a strong national entity.

22.4 German Unification

How did Otto von Bismarck use war as a tool for achieving German unification?

German unification was the most important political development in Europe between 1848 and 1914. (See Map 22–3.) It transformed the balance of economic, military, and international power. Moreover, the way it was unified largely determined the character of the new German state. Germany's unification was masterminded by Otto von Bismarck, the conservative prime minister of Prussia, who wanted to outflank Prussian liberals and prevent a more radical version of a unified Germany by revolution from below. The prime minister was aided by the army and the monarchy. Although he had no master plan for German unification, he used every opportunity to secure the continued dominance of Prussia within Germany and the power of the Prussian monarch. A unified Germany, which two

generations of German liberals had sought, was achieved for the most illiberal of reasons.

During the 1850s, German unification seemed remote. The political structure of the German-speaking lands was the German Confederation, which had been established at the Congress of Vienna. It was a loose federation of thirty-nine states of differing size and strength whose appointed representatives met in a central diet in Frankfurt. The two by far strongest states were Austria and Prussia. During the 1850s, Austria presided over the diet of the German Confederation. The major states continued to trade with each other through the Zollverein (tariff union), and railways linked their economies. Frederick William IV of Prussia had rejected overtures toward unification under Prussian leadership. Austria continued to oppose any union. If a union included Austrian Germans, the empire would be split in half; if it excluded them, Austria's influence within Germany would diminish. Liberal nationalists had not recovered from the humiliations of 1848 and 1849 and did not have the political power to push for unification.

What quickly overturned this static situation was a series of domestic political changes and problems within Prussia.

In 1858, Frederick William IV was judged insane, and his brother William assumed the regency. William I (r. 1861–1888), who became king in his own right in 1861, was less idealistic than his brother and more of a Prussian patriot. In the usual Hohenzollern tradition, his first concern was to strengthen the Prussian army. In 1860, his war minister and chief of staff proposed enlarging the army, increasing the number of officers, and extending the period of conscription from two to three years. The Prussian Parliament, created by the Constitution of 1850, refused to approve the necessary taxes. The liberals, who dominated the body, sought to avoid placing additional power in the hands of the monarchy. For two years, monarch and parliament were deadlocked.

22.4.1 Bismarck

In September 1862, William I turned for help to the person who, more than any other single individual, shaped the next thirty years of European history: Otto von Bismarck (1815–1898). Bismarck came from the landed nobility (Ger. *Junker*). During the 1840s, he was elected to the provincial diet, where he was so reactionary he disturbed even the king. Yet he had made his mark. From 1851 to 1859, Bismarck served as the Prussian representative to the German Confederation. There he was an outspoken opponent of Austria. Later he became Prussian ambassador to Russia and was ambassador to France when William I appointed him prime minister.

Upon becoming prime minister in 1862, Bismarck immediately moved against the liberal parliament. He contended that even without new financial levies, the Prussian constitution permitted the government to carry out its functions based on previously granted taxes. Therefore, taxes could be collected and spent despite parliamentary refusal to vote them. The army and most of the bureaucracy supported this interpretation of the constitution. In 1863, however, new elections sustained the liberal majority in the parliament. Bismarck needed to attract popular support away from the liberals and toward the monarchy and the army. He therefore set about uniting Germany through the conservative institutions of Prussia. In effect, Bismarck embraced German nationalism as a strategy to enable Prussian conservatives to outmaneuver Prussian liberals.

Although Bismarck never abandoned his fundamental conservatism, he recognized that the only successful way to prevent the change he did not want was to lead Prussia toward change compatible with his basic values: monarchism and Prussian strength. Because the transformations in German history that Bismarck oversaw amounted to a revolution with the aim of protecting core conservative values, he has been called a "white revolutionary."[3] He opposed parliamentary government but not a constitutionalism that preserved a strong monarchy. He understood that

Prussia—and later, Germany—must have a strong industrial base. His years in Frankfurt arguing with his Austrian counterpart had hardened his Prussian patriotism. In politics, he was a pragmatist who put more trust in power and action than in ideas.

As he declared in his first speech as prime minister, "Germany is not looking to Prussia's liberalism but to her power. . . . The great questions of the day will not be decided by speeches and majority decisions—that was the mistake of 1848–1849—but by iron and blood."[4] After German unification, Bismarck became a dedicated advocate of preserving European peace. He served as an important check on the ambitions of his king. But during the process of unification, Bismarck was willing to go to war to achieve his goals. Germany was unified over the course of three wars, each of which Bismarck could have prevented had he not considered them useful.

22.4.1.1 THE DANISH WAR (1864) Bismarck's vision of a united Germany did not include all German-speaking lands. He pursued a *kleindeutsch*, or small German, solution to unification. He intended to exclude Austria from any future united German state. This goal required complex diplomacy.

The Schleswig-Holstein problem gave Bismarck an opportunity to antagonize Austria. The kings of Denmark had long ruled these two northern duchies, which had never actually become part of Denmark itself, and which were inhabited by both Germans and Danes. Holstein, where Germans predominated, belonged to the German Confederation. In 1863, the Danish Parliament moved to incorporate both duchies into Denmark. The smaller states of the German Confederation proposed an all-German war to halt this move. Bismarck proposed a war against Denmark—the **Danish War**—waged by Prussia allied with Austria, excluding the smaller German states. Together, the two large states easily defeated Denmark in 1864.

Over the next two years, Bismarck managed to maneuver Austria into war with Prussia. In August 1865, the two powers negotiated the Convention of Gastein, which put Austria in charge of Holstein and Prussia in charge of Schleswig. Bismarck then needed to prepare a second, more decisive conflict with Austria. First, he established international support for Prussia. He had gained Russian sympathy in 1863 by supporting Russia's suppression of a Polish revolt, and he persuaded Napoleon III to promise neutrality in an Austro-Prussian conflict. In April 1866, Bismarck promised Venetia to the new Kingdom of Italy if it attacked Austria in support of Prussia when war broke out. Now Bismarck had to provoke his war.

22.4.1.2 THE AUSTRO–PRUSSIAN WAR (1866) Constant Austro–Prussian tensions had arisen over the administration of Schleswig and Holstein. Bismarck ordered the Prussian forces to be as obnoxious as possible to the Austrians.

On June 1, 1866, Austria appealed to the German Confederation to intervene in the dispute. Bismarck claimed that this request violated the 1864 alliance and the Convention of Gastein. The result was the Seven Weeks' War, which began in the summer of 1866. Nationalists were horrified by this German "civil war." Although the smaller German states sided with Austria, Prussia decisively defeated Austria and its allies at Königgrätz in Bohemia.

The Treaty of Prague, which ended the conflict on August 23, was lenient toward Austria, which only lost Venetia, and permanently excluded the Austrian Habsburgs from German affairs. Prussia had thus established itself as the only major power among the German states. The nationalists who had objected to Bismarck's fostering of conflict with Austria now celebrated "the god of the moment: success."[5]

22.4.1.3 THE NORTH GERMAN CONFEDERATION

In 1867, Prussia annexed Hanover, Hesse-Kassel, Nassau, and the city of Frankfurt, all of which had supported Austria during the war and deposed their rulers. Under Prussian leadership, the German states north of the Main River now formed the North German Confederation. Each state retained its own government, but all military forces were under federal control. The president of the federation was the king of Prussia, represented by his chancellor, Bismarck. A legislature consisted of two houses: a federal council, or *Bundesrat*, comprised of members appointed by the governments of the states, and a lower house, or *Reichstag*, chosen by universal male suffrage.

Bismarck embraced a democratic franchise because he anticipated that the peasants would vote for conservatives. Moreover, the Reichstag had little real power because the ministers were responsible only to the monarch. The Reichstag could not even originate legislation. The constitution of the North German Confederation, which after 1871 became the constitution of the German Empire, had the appearances, but none of the substance, of liberalism. Germany was, in effect, a conservative monarchy supported by the landed aristocracy and the military.

Bismarck's spectacular successes overwhelmed the liberal opposition in the Prussian Parliament. The liberals were split between those who prized the principles of liberalism and those whose primary goal was national unification. In the end, nationalism proved more attractive. Bismarck had crushed the Prussian liberals by making the monarchy and the army the most popular institutions in the country. The drive toward German national unification had achieved his domestic Prussian political goal.

22.4.2 The Franco-Prussian War and the German Empire (1870–1871)

Bismarck now wanted to complete unification by bringing the states of southern Germany—Bavaria, Württemberg, Baden, and Hesse-Darmstadt—into the newly established confederation. Spain gave him the excuse. In 1868, a military coup deposed the corrupt Bourbon queen of Spain, Isabella II (r. 1833–1868). To replace her, the Spaniards chose Prince Leopold of Hohenzollern-Sigmaringen, a Catholic cousin of William I of Prussia. On June 19, 1870, Leopold accepted the Spanish crown with Prussian blessings. Bismarck knew that France would object strongly to a Hohenzollern Spain.

PROCLAMATION OF THE GERMAN EMPIRE, 1871 Shown here is the proclamation of the German Empire in the Hall of Mirrors at Versailles, January 18, 1871, after the defeat of France in the Franco-Prussian War. Kaiser Wilhelm I stands at the top of the steps under the flags, but viewers are drawn to Bismarck, who stands in the center in a white uniform.
SOURCE: bpk Bildagentur/Art Resource, NY

On July 12, Leopold's father renounced his son's candidacy for the Spanish throne, fearing the issue would cause war between Prussia and France.

The matter might have ended there, had it not been for the impetuosity of the French and the guile of Bismarck. On July 13, the French government instructed its ambassador, Count Vincent Benedetti, to ensure William would not tolerate any future Spanish candidacy for Leopold. The king refused but said he might take the question under further consideration. Later that day he sent Bismarck, who was in Berlin, a telegram reporting the substance of the meeting. The peaceful resolution of the controversy disappointed Bismarck, who desperately wanted a war with France to complete unification. William's telegram gave him a new opportunity to provoke war. Bismarck released an edited version of the dispatch. The revised Ems dispatch made it appear that William had insulted the French ambassador. The idea was to goad France into declaring war.

The French government fell for Bismarck's bait and declared war on July 19. Napoleon III was sick and not eager for war, but his government believed victory over the North German Confederation would renew popular support for the empire. Once the conflict erupted, the southern German states, honoring treaties of 1866, joined Prussia against France, whose defeat was not long in coming. On September 1, at the Battle of Sedan, German forces not only beat the French army but also captured Napoleon III. By late September, Paris was besieged; it finally capitulated on January 28, 1871.

Ten days earlier, in the Hall of Mirrors at the Palace of Versailles, the German Empire had been proclaimed. The German princes asked William to accept the title of German emperor. The princes remained heads of their respective states within the new empire. Through the peace settlement with France, Germany annexed Alsace and part of Lorraine and forced the French to pay a large indemnity.

Both the fact and the manner of German unification produced long-range effects in Europe. A powerful new state had been created in north central Europe. It was rich in natural resources and talented citizens and had an advanced educational system. Militarily and economically, the German Empire would be far stronger than Prussia had been alone. The unification of Germany was also a blow to European liberalism because the new state was a conservative creation. Conservative politics were now backed not by a weak Austria or an economically underdeveloped Russia but by the strongest military and economic state on the Continent.

The two nations most immediately affected by German and Italian unification were France and Austria. The emergence of the two new unified states revealed French and Habsburg weaknesses. Each had to change. France returned to republican government, and the Habsburgs undertook a major domestic restructuring.

KEY EVENTS OF GERMAN AND ITALIAN UNIFICATION	
1854	Crimean War begins
1855	Cavour leads Piedmont into the war on the side of France and Britain
1856	Treaty of Paris concludes the Crimean War
1858 (January 14)	Attempt to assassinate Napoleon III
1858 (July 20)	Secret conference between Napoleon III and Cavour at Plombières
1859	War of Piedmont and France against Austria
1860	Garibaldi lands his forces in Sicily and invades southern Italy
1861 (March 17)	Proclamation of the Kingdom of Italy
1861 (June 6)	Death of Cavour
1862	Bismarck becomes prime minister of Prussia
1864	Danish War
1865	Convention of Gastein
1866	Seven Weeks' War between Prussia and Austria
1866	Austria cedes Venetia to Italy
1867	North German Confederation formed
1870 (June 19–July 12)	Crisis over Hohenzollern candidacy for the Spanish throne
1870 (July 13)	Bismarck publishes the edited Ems dispatch
1870 (July 19)	France declares war on Prussia
1870 (September 1)	German forces defeat France at Sedan and capture Napoleon III
1870 (September 4)	French Republic proclaimed
1870 (October 2)	Italian state annexes Rome
1871 (January 18)	Proclamation of the German Empire at Versailles
1871 (March 28–May 28)	Paris Commune
1871 (May 23)	Treaty of Frankfurt ratified between France and Germany

22.5 France: From Liberal Empire to the Third Republic

What event led to the establishment of a Third Republic in France?

Historians divide the reign of Napoleon III (r. 1852–1870) into the years of the authoritarian empire and those of the liberal empire. The year of division is 1860. After the coup in December 1851, Napoleon III had controlled the legislature, censored the press, and harassed political dissidents. His support came from the army, property owners, the French Catholic Church, peasants, and businesspeople. They approved the security he ensured for property, his protection of the pope, and his economic program. French victory in the Crimean War had confirmed the emperor's popularity.

From the late 1850s onward, Napoleon III modified his authoritarian policy. In 1860, he concluded a free-trade treaty with Britain and permitted freer debate in the legislature. By the late 1860s, he had relaxed the press laws and permitted labor unions. In 1870, he allowed the leaders of the moderates in the legislature to form a ministry, and he also agreed to a liberal constitution that made the ministers responsible to the legislature.

Napoleon III's liberal concessions were an attempt to shore up domestic support to compensate for his failures in foreign policy. By 1860, he had lost control of the diplomacy of Italian unification. Between 1861 and 1867, he had supported a disastrous military expedition against Mexico. In 1866, France had watched passively while Bismarck and Prussia reorganized German affairs. The Franco–Prussian War of 1870 had been the French government's last and most disastrous attempt to demonstrate strength in international affairs to secure domestic popularity.

The Second Empire came to an inglorious end with the Battle of Sedan in September 1870. The emperor was captured and then allowed to go to England, where he died in 1873. Shortly after news of Sedan reached Paris, a republic was proclaimed and a government of national defense established. Paris itself was soon under Prussian siege, and the government moved to Bordeaux. Paris finally surrendered in January 1871, but France had been ready to sue for peace long before.

22.5.1 The Paris Commune

The division between the provinces and Paris became sharper after the fighting with Germany stopped. Monarchists dominated the new National Assembly elected in February. For the time being, the assembly gave executive power to Adolphe Thiers (1797–1877), who had been active in French politics since 1830. He negotiated a settlement with Prussia, the Treaty of Frankfurt, which was officially ratified on May 23.

Many Parisians, having suffered during the siege, resented what they regarded as a betrayal by the monarchist National Assembly sitting at Versailles. The Parisians elected a new municipal government, called the **Paris Commune**, which was formally proclaimed on March 28, 1871. The commune intended to administer Paris separately from the rest of France. Radicals and socialists of all stripes participated in the commune. In April, the National Assembly surrounded Paris with an army and on May 8, bombarded the city. On May 21, it broke through the city's defenses. During the next seven days, the troops killed about 20,000 inhabitants while the communards shot scores of hostages.

The Paris Commune became a legend throughout Europe. Marxists regarded it as a genuine proletarian government that the French bourgeoisie had suppressed. This interpretation is mistaken. The commune, though of shifting composition, was dominated by petty bourgeois members.

The socialism of the commune had its roots in Blanqui's and Proudhon's anarchism rather than in Marx's concept of class conflict. The commune did not want a nation of workers but of relatively independent, radically democratic enclaves. Its suppression thus represented not only the protection of property but also the triumph of the centralized nation-state. Just as the armies of Piedmont and Prussia had united the small states of Italy and Germany, the army of the French National Assembly destroyed the particularistic political tendencies of Paris and, by implication, those of any other French community.

22.5.2 The Third Republic

The National Assembly backed into a republican form of government against its will. Its monarchist majority was divided in loyalty between the House of Bourbon and the House of Orléans.

While the monarchists quarreled among themselves, events marched on. By September 1873, the indemnity had been paid, and the Prussian occupation troops had withdrawn. Thiers was ousted from office because he had displayed clear republican sentiments. A conservative army officer, Marshal Patrice MacMahon (1808–1893), was elected president and expected to prepare for a monarchist restoration. In 1875, the National Assembly, still monarchist in sentiment but unable to find a king, adopted a law that provided for a Chamber of Deputies elected by universal male suffrage, a senate chosen indirectly, and a president elected by the two legislative houses. This rather simple republican system had resulted from the bickering and frustration of the monarchists.

After numerous quarrels with the Chamber of Deputies, MacMahon resigned in 1879. His departure meant that dedicated republicans controlled the national government despite lingering opposition from the church, wealthy families, and a part of the army.

The political structure of the **Third Republic** proved much stronger than many citizens suspected at the time. It survived challenges from persons such as General Georges Boulanger (1837–1891), who would have imposed stronger executive authority. It also survived several scandals, such as those involving sales of awards of the Legion of Honor and widespread corruption of politicians and journalists by a company that tried to construct a canal in Panama. The institutions of the republic, however, allowed new ministers to replace those whose corruption was exposed without revolution.

22.6 The Habsburg Empire

Why was nationalism such a threat to the Habsburg Empire?

At the beginning of the nineteenth century, Austria was still considered the most powerful state in central Europe. A series of defeats and mismanaged diplomatic conflicts had revealed

FRANCIS JOSEPH Francis Joseph (1830–1916) ruled Austria and then Austria-Hungary from 1848 until his death. In this 1865 photo, the young emperor is shown in military gala attire, one of his preferred uniforms. His devotion to the Austrian army made it difficult for him to share control over the military with parliament, which contributed to chronic underfunding.
SOURCE: Sueddeutsche Zeitung Photo/Alamy Stock Photo

KEY DATES IN THE LATE-NINETEENTH-CENTURY HABSBURG EMPIRE	
1848	Francis Joseph becomes emperor at age 18
1859	Defeat by France and Piedmont
1860	October Diploma
1861	February Patent
1866	Defeat by Prussia
1867	Compromise between emperor and Hungary, establishing the dual monarchy
1897	Ordinances giving equality of language between Germans and Czechs in Austria
1907	Universal male suffrage introduced for Austria

power encountered tremendous resentment. They eventually floundered because of setbacks in foreign affairs.

Austrian refusal to support Russia during the Crimean War meant the new tsar Alexander II (r. 1855–1881) would no longer help preserve Habsburg rule in Hungary, as Nicholas I had done in 1849. Austria lost Russian support without gaining the support of France or Great Britain. The Austrian defeat in 1859 at the hands of France and Piedmont, the subsequent loss of territory in Italy, and later the defeat at the hands of Prussia in 1866 confirmed the necessity for a new domestic policy. The emperor, his civil servants, aristocrats, and politicians tried to construct a viable system of government that would maintain the integrity of the empire while meeting regional demands for self-governance.

22.6.1 Formation of the Dual Monarchy

In 1860, Francis Joseph put his attempts at centralization aside and issued the October Diploma, which created a federation among the states and provinces of the empire. There were to be local diets dominated by the landed classes and a single imperial parliament. The Hungarian nobility, however, rejected the plan.

Consequently, in 1861, the emperor issued the February Patent, which set up an entirely different form of government. It established a bicameral imperial parliament, or *Reichsrat*, with an upper chamber appointed by the emperor and an indirectly elected lower chamber. Again, the Hungarians refused to cooperate in a system that denied them full control over historic Hungarian territory. Nevertheless, for six years, the February Patent governed the empire. Ministers were responsible to the emperor, not the Reichsrat, and civil liberties were not guaranteed. Armies could be levied and taxes raised without parliamentary consent. When the Reichsrat was not in session, the emperor could rule by decree.

Meanwhile, secret negotiations between the emperor and the Hungarians produced no concrete result until the Prussian defeat of Austria in the summer of 1866 and the consequent exclusion of Austria from German affairs. Francis Joseph now had to come to terms with the Hungarians. The subsequent

Austria's weakness relative to France, Russia, Germany, and even Italy, and left it isolated. An ungenerous critic remarked that a standing army of soldiers, a kneeling army of priests, and a crawling army of informers supported the empire. In the age of national states, liberal institutions, and industrialism, the Habsburg domains remained primarily dynastic, absolutist, and agrarian. The Habsburg response to the revolts of 184 through 1849 had been to reassert absolutism. **Emperor Francis Joseph** (r. 1848–1916) was honest, conscientious, and hardworking, but unimaginative and deeply committed to dynastic tradition. He did not have an advisor like Bismarck or Cavour who could show him the path to managing inevitable change. Instead, he held on to tradition as long as possible, only reacting to events as he was forced to do so.

During the 1850s, his ministers attempted to impose a centralized administration on the empire. The Vienna government abolished internal tariffs in the empire. It divided Hungary, which had been so revolutionary in 1848, into military districts. The Roman Catholic Church acquired control of education. In a country in which traditional local privileges held by powerful aristocratic interests had so much historical power, these attempts to increase central

Ausgleich, or Compromise, of 1867 transformed the Habsburg Empire into a dual monarchy known as Austria-Hungary.

Francis Joseph was crowned king of Hungary in Budapest in 1867. Except for the common monarch, army, and foreign relations, Austria and Hungary became almost wholly separate states.

22.6.2 Unrest of Nationalities

The Compromise of 1867 introduced two different principles of political legitimacy into the two sections of the Habsburg Empire. In Hungary, political loyalty was based on nationality because Hungary had been recognized as a distinct part of the monarchy on the basis of nationalism. In the rest of the Habsburg domains, the principle of legitimacy meant dynastic loyalty to the emperor. Nationalists

who claimed to represent other peoples within the empire wished to achieve the same type of settlement that the Hungarians had won; to govern themselves; or as time went on, to unite with fellow nationals outside the empire.

Nationalists claiming to represent Czechs, Poles, Ukrainians, Romanians, Croats, and Italians complained that the Compromise of 1867 permitted the German-speaking Austrians and the Hungarians to dominate all other nationalities within their respective "halves" of the empire. The most vocal critics were the Czechs of Bohemia. They favored a policy of "trialism," or triple monarchy, in which the Czechs would have a position similar to that of the Hungarians. In 1871, Francis Joseph was willing to accept this concept. The Hungarians, however, vetoed; they did not want to be forced to make similar concessions to their own subject nationalities. Furthermore,

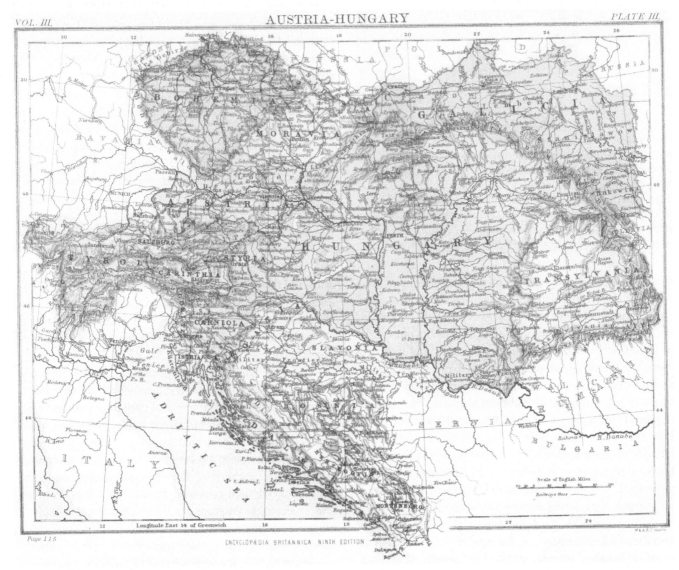

NATIONALITIES WITHIN THE HABSBURG EMPIRE The Habsburg census forced residents to choose one "language of daily use." Many bilingual people in the empire were thus statistically represented as members of a single nationality. As a result, in ethnolinguistic maps of the time, the empire appeared as a patchwork of many different nationalities—Bohemian, Moravian, Galician, Austrian, Hungarian, Transylvanian, Tyrolian, Carpathian, etc.—which both underestimated the sense of unity within the empire and overestimated the homogeneity of various "national" regions. This map, from a 1905 French school textbook, illustrates this phenomenon.
SOURCE: Antiqua Print Gallery/Alamy Stock Photo

German-speakers in Bohemia were afraid the Czech language would be imposed on them.

At the same time the compromise between Austria and Hungary was introduced, the emperor proclaimed a new constitution, called the "Basic Law," that would apply in Austria. It guaranteed Austrians basic civil rights. The liberal provisions of the constitution, however, did not satisfy nationalists within the empire. By the 1890s, however, Czech nationalism was particularly strident. In 1897, Francis Joseph's prime minister, Count Casimir Badeni, made the Czech and German languages equal in Bohemia. This would in effect require that all civil servants in Bohemia be bilingual. Both German and Czech nationalists in the Austrian Reichsrat opposed these measures by disrupting parliament. By the turn of the century, this obstructionism, which included the playing of musical instruments in the Reichsrat, had paralyzed parliamentary life. With parliament unable to pass legislation, the emperor ruled by imperial decree through the bureaucracy. In 1907, Francis Joseph introduced universal male suffrage in Austria (but not in Hungary), but this action did not eliminate the chaos in the Reichsrat. Parliament's problems diminished many Austrians' faith in the effectiveness of constitutional rule.

Interest in nationalism became more widespread during the last quarter of the nineteenth century, but even then many Austrians continued to place greater importance in dynastic loyalty, religion, or local identity. Language became the single most important factor in defining a nation. The expansion of education made this possible. In all countries where nationalist groups prospered, their membership was dominated by intellectuals, students, and educated members of the middle class, all of whom were familiar with the literary version of particular national languages.

The agitation of nationalists within the Habsburg Empire not only caused internal political difficulties but also became a major source of political instability for central and eastern Europe. Each of the nationality problems normally had ramifications for both foreign and domestic policy. Poles wanted an independent state with their fellow nationals who lived in the Russian Empire and Germany. Even Poles who argued for autonomy within the Austrian Empire used nationalist language that seemed to undermine the idea of a unified empire. But it was not in the Austrian emperor's power to authorize greater links among the various parts of the former Polish–Lithuanian Commonwealth. Italian nationalists in Trieste and Southern Tyrol/Trent demanded unification with the Kingdom of Italy, exacerbating tensions between Austria and Italy. Many of the Slavic nationalities, especially in the South, looked to Russia to protect their interests or influence the government in Vienna. Romania was concerned about the Romanian minority in Hungary. Serbia sought to expand its borders to include Serbs who lived within Habsburg or Ottoman territory. From these Balkan tensions emerged much of the turmoil that would spark World War I.

Although nationalistic tensions within Austria-Hungary were a significant contributor to the political instability of the empire and the international tensions that led to World War I, they should not be overestimated. Nationalists dominated the press and politics, but their views were not universally shared. Many subjects of the Habsburg emperor remained loyal to the dynasty and the idea of a multinational empire until the very last months of World War I.

Whatever the private sentiments of the citizenry, however, nationality problems touched all four of the great central and eastern European empires—the German, the Russian, the Austrian, and the Ottoman. All four contained many minority groups, including, in the case of the first three, large Polish populations. The weakness of the Ottoman Empire allowed both Austria and Russia to compete in the Balkans for influence and thus further inflame nationalist resentments. Such nationalist stirrings affected the fate of all four empires from the 1860s through the outbreak of World War I. The government of each of these empires would be overturned during the war, and the Habsburg monarchy and the Ottoman Empire would disappear.

22.7 Russia: Emancipation and Revolutionary Stirrings

Why did reform in Russia fail to produce political stability?

Russia changed remarkably during the last half of the nineteenth century. The government finally addressed the long-standing problem of serfdom and undertook a broad range of administrative reforms. During the same period, however, radical revolutionary groups began to organize. These groups tried to draw the peasants into revolutionary activity and assassinated government officials, including the tsar. The government's response was renewed repression.

KEY DATES IN LATE-NINETEENTH-CENTURY RUSSIA	
1855	Alexander II becomes tsar
1856	Defeat in Crimean War
1861	Serfdom abolished
1863	Suppression of Polish rebellion
1864	Reorganization of local government
1864	Reform of judicial system
1874	Military enlistment period reduced
1878	Attempted assassination of military governor of Saint Petersburg
1879	Land and Freedom splits
1881	The People's Will assassinates Alexander II
1881	Alexander III becomes tsar
1894	Nicholas II becomes tsar

22.7.1 Reforms of Alexander II

Russia's defeat in the Crimean War and its humiliation in the Treaty of Paris compelled the government to reconsider its domestic policies. The debacle of the war had made reform both necessary and possible. Alexander II took advantage of this turn of events to institute the most extensive restructuring of Russian society and administration since Peter the Great. Like Peter, Alexander imposed his reforms from the top.

22.7.1.1 ABOLITION OF SERFDOM

In every area of economic and public life, a profound cultural gap separated Russia from the rest of Europe. Nowhere was this more apparent than in the survival of serfdom. In Russia, the institution had changed little since the eighteenth century, although every other nation on the Continent had abandoned it. Russian landowners still had a free hand with their serfs, and the serfs had little recourse against the landlords. In March 1856, at the conclusion of the Crimean War, Alexander II announced his intention to abolish serfdom. He had decided that its abolition was necessary if Russia was to remain a great power.

Serfdom was economically inefficient. There was always the threat of revolt, and the serfs forced into the army had performed poorly in the Crimean War. Moreover, nineteenth-century moral opinion condemned serfdom. For five years, government commissions wrestled over how to implement the tsar's desire. Finally, in February 1861, despite opposition from the nobility and the landlords, Alexander II ended serfdom.

The emancipation law was a disappointment, however, because land did not accompany freedom. Serfs immediately received the personal right to marry without their landlord's permission, as well as the rights to buy and sell property, to sue in court, and to pursue trades. What they did not receive was free title to their land. They had to pay the landlords over a period of forty-nine years for allotments of land that were frequently too small to support them. The former serfs, who were now free peasant farmers, made the payments to the government, which had already reimbursed the landlords for their losses. The peasants would not receive title to their land until the debts were paid. Although peasants were no longer personally bonded to their landlords, restrictions on individual freedom continued. What the landlord no longer controlled was now controlled by the communes and the elders who oversaw their management and governance. Redemption payments, taxes, and rights to land use were all collective and controlled by village elders, whose permission was even required if a peasant wanted to leave the commune.

The procedures were so complicated and the results so limited that many serfs believed real emancipation was still to come. The redemption payments led to almost unending difficulty. Poor harvests made it impossible for many peasants to make the payments, and they fell increasingly behind in their debt. The situation was not remedied until 1906, when during the widespread revolutionary unrest following the Japanese defeat of Russia in 1905, the government grudgingly canceled the remaining debts.

22.7.1.2 REFORM OF LOCAL GOVERNMENT, THE JUDICIAL SYSTEM, AND THE MILITARY

The abolition of serfdom required the reorganization of local government and the judicial system. The authority of village communes replaced that of the landlord over the peasant. The village elders settled family quarrels, imposed fines, issued internal passports that were legally required for peasants to move from one locale to another, and collected taxes. Often the village commune, not individual peasants, owned the land. The nobility was given a larger role in local administration through a system of provincial and county *zemstvos*, or councils, organized in 1864. These councils were to oversee local matters, such as bridge and road repair, education, and agricultural improvement. The zemstvos were underfunded and many of them remained ineffective.

In 1864, Alexander II issued a new statute on the judiciary that for the first time introduced Western European legal principles into Russia. These included equality before the law, impartial hearings, uniform procedures, judicial independence, and trial by jury. The new system was far from perfect. The judges were not genuinely independent, and the tsar could increase as well as reduce sentences. Nonetheless, the new courts were both more efficient and less corrupt than the old system.

The government also reformed the army. Russia possessed the largest army on the Continent, but it had floundered badly in the Crimean War. The usual period of service for a soldier was twenty-five years. Villages had to provide quotas of serfs to serve in the army. Once in the army, recruits rarely saw their homes again. Life in the army was harsh, even by the brutal standards of most mid-century armies. In the 1860s, the army lowered the period of service to fifteen years and relaxed discipline slightly. In 1874, the enlistment period was lowered to six years of active duty and nine years in the reserves. All males were subject to military service after the age of twenty.

22.7.1.3 REPRESSION IN POLAND

Alexander's reforms became more measured shortly after the Polish January Insurrection of 1863. As in 1830, Polish nationalists attempted to overthrow Russian dominance. Once again, the Russian army suppressed the rebellion. Alexander II then moved to Russify Poland. In 1864, he emancipated the Polish serfs to punish the politically restive Polish nobility. Russian law, language, and administration were imposed on all areas of Polish life.

As the Polish suppression demonstrated, Alexander II was a reformer only within the limits of his own autocracy. His changes in Russian life failed to create new loyalty to, or gratitude for, the government among his subjects. The serfs felt their emancipation had been inadequate. The nobles and the wealthier educated segments of Russian society resented the tsar's persistent refusal to allow them a meaningful role in government and policymaking. Consequently, although Alexander II became known as the Tsar Liberator, he was never popular. He became even more indecisive and closed-minded after an attempt was made on his life in 1866. Thereafter, Russia increasingly became a police state. This new repression fueled the activity of radical groups within Russia. Their actions, in turn, made the autocracy more reactionary.

22.7.2 Revolutionaries

Many critics, both inside and outside Russia, targeted the tsarist regime. One of the most prominent was Alexander Herzen (1812–1870), who lived in exile. Russian students and intellectuals who had greeted Alexander II's initial reforms enthusiastically soon became discontented with their limited character. Drawing on the ideas of Herzen and other radicals, these students formed a revolutionary movement known as populism. They sought a social revolution based on the communal life of the Russian peasants. The chief radical society was called Land and Freedom.

In the early 1870s, hundreds of young Russian men and women took their revolutionary message to the countryside. They intended to live with the peasants, to gain their trust, and to teach them about the peasant's role in the coming revolution. The bewildered and distrustful peasants turned most of the youths over to the police. In the winter of 1877 to 1878, almost 200 students were tried. Most were acquitted or

given light sentences because they had been held for months in preventive detention and because the court believed a display of mercy might lessen public sympathy for the revolutionaries. The court even suggested the tsar might wish to pardon those students given heavier sentences. The tsar refused and let it be known he favored heavy penalties for all persons involved in revolutionary activity.

Thereafter, the revolutionaries decided the tsarist regime must be attacked directly. They adopted a policy of terrorism. In January 1878, Vera Zasulich (1849–1919) attempted to assassinate the military governor of Saint Petersburg. A jury acquitted her because the governor she had shot had a reputation for brutality. Some people also believed Zasulich had a personal rather than a political grievance against her victim. Nonetheless, the verdict further encouraged the terrorists.

In 1879, a group known as The People's Will split off from Land and Freedom. It was dedicated to the overthrow of the autocracy. Its members decided to assassinate the tsar himself. Several attempts failed, but on March 1, 1881, a bomb hurled by a member of The People's Will killed Alexander II. Four men and two women were sentenced to death for the deed. All of them had been willing to die for their cause. The emergence of dedicated revolutionary opposition was as much a part of the reign of Alexander II as were his reforms.

The reign of Alexander III (r. 1881–1894) strengthened that pessimism. He possessed all the autocratic and repressive characteristics of his grandfather, Nicholas I. Alexander III sought primarily to roll back his father's

ASSASSINATION OF ALEXANDER II, 1881 Tsar Alexander II (r. 1855–1881) was assassinated on March 1, 1881. The assassins first threw a bomb that wounded several imperial guards. When the tsar stopped his carriage to see the injured, the assassins threw a second bomb, killing him.
SOURCE: bpk Bildagentur/Art Resource, NY

reforms. He favored the centralized bureaucracy over the *zemstvos*. He strengthened the secret police and increased censorship of the press. In effect, he confirmed all the evils that the revolutionaries saw as inherent in autocratic government. His son, Nicholas II (r. 1894–1917), would discover that autocracy could not survive the pressures of the twentieth century.

22.8 Great Britain: Toward Democracy

What forces led to the expansion of democracy in Great Britain?

While the continental nations became unified and struggled toward internal political restructuring, Great Britain symbolized the confident liberal state. Britain faced its own difficulties and domestic conflicts, but it seemed able to deal with them through its existing political institutions. The general prosperity of the third quarter of the century mitigated the social hostility of the 1840s. Even the leaders of trade unions during these years asked mainly to receive more of the fruits of prosperity and to have their social respectability acknowledged. Parliament itself remained an institution through which new groups and interests were absorbed into the existing political processes. (See the "Encountering the Past" sidebar on the penny postage, which follows below.)

22.8.1 The Second Reform Act (1867)

By the early 1860s, most observers realized that the franchise—the right to vote—would again have to be expanded. Many politicians came to believe that the only way to win over the workers' loyalty to the existing system was to accept their demands for the right to vote. Organizations such as the Reform League, led by John Bright (1811–1889), agitated for parliamentary action. In 1866, Lord Russell's liberal ministry introduced a reform bill that a coalition of traditional conservatives and antidemocratic liberals defeated. Russell resigned, and the conservative Lord Derby (1799–1869) replaced him.

The Conservative ministry, led in the House of Commons by **Benjamin Disraeli** (1804–1881), introduced its own reform bill, **the Second Reform Act**, in 1867. As the debate proceeded, Disraeli accepted one amendment after another and expanded the electorate well beyond the limits the liberals had earlier proposed. The final measure increased the number of voters from approximately 1,430,000 to 2,470,000. Although Britain was not a democracy, the admission of large numbers of male working-class voters represented a large step in that direction. As was the case elsewhere in Europe where the franchise was extended, however, women continued to have

no political rights. Across Europe, the franchise was becoming a male prerogative instead of an upper-class one.

Like his contemporary Bismarck, Disraeli thought democracy could be a conservative tool. He believed that eventually significant portions of the working class would support conservative candidates who were responsive to social issues. Because reform was inevitable, it was best for the conservatives to enjoy the credit for it. He also thought the growing suburban middle class would become more conservative. In the long run, his intuition proved correct. The Conservative Party dominated British politics in the twentieth century.

The immediate election of 1868, however, dashed Disraeli's hopes. **William Gladstone** (1809–1898) became the new prime minister. Gladstone had begun political life in 1833 as a strong Tory, but over the next thirty-five years, he became steadily more liberal. He had supported Robert Peel, free trade, repeal of the Corn Laws, and efficient administration. As chancellor of the exchequer (finance minister) during the 1850s and early 1860s, he had lowered taxes and government expenditures. In 1866, he had been Russell's spokesperson in the House of Commons for the unsuccessful liberal reform bill.

22.8.2 Gladstone's Great Ministry (1868–1874)

Gladstone's ministry of 1868 to 1874 witnessed the culmination of classical British liberalism. Those institutions that remained the preserve of the aristocracy and the Anglican church were opened to people from other classes and religious denominations. In 1870, competitive examinations for the civil service replaced patronage. In 1871, the purchase of officers' commissions in the army was abolished. The same year, Anglican religious requirements for the faculties of Oxford and Cambridge universities were removed. The Ballot Act of 1872 introduced voting by secret ballot.

The most momentous measure of Gladstone's first ministry was the **Education Act of 1870**. For the first time in British history, the government assumed the responsibility for establishing and running elementary schools. Previously, British education had been a task relegated to the religious denominations, which received small amounts of state support for the purpose. Now the government could establish schools where religious denominations had not done so.

These reforms were typically liberal. They removed abuses without destroying institutions and permitted all able citizens to compete on the grounds of ability and merit. They tried to avoid the potential danger to a democratic state of an illiterate citizenry. At the same time, they reinforced loyalty to the nation by abolishing sources of discontent.

22.8.3 Disraeli in Office (1874–1880)

Disraeli succeeded Gladstone as prime minister in 1874. The two men differed on most issues. Whereas Gladstone

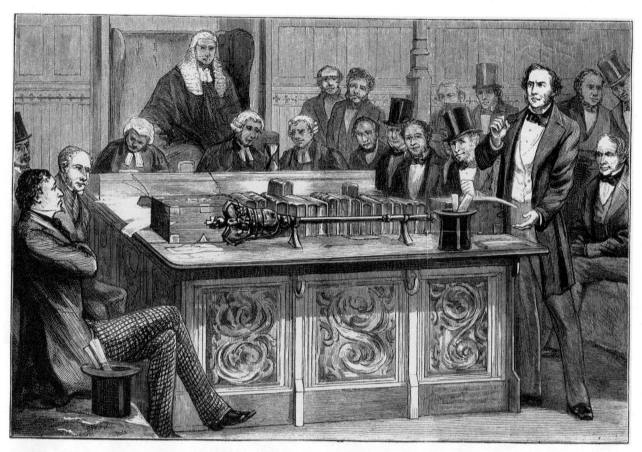

A HOUSE OF COMMONS DEBATE William Gladstone (1809–1898), standing on the right, served in the British Parliament from the 1830s through the 1890s. Four times the Liberal Party prime minister, he was responsible for guiding major reforms through Parliament. Benjamin Disraeli (1804–1881), sitting on left with folded arms, is regarded as the founder of modern British conservatism. He was twice prime minister, in 1868 and from 1874 to 1880. The illustration conveys something of the long-standing hostility between the two statesmen.
SOURCE: Artokoloro Quint Lox Limited/Alamy Stock Photo

looked to individualism, free trade, and competition to solve social problems, Disraeli believed in paternalistic legislation to protect the weak and ease class antagonisms.

Disraeli had few specific programs or ideas. The significant social legislation of his ministry stemmed primarily from the efforts of his home secretary, Richard Cross (1823–1914). The **Public Health Act** of 1875 consolidated previous legislation on sanitation and reaffirmed the duty of the state to interfere with private property to protect health and physical well-being. Through the Artisan Dwelling Act of 1875, the government became actively involved in providing housing for the working class. That same year, in an important symbolic gesture, the conservative majority in Parliament gave new protection to British trade unions and allowed them to raise picket lines. The Gladstone ministry, although recognizing the legality of unions, had refused such protection.

22.8.4 The Irish Question

From the late 1860s onward, Irish nationalists had sought **home rule** for Ireland, meaning Irish control of local

government. The Irish question became the major issue of the 1880s, during Gladstone's second ministry.

During his first ministry, Gladstone addressed the Irish question through two major pieces of legislation. In 1869, he disestablished the Church of Ireland, the Irish branch of the Anglican church. Henceforth, Irish Roman Catholics would not pay taxes to support the hated Protestant church, to which few of the Irish belonged. Second, in 1870, the liberal ministry sponsored a land act that provided compensation to those Irish tenant farmers who were evicted and loans for those who wished to purchase their land. Throughout the 1870s, the Irish question continued to fester. Land remained the center of the agitation. The organization of the Irish Land League in the late 1870s led to intense agitation and intimidation of landlords, who were often Protestants of English descent. The leader of the Irish movement for a just land settlement and for home rule was Charles Stewart Parnell (1846–1891). In 1881, the second Gladstone ministry passed another Irish land act that strengthened tenant rights. It was accompanied, however, by a Coercion Act to restore law and order to Ireland.

By 1885, Parnell had organized eighty-five Irish members of the House of Commons into a tightly disciplined

Encountering the Past

The Arrival of Penny Postage

WHILE THE ARMIES of the great powers were redrawing the map of Europe during the middle of the nineteenth century, new forms of administration were drawing people closer together. One of the most important of these innovations was the development of postal systems for delivering mail inexpensively. The British government took the lead.

SORTING THE MAIL With the new British postal system, the volume of mail vastly increased, as did the number of postal workers involved in sorting and delivering it. This illustration of the stamping and sorting room in the General Post Office in London dates from 1875.
SOURCE: Print Collector/Getty Images

Sending letters and newspapers through the mail had become increasingly expensive, and the British postal service ran large deficits. Other countries had similar problems. At that time the weight of the item to be mailed and the distance over which it had to be carried determined how much it cost to mail it. Furthermore, the person receiving the letter or packet, not the sender, had to pay the postage. Many officials had the privilege of franking their letters and thus paying nothing. The system encouraged schemes to avoid paying postage. Some people could not afford the postage on letters sent to them. Others put symbols on the outside of their letters, so recipients could refuse to accept letters but still "get the message."

Rowland Hill (1795–1879), an English reformer, proposed a simple new procedure in 1837. The price of postage would be lowered, would be uniform for most letters and newspapers regardless of distance, and would be prepaid by the sender. Franking by government officials would also end.

In 1840, the system, known as the Uniform Penny Post, began. Within two years the volume of British mail grew from approximately 75 million items to 196.5 million and by 1849, to 329 million. The reduced cost of postage meant almost everyone could afford to send letters and postcards. It also led to a huge increase in the size of the government workforce. In Britain and most other countries, the number of postal workers was soon rivaled only by the number of soldiers and sailors.

Hill had also suggested a small, self-adhesive stamp be attached to a letter to indicate the postage had been paid. The first such stamp bore only the words *postage one penny*. It paid for letters up to one-half ounce. A two-penny stamp was used for letters that weighed an ounce.

Other nations soon issued their own stamps. It became as important for governments to prevent the forging of postage stamps as currency. Consequently, stamps were printed from engraved steel plates to which small changes were made from time to time. Those changes, introduced to prevent fraud or to commemorate famous people and events, together with the sheer number of national postal systems with their own stamps, gave rise to the hobby of stamp collecting.

The rise of the modern postal system also fostered international cooperation. A treaty signed in Berne, Switzerland, in 1874, established what became the Universal Postal Union, which is still functioning. It mandates that the postage paid in the sender's nation ensures delivery of a letter or package anywhere in the world.

Questions

1. What changes did Rowland Hill introduce to the British postal service?
2. How did those changes affect the quantity of mail and the size of the government workforce?

SOURCES: M. J. Daunton, "Rowland Hill and the Penny Post," *History Today*, August 1985; "Post, and Postal Service," *Encyclopedia Britannica*, 11th ed.

party that often voted as a bloc. They frequently disrupted Parliament to gain attention for the cause of home rule. In the election of 1885, the Irish Party emerged holding the balance of power between the English liberals and conservatives. Irish support could decide which party took office. In December 1885, Gladstone announced his support of home rule for Ireland and Parnell gave his votes to a liberal ministry. The home rule issue then split the Liberal Party. In 1886, a group known as the Liberal Unionists joined with the conservatives to defeat home rule. Gladstone called for a new election, but the liberals were defeated. They remained divided, and Ireland remained firmly under English administration.

The new conservative ministry of Lord Salisbury (1830–1903) attempted to reconcile the Irish to British rule through public works and administrative reform. The policy, which was tied to further coercion, had only marginal success. In 1892, Gladstone returned to power. A second Home Rule Bill passed the House of Commons but was defeated in the House of Lords. There the Irish question stood until after the turn of the century. The conservatives sponsored a land act in 1903 that carried out the final transfer of land to tenant ownership. Ireland became a country of small farms. In 1912, a liberal ministry passed the third Home Rule Bill. Under the provisions of the House of Lords Act of 1911, which curbed the power of the Lords, the bill had to pass the Commons three times over the Lords' veto to become law. The third passage occurred in the summer of 1914, but the implementation of home rule was suspended for the duration of World War I.

The Irish question affected British politics in a manner not unlike that of the Austrian nationalities problem. Normal British domestic issues could not be resolved because of the political divisions Ireland created. The split of the Liberal Party proved especially harmful to the cause of further social and political reform. People who could agree about reform could not agree about Ireland, and the Irish problem seemed more important. Because the two traditional parties failed to deal with the social questions by the turn of the century, a newly organized Labour Party began to fill the vacuum.

KEY DATES IN LATE-NINETEENTH-CENTURY BRITAIN	
1867	Second Reform Act
1868	Gladstone becomes prime minister
1869	Disestablishment of Church of Ireland
1870	Education Act and first Irish Land Act
1871	Purchase of army officers' commissions abolished
1871	Religious tests abolished at Oxford and Cambridge
1872	Secret Ballot Act
1874	Disraeli becomes prime minister
1875	Public Health Act and Artisan Dwelling Act
1880	Beginning of Gladstone's second ministry
1881	Second Irish Land Act and Irish Coercion Act
1884	Third Reform Act
1885	Gladstone announces support of Irish home rule
1886	Home Rule Bill defeated and Lord Salisbury becomes the conservative prime minister
1892	Gladstone begins his third ministry; second Irish Home Rule Bill defeated
1903	Third Irish Land Act
1912	Third Irish Home Rule Bill passed
1914	Provisions of Irish Home Rule Bill suspended because of the outbreak of World War I

The Chapter in Perspective

Between 1850 and 1875, the major contours of the political systems that would dominate Europe until World War I had been drawn. These systems and political arrangements solved, as far as such matters can be solved, many of the

political problems that had troubled Europeans during the first half of the nineteenth century. On the whole, the concept of the nation-state had triumphed. Support for governments no longer stemmed from loyalty to dynasties but from citizen participation. Moreover, the unity of nations was now based on cultural, linguistic, and historical bonds. Both parliamentary governments and monarchies had been compelled to recognize the force of nationalism and the larger role of citizens in political affairs. Only Russia failed to make such concessions. In Russia the only concession to popular opinion had been the emancipation of the serfs.

Future discontent would arise primarily from the demands of labor to enter the political arena and the unsatisfied aspirations of subject nationalities. These two sources of unrest would trouble Europe for the next forty years and would eventually undermine the political structures created during the late nineteenth century.

The Chapter in Review

Review Questions

1. Why did the Ottoman Empire attempt reform between 1839 and 1914? What was the result of these efforts?
2. Why was it so difficult to unify Italy? What groups wanted unification? Why did Cavour succeed? What did Garibaldi contribute to Italian unification?
3. How and why did Bismarck unify Germany? Why had earlier attempts failed? How did German unification affect the rest of Europe?
4. What events led to the establishment of the Third Republic in France? What were the objectives of the Paris Commune?
5. Why did the Habsburgs agree to the Compromise of 1867? Was it a success?
6. What reforms did Alexander II institute in Russia? Did they solve Russia's domestic problems? Why did the abolition of serfdom not satisfy the peasants? What were the goals of The People's Will?
7. How did the policies of the British Liberal and Conservative parties differ between 1860 and 1890? Why was Irish home rule such a divisive issue in British politics?

Key Terms

Austro-Prussian War The Seven Weeks' War in 1866 provoked by Bismarck and that resulted in Prussia's decisive defeat of Austria and its allies at Königgrätz in Bohemia.

Benjamin Disraeli (1804–1881) Prime minister of the United Kingdom from 1874 to 1880, who believed in paternalistic legislation to protect the weak and ease class antagonisms.

Count Camillo Cavour (1810–1861) Italian statesman and a leading figure in the movement toward the unification of Italy.

Crimean War A military conflict from 1853 to 1856 that ended with the defeat of the Russian Empire by an alliance of the Ottoman Empire and the forces of France, Britain, and Austria.

Danish War A successful conflict fought by Prussia against Denmark in 1864 under the leadership of Bismarck.

Education Act of 1870 For the first time in British history, government assuming responsibility for setting up and running elementary schools.

Emperor Francis Joseph (1830–1916) Ruled Austria and then Austria-Hungary as king from 1848 till his death.

Franco-Prussian War Fought from 1870 to 1871 between France and Prussia led by Bismarck, which resulted in the defeat of France and the establishment of the German Empire.

Giuseppe Garibaldi (1807–1882) Italian general, politician, and nationalist and one of the great figures in the history of Italy.

Giuseppe Mazzini (1805–1872) Activist for the unification of Italy and one of the leaders of romantic republican nationalism.

home rule The advocacy of a large measure of administrative autonomy for Ireland within the British Empire between the 1880s and 1914.

Italia irredenta Meaning "unredeemed Italy." The areas with large Italian-speaking populations that remained outside Italy, such as the province of Trent and the city of Trieste.

Paris Commune The new municipal government proclaimed March 28, 1871, elected by Parisians to administer Paris separately from the rest of France.

Public Health Act of 1875 Reaffirmed the duty of the British state to interfere with private property to protect health and physical well-being.

romantic republicanism One approach used to unite the small, mostly absolutist principalities of the Italian peninsula into a single state.

Second Reform Act A reform bill introduced by the conservative ministry in 1867 in the United Kingdom; admitted large numbers of male working-class voters.

Third Republic The French republican form of government from 1870 to 1940 that came about after the suppression of the Paris Commune and the collapse of the Second French Empire.

Vittorio Emanuele II (1820–1878) King of Sardinia (r. 1849–1861) who became the first king of a unified Italy in the modern period (1861–1878).

William Gladstone (1809–1898) British prime minister from 1868 to 1874 whose ministry saw the culmination of classical British liberalism; looked to individualism, free trade, and competition to solve social problems.

Young Turks A group of reformist officers in the Ottoman Empire who sought to modernize the empire.

Notes

1. *The New Cambridge Modern History*, Vol. 10 (Cambridge, UK: Cambridge University Press, 1967), p. 273.
2. William L. Langer, *Political and Social Upheaval, 1832–1852* (New York: Harper Torchbooks, 1969), p. 115.
3. Henry Kissinger, "The White Revolutionary: Reflections on Bismarck," *Daedalus* 97 (Summer 1968): 888.
4. Otto Pflanze, *Bismarck and the Development of Germany: The Period of Unification: 1815–1871* (Princeton, NJ: Princeton University Press, 1963), p. 177.
5. Jonathan Steinberg, *Bismarck: A Life* (Oxford, UK: Oxford University Press, 2011), p. 263.

Chapter 23
The Building of European Supremacy: Society and Politics to World War I

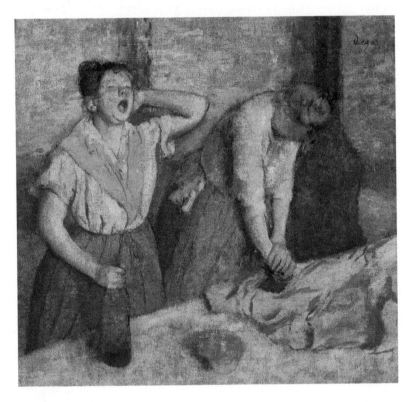

LAUNDRESSES AT WORK Although new opportunities opened to them in the late nineteenth century, many working-class women, like these women ironing in a laundry, remained in traditional occupations. The most common occupation for urban working-class women in the late nineteenth century, up until World War I, remained domestic service. As the wine bottle suggests, alcoholism was a problem for women as well as men engaged in tedious work.
SOURCE: RMN-Grand Palais/Art Resource, NY

 ## Contents and Focus Questions

The Chapter in Brief

THE GROWTH OF industrialism between 1860 and 1914 increased Europe's productive capacity to unprecedented and unparalleled levels. New steel mills, railways, shipyards, and chemical plants reflected an expanding supply of capital goods in the second half of the nineteenth century. By the first decade of the twentieth century, the age of the automobile, the airplane, the bicycle, the refrigerated ship, the telephone, the radio, the typewriter, and the electric light bulb had dawned. The world's economies, based on the gold standard, became increasingly interdependent. Europe's political, economic, and cultural reach extended across much of the inhabited world as European empires established global empires. European manufactured goods and financial capital flowed into markets all over the globe. In turn, Europeans imported foreign raw materials and foodstuffs. Within Europe itself, the eastern and southern European countries tended to import finished goods from the west and the north and to export agricultural products. While European societies remained divided over questions like workers' and women's rights, most Europeans took pride in what they believed was their superior "civilization" compared to the peoples they encountered in Africa and Asia. Political leaders took advantage of the popularity of imperialism to distract the ever-expanding electorate from dissatisfaction at home.

Within Europe, nation-states with large electorates, political parties, and centralized bureaucracies emerged. Business adopted large-scale corporate structures, and the labor force organized itself into trade unions. The number of white-collar workers increased. Western Europe became predominantly urban. Socialism strongly affected the political life of all nations. The foundations of the welfare state and of vast military establishments were laid. Taxation increased accordingly.

Europe had also quietly become dependent on the resources and markets of the rest of the world. Changes in the weather in Kansas, Argentina, or New Zealand might now affect the European economy. Before World War I, however, Europe's industrial, military, and financial supremacy concealed that dependency. Many Europeans assumed their supremacy to be natural and permanent, but the twentieth century would reveal it to have been temporary.

23.1 Population Trends and Migration

Why were so many Europeans on the move in the late nineteenth century?

The proportion of Europeans in the world's total population was apparently greater around 1900—estimated at about 20 percent—than ever before or since. The number of Europeans had risen from approximately 266 million in 1850 to 401 million in 1900 and to 447 million in 1910. Thereafter, birth and death rates declined or stabilized in Europe and other developed regions, and population growth began to slow.

Europe's peoples were on the move in the latter half-century as never before. (See Map 23–1.) The mid-century emancipation of peasants made legal movement and migration easier. Railways, steamships, and better roads increased mobility. Cheap land and better wages accompanied economic development in parts of Europe, North America, Latin America, and Australia, enticing people to move from regions where they had little prospect of improving their lives to regions that held or seemed to hold opportunity. In Europe itself the main migration continued to be from the countryside into urban areas. During this era, Europeans also left their own continent in record numbers. Between 1846 and 1932, more than 50 million Europeans left their homelands. The major areas to benefit from this movement were the United States, Canada, Australia, South Africa, Brazil, Algeria, and Argentina. At mid-century, most of the emigrants were from Great Britain (especially Ireland), the German states, and Scandinavia. After 1885, migration from southern and eastern Europe rose. This exodus helped relieve the social and population pressures on the Continent. Although much of this migration was permanent, even Europeans who remained in the countries of their birth were more likely to move seasonally or temporarily than ever before.

23.2 The Second Industrial Revolution

How did the Second Industrial Revolution transform European life?

During the third quarter of the nineteenth century, the gap that had long existed between British and continental economic development closed. (See Map 23–2.) The basic heavy

Map 23–1   PATTERNS OF GLOBAL MIGRATION, 1840–1900

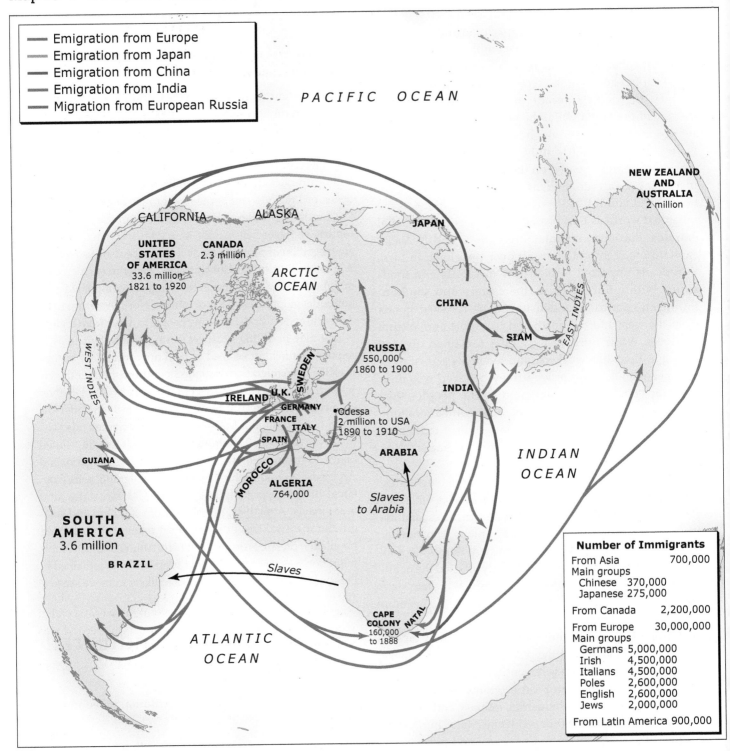

Emigration from Europe
Emigration from Japan
Emigration from China
Emigration from India
Migration from European Russia

PACIFIC OCEAN

NEW ZEALAND
AND
AUSTRALIA
2 million

CALIFORNIA   ALASKA

JAPAN

UNITED
STATES
OF AMERICA
33.6 million
1821 to 1920

CANADA
2.3 million

ARCTIC
OCEAN

CHINA

SIAM

EAST INDIES

WEST INDIES

RUSSIA
550,000
1860 to 1900

SWEDEN

IRELAND   U.K.

GERMANY

FRANCE

ITALY

SPAIN

•Odessa
2 million to USA
1890 to 1910

INDIA

INDIAN

OCEAN

GUIANA

ARABIA

MOROCCO

ALGERIA
764,000

Slaves
to Arabia

SOUTH
AMERICA
3.6 million

BRAZIL

Slaves

CAPE
COLONY
160,000
to 1888

NATAL

ATLANTIC
OCEAN

Number of Immigrants

From Asia	700,000
Main groups	
Chinese	370,000
Japanese	275,000
From Canada	2,200,000
From Europe	30,000,000
Main groups	
Germans	5,000,000
Irish	4,500,000
Italians	4,500,000
Poles	2,600,000
English	2,600,000
Jews	2,000,000
From Latin America	900,000

Emigration was a global process by the late nineteenth century, but more immigrants went to the United States than to all other nations combined.

Map 23–2 EUROPEAN INDUSTRIALIZATION, 1860–1913

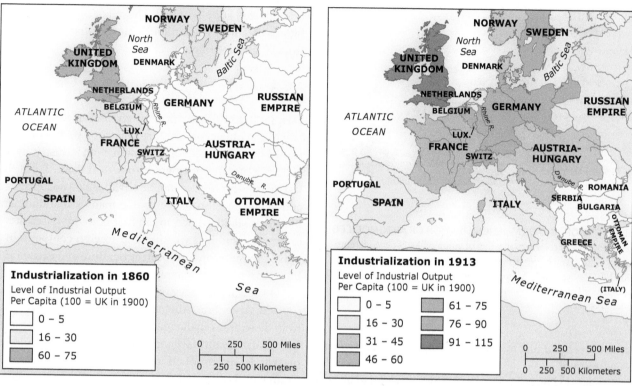

In 1860 Britain was far more industrialized than other European countries. In the following half-century, industrial output rose significantly, if unevenly, across much of Western Europe, especially in the new German Empire. The economies of the Balkan states and the Ottoman Empire, however, remained largely agricultural.

industries of Belgium, France, and Germany expanded rapidly. In particular, the growth of German industry was stunning. German steel production surpassed Britain's in 1893 and was nearly twice that of Britain by the outbreak of World War I. The emergence of an industrial Germany was the major factor in European economic and political life at the turn of the century, contributing to British fear of German power.

KEY DATES IN THE SECOND INDUSTRIAL REVOLUTION	
1856–1870	Passage of laws permitting joint stock companies: 1856, Britain; 1863, France; 1870, Prussia
1857	Bessemer process for making steel
1873	Panic of 1873 triggers major international economic depression
1876	Alexander Graham Bell invents the telephone
1879	Edison perfects the electric light bulb
1881	First electric power plant in Britain
1885	Gottlieb Daimler invents the internal combustion engine
1889	Daimler's first automobile
1895	Diesel engine invented
1895	Wireless telegraphy invented
1890s	First major impact of petroleum
1903	Wright brothers make first successful airplane flight
1909	Henry Ford manufactures the Model T

23.2.1 New Industries

Initially, the economic expansion of the third quarter of the century involved industries similar to those pioneered earlier in Great Britain. In particular, the expansion of railway systems on the Continent spurred economic growth. Thereafter, however, wholly new industries emerged. This latter development is usually termed the **Second Industrial Revolution**. The first Industrial Revolution was associated with textiles, steam, and iron; by contrast, the second was associated with steel, chemicals, electricity, and oil.

In the 1850s, Henry Bessemer (1830–1898), an English engineer, discovered a new process, named after him, for manufacturing steel cheaply in large quantities. In 1860, Great Britain, Belgium, France, and Germany combined produced 125,000 tons of steel. By 1913, the figure had risen to more than 32 million tons.

The chemical industry also came of age during this period. The Solvay process of alkali production allowed for the recovery of more chemical by-products and for increased production of sulfuric acid and laundry soap. New dyestuffs and plastics were also developed. Formal scientific research played an important role in this growth of the chemical industry, marking the beginning of a direct link between science and industrial development. As in so many aspects of the Second Industrial Revolution, Germany

458 M. FOURNIER'S "MORS."
The Winner of the Race from Paris
to Berlin. 1901.

THE INVENTION AND COMMERCIALIZATION OF AUTOMOBILES
The invention and commercialization of automobiles soon led to auto
races in Europe and North America. Here Henri Fournier, the winner
of the 1901 Paris to Berlin Motor Car Race, sits in his winning racing car
manufactured by the Paris-based auto firm of Emile and Louis Mors.
SOURCE: Hulton Archive/Stringer/Getty Images

was a leader in forging this link, fostering scientific research
and education.

The most significant change for industry and eventually for everyday life involved the application of electrical
energy to production. Electricity was the most versatile
and transportable source of power ever discovered. It
could be delivered almost anywhere to run either large
or small machinery, making the locations of factories
more flexible and factory construction more efficient. The
first major public power plant was constructed in 1881 in
Great Britain. Soon electric poles, lines, and generating
stations dotted the European landscape. Homes began to
use electric lights, and streetcar and subway systems were
electrified.

In the 1850s, an Austrian inventor created a new lamp
that could burn kerosene safely. Advances in refining and
lamp design created a market for petroleum, which was
useful as a lighting material and lubricant for decades
before its use in internal combustion engines became
widespread. In 1885, German engineer **Gottlieb Daimler**
(1834–1900), improving a previous prototype, invented
the modern internal combustion engine. By 1889, he had
mounted it on a carriage body specifically designed to
incorporate a still more improved internal combustion
engine, and the automobile was born. For many years, the
car remained a novelty item that only the wealthy could
afford. It was the American, Henry Ford (1863–1947), who
later made the automobile accessible to the masses. No
single invention so transformed the mobility of large numbers of people, first through the automobile itself and then
through trolleys and buses. The only European countries

with major domestic sources of oil production were Russia and Austria-Hungary. Then as now, Europe depended
on imported supplies of oil. The major oil companies were
Standard Oil of the United States, British Shell Oil, and
Royal Dutch Petroleum.

23.2.2 Economic Difficulties

Despite the multiplication of new industries, the second
half of the nineteenth century was not a period of uninterrupted or smooth economic growth. Both industry and agriculture generally prospered from 1850 to 1873, but in the
last quarter-century, economic advance slowed. Speculation
and overexpansion, as well as Germany's abandonment of
the silver standard, led to the first of many crises of modern capitalism. Bad weather and foreign competition put
grave pressures on European agriculture and caused many
European peasants to emigrate to other parts of the world.

As new farming regions developed in the United States,
Canada, Argentina, Australia, and New Zealand, products
from those areas challenged the market for home-produced
European agricultural goods. Refrigerated ships could bring
meat and dairy products to Europe from all over the world.
Grain could be grown more economically on the plains of
North America, Argentina, and Ukraine than it could in
Western Europe, and railways and steamships made it easy
and cheap to ship it across continents and oceans. These
developments lowered the prices of consumer goods but
put great pressure on European agriculture.

Several large banks failed in 1873, and the rate of capital investment slowed. Some industries then entered a two-
decade-long period of stagnation that many contemporaries
regarded as a depression. Although the general standard
of living in the industrialized nations improved in the second half of the nineteenth century, many workers still lived
and labored in abysmal conditions. There were pockets of
unemployment (a word that was coined during this period),
and strikes and other forms of labor unrest were common.
These economic difficulties fed the growth of trade unions
and Socialist political parties.

The new industries produced consumer goods, and
expansion in consumer demand brought the economy out
of stagnation by the end of the century. (See "Encountering
the Past" sidebar on bicycles, which follows below.) Lower
food prices eventually allowed all classes to spend more on
consumer goods. Urbanization created larger markets by
exposing people to more commodities than they would have
encountered in the countryside. New forms of retailing and
marketing appeared—department stores, chain stores, mail-
order catalogs, and advertising—simultaneously stimulating and feeding consumer demand. Imperialism also opened
new markets overseas for European consumer goods.

Encountering the Past

Bicycles: Transportation, Freedom, and Sport

BEFORE THE CAR came the bicycle. Bicycles were the first mass-produced, affordable machines for individual travel. Between 1880 and 1900, they took Europe and North America by storm. For the first time in history, individual men and, significantly, women had machines that enabled them to travel on their own for work or pleasure. Bicycles had an immense impact on Western society.

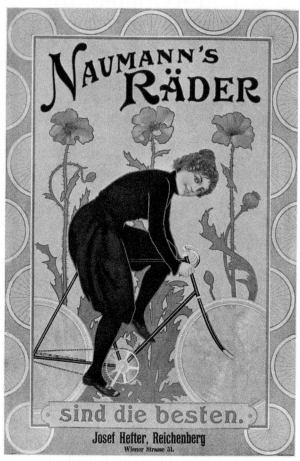

NAUMANN'S BICYCLES ARE THE BEST In many respects, the bicycle revolutionized society. Among other things, it gave women greater freedom and influenced women's fashion.
SOURCE: Lebrecht Music and Arts Photo Library/Alamy Stock Photo

The first functioning bicycles had been invented in Germany about 1817, but they were clumsy and dangerous. Made of wood, these machines lacked pedals and tires. They had to be pushed along the ground, and their riders could not control their speed. It took another eighty years for the modern bicycle to take shape. Pedals were introduced in the 1860s. Metal frames, solid rubber tires, and chain drives, which increased speed, appeared in the 1870s. In the 1880s, the ride became much smoother when John Boyd Dunlop, an Irish physician, invented the pneumatic tire, and in France, the Michelin brothers introduced the inner tube. (Before then, the ride was so rough that bicycles were sometimes called "boneshakers.") By the 1890s, the "safety bicycle" with its now familiar triangular frame and chain drive attached to the pedal and back wheel was being mass-produced across Europe and North America, and men and women of the working class could afford them. By 1900, male workers of modest means across Europe were riding bicycles to work.

By increasing individual mobility, the bicycle made it easier to get to work, to hold a job farther from home, and to move about one's city or town or reach the countryside. New clothing designs, especially "bloomers," trousers worn under skirts (designed before the bicycle), permitted women to bicycle while maintaining modesty. In the 1890s, feminists like Maria Pognon in France and Susan B. Anthony in the United States hailed the "egalitarian and leveling bicycle" for the freedom it gave women.

By 1914, there were millions of cyclists across the transatlantic world. Europeans and Americans organized cycling clubs with distinctive uniforms. Some of these clubs, such as the English Clarion Cycling Clubs, the French *Union Sportive du Parti Socialiste*, and the German *Solidaritet*, used cycling trips to spread literature for left-wing causes. Other groups cycled for pleasure. The kinds of touring clubs that now exist for automobiles were first organized for cyclists, as were many of the early European travel guides such as the French *Guides Michelin*, which first appeared in 1900. Then as now, Michelin made tires and stood to sell more of them the more people toured the countryside.

Bicycle racing quickly became a competitive sport. The most famous professional racer in the world was Marshall Walter "Major" Taylor, an African American who raced in both the United States and Europe. Paris and other French cities built velodromes for indoor cycle racing, which was one of the official sports of the first modern Olympics in 1896. In 1903, *L'Auto*, a French sports paper, organized the first Tour de France race to increase its circulation. Six riders raced a 2,500-km course for more than nineteen days.

Questions

1. Why did bicycles become so popular in Europe in the late nineteenth century?
2. What advantages did bicycles have for women?

SOURCES: Eugen Weber, *France: Fin de Siècle* (Cambridge, MA: Harvard University Press, 1986), pp. 103–104, 195–206; Will and Terra Hanger, "Bicycles," *History Magazine* (October/November 2001).

23.3 The Middle Classes in Ascendancy

What explains the prominence of the middle class in late-nineteenth-century Europe?

The sixty years before World War I were the age of the middle classes. The **London Great Exhibition** of 1851 held in the Crystal Palace displayed the products and the new material life they had forged. Thereafter, the middle classes became the arbiter of consumer taste. After the revolutions of 1848, the middle classes ceased to be a revolutionary group. Once the question of social equality and equality of property had been raised, large and small property owners across the Continent moved to protect what they possessed against demands from Socialists and other working-class groups.

23.3.1 Social Distinctions Within the Middle Classes

The middle classes, never perfectly homogeneous, grew increasingly diverse. Their most prosperous members—the owners and managers of great businesses and banks—lived in splendor that rivaled, and sometimes exceeded, that of the aristocracy. In Britain some of them, such as W. H. Smith (1825–1891), the owner of railway newsstands, were made members of the House of Lords. The Krupp family of Germany, who owned huge steel works in the Rhineland, were pillars of the state and were ennobled by the German emperor and received visits from the imperial court.

Only a few hundred families gained such wealth. Beneath them were the comfortable small entrepreneurs and professional people, whose incomes permitted private homes, large quantities of furniture, pianos, pictures, books, journals, education for their children, and vacations. Also in this group were the shopkeepers, schoolteachers, librarians, and others who had either a bit of property or a skill they had learned that provided respectable nonmanual employment.

Finally, there was a whole new element—"white-collar workers"—who formed the lower middle class, or *petite bourgeoisie.* They included secretaries, retail clerks, and lower-level bureaucrats in business and government. They often had working-class origins and might even belong to unions, but they had middle-class aspirations and consciously sought to distance themselves from a working-class lifestyle. They pursued educational opportunities and chances for even the slightest career advancement for themselves and their children. Many of them spent much of their disposable income on consumer goods, such as stylish clothing and furniture, that were distinctively middle class in appearance. Significant tensions and social anxieties marked relations among the various middle-class groups. Small shopkeepers resented the power of the great capitalists, with their department stores and mail-order catalogs. There is some evidence that the professions were becoming overcrowded. People who had only recently attained middle-class lifestyles feared losing it in bad economic times.

23.4 Late-Nineteenth-Century Urban Life

What forces shaped the development of European cities?

Europe became more urbanized than ever in the latter half of the nineteenth century as migration to the cities continued. Between 1850 and 1911, urban dwellers rose from 25 to 44 percent of the population in France and from 30 to 60 percent of the population in Germany. Similar increases occurred in other Western European countries.

The rural migrants to the cities were largely uprooted from traditional social ties. They often faced poor housing, social anonymity, and unemployment. People from different regional backgrounds, sometimes speaking different languages and practicing different religions, found themselves in proximity to one another and had difficulty mixing socially. Competition for jobs generated new varieties of political and social discontent, such as the anti-Semitism directed at the thousands of Russian Jews who had migrated to Western Europe. Indeed, much of the political anti-Semitism of the latter part of the century had its roots in the problems urban migration generated.

23.4.1 The Redesign of Cities

The inward urban migration placed new social and economic demands on already strained city resources and gradually transformed the patterns of urban living. National and municipal governments redesigned the central portions of many large European cities during the second half-century.

23.4.1.1 THE NEW PARIS The most famous and extensive transformation of a major city occurred in Paris. Like many other European cities, Paris had expanded from the Middle Ages onward with little or no planning. Great public buildings and squalid hovels stood near each other. The Seine River was an open sewer. The streets were narrow, crooked, and crowded. It was impossible to cross easily from one part of the city to another either on foot or by carriage. In 1850, an accurate map of the city did not even exist. Of more concern to the government of Napoleon III (r. 1852–1870), the city's streets were battlegrounds for urban insurrections that had threatened or toppled French governments on numerous occasions, most recently in 1848.

Napoleon III personally determined to redesign Paris. He appointed Baron Georges Haussmann (1809–1891), who, as prefect of the Seine from 1853 to 1870, oversaw a vast urban reconstruction program. Whole districts were destroyed to open the way for the broad boulevards and streets that became the hallmark of modern Paris. Much, though not all, of the purpose of this street planning was political. The wide vistas not only were beautiful but also allowed for the quick deployment of troops to put down riots. The eradication of the many small streets and alleys removed areas where barricades could be, and had been, erected.

Further rebuilding and redesign occurred under the Third Republic after the destruction that accompanied the suppression of the Paris Commune in 1871. Many department stores, office complexes, and largely middle-class apartment buildings were constructed. By the late 1870s, mechanical trams were operating in Paris. After much debate, construction of a subway system (the *métro*) began in 1895. Near the close of the century, new railway stations were also erected to link the refurbished central city to the suburbs.

23.4.1.2 DEVELOPMENT OF SUBURBS Commercial development, railway construction, and slum clearance displaced many city dwellers and raised urban land values and rents. Consequently, both the middle classes and the working class began to seek housing elsewhere. The middle classes looked for neighborhoods removed from urban congestion. The working class looked for affordable housing. The result, in virtually all countries, was the development of suburbs surrounding the city proper. These suburbs housed families whose breadwinners worked in the central city or in a factory located within the city limits.

The expansion of railways with cheap workday fares and the introduction of mechanical and later electric tramways, as well as subways, allowed tens of thousands of workers from all classes to move daily between the city and the outlying suburbs. For hundreds of thousands of Europeans, home and work became more physically separated than ever before.

23.4.2 Urban Sanitation

The efforts of governments and of the increasingly conservative middle classes to maintain public order after 1848 led to a growing concern with the problems of public health and housing for the poor. Many believed that only when the health and housing of the working class were improved would middle-class health also be secure and the political order stable.

23.4.2.1 IMPACT OF CHOLERA Concerns with health and housing first developed as a result of the great cholera epidemics of the 1830s and 1840s. Unlike many other common deadly diseases of the day that touched only the poor, cholera struck all classes, and the middle class demanded a solution. Before the development of the bacterial theory of disease late in the century, physicians and sanitary reformers believed that miasmas in the air spread the infections that led to cholera and other diseases. These miasmas, which could be detected by their foul odors, were believed to arise from filth. The way to get rid of the dangerous, foul-smelling air was to clean up the cities.

During the 1840s, many physicians and some government officials began to publicize the dangerous, unsanitary conditions associated with overcrowding in cities and with businesses such as basement slaughterhouses. These and various other private reports and those by public commissions closely linked the issues of wretched living conditions and public health. They also argued that sanitary reform would remove the dangers.

23.4.2.2 NEW WATER AND SEWER SYSTEMS The proposed solution to the health hazard was cleanliness, to be achieved through new water and sewer systems. These facilities were constructed slowly, usually first in capital cities and then much later in provincial centers. Some major urban areas did not have good water systems until after 1900. Nonetheless, the building of such systems was one of the major health and engineering achievements of the second half of the nineteenth century. The sewer system of Paris was a famous part of Haussmann's rebuilding program. In London, the construction of the Albert Embankment along the Thames involved not only large sewers discharging into the river but also gas mains and water pipes; all were encased in thick walls of granite and concrete, one of the new building materials of the day. Wherever these sanitary facilities were installed, the mortality rate dropped considerably—not because they prevented miasmas but because they disposed of human

Table 23–1 POPULATION OF MAJOR EUROPEAN CITIES (in thousands)

City	1850	1880	1910
Berlin	419	1,122	2,071
Birmingham	233	437	840
Frankfurt	65	137	415
London	2,685	4,470	7,256
Madrid	281	398	600
Moscow	365	748	1,533
Paris	1,053	2,269	2,888
Rome	175	300	542
St. Petersburg	485	877	1,962
Vienna	444	1,104	2,031
Warsaw	160	339	872

waste and provided clean water free of harmful bacteria for people to drink, cook with, and bathe in.

KEY DATES IN SANITATION REFORM	
1830s and 1840s	Cholera epidemics
1840	Villermé's *Catalog of the Physical and Moral State of Workers*
1842	Chadwick's *Report on the Sanitary Condition of the Labouring Population*
1848	British Public Health Act
1851	French Melun Act

23.4.2.3 EXPANDED GOVERNMENT INVOLVEMENT IN PUBLIC HEALTH   The concern with public health led to an expansion of governmental power on various levels. In Britain the Public Health Act of 1848, in France the Melun Act of 1851, and various laws in the still independent German states, as well as later legislation, introduced new restraints on private life and enterprise. This legislation allowed medical officers and building inspectors to enter homes and businesses in the name of public health. The state could condemn private property for posing health hazards. Private land could be excavated to construct the sewers and water mains required to protect the public. New building regulations restrained the activities of private contractors.

Acceptance at the close of the century of the bacterial theory of disease associated with the discoveries of **Louis Pasteur** (1822–1895) in France, Robert Koch (1843–1910) in Germany, and Joseph Lister (1827–1912) in Britain increased public concern about cleanliness. Throughout Europe, issues related to the maintenance of public health and the physical well-being of the population repeatedly permitted new modes of government intervention in the lives of citizens.

23.4.3 Housing Reform and Middle-Class Values

The newly available information about working-class living conditions also led to heated debates over the housing problem. The wretched dwellings of the poor were themselves a cause of poor sanitation and thus became a newly perceived health hazard. Furthermore, the domestic arrangements of the poor, whose large families might live in a single room without any personal privacy, shocked middle-class reformers and bureaucrats. A single toilet might serve a whole block of tenements. After the revolutions of 1848, the overcrowding in housing and the social discontent that it generated were also seen to pose a political danger.

Middle-class reformers thus turned to housing reform to solve the medical, moral, and political dangers slums posed. Decent housing would foster a good home life, in turn leading to a healthy, moral, and politically stable population. As A. V. Huber, one of the early German housing reformers, declared,

Certainly it would not be too much to say that the home is the communal embodiment of family life. Thus the purity of the dwelling is almost as important for the family as is the cleanliness of the body for the individual. Good or bad housing is a question of life and death if ever there was one.[1]

Later advocates of housing reform, such as Jules Simon (1814–1896) in France, saw good housing as leading to good family life and ultimately to strong patriotic feeling. It was widely believed that providing the poor and the working class with adequate, respectable, cheap housing would alleviate social and political discontent. It was also believed that the personal saving and investment that were required to own a home would lead the working class to adopt the thrifty habits of the middle classes.

Private philanthropy funded the first initiatives to address the housing problem. Companies operating on low profit margins or making low-interest loans encouraged housing for the poor. Firms such as the German Krupp Armaments concern, which sought to ensure a contented, healthy, and stable workforce, constructed model housing projects and industrial communities.

By the mid-1880s, the migration into cities had made housing a political issue. Legislation in England in 1885 lowered the interest rates to construct cheap housing, and soon thereafter local governments began public housing projects. In Germany, action on housing came later in the century through the initiative of local municipalities. In 1894, France made inexpensive credit available to construct housing for the poor. None of these governments, however, adopted widescale housing experiments.

Nonetheless, by 1914, the housing problem had been fully recognized if not adequately addressed. The goal of housing reform across Western Europe came to be to provide homes for the members of the working class that would allow them to enjoy a family life more or less like that of the middle class. Such a home would be in the form of a detached house or an affordable city apartment with several rooms, a private entrance, and separate toilet facilities.

23.5 Varieties of Late-Nineteenth-Century Women's Experience

What was life like for women in late-nineteenth-century Europe?

Late-nineteenth-century women and men led lives that reflected their social rank. Yet, within each rank, the experience of women was distinct from that of men. Women had no voting rights and limited opportunities to assert their economic and legal rights. They remained, in general, economically dependent on men, whatever their social class be.

EMMELINE PANKHURST Emmeline Pankhurst (1857–1928) was frequently arrested for forcefully advocating votes for British women.
SOURCE: Jimmy Sime/Stringer/Getty Images

23.5.1 Women's Social Disabilities

In the mid-nineteenth century, virtually all European women faced social and legal disabilities in three areas: property rights, family law, and education. By the close of the century, there had been some improvement in each area.

23.5.1.1 WOMEN AND PROPERTY   Until the last quarter-century in most European countries, married women could not own property in their own names, no matter what their social class. For all practical purposes, upon marriage, women lost to their husbands' control any property they owned, might inherit, or earn by their own labor. Their legal identities were subsumed in their husbands' identities, and they had no independent standing before the law. The courts saw the theft of a woman's purse as a theft of her husband's property. Because private property and wage earning were the bases of European society, these inequalities put married women at a great disadvantage, limiting their freedom to work, to save, and to move from one location to another.

Reform of women's property rights came slowly. By 1882, Great Britain had passed the **Married Woman's Property Act,** which allowed married women to own property in their own right. In France, however, a married woman could not even open a savings account in her own name until 1895, and married French women did not gain possession of the wages they earned until 1907. In 1900, Germany allowed women to take jobs without their husbands' permission, but except for her wages, a German husband retained control of most of his wife's property. Similar laws prevailed elsewhere in Europe.

23.5.1.2 FAMILY LAW   European family law also disadvantaged women. Legal codes required wives to "give obedience" to their husbands. The Napoleonic Code and the remnants of Roman law still in effect made women legal minors throughout Europe. Divorce was difficult everywhere for most of the century. In England before 1857, each divorce required a separate act of Parliament. Thereafter, couples could divorce, with difficulty, through the Court of Matrimonial Causes. Most nations did not permit divorce by mutual consent. French law forbade divorce between 1816 and 1884. Thereafter, most nations recognized a legal cause for divorce—cruelty or injury—which had to be proven in court. Across Europe, some version of the double standard prevailed whereby husbands' extramarital sexual relations were tolerated to a much greater degree than those of wives. Everywhere, divorce required hearings in court and the presentation of legal proof, making the process expensive and more difficult for women, who did not control their own property.

The authority of husbands also extended to children. A husband could take children away from their mother and give them to someone else to rear. Only a father, in most countries, could permit his daughter to marry. In some countries, he could force his daughter to marry the man of his choice. In cases of divorce and separation, courts normally awarded the husband authority over and custody of children, no matter how he had treated them previously.

Issues surrounding the sexual and reproductive rights of women could hardly be discussed in the nineteenth century. Until well into the twentieth century, both contraception and abortion were illegal. The law surrounding rape normally worked to the disadvantage of women. Whether they turned to physicians or lawyers, women confronted a world that men almost wholly populated and controlled.

23.5.1.3 EDUCATIONAL BARRIERS   Throughout the nineteenth century, women had less access to education than men had, and the education available to them was inferior to that available to men. Not surprisingly, there were many more illiterate women than men. Most women were educated only enough for the domestic lives they were expected to lead. University and professional education remained reserved for men until at least the third quarter of the century.

The absence of a system of secondary education for women denied most of them the qualifications they needed to enter a university, whether or not the university prohibited them. Educated, professional men feared that admitting women to universities would overcrowd their professions. Women who attended universities and medical schools were sometimes labeled political radicals.

By the turn of the century, some male educated elites believed educating women would threaten their traditional gender roles in the home and workplace. Restricting women's access to secondary and university education helped bar them from social and economic advancement. Women would benefit only marginally from the expansion of professional employment that occurred during the late nineteenth and early twentieth centuries. Very few women did enter the professions, particularly medicine. Most nations refused to allow women to become lawyers until after World War I.

School teaching at the elementary level, which had come to be seen as a "female job" because of its association with the nurturing of children, became a professional haven for women. Trained at institutions designed particularly for elementary schoolteachers, usually known as normal schools, women schoolteachers at the elementary level were regarded as educated, but not as university educated. Higher education remained largely the province of men.

The few women who pioneered in the professions and on government commissions and school boards, or who circulated birth control information, faced social obstacles, humiliation, and often outright bigotry. These women and their male supporters were challenging the clear separation into male and female spheres that had emerged in middle-class European social life during the nineteenth century. Women were often hesitant to support feminist causes or expanded opportunities for females because they had been so thoroughly acculturated into stereotyped roles. Many women, as well as men, saw a real conflict between family responsibilities and feminism.

23.5.2 New Employment Patterns for Women

During the Second Industrial Revolution, two major developments affected the economic lives of women. The first was the large-scale expansion in the variety of jobs available to women outside the better-paying learned professions. The second was the withdrawal of many married women from the workforce. These two seemingly contradictory developments require explanation.

23.5.2.1 AVAILABILITY OF NEW JOBS The expansion of governmental bureaucracies, the emergence of corporations and other large businesses, and the vast growth of retail stores created many new employment opportunities for women. The need for elementary school teachers, usually women, grew as governments adopted compulsory education laws. Technological inventions and innovations, such as the typewriter and eventually the telephone exchange, also fostered female employment. Women by the thousands became secretaries and clerks for governments and private businesses. Thousands more became shop assistants.

Although these jobs did open new and often better employment opportunities for women, they nonetheless

CENTRAL TELEPHONE EXCHANGE Shown here, in a photograph from around 1903, women work in the London Central Telephone Exchange. The invention of the telephone opened new employment opportunities for women.
SOURCE: Heritage Image Partnership Ltd/Alamy Stock Photo

required low-level skills and involved minimal training. They were occupied primarily by unmarried women or widows. Women rarely occupied more prominent positions.

Employers continued to pay women low wages because, although they often knew better, a woman did not need to live on what she herself earned but could expect additional financial support from her father or her husband. Consequently, a woman who did need to support herself independently could seldom find a job that paid an adequate income—or a position that paid as well as one a man supporting himself held.

23.5.2.2 WITHDRAWAL FROM THE LABOR FORCE Most of the women filling the new service positions were young and unmarried. Upon marriage, or certainly after the birth of her first child, a woman normally withdrew from the labor force. Either she did not work or she worked at some occupation she could pursue at home. This pattern was not new, but it had become significantly more common by the end of the nineteenth century. The kinds of industrial occupations that women had filled in the mid-nineteenth century, especially textile and garment making, were shrinking. Married or unmarried women thus had fewer opportunities for employment in those industries. Employers in offices and retail stores preferred young, unmarried women whose family responsibilities would not interfere with their work.

The cultural dominance of the middle class established a pattern of social expectations, especially for wives. The more prosperous a working-class family became, the less involved in employment its women were supposed to be. Indeed, the less income-producing work a wife did, the more prosperous and stable the family was considered.

Despite these generalities, women encountered an enormous variety of social and economic experiences in the late nineteenth century. As might be expected, the chief determinant of these individual experiences was social class.

23.5.3 Working-Class Women

Although the textile industry and garment making were much less dominant than earlier in the century, they continued to employ many women. The German clothing-making trade illustrates the kind of vulnerable economic situation that women could encounter as a result of their limited skills and the way the trade was organized. The system of manufacturing mass-made clothes of uniform sizes in Germany was designed to require minimal capital investment by manufacturers and to protect them from risk. A major manufacturer would produce clothing through what was called a **putting-out system**. The manufacturer would purchase the material and then put it out for tailoring. Usually, numerous independently owned small sweatshops or women working in their homes made the clothing. It was seldom made in a factory.

In Berlin in 1896, this system employed more than 80,000 garment workers. When business was good and demand strong, employment for these women was high. As the seasons shifted or business slackened, however, less and less work was put out, idling many of them. In effect, the workers who sewed the clothing carried much of the risk of the enterprise.

The expectation of separate social and economic spheres for men and women and the definition of women's chief work as pertaining to the home contributed mightily to the exploitation of women workers outside the home. Because their wages were regarded merely as supplementing their husbands' wages, they became particularly vulnerable to the kind of economic exploitation that characterized the German putting-out system for clothing production and similar systems elsewhere. Women were nearly always treated as casual workers everywhere in Europe.

23.5.4 Poverty and Prostitution

A major, but little recognized, social fact of most nineteenth-century cities was the presence of a surplus of working

POVERTY AND PROSTITUTION In Drury Lane in London during the latter part of the nineteenth century young women and even younger girls, advertising their availability, dance as a crowd of spectators, made up mostly of men, watch.
SOURCE: Museum of London/Heritage Image/AGE Fotostock

women who did not fit the stereotype of wife or daughter supplementing a family's income. Almost always many more women were seeking employment than there were jobs. The economic vulnerability of women and the consequent poverty many of them faced were among the chief causes of prostitution. Every major late-nineteenth-century European city had thousands of prostitutes.

On the Continent, prostitution was generally legalized and subject to governmental and municipal regulations that male legislatures and councils passed and male police and physicians enforced. In Britain, prostitution received only minimal regulation.

Many myths and misunderstandings have surrounded the subject of prostitution. The most recent studies of prostitution in England emphasize that most prostitutes were active on the streets for only a few years, from their late teens to about age twenty-five. Many were poor women who had recently migrated from nearby rural areas. Others were born in the towns where they became prostitutes. Certain cities—those with large army garrisons or naval bases or those like London with large transient populations—attracted prostitutes. Far fewer prostitutes worked in manufacturing towns, where there were more opportunities for steady employment and community life was more stable.

Women who became prostitutes usually came from families of unskilled workers, and they had minimal skills and education. Many had been servants. They also often were orphans or came from broken homes. Working-class women were always potentially subject to sexual exploitation, whether they became prostitutes or not.

23.5.5 Women of the Middle Class

A vast social gap separated poor working-class women from their middle-class counterparts. As their fathers' and husbands' incomes permitted, middle-class women participated in the expansion of consumerism and domestic comfort that marked the late nineteenth and the early twentieth centuries. They filled their homes with manufactured items, including clothing, china, furniture, carpets, drapery, wallpaper, and prints. They enjoyed all the improvements of sanitation and electricity. They could command the services of numerous domestic servants. They moved into the fashionable new houses being constructed in the rapidly expanding suburbs.

23.5.5.1 THE CULT OF DOMESTICITY For the middle classes, the distinction between work and family, defined by gender, had become complete and constituted the model for all other social groups. Middle-class women, if possible, did not work. More than any other women, they became limited to the roles of wife and mother. As a result, they might enjoy great domestic luxury and comfort, but their lives, talents, ambitions, and opportunities for applying their intelligence were sharply circumscribed.

Middle-class women became, in large measure, the product of a particular understanding of social life. Home life was to be a private place of refuge from the life of business and the marketplace. Within the home, a middle-class woman largely directed the household. She supervised all domestic management and child care. She was in charge of the home as a unit of consumption, which is why so much advertising was directed toward women. This domestic activity, however, occurred within the bounds of the approved middle-class lifestyle that set strict limits on a woman's initiative. In her conspicuous position within the home and family, a woman symbolized first her father's and then her husband's worldly success.

23.5.5.2 RELIGIOUS AND CHARITABLE ACTIVITIES Throughout Europe, religion and religious activities became part of the expected work of women. They internalized those portions of the Christian religion that stressed meekness and passivity. This close association between religion and a strict domestic life for women was one reason for later tension between feminism and religious authorities.

Another important role for middle-class women was the administration of charity. Women were considered especially qualified for this work because of their presumed innate spirituality and their capacity to instill domestic and personal discipline. Women were supposed to be particularly interested in the problems of poor women, their families, and their children. By the end of the century, middle-class women seeking to expand their spheres of activity became social workers for the church, for private charities, or for the government. These vocations were a natural extension of the roles society assigned to them.

The following obituary of a French lady who died in the late nineteenth century illustrates how these vocations and virtues received public praise for women who fulfilled them:

> The poor were the object of her affectionate interest, especially the shameful poor, the fallen people. She sought them out and helped them with perfect discretion which doubled the value of her benevolent interest. To those whom she could approach without fear of bruising their dignity, she brought, along with alms to assure their existence, consolation of the most serious sort—she raised their courage and their hopes. To others, each Sunday, she opened all the doors of her home, above all when her children were still young. In making them distribute these alms with her, she hoped to initiate them early into practices of charity.[2]

Many ideas and social forces would challenge the values this obituary celebrates, but the role of upper-middle-class women that it illustrates would dominate European life for decades to come.

23.5.5.3 SEXUALITY AND FAMILY SIZE Historians have come to realize that the world of the middle-class wife and her family was much more complicated than they once thought. Neither all wives nor their families conformed

to the stereotypes. Recent studies suggest that the middle classes of the nineteenth century enjoyed sexual relations within marriage far more than was once thought. Diaries, letters, and even early medical and sociological sex surveys indicate that sexual enjoyment rather than sexual repression was fundamental to middle-class marriages. Much of the inhibition about sexuality stemmed from the dangers of childbirth, which, in an age of limited sanitation and anesthesia, were widely and rightly feared, rather than from any dislike or disapproval of sex itself.

One of the major changes in this regard during the second half of the century was the acceptance of a small family size among the middle classes. The birthrate in France dropped throughout the nineteenth century. It began to fall in England steadily from the 1870s onward. During the last decades of the century, new contraceptive devices became available, which middle-class couples used. One of the reasons for the apparently conscious decision of couples to limit their family size was to maintain a relatively high level of material consumption.

23.5.6 The Rise of Political Feminism

Liberal society and its values had neither automatically nor inevitably improved the lot of women. In particular, they did not give women the vote or access to political activity. In Catholic countries, male liberals feared that granting the vote to women would benefit political conservatives because men thought that priests exercised undue control over women. A similar apprehension existed about the alleged influence of the Anglican clergy over women in England and of Protestant pastors in parts of Germany. Consequently, anticlerical liberals often refused to cooperate with feminists.

KEY DATES IN WOMEN'S HISTORY, 1850s–1920s	
1857	Revised English divorce law
1865	University of Zurich admits women for degrees
1869	John Stuart Mill's *The Subjection of Women*
1878	University of London admits women as candidates for degrees
1882	English Married Woman's Property Act
1894	Union of German Women's Organizations founded
1901	National Council of French Women founded
1903	British Women's Social and Political Union founded
1907	Norway permits women to vote on national issues
1910	British suffragettes adopt radical tactics
1918	Vote extended to some British women
1919	Weimar constitution allows German women to vote
1920	Ratification of Nineteenth Amendment grants women right to vote in United States
1920–1921	Oxford and Cambridge Universities award degrees to women
1922	French Senate defeats bill extending vote to women
1928	Britain extends vote to women on same basis as men

23.5.6.1 OBSTACLES TO ACHIEVING EQUALITY Many women were reluctant to support feminist causes. Political issues relating to gender were only one of several priorities for women. Some were sensitive to their class and economic interests. Others subordinated feminist political issues to national unity and patriotism. Still others would not support particular feminist organizations because they objected to their tactics. The various social and tactical differences among women often led to sharp divisions within the feminists' own ranks. Except in England, it was often difficult for working-class and middle-class women to cooperate. Roman Catholic feminists were uncomfortable with radical secularist feminists. There were other disagreements about the goals that were most important for improving women's legal and social conditions.

Although liberal society and law presented women with many obstacles, they also provided feminists with many of their intellectual and political tools. As early as 1792 in Britain, Mary Wollstonecraft (1759–1797), in *The Vindication of the Rights of Woman*, had applied the revolutionary doctrines of the rights of man to the predicament of the members of her own sex (see Chapter 17). John Stuart Mill (1806–1873) and Harriet Taylor (1804–1858) extended the logic of liberal freedom to the position of women in *The Subjection of Women* (1869). The arguments for utility and efficiency so dear to middle-class liberals were used to expose the human and social waste implicit in the inferior role assigned to women.

Furthermore, the Socialist criticism of capitalist society often, though by no means always, included a harsh indictment of the social and economic position to which women had been relegated. The earliest statements in support of feminism arose from critics of the existing order who had unorthodox opinions about sexuality, family life, and property. This hardened resistance to the feminist message.

23.5.6.2 VOTES FOR WOMEN IN BRITAIN Europe's most dynamic women's movement was in Britain. There, Millicent Fawcett (1847–1929) led the moderate National Union of Women's Suffrage Societies. She believed Parliament would grant women the vote only if it were convinced they would be respectable and responsible in their political activity. In 1908, the National Union could rally almost half a million women in London. Fawcett's tactics were those of English liberals. Her husband, Henry Fawcett (1833–1884), was a Liberal Party cabinet minister and economist who also supported women's suffrage.

Emmeline Pankhurst (1858–1928) led a much more radical branch of British feminists. In 1903, Pankhurst and her daughters, Christabel and Sylvia, founded the Women's Social and Political Union. For years they and their followers, known derisively as **suffragettes**, lobbied publicly and privately for extending the vote to women. By 1910, having failed to move the government, they turned to the violent

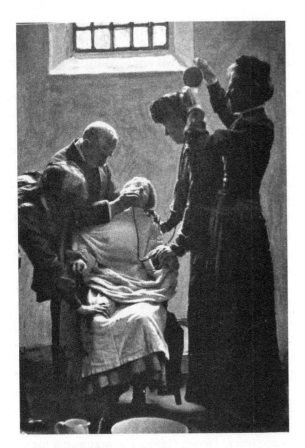

THE FIGHT FOR WOMEN'S RIGHTS When advocates of women's suffrage went on hunger strike, they were forcibly fed in prison. When they refused to open their mouths, feeding tubes were inserted into their nostrils, as in this 1909 photograph taken in Holloway Prison in London.

SOURCE: Private Collection/The Stapleton Collection/Bridgeman Images

tactics of arson, breaking windows, and sabotage of postal boxes. They marched en masse on Parliament. The liberal government of Prime Minister Herbert Asquith (1852–1928) imprisoned demonstrators and force-fed those who went on hunger strikes in jail. The government refused to extend the franchise. Only in 1918, and then as a result of their contribution to the war effort in World War I, did British women over age thirty receive the vote. Men could vote at age twenty-one.

23.5.6.3 POLITICAL FEMINISM ON THE CONTINENT Women's movements on the Continent tended to be much smaller than in Britain. In France, when Hubertine Auclert (1848–1914) began campaigning for the vote in the 1880s, she stood virtually alone. During the 1890s, several women's organizations emerged. In 1901, the National Council of French Women (CNFF) was organized among upper-middle-class women, but it did not support the vote for women for several years. French Roman Catholic feminists such as Marie Maugueret (1844–1928) supported the franchise.

Almost all French feminists, however, rejected violence and believed women could achieve the vote through careful legalism. In 1919, the French Chamber of Deputies passed a bill granting the vote to women, but in 1922, the French Senate defeated the bill. French women did not receive the right to vote until after World War II.

In Germany, feminist awareness and action faced great challenges. Louise Otto (1819–1895) had pioneered the German women's movement in the 1840s but was forced to withdraw from political life during the backlash after 1848. German law forbade German women from engaging in political activity. In 1894, Otto's friend, Auguste Schmidt (1833–1902), together with several other women, founded the Union of German Women's Organizations (BDF). By 1902, the German women's movement, which had begun with demands for better education for women, was supporting the right to vote. But its main concern remained improving women's social conditions, increasing their access to education, and extending their right to other protections. The BDF also tried to gain women's admittance to political or civic activity on the municipal level. Its work usually included education, child welfare, charity, and public health. The German Social Democratic Party supported women's suffrage, but the German authorities and German Roman Catholics so disdained the Socialists that its support only made suffrage more suspect in their eyes. Women received the vote in Germany only in 1919, under the constitution of the Weimar Republic after the German defeat in war and revolution at home.

Throughout Europe before World War I, women demanded rights widely and vocally. Their tactics and the success they achieved, however, varied from country to country depending on political and class structures. Before World War I, only Norway (1907) and Finland (1906) allowed women to vote on national issues.

23.6 Jewish Emancipation

How did Jewish life in Europe change in the late nineteenth century?

The emancipation of European Jews from the narrow life of the ghetto into a world of equal or nearly equal citizenship and social status was a major accomplishment of political liberalism and had an enduring impact on European life. Emancipation, slow and never fully completed, began in the late eighteenth century and continued throughout the nineteenth. It moved at different paces in different countries.

23.6.1 Differing Degrees of Citizenship

In 1781 and 1782, Joseph II, the Habsburg emperor, issued decrees that placed Jews, Orthodox Christians, and Protestants in his empire under the same laws as Catholics. In France, the National Assembly recognized Jews as French citizens in 1789. During the turmoil of the Napoleonic Wars, Jewish communities in Italy and the German states were generally on equal footing with the Christian population. These steps toward political emancipation were always uncertain and were frequently limited or abrogated when rulers or governments changed. Certain freedoms were granted, only to be partially withdrawn later. Even countries that had given Jews political rights did not permit them to own land and often subjected them to discriminatory taxes. Nonetheless, during the first half of the century, Jews began to gain equal or more nearly equal citizenship.

In Russia, and in Poland under Russian rule, the traditional modes of prejudice and discrimination continued unabated until World War I. Russian rule treated Jews as aliens. The government undermined Jewish community life, limited the publication of Jewish books, restricted areas where Jews could live, required them to have internal passports to move about the country, banned them from many forms of state service, and excluded them from many institutions of higher education. The state allowed the police and right-wing nationalist groups to conduct *pogroms*—organized riots—against Jewish neighborhoods and villages.

23.6.2 Broadened Opportunities

After the revolutions of 1848, European Jews saw a general improvement in their situation that lasted for several decades. In various German states, Italy, the Low Countries, and Scandinavia, Jews attained full citizenship. After 1858, Jews in Great Britain could sit in Parliament. Austria-Hungary extended full legal rights to Jews in 1867. Indeed, from about 1850 to 1880, relatively little organized or overt prejudice was expressed against Jews in non-Russian Europe. They entered the professions and other occupations once closed to them. They participated fully in literary and cultural life and were active in the arts and music. They became leaders in science and education. Jews intermarried freely with non-Jews as legal, secular prohibitions against such marriages were repealed during the last quarter-century.

Outside of Russia, Jewish politicians entered cabinets and served in the highest offices of the state. Politically, Jews often were aligned with liberal parties because these groups had championed equal rights. Later in the century,

LIONEL ROTHSCHILD Because many major financial institutions of nineteenth-century Europe were owned by wealthy Jewish families, anti-Semitic political figures often blamed them for economic hard times. The most famous family was the Rothschild family, who controlled banks in several countries. The head of the London branch was **Lionel Rothschild** (1808–1879). He was elected to Parliament several times but was not seated because he would not take the required Christian oath. After the requirement of that oath was abolished in 1858, he sat in Parliament from 1858 until 1874.
SOURCE: Hulton Archive/Stringer/Archive Photos/Getty Images

especially in eastern Europe, many Jews became associated with Socialist parties.

The prejudice that had been associated with Christian religious attitudes toward Jews seemed to have largely dissipated. Hundreds of thousands of European Jews migrated from Russia's Pale of Settlement (the only part of Russia where Jews were permitted to live) to Western Europe and the United States. Almost anywhere in Europe, Jews might encounter prejudice on a personal level. Yet in England, France, Italy, Germany, the Low Countries, and Austria, the legalized persecution and discrimination that had so haunted Jews in the past seemed to have ended.

That newfound security began to erode during the last two decades of the nineteenth century. Anti-Semitic voices began to be heard in the 1870s, attributing the economic stagnation of the decade to Jewish bankers and financial interests. In the 1880s, organized **anti-Semitism** erupted in Germany, as it did in France at the time of the Dreyfus affair. Most Jewish leaders believed the attacks on Jewish life were merely temporary recurrences of older forms of prejudice; they felt their communities would remain safe under the liberal legal protections that had been extended during the century.

23.7 Labor, Socialism, and Politics to World War I

What role did the Socialist and labor movements play in late-nineteenth-century politics?

The late-century industrial expansion further changed the life of the labor force. In all industrializing continental countries, the numbers of the urban proletariat rose. The proportion of artisans and highly skilled workers declined, and for the first time, factory wage earners predominated. The number of unskilled workers in shipping, transportation, and building also grew.

After 1848, however, European workers stopped rioting in the streets to voice their grievances. After mid-century, workers turned to new institutions and ideologies. Chief among these were trade unions, democratic political parties, and socialism.

CERTIFICATE OF UNION MEMBERSHIP As the number of workers grew, they began to organize. The number of trade unions increased in the latter part of the nineteenth century, especially after governments recognized their legal status. Unions often had elaborate membership certificates such as this one from the Amalgamated Society of Railway Servants of Great Britain and Ireland.
SOURCE: Chronicle/Alamy Stock Photo

23.7.1 Trade Unionism

Trade unionism came of age when governments extended legal protections to unions during the second half-century. Unions became fully legal in Great Britain in 1871 and were allowed to picket in 1875. The Third French Republic fully legalized unions in 1884. In Germany, unions were permitted to function with little disturbance after 1890. As long as the representatives of the traditional governing classes looked after labor interests, members of the working class rarely sought office themselves.

Unions directed their mid-century organizational efforts toward skilled workers and the immediate improvement of wages and working conditions. By the close of the century, industrial unions for unskilled workers were being organized. Employers intensely opposed these large unions of thousands of workers. Unions frequently had to engage in long strikes to convince employers to accept their demands. Europe experienced a rash of strikes in the decade before World War I as unions sought to keep wages in line with inflation. Despite union advances, however, and the growth of union membership (in 1910 to approximately 3 million in Britain, 2 million in Germany, and 977,000 in France), most of Europe's labor force was never unionized in this period. Unions represented a new collective form of association for workers to confront economic difficulties and improve security.

23.7.2 Democracy and Political Parties

Except for Russia, all the major European states adopted broad-based, if not perfectly democratic, electoral systems in the late nineteenth century. Great Britain passed its second voting reform act in 1867 and its third in 1884. Bismarck brought universal male suffrage to the German Empire in 1871. The French Chamber of Deputies was democratically elected. Universal male suffrage was adopted in Switzerland in 1879, in Spain in 1890, in Belgium in 1893, in the Netherlands in 1896, in Norway in 1898, in Austria in 1907, and in Italy in 1912. The broadened franchise meant politicians could no longer ignore workers, and discontented groups could now voice their grievances and advocate their programs within the institutions of government rather than from the outside.

The advent of democracy brought organized mass political parties to Europe for the first time. The expansion of the electorate brought into the political process many people whose level of political consciousness, awareness, and interest was low. This electorate had to be organized and taught about power and influence in the liberal democratic state.

The organized political party—with its workers, newspapers, offices, social life, and discipline—was the vehicle that mobilized the new voters. The largest single group in these mass electorates was the working class. The democratization of politics presented the Socialists with opportunities and required the traditional ruling classes to vie with the Socialists for support of the new voters.

During these years, socialism as a political ideology and plan of action opposed nationalism. The problems of class were supposed to be transnational, and socialism was supposed to unite the working classes across national borders. European Socialists, however, badly underestimated the emotional power of nationalism. Many workers had both Socialist and nationalist sympathies, which were rarely in conflict with each other. When the outbreak of war in 1914 did bring them into conflict, however, nationalist feelings prevailed.

The major question for late-century Socialist parties throughout Europe was whether revolution or democratic reform would improve the life of the working class. This question sharply divided all Socialist parties and especially those whose leadership adhered to the intellectual legacy of Karl Marx. The Bolshevik Revolution of November 1917 would transform Socialist debates and actions and render many of the prewar disputes moot.

23.7.3 Karl Marx and the First International

In 1864, a group of British and French trade unionists founded the **International Working Men's Association.** Known as the First International, its membership encompassed a vast array of radical political types, including Socialists, anarchists, and Polish nationalists. In the inaugural address for the First International, Marx approved workers' and trade unions' efforts to reform the conditions of labor within the existing political and economic processes. In his private writings he often criticized such reformist activity, but these writings were not made public until near the end of the century, years after his death.

The violence involved in the rise and suppression of the Paris Commune, which Marx had declared a genuine proletarian uprising, cast a pall over socialism throughout Europe. British trade unionists, who received legal protections in 1871, wanted no connection with the events in Paris. The French authorities used the uprising to suppress Socialist activity. Under these pressures, the First International held its last European congress in 1873. It soon transferred its offices to the United States, where it was dissolved in 1876.

The short-lived First International had a disproportionately great impact on the future of European socialism. Throughout the late 1860s, the organization gathered statistics, kept labor groups informed of mutual problems, provided a forum to debate Socialist doctrine, and overstated its own influence over contemporary events. From these debates and activities, Marxism emerged as the single most important strand of Socialism. Marx and his supporters defeated or drove out anarchists and advocates of other forms of Socialism. The apparently scientific character of Marxism made it attractive at a time when science was more influential than at any previous period in European history. Marx's thought deeply impressed German Socialists, who were to establish the most powerful Socialist party in Europe and became the chief vehicle for preserving and developing it. The full development of German socialism, however, also involved the influence of non-Marxist Socialists in Great Britain.

23.7.4 Great Britain: Fabianism and Early Welfare Programs

Neither Marxism nor any other form of socialism made significant progress in Great Britain, the most industrial society of the day. Trade unions grew steadily, and their members normally supported Liberal Party candidates. The "new unionism" of the late 1880s and the 1890s organized the dockworkers, the gas workers, and similar unskilled groups. In 1892, Keir Hardie (1856–1915) became the first independent working man to be elected to Parliament. Until 1901, labor's general political activity remained limited. In that year, however, the House of Lords, which also acts as Britain's highest court, removed the legal protection previously accorded union funds through the Taff Vale decision. The Trades Union Congress responded by launching the Labour Party. In the election of 1906, the fledgling party sent twenty-nine members to Parliament. Although the British labor movement became more militant in this period, its goals did not include socialism. In scores of strikes before the war, workers fought for wages to meet the rising cost of living. The government took a larger role than ever before in mediating these strikes, which in 1911 and 1912 involved the railways, the docks, and the coal mines.

British socialism itself remained primarily the preserve of non-Marxist intellectuals. The **Fabian Society**, founded in 1884, was Britain's most influential Socialist group. The

BEATRICE AND SIDNEY WEBB Beatrice and Sidney Webb, shown in this photograph from the 1920s, were the most influential British Fabian Socialists. They wrote many books on governmental and economic matters, served on special parliamentary commissions, and agitated for the enactment of Socialist policies.
SOURCE: Hulton Archive/Stringer/Getty Images

society took its name from Q. Fabius Maximus (d. 203 B.C.E.), the Roman general whose tactics against Hannibal involved avoiding direct conflict that might lead to defeat. Many Fabians were civil servants who believed the problems of industry could be solved and achieved gradually, peacefully, and democratically. They sought to educate the country about the rational wisdom of socialism. They were particularly interested in modes of collective ownership on the municipal level, the so-called gas-and-water socialism.

The British government responded slowly to these pressures. After 1906, the Liberal Party, led by Sir Henry Campbell-Bannerman (1836–1908) and, after 1908, by Herbert Asquith, pursued a two-pronged policy. Fearful of losing seats in Parliament to the new Labour Party, they restored the former protection of the unions. Then, after 1909, under the leadership of Chancellor of the Exchequer David Lloyd George (1863–1945), the liberal ministry undertook a broad program of social legislation that included establishing labor exchanges; regulating certain trades, such as tailoring and lace making; and passing the National Insurance Act of 1911, which provided unemployment benefits and health care.

The financing of these programs brought the liberal majority in the House of Commons into conflict with the Conservative-dominated House of Lords. The result was the Parliament Act of 1911, which allowed the Commons to override the legislative veto of the upper chamber. The new taxes and social programs meant that in Britain, the home of nineteenth-century liberalism, the state was taking on an expanded role in the life of its citizens. The early welfare legislation was only marginally satisfactory to labor, many of whose members still thought they could gain more from the direct action of strikes.

23.7.5 France: "Opportunism" Rejected

French socialism was a less united and more politically factionalized movement than socialism in other countries. At the turn of the century, Jean Jaurès (1859–1914) and Jules Guesde (1845–1922) led the two major factions of French Socialists. Jaurès believed Socialists should cooperate with middle-class radical ministries to ensure the enactment of needed Social legislation. Guesde opposed this policy, arguing that Socialists could not, with integrity, support a bourgeois cabinet they were theoretically dedicated to overthrowing.

The Second International had been founded in 1889 in a new effort to unify the various national Socialist parties and trade unions. By 1904, the Amsterdam Congress of the Second International debated the issue of opportunism, as such participation by Socialists in cabinets was termed. The Congress condemned opportunism in France and ordered French Socialists to form a single party. Jaurès accepted the decision. Thereafter French Socialists began to work together, and by 1914 the recently united Socialist Party had become the second largest group in the Chamber of Deputies.

The French labor movement, with deep roots in anarchism, was uninterested in either politics or socialism. French workers usually voted Socialist, but the unions themselves, unlike those in Britain, avoided active political participation. The main labor union, Confédération Générale du Travail, founded in 1895, regarded itself as a rival to the Socialist parties. Its leaders sought to improve the workers' conditions through direct action. The strike tactic often conflicted with the Socialist belief in aiding labor through state action. Strikes were common in France between 1905 and 1914, and the middle-class radical ministry repeatedly used troops to suppress them.

23.7.6 Germany: Social Democrats and Revisionism

The negative judgment the Second International rendered against French Socialist participation in bourgeois ministries reflected a policy of permanent hostility to nonsocialist governments that the German Social Democratic Party, or SPD,

had already adopted. The organizational success of this party, more than any other single factor, kept Marxist Socialism alive during the late nineteenth and early twentieth centuries.

The SPD had been founded in 1875. Its origins lay in the labor agitation of Ferdinand Lassalle (1825–1864), who wanted workers to participate in German politics. Wilhelm Liebknecht (1826–1900) and August Bebel (1840–1913), who were Marxists who opposed reformist politics, soon joined the party. Thus, from its founding, the SPD was divided between those who advocated reform and those who advocated revolution.

23.7.6.1 BISMARCK'S REPRESSION OF THE SPD Twelve years of persecution under Bismarck forged the character of the SPD. The so-called Iron Chancellor believed socialism would undermine German politics and society. He used an assassination attempt on Emperor William I (r. 1861–1888) in 1878, in which the Socialists were not actually involved, to steer anti-Socialist laws through the Reichstag. The measures suppressed the organization, meetings, newspapers, and other public activities of the SPD. Thereafter, to remain a Socialist meant to remove oneself from the mainstream of respectable German life and possibly to lose one's job. The anti-Socialist legislation proved politically counterproductive. Even under the repressive laws, members of the SPD could sit in the Reichstag. From the early 1880s onward, the SPD steadily polled more and more votes in elections to the Reichstag.

As simple repression failed to wean German workers from Socialist loyalties, Bismarck undertook a program of social welfare legislation. In 1883, the German Empire adopted a health insurance measure. The next year the Reichstag enacted accident insurance legislation. Finally, in 1889, Bismarck sponsored a plan for old age and disability pensions. These programs, to which both workers and employers contributed, represented a paternalistic, conservative alternative to socialism. The state itself would organize a system of social security that did not require any change in the system of property holding or politics. Germany became the first major industrial nation to employ and benefit from this kind of welfare program.

23.7.6.2 THE ERFURT PROGRAM After forcing Bismarck's resignation mainly because of differences over foreign policy, Emperor William II (r. 1888–1918) allowed the anti-Socialist legislation to expire, hoping to build new political support among the working class. With the repressive measures lifted, the party needed to decide what attitude to assume toward the German Empire.

The answer came in the **Erfurt Program** of 1891. The program insisted on Socialist ownership of the means of production. The party intended to pursue these goals through legal political participation rather than revolutionary activity. So although in theory the SPD was vehemently hostile to the German Empire, in practice the party functioned within the empire's institutions. The SPD members of the Reichstag maintained clear political consciences by refusing to enter the cabinet (to which they were not invited anyway) and by refraining for many years from voting in favor of the military budget. In this way, they used their political positions to benefit the workers they represented, without strengthening the political and economic system they opposed.

23.7.6.3 THE DEBATE OVER REVISIONISM

The dilemma of the SPD, however, generated the most important challenge within the Socialist movement to the orthodox Marxist analysis of capitalism and the Socialist revolution. The author of this Socialist heresy, Eduard Bernstein (1850–1932), had lived in Britain and was familiar with the Fabians. Bernstein questioned whether Marx and his later orthodox followers, such as Karl Kautsky, had been correct in their pessimistic appraisal of capitalism and their necessity for revolution. In *Evolutionary Socialism* (1899), Bernstein pointed to conditions that did not meet orthodox Marxists' expectations. The standard of living was rising in Europe. Stockholding was making the ownership of capitalist industry more widespread. The inner contradictions of capitalism had not developed the way Marx had predicted. Moreover, the extension of the franchise to the working class meant that parliamentary methods might achieve revolutionary social change. For Bernstein, social reform through democratic institutions replaced revolution as the path to a humane Socialist society.

Bernstein's doctrines, known as revisionism, generated heated debate among German Socialists, who finally condemned them. His critics argued that evolution toward social democracy might be possible in liberal, parliamentary Britain, but not in conservative Germany, with its feeble Reichstag. Nonetheless, while still calling for revolution, the SPD pursued a course of action similar to Bernstein's. Its trade union members, prospering within the German economy, did not want revolution. Its grassroots members wanted to be patriotic Germans as well as good Socialists. Its leaders feared anything that might renew the persecution they had experienced under Bismarck.

Consequently, the SPD worked for electoral gains, expansion of its membership, and short-term political and social reform. It prospered and became one of the most important institutions of imperial Germany. Even middle-class Germans voted for it to oppose the illiberal institutions of the empire. In August 1914, after long internal debate, the SPD members of the Reichstag unanimously voted for the war credits that would finance Germany's participation in World War I.

23.7.7 Russia: Industrial Development and the Birth of Bolshevism

In the 1890s, Russia entered the industrial age and confronted many of the problems that other nations of the Continent had experienced fifty or seventy-five years earlier. Unlike those other countries, Russia had to deal with political discontent and economic development simultaneously. Russian socialism reflected that peculiar situation.

KEY DATES IN RUSSIAN HISTORY, 1890s–1910s	
1892	Witte appointed finance minister
1895	Lenin arrested and sent to Siberia
1897	11.5-hour workday established
1898	Russian Social Democratic Party founded
1900	Lenin leaves Russia for Western Europe
1901	Social Revolutionary Party founded
1903	Constitutional Democratic Party (Cadets) founded
1903	Bolshevik–Menshevik split
1903	Witte dismissed
1904	Russo-Japanese War begins
(January 22) 1905	Revolution breaks out in St. Petersburg after Bloody Sunday
(August) 1905	Japan defeats Russia
(October 20) 1905	General strike
(October 26) 1905	October Manifesto establishes constitutional government
(May 10) 1906	First Duma meets
(June) 1906	Stolypin appointed prime minister
(July 21) 1906	Dissolution of first Duma
(November) 1906	Land redemption payments canceled for peasants
(March 5–16) 1907	Second Duma seated and dismissed in June
1907	Franchise changed; third Duma elected, which sits until 1912
1911	Stolypin assassinated by a Social Revolutionary
1912	Fourth Duma elected
1914	World War I breaks out

23.7.7.1 WITTE'S PROGRAM FOR INDUSTRIAL GROWTH

Tsar Alexander III (r. 1881–1894) and, after him, Nicholas II (r. 1894–1917) were determined that Russia should become an industrial power. Only by doing so, they believed, could the country maintain its position as a great power. Count **Sergei Witte** (1849–1915) led Russia into the industrial age. After a career in railways and other private business, he was appointed first minister of communications and then finance minister in 1892. Witte, who pursued a policy of planned economic development, protective tariffs, high taxes, putting Russia's currency on the gold standard, and efficiency in government and business, epitomized the nineteenth-century modernizer. He established a strong financial relationship with the French money market, which enabled Russia to finance its modernization program with French loans and later led to diplomatic cooperation and an alliance between Russia and France.

Witte favored heavy industries. Between 1890 and 1904, the Russian railway system grew from 30,596 to 59,616 kilometers. The 5,000-mile-long Trans-Siberian Railroad was completed in 1903. Coal output more than tripled during the same period. Pig-iron production increased from 928,000 tons in 1890 to 4,641,000 tons in 1913. During the same period, steel production rose from 378,000 to 4,918,000 tons. Textile manufacturing continued to expand and was still the single largest industry. The factory system spread extensively.

Industrialism, however, also brought social discontent to Russia, as it had elsewhere. Landowners felt that foreign capitalists were earning too much of the profit. The peasants saw their grain exports and tax payments finance development that did not measurably improve their lives. A small, but significant, industrial proletariat emerged. In 1900, Russia had approximately three million factory workers. Their working and living conditions were poor. They enjoyed little state protection, and trade unions were illegal. In 1897, Witte did enact an eleven-and-one-half-hour workday, but still, discontent and strikes continued.

Similar social and economic problems arose in the countryside. Russian agriculture had not prospered after the emancipation of the serfs in 1861. The peasants remained burdened with redemption payments for the land they farmed, local taxes, excessive national taxes, and falling grain prices. Peasants did not own their land as individuals, but communally through the *mir*, or village. They farmed the land inefficiently through strip farming or by tilling small plots. Many free peasants with too little land to support their families had to work on large estates owned by nobles or for more prosperous peasant farmers, known as *kulaks*. Between 1860 and 1914, the population of European Russia rose from about 50 million to around 103 million people. Land hunger and discontent spread among the peasants and sparked frequent uprisings in the countryside.

New political developments accompanied economic changes. The membership and intellectual roots of the Social Revolutionary Party, founded in 1901, reached back to the Populists of the 1870s. The new party opposed industrialism and looked to the communal life of rural Russia as a model for the future. In 1903, the Constitutional Democratic Party, or Cadets, was formed. This liberal party drew its members from those who participated in local councils called zemstvos. Modeled on the liberal parties of Western Europe, the Cadets wanted a constitutional monarchy under a parliamentary regime with civil liberties and economic progress.

23.7.7.2 LENIN'S EARLY THOUGHT AND CAREER The situation of Russian Socialists differed radically from that of Socialists in other major European countries. Russia had no representative institutions and only a small working class. The compromises and accommodations achieved elsewhere were meaningless in Russia where Socialists believed in both theory and practice that they must be revolutionary. The repressive policies of the tsarist regime required the Russian Social Democratic Party, founded in 1898, to function in exile. The party members greatly admired the German Social Democratic Party and adopted its Marxist ideology.

The leading late-nineteenth-century Russian Marxist was Gregory Plekhanov (1857–1918), who wrote from exile in Switzerland. At the turn of the century, his chief disciple was **Vladimir Ilyich Ulyanov** (1870–1924), who later took the name of Lenin. The future leader of the Communist revolution was the son of a high bureaucrat. His older brother, while a student in St. Petersburg, had become involved in radical politics; arrested for participating in a plot against Alexander III, he was executed in 1887. In 1893, Lenin moved to St. Petersburg, where he studied law. Soon he too was drawn to the revolutionary groups among the factory workers. He was arrested in 1895 and exiled to Siberia. In 1900, after his release, Lenin left Russia for the West. He spent most of the next seventeen years in Switzerland.

There, Lenin became deeply involved in the disputes of the exiled Russian Social Democrats. They all considered themselves Marxists, but they differed on what a Marxist revolution would mean for primarily rural Russia and on how to structure their own party. The Social Democrats favored industrial development and did not idolize Russia's agricultural past. Most Russian Social Democrats believed Russia had to develop a large proletariat before the Marxist revolution could come. They also hoped to build a mass political party like the German SPD.

Lenin dissented from both these ideas. In *What Is to Be Done?* (1902), he condemned cooperation with existing governments, such as those of the German SPD as well as trade unionism that settled for short-term reformist gains. Lenin further rejected the concept of a mass democratic party comprised of workers. Instead, he declared that revolutionary consciousness would not arise spontaneously from the working class. Rather, "people who make revolutionary activity their profession" must carry that consciousness

LENIN When a warrant for his arrest was issued, Lenin (1870–1924) traveled to Finland in disguise under an assumed name, using this fake passport. Later, in the fall of 1917, he led the Bolsheviks in a successful revolution.
SOURCE: Hulton-Deutsch/Getty Images

to the workers.[3] Only a small, tightly organized elite party could dedicate themselves to revolution and resist penetration by police spies. The guiding principle of that party should be "the strictest secrecy, the strictest selection of members, and the training of professional revolutionaries."[4] Lenin thus rejected both Kautsky's view that revolution was inevitable and Bernstein's view that democratic means could achieve revolutionary goals. Lenin substituted the small, professional, nondemocratic revolutionary party for Marx's proletariat as the instrument of revolutionary change. (For more on the tactics of European socialism, see this chapter's "Compare and Connect" sidebar, which follows below.)

Compare and Connect

Bernstein and Lenin Debate the Tactics of European Socialism

BY THE CLOSE of the nineteenth century the European Socialist movement found itself sharply divided over its future goals and tactics. Some Socialists, including Eduard Bernstein, came to reject Karl Marx's emphasis on a proletarian revolution and embraced democratic politics as the best way to realize their goals of improving the life of the working class. A minority, including Lenin, rejected democracy and embraced the concept of violent revolution achieved by a small professional elite rather than by a spontaneous proletarian uprising. After the 1917 Bolshevik Revolution in Russia, these divisions would play themselves out in an enormously hostile conflict between Democratic Socialists in Western Europe and Communists in the Soviet Union and those Communists in Western Europe dominated by the Soviet Union.

KRUPP STEEL WORKS By the close of the nineteenth century, European Socialists had come to doubt whether the industrial proletariat around the world, such as these workers in the Krupp steel works around 1910, could bring about a revolution as predicted by Marx. Eduard Bernstein thought democratic social change would improve the lot of workers. Lenin believed an elite revolutionary party would produce such radical change. Krupp was one of many Germany companies that introduced paternalistic benefits to workers, such as subsidized modern housing projects, to show that cooperation improved workers' lives more than violent revolution would.
SOURCE: Hulton Archive/Stringer/Getty Images

Before Reading

• Think about how and why Lenin's ideas about democracy and revolution differ from those of Eduard Bernstein and Marx.

Questions

1. According to Bernstein, what specific predictions in the *Communist Manifesto* failed to materialize?
2. Why is the advance of democracy important to Bernstein's argument? Why does he renounce the concept of a "dictatorship of the proletariat"?

3. What does Lenin mean by "professional revolutionaries"? Why does he believe Russia needs such revolutionaries?
4. How does Lenin reconcile his antidemocratic views with the goal of aiding the working class?
5. How could the ideas of both Bernstein and Lenin be viewed as departures from Marx's own thinking?

I. BERNSTEIN URGES SOCIALISTS TO EMBRACE DEMOCRACY

Eduard Bernstein was responsible for the emergence of Revisionism within the German Social Democratic Party. He was a dedicated Socialist, but was convinced that Marx's Communist Manifesto *(1848) had not predicted the future of the European working classes. Bernstein did not believe the capitalist system would suddenly collapse. He urged Socialists to change their tactics to achieve democratic political rights and pursue reform instead of revolution.*

Social conditions have not developed to such an acute opposition of things and classes as is depicted in the [*Communist*] *Manifesto*. . . . The number of members of the possessing classes is today not smaller but larger. The enormous increase of social wealth is not accompanied by a decreasing number of large capitalists but by an increasing number of capitalists of all degrees. . . .

In all advanced countries we see the privileges of the capitalist bourgeoisie yielding step by step to democratic organizations. . . .

The conquest of political power by the working classes, the expropriation of capitalists, are not ends in themselves but only means for the accomplishment of certain aims and endeavours. . . .

Democracy is in principle the suppression of class government, though it is not yet the actual suppression of classes. . . . The right to vote in a democracy makes its members virtually partners in the community, and this virtual partnership must in the end lead to real partnership. . . .

Universal franchise is, from two sides, the alternative to a violent revolution. But universal suffrage is only a part of democracy, although a part which in time must draw the other parts after it as the magnet attracts to itself the scattered portions of iron. It certainly proceeds more slowly than many would wish, but in spite of that it is at work. And social democracy cannot further this work better than by taking its stand unreserved only the theory of democracy—on the ground of universal suffrage with all the consequences resulting therefrom to its tactics. . . .

Is there any sense . . . in maintaining the phrase of the 'dictatorship of the proletariat' at a time when in all possible places representatives of social democracy have placed themselves practically in the arena of Parliamentary work, have declared for the proportional representation of the people, and for direct legislation—all of which is inconsistent with a dictatorship.

The phrase is today so antiquated that it is only to be reconciled with reality by stripping the word dictatorship of its actual meaning and attaching to it some kind of weakened interpretation. The whole practical activity of social democracy is directed towards creating circumstances and conditions which shall render possible and secure a transition (free from convulsive outbursts) of the modern social order to a higher one.

II. LENIN ARGUES FOR A SECRET AND ELITE PARTY OF PROFESSIONAL REVOLUTIONARIES

Social democratic parties in Western Europe had mass memberships and were generally democratic organizations. In this passage from What Is to Be Done? *(1902), Lenin explains why the autocratic political conditions of Russia demanded a different kind of organization for the Russian Social Democratic Party. Lenin's ideas became the guiding principles of Bolshevik organization. Lenin departed from Marx's thought by urging the necessity of fulminating revolution rather than waiting for it to occur as a necessary result of the collapse of capitalism.*

I assert that it is far more difficult [for government police] to unearth a dozen wise men than a hundred fools. This position I will defend, no matter how much you instigate the masses against me for my "anti-democratic" views, etc. As I have stated repeatedly, by "wise men," in connection with organization, I mean professional revolutionaries, irrespective of whether they have developed from among students or working men. I assert: (1) that no revolutionary movement can endure without a stable organization of leaders maintaining continuity; (2) that the broader the popular mass drawn spontaneously into the struggle, which forms the basis of the movement and participates in it, the more urgent the need for such an organization, and the more solid this organization must be . . . ; (3) that such an organization must consist chiefly of people professionally engaged in revolutionary activity; (4) that in an autocratic state [such as Russia], the more we confine the membership of such an organization to people who are professionally engaged in revolutionary activity and who have been professionally trained in the art of combating the political police, the more difficult will it be to unearth the organization; and (5) the greater will be the number of people from the working class and from other social classes who will be able to join the movement and perform active work in it. . . .

The only serious organization principle for the active workers of our movement should be the strictest secrecy, the strictest selection of members, and the training of professional revolutionaries.

SOURCES: (I) From Eduard Bernstein, *Evolutionary Socialism: A Criticism and Affirmation, 1899* (New York: Schocken Books, 1961), pp. xxiv–xxv, xxix, 143–146. (II) From Albert Fried and Ronald Sanders, eds. *Socialist Thought: A Documentary History* (Garden City, NY: Anchor Doubleday, 1964), pp. 460, 468.

In 1903, at the London Congress of the Russian Social Democratic Party, Lenin forced a split in the party ranks. He and his followers lost many votes on questions put before the congress, but near its close they mustered a slim majority. Thereafter Lenin's faction assumed the name **Bolsheviks**, meaning "majority," and the other, more moderate, democratic revolutionary faction came to be known as the **Mensheviks**, or "minority." There was, of course, a considerable public relations advantage to the name Bolshevik.

A fundamental organizational difference had existed between the two chief factions of the Russian Social Democratic Party. The **Mensheviks** wanted a party with mass membership, similar to the German SPD and other West European Socialist parties, which would function democratically. The Bolsheviks intended their party to consist of elite professional revolutionaries who would provide centralized leadership for the working class.

In 1905, Lenin complemented his organizational theory with a program for revolution in Russia. In *Two Tactics of Social Democracy in the Bourgeois-Democratic Revolution*, he urged the Socialist revolution to unite the proletariat and the peasantry. Lenin grasped better than any other revolutionary the profound discontent in the Russian countryside. He believed the tsarist government probably could not suppress an alliance of workers and peasants in rebellion.

Lenin's two principles—an elite party and a dual social revolution—guided later Bolshevik activity. In 1912, the Bolsheviks organized as a separate party. The Bolsheviks ultimately seized power in November 1917, transforming the political landscape of the twentieth century, but they did so only after the turmoil of World War I had undermined support for the tsar and other political forces had already toppled the tsarist government in February 1917. Before World War I, the Bolsheviks constituted the odd man out in European Socialist politics; they exerted no significant prewar influence on members of other Socialist groups. The Bolsheviks responded by scorning the West European Socialist parties that worked within their nations' political systems.

23.7.7.3 THE REVOLUTION OF 1905 AND ITS AFTERMATH
The quarrels among the exiled Russian Socialists and Lenin's doctrines had no immediate influence on events in Russia. Industrialization continued to stir resentment. In 1903, Nicholas II dismissed Witte, hoping to quell the criticism. The next year, in response to conflicts over Manchuria and Korea, Russia went to war against Japan, partly in hopes the conflict would rally public opinion to the tsar. Instead, the Russians lost the war, and the government faced an internal political crisis. The Japanese captured Port Arthur, Russia's naval base on the coast of China, early in 1905. A few days later, on January 22, a Russian Orthodox priest named Father George Gapon led several hundred workers to petition the tsar to improve industrial conditions. The petitioners did not know the tsar was not even in St. Petersburg, but as they approached the Winter Palace, troops opened fire, killing approximately forty people and wounding hundreds of others. As word of this massacre spread and large, angry crowds gathered elsewhere in the city, the military shot more people. The final death toll was approximately 200 killed and 800 wounded, though at the time numbers were rumored to be much larger. The day, soon known as **Bloody Sunday**, marked a turning point, as ordinary Russians came to believe they could no longer trust the tsar or his government. (For more about the events of Bloody Sunday, see the "Closer Look" sidebar, which follows below.)

During the next ten months, revolutionary disturbances spread throughout Russia. Sailors mutinied, workers went on strike, peasants revolted, and property was attacked. The uncle of Nicholas II was assassinated in Moscow. Liberal leaders of the Constitutional Democratic Party from the zemstvos demanded political reform. University students went on strike. Social Revolutionaries and Social Democrats agitated among urban working groups. In early October 1905, strikes broke out in St. Petersburg, and for all practical purposes, worker councils, called *soviets*, controlled the city. Nicholas II issued the October Manifesto, which promised Russia a constitutional government.

Early in 1906, Nicholas II announced the creation of a representative body, the *Duma*, with two chambers. He reserved to himself, however, ministerial appointments, financial policy, and military and foreign affairs. The April elections returned a highly radical group of representatives. The tsar appointed Piotr Stolypin (1862–1911), who had little sympathy for parliamentary government, as prime minister. Stolypin persuaded Nicholas to dissolve the Duma. A second assembly was elected in February 1907. Again, cooperation proved impossible, and the tsar dissolved that Duma in June. A third Duma, elected in late 1907 based on a more conservative franchise, proved sufficiently pliable for the tsar and Stolypin. Thus, within two years of the 1905 Revolution, Nicholas II had recaptured much of the ground he had conceded.

Stolypin set about repressing rebellion, removing some causes of the revolt, and rallying property owners behind the tsarist regime. Early in 1907, special field courts-martial condemned almost 700 rebellious peasants to death. Before undertaking this repression, Stolypin, in November 1906, had canceled any redemptive payments that the peasants still owed the government from the emancipation of the serfs in 1861. He took this step to encourage peasants to assume individual proprietorship of the land they farmed and to abandon the communal system of shared village ownership. Stolypin believed farmers would be more productive working for themselves. Combined with a program to instruct peasants on how to farm more efficiently, this policy improved agricultural production. However, many peasant small-holders sold their land and joined the industrial labor force.

A Closer Look

Bloody Sunday, St. Petersburg, 1905

ON BLOODY SUNDAY, January 22, 1905, troops of Tsar Nicholas II fired on a peaceful procession of workers at the Winter Palace presenting a petition for better working and living conditions. The scene in St. Petersburg square portrayed here, which can still be visited today, depicts one of the enduring images of events leading to the subsequent Russian Revolutions of 1905 and 1917. It was used in at least two movies: the 1925 antitsarist Soviet silent film *The Ninth of January*, and *Nicholas and Alexandra*, the lavish 1971 movie that was sympathetic to the tsar and blamed Bloody Sunday on frightened and incompetent officials. Although Nicholas had not ordered the troops to fire and was not even in St. Petersburg on Bloody Sunday, the event all but destroyed the chance of reconciliation between the tsarist government and the Russian working class.

Visibly defenseless workers scatter as security forces prepare to shoot.

The large square in front of the Winter Palace affords no protection to the unarmed petitioners.

The Winter Palace, facing the backs of the troops, is just out of view.

RUSSIAN TROOPS ON BLOODY SUNDAY N/A
SOURCE: bpk Bildagentur/Art Resource, NY

Questions

1. How did the invention of photography and the making of movies transform the recording and interpretation of the past?
2. Do you think the firing on the crowd on January 22,1905, was as orderly as this still from a later Bolshevik film made it appear?
3. How did the ongoing reenactment of Bloody Sunday continue to discredit the tsarist government and to champion the later Bolshevik Revolution?

The moderate liberals who sat in the Duma approved of the new land measures promoting competition and individual property ownership. The Constitutional Democrats wanted a more genuinely parliamentary mode of government, but they compromised out of fear of new revolutionary disturbances. Hatred of Stolypin was still widespread, however, among the country's older conservative groups, and industrial workers remained antagonistic to the tsar. In 1911, Stolypin was assassinated by a Social Revolutionary, who may have been a police agent in the pay of conservatives. Nicholas II found no worthy successor. His government simply muddled along.

Meanwhile, at court, the monk Grigory Yefimovich Rasputin (1871–1916) gained ascendancy with the tsar and his wife because of his alleged power to heal the tsar's hemophilic son Alexis, the heir to the throne, when medicine proved unable to help the boy. Popular resentment of Rasputin's undue influence, as well as continued social discontent and conservative resistance to any further liberal reforms, undermined the position of the tsar and his government after 1911. Once again, as in 1904, Nicholas II and his ministers thought that a bold move in foreign policy might bring the regime the popular support it desperately needed.

The Chapter in Perspective

From 1860 through 1914, two apparently contradictory developments emerged in European social life. On the one hand, the lifestyle of the urban middle classes was one to which much of society aspired. The characteristics of this lifestyle included a relatively small family living in its own house or large apartment, servants, and a wife who did not earn an income. The middle classes, in general, benefited from the many material comforts that the Second Industrial Revolution had generated.

During the same period, the forces of socialism and labor unions assumed a new and major role in European political life. Their leaders demanded greater social justice and a fairer distribution of the vast quantities of consumer goods Europe was producing. Some Socialists sought in one way or another to work within existing political systems. Others—particularly, those in Russia—advocated revolution. The growth in wealth and the availability of new goods and services magnified the injustices the poor suffered, and the contrast between them and the middle classes made the demands of labor and the Socialists more strident. In Russia, the strains of the early stages of industrialization intensified social unrest. These strains, compounded by the humiliating defeat in a war against Japan, triggered the unsuccessful revolution of 1905.

The working class, however, was not alone in seeking change. Women, for the first time in European history, began in significant ways to demand a political role and to protest the gender inequalities embedded in law and family life. They were beginning to enter the professions and were taking a significant role in the service economy, such as the new telephone companies. These changes, as much as the demands of Socialists, would in time raise questions about the adequacy of the much admired late-nineteenth-century middle-class lifestyle.

The Chapter in Review

Review Questions

1. What new industries developed during the Second Industrial Revolution, and which do you think had the greatest impact in the twentieth century? Why did European economic growth slacken in the second half of the nineteenth century?

2. Why were European cities redesigned during the late nineteenth century? Why were housing and health key issues for urban reform?

3. What was the status of European women in the second half of the nineteenth century? Why did they grow discontented? What factors led to change? To what extent had they improved their position by 1914? What tactics did they use to effect change? Was the emancipation of women inevitable? How did women approach their situation differently from country to country?

4. What were the major characteristics of Jewish emancipation in the nineteenth century?

5. What was the status of the European working classes in 1860? Had it improved by 1914? Why did trade unions and organized mass political parties grow? Why were the debates over "opportunism" and "revisionism" important to the Western European Socialist parties?

6. What were the benefits and drawbacks of industrialization for Russia? Were the tsars wise to attempt to modernize their country or should they have left it as it was? How did Lenin's view of socialism differ from that of the Socialists in Western Europe?

Key Terms

anti-Semitism Prejudice, hostility, or legal discrimination against Jews.

Bloody Sunday At St. Petersburg on January 22, 1905, a massacre in which troops of Tsar Nicholas II fired on workers at the Winter Palace petitioning for better working and living conditions.

Bolsheviks Meaning the "majority." Term Lenin applied to his faction of the Russian Social Democratic Party, which became the Communist Party of the Soviet Union after the Russian Revolution.

Emmeline Pankhurst (1857–1928) Founder of the Women's Social and Political Union, a radical branch of British feminists.

Erfurt Program The program in Germany of 1891 that insisted on the necessity of Socialist ownership of the means of production.

Fabian Society Founded in 1884, Britain's most influential Socialist group that sought to educate the country about the rational wisdom of socialism.

Gottlieb Daimler (1834–1900) The inventor of the internal combustion engine.

International Working Men's Association Founded in 1864 by British and French trade unionists, known as the First International; gathered statistics, kept labor groups informed of mutual problems, and provided a forum to debate Socialist doctrine.

Lionel Rothschild (1808–1879) The British banker, politician, and philanthropist who was a member of the prominent Rothschild banking family of England.

London Great Exhibition The exhibition held in 1851 in the Crystal Palace that displayed the products and the new material life of the middle classes.

Louis Pasteur (1822–1895) French biologist, microbiologist, and chemist, whose discoveries led to the full acceptance of the bacterial theory of disease.

Married Woman's Property Act Legislation in Great Britain in 1882 that allowed married women to own property.

Mensheviks Meaning the "minority." Term Lenin applied to the majority moderate faction of the Russian Social Democratic Party opposed to him and the Bolsheviks.

petite bourgeoisie **(peh-TEET BOOSH-schwa-zee)** The lower middle class.

pogroms **(PO-grohms)** Organized riots against Jews in the Russian Empire.

putting-out system A method of producing clothing in which the manufacturer would purchase the material and then put it out for tailoring.

Second Industrial Revolution The emergence of new industries and the spread of industrialization from Britain to other countries, especially Germany and the United States, in the second half of the nineteenth century.

Sergei Witte (1849–1915) An economist in imperial Russia who led the country into the industrial age.

Suffragettes British women who lobbied and agitated for the right to vote in the early twentieth century.

Vladimir Ilyich Ulyanov (1870–1924) The leader of the Communist revolution in Russia who later took the name of Lenin.

Notes

1. Nicholas Bullock and James Read, *The Movement for Housing Reform in Germany and France, 1840–1914* (Cambridge, UK: Cambridge University Press, 1985), p. 42.
2. Bonnie G. Smith, *Ladies of the Leisure Class: The Bourgeoises of Northern France in the Nineteenth Century* (Princeton, NJ: Princeton University Press, 1981), pp. 147–148. Copyright © 1981 by Princeton University Press. Reprinted by permission of Princeton University Press.
3. Albert Fried and Ronald Sanders, eds., *Socialist Thought: A Documentary History* (Garden City, NY: Anchor Doubleday, 1964), p. 459.
4. Fried and Sanders, *Socialist Thought*, p. 468.

Chapter 24
The Birth of Modern European Thought

THE EVOLUTION OF MANKIND Darwin's theories about the evolution of humankind from the higher primates aroused enormous controversy. This caricature shows him with a monkey's body holding a mirror to an apelike creature.
SOURCE: National History Museum, London, UK/Bridgeman Images

 ## Contents and Focus Questions

The Chapter in Brief

DURING THE SAME period that the modern nation-state developed and the Second Industrial Revolution laid the foundations for modern life, the ideas that marked European thought for much of the twentieth century and beyond took shape. Like previous intellectual changes, these arose from earlier patterns of thought. The Enlightenment provided late-nineteenth-century Europeans with a heritage of rationalism, toleration, cosmopolitanism, and an appreciation of science. Romanticism led them to value feelings, imagination, national identity, and the autonomy of the artistic experience.

By 1900, these strands of thought had become woven into a new fabric. Many of the traditional intellectual signposts were disappearing. Christianity had experienced the most severe intellectual attack in its history. The picture of the physical world that had prevailed since Newton had undergone major modification. Darwin and Freud had challenged the special place that Western thinkers had assigned to humankind. Writers began to question rationality. The humanitarian ideals of liberalism and Socialism gave way to aggressive nationalism. European intellectuals were more daring than ever before, but they were also probably less certain and optimistic.

24.1 The New Reading Public

What effect did state-financed education have on literacy in late-nineteenth-century Europe?

The social context of intellectual life changed in the latter part of the nineteenth century. For the first time in Europe, a mass reading public developed as more people than ever before were drawn into the world of print culture. In 1850, about one-half the population of Western Europe and a much higher proportion of Russians were illiterate. That situation changed during the next half-century.

24.1.1 Advances in Primary Education

Literacy on the Continent improved steadily from the 1860s onward as governments financed education. Austria mandated elementary education in 1775, Hungary provided elementary education in 1868, Britain in 1870, Switzerland in 1874, Italy in 1877, and France between 1878 and 1881. The already advanced education system of Prussia was

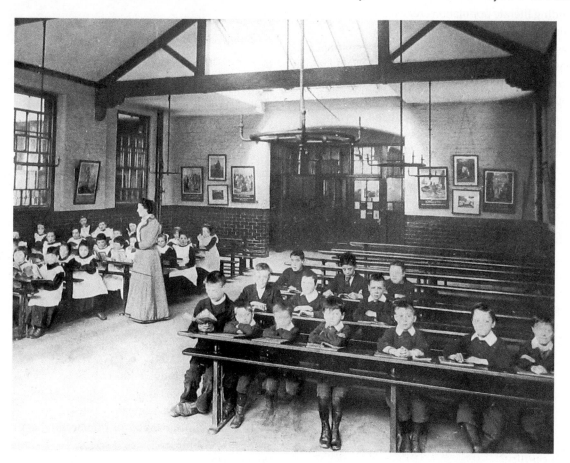

PUBLIC EDUCATION IN 1905 Public education became widespread in Europe during the second half of the nineteenth century. Women came to dominate the teaching profession at the elementary level. Shown here, a photograph of a classroom in Victorian England.
SOURCE: KGPA Ltd/Alamy Stock Photo

extended throughout the German Empire after 1871. By 1900, in Britain, France, Belgium, the Netherlands, Germany, and Scandinavia, approximately 85 percent or more of the people could read. Literacy rates in Austria-Hungary varied from very high in certain urban areas to very low in the eastern and southernmost provinces. Italy, Spain, Russia, and the Balkans had illiteracy rates of between 30 and 60 percent.

The new primary education in the basic skills of reading, writing, and elementary arithmetic reflected and generated social change. Both liberals and conservatives regarded such minimal training as necessary for orderly political behavior by the newly enfranchised voters. They also hoped that literacy would create a more productive labor force.

The school-teaching profession grew rapidly in numbers and became a major area for the employment of women. Having created systems of primary education, the major nations had to give further attention to secondary education by the time of World War I. In another generation, the question would become one of democratic university instruction.

24.1.2 Reading Material for the Mass Audience

The expanding literate population created a vast market for new reading material. The number of newspapers, books, magazines, mail-order catalogs, and libraries grew rapidly. Cheap mass-circulation newspapers, such as *Le Petit Journal* of Paris and the *Daily Mail* of London, enjoyed their first heyday. Such newspapers advertised new consumer products to readers. Other publishers produced newspapers with specialized political or religious viewpoints. The number of monthly and quarterly journals for families, women, and freethinking intellectuals increased. Probably more people could get their ideas into print in the late nineteenth century than ever before in European history.

Many of the new readers were only marginally literate and ill-informed about some subjects. Cheap newspapers prospered on stories of sensational crimes and political scandal and on pages of advertisements. Religious journals depended on denominational rivalry. A brisk market existed for pornography. Newspapers with editorials on the front page became major factors in the emerging mass politics.

24.2 Science at Mid-Century

What role did science play in the second half of the nineteenth century?

In about 1850, learned persons regarded the physical world as rational, mechanical, and dependable. Experiment and observation could reveal their laws objectively. Scientific

AUGUSTE COMTE The French philosopher Auguste Comte (1798–1857) is regarded as the founder of positivism, which was influential during the second half of the nineteenth century. His attention to the social aspects of science paved the way for the development of sociology.
SOURCE: Art Collection 2/Alamy Stock Photo

theory purportedly described physical nature as it really existed. Moreover, by 1850, science had a strong institutional life in French and German universities and in new professional societies. William Whewell of Cambridge University had invented the word *scientist* in the early 1830s, and it was in common use by the end of the century. (See the "Encountering the Past" sidebar on the birth of science fiction, which follows below.)

24.2.1 Comte, Positivism, and the Prestige of Science

During the early nineteenth century, science had continued to establish itself as the model for all human knowledge. French philosopher Auguste Comte (1798–1857) developed **positivism**, a philosophy of human intellectual development that culminated in science. In *The Positive Philosophy* (1830–1842), Comte argued that human thought had developed in three stages. In the first, or theological, stage, physical nature was explained in terms of the action of divinities or spirits. In the second, or metaphysical, stage, nature

Encountering the Past

The Birth of Science Fiction

DURING THE RENAISSANCE many European writers composed works about fantasy voyages to distant lands. In the seventeenth century, authors published some 200 accounts of trips to the moon. Throughout the nineteenth century, other authors told tales of fantastic voyages into space or beneath the earth. Mary Shelley's *Frankenstein* displayed many of the characteristics of science fiction, with themes pushing the boundary of what was technologically possible at the time it was written.

However, the real father of today's works of popular science fiction was Jules Verne (1828–1905). His *Five Weeks in a Balloon* (1863), a tale of a balloon trip across Africa, sold so well that a French publisher immediately gave Verne a contract to write two such stories each year for a magazine. In 1865, he published a fanciful story about a trip to the moon in a projectile launched from a cannon, *From the Earth to the Moon*. This story influenced another pioneer in science fiction, French filmmaker George Méliès, whose 1902 film *A Trip to the Moon* is indebted to Verne. So influential was Verne's image of the future that the United States named its first atomic submarine the *Nautilus* after the vessel the mysterious Captain Nemo commanded in Verne's *Twenty Thousand Leagues under the Sea* (1870).

Verne prided himself on his scientific veracity. He also located his stories in his own age. Readers felt they were experiencing a contemporary adventure.

Toward the turn of the century, science fiction found another master in English novelist H. G. Wells (1866–1946), who in 1895 published *The Time Machine* in which the characters travel through time. Wells's first success was rapidly followed by *The Island of Dr. Moreau* (1896) about a mad surgeon's inhuman experiments on animals, and *The War of the Worlds* (1898) about a Martian invasion of the earth. Wells invented many narrative devices, such as new stars appearing near the solar system, Martians and other planetary creatures unfriendly to humans, machinery that goes astray, and strange diseases, that would become the stock in trade for later science fiction writers.

Verne, Wells, and their many imitators published their stories in cheap illustrated magazines with mass circulations. Consequently, science fiction immediately entered

SCIENCE FICTION À LA JULES VERNE A pioneer in science fiction, the French author Jules Verne (1828–1905) wrote novels that stretched the imagination and inspired generations of budding scientists. He predicted many inventions and breakthroughs of the twentieth century: submarines, skyscrapers, flying vehicles, and space travel. Illustrated here, a printed page from *From the Earth to the Moon*, Verne's 1865 novel, which depicts the passengers in a spaceship enjoying the experience of weightlessness.
SOURCE: Science History Images/Alamy Stock Photo

popular culture. Throughout the twentieth century popular movies and television series were made based on the stories of both Verne and Wells. In 1938, when Orson Welles (1915–1985) broadcast *War of the Worlds* over the radio, many Americans believed Martians had landed in New Jersey. The works of Verne and Wells continue to influence the writing of science fiction.

Questions

1. Why is Jules Verne considered the father of modern science fiction?
2. What enduring plot devices did H. G. Wells introduce?
3. Why did science fiction become so popular?

SOURCES: P. Nichols and J. Clute, *The Encyclopedia of Science Fiction* (New York: St. Martin's Press, 1995); Dieter Wuckel and Bruce Cassidy, *The Illustrated History of Science Fiction* (New York: Ungar, 1986); David Kyle, *A Pictorial History of Science Fiction* (London: Hamlyn, 1976).

could be described by abstract principles. In the final, or positive, stage, explanations of nature were based on exact description of phenomena.

Comte believed that positive laws of social behavior could be discovered in the same way as laws of physical nature. He is thus generally regarded as the father of sociology. Works like Comte's helped convince learned Europeans that all knowledge must resemble scientific knowledge.

24.2.2 New Theories of Evolution: Lamarck, Lyell, Darwin, Wallace

The first modern European thinker to develop a comprehensive theory of evolutionary change was Jean-Baptiste Lamarck (1744–1829). Lamarck denied the possibility of extinction, that geological forms changed gradually over time, and that living organisms had to match their environments. From these premises, the notion that living organisms also changed gradually over time seemed a necessary conclusion. Organisms were forced to change their habits in response to changes in their environments, and new habits led to new forms. Lamarck is best remembered today for his idea that acquired characteristics could be inherited, that is, a blacksmith's son could be born with a stronger arm because of his father's lifelong muscular use of that arm. While this notion has since been largely rejected, Lamarck's broader ideas about evolutionary change proved very influential.

Another major contributor to new theories of evolution in the nineteenth century was geologist Charles Lyell (1797–1875). Lyell published *Principles of Geology* in three volumes between 1830 and 1833. In it, he developed the older theory of "uniformitarianism." According to uniformitarianism, the same natural laws that govern the universe in the present have always governed the universe and that they are consistent across both time and space. It also holds that change is gradual and uniform. Lyell's theory of gradual change and of using present-day observation to explain phenomena in the deep past profoundly influenced Charles Darwin (1809–1882), who wrote in 1844 that "I always feel as if my books came half out of Lyell's brains."[1]

In 1859, Darwin published *On the Origin of Species*, which carried the mechanical interpretation of physical nature into the world of living things. The book was one of the seminal works of Western thought. Both Darwin and his book have been much misunderstood. He did not originate the concept of evolution, which had been discussed widely before he wrote. Alfred Russel Wallace (1823–1913) came to many of the same conclusions as Darwin independently and based on his own field research. Both men separately formulated variations of the principle of natural selection, which explained how species had changed or evolved over

time. Earlier writers had believed evolution might occur; Darwin and Wallace explained how it could occur.

Drawing on Malthus, the two scientists contended that more living organisms come into existence than can survive in their environment. According to Darwin, the organisms with a marginal advantage in the struggle for existence are able to survive (the "survival of the fittest") and live long enough to reproduce, which principle he called **natural selection**. It was naturalistic and mechanistic, requiring no guiding mind behind the development in organic nature. What neither Darwin nor anyone else in his day could explain was the origin of those chance variations that provided some living things with the marginal chance for survival. Only after 1900, when the work on heredity of Austrian monk Gregor Mendel (1822–1884) received public attention, did the mystery of those variations begin to be unraveled.

Darwin and Wallace's theory represented the triumph of naturalistic explanation, which removed the idea of purpose from organic nature. Eyes were not made for seeing according to the rational wisdom and purpose of God but had developed mechanistically over time. Thus, the theory of evolution through natural selection not only contradicted the biblical narrative of the creation but also undermined the deistic argument for the existence of God from the design of the universe and the concept of fixity in nature or the universe at large. The idea that physical and organic nature might be constantly changing allowed people to believe that society, values, customs, and beliefs should also change.

In 1871, in *The Descent of Man*, Darwin applied the principle of evolution by natural selection to human beings. Darwin was not the first person to treat human beings as animals, but he contended that humankind's moral nature and religious sentiments, as well as its physical frame, had developed naturalistically in response to the requirements of survival. Neither the origin nor the character of humankind, in Darwin's view, required the existence of a god for their explanation.

Darwin's theory of evolution by natural selection was controversial from the moment *On the Origin of Species* appeared. It encountered criticism from both the religious and the scientific communities. By the end of the century, scientists widely accepted the concept of evolution, but not yet Darwin's idea of natural selection, whose acceptance dates from the 1920s and 1930s, when his theory was combined with modern genetics.

24.2.3 Science and Ethics: Social Darwinism

One area in which science came to have a new significance was social thought and ethics. Philosophers applied the concept of the struggle for survival to human social relationships. The phrase "survival of the fittest" predated

Darwin and reflected the competitive outlook of classical economics. Darwin's use of the phrase gave it the prestige associated with advanced science.

The most famous advocate of evolutionary ethics was Herbert Spencer (1820–1903), a British philosopher. Spencer, a strong individualist, believed human society progresses through competition. If the weak receive too much protection, the rest of humankind loses. The concept could be (and was) used to justify not aiding the poor and the working class, to justify the domination of colonial peoples, or to advocate aggressive competition among nations. Evolutionary ethics and similar concepts, all of which are usually termed **social Darwinism**, often came close to saying that "might makes right."

One of the chief opponents of such thinking was Thomas Henry Huxley, the great defender of Darwin. In 1893, Huxley declared that the physical process of evolution was at odds with human ethical development. The struggle in nature only showed how human beings should not behave. Despite Huxley's arguments, the ideas of social Darwinism continued to influence thought and public policy on both sides of the Atlantic.

24.3 Christianity and the Church Under Siege

What challenges did European Christianity face in the late nineteenth century?

The nineteenth century was one of the most difficult periods in the history of organized Christian churches. Many European intellectuals left the faith. Secular, liberal nation-states attacked the influence of the church. The expansion of population and the growth of cities challenged its organizational capacity. Yet during all this turmoil, the Protestant and Catholic churches continued to draw popular support and personal religious devotion. Nonetheless, the development of an overwhelmingly secular European society had its roots in the late nineteenth century.

24.3.1 Intellectual Skepticism

The intellectual attack on Christianity challenged its historical credibility, its scientific accuracy, and its morality. The philosophes of the Enlightenment had delighted in pointing out contradictions in the Bible. The historical scholarship of the nineteenth century brought new issues to the foreground.

24.3.1.1 HISTORY In 1835, David Friedrich Strauss (1808–1874) published *The Life of Jesus*, in which he questioned whether the Bible provides any genuine historical evidence about Jesus. Strauss contended the story of Jesus was a myth stemming from the particular social and intellectual

conditions of first-century Palestine. Jesus's character and life represented the aspirations of the people of that time and place, rather than events that actually occurred.

During the second half-century, scholars such as Julius Wellhausen (1844–1918) in Germany, Ernst Renan (1823–1892) in France, and Matthew Arnold (1822–1888) in Great Britain contended that human authors had written and revised the books of the Bible with the problems of Jewish society and politics in mind. These writers made the Bible appear like a series of books written by normal human beings in an ancient civilization, much like the Homeric epics. This questioning of the historical validity of the Bible caused more literate men and women to lose faith in Christianity than any other single cause. (See the "Compare and Connect" sidebar, which follows below, on Christian critics of Darwin's theory of evolution.)

24.3.1.2 SCIENCE Nineteenth-century science also undermined Christianity and faith in the validity of biblical narratives, although eighteenth-century writers had led Christians to believe the scientific examination of nature buttressed their faith. The geology of Charles Lyell suggested that the earth was much older than biblical records contended. By looking to natural causes to explain floods, mountains, and valleys, Lyell removed the miraculous hand of God from the physical development of the earth. Darwin's theory cast doubt on the creation. Anthropologists, psychologists, and sociologists proposed that religious sentiments were just one more set of natural phenomena.

24.3.1.3 MORALITY Other intellectuals questioned the morality of Christianity. The issue of immoral biblical stories was again raised. The morality of the Old Testament God, his cruelty and unpredictability, did not fit well with the tolerant, rational values of liberals. They also wondered about the morality of the New Testament God, who would sacrifice for his own satisfaction the only perfect being ever to walk the earth. Even some clergy began to question if they could preach doctrines they felt to be immoral.

Other writers like **Friedrich Nietzsche** (1844–1900) in Germany portrayed Christianity as a religion that glorified weakness rather than the strength life required. Christianity, he claimed, demanded a useless and debilitating sacrifice of the flesh and spirit, rather than heroic living and daring. Nietzsche once observed, "War and courage have accomplished more great things than love of neighbor."[2]

These skeptical currents created a climate in which Christianity lost much of its intellectual respectability. But the secularism of everyday life proved as harmful to the faith as the direct attacks. This situation was especially prevalent in the cities, which were growing faster than the capacity of the churches to meet the challenge. Whole generations of the urban poor grew up with little or no experience of the church as an institution or of Christianity as a religious faith.

Compare and Connect

Charles Darwin's Christian Critics

IN THE EYES OF MANY nineteenth-century observers, Charles Darwin's theory of evolution was a direct assault on long venerated Christian teachings. On its face, it seemed to contradict biblical teachings on creation. Moreover, Darwin made no distinction between human beings and other living creatures, suggesting that, at least with respect to evolution, humans were nothing more than another species of animal. Not all Christian commentators, however, agreed on this subject. Some sought to correct Darwin, arguing that he was mistaken on a number of key points. Others, however, saw no inconsistency between Darwin's theory and the teachings of the Bible and celebrated Darwin's insights. The excerpts below provide examples of these two positions.

MAN IS BUT A WORM The British naturalist Charles Darwin (1809–1882) was a pioneering figure in the development of the theory of evolution. His ideas challenged creationism, which held that God created the universe. Darwin's ideas were often parodied by his critics, as in 1882 *Punch* cover illustrates.
SOURCE: Chronicle/Alamy Stock Photo

Before Reading

- Consider the intellectual and religious contexts of the second half of the nineteenth century.
- Think about Charles Darwin's view on religion and science.
- Note the basic assumptions made by Samuel Wilberforce and J. H. Gladstone.

Questions

1. Why did Wilberforce reject efforts to reconcile science and scripture?
2. On what basis did Wilberforce argue that Darwin's theory was incorrect?
3. How might Gladstone have responded to Wilberforce's argument?

I. SAMUEL WILBERFORCE DISPUTES DARWIN'S CLAIMS (1860)

Few things have more deeply injured the cause of religion than the busy fussy energy with which men, narrow and feeble alike in faith and in science, have bustled forth to reconcile all new discoveries in physics with the word of inspiration. For it continually happens that some larger collection of facts, or some wider view of the phenomena of nature, alter the whole philosophic scheme; whilst revelation has been committed to declare an absolute agreement with what turns out after all to have been a misconception or an error. We cannot, therefore, consent to test the truth of natural science by the word of revelation. But this does not make it the less important to point out on scientific grounds scientific errors, when those errors tend to limit God's glory in creation, or to gainsay the revealed relations of that creation to Himself. To both these classes of error, though, we doubt not, quite unintentionally on his part, we think that Mr. Darwin's speculations directly tend.

Mr. Darwin writes as a Christian, and we doubt not that he is one. We do not for a moment believe him to be one of those who retain in some corner of their hearts a secret unbelief which they dare not vent; and we therefore pray him to consider well the grounds on which we brand his speculations with the charge of such a tendency. First, then, he not obscurely declares that he applies his scheme of the action of the principle of natural selection to man himself, as well as to the animals around him. Now, we must say at once, and openly, that such a notion is absolutely incompatible not only with single expressions in the word of God on that subject of natural science with which it is not immediately concerned, but, which in our judgment is of far more importance, with the whole representation of that moral and spiritual condition of man which is its proper subject matter. Man's derived supremacy over the earth; man's power of articulate speech; man's gift of reason; man's free will and responsibility; man's fall and man's redemption; the incarnation of the Eternal Son; the indwelling of the Eternal Spirit–all are equally and utterly irreconcilable with the degrading notion of the brute origin of him who was created in the image of God, and redeemed by the Eternal Son assuming to himself His nature. Equally inconsistent, too, not with any passing expressions, but with the whole scheme of God's dealings with man as recorded in His word, is Mr. Darwin's daring notion of man's further development into some unknown extent of powers and shape, and size, through natural selection acting through that long vista of ages which He casts mistily over the earth upon the most favored individuals of His species. . . .

Nor can we doubt, secondly, that this view, which thus contradicts the revealed relation of creation to its Creator, is equally inconsistent with the fullness of His glory. It is, in truth, an ingenious theory for diffusing throughout creation the working and so the personality of the Creator. And thus, however unconsciously to him who holds them, such views really tend inevitably to banish from the mind most of the peculiar attributes of the Almighty.

II. J. H. GLADSTONE DEFENDS THE THEORY OF EVOLUTION (1872)

[T]he science of biology has recently caused no small anxiety to some believers and afforded no small triumph to some unbelievers. I allude to the doctrine of the evolution of living things. How this question presents itself to my mind will be best explained by putting myself into the confessional. When Darwin's book on The Origen of Species made its appearance, I read it with great interest and pleasure. Previous theories of development had appeared very unsatisfactory to me, but the additional arguments of that book, and the exposition of natural selection, made me entertain a different idea of the probabilities of the case. Though Darwin in that work treats only of the lower animals, it was perfectly plain that the argument must also include the genus Homo, as far as his bodily frame and instincts are concerned. Nevertheless, I felt no shock to my religious faith: indeed the progressive development of animated nature seemed to harmonize with that gradual unveiling of the divine plan which I had loved to trace in the Bible, while it offered a satisfactory explanation of those rudimentary or abortive organs which had puzzled me as a student of natural theology. . . .

The problem of the method of creation is a grand one, and modern science lures us on with the hope of a solution. At present we are in the early stage of crude guesses, or at best of partial glimpses; yet whatever further insight may be gained, we may rest assured that the Christian will continue to exclaim as the Psalmist did when reviewing the animate world, but with an ever widening intelligence, "O Lord, how manifold are Thy works; in wisdom hast Thou made them all!"

SOURCES: (I) From Samuel Wilberforce, *Essays Contributed to the Quarterly Review*, 2 Vols. (London, 1874), pp. 92–95. (II) From J. H. Gladstone, *The Christian Evidence Society, Faith and Free Thought: A Second Course of Lectures Delivered at the Request of the Christian Evidence Society* (New York: Christian Evidence Society, 1872), pp. 136–160.

24.3.2 Conflict Between Church and State

The secular states of late-nineteenth-century Europe clashed with both the Protestant and the Roman Catholic churches. Liberals, including those who were religiously observant, disliked the dogma and the political privileges of the established churches. National states were often suspicious of the supranational character of the Roman Catholic Church. The primary area of conflict between the state and the churches, however, was education. Previously, most education in Europe had taken place in church schools. The churches feared that future generations would emerge from the new state-financed schools without any religious teaching. From 1870 through the turn of the century, all the major countries debated religious education.

24.3.2.1 GREAT BRITAIN In Great Britain, the Education Act of 1870 provided for state-supported schools run by elected school boards, whereas earlier the government had given small grants to religious schools. The new schools were to be built in areas where the religious denominations did not provide satisfactory education. All the churches opposed improvements in education because these increased the costs of church schools. In the Education Act of 1902, the government provided state support for both religious and nonreligious schools but imposed the same educational standards on each.

24.3.2.2 FRANCE France had a dual system of Catholic and public schools. Under the Falloux Law of 1850, local priests provided religious education in public schools. Between 1878 and 1886, a series of educational laws sponsored by

Jules Ferry (1832–1893) replaced religious instruction in the public schools with civic training. The number of public schools was expanded, and members of religious orders could no longer teach in them. After the Dreyfus affair, the French Catholic Church paid a price for its reactionary politics. The radical government of Pierre Waldeck-Rousseau (1846–1904), drawn from pro-Dreyfus groups, suppressed the religious orders. In 1905, church and state were formally separated.

24.3.2.3 GERMANY The most extreme and violent church–state conflict occurred in Germany during the 1870s. The *Kulturkampf* or clash of civilizations, as it was called, pitted Bismarck and German liberals against the Catholic Church in Germany. From the start, the conflict was more political than religious. Bismarck and German liberals had different reasons for their suspicion of the power of the Roman Catholic Church in Germany. Bismarck was suspicious of the loyalties of the many Polish-speaking Catholics in Prussia. Liberals were appalled by the Pope's pronouncement of papal infallibility in 1870 and thought Catholics represented a "backward" opposition to progress. They both feared the power of the Catholic Center Party, a political party dedicated to protecting the liberty of the Catholic Church within unified Germany. In 1870 and 1871, Bismarck removed the clergy from overseeing local education in Prussia. This secularization of education represented the beginning of a concerted attack on the Catholic Church in Germany.

The "May Laws" of 1873, which applied to Prussia but not to the entire German Empire, required priests to be educated in German schools and universities and to pass state examinations. The state could veto the appointments of priests. The legislation abolished the disciplinary power of the pope and the church over the clergy and transferred it to the state. Many of the clergy refused to obey, and new laws allowed their property to be seized, their pay to be stopped, and for them to be held in prison. Thousands of priests and bishops were arrested or exiled from Prussia.

By the end of the 1870s, Bismarck had abandoned his attack on the Catholic Church. He had gained state control of education and civil laws governing marriage only at the price of provoking Catholic resentment against the German state.

24.3.3 Areas of Religious Revival

The German Catholic resistance to the intrusions of the secular state illustrates the continuing vitality of Christianity during this period of intellectual and political hardship.

The last half of the nineteenth century witnessed the final great effort to Christianize Europe. It was well organized, well led, and well financed. It failed only because the population of Europe had outstripped the resources of the churches. (See the "Closer Look" sidebar, which follows below, for a visual take on pilgrimages, one popular form of religious revival.)

24.3.3.1 THE ROMAN CATHOLIC CHURCH AND THE MODERN WORLD The most striking feature of Christian religious revival was the resilience of the papacy. The brief hope for a liberal pontificate from Pope Pius IX (r. 1846–1878) vanished when he fled the turmoil of Rome in November 1848. In the 1860s, embittered by the process of Italian unification, he launched a counteroffensive against liberalism. In 1864, he issued the *Syllabus of Errors*, in which he described as false the statement that "the Roman Pontiff can, and ought to, reconcile himself, and come to terms with, progress, liberalism and modern civilization."[3]

In 1869, the pope summoned the First Vatican Council. The next year, the council promulgated the dogma of **papal infallibility** when speaking officially on matters of faith and morals. No earlier pope had asserted such centralized authority within the church. The First Vatican Council ended in 1870, when Italian troops occupied Rome at the outbreak of the Franco–Prussian War. Thereafter the territory of the papacy was limited to the Vatican City, but the papacy made no formal accommodation to the Italian state until 1929. The spiritual authority of the papacy became a substitute for its lost political and temporal authority.

Pius IX was succeeded by Leo XIII (r. 1878–1903). Leo, who was sixty-eight years old at the time of his election, wished to make accommodations to the modern age and to address its great social questions. Leo XIII's most important pronouncement on public issues was the encyclical *Rerum Novarum* (1891). In that document, he defended private property, religious education, and religious control of the marriage laws; condemned Socialism and Marxism; and also declared that employers should treat their employees justly, pay them proper wages, and permit them to organize labor unions. The pope urged that modern society be organized into corporate groups that would include people from various classes who would cooperate with Christian principles. The corporate society, based on medieval social organization, was to be an alternative to both Socialism and competitive capitalism. Based on Leo XIII's pronouncements, democratic Catholic political parties and Catholic trade unions were founded throughout Europe.

Leo's successor Pius X (r. 1903–1914) hoped to resist modern thought and restore traditional devotional life. Between 1903 and 1907, he condemned Catholic modernism, a movement of modern biblical criticism within the church, and in 1910 he required all priests to take an anti-modernist oath. The struggle between Catholicism and modern thought was resumed.

A Closer Look

Popular Religion and Pilgrimage

THE NINETEENTH CENTURY WAS A PERIOD of great challenge for the Roman Catholic Church in Europe, but it also witnessed a revival in popular religiosity and in the practice of pilgrimage. Pilgrimage had been common in the medieval and early modern periods but had come under attack during the Enlightenment. The formal proclamation of the doctrine of the Immaculate

In Lourdes (France), between February 11 and July 16, 1858, a poor teenage girl saw eighteen apparitions of a "beautiful lady" claiming to be the Blessed Virgin Mary. In 1862, after a thorough investigation, the Catholic Church officially recognized the apparitions and authorized the creation of a sanctuary and pilgrimage site in that location. After Rome, the sanctuary at Lourdes has become the most visited pilgrimage site in Christian Europe.

Pilgrims traveled to Lourdes from all parts of Europe. While pilgrimage sites could take on a national character, they were overwhelmingly supranational. Long-distance travel to pilgrimage sites was made more feasible by the introduction of the railroad and the spread of railroad networks to the provinces

Women made frequent pilgrimages. Although men and women were often separated during transit, pilgrimages to Lourdes presented opportunities for them to mingle outside the confines of the family home.

Many pilgrims to Lourdes hoped that physical infirmities could be cured through the intercession of Christian saints and the Blessed Virgin Mary.

Groups of lay pilgrims were often led on tours of Lourdes by priests.

ON PILGRIMAGE TO LOURDES The town of Lourdes in France was a popular destination for pilgrims, many of whom were women, invalids, and members of the clergy. Illustrated here, an 1873 engraving of pilgrims arriving at a train station near Lourdes.
This engraving shows pilgrims who have arrived in a train station near Lourdes preparing to proceed to their destination on foot.
SOURCE: Artokoloro Quint Lox Limited / Alamy Stock Photo

Questions

1. How is the diversity of pilgrims represented in this image? What sort of people went on pilgrimage?
2. What is the mood of the pilgrims as they anticipate their arrival in Lourdes?
3. What sort of journey could nineteenth-century pilgrims expect, and how had it changed since the medieval and early modern periods?

24.3.3.2 ISLAM AND LATE-NINETEENTH-CENTURY EUROPEAN THOUGHT The few European thinkers who wrote about Islam in the late nineteenth century used the same scientific and naturalistic scholarly methods they applied to Christianity and Judaism. They interpreted Islam as a historical phenomenon without any reference to the supernatural, and the *Qur'an* received the same kind of critical historical analysis that was being directed toward the Bible. In the works of scholars such as influential French writer Ernest Renan, Islam was, like Judaism, a manifestation of the ancient Semitic mentality, which had given rise to a powerful monotheistic vision. Renan and sociologists such as Max Weber also falsely described Islam as a religion and culture incapable of developing science. The European racial and cultural outlooks that denigrated nonwhite peoples and their civilizations were also directed toward the Arab world.

Christian missionaries reinforced these anti-Islamic attitudes. They blamed Islam for Arab economic backwardness, for mistreating women, and for condoning slavery. Missionaries founded schools and hospitals, hoping these Christian foundations would eventually lead some Muslims to Christianity. Few Muslims converted, but these institutions did educate young Arabs in Western science and medicine, and many of their students became leaders in the Middle East.

Within the Islamic world, and especially in the decaying Ottoman Empire, political leaders championing Western scientific education and technology confronted a variety of responses from Islamic religious thinkers. Some of these thinkers sought to combine modern thought with Islam. For example, the Salafi, or the *salafiyya* movement, believed there was no inherent contradiction between science and Islam.

Other Islamic religious leaders simply rejected the West and modern thought. They included the Mahdist movement in Sudan, the Sanussiya in Libya, and the Wahhabi movement in the Arabian peninsula. Such religious-based opposition was strongest in those portions of the Middle East where the European presence was least direct, outside of Morocco, Algeria, Egypt, and Tunisia, which for all intents and purposes were under the control of Western powers by 1900, and Turkey, where Ottoman leaders had long been deeply involved with the West.

24.4 Toward a Twentieth-Century Frame of Mind

How did developments in art, psychology, and science reflect a profound shift in Western thought?

The last quarter of the nineteenth century and the first decade of the twentieth century were the crucible of modern Western thought. Philosophers, scientists, psychologists, and artists portrayed physical reality, human nature, and society in ways different from those of the past. Their new concepts challenged the major presuppositions of mid-nineteenth-century science, rationalism, liberalism, and bourgeois morality.

24.4.1 Science: The Revolution in Physics

The changes in the scientific worldview originated within the scientific community itself. By the late 1870s, discontent existed over the excessive realism of mid-century science. It was thought that many scientists believed their mechanistic models, solid atoms, and absolute time and space actually described the real universe.

In 1883, Ernst Mach (1838–1916) published *The Science of Mechanics*, in which he urged that scientists consider their concepts descriptive not of the physical world but of the sensations the scientific observer experiences. Scientists could describe only the sensations not the physical world that underlay those sensations. In line with Mach, French scientist Henri Poincaré (1854–1912) urged that the theories of scientists be regarded as hypothetical constructs of the human mind rather than as true descriptions of nature. In 1911, Hans Vaihinger (1852–1933) suggested the concepts of science be considered "as if" descriptions of the physical world. By World War I, few scientists believed they could portray the truth about physical reality. Rather, they saw themselves as recording the observations with instruments and as offering useful hypothetical or symbolic models of nature.

24.4.1.1 X-RAYS AND RADIATION Discoveries in the laboratory paralleled the philosophical challenge to nineteenth-century science. With those discoveries, the comfortable world of supposedly "complete" nineteenth-century physics vanished forever. In December 1895, Wilhelm Roentgen (1845–1923) published a paper on his discovery of X-rays, a form of energy that penetrated various opaque materials. Major steps in the exploration of radioactivity followed within months of the publication of his paper.

In 1896, Henri Becquerel (1852–1908) discovered that uranium emitted a similar form of energy. The next year, J. J. Thomson (1856–1940), at Cambridge University, formulated the theory of the electron. The interior world of the atom had become a new area for human exploration. In 1902, Ernest Rutherford (1871–1937) explained the cause of radiation through the disintegration of the atoms of radioactive materials. Shortly thereafter, he speculated on the immense store of energy present in the atom.

24.4.1.2 THEORIES OF QUANTUM ENERGY, RELATIVITY, AND UNCERTAINTY The discovery of radioactivity and discontent with the existing mechanical models led to revolutionary theories in physics. In 1900, **Max Planck** (1858–1947) pioneered the articulation of the quantum theory of energy, according to which energy is a series of discrete quantities, or packets, rather than a continuous stream. In 1905, Albert Einstein (1879–1955) published his

MARIE SKŁODOWSKA CURIE AND PIERRE CURIE Marie Skłodowska Curie (1869–1934) and Pierre Curie (1859–1906) were two of the most important figures in the fields of physics and chemistry. Skłodowska Curie was born in Warsaw (Russian Poland) but worked in France for most of her life. She is credited with the discovery of radium, for which she was awarded the Nobel Prize in Chemistry in 1911.
SOURCE: Pictorial Press Ltd/Alamy Stock Photo

first epoch-making papers on relativity in which he contended that time and space exist not separately but rather as a combined continuum. Moreover, the measurement of time and space depended on the observer as well as on the entities being measured.

In 1927, Werner Heisenberg (1901–1976) set forth his uncertainty principle, according to which the behavior of subatomic particles is a matter of statistical probability rather than of exactly determinable cause and effect. Much that had seemed unquestionable about the physical universe had now become ambiguous.

The mathematical complexity of twentieth-century physics meant science would rarely be successfully popularized. At the same time, science affected daily living more than ever before. Scientists from the late nineteenth century onward became the most successful group of Western intellectuals in gaining the financial support of governments and private institutions for their research. They did so by relating the success of science to the economic progress, military security, and the health of their nations.

24.4.2 Literature: Realism and Naturalism

Between 1850 and 1914, the moral certainties of middle-class Europeans changed no less radically than their concepts of the physical universe. The realist movement in literature portrayed the hypocrisy, brutality, and the dullness that underlay bourgeois life. By using the mid-century cult of science so vital to the middle class, **realist** writers confronted readers with the harsh realities of life. Realism rejected the romantic idealization of nature, the poor, love, and polite society and instead portrayed the dark side of life.

The major figures of late-century realism examined the dreary and unseemly side of life without being certain whether a better life was possible. They portrayed human beings as subject to the passions, the materialistic determinism, and the pressures of the environment like any other animals. Most of them, however, also saw society itself as perpetuating evil.

KEY PUBLICATION DATES OF MAJOR WORKS OF FICTION	
1857	Flaubert, *Madame Bovary*
1877	Zola, *L'Assommoir*
1879	Ibsen, *A Doll's House*
1880	Zola, *Nana*
1881	Ibsen, *Ghosts*
1892	Ibsen, *The Master Builder*
1893	Shaw, *Mrs. Warren's Profession*
1894	Shaw, *Arms and the Man*
1901	Mann, *Buddenbrooks*
1903	Shaw, *Man and Superman*
1913	Shaw, *Androcles and the Lion*
1913	Proust, first volume of *In Search of Time Past*
1922	Joyce, *Ulysses*
1924	Mann, *The Magic Mountain*
1925	Woolf, *Mrs. Dalloway*
1927	Woolf, *To the Lighthouse*

24.4.2.1 FLAUBERT AND ZOLA Critics have often considered Gustave Flaubert's (1821–1880) *Madame Bovary* (1857), with its story of colorless provincial life and a woman's hapless search for love in and outside of marriage, as the first genuinely realistic novel. The work portrayed life without heroism, purpose, or even civility.

The author who turned realism into a movement, however, was Émile Zola (1840–1902). He believed absolute physical and psychological determinism ruled human events in the way it did the physical world.

Between 1871 and 1893, Zola published twenty novels exploring subjects normally untouched by writers: alcoholism, prostitution, adultery, labor strife. He refused to turn his readers' thoughts away from the ugly aspects of life. Nothing in his purview received the light of hope or the aura of romance. Although critics faulted his taste and moralists condemned his subject matter, Zola enjoyed a worldwide following.

24.4.2.2 IBSEN AND SHAW Norwegian playwright Henrik Ibsen (1828–1906) carried realism into the dramatic presentation of domestic life. He sought to strip away the illusory mask of middle-class morality. His most famous play is *A Doll's House* (1879). Its chief character, Nora, has a narrow-minded husband who cannot tolerate independence of character or thought on her part. Ibsen's works were controversial. He dared to attack sentimentality, the ideal of the female "angel of the house," and the cloak of respectability that hung so insecurely over the middle-class family.

One of Ibsen's greatest champions was Irish writer George Bernard Shaw (1856–1950), who spent most of his life in England. Shaw defended Ibsen's work and carried out his own realistic onslaught against romanticism and false respectability. In *Mrs. Warren's Profession* (1893), he dealt with prostitution. In *Arms and the Man* (1894) and *Man and Superman* (1903), he heaped scorn on the romantic ideals of love and war, and in *Androcles and the Lion* (1913), he pilloried Christianity.

Realist writers believed it was their duty to portray reality and the commonplace. In dissecting what they considered the real world, they helped change the moral perception of the good life. They refused to let public opinion dictate what they wrote about or how they treated their subjects. By presenting their audiences with unmentionable subjects, they sought to remove the veneer of hypocrisy that had forbidden such discussion. They hoped to destroy illusions and compel the public to face reality. Few of the realist writers who raised these problems posed solutions to them. They often left their readers unable to sustain old values and uncertain about where to find new ones.

24.4.3 Modernism in Literature

From the 1870s onward throughout Europe, a new multifaceted movement, usually called **modernism**, touched all the arts. Like realism, modernism was critical of middle-class society and morality. Modernism, however, was not deeply concerned with social issues. What drove the modernists was a concern for the aesthetic or the beautiful. Across the spectrum of the arts, modernists tried to break the received forms and to create new forms."

Among the chief proponents of modernism in England were the members of the Bloomsbury Group, including authors Virginia Woolf (1882–1941) and Leonard Woolf (1880–1969); artists Vanessa Bell (1879–1961) and Duncan Grant (1885–1978); historian and literary critic Lytton Strachey (1880–1932); and economist John Maynard Keynes (1883–1946). These authors challenged the values of their Victorian forebears. In *Eminent Victorians* (1918), Strachey used a series of biographical sketches to heap contempt on his subjects. Keynesian economics eventually challenged much of the structure of nineteenth-century economic theory. In both personal practice and theory, the Bloomsbury Group rejected what they regarded as the repressive sexual morality of their parents' generation.

No one charted these changing sensibilities with more eloquence than Virginia Woolf. Her novels, such as *Mrs. Dalloway* (1925) and *To the Lighthouse* (1927), portrayed individuals trying to find their way in a world with most of the nineteenth-century social and moral certainties removed.

On the Continent, one of the major literary modernists was Marcel Proust (1871–1922). In his seven-volume novel *In Search of Time Past* (*A la Recherche du Temps Perdu*), published between 1913 and 1927, he adopted a stream-of-consciousness format that allowed him to explore his memories. To do this he would concentrate on a single experience or object and then allow his mind to wander through all the thoughts and memories it evoked. In Germany, Thomas Mann (1875–1955), through a long series of novels, the most famous of which were *Buddenbrooks* (1901) and *The Magic Mountain* (1924), explored both the social experience of middle-class Germans and how they dealt with the intellectual heritage of the nineteenth century. In *Ulysses* (1922), James Joyce (1882–1941), who was born in Ireland but spent much of his life on the Continent, transformed not only the novel but also the structure of the paragraph.

Modernism in literature began before World War I and flourished after the war, nourished by the turmoil and social dislocation it created. The war removed many of the old political structures and social expectations. After its appalling violence, readers were much less shocked by upheavals in literary forms and the moral content of novels and poetry.

24.4.4 The Coming of Modern Art

The last quarter of the nineteenth century witnessed a series of new departures in Western art that transformed painting and later sculpture in a revolutionary manner that has continued to the present day.

24.4.4.1 IMPRESSIONISM This fundamental change in European painting arose primarily in Paris. Two major characteristics marked this new style of painting. First, instead of portraying religious, mythological, and historical themes, painters began to depict modern life itself, focusing on the social life and leisure activities of the urban middle and lower middle classes. Second, many of these artists were fascinated with light, color, and the representation through painting of momentary, largely unfocused, visual experience.

The new paintings of modern life by the impressionists, including Édouard Manet (1837–1883), **Claude Monet** (1840–1926), Camille Pissarro (1830–1903), Pierre-Auguste Renoir (1841–1919), and Edgar Degas (1834–1917), recorded Parisians attending cafés, dance halls, concerts, picnics, horse races, boating excursions, and beach parties. The backdrop for these works was Paris as it had been reconstructed under Napoleon III (r. 1852–1870) into a city of wide boulevards, parks, and places for middle-class leisure.

The sites included in these paintings allowed people from different classes to mix socially while pursuing a leisure activity. One such meeting place was the Folies-Bergère, one of many Parisian cafés/concert halls where patrons could enjoy a variety of popular entertainment, including singers, musicians, dancers, gymnasts, and animal shows.

In *A Bar at the Folies-Bergère*, first displayed in 1882, Édouard Manet painted a young barmaid standing behind a table holding liquor and wine bottles in front of a large mirror that reflects the activity occurring in front of her.

(Manet actually painted this picture in his studio with a woman who worked as a barmaid posing as his model.) The table, together with its bottles, fruit, vase, and flowers, constitutes a formal still-life composition, but unlike traditional still life, it shows objects of commercial consumption in a setting where leisure itself is commercially consumed. The mirror reflects the table and its contents, the music hall with the legs of a trapeze artist appearing in the top left corner, the audience, the back of the barmaid, and a man she is serving. Manet took great pains to paint the interior light of the hall, which appears to emanate from the newly invented electric light bulbs.

24.4.4.2 POSTIMPRESSIONISM By the 1880s, the impressionists had had an enormous impact on contemporary art. Their work was followed by that of younger artists who drew upon their techniques but also attempted often to relate impressionism to earlier artistic traditions. Form and structure rather than the effort to record the impression of the moment played a major role in their work. This later type of art has been described as **Postimpressionism,** though it should best be understood as a continuation of the

A BAR AT THE FOLIES-BERGÈRE Édouard Manet (1832–1883), *A Bar at the Folies-Bergère*, 1882.
SOURCE: Ian Dagnall/Alamy Stock Photo

previous movement rather than a reaction against it. The chief figures associated with Postimpressionism are Georges Seurat, Paul Cézanne, Vincent van Gogh, and Paul Gauguin.

Georges Seurat (1859–1891) was a young French painter who read extensively in contemporary scientific works about light, color, and vision. These studies led him to a technique of painting known as pointillism whereby the artist applied small dots or points of paint to the canvas. Through this laborious process Seurat hoped to decompose colors into their basic units, leaving it to the viewer to mix those dots into the desired color or shade of color. Seurat is counted among the first Postimpressionists because he saw himself bringing the new painting of modern life back into touch with earlier artistic traditions.

Seurat also introduced implicit social commentary into the previous impressionist portrayal of leisured activity. The Grande Jatte was an island in the Seine beyond Paris where on Sundays Parisians would gather. In Seurat's painting, *A Sunday Afternoon on the Island of La Grande Jatte*, shadows in the foreground suggest that it is not entirely sunny for the largely middle-class afternoon crowd. The boatman smoking a pipe indicates a brooding working-class presence in the foreground of their lives. All the figures resemble mannequins that appeared in the fashionable new Paris department stores. Except for one child who is running, the figures appear mechanical, like the manufacturing processes that produced their clothing and their other domestic consumer goods. Compared by one contemporary critic to lead soldiers, they stand bored and perhaps puzzled by their situation of comfort, leisure, and ease.

In reaction to the impressionists' fascination with light, Paul Cézanne (1839–1906), working largely in isolation, brought form and solidity back into his paintings of still life and of the landscape of Provence. Displaying a new sensitivity to non-Western peoples and their art, Paul Gauguin (1848–1903) produced works portraying peoples living in the South Pacific. Other artists collected African masks or studied such objects in the anthropological museum in Paris. The art of Africa and of the Pacific gave artists examples of remarkable works that had no relationship to the long-standing Western artistic tradition.

24.4.4.3 CUBISM The single most radical new departure in early-twentieth-century Western art was **cubism**, a term first coined to describe the paintings of Pablo Picasso (1881–1973) and Georges Braque (1882–1963).

A SUNDAY AFTERNOON ON THE ISLAND OF LA GRANDE JATTE Georges Seurat (1859–1891) pioneered a technique that came to be called pointillism. His masterpiece, *A Sunday Afternoon on the Island of La Grande Jatte*, demonstrated technical mastery and also offered a critical commentary on Parisian society.
SOURCE: Artepics/Alamy Stock Photo

For over 500 years, painting in the West had sought to reproduce the appearance of reality. From the time of the Renaissance, paintings were a kind of window into an artistic depiction of the real world. Even the impressionists and Postimpressionists painted in this tradition.

Beginning in 1907, Picasso and Braque rejected the idea of a painting as a window into the real world. Rather, they saw painting as an autonomous realm of art with no purpose beyond itself. Braque once commented, "The painter thinks in forms and colors. The aim is not to reconstitute an anecdotal fact but to constitute a pictorial fact. . . . One does not imitate the appearance; the appearance is the result."[4] Echoing the art of ancient Egypt, medieval primitives, and Africa, Picasso and Braque represented only two dimensions in their painting. They made little or no effort to go beyond the flatness of the surface itself. They attempted to include at one time on a single surface as many different perspectives, angles, or views of the object painted as possible. "Reality" was the construction of their experience of multiple perceptions.

Braque's still life *Violin and Palette* (1909 and 1910) represents the cubist determination to present "a new, completely non-illusionistic and non-imitative method of depicting the visual world."[5] Various shapes seem to flow into other shapes. Portions of the violin and of the palette are recognizable, but as shapes, not as objects themselves. The violin appears at one moment from a variety of perspectives. As the viewer moves to the right of the painting, there are no recognizable objects. Throughout the painting Braque literally takes apart the violin and other objects so that he and the viewer can analyze them. The palette, the violin, and the notes of a musical score floating on folded paper tents give interest and meaning to this painting only because they are in the painting not because they are imitations of a violin, a palette, or a musical score.

The cubist painters redirected the artistic portrayal of reality in the same manner that literary modernists had reshaped the portrayal of social and moral experience and the new physics had reconceptualized nature itself.

24.4.5 Friedrich Nietzsche and the Revolt Against Reason

During the second half of the century, philosophers began to question the adequacy of rational thinking to address the human situation. No writer better exemplified this new attitude than German philosopher Friedrich Nietzsche (1844–1900). Wholly at odds with the values of the age, he attacked Christianity, democracy, nationalism, rationality, science, and progress. He sought less to change values than to understand their sources in the human character.

His first important work was *The Birth of Tragedy* (1872) in which he urged that the nonrational aspects of human nature are as important and noble as the rational characteristics. He insisted on the positive function of instinct and ecstasy in human life. To limit human activity to strictly rational behavior was to impoverish human life. In Nietzsche's view, the strength for the heroic life and for the highest artistic achievement arises from sources beyond rationality.

In later works, such as the prose poem *Thus Spake Zarathustra* (1883), Nietzsche criticized democracy and Christianity, claiming both would lead only to the mediocrity of sheepish masses. He announced the death of God and proclaimed the coming of the *Superman* (*Übermensch*), who would embody heroism and greatness. The term was frequently interpreted as some mode of super human or super race, but this was not Nietzsche's intention. He was critical of contemporary racism and anti-Semitism. He sought a return to the heroism that he associated with Greek life in the Homeric age. He thought the values of Christianity and of bourgeois morality prevented humankind from achieving life on a heroic level.

Two of Nietzsche's most profound works are *Beyond Good and Evil* (1886) and *The Genealogy of Morals* (1887). Nietzsche sought to discover not what is good and what is evil, but the social and psychological sources of the judgment of good and evil. He declared, "There are no moral phenomena at all, but only a moral interpretation of phenomena."[6] He dared to raise the question of whether morality itself was valuable: "We need a critique of moral values; the value of these values themselves must first be called in question."[7] In Nietzsche's view, morality was a human convention that had no independent existence. For Nietzsche, this discovery liberated human beings to create life-affirming values instead. Christianity, utilitarianism, and middle-class respectability could, in good conscience, be abandoned. Human beings could create a new moral order that would glorify pride, assertiveness, and strength rather than meekness, humility, and weakness.

In his appeal to feelings and emotions and in his questioning of the adequacy of rationalism, Nietzsche drew on the romantic tradition. The kind of creative impulse that earlier romantics had considered the gift of artists Nietzsche saw as the burden of all human beings. The character of the human situation that this philosophy urged on its contemporaries was that of an ever-changing flux in which nothing but change itself was permanent. Human beings had to forge from their own will and determination the values that were to exist in the world.

KEY PUBLICATION DATES OF MAJOR NONFICTION WORKS	
1830	Lyell, *Principles of Geology*
1830–1842	Comte, *The Positive Philosophy*
1835	Strauss, *The Life of Jesus*
1853–1854	Gobineau, *Essay on the Inequality of the Human Races*
1859	Darwin, *The Origin of Species*
1864	Pius IX, *Syllabus of Errors*
1865	Bernard, *An Introduction to the Study of Experimental Medicine*
1871	Darwin, *The Descent of Man*
1872	Nietzsche, *The Birth of Tragedy*
1883	Mach, *The Science of Mechanics*
1883	Nietzsche, *Thus Spake Zarathustra*
1891	Leo XIII, *Rerum Novarum*
1893	Huxley, *Evolution and Ethics*
1896	Herzl, *The Jewish State*
1899	Chamberlain, *The Foundations of the Nineteenth Century*
1900	Freud, *The Interpretation of Dreams*
1900	Key, *The Century of the Child*
1905	Weber, *The Protestant Ethic and the Spirit of Capitalism*
1908	Sorel, *Reflections on Violence*
1929	Woolf, *A Room of One's Own*
1933	Jung, *Modern Man in Search of a Soul*

24.4.6 The Birth of Psychoanalysis

A determination to probe beneath the surface or public appearance united the major figures of late-nineteenth-century science, art, and philosophy. They sought to discern the undercurrents, tensions, and complexities that lay beneath the calm surfaces of hard atoms, respectable families, rationality, and social relationships. Because of their theories and discoveries, educated Europeans could never again view life with complacency or even with much confidence. No intellectual development more exemplified this trend than psychoanalysis through the work of Sigmund Freud (1856–1939).

24.4.6.1 DEVELOPMENT OF FREUD'S EARLY THEORIES

Freud was born in Moravia into an Austrian Jewish family that settled in Vienna. He planned to become a lawyer but soon decided to study physiology and medicine. In 1886, he opened his medical practice in Vienna, where he lived until the Nazis drove him out in 1938. Freud sought to apply the critical method of science to the study of psychic disorders. He collaborated with another physician, Josef Breuer (1842–1925), and in 1895 they published *Studies in Hysteria*.

In the mid-1890s, Freud abandoned the hypnosis he had learned during a year in Paris and allowed his patients

SIGMUND FREUD IN AMERICA, 1909 In 1909, Sigmund Freud (1856–1939) and his then-devoted disciple Carl Jung (1875–1961) visited Clark University in Worcester, Massachusetts, during Freud's only trip to the United States. Freud, holding a cane, sits on the left. Jung is seated on the far right.
SOURCE: World History Archive/Alamy Stock Photo

to talk freely and spontaneously about themselves. He found that they associated their neurotic symptoms with experiences related to earlier experiences, going back to childhood. He also noted that sexual matters were significant in his patients' problems. For a time, he thought that perhaps sexual incidents during childhood accounted for their illnesses.

By 1897, however, Freud had rejected this view. In its place he formulated a theory of infantile sexuality, according to which sexual drives and energy already exist in infants and do not simply emerge at puberty. Freud thus questioned in the most radical manner the concept of childhood innocence.

24.4.6.2 FREUD'S CONCERN WITH DREAMS During the same decade, Freud also examined the psychic phenomena of dreams. Romantic writers had taken dreams seriously, but few psychologists had examined them scientifically. Freud believed the seemingly irrational content of dreams must have a reasonable, scientific explanation. He concluded that dreams allow unconscious wishes, desires, and drives that had been excluded from everyday conscious life to enjoy freer play in the mind. "The dream," he wrote, "is the [disguised] fulfillment of a [suppressed, repressed] wish."[8] During the waking hours, the mind represses or censors certain wishes, Freud claimed, which are as important to the individual's psychological makeup as conscious thought is. Freud developed these concepts and related them to his idea of infantile sexuality in his most important book, *The Interpretation of Dreams*, published in 1900.

24.4.6.3 FREUD'S LATER THOUGHT In later books and essays, Freud developed a new model of the internal organization of the mind as an arena of struggle and conflict among three entities: the id, the superego, and the ego. The **id** consists of amoral, irrational, driving instincts for sexual gratification, aggression, and general physical and sensual pleasure. The **superego** embodies the external moral imperatives and expectations imposed on the personality by society and culture. The **ego** mediates between the impulses of the id and the asceticism of the superego and allows the personality to cope with the inner and outer demands of its existence. Consequently, everyday behavior displays the activity of the personality as its inner drives are partially repressed through the ego's coping with external moral expectations, as interpreted by the superego.

In his acknowledgment of the roles of instinct, will, dreams, and sexuality, Freud reflected the romantic tradition of the nineteenth century. In other respects, however, he was a son of the Enlightenment. Like the philosophes, he was a realist who wanted human beings to live free of fear and illusions by rationally understanding themselves and their world. He saw the personalities of human beings

as being determined by finite physical and mental forces in a finite world. He was hostile to religion and spoke of it as an illusion. Freud, like the writers of the eighteenth century, wished to see civilization and humane behavior prevail. More fully than those predecessors, however, he understood the immense sacrifice of instinctual drives required for rational civilized behavior. Some misunderstand Freud as urging humankind to thrust off all repression. He did indeed believe that excessive repression could lead to a mental disorder, but he also believed civilization and the survival of humankind required some repression of sexuality and aggression. Freud thought the sacrifice and struggle were worthwhile, but he was pessimistic about the future of civilization in the West.

24.4.6.4 DIVISIONS IN THE PSYCHOANALYTIC MOVEMENT By 1910, Freud had gathered around him a small group of disciples. Several of his early followers soon moved toward theories of which Freud disapproved. The most important of these dissenters was Carl Jung (1875–1961), a Swiss whom for many years Freud regarded as his most promising student. Jung questioned the primacy of sexual drives in forming personality and in contributing to mental disorder. He also put less faith in reason.

Jung believed the human subconscious contains inherited memories from previous generations. These collective memories, as well as the personal experience of an individual, constitute his or her soul. Jung regarded human beings in the twentieth century as alienated from these useful collective memories. Freud was highly critical of most of Jung's work. If Freud's thought derived primarily from the Enlightenment, Jung's was more dependent on romanticism.

By the 1920s, the psychoanalytic movement had become even more fragmented. Nonetheless, it influenced not only psychology but also sociology, anthropology, religious studies, and literary theory.

24.4.7 Retreat from Rationalism in Politics

Nineteenth-century liberals and Socialists agreed that rational analysis could discern the problems of society and propose solutions. These thinkers felt that, once given the vote, individuals would behave according to their rational political self-interest. Education would improve the human condition. By 1900, these views had come under attack. Political scientists and sociologists painted politics as frequently irrational. Racial theorists questioned whether rationality and education could affect human society at all.

24.4.7.1 WEBER German sociologist **Max Weber** (1864–1920) regarded the emergence of rationalism throughout society as the major development of human history. Such rationalization displayed itself in the rise of both scientific knowledge and bureaucratic organization.

Weber saw bureaucratization as the basic feature of modern social life. He used this view to oppose Marx's concept of the development of capitalism as the driving force in modern society. Bureaucratization involved the division of labor, with each individual fitting into a particular role in much larger organizations. Furthermore, Weber believed that in modern society people derive their own self-images and sense of personal worth from their positions in these organizations.

Weber also contended—again, in contrast to Marx—that noneconomic factors might account for major developments in human history. For example, in his best-known essay, *The Protestant Ethic and the Spirit of Capitalism* (1905), Weber traced much of the rational character of capitalist enterprise to the ascetic religious doctrines of puritanism. The puritans, in his opinion, worked for worldly success less for its own sake than to ensure that they stood among the elect of God.

24.4.7.2 THEORISTS OF COLLECTIVE BEHAVIOR In his emphasis on the individual and on the dominant role of rationality, Weber differed from many contemporary social scientists who explored the activity of crowds and mobs. In *Reflections on Violence* (1908), Georges Sorel (1847–1922) argued that people do not pursue rationally perceived goals but are led to action by collectively shared ideals. Émile Durkheim (1858–1917) and Graham Wallas (1858–1932) became deeply interested in the necessity of shared values and activities in a society. Besides playing down the function of reason in society, these theorists emphasized the role of collective groups in politics rather than that of the individual, formerly championed by liberals.

24.4.8 Racism

The same tendencies to question or even to deny the constructive activity of reason in human affairs and to sacrifice the individual to the group were manifested in theories of race. **Racism** had long existed in Europe. Renaissance explorers had displayed prejudice against nonwhite peoples. Since at least the eighteenth century, biologists and anthropologists had classified human beings according to the color of their skin, their language, and their stage of civilization. After late-eighteenth-century linguistic scholars observed similarities between many of the European languages and Sanskrit and they postulated the existence of an ancient race called the Aryans, who had spoken the original language from which the rest derived. During the romantic period, writers had called the different cultures of Europe "races."

What transformed racial thinking at the end of the century was its association with the biological sciences. The prestige associated with biology and science in general became transferred to racial thinking, whose advocates now claimed to possess a materialistic, scientific basis for their thought. They argued that racial science could support a hierarchy of superior and inferior races within Europe and among the various peoples outside Europe.

24.4.8.1 GOBINEAU Count Arthur de Gobineau (1816–1882), a reactionary French diplomat, enunciated the first important theory of race as the major determinant of human history. In his four-volume *Essay on the Inequality of the Human Races* (1853–1854), Gobineau portrayed the troubles of Western civilization as the result of the long degeneration of the original white Aryan race. He claimed it had unwisely intermarried with the inferior yellow and black races, thus diluting the greatness and ability that originally existed in its blood. Gobineau saw no way to reverse this degeneration.

Gobineau's essay remained little known for years. However, a growing literature by anthropologists and explorers spread racial thinking. In the wake of Darwin's theory, thinkers applied the concept of survival of the fittest to races and nations. The recognition of the animal nature of humankind made the racial idea even more persuasive.

24.4.8.2 CHAMBERLAIN At the close of the century, **Houston Stewart Chamberlain** (1855–1927), an Englishman who settled in Germany, wove together these strands of racial thought into the two volumes of his *Foundations of the Nineteenth Century* (1899). He championed the concept of biological determinism through race but believed that through genetics the human race could be improved and even that a superior race could be developed.

Chamberlain was anti-Semitic. He pointed to the Jews as the major enemy of European racial regeneration. Chamberlain's book and the works on which it drew aided the spread of anti-Semitism in European political life.

24.4.8.3 LATE-CENTURY NATIONALISM Racial thinking was one part of a wider late-century movement toward more aggressive nationalism. Previously, nationalism had in general been a movement among European literary figures and liberals.

From the 1870s onward, however, nationalism became a movement with mass support, well-financed organizations, and political parties. Nationalists often redefined nationality in terms of race and blood. The new nationalism opposed the internationalism of both liberalism and Socialism. The ideal of nationality was used to overcome the pluralism of class, religion, and geography. The nation became a secular religion in the hands of state schoolteachers, who were replacing the clergy as the instructors of youth. Nationalism of this aggressive, racist variety became the most powerful ideology of the early twentieth century.

Some Europeans also used racial theory to support harsh, condescending treatment of colonial peoples in the late nineteenth and early twentieth centuries. They were convinced that white Europeans were racially superior to the peoples of color whom they governed. Similar racial theory also informed attitudes toward peoples of color in the West itself, as was the case with the inferiority ascribed to African Americans and Native Americans in the United States.

24.4.9 Anti-Semitism and the Birth of Zionism

Political and racial anti-Semitism, which cast such dark shadows across the twentieth century, developed in part from the prevailing atmosphere of racial thought and the retreat from rationality in politics. Religious anti-Semitism dated from at least the Middle Ages. Since the French Revolution, West European Jews had gradually gained entry into civil life. Popular anti-Semitism, however, survived, with the Jewish community being identified with money and banking interests. During the last third of the century, as finance capitalism changed the economic structure of Europe, many non-Jewish Europeans threatened by the changes became hostile toward the Jewish community.

24.4.9.1 THE DREYFUS AFFAIR In Vienna, Mayor Karl Lueger (1844–1910) used anti-Semitism as a major attraction for his Christian Socialist Party. In Germany, ultraconservative Lutheran chaplain Adolf Stoecker (1835–1909) revived anti-Semitism. Nowhere, however, did nineteenth-century anti-Semitism create a greater political crisis than the one caused by the Dreyfus affair in France.

On December 22, 1894, a French military court found Captain **Alfred Dreyfus** (1859–1935) guilty of passing secret information to the German army. The evidence against him was flimsy and was later revealed to have been forged. Someone in the officer corps had been passing documents to the Germans, and it suited the army investigators to accuse Dreyfus, who was Jewish. Even after Dreyfus was sent to Devil's Island, a notorious prison in French Guiana, secrets were uncovered to the German army. In 1896, a new head of French counterintelligence reexamined the Dreyfus file and found evidence of forgery. A different officer was implicated, but a military court acquitted him of all charges.

ALFRED DREYFUS These photographs of Alfred Dreyfus (1859–1935), in uniform but stripped of all the signs and insignia of his captain's rank, were taken in January 1895, after he was sentenced, in 1894, to life imprisonment for treason. His trial and conviction provoked a deeply troubling crisis in the French republic.
SOURCE: Apic/RETIRED/Getty Images

By then the affair had provoked near-hysterical public debate. The army, the French Catholic Church, political conservatives, and vehemently anti-Semitic newspapers contended that Dreyfus was guilty despite mounting evidence of his innocence. Anti-Dreyfus opinion was dominant at the beginning of the affair. In 1898, however, the novelist Émile Zola (1840–1902) published a newspaper article, "*J'accuse*" ("I accuse"), in which he contended that the army had denied due process to Dreyfus and had suppressed or forged evidence. Zola was convicted of libel and fled to England to avoid serving a one-year prison sentence.

Zola was only one of numerous liberals, radicals, and Socialists who had begun to demand a new trial for Dreyfus. Although these leftists had come to Dreyfus's support rather slowly, they soon realized his cause could aid their own public image. They blamed the conservative institutions of the nation for denying Dreyfus the rights belonging to any citizen of the republic. They also claimed, and properly so, that Dreyfus had been framed to protect the guilty persons, who were still in the army. In August 1898, further evidence of forged material came to light. The officer responsible for those forgeries committed suicide in jail, but a new military trial again convicted Dreyfus. The president of France immediately pardoned him in 1906, and a civilian court set aside the results of both military trials.

To this ugly atmosphere, racial thought contributed the belief that no matter to what extent Jews assimilated into the culture of their countries, their Jewishness—and thus their alleged danger to society—would remain. For racial thinkers, the problem of race was not in the character but in the blood of the Jew. An important Jewish response to this new, rabid outbreak of anti-Semitism was the launching in

1896 of the **Zionist** movement to found a separate Jewish state. Its founder was the Austro-Hungarian Theodor Herzl (1860–1904).

24.4.9.2 HERZL'S RESPONSE The conviction in 1894 of Captain Dreyfus in France and the election of Karl Lueger in 1895 as mayor of Vienna, as well as personal experiences of discrimination, convinced Herzl that liberal politics and the institutions of the liberal state could not protect the Jews in Europe or ensure that they would be treated justly. In 1896, Herzl published *The Jewish State*, in which he called for a separate state in which all Jews might be ensured of those rights and liberties that they should be enjoying in the liberal states of Europe. Furthermore, Herzl followed the tactics of late-century mass democratic politics by directing his appeal particularly to the poor Jews who lived in the ghettos of Eastern Europe and the slums of Western Europe. The original call to Zionism thus combined a rejection of the anti-Semitism of Europe and a desire to realize some of the ideals of both liberalism and Socialism in a state outside Europe.

24.5 Women and Modern Thought

How did women challenge gender stereotypes in the late nineteenth and early twentieth centuries?

The ideas that so shook Europe from the publication of *The Origin of Species* through the opening of World War I produced, at best, mixed results for women. Within the often radically new ways of thinking about the world, views of women and their roles in society often remained remarkably unchanged.

24.5.1 Antifeminism in Late-Century Thought

The influence of biology on the thinking of intellectuals during the late nineteenth century and their interest in the nonrational side of human behavior led many of them to sustain what had become stereotyped views of women. The emphasis on biology, evolution, and reproduction led intellectuals to concentrate on women's mothering role. Their interest in the nonrational led them to reassert the traditional view that feeling and the nurturing instinct are basic to women's nature. Many late-century thinkers and writers of fiction also often displayed fear and hostility toward women, portraying them as creatures susceptible to overwhelming and often destructive feelings and instincts. A genuinely misogynist strain emerged in late-century fiction and painting.

VIRGINIA WOOLF Virginia Woolf charted the changing sentiments of a world with most of the nineteenth-century social and moral certainties removed. In *A Room of One's Own*, she also challenged some of the accepted notions of feminist thought, asking whether women writers should bring to their work any separate qualities as women and concluding that men and women writers should share each other's sensibilities.
SOURCE: George C. Beresford/Stringer/Getty Images

This conservative and hostile perception of women manifested itself in several ways within the scientific community. In London in 1860, the Ethnological Society excluded women from its discussions on the grounds that the subject matter of the customs of primitive peoples was unfit for women and that women were amateurs whose presence would lower the level of the discussion. T. H. Huxley, in public lectures, claimed to have found scientific evidence of the inferiority of women to men. Karl Vogt (1817–1895), a leading German anthropologist, held similar views about the character of women. Darwin would repeat the ideas of both Huxley and Vogt in his *Descent of Man*. Late-Victorian anthropologists tended likewise to assign women, as well as nonwhite races, an inferior place in the human family. Still, despite their otherwise conservative views on gender, both Darwin and Huxley supported the expansion of education for women.

Freud, too, portrayed women as incomplete human beings who might be inevitably destined to unhappy mental lives. He saw the natural destiny of women as motherhood and the rearing of sons as their greatest fulfillment. The first psychoanalysts were trained as medical doctors, and their views of women reflected contemporary medical education, which, like much of the scientific establishment, tended to portray women as inferior. Distinguished women psychoanalysts, such as Karen Horney (1885–1952) and Melanie Klein (1882–1960), would later challenge Freud's views on women, and other writers would try to establish a psychoanalytic basis for feminism. Nonetheless, the psychoanalytic profession would remain dominated by men, as would academic psychology.

The social sciences of the late nineteenth and early twentieth centuries similarly reinforced traditional gender roles. Most major theorists believed that women's role in reproduction and childrearing demanded a social position inferior to men. Auguste Comte, whose thought in this area owed much to Jean-Jacques Rousseau, portrayed women as biologically and intellectually inferior to men. Herbert Spencer, although an advocate for improving women's lot, thought they could never achieve equality with men. Émile Durkheim portrayed women as creatures of feeling and family rather than of intellect. Max Weber favored improvements in the condition of women but did not support significant changes in their social roles or in their relationship to men. Virtually all the early sociologists took a conservative view of marriage, the family, childrearing, and divorce.

24.5.2 New Directions in Feminism

The close of the century witnessed a revival of feminist thought in Europe. The role of feminist writers during these years was difficult. Many women's organizations concentrated on achieving the vote for women, but feminist writers and activists raised other questions as well. Some organizations redefined ways of thinking about women and their relationships to men and society. Few of these groups were large, and their victories were rare. Nonetheless, by the early 1900s, they had defined the issues that would become more fully and successfully explored after World War II.

24.5.2.1 SEXUAL MORALITY AND THE FAMILY In various nations, middle-class women began to challenge the double standard of sexual morality and the traditional male-dominated family. This often meant challenging laws about prostitution.

Between 1864 and 1886, English prostitutes were subject to the Contagious Diseases Acts. Police in certain cities with naval or military bases could require any woman identified as, or suspected of being, a prostitute to undergo an immediate internal medical examination for venereal disease. Those found to have a disease could be confined for months to locked hospitals without legal recourse. The law took no action against their male customers. Indeed, the purpose of the laws was to protect men, presumably sailors and soldiers, and not the women, from infection.

These laws angered English middle-class women who believed the harsh working conditions and the poverty imposed on many working-class women were the true causes of prostitution. They framed the issue in the context of their own efforts to prove that women were as human and rational as men and thus subject to equal treatment. They saw poor women as victims of the same kind of discrimination that prevented women of their class from entering the universities and professions. The Contagious Diseases Acts assumed that women were inferior to men and treated them as less than rational human beings. The laws literally put women's bodies under the control of male customers, male physicians, and male law-enforcement personnel. They denied to poor women the freedoms that all men enjoyed in English society.

By 1869, the Ladies' National Association for the Repeal of the Contagious Diseases Acts, a distinctly middle-class organization led by Josephine Butler (1828–1906), began actively to oppose those laws. The group achieved the suspension of the acts in 1883 and their repeal in 1886. Government and police regulation of prostitution roused similar movements in other nations, which adopted the English movement as a model.

The feminist groups that demanded the abolition of laws punishing prostitutes without questioning the behavior of their customers were challenging the double standard and, by extension, the traditional relationship of men and women in marriage. In their view, marriage should be a free union of equals, with men and women sharing responsibility for their children. In Germany, the Mothers' Protection League*Bund für Mutterschutz*, contended that both married and unmarried mothers required the help of the state, including leaves for pregnancy and child care. This radical group emphasized the need to rethink all sexual morality. In Sweden, Ellen Key (1849–1926), in *The Century of the Child* (1900) and *The Renaissance of Motherhood* (1914), maintained that motherhood was so crucial to society that the government, rather than husbands, should support mothers and their children. All turn-of-the-century feminists in one way or another supported increased sexual freedom for women, often claiming it would benefit society as well as improve women's lives.

24.5.2.2 WOMEN DEFINING THEIR OWN LIVES For Josephine Butler and Auguste Fickert, as well as other continental feminists, achieving legal and social equality for women would be one step toward transforming Europe from a male-dominated society to one in which both men and women could control their own destinies. Fickert wrote, "Our final goal is therefore not the acknowledgement of rights, but the elevation of our intellectual and moral level, the development of our personality."[9] Increasingly, feminists would concentrate on freeing and developing women's personalities through better education and government financial support for women engaged in traditional social roles, whether or not they had gained the vote.

Some women also became active within Socialist circles. There they argued that the Socialist transformation of society should include major reforms for women. Socialist parties usually had all-male leadership. By the close of the century, most male Socialist leaders, including Lenin and later Stalin, were intolerant of demands for changes in the family or greater sexual freedom for either men or women. Nonetheless, Socialist writings began to include calls for improvements in the economic situation of women that were compatible with more advanced feminist ideals.

It was within literary circles, however, that feminist writers most clearly articulated the problems that they now understood themselves to face. Virginia Woolf's *A Room of One's Own* (1929) became one of the fundamental texts of twentieth-century feminist literature. In it, she meditated first on the difficulties that women of both brilliance and social standing encountered as writers and intellectuals. She concluded that a woman who wishes to write required both a room of her own, meaning a space not dominated by male institutions, and an adequate independent income. Woolf, however, was concerned with more than the right of women to participate in intellectual life. Establishing a new stance for feminist writers, she asked whether women, as writers, must imitate men or use the intellectual and psychological qualities they possessed as women. Just as she had challenged the literary conventions of the traditional novel in her fiction, she challenged the accepted notions of feminist thought in *A Room of One's Own*, concluding that male and female writers need to think as both men and women and share the sensibilities of each. In this sense, she raised the question of gender definition.

By World War I, feminism in Europe, fairly or not, had become associated in the popular imagination with challenges to traditional gender roles and sexual morality and with either Socialism or political radicalism. When extremely conservative political movements developed between the world wars, their leaders often emphasized traditional roles for women and traditional ideas about sexual morality.

The Chapter in Perspective

By the opening of the twentieth century, European thought had contours that seem familiar to us today. Science had revolutionized thinking about nature. Physicists had transformed the traditional views of matter and energy as they probed the mysteries of the atom. Evolutionary biology had revealed that human beings were not distinct from the natural order. Many believed science would provide a new basis for ethics and morality. Christianity had experienced its most severe challenge in modern times from science, history, philosophy, and the secular national states.

Nonreligious thinkers and writers also assailed the primacy of reason. Nietzsche and Freud, in their different ways, questioned whether human beings were rational creatures at all. Weber and other social and political theorists doubted that politics could ever be entirely rational. All these developments challenged the rational values of the Enlightenment.

Racial theorists questioned whether mind and character were as important as racial characteristics allegedly carried in the blood. Racial thinking also allowed some Europeans to believe they were inherently superior to non-Europeans, Jews, and ethnic minorities in Europe itself.

Turn-of-the-century feminists demanded equal treatment for women under the law and contended that the relationship between men and women within marriage required rethinking. They thereby set much of the feminist agenda for the twentieth century.

The Chapter in Review

Review Questions

1. Why was science dominant in the second half of the nineteenth century? How did the scientific outlook change between 1850 and 1914? What was positivism? How did Darwin and Wallace's theory of natural selection affect ethics, Christianity, and European views of human nature?
2. Why was Christianity attacked in the late nineteenth century? Why was Leo XIII regarded as a liberal pope? Why was the papacy itself so resilient?
3. Why did Europeans feel superior toward Islam? How did Islamic thinkers respond to the European challenge?
4. How did social conditions of literature change in the late nineteenth century? What was the significance of the explosion of literary matter? How did the realists undermine middle-class morality? How did literary modernism differ from realism?

5. What were the major movements associated with the rise of modern art?
6. Why were many late-nineteenth-century intellectuals afraid of and hostile to women? How did Freud view the position of women? What social and political issues affected women in the late nineteenth and early twentieth centuries? What new directions did feminism take?
7. What was the character of late-nineteenth-century racism? How did it become associated with anti-Semitism?
8. How did many ideas associated with modernism conflict with feminist goals? What were new departures in turn-of-the-century feminism?

Key Terms

Alfred Dreyfus (1859–1935) French Jewish artillery officer and a victim of violent anti-Semitism in France; convicted on charges of treason in 1894 based on false evidence; divided France as no other issue since the Paris Commune.

Claude Monet (1840–1926) One of the leading French artists to transform painting and later sculpture through his use of light and color to represent modern life.

cubism A radical new departure in early-twentieth-century Western art whose name was first coined to describe the paintings of Pablo Picasso and Georges Braque.

ego One of the three entities in Sigmund Freud's model of the internal organization of the human mind; mediates between the id and superego and allows the personality to cope with the internal and external demands of its existence.

Friedrich Nietzsche (1844–1900) German philosopher who drew on the romantic tradition to question the adequacy of rationalism to address the human situation.

Houston Stewart Chamberlain (1855–1927) British-born philosopher who championed the concept of biological determinism but believed that through genetics the human race could be improved and even that a superior race could be developed.

id One of the three entities in Sigmund Freud's model of the internal organization of the human mind; consists of the amoral, irrational instincts for self-gratification.

Kulturkampf **(cool-TOOR-cahmff)** Meaning the "battle for culture." The conflict between the Roman Catholic Church and the government of the German Empire in the 1870s.

Max Planck (1858–1947) German theoretical physicist who was the first scientist to articulate the quantum theory of energy.

Max Weber (1864–1920) German sociologist who saw the advent of rationalism, as shown in the rise of both scientific knowledge and bureaucratic organization, as the major advance of human history.

modernism The movement in the arts and literature in the late nineteenth and early twentieth centuries to create new aesthetic forms and to elevate the aesthetic experience of a work of art above the attempt to portray reality as accurately as possible.

natural selection The theory originating with Darwin that organisms evolve through a struggle for existence in which those that have a marginal advantage live long enough to propagate their kind.

papal infallibility The doctrine that the pope is infallible when pronouncing officially in his capacity as head of the church on matters of faith and morals, enumerated by the First Vatican Council in 1870.

positivism The philosophy of Auguste Comte that science is the final, or positive, stage of human intellectual development because it involves exact descriptions of phenomena, without recourse to unobservable operative principles, such as gods or spirits.

Postimpressionism A term used to describe European painting that followed impressionism; applies to several styles of art, all of which to some extent derived from impressionism or were a reaction to impressionism.

racism The pseudoscientific theory that biological features of race determine human character and worth.

realist The style of art and literature that depicts the physical world and human life with scientific objectivity and detached observation.

social Darwinism The application of Darwin's concept of "the survival of the fittest" to relate evolution in nature to human social relationships.

superego One of the three entities in Sigmund Freud's model of the internal organization of the human mind; embodies the external morality imposed on the personality by society.

Zionist The movement to create a Jewish state in Palestine (the Biblical Zion).

Notes

1. Stephen Jay Gould, *The Structure of Evolutionary Theory* (Cambridge, MA: Harvard University Press, 2002), p. 94.
2. Walter Kaufmann, ed. and trans., *The Portable Nietzsche* (New York: Viking, 1967), p. 159.
3. W. F. Hogan, "Syllabus of Errors," *The New Catholic Encyclopedia*, Vol. 13, 2nd edition (Detroit, MI: Gale, 2003), p. 652.
4. Max Kozloff, *Cubism/Futurism* (New York: Charterhouse, 1973), p. 11.
5. Edward F. Fry, *Cubism* (New York: McGraw-Hill, 1966), p. 38.
6. *The Basic Writings of Nietzsche*, ed. and trans. by Walter Kaufman (New York: The Modern Library, 1968), p. 275.
7. Kaufman, *The Basic Writings of Nietzsche*, p. 456.
8. *The Basic Writings of Sigmund Freud*, trans. by A. A. Brill (New York: The Modern Library, 1938), p. 235.
9. Harriet Anderson, *Utopian Feminism: Women's Movements in Fin-de-Siècle Vienna* (New Haven, CT: Yale University Press, 1992), p. 13.

Chapter 25
The Age of Western Imperialism

The British Dominions Beyond the Seas: Natives of the Greatest Empire the World has ever Known.

SPECIALLY PAINTED FOR "THE ILLUSTRATED LONDON NEWS."

(For Details, see the Key on the Opposite Page and the Appendix)

"THE GREATEST EMPIRE THE WORLD HAS EVER KNOWN"
The global British Empire dominated the nineteenth-century European imperial experience. The empire was popularized in newspapers, books, and in thousands of illustrations and photographs. This illustration shows the British Empire's worldwide reach, the varied peoples it governed abroad and, as seen in the title, its national pride in its imperial achievement. Similar illustrations portray the empires of France, Germany, the Netherlands, Belgium, and Russia.
SOURCE: Chronicle/Alamy Stock Photo

 ## Contents and Focus Questions

The Chapter in Brief

THE HALF-CENTURY between the beginning of the American Revolution and the end of the Latin American Wars of Independence (1775–1830) marked the end of the early modern era of European interaction with the wider world that had begun in the late fifteenth century. The second and third quarters of the nineteenth century witnessed the high age of the British Empire. During that time other European nations had fewer interests in the non-Western world. This situation began to change in the 1870s, however, with the dawn of the period historians call the **New Imperialism**. For the next half-century, until the outbreak of World War I in 1914, European powers dominated and controlled much of the world. During this period the United States and Japan also first appeared as major players on the world stage.

The word **imperialism** is now used so loosely in political debate that it has almost lost meaning. To analyze events in the nineteenth century, it may be useful to define imperialism as "the policy of extending a nation's authority by territorial acquisition or by establishing economic and political hegemony over other nations."[1] That definition seems to apply equally well to ancient Egypt and Mesopotamia and to European domination in the nineteenth century, but the latter case had new elements. Previous imperialisms had either seized land and settled it with the conqueror's people or established trading centers to exploit the resources of the dominated area. Nineteenth-century Western imperialism did not abandon these methods, but it introduced new ones. Moreover, modern Western imperial powers benefited from the advanced economies and technologies that they had developed since the late eighteenth century.

Nonetheless, as we shall see, the age of modern imperialism and the interactions of Western nations with other parts of the world displayed many of the themes we have already discussed. The challenges of governing and administering empires led to constitutional issues. The technology that enabled Europeans to build empires displayed the impact of scientific knowledge on Western society and industry and Westerners' ability to use that knowledge to dominate other parts of the world. The activities of missionaries and their frequent conflict with colonial administrators reflected the struggles that had long disturbed church-state relations in their home countries. The criticism of imperial ventures by some Westerners manifested the critical spirit that has informed so much of the Western experience. The economic exploitation of and cultural disrespect for other peoples reflected the limits of Europeans' commitment to equality.

The legacies of nineteenth-century Western imperialism still affect our world today. The emergence of independent states in Asia and Africa from former colonies after World War II, the Vietnam War, the establishment of Communism in China, the rise and fall of apartheid in South Africa, and the turbulence in the Middle East all flow directly from the imperial encounters of the nineteenth and early twentieth centuries. So do much of the present-day economic structure and agricultural production of the non-Western world. Furthermore, the current tensions between Christian churches of the northern and southern hemispheres would not exist if missionaries had not planted new Christian communities in Africa and Asia during the nineteenth century. The existence of Canada, Australia, and New Zealand as self-governing nations is also the result of nineteenth-century British imperial policy. Consequently, the subjects discussed in this chapter are important for understanding both the political rivalries among European nations that led to World War I and the world today.

25.1 The Close of the Age of Early Modern Colonization

How did early modern colonization differ from nineteenth-century Western imperialism?

The era of early modern European expansion that lasted from the late fifteenth to the late eighteenth centuries had witnessed the encounter, conquest, settlement, and exploitation of the American continents by the Spanish, Portuguese, French, and English; the establishment of modest trading posts by European countries in Africa and Asia; Dutch dominance in the East Indies (modern Indonesia); and British domination of India. During these three centuries, the European powers had largely conducted their colonial rivalries within the context of mercantilist economic assumptions. Each empire was, at least in theory and largely in fact, closed to the commerce of other nations. Furthermore, in the Americas, from New England to the Caribbean and then throughout Latin America, slavery was a major fact of economic life, with most slaves imported from Africa.

Early European colonial rivalry had occurred primarily within the transatlantic world. By the early eighteenth century, the following patterns of European domination prevailed in the Americas: The Spanish Empire extended from California and Texas to Argentina. The Spanish also claimed Florida. Portugal controlled Brazil. The Dutch, French, Spanish, and British exploited the rich sugar islands of the Caribbean. France loosely controlled the Saint Lawrence and Mississippi River Valleys and the upper Atlantic coast. The British had settled the Atlantic coast from Maine to Georgia.

Between the mid-eighteenth and the early nineteenth centuries, a vast political transformation occurred in these regions. The French lost their North American Empire to the British. The American Revolution drove the British from their Atlantic coastal colonies, which became the United States. Thousands of American loyalists fled to Canada, which developed a closer relationship with Britain. Warfare shifted the ownership of the Caribbean islands from one country to another, with Haiti by 1804 establishing its independence from France. In 1803, Napoleon sold the Louisiana Territory to the United States. In the 1820s Latin America shook off Spanish and Portuguese control. Except for Canada, the Caribbean islands, and a few toeholds on the coasts of Central and South America, European rule in the Americas had ended. The **Monroe Doctrine**, which the United States announced in 1823 and the British navy enforced, closed the Americas to European colonialism.

In contrast to early modern European empires, slavery was absent from those of the nineteenth century. In 1807 Britain had banned the slave trade and had abolished slavery itself in its own colonies from 1833 to 1834. Thereafter, the British navy worked to close down the slave trade of other nations. Consequently, although economic inequality and forced labor were common in the European empires of the late nineteenth century, the institution of slavery, which had been the chief characteristic of the earlier imperial transatlantic plantation economies, had disappeared.

Roman Catholicism had been the driving religious influence among the early modern transatlantic empires. Almost from the moment Europeans first reached the Americas in the 1490s, Catholic priests, friars, and nuns had worked relentlessly to convert the indigenous peoples of the Caribbean, Latin America, and French Canada. These regions remain overwhelmingly Catholic. The largely Protestant settlers of the British colonies had been religiously zealous, but their missionary impulse was less strong, and there were fewer indigenous people along the Atlantic seaboard for them to convert. By contrast, during the nineteenth century, evangelical Protestants from Britain and the societies that backed them set the pace for missionary enterprises that other Western nations imitated, including those that sponsored Roman Catholic missions.

25.2 The Age of British Imperial Dominance

How did Britain use its economic might to extend its influence around the world?

During the first half of the nineteenth century, no one doubted that Great Britain was the only power that could exert its influence around the world. During this half-century, Britain fostered the settlements that became the nations of Canada, Australia, and New Zealand and expanded its control of India. The early nineteenth-century British Empire also included smaller colonies and islands in the Caribbean and the Pacific and Indian Oceans. However, until the 1860s and 1870s, except in India and Western Canada, Britain did not seek additional territory. Rather, it extended its influence through what historians call the **Imperialism of Free Trade**.

25.2.1 The Imperialism of Free Trade

Nineteenth-century British imperial economic ideas differed sharply from the mercantilist doctrines that had dominated previous centuries. Mercantile economic doctrine had asserted that a nation measured its wealth in terms of the amount of gold and silver it amassed and that the amount of trade was finite: If one nation's trade increased, another nation's trade had to decrease. But in the 1770s, economic thinkers such as Adam Smith argued that empires would best prosper by abandoning closed imperial systems in favor of free trade: by fostering the exchange of goods across borders and oceans with minimal government regulation and tariff barriers. Free traders argued that this would allow trade to grow upon itself—that the amount of trade was potentially infinite—and would ensure the lowest prices for consumers. This outlook still dominates economic theory in the West and provides the theoretical foundation for economic globalism.

As a result of the productive energies that the Industrial Revolution of the late eighteenth and early nineteenth centuries unleashed, Britain became "the workshop of the world." It produced more manufactured goods than its population could absorb on its own, and it did so more cheaply than anyone else. To dominate a foreign market, British merchants needed only the ability to trade without government interference in the form of tariffs, subsidies, or price controls. Until at least the 1870s, free trade alone allowed Britain to dominate economically one region of the world after another without the need to establish a formal colonial administration.

Although nineteenth-century liberals believed that free trade fostered peace, it could and did lead to warfare.

The most important example of this concerned the opium trade between British merchants operating out of India and their potential Chinese customers. China had never been an extensive market for Western goods. Nonetheless, Europeans and Americans wanted to import Chinese goods, especially tea, silk, and porcelain, in large quantities. With the Chinese uninterested in buying Western manufactured goods, British merchants looked for another product to sell to the Chinese market. They found it in the opium produced in India. The Chinese government resisted the import of opium to prevent addiction among its people.

Between 1839 and 1842 and again between 1856 and 1860, the British went to war to impose a free trade in opium on China. At the conclusion of the first of these **Opium Wars**, the British gained control of Hong Kong, and forced the Chinese to allow Christian missionaries to operate in China, to open various ports to British merchants who remained subject to British rather than Chinese law, and to pay substantial reparations. During the Second Opium War, Britain, in alliance with France, forced the Chinese to allow foreign envoys to establish embassies in Beijing, to open more ports and areas to foreign trade, and to permit Christian missionaries to operate even more freely in China. The British were prepared to enforce free trade and their merchants' access to foreign markets even if the products those merchants sold poisoned buyers.

25.2.2 British Settler Colonies

During the early nineteenth century, Britain oversaw the settlement and economic development of three regions that had come under its domination in the eighteenth century: Canada, Australia, and New Zealand. Warfare had won Canada. Captain James Cook's voyages of exploration in the 1770s established British claims to Australia and New Zealand. Australia was first settled as a colony for British convicts. Missionaries led the colonization of New Zealand. The settlement of these lands, which attracted millions of immigrants from Britain and other European nations, resembled the westward movement in the United States during the same period. In both cases, native peoples paid the cost—in land, lives, and liberty—for European settlement.

The British assumed that eventually these regions would have some form of self-government and be a market for British goods. And in fact, during the nineteenth century, each of these colonies did establish self-government based on British law and political institutions. The British system of self-government based on an increasingly inclusive franchise was thus transferred to large parts of the world.

25.3 India: The Jewel in the Crown of the British Empire

Why was India such an important part of the British Empire?

Except for Canada, nineteenth-century British colonial interest shifted from the Atlantic world to Asia and the Indian and Pacific Oceans. During the same years that Britain had lost its North American colonies (1775–1783), it had established itself as the ruler of India. British India encompassed what is today India, Pakistan, and Bangladesh. From the late eighteenth century until its independence in 1947, India was the most important part of the British Empire and provided the base for British military and economic power throughout Asia. The protection of the commercial and military routes to India would be the chief concern of British imperial strategy during the nineteenth century. Other nations, particularly Russia, believed they could threaten Britain by bringing military pressure to bear on India. As we shall see later in the chapter, Britain largely became involved in Africa in the late nineteenth century to protect India.

Control of India meant that Britain had to dominate and govern not a land of settler-farmers, most of whom had emigrated from Britain and shared British values, but rather a vast heterogeneous nonwhite population with numerous political allegiances, complex economic and social conditions, and non-Western religions, particularly Islam and Hinduism.

In theory until 1857, India was still ruled by the Mughal Empire, which had governed the region since the 1500s. But that empire was only a shadow of its former self. Local rulers, called nawabs or maharajahs, paid little attention to the Mughal emperor who still resided in Delhi, the old imperial capital.

25.3.1 British East India Company

Initially the British achieved their domination of India through the East India Company, which was a private company of merchants chartered by Parliament in 1600. In the late eighteenth and early nineteenth centuries, the Company expanded its authority across India by warfare and negotiation. By the 1830s, British control over India was essentially complete. The willingness of Indians to defer to British authority rather than accept the dominance of other Indians made British rule possible. Like the Romans, the

Map 25–1   BRITISH INDIA, 1820 AND 1856

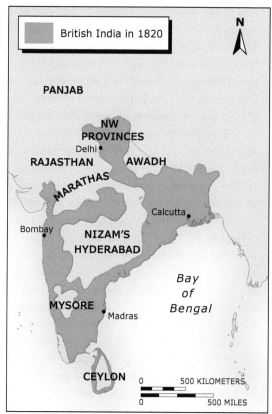

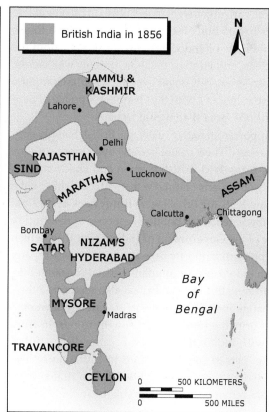

British had perfected the imperial art of dividing and conquering. (See Map 25–1.)

The rationale for British rule in India changed over time. The East India Company essentially saw India as a place to make money through economic exploitation. By the early nineteenth century, while still hoping to make India profitable, the British saw themselves as bringing wise administration to a subcontinent where local authority was in disarray. In 1813, Parliament permitted British Christian missionaries to work in India. Their presence meant that for the first time Britain would challenge the religious customs of Indian Hindus and Muslims. Some British administrators cooperated with missionaries to bring the "Enlightenment" of Western values to India. For example, the British prohibited the practice of *suttee*: Hindu widows burning themselves to death on their husband's funeral pyres. English became the official administrative language of India. Such intrusions suggested that British administrators believed they could raise India to what they considered to be a higher rung on the ladder of civilization. In their own colonial empire, the French would later call this belief in the spread of Western values the **civilizing mission**.

In 1857, however, India witnessed the most extensive resistance against any European power that occurred in the nineteenth century. The sepoy rebellion or mutiny (Indian troops were called sepoys) was all the more frightening to the British because it occurred within the Indian army itself. The precipitating cause of the mutiny was the East India Company's introduction of new cartridges for its soldiers' muskets that the sepoys believed were lubricated with pork or beef fat (the cartridges were in fact coated with vegetable oil). Soldiers had to bite off the end of the cartridge to use it. This would have offended both Muslims, for whom the pig was unclean, and Hindus, to whom the cow was sacred. There was also simmering anger over the way the Company treated native rulers and with the Company's policy of paying British troops more than it paid Indians.

With support from native rulers, the British harshly suppressed the rebels. Their tactics became even more ruthless after sepoys massacred British women and children. Tens of thousands of Indians and more than 10,000 British were killed. By June 1858, the British were firmly back in control.

The immediate British political response to the mutiny was passage of the **Government of India Act** in 1858, which transferred political authority from the East India Company to the British crown. Many company officials became British crown administrators. The British also restrained their efforts to change India or to move it "toward civilization." Instead, the British administration sought to refrain from interfering with Indian religion and became distrustful of missionary efforts to convert Indians to Christianity. The British also worked more closely with Indian rulers. One-third of India remained under the rule of Indian princes

who swore allegiance to the British crown and were advised by British officials. More British troops were also stationed in India, and Indian troops were not allowed artillery. Finally, in 1877, Prime Minister Benjamin Disraeli pushed through an act of Parliament that declared **Queen Victoria** (r. 1837–1901) Empress of India.

Indians did not sit passively while Britain revised its policies. In 1885, Hindus founded the Indian National Congress with the goals of modernizing Indian life and liberalizing British policy. Muslims organized the Muslim League in 1887, which for a time cooperated with the National Congress, but eventually sought an independent Muslim state.

25.4 The "New Imperialism," 1870–1914

What was new about the "New Imperialism"?

Whereas in the first three quarters of the nineteenth century Britain had largely dominated the world stage, between 1870 and 1914 other Western powers undertook colonial ventures with remarkable results. During this half-century, Western nations including the United States and Japan, which had industrialized and modernized its government and armed forces along Western lines between the 1860s and the 1880s, achieved unprecedented influence and control over the rest of the world and provoked intense colonial rivalries. Between 1870 and 1900, Western states controlled more than 10 million square miles and 150 million people—about one-fifth of the world's land area and one-tenth of its population. During this period, imperial expansion went forward with great speed, and empire was regarded as necessary for a great power. Because of the numerous actors, the speed, the extent, and the many nations involved, historians regard this era as constituting a "New Imperialism" different from the imperialism of the early nineteenth century. New Imperialism is a term of convenience that covered many diverse and even conflicting actions, ideas, and activities.

Why were the imperial encounters of this era perceived to be "new"? First, they were more intentionally imperial and involved direct political and administrative control of non-Westerners by the Western powers. With a few notable exceptions, including Western influence over China and European and American economic dominance in Latin America, free-trade imperialism and informal empire were abandoned. In their place arose a variety of devices for formal empire or imperial control through **protectorates** and **spheres of influence**. In a protectorate a Western nation placed officials in a foreign state to oversee its government without formally assuming responsibility for administration. In other instances, a European state, the United States, or Japan established spheres of influence in which it received special commercial and legal privileges in part of an Asian or African state without direct political involvement. These late-century imperial changes encompassed the British crown taking over direct administration of India; the British and French establishing protectorates over Egypt and Tunisia, respectively; the establishment of direct French rule in Vietnam; the division of Africa into colonies ruled by a half dozen European powers; the division of Persia (Iran) into Russian- and British-dominated zones; Japanese annexation of Korea and Taiwan; and the United States annexing Hawaii and taking control of the Philippines from Spain.

Second, the New Imperialism occurred over a relatively brief period and involved an unprecedented number of nations. In addition to the older imperial powers—Britain, France, Russia, the Netherlands, Spain, and Portugal—the newly united Germany and Italy and the Belgian monarchy, which had only existed since 1830, sought to achieve empires as did the United States and Japan.

Third, virtually none of the numerous imperial ventures of this era involved significant numbers of immigrants as settlers. Rather, Westerners came to govern directly or indirectly vast numbers of non-European peoples. Fourth, during these decades Europeans at home and in colonial settings exhibited a cultural confidence and racial arrogance that marked a departure from previous eras when persons associated with European empires esteemed indigenous cultures or assumed that these cultures could climb the ladder of civilization. Fifth, despite its worldwide scope and especially the establishment of French rule in Indochina, the New Imperialism focused to an unprecedented degree on Africa, with the European powers partitioning Africa among themselves. The boundaries they established still determine Africa's political divisions.

Two other points should be noted about the New Imperialism. First, the number of Westerners carrying it out was relatively small. Except for soldiers and sailors, only a few thousand administrators, merchants, and missionaries were associated with empire. Second, the empires created by the New Imperialism were short-lived, in most cases lasting less than a century.

25.5 Motives for the New Imperialism

What were the motives for the New Imperialism?

Until the mid-twentieth century, the predominant interpretation of the motives for the New Imperialism was economic. This view originated in a book titled *Imperialism: A Study* published in 1902 by English economist and journalist J. A. Hobson (1858–1940). Hobson had opposed Britain's conquest of the Dutch-speaking, white-ruled Afrikaner republics in South Africa during the Boer War (1899–1902), which he blamed on the influence of capitalists and bankers. He saw the same influences motivating the imperialist ambitions of other European states. According to Hobson, capitalist economies overproduced, which caused manufacturers, bankers, and financiers to press governments into imperial ventures to provide new markets for their excess goods and capital.[2] Hobson, who was a radical but not a Marxist critic of capitalism, believed that European economies should be restructured to make imperialism as he understood it unnecessary.

In 1916 Lenin adopted and modified Hobson's ideas in his book *Imperialism, the Highest Stage of Capitalism*. There Lenin maintained, "Imperialism is the monopoly stage of capitalism," the last stage of a dying system.[3] He argued that competition inevitably eliminates inefficient capitalists and therefore leads to monopoly. Powerful industrial and financial capitalists, he claimed, soon run out of profitable investments in their own countries and persuade their governments to gain colonies in "less developed" countries. Here they can find higher profits, new markets for their products, and safe sources of raw materials. For Lenin, capitalism could not be reformed. Revolution was needed. Lenin's concept of imperialism after the Russian Revolution of 1917 became dogma in the Soviet Bloc and influenced the thinking of Marxist historians in Western countries for decades.

Hobson and Lenin presumed that something inherent in the economic and political character of capitalist states caused them to undertake imperial ventures. Each writer developed a broad theory about the New Imperialism that was based on their need to support their own political agenda—opposition to the Boer War for Hobson and the necessity for revolution for Lenin.

The history of the Western imperial advance does not support the theories of Hobson and Lenin. European powers did invest considerable capital abroad and did seek markets, but not in a way that fits the Hobson-Lenin model. Britain, for example, made heavier investments abroad before 1875, when it was not actively acquiring new colonies, than during the next two decades when it was expanding its empire. Only a small percentage of British and European overseas investments, moreover, went to their new colonies. Most capital went into other European countries or to older, well-established states like the United States and Argentina and to the settler colonies of Canada, Australia, and New Zealand. Even when Western countries did invest in new colonies, they often did not invest in their own colonies.

The facts are equally discouraging for those who try to explain the New Imperialism by emphasizing the need for markets and raw materials. While some European businesspeople and politicians hoped that colonial expansion would cure the great depression of 1873 to 1896, few colonies were important markets for the great imperial nations. Instead these states were forced to rely on areas they did not control for sources of vital raw materials. It is not even clear that control of the new colonies was particularly profitable, with the notable exception of India. Nevertheless, as one of the leading students of the subject has said, "No one can determine whether the accounts of empire ultimately closed with a favorable cash balance."[4] This is true of the European imperial nations collectively, but for some of them, like Italy and Germany, empire was a losing proposition. Some individuals, such as **King Leopold II** of the Belgians, in the Congo, and companies, of course, made great profits from colonial ventures, but they were not always able to influence national policy. Economics certainly played a part, but a full understanding of the New Imperialism requires a search for other motives as well.

At the time, advocates of imperialism justified it in various ways. Some, embracing what they called the "**civilizing mission**," argued that the European nations had a duty to bring benefits of their higher culture and superior civilization to "backward" peoples. Religious groups demanded that Western governments support Christian missionaries politically and even militarily. Some politicians and diplomats supported imperialism as a tool for social policy. In Germany, for instance, conservative nationalists hoped that imperial expansion would deflect public interest away from demands for social reform. Yet Germany acquired few colonies, and such considerations played little, if any, role in its colonial policy. In Britain, Joseph Chamberlain (1836–1914), the colonial secretary from 1895 to 1903, argued for the empire as a source of profit and economic security that would finance a great program of domestic reform, but he made these arguments well after Britain had acquired most of its empire. Another apparently plausible justification for imperialism was that colonies would attract a European country's surplus population. But most continental European emigrants went to the Americas and Australia, areas their home countries did not control. (See the "Compare and Connect" sidebar, which follows below, for two of many views on the purpose of New Imperialism.)

Three motives seem to have strongly influenced the imperial policies of each of the major European nations. First, after 1870, many political leaders came to believe that the possession of colonies or of imperial influence was an important and even necessary characteristic of a great European power. Here they were clearly following the British example. By the 1880s French politicians believed that colonies could compensate for France's loss of prestige and territory in the Franco–Prussian War of 1870 to 1871. Similar motives drove Russia's advance into Asia following its defeat in the Crimean War (1854–1856). As a result, huge French and Russian empires were created. Two newly created European states also embraced imperial ventures: Italy believed it must secure colonies to prove that it was a great power but did so with only modest success; Germany created a more significant, if short-lived, empire. The United States at the time of the Spanish-American War in 1898 also came to believe that possession of colonies was essential to its world status. So did Japan, which became a major imperial power in Asia, acquiring Taiwan in 1895 after defeating China and annexing the independent kingdom of Korea in 1910.

Second, much of the territorial acquisitions associated with the New Imperialism as well as subsequent Western involvement in the Middle East arose in anticipation of the decay of the Ottoman Empire. In European diplomacy this became known as the Eastern Question. The Ottoman Empire at its height in the seventeenth century had extended from Algeria to the Balkans, Mesopotamia, and the Arabian Peninsula. Throughout the nineteenth century, however, the Ottoman government in Istanbul slowly but steadily lost province after province to Western powers or nationalist revolts. European powers were anxious that their rivals might profit from the weakness of the Ottoman Empire, and became directly involved in both precipitating and trying to control the loss of Ottoman authority. Tension between the Russian and Austrian empires over former Ottoman territory in the Balkans, for example, provided the catalyst for World War I, and the turmoil that has characterized much of the Middle East since 1945 originated in the collapse of Ottoman power in that area.

Third, the geopolitical assumptions of European statesmen led them to deeper and deeper involvements from the eastern Mediterranean to Africa. European powers often intruded into other regions of the world to protect what they regarded as their strategic interests and then had to decide how to manage administering them.

One final comment should be made about the motives for the New Imperialism. Western governments often found themselves reacting to events on the spot rather than determining their actions in advance. In one region after another, a colonial administrator, military commander, group of missionaries, or business concern would act without prior authorization from the governments in Europe. This then created a situation in which governments had to respond, leading to greater involvement in an area than European governments had ever intended.

Compare and Connect

Two Views of Turn-of-the-Twentieth-Century Imperial Expansion

THROUGHOUT THE AGE of the most active European expansion, political and popular opinion was divided over whether imperialism was desirable and morally right for the major European powers. Gustav Schmoller, a German political economist, presented his argument in favor of imperial expansion around 1900. Four years later, French Socialist and novelist Anatole France attacked imperialism.

ARRIVAL IN SAIGON Arrival in Saigon of Paul Beau (1857–1927), governor general of Indo-China (1902–1907), an illustration from *Le Petit Journal*, November 1902.

SOURCE: Private CollectionArchives Charmet/Bridgeman Images

Before Reading

- Consider how Gustav Schmoller describes imperial powers.
- Think about the reasons why Anatole France sees little value in imperialism.

Questions

1. What are the characteristics that Schmoller ascribes to other contemporary imperial powers?
2. What are the benefits Schmoller sees from acquiring colonies?
3. Why does France equate imperialism with barbarism? Why does France believe that no benefits result from imperialism?
4. How could two writers come to such different conclusions about the European imperial enterprise? What values inform the views of each writer?

I. GUSTAV SCHMOLLER MAKES THE CASE FOR GERMAN IMPERIAL EXPANSION

Gustav Schmoller (1838–1917) was a highly respected German economist and active political figure who served in the Prussian Privy Council and as a member of the Upper Chamber in the Prussian Diet. In this lecture from around the turn of the century, Schmoller presents Germany as surrounded on the world scene by aggressive imperial powers and argues that Germany must become an imperial power and create its own strong navy and overseas empire. Schmoller attaches great importance to the victory of the United States in the Spanish-American War and portrays Spain as an unsuccessful imperial power.

In various States, arrogant, reckless, cold-blooded daring bullies, men who possess the morals of a captain of pirates . . . push themselves more and more forward into the Government. . . . We must not forget that it is in the freest States, England and North America, where the tendencies of conquest, Imperial schemes, and hatred against new economic competitors are growing up amongst the masses. The leaders of these agitations are great speculators, who have the morals of a pirate, and who are at the same time party leaders and Ministers of State. . . . The conquest of Cuba and the Philippines by the United States alters their political and economical basis. Their tendency to exclude Europe from the North and South American markets must needs lead to new great conflicts. . . . These bullies, these pirates and speculators *à la* Cecil Rhodes, act like poison within their State. They buy the press, corrupt ministers and the aristocracy, and bring on wars for the benefit of a bankrupt company or for the gain of filthy lucre. . . . We mean to extend our trade and industries far enough to enable us to live and sustain a growing population. We mean to defend our colonies, and, if possible, to acquire somewhere agricultural colonies. We mean to prevent extravagant mercantilism everywhere, and to prevent the division of the earth among the three world powers, which would exclude all other countries and destroy their trade. In order to attain this modest gain we require today so badly a large fleet. The German Empire must become the centre of a coalition of States, chiefly in order to be able to hold the balance in the death-struggle between Russia and England, but that is only possible if we possess a stronger fleet than that of today. . . . We must wish that at any price a German country, peopled by twenty to thirty million Germans, should grow up in Southern Brazil. Without the possibility of energetic proceedings on the part of Germany our future over there is threatened. . . . We do not mean to press for an economic alliance with Holland, but if the Dutch are wise, if they do not want to lose their colonies someday, as Spain did, they will hasten to seek our alliance.

II. ANATOLE FRANCE DENOUNCES IMPERIALISM

Anatole France (1844–1924) was a famous late-century French novelist who was also active in the French Socialist movement. Many Socialists across Europe criticized the imperial ventures of their governments. In this passage France provides both a moral and a utilitarian critique of French imperialism around the world. He associates it with ambitious military figures, greedy businessmen, and corrupt politicians. He also contends that imperialism brings nothing of value to France. Similar critiques appeared among other liberal, Socialist, and radical politicians and political commentators across Europe and in the United States and would continue until the close of the colonial age during the last quarter of the twentieth century. Like Schmoller, France sees imperialism as characterizing all the major powers.

Imperialism is the most recent form of barbarism, the end of the line for civilization. I do not distinguish between the two terms—imperialism and barbarism—for they mean the same thing.

We Frenchmen, a thrifty people, who see to it that we have no more children than we are able to support easily, careful of adventuring into foreign lands, we Frenchmen who hardly ever leave our own gardens, for what in the world do we need colonies? What can we do with them? What are the benefits for us? It has cost France much in lives and money so that the Congo, Cochinchina, Annam, Tonkin, Guinea, and Madagascar may be able to buy cotton from Manchester, liquors from Danzig, and wine from Hamburg. For the last seventy years France has attacked and persecuted the Arabs so that Algeria might be inhabited by Italians and Spaniards!

The French people get nothing from the colonial lands of Africa and Asia. But their government finds it profitable. Through colonial conquest the military people get promotions, pensions, and awards, in addition to the glory gained by quelling the natives. Shipowners, army contractors, and shady politicians prosper. The ignorant mob is flattered because it believes that an overseas empire will make the British and Germans green with envy.

Will this colonial madness never end? I know well that nations are not reasonable. Considering their composition, it would be strange, indeed, if they were. But sometimes they know instinctively what is bad for them. Through long and bitter experience they will come to see the mistakes they have made. And, one day, they will realize that colonies bring only danger and ruin.

SOURCES: (I) Gustav Schmoller lecture of about 1900, quoted in J. Ellis Barker, *Modern Germany: Her Political and Economic Problems, Her Foreign and Domestic Policy, Her Ambitions, and the Causes of Her Success*, 2nd ed. (London: Smith, Elder, & Co., 1907), pp. 139–140. (II) Anatole France, "The Colonial Folly," (1904), as quoted in Louis L. Snyder, *The Imperialism Reader: Documents and Readings on Modern Expansionism* (New York: D. Van Nostrand Company, Inc., 1962), pp. 155–156.

25.6 The Partition of Africa

How did European politics contribute to the "Scramble for Africa"?

For almost fifty years inter-European rivalries played out in regions far away from Europe itself and nowhere more intensely than in Africa. During the so-called "Scramble for Africa," which occurred between the late 1870s and about 1912, the European powers sought to maximize their strategic control of African territory, markets, and raw materials. Motivated by intense competition, the imperial powers eventually divided almost the entire continent among themselves. (See Map 25–2.) The short- and long-term consequences were devastating for the Africans. Among the long-term

Map 25–2 IMPERIAL EXPANSION IN AFRICA TO 1880

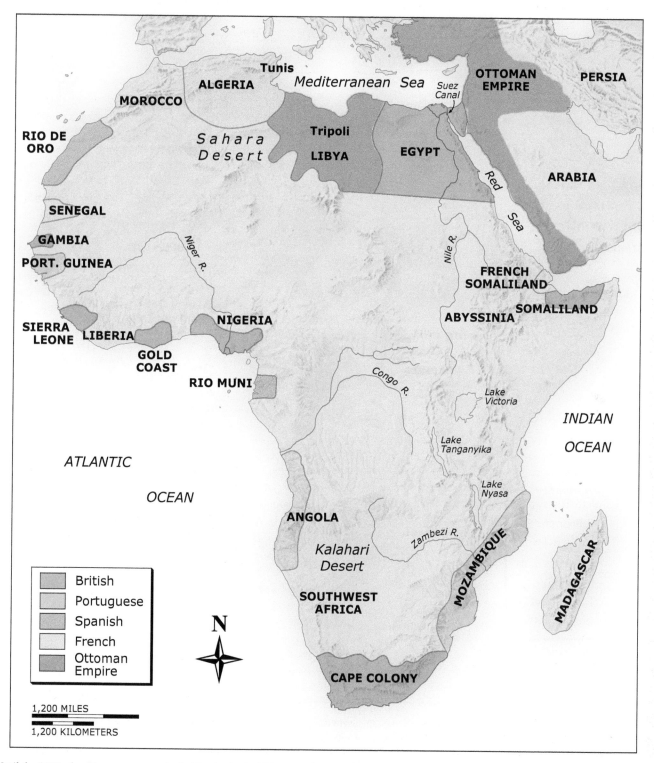

Until the 1880s, few European countries held colonies in Africa, mostly on its fringes.

effects was that European control forcibly integrated largely agrarian African societies into the modern world industrial economy. In the process, new forms of agrarian production, market economies, social organizations, political structures, and religious allegiances emerged that would form the basis for the postcolonial African nations. (See Map 25–3.)

The European partition of Africa was not based on a universal policy, and each power acquired and administered

Map 25–3 PARTITION OF AFRICA, 1880–1914

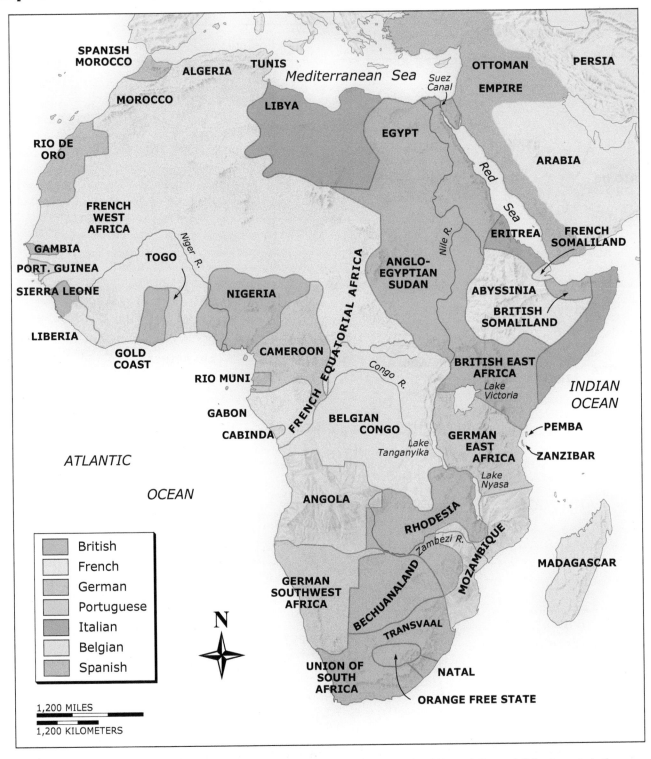

Before 1880, the European presence in Africa was largely the remains of early exploration by old imperialists and did not penetrate the heart of the Continent. By 1914, the occupying powers included most large European states; only Liberia and Abyssinia (Ethiopia) remained independent.

its new possessions in different ways. Their goals, however, were the same: to gain control, or at least dominance, through diplomacy or force and then either to place Europeans directly in charge of administering the territories or to compel local rulers to accept European advisers who would exercise real authority.

25.6.1 Algeria, Tunisia, Morocco, and Libya

France left the Congress of Vienna in 1815 with only a few small colonies and trading posts. For a time French popular opinion seems to have resisted further colonial ventures. Then, in 1830, the government of **Charles X** (r. 1824–1830) launched a military expedition against Algiers. Following the Revolution of 1830, which deposed Charles, France did not pull back from Algeria. French governments saw Algeria's fertile coastal regions as providing land for a settler colony. By 1871, more than 275,000 French settlers lived there. Over the decades, France pushed beyond the coast into the Sahara Desert where its forces established their authority over various nomadic Muslim peoples. The French came to regard Algeria as an integral part of France, and the European inhabitants there were French citizens who elected representatives to the Parliament in Paris. Civilian French officials administered the coastal districts of Algeria, where most of the Europeans lived, as if they were part of France itself. Algeria was

the most important portion of the French Empire, and it was the part of Africa that a European nation most fully and directly ruled.

From 1881 to 1882, the French also established a protectorate over Tunisia, which was nominally a province of the Ottoman Empire, and then between 1901 and 1912, set up another protectorate in Morocco. In both Tunisia and Morocco, the French retained the local rulers as puppet monarchs. (See the "Closer Look" sidebar, which follows below, to examine a French magazine's depiction of French imperialism in Morocco.)

Italy, having failed to conquer Ethiopia in 1896, seized Libya from Turkey from 1911 to 1912, establishing its most important colony. These French and Italian colonial advances in North Africa demonstrated the profound weakness of the Ottoman Empire. Thus, by the outbreak of World War I, all North Africa lay under some form of European control. In each of these cases a Western power dominated a largely Muslim population.

25.6.2 Egypt and British Strategic Concern about the Upper Nile

Like Tunisia, Egypt, the richest and most populous region of North Africa, was a semi-independent province of the Ottoman Empire under the hereditary rule of a Muslim dynasty. After the failed Napoleonic invasion in 1798, the Khedives, as Egyptian rulers were titled, had tried to modernize Egypt

INAUGURATION PROCESSION AT THE OPENING OF THE SUEZ CANAL The opening of the Suez Canal in 1869, linking Asia and Europe, was a great engineering achievement. It also became a major international waterway, reducing the distance from London to Bombay by half.
SOURCE: Riou/Edouard/Bridgeman Images

A Closer Look

The French in Morocco

MANY IMPERIALISTS—EUROPEAN, American, and Asian—claimed altruistic motives for their acquisition of colonies. The French took pride in bringing French civilization to the lands France ruled. This cover of a French magazine appeared in November 1911, when the French decision to extend and tighten their control of Morocco sparked an international crisis. It illustrates literally how France justified its colonial empire as a *mission civilisatrice*, a mission to bring civilization to "backward" peoples.

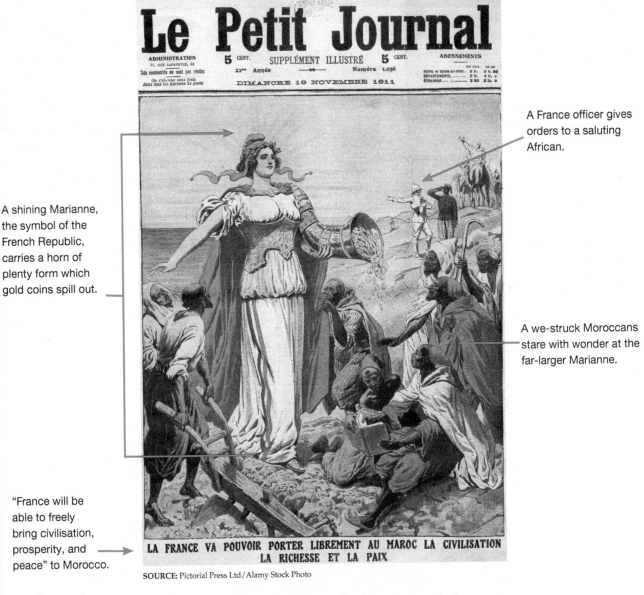

A France officer gives orders to a saluting African.

A shining Marianne, the symbol of the French Republic, carries a horn of plenty form which gold coins spill out.

A we-struck Moroccans stare with wonder at the far-larger Marianne.

"France will be able to freely bring civilisation, prosperity, and peace" to Morocco.

LA FRANCE VA POUVOIR PORTER LIBREMENT AU MAROC LA CIVILISATION LA RICHESSE ET LA PAIX

SOURCE: Pictorial Press Ltd / Alamy Stock Photo

Questions

1. Who is the intended audience for this image?
2. How does this image of the effect of French imperialism serve France's domestic political interests?
3. What are the trappings of civilization emphasized in this image?

by building new harbors, roads, and a modern army. Egypt also sought to expand its rule into the Sudan. To pay for these projects, the Khedives borrowed money from European creditors. To earn the money to repay these loans,

they forced farmers to plant cash crops, particularly cotton, which could be sold on the international market. The Egyptian government became utterly dependent on European creditors for new loans at exorbitant rates of interest.

The construction of the **Suez Canal** was the final blow to Egypt's finances.

The Suez Canal was opened in 1869. Built by French engineers with European capital, it was one of the most remarkable engineering feats of the day. The canal connected the Mediterranean to the Red Sea, which meant that ships from Europe no longer had to sail around Africa to reach Asia. The canal also reduced the shipping distance from India to Britain from about 12,000 miles to 7,000 miles. The canal increased the speed of international contacts and, by reducing shipping costs, made many goods on the world market more affordable. India thus became an even more important market for British goods. Yet the tangible benefits to Egypt itself were not immediately clear. By 1875, the Khedive was bankrupt, and that year Prime Minister Benjamin Disraeli purchased the Khedive's shares in the canal to give the British government a controlling interest in its management. Egypt's European creditors were taking more than 50 percent of Egyptian revenue each year to repay their loans, and they forced the Egyptian government to increase taxes to raise more revenue. This provoked a nationalist rebellion, and in 1881, the Egyptian army took over the government to defend Egypt from foreign exploitation. An uncooperative, nationalist Egypt was, however, not in the interests of the European powers. In 1882 Britain sent a fleet and army to Egypt that easily defeated the Egyptians and established seventy years of British supremacy in the country. A European power was thus established into the Middle East as never before.

Egypt was never an official part of the British Empire. The Khedives, who became kings after Egypt severed its ties with Turkey during World War I, continued to reign, but a small number of British officials dominated the Egyptian administration. The British used their experience "advising" the Indian princes to run Egypt behind the facade of the Khedive's government.

Britain's primary goal in Egypt was political and military stability. Egypt had to repay its debts, and Britain was to retain control of the Suez Canal. The British built a naval base at Alexandria and installed a large garrison in Cairo. They established municipal governments that were responsible for taxation and public services and further expanded cotton cultivation. They also prevented the Egyptians from establishing a textile industry that would compete with Britain's own mills.

Economically, this meant that while the Egyptian economy grew and tax revenues increased, per capita income actually declined among Egyptians, most of whom were peasants who owned little or no land. Politically, it led to the growth of Egyptian nationalism, to Islamic militancy, and to demands that the British leave Egypt. Egyptian Islamic militants, organized into the Muslim Brotherhood in the late 1920s, would provide many of the anti-Western ideas that inspire radical Islam today.

The British occupation of Egypt quickly drew Britain even deeper into Africa along the Nile. Control of the upper Nile had been understood to be essential to the security of Egypt since ancient times. The collapse of the Khedive's

BATTLE OF OMDURMAN The Battle of Omdurman, fought near Khartoum on September 2, 1898, demonstrated the capacity of European forces armed with the most modern weapons—in this case, a British army of British, Egyptian, and Sudanese troops, commanded by Horatio Herbert Kitchener—to decimate a vast Sudanese force armed with less advanced weapons. Approximately 10,000 African warriors were killed, while British losses numbered forty-eight men.
SOURCE: Tacconi/Ferdinando/Bridgeman Images

authority in Cairo in 1881 had led to a similar collapse of Egyptian authority in the Sudan. The Sudan remained in turmoil until 1898 when an Anglo-Egyptian army under General later Lord) Horatio Herbert Kitchener (1850–1916), conquered it in a remarkably violent campaign during which 11,000 Sudanese troops were killed and 16,000 were wounded by modern weaponry in a single battle at Omdurman. The British lost only forty-eight men in the battle. The number of casualties at Omdurman would not be matched in a single day until European armies turned modern weapons on each other during World War I.

The British determination to secure the upper Nile and the Sudan led to one of the major crises of the imperial age. Although the French had refused to participate when British forces invaded Egypt in 1882, they retained large investments there and still hoped to influence Egyptian affairs by controlling the upper Nile. In the summer of 1898, a small French military force from West Africa reached the upper Nile at an unimportant location called Fashoda. As Kitchener's forces moved south, he confronted the French. War seemed possible until Paris ordered the French to withdraw. Instead of fighting, France and Britain eventually resolved their imperial rivalries. France acquiesced to Britain's domination of Egypt, and Britain agreed to support French ambitions in Morocco. The peaceful resolution of the Fashoda incident and other imperial disputes was essential to the formation of the loose alliance called the Anglo-French Entente in 1904 and to the two countries fighting as allies in World War I.

25.6.3 West Africa

France could surrender hope of dominating Egypt because it already controlled much of sub-Saharan Africa. West Africa, in particular, was a key area for French imperialism. In 1895 French West Africa included 12 million inhabitants and was eight times larger than France itself.

The British had four West African colonies: Sierra Leone, which was originally a home for freed slaves; Gambia; the Gold Coast (now Ghana); and Nigeria, the largest and most populous black African colony possessed by a European power. British slavers had worked on the Nigerian coast during the eighteenth century, and Britain had moved steadily into the Nigerian interior since the 1840s, seeking to establish trade and acquire tropical products, especially palm oil and cotton. The British annexed the port of Lagos in 1861. Various British trading companies operated on the Niger River with the Royal Niger Company, the most important of them, founded in 1886. Over time the British established protectorates over the Muslim emirates in northern Nigeria and direct control over other areas. In 1914, they combined these territories into a single administrative unit, which they called the colony of Nigeria. To prevent indigenous resistance, British officials ran the country through local rulers,

PUNCH, OR THE LONDON CHARIVARI.—November 28, 1906.

IN THE RUBBER COILS.

Scene—The Congo "Free" State.

THE CONGO IN COILS In this 1906 cartoon, King Leopold II is depicted as a snake squeezing a Congolese rubber worker to death in his coils. In the background, a woman flees in horror, clutching a baby. Leopold's policies in Belgium led to the death of one-half the native population of his territory in only thirty years.
SOURCE: Chronicle / Alamy Stock Photo

a policy known as indirect rule. Nigeria also became one of the most successful regions for British missionaries and has one of the largest Christian populations in Africa.

25.6.4 The Belgian Congo

Perhaps the most remarkable story in the European Scramble for Africa was the acquisition of the Belgian Congo. In the 1880s, the lands drained by the vast Congo River and its tributaries became the personal property of King Leopold II of Belgium (r. 1865–1909). As a young monarch, he had become determined that Belgium, despite its small territory, must acquire colonies. No doubt he was inspired by the great commercial wealth that the neighboring Netherlands had accumulated from its long history of trade and empire in the East Indies.

The Belgian government, however, had no interest in colonies. So despite being a constitutional monarch, Leopold used his own wealth and political guile to realize his colonial ambitions. He did so under the guise of humanitarian concern for Africans. In 1876, he gathered explorers, geographers, and antislavery reformers in Brussels and formed the International African Association. He then recruited English-born journalist and explorer Henry Morton Stanley (1841–1904) to undertake an expedition into the Congo. Stanley had previously made a great reputation by crossing Africa from east to west. Between 1879 and 1884, he explored the Congo and on Leopold's behalf made "treaties" with African rulers who had no idea what they were signing. Leopold then won diplomatic recognition for those treaties and for his own allegedly humanitarian efforts in the region. Leopold thus personally became the ruler of an African domain that was more than seventy times the size of Belgium.

Although Leopold cultivated the image of a humanitarian ruler by sponsoring antislavery conferences and manipulating public relations, his goal in the Congo was brutal economic exploitation. Leopold's administrators used slave labor, intimidation, torture, mutilation, and mass murder to extract rubber and ivory from what became known as the Congo Free State. Eventually, beginning with African American reporter George Washington Williams (1849–1891) and culminating with an international outcry led by English journalist E. D. Morel (1873–1924) and diplomat Roger Casement (1864–1916), Leopold's crimes were exposed, and he formally turned the Congo over to Belgium in 1908, the year before he died.

The cruelties in the Congo, which became the basis for Joseph Conrad's classic novel *Heart of Darkness* (1902), were recorded in photographs, eyewitness accounts, and newspaper articles and by an official Belgian commission. The most responsible historical estimates suggest that Leopold's exploitation halved the population of the Congo in about thirty years. Millions of Africans were murdered or died from overwork, starvation, and disease.

25.6.5 German Empire in Africa

German chancellor Otto von Bismarck appears to have pursued an imperial policy, however briefly, with coldly political motives and only modest enthusiasm. Bismarck had initially been dismissive of colonial ventures. By the mid-1880s, however, he had changed his mind. In 1884 and 1885, Germany declared protectorates over South-West Africa (today the country of Namibia), Togoland, and the Cameroons in West Africa, and Tanganyika in East Africa. None of these places was particularly valuable or strategically important. Bismarck acquired colonies chiefly to improve Germany's diplomatic position in Europe and to divert France to colonial expansion and away from hostility to Germany. He also used German colonial activities in Africa to pressure the British to be reasonable about European affairs.

25.6.5.1 THE BERLIN CONFERENCE Bismarck called the Berlin Conference in 1884 (not to be confused with the Congress of Berlin, which sought to settle the Eastern Question in 1879). At the Berlin Conference the major European powers decided on a process of power-sharing in Africa that would

eventually lead to the formal partition of nearly the entire continent. That was not, however, their intent. The diplomatic representatives sat in a room where a large map of Africa hung on a wall, leading to the myth that they glanced at the map and divided up their interests in the Continent. It is true that by 1890 almost all the Continent had been parceled out. Great powers and small ones expanded into areas neither profitable nor strategic for reasons that were less calculating and rational than Bismarck's. But at the Berlin Conference itself, representatives of the assembled powers believed they were setting guidelines that would bring civilization, Christianity, and commerce to Africa without formal partitions. Just how mistaken they were would be revealed by the terrible fate of Congo in the hands of Leopold II.

Germany's proved to be the shortest lived of any of the European colonial ventures. German imperialism involved few Germans and produced no significant economic returns. At the end of World War I, the Allies stripped Germany of its colonial holdings. This meant that Germany was the only major West European state not drawn into the struggles of decolonization after World War II. But the German entry into the arena of imperial competition did contribute to the tensions that led to World War I.

25.6.5.2 GENOCIDE IN SOUTH-WEST AFRICA The German Empire lasted for only about three decades, but in that time German administrators carried out a major atrocity against indigenous peoples in German South-West Africa. The Germans had occupied the region because the British were not interested in it and because parts of it appeared suitable for settlement. As German administrators seized more land and used natives as virtual slave labor, resistance mounted and German settlers were killed.

In 1904 the Herero people in the colony revolted, and the Germans decided to take severe action. They announced that the Hereros had to leave their land, and German commander General Lothar von Trotha authorized the killing of all male Hereros. Germans drove Herero women and children into the desert. Herero prisoners were placed in concentration camps where the death rates from disease were high, although the Germans ran the camps with meticulous bureaucratic attention to detail. A United Nations report in 1985 concluded that by the time the Germans suppressed the revolt in 1908, 80 percent of the Herero population had died.

25.6.6 Southern Africa

Except for coastal Algeria, only South Africa had attracted large numbers of European settlers. The Dutch had begun to settle there in the mid-1600s. By 1800, Cape Town had become an important port for ships on their way to Asia. During the Napoleonic Wars the British captured Cape Town from the Dutch. British settlers began to arrive, and British economic and cultural influence soon predominated on the Cape. Even though the British abolished slavery

DIAMOND MINING IN SOUTH AFRICA Diamond mining in South Africa took off in the late 1860s. By 1880 Kimberly, the biggest mine in the region, had 30,000 people, second only to Cape Town. Whites monopolized the well-paid, skilled jobs, while black Africans undertook dangerous work in the mines. This photograph was taken around 1900, when the De Beers diamond mines employed nearly 4,000 people.
SOURCE: Chris Howes/Wild Places Photography/Alamy Stock Photo

throughout the empire in 1834, African workers at the Cape remained subject to strict discriminatory legislation.

Not surprisingly, the Dutch resented British control. During the 1830s and 1840s, the **Boers** or Afrikaners, as the descendants of the Dutch were known, undertook the **Great Trek** during which they moved north and east of the Cape. This migration was key in the forging of Afrikaner national consciousness. They founded states outside British control that would become Natal, Transvaal, and the Orange Free State. During the Great Trek the Boers also fought the Zulu people, who were themselves building an empire over other Africans. In 1843 the British annexed Natal, but the other two Boer republics remained independent.

In 1886 gold was discovered in the Transvaal, and 50,000 miners rushed to Johannesburg. There were now more non-Boer white settlers in the Transvaal than Boers, but the government refused to allow non-Boers the right to vote. In 1895, Cecil Rhodes (1853–1902), prime minister of the Cape Colony, supported a conspiracy to install a British government in the Transvaal. The conspiracy failed and Rhodes was forced to resign, but tensions mounted between Britain and the Boers. In 1899 war broke out. Although the British finally won the Boer War in 1902, they were surprised by the strength of Boer resistance. When the Boers resorted to guerrilla tactics, the British gathered Boer women and children into what they called **concentration camps** where many died from disease and exposure.

In 1910, the British combined the colonies in South Africa into a confederation whose constitution guaranteed the rule of the European minority over the majority black and nonwhite population. Africans and people of mixed race whom the British referred to as "colored" were forbidden to own land, denied the right to vote, and excluded from positions of power. To preserve their political power and economic privileges, the white elite of South Africa eventually enforced a policy of racial **apartheid**—"separateness"—that turned the country into a totally segregated land until the 1990s. The result was decades of oppression, racial tensions, and economic exploitation.

25.7 Russian Expansion in Mainland Asia

How did Russia come to control a vast and diverse Asian empire, and what developments facilitated Western penetration and control of Asia?

The British presence in India was intimately related to Russian expansion across mainland Asia in the nineteenth century, which eventually brought huge territories and millions of people of a variety of ethnicities and religions under tsarist rule. This expansion of Russian imperialism is one of the chief sources of tensions that exist today between the Russian Federation and Chechnya and other parts of the Caucasus.

During the early eighteenth century, the tsars had consolidated their control around the Baltic Sea. Catherine the Great (r. 1762–1796) had gained much of southern Ukraine and opened the regions around the Black Sea to Russian control at the cost of Ottoman influence. The partitions of Poland had extended Russian authority toward the west. During the nineteenth century the Russian government would look to the east where no major state could oppose its advance and where the weakness of the Ottoman Empire and China worked to Russian advantage.

Even during the eighteenth century, the tsarist government had ruled extremely diverse groups of people who were not Russian by language, religion, or cultural heritage. The Russians had generally approached these peoples in a pragmatic way, tolerating their religions and recognizing their social elites in exchange for loyalty to the tsar.

Beginning in the late eighteenth century, however, the tsarist government began to regard the nomadic societies or communities who lived in the mountainous regions to the south and east as *inorodtsy*, meaning foreigners. Moreover, the government drew upon the Enlightenment four-stage theory of social development to distinguish sedentary peoples as superior to those who lived as hunters, gatherers, fishermen, or nomads. One of the purposes thereafter of Russian expansion was, like that of early Victorian British administrators in India, to raise these people on the ladder of civilization.

CHAIN-CLAD WARRIORS FROM THE KHEVSURETI REGION OF GEORGIA The Russians largely subdued the Caucasus region by the 1860s—with a Muslim separatist movement led by Imam Shamil put down only after decades of struggle. This photograph, taken around 1890, shows a group of chain-clad warriors from the Khevsureti region of Georgia, which had been incorporated into the Russian Empire early in the nineteenth century. With their primitive firearms, swords, and shields, these fighting men appear to be no match for mechanized firepower, but the many ethnic groups of this rugged mountain region remained free of governmental authority until well into the twentieth century. **SOURCE:** Library of Congress Prints and Photographs Division

Russian governors would henceforth rarely, if ever, consider conquered peoples to be their social or cultural equals.

The nineteenth century saw Russia extend its authority in three distinct areas of mainland Asia. The first was in the Transcaucasus. This expansion came at the cost of Persia and the Ottoman Empire. The tsarist government presented these conquests as moves to protect Christian Georgians and Armenians from Muslim rule. It never securely incorporated these regions into the Russian Empire because their elites were not willing to be co-opted. By the late nineteenth century, nationalist unrest was rising among Georgians, Armenians, and Azerbaijanis.

The Russians were also only modestly successful in subjugating the Muslim peoples living in the Caucasus regions of Chechnya, Dagestan, and Circassia. Between 1817 and 1865, the Russians had to fight a brutal guerrilla war in these areas led by Imam Shamil (1797–1871). Once the Russian government had suppressed this resistance, it pursued its usual policy of seeking to gain the support of local aristocrats by recognizing their privileges and not disturbing their religion. Again this policy was only partially successful.

The second prong of Russian imperial advance occurred in the vast steppes of Central Asia where various nomadic peoples, including Kazakhs, lived.

The final area of Russian imperial conquest occurred in southern Middle Asia from the 1860s to the 1880s. This is the region of present-day Uzbekistan, Turkistan, and the areas bordering Afghanistan, all of which are primarily Muslim.

Here the Russians established protectorates under the nominal authority of the local rulers known as khans. Expansion in this area followed Russia's defeat in the Crimean War and sought to demonstrate that Russia could still exert imperial influence in Asia and counter the British presence in India. The Russian-British rivalry over these regions, particularly over Afghanistan, became known in journalism and fiction as "the Great Game." It sometimes brought Russia and Britain to the edge of war until the early twentieth century when both powers became more concerned about German influence in the Ottoman Empire that they were about one another. The Anglo-Russian Convention of 1907 ended their Central Asian rivalry and gave each power spheres of influence in Persia. Like the settlement of colonial claims between Britain and France, the end of this imperial contest also paved the way for Britain and Russia to become allies against Germany during World War I.

25.8 Western Powers in Asia

What role did Western powers such as France and the United States play in Asia?

While merchants had established the British interest in India and South Asia, French interest in Indochina arose because of the activity of Roman Catholic missionaries.

The French domain in Indochina eventually consisted of Vietnam, Cambodia, and Laos.

25.8.1 France in Asia

French missionaries had been active in Vietnam as early as the seventeenth century. However, with papal support, they gained ground in Indochina and elsewhere in Asia in the 1830s and 1840s. Persecution soon followed. In 1856, Napoleon III (r. 1852–1870), whose troops protected the Pope in Rome and whose wife was a fervent Roman Catholic, sent forces to Vietnam to protect the missionaries and give France a base from which the French navy could operate in the Far East and French commerce could expand in Asia. By 1862, French forces controlled Saigon and the area around it. By the 1880s, France controlled all of Vietnam and had made Cambodia a protectorate. In 1896, Laos also became a French protectorate. Missionary work continued throughout Indochina, especially in Vietnam where Catholics became and remain a significant minority.

25.8.2 U.S. Actions in Asia, the Pacific, and Latin America

In 1853, a U.S. naval squadron under Commodore Matthew C. Perry (1794–1858) arrived in Japanese waters to open Japanese markets to American goods. In 1867, American interest in the Pacific again manifested itself when the United States bought Alaska from Russia. For the next twenty-five years, the United States assumed a fairly passive role in foreign affairs, but it had established its presence in the Pacific.

Cuba's revolt against Spain in the 1890s ended this passivity and provided the impetus for the creation of an American Empire. Sympathy for the Cuban cause, investments on the island, the desire for Cuban sugar, and concern over Cuba's strategic importance all helped drive the United States to fight Spain.

Victory in the brief Spanish-American War of 1898 brought the United States an informal protectorate over Cuba, and the annexation of Puerto Rico ended 400 years of Spanish rule in the Western Hemisphere. The United States also forced Spain to sell it the Philippines and Guam, while Germany bought the other Spanish islands in the Pacific. The United States and Germany divided Samoa between them. In 1898 the United States also annexed Hawaii five years after an American-backed coup had overthrown the native Hawaiian monarchy. In 1903, President Theodore Roosevelt supported U.S. efforts to acquire the rights to build and control the Panama Canal. When Colombia refused to ratify an agreement granting these rights to the United States, Roosevelt supported Panama's separation from Colombia. A treaty was subsequently signed with a representative of the new independent state of Panama, and the United States commenced building, using equipment purchased from an earlier French effort, in 1904. This burst of activity made the United States an imperial power. This status was confirmed when Roosevelt sent an American fleet around the world between 1907 and 1909 and when the U.S.-built Panama Canal opened in 1914.

25.8.3 The Boxer Rebellion

By the close of the nineteenth century, Western powers had forced the Chinese government to give them privileged status in Chinese markets. With the backing of their governments, Christian missionaries were operating in much of China. The Qing dynasty, which had ruled China since 1644, was in a state of near collapse, and its decay both enabled Western penetration and was exacerbated by it.

The United States feared that the European powers and Japan would soon carve up China and close its lucrative markets and investment opportunities to American interests. In 1899, to prevent this, the United States proposed the **Open Door Policy**, which was designed to prevent formal foreign annexations of Chinese territory and to allow businesspeople from all nations to trade in China on equal terms. Although all powers except Russia eventually agreed to this policy in principle, they nonetheless carved out spheres of influence in China, and France, Britain, Germany, and Russia established naval bases on the Chinese coast. (See Map 25–4.)

Although the Qing government was too feeble to resist Western bullying, hatred of foreigners and resentment of their presence were strong. From late 1899 through the autumn of 1901, a Chinese group called the Righteous and Harmonious Society of Fists, better known in the West as the Boxers, attempted to resist the Western incursions. The Boxers, who were supported by a faction at the Qing court, hated missionaries, whom they regarded as agents of the imperial powers that had killed thousands of their Chinese converts.

For the imperial powers, the key moment in the **Boxer Rebellion** was the attacks on the foreign diplomatic missions in Beijing, which lasted off and on for three months in 1900 until an international army occupied the Chinese capital in August 1900. For the second time in less than a half-century, Western troops had seized Beijing. In September 1901, the Chinese government agreed to execute officials who had helped the Boxers and pay large reparations to the Western powers and Japan.

The suppression of the Boxer Rebellion had demonstrated that even without formal empire Western powers could freely intervene in China. It set the stage for the collapse of the Qing dynasty in 1912 and introduced China to

Map 25–4 ASIA, 1880–1914

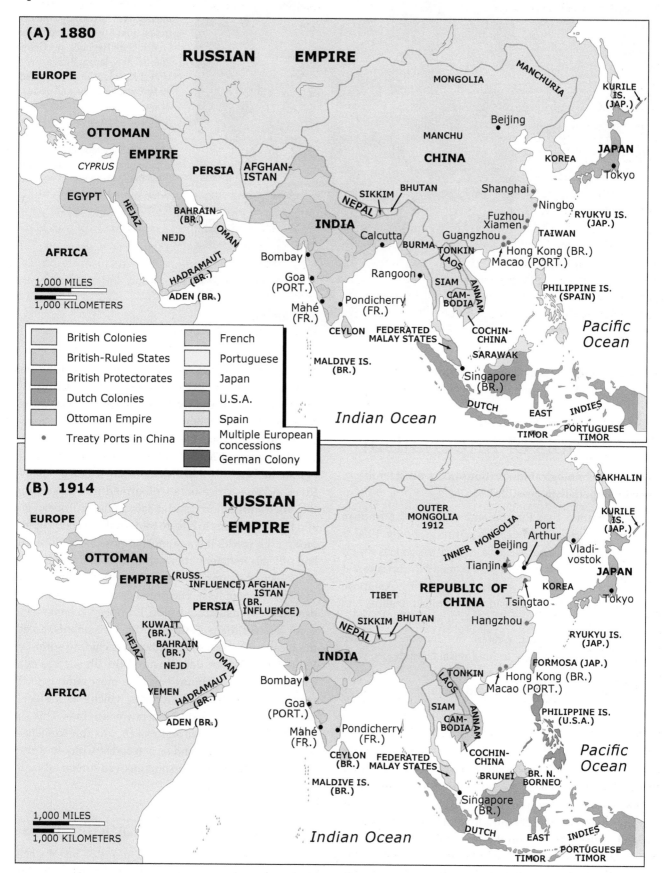

(A) 1880

EUROPE

RUSSIAN EMPIRE

MONGOLIA

MANCHURIA

KURILE IS. (JAP.)

OTTOMAN EMPIRE

CYPRUS

PERSIA

AFGHAN-ISTAN

Beijing

MANCHU

CHINA

KOREA

JAPAN

Tokyo

EGYPT

HEJAZ

BAHRAIN (BR.)

OMAN

NEJD

SIKKIM

NEPAL

BHUTAN

Shanghai

Ningbo

Fuzhou

Xiamen

RYUKYU IS. (JAP.)

INDIA

TAIWAN

AFRICA

HADRAMAUT (BR.)

ADEN (BR.)

Calcutta

Guangzhou

Hong Kong (BR.)

Macao (PORT.)

1,000 MILES

1,000 KILOMETERS

Bombay

Goa (PORT.)

Mahé (FR.)

BURMA

Rangoon

Pondicherry (FR.)

TONKIN

LAOS

SIAM

CAM-BODIA

ANNAM

PHILIPPINE IS. (SPAIN)

Pacific Ocean

CEYLON

MALDIVE IS. (BR.)

FEDERATED MALAY STATES

COCHIN-CHINA

SARAWAK

Indian Ocean

Singapore (BR.)

DUTCH

EAST INDIES

PORTUGUESE TIMOR

TIMOR

Legend:
- British Colonies
- British-Ruled States
- British Protectorates
- Dutch Colonies
- Ottoman Empire
- • Treaty Ports in China
- French
- Portuguese
- Japan
- U.S.A.
- Spain
- Multiple European concessions
- German Colony

(B) 1914

SAKHALIN

EUROPE

RUSSIAN EMPIRE

OUTER MONGOLIA 1912

KURILE IS. (JAP.)

OTTOMAN EMPIRE

(RUSS. INFLUENCE)

AFGHAN-ISTAN (BR. INFLUENCE)

INNER MONGOLIA

Beijing

Port Arthur

Vladi-vostok

PERSIA

Tianjin

REPUBLIC OF CHINA

KOREA

JAPAN

TIBET

Tsingtao

Tokyo

KUWAIT (BR.)

BAHRAIN (BR.)

OMAN

HEJAZ

NEJD

SIKKIM

NEPAL

BHUTAN

Hangzhou

RYUKYU IS. (JAP.)

AFRICA

YEMEN

HADRAMAUT (BR.)

INDIA

Bombay

TONKIN

FORMOSA (JAP.)

Hong Kong (BR.)

Macao (PORT.)

ADEN (BR.)

Goa (PORT.)

Mahé (FR.)

Pondicherry (FR.)

LAOS

SIAM

CAM-BODIA

ANNAM

PHILIPPINE IS. (U.S.A.)

Pacific Ocean

CEYLON (BR.)

FEDERATED MALAY STATES

COCHIN-CHINA

1,000 MILES

1,000 KILOMETERS

MALDIVE IS. (BR.)

BRUNEI

BR. N. BORNEO

Singapore (BR.)

DUTCH

EAST INDIES

Indian Ocean

PORTUGUESE TIMOR

TIMOR

As in Africa, in the decades before World War I, imperialism spread widely and rapidly in Asia. Two new powers, Japan and the United States, joined the British, French, and Dutch in extending control both to islands and to the mainland and in exploiting an enfeebled China.

SUPPRESSING THE BOXER REBELLION In August 1900, an international force comprised of troops from Austria-Hungary, the French Third Republic, the German Empire, Italy, Japan, Russia, the United Kingdom, and the United States invaded China and occupied Beijing to suppress the Boxer Rebellion, which had endangered Western missionaries and Western interests in China. This contemporary print presents a romanticized heroic assault by these foreign troops.
SOURCE: Library of Congress Prints and Photographs Division

decades of internal turmoil, foreign invasion, civil war, and eventually in 1949 a Communist Revolution.

25.9 Tools of Imperialism

How did technological innovations make nineteenth-century imperialism possible?

The domination that Europe and peoples of European descent came to exert over the entire globe by 1900 is extraordinary. It had not existed a century earlier and would not exist a century later. At the time, many Europeans and Americans worked their way across the North American Continent in what was considered manifest destiny, and they saw this domination as evidence of their cultural or racial superiority. In fact, Western domination was based on distinct and temporary technological advantages, what one historian called the "tools of empire."[5] These tools enabled Westerners to conquer and dominate vast areas of the world.

25.9.1 Steamboats

Europeans had long possessed naval superiority on the high seas. The power of those navies and of commercial sailing vessels had supported the early modern European empires and protected their trade routes across the Atlantic and around Africa into the Indian Ocean. That naval superiority persisted in the early nineteenth century, but it only allowed the European navies to attack and control coastal cities and strategic islands in the Indian and Pacific Oceans.

Robert Fulton, an American, had invented the steamboat in 1807. By the 1830s, steam power enabled warships to penetrate the inland rivers and shallow coastal waters of Asia and Africa, leading to the coinage of Western power as **gunboat diplomacy**.

By the late 1820s, steamboats were being constructed of iron. In the 1830s, a British merchant sailed up the Niger River in West Africa on a well-armed iron steamship. In the nineteenth century, such boats carried European goods and European arms to ensure trade in those goods up rivers around the world. It was almost impossible for local rulers and officials to defend themselves against iron warships.

Western steamboats were particularly effective along the vast rivers of Asia. The presence of gunboats on a river beside a city usually ensured European merchants and, especially for many decades, British merchants, access to the local markets. Iron steamboats, including some of the largest built to that date, ensured British success against China in the first Opium War. The most famous of these new iron warships was the *Nemesis*, which was 184 feet long and employed two sixty-horsepower engines. This single ship armed with cannon and rockets was able to silence the guns of Chinese forts and sink wooden Chinese warships with impunity. French warships enjoyed similar advantages in Indochina.

25.9.2 Conquest of Tropical Diseases

Tropical diseases often proved more of an obstacle to European conquest than African or Asian armed forces. For centuries, diseases, especially malaria, had prevented Europeans from penetrating deep into the forests of sub-Saharan Africa. Often as many as one-third to one-half of the European traders and soldiers stationed in trading bases on the West African coast would die from disease each year.

To move inland and increase their profits from commerce, especially after the formal end of the slave trade in the early nineteenth century, Europeans had to find a way around the malaria problem. The solution was quinine. French chemists had isolated quinine from cinchona bark as early as 1820. Slowly Western doctors began to recognize its medicinal qualities. The triumph of quinine came in 1854 when a British steamship, the *Pleiad*, under the command of a captain who was also a physician, steamed up the Niger River in West Africa with all its crew and passengers taking quinine pills and returned with no loss of life.

Quinine pills made possible the rapid exploration and eventual partition of Africa. Moreover, the demand for quinine transformed its area of production. Originally cinchona bark had been grown in Peru. By the late nineteenth century, its chief regions of cultivation were Dutch plantations in the East Indies and British plantations in India.

25.9.3 Firearms

During the nineteenth century momentous changes occurred in the technology of Western firearms. These changes gave Western nations an overwhelming advantage over non-Western peoples.

The rifle was improved so that bullets would spin more rapidly and move in a straighter direction. Early in the century Thomas Shaw invented the percussion cap for bullets. Unlike the earlier flintlock rifles, the percussion caps could easily be used in wet weather. The design of bullets themselves changed to allow greater speed and precision. By the mid-1850s, the British had adopted the Enfield rifle, which incorporated all the new technologies and was manufactured with interchangeable parts. These guns were accurate at several hundred yards. The invention of the breechloader in the 1860s brought still greater distance and precision in firepower for both rifles and artillery. Later in the century smokeless gunpowder and repeating mechanisms further enhanced accuracy and firepower.

These technological changes were incorporated into the development of the machine gun. By 1900, the machine gun had become arguably the single most important weapon in colonial warfare and accounted for the deaths of tens of thousands of non-European peoples. Europeans also used expanding bullets, which exploded inside a wound, against native peoples when they would not use them against other Europeans.

Repeatedly in late-century colonial military campaigns, native peoples' guns, when they had any, were no match for European weapons. European nations also attempted to prevent new kinds of guns from being sold in Africa or other parts of the imperial world. A relatively small European force armed with the new rifles, cannon, and machine guns could overcome local armies that greatly outnumbered them. Such weaponry permitted Kitchener's overwhelming victory in the Sudan in 1898. Often Europeans ascribed their victories to their supposedly advanced civilization or racial superiority rather than to to their superior firepower.

When African and Asian states did secure advanced weapons, they could either defeat European armies or carry out prolonged resistance. For example, in 1896, an Ethiopian army armed in part with modern rifles purchased from the French annihilated an invading Italian force at the Battle of Aduwa. (See the "Encountering the Past" sidebar on the invention of the Maxim machine gun, which follows below.)

25.10 The Missionary Factor

What was the relationship between missionaries and their home governments?

The modern Western missionary movement, which continues to the present day, originated in Great Britain in the late eighteenth century as a direct outgrowth of evangelical Christianity. Evangelicalism, which influenced Protestant communities from central Europe to the United States, emphasized the authority of the Bible, the importance of a personal conversion experience, and the duty to spread the Gospel. Many Evangelicals also hoped to prepare the world for the Second Coming of Jesus by carrying the message of Christian redemption to peoples who had not heard it. British Evangelicals first looked to unchurched groups in their own nation as the primary field for bearing Christian witness, but by the close of the eighteenth century, in a largely new departure for Protestants, small groups of Evangelicals began to be active in the non-Western world. Roman Catholics later copied these early Protestant missionary efforts. The result of this widespread nineteenth-century missionary campaign was the establishment of large Christian communities in Africa and Asia.

25.10.1 Missionary Movements

The missionary movements in areas such as India sought to carry the Christian faith to non-Western peoples overseas. The work of the evangelicals coincided with the consolidation of British control of India and what would become a century of unprecedented imperial expansion.

25.10.1.1 EVANGELICAL PROTESTANT MISSIONARIES The chief moving forces in the British missionary movement were the Baptist Missionary Society, the London Missionary Society, the Edinburgh and Glasgow Missionary Societies, and the Church [of England] Missionary Society, all founded in the 1790s. American Protestant missionary

Encountering the Past

Hiram Maxim and the Maxim Gun

BORN IN MAINE IN 1840, HIRAM MAXIM was a mechanical engineer and inventor. He had a wide variety of interests, and this was reflected in his many inventions, which included everything from an electric curling iron, to coffee substitutes, to the first

THE MAXIM The Maxim was the first wholly portable machine gun, pictured here with its American-born inventor Hiram Stevens Maxim (1840–1916), who became a British citizen. Technological superiority in weaponry and naval ships accounted in large measure for the success of Western imperialism in the nineteenth century. From the beginning, the Maxim gun was closely associated with European colonization in Africa and Asia. A prototype of the gun was given by Maxim in 1886 to the Emin Pasha Relief Expedition into the interior of central Africa, led by Henry Stanley, which contributed to the gun's fame.
SOURCE: Roger Viollet/The Image Works

automatic fire sprinkler system. In the 1870s he installed the first electric lights in a New York City building, and vigorously disputed Thomas Edison's claim to have invented the light bulb. He was deeply interested in powered flight and attempted a number of trial flights in the 1890s with a flying machine powered by two steam engines.

It was the Maxim gun, however, that made his fortune. Maxim's business brought him to Europe on a regular basis, and he became convinced that there was almost limitless money to be made selling advanced weaponry to European armies. Between 1883 and 1885, he filed a series of patents that would culminate in the world's first portable, fully automatic machine gun. His Maxim gun was a huge improvement over earlier machine guns, and he was able to secure the backing of the British steel manufacturer Edward Vickers to produce Maxim guns on an industrial scale. The gun's effectiveness in Britain's colonial wars made Maxim a celebrity. In 1899 he became a naturalized British citizen, and two years later he was knighted for his contribution to British military might.

In the decades following the invention of the Maxim gun, its successful use by the British inspired other nations to adopt the machine gun. Some purchased Maxims, and others pursued machine gun designs of their own. In 1912 an improved version of the Maxim gun called the Vickers machine gun became the standard machine gun of the

British army. It would remain in use until 1968. The Vickers machine gun, along with the machine guns used by other European nations, would have a profound impact on the course of World War I. Ironically, a weapon that delivered quick and decisive victories in Africa and Asia contributed to the long and bloody stalemate on the Western front. The machine gun gave defending armies an enormous advantage, making it extraordinarily difficult for attacking armies to gain significant ground. After the initial German offensive in 1914, neither side was able to launch a successful offensive until the arrival of fresh American troops in 1917.

Questions

1. What prompted Hiram Maxim to invent the Maxim gun?
2. How did the Maxim gun affect British imperialism in the late nineteenth century?

---

societies soon followed. Initially the missionary societies, who often competed with each other along denominational lines, floundered and attracted little support, but by the mid-1820s, they were firmly established and growing enterprises. By 1900, British missionary societies employed approximately 10,000 missionaries.

German Protestants also embraced the missionary impulse. The earliest German societies such as the Leipzig Mission, founded in 1836, devoted their efforts to India. The

Rhenish Missionary Society, founded in 1828, established itself in East Africa and supported German colonial claims there in the 1880s. As early as 1833, the Berlin Missionary Society sent missionaries to South Africa; by 1869, it was also working in China.

25.10.1.2 ROMAN CATHOLIC MISSIONARY
ADVANCE The nineteenth-century French Roman Catholic missionary effort was also enormous. It reflected the

resurgence of the Catholic Church in France in the decades following the French Revolution and Napoleon. The Society for the Propagation of the Faith, the largest French missionary society, was founded in 1822. By the 1860s, it had over a million members. Its earliest missionaries went to China and Vietnam. Over time, however, French Catholic missionaries worked on every continent, including the islands of the Pacific.

25.10.1.3 WOMEN AND MISSIONARY ACTIVITY As Europeans traveled around the world, they often commented on the status and treatment of women in other societies. In the Ottoman Empire, affluent women lived in separate portions of the house called harems. In India, sati, a practice whereby widows immolated themselves on their deceased husbands' funeral pyres, existed in some communities. In China, some young girls were encouraged to bind their feet to prevent their full growth, leading to painful, deformed feet and limited mobility. European observers made broad generalizations about the position of women in other societies based on their limited understanding of these practices. They often believed that their "civilizing" interventions in other societies would be particularly beneficial to women and girls. Much of the activity intended to improve the status and quality of life of women was led by missionaries. In India, for example, missionaries founded women's colleges. As missionary groups became more directly associated with education, the number of women missionaries in India grew, and by the early twentieth century, most missionaries there were women. Women also

played a large role in missionary activity in Africa and elsewhere. This missionary activity gave married and unmarried women the opportunity to travel and experience the world outside Europe firsthand. Some of these women carried their impressions back to their home countries, hoping to take a larger role in politics.

25.10.2 Tensions Between Missionaries and Imperial Administrators

The mission societies and their missionaries had a complex relationship with their home governments. Missionary work did not necessarily support imperial missions. Missionaries from both Europe and America often settled in regions their governments did not control, and missionary societies often employed missionaries who came from countries other than the one sponsoring their mission. Nonetheless, the missionaries developed many links with Western governments. The British missionary movement often saw the expansion of the British Empire as facilitating the spread of the Gospel. They viewed the spread of Western commerce as both financially beneficial for missions and as opening up new areas for the missionary enterprise. During the Opium Wars, for example, missionary societies demanded that the British government negotiate access for missionaries as well as traders and merchandise into China. Missionaries and advocates of free-trade imperialism thus could have a mutually supportive relationship. This relationship

WOMEN OF THE FOOCHOW MISSION, FUZHOU SHI, CHINA Women played a prominent role as teachers in the Western foreign missionary effort. Miss Emily Hartwell was a turn-of-the-century, American-born Protestant missionary to the Foochow Mission in Fuzhou Shi, China. Here, in a photo from the missionary magazine *Light and Life,* she is pictured with one of her Bible classes composed of Chinese women. Her letters home spoke of the disadvantages of women in Chinese culture.
SOURCE: Library of Congress Prints and Photographs Division

softened toward the close of the century when missionary societies defined themselves more strictly in terms of the spiritual mission of bearing witness to the Gospel.

Colonial administrators frequently resisted the introduction of missionaries into their territories, fearing the missionaries would be a destabilizing force as they challenged traditional religions and cultural values. Missionaries might defend the rights of native peoples against official imperial policy or commercial interests' efforts to increase their profits. In the settlement colonies, missionaries often clashed with settlers who wanted to prevent native peoples from gaining skills that would enable them to compete with whites. Colonial officials were also concerned about conflicts among Christian converts from different denominations. Furthermore, missionaries frequently educated persons from the lower levels of society who might resent colonial rule and the authority of native elites. The Christian vision of equality before God could, though it did not always, undermine the hierarchies of colonial authority. As one historian has commented, in India "there were always prominent missionaries prepared to challenge or ignore the imperial system and their own ecclesiastical authorities."[6]

But even when colonial officials disliked them, missionaries nonetheless provided much of the educational infrastructure of imperialism, particularly in India. At the village level their schools provided instruction in the local languages and English. Some of these schools received government financial support and became part of the administrative system. Missionaries also established institutions of higher education. These colleges trained primarily members of the Indian elite, both Hindu and Muslim. Instruction was invariably in English because the elites knew English was essential to their status in imperial India.

The relationship of French Roman Catholic missionaries to imperialism was complicated because the governments of the Third Republic in France were usually anticlerical after the 1870s. Yet although the republican government often clashed with the Catholic Church in France, it frequently supported missionary activity abroad as a way of extending French national interests. For example, France remained the official protector of Roman Catholics in the Ottoman Empire even after the French government broke diplomatic ties with the Vatican in 1905. In some cases the government in Paris or local colonial administrators encouraged French missionary activity to make native peoples sympathetic to French rule or to block the advance of other European powers. By teaching the French language, French missionaries also made it easier for French commercial interests to operate in a territory.

By 1900, approximately 58,000 French priests, religious brothers, and nuns were involved in the missionary enterprise. Like their British and German counterparts, French missionaries also often experienced tense relations with colonial administrators. Sometimes the colonial government

pressed the civilizing mission through secular physicians, teachers, and agricultural consultants to counter the religious influence of missionaries. At the same time, however, the success of the French Catholic missionary effort meant that colonial officials in Vietnam and parts of Africa and the Pacific had to deal with large numbers of native Roman Catholics who supported and admired the missionaries. Yet by the early twentieth century, French missionaries increasingly saw their role not only as winning converts but also as molding native cultures in the image of France. As one historian has written, "Spreading civilization, which missionaries had long considered simply a fortunate by-product of evangelizing, came to the fore in Catholic propaganda as the movement's chief goal. From the 1890s forward, missionary publications increasingly chronicled the lives and tribulations of missionaries committed not only to God but also to the *patrie* [the French fatherland] and a specifically French civilizing mission."[7]

However sympathetic missionaries might become to indigenous peoples, they remained spokespersons for Western civilization. Because missionaries wished to convert indigenous peoples to Western Christianity, they implicitly shared with colonial officials the general cultural assumption of Western superiority. Even when missionaries were not formal agents of empire, they introduced Western cultural values, manners, and outlooks. While colonial governments might be associated with more advanced military and transportation technology, missionaries might be associated with more advanced medicine or agriculture in the hospitals and mission stations they ran. And missionaries, like colonial officials, generally assumed that native peoples were inferior to Westerners. While a few missionaries by 1900 believed that Christians and persons of other religions could learn from each other, most missionaries regarded non-Christians simply as heathens. That outlook, like the attitudes of secular administrators, generated its own sets of reactions.

25.10.3 Missionaries and Indigenous Religious Movements

Just as colonial administrations during the nineteenth century gave rise to various nationalist movements or movements promoting the rights and interests of native peoples, the missionary activities gave rise to Asian and African religious movements that challenged the dominance of Western missionaries. The founding of new African and Asian Christian churches was a result of the rejection of racial and cultural assumptions of Western missionaries and as a means of reconciling Christianity with long-standing cultural practices, such as polygamy in Africa. The most important fact about the independent churches of Africa was that their leaders were African. For example, in 1888 David Brown Vincent established the Native Baptist Church in Lagos, Nigeria, after leaving the American-founded Baptist Church there. Not long thereafter, in South Africa, Mangena Makone broke with the methodists to found the Ethiopian Church. In Kenya, Christian members of the Kikuyu tribe split with the Church of Scotland Mission. In the early twentieth century, Christian Pentecostal groups arose among African Christians, as did other churches associated with gifts of healing or prophecy.

How can we describe the interrelationship of the missionary movement and colonialism? First, it was dynamic and changed during the nineteenth century as missionary goals and sensibilities changed from one generation to another. Second, the missionary movement gained publicity in the form of newspaper and journal articles, missionary society publications, and missionary narratives and autobiographies. These materials publicized the vision of empire and raised interest in the West about the non-Western world. They also strongly influenced popular culture at a time when the churches were more influential than they are today, especially in Europe. Third, the missionary societies and the churches with which they were associated became skilled at pressuring their governments. Initially they directed their efforts at permitting and protecting missionary activities. By the early twentieth century, however, many missionaries were supporting native peoples in their opposition to colonial authorities. Fourth, the religious effects of the missions were a two-way street. While Westerners brought Christianity to Africa and Asia, by 1900, non-Western Christians were beginning to move Christianity away from its dominance by Europeans and Americans. This process is still going on today. Finally, the nineteenth-century missionary movement made Christianity a genuinely worldwide religion for the first time. The spread of Christianity, like the development of self-government in the British settler colonies, was thus a major element of the extension of Western civilization around the globe.

25.11 Science and Imperialism

How did science increase imperialism's appeal to domestic audiences in Europe?

The early modern European encounter with the non-Western world from the fifteenth-century voyages of discovery onward had been associated with the expansion of natural knowledge. The same would be true of Western imperialism in the nineteenth and early twentieth centuries. Commencing in 1768, Captain James Cook (1728–1779) had undertaken his famous voyages to the South Pacific under the patronage of the Royal Society of London to observe the transit of the planet Venus. Sir Joseph Banks (1744–1820),

later president of the Royal Society, went with him to collect specimens of plants and animals unknown in Europe. Other British, French, and Spanish naval expeditions also carried scientists with their crews. Scientific societies often cooperated with military forces to carry out their research. For example, dozens of French scholars accompanied Napoleon's invasion of Egypt in 1798.

Geography was an expanding scientific discipline in the nineteenth century. Explorers wrote of their discoveries and adventures in Africa and Asia. Some explorers, such as Scottish Presbyterian David Livingstone (1813–1873) and French Jesuit Armand David (1829–1900), were also missionaries. Explorers portrayed themselves as pioneers who opened wild and savage spaces for commerce, religion, and ultimately civilization. Consequently, scientific and geographical societies generally supported their nations' imperialist goals and saw their research as benefitting from it. Scientific institutes, especially astronomical observatories, were set up in colonies. Colonial administrations also employed large numbers of engineers who planned and oversaw the construction of railways, roads, bridges, harbors, dams, and telegraph lines throughout the European empires. Geologists working for governments and private companies surveyed the mineral resources of newly acquired empires. As one British historian put it, "Natural scientists formed . . . [an] important . . . category of professional 'collaborators': an interest group central to the weaving of Africa, Asia, and the Americas into the fabric of national life."[8]

Four areas of scientific research deserve particular mention because they demonstrate how imperialism filtered into the wider European culture and captured the imagination of domestic audiences who never set foot outside Europe. These are botany, zoology, medicine, and anthropology.

25.11.1 Botany

Botany was the nineteenth-century colonial science par excellence, reflecting and nurturing the vast expansion of agriculture around the globe. This expansion brought millions of acres of new land under cultivation in the Americas, Australia, New Zealand, and Algeria. Colonial officials and Western investors also forced or induced colonial peoples, mainly in the tropics, to grow cash crops—such as coffee, sugar, tea, rubber, jute, cotton, bananas, and cocoa—for export to Europe.

European botanists were intensely interested in the plants they might discover abroad. Their interest ranged from the discovery of previously unknown specimens to the development of new crops that would improve agriculture. Changes in taste, like the spread of tea and coffee drinking, and in technology, like the demand for rubber for bicycle and motorcar tires, created demands for colonial agricultural products.

KEW GARDEN Kew Garden near London was the center of botanical research. Joseph Dalton Hooker, its director, persuaded collectors from around the world to send specimens to Kew. Tropical plants were grown in its greenhouse, where British citizens could visit the grounds and see plants that populated the far regions of the British Empire. This photo shows Kew Palace, located in Kew Garden.
SOURCE: Jamie Marshall/Dorling Kindersley Ltd

British colonies almost invariably had a large botanical garden to develop useful plants. The Royal Botanical Garden at Kew, near London, was the hub of a large network of imperial gardens dedicated to the advancement of agriculture.

Gardens such as Kew and the *Jardin des Plantes* in Paris also allowed the public to encounter a soft and inviting side of empire. Visitors could experience different parts of the empire in a pleasant setting as they strolled along flowerbeds, under trees, or through greenhouses. These great gardens made empire appear benign and far removed from the difficulties of its administration, the oppression of its indigenous peoples, or the havoc that empire may have wreaked on the peasant farmers of faraway places. These gardens and the new products and foods that Europeans and Americans consumed persuaded visitors that empire was part of the general progress of the age, which they associated with science.

The gardens with their research staffs also helped transform economies. The same spirit of agricultural improvement that had begun in Britain in the eighteenth century was carried throughout the empire. Botanists worked as economic innovators to enable intercontinental transfers of plants to secure products for their home countries and to develop colonial economies. In India, the British pushed farmers to grow cotton, hemp, tea, and cinchona trees. French botanists helped change the agricultural economy of Algeria from producing grain, which France already had

in abundance, to growing wine grapes, fruit, and olives, which had ready markets in France.

As plant commodities fell in value in one part of the British Empire, British administrators and merchants would contact Kew Garden for suggestions of other profitable crops. The botanists thus profited from empire as experts for the economic development of colonies after they had been annexed or after the crops that had once supported them were no longer profitable. Planters associations in the European colonies also established their own experimental stations to improve existing crops or develop new ones for cultivation.

25.11.2 Zoology

In the eighteenth century some European monarchs, such as the Habsburg emperors in Vienna and the French kings in Paris, had established collections of exotic animals. In the nineteenth century zoos and zoological gardens were founded in major European and American cities. These zoos displayed animals from around the world that expeditions acquired from the regions affected by European imperialism.

Other scientists would collect specimens of animals, particularly birds, which they killed and brought back from the colonies to Europe to be placed in natural history museums. These museums became increasingly popular in the late nineteenth century.

25.11.3 Medicine

Medical science was an integral part of the imperial enterprise on several different levels. As already noted, Westerners had to overcome various tropical diseases, especially malaria, that prevented them from surviving in the tropics. But Western medicine also became a fundamental feature of the civilizing mission of colonial administrators and missionaries, many of whom were physicians. The spread of Western medicine justified colonial rule and helped win converts. The primary diseases that Western doctors battled in the tropical colonies were yellow fever, sleeping sickness, smallpox, hookworm, and leprosy.

Missionaries pioneered Western medicine in the colonial setting. They presented themselves as healers of both body and soul. Some missionaries thought they could convert native peoples to Christianity by first demonstrating the power of Western medicine. In Africa various forms of surgery and the removal of cataracts, which restored sight, became powerful tools of conversion.

Physicians and medical researchers hoped to win government financial support by demonstrating that modern medicine could cure the endemic diseases that ravaged colonial peoples. Among the most influential colonial medical institutions were the Pasteur Institutes, named after Louis Pasteur (1822–1895), the French scientist who had found a cure for rabies and other diseases. The first overseas Pasteur Institute was founded in Saigon in 1891; others followed across the French Empire.

In general in the colonial world, Western science became a vehicle for what is often termed *cultural imperialism*. Medical advances allowed Western penetration of the tropics and then underpinned Western cultural and political domination. European medical institutions controlled research in the colonies. Westerners seldom had respect for Asian and African medical personnel no matter how well they were trained. At the same time, Western medicine either eradicated or lessened the impact of diseases that had ravaged the non-Western world for centuries.

25.11.4 Anthropology

Almost immediately from Christopher Columbus's first encounter with the Americas in 1492, European observers began to record and analyze the character of the non-European peoples they confronted and conquered. This interest never ceased, but in the late nineteenth century, the study of non-Western peoples became associated with the science of anthropology.

Anthropological societies were founded in Paris in 1859, London in 1863, and Berlin in 1870. The leaders of these new societies were convinced of the multiple origins

AT THE ST. LOUIS WORLD'S FAIR, 1904 Peoples from colonized nations were transported to world's fairs and similar exhibitions during the late nineteenth and early twentieth centuries. At the St. Louis World's Fair of 1904, African Pygmies, pictured above, demonstrated beheading. Native peoples constituted living exhibitions and were frequently presented in demeaning roles, fulfilling Western spectators' expectations of "exotic" behavior and convincing them of their superior civilization.
SOURCE: Library of Congress Prints and Photographs Division

of the races of humankind, a theory termed *polygenesis*, and of the inherent inequality of races. The concept of multiple origins had originated earlier in the nineteenth century in the United States where it had been an argument in defense of slavery. Polygenesis was one of many scientific theories that supported a hierarchy of unequal races at the top of which Westerners always placed the white races.

Many anthropologists believed that such factors as skull type determined human character, another idea originating in the United States. Paul Broca (1824–1880), a French physician who specialized in the brain, measured the skulls of human beings from different races and assigned them intellectual capacity based on brain size. Other European and American scientists followed his lead. Anthropologists who studied colonial societies incorporated these ideas in their research.

Anthropology as a social science infused with racial thinking had become organized in Western Europe on the eve of the Scramble for Africa. Anthropologists from then through World War II rode the wave of imperial enthusiasm. They worked closely with colonial administrations and encouraged expeditions to explore Africa. Even anthropologists who opposed colonialism cooperated with administrators once colonial empires had been created. Moreover, whatever their private doubts about racial theory may have been, anthropologists eagerly pursued university professorships in the colonies and government funding for research on the grounds that their research supported colonialism.

In fact, colonial officials rarely sought anthropologists' advice. Instead, anthropologists influenced imperial policies through their books, lectures, and university classes. European and American readers and students were taught that non-Western peoples were inferior; that their economies were underdeveloped; that their societies were corrupt, decadent, or primitive; and that their religions were dangerous and false. These factors proved the need for Western administration and control.

Many of these same attitudes informed the creation of the great anthropological museums in Europe and the United States. These popular museums often presented artifacts of African and Asian culture that explorers, travelers, or researchers had brought home. These exhibitions, like the botanical gardens, zoos, and museums of natural history, introduced Western audiences to what was considered to be the exotic features and otherness of non-Western peoples and cultures.

The idea of museums or zoos to display exotic creatures was also extended to human beings in both Europe and the United States. Showmen such as the American P. T. Barnum would exhibit Africans, Asians, and Native Americans. Carl Hagenbeck, a German, brought Polynesians, Sudanese, and Inuits from Canada to live in "native villages" in the Hamburg Zoo. In the thirty years before World War I, the Paris Zoo staged over twenty-five such exhibitions. At world's fairs, millions of Europeans and Americans paid to view native peoples.

The Chapter in Perspective

Western imperialism during the nineteenth and early twentieth centuries reshaped the world in ways that still affect us today. The productive capacity, military superiority, and technological prowess first of the European powers and later of the United States allowed those nations to dominate the world as they had never been able to do before. For some Europeans, the ability to rule others was itself the only justification for rule required. Their dominance would last for about a century. Western influence arose from decades of free-trade imperialism in the early nineteenth century marked in general by the absence of formal imperial government except for Britain in India and its settler colonies. The New Imperialism began in the 1870s largely as a result of the political changes that had occurred in Europe since the 1850s: the defeat of Russia in the Crimean War, the unification of Italy and Germany, and the defeat of France by Germany in 1870. These changes upset the balance of power and heightened tensions and competition among the great powers who increasingly sought to ensure their control by expanding into the non-Western

world. The New Imperialism thus involved the creation of formal empires as a sign of great power status, the protection of what were seen as vital geopolitical interests, an assertion of white racial superiority, and the partition of Africa. All these ideas and events led the European powers into overseas imperial rivalries that contributed to the tensions resulting in the outbreak of World War I in 1914.

Western imperialism found many supporters. Manufacturers and merchants sought markets for their goods and sources of tropical raw materials. Missionaries sought to evangelize the parts of Africa and Asia previously closed to Christianity. Scientists saw the imperial mission as creating networks for research and a new appreciation of their own efforts as supporters of their national governments. Army and navy officers looked to colonial wars as avenues for professional advancement.

For more than a century, from the 1830s to the 1940s, the peoples of the non-Western world found themselves generally acted upon by foreign political, economic, and military forces that they could not effectively resist.

Many of these non-Western peoples sought to work with Westerners for their own advantage. Indeed, the Western colonial empires could not have functioned without African and Asian collaborators. By the outbreak of World War I, however, discontent was stirring throughout the colonial world, and the leaders of the post-World War II movement for decolonization and independence had begun to emerge.

The Chapter in Review

Review Questions

1. What was the New Imperialism? How was it different from free-trade imperialism? Why was Britain the dominant world power until the late nineteenth century? What were the Opium Wars?

2. How did the British come to dominate India? What were the causes of the Indian rebellion of 1857? How did British rule in India change after the rebellion? Why was India so important to Britain?

3. What were the motives of the New Imperialism? To what extent was the New Imperialism related to the capitalist search for higher profits and new markets? How did colonial officials and businesspeople influence the growth of colonial empires?

4. Why was Algeria the most important part of the French Empire? What parts of the Ottoman Empire fell under European rule between the 1880s and 1914? Why did Britain come to dominate Egypt? Why did Germany and Italy acquire colonies? Why did Leopold II build an empire in the Congo? What was the Scramble for Africa?

5. How did France gain control of Indochina? How did the United States become an imperial power? Where did Russia expand in mainland Asia? What were the consequences of Western imperialism in China?

6. What were the "tools of imperialism"? Why was quinine so important for the spread of empires? What technological improvements enabled Western powers to dominate so much of the non-Western world? Why were the new colonial empires so short-lived?

7. Why did Western missionary efforts expand in the nineteenth century? Why was the relationship between Western missionaries and colonial officials so complicated? Why did Africans want to found their own churches? How has the spread of Christianity in the non-Western world affected the Christian churches?

8. How did Westerners justify imperialism? What was the civilizing mission? What sciences were most associated with the New Imperialism? What role did racism play in the New Imperialism?

Key Terms

apartheid (a-PAR-tid) An official policy of segregation, assignment of peoples to distinct regions, and other forms of social, political, and economic discrimination based on race associated primarily with South Africa.

Boers Afrikaners, as the descendants of the Dutch in South Africa were known, who undertook the Great Trek during the 1830s and 1840s, moving north and east of the Cape; founded three states outside British control, two of which remained independent republics.

Boxer Rebellion (1899–1901) The attempt by a Chinese group, the Righteous and Harmonious Society of Fists, better known as the Boxers, to resist Western incursions.

Charles X (r. 1824–1830) French king who launched a military expedition against Algiers.

civilizing mission The concept that Western nations could bring advanced science and economic development to non-Western parts of the world that justified imperial administration.

concentration camps Camps first established by Great Britain in South Africa during the Boer War to incarcerate noncombatant civilians; later, camps established for political prisoners and other persons deemed dangerous to the state in the Soviet Union and Nazi Germany; term now primarily associated with the camps established by the Nazis during the Holocaust.

Government of India Act (1858) The British response to the mutiny within the Indian Army, which transferred authority from the East India Company to the British Crown.

Great Trek The migration by Boer (Dutch) farmers during the 1830s and 1840s from regions around Cape Town into the eastern and northeastern regions of South Africa that ultimately resulted in the founding of the Orange Free State and Transvaal.

gunboat diplomacy The projection of Western force through steam power, which enabled warships to penetrate the inland rivers and shallow coastal waters of Africa and Asia.

imperialism The extension of a nation's authority over other nations or areas through conquest or political or economic hegemony.

Imperialism of Free Trade The advance of European economic and political interests in the nineteenth century by demanding that non-European nations allow European nations, most particularly Great Britain, to introduce their manufactured goods freely into all nations or to introduce other goods, such as opium into China, that allowed those nations to establish economic influence and to determine the terms of trade.

King Leopold II (r. 1865–1909) The Belgian monarch determined to acquire colonies in the Congo, despite the lack of interest by his government.

Monroe Doctrine (1823) The policy of the United States that closed the Americas to European colonialism.

New Imperialism The extension in the late nineteenth and early twentieth centuries of Western political and economic dominance to Asia, the Middle East, and Africa.

Open Door Policy (1899) The policy of the United States designed to prevent formal annexations of Chinese territory and to allow all nations to trade in China on equal terms.

Opium Wars (1839–1842; 1856–1860) A series of wars waged by the British to impose a free trade in opium on China.

protectorates (pro-TEC-tor-ates) Non-Western territories administered by Western nations without formal conquest or annexation, usually de facto colonies.

Queen Victoria (r. 1837–1901) The British monarch who became empress of India in 1877 through an act of Parliament.

spheres of influence Regions, cities, or territories where non-Western nations exercised informal administrative influence through economic, diplomatic, or military advisers.

Suez Canal Opened in 1869, the canal that connected the Mediterranean to the Red Sea, so that ships from Europe no longer had to sail around Africa to reach Asia.

Notes

1. *American Heritage Dictionary of the English Language*, 3rd ed. (New York: Houghton Mifflin, 1993), p. 681.

2. J. A. Hobson, *Imperialism: A Study* (London: James Nisbet, 1902), p. 85, as quoted in H. L. Wesseling, *The European Colonial Empires* (London: Longman, 2004), p. 129.

3. V. I. Lenin, *Imperialism, the Highest Stage of Capitalism* (New York: International Publishers, 1939), p. 88.

4. D. K. Fieldhouse, *The Colonial Empires* (New York: Delacorte, 1966), p. 393.

5. Daniel Headrick, *Tools of Empire: Technology and European Imperialism in the Nineteenth Century* (New York: Oxford University Press, 1981). The authors wish to acknowledge their indebtedness to Headrick's scholarship in this section.

6. J. P. Daughton, *An Empire Divided: Religion, Republicanism, and the Making of French Colonialism, 1880–1914* (New York: Oxford University Press, 2006), p. 18.

7. Robert Frykenberg, "Christian Missions and the Raj," in Norman Etherington, ed., *Missions and Empire* (New York: Oxford University Press, 2005), p. 129.

8. Richard Drayton, *Nature's Government: Science, Imperial Britain, and the "Improvement" of the World* (New Haven, CT: Yale University Press, 2000), p. 171.

Chapter 26
Alliances, War, and a Troubled Peace

IN THE TRENCHES ON THE EASTERN FRONT World War I produced unprecedented destruction and loss of life. Unlike a war of rapid movement, much combat occurred along stationary trenches dug in both Western and Eastern Europe. Here, Austro-Hungarian troops fight from trenches on the eastern front wearing gas masks. The use of poison gas, one of the innovations of the war, was generally condemned after the war.
SOURCE: National Archives and Records Administration

 Contents and Focus Questions

The Chapter in Brief

IN THE SUMMER of 1914, the **Archduke Francis Ferdinand**, heir to the throne of Austria-Hungary, was assassinated in Sarajevo, Bosnia. This act of political violence set off a crisis that concluded with the outbreak of a European war that became a worldwide conflict involving numerous colonies of the European imperial powers and the United States. Originally known as the Great War, World War I witnessed unprecedented loss of life and destruction of property. The war constituted the defining event of the twentieth century from which followed revolution first in Russia and later in Germany and Austria. The Ottoman Empire would also collapse. From that time to the present day the vast semicircle of territories commencing in Germany in central Europe, passing through eastern Europe and the Balkans into Turkey, and then across northeastern Africa into the Arab Peninsula has for almost a century witnessed violent shifts in political power and political ideologies.

Moreover, the deeply flawed peace settlement that ended World War I planted the seeds of ongoing European international tension, economic dislocation, and conflict. That settlement treated Germany harshly, though presumably no more harshly than Germany would have treated its foes had it been victorious. Despite the severity of the settlement toward Germany, the new international system failed to provide realistic and effective safeguards against a return to power by a vengeful Germany. The withdrawal of the United States into a disdainful isolation from world affairs further destroyed the basis for keeping the peace on which Britain and France relied. The peace settlement also produced domestic economic problems that played into the hands of extreme political parties that wished to overturn the post–World War I peace settlement.

World War I, which produced these extensive ongoing destructive results, originated in the domestic unrest among subject nationalities on the Continent and the imperial rivalries among the great powers that built up in the decades after the unification of Germany and Italy. The ferocity of the conflict was the result of the modern armament of European nations made possible by the Second Industrial Revolution. The conflict reached its worldwide extent because of the empires created by European states in the nineteenth century and the rise to the status of a great power by the United States.

For more than two decades after 1871 European diplomats and political leaders through various alliances had been able to contain and resolve those domestic and international tensions while Europe prospered and exerted vast global influence. After 1890, however, Europe witnessed a series of international crises that might have but did not lead to war. It also witnessed important diplomatic realignments. Then in the summer of 1914 the crisis in the Balkans following the assassination of heir to the throne of Austria-Hungary erupted into a conflict of previously unimaginable extent, destruction, and political upheaval that lasted until 1918.

26.1 Emergence of the German Empire and the Alliance Systems (1873–1890)

Why did the alliance system fail?

Prussia's victories over Austria and France and its creation of a large, powerful German Empire in 1871 revolutionized European diplomacy. A vast new political unit had united the majority of Germans to form a nation of great and growing population, wealth, industrial capacity, and military power. Its sudden appearance created new problems and upset the balance of power that the Congress of Vienna had forged. Britain and Russia retained their positions, although the Crimean War had weakened the latter.

Austria, however, had been severely weakened, and the forces of nationalism threatened it with disintegration. The Franco-Prussian War and the German annexation of Alsace-Lorraine badly damaged French power and prestige. The French were afraid of their powerful new neighbor as well as resentful of their defeat, their loss of territory, and the loss of their traditional position as the dominant Western European power.

26.1.1 Bismarck's Leadership

Until 1890, Bismarck continued to guide German policy. After 1871, he insisted Germany was a satisfied power and wanted no further territorial gains, and he meant it. He wanted to avoid a new war that might undo his achievement. He tried to assuage French resentment by pursuing friendly relations and by supporting French colonial aspirations. He also prepared for the worst. If France could not be conciliated, it must be isolated. Bismarck sought to prevent an alliance between France and any other European power—especially Austria or Russia—that would threaten Germany with a war on two fronts.

26.1.1.1 WAR IN THE BALKANS Bismarck's first move was to establish the Three Emperors' League in 1873. The league brought together the three great conservative empires of Germany, Austria, and Russia. The league soon collapsed over Austro-Russian rivalry in the Balkans stemming from the Russo-Turkish War that broke out in 1877. The tottering Ottoman Empire was held together chiefly because the European powers could not agree about how

BISMARCK WITH THE KAISER Bismarck and the young Kaiser William II meet in 1888. The two disagreed over many issues, and in 1890 William dismissed the aged chancellor.
SOURCE: Classic Image/Alamy Stock Photo

to partition it. Ottoman weakness encouraged Serbia and Montenegro to come to the aid of their fellow Slavs in Bosnia and Herzegovina when they revolted against Turkish rule. Soon the rebellion spread to Bulgaria.

Then Russia entered the fray and turned it into a major international crisis. The Russians hoped to pursue their traditional policy of expansion at Ottoman expense and especially to gain control of Constantinople and the Dardanelles. Russian intervention also reflected the influence of the Pan-Slavic movement, which sought to unite all the Slavic peoples, even those under Austrian or Ottoman rule, under the protection of Holy Mother Russia.

The Ottoman Empire was soon forced to sue for peace. The Treaty of San Stefano of March 1878 was a Russian triumph. The Slavic states in the Balkans were freed of Ottoman rule, and Russia itself obtained territory and a large monetary indemnity. The settlement, however, alarmed the other great powers. Austria feared that the Slavic victory and the

increase in Russian influence in the Balkans would threaten its own Balkan provinces. The British were alarmed both by the effect of the Russian victory on the European balance of power and by the possibility of Russian control of the Dardanelles, which would make Russia a Mediterranean power and threaten Britain's control of the Suez Canal.

26.1.1.2 THE CONGRESS OF BERLIN Britain and Austria forced Russia to agree to an international conference at which the other great powers would review the provisions of San Stefano. The resulting **Congress of Berlin** met in June and July 1878 under the presidency of Bismarck. The choice of site and presiding officer were a clear recognition of Germany's new importance and of Bismarck's claim that Germany wanted no new territory and sought to preserve the peace.

The decisions of the congress were a blow to Russian ambitions. Bulgaria, a Russian client, was reduced in size by two-thirds and deprived of access to the Aegean Sea. Austria-Hungary was given Bosnia and Herzegovina to "occupy and administer," although those provinces remained formally under Ottoman rule. Britain received Cyprus, and France was encouraged to occupy Tunisia. These territories were compensation for the gains that Russia was permitted to keep. Germany asked for nothing but still earned Russian resentment. The Russians believed they had saved Prussia in 1807 from complete destruction by Napoleon and had expected German gratitude. They were bitterly disappointed, and the Three Emperors' League was dead.

The Berlin settlement also annoyed the Balkan states. Romania wanted Bessarabia, which Russia kept; Bulgaria wanted the borders of the Treaty of San Stefano; and Greece wanted more Ottoman territory. The major trouble spot, however, was in the south Slavic states of Serbia and Montenegro. They resented the Austrian occupation of Bosnia and Herzegovina, as did many of the natives of those provinces. The south Slavic question, no less than the estrangement between Russia and Germany, was a threat to the peace of Europe.

26.1.1.3 GERMAN ALLIANCES WITH RUSSIA AND AUSTRIA For the moment, Bismarck could ignore the Balkans, but he could not ignore the breach in his eastern alliance system. With Russia alienated, he concluded a secret treaty with Austria in 1879. This Dual Alliance provided that Germany and Austria would come to one another's aid if Russia attacked either of them. If another country attacked one of them, each promised at least to maintain neutrality.

The treaty was for five years and was renewed regularly until 1918. As the anchor of German policy, it was criticized at the time, and in retrospect, some have considered it an error. It appeared to tie German fortunes to those of the troubled Austro-Hungarian Empire and thus to borrow trouble for Germany. That is, Germany was much more likely to be drawn into aiding Austria-Hungary than the reverse. In addition, by isolating the Russians, the Dual Alliance pushed them to seek alliances in the West.

Bismarck was fully aware of these dangers but discounted them with good reason. He personally never allowed the alliance to drag Germany into Austria's Balkan quarrels. As he put it, in any alliance there is a horse and a rider, and he meant Germany to be the rider. He made it clear to the Austrians that the alliance was purely defensive and Germany would never be a party to an attack on Russia. "For us," he said, "Balkan questions can never be a motive for war."

Bismarck believed that monarchical, reactionary Russia would not seek an alliance either with republican, revolutionary France or with increasingly democratic Britain. In fact, he expected the Austro-German negotiations to frighten Russia into seeking closer relations with Germany, and he was right. By 1881, he had renewed the Three Emperors' League on a firmer basis.

26.1.1.4 THE TRIPLE ALLIANCE In 1882, Italy, ambitious for colonial expansion and angered by the French occupation of Tunisia, asked to join the Dual Alliance. The provisions of its entry were defensive and directed against France. Bismarck's policy was now a complete success. He was allied with three of the great powers and friendly with the other, Great Britain, which held aloof from all alliances. France was isolated and no threat. Bismarck's diplomacy was a great achievement, but an even greater challenge was to maintain this complicated system of secret alliances in the face of the continuing rivalries among Germany's allies. Despite a war in 1885 between Serbia and Bulgaria that again estranged Austria and Russia, Bismarck succeeded.

Although the Three Emperors' League lapsed, the Triple Alliance (Germany, Austria, and Italy) was renewed for another five years. To restore German relations with Russia, Bismarck negotiated the Reinsurance Treaty of 1887, in which both powers promised to remain neutral if either was attacked. All seemed smooth, but a change in the German monarchy upset Bismarck's arrangements.

In 1888, William II (r. 1888–1918) came to the German throne. He was twenty-nine years old, ambitious, and impetuous. He was imperious by temperament and believed he ruled by divine right. An injury at birth had left him with a withered left arm. He compensated for this disability with vigorous exercise, a military bearing, and an often embarrassingly bombastic rhetoric.

Like many Germans of his generation, William II was filled with a sense of Germany's destiny as the leading power of Europe. He wanted recognition of at least equality with Britain, the land of his mother and of his grandmother, Queen Victoria. To achieve a "place in the sun," he and his contemporaries wanted a navy and colonies like

Britain's. These aims, of course, ran counter to Bismarck's limited continental policy. When William argued for a navy as a defense against a British landing in North Germany, Bismarck replied, "If the British should land on our soil, I should have them arrested." This was only one example of the great distance between the young emperor, or kaiser, and his chancellor. In 1890, William used a disagreement over domestic policy to dismiss Bismarck.

As long as Bismarck held power, Germany was secure, and the great European powers remained at peace. Although he made mistakes, his understanding and management of international relations in the real world was admirable. He had a clear and limited idea of his nation's goals, and he resisted pressures for further expansion with few and insignificant exceptions. Bismarck understood and used the full range of diplomatic weapons: appeasement and deterrence, threats and promises, secrecy and openness. He tried to help other countries satisfy their needs or used those countries to his advantage. His system of alliances created a stalemate in the Balkans and ensured German security.

During Bismarck's time, Germany was increasingly understood to be a force for European peace. This position would not, of course, have been possible without its great military power. It also required, however, the leadership of a statesman able to exercise restraint and understand what his country needed and what was possible.

26.1.2 Forging the Triple Entente (1890–1907)

Almost immediately after Bismarck's retirement, his system of alliances collapsed. His successor was General Leo von Caprivi (1831–1899), who had once asked, "What kind of jackass will dare to be Bismarck's successor?" Caprivi refused the Russian request to renew the Reinsurance Treaty, in part because he felt incompetent to continue Bismarck's complicated policy and in part because he wished to draw Germany closer to Britain. But Britain remained aloof, and Russia was alienated.

26.1.2.1 FRANCO–RUSSIAN ALLIANCE Even Bismarck had assumed that ideological differences would prevent a Franco–Russian alliance. Political isolation and the need for foreign capital, however, drove the Russians toward France. The French, who were even more isolated, encouraged their investors to pour capital into Russia if such investment would ensure security against Germany. In 1894, France and Russia signed a defensive alliance against Germany.

26.1.2.2 BRITAIN AND GERMANY Britain now became the key to the international situation. Colonial rivalries pitted the British against the Russians in Central Asia and against the French in Africa. Traditionally, Britain had also opposed Russian control of Constantinople and the Dardanelles and French control of the Low Countries. There was no reason to think Britain would soon become friendly with its traditional rivals or abandon its accustomed friendliness toward the Germans.

Yet within a decade of William II's accession, Germany had become the enemy in British minds. Before the turn of the century, popular British thrillers about imaginary wars portrayed the French as the invader; after the turn of the century, the enemy was usually Germany. This remarkable transformation has often been attributed to economic rivalry between Germany and Britain, in which Germany challenged and even overtook British production in various materials and markets. Certainly, Germany was economically superior, and the British resented them. Yet the economic problem was not a serious cause of hostility, and it waned during the first decade of the century. The real problem lay in the foreign and naval policies of the German emperor and his ministers.

William II admired Britain's colonial empire and mighty fleet. At first, Germany tried to win the British over to the Triple Alliance, but when Britain clung to its "splendid isolation," German policy changed. The idea was to demonstrate Germany's worth as an ally by withdrawing support and even making trouble for Britain. This odd manner of gaining an ally reflected the kaiser's confused feelings toward Britain, which mixed dislike and jealousy with admiration. Many Germans, especially in the intellectual community, shared these feelings. Like William, they were eager for Germany to pursue a world policy rather than Bismarck's limited one that confined German interests to Europe. They too saw England as the barrier to German ambitions. Their influence in schools, universities, and the press guaranteed popular approval of hostility to Britain.

In Africa, the Germans blocked British attempts to build a railroad from Cape Town to Cairo. They also openly sympathized with the Boers of South Africa in their resistance to British expansion. In 1896, William congratulated Paul Kruger (1825–1904), president of the Boer Transvaal Republic, for repulsing a British raid "without having to appeal to friendly powers [i.e., Germany] for assistance."

In 1898, William began to realize his dream of a German navy with the passage of a naval law providing for the construction of nineteen battleships. In 1900, a second law doubled that figure. The architect of the new navy was Admiral Alfred von Tirpitz (1849–1930), who openly proclaimed that Germany's naval policy was aimed at Britain.

The naval policy was a failure. It wasted German resources and began a great naval race with Britain. Eventually, the threat the German navy posed so antagonized and alarmed the British that they abandoned their traditional policies of avoiding alliances.

26.1.2.3 THE ENTENTE CORDIALE The first breach of Britain's isolation came in 1902, when it concluded an alliance with Japan to defend British interests in the Far East

against Russia. Next, Britain abandoned its traditional antagonism toward France and in 1904 concluded a series of agreements with the French, collectively known as the **Entente Cordiale**. It was not a formal treaty and had no military provisions, but it settled outstanding colonial differences between the two nations. In particular, Britain gave France a free hand in Morocco in return for French recognition of British control over Egypt. The Entente Cordiale was a long step toward aligning the British with Germany's great potential enemy.

Britain's new relationship with France was surprising, but in 1904, hardly anyone believed the British whale and the Russian bear would ever come together. The **Russo–Japanese War** of 1904–1905 made such a development seem even less likely because Britain was allied with Russia's enemy, but Britain had behaved with restraint, and their unexpected defeat, which also led to the Russian Revolution of 1905, humiliated the Russians. Although the revolution was put down, it weakened Russia and reduced British apprehensions about Russian power. The British also became concerned that Russia might again drift into the German orbit.

26.1.2.4 THE FIRST MOROCCAN CRISIS At this point, Germany decided to test the new understanding between Britain and France. In March 1905, Emperor William II landed at Tangier, made a speech in favor of Moroccan independence, and by implication asserted Germany's right to participate in Morocco's destiny. This speech was a challenge to France.

The Germans demanded an international conference to show their power more dramatically. The conference met in 1906 at Algeciras in Spain. Austria sided with its German ally, but Spain, which also had claims in Morocco, Italy, Russia, and the United States, voted with Britain and France. The Germans had overplayed their hand, receiving trivial concessions, and the French position in Morocco was confirmed. German bullying had, moreover, driven Britain and France closer together. Facing a possible German attack on France, Sir Edward Grey (1862–1933), the British foreign secretary, without making a firm commitment, authorized conversations between the British and French general staffs. Their agreements became morally binding as the years passed. By 1914, French and British military and naval plans were so mutually dependent that the two countries were effectively, if not formally, allies.

26.1.2.5 BRITISH AGREEMENT WITH RUSSIA Britain's fear of Germany's growing naval power; its concern over German ambitions in the Near East, as represented by the German-sponsored plan to build a railroad from Berlin to Baghdad; and its closer relations with France made it desirable for Britain to become more friendly with France's ally, Russia. With French support, in 1907 the British concluded an agreement with Russia much like the Entente Cordiale with France. It settled Russo–British quarrels in

Central Asia and opened the door for wider cooperation. The Triple Entente, an informal but powerful association of Britain, France, and Russia, was now ranged against the Triple Alliance. Italy was an unreliable ally, however, which meant two great land powers and Great Britain encircled Germany and Austria-Hungary.

William II and his ministers had turned Bismarck's nightmare of the prospect of a two-front war with France and Russia into a reality. They had made it even worse by adding Britain to their foes. The equilibrium that Bismarck had worked so hard to achieve was destroyed. Britain would no longer support Austria in restraining Russian ambitions in the Balkans. Germany, increasingly alarmed

by a sense of being encircled, was less willing to restrain the Austrians for fear of alienating them too.

26.2 World War I

How did conflict in the Balkans lead to the outbreak of general war in Europe?

Bismarck had built his alliance system to maintain peace, but the new alliance of Britain, France, and Russia increased the risk of war and made the Balkans a likely spot for it to break out. Bismarck's diplomacy had left France isolated and impotent. The new alliance associated France with

PUNCH, OR THE LONDON CHARIVARI.—October 2, 1912.

THE BOILING POINT.

THE BOILING POINT As this aptly titled cartoon from an October 2, 1912, issue of the British magazine *Punch* illustrates, tensions in the Balkans reached a boiling point in the years leading up to the outbreak of World War I. The men atop the bubbling cauldron of "Balkan Troubles" represent the leaders of Europe trying to keep the lid on an explosive situation.
SOURCE: Heritage Image Partnership Ltd/Alamy Stock Photo

the two greatest powers in Europe besides Germany. The Germans could rely only on Austria, and Austria was less likely to provide aid than to need it.

26.2.1 The Road to War (1908–1914)

The weak Ottoman Empire still controlled the central strip of the Balkan Peninsula running west from Constantinople to the Adriatic. North and south of it were the independent states of Romania, Serbia, Montenegro, and Greece, as well as Bulgaria, technically still part of the empire but legally autonomous and practically independent. The Austro-Hungarian Empire included Croatia and Slovenia and since 1878, had "occupied and administered" Bosnia and Herzegovina.

Except for the Greeks and the Romanians, most of the inhabitants of the Balkans spoke variants of the same Slavic language and felt a cultural and historical kinship with each another. For centuries Austrians, Hungarians, or Turks had ruled them, and the nationalism that characterized late-nineteenth-century Europe made many of them eager for independence. The more radical among them longed for a union of the south Slavic, or Yugoslav, peoples in a single nation. They looked to independent Serbia as the center of the new nation and hoped to detach all the Slavic provinces, especially Bosnia, which bordered on Serbia, from Austria. Serbia believed its destiny was to unite the Slavs at the expense of Austria, as Piedmont had united the Italians and Prussia the Germans.

KEY EVENTS IN THE RUN-UP TO WORLD WAR I	
1871	The end of the Franco-Prussian War; creation of the German Empire; German annexation of Alsace-Lorraine
1873	The Three Emperors' League (Germany, Russia, and Austria-Hungary)
1877–1878	The Russo–Turkish War
1878	The Congress of Berlin
1879	The Dual Alliance between Germany and Austria
1881	The Three Emperors' League is renewed
1882	Italy joins Germany and Austria in the Triple Alliance
1888	William II becomes the German emperor
1890	Bismarck is dismissed
1894	The Franco–Russian alliance
1898	Germany begins to build a battleship navy
1899–1902	Boer War
1902	The British alliance with Japan
1904	The Entente Cordiale between Britain and France
1904–1905	The Russo–Japanese War
1905–1906	The first Moroccan crisis
1907	The British agreement with Russia
1908–1909	The Bosnian crisis
1911	The second Moroccan crisis
1911	Italy attacks Turkey
1912–1913	The First and Second Balkan Wars
1914	Outbreak of World War I

In 1908, a group of modernizing reformers called the Young Turks seized power in the Ottoman Empire. Their actions threatened to breathe new life into the empire and to interfere with the plans of the European jackals to pounce on the Ottoman corpse. These events brought on the first of a series of Balkan crises that would eventually lead to war.

26.2.1.1 THE BOSNIAN CRISIS
In 1908, the Austrian and Russian governments decided to act quickly before Turkey became strong enough to resist. They struck a bargain in which Russia agreed to support the Austrian annexation of Bosnia and Herzegovina in return for Austrian backing for opening the Dardanelles to Russian warships.

Austria, however, declared the annexation before the Russians could act. The British and French, eager for the favor of the Young Turks, refused to agree to the Russian demand to open the Dardanelles. The Russians were humiliated and furious but too weak to do anything but protest. The Austrian annexation of Bosnia enraged Russia's "little brothers," the Serbs.

Germany had not been warned of Austria's plans and was unhappy because the action threatened their relations with Russia and Turkey. Germany felt so dependent on the Dual Alliance, however, that it nevertheless assured Austria of its support. Austria had been given a free hand, and to some extent, Vienna was now making German policy. It was a dangerous precedent. In addition, the failure of Britain and France to support Russia strained the Triple Entente. This made it harder for them to oppose Russian interests in the future if they were to keep Russian friendship.

26.2.1.2 THE SECOND MOROCCAN CRISIS
The second Moroccan crisis in 1911 emphasized the French and British need for mutual support. When France sent an army to Morocco, Germany took the opportunity to "protect German interests" there as a means to extort colonial concessions in the French Congo. To add force to their demands, the Germans sent the gunboat *Panther* to the Moroccan port of Agadir, purportedly to protect German citizens there. Once again, as in 1905, the Germans went too far. The *Panther*'s visit to Agadir provoked a strong reaction in Britain. For some time Anglo-German relations had been growing worse, chiefly because the naval race had intensified. In 1907, Germany had built its first dreadnought, a new type of battleship that Britain had launched in 1906. In 1908, Germany had passed still another naval law that accelerated the challenge to British naval supremacy.

These actions threatened Britain's security. Britain had to increase taxes to pay for new armaments just when its liberal government was launching its expensive program of social legislation. Negotiations failed to persuade William II and Tirpitz to slow down naval construction.

In this atmosphere, when the British learned of the *Panther's* arrival in Morocco, they wrongly believed the Germans meant to turn Agadir into a naval base on the Atlantic. The crisis passed when France yielded some insignificant bits of the Congo and Germany recognized the French protectorate over Morocco. Britain drew closer to France. The British made plans to send an expeditionary force to defend France in case Germany attacked, and the British and French navies agreed to cooperate. Without any formal treaty, the German naval construction and the Agadir crisis had turned the Entente Cordiale into a de facto alliance. If Germany attacked France, Britain would now have to defend the French, as the security of each was inextricably tied up with the other.

26.2.1.3 WAR IN THE BALKANS The second Moroccan crisis also provoked another conflict in the Balkans. Italy sought to gain colonies and to take its place among the great powers. It wanted Libya, which, though worth little before the discovery of oil in the 1950s, was at least available. Italy feared that the recognition of the French protectorate in Morocco would encourage France to move into Libya also. In 1911, Italy attacked the Ottoman Empire to preempt the French and forced Turkey to cede Libya and the Dodecanese Islands in the Aegean. The Italian victory encouraged the Balkan states to try their luck. In 1912, Bulgaria, Greece, Montenegro, and Serbia jointly attacked the Ottoman Empire and won easily. (See Map 26–1.) After this First Balkan War, the victors fell out among themselves over the division of Macedonia, and in 1913 a Second Balkan War erupted. This time, Turkey and Romania joined Serbia and Greece against Bulgaria and stripped away much of what the Bulgarians had gained in 1878 and 1912.

After the First Balkan War, the alarmed Austrians were determined to limit Serbian gains and especially to prevent the Serbs from gaining a port on the Adriatic. This policy meant keeping Serbia out of Albania, but the Russians backed the Serbs and tensions mounted. An international conference sponsored by Britain in early 1913 resolved the dispute in Austria's favor and called for an independent principality of Albania. Austria, however, felt humiliated by the public airing of Serbian demands, and the Serbs defied the powers and continued to occupy parts of Albania. Finally, in October 1913, Austria issued an ultimatum, and Serbia withdrew its forces from Albania.

The lessons learned from this crisis of 1913 influenced behavior in the final crisis in 1914. As in 1908, the Russians had been embarrassed by their passivity, and their allies were more reluctant to restrain them again. The Austrians were embarrassed by the results of accepting an international conference and were determined not to do it again. They had gotten better results from threatening to use force; they and their German allies did not disregard this lesson.

26.2.2 Sarajevo and the Outbreak of War (June–August 1914)

The assassination of the Austrian archduke set in motion a chain of events that culminated in the outbreak of the war. On the one hand, the incident provided a desired pretext for Austria to attack Serbia. But the need for support from Germany and the complex relations among the great powers complicated the picture.

Map 26–1 THE BALKANS, 1912–1913

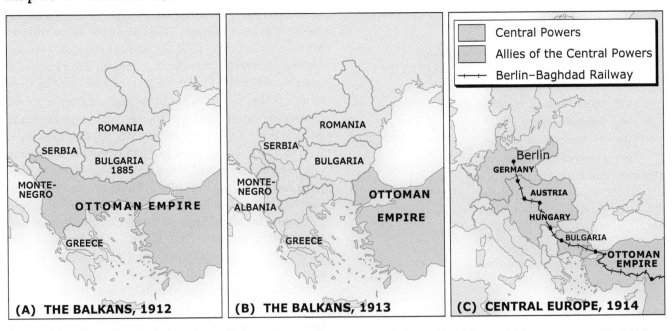

(A) THE BALKANS, 1912

(B) THE BALKANS, 1913

(C) CENTRAL EUROPE, 1914

Central Powers
Allies of the Central Powers
Berlin–Baghdad Railway

The first two maps show the Balkans before and after the two Balkan wars; note the Ottoman retreat. The third map shows the geographical relationship of the Central Powers and their Bulgarian and Turkish allies.

26.2.2.1 THE ASSASSINATION

On June 28, 1914, a nine-teen-year-old Serbian nationalist shot and killed Archduke Francis Ferdinand, heir to the Austrian throne, and his wife as they drove in an open car through the Bosnian capital of Sarajevo. The assassin was a member of a conspiracy hatched by a political terrorist society called Union or Death, better known as the **Black Hand.** The chief of intelligence of the Serbian army's general staff had helped plan the crime. Though his role was not known at the time, it was generally believed throughout Europe that Serbian officials were involved. The glee of the Serbian press after the assassination lent support to that belief.

The archduke was not popular in Austria, and his funeral evoked little grief. He had been known to favor a form of federal government for Austria that would have raised the status of the Slavs in the empire. This position alienated the conservatives among the Habsburg officials and the Hungarians. It also threatened the radical nationalists' dream of an independent south Slav state.

26.2.2.2 GERMANY AND AUSTRIA'S RESPONSE

News of the assassination produced outrage everywhere in Europe except in Serbia. To those Austrians who had long favored an attack on Serbia, the opportunity seemed irresistible, but it was never easy for the Dual Monarchy to make a decision. Conrad von Hotzendorf (1852–1925), chief of the Austrian general staff, urged an attack, as he had often done. Count Stefan Tisza (1861–1918), speaking for Hungary, resisted. Count Leopold von Berchtold (1863–1942), the Austro-Hungarian foreign minister, felt the need for strong action, but he knew German support would be required in the likely event that Russia should intervene to protect Serbia. Moreover, nothing could be done without Tisza's approval, and only German support could persuade the Hungarians

to accept a war. The question of peace or war against Serbia, therefore, had to be answered in Berlin.

William II and Chancellor Theobald von Bethmann-Hollweg (1856–1921) readily promised German support for an attack on Serbia. It has often been said that they gave the Austrians a "blank check," but their message was more specific than that. They urged the Austrians to move swiftly while the other powers were still angry at Serbia. They also made the Austrians feel that a failure to act would be evidence of Austria-Hungary's weakness and uselessness as an ally. Therefore, the Austrians never wavered in their determination to make war on Serbia. They hoped, with the protection of Germany, to fight Serbia alone, but they were prepared to risk a general European conflict. The Germans also knew they risked a general war, but they too hoped to "localize" the fight between Austria and Serbia.

Some scholars believe Germany had long been plotting war, and some even think a specific plan for war in 1914 was set in motion as early as 1912. The vast body of evidence on the crisis of 1914, however, gives little support to such notions. The German leaders plainly reacted to a crisis they had not foreseen and just as plainly made decisions in response to events. The decision to support Austria, however, made war difficult, if not impossible, to avoid. The emperor and chancellor made that decision without consulting either their military or diplomatic advisers.

William II reacted violently to the assassination. He was moved by his friendship for the archduke and by outrage at an attack on royalty. A different provocation would probably not have moved him so much. Bethmann-Hollweg was less emotional but under severe pressure. To resist the decision would have meant flatly opposing the emperor. The German army suspected the chancellor of being soft. It would have been difficult for him to take a conciliatory

THE ASSASSINATION OF ARCHDUKE FERDINAND AND HIS WIFE The Austrian archduke Francis Ferdinand and his wife descend to an awaiting motorcar on June 28, 1914, in Sarajevo (left). Later that day, the royal couple was killed by young revolutionaries trained in and supplied by Serbia, igniting the crisis that led to World War I. Moments after the assassination, the Austrian police captured one of the assassins (right).
SOURCE: Pictorial Press Ltd/Alamy Stock Photo

position. Important military leaders, especially General Helmut von Moltke (1848–1916), Chief of the General Staff since 1906, had come to believe that the growing power of Russia threatened Germany. Moltke repeatedly spoke of the need for a decisive war against Russia, and its allies if necessary, "the sooner the better." His influence would be important at key moments during the crisis.

Bethmann-Hollweg, like many other Germans, also feared for the future. Russia was recovering its strength and would reach a military peak in 1917. The Triple Entente was growing closer and more powerful, and Germany's only reliable ally was Austria. The chancellor recognized the danger of supporting Austria, but he believed it even more dangerous to withhold that support. If Austria did not crush Serbia, it might collapse before the onslaught of Slavic nationalism backed by Russia. If Germany did not defend its ally, the Austrians might look elsewhere for help. His policy was one of calculated risk.

Unfortunately, the calculations proved to be incorrect. Bethmann-Hollweg hoped the Austrians would strike swiftly, presenting the powers with a fait accompli while the outrage of the assassination was still fresh and that German support would deter Russia. Failing that, he was prepared for a continental war against France and Russia. This policy, though, depended on British neutrality, and the German chancellor convinced himself the British would stand aloof.

The Austrians, however, were slow to act. They did not even deliver their deliberately unacceptable ultimatum to Serbia until July 23, when general hostility toward Serbia had begun to subside. Serbia further embarrassed the Austrians by returning so soft and conciliatory an answer that even the mercurial German emperor thought it removed all reason for war, but the Austrians were determined not to turn back. On July 28, they declared war on Serbia, even though the army would not be ready to attack until mid-August.

26.2.2.3 THE TRIPLE ENTENTE'S RESPONSE The
Russians, previously so often forced to back off, responded angrily to the Austrian demands on Serbia. The most conservative elements of the Russian government feared that war would lead to revolution, as it had in 1905, but nationalists, Pan-Slavs, and most of the politically conscious classes in general demanded action. The government responded by ordering partial mobilization against Austria only. This policy was militarily impossible, but its intention was to put diplomatic pressure on Austria to refrain from attacking Serbia.

Mobilization of any kind, however, was a dangerous weapon because it was generally understood to be equivalent to an act of war. In fact, only Germany's war plan made mobilization the first and irrevocable start of a war. It required a quick victory in the west before the Russians were ready to act. Even partial Russian mobilization seemed

to jeopardize this plan and put Germany in great danger. From this point on, the General Staff pressed for German mobilization and war, and their claim of military necessity soon became irresistible.

France and Britain were not eager for war. France's president and prime minister were on their way back from a long-planned state visit to Russia when the crisis flared on July 23. In their absence and without consulting his government, the French ambassador to Russia assured the Russians of support as Germany had for Austria. The British worked hard to resolve the crisis by traditional means: a conference of the powers. Austria, still smarting from its humiliation after the London Conference of 1913, would not hear of it. The Germans privately supported the Austrians but publicly took on a conciliatory tone to placate the British.

On July 30, Austria ordered mobilization against Russia. Bethmann-Hollweg resisted the enormous pressure to mobilize not because he hoped to avoid war but because he wanted Russia to mobilize against Germany first and appear to be the aggressor. Only in that way could he win the support of the German nation for war, especially the backing of pacifist Social Democrats. His luck was good for a change. The news of Russian general mobilization came only minutes before Germany would have mobilized in any case. Germany then declared war on Russia on August 1. The Schlieffen Plan went into effect. The Germans occupied Luxembourg on August 2 and invaded Belgium, which resisted, on August 3—the same day Germany declared war on France. The invasion of Belgium violated the treaty of 1839 in which the British had joined the other powers in guaranteeing Belgian neutrality. This factor undermined sentiment in Britain for neutrality and united the nation against Germany, which then invaded France. On August 4, Britain declared war on Germany.

The Great War had begun. As Sir Edward Grey, the British foreign secretary, put it, the lights were going out all over Europe. They would come on again, but Europe would never be the same.

Although debate on the causes of the war continues, the most common opinion today is that German ambitions for a higher place in the international order under the new **kaiser William II** led to a new challenge to the status quo. German bullying resulted in a series of crises that led to the final crisis in July 1914, when Germany supported—indeed, pushed—its only reliable ally Austria into a war against Serbia that touched off the world war.

The deeper causes of that war are seen to be Germany's new ambitions to become a world power like Great Britain and to become the dominant power on the European continent. Germany's decision to build a battleship navy threatened Britain's interests and security. In response, the British launched an expensive and unwelcome naval race to maintain their superiority at sea and abandoned their cherished "splendid isolation" and long-standing competitions with France and Russia. In an unprecedented reversal of policy, they made an alliance with Japan and agreements with France and Russia to form the Triple Entente, which grew from a set of colonial accords to an informal, but visible, check on German ambitions. This new international configuration alarmed Germany, which complained that jealous and hostile forces were encircling it. The Germans feared the growing power of the its enemies, but Germany did not seriously attempt to ease the tension. Instead, a new arms race ensued, and Germany assumed a rigid stance in the final crisis that ended in war.

26.2.3 Strategies and Stalemate: 1914–1917

Throughout Europe, jubilation greeted the outbreak of war. No general war had been fought since Napoleon, and few understood the horrors of modern warfare. The dominant memory was of Bismarck's swift and decisive campaigns, in which the costs and casualties were light and the rewards great. After years of crises and resentments, war came as a

release of tension. The popular press had increased public awareness of, and interest in, foreign affairs and had fanned the flames of patriotism. The prospect of war moved even a rational man of science like Sigmund Freud to say, "My whole libido goes out to Austria-Hungary."

The Triple Entente powers—or the Allies, as they called themselves—held superiority in numbers and financial resources, as well as command of the sea (see Figure 26–1). Germany and Austria, the Central Powers, had the advantages of possessing internal lines of communication and having launched their attack first.

26.2.3.1 A NEW STYLE OF WAR Both sides expected a war of movement, like the European wars of the later nineteenth century, that would end quickly with a few battles that would prove decisive. The American Civil War, where improved weapons produced enormous casualties that, in turn, caused the armies to dig lines of trenches and erect field fortifications, was a terrible war that lasted for four years. The Europeans took little notice. Both sides continued to believe in the decisiveness of the offensive and planned for a quick victory. The development of ever more powerful

Figure 26–1 RELATIVE STRENGTHS OF THE COMBATANTS IN WORLD WAR I

	POPULATION (TOTAL)	SOLDIERS POTENTIALLY AVAILABLE	MILITARY EXPENDITURES (1913–1914)	BATTLESHIPS IN SERVICE OR BEING BUILT	CRUISERS	SUBMARINES	MERCHANT SHIPS (TONS)
GREAT BRITAIN	Overseas Emp. 390 Million 45,000,000	711,000	250,000,000	64	121	64	20,000,000
FRANCE	Overseas Emp. 58 Million 40,000,000	1,250,000	185,000,000	28	34	73	2,000,000
ITALY	Overseas Emp. 2 Million 35,000,000	750,000	50,000,000	14	22	12	1,750,000
RUSSIA	164,000,000	1,200,000	335,000,000	16	14	29	750,000
BELGIUM	7,500,000	180,000	13,750,000				
ROMANIA	7,500,000	420,000	15,000,000				
GREECE	5,000,000	120,000	3,750,000				
SERBIA	5,000,000	195,000	5,250,000				
MONTE-NEGRO	500,000						
UNITED STATES	92,000,000	150,000	150,000,000	37	35	25	4,500,000
GERMANY	65,000,000	2,200,000	300,000,000	40	57	23	5,000,000
AUSTRIA-HUNGARY	50,000,000	810,000	110,000,000	16	12	6	1,000,000
OTTOMAN EMPIRE	20,000,000	360,000	40,000,000				
BULGARIA	4,500,000	340,000	5,500,000				

The Triple Entente powers—or the Allies, as they called themselves—held superiority in numbers and financial resources, as well as command of the sea.

BLINDED BY MUSTARD GAS The use of poison gas (by both sides) during World War I and its dreadful effects—blinding, asphyxiation, burned lungs—came to symbolize the horrors of modern war. This painting shows a group of British soldiers being guided to the rear after they were blinded by mustard gas on the western front.
SOURCE: Christie's Images/Bridgeman Images.

artillery, rifles with greater range and accuracy, and especially machine guns, however, gave the advantage to the defense. The German offensive in the west failed to break the Allied forces; both sides were forced to dig deep trenches protected by barbed wire and machine guns. Over time, airplanes and tanks were introduced, bringing warfare into the machine age, and casualties were terribly numerous. The armies were raised by conscription, even in Britain for the first time, making the conflict a total war. The number of casualties among the fighting forces was terrible, but the burden on the civilian population was also enormous.

26.2.3.2 THE HOME FRONT As the war continued, the demand for foodstuffs, supplies, and other necessities and their destruction on land and sea made it a war of exhaustion as well as of annihilation. Dangers and shortages of every kind plagued the people at home and forced important changes on them. Women, especially, encountered new opportunities and faced great challenges. With so many men off in the armed services, many of them had to take on the responsibilities of the head of the household as well as their usual duties. Soon, more and more women were drawn into jobs away from home, such as conducting streetcars, that were more demanding than the traditional limited sphere thought suitable for women but also better paying. As the demand for greater production grew, women were hired to do hard manual labor in munitions plants and other factories that had been thought to be for men only. These wartime experiences surely helped change society's view of the proper role of women.

26.2.3.3 GOVERNMENT CONTROL Early in the war, business and production continued in the usual way, but within months its inefficiency and inadequacy to deal with the new demands became obvious. Shortages, especially in munitions

and other military needs, led governments to intervene in the economy, production, and other aspects of life and increasingly to control the lives of their subjects and citizens. Shortages led to the rationing of food and other needed items. Germany, which relied heavily on imports to feed its people, blockaded by the Allies' navies, suffered especially, and the Germans' submarine campaign forced even Britain to resort to food rationing in the last years of the war.

The shortages also encouraged higher prices and black markets. Governments intervened to control prices and wages, but inflation pressed hard on the workers. In the early years of the war patriotism had prevented strikes and unrest, but growing hardship undermined class unity and led to renewed union activity and great numbers of strikes and protests that took a political turn. Governments on both sides suppressed and punished criticism, imposed censorship, and curtailed civil liberties.

26.2.3.4 THE CONDUCT OF THE WAR Germany's war plan was based on ideas developed by **Count Alfred von Schlieffen** (1833–1913), chief of the German general staff from 1891 to 1906. (See Map 26–2.) It aimed to outflank the French frontier defenses by sweeping through Belgium to the Channel and then wheeling to the south and east to envelop the French and crush them against the German fortresses in Lorraine. The secret of its success lay in making the right wing of the advancing German army immensely strong and deliberately weakening the left opposite the French frontier. The weakness of the left was meant to draw the French into attacking the wrong place while the war was decided on the German right. In the east, the Germans planned to stand on the defensive against Russia until France had been crushed, a task they thought would take only six weeks.

WOMEN MUNITIONS WORKERS IN ENGLAND World War I demanded more from civilian populations than had previous wars, resulting in important social changes. The demands of the munitions industries and a shortage of men (so many of whom were in uniform) brought many women out of traditional roles at home and into factories and other war-related work.
SOURCE: Hulton Archive/Stringer/Getty Images

Map 26–2   THE SCHLIEFFEN PLAN OF 1905

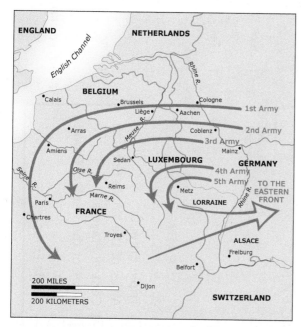

Germany's grand strategy for quickly winning the war against France in 1914 is shown by the wheeling arrows on the map. In the original plan, the crushing blows at France were to be followed by the release of troops for use against Russia on Germany's eastern front. The plan, however, was not adequately implemented. Instead the war on the western front became a long contest in place.

The apparent risk, besides the violation of Belgian neutrality and the consequent alienation of Britain, lay in weakening the German defenses against a direct attack across the frontier. The strength of German fortresses and the superior firepower of German howitzers made that risk more theoretical than real. The true danger was that the German striking force on the right through Belgium would not be powerful enough to make the swift progress vital to success. The execution of the plan fell to Count Helmuth von Moltke, the nephew of Bismarck's most effective general. Moltke added divisions to the left wing and even weakened the Russian front for the same purpose. For reasons still debated, the plan failed by a narrow margin.

26.2.3.5 THE WAR IN THE WEST   The French had also put their faith in the offensive, but with less reason than the Germans. They underestimated the numbers and effectiveness of the German reserves and overestimated the courage and spirit of their own troops. Courage and spirit could not defeat machine guns and heavy artillery. The French offensive on Germany's western frontier failed totally. This defeat probably was preferable to a partial success because it released troops for use against the main German army. As a result, the French and the British were able to stop the German advance on Paris at the **Battle of the Marne** in September 1914. (See Map 26–3 and Map 26–4.)

Map 26–3 WORLD WAR I IN EUROPE

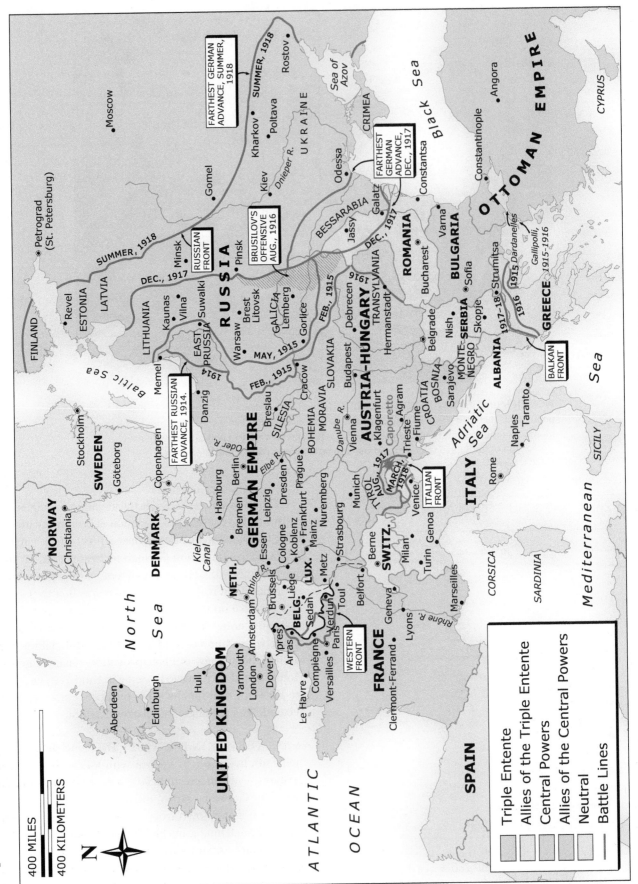

400 MILES

400 KILOMETERS

N

FARTHEST GERMAN ADVANCE, SUMMER, 1918

SUMMER, 1918

Moscow

Rostov

Sea of Azov

Petrograd (St. Petersburg)

FINLAND

SUMMER, 1918

Gomel

Kharkov

Poltava

FARTHEST GERMAN ADVANCE, DEC., 1917

UKRAINE

Kiev

Dnieper R.

Odessa

Angora

CYPRUS

OTTOMAN EMPIRE

Constantinople

Black Sea

DEC., 1917

RUSSIAN FRONT

Minsk

Pinsk

BRUSILOV'S OFFENSIVE AUG., 1916

BESSARABIA

Galatz

Constantsa

Varna

BULGARIA

Sofia

NORWAY

Christiania

SWEDEN

Stockholm

Göteborg

Revel

ESTONIA

LATVIA

Kaunas

Vilna

LITHUANIA

Suwalki

EAST PRUSSIA

1914

Brest Litovsk

RUSSIA

Jassy

Debrecen

TRANSYLVANIA

1916

ROMANIA

Bucharest

Hermanstadt

Nish

Strumitsa

1915

1916

1917–18

GREECE

Dardanelles

Gallipoli, 1915–1916

BALKAN FRONT

Copenhagen

DENMARK

Kiel Canal

Hamburg

Bremen

Berlin

Memel

Danzig

FARTHEST RUSSIAN ADVANCE, 1914.

Warsaw

MAY, 1915

FEB. 1915

Cracow

Breslau

SILESIA

Oder R.

Gorlice

Lemberg

GALICIA

FEB., 1915

SLOVAKIA

MORAVIA

BOHEMIA

Prague

GERMAN EMPIRE

Leipzig

Dresden

Essen

Cologne

Frankfurt

Nuremberg

Mainz

Koblenz

Munich

Vienna

Budapest

Klagenfurt

AUSTRIA-HUNGARY

Agram

CROATIA

Belgrade

Sarajevo

BOSNIA

SERBIA

MONTE-NEGRO

Skopje

ALBANIA

Taranto

Naples

ITALY

Rome

North Sea

UNITED KINGDOM

Aberdeen

Edinburgh

Hull

Yarmouth

London

Dover

Le Havre

Amsterdam

NETH.

Brussels

Liège

BELG.

Ypres

Arras

Sedan

Compiègne

Versailles

Paris

WESTERN FRONT

Verdun

Toul

Belfort

Strasbourg

Metz

LUX.

Rhine R.

Nancy

Geneva

SWITZ.

Berne

Milan

Turin

Genoa

TYROL

AUG., 1917

MARCH, 1918

Caporetto

ITALIAN FRONT

Venice

Trieste

Fiume

Adriatic Sea

CORSICA

SARDINIA

Mediterranean Sea

SICILY

Marseilles

Lyons

Clermont-Ferrand

Rhône R.

FRANCE

SPAIN

ATLANTIC OCEAN

Baltic Sea

Elbe R.

Danube R.

Kaunas

Strasbourg

Triple Entente

Allies of the Triple Entente

Central Powers

Allies of the Central Powers

Neutral

Battle Lines

Despite the importance of military action in the Far East, in the Arab world, and at sea, the main theaters of activity in World War I were in Europe.

Map 26–4 THE WESTERN FRONT, 1914–1918

This map shows the crucial western front in detail.

Thereafter, the nature of the war in the west became one of position instead of movement. Both sides dug in behind a wall of trenches protected by barbed wire that stretched from the North Sea to Switzerland. Strategically placed machine-gun nests made assaults difficult and dangerous. Both sides nonetheless attempted massive attacks preceded by artillery bombardments of unprecedented and horrible force and duration. Still, the defense was always able to recover and to bring up reserves fast enough to prevent a breakthrough.

Assaults that cost hundreds of thousands of lives produced advances of only hundreds of yards. Even poison gas proved ineffective. In 1916, the British introduced the tank, which eventually proved to be the answer to the machine gun. (See the "Closer Look" sidebar, which follows below, for a detailed look at the armored tank and its significance.) The Allied command was slow to understand this, however, and until the end of the war, defense was supreme. For three years after its establishment, the western front moved only a few miles in either direction.

26.2.3.6 THE WAR IN THE EAST In the east, the war began auspiciously for the Allies. The Russians advanced

into Austrian territory and inflicted heavy casualties, but Russian incompetence and German energy soon reversed the situation. In 1915, the Central Powers pressed their advantage in the east and drove into the Baltic states and Russian Poland, inflicting more than two million casualties in a single year.

As the battle lines hardened, both sides sought new allies. Turkey, because of its hostility to Russia, and Bulgaria, the enemy of Serbia, joined the Central Powers. Both sides bid for Italian support with promises of the spoils of victory. Because the Austrians held what the Italians wanted most, the Allies could promise more. In a secret treaty of 1915, they agreed to deliver to Italy after victory most of *Italia irredenta* (the South Tyrol, Trieste, and some of the Dalmatian Islands), plus colonies in Africa and a share of the Turkish Empire. By the spring of 1915, Italy was engaging Austrian armies. The Italian campaign weakened Austria and diverted some German troops, but the Italian alliance never produced significant results. Romania joined the Allies in 1916 but was quickly defeated and driven from the war.

In the Far East, Japan honored its alliance with Britain and entered the war. The Japanese quickly overran the German colonies in China and the Pacific and used the opportunity to put pressure on China. Both sides also appealed to nationalistic sentiment in areas the enemy held. The Germans supported nationalist movements among the Irish, the Flemings in Belgium, and the Poles and Ukrainians under Russian rule. They even tried to persuade the Turks to lead a Muslim uprising against the British in Egypt and India and against the French and Italians in North Africa. The Allies made the same appeals with greater success. They sponsored movements of national autonomy for the Czechs, the Slovaks, the south Slavs, and against the Poles who were under Austrian rule. They also favored a movement of Arab independence from Turkey. Guided by Colonel T. E. Lawrence (1888–1935), this last scheme proved especially successful later in the war.

In 1915, the Allies tried to break the deadlock on the western front by going around it. The idea came chiefly from **Winston Churchill** (1874–1965), first lord of the British admiralty. He proposed to attack the Dardanelles and capture Constantinople. This policy supposedly would knock Turkey from the war, bring help to the Balkan front, and ease communications with Russia.

The success of Churchill's plan depended on timing, speed, and daring leadership, but all of these were lacking. Worse, the execution of the attack was inept and overly cautious. Before the campaign was abandoned, the Allies lost almost 150,000 men and diverted three times that number from more useful occupations.

A Closer Look

The Development of the Armored Tank

WARFARE FREQUENTLY leads to technological innovation. This was true of World War I, which witnessed the development of numerous new weapons. Among the most important of these was the tank—an armored vehicle using a caterpillar track rather than wheels for transport. The caterpillar track had been invented in Great Britain but was then purchased by the American Holt tractor company. In the first decade of the century it devised a caterpillar tractor to cultivate areas with wet or loose earth where a wheeled vehicle would sink into the ground. During World War I the British modified the caterpillar tractor by introducing a heavily armored closed compartment for a crew armed with machine guns. These early slow-moving tanks could drive over trenches, small hills, and rough terrain and through mud, thus bringing mobility to combat zones where trench warfare had made effective assault on enemy troops difficult. The tank was used primarily by Britain, France, and the United States in relatively small numbers in World War I, but rapidly moving tanks became one of the major weapons of later twentieth-century warfare.

The design of the driver's cabin, intended to allow for the widest area of vision on all sides, was fully exposed.

The caterpillar track enabled the tractor to move over loose or wet soil without sinking.

A CATERPILLAR TRACTOR FOR CULTIVATION
SOURCE: Library of Congress Prints and Photographs Division

The opening on the top permitted the mounting of a machine gun.

Armored and enclosed, the tank protected the crew from small-arms fire.

A MODIFIED CATERPILLAR TRACTOR FOR WARFARE
SOURCE: Topical Press Agency/Stringer/Getty Images

Questions

1. What technological developments prior to World War I made tank warfare possible? What military developments made it desirable?
2. What advantages did tank warfare offer?
3. How did tanks interact with other military units to achieve success?
4. What devices and tactics have modern armies developed to combat the tank?

26.2.3.7 RETURN TO THE WEST Both sides turned back to the west in 1916. General Erich von Falkenhayn (1861–1922), who had succeeded Moltke in September 1914, attacked the French stronghold of Verdun. His plan was not to break through the French line, but to inflict enormous casualties on the French, who would have to defend Verdun against superior firepower from several directions. He too underestimated the superiority of the defense. The French held Verdun with comparatively few men and inflicted almost as many casualties as they suffered. The commander of Verdun, Henri Pétain (1856–1951), became a national hero and "They shall not pass" a slogan of national defiance.

The Allies tried to end the impasse by launching a major offensive along the River Somme in July. Aided by a Russian attack in the east that drew off some German strength and by an enormous artillery bombardment, they hoped at last to break through. Once again, the defense was superior. Enormous casualties on both sides brought no result. The war on land dragged on with no end in sight. (See the "Compare and Connect" sidebar, which follows below, for the perspective of two soldiers on the fighting.)

26.2.3.8 THE WAR AT SEA As the war continued, control of the sea became more important. The British imposed a strict blockade meant to starve out the enemy, regardless of international law. The Germans responded with submarine warfare meant to destroy British shipping and starve the British. They declared the waters around the British Isles a war zone, where even neutral ships would not be safe. Both policies were unwelcomed by neutrals, and especially to the United States, which conducted extensive trade in the Atlantic. Yet the sinking of neutral ships by German submarines was both more dramatic and more offensive than the British blockade.

In May 1915, a German submarine torpedoed the British liner *Lusitania*. Among the 1,200 who drowned were 118 Americans. President Woodrow Wilson (1856–1924) warned Germany that another such attack would have grave consequences; the Germans desisted for the time being, rather than further anger the United States.

26.2.3.9 AMERICA ENTERS THE WAR In December 1916, President Wilson intervened to try to bring about a negotiated peace. Neither side, however, was willing to renounce war aims that its opponent found acceptable. The war seemed likely to continue until one or both sides reached exhaustion.

Two events early in 1917 changed the situation radically. On February 1, the Germans announced the resumption of unrestricted submarine warfare, which led the United States to break off diplomatic relations. On April 6, the United States declared war on Germany. One of the deterrents to

an earlier American intervention had been the presence of the autocratic tsarist Russia among the Allies. Wilson could conceive of the war only as an idealistic crusade "to make the world safe for democracy." That problem was resolved in March 1917 by a revolution in Russia that overthrew the tsarist government.

26.3 The Russian Revolution

What factors made the rise of the Bolsheviks to power in Russia possible?

World War I had many unexpected consequences, reshaping both Europe and the rest of the world in ways that could not have been anticipated in 1910. For the rest of European history in the twentieth century no such unexpected event produced so many long-term results as the revolution that occurred in Russia in 1917. That revolution changed the course of the war and the future course of Europe by setting a Communist government in charge of a major European state and empire.

The Russian Revolution of 1917, which impacted the world for years, went through two distinct stages. In March of that year the government of Tsar Nicholas II collapsed in the wake of popular demonstrations against the war, its casualties, and the economic and social conditions flowing from Russian participation in the conflict. Then in November a second unforeseen event occurred. The previously largely obscure and ignored **Bolshevik Party** led by V. I. Lenin seized power from the provisional government. The Bolsheviks would quickly take Russia out of the war and then proceed to establish their own domestic Communist Party dictatorship.

No political faction planned or led the **March Revolution** in Russia. It was the result of the collapse of the monarchy's ability to govern. Although public opinion in Russia had strongly supported the country's entry into the war, the conflict overtaxed Russia's resources and the efficiency of the tsarist government.

Nicholas II was weak and incompetent and suspected of being dominated by his German wife and the insidious peasant faith healer Rasputin, whom a group of Russian noblemen assassinated in 1916. Military and domestic failures produced massive casualties, widespread hunger, strikes by workers, and disorganization in the army. The peasant discontent that had plagued the countryside before 1914 did not subside during the conflict. In 1915, the tsar took personal command of the armies on the German front, which kept him away from the capital. In his absence,

Compare and Connect

War Poets on the Western Front

WORLD WAR I USHERED IN A NEW ERA of industrial conflict. The European wars of the previous century had been short, decisive affairs with relatively few casualties. At the onset of the fighting, many observers assumed this latest war would be no different. They were mistaken. As the western front settled into a bloody stalemate, and the number of dead and wounded increased, soldiers and civilians alike reflected on the meaning of the carnage. The poems below were written by Allied soldiers who served on the western front. John McCrae survived the war, only to succumb to the influenza epidemic that swept across the world in 1919. Wilfred Owen was killed in battle in November 1918, just one week before the armistice.

GERMAN CASUALTIES AT THE SOMME With over a million men killed or wounded, the Battle of the Somme on the western front stands out as one of the bloodiest of World War I. For five months in the second half of 1916, British and French forces fought the Germans in a ruthless battle of attrition.
SOURCE: Universal Images Group North America LLC / Alamy Stock Photo

Before Reading

- Consider the nature of the fighting on the western front.
- Think about the mood in Europe at the onset of the war.
- Ask yourself how poems such as these might have been received by other soldiers.

Questions

1. What beliefs and values are reflected in John McCrae's "In Flanders Fields"?
2. How might Wilfred Owen have responded to McCrae's poem?
3. What is the central message of Owen's "Dulce et Decorum est"?

I. JOHN MCCRAE, "IN FLANDERS FIELDS"

In Flanders fields the poppies blow
Between the crosses, row on row
That mark our place; and in the sky
The larks, still bravely singing, fly
Scarce heard amid the guns below.
We are the Dead. Short days ago
We lived, felt dawn, saw sunset glow,
Loved and were loved, and now we lie
In Flanders fields.
Take up our quarrel with the foe:

To you from failing hands we throw
The torch; be yours to hold it high.
If ye break faith with us who die
We shall not sleep, though poppies grow
In Flanders fields.

II. WILFRED OWEN, "DULCE ET DECORUM EST"

Bent double, like old beggars under sacks,
Knock-kneed, coughing like hags, we cursed through sludge,
Till on the haunting flares we turned our backs
And towards our distant rest began to trudge.
Men marched asleep. Many had lost their boots
But limped on, blood-shod. All went lame; all blind;
Drunk with fatigue; deaf even to the hoots
Of tired, outstripped Five-Nines that dropped behind.
Gas! GAS! Quick, boys! -- An ecstasy of fumbling,
Fitting the clumsy helmets just in time;
But someone still was yelling out and stumbling
And flound'ring like a man in fire or lime . . .
Dim, through the misty panes and thick green light,
As under I green sea, I saw him drowning.
In all my dreams, before my helpless sight,
He plunges at me, guttering, choking, drowning.
If in some smothering dreams you too could pace
Behind the wagon that we flung him in,
And watch the white eyes writhing in his face,
His hanging face, like a devil's sick of sin;
If you could hear, at every jolt, the blood
Come gargling from the froth-corrupted lungs,
Obscene as cancer, bitter as the cud
Of vile, incurable sores on innocent tongues, --
My friend, you would not tell with such high zest
To children ardent for some desperate glory,
The old lie: *Dulce et decorum est*
Pro patria mori. [It is sweet and proper to die for the fatherland.]

SOURCES: (I) John McCrae, *In Flanders Fields and Other Poems,* (London: G. P. Putnam's Sons, 1919), p. 3. (II) Wilfred Owen, *Poems* (New York: Viking Press, 1921), p. 15.

corrupt and incompetent ministers increasingly discredited the government even in the eyes of conservative monarchists. All political factions in the Duma, Russia's parliament, were discontented.

26.3.1 The Provisional Government

In early March 1917, strikes and worker demonstrations erupted in Petrograd, as Saint Petersburg had been renamed. The ill-disciplined troops in the city refused to fire on the demonstrators. The tsar abdicated on March 15, and the government of Russia fell into the hands of members of the Duma, who soon formed a provisional government comprised chiefly of Constitutional Democrats (Cadets) with Western sympathies.

At the same time, the various Socialist groups, including both Social Revolutionaries and Social Democrats of the Menshevik wing, began to organize soviets, councils of workers and soldiers. Initially, they allowed the provisional government to function without actually supporting it, but they became estranged when the Cadets failed to control the army or to purge reactionaries from the government.

In this climate, the provisional government decided to remain loyal to Russia's alliances and continue the war. The provisional government thus accepted tsarist foreign policy and associated itself with the main source of domestic suffering and discontent. The collapse of the last Russian offensive in the summer of 1917 sealed its fate. Disillusionment with the war, shortages of food and other necessities at home, and the peasants' demands for land reform undermined the government. Moreover, discipline in the army had disintegrated. This failure of the provisional government occurred even after moderate Socialist Alexander Kerensky (1881–1970) became prime minister.

THE BOLSHEVIKS The year 1917 witnessed revolutionary upheaval in Russia and the rise of the Bolsheviks. In this photograph, the Bolsheviks, in a show of force, parade through the streets shortly after the collapse of the monarchy in the early spring. Later that fall, the Bolsheviks would topple a provisional government, which was established after Nicholas II was forced to abdicate.

SOURCE: Everett Collection Historical/Alamy Stock Photo

26.3.2 Lenin and the Bolsheviks

Ever since April, the Bolshevik wing of the Social Democratic Party had been working against the provisional government. The Germans, in their most successful attempt at subversion, had rushed the brilliant Bolshevik leader Lenin (1870–1924) in a sealed train from his exile in Switzerland across Germany to Petrograd. They hoped he would cause trouble for the revolutionary government.

Lenin saw the opportunity to achieve the political alliance of workers and peasants he had advocated before the war. In speech after speech, he hammered away on the theme of peace, bread, and land. The Bolsheviks demanded that all political power go to the soviets, which they controlled. The failure of the summer offensive encouraged them to attempt a coup, but the effort was a failure. Lenin fled to Finland, and his chief collaborator, **Leon Trotsky** (1879–1940), was imprisoned.

The failure of a right-wing countercoup gave the Bolsheviks another chance. Trotsky, released from prison, led the powerful Petrograd soviet. Lenin returned in October, insisted to his doubting colleagues that the time was ripe to take power, and by the extraordinary force of his personality persuaded them to act. Trotsky organized the

coup that took place on November 6 and concluded with an armed assault on the provisional government. The Bolsheviks, as much to their astonishment as to that of the rest of the world, had come to rule Russia.

26.3.3 The Communist Dictatorship

The victors moved to fulfill their promises and ensure their security. The provisional government had decreed an election for late November to select a Constituent Assembly. The Social Revolutionaries won a large majority over the Bolsheviks. When the assembly gathered in January, it met for only a day before the Red Army, controlled by the Bolsheviks, dispersed it. All other political parties also ceased to function in any meaningful fashion. In November and January, the Bolshevik government nationalized the land and turned it over to its peasant proprietors. Factory workers were put in charge of their plants. The state seized banks and repudiated the debt of the tsarist government. Property of the church reverted to the state.

The Bolshevik government also took Russia out of the war, which they believed benefited only capitalism. They signed an armistice with Germany in December 1917 and in March 1918 accepted the Treaty of Brest-Litovsk, by which

Russia yielded Poland, Finland, the Baltic states, and Ukraine. Some territory in the Transcaucasus region went to Turkey. The Bolsheviks also agreed to pay a heavy war indemnity.

These terms were a high price to pay for peace, but Lenin had no choice. Russia was incapable of renewing the war effort, and the Bolsheviks needed time to impose their rule. Moreover, Lenin believed that the war and the Russian example would soon lead to Communist revolutions across Europe.

The new Bolshevik government met major domestic resistance. Civil war erupted between Red Russians, who supported the revolution, and White Russians, who opposed it. In the summer of 1918, the Bolsheviks murdered the tsar and his family. Loyal army officers continued to fight the revolution and received aid from Allied armies. Under the leadership of Trotsky, however, the Red Army eventually overcame domestic opposition. By 1921, Lenin and his supporters were in firm control.

26.4 The End of World War I

What were the immediate consequences of the end of World War I?

The collapse of Russia and the Treaty of Brest-Litovsk were the zenith of German success. The Germans controlled eastern Europe and its resources, especially food, and by 1918 they were free to concentrate their forces on the western front. These developments would probably have been decisive without American intervention. Still, American troops would not arrive in significant numbers for about a year, and both sides tried to win the war in 1917.

An Allied attempt to break through in the west failed disastrously. Losses were heavy and the French army mutinied. The Austrians, supported by the Germans, defeated the Italians at Caporetto and threatened to overrun northern Italy, until they were checked with the aid of Allied troops. The deadlock continued, but time was running out for the Central Powers.

26.4.1 Germany's Last Offensive

In March 1918, the Germans decided to gamble everything on one last offensive. The German army reached the Marne again but got no farther. They had no more reserves, and the entire nation was exhausted. In contrast, the arrival of American troops in ever-increasing numbers bolstered the Allies. An Allied counteroffensive proved irresistible. As the exhausted Austrians collapsed in Italy, and Bulgaria and Turkey dropped out of the war, the German high command knew the end was imminent.

Ludendorff was determined to make peace before the German army was thoroughly defeated in the field and to make civilians responsible for ending the war. For some time,

he had been the effective ruler of Germany under the aegis of the emperor. He now allowed a new government to be established on democratic principles and to seek peace immediately. The new government, under Prince Max of Baden, asked for peace on the basis of the **Fourteen Points** that President Wilson had declared as the American war aims. These were idealistic principles, including self-determination for nationalities, open diplomacy, freedom of the seas, disarmament, and the establishment of the **League of Nations** to keep the peace. Wilson insisted he would work only with a democratic German government to be sure he was dealing with the German people and not merely their rulers.

26.4.2 The Armistice

The disintegration of the German army forced William II to abdicate on November 9, 1918. The majority branch of the Social Democratic Party proclaimed a republic to prevent their radical Leninist wing from setting up a soviet government. Two days later, this republican, Socialist-led government signed the armistice that ended the war by accepting German defeat. The German people were, in general, unaware their army had been defeated and was crumbling. No foreign soldier stood on German soil. Many Germans expected a negotiated and mild settlement, but the real peace embittered the Germans. Many of them came to believe Germany had not been defeated but had been tricked by the enemy and betrayed—even stabbed in the back—by republicans and Socialists at home.

The victors rejoiced, but they also had much to mourn. The casualties on all sides came to about 10 million dead and twice as many wounded. The economic and financial resources of the European states were badly strained. The victorious Allies, formerly creditors to the world, became debtors to the new American colossus, which the calamities of war had barely touched.

World War I, or the Great War, as contemporaries called it, for those who lived through its horrible offspring, lasted more than four years, doing terrible damage. Battle casualties alone counted more than 4 million dead and 8.3 million wounded among the Central Powers and 5.4 million dead and 7 million wounded from their opponents; millions of civilians died from the war and causes arising from it. Among the casualties also were the German, Austro-Hungarian, Russian, and Turkish empires. The American intervention in 1917 thrust the United States into European affairs with a vengeance, and the collapse of the Russian autocracy brought the Bolshevik Revolution and the reality of a great Communist state. Disappointment, resentment, and economic dislocations caused by the war brought various forms of Fascism to Italy, Germany, and other countries. The comfortable nineteenth-century assumptions of inevitable progress based on reason, science and technology, individual freedom, democracy, and free enterprise gave way in many places to cynicism, nihilism, dictatorship, statism, official racism, and class warfare. It is widely agreed that the First World War was the mother of the Second and of most of the horrors of the remainder of the century.

These changes affected the colonial peoples the European powers ruled, and overseas empires would never be as secure as they had seemed before the war. Europe was no longer the center of the world, free to interfere with or to ignore the rest of the world if it chose. The memory of the war lived on to shake the nerve of the victorious Western powers as they faced the conditions of the postwar world.

KEY CAMPAIGNS AND EVENTS OF WORLD WAR I	
August 1914	Germans attack in West
August–September	First Battle of the Marne
1914	Battles of Tannenberg and the Masurian Lakes
April 1915	British land at Gallipoli; start of Dardanelles campaign
May 1915	Germans sink British ship *Lusitania*
February 1916	Germans attack Verdun
May–June 1916	Battle of Jutland
July–November 1916	Battle of the Somme
February 1917	Germans declare unrestricted submarine warfare
March 1917	Russian Revolution
April 1917	United States enters war
November 1917	Bolsheviks seize power in Russia
March 1918	Treaty of Brest-Litovsk
March 1918	German offensive in the West
November 1918	Armistice

26.4.3 The End of the Ottoman Empire

At the outbreak of World War I in August 1914, the Ottoman Empire was neutral, but many military officers, the so-called Young Turks who had taken control of the Ottoman government in 1909, were pro-German. After hesitating for three months, the Turks entered the war on the German side in November 1914. This decision ultimately brought about the end of the Ottoman Empire. Early victories gave way to defeat after defeat at the hands of the Russians and the British, the latter assisted by Arabs from the Arabian Peninsula and neighboring lands, most notably Hussein (1856–1931), *sherif* (ruler or emir) of Mecca, the city of Muhammad. The British drove the Ottomans out of Palestine and advanced deep into Mesopotamia, as far north as the oil fields of Mosul in modern Iraq. By October 30, 1918, Turkey was out of the war. In November, an Allied fleet sailed into the harbor of Constantinople and landed troops who occupied the city. The Ottoman government was helpless.

The peace treaty signed in Paris in 1920 between Turkey and the Allies dismembered the Ottoman Empire, placing large parts of it, particularly the areas Arabs inhabited, under the control of Britain and France. In Mesopotamia the British created the state of Iraq which along with Palestine became British mandates. Syria and Lebanon became French mandates. **Mandates** were territories legally administered under the auspices of the League of Nations but in effect ruled as colonies. A Greek invasion of the Turkish homeland in Anatolia in 1919 provoked a

OPPONENTS OF THE OTTOMANS AT PARIS PEACE CONFERENCE, 1919 The Allies promoted Arab efforts to secure independence from Turkey in an effort to remove Turkey from the war. Delegates to the Paris Peace Conference of 1919 included British colonel T. E. Lawrence, who helped lead the rebellion, and representatives from the Middle Eastern region. Prince Feisal, the third son of King Hussein, stands in the foreground of this picture; Colonel T. E. Lawrence is in the middle row, second from the right; and Brigadier General Nuri Pasha Said of Baghdad is second from the left.
SOURCE: Pictorial Press Ltd/Alamy Stock Photo

nationalist reaction, bringing the young general Mustafa Kemal (1881–1938), who later took the name **Ataturk**, meaning "Father of the Turks," to power. He drove the Greeks out of Anatolia and compelled the victorious powers to make a new arrangement sealed by the treaty of Lausanne in 1923. Ataturk abolished the Ottoman sultanate and deposed the last caliph. The new Republic of Turkey abandoned most of the old Ottoman Empire but became fully independent of control by the European powers and sovereign in its Anatolian homeland. Under Ataturk and his successors, Turkey, although its population was overwhelmingly Muslim, became a secular state and a force for stability in the region.

The Arab portions of the old empire, however, were a different story. Divided into a collection of artificial states that had no historical reality, governed or dominated as client regimes by the British and French, they were relatively quiet during the 1920s and 1930s. The weakening of Britain and France during and after World War II, however, and their subsequent abandonment of control in the Middle East would create problems in the latter part of the century.

26.5 The Settlement at Paris

What were the key weaknesses of the Paris peace settlement?

The representatives of the victorious states gathered at Versailles and other Parisian suburbs in the first half of 1919. Wilson speaking for the United States, David Lloyd George (1863–1945) for Britain, Georges Clemenceau (1841–1929) for France, and Vittorio Emanuele Orlando (1860–1952) for Italy made up the Big Four. Japan also had an important part in the discussions. The diplomats who met in Paris had a far more difficult task than those who had met in Vienna a century earlier. Both groups attempted to restore order to the world after long and costly wars. At Vienna, however, Metternich and his associates could confine their thoughts to Europe. France had acknowledged defeat and was willing to uphold the Vienna settlement. The diplomats at Vienna were not much affected by public opinion, and

THE BIG FOUR The Big Four attended the Paris Peace Conference: Vittorio Orlando, premier of Italy; David Lloyd George, prime minister of Great Britain; Georges Clemenceau, premier of France; and Woodrow Wilson, president of the United States (left to right).

SOURCE: National Archives and Records Administration

they could draw the new map of Europe along practical lines determined by the realities of power and softened by compromise.

26.5.1 Obstacles the Peacemakers Faced

The negotiators at Paris in 1919 were less fortunate. They represented constitutional, generally democratic governments, and public opinion had become a mighty force. Though there were secret sessions, the conference often worked in the full glare of publicity. Nationalism had become almost a secular religion, and Europe's many ethnic groups could not be relied on to remain quiet while the great powers distributed them on the map. Moreover, propaganda and especially the intervention of Woodrow Wilson had transformed World War I into a moral crusade to achieve a peace that would be just as well as secure. (See the "Encountering the Past" sidebar, which follows below, for an examination of war propaganda and the movies.) The Fourteen Points set forth the right of nationalities to self-determination as an absolute value, but in fact no one could draw the map of Europe to match ethnic groups perfectly with their homelands. All these elements made compromise difficult.

Wilson's idealism, moreover, came into conflict with the more practical war aims of the victorious powers and with many of the secret treaties that had been made before and during the war. The British and French people had been told that Germany would be made to pay for the war. Russia had been promised control of Constantinople in return for recognizing the French claim to Alsace-Lorraine and British control of Egypt. Romania had been promised Transylvania at the expense of Hungary.

Some of the agreements contradicted others. Italy and Serbia had competing claims in the Adriatic. During the war, the British had encouraged Arab hopes of an independent Arab state carved out of the Ottoman Empire. Those plans, however, contradicted the Balfour Declaration (1917), in which the British seemed to accept Zionist ideology and to promise the Jews a national home in Palestine. Both these plans conflicted with an Anglo-French agreement to divide the Near East between themselves.

The continuing national goals of the victors presented further obstacles to an idealistic "peace without victors." France was painfully conscious of its numerical inferiority to Germany and of the low birthrate that would keep it inferior, and it was naturally eager to weaken Germany permanently and preserve French superiority. Italy continued to seek *Italia irredenta*, Britain looked to its imperial interests, and Japan pursued its own advantage in Asia. The United States insisted on freedom of the seas, which favored American commerce, and on its right to maintain the Monroe Doctrine.

Finally, the peacemakers of 1919 faced a world still in turmoil. The greatest immediate threat appeared to be the spread of Bolshevism. While civil war distracted Lenin and his colleagues, the Allies landed small armies in Russia to help overthrow the Bolshevik regime. The revolution seemed likely to spread as Communist governments were established in Bavaria and Hungary. A Communist uprising led by the "Spartacus group" had to be suppressed in Berlin. The worried Allies even allowed an army of German volunteers to fight the Bolsheviks in the Baltic states.

26.5.2 The Peace

The Paris settlement consisted of five separate treaties between the victors and the defeated powers. Formal sessions began on January 18, 1919, and the last treaty was signed on August 10, 1920. (See Map 26–5.) Wilson arrived in Europe to unprecedented popular acclaim. Liberals and idealists expected a new kind of international order achieved in a new and better way, but they were soon disillusioned. "Open covenants openly arrived at" soon gave way to closed sessions in which Wilson, Clemenceau, and Lloyd George made arrangements that seemed cynical to outsiders.

The notion of "a peace without victors" became a mockery when the Soviet Union (as Russia was now called) and Germany were excluded from the peace conference. The Germans were simply presented with a treaty and compelled to accept it, fully justified in their complaint that the treaty had been dictated, not negotiated. The principle of national self-determination was violated many times and was unavoidable. Still, their exclusion from decisions angered the diplomats from the small nations. The undeserved adulation accorded Wilson on his arrival gradually turned into equally undeserved scorn. He had not abandoned his ideals lightly but had merely given way to the irresistible force of reality.

26.5.2.1 THE LEAGUE OF NATIONS Wilson could make unpalatable concessions without abandoning his ideals because he put great faith in a new instrument for peace and justice: the **League of Nations**. Its covenant was an essential part of the peace treaty. The league was to be, not an international government, but a body of sovereign states that agreed to pursue common policies and to consult in the common interest, especially when war threatened. The members promised to submit differences among themselves to arbitration, an international court, or the League Council. Refusal to abide by the results would justify economic sanctions and even military intervention by the league. The league was unlikely to be effective, however, because it had no armed forces at its disposal. Furthermore, any action required the unanimous consent of its council, consisting permanently of Britain, France, Italy, the United States, and Japan, as well as four other states that had temporary seats.

Encountering the Past

War Propaganda and the Movies: Charlie Chaplin

THE VAST SCOPE of World War I required support. As the war stretched on and its costs increased, competing nations intensified propaganda campaigns to justify the huge expenditure of lives and resources. Sometimes this took the form of painting the enemy in brutal and lurid colors to provoke hatred; other times it took the form of sympathetic images of patriotism and sacrifice for a noble cause. These efforts, sponsored both by government and private agencies, saturated the lives of everyone—men, women, and even children—while the war lasted.

At first, most propaganda was in the form of writing—newspaper articles and pamphlets—justifying the war and demonizing the enemy. Soon, however, verbal efforts gave way to more emotionally powerful visual devices such as posters, cartoons, and caricatures. By the middle of the war, however, the relatively new medium of film became the most powerful weapon of propaganda. Graphically and dramatically, movies showed the enemy as either horrible or ridiculous and one's own soldiers as brave and noble. Such images could reach rich and poor, literate and illiterate, and young and old, with great emotional effect.

Both sides produced films that became enormously popular but none more so than those Charlie Chaplin (1889–1977) did for the Allies. Born in England, he came to America as a vaudeville star in 1914 and was already famous when the war broke out. His tragicomic character, the tramp, in many variations, had universal appeal. His wartime films had amazing effects: they helped sell great quantities of Liberty Bonds, which the American government used to help pay for its involvement in the war; raised the morale of civilians; and even eased the miseries of shell-shocked soldiers.

Chaplin's 1918 movie *Shoulder Arms* was his greatest wartime success. It was a comic portrait of the difficulties of basic training for American recruits and of the Germans as bumbling fools. In the film, Chaplin's character, exhausted by the rigors of drilling, falls asleep. He wakes up at the front, where he deceives the enemy by pretending to be a tree and captures first a German unit and finally the kaiser all by himself.

The Germans, too, soon learned the propaganda value of films, which were controlled more by the government than those made in the Allied states. The German army made comedies, melodramas, and newsreels and showed them both to the troops and the civilian public. The German government thought movies so important that even during the freezing, brutal winter of 1917 to 1918 when fuel supplies were at a premium, it gave movie theaters special priority to use coal and electricity. But there was no German Charlie Chaplin.

CHARLIE CHAPLIN IN *SHOULDER ARMS* In *Shoulder Arms* (1918), Charlie Chaplin (1889–1977) brought humor to a war that had ravaged the world for four years.
SOURCE: AF archive/Alamy Stock Photo

Questions

1. What were the purposes of propaganda during the war?
2. What were the advantages of using movies in the war effort?

Map 26–5 WORLD WAR I PEACE SETTLEMENT IN EUROPE AND THE MIDDLE EAST

The map of central and eastern Europe, as well as that of the Middle East, underwent drastic revision after World War I. The enormous territorial losses suffered by Germany, Austria-Hungary, the Ottoman Empire, Bulgaria, and Russia were matched by gains for France, Italy, Greece, and Romania and by the appearance or reappearance of at least eight new independent states from Finland in the north to Yugoslavia in the south. The mandate system for former Ottoman territories outside Turkey proper laid foundations for several new, mostly Arab, states in the Middle East. In Africa, the mandate system placed the former German colonies under British, French, and South African rule.

The Covenant of the League bound its members to "respect and preserve" the territorial integrity of all its members; this was generally seen as a device to ensure the security of the victorious powers. The exclusion of Germany and the Soviet Union from the League Assembly further undermined its claim to evenhandedness.

Members of the League of Nations remained fully sovereign and continued to pursue their national interests. Only Wilson put much faith in the league's future ability to produce peace and justice. To get the other states to agree to the league, he approved territorial settlements that violated his own principles.

26.5.2.2 GERMANY In the West, the main territorial issue was the fate of Germany. Although a united Germany was less than fifty years old, no one seems to have thought of undoing Bismarck's work and dividing the country into its component parts. The French wanted to set the Rhineland up as a separate buffer state, but Lloyd George and Wilson would not permit it. Still, they could not ignore France's need for protection against a resurgent Germany. France received Alsace-Lorraine and the right to work the coal mines of the Saar for fifteen years. Germany west of the Rhine and fifty kilometers east of it was to be a demilitarized zone. Allied troops could stay on the west bank for fifteen years.

The treaty also provided that Britain and the United States would help France if Germany attacked it. Such an attack was made more unlikely by the permanent disarmament of Germany. Its army was limited to 100,000 men on long-term service, its fleet was reduced to a coastal defense force, and it was forbidden to have warplanes, submarines, tanks, heavy artillery, or poison gas. If these provisions were observed, France would be safe.

26.5.2.3 THE EAST The settlement in the East reflected the collapse of the great defeated empires that had ruled it for centuries. Germany lost part of Silesia, and East Prussia was cut off from the rest of Germany by a corridor carved out to give the revived state of Poland access to the sea. The Austro-Hungarian Empire disappeared entirely, giving way to five small successor states. Most of its German-speaking people were gathered in the Republic of Austria, cut off from the Germans of Bohemia and forbidden to unite with Germany.

The Magyars were left with the much-reduced kingdom of Hungary. The Czechs of Bohemia and Moravia joined with the Slovaks and Ruthenians to the east to form Czechoslovakia, and this new state included several million unhappy Germans plus Poles, Magyars, and Ukrainians. The southern Slavs were united in the kingdom of Serbs, Croats, and Slovenes, or Yugoslavia. Italy gained Trentino, which included tens of thousands of German speakers, and the port of Trieste. Romania was enlarged by receiving Transylvania from Hungary and Bessarabia from Russia. Bulgaria lost territory to Greece and Yugoslavia. Russia lost vast territories in the west. Finland, Estonia, Latvia, and Lithuania became independent states, and most of Poland was carved out of formerly Russian soil.

26.5.2.4 REPARATIONS Perhaps the most debated part of the peace settlement dealt with reparations for the damage Germany did during the war. Before the armistice, the Germans promised to pay compensation "for all damages done to the civilian population of the Allies and their property." The Americans judged the amount would be between $15 billion and $25 billion and that Germany would be able to pay that amount. France and Britain, however, who worried about repaying their war debts to the United States, were eager to have Germany pay the full cost of the war, including pensions to survivors and dependents.

There was a general agreement that Germany could not afford to pay such a huge sum, whatever it might be, and the conference did not specify an amount. In the meantime, Germany was to pay $5 billion annually until 1921. At that time, a final figure would be set, which Germany would have to pay in thirty years. The French did not regret this outcome. Either Germany would pay and be bled into impotence, or Germany would refuse to pay and French intervention would be warranted.

To justify these huge reparation payments, the Allies inserted the notorious **war guilt clause** (Clause 231) into the treaty:

> The Allied and Associated Governments affirm, and Germany accepts, the responsibility of Germany and her allies for causing all the loss and damage to which the Allied and Associated Governments and their nationals have been subjected as a consequence of the war imposed upon them by aggression of Germany and her allies.

The Germans, of course, did not believe they were solely responsible for the war and bitterly resented the charge. They had lost territories containing badly needed natural resources. Yet they were presented with an astronomical and apparently unlimited reparations bill. To add insult to injury, they were required to admit to a war guilt they did not feel.

Finally, to heap insult upon insult, they were required to accept the entire treaty as the victors wrote it, without negotiation. The Social Democrats and the Catholic Center Party formed a new government, and their representatives signed the treaty. These parties formed the backbone of the Weimar government that ruled Germany until 1933. They never overcame the stigma of having accepted the Treaty of Versailles.

26.5.3 World War I and Colonial Empires

World War I and the peace settlement introduced numerous changes and transformations to the European colonial world. In fact, the struggles regarding colonies helped shape the course of the Great War and its aftermath. This can be seen in the establishment of mandates within former colonies and the regions that the empires governed.

26.5.3.1 REDISTRIBUTION OF COLONIES INTO MANDATES

The rivalries over empire that had predated the outbreak of the war and had contributed so mightily to prewar tensions continued throughout the conflict. In effect, the war had opened the possibility for whoever won it to expand their empires at the cost of the defeated powers. As a result, the single most important imperial consequence of World War I was Germany being stripped of its colonies and the Ottoman Empire of regions it had formerly governed.

The Covenant of the League of Nations established mandates within these former colonies and regions. These mandates, located in the Middle East, Africa, and the Pacific, were placed under the "tutelage" of one of the great powers under League of Nations supervision and encouraged to become independent. Britain and France became the chief mandate administrators and were consequently drawn more deeply into new regions of the world, most particularly the Middle East. In effect, the mandates became colonies of the administering powers. Some mandates, most notably Iraq, became independent between the wars. Other mandates became independent often with considerable conflict from the closing years of World War II through the third quarter of the twentieth century. Some of these latter mandates included Palestine, Syria, Lebanon, Transjordan, Tanganyka, Kamerun, Southwest Africa, and German New Guinea.

26.5.3.2 COLONIAL PARTICIPATION

Colonial peoples themselves had played a significant role in World War I. Germany itself did not call upon troops from its colonies. The war led Britain and France, however, to view their empires in new ways as sources of military as well as economic support. The French government recruited tens of thousands of Algerians into its armed forces and over 150,000 West Africans. It is estimated that more than 2.5 million British colonial troops participated in the war. More than 1.25 million Indian troops were involved either directly in combat or as laborers working for cheap wages. Canada, Australia, New Zealand, and South Africa sent hundreds of thousands of troops into the war and experienced very significant losses. The presence of so many non-European troops on the European continent even before the arrival of U.S. troops was one of the factors that made the war a genuinely world conflict. Both colonial troops of color and United States troops of color encountered significant racial prejudice in Europe.

What Europeans had learned from the wartime experience was the value of their colonies in terms of troops to be recruited and natural resources to be devoted to the war effort, and they tended to seek ways to draw them into closer relations. In this respect, the years after the war were in some ways the period of most extensive direct colonial involvement by Great Britain and France and the ongoing desire for empire on the part of Italy. When World War II broke out, both nations would encounter much more nationalist resistance that after the war would culminate in decolonization.

26.5.3.3 IMPACT OF THE PEACE SETTLEMENT ON FUTURE COLONIAL RELATIONS

Many native colonial leaders in Africa and Asia had supported the Allied war effort in the hope that their peoples would be rewarded with greater independence and better economic relations with Europe. These hopes were dashed at the peace conference and in the years thereafter. These colonial leaders had hoped they might be allowed to put their case for independence or major administrative reform before the conference, and they had been denied that opportunity. Their disappointment led them over the years to reject engagement with the existing international order and to move in various new directions of disruptive and ultimately successful national anticolonialism.

The European powers themselves had directly contributed to these developments in another fashion. They had sought to stir nationalist uprisings in the lands of their opponents. The most significant effort took place among Arab peoples governed by the Ottoman Empire, which had sided with Germany. The British led Arab nationalist groups to believe that they might achieve independence in the wake of an Allied victory. T. E. Lawrence, later known popularly as Lawrence of Arabia, led much of this effort on behalf of the British. For their part the Germans had attempted to stir unrest in northern Africa.

A glance at the new map of the world after World War I could give the impression that the old imperial nations, especially Britain and France, were more powerful than ever but that impression would be superficial and misleading. The great Western European powers had paid an enormous price in lives, money, and will for their victory. Colonial peoples pressed for the rights that the West proclaimed as universal but denied to their colonies, and some influential minorities in the countries that ruled those colonies sympathized with colonial aspirations for independence. Tension between colonies and their ruling nations was a cause of serious instability in the world the Paris treaties of 1919 created.

26.5.4 Evaluating the Peace

Few peace settlements have undergone more severe attacks than the one negotiated in Paris in 1919. It was natural that the defeated powers should object to it, but the peace soon came under bitter criticism in the victorious countries as well. Many of the French objected that the treaty tied French security to promises of aid from the unreliable Anglo-Saxon countries. In England and the United States, a wave of bitter criticism arose in liberal quarters because the treaty seemed to violate the idealistic and liberal aims that the Western leaders had professed.

It was not a peace without victors. It did not put an end to imperialism but attempted to promote the national interests of the winning nations. It violated the principles of national self-determination by leaving significant pockets of minorities outside the borders of their national homelands.

26.5.4.1 THE ECONOMIC CONSEQUENCES OF THE PEACE
The most influential economic critic of the treaty was John Maynard Keynes (1883–1946), a brilliant British economist who took part in the peace conference. He resigned in disgust when he saw the direction it was taking. His book *The Economic Consequences of the Peace* (1920) was a scathing attack, especially on reparations and the other economic aspects of the peace. It was also a skillful assault on the negotiators and particularly on Wilson, whom Keynes depicted as a fool and a hypocrite. Keynes argued that the Treaty of Versailles was both immoral and unworkable. He called it a Carthaginian peace, referring to Rome's destruction of Carthage after the Third Punic War. He argued that such a peace would bring economic ruin and war to Europe unless it was repudiated.

Keynes's argument had a great effect on the British, who were already suspicious of France and glad of an excuse to withdraw from continental affairs. The decent and respectable position came to be one that supported revision of the treaty in favor of Germany. In the United States, the book fed the traditional tendency toward isolationism and gave powerful weapons to Wilson's enemies. Wilson's own political mistakes helped prevent American ratification of the treaty. Thus, America was out of the League of Nations and not bound to defend France. Britain, therefore, was also free from its obligation to France. France was left to protect itself without adequate means to do so for long.

Many of the attacks on the Treaty of Versailles are unjustified. It was not a Carthaginian peace. Germany was neither dismembered nor ruined. Reparations could be and were scaled down. Until the great world depression of the 1930s, the Germans recovered prosperity. When measured against the peace that the victorious Germans had imposed on Russia at Brest-Litovsk and their plans for a European settlement if they had won, the Treaty of Versailles was far less severe. The attempt to achieve self-determination for nationalities was less than perfect, but it was the best effort Europe had ever made to do so.

26.5.4.2 DIVISIVE NEW BOUNDARIES AND TARIFF WALLS
The peace nevertheless was unsatisfactory in important ways. The elimination of the Austro-Hungarian Empire, however inevitable, created serious problems. Economically, it was disastrous. New borders and tariff walls separated raw materials from manufacturing areas and producers from their markets. In hard times, this separation created friction and hostility that aggravated other quarrels the peace treaties also created. Poland contained unhappy German, Lithuanian, and Ukrainian minorities, and Czechoslovakia and Yugoslavia were collections of nationalities that did not find it easy to live together. Territorial disputes in eastern Europe promoted further tension.

Moreover, the peace rested on a victory that Germany did not admit. The Germans felt cheated rather than defeated. The high moral principles the Allies proclaimed undercut the validity of the peace, for it plainly fell far short of those principles.

26.5.4.3 FAILURE TO ACCEPT REALITY
Finally, the great weakness of the peace was its failure to accept reality. Germany and Russia would inevitably play an important part in European affairs, yet the settlement and the League of Nations excluded them. Given the many discontented parties, the peace was not self-enforcing, yet no satisfactory machinery to enforce it was established. The League of Nations was never a serious force for this purpose. It was left to France, with no guarantee of support from Britain and no hope of help from the United States, to defend the new arrangements. Finland, the Baltic states, Poland, Romania, Czechoslovakia, and Yugoslavia were expected to be a barrier to the westward expansion of Russian Communism and to help deter a revival of German power. Most of these states, however, would have to rely on France in case of danger, and France was simply not strong enough to protect them if Germany revived.

The tragedy of the Treaty of Versailles was that it was neither conciliatory enough to remove the desire for revision, even at the cost of war, nor harsh enough to make another war impossible. The only hope for a lasting peace was that Germany would remain disarmed while the more obnoxious clauses of the peace treaty were revised. Such a policy required continued attention to the problem, unity among the victors, and farsighted leadership; none of these was consistently present during the next two decades.

The Chapter in Perspective

The unification of Germany in 1871 transformed the European international order. For twenty years a series of alliances and an ongoing process of shrewd negotiation on the part of Bismarck had brought a fragile stability to European diplomatic relations. In the years after Bismarck was forced from office in 1890, Kaiser Wilhelm and the German military pursued expansively aggressive policies that destabilized European diplomatic relations. Germany became overly dependent upon its alliance with Austria. Britain, France, and Russia by the first decade of the twentieth century had forged the very kind of friendly diplomatic understandings that Bismarck had sought to avoid.

The first fifteen years of the twentieth century saw a number of European diplomatic crises related to imperial concerns and rivalries in the Balkan Peninsula. These crises increased distrust between Germany and other European powers and cemented the understandings among Britain, France, and Russia. The assassination of Archduke Francis Ferdinand in the summer of 1914 sparked a Balkans crisis that could not be contained. The initial conflict between Serbia and Austria-Hungry soon drew in Russia in support of the former and Germany in support of the latter. Thereafter, the other alliances and understandings of mutual support came into play. The war plans of the various powers quickly led to the most extensive war Europe had experienced in a century.

Other unexpected transformative events followed the military stalemate. In March 1917 revolution overthrew the tsarist government of Russia. The next month the United States entered the war. In November 1917 the Bolsheviks seized power in Russia and rapidly withdrew Russia from the conflict. By November 1918 Germany surrendered. In both Germany and Austria-Hungary, the governments that had led their nations into the war had collapsed.

At the Paris Peace Conference of 1919 the victorious allies redrew the map of Europe, rearranged much of the European colonial world, established the League of Nations, and imposed a war guilt clause and high reparations on Germany. The United States refused to ratify the treaty and for two decades largely withdrew from European affairs. The peace settlement planted the seeds of ongoing resentment and nationalist unrest in Europe.

The Chapter in Review

Review Questions

1. What role in the world did Bismarck envisage for the new Germany after 1871? How successful was he in carrying out his vision? Was he wise to tie Germany to Austria-Hungary?

2. Why and in what stages did Britain abandon its policy of "splendid isolation" at the turn of the century? Were the policies it pursued instead wise ones, or should Britain have followed a different course altogether?

3. How did developments in the Balkans lead to the outbreak of World War I? What was the role of Serbia? Of Austria? Of Russia? What was the aim of German policy in July 1914? Did Germany want a general war?

4. What were the benefits of the Treaty of Versailles to Europe, and what were its drawbacks? Was the settlement too harsh or too conciliatory? Could it have secured lasting peace in Europe? How might it have been improved?

5. Why did Lenin succeed in establishing Bolshevik rule in Russia? What role did Trotsky play? Was it wise policy for Lenin to take Russia out of the war?

6. How had imperialism contributed to pre–World War I rivalries? How did the war and the peace settlement change European colonialism and plant seeds for further colonial discontent?

Key Terms

Archduke Francis Ferdinand (1863–1914) An archduke of Austria-Este, whose murder led to Austria's declaration of war against Serbia and resulted in the Central Powers and Serbia's allies declaring war on each other and starting World War I.

Ataturk (1881–1938) A Turkish army officer and the founder of the Republic of Turkey, who sought to modernize his country by forcing the Turks to adopt Western ways.

Battle of the Marne (September 6–10, 1914) Battle in which the fighting resulted in an Allied victory over the German armies in the West to stop the German advance on Paris.

Black Hand The political terror society, which killed Francis Ferdinand, also known as Union or Death.

Bolshevik Party The Russian party led by Lenin, which seized power from the provisional government after the March Revolution.

Bosnian crisis The crisis that erupted in 1908 when Austria annexed the Ottoman territories of Bosnia and Herzegovina.

Congress of Berlin (June 13–July 13, 1878) The meeting of the six great powers following the Russo-Turkish War, which ended with the treaty of Berlin replacing the Treaty of San Stefano and determined the territories of the Balkan states.

Count Alfred von Schlieffen (1833–1913) The chief of the German general staff whose ideas formed the basis for Germany's war plan for a quick victory against France in 1914.

Entente Cordiale A series of agreements in 1904 in which Britain abandoned its traditional antagonism toward France.

Fourteen Points President Woodrow Wilson's (1856–1924) idealistic war aims.

Italia irredenta (1915) The territories (i.e., the South Tyrol, Trieste and some of the Dalmatian Islands) that the Allies agreed to deliver to Italy in exchange for Italian support in the war.

Kaiser William II (r. 1888–1918) Came to the German throne in 1888 as an ambitious and imperious young man of twenty-nine, who believed he ruled by divine right; wanted a navy and colonies to rival Britain and establish Germany as the leading power of Europe; his aims ran counter to Bismarck's limited continental policy.

League of Nations The association of sovereign states set up after World War I to pursue common policies and avert international aggression.

Leon Trotsky (1879–1940) Lenin's chief collaborator who organized a coup against the provisional government on November 6, 1917, which resulted in the establishment of Bolshevik rule in Russia.

mandates The assigning of the former German colonies and Turkish territories in the Middle East to Britain, France, Japan, Belgium, Australia, and South Africa as de facto colonies under the vague supervision of the League of Nations with the hope that the territories would advance to independence.

March Revolution The revolution of March 1917, in which the government of Tsar Nicholas II collapsed in the wake of popular protests against the war, its casualties, and the economic and social damage it caused to the country.

Russo-Japanese War (1904–1905) War in which the empires of Russia and Japan fought over territories in Manchuria and Korea and in which the complete defeat of Russia changed the balance of power in East Asia and elevated Japan's status to that of world superpower.

war guilt clause Clause 231 of the Treaty of Versailles, which assigned responsibility for World War I solely to Germany.

Winston Churchill (1874–1965) First lord of the British admiralty who, during World War I, proposed a daring plan to drive Turkey from the war and help the Balkan front by attacking the Dardanelles and capturing Constantinople; his poor execution of the attack forced the abandonment of the campaign.

Chapter 27
The Interwar Years: The Challenge of Dictators and Depression

THE FIRST FIVE-YEAR PLAN, 1932 This 1932 poster shows an idealized Soviet collective farm on which state-owned tractors have replaced peasant labor. In reality, collectivization provoked fierce resistance and caused famines in which millions of peasants died.
SOURCE: Deutsches Plakat Museum, Essen, Germany Archives Charmet/ Bridgeman

Contents and Focus Questions

27.1 After Versailles: Demands for Revision and Enforcement
Why did the Paris settlement fail to bring peace and prosperity to Europe?

27.2 Toward the Great Depression in Europe
What key factors combined to produce the Great Depression?

The Chapter in Brief

DURING THE TWO decades that followed the Paris settlement, Europe saw bold experiments in politics and economic life. Two broad sets of factors accounted for these experiments. First, the war, the Russian Revolution, and the peace treaty had transformed the political face of Europe. New political regimes had emerged in the wake of the collapse of the monarchies of Germany, Austria-Hungary, and Russia. These were the Weimar Republic in Germany, a host of successor states to the Austro-Hungarian and Russian Empires, and the Communist Soviet Union. In Great Britain, most of Ireland established itself as, in effect, an independent nation. These new governments immediately faced the problems of postwar reconstruction, economic dislocation, and nationalistic resentment. Most of these nations also included large groups who questioned the legitimacy of their governments. All the governments and societies of both Western and eastern Europe believed they were profoundly threatened by the Soviet Union. The Russian Revolution was thus a pivotal factor in the rise of right-wing and Fascist dictators, who often based their power on their firm opposition to the "Red Menace" and to the growing popularity of Socialism and Communism in many European countries during the economic crisis of the 1930s.

Second, beginning in the early twenties, economic dislocations leading to the economic downturn that became known as the Great Depression spread across the world. The economic troubles were caused by financial turmoil in the industrialized nations and a collapse of commodity prices that hurt the economies of the countries that exported raw materials. Faced with political instability and economic crisis, governments contrived various responses. The Great Depression, itself, which began in 1929, was the most severe downturn capitalist economies had ever experienced. High unemployment, low production, financial instability, and shrinking trade arrived and would not depart. Business and political leaders despaired over the market's seeming inability to resolve the crisis. Marxists and indeed many other observers thought the final downfall of capitalism was at hand.

European voters looked for new ways out of the doldrums, and politicians sought to escape the pressures that the Depression had brought on them. One result of the fight for economic security was the establishment of the Nazi dictatorship in Germany. Another was the piecemeal construction of what became known as the mixed economy; that is, governments became directly involved in making economic decisions alongside business and labor. In both cases, most of the political and economic guidelines of nineteenth-century liberalism were abandoned and so were decency and civility in political life. Authoritarianism and aggression were not the inescapable destiny of Europe. They emerged from the failure to secure alternative modes of democratic political life and stable international relations and from the inability to achieve long-term economic prosperity.

27.1 After Versailles: Demands for Revision and Enforcement

Why did the Paris settlement fail to bring peace and prosperity to Europe?

The Paris settlement fostered both resentments and discontent. Those resentments counted among the chief political factors in Europe for the next two decades. Germany had been humiliated. The arrangements for reparations led to endless haggling over payments. Many national groups in the successor states of the Austro-Hungarian Empire felt that their rights to self-determination had been violated or ignored. There were strident demands for further border adjustments because significant national minorities, particularly Germans and Magyars, resided outside the national boundaries drawn in Paris. On the other side, the victorious powers, especially France, often believed that the provisions of the treaties were being inadequately enforced. Consequently, throughout the 1920s and into the 1930s, demands either to revise or to enforce the Paris treaties contributed to domestic political turmoil across the Continent.

THE GREAT DEPRESSION IN FRANCE American credit played a vital role in Europe's postwar economic recovery. Thus, when the Great Depression hit, the bottom fell out not only of the American but of the European economy as well. In Paris, in 1933, the unemployed and the hungry marched in the streets to demand relief.

SOURCE: Sueddeutsche Zeitung Photo/Alamy Stock Photo

27.2 Toward the Great Depression in Europe

What key factors combined to produce the Great Depression?

Along with the move toward political experimentation and the demands for revision of the new international order, there was a widespread yearning to return to the economic prosperity of the prewar years. After 1918, however, it was impossible to restore to the economic realm what U.S. president Warren Harding (1865–1923) would term *normalcy*. During the Great War, Europeans had turned the military and industrial power that they had created during the previous century against themselves. What had been normal in economic and social life before 1914 could not be reestablished.

The casualties from the war numbered in the millions. (See Table 27–1.) This represented not only a waste of human life and talent but also the loss of producers and consumers.

Three factors originating in the 1920s combined to bring about the intense severity and the extended length of the **Great Depression**. First, a financial crisis stemmed directly from the war and the peace settlement. To this was added a crisis in the production and distribution of goods in the world market. These two problems became intertwined in 1929, and in Europe they reached the breaking point in 1931. Finally, both of these difficulties worsened because no major Western European country or the United States provided strong, responsible economic leadership that might have resulted in some form of cooperation to face the challenge of the Depression.

Table 27–1 TOTAL CASUALTIES IN THE FIRST WORLD WAR

Country	Dead	Wounded	Total Killed (% of population)
Germany	2,037,000	4,207,000	3.0
Russia	1,811,000	1,450,000	1.1
France	1,398,000	2,000,000	3.4
Austria-Hungary	1,100,000	3,620,000	1.9
British Empire	921,000	2,090,000	1.7
Turkey	804,000	400,000	3.7
Italy	578,000	947,000	1.6
Serbia	278,000	133,000	5.7
Romania	250,000	120,000	3.3
United States	114,000	206,000	0.1
Bulgaria	88,000	152,000	1.9
Belgium	38,000	44,700	0.5

SOURCE: Niall Ferguson, *The Pity of War* (New York: Basic Books, 1998).

27.2.1 Financial Tailspin

As one of the chief victors in the war, France was determined to collect reparations from Germany for the destruction the war had caused in northern France. The United States was no less determined that its allies repay the money it had lent them during the war. The European allies also owed debts to each other. German reparations were to provide the means of repaying these debts. Most of the money that the Allies collected from each other also went to the United States.

The quest for payment of German reparations caused one of the major diplomatic crises of the 1920s; that crisis itself resulted in further economic upheaval. In early 1923 the Allies—France in particular—declared Germany to be in technical default of its reparation payments. On January 11, to ensure receipt of the hard-won reparations, French and Belgian troops occupied the Ruhr mining and manufacturing district. The **Weimar Republic** ordered passive resistance that amounted to a general strike in Germany's largest industrial region. Confronted with this tactic, the French sent technicians and engineers to run the German mines and railroads. France got its way. The Germans paid, but its victory cost France dearly. The British were alienated by the French heavy-handedness and took no part in the occupation; they became more suspicious of France and more sympathetic to Germany. The cost of the Ruhr occupation, moreover, vastly increased French as well as German inflation and damaged the French economy.

The political and economic turmoil of the Ruhr invasion led to international attempts to ease the German payment of reparations. At the same time, American investment capital was pouring into Europe. However, by 1928 this investment decreased as American money was diverted into the booming New York stock market. The crash of Wall Street in October 1929—the result of virtually unregulated financial speculation—led to the loss of large amounts of money. Credit sharply contracted in the United States as numerous banks failed. Thereafter, little American capital was available for investment in Europe.

As American credit for Europe began to run out, a major financial crisis struck the Continent. In May 1931 the Kreditanstalt bank in Austria collapsed. The Kreditanstalt was a primary financial institution for much of central and eastern Europe. Its collapse put severe pressure on the German banking system, which was saved only through government guarantees. As the German difficulties increased, U.S. president Herbert Hoover (1874–1964) announced in June 1931 a one-year moratorium on all payments of international debts. The Hoover moratorium was a prelude to the end of reparations. The Lausanne Conference in the summer of 1932 brought, in effect, the era of reparations to a close. The next year the debts owed to the United States were settled either through small token payments or simply through default.

27.2.2 Problems in Agricultural Commodities

In the 1920s the market demand for European goods shrank, leaving much of the Continent's productive capacity idle or underused. This problem originated both within and outside Europe. In both instances the difficulty arose from agriculture. Better methods of farming, improved strains of wheat, expanded acreage under the plow, and more extensive transport facilities vastly increased the quantity of grain produced by farmers around the world. World wheat prices fell to record lows. Although this helped consumers, it decreased the income of European farmers. At the same time, higher industrial wages raised the cost of the industrial goods that farmers or peasants used. Consequently, they had great difficulty paying off their mortgages and loans for normal operating costs. These problems were especially acute in central and eastern Europe and increased farmers' disillusionment with liberal politics. German farmers, for example, would become prime supporters of the National Socialist Workers Party or Nazis.

Outside Europe similar problems affected other producers of agricultural commodities. The prices they received for their products plummeted. Government-held reserves of raw materials reached record levels. This glut of major world commodities involved wheat, sugar, coffee, rubber, wool, and lard. The people who produced these goods in underdeveloped nations could no longer make enough money to buy goods from industrial Europe. As world credit collapsed, the economic position of these commodity producers worsened. Commodity production had simply outstripped world demand.

The results of the collapse in the agricultural sector of the world economy and the financial turmoil were stagnation and depression for European industry. Coal, iron, and textiles had depended largely on international markets. Unemployment spread from these industries to those producing consumer goods. Persistent unemployment in Great Britain and to a lesser extent in Germany during the 1920s had created "soft" domestic markets. The policies of reduced spending with which the governments confronted the Depression further weakened domestic demand. By the early 1930s the Depression was feeding on itself.

27.2.3 Depression and Government Policy in Britain and France

The Depression did not mean absolute economic decline or total unemployment. But the economic downturn spread potential as well as real insecurity. People in nearly all walks of life feared the loss of their economic security. The Depression also frustrated normal social and economic expectations. Even the employed often seemed to make no progress; and their anxieties created a major source of discontent.

The governments of the late 1920s and the early 1930s were not well suited in either structure or ideology to confront these problems. The electorates demanded action. The governments' responses depended largely on the severity of the Depression in a particular country and on the self-confidence of the nation's political system.

Because their vast empires commanded very large economies, Great Britain and France undertook moderate political experiments. In 1924 the Labour Party in Great Britain was established as a viable governing party by forming a short-lived government. It again formed a ministry in 1929. Under the pressure of the Depression and at the urging of King George V (r. 1910–1936), Labour prime minister Ramsay MacDonald (1866–1937) organized a national government, which was a coalition of the Labour, Conservative, and Liberal Parties.

The 1920s also saw the establishment of an independent Irish state. On Easter Monday in April 1916, a nationalist uprising occurred in Dublin. The British suppressed the uprising but made martyrs of its leaders by executing several of them. Leadership of the nationalist cause quickly shifted from the Irish Party in Parliament to the extremist **Sinn Fein**, or "Ourselves Alone," movement. On January 21, 1919, they declared Irish independence. Thereafter a civil war broke out between the military wing of Sinn Fein, which became the Irish Republican Army (IRA), and the British army. The conflict ended with a treaty in December 1921, which established the Irish Free State as one of the dominions in the British Commonwealth. The six, predominantly Protestant, counties of Ulster, or Northern Ireland,

were permitted to remain part of what was now called the United Kingdom of Great Britain and Northern Ireland, with provisions for home rule. In the 1920s and 1930s, the Free State gradually severed its ties to Britain. It remained neutral during World War II and declared itself an independent republic in 1949.

The most important French interwar political experiment was the **Popular Front**, which came to office in 1936. It was composed of Socialists, Radicals, and Communists: despite fierce resistance from business and conservative groups, the Popular Front enacted major social and economic reforms, including the forty-hour week, paid vacations for workers, and compulsory arbitration of labor disputes. But its parliamentary support gradually faded until its final collapse in October 1938.

The political changes in Britain and France were essentially of domestic significance. But the political experiments of the 1920s and 1930s that reshaped world history and civilization involved the establishment of a Soviet government in Russia, a Fascist regime in Italy, and a Nazi dictatorship in Germany.

27.3 The Soviet Experiment

What was the relationship between politics and economics in the early decades of the Soviet Union?

The consolidation of the Bolshevik Revolution in Russia established the most extensive and durable of all twentieth-century authoritarian governments. The Communist Party of the Soviet Union retained power from 1917 until the end of 1991, and its presence influenced the political history of Europe and much of the rest of the world as did no other single factor. Unlike the Italian Fascists or the German National Socialists, the Bolsheviks seized power violently through revolution. For several years they confronted civil war, and their leaders long felt insecure about their hold on the country. The Communist Party was neither a mass party nor a nationalistic one. Its early membership rarely exceeded more than 1 percent of the Russian population. The Bolsheviks confronted a much less industrialized economy than that in Italy or Germany. They believed in and practiced the collectivization of economic life. The Marxist–Leninist ideology had vastly more international appeal than the nationalism of the Fascists and the racism of the Nazis. Communism was an exportable commodity. The Communists did not regard their government and revolution only as part of Russian history, but rather as epoch-making events in the history of the world and the development of humanity. Fear of Communism and determination to stop its spread became one of the leading political forces in Western Europe and the United States for most of the rest of

LENIN, REVOLUTIONARY HERO Anxiety about the Bolshevik Revolution was a significant factor in European politics during the 1920s and 1930s. Images like this Soviet portrait of Lenin as a heroic revolutionary conjured fears in the rest of Europe of a political force determined to overturn their social, political, and economic institutions.
SOURCE: bpk Bildagentur/Art Resource, NY

the century. Policies stemming from that opposition would influence European and American relationships with much of the rest of the world.

27.3.1 War Communism

Within the Soviet Union the Red Army under the organizational genius of Leon Trotsky (1879–1940) had suppressed internal and foreign military opposition to the new government during the civil war that raged from 1918 to 1920. Within months of the revolution, a new secret police, known as *Cheka*, appeared. Throughout the civil war Lenin (1870–1924) had declared that the Bolshevik Party, as the vanguard of the revolution, was imposing the dictatorship of the proletariat. Political and economic administration became highly centralized. All major decisions flowed from the top in a nondemocratic manner. Under the economic policy of **War Communism**, the revolutionary government confiscated and then operated the banks, the transport facilities, and heavy industry. The state also forcibly requisitioned grain and shipped it from the countryside to feed

the army and the urban workers. The Bolsheviks used the civil war as justification for suppressing any resistance to these economic policies.

War Communism helped the Red Army defeat its opponents. The revolution had survived and triumphed. The policy, however, generated domestic opposition to the Bolsheviks, who in 1920 numbered only about 600,000. The alliance of workers and peasants forged in 1917 by the Bolsheviks' slogan of "Peace, Bread, and Land" had begun to dissolve. Many Russians were no longer willing to make the sacrifices demanded by the central party bureaucrats. In 1920 and 1921, serious strikes occurred. Peasants were discontented and resisted the requisition of grain. In March 1921, the sailors mutinied at the Kronstadt naval base on the Baltic. The Red Army crushed the rebellion with grave loss of life. These acts of opposition suggested that the proletariat itself was opposing the dictatorship of the proletariat. Also, by late 1920 it had become clear that revolution was not going to sweep across the rest of Europe. For the time being, the Soviet Union would constitute a vast island of revolutionary Socialism in the larger sea of world capitalism.

27.3.2 The New Economic Policy

Under these difficult conditions Lenin made a strategic retreat. In March 1921, following the Kronstadt mutiny, he outlined the **New Economic Policy**, or NEP. Apart from what he termed "the commanding heights" of banking, heavy industry, transportation, and international commerce, considerable private economic enterprise was allowed. In particular, peasants could farm for a profit. They would pay taxes like other citizens, but they could sell their surplus grain on the open market. The NEP was consistent with Lenin's earlier conviction that the Russian peasantry held the key to the success of the revolution, but the changes came too late to avert the famine of 1921 to1922 in which perhaps five million people died. After 1921 the countryside did become more stable, and a secure food supply seemed ensured for the cities. Similar free enterprise flourished within light industry and the domestic retail trade. By 1927 industrial production had reached its 1913 level. The revolution seemed to have transformed Russia into a land of small farms and privately owned shops and businesses.

27.3.3 The Third International

The onset and consolidation of the Bolshevik Revolution in Russia was a transforming event for the history of Socialism as well as for Russia and international affairs. In the West, before the war, Social Democratic parties had regarded the Russian Bolsheviks as eccentric, politically marginal Marxist extremists. The Bolshevik victory forced West European Social Democrats to rethink their position within the world of international Socialism. For their part, the Bolsheviks intended to establish themselves as the international leaders of Marxism and regarded reformist Social Democrats as enemies and rivals.

In 1919, the Soviet Communists founded the Third International of the European Socialist movement, better known as the *Comintern*. The Comintern worked to make the Bolshevik model of Socialism, as Lenin had developed it, the rule for all Socialist parties outside the Soviet Union. In 1920, the Comintern imposed its Twenty-one Conditions on any Socialist party that wished to join it. These conditions included acknowledging Moscow's leadership, rejecting reformist or revisionist Socialism, repudiating previous Socialist leaders, and adopting the Communist Party name. In effect, the Comintern sought to destroy democratic Socialism, which it accused of having betrayed the working class through reform policies and parliamentary accommodation.

The decision whether to accept these conditions split every major European Socialist party. As a result, separate Communist and Social Democratic parties emerged in most countries, and they fought each other more intensely than they fought either capitalism or conservative political parties. Their fierce conflict was one of the fundamental features of the interwar European political landscape.

These Comintern polices and the resulting divisions of the Socialist parties directly affected the rise of the Fascists and the Nazis in Western Europe. It is difficult to overestimate the fears that Soviet political rhetoric and Communist Party activity aroused in Europe during the 1920s and 1930s. Conservative and right-wing political groups manipulated and exaggerated these fears. The presence of separate Communist parties in Western Europe meant that right-wing politicians always had a convenient target they could justly accuse of seeking to overthrow the government and to impose Soviet-style political, social, and economic systems in their nations. Furthermore, right-wing politicians also accused the Democratic Socialists of supporting policies that might facilitate a Communist takeover. The divisions between Communists and Democratic Socialists also meant that right-wing political movements rarely had to confront a united left.

27.3.4 Stalin versus Trotsky

The NEP had caused sharp disputes within the Politburo, the highest governing committee of the Communist Party. The partial return to capitalism seemed to some members nothing less than a betrayal of sound Marxist principles. These frictions increased as Lenin's firm hand disappeared. After suffering a stroke in 1922, he never again dominated party affairs and died in 1924. In the ensuing power vacuum, an intense struggle for leadership of the party commenced. Two factions emerged. One was led by Trotsky, the other by Joseph Stalin (1879–1953), who had become general secretary of the party in 1922.

Each faction wanted to control the party and thus also the state, but the struggle was fought over the question of Russia's path toward industrialization and the future of the Communist revolutionary movement. Trotsky, speaking for what became known as the left wing, urged rapid industrialization and looked to voluntary collectivization of farming by poor peasants as a means of increasing agricultural production. He further argued that the revolution in Russia could succeed only if new revolutions took place elsewhere.

A right-wing faction opposed Trotsky, and Stalin was its true political manipulator. In the mid-1920s this group pressed for the continuation of Lenin's NEP and relatively slow industrialization.

Stalin was the ultimate victor in these intraparty rivalries. Unlike the other early Bolshevik leaders, he had not spent a long exile in Western Europe. He was much less an intellectual and internationalist. He was also much more brutal. His handling of various recalcitrant national groups within Russia after the revolution had shocked even Lenin. Stalin's power lay in his command of bureaucratic and administrative methods. He was neither a brilliant writer nor an effective public speaker; however, he mastered the crucial, if dull, details of party structure, including admission, promotion, and rewards. That mastery meant that he could draw on the support of the lower levels of the party apparatus when he clashed with other leaders.

In the mid-1920s Stalin supported Nikolai Bukharin's position on economic development. In 1924 he also enunciated, in opposition to Trotsky, the doctrine of "Socialism in one country." He urged that Socialism could be achieved in Russia alone. Russian success did not depend on the fate of the revolution elsewhere. Stalin thus nationalized the previously international scope of the Marxist revolution. He cunningly used the apparatus of the party and his control over its Central Committee to edge out Trotsky and his supporters. By 1927 Trotsky had been removed from all his offices, ousted from the party, and exiled. In 1929 he was expelled from Russia and eventually moved to Mexico, where he was murdered in 1940 by one of Stalin's agents. With the removal of Trotsky, Stalin was firmly in control of the Soviet state. It remained to be seen what "Socialism in one country" would mean in practice.

27.3.5 The Decision for Rapid Industrialization

In 1927 the Party Congress decided to push for rapid industrialization. Implemented through what has been termed "industrialization by political mobilization," this policy marked a sharp departure from the NEP and a rejection of the pockets of relatively free-market operations within the larger Soviet economy.[1]

Stalin's goal was to have the Soviet Union overtake the productive capacity of its enemies, the capitalist nations. This

MAGNITOGORSK, STALIN'S CITY OF STEEL Magnitogorsk was a city that became a monument to Stalin's drive toward rapid industrialization. Located in the Ural Mountains near a vast supply of iron ore, the city became the site of major iron and steel production. It was one of the new industrial cities founded under the Five-Year Plan to challenge capitalist production of Western nations.
SOURCE: National Archives

policy required the rapid construction of heavy industries, such as iron, steel, and machine tool making; building electricity-generating stations; and manufacturing tractors. Stalin's organizational vehicle for industrialization was a series of Five-Year Plans, starting in 1928. The State Planning Commission, or *Gosplan*, set goals for production in every area of economic life and attempted to organize the economy to meet them. The task of coordinating all facets of production was immensely complicated. Deliveries of materials from mines or factories had to be ensured before the next unit could carry out its part of the plan. Enormous economic disruption occurred as the *Gosplan* built power plants and steel mills and increased the output of mines. The plans consistently favored capital projects over the production of consumer goods. The number of centralized agencies and ministries involved in planning soared, and they often competed with each other.

The rapid expansion of the industrial base created the first genuinely large factory labor force in what had been Russia. Workers were recruited from the countryside and from the urban unemployed. New cities and industrial districts in existing cities arose. Most workers were crowded into shoddy buildings with inadequate sanitation, living space, and nourishment. Their lives were as bad as or worse than anything Marx and Engels had decried in the nineteenth century.

The government and the Communist Party undertook a vast program of propaganda to sell the Five-Year Plans to the Russian people and to elicit their cooperation. The government boasted of the sheer size of the plants and new towns being constructed. Such propaganda was necessary because most industrial workers were displaced peasants who had never worked in a factory and often resisted industrial discipline. The party appealed to the idealism of the young by proclaiming its goals of rapidly modernizing the nation. Workers, such as a legendary coal miner named Stakhanov, who exceeded their assigned goals received rewards and publicity.

The results were impressive. Soviet industrial production rose approximately 400 percent between 1928 and 1940. Industries that had never existed in Russia challenged their foreign counterparts. Hundreds of thousands of people populated new industrial cities. The social and human cost of this effort had, however, been appalling.

27.3.6 The Collectivization of Agriculture

Agricultural productivity had always been a core problem for the emerging Soviet economy. Under the NEP the government purchased a certain amount of grain at prices it set itself. The rest of the grain was then supposed to be sold at market prices, which were higher than the government-set prices. Peasant farmers of all levels of wealth tried to circumvent this system, often by keeping grain off the market in hopes that its price would rise. The scarcity of consumer goods available for purchase in the countryside also encouraged hoarding. With little to buy from what they earned by selling their grain, farmers had little incentive to sell it. Instead, many of them refused to sell grain to the government at the low prices it set and insisted on selling it at the market price, which the government refused to accept. In 1928 and 1929, as a result, the Soviet government confronted shortfalls of grain on the market and the prospect of food shortages in the cities and social unrest.

Stalin therefore decided to reverse the agricultural policies of the NEP. Toward the end of the 1920s, Soviet economists and party officials devised an explanation for the difficulties they confronted in the agricultural sector. First, they asserted that traditional peasant holdings were too small to produce enough grain to meet the country's needs. Second, they claimed that a class-enemy was responsible for the hoarding and for what they regarded as speculation in the grain trade. This enemy was the group of relatively prosperous peasants, known as *kulaks*, who numbered somewhat less than 5 percent of the rural population and were often the most productive and efficient farmers. Based on these ideas, Stalin decided that Soviet agriculture must be collectivized to produce enough grain for domestic food and foreign export. **Collectivization**—the replacement of private peasant farms with huge state-run and state-owned farms called collectives—would also put the Communist Party firmly in control of the farm sector of the economy and free up peasant labor to work in the expanding industrial sector. To carry out this policy, Stalin blamed the kulaks for the agricultural problems.

THE DRIVE TO COLLECTIVIZE Stalin used intimidation and propaganda to support his drive to collectivize Soviet agriculture. Communist Party agitators led groups of peasants to demand the seizure of the farms worked by kulaks, members of the Russian peasant class who were targeted for having excess wealth.
SOURCE: Everett Historical/Shutterstock

Party officials carried out the initial campaign of dekulakization and collectivization. Usually they would seek first to remove kulaks from a village while confiscating their land and then attempt to coerce the remaining peasants into organizing a collective farm. Enormous turmoil and violence resulted.

Peasants determined to keep their land, often with women in the lead, had sabotaged collectivization by slaughtering millions of livestock between 1929 and 1933. Peasants who resisted were killed outright. Others starved to death on their own farms when all the grain that they had produced was seized. Over two million peasants were forcibly removed from their homes and deported to distant areas of the Soviet Union or to prison camps where many died from disease, exposure, and malnutrition. Even if they survived that ordeal, the peasants had to patch together some kind of life as industrial workers or miners in Siberia or another inhospitable province. Their children were treated as class-enemies and political traitors. Much of the violence of collectivization occurred in Ukraine, where Stalin used the process not only to restructure agricultural production but also to crush any vestiges of Ukrainian nationalism, and many millions of lives were lost as a result.

During the drive toward collectivization, the Communist Party also targeted priests of the Russian Orthodox Church. The party, atheistic in its ideology, had always opposed religion, but only with collectivization were many rural priests attacked and churches closed or vandalized. Between 1926 and 1937, the number of priests recorded in the Soviet census dropped by more than one-half. Rabbis, Catholic priests, Protestant ministers, and mullahs received the same harsh treatment.

At the cost of millions of peasant lives, Stalin and the Communist Party had won the battle of the grain fields, but they had not solved the problem of producing enough food. That difficulty would plague the Soviet Union until its collapse in 1991 and remains a problem for its successor states.

27.3.7 The Purges

In 1933, with turmoil in the countryside and economic dislocation caused by industrialization, Stalin and others in the central Soviet bureaucracy began to fear they were losing control of the country and the party apparatus and that effective rivals to their power and policies might emerge. These apprehensions were largely a figment of Stalin's own paranoia and lust for power, but they resulted in the **Great Purges**, which remain one of the most mysterious and horrendous political events of the twentieth century. Few observers understood the purges at the time, and despite the recent opening of Soviet archives, they have still not been fully comprehended, either inside or outside the former Soviet Union.

The pretext for the onset of the purges was the assassination on December 1, 1934, of Sergei Kirov (1888–1934), the popular party chief of Leningrad and a member of the Politburo. In the wake of the shooting, thousands of people were arrested and still more were expelled from the party and sent to labor camps. At the time, many thought that opponents of the regime had murdered Kirov, and Stalin routinely accused those he attacked of complicity in the crime. Today, many scholars believe that Stalin himself authorized Kirov's assassination because he was afraid of him. The available documentary evidence does not allow us to know for sure whether Stalin was involved, but he quickly used Kirov's death for his own purposes.

The purges that took place immediately after Kirov's death were just the beginning of a larger and longer process. Between 1936 and 1938, a series of spectacular show trials were held in Moscow. Former high Soviet leaders, including members of the Politburo, such as Bukharin, publicly confessed to political crimes and were convicted and executed. It is still not certain why they made these obviously false confessions, although ritual confession of faults and shortcomings had long characterized internal Communist Party life. They had also been interrogated under the most difficult conditions, including torture, and feared for their families' lives. (Stalin regularly arrested the wives, children, siblings, and in-laws of "traitors" and had them shot or sent to die in labor camps.) Other lower-level party members were tried in private and shot. Hundreds of thousands, perhaps millions, of ordinary Soviet citizens received no trial at all and were either executed or deported to slave labor camps where many died. Within the party itself, thousands of members were expelled, and applicants for membership were removed from the rolls. After the civilian party members and leaders had been purged, the prosecutors turned against the government bureaucracy and the Soviet army and navy, convicting and executing thousands of officials and officers, including heroes of the civil war. The exact number of executions, imprisonments, interrogations, and expulsions is unknown, but it ran well into the millions. While the purges went on, no one in the Soviet Union, except Stalin himself, was safe.

The rational explanations of the purges—to the extent that mass murder can ever be rationally explained—probably lie in two directions. First, different portions of the party leadership moved against others during the several years the purges lasted. Initially, Stalin and the central Moscow leadership used the purges to settle old scores and to discipline and gain more control over lower levels of the party in the far-flung regions of the Soviet Union. In addition to increasing Stalin's authority, these central bureaucratic groups wanted to eliminate any opposition to their own positions or policies. By 1937, however, Stalin seems to have become distrustful of the central party elite, his own supporters, and began to find or pretend to find enemies within its ranks. Moreover, by that date, local Communist groups were allowed to designate their own victims with little direction from Moscow. Thereafter, a self-destructive cascade of accusations, imprisonments, and executions occurred throughout the party and within its highest levels. The Communist Party leadership at all levels appeared to be consuming itself in an atmosphere of terror for its own sake. This situation has been termed "centrally authorized chaos."[2]

Second, no matter how much tension and rivalry there were among the different levels and regions of the Communist Party, Stalin's primary motive for the purges was almost certainly fear for his own power and a ruthless determination to preserve and increase it. He and the deputies whom he allowed to survive the purges personally selected certain victims and determined the fate of their families. In effect, the purges created a new Communist Party that was absolutely subservient and loyal to Stalin. The "old Bolsheviks" of the October Revolution in 1917 were among his earliest targets. They and others active in the first years of the revolution knew how far Stalin had moved away from Lenin's policies. New, younger recruits replaced the party members, who were executed or expelled. The newcomers knew little about old Russia or the ideals of the original Bolsheviks. They had not been loyal to Lenin, Trotsky, Bukharin, or any other Soviet leader except Stalin himself.

The internal difficulties of collectivization and industrialization and his worries about internal opposition led Stalin to make an important shift in foreign policy. In 1934, he began to fear the nation might be left isolated against aggression by Nazi Germany. The Soviet Union was not yet strong enough to withstand such an attack. That year Stalin ordered the Comintern to permit Communist parties in other countries to cooperate with non-Communist parties against Nazism and Fascism. This reversed the Comintern policy Lenin established as part of the Twenty-one Conditions in 1919. The new Stalinist policy allowed the Popular Front Government in France to come to power.

27.4 The Fascist Experiment in Italy

What did Fascism mean to Mussolini and his supporters?

The first authoritarian political experiment in Western Europe that arose in part from fears of the spread of Bolshevism beyond the Soviet Union occurred in Italy. The general term *Fascist*, which has been used to describe the various right-wing dictatorships that arose between the wars, was derived from the Italian Fascist movement of **Benito Mussolini** (1883–1945).

While scholars still dispute the exact meaning of **Fascism** as a political term, the governments regarded as Fascist were antidemocratic, anti-Marxist, antiparliamentary, and frequently anti-Semitic. They hoped to hold back the spread of Bolshevism, which seemed a real threat at the time. They sought a world that would be safe for the middle class, small businesses, owners of moderate amounts of property, and small farmers. The Fascist regimes rejected the political inheritance of the French Revolution and of nineteenth-century liberalism. Their adherents believed that normal parliamentary politics and parties sacrificed national honor and greatness to petty party disputes. They wanted to overcome the class conflict of Marxism and the party conflict of liberalism by consolidating the various groups and classes within the nation for great national purposes. As Mussolini declared in 1931, "The fascist conception of the state is all-embracing, and outside of the state no human or spiritual values can exist, let alone be desirable."[3] Fascist governments were usually single-party dictatorships characterized by terrorism against and police surveillance of both opponents and the general citizenry. These dictatorships were rooted in the base of mass political parties.

27.4.1 The Rise of Mussolini

The Italian *Fasci di Combattimento* ("Band of Combat") was founded in 1919 in Milan. Most of its members were war veterans who felt that the sacrifices Italy had made in World War I had been in vain. They resented Italy's failure to gain the city of Fiume, toward the northern end of the Adriatic Sea, and other territories at the Paris conference. They feared Socialism, inflation, and labor unrest.

Their leader or **Il Duce**, Benito Mussolini, was just another Italian politician. His Fascist organization was one of many small political groups in a country characterized by such entities. As a politician, Mussolini was an opportunist par excellence. He could change his ideas and principles to suit every new occasion. Action for him was always more important than thought or rational justification. His one real rule was political survival.

Postwar Italian politics was a muddle. Many Italians were dissatisfied with the parliamentary system as it then existed. They felt that Italy had emerged from the war as less than a victorious nation, had not been treated as a great power at the Paris peace conference, and had not received the rewards it deserved. The main spokesman for this discontent was extreme nationalist writer Gabriele D'Annunzio (1863–1938). In 1919 he captured Fiume with a force of patriotic Italians. The Italian army, enforcing the terms of the Versailles Treaty, eventually drove him out. D'Annunzio had provided the example of the political use

BENITO MUSSOLINI Benito Mussolini became famous for bombastic public speeches delivered in settings surrounded by his Fascist followers and military supporters.
SOURCE: Associated Press

of a nongovernmental military force. Removing him from Fiume made the parliamentary ministry seem unpatriotic.

Between 1919 and 1921 Italy was also wracked by social turmoil. Numerous industrial strikes occurred, and workers occupied factories. Peasants seized uncultivated land from large estates. Parliamentary and constitutional government seemed incapable of dealing with this unrest. The Socialist Party had captured a plurality of seats in the Chamber of Deputies in 1919. A new Catholic Popular Party had also done well. Both appealed to the working and agrarian classes. However, neither party would cooperate with the other, and parliamentary deadlock resulted. Under these conditions, many Italians honestly—and still others conveniently—believed that a Communist revolution might break out.

Initially, Mussolini was uncertain which way the political winds were blowing. He first supported the factory occupations and land seizures. Never one to be concerned with consistency, however, he soon reversed himself. He had discovered that many upper- and middle-class Italians who were hurt by inflation and who feared the loss of their property had no sympathy for the workers or the peasants. They wanted order rather than some vague social justice that might harm their own interests. Consequently, Mussolini and his Fascists took direct action in the face of the government's inaction. They formed local squads who terrorized Socialists. They attacked strikers and farm workers and protected strikebreakers. Conservative land and factory owners were grateful to the terrorists. The officers of the law simply ignored these crimes. By early 1922 the Fascists controlled local government in many parts of northern Italy.

In 1921 Mussolini and thirty-four of his followers had been elected to the Chamber of Deputies. Their importance grew as the local Fascists gained more direct power. The Fascist movement now had hundreds of thousands of supporters. In October 1922 the Fascists, dressed in their characteristic black shirts, began a march on Rome. Intimidated, King Victor Emmanuel III (r. 1900–1946) refused to authorize an army against the marchers. No other single decision so ensured a Fascist seizure of power. The cabinet resigned in protest. On October 29 the monarch telegraphed Mussolini in Milan and asked him to become prime minister. The next day Mussolini arrived in Rome by sleeping car and, as head of the government, greeted his followers when they entered the city.

Technically, Mussolini had come into office by legal means. The monarch did have the power to appoint the prime minister. Mussolini, however, had no majority in the Chamber of Deputies. Behind the legal façade of his assumption of power lay months of terrorist disruption and intimidation and the threat of the Fascists' October march.

27.4.2 The Fascists in Power

Mussolini had not really expected to be appointed prime minister. He moved cautiously to consolidate his power. He succeeded because of the impotence of his rivals, his effective use of his office, his power over the masses, and his sheer ruthlessness. On November 23, 1922, the king and Parliament granted Mussolini dictatorial authority for one year to bring order to the lower levels of the government. Wherever possible, Mussolini appointed Fascists to office. Late in 1924, at Mussolini's behest, Parliament changed the election law. Previously parties had been represented in the Chamber of Deputies in proportion to the popular vote cast for them. According to the new election law, the party that gained the largest popular vote (with a minimum of at least 25 percent) received two-thirds of the seats in the chamber. Coalition government, with all its compromises and hesitations, would no longer be necessary. In the election of 1924 the Fascists won a great victory and complete control of the Chamber of Deputies. They used that majority to end legitimate parliamentary life. A series of laws passed in 1925 and 1926 permitted Mussolini, in effect, to rule by decree. In 1926 all other political parties were dissolved, and Italy was transformed into a single-party, dictatorial state.

The Italian dictator made one important domestic departure that brought him significant political dividends. Through the Lateran Accord he signed with the Vatican in February 1929, the Roman Catholic Church and the Italian state made peace with each other. Ever since the armies of Italian unification had seized papal lands in the 1860s, the church had been hostile to the state. The popes had virtually secluded themselves in the Vatican after 1870. The agreement of 1929 recognized the pope as the temporal ruler of the mini-state of Vatican City. The Italian government agreed to pay an indemnity to the papacy for confiscated land. The state also recognized Catholicism as the religion of the nation, exempted church property from taxes, and allowed church law to govern marriage. The Lateran Accord brought further respectability to Mussolini's authoritarian regime.

27.5 German Democracy and Dictatorship

Why did democracy fail to thrive in postwar Germany?

The Weimar Republic was born from the defeat of the imperial army, the revolution of 1918 against the Hohenzollerns, and the hopes of German Liberals and Social Democrats. Its name derived from the city in which its constitution was written and promulgated in August 1919. While the constitution was being debated, the republic, headed by the Social Democrats, accepted the humiliating terms of the Treaty of Versailles. Although its officials had signed only under the threat of an Allied invasion, the republic was nevertheless permanently associated with the national disgrace and the economic burdens of the treaty.

27.5.1 The Weimar Republic

Throughout the 1920s the government of the republic was required to fulfill the economic and military provisions imposed by the Paris settlement. It became all too easy for nationalists and military figures whose policies had brought on the tragedy and defeat of the war to blame the young republic and the Socialists for the results of the conflict. In Germany, more than in other countries, the desire to revise the treaty was closely related to a desire to change the mode of domestic government.

GUSTAV STRESEMANN Gustav Stresemann (1878–1929) played an instrumental role in the restoration of Germany's international status following World War I. He was awarded the Nobel Peace Prize in 1926 for his policy of détente but died young, at fifty-one in 1929, before the National Socialists came to power in Germany.
SOURCE: Lebrecht Music and Arts Photo Library/Alamy Stock Photo

The Weimar Constitution was a highly enlightened document. It guaranteed civil liberties and provided for direct election, by universal suffrage, of the *Reichstag* and the president. It also, however, contained crucial structural flaws that eventually allowed it to be overthrown. Seats in the Reichstag were allotted according to a complicated system of proportional representation. This made it relatively easy for small political parties to gain seats and resulted in shifting party combinations that led to eleven governments in thirteen years. Ministers were technically responsible to the Reichstag, but the president appointed and removed the chancellor, the head of the cabinet. Perhaps most important, Article 48 allowed the president, in an emergency, to rule by decree. The constitution thus permitted the possibility of presidential dictatorship.

The new government suffered major and minor humiliations as well as considerable economic instability. In March

1920 the right-wing Kapp Putsch, or armed insurrection, erupted in Berlin. Led by a conservative civil servant and supported by army officers, the attempted coup failed, but only after government officials had fled the city and workers had carried out a general strike. In the same month, strikes took place in the Ruhr mining district. The government sent in troops. Such extremism from both the left and the right would haunt the republic for all its days. In May 1921 the Allies presented a reparations bill for 132 billion gold marks. The German Republican government accepted this preposterous demand only after new Allied threats of occupation. Throughout the early 1920s there were numerous assassinations or attempted assassinations of important Republican leaders. Violence was the hallmark of the first five years of the republic.

27.5.1.1 INVASION OF THE RUHR AND INFLATION

Inflation brought on the major crisis of this period. The financing of the war and continued postwar deficit spending generated a colossal rise in prices. Consequently, the value of German currency fell. By early 1921 the German mark traded against the American dollar at a ratio of 64 to 1, compared with a ratio of 4.2 to 1 in 1914. The German

WORTHLESS PAPER In 1923, Germany suffered from enormous inflation. Paper money became worthless—not worth the paper it was printed on. It was used instead as fuel to light kitchen stoves.
SOURCE: Library of Congress Prints and Photographs Division [LC-USZ62-52900]

financial community contended that the value of the currency could not be stabilized until the reparations issue had been solved. In the meantime, the printing presses kept pouring out paper money, which was used to redeem government bonds as they were due.

The French invasion of the Ruhr in January 1923 to secure payment of reparations and the German response of passive economic resistance produced cataclysmic inflation. The Weimar government paid subsidies to the Ruhr labor force, who had laid down their tools. Unemployment soon spread from the Ruhr to other parts of the country, creating a new drain on the treasury and also reducing tax revenues. Money was literally not worth the paper it was printed on. Stores were unwilling to exchange goods for the worthless currency, and farmers withheld produce from the market.

The moral and social values of thrift and prudence were thoroughly undermined. Middle-class savings, pensions, and insurance policies were wiped out, as were investments in government bonds. Simultaneously, debts and mortgages could not be paid off. Speculators in land, real estate, and industry made fortunes. Union contracts generally allowed workers to keep up with rising prices. Thus, inflation was not a disaster for everyone. To the middle and lower middle classes, however, inflation was another trauma coming hard on the heels of the military defeat and the peace treaty. Only when the social and economic upheaval of these months is grasped can one understand the German desire for order and security at almost any cost.

27.5.1.2 HITLER'S EARLY CAREER

Late in 1923 **Adolf Hitler** (1889–1945) made his first significant appearance on the German political scene. The son of a minor Austrian customs official, he had gone to Vienna, where his hopes of gaining admission to an elite art school were soon dashed. Hitler absorbed the rabid German nationalism and extreme anti-Semitism that flourished in Vienna. He came to hate Marxism, which he associated with Jews. During World War I, Hitler fought in the German army, was wounded, rose to the rank of corporal, and won the Iron Cross for bravery. The war gave him his first sense of purpose.

After the conflict, Hitler settled in Munich. He soon became associated with a small nationalistic, anti-Semitic political party that in 1920 adopted the name of National Socialist German Workers Party, better known simply as the **Nazis**. In the same year the group began to parade under a red-and-white banner with a black swastika. It issued a platform, or program, of Twenty-Five Points. Among other things, this platform called for the repudiation of the Versailles Treaty, the unification of Austria and Germany, the exclusion of Jews from German citizenship, agrarian reform, the prohibition of land speculation, the confiscation of war profits, state administration of the giant cartels, and the replacement of department stores with small retail shops. Originally the Nazis had called for a broad program of nationalization of industry in an attempt to compete directly with the Marxist political parties for the vote of the workers. As the tactic failed, the Nazis redefined the meaning of the word *Socialist* in the party name so that it suggested a nationalistic outlook. In 1922, Hitler said,

> Whoever is prepared to make the national cause his own to such an extent that he knows no higher ideal than the welfare of his nation; whoever has understood our great national anthem, *Deutschland, Deutschland, über Alles* ["Germany, Germany, over All"], to mean that nothing in the wide world surpasses in his eyes this Germany, people and land, land and people—that man is a Socialist.[4]

This definition, of course, had nothing to do with traditional German Socialism. The Socialism that Hitler and the Nazis had in mind was not state ownership of the means of production, but the subordination of all economic enterprise to the welfare of the nation. It often implied protection for small economic enterprises. Increasingly, the Nazis discovered their party appealed to virtually any economic group that was at risk and under pressure, and they often tailored their messages to the particular local problems these groups confronted in different parts of Germany. The Nazis also found considerable support among war veterans, who faced economic and social displacement in Weimar society.

Soon after the promulgation of the Twenty-Five Points, the storm troopers, or **SA (Sturm Abteilung)**, were organized under the leadership of Captain Ernst Roehm (1887–1934). It was a paramilitary organization that initially provided its members with food and uniforms and, later in the decade, with wages. In the mid-1920s the SA adopted its famous brown-shirted uniform. The storm troopers were the chief Nazi instrument for terror and intimidation before the party controlled the government. They were a law unto themselves. The organization constituted a means of preserving military discipline and values outside the small army permitted by the Paris settlement. The existence of such a private party army and of a similar one run by the Communists was a sign of the potential for violence in the Weimar Republic and the widespread contempt for the law and the institutions of the republic.

The social and economic turmoil following the French occupation of the Ruhr and the German inflation gave the fledgling party an opportunity for direct action against the Weimar Republic, which seemed incapable of providing military or economic security. By this time, because of his immense oratorical skills and organizational abilities, Hitler personally dominated the Nazi Party. As he established his dominance within the party, he clearly had the model of Mussolini in mind and spoke of the Italian dictator's accomplishments in glowing terms. Both men recruited from disillusioned veterans of the World War. Both adopted paramilitary modes of organization. Both disparaged liberal politics as incapable of achieving great national ends and

righting the wrongs of the peace settlement. Both exalted the principle of obedience to the heroic leader. In late 1923, with the memory of Mussolini's march on Rome still fresh, Hitler attempted to seize power by force.

On November 9, 1923, Hitler and a band of followers, accompanied by General Erich Ludendorff (1865–1937), attempted an unsuccessful putsch from a beer hall in Munich. When the local authorities crushed the rising, sixteen Nazis were killed. Hitler and Ludendorff were arrested and tried for treason. The general was acquitted. Hitler used the trial to make himself into a national figure. He condemned the republic, the Versailles Treaty, the Jews, and the weakened condition of his adopted country. He was convicted and sentenced to five years in prison, but he actually spent only a few months in jail before being paroled. During this time, he dictated *Mein Kampf* ("My Struggle"), from which he eventually made a good deal of money. In this book, not taken seriously enough at the time, he outlined key political views from which he never swerved, including a fierce racial anti-Semitism; opposition to Bolshevism, which he associated with Jews; and a conviction that Germany must expand eastward into Poland and Ukraine to achieve greater "living space." Such expansion assumed the resurgence of German military might. In effect, Hitler transferred the foreign policy goals and racial outlooks previously associated with German overseas imperialism to the politics of central and eastern Europe. The natural targets of implementing these ideas would be Jews, the successor states of eastern Europe, the Soviet Union, and any groups within Germany that opposed Hitler's vision of national unity and purpose. In the mid-1920s, most observers discounted the likelihood of any German political party's carrying out such policies.

During his imprisonment, Hitler reached two other decisions. First, it appears that this was the moment when he came to see himself as the leader who could transform Germany from a position of weakness to strength. Second, he decided that he and the party must pursue power by legal means, but as Hitler emerged from prison, he was still a regional politician (albeit one who was transforming himself into a national figure).

27.5.1.3 THE STRESEMANN YEARS The officials of the republic attempted to repair the damage from the inflation. Gustav Stresemann (1878–1929) was responsible primarily for reconstruction of the republic and for its achievement of a sense of self-confidence. Stresemann abandoned the policy of passive resistance in the Ruhr. The country simply could not afford it. Then, with the aid of banker Hjalmar Schacht (1877–1970), he introduced a new German currency. The rate of exchange was one trillion of the old German marks for one new Rentenmark. Stresemann also moved against challenges from both the left and the right. He supported the crushing of both Hitler's abortive putsch and smaller Communist disturbances. In late November 1923, after four months as chancellor, he resigned to become foreign minister, a post he held until his death in 1929. In that office he continued to influence the affairs of the republic.

In 1924 the Weimar Republic and the Allies renegotiated the reparation payments. The Dawes Plan lowered the annual payments and allowed them to fluctuate according to the fortunes of the German economy. The last French troops left the Ruhr in 1925. (See Map 27–1.) The same year,

Map 27–1 GERMANY'S WESTERN FRONTIER

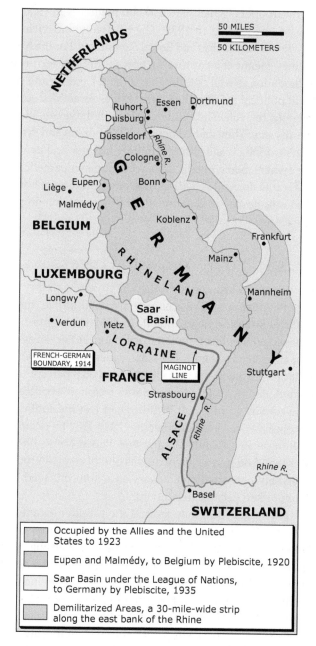

The French–Belgian–German border area between the two world wars was sensitive. Despite efforts to restrain tensions, there were persistent difficulties related to the Ruhr, Rhineland, Saar, and Eupen-Malmédy regions that required strong defenses.

Field Marshal Paul von Hindenburg (1847–1934), a military hero and a conservative monarchist, was elected president of the republic. He governed in strict accordance with the constitution, but his election suggested that German politics had become more conservative. Conservative Germans seemed reconciled to the republic. This conservatism was in line with the prosperity of the latter 1920s. Foreign capital flowed into Germany, and employment, which had been poor throughout most of the postwar years, improved smartly. Giant industrial combines spread. The prosperity helped to establish broader acceptance and appreciation of the republic.

In foreign affairs, Stresemann pursued a conciliatory course. He fulfilled the provisions of the Versailles Treaty even as he attempted to revise it through diplomacy. He was willing to accept the settlement in the west but was a determined, if sometimes secret, revisionist in the east. He aimed to recover German-speaking territories lost to Poland and Czechoslovakia and possibly to unite with Austria, chiefly by diplomatic means. The first step, however, was to achieve respectability and economic recovery. That goal required a policy of accommodation and "fulfillment," for the moment at least.

27.5.1.4 LOCARNO These developments led to the Locarno Agreements of October 1925. The spirit of conciliation led foreign ministers Austen Chamberlain (1863–1937) for Britain and Aristide Briand (1862–1932) for France to accept Stresemann's proposal for a fresh start. France and Germany both accepted the western frontier established at Versailles as legitimate. Britain and Italy agreed to intervene against the aggressor if either side violated the frontier or if Germany sent troops into the demilitarized Rhineland. Significantly, no such agreement was made about Germany's eastern frontier, but the Germans made treaties of arbitration with Poland and Czechoslovakia, and France strengthened its ties with those countries. France supported German membership in the League of Nations and agreed to withdraw its occupation troops from the Rhineland in 1930, five years earlier than specified at Versailles.

Germany was pleased to have achieved respectability and a guarantee against another Ruhr occupation, as well as the possibility of revision in the east. Britain enjoyed playing a more evenhanded role. Italy was glad to be recognized as a great power. The French were happy, too, because the Germans voluntarily accepted the permanence of their western frontier, which was also guaranteed by Britain and Italy, and France maintained its alliances in the east.

The Locarno Agreements brought new hope to Europe. Germany's entry into the League of Nations was greeted with enthusiasm. Chamberlain, Briand, and Stresemann all received the Nobel Peace Prize in 1925 and 1926. The spirit of Locarno was carried even further when the leading European states, Japan, and the United States signed the Kellogg-Briand Pact in 1928, renouncing "war as an instrument of national policy." The joy and optimism were not justified. France had merely recognized its inability to coerce Germany without help. Britain had shown its unwillingness to uphold the settlement in the east. Chamberlain declared that no British government would ever "risk the bones of a British grenadier" for the Polish Corridor. Germany was not reconciled to the eastern settlement. It maintained clandestine military connections with the Soviet Union and planned to continue to press for revision.

In both France and Germany, moreover, the conciliatory politicians represented only a part of the nation. In Germany especially, most people continued to reject the Versailles treaty and regarded Locarno as only an extension of it. When the Dawes Plan ran out in 1929 it was replaced by the Young Plan, which lowered the reparation payments, put a term on how long they must be made, and removed Germany entirely from outside supervision and control. The intensity of the outcry in Germany against the continuation of any reparations showed how far the Germans were from accepting their situation. Despite these problems, war was by no means inevitable. Europe, aided by American loans, was returning to prosperity. German leaders like Stresemann would certainly have continued to press for change, but there is little reason to think that they would have resorted to force, much less to a general war. Continued prosperity and diplomatic success might have won the loyalty of the German people for the Weimar Republic and moderate revisionism, but the Great Depression of the 1930s brought new forces to power.

27.5.2 Depression and Political Deadlock

The outflow of foreign, and especially American, capital from Germany that began in 1928 undermined the economic prosperity of the Weimar Republic. The resulting economic crisis brought parliamentary government to a halt. In 1928 a coalition of center parties and the Social Democrats governed. All went reasonably well until the Depression struck. Then the coalition partners differed sharply on economic policy. The Social Democrats refused to reduce social and unemployment insurance. The more conservative parties, remembering the inflation of 1923, insisted on a balanced budget. The coalition dissolved in March 1930. To resolve the parliamentary deadlock in the Reichstag, President von Hindenburg appointed Heinrich Brüning (1885–1970) as chancellor. Lacking a majority in the Reichstag, the new chancellor governed through emergency presidential decrees, as authorized by Article 48 of the constitution. Party divisions prevented the Reichstag from overriding the decrees. The Weimar Republic had become a presidential dictatorship.

German unemployment rose from 2,258,000 in March 1930 to over 6,000,000 in March 1932. There had been persistent unemployment during the 1920s, but nothing of such magnitude or duration. The economic downturn and the parliamentary deadlock worked to the advantage of the more extreme political parties. In the election of 1928 the Nazis had won only twelve seats in the Reichstag, and the Communists had won fifty-four seats. Two years later, after the election of 1930, the Nazis held 107 seats and the Communists seventy-seven.

The power of the Nazis in the streets was also on the rise. The unemployment fed thousands of men into the storm troopers, which had 100,000 members in 1930 and almost one million in 1933. The SA freely and viciously attacked Communists and Social Democrats. For the Nazis, politics meant the capture of power through terror and intimidation as well as through elections. Decency and civility in political life vanished. Nazi rallies resembled secular religious revivals. They paraded through the streets and the countryside. They gained powerful supporters and sympathizers among businessmen, military officers, and newspaper owners. Some intellectuals were also sympathetic. The Nazis transformed this discipline and enthusiasm born of economic despair and nationalistic frustration into impressive electoral results.

27.5.3 Hitler Comes to Power

For two years Brüning continued to govern with the backing of Hindenburg. The economy did not improve, and the political situation deteriorated. In 1932 the eighty-three-year-old Hindenburg stood for reelection. Hitler ran against him and forced a runoff. The Nazi leader garnered 30.1 percent of the vote in the first election and 36.8 percent in the second. Although Hindenburg was returned to office, the vote convinced him that Brüning had lost the confidence of conservative German voters. In May 1932 he dismissed Brüning and appointed Franz von Papen (1878–1969) in his place. The new chancellor was one of a small group of extremely conservative advisers on whom the aged Hindenburg had become dependent.

Papen and the circle around the president wanted to draw the Nazis into cooperation with them without giving Hitler effective power. The government needed the popular support on the right that only the Nazis seemed able to generate. The Hindenburg circle decided to convince Hitler that the Nazis could not come to power on their own. Papen removed the ban on Nazi meetings that Brüning had imposed and then called a Reichstag election for July 1932. The Nazis won 230 seats and polled 37.2 percent of the vote. Hitler would only enter the cabinet if he were made chancellor. Hindenburg refused. Another election was called in November, partly to wear down the Nazis' financial resources. The Nazis won only 196 seats, and their percentage of the popular vote dipped to 33.1 percent. Hindenburg's advisers still refused to appoint Hitler to office.

In early December 1932 Papen resigned, and General Kurt von Schleicher (1882–1934) became chancellor. People were now afraid of civil war between the extreme left and the far right. Schleicher decided to try and fashion a broad-based coalition of conservative groups and trade unionists. The prospect of such a coalition, including groups from the political left, frightened the Hindenburg circle even more than the prospect of Hitler. They did not trust Schleicher's motives, which have never been clear. Consequently, they persuaded Hindenburg to appoint Hitler chancellor. To control Hitler and to see that he did little mischief, Papen was named vice chancellor, and other traditional conservatives were appointed to the cabinet. On January 30, 1933, Adolf Hitler became the chancellor of Germany.

It is important to emphasize that this outcome had not been inevitable. As his most distinguished biographer has observed, "Hitler's rise from humble beginnings to 'seize' power by 'triumph of the will' was the stuff of Nazi legend. In fact, political miscalculation by those with regular access to the corridors of power rather than any actions on the part of the Nazi leader played a larger role in placing him in the Chancellor's seat."[5] Hitler did not come to office on the tide of history, but through the blunders of conservative German politicians who hated the Weimar Republic and its rejection of traditional German political elites and who feared the domestic political turmoil the Depression had spawned.

Like Mussolini, Hitler had, however, technically become head of the government by legal means. All the proper legal forms and procedures had been observed. As a result, the civil service, the courts, and the other agencies of the government could support him in good conscience. He had forged a rigidly disciplined party structure and had mastered the techniques of mass politics and propaganda. (See the "Encountering the Past" sidebar, which follows below, for an examination of a particularly effective propaganda tool.) He understood how to touch the raw social and political nerves of the electorate. His support appears to have come from across the social spectrum and not, as historians once thought, just from the lower middle class. Pockets of resistance appeared among Roman Catholic voters in the countryside and small towns. Otherwise, support for Hitler was particularly strong among groups such as farmers, war veterans, and the young, whom the insecurity of the 1920s and the Depression of the early 1930s had badly hurt. Hitler promised them security against Communists and Socialists, effective government in place of the petty politics of the other parties, and a strong, restored, purposeful Germany.

German big business once received much of the blame for the rise of Hitler. There is little evidence, however, that business contributions made any crucial difference to the Nazis' success or failure. Hitler's supporters were frequently suspicious of big business and capitalism. They wanted a simpler world, one in which small property would be safe from both Socialism and big business. They supported Hitler and the Nazis rather than the Social Democrats because the latter were not sufficiently nationalistic. The Nazis won out over other conservative nationalistic parties because, unlike those conservatives, the Nazis addressed social insecurities.

27.5.4 Hitler's Consolidation of Power

Once in office, Hitler consolidated his control with almost lightning speed. This process had three facets: the capture of full legal authority, the crushing of alternative political groups, and the purging of rivals within the Nazi Party itself. On February 27, 1933, a mentally ill Dutch Communist set fire to the Reichstag building in Berlin. The Nazis quickly turned the incident to their own advantage by claiming that the fire proved the existence of an immediate Communist threat against the government. To the public, it seemed plausible that the Communists might attempt some action against the state now that the Nazis were in power. Under Article 48, Hitler issued an Emergency Decree suspending civil liberties and proceeded to arrest Communists or alleged Communists. This decree remained in force as long as Hitler ruled Germany.

In early March another Reichstag election took place. The Nazis still received only 43.9 percent of the vote. However, the arrest of the newly elected Communist deputies and the political fear aroused by the fire meant that Hitler could control the Reichstag. On March 23, 1933, the Reichstag passed an Enabling Act that permitted Hitler to rule by decree. Thereafter, there were no legal limits on his exercise of power. The Weimar Constitution was never formally repealed or amended. It had simply been supplanted by the February Emergency Decree and the March Enabling Act, which together made the constitution a dead letter.

Perhaps better than anyone else, Hitler understood that he and his party had not inevitably come to power. His potential opponents had been divided from 1929 to 1933, and he intended to prevent them from regrouping. In a series of complex moves, Hitler outlawed or undermined various German institutions that might have served as rallying points for opposition. In early May 1933 the offices, banks, and newspapers of the free trade unions were seized and their leaders arrested. The Nazi Party itself, rather than any government agency, undertook this action. In late June and early July, the other German political parties were outlawed. By July 14, 1933, the National Socialists were the only legal party in Germany. During the same months the Nazis had taken control of the governments of the individual federal states in Germany. By the close of 1933, all major institutions of potential opposition had been eliminated.

Encountering the Past

Cinema of the Political Left and Right

BEFORE THE INVENTION of television, the cinema was the most powerful cultural vehicle for political regimes to project their power. Film directors of genius were drawn to the authoritarian governments of both the left and the right, and the films they made for these regimes, especially those of Soviet Russia and Nazi Germany, still impress moviegoers.

BERLIN, 1936 A pioneer in cinematic techniques, German film director Leni Riefenstahl (1902–2003) is best known for producing propaganda films for the Nazis. She won international acclaim as director of *Olympia* (1938), a film on the Olympic Games of 1936 in Berlin. During the opening of the games, Riefenstahl occupied a space on the reviewing standing. See her at right, under the camera.
SOURCE: Sueddeutsche Zeitung Photo/Alamy Stock Photo

During the 1920s, the Soviet Union promoted the cinema as a propaganda tool. The greatest Soviet film director was Sergei Eisenstein (1898–1948). His most famous film, *The Battleship Potemkin*, which critics regard as one of the most important films of all time, depicts a mutiny on a warship during the Russian Revolution of 1905. In *Potemkin*, Eisenstein portrayed the working class as the hero both of the film and, true to Marxist doctrine, of history itself.

As Stalin gained more and more power from the mid-1920s onward, he imposed rigid censorship on the arts. To work in the Soviet Union, Eisenstein had to make films that pleased Stalin and thus he did. Still, Eisenstein made two movies that many film scholars consider masterpieces: *Alexander Nevsky*, which depicts the victory of a medieval Russian prince over invading Germans, and *Ivan the Terrible*, which some see, in its depiction of the sixteenth-century despotic tsar whom Stalin admired, as Eisenstein's surrender to Stalin.

Leni Riefenstahl (1902–2003) was by the early 1930s the most skilled documentary filmmaker in Germany and perhaps the world—an extraordinary accomplishment for a woman in a field dominated by men. Adolf Hitler asked her to make a documentary extolling the Third Reich after the Nazis took power in 1933. The results were *Triumph of the Will* (1934), about a Nazi Party rally, and *Olympia* (1938), about the Olympic Games held in Berlin in 1936. Both films display innovative, dramatically effective cinematic techniques and also the skilled political theatricality of the Nazi regime. These films dazzled audiences and are still shown in film classes as major works of twentieth-century cinematic art. Yet despite her artistry, Riefenstahl became labeled —no matter how much she protested that she was a "pure" artist—as a producer of Nazi propaganda films. No American film studio would distribute her films to U.S. audiences.

After the defeat of Germany in 1945, Riefenstahl was imprisoned by the Allies under their de-Nazification program before being released in 1949. Thereafter, she attempted to rescue her career as a filmmaker, but the Nazi taint proved indelible. Instead, she became a noted photographer, especially of underwater photography. To the end of her life, Riefenstahl defended her films for the Third Reich as art, not propaganda.

Questions

1. Why were the Soviet and Nazi regimes so interested in the cinema?
2. How did Leni Riefenstahl's films of Hitler and Nazi rallies affect her later career?

The final element in Hitler's personal consolidation of power involved the Nazi Party itself. By late 1933 the SA consisted of approximately one million active members and a larger number of reserves. The commander of this party army was Ernst Roehm, a possible rival to Hitler himself. The German army officer corps, on whom Hitler depended to rebuild the national army, was jealous of the SA. Consequently, to protect his own position and to shore up support with the regular army, on June 30, 1934, Hitler ordered the murder of key SA officers, including Roehm. The German army, which was the only institution in the nation that might have prevented the murders, did nothing. A month later, on August 2, 1934, President Hindenburg died. Thereafter, the offices of chancellor and president were combined. Hitler was now the *führer*, or sole ruler, of Germany and of the Nazi Party.

27.5.5 Anti-Semitism and the Police State

Terror and intimidation had helped propel the Nazis to office. As Hitler consolidated his power, he oversaw the organization of a police state. The chief vehicle of police surveillance was the **SS (*Schutzstaffel*)**, or security units, commanded by Heinrich Himmler (1900–1945). This group had originated in the mid-1920s as a bodyguard for Hitler and had become a more elite paramilitary organization than the larger SA. In 1933 the SS had approximately 52,000 members. It was the instrument that carried out the blood purges of the party in 1934. By 1936 Himmler had become head of all police matters in Germany.

27.5.5.1 ATTACK ON JEWISH ECONOMIC LIFE The police character of the Nazi regime was all-pervasive, but the people who most consistently experienced its terror were the German Jews. Anti-Semitism had been a key plank of the Nazi program—anti-Semitism based on biological racial theories stemming from late-nineteenth-century thought rather than from religious discrimination. Before World War II the Nazi attack on the Jews went through three stages of increasing intensity. In 1933, shortly after assuming power, the Nazis excluded Jews from the civil service.

For a time they also attempted to enforce boycotts of Jewish shops and businesses. The boycotts won relatively little public support.

27.5.5.2 RACIAL LEGISLATION Then in 1935, a series of measures known as the Nuremberg Laws robbed German Jews of their citizenship. The professions and the major occupations were closed to those defined as Jews. Marriage and sexual intercourse between Jews and non-Jews were

BOYCOTT OF JEWISH BUSINESSES Soon after seizing power, the Nazi government began harassing German Jewish businesses. Non-Jewish German citizens were urged not to buy merchandise from shops owned by Jews.

SOURCE: bpk Bildagentur/Art Resource, NY

prohibited. Legal exclusion and humiliation of the Jews became the order of the day.

27.5.5.3 KRISTALLNACHT The persecution of the Jews increased again in 1938. Business careers were forbidden. In November 1938, under orders from the Nazi Party, thousands of Jewish stores and synagogues were burned or otherwise destroyed. The Jewish community itself had to pay for the damage that occurred on this *Kristallnacht* or "Night of Smashed Glass" because the government confiscated the insurance money. In many other ways, large and petty, the German Jews were harassed. This persecution allowed the Nazis to inculcate the rest of the population with the concept of a master race of pure German "Aryans" and also to display their own contempt for civil liberties.

27.5.5.4 THE FINAL SOLUTION After the war broke out, Hitler decided in 1942 to destroy the Jews in Europe. It is thought that over six million Jews, mostly from eastern European nations, died as a result of that staggering decision, unprecedented in its scope and implementation. (This subject is more fully treated in the next chapter.)

27.5.6 Racial Ideology and the Lives of Women

Hitler and other Nazis were less interested in increasing the national population, which was Mussolini's policy in Italy, than in producing racially pure Germans. In their role as mothers, German women had the special task of preserving racial purity and giving birth to pure Germans who were healthy in mind and body. Nazi journalists often compared the role of women in childbirth to that of men in battle. Each served the state in particular social and gender roles. In both cases, the good of the nation was more important than that of the individual. (See the "Compare and Connect" sidebar, which follows below, to learn about Nazi and Soviet policies on the role of women.)

Nazi policy favored motherhood only for those regarded as racially fit for it. As early as late 1933, the government raised the issue of what kind of persons were fit to bear children for the nation. This policy disapproved of motherhood among those people Nazi racism condemned—particularly the Jews, but also Slavs and Gypsies. During the mass executions of Jews in the Holocaust, Jewish women were specifically targeted for death, in part to prevent them from bearing a new generation.

Nazi theorists also discriminated between the healthy and unhealthy, the desirable and undesirable, in the German population itself. The government sought to prevent "undesirables" from reproducing, a policy that led to both the sterilization and death of many women, often because of an alleged mental "degeneracy." Some pregnant women were forced to have abortions. The Nazis' population policy was,

in effect, one of selective breeding, or antenatalism, that profoundly affected the lives of women.

To support motherhood among those whom they believed should have children, the Nazis provided loans to encourage early marriage, tax breaks for families with children, and child allowances. In this respect, Nazi legislation resembled that passed elsewhere in Europe during the decade. The subsidies and other family payments were sent to husbands rather than wives, to make married fatherhood seem preferable to bachelorhood. Furthermore, these policies were administered on the premise that only racially and physically desirable children received support.

Although Nazi ideology emphasized motherhood, in 1930 the party vowed to protect the jobs of working women, and the number of women working in Germany rose steadily under the Nazi regime. The Nazis recognized that in the midst of the Depression many women needed to work, but the party urged them to pursue employment that was "natural" to their character as women. Such employment included agricultural labor, teaching, nursing, social service, and domestic service. The Nazis also intended women to be educators of the young. In that role, whether as mothers or as members of the serving professions, women became special protectors of German cultural values. Through cooking, dress, music, and stories, mothers were to instill a love for the nation in their children. As consumers for the home, women were to support German-owned shops, buy German-made goods, and boycott Jewish merchants.

27.5.7 Nazi Economic Policy

Besides consolidating political authority and pursuing anti-Semitic policies, Hitler still had to confront the Great Depression. German unemployment had helped propel him to power. The Nazis attacked this problem with a success that astonished and frightened Europe. (See the "Closer Look" sidebar, which follows below, for a perspective on staged public rallies as instruments of Nazi solidarity and success.) By 1936, while the rest of the European economy remained stagnant, the specter of unemployment and other difficulties associated with the Great Depression no longer haunted Germany.

As far as the economic crisis was concerned, Hitler had become the most effective political leader in Europe. This success was perhaps the most important reason Germans supported his tyrannical regime. The Nazi success against the Great Depression gave the regime credibility. Underlying both business and labor were the Nazi terror and police. The Nazi economic experiment proved that, by sacrificing all political and civil liberty, destroying a free trade-union movement, limiting the private exercise of capital, and ignoring consumer satisfaction, a government could achieve full employment to prepare for war and aggression.

Compare and Connect

The Soviets and the Nazis Confront the Issues of Women and the Family

BOTH THE SOVIET and Nazi dictatorships intruded deeply into the private lives of their citizens. Some Communist writers in the Soviet Union, such as Alexandra Kollontai, imagined utopian changes to traditional family life and traditional roles for women.

In Germany under Hitler's leadership the state imposed policies that would make women's roles as wives and mothers serve the larger political and ideological goals of the Nazi Party. As illustrated in the passages below, although the policies of the two dictatorships were different, both challenged the social roles of women that were emerging in Western Europe and in the United States.

EMANCIPATION OF WOMEN A celebration of International Women's Day, this Soviet poster, from 1932, illustrates the significant role of women in Communist society in industrial and agricultural development and progress. It differed greatly from the traditional role assigned to women in Nazi ideology.

SOURCE: Heritage Image Partnership Ltd/Alamy Stock Photo

Before Reading

- Consider the arguments of Alexandra Kollontai in favor of reforming the family.
- Think about how Hitler viewed the role of women in Nazi society.
- Compare the competing visions of women in Communist and Nazi policy.

Questions

1. Why did Kollontai see the restructuring of the family as essential to a new kind of Communist society? Would these changes make people loyal to that society?
2. What changes in society did the economic independence Kollontai wanted for women presuppose? What might childhood be like in this society?
3. What social tasks did Hitler assign to women? How did he attempt to subordinate the lives of women to the supremacy of the state?
4. Why did Hitler associate the emancipation of women with Jews and intellectuals?
5. Why was the present and future role of women such an important topic for both the Communist and the Nazi governments?

I. A COMMUNIST WOMAN DEMANDS A NEW FAMILY LIFE

While Lenin sought to consolidate the Bolshevik Revolution against internal and external enemies, there existed within the young Soviet Union a utopian impulse to change and reform every social institution that had existed before the revolution or the Communists associated with capitalist society. Alexandra Kollontai (1872–1952) was a spokesperson of the extreme political left during the early Soviet Union. There had been much speculation on how the end of bourgeois society might change the structure of the family and the position of women. In this passage written in 1920, Kollontai defines one of the most radically utopian visions of this change. During the years immediately after the revolution, rumors circulated in both Europe and America about sexual and family experimentation in the Soviet Union. Statements such as Kollontai's fostered such rumors. Kollontai herself later became a supporter of Stalin and a Soviet diplomat.

There is no escaping the fact: the old type of family has seen its day. It is not the fault of the Communist State, it is the result of the changed conditions of life. The family is ceasing to be a necessity of the State, as it was in the past; on the contrary, it is worse than useless, since it needlessly holds back the female workers from more productive and far more serious work. . . . But on the ruins of the former family we shall soon see a new form rising which will involve altogether different relations between men and women, and which will be a union of affection and comradeship, a union of two equal members of the Communist society, both of them free, both of them independent, both of them workers. No more domestic "servitude" of women. No more inequality within the family. No more fear on the part of the woman lest she remain without support or aid with little ones in her arms if her husband should desert her. The woman in the Communist city no longer depends on her husband but on her work. It is not her husband but her robust arms which will support her. There will be no more anxiety as to the fate of her children. The State of the Workers will assume responsibility for these. Marriage will be purified of all its material elements, of all money calculations, which constitute a hideous blemish on family life in our days. . . .

The woman who is called upon to struggle in the great cause of the liberation of the workers—such a woman should know that in the new State there will be no more room for such petty divisions as were formerly understood: "These are my own children, to them I owe all my maternal solicitude, all my affection; those are your children, my neighbour's children; I am not concerned with them. I have enough to do with my own." Henceforth the worker-mother, who is conscious of her social function, will rise to a point where she no longer differentiates between yours and mine; she must remember that there are henceforth only our children, those of the Communist State, the common possession of all the workers.

The Worker's State has need of a new form of relation between the sexes. The narrow and exclusive affection of the mother for her own children must expand until it embraces all the children of the great proletarian family. In place of the indissoluble marriage based on the servitude of woman, we shall see rise the free union, fortified by the love and mutual respect of the two members of the Workers' State, equal in their rights and in their obligations. In place of the individual and egotistic family there will arise a great universal family of workers, in which all the workers, men and women, will be, above all, workers, comrades.

II. HITLER REJECTS THE EMANCIPATION OF WOMEN

According to Nazi ideology, women's place was in the home producing and rearing children and supporting their husbands. In this speech, Hitler encourages this view of the role of women. He uses anti-Semitism to discredit those writers who had supported the emancipation of women from their traditional roles and occupations. Hitler returns here to the concept of "separate spheres" for men and women. His traditional outlook of women opposed views associated with the Soviet experiment during the interwar years. Ironically, once World War II began, Nazi leadership demanded that women leave the home and work in factories to support the war effort.

The slogan "Emancipation of women" was invented by Jewish intellectuals and its content was formed by the same spirit. In the really good times of German life the German woman had no need to emancipate herself. She possessed exactly what nature had necessarily given her to administer and preserve; just as the man in his good times had no need to fear that he would be ousted from his position in relation to the woman. . . .

If the man's world is said to be the State, his struggle, his readiness to devote his powers to the service of the community, then it may perhaps be said that the woman's is a smaller world. For her world is her husband, her family, her children, and her home. But what would become of the greater world if there were no one to tend and care for the smaller one? How could the greater world survive if there were no one to make the cares of the smaller world the content of their lives? No, the greater world is built on the foundation of this smaller world. This great world cannot survive if the smaller world is not stable. Providence has entrusted to the woman the cares of that world which is her very own, and only on the basis of this smaller world can the man's world be formed and built up. The two worlds are not antagonistic. They complement each other, they belong together just as man and woman belong together.

We do not consider it correct for the woman to interfere in the world of the man, in his main sphere. We consider it natural if these two worlds remain distinct. To the one belongs the strength of feeling, the strength of the soul. To the other belongs the strength of vision, of toughness, of decision, and of the willingness to act. In the one case this strength demands the willingness of the woman to risk her life to preserve this important cell and to multiply it, and in the other case it demands from the man the readiness to safeguard life. . . .

So our women's movement is for us not something which inscribes on its banner as its programme the fight against men, but something which has as its programme the common fight together with men. For the new National Socialist national community acquires a firm basis precisely because we have gained the trust of millions of women as fanatical fellow-combatants, women who have fought for the common life in the service of the common task of preserving life. . . .

Whereas previously the programmes of the liberal, intellectualist women's movements contained many points, the programme of our National Socialist Women's movement has in reality but one single point, and that point is the child, that tiny creature which must be born and grow strong and which alone gives meaning to the whole life-struggle.

SOURCE: (I) From Alexandra Kollontai, *Communism and the Family*, as reprinted in Rudolf Schlesinger, ed. and trans., *The Family in the USSR* (London: Routledge and Kegan Paul, 1949), pp. 67–69. Reprinted by permission. (II) From J. Noakes and G. Pridham, eds., *Nazism, 1919–1945*, Vol. 2, *State, Economy and Society, 1933–39: A Documentary Reader*, Exeter Studies in History No. 8 (University of Exeter Press, 1984), pp. 449–450.

Nazi economic policies supported private property and private capitalism but subordinated all significant economic enterprise and decisions about prices and investment to the goals of the state. Hitler reversed the deflationary policy of the cabinets that had preceded him. He instituted a massive program of public works and vast military spending. From the earliest years of the Nazi regime, government spending and other economic policies served the cause of rearmament. The government built canals, reclaimed land, and constructed an extensive highway system for clear military uses. It also sent unemployed workers back to farms if they had originally come from them. Other laborers were not permitted to change jobs without official permission.

In 1935, the renunciation of the military provisions of the Versailles treaty led to open rearmament and military expansion with little opposition. These measures essentially restored full employment. In 1936, Hitler instructed Hermann Göring (1893–1946), who had headed the air force since 1933, to undertake a four-year plan to prepare the army and the economy for war. The government determined that Germany must be economically self-sufficient. Armaments received top priority. This economic program satisfied both the yearning for social and economic security and the desire for national fulfillment.

With the crushing of the trade unions in 1933, strikes became illegal. There was no genuine collective bargaining. The government handled labor disputes through compulsory arbitration. It also required workers and employers to participate in the Labor Front, an organization intended to demonstrate that class conflict had ended. The Labor Front sponsored a "Strength Through Joy" program that provided vacations and other forms of recreation for workers and farmers.

27.6 Trials of the Successor States in Eastern Europe

What shared challenges did the successor states face in eastern Europe?

It had been an article of faith among nineteenth-century liberals sympathetic to nationalism that only good could come from the demise of Austria-Hungary, the restoration of Poland, and the establishment of nation-states throughout eastern Europe. These new states were to embody the principle of national self-determination and to provide a buffer against the westward spread of Bolshevism. They were, however, in trouble from the beginning.

27.6.1 Economic and Ethnic Pressures

All the new states faced immense postwar economic difficulties. None of them possessed the kind of strong economy that nation-states such as France and Germany had developed in the nineteenth century. Indeed, political

A Closer Look

The Nazi Party Rally

NAZI RALLIES WERE INTENDED to generate nationalistic group solidarity that would demonstrate that loyalty to the Nazi Party and to the nation was more important than any other group loyalty. The image below of a 1938 rally illustrates the gender divisions Nazi ideology fostered. Men were portrayed as defenders of the homeland, and women were to pursue traditional domestic roles and to bear children for the nation.

The ever-present Swastika (or hooked cross) had been used as a symbol of "Aryan identity" by the Nazis since 1920. Hitler claimed to have chosen the symbol, which he and other Nazis associated with an allegedly racially pure Aryan past. In fact, many cultures had used the Swastika as a symbol.

The Nazis adopted the Swastika as the German national flag in 1935.

Young women in folk costumes, an expression of national identity, are enthusiastic supporters among the crowd extending the Nazi salute.

Young men in uniform are stoic defenders of the nation.

NATIONALIST SOLIDARITY
SOURCE: bpk Bildagentur/Art Resource, NY

Questions

1. How might rallies have given the sense that loyalty to the Nazi Party and the nation overrode all other social and political loyalties?
2. How could attending Nazi rallies or viewing them through movies or newsreels convey to the German and non-German public throughout Europe a sense of inevitable Nazi success and widespread support?
3. What events or experiences at Nazi rallies might not have been captured in photographs? How could photographs be used to shape the news in the 1930s and later?

independence disrupted the previous economic relationships that each of them had developed as part of one of the prewar empires. None of the new states was financially independent; except for Czechoslovakia, all of them depended on foreign loans to finance economic development. Nationalistic antagonisms often prevented these states from trading with each other, and as a consequence, most became highly dependent on trade with Germany. The successor states of eastern Europe were poor and

overwhelmingly rural nations in an industrialized world. The Depression hit them especially hard because they had to import finished goods for which they paid with agricultural exports whose value was falling sharply.

Finally, throughout eastern Europe, the collapse of the old German, Russian, and Austrian empires allowed various ethnic groups—large and small—to pursue nationalistic goals unchecked by any great power or central political authority. The major social and political groups in these countries were generally unwilling to make compromises lest they undermine their nationalist identity and independence. Each state included minority groups that wanted to be independent or to become part of a different nation in the region. Again, except for Czechoslovakia, all these states succumbed to some form of domestic authoritarian government.

27.6.2 Poland: Democracy to Military Rule

The nation whose postwar fortunes probably most disappointed liberal Europeans was Poland. For more than a hundred years, the country had been erased from the map. When the country was restored in 1919, nationalism proved an insufficient bond to overcome political disagreements stemming from class differences, diverse economic interests, and regionalism. Furthermore, large Ukrainian, Jewish, Lithuanian, and German minorities distrusted the Polish government and resented attempts to force them to adopt Polish culture. The new Poland had been constructed from portions governed by Germany, Russia, and Austria for more than a century. Each of those regions of partitioned Poland had different administrative systems and laws, different economies, and different degrees of experience with electoral institutions. A host of small political parties bedeviled the new Polish Parliament, and the executive was weak. In 1926, Marshal Josef Pilsudski (1867–1935) carried out a military coup. Thereafter, he ruled, in effect, personally until his death, when the government passed into the hands of a group of his military followers. The government became increasingly anti-Semitic, and non-Polish minorities suffered various forms of discrimination.

27.6.3 Czechoslovakia: A Viable Democratic Experiment

Only one central European successor state escaped the fate of self-imposed authoritarian government. Czechoslovakia possessed a strong industrial base, a substantial middle class, and a tradition of liberal values. After the war, the new government had broken up large estates in favor of small peasant holdings. Tomas Masaryk (1850–1937) was a gifted leader of immense integrity and fairness. The country had a real chance of becoming a viable modern nation-state.

There were, however, tensions between the Czechs and the Slovaks, who were poorer and more rural. Moreover, other non-Czech national groups, including Poles, Magyars, Ukrainians, and especially the Germans of the Sudetenland, which the Paris settlement had placed within Czech borders, resented being part of Czechoslovakia. The parliamentary regime might have been able to work through these problems, but extreme German nationalists in the Sudetenland looked to Hitler, who wanted to expand into eastern Europe, for help. In 1938, at Munich, the great powers first divided liberal Czechoslovakia to appease Hitler's aggressive instincts and then watched passively in early 1939 as he occupied much of the country, gave parts to Poland and Hungary, and manipulated a Slovak puppet state.

27.6.4 Hungary: Turn to Authoritarianism

Hungary was one of the defeated powers of World War I. In that defeat, it achieved its long-desired separation from Austria but at a high political and economic price. In Hungary during 1919, Bela Kun (1885–1937), a Communist, established a short-lived Hungarian Soviet Republic, which received Socialist support. The Allies authorized an invasion by Romanian troops to remove the Communist danger. The Hungarian landowners then established Admiral Miklós Horthy (1868–1957) as regent for the Habsburg monarch who could not return to his throne—a position Horthy held until 1944. After the collapse of the Kun government, thousands of Hungarians were either executed or imprisoned.

The Hungarians also deeply resented the territory Hungary had lost in the Paris settlement. The largely agrarian Hungarian economy suffered from a general stagnation. During the 1920s, the effective ruler of Hungary was Count Stephen Bethlen (1874–1947). He presided over a government that was parliamentary in form but aristocratic in character. In 1932, he was succeeded by General Julius Gömbös (1886–1936), who pursued anti-Semitic policies and rigged elections. No matter how the popular vote turned out, the Gömbös party controlled Parliament. After his death in 1936, anti-Semitism lingered in Hungarian politics.

27.6.5 Austria: Political Turmoil and Nazi Occupation

Austria's situation was little better than that of the other successor states. A quarter of the eight million Austrians lived in Vienna. Viable economic life was almost impossible, and the Paris settlement forbade union with Germany. Throughout the 1920s, the leftist Social Democrats and the conservative Christian Socialists contended for power. Both groups employed small armies to terrorize their opponents and to impress their followers.

In 1933, Christian Socialist Engelbert Dollfuss (1892–1934) became chancellor. He tried to steer a course between the Austrian Social Democrats and the German Nazis, who had surfaced in Austria. In 1934, he outlawed all political parties except the Christian Socialists, the agrarians, and the paramilitary groups that composed his own Fatherland Front. He used troops against the Social Democrats but was murdered later that year during an unsuccessful Nazi coup. His successor, Kurt von Schuschnigg (1897–1977), presided over Austria until Hitler annexed it in 1938.

27.6.6 Southeastern Europe: Royal Dictatorships

In southeastern Europe, revision of the arrangements in the Paris settlement was less of an issue. Parliamentary government floundered there nevertheless. Yugoslavia had been founded by the Corfu Agreement of 1917 and was known as the Kingdom of the Serbs, Croats, and Slovenes until 1929. Throughout the interwar period, the Serbs dominated the government and were opposed by the Croats. The two groups clashed violently, but the Serbs had the advantage of having had an independent state with an army prior to World War I, whereas the Croats and Slovenes had been part of the Austro-Hungarian Empire. The Croats generally were Roman Catholic, better educated, and accustomed to reasonably incorrupt government administration. The Serbs were Orthodox, less well educated, and considered corrupt administrators by the Croats. Furthermore, although each group predominated in certain areas of the country, each had isolated enclaves in other parts of the nation. Bosnia-Herzegovina, in addition to Serbs and Croats, had a significant Muslim population. The Slovenes, Muslims, Albanians, and other small national groups often played the Serbs and the Croats against each other. All the political parties except the small Communist Party represented a particular ethnic group rather than the nation of Yugoslavia. The violent clash of nationalities eventually led to a royal dictatorship in 1929 under King Alexander I (r. 1921–1934), himself a Serb. He outlawed political parties and jailed popular politicians. Alexander was assassinated in 1934, but the authoritarian government continued under a regency for his son.

Other royal dictatorships were imposed elsewhere in the Balkans: in Romania by King Carol II (r. 1930–1940) and in Bulgaria by King Boris III (r. 1918–1943). They regarded their own illiberal regimes as preventing the seizure of power by more extreme antiparliamentary movements and as quieting the discontent of the varied nationalities within their borders. In Greece, the parliamentary monarchy floundered amid military coups and calls for a republic. In 1936, General John Metaxas (1871–1941) instituted a dictatorship under King George II (r. 1935–1947) that, for the time being, ended parliamentary life in Greece.

KEY POLITICAL EVENTS OF THE 1920s AND 1930s	
1919 (August)	Constitution of the Weimar Republic promulgated
1920	Kapp Putsch in Berlin
1921 (March)	Kronstadt mutiny leads Lenin to initiate his New Economic Policy
1922 (October)	Fascist march on Rome leads to Mussolini's assumption of power
1923 (January)	France invades the Ruhr
1923 (November)	Hitler's Beer Hall Putsch
1924	Death of Lenin
1925	Locarno Agreements
1928	Kellogg-Briand Pact; first Five-Year Plan launched in USSR
1929 (January)	Trotsky expelled from USSR
1929 (February)	Lateran Accord between the Vatican and the Italian state
1929 (April)	Bukharin expelled from his offices in the Soviet Union; Stalin's central position thus affirmed
1929 (October)	New York stock market crash
1930 (March)	Brüning government begins in Germany Stalin calls for moderation in his policy of agricultural collectivization because of "dizziness from success"
1930 (September)	Nazis capture 107 seats in German Reichstag
1931 (August)	National Government formed in Britain
1932 (March 13)	Hindenburg defeats Hitler for German presidency
1932 (May 31)	Franz von Papen forms German cabinet
1932 (July 31)	German Reichstag election
1932 (November 6)	German Reichstag election
1932 (December 2)	Kurt von Schleicher forms German cabinet
1933 (January 30)	Hitler made German chancellor
1933 (February 27)	Reichstag fire
1932 (March 5)	Reichstag election
1932 (August)	Enabling Act consolidates Nazi power
1934 (June 30)	Blood purge of the Nazi Party
1934 (August 2)	Death of Hindenburg
1934 (December 1)	Assassination of Kirov leads to the beginning of Stalin's purges
1936 (May)	Popular Front government in France
1936 (July–August)	Most famous of public purge trials in Russia

The Chapter in Perspective

By the mid-1930s, dictators of the right and the left were established across much of Europe. Political tyranny was hardly new to Europe, but several factors combined to give these rulers unique characteristics. They drew their immediate support from well-organized political parties. Except for the Bolsheviks, these were mass parties. The roots of support for the dictators lay in nationalism, the social and economic frustration of the Great Depression, and political ideologies that promised to transform the social and political order. As long as the new rulers seemed successful, they did not lack support. Many citizens believed these leaders had ended the pettiness of everyday politics.

After coming to power, the dictators possessed a practical monopoly over mass communications. Through armies, police forces, and party discipline, they also monopolized terror and coercive power. They could propagandize large populations and compel people to obey them and their followers. Finally, as a result of the Second Industrial Revolution, they commanded a great amount of technology and a capacity for immense destruction. Earlier rulers in Europe may have shared the ruthless ambitions of Hitler, Mussolini, and Stalin, but they had lacked the ready implements of physical force to impose their wills.

Mass political support, the monopoly of police and military power, and technological capacity meant the dictators of the 1930s held more extensive sway over their nations than any other group of rulers who had governed on the Continent. Soon the issue would become whether they would be able to maintain peace among themselves and with their democratic neighbors.

The Chapter in Review

Review Questions

1. What caused the Great Depression? Why was it more severe, and why did it last longer than previous economic downturns? Could it have been avoided?
2. How did Stalin achieve supreme power in the Soviet Union? Why did he decide that Russia had to industrialize rapidly? Why did this require the collectivization of agriculture? Was the policy a success? How did it affect the Russian people? Why did Stalin carry out the great purges?
3. Why was Italy dissatisfied and unstable after World War I? How did Mussolini achieve power? What were the characteristics of the Fascist state?
4. Why did the Weimar Republic collapse in Germany? How did Hitler come to power? Which groups in Germany supported Hitler and why were they pro-Nazi? How did he consolidate his power? Why was anti-Semitism central to Nazi policy?
5. What characteristics did the authoritarian regimes in the Soviet Union, Italy, and Germany have in common?
6. Why did liberal democracy fail in the successor states of Eastern Europe?

Key Terms

Adolf Hitler (1889–1945) A German dictator and the leader of the Nazi Party, whose invasion of Poland in September 1939 led to the outbreak of World War II in Europe and who was a central figure in the Holocaust.

Benito Mussolini (1883–1945) An Italian politician and leader of the National Fascist Party, who ruled Italy as a dictator from 1925 to 1943; signed Lateran Accord with the Vatican, allowing the Roman Catholic Church and the Italian state to make peace with one another.

collectivization The bedrock of Stalinist agriculture, which forced Russian peasants to give up their private farms and work as members of collectives, large agricultural units controlled by the state.

Il Duce (DO-chay) Meaning "leader." Mussolini's title as head of the Fascist Party.

Fascism Political movements that tend to be antidemocratic, anti-Marxist, antiparliamentary, often anti-Semitic, invariably nationalistic and exalt the nation over the individual; supported the interests of the middle class and rejected the ideas of the French Revolution and nineteenth-century liberalism; first Fascist regime founded by Benito Mussolini (1883–1945) in Italy in the 1920s.

führer Meaning "leader." The title taken by Hitler when he became dictator of Germany.

Great Depression A prolonged worldwide economic downturn that began in 1929 with the collapse of the New York Stock Exchange.

Great Purges The imprisonment and execution of millions of Soviet citizens by Stalin between 1934 and 1939.

Kristallnacht (KRIS-tahl-NAHKT) Meaning "crystal night" because of the broken glass that littered German streets after the looting and destruction of Jewish homes, businesses, and synagogues across Germany on the orders of the Nazi Party in November 1938.

Mein Kampf (MINE KAHMFF) Meaning "My Struggle." Hitler's statement of his political program, published in 1924.

Nazis The German Nationalist Socialist Party.

New Economic Policy (NEP) A limited revival of capitalism, especially in light industry and agriculture, introduced by Lenin in 1921 to repair the damage inflicted on the Russian economy by the Civil War and the policy of War Communism.

Popular Front A government of all left-wing parties that took power in France in 1936 to enact social and economic reforms.

Reichstag (RIKES-stahg) The German parliament, which existed in various forms, until 1945.

SA (*Sturm Abteilung*) The Nazi parliamentary forces, or storm troopers.

Sinn Fein   An Irish political party that led the nationalist cause after World War I; its military wing, which became the Irish Republican Army, fought against the British army for the independence of the Free Irish State.

SS (*Schutzstaffel*)   The chief security units of the Nazi state.

War Communism   The economic policy adopted by the Bolsheviks during the Russian Civil War to seize the banks, heavy industry, railroads, and grain.

Weimar Republic (Why-mar)   The German democratic regime that existed between the end of World War I and Hitler's coming to power in 1933.

Notes

1. Vladimir Andrle, *A Social History of Twentieth-Century Russia* (London: Arnold, 1994), p. 161.
2. J. Arch Getty and Oleg V. Naumov, *The Road to Terror: Stalin and the Self-Destruction of the Bolsheviks, 1932–1939*, trans. by Benjamin Sher (New Haven, CT: Yale University Press, 1999), p. 583.
3. Denis Mack Smith, *Italy: A Modern History* (Ann Arbor: University of Michigan Press, 1959), p. 412.
4. Alan Bullock, *Hitler: A Study in Tyranny*, rev. ed. (New York: Harper & Row, 1964), p. 76.
5. Ian Kershaw, *Hitler 1889–1936: Hubris* (New York: W. W. Norton & Company, 1999), p. 424.

The West and the World

Imperialism: Ancient and Modern

THE CLASH OF EMPIRES The ancient world was fascinated by the clash of empires that marked its history. The Romans created the grandest of the ancient empires, but they knew theirs had been preceded by others. This ancient mosaic, which resides on the walls of the House of the Faun in Pompeii, depicts the Battle of Issus (333 B.C.E.), when the Macedonian Alexander the Great defeated the Persian Empire ruled by Darius III. Alexander appears on the left of the mosaic and Darius appears on his chariot. The mosaic, based on a still more ancient lost painting, probably dates from the second century B.C.E. and was rediscovered in 1831.
SOURCE Alinari/Art Resource, NY

THE CONCEPT OF "empire" does not win favor today, and the word *imperialism*, derived from it, has carried an increasingly pejorative meaning since it was coined in the nineteenth century. Both words imply forcible domination by a nation or a state that exploits an alien people for its own benefit. Although, in our time, the charge of imperialism arises whenever a large and powerful nation influences weaker ones, exertion of influence alone is not imperialism. To be true to historical experience, one nation's actions toward another are imperialistic only if the dominant nation exerts both political and military control over the weaker one. In that sense, the last great empire in the modern world was the conglomeration of republics and ostensibly independent satellite states dominated by Russia prior to the USSR's collapse, but the Russians and the other imperial powers after World War II took no public pride in their domination. In our day, ruling an "empire" or engaging in "imperialism" is generally considered among the worst acts a nation can commit.

Such views are rare, perhaps unique, in the history of civilization. A major source for this opinion is the Christian religious tradition, especially parts of the New Testament that deprecate power and worldly glory and praise humility. In fact, Christianity was not hostile to power and empire, for it took control of the Roman Empire in the fourth century C.E. and has lived comfortably with "empire" until our own century. The rise of democracy and nationalism in the last two centuries may have been more influential in changing attitudes toward imperialism because these movements exalt the freedom and autonomy of a people. Perhaps the modern disdain for empire building has its principal origins in the extraordinary horror of modern warfare and the historical knowledge that competition for empire has often led to war.

If, however, we are to understand the widespread experience of empire throughout history, we must be alert to the great gap that separates the views of most people throughout history from our current opinions. The earliest empires go back more than 4,000 years to the valleys of the Nile and the Tigris-Euphrates, and empires arose later in China, Japan, India, Iran, and Central and South America, among other areas. Typically, they were led by rulers who were believed to be gods or the representatives of gods, or at least were godlike in their ability to rule over many people. To their own people they brought wealth and prosperity, power, and reflected glory, all considered highly desirable. No one appears to have questioned the propriety of conquering another people and taking their lands, property, and persons to benefit the conquerors. Empire seemed to be part of the order of things—good for the rulers, usually bad for the ruled.

The Greeks: Ambiguities of Power

In most respects, the Greeks resembled other ancient peoples in their attitudes toward power, conquest, empire, and the benefits that came with them. Their Olympian gods held sway over earth, heaven, and the underworld because of victorious wars over other deities, and they gloried in their rule. The heroes in the epic poems that formed the Greek system of values won glory and honor through battle, conquest, and rule over other people. They viewed the world as a place of intense competition in which victory and domination, which brought fame and glory, were the highest goals, whereas defeat and subordination brought ignominy and shame.

When the legendary world of aristocratic heroes gave way to the world of city-states (poleis), competition was elevated from contests among individuals, households, and clans to contests and wars among poleis. In 416 B.C.E., more than a decade after the death of Pericles (c. 490–429 B.C.E.), Athenian spokesmen explained to some Melian officials their view of international relations: "Of the gods we believe, and of men we know, that by a necessity of their nature they always rule wherever they have the power."[1] Although their language was shockingly blunt, it reflected the views of most Greeks.

Yet this was also a dramatic presentation of the morally problematic status of the Athenian Empire. The Athenians' harsh statement would have struck a sympathetic chord among the Greeks. They appreciated power and the security and glory it can bring, but their own historical experience was different from that of other ancient nations. Their culture had been shaped by small, autonomous, independent city-states, and they considered freedom natural for people raised in such an environment. Citizens, they believed, should be free in their persons; free to maintain their own constitutions, laws, and customs; and their city-states should be free to conduct their own foreign relations and to compete for power and glory. The free, autonomous polis, they thought, was greater than the mightiest powers in the world, and the sixth-century B.C.E. poet Phocylides was prepared to compare it to the great Assyrian Empire: "A little polis living orderly in a high place is greater than block-headed Nineveh" (Fragment 5).

When poleis fought one another, the victor typically took control of a piece of borderland that was usually the source of the dispute. They did not normally enslave the defeated enemy or annex and occupy its land. In these matters, as in many others, the Greeks distinguished themselves from alien peoples who did not speak Greek and were not shaped by the Greek cultural tradition. These people were called barbarians, *barbaroi*, because their speech sounded to the Greeks like "bar bar." Because they had not been raised as people in free communities but lived as subjects to a ruler, they were, it seemed, slaves by nature. To the Greeks, then, dominating and enslaving such people was perfectly acceptable. Greeks, however, viewed themselves as naturally free, as they demonstrated by creating and living in the free institutions of the polis. To rule over such people, to deny them their freedom and autonomy, would be wrong—so the Greeks thought, but they did not always act accordingly. The early Spartans, for instance, had changed the status of the conquered Greeks of Laconia and Messenia to *Helots*, or slaves of the state.

The Greeks shared still another belief that interfered with the comfortable acceptance of great power and empire: They thought any good thing amassed by humans to excess, beyond moderation, eventually led to *hubris*, a condition of wanton violence arising from arrogant pride in one's greatness. Those overcome by hubris were thought to have overstepped the limits established for human beings, to have shown contempt for the gods, and, thereby, to have incurred *nemesis*, or divine anger and retribution. The great example to the Greeks of the fifth century B.C.E. of the workings of hubris and nemesis was the fate of Xerxes (r. 486–465 B.C.E.), great king of the Persian Empire. His power became so great, it filled him with a blind arrogance that led him to try to extend his rule over the Greek mainland and thus brought disaster to himself and his people. When, therefore, the Athenians undertook the leadership of a Greek alliance after the Persian War, and that leadership brought them wealth and power and, in fact, became what was frankly acknowledged to be an empire, their response was ambiguous and contradictory. These developments were a source of pride and gratification but also of embarrassment and, to some Athenians, shame.

The Macedonian conquest of the Greek city-states in 338 B.C.E. marked a return to an older attitude toward empire. Alexander the Great (r. 340–323 B.C.E.) conquered the vast Persian Empire, itself the successor of empires that had stretched from the Nile to the Indus valley. The death of Alexander led to its division and eventual absorption by the emergent Roman Empire by the second century B.C.E.

The Romans: A Theory of Empire

The Romans had fewer hesitations about the desirability of imperial power than the Greeks. Their culture, which arose from a world of farmers accustomed to hard work, deprivation, and subordination to authority, venerated the military virtues. Roman society valued power, glory, and the responsibilities of leadership, even domination, without embarrassment. In time, the Romans formulated a theory of empire that claimed Roman rule brought great advantages to its subjects: prosperity, justice, the rule of law, and most valuable of all, peace. In the words of their great epic poet Virgil (70–19 B.C.E.), it was the Roman practice "to humble the arrogant and be sparing to their subjects."[2] These claims had considerable foundation, and the Romans could not have ruled so vast an empire with a relatively small army

SULEYMAN THE MAGNIFICENT IN BATTLE The Ottoman Turks began to overrun the Balkans in the mid-1300s. In 1526, Sultan Suleyman the Magnificent destroyed a Hungarian army at the Battle of Mohacs. The Ottoman Empire ruled most of the Balkans until the late nineteenth century.
SOURCE: Bridgeman-Giraudon/Art Resource, NY

for more than half a millennium if their subjects had not enjoyed these benefits. Some of the conquered had a different viewpoint, however. As one British chieftain put it in the first century C.E.: "They make a wilderness and call it peace."[3]

Muslims, Mongols, and Ottomans

The rise of Islam in the seventh century C.E. produced a new kind of empire that derived its energy from religious zeal. Bursting out of Arabia, the Muslim armies swiftly gained control of most of the territory held by the old Persian Empire, North Africa, and Spain.

In the twelfth and thirteenth centuries, the great Mongol Empire, at its height, dominated Eurasia from the Pacific to central Europe, ruling Russia for more than two centuries. As in most ancient empires, the Mongols demanded taxes and military service from the conquered. They also imposed their rule over the mighty and long-standing Chinese Empire, parts of India, and much of the Islamic world before their power declined.

Still another great empire that spanned Europe and Asia was that of the Ottomans, a Turkish people, originally from central Asia. In the fourteenth century, they established a kingdom in Anatolia (Asia Minor) and soon conquered the ancient Byzantine Empire, seizing Constantinople in 1453. In the next century, the Ottoman Empire dominated southeastern Europe, the Black Sea, North Africa from Morocco to Egypt, Palestine, Syria and Arabia, Mesopotamia and Iraq, and Kurdistan and Georgia in the Caucasus. As late as 1683, Ottoman armies threatened to take Vienna and push into Western Europe. Over the next two centuries, however, Ottoman power declined as the European national states grew stronger. Russia, in particular, inflicted defeats that left Turkey in the late nineteenth century, "the sick man of Europe."

European Expansion

Europe, divided first by feudalism, then by the emergence of multiple nascent national states, had been the victim of Islamic imperial expansion during the Middle Ages, first at the hands of the Arabs, then the Turks. The crusades had produced small and transitory conquests. It was only in the late 1400s that Europeans began the economic and political expansion that culminated in their command of much of the planet by 1900. The first phase of European expansion involved the "discovery," exploration, conquest, exploitation, and settlement of the Americas. It was made possible by important developments in naval and military technology, the dynamism inherent in early commercial and financial capitalism, and the freedom to compete for wealth and power unleashed by the division into separate states.

MASSACRE AT ARMRITSAR European imperialism ultimately rested on the willingness to use force. When anti-British agitation increased in India after World War I, General Reginald Dyer's troops fired on unarmed Indian demonstrators at Amritsar. More than 300 Indians were killed.
SOURCE: CSP_imagex/Fotosearch LBRF/AGE Fotostock

Spain and Portugal took the lead, founding empires in Central and South America, sometimes conquering existing empires ruled by native peoples. In Central America, the Aztecs exacted labor and taxes from their subject peoples, using some of them as human sacrifices. In the Andes, the Incas ruled a great empire that also required military service and forced labor from its subjects. Both Native American empires were overthrown by Spain, which then established a large American empire whose resources, especially gold and silver, formed the basis of the great Spanish Empire in Europe. Portugal exploited the agricultural and mineral riches of Brazil using slaves imported from Africa.

The seventeenth century saw the establishment of European trading posts and then colonies on the Indian subcontinent and in the East Indies, chiefly by the Dutch, British, and French. In North America, Spain held Mexico, Florida, and California. Of more lasting significance were French and British settlements in Canada and what was to become the United States. The British colonies especially represented a kind of European overseas settlement in which concern for commerce was less important than the acquisition of land for farming.

The wars of the eighteenth century ultimately cleared North America and India of French competition, leaving both as British monopolies and important bases of what would become a worldwide British Empire. The largest and most populous empire in the history of the world, it included colonies on all the inhabited continents; "the sun," as the saying went, "never set on the British Empire." Whether European colonialism was profitable for the imperial powers is still controversial, but Great Britain certainly benefited more than the others. Unlike most colonial powers, the British imported great quantities of natural resources from their colonies and carried on a high percentage of their trade with them. Even more singular, the British Empire included such self-governing areas as Canada, Australia, New Zealand, and South Africa, ruled by emigrants from Britain who remained loyal to the mother country and were willing to assist it in wartime. "The jewel in Britain's imperial crown," as another saying went, "was India." With a population of some 300 million, it contained perhaps 80 percent of the empire's subjects and provided much of the imperial profit.

At the height of its power in the mid-nineteenth century, it is remarkable how little money and effort Britain needed to spend to maintain these desired conditions. The cost of its armed services, including its great navy, during these years was only about 2–3 percent of its gross national product—a low figure compared with other nations and incredibly low considering Britain's status as the world's greatest empire. The British army was the smallest among the European powers: By 1880 it numbered fewer than a quarter of a million men—less than half the size of France's and barely a quarter of Russia's.

France returned to its imperial pursuits after its defeat in the Napoleonic Wars, especially in North Africa and Southeast Asia, and in the last quarter of the century, Germany and Italy joined the competition for colonies. The latter part of the century brought the European partition of Africa and the establishment of European economic and political power throughout Asia. Modernized Japan, too, became a colonial power, modeling itself on the imperialist policies of the European powers.

By the next century, European dominance had created a single global economy and had made events in any corner of the world significant thousands of miles away. The possession of colonies became part of the definition of a great power, and the competition for colonies helped bring on World War I.

Toward Decolonization

The weakening of the European colonial powers in World War II began the process of decolonization. The economic value of most colonies had proved to be much smaller than anticipated, and the colonial powers lacked both the capacity and the incentive to restore their former rule. Nationalist movements in the old colonies, moreover, would make such attempts costly and unpleasant. These movements flourished under the banner of national self-determination, self-government, and independence, ideas that came from and were cherished by the European colonial powers themselves. The example of Nazi Germany, moreover, had discredited theories of racial superiority that had justified much of European imperial rule. For European imperialism the handwriting was on the wall, although some colonial powers held on more fiercely than others. The French, for instance, fought at great cost—but in vain—to retain Algeria and Indochina. By the 1970s, a postcolonial world had emerged, and the concept of empire had become unclean.

Questions

1. What were the major ancient attitudes toward imperialism? What are the main modern attitudes? Do you think ancient and modern reasons for imperialism are fundamentally different? How do you account for the differences?

2. What justifications and explanations have modern people used regarding imperialism? Which do you think are the most important?

Notes

1. Thucydides 5.105
2. Virgil *Aeneid* 6.850
3. Tacitus *Agricola* 30

Chapter 28
World War II

DROPPING THE BOMB In August 1945, the United States exploded atomic bombs on the Japanese cities of Hiroshima and Nagasaki. A week later Japan surrendered. Without the bombs, the United States would almost certainly have had to invade Japan, and tens of thousands of Americans would have been killed. Still, the decision to use the bomb remains controversial.
SOURCE: Cultura RM/Alamy Stock Photo

Contents and Focus Questions

The Chapter in Brief

THE MORE IDEALISTIC survivors of World War I, especially in the United States and Great Britain, thought of it as "the war to end all wars" and a war "to make the world safe for democracy." Only thus could they justify the slaughter, expense, and upheaval of that terrible conflict. How appalled they would have been had they known that only twenty years after the peace treaties a second great war would break out, more global than the first. In this war,

758

the democracies would be fighting for their lives against militaristic, nationalistic, authoritarian, and totalitarian states in Europe and Asia, and they would be allied with the Communist Soviet Union in the struggle. The defeat of the militarists and dictators would not bring the peace they longed for, but instead the Cold War, in which the European states would become powers of the second class, subordinate to two new superpowers, partially or fully non-European: the Soviet Union and the United States.

28.1 Again the Road to War (1933–1939)

How did World War I sow the seeds of World War II?

World War I and the Versailles treaty had only a marginal relationship to the world depression of the 1930s. In Germany, however, where the reparations settlement had contributed to the vast inflation of 1923, economic and social discontent focused on the Versailles settlement as the cause of all ills. Throughout the late 1920s, Adolf Hitler and the Nazi Party denounced Versailles as the source of Germany's troubles. The economic woes of the early 1930s seemed to bear them out. Nationalism and attention to the social question, along with party discipline, had been the sources of Nazi success. They continued to influence Hitler's foreign policy after he became chancellor in January 1933. Moreover, the Nazi destruction of the Weimar constitution and of political opposition meant that Hitler himself totally dominated German foreign policy. Consequently, it is important to know what his goals were and how he planned to achieve them.

KEY EVENTS IN THE RUN-UP TO WORLD WAR II	
June 1919	The Versailles Treaty
January 1923	France occupies the Ruhr
October 1925	The Locarno Agreements
Spring 1931	Onset of the Great Depression in Europe
September 1931	Japan occupies Manchuria
January 1933	Hitler comes to power
October 1933	Germany withdraws from the League of Nations
March 1935	Hitler renounces disarmament, starts an air force, and begins conscription
October 1935	Mussolini attacks Ethiopia
March 1936	Germany reoccupies and remilitarizes the Rhineland
July 1936	Outbreak of the Spanish Civil War
October 1936	Formation of the Rome–Berlin Axis
March 1938	*Anschluss* with Austria
September 1938	The Munich conference and the partition of Czechoslovakia
March 1939	Hitler occupies Prague; France and Great Britain guarantee Polish independence
August 1939	The Nazi–Soviet pact
September 1 1939	Germany invades Poland
September 3 1939	Britain and France declare war on Germany

28.1.1 Hitler's Goals

From the first expression of his goals in a book written in jail, *Mein Kampf (My Struggle)*, to his last days in the underground bunker in Berlin where he killed himself, Hitler's racial theories and goals were at the center of his thought. He meant to go far beyond Germany's 1914 boundaries which were the limit of the vision of his predecessors. He meant to bring the entire German people—the *Volk*—understood as a racial group, together into a single nation.

The new Germany would include all the Germanic parts of the old Habsburg Empire, including Austria. This virile and growing nation would need more space to live, or **Lebensraum**, that would be taken from the Slavs, who according to Nazi theory, were a lesser race fit only for servitude. The removal of the Jews, another inferior race according to Nazi theory would purify the new Germany. The plans required conquering Poland and Ukraine as the primary areas for German settlement and providing badly needed food. Neither *Mein Kampf* nor later statements of policy were blueprints for action. Rather, Hitler was a brilliant improviser who exploited opportunities as they arose. He never lost sight of his goal, however, which would almost certainly require a major war.

28.1.1.1 GERMANY REARMS When Hitler came to power, Germany was far too weak to permit a direct approach to reach his aims. The first problem he set out to resolve was to shake off the fetters of Versailles and to make Germany a formidable military power. In October 1933, Germany withdrew from an international disarmament conference and also from the League of Nations. These acts alarmed the French but were merely symbolic. In January 1934, Germany signed a nonaggression pact with Poland that was of greater concern to France, for it undermined France's chief means of containing the Germans. At last, in March 1935, Hitler formally renounced the disarmament provisions of the Versailles treaty with the formation of a German air force, and soon he reinstated conscription, which aimed at an army of half a million men.

28.1.1.2 THE LEAGUE OF NATIONS FAILS Growing evidence that the League of Nations could not keep the peace and that collective security was a myth made Hitler's path easier. In September 1931, Japan occupied Manchuria. China appealed to the League of Nations. The league dispatched a commission under a British diplomat, the earl of Lytton (1876–1951). The *Lytton Report* condemned the Japanese for resorting to force, but the powers were unwilling to impose sanctions. Japan withdrew from the league and kept control of Manchuria.

When Hitler announced his decision to rearm Germany, the league formally condemned that action, but it took no steps to prevent it. France and Britain felt unable to object forcefully because they had not carried out their own promises to disarm. Instead, they met with Mussolini in June 1935 to form the so-called Stresa Front, promising to use force to maintain the status quo in Europe. This show of unity was short-lived, however. Britain, desperate to maintain superiority at sea, violated the spirit of the Stresa accords and sacrificed French security to make a separate naval agreement with Hitler. The pact allowed him to rebuild the German fleet to 35 percent of the British navy. Hitler had taken a major step toward his goal without provoking serious opposition. Italy's expansionist ambitions in Africa, however, soon brought it into conflict with the Western powers.

28.1.2 Italy Attacks Ethiopia

In October 1935, Mussolini, using a border incident as an excuse, attacked Ethiopia. This attack made the impotence of the League of Nations and the timidity of the Allies clear. Mussolini's purposes were to avenge a humiliating defeat that the Italians had suffered in Ethiopia in 1896, to restore Roman imperial glory, and perhaps to distract Italian public opinion from domestic problems.

The League of Nations condemned Italian aggression and for the first time voted economic sanctions. It imposed an arms embargo that limited loans and credits to, and imports from, Italy. To avoid alienating Mussolini, however, Britain and France refused to embargo oil, the one economic sanction that could have prevented Italian victory. Even more important, Britain allowed Italian troops and munitions to reach Ethiopia through the Suez Canal. The results of this policy were disastrous. The League of Nations and collective security were discredited, and Mussolini was alienated. He now turned to Germany, and by November 1, 1936, he spoke publicly of a Rome–Berlin **Axis**.

28.1.3 Remilitarization of the Rhineland

The Ethiopian affair also convinced Hitler that the Western powers were too timid to oppose him forcefully. On March 7, 1936, he took his greatest risk yet, sending a small armed force into the demilitarized Rhineland. This was a breach not only of the Versailles treaty but also of the **Locarno Agreements** of 1925—agreements Germany had made voluntarily. It also removed a crucial element of French security. France and Britain had every right to resist, and the French especially had a claim to retain the only element of security left to them after the failure to

guarantee France's defense. Yet neither power did anything but register a feeble protest with the League of Nations. British opinion would not permit support for France, and the French would not act alone. Internal division and a military doctrine that stressed defense and shunned the offensive paralyzed them. A growing pacifism further weakened both countries.

In retrospect, the Allies lost a great opportunity in the Rhineland to stop Hitler before he became a serious menace. The failure of his gamble, taken against his generals' advice, might have led to his overthrow; at the least, it would have made German expansion to the east dangerous if not impossible. Nor is there reason to doubt that the French army could easily have routed the tiny German force in the Rhineland. As the German general Alfred Jodl (1890–1946) said some years later, "The French covering army would have blown us to bits."[1]

A Germany that was rapidly rearming and had a defensible western frontier presented a completely new problem to the Western powers. They responded with the policy of **appeasement**, based on the assumption that Germany had real grievances and that Hitler's goals were limited and ultimately acceptable. They set out to negotiate and make concessions before a crisis could lead to war.

Underlying this approach was the universal dread of another war. Memories of the horrors of the last war were still vivid, and the prospect of aerial bombardment made the thought of a new war even more terrifying. A firmer policy, moreover, would have required rapid rearmament. British leaders especially were reluctant to pursue this path because of the expense and the widespread belief that the arms race had been a major cause of the last war. As Germany armed, the French huddled behind their newly constructed defensive wall, the **Maginot Line**, and the British hoped for the best.

28.1.4 The Spanish Civil War

The Spanish Civil War, which broke out in July 1936, made the new European alignment with the Western democracies on one side and the Fascist states on the other clearer. (See Map 28–1.) In 1931, the monarchy had collapsed, and Spain became a democratic republic. The new government followed a program of moderate reform that antagonized landowners, the Catholic Church, nationalists, and conservatives without satisfying the demands of peasants, workers, Catalán separatists, or radicals. Elections in February 1936 brought to power a Spanish Popular Front government ranging from republicans of the left to Communists and anarchists. The losers, especially the Falangists, the Spanish Fascists, would not accept defeat at the polls. In July, the

A BLOODY CIVIL WAR IN SPAIN This poster supports General Francisco Franco's nationalists in the bloody Spanish Civil War, which lasted almost three years and claimed hundreds of thousands of lives.
SOURCE: Library of Congress

army, later led by General Francisco Franco (1892–1975), invaded from Spanish Morocco and began a civil war against the republic.

The Spanish Civil War, which lasted almost three years, cost hundreds of thousands of lives and provided a training ground for World War II. Germany and Italy supported Franco with troops, airplanes, and supplies. The Soviet Union sent equipment and advisers to the republicans. Liberals and leftists from Europe and America volunteered to fight in the republican ranks against Fascism.

The civil war, fought on blatantly ideological lines, profoundly affected world politics. It brought Germany and Italy closer together, leading to the Rome–Berlin Axis Pact in 1936. Japan joined the Axis powers in the Anti-Comintern Pact, ostensibly directed against international Communism but really a new and powerful diplomatic alliance. Western

Europe, especially France, had a great interest in preventing Spain from falling into the hands of a Fascist regime closely allied with Germany and Italy. Appeasement reigned, however. Although international law permitted the sale of weapons and munitions to the legitimate republican government, France and Britain forbade the export of war materials to either side, and the United States passed new neutrality legislation to the same end. When Barcelona fell to Franco early in 1939, the Fascists had won effective control of Spain.

28.1.5 Austria and Czechoslovakia

Hitler made good use of his new friendship with Mussolini. He had always planned to annex his native Austria. In 1934, the Nazi Party in Austria assassinated the prime minister and tried to seize power. Mussolini had not yet allied with Hitler and was suspicious of German intentions. He quickly moved an army to the Austrian border, preventing German intervention and causing the coup to fail.

In 1938, the new diplomatic situation encouraged Hitler to try again. He perhaps hoped to achieve his goal by propaganda, bullying, and threats, but Austrian chancellor Kurt von Schuschnigg (1897–1977) refused to be intimidated. Schuschnigg announced a plebiscite for March 13, in which the Austrian people themselves could decide whether to unite with Germany. To forestall the plebiscite, Hitler sent his army into Austria on March 12. To his relief, Mussolini did not object, and Hitler rode to Vienna amid the cheers of his Austrian sympathizers.

The *Anschluss*, or union of Germany and Austria, was another clear violation of Versailles. The treaty, however, was now a dead letter, and the West remained passive. The Anschluss had great strategic significance, however, because Germany now surrounded Czechoslovakia, one of the bulwarks of French security, on three sides.

In fact, the very existence of Czechoslovakia was an affront to Hitler. It was democratic and pro-Western; it had been created partly to check Germany and was allied both to France and to the Soviet Union. It also contained about 3.5 million Germans who lived in the Sudetenland, near the German border. These Germans had belonged to the dominant nationality group in the old Austro-Hungarian Empire and resented their new minority position. Supported by Hitler and led by Konrad Henlein (1898–1945), they made ever-increasing demands for privileges and autonomy within the Czech state. The Czechs made concessions, but Hitler really wanted to destroy Czechoslovakia. He told Henlein, "We must always demand so much that we can never be satisfied."[2]

Map 28–1 THE SPANISH CIVIL WAR, 1936–1939

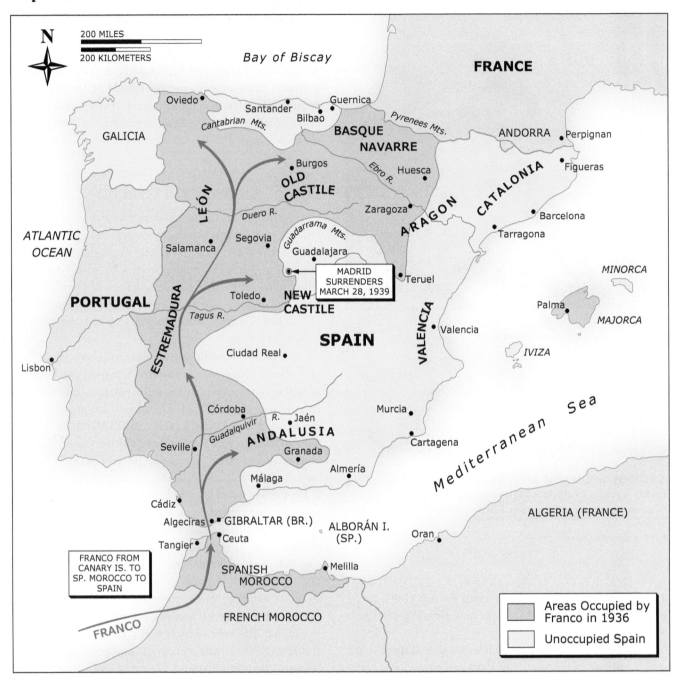

The purple area on the map shows the large portion of Spain quickly overrun by Franco's insurgent armies during the first year of the Spanish Civil War. In the next two years, progress was slower for the Fascists as the war became a kind of international rehearsal for the coming World War II. Madrid's fall to Franco in the spring of 1939 had been preceded by that of Barcelona a few weeks earlier.

On September 12, 1938, Hitler made a provocative speech at the Nuremberg Nazi Party rally. His rhetoric led to rioting in the Sudetenland, and the Czechs declared martial law. German intervention seemed imminent. British prime minister **Neville Chamberlain**, aged sixty-nine, who had never flown before, made three flights to Germany between September 15 and September 29 in an attempt to appease Hitler at Czech expense and thus to avoid war. At Hitler's mountain retreat, Berchtesgaden, on September 15, Chamberlain accepted the separation of the Sudetenland from Czechoslovakia, and he and the French premier, Edouard Daladier (1884–1970), forced the Czechs to agree by threatening to abandon them. A week later, Chamberlain flew yet again to Germany, only to find that Hitler had raised his demands. He wanted cession of the Sudetenland in three days and immediate occupation by the German army.

28.1.6 Munich

Chamberlain returned to England, and France and Britain prepared for war. At Chamberlain's request and at the last moment, Mussolini proposed a conference of Germany, Italy, France, and Britain. It met on September 29 at Munich. Hitler received almost everything he had demanded. (See Map 28–2.) The Sudetenland, the key to Czech security, became part of Germany, thus depriving the Czechs of any chance of self-defense. In return, Hitler agreed to spare the rest of Czechoslovakia. He promised, "I have no more territorial demands to make in Europe." Chamberlain returned to England with the Munich agreement and told a cheering crowd that he had brought "peace with honor" and he believed it was "peace for our time." (For two views of the Munich agreement, see the "Compare and Connect" sidebar, which follows below.)

Even in the short run, the appeasement of Hitler at Munich was a failure. Czechoslovakia did not survive. Soon Poland and Hungary took more territory from it, and the Slovaks demanded a state of their own. Finally, on March 15, 1939, Hitler broke his promise and occupied Prague, putting an end to the Czech state and to illusions that his only goal was to restore Germans to the Reich.

If the French and the British had been willing to attack Germany from the west while the Czechs fought in their own defense, their efforts might have been successful. High officers in the German army were opposed to Hitler's risky policies and might have overthrown him. Even failing such developments, a war begun in October 1938 would have forced Hitler to fight without the friendly neutrality and material assistance of the Soviet Union—and without the resources of Eastern Europe that became available to him as a result of appeasement and Soviet cooperation. If, moreover, the West ever had a chance of concluding an alliance with the Soviet Union against Hitler, the exclusion of the Russians from Munich and the appeasement

Map 28–2   PARTITIONS OF CZECHOSLOVAKIA AND POLAND, 1938–1939

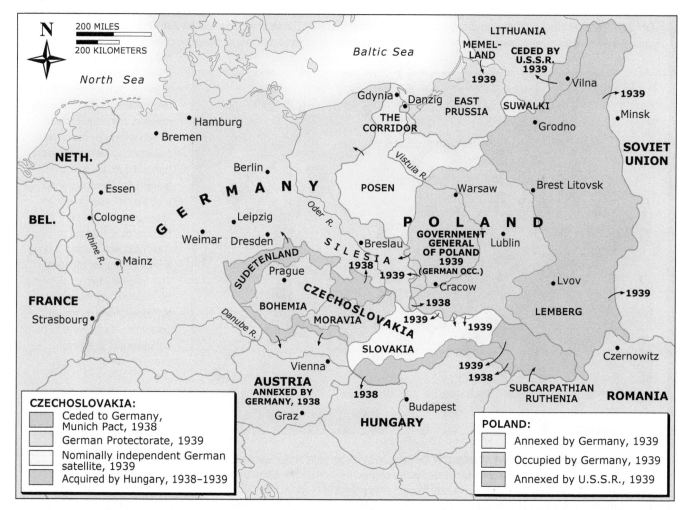

The immediate background of World War II is found in the complex international drama unfolding on Germany's eastern frontier in 1938 and 1939. Germany's expansion inevitably meant the victimization of Austria, Czechoslovakia, and Poland. With the failure of the Western powers' appeasement policy and the signing of a German–Soviet pact, the stage for the war was set.

policy helped destroy it. Munich remains an example of shortsighted policy that helped bring on war in disadvantageous circumstances because of the very fear of war and the failure to prepare for it.

Poland was the next target of German expansion. In the spring of 1939, the Germans put pressure on Poland to restore the formerly German city of Danzig and to allow a railroad and a highway through the Polish Corridor to connect East Prussia with the rest of Germany. When the Poles would not yield, the usual propaganda campaign began and the pressure mounted. On March 31, Chamberlain announced a Franco–British guarantee of Polish independence. Hitler appears to have expected to fight a war with Poland but not with the Western allies, for he did not take their guarantee seriously and had come to hold their leaders in contempt. He knew both countries were unprepared for

war and that large segments of their populations opposed fighting for Poland.

Moreover, France and Britain had no means to get effective help to the Poles. The French, still dominated by the defensive mentality of the Maginot Line, had no intention of attacking Germany. The only way to defend Poland was to bring Russia into the alliance against Hitler, but a Russian alliance posed many problems. Each side was profoundly suspicious of the other. The French and the British were hostile to Communism, and since Stalin's purge of the Red Army, they were skeptical of the military value of a Russian alliance. Besides, the Russians could not help Poland without being given the right to enter Poland and Romania. Both nations, suspicious of Russian intentions—and with good reason—refused to grant these rights. As a result, Western negotiations for an alliance with Russia made little progress.

Compare and Connect

The Munich Settlement

ON SEPTEMBER 29–30, 1938, Germany's dictator Adolf Hitler met with British prime minister Neville Chamberlain, Italy's dictator Benito Mussolini, and France's prime minister Edouard Daladier to settle the fate of Czechoslovakia. The Czechs were

not permitted to take part. It was the height of the Western democracies' effort to appease the dictators and resulted in the partition of Czechoslovakia; the region called the Sudetenland was handed over to Germany, leaving the Czechs without a viable defense. Although Hitler promised to stop there, he took over the rest of Czechoslovakia without firing a shot on March 15, 1939. The following two documents, by Neville Chamberlain and Winston Churchill, present opposite views on the achievement at Munich.

THE APPEASEMENT OF HITLER AT MUNICH On September 29–30, 1938, Hitler met with the leaders of Britain and France at Munich to decide the fate of Czechoslovakia. The Allied leaders abandoned the small democratic nation in a vain attempt to appease Hitler and avoid war. From left to right in the foreground: British prime minister Neville Chamberlain, French prime minister Edouard Daladier, Adolf Hitler, Benito Mussolini, and Italian minister of foreign affairs, and Mussolini's son-in-law, Count Ciano.
SOURCE: National Archives

Before Reading

- Notice that Neville Chamberlain considers his policy a success at Munich.
- Consider the grounds on which Winston Churchill objects to the policy of appeasement.

Questions

1. Why did Chamberlain think the meeting at Munich was a success for Britain?
2. How would Chamberlain defend his policy of appeasement?
3. What were Churchill's objections to the Munich agreement?
4. What critique would Churchill make of the appeasement policy?
5. Who do you think was right? Why?

I. NEVILLE CHAMBERLAIN'S EVALUATION

The following is an account of Neville Chamberlain's return to England the day after the Munich conference. He was greeted like a hero at the airport by a big crowd. Later that day he stood outside Number 10 Downing Street where again he read from the document and declared that he had brought back "peace with honour. I believe it is peace for our time."

"The settlement of the Czech problem, which has now been achieved, is, in my view only the prelude to a larger settlement in which all Europe may find peace" (people cheer at this). "This morning I had another talk with the German Chancellor Herr Hitler and here is the paper which bears his name upon it as well as mine" (he holds paper up and waves it about, people cheer again). "Some of you perhaps have already heard what it contains, but I would just like to read it to you." (He reads) "We, the German Fuhrer and Chancellor and the British Prime Minister, have had a further meeting today and are agreed in recognising that the question of Anglo-German relations is of the first importance for the two countries, and for Europe. We regard the agreement signed last night and the Anglo-German naval agreement, as symbolic of the desire of our two peoples never to go to war with one another again" (everyone cheers). "We are resolved that the method of consultation shall be the method adopted to deal with any other questions that may concern our two countries, and we are determined to continue our efforts to remove possible sources of difference and thus to continue to assure the peace of Europe." (Everyone cheers and someone shouts "three cheers for Chamberlain" which they all do as he walks away and gets into the car. Everyone waves as he drives away.)

II. WINSTON CHURCHILL'S RESPONSE TO MUNICH

In the parliamentary debate that followed the Munich conference at the end of September 1938, Winston Churchill was one of the few who criticized what had been accomplished. In the following selections from his speech, he expresses his concerns.

I will begin by saying what everybody would like to ignore or forget but which must nevertheless be stated, namely, that we have sustained a total and unmitigated defeat, and that France has suffered even more than we have. . . .

We really must not waste time after all this long Debate upon the difference between the positions reached at Berch-tesgaden, at Godesberg and at Munich. They can be very simply epitomized, if the House will permit me to vary the metaphor. One pound was demanded at the pistol's point. When it was given, £2 were demanded at the pistol's point. Finally, the dictator consented to take £1 17s. 6d. and the rest in promises of good will for the future. . . .

All is over. Silent, mournful, abandoned, broken, Czechoslovakia recedes into the darkness. She has suffered in every respect by her association with the Western democracies and with the League of Nations, of which she has always been an obedient servant. . . .

We have been reduced in these five years from a position of security so overwhelming and so unchallengeable that we never cared to think about it. We have been reduced from a position where the very word "war" was considered one which could be used only by persons qualifying for a lunatic asylum. We have been reduced from a position of safety and power—power to do good, power to be generous to a beaten foe, power to make terms with Germany, power to give her proper redress for her grievances, power to stop her arming if we chose, power to take any step in strength or mercy or justice which we thought right—reduced in five years from a position safe and unchallenged to where we stand now. . . .

[T]he responsibility must rest with those who have had the undisputed control of our political affairs. They neither prevented Germany from rearming, nor did they rearm ourselves in time. They quarreled with Italy without saving Ethiopia. They exploited and discredited the vast institution of the League of Nations and they neglected to make alliances and combinations which might have repaired previous errors, and thus they left us in the hour of trial without adequate national defense or effective international security. . . .

We are in the presence of a disaster of the first magnitude which has befallen Great Britain and France. Do not let us blind ourselves to that. It must now be accepted that all the countries of Central and Eastern Europe will make the best terms they can with the triumphant Nazi power. The system of alliances in Central Europe upon which France has relied for her safety has been swept away, and I can see no means by which it can be reconstituted. The road down the Danube Valley to the Black Sea, the road which leads as far as Turkey, has been opened.

SOURCES: (I) From British Pathe.com Peace Four Power Conference 983.14. (II) From *Parliamentary Debates*, 5th series, vol. 339 (1938).

28.1.7 The Nazi–Soviet Pact

The Russians had at least equally good reason to hesitate. They resented being left out of the Munich agreement. The low priority that the West gave to negotiations with Russia, compared with the urgency with which Britain and France dealt with Hitler, annoyed them. The Russians feared rightly that the Western powers meant them to bear the burden of the war against Germany. As a result, they opened negotiations with Hitler, and on August 23, 1939, the world was shocked to learn of a Nazi–Soviet nonaggression pact.

The secret provisions of the pact, which were easily guessed and soon carried out, divided Poland between the two powers and allowed Russia to occupy the Baltic states and to take Bessarabia from Romania. The most bitter ideological enemies had become allies. Communist parties in the West changed overnight from ardently advocating resistance to Hitler to a policy of peace and quiet. Ideology gave way to political and military reality. The West offered the Russians immediate danger without much prospect of gain. Hitler offered Stalin short-term gain without immediate danger. There could be little doubt about Stalin's decision.

The Nazi–Soviet pact sealed the fate of Poland, and the Franco–British commitment guaranteed a general war. On September 1, 1939, the Germans invaded Poland. Two days later, Britain and France declared war on Germany. World War II had begun.

28.2 World War II (1939–1945)

In what ways was World War II a "total" war?

World War II was truly global. Fighting took place in Europe, North Africa, and Asia, on the Atlantic and the Pacific Oceans, and in the northern and southern hemispheres. The demand for the fullest exploitation of material and human resources for increased production, the use of blockades, and the intensive bombing of civilian targets made the war of 1939 even more "total"—that is, comprehensive and intense—than that of 1914.

KEY CAMPAIGNS AND EVENTS OF WORLD WAR II	
September 1939	Germany and the Soviet Union invade Poland
November 1939	The Soviet Union invades Finland
April 1940	Germany invades Denmark and Norway
May 1940	Germany invades Belgium, the Netherlands, Luxembourg, and France
June 1940	Fall of France
August 1940	Battle of Britain begins
June 1941	Germany invades the Soviet Union
July 1941	Japan takes Indochina
December 1941	Japan attacks Pearl Harbor; United States enters war against Axis powers
June 1942	Battle of Midway Island
November 1942	Battle of Stalingrad begins
July–August 1943	Allies take Sicily, land in Italy
June 1944	Allies land in Normandy
May 1945	Germany surrenders
August 1945	Atomic bombs dropped on Hiroshima and Nagasaki
September 1945	Japan formally surrenders

28.2.1 The German Conquest of Europe

The German attack on Poland produced swift success. The new style of "lightning warfare," or *blitzkrieg*, employed fast-moving, massed armored columns supported by airpower. The Poles had few planes and fewer tanks, and their defense soon collapsed. The speed of the German victory astonished the Russians, who hastened to collect their share of the booty before Hitler could deprive them of it.

On September 17, Russia invaded Poland from the east, dividing the country with the Germans. The Red Army then occupied the encircled Baltic countries. By July 1940, Estonia, Latvia, and Lithuania had become puppet republics within the Soviet Union. In June 1940, the Russians forced Romania to cede Bessarabia. In November 1939, the Russians invaded Finland, but the Finns resisted fiercely for six months. Although they were finally worn down and compelled to yield territory and bases to Russia, the Finns remained independent. Russian expansionism and the poor

***BLITZKRIEG*, OR "LIGHTNING WARFARE"** The German tactic of lightning warfare known as blitzkrieg relied on tanks, planes, and artillery to break through defensive lines. The tactic proved particularly effective in the first few years of the war, allowing Germany to bring most of continental Europe under its control.
SOURCE: World History Archive/Alamy Stock Photo

performance of the Red Army in Finland may well have encouraged Hitler to invade the Soviet Union in June 1941, just twenty-two months after the 1939 treaty.

Until the spring of 1940, the western front was quiet. The French remained behind the Maginot Line while Hitler and Stalin swallowed Poland and the Baltic states. Britain rearmed hastily, and the British navy blockaded Germany. Cynics in the West called it the phony war, or *Sitzkrieg*, but Hitler shattered the stillness in the spring of 1940. In April, without warning and with swift success, the Germans invaded Denmark and Norway. Hitler's northern front was secure, and he now had both air and naval bases closer to Britain. A month later, a combined land and air attack struck Belgium, the Netherlands, and Luxembourg. German airpower and armored divisions were irresistible. The Dutch surrendered in a few days; the Belgians, though aided by the French and the British, gave up less than two weeks later.

The British and French armies in Belgium were forced to flee to the English Channel to seek escape on the beaches of Dunkirk. The heroic efforts of hundreds of Britons manning small boats saved more than 200,000 British and 100,000 French soldiers. Casualties, however, were high, and valuable equipment was abandoned.

The Maginot Line ran from Switzerland to the Belgian frontier. Until 1936, the French had expected the Belgians to continue the fortifications along their German border. After Hitler remilitarized the Rhineland without opposition, the

Belgians lost faith in their French alliance and proclaimed their neutrality, leaving the Maginot Line exposed on its left flank. Hitler's swift advance through Belgium, therefore, circumvented France's main line of defense.

The French army, poorly and hesitantly led by aged generals who did not understand how to use tanks and planes, collapsed. Mussolini, eager to claim the spoils of victory when he thought it was safe to do so, invaded southern France on June 10. Less than a week later, the new French government, under the ancient hero of Verdun, Marshal Henri Philippe Pétain (1856–1951), asked for an armistice. In two months Hitler had accomplished what Germany had failed to achieve in four years of bitter fighting in the previous war.

28.2.2 The Battle of Britain

The fall of France left Britain isolated, and Hitler expected the British to come to terms. He was prepared to allow Britain to retain its empire in return for a free hand for Germany on the Continent. The British had never been willing to accept such an arrangement and had fought the long and difficult war against Napoleon to prevent a single power from dominating the Continent. If there was any chance the British would consider such terms, it disappeared when Winston Churchill (1874–1965) replaced Chamberlain as prime minister in May 1940.

Churchill had been an early and forceful critic of Hitler, the Nazis, and the policy of appeasement. He was a descendant and biographer of the Duke of Marlborough (1650–1722), who had fought Louis XIV in the eighteenth century. Churchill's sense of history, his feeling for British greatness, and his hatred of tyranny and love of freedom made him reject any compromise with Hitler. His skill as a speaker and a writer enabled him to inspire the British people with own courage and determination and to undertake what seemed a hopeless fight. Hitler and his allies, including the Soviet Union, controlled all of Europe. Japan was having its way in Asia. The United States was neutral, dominated by isolationist sentiment, and determined to avoid involvement outside the Western Hemisphere.

One of Churchill's greatest achievements was establishing a close relationship with U.S. president **Franklin D. Roosevelt** (1882–1945). Roosevelt found ways to help the British despite strong political opposition. In 1940 and 1941, before the United States was at war, America sent military supplies, traded badly needed warships for leases on British naval bases, and even convoyed ships across the Atlantic to help the British survive.

As weeks passed and Britain remained defiant, Hitler was forced to contemplate an invasion and that required control of the air. The first strikes by the German *Luftwaffe*, or air force, directed against the airfields and fighter planes in southeast England, began in August 1940. If these attacks had continued, Germany might have gained control of the air and with it the chance of a successful invasion.

In early September, however, seeking revenge for some British bombing raids on German cities, the Luftwaffe switched its main attacks to London. For two months, it bombed London every night. Much of the city was destroyed, and about 15,000 people were killed. The theories of victory through airpower alone, however, proved false. Casualties were much fewer than expected, and

morale was not shattered. In fact, the bombings united the British people and made them more resolute.

The Royal Air Force (RAF) inflicted heavy losses on the Luftwaffe. Aided by the newly developed radar and excellent communications, the British Spitfire and Hurricane fighter planes destroyed more than twice as many enemy planes as the RAF lost. Hitler had lost the Battle of Britain in the air and was forced to abandon his plans for invasion.

28.2.3 The German Attack on Russia

The defeat of Russia and the conquest of the Ukraine to provide Lebensraum for the German people had always been a major goal for Hitler. Even before the assault on Britain, he had informed his staff of his intention to attack Russia as soon as conditions were favorable. In December 1940, even while the bombing of England continued, he ordered his generals to prepare to invade Russia by May 15, 1941. He apparently thought a blitzkrieg victory in the east would also destroy the British hope of resistance. (See Map 28–3.)

Operation Barbarossa, the code name for the invasion of Russia, was aimed to destroy Russia before winter could set in. Success depended, in part, on an early start, but here Hitler's Italian alliance proved costly. Mussolini was jealous of Hitler's success and annoyed by how the German dictator had treated him. His invasion of France was a fiasco, even though the Germans were simultaneously crushing the main French forces. Hitler did not allow Mussolini to annex French territory in Europe or North Africa. Mussolini instead attacked the British in Egypt and drove them back some sixty miles. Encouraged by this success, he also invaded Greece from his base in Albania, which he had seized in 1939. As he told his son-in-law, Count Ciano: "Hitler always faces me with a fait accompli. This time I am

STALINGRAD In the battle of Stalingrad, Russian troops contested every street and building. Although the city was all but destroyed and Russian casualties were enormous, the German army in the east never recovered from the defeat it suffered there.
SOURCE: Hulton Archive/Stringer/Getty Images.

Map 28–3 AXIS EUROPE, EVE OF GERMAN INVASION OF THE SOVIET UNION, 1941

On the eve of the German invasion of the Soviet Union, the Germany–Italy Axis occupied most of Western Europe by annexation, occupation, or alliance—from Norway and Finland in the north to Greece in the south and from Poland to France. Britain, the Soviets, a number of insurgent groups, and finally America had before them the long struggle of conquering this Axis.

going to pay him back in his own coin. He will find out in the newspapers that I have occupied Greece."[3]

In North Africa, however, the British counterattacked and invaded Libya. The Greeks themselves pushed into Albania. In March 1941, the British sent help to the Greeks, and Hitler was forced to divert his attention to the Balkans and Africa. General **Erwin Rommel** (1891–1944), later to earn the title of "Desert Fox," went to Africa and soon drove

the British back into Egypt. In the Balkans, the German army swiftly occupied Yugoslavia and crushed Greek resistance. The price, however, was a delay of six weeks. The diversion Mussolini's vanity caused proved to be costly the following winter in the Russian campaign.

Operation Barbarossa was launched against Russia on June 22, 1941, and it almost succeeded. Despite their deep suspicion of Germany , and the excuse later given by apologists for the Soviet Union that the Nazi–Soviet pact was meant to give Russia time to prepare, the Russians were taken quite by surprise. Stalin appears to have panicked. He had not fortified his frontier nor did he order his troops to withdraw when attacked. In the first two days, the Germans destroyed 2,000 Russian planes on the ground. By November, the German army stood at the gates of Leningrad, on the outskirts of Moscow, and on the Don River. Of the 4.5 million troops with which the Russians had begun the fighting, they had lost 2.5 million; of their 15,000 tanks, only 700 were left. Moscow was in panic, and a German victory seemed imminent.

Yet the Germans could not deliver the final blow. In August, they delayed their advance while Hitler decided strategy. The German general staff wanted to take Moscow before winter. This plan probably would have brought victory. Unlike in Napoleon's time, Moscow was the hub of the Russian transportation system. Hitler, however, diverted a significant force to the south. By the time he was ready to return to the offensive near Moscow, it was too late. Winter devastated the German army, which was not equipped to face it.

Given precious time, Stalin restored order and built defenses for the city. Even more importantly, troops arrived from Siberia, where they had been placed to check a possible Japanese attack. In November and December, the Russians counterattacked. The blitzkrieg had turned into a war of attrition, and the Germans began to have nightmares of duplicating Napoleon's retreat.

28.2.4 Hitler's Plans for Europe

Hitler often spoke of the "new order" that he meant to impose after he had established his **Third Reich**, or empire, throughout Europe. The first two German empires were those of Charlemagne in the ninth century and Bismarck in the nineteenth. Hitler predicted that his own would last for a thousand years. His organization of Germany before the war was not based on a single plan of government but relied on intuition and pragmatism. His organization of a conquered Europe had the same patchwork characteristics. Some conquered territory was annexed to Germany, some was not annexed but administered directly by German officials, and other lands were nominally autonomous but ruled by puppet governments.

Hitler's regime was probably unmatched in history for carefully planned terror and inhumanity. His plan of giving Lebensraum to the Germans was to be accomplished at the expense of people he deemed inferior. Hitler established colonies of Germans in parts of Poland, driving the local people from their land and employing them as cheap, virtually slave labor. He had similar plans on an even greater scale for Russia. The Russians would be driven back to Central Asia and Siberia. Frontier colonies of German war veterans would keep them in check while Germans settled European Russia.

Hitler's long-range plans included germanization as well as colonization. In lands people racially akin to the Germans inhabited, like the Scandinavian countries, the Netherlands, and Switzerland, the German nation would absorb the natives. Such peoples would be reeducated and purged of dissenting elements, but there would be little or no colonization. Hitler even had plans to adopt selected people from the lesser races into the master race. For example, the Nazis planned to bring half a million Ukrainian girls to Germany as servants and find German husbands for them.

Hitler regarded the conquered lands as a source of plunder. From Eastern Europe, he removed everything useful, including entire industries. In Russia and Poland, the Germans simply confiscated the land itself. In the West, the conquered countries had to support the occupying army at a rate several times above the real cost. The Germans used the profits to buy up everything desirable, stripping the conquered peoples of most necessities. The Nazis were frank about their policies. One of Hitler's high officials said, "Whether nations live in prosperity or starve to death interests me only insofar as we need them as slaves for our culture."[4]

28.2.5 Japan and the United States Enter the War

The American government was pro-British. The assistance that Roosevelt gave Britain would have justified a German declaration of war. Hitler, however, held back. The U.S. government might not have overcome its isolationist sentiment and entered the war in the Atlantic if war had not been thrust on America in the Pacific.

Since the Japanese conquest of Manchuria in 1931, American policy toward Japan had been suspicious and unfriendly. The outbreak of the war in Europe accelerated the Japanese drive to dominate Asia. They allied themselves with Germany and Italy, made a treaty of neutrality with the Soviet Union, and forced defeated France to give them bases in Indochina. They also continued their war in China and planned to gain control of Malaya and the East Indies (Indonesia) at the expense of beleaguered Britain and the conquered Netherlands. The only barrier to Japanese expansion was the United States.

The Americans had temporized, unwilling to cut off vital supplies of oil and other materials for fear of provoking a Japanese attack on Southeast Asia and the East Indies. The Japanese occupation of Indochina in July 1941 changed that policy, which had already begun to stiffen. The United States froze Japanese assets and cut off oil supplies; the British and Dutch did the same. Japanese plans for expansion could not continue without the conquest of the Indonesian oil fields and Malayan rubber and tin.

THE ATTACK ON PEARL HARBOR The successful Japanese attack on the American base at Pearl Harbor in Hawaii on December 7, 1941, together with simultaneous attacks on other Pacific bases, brought the United States into war with the Axis powers. This picture shows the battleships USS *West Virginia* and USS *Tennessee* in flames as a small boat rescues a man from the water.
SOURCE: United States Army Central

In October, a war faction led by General Hideki Tojo (1885–1948) took power in Japan and decided to risk a war rather than yield. On Sunday morning, December 7, 1941, while Japanese representatives were in Washington to discuss a settlement, Japan launched an air attack on Pearl Harbor, Hawaii, the chief American naval base in the Pacific. The technique was similar to the one Japan had used against the Russian fleet at Port Arthur in 1904, and it caught the Americans equally by surprise. The attack destroyed much of the American fleet and many airplanes, and the American capacity to wage war in the Pacific was negated for the time being. The next day, the United States and Britain declared war on Japan. Three days later, Germany and Italy declared war on the United States.

28.2.6 The Tide Turns

The potential power of the United States was enormous, but America was ill prepared for war. The army was tiny, inexperienced, and poorly supplied. American industry was not ready for war. The Japanese swiftly captured Guam, Wake Island, and the Philippine Islands. By the spring of 1942, they had conquered Hong Kong, Malaya, Burma, and the Dutch East Indies. They controlled the southwest Pacific as far as New Guinea and were poised for an attack on Australia. It seemed that nothing could stop them.

In 1942, the Germans also advanced deeper into Russia, while in Africa Rommel drove the British back into Egypt until they stopped him at **El Alamein**, only seventy miles from Alexandria. Relations between the democracies and their Soviet ally were not close. German submarine warfare was threatening British supplies. The Allies were being thrown back on every front, and the future looked bleak.

The first good news for the Allied cause in the Pacific came in the spring of 1942. A naval battle in the Coral Sea sank many Japanese ships and gave security to Australia. A month later, the United States defeated the Japanese in a fierce air and naval battle off Midway Island. This victory blunted the chance of another assault on Hawaii and did enough damage to halt the Japanese advance. Soon American marines landed on Guadalcanal in the Solomon Islands and began to reverse the momentum of the war. The war in the Pacific was far from over, but the check to Japan allowed the Allies to concentrate their efforts on Europe.

In 1942, American preparation and production were inadequate to invade Europe. German submarines made it dangerous to ship the vast numbers of troops such an invasion needed across the Atlantic. Not until 1944 were conditions right for the invasion, but in the meantime other developments forecast the doom of the Axis.

28.2.6.1 ALLIED LANDINGS IN AFRICA, SICILY, AND ITALY
In November 1942, an Allied force landed in French North Africa. (See Map 28–4.) Even before that landing, after stopping Rommel at El Alamein, British field marshal Bernard Montgomery (1887–1976) had begun a drive to the west. Now, the Americans pushed eastward through Morocco and Algeria. The two armies caught the German army between

them in Tunisia and crushed it. The Allies now controlled the Mediterranean and could attack southern Europe.

In July and August 1943, the Allies took Sicily. A coup toppled Mussolini, but the Germans occupied Italy. The Allies landed in Italy, and Marshal Pietro Badoglio (1871–1956), the leader of the new Italian government, declared war on Germany. Churchill had spoken of Italy as the "soft underbelly" of the Axis, but the Germans there resisted fiercely. Still, the need to defend Italy weakened the Germans on other fronts.

28.2.6.2 BATTLE OF STALINGRAD
The Russian campaign became especially demanding. In the summer of 1942, the Germans resumed the offensive on all fronts but were unable to get far except in the south. (See Map 28–5.) Their goal was the oil fields near the Caspian Sea. Stalingrad, on the Volga, was a key point on the flank of the German army in the south. Hitler was determined to take the city, and Stalin was equally determined to hold it. The **Battle of Stalingrad** raged for months with unexampled

Map 28–4 NORTH AFRICAN CAMPAIGNS, 1942–1945

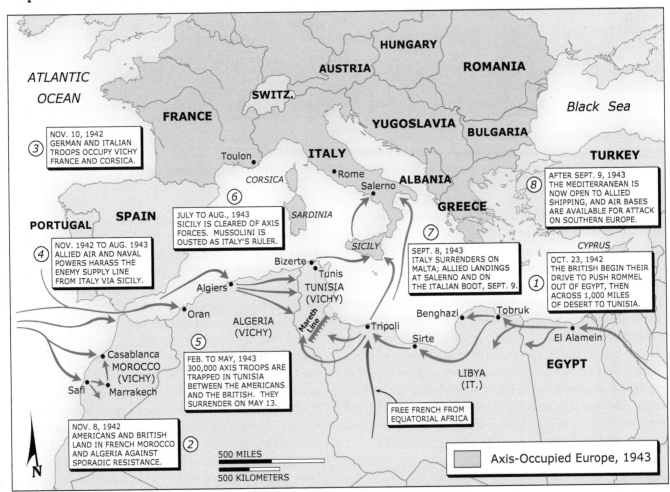

Control of North Africa would give the Allies access to Europe from the south. Illustrated here is the theater of the war from Morocco to Egypt and the Suez Canal.

Map 28-5 DEFEAT OF THE AXIS IN EUROPE, 1942–1945

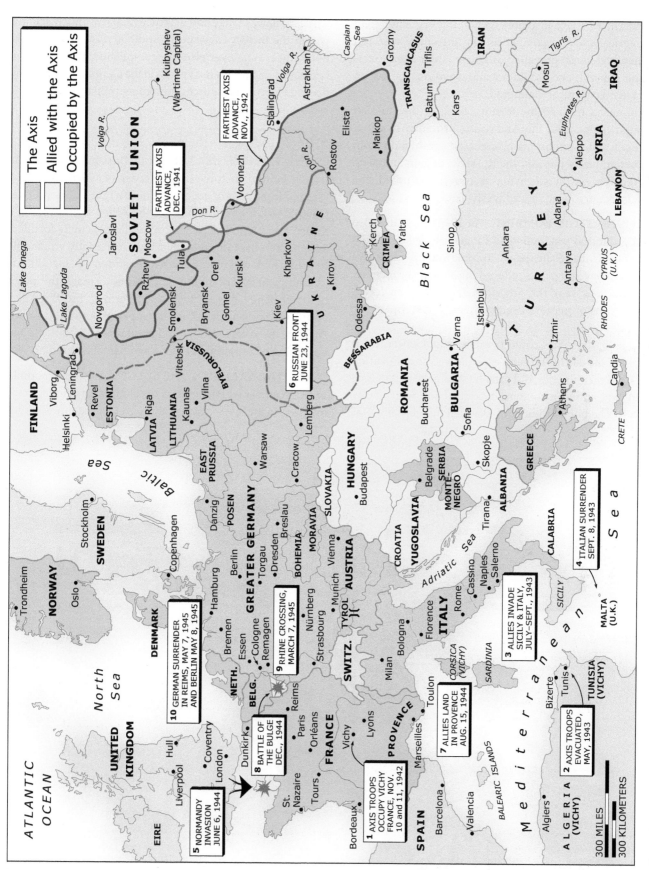

The Axis
Allied with the Axis
Occupied by the Axis

FARTHEST AXIS ADVANCE, NOV., 1942

FARTHEST AXIS ADVANCE, DEC., 1941

6 RUSSIAN FRONT JUNE 23, 1944

10 GERMAN SURRENDER IN REIMS, MAY 7, 1945 AND BERLIN MAY 8, 1945

9 RHINE CROSSING, MARCH 7, 1945

8 BATTLE OF THE BULGE DEC., 1944

5 NORMANDY INVASION JUNE 6, 1944

1 AXIS TROOPS OCCUPY VICHY FRANCE, NOV. 10 and 11, 1942

7 ALLIES LAND IN PROVENCE AUG. 15, 1944

3 ALLIES INVADE SICILY & ITALY, JULY–SEPT., 1943

4 ITALIAN SURRENDER SEPT. 8, 1943

2 AXIS TROOPS EVACUATED, MAY, 1943

300 MILES

300 KILOMETERS

Shown here are some of the major steps toward Allied victory against Axis Europe. From the south through Italy, the west through France, and the east through Russia, the Allies gradually conquered the Continent to bring the war in Europe to a close.

ferocity. The Russians lost more men in this one battle than the Americans lost in combat during the entire war, but their heroic defense prevailed. Because Hitler again overruled his generals and would not allow a retreat, he lost an entire German army at Stalingrad.

Stalingrad marked the turning point of the Russian campaign. Thereafter, the Americans provided material help. Even more importantly, increased production from their own industry allowed the Russians to gain and keep the offensive. As the Germans' resources dwindled, the Russians inexorably advanced westward.

28.2.6.3 STRATEGIC BOMBING In 1943, the Allies also gained ground in production and logistics. The industrial might of the United States began to come into full force, and new technology and tactics reduced the submarine menace.

In the same year, the American and British air forces began a series of massive bombardments of Germany by night and day.

By 1945, the Allies could bomb at will. Concentrated attacks on industrial targets, especially communication centers and oil refineries, did extensive damage and helped shorten the war. Terror bombing continued, too, with no useful result. The bombardment of Dresden in February 1945 was especially savage and destructive. It was much debated within the British government and has raised moral questions since. Whatever else it accomplished, the aerial war over Germany took a heavy toll on the German air force and diverted German resources from other military purposes.

28.2.7 The Defeat of Nazi Germany

On June 6, 1944, "D-day," American, British, and Canadian troops landed in force on the coast of Normandy. The "second front" was opened. General **Dwight D. Eisenhower** (1890–1969), the commander of the Allied armies, faced a difficult problem. The European coast was heavily fortified. Amphibious assaults, moreover, were especially vulnerable to wind and weather. Success depended on meticulous planning, heavy bombing, and feints to mask the point of attack. The German defense was strong, but the Allies established a beachhead and then broke out of it. In mid-August, the Allies also landed in southern France. By the beginning of September, France had been liberated.

28.2.7.1 THE BATTLE OF THE BULGE All went smoothly until December when the Germans launched a counterattack in Belgium and Luxembourg through the Ardennes Forest.

OMAHA BEACH, D-DAY American soldiers land at Omaha Beach in Normandy on D-day, June 6, 1944.
SOURCE: Library of Congress

Because the Germans pushed forward into the Allied line, this was called the Battle of the Bulge. Although the Allies suffered heavy losses, the Bulge was the last gasp for the Germans in the West. The Allies crossed the Rhine in March 1945, and German resistance crumbled. This time there could be no doubt the Germans had lost the war on the battlefield.

28.2.7.2 THE CAPTURE OF BERLIN In the east, the Russians swept forward no less swiftly despite fierce German resistance. By March 1945, they were near Berlin. Because the Allies insisted on unconditional surrender, the Germans fought on until May. Hitler committed suicide in an underground bunker in Berlin on April 30, 1945. The Russians occupied Berlin by agreement with their Western allies. The Third Reich lasted only a dozen years instead of the thousand Hitler had predicted.

28.2.8 Fall of the Japanese Empire

The war in Europe ended on May 8, 1945 and by then, victory over Japan was also in sight. The original Japanese attack on the United States had been a calculated risk against the odds. Japan was inherently weaker than the United States. The longer the war lasted, the more American superiority in industrial production and population counted.

28.2.8.1 AMERICANS RECAPTURE THE PACIFIC ISLANDS In 1943, the American forces, still small in number, began a campaign of "island hopping." They did not try to recapture every Pacific island the Japanese held but selected major bases and strategic sites along the enemy supply line. (See Map 28–6.) Starting from the Solomon Islands, they moved northeast toward Japan itself. By

Map 28–6 WORLD WAR II IN THE PACIFIC

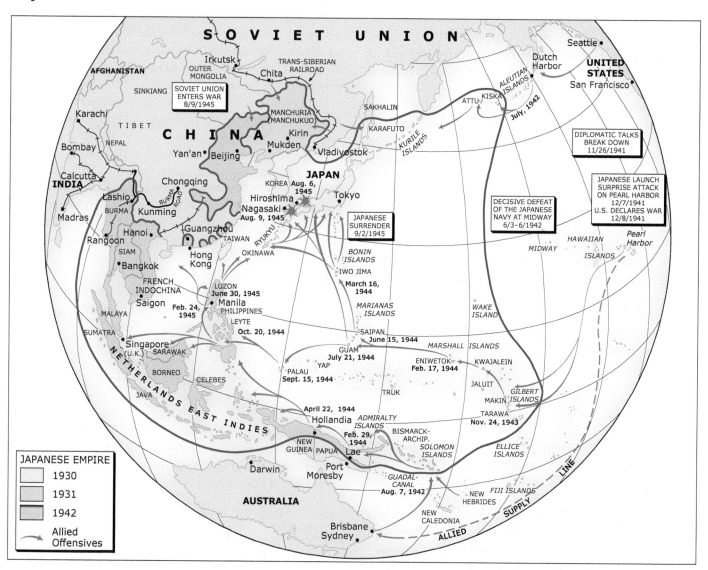

As in Europe, the Pacific war involved Allied recapture of areas that had been quickly taken earlier by the enemy. The enormous area represented by this map shows the initial expansion of Japanese holdings to cover half the Pacific and its islands, as well as huge sections of eastern Asia, and the long struggle to push the Japanese back to their homeland and defeat them by the summer of 1945.

June 1944, they had reached the Mariana Islands, usable as bases to bomb the Japanese in the Philippines, China, and Japan itself.

In October of the same year, the Americans recaptured most of the Philippines and drove the Japanese fleet back into its home waters. In 1945, Iwo Jima and Okinawa fell, despite fierce Japanese resistance that included kamikaze attacks, namely, suicide missions in which pilots deliberately flew their explosive-filled planes into American warships. From these new bases closer to Japan, the Americans launched a terrible wave of bombings that destroyed Japanese industry and disabled the Japanese navy. Still, the Japanese government, dominated by a military clique, refused to surrender.

Confronted with Japan's determination, the Americans made plans for a frontal assault on the Japanese homeland. They calculated it might cost a million American casualties and even greater losses for the Japanese. At this point, science and technology presented the Americans with another choice.

28.2.8.2 THE ATOMIC BOMB Since early in the war, a secret program had been in progress. Its staff, many of whom were exiles from Hitler's Europe, was working to use atomic energy for military purposes. On August 6, 1945, an American plane dropped an atomic bomb on the Japanese city of Hiroshima. The city was destroyed and more than 70,000 of its 200,000 residents were killed. Two days later, the Soviet Union declared war on Japan and invaded Manchuria. The next day, a second atomic bomb hit Nagasaki. Even then, the Japanese cabinet was prepared to face an invasion rather than give up.

The unprecedented intervention of Emperor Hirohito (r. 1926–1989) finally forced the government to surrender on August 14 on the condition that Japan retain the emperor. Although the Allies had continued to insist on unconditional surrender, President **Harry S. Truman** (1884–1972), who had come to office on April 12, 1945, upon the death of Franklin D. Roosevelt, accepted the condition. Peace was formally signed aboard the USS *Missouri* in Tokyo Bay on September 2, 1945.

28.2.9 The Cost of War

World War II was the most terrible war in history. Military deaths are estimated at some 15 million, and at least as many civilians were killed. Including deaths linked indirectly to the war, from disease, hunger, and other causes, the number of victims might reach 40 million. Most of Europe and large parts of Asia were devastated. Yet the end of so terrible a war brought little opportunity to relax. The dawn of the atomic age made people conscious that another major war might extinguish humanity. Everything depended on concluding a stable peace, but even as the fighting ended, conflicts among the victors made the prospects of a lasting peace doubtful.

28.3 Racism and the Holocaust

What was the Holocaust?

The most horrible aspect of the Nazi rule in Europe arose not from military or economic necessity but from the inhumanity and brutality inherent in Hitler's racial doctrines. These affected several groups of people in Eastern Europe.

Hitler considered the Slavs *Untermenschen* ("subhuman"). In parts of Poland, the upper and professional classes were entirely removed—jailed, deported, or killed. Schools and churches were closed. The Nazis limited marriage to keep down the Polish birthrate and imposed harsh living conditions.

In Russia, things were even worse. Hitler spoke of his Russian campaign as a war of extermination. Heinrich Himmler (1900–1945), head of Hitler's elite SS formations, planned to eliminate 30 million Slavs to make room for Germans; he formed extermination squads for this purpose. Six million Russian prisoners of war and deported civilians may have died under Nazi rule.

Hitler, however, had envisioned a special fate for the Jews. He meant to make all Europe *Judenrein*, or "free of Jews." For a time, he considered sending them to the island of Madagascar. Later, he arrived at the "final solution of the Jewish problem"—extermination. The Nazis built extermination camps in Germany and Poland and used the latest technology to efficiently kill millions of men, women, and children simply because they were Jews. The most extensive destruction occurred in Eastern Europe and Russia, but the Nazis and their collaborators in occupied areas of Western Europe, including France, the Netherlands, Italy, and Belgium, also deported Jews from these nations to almost certain death in the east. Before the war was over, perhaps six million Jews had died in what has come to be called the **Holocaust**. Only about a million European Jews survived, most of them in pitiable condition. (See Map 28-7.)

It is difficult to comprehend the massive Nazi effort to eradicate the Jews of Europe. This destruction took different forms in different regions of the Continent. To explore this central event of twentieth-century European history, we examine the fate of the Polish Jewish community, which before World War II was the largest in Europe, consisting of 10 percent of Poland's population.

28.3.1 The Destruction of the Polish Jewish Community

A large Jewish community had dwelled within Poland for centuries, often in a climate of religious and cultural anti-Semitism. As a result of this anti-Semitism, Polish Jews had

UNTERMENSCHEN (THE SUBHUMAN) World War II resulted in the near-total destruction of European Jews, victims of the Holocaust spawned by Hitler's racial theories of the superiority and inferiority of particular ethnic groups. Hitler especially emphasized the need to exterminate the Jews, to whom he attributed particular wickedness. Shown here are Hungarian Jewish women, after "disinfection" and head shaving, marching to the death camp at Auschwitz-Birkenau, Poland.
SOURCE: Library of Congress

long lived in their own villages and later in their own urban neighborhoods. After the late-eighteenth-century partitions of Poland and the Congress of Vienna, most of Poland came under Russian rule. Through the policy of Official Nationalism, the nineteenth-century tsars identified loyalty to their government with membership in the Russian Orthodox Church. Other Christian groups, such as Lutherans and Roman Catholics, were often treated with suspicion. Jews were treated worse and were subject to a wide variety of discriminatory legislation. Polish Jews did not experience any of the forms of Jewish emancipation that occurred in Western Europe.

Language, food, dress, and place of residence as well as religion distinguished Jews from the rest of the Polish population, almost all of whom were Roman Catholics. Hebrew was the Polish Jews' chief written language and Yiddish their primary spoken language. Many Jews, particularly older ones, wore distinctive dress. They ate food different from that of most Poles. Many Polish Jews also moved to cities, and Jews were regarded as an urban people in a predominantly rural nation. Moreover, Jews were among the poorest people in Poland, often working as self-employed

merchants, peddlers, and craftspeople, or in industries such as textiles, clothing, and paper, that other Poles identified as Jewish-dominated. Few Polish Jews belonged to trade unions. These conditions made them vulnerable during the economic turmoil of the 1920s and especially of the 1930s.

28.3.2 Polish Anti-Semitism Between the Wars

Discrimination against Jews existed throughout the culture and politics of interwar Poland. During those years, the Polish government, supported by spokesmen for the Polish Roman Catholic Church, pursued policies that were anti-Semitic. The Polish government nationalized the matches, salt, tobacco, and alcohol industries and then enacted legislation that discriminated against hiring Jews for these government monopolies. Other laws made it difficult for Jews to observe the Sabbath while keeping their jobs. Regulations requiring businesses to be closed on Sunday meant Jewish shops had to close two days of the week. By the late 1930s, as ethnic nationalism became stronger, the government required businesses to display their owners'

Map 28–7 THE HOLOCAUST

Legend	
Extent of German Reich, 1942	
■	Concentration camp
11,750	Estimated number of Jews murdered in Holocaust
	Percentage of total population of Jews murdered in Holocaust (where available)

The Nazi policy of ethnic cleansing—targeting Jews, Gypsies, political dissidents, and "social deviants"—began with imprisoning them in concentration camps, but by 1943 the *Endlösung*, or Final Solution, called for the systematic extermination of "undesirables."

and culture in Poland. These divisions made the Jews of Poland more vulnerable when World War II broke out in 1939.

Whatever active anti-Semitism existed in Poland before the German invasion of 1939, it was the Nazis who tried to destroy the Polish Jewish community and Jewish communities elsewhere in Europe that fell under German control. In that respect, the Holocaust constitutes an event driven by German policy within the larger event of World War II.

28.3.3 The Nazi Assault on the Jews of Poland

The joint German–Soviet invasion of Poland brought millions of Jews under either German or Soviet authority. By conquering Poland, the Nazi government could carry out the destruction of Jewish communities to an extent far beyond anything possible in Germany itself. From the Nazi standpoint, the destruction of the Polish Jewish community held special importance. Polish Jewry was large and had produced many religious, cultural, and political leaders. It also constituted the single most important source for Jewish emigration beyond Eastern Europe. For the Nazis, Poland was the chief breeding ground for world Jewry.

By late autumn 1939, the Germans had begun to move against Polish Jews. The Nazi government first thought it might herd virtually all the Jews of occupied Europe into the Lublin region of Poland. By early 1940, the Nazis decided to move as many Jews as possible into ghettos, where they would be separated from the rest of the Polish population. The largest ghettos were Lodz and Warsaw, each of which had populations of several hundred thousand. The Nazis moved Jews from all over Poland and eventually other occupied regions by rail into these ghettos and then sealed them off with police guards and walls. Jewish councils, torn between responsibility to their communities and the need to respond to German orders, administered the ghettos. The Nazis confiscated and sold the personal property and businesses of the Jews who were herded into the ghettos. Jewish laborers were sent out to work as contract labor while their families remained in the ghettos. By 1941, the Polish Jews had lost their civic standing and property. They had been

names prominently, which made it easy for people to avoid Jewish shops. Because Jews were excluded from the civil service, they moved into law and medicine, which provoked further resentment.

Assimilation into the larger culture that many European Jewish leaders had advocated during the nineteenth century hit a dead end in Poland because many Poles refused to regard even secular, assimilated Jews as fellow Poles. Nonetheless, many Jews attempted to embrace the social practices, dress, and language of the Polish majority, without expecting to be considered Polish, and to move from a traditional style of life to a more modern and Polish one. Jewish newspapers and other magazines began to be published in Polish. Jews took advantage of their right to political participation, but they were divided into different factions and could not agree on how to defend Jewish life relocated in segregated communities within Poland where disease was rampant and the food supply meager. Approximately 20 percent of the population of both the Lodz and Warsaw ghettos died of disease and malnourishment.

The German invasion of the Soviet Union in June 1941 made the situation of Jews in Poland even worse. The advancing German forces killed tens of thousands of Jews in the Soviet Union during 1941 and hundreds of thousands more the next year. Bolsheviks and Jews became conflated in German thinking and propaganda. During the second half of 1941, the Nazi government decided to exterminate the Jews of Europe. From late 1941 through 1944, the Germans transported Jews from the ghettos by rail to death camps in Poland, including Kulmhof, Belsen, Sobibor, Treblinka, Birkenau, and Auschwitz. One or more of the camps were in operation from 1941 to 1944, with Auschwitz being the last closed. In these camps, Jews were systematically killed in gas chambers.

By 1945, approximately 90 percent of the pre-1939 Jewish population of Poland had been destroyed. The tiny minority of Polish Jews who had survived faced bitter anti-Semitism under the postwar Soviet-dominated government. Many immigrated to Israel, leaving only a few thousand Jews within the borders of a nation where they had numbered in the millions and where they had created a rich religious, cultural, and political community. The largest Jewish community in Europe had ceased to exist.

28.3.4 Explanations of the Holocaust

As interest in the Holocaust has grown since the 1960s, so has debate about its character and meaning. Was it a unique event of unprecedented and unparalleled evil, or was it one specific instance of a more general human wickedness that found expression throughout history? Are its roots to be found in flaws in human nature, or are they unique to the experience of the West or perhaps to the German people?

Perhaps we should think of the problem from the standpoint of two questions: Why were the Jews the main target of Hitler's policy of extermination? How was it possible to carry out such a mass murder? Surely, an essential part of an answer to the first question is the persistence of anti-Semitism in Christianity and Western culture, from the Church Fathers to Luther and to the teachings of churches in modern times. Some would combine this religious and historical anti-Semitism with the coming of the Enlightenment and the social sciences, which gave rise to pseudoscientific racial theories that lent a new twist to the old hatred of the Jews. Pseudoscientific racism appears to have been the most powerful influence on Hitler, but it could not have found widespread support without deeply rooted religious and social anti-Semitism.

For example, in at least one instance in Poland, Poles turned against their Jewish neighbors in outbursts of localized anti-Semitic violence. In July 1941, in the town of Jedwabne in northeast Poland, non-Jewish Poles killed approximately 1,600 of their Jewish fellow townspeople. This horrendous incident suggests that although the Nazis carried out most of the atrocities against the Jews, a climate of either indifference or outright support existed in Poland as well as in other parts of Nazi-occupied Europe. Yet it must also be noted that between 1942 and 1945 the Council for Aid to Jews in Occupied Poland, known as ZEGOTA and sponsored by the Polish government in exile, protected and aided the escape of many thousands of Polish Jews.

As to how it was possible to murder six million people, part of the answer must lie in the parochial nationalism that arose during and after the French Revolution. For many, nationalism divided the world into one's fellow nationals and all others. It encouraged, excused, and even justified terrible and violent acts performed on behalf of one's homeland. Another part of the answer may derive from the utopian visions also unleashed by some Enlightenment writers, who promised to achieve perfect societies through social engineering regardless of the human cost. To this were added the scientific and technological advances that gave the modern state new power to command its people, to persuade them to obey by controlling propaganda, and to enforce its will with efficient brutality. All these permitted the creation of a totalitarian state that, for the first time in history, could conduct mass murder on the scale of the Holocaust.

These questions and their possible answers are suggestions meant to encourage further and deeper thought in what will be a continuing debate among scholars and the general public.

The victorious Western allies were shocked by what they saw when they came upon the Nazi extermination camps and their pitiful survivors. It was little wonder that they were convinced the effort to resist the Nazis and all the pain it had cost were well worth it.

28.4 The Domestic Fronts

What impact did World War II have on European society?

World War II represented an effort at total war by all the belligerents. Never in European or world history had so many men and women and such resources been devoted to military effort. One result was the carnage of the fighting. Another was the unprecedented mobilization of civilians at home. Each domestic effort and experience was different, but few escaped the impact of the conflict. Everywhere there were shortages, propaganda campaigns, and new political developments. (To learn more about women workers who flocked to jobs in U.S. defense industries, see the "Encountering the Past" sidebar, which follows below.)

Encountering the Past

American Women in the Workforce

THE INDUCTION OF millions of men into the armed forces created a demand for new workers, especially in the defense industries. In response, millions of women entered the labor force, some taking jobs in defense plants to do work only men usually did. Economic pressures caused by the Great Depression of the 1930s had already brought many more women into the workforce than before. Most came from poor families and worked in blue-collar jobs to support themselves or to help their families eke out a living. Even so, the heavy burden of housework and the widespread hostility to women working outside the home kept most women at home.

America's entry into the war changed things quickly. The need for vast amounts of equipment to wage the war called for and attracted new groups to seek work in the many enlarged and new factories. African Americans from the south came to northern and western cities to seek well-paying jobs, and women too came forward in greater numbers than ever before. Prejudices had kept them from many opportunities, but the needs of war were too important. In October 1942, President Roosevelt made the new situation clear: "In some communities employers dislike to hire women. In others they are reluctant to hire Negroes. We can no longer afford to indulge such prejudice."

Many women changed jobs to work in the defense industries; others entered the workforce for the first time, lured less by wages than by patriotism. Their brothers and boyfriends were risking their lives for their country and its ideals of freedom and democracy. They were eager to do their part to support them, to be, in the words of a current song, the woman "behind the man behind the gun." Another popular song, "Rosie the Riveter," told of a young woman working in an aircraft factory to provide protection for her boyfriend in the Marines. Rosie became one of the best-known symbols of the war effort when she appeared on the cover of the *Saturday Evening Post* in a painting by Norman Rockwell. With her rivet gun on her lap she stamps on a copy of Hitler's *Mein Kampf*, the hated symbol of the evil enemy.

ROSIE THE RIVETER Rosie the Riveter symbolized women's contribution to the U.S. war effort in World War II. In this cover illustration for the *Saturday Evening Post*, from May 29, 1943, Norman Rockwell captures the iconic Rosie during a lunch break. Notice all the details, including the copy of *Mein Kampf* underfoot, which suggest that women defense workers were on the job for more than a paycheck.
SOURCE: Photo 12/Alamy Stock Photo

Questions

1. How did the war change women's place in American society?
2. What attitudes had to be overcome for this change to occur?

28.4.1 Germany: From Apparent Victory to Defeat

Hitler had expected to defeat all his enemies by rapid strokes, or blitzkriegs. Such campaigns would have required little change in Germany's society and economy. During the first two years of the war, in fact, Hitler demanded few sacrifices from the German people. Spending on domestic projects continued, and food was plentiful; the economy was not on a full wartime footing. Germany's failure to quickly overwhelm the Soviet Union changed everything. Food was no longer available from the east in needed quantities, Germany had to mobilize for total war, and the government demanded major sacrifices.

A great expansion of the army and of military production began in 1942. As minister for armaments and munitions, Albert Speer (1905–1981) directed the economy, and Germany met its military needs. The government sought the cooperation of major German businesses to increase wartime production. Between 1942 and late 1944, the output of military products tripled. As the war went on, more men were drafted from industry into the army, and military production suffered.

As the manufacture of armaments replaced the production of consumer goods, shortages of everyday products became serious. Prices and wages were controlled, but the standard of living of German workers fell. Food rationing began in April 1942, and shortages were severe until the Nazi government seized more food from occupied Europe.

By 1943, labor shortages became severe. The Nazis required German teenagers and retired men to work in the factories, and many women joined them. To achieve total mobilization, the Germans closed retail businesses, raised the age of eligibility of women for compulsory service, shifted non-German domestic workers to wartime industry, moved artists and entertainers into military service, closed theaters, and reduced such basic public services as mail and railways. Finally, the Nazis compelled thousands of non-Germans to do forced labor in Germany.

Hitler assigned women a special place in the war effort. The celebration of motherhood continued, with an emphasis on women who were the mothers of important military figures. Films portrayed ordinary women who were brave and patriotic during the war and remained faithful to their husbands who were at the front. Women were shown as mothers and wives who sent their sons and husbands off to war. The government pictured other wartime activities of women as the natural fulfillment of their maternal roles. As air-raid wardens, they protected their families; as factory workers in munitions plants, they aided their sons on the front lines. Women working on farms were providing for their soldier sons and husbands; as housewives, they were helping to win the war by conserving food. Finally, by their faithful chastity, German women were protecting racial purity. They were not to marry or to have sex with non-Germans.

During the war domestic political propaganda went beyond that of other countries. Hitler and other Germans genuinely believed that weak domestic support had led to Germany's defeat in World War I; they were determined not to let this happen again. Nazi propaganda blamed the outbreak of the war on the British and the Jews and its prolongation on Germany's opponents. It also stressed the power of Germany and the inferiority of its foes.

Propaganda minister Josef Goebbels (1897–1945) used both radio and films to boost the Nazi cause. Movies of the collapse of Poland, Belgium, Holland, and France showed German military might. Throughout the conquered territories, the Nazis used the same mass media to frighten inhabitants about the possible consequences of an Allied victory. Later in the war, Goebbels broadcast exaggerated claims of Nazi victories. As the German armies were checked on the battlefield, especially in Russia, propaganda became a substitute for victory. To stiffen German resolve, propaganda now aimed to frighten Germans about the consequences of defeat.

After May 1943, when the Allies began their major bombing offensive over Germany, the German people had much to fear. The bombing devastated one German city after another but did not undermine German morale. The bombing may even have increased German resistance by seeming to confirm the regime's propaganda about the ruthlessness of Germany's opponents.

World War II increased the power of the Nazi Party in Germany. Every area of the economy and society came under the direct influence or control of the party. The Nazis were determined that they, rather than the traditionally honored German officer corps, would profit from the new authority the war effort was giving to the central government. There was no serious opposition to Hitler or his ministers. In July 1944, a group of army officers attempted to assassinate Hitler; the effort failed, and there was little popular support for this attempt.

The war brought great changes to Germany, but the most powerful was the experience of physical destruction, invasion, and occupation. Hitler and the Nazis had brought Germany to such a complete and disastrous defeat that only a new kind of state with new political structures could emerge.

28.4.2 France: Defeat, Collaboration, and Resistance

The terms of the 1940 armistice between France, under Marshal Pétain, and Germany, signed June 22, allowed the Germans to occupy more than half of France, including the Atlantic and English Channel coasts. To prevent the French from continuing the fight from North Africa, and even more to prevent them from turning their fleet over to Britain, Hitler left southern France unoccupied until November 1942. Pétain set up a dictatorial regime at the resort city of **Vichy** and collaborated with the Germans in hopes of preserving as much autonomy as possible.

Some of the collaborators believed the Germans were sure to win the war and wanted to be on the victorious side. A few sympathized with Nazi ideas and plans. Many conservatives judged the French defeat as a corrupt, secularized, liberal Third Republic. Most of the French were not active collaborators but were demoralized by defeat and German power.

Many conservatives and extreme rightists saw in the Vichy government a way to reshape the French national character and to halt the decadence they associated with political and religious liberalism. The Roman Catholic clergy, which had lost power and influence under the Third Republic, gained status under Vichy. The church supported Pétain, and his government restored religious instruction in the state-run schools and increased financial support for Catholic schools. Vichy adopted the church's views on the importance of family and spiritual values. The government made divorce difficult and forbade it entirely during the first three years of marriage. The state encouraged and subsidized large families. (In this chapter's "Closer Look" sidebar, a poster extols the Vichy regime and pans the Third Republic.)

The Vichy regime also encouraged an intense, chauvinistic nationalism. It exploited prejudice against foreigners working in France and fostered resentment even against French men and women whom it regarded as not genuinely "French," especially French Jews. Even before Germany undertook Hitler's "final solution" in 1942, the French had begun to remove Jews from positions of influence in government, education, and publishing. In 1941, the Germans began to intern Jews living in occupied France; soon they murdered individual Jews and imposed large fines collectively on the Jews of the occupied zone. In the spring of 1942, they began to deport Jews from France—ultimately more than 60,000—to the extermination camps of Eastern Europe. The Vichy government had no part in these decisions, but it made no protest, and its own anti-Semitic policies made the process easier to carry out. The great majority of Frenchmen, who were not Jewish, also suffered greatly.

The absence of some two million men who were prisoners of war compelled the women of France to carry on much of the labor normally done by men. All the French suffered shortages of consumer goods under a strict and mismanaged rationing system. The Germans seized about 20 percent of the French food production, and French farm production fell by half because of lack of fuel, fertilizer, and workers. Food shortages were most acute in large cities. Farmers did better, but the official ration provided starvation-level diets of 1,300 or fewer calories a day.

Some French men and women, notably General Charles de Gaulle (1890–1969), fled to Britain after the defeat of France. There they organized the French National Committee of Liberation, or "Free French." Until the end of 1942, the Vichy government controlled French North Africa and the navy, but the Free French began operating in Central Africa. From London, they broadcast hope and defiance to their compatriots in France. Serious internal resistance to the German occupiers and the Vichy government, however, began to develop only late in 1942. The Germans tried to force young people in occupied France to work in German factories; some of them joined the resistance, but the number of the resisters was small. Fear of German retaliation deterred many. Others disliked the violence that resistance to a powerful ruthless nation inevitably entailed. As long as it appeared the Germans would win the war, moreover, resistance seemed imprudent and futile. For these reasons, the organized resistance never attracted more than 5 percent of the adult French population.

By early 1944, the tide of battle had shifted. The Allies seemed sure to win, and the Vichy government would clearly not survive; only then did a large-scale active movement of resistance assert itself. General de Gaulle spoke confidently for Free France from his base in London and urged the French people to resist their conquerors and the German lackeys in the Vichy government. Within France, resistance groups joined forces to plan for a better day. From Algiers on August 9, 1944, the Committee of National Liberation declared the authority of Vichy illegitimate. French soldiers joined in the liberation of Paris and established a government for Free France. On October 21, 1945, France voted to end the Third Republic and adopted a new constitution as the basis of the Fourth Republic. The French people had experienced defeat, disgrace, deprivation, and suffering. Hostility and quarrels over who had done what during the occupation and under Vichy divided them for decades.

A Closer Look

The Vichy Regime in France

AFTER THEIR SURPRISINGLY swift conquest of France in 1940, the Germans ruled one part of it directly from Paris, leaving the rest unoccupied until 1942, but firmly under the control of a collaborationist French government under Marshal Henri Philippe Pétain (1856–1951). (Refer again to Map 28–3.) This regime, based in the city of Vichy, pursued a reactionary policy, turning away from the democratic ways of the defeated Third Republic. The "Propaganda Centers of the National Revolution" published the poster shown in the photo. "The National Revolution" was the Vichy regime's name for its program to remake France.

In the poster, the house on the left, representing the Third Republic, carries the name "France and Company" and implies that the Third Republic was run like a corrupt business. It tilts precariously on shaky supports: egoism, radicalism, capitalism, communism, Jewry, antimilitarism, parliament, and disorder. These, in turn, rest on what Vichy considered the republic's basic flaws: laziness, demagogy, and internationalism instead of French patriotism.

The house on the right represents the Vichy government. Its name is "France," pure and simple. It sits, safe, strong, neat, and orderly on solid columns: school, craftsmanship, the peasantry, and the military. These rest on equally firm bases: discipline, order, thrift, and courage. Underlying all are the three basic values—work, family, and fatherland—that Vichy made its national slogan to replace the "liberty, equality, and fraternity" motto of French republican regimes since the French Revolution.

The Third Republic tilts precariously on shaky supports.

The Republic's basic flaws according to Vichy? paresse (laziness), demagogie, and internationalisme.

Vichy France rests on a solid foundation of discipline, ordre, épargne (thrift), and courage.

TRAVAIL, FAMILLE, PATRIE
SOURCE: Photo 12/Alamy Stock Photo

Questions

1. What were the political differences between the Vichy regime and its critics?
2. Why would the Vichy regime replace the traditional slogan of the French Revolution with a new one?
3. What events in the twentieth century might justify the change?

28.4.3 Great Britain: Organization for Victory

On May 22, 1940, the British Parliament gave the government emergency powers. Together with others already in effect, this measure allowed the government to institute compulsory military service, rationing, and economic controls.

To deal with the crisis, all British political parties joined in a national government under Winston Churchill. Churchill and the British war cabinet moved as quickly as possible to mobilize the nation. The demand for more planes and other armaments inspired a campaign to reclaim scrap metal. Wrought-iron fences, kitchen pots and pans, and every conceivable metal object were collected for the war effort. This was only one successful example of the many ways the civilian population enthusiastically engaged in the struggle.

By the end of 1941, British production had already surpassed Germany's. To meet the heavy demands on the labor force, factory hours were extended and many women joined the workforce. Unemployment disappeared, and the working classes had more money to spend than they had enjoyed for many years. To avoid inflation caused by increased demand for an inadequate supply of consumer goods, savings were encouraged, and taxes were raised to absorb the excess purchasing power.

The "blitz" air attacks from 1940 to 1941 were the most immediate and dramatic experience of the war for the British people. The German air raids killed thousands of people and left many others homeless. Once the bombing began, many families moved their children to the countryside. Ironically, the rescue effort improved the standard of living of many children, for the government paid for their food and medication. The government issued gas masks to thousands of city dwellers, who were frequently compelled to take shelter from the bombs in the London subways.

After the spring of 1941, Hitler needed most of his air force on the Russian front, but the bombing of Britain continued, killing more than 30,000 people by the end of the war. Terrible as it was, this toll was much smaller than the number of Germans killed by Allied bombing. In England, as in Germany, however, the bombing may have made people more determined.

The British made many sacrifices. Transportation facilities were strained simply from carrying enough coal to heat homes and run factories. Food and clothing for civilians were scarce and strictly rationed. Every scrap of land was farmed, increasing the productive portion by almost four million acres. Gasoline was scarce, and private vehicles almost vanished.

THE BLITZ Fire engulfs a building in London, England, during the German air raids. Despite many casualties and widespread devastation, the German bombing of London did not break British morale or prevent the city from functioning.
SOURCE: Hulton Archive/Stringer/Getty Images

The British established their own propaganda machine to influence the Continent. The British Broadcasting Company (BBC) sent programs to every country in Europe in the local language to encourage resistance to the Nazis. At home, the government used the radio to unify the nation. Soldiers at the front heard the same programs their families did at home. The most famous program, second only to Churchill's speeches, was *It's That Man Again*, a humorous broadcast filled with imaginary figures that the entire nation came to treasure.

Strangely, for the broad mass of the population, the standard of living improved during the war. The general health of the nation also improved, for reasons that are still not clear. These improvements should not be exaggerated, but they did occur, and many connected them with the active involvement of the government in the economy and in the lives of the citizens. This wartime experience may have contributed to the Labour Party's victory in 1945; many feared a return to Conservative Party rule would also mean a return to the economic problems and unemployment of the 1930s.

28.4.4 The Soviet Union: "The Great Patriotic War"

The war against Germany came as a great surprise to Stalin and the Soviet Union. The German attack violated the 1939 pact with Hitler and put the government of the Soviet Union on the defensive militarily and politically. It showed the failure of Stalin's foreign policy and the ineptness of his preparation for war. Within days, German troops occupied much of the western Soviet Union. The Communist government feared that Soviet citizens in the occupied zones—many of whom were not ethnic Russians—might welcome the Germans as liberators. The Stalinist regime had harshly oppressed these Soviet citizens.

No nation suffered more during World War II than the Soviet Union. Perhaps as many as 16 million people were killed, and vast numbers of Soviet troops were taken prisoner. Hundreds of cities and towns and more than one-half of the industrial and transportation facilities of the country were devastated. From 1942, thousands of Soviet prisoners worked in German factories as forced labor. The Germans also seized grain, mineral resources, and oil from the Soviet Union.

Stalin conducted the war as the virtual chief of the armed forces, and the State Committee for Defense provided strong central coordination. In the decade before the war, Stalin had already made the Soviet Union a highly centralized state; he had tried to manage the entire economy from Moscow through the Five-Year Plan, the collectivization of agriculture and the purges. The country was thus already on what amounted to a wartime footing long before the conflict erupted. When the war began, millions of citizens entered the army, but the army itself did not grow in influence at the expense of the state and the Communist Party—that is, of Stalin. He was suspicious of the generals, though he had presumably eliminated officers of doubtful loyalty in the purges of the late 1930s. As the war continued, however, the army gained more freedom, and eventually the generals were no longer subservient to party commissars. The power of Stalin and the nature of Soviet government and society, however, still sharply limited the army.

Soviet propaganda was different from that of other nations. Because the Soviet government distrusted its citizens' loyalty, it confiscated radios to prevent the people from listening to German or British propaganda. In cities, the government broadcast to the people over loudspeakers in place of radios. During the war, Soviet propaganda emphasized Russian patriotism rather than traditional Marxist themes that stressed class conflict. The struggle against the Germans was called "the Great Patriotic War."

The regime republished great Russian novels of the past and printed more than half a million copies of Tolstoy's *War and Peace*, which was set during Napoleon's invasion of Russia, during the siege of Leningrad (Saint Petersburg). Authors wrote straightforward propaganda fostering hatred of the Germans. Serge Eisenstein (1898–1948), the great filmmaker, produced the epic *Ivan the Terrible*, which glorified this brutal sixteenth-century tsar. Composers wrote music to evoke heroic emotions. The most important composition was Dimitri Shostakovich's (1906–1975) *Leningrad Symphony*.

The pressure of war led Stalin to make peace with the Russian Orthodox Church, and the Patriarch of Moscow urged resistance to the Germans. Stalin hoped this new policy would increase his support at home and in Eastern Europe, where the Orthodox Church predominated.

Within occupied portions of the western Soviet Union, an active resistance movement harassed the Germans. The swiftness of the German invasion had stranded thousands of Soviet troops behind German lines. Some escaped and carried on guerrilla warfare behind enemy lines. Stalin supported partisan forces in lands the enemy held for two reasons: He wanted to cause as much difficulty as possible for the Germans, and Soviet-sponsored resistance reminded the peasants that the Soviet government had not disappeared. Stalin feared the peasants' hatred of the Communist government and collectivization might lead them to collaborate with the invaders. When the Soviet army moved westward, it incorporated the partisans into the regular army.

As its armies reclaimed the occupied areas and then moved across Eastern and central Europe, the Soviet Union established itself as a world power second only to the United States. Stalin had entered the war a reluctant belligerent but had emerged a major victor. In that respect, the war and the extraordinary sacrifice it generated consolidated the power of Stalin and the party more effectively than the political and social policies of the previous decade.

28.5 Preparations for Peace

How did the Allies prepare for a postwar Europe?

The split between the Soviet Union and its wartime allies should cause no surprise. As the self-proclaimed center of world Communism, the Soviet Union was openly dedicated to the overthrow of the capitalist nations. The Soviets muted this message, however, when the occasion demanded. On the other side, the Western allies were no less open about their hostility to Communism and its chief purveyor, the Soviet Union.

Nonetheless, the need to cooperate against a common enemy and strenuous propaganda efforts helped improve Western feeling toward the Soviet ally. Still, Stalin remained suspicious and critical of the Western war effort, and Churchill was determined to contain the Soviet advance into Europe. Roosevelt perhaps had been more hopeful that the Allies could continue to work together after the war, but even he was losing faith by 1945. Differences in historical development and ideology, as well as traditional conflicts over political power and influence, soon dashed hopes of a mutually satisfactory peace settlement and continued cooperation to uphold it.

KEY EVENTS IN NEGOTIATIONS AMONG THE ALLIES	
August 1941	Churchill and Roosevelt meet off Newfoundland to sign Atlantic Charter
October 1943	American, British, and Soviet foreign ministers meet in Moscow
November 1943	Churchill, Roosevelt, and Stalin meet at Tehran
October 1944	Churchill meets with Stalin in Moscow
February 1945	Churchill, Roosevelt, and Stalin meet at Yalta
July 1945	Attlee, Stalin, and Truman meet at Potsdam

28.5.1 The Atlantic Charter

In August 1941, even before the Americans were at war, Roosevelt and Churchill met on a ship off Newfoundland and agreed to the Atlantic Charter. This broad set of principles in the spirit of Wilson's Fourteen Points provided a theoretical basis for the peace they sought. When Russia and the United States joined Britain in the war, the three powers entered a purely military alliance in January 1942, leaving all political questions aside. The first political conference was the meeting of foreign ministers in Moscow in October 1943. The ministers reaffirmed earlier agreements to fight on until the enemy surrendered unconditionally and to continue cooperating after the war in a united-nations organization.

28.5.2 Tehran: Agreement on a Second Front

The first meeting of the leaders of the "Big Three" (the USSR, Britain, and the United States) took place at Tehran, the capital of Iran, in 1943. Western promises to open a second front in France the summer of 1944 and Stalin's agreement to fight Japan when Germany was defeated created an atmosphere of goodwill in which to discuss a postwar settlement. Stalin wanted to retain what he had gained in his pact with Hitler and to dismember Germany. Roosevelt and Churchill were conciliatory but made no firm commitments.

The most important decision was choosing Europe's west coast as the main point of attack instead of the Mediterranean. That meant, in retrospect, that Soviet forces would occupy Eastern Europe and control its destiny. At Tehran in 1943, the Western allies did not foresee this clearly, for the Russians were still fighting deep within their own frontiers, and military considerations were paramount.

28.5.2.1 CHURCHILL AND STALIN By 1944, the situation had changed. In August, Soviet armies were before Warsaw, which had revolted against the Germans in expectation of liberation, but the Russians halted and turned south into the Balkans, allowing the Germans to annihilate the Poles. The Russians gained control of Romania, Bulgaria, and Hungary, advances that centuries of expansionist tsars had only dreamed of achieving. Alarmed by these developments, Churchill went to Moscow and met with Stalin in October. They agreed to share power in the Balkans on the basis of Soviet predominance in Romania and Bulgaria, Western predominance in Greece, and equality of influence in Yugoslavia and Hungary. These agreements were not enforceable without American approval, and the Americans were hostile to such un-Wilsonian devices as "spheres of influence."

28.5.2.2 GERMANY The three powers easily agreed on Germany—its disarmament, de-Nazification, and division into four zones of occupation by France and the Big Three. Churchill, however, balked at Stalin's demand for $20 billion in reparations as well as forced labor from all the zones, with Russia to get half of everything. These matters festered and caused dissension in the future.

28.5.2.3 EASTERN EUROPE The settlement of Eastern Europe was equally thorny. Everyone agreed the Soviet Union deserved to have friendly neighboring governments, but the West insisted they also be autonomous and democratic. The Western leaders, particularly Churchill, were not eager to see Russia dominate Eastern Europe. They were also, especially Roosevelt, committed to democracy and self-determination.

Stalin, however, knew that independent, freely elected governments in Poland, Hungary, and Romania would not be friendly to Russia. He had already established a

STALIN, ROOSEVELT, AND CHURCHILL AT YALTA In February 1945, Churchill, Roosevelt, and Stalin the Big Three met at Yalta in the Crimea to plan the organization of Europe at the end of the war. Seated from left to right are Stalin, Roosevelt, and Churchill. Standing behind President Roosevelt is Admiral William D. Leahy. Behind the prime minister are Admiral Sir Andrew Cunningham and Air Marshal Portal.
SOURCE: U.S. Army Photograph

puppet government in Poland in competition with the Polish government-in-exile in London. Under pressure from the Western leaders, however, he agreed to include some Poles friendly to the West in it. He also signed a Declaration on Liberated Europe, promising self-determination and free democratic elections.

Stalin may have been eager to avoid conflict before the war with Germany was over. He was always afraid the Allies would make a separate peace with Germany and betray him, and he probably thought it worth endorsing some hollow principles as the price of continued harmony. In any case, he wasted little time violating these agreements.

28.5.3 Yalta

The next meeting of the Big Three was at Yalta in Crimea in February 1945. The Western armies had not

yet crossed the Rhine, but the Soviet army was within a hundred miles of Berlin. (See Map 28–8.) The war with Japan continued, and no atomic explosion had yet taken place. Roosevelt, faced with a prospective invasion of Japan and heavy losses, was eager to bring the Russians into the Pacific war as soon as possible. As a true Wilsonian, he also suspected Churchill's determination to maintain the British Empire and Britain's colonial advantages. The Americans thought Churchill's plan to set up British spheres of influence in Europe would encourage the Russians to do the same and would lead to friction and war. To encourage Russian participation in the war against Japan, Roosevelt and Churchill made extensive concessions to Russia, ceding the Soviets Sakhalin and the Kurile Islands, and accommodating some of their desires in Korea and in Manchuria.

Again in the tradition of Wilson, Roosevelt emphasized a united-nations organization: "Through the United

Map 28–8 YALTA TO THE SURRENDER

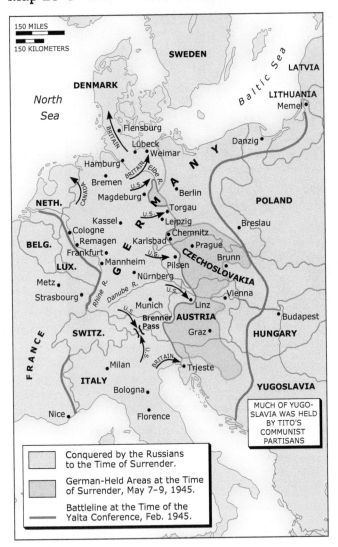

The Big Three—Roosevelt, Churchill, and Stalin—met at Yalta in the Crimea in February 1945. At the meeting, concessions were made to Stalin concerning the settlement of Eastern Europe because Roosevelt was eager to bring the Russians into the Pacific war as soon as possible. This map shows the positions held by the victors when Germany surrendered.

Nations, he hoped to achieve a self-enforcing peace settlement that would not require American troops, as well as an open world without spheres of influence in which American enterprise could work freely."[5] Soviet agreement on these points seemed worth concessions elsewhere.

28.5.4 Potsdam

The Big Three met for the last time in the Berlin suburb of Potsdam in July 1945. Much had changed since the previous conference. Germany had been defeated, and news of the successful explosion of an atomic weapon reached the American president during the meetings. The cast of characters was also different: President Truman replaced the deceased Roosevelt, and Clement Attlee (1883–1967), leader of the Labour Party that had just won a general election, replaced Churchill as Britain's spokesperson during the conference. Previous agreements were reaffirmed, but progress on undecided questions was slow.

Russia's western frontier was moved far into what had been Poland and included most of German East Prussia. In compensation, Poland was allowed "temporary administration" over the rest of East Prussia and Germany east of the Oder-Neisse River, a condition that became permanent. In effect, Poland was moved about a hundred miles west, at the expense of Germany, to accommodate the Soviet Union. The Allies agreed to divide Germany into occupation zones until the final peace treaty was signed. Germany remained divided until 1990.

A Council of Foreign Ministers was established to draft peace treaties for Germany's allies. Growing disagreements made the job difficult, and Italy, Romania, Hungary, Bulgaria, and Finland did not sign treaties until February 1947. The Russians were dissatisfied with the treaty that the United States made with Japan in 1951 and signed their own agreements with the Japanese in 1956. These disagreements were foreshadowed at Potsdam.

The Chapter in Perspective

The second great war of the twentieth century (1939–1945) grew out of the unsatisfactory resolution of the first. In retrospect, the two wars appear to some to be one continuous conflict, a kind of twentieth-century "Thirty Years' War," with two main periods of fighting separated by an uneasy truce. To others, this point of view oversimplifies by implying the second war was the inevitable result of the first and its inadequate peace treaties. The latter opinion seems more sound, for, whatever the flaws of the treaties of Paris, the world suffered an even more terrible war than the first

because of failures of judgment and will by the victorious democratic powers.

Between the two wars, the United States, which had become the wealthiest and potentially the strongest nation in the world, disarmed almost entirely and withdrew into a shortsighted and foolish isolation. Therefore, it played no important part in restraining the angry and ambitious dictators who brought on the war. Britain and France refused to face the threat of the Axis powers until the most deadly war in history was required to put it down. If the victorious democracies had remained strong, responsible, and realistic, they could have remedied the injustices or mistakes of the treaties without endangering the peace.

The second war itself was so plainly a world war that little need be said about its global character. If the Japanese occupation of Manchuria in 1931 was not technically a part of that war, it was a significant precursor. Moreover, there were Italy's attack on the African nation of Ethiopia in 1935; the Italian, German, and Soviet interventions in the Spanish Civil War (1936–1939); and Japan's attack on China in 1937. These acts revealed that aggressive forces were on the march around the globe and the defenders of the world order lacked the will to stop them. The formation of the Axis incorporating Germany, Italy, and Japan guaranteed that when the war came, it would be fought around the world.

There were fighting and suffering in Asia, Africa, the Pacific islands, and Europe, and men and women from all the inhabited continents took part in them. The use of atomic weapons brought the frightful struggle to a close. Still, conventional weapons did almost all the damage; their level of destructiveness threatened the survival of civilization, even without the use of atomic or nuclear devices.

World War II ended not with unsatisfactory peace treaties but with no treaty at all in the European arena, where the war had begun. The world quickly split into two unfriendly camps: the Western, led by the United States, and the eastern, led by the Soviet Union. This division, among other things, hastened the liberation of former colonial territories. The bargaining power of the new nations was temporarily increased as the two rival superpowers tried to gain their friendship or allegiance. It became customary to refer to these nations as "the Third World" or "developing countries," with the former Soviet Union and the United States and their respective allies being the first two. Time has shown that the differences among Third World nations are so great that the term is all but meaningless.

The surprising treatment the defeated powers of World War II received was also largely the result of the emergence of the Cold War. Instead of holding them back, the Western powers installed democratic governments in Italy, West Germany, and Japan, took them into the Western alliances designed to contain Communism, and helped them recover economically. All three are now among the richest nations in the world.

The Chapter in Review

Review Questions

1. What were Hitler's foreign policy aims? Was he bent on conquest, or did he simply want to return Germany to its 1914 boundaries?
2. Why did Britain and France adopt a policy of appeasement in the 1930s? Did the West buy valuable time to rearm at Munich in 1938?
3. How was Hitler able to defeat France so easily in 1940? Why did the air war against Britain fail? Why did Hitler invade Russia? Could the invasion have succeeded?
4. Why did Japan attack the United States at Pearl Harbor? How important was American intervention in the war? Why did the United States drop atomic bombs on Japan? Was President Truman right to use the bombs?
5. How did experiences on the domestic front in Britain differ from those in Germany and France?
6. What was Hitler's final solution to the Jewish question? Why did he want to eliminate Slavs as well? To what extent can it be said the Holocaust was the defining event of the twentieth century?

Key Terms

Anschluss (**AHN-shluz**) Meaning "union." The annexation of Austria by Germany in March 1938.

appeasement The Anglo-French policy of making concessions to Germany in the 1930s to avoid a crisis that would lead to war and that assumed that Germany had real grievances and Hitler's aims were limited and ultimately acceptable.

Axis The alliance between Nazi Germany and Fascist Italy. Also called the Pact of Steel.

Battle of Stalingrad A ferocious battle in summer 1942 that marked the turning point of the Russian campaign against the Nazis, in which Hitler lost an entire German army when he refused to allow a retreat.

blitzkrieg (**BLITZ-kreeg**) Meaning "lightning war." The German tactic early in World War II of employing fast-moving, massed armored columns supported by airpower to overwhelm the enemy.

Dwight D. Eisenhower (1890–1969) American Army general and the commander of the Allied forces who was responsible for the "D-day" landing of American, British, and Canadian troops on the coast of Normandy.

El Alamein A town on Egypt's Mediterranean coast where a decisive battle took place in 1942 between British and

German forces and in which the Allied victory led to the German surrender in North Africa.

Erwin Rommel   (1891–1944) German general and military theorist, known as the "Desert Fox" for his capable leadership of the German and Italian forces in the North African Campaign; also commanded the German forces opposing the Allied invasion of Normandy.

Franklin D. Roosevelt   (1882–1945) U.S. president who supported the British before the United States entered the war despite strong political opposition at home.

Harry S. Truman   (1884–1972) The U.S. president at the end of the war following the death of Franklin D. Roosevelt and who approved attacking Japan with atomic bombs to end the war.

Holocaust   The Nazi extermination of millions of European Jews between 1940 and 1945; also called the "final solution to the Jewish problem."

Lebensraum **(LAY-benz-rauhm)**   Meaning "living space." The Nazi plan to colonize and exploit the Slavic areas of Eastern Europe for the benefit of Germany.

Locarno Agreements   The seven agreements of 1925 designed to secure the territorial settlement after World War I between the Western European Allied powers and the new states of central and Eastern Europe.

Luftwaffe **(LUFT-vaff-uh)**   The German air force in World War II.

Maginot Line   Built in the 1930s on the French side of its borders with Switzerland, Germany, and Luxembourg and designed by the French with concrete fortifications, obstacles and weapons installations to deter invasion by Germany.

Neville Chamberlain   (1869–1940) The British prime minister who sought to prevent Britain going to war through the policy of appeasement with Hitler.

Operation Barbarossa   The code name for the Axis invasion of Russia, which aimed to destroy Russia before winter could set in.

Third Reich (RIKE)   Hitler's regime in Germany, which lasted from 1933 to 1945.

Vichy   The French resort city where Marshall Pétain set up a dictatorial regime and collaborated with the Germans in hopes of preserving as much autonomy as possible.

Notes

1. W. L. Shirer, *The Collapse of the Third Republic* (New York: Simon & Schuster, 1969), p. 281.

2. Alan Bullock, *Hitler, a Study in Tyranny* (New York: Harper & Row, 1962), p. 443.

3. Gordon Wright, *The Ordeal of Total War, 1939–1945* (New York: Harper & Row, 1968), pp. 35–36.

4. Wright, *The Ordeal of Total War*, p. 117.

5. Robert O. Paxton, *Europe in the Twentieth Century* (New York: Harcourt Brace Jovanovich, 1975), p. 487.

Chapter 29

The Cold War Era, Decolonization, and the Emergence of a New Europe

THE TRANSITION TO INDEPENDENCE IN GUYANA
A statue of Queen Victoria is removed from the front of the Supreme Court building in Georgetown, former capital of the British colony of Guyana, in February 1970, in preparation for the transition to independence. Decolonization represented as dramatic a transition in world political relations as the establishment of European empires had in the nineteenth-century Victorian age.
SOURCE: Bettmann/Contributor/Getty Images

 ## Contents and Focus Questions

The Chapter in Brief

SINCE THE END of World War II in 1945, two often inter-related sets of fundamental, international political relationships have shaped the experience of Europe, the United States, and the wider global community. These were the Cold War between the United States and the Soviet Union and the long process of **decolonization**, whereby the peoples of those regions of the world formally or informally dominated by European nations and later by the United States have rejected that domination.

From the end of World War II in 1945 until the collapse of Communist regimes in Eastern Europe between 1989 and 1991, the Soviet Union and the United States—two nuclear-armed superpowers—confronted one another in a simmering conflict known as the **Cold War**. While it lasted, this conflict dominated global politics and threatened the peace of Europe, which stood divided between the U.S.-dominated North Atlantic Treaty Organization **(NATO)** and the Soviet-dominated **Warsaw Pact**.

Decolonization very rapidly became enmeshed with the Cold War. As the nations of Europe retreated from empire, the rivalry between the two superpowers expanded into a contest for dominance in the postcolonial world. Superpower intervention aggravated local conflicts on every continent. In its efforts to limit Communism, the United States became embroiled in bitter wars in Korea and Vietnam. The struggle between Israel and the Arab nations likewise became an arena of superpower conflict.

In the almost two decades since the collapse of the Soviet Union, the United States has remained the world's single superpower. It has become symbolically identified as embodying the political, economic, and cultural values of modern Western civilization. In this role, it has replaced Europe as the object of anti-Western resistance. One of the numerous results of this transformation is the clash between the United States and radical political Islamism. The result has been the terrorist attacks on the United States on September 11, 2001, and the subsequent American intervention in Afghanistan and Iraq.

One way to think of the past sixty years is to see the history of Western civilization as entering a new global era. Europe and later the United States had been active across the world scene since the end of the fifteenth century. Europe had created formal and informal regions of empire by the early twentieth century. However, beginning in the 1930s and continuing to the present day, those once colonially dominated areas of the world have influenced the international relations and domestic politics of many European nations and of the United States rather than remaining regions largely subject to Western economic, political, and military influence. The give-and-take of political, economic, military, and cultural power has become far more reciprocal between the West and the rest of the global community.

29.1   The Emergence of the Cold War

What were the origins of the Cold War?

The tense relationship between the United States and the Soviet Union began in the closing months of World War II. In part, the coldness between the Allies arose from the mutual feeling that each had violated previous agreements. The Russians were plainly asserting permanent control of Poland and Romania under puppet Communist governments. The United States was taking a harder line about German reparation payments to the Soviet Union.

In retrospect, however, and as more information emerges from the previously closed Soviet archives, it appears unlikely that friendlier styles on either side could have avoided a split that arose from basic differences of ideology and interest. The Soviet Union's attempt to extend its control westward into central Europe and the Balkans and southward into the Middle East continued the general thrust of the foreign policy of tsarist Russia. Britain had traditionally tried to restrain Russian expansion into these areas, and the United States inherited that task as Britain's power waned.

Beyond considerations of traditional power politics and international rivalries lay the special problem posed by contradictory ideologies firmly held by the two great victorious nations. The Soviet Union was a Communist autocracy that had long proclaimed its intention to bring its economic, social, and political system to the rest of the world and to eliminate the democratic, capitalistic world order. The United States was no less eager to encourage and foster democracy and free enterprise and especially to prevent the Soviets from dominating Europe. In light of that conflict it is hard to see how serious competition could have been avoided. What is truly remarkable is that such a contest could go on for decades without direct military conflict between the antagonists.

The Americans made no attempt to roll back Soviet power where it existed at the close of World War II. (See Map 29–1.) At the time, American military forces were the greatest in U.S. history, American industrial power was unmatched in the world, and atomic weapons were an American monopoly. In less than a year from the war's end, the Americans had reduced their forces in Europe from 3.5 million to 500,000. The speed of the withdrawal reflected domestic pressure to "get the boys home" but was also fully in accord with America's peacetime plans and goals, which included support for self-determination, autonomy, and democracy in the political sphere, and free trade, freedom of the seas, no barriers to investment, and an Open Door policy in the economic sphere. These goals reflected American principles and served American interests well. As the strongest, richest nation in the world—the one with the greatest industrial base and the strongest currency—the United States would benefit handsomely from an international order based on such goals.

Although postwar American hostility to colonial empires created tensions with France and Britain, the main conflict lay with the Soviet Union. The growth in France and Italy of large popular Communist parties taking orders from Moscow led Americans to believe that Stalin was engaged in a worldwide plot to subvert capitalism and democracy. From the Soviet perspective, extending the borders of the USSR and dominating the formerly independent successor states of Eastern Europe would provide security and compensate for the fearful losses the Soviet people had endured in the war. The Soviets could thus see American resistance to their expansion as a threat to their security and their legitimate aims. They considered American objections to Soviet actions in Poland and other states as an effort to undermine regimes friendly to Russia and to encircle the

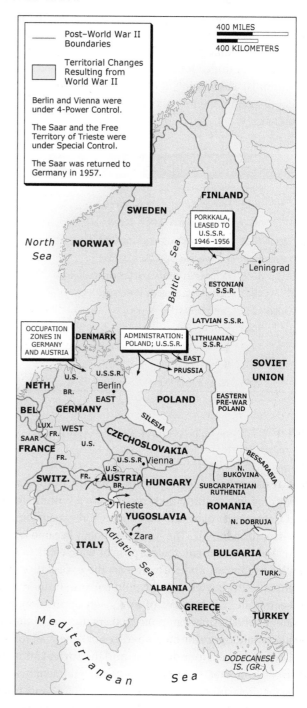

Map 29–1 TERRITORIAL CHANGES IN EUROPE AFTER WORLD WAR II

Shown here are the shifts in territory that followed the defeat of the Axis. No treaty of peace formally ended the war with Germany.

Soviet Union with hostile neighbors. The Soviets could also use this point of view to justify their attempts to overthrow regimes friendly to the United States in Western Europe and elsewhere.

Evidence of the new mood of postwar hostility between the former Allies was soon apparent. In February 1946, both Stalin and his foreign minister, Vyacheslav Molotov (1890–1986), publicly spoke of the Western democracies as enemies. A month later, Churchill gave a speech in Fulton, Missouri, in which he declared that an **"Iron Curtain"** had descended on Europe, dividing a free and democratic West from an East under totalitarian rule. He warned against Communist subversion and urged Western unity and strength against the new menace. In this atmosphere, difficulties grew.

KEY EVENTS OF THE EARLY COLD WAR YEARS	
1945	Yalta Conference
1945	Founding of the United Nations
1946	Churchill's Iron Curtain speech
March 1947	Truman Doctrine regarding Greece and Turkey
June 1947	Announcement of Marshall Plan
1948	Communist takeover in Czechoslovakia
1948	Communist takeover in Hungary
1948–1949	Berlin blockade
1949	NATO founded
1949	East and West Germany emerge as separate states
1950–1953	Korean conflict
1955	Warsaw Pact founded

29.1.1 Containment in American Foreign Policy

The resistance of Americans and Western Europeans to what they increasingly perceived as Soviet intransigence and Communist plans for subversion and expansion took a clearer form in 1947. The American policy became known as one of **containment**, the purpose of which was to resist Soviet expansion and influence in the expectation that eventually the Soviet Union would collapse from internal pressures and the burdens of its foreign oppression. This strategy, which American policymakers devised in the late 1940s, would direct the broad outlines of American foreign policy for the next four decades, until the Soviet Union did collapse from exactly such pressures. Containment marked a major departure in American foreign policy and transformed the international situation during the second half of the twentieth century. The execution of the policy led the United States to enter overseas alliances, to make formal and informal commitments of support to regimes around the world it perceived as being anti-Communist, to undertake enormous military expenditures, and to send large amounts of money abroad. In these respects, the United States assumed unprecedented long-term foreign policy responsibilities. The United States thus became a permanent player in European international relations and in areas of the world where only European nations had been involved earlier in the century.

29.1.1.1 THE TRUMAN DOCTRINE Since 1944, civil war had been raging in Greece between the royalist government restored by Britain and insurgents supported by the Communist countries, chiefly Yugoslavia. In 1947, Britain informed the United States it could no longer financially support its Greek allies. On March 12, President Truman asked Congress to provide funds to support Greece and Turkey, which was then under Soviet pressure to yield control of the Dardanelles, and Congress complied. In a speech to Congress that gave these actions much broader significance, the president set forth what came to be called the Truman Doctrine. He advocated a policy of support for "free people who are resisting attempted subjugation by armed minorities or by outside pressures," by implication, anywhere in the world.

29.1.1.2 THE MARSHALL PLAN American aid to Greece and Turkey took the form of military equipment and advisers. For Western Europe, where postwar poverty and hunger fueled the menacing growth of Communist parties, the Americans devised the European Recovery Program. Named the **Marshall Plan** after George C. Marshall (1880–1959), the secretary of state who introduced it, this program provided broad economic aid to European states on the sole condition that they work together for their mutual benefit. The Soviet Union and its satellites were invited to participate. Finland and Czechoslovakia were willing to do so, and Poland and Hungary showed interest. The Soviets, however, forbade them to take part.

The Marshall Plan restored prosperity to Western Europe and set the stage for Europe's unprecedented postwar economic growth. In addition to the vast program of American economic aid, the strong Christian Democratic movement that dominated the politics of Italy, France, and West Germany worked to keep Communist influence at bay outside the Soviet sphere in Eastern Europe.

Following the declaration of the Truman Doctrine and the announcement of the Marshall Plan, the Soviet Union defined a new era of conflict between the United States and itself.

29.1.2 Soviet Domination of Eastern Europe

The Soviet determination to control Eastern Europe had both historical and ideological roots. Western European powers had invaded Russia twice in the nineteenth century, under Napoleon in 1812 and during the Crimean War of 1854–1856, and already twice more in the twentieth century. Tsarist Russia had governed most of Poland from the 1790s to 1915 and had intervened at the request of the Austrian Empire to put down the Hungarian revolution in 1849. Russia's interests in Turkey and the lands around the Black Sea were similarly long-standing. Given this history and the

THE ARCHITECTS OF U.S. FOREIGN POLICY AT THE START OF THE COLD WAR President Harry Truman, left, greets Secretary of State George Marshall, right, returning from Europe. Truman and Marshall were the architects of American foreign policy during the early years of the Cold War.
SOURCE: Hulton Archive/Staff/Getty Images.

Soviet Union's extraordinary losses in World War II, it is not surprising that Soviet leaders sought to use their Eastern European satellites as a buffer against future invasions.

Stalin may have seen containment as a renewed Western attempt to isolate and encircle the USSR. In Eastern Europe, the Soviet Union found numerous supporters among those who had opposed the various right-wing movements in those countries before the war and who had fought the Nazis during the war. In the autumn of 1947, Stalin called a meeting in Warsaw of all Communist parties from around the globe. There they organized the Communist Information Bureau (Cominform), a revival of the old Comintern, dedicated to spreading revolutionary Communism throughout the world. In Western Europe the establishment of the Cominform officially ended the era of the popular front during which Communists had cooperated with non-Communist parties. Hard-liners who supported the Soviet line on every issue replaced Communist leaders in the West who favored collaboration and reform. (See the "Compare and Connect" sidebar, which follows below, for statements by the Cominform and the U.S. National Security Council defining their global ideologies and policies on containment.)

During the late 1940s, the Soviet Union required the other subject governments in Eastern Europe to impose Stalinist policies, including one-party political systems, close military cooperation with the Soviet Union, the collectivization of agriculture, Communist Party domination of education, and attacks on the churches. Longtime

Communist Party officials were purged and condemned in show trials like those that had taken place in Moscow during the late 1930s. The catalyst for this policy probably was the success of Marshal Josip (Broz) Tito (1892–1980), the leader of Communist Yugoslavia, in freeing his country from Soviet domination. Stalin wanted to prevent other Eastern European states from following the Yugoslav example.

29.1.3 The Postwar Division of Germany

Soviet actions, especially those in Czechoslovakia, increased the determination of the United States to proceed with its own arrangements in Germany. The question of the dismemberment of Germany and of how to deal with the German economy divided the Allies. The United States thought that an independent Germany suited Western interests much better than a country deprived of its former industrial strength.

29.1.3.1 DISAGREEMENTS OVER GERMANY During the war, the Allies had never decided how to treat Germany after its defeat. At first they agreed it should be dismembered but they differed on how. By the time of Yalta, Churchill had come to fear Russian control of Eastern and central Europe and began to oppose dismemberment.

The Allies also differed on economic policy. The Russians swiftly dismantled German industry in the eastern zone, but

Compare and Connect

Drawing the Lines of the Cold War

BETWEEN 1945 AND 1950, the tension between the United States and the Soviet Union became known as the Cold War. Each country quickly came to define the other as its principal enemy on the world scene. The following two documents illustrate how each nation defined its conflict with the other within a larger framework of ideological and political rivalry. The rhetoric of these documents would characterize the Cold War from its inception until the collapse of the Soviet Union.

ALLIED AIRLIFT OVER BERLIN With Berlin deep in the Soviet zone, Stalin expected that the blockade he had imposed would end the Western presence in Berlin. The Berlin Airlift, however, circumvented the blockade. Every day, for almost a year, Western planes supplied Berlin until Stalin lifted the blockade in May 1949.
SOURCE: Everett Collection Historical/Alamy Stock Photo

Before Reading

- Notice the ways in which the restraint advocated in these texts both limits the exercise of power and justifies it when applied.
- Think about the use of the terms *democratic* and *imperialist* by the Cominform.
- Consider the Cominform's view of the Marshall Plan in comparison with the goals that the National Security Council hoped to attain through containment.

Questions

1. How did the Cominform use the terms *democratic* and *imperialist* to its advantage?
2. Why did it see the Marshall Plan as an act of aggression?
3. How did the National Security Council characterize Soviet policy?
4. What were the goals of containment?
5. Why did the council urge that the Soviet Union be given opportunity to save face and to back down with dignity?
6. How did each document indicate that both the Soviet Union and the United States regarded their conflict as part of a wider global political scene?

I. THE COMINFORM DEFINES CONFLICT BETWEEN THE SOVIET UNION AND THE UNITED STATES

In 1947, under the leadership of the Soviet Union, the leaders of the Soviet and East European Communist parties formed the Communist Information Bureau, which became known as the Cominform. It was organized in the wake of the Truman Doctrine and Marshall Plan. In September 1947, the Communist parties constituting the Cominform issued a statement presenting their view of the emerging conflict between the Soviet bloc and the United States. In it they attacked not only the United States but also the democratic Socialist parties of Western Europe that the Soviet Union had seen as an enemy since the days of Lenin.

Fundamental changes have taken place in the international situation as a result of the Second World War and in the post-war period.

These changes are characterized by a new disposition of the basic political forces operating in the world arena, by a change in the relations among the victor states in the Second World War, and their realignment.

. . . The Soviet Union and the other democratic countries regarded as their basic war aims the restoration and consolidation of democratic order in Europe, the eradication of fascism and the prevention of the possibility of new aggression on the part of Germany, and the establishment of a lasting all-round cooperation among the nations of Europe. The United States of America, and Britain in agreement with them, set themselves another aim in the war: to rid themselves of competitors on the markets (Germany and Japan) and to establish their dominant position. . . .

Thus two camps were formed—the imperialist and anti-democratic camp having as its basic aim the establishment of world domination of American imperialism and the smashing of democracy, and the anti-imperialist and democratic camp having as its basic aim the undermining of imperialism, the consolidation of democracy, and the eradication of the remnants of fascism. . . .

. . . the imperialist camp and its leading force, the United States, are displaying particularly aggressive activity. . . . The Truman-Marshall Plan is only a constituent part. . . . of the general plan for the policy of global expansion pursued by the United States in all parts of the World. . . .

To frustrate the plan of imperialist aggression the efforts of all the democratic anti-imperialist forces of Europe are necessary. The right-wing Socialists are traitors to this cause. . . . and primarily the French Socialists and the British Labourites . . . by their servility and sycophancy are helping American capital to achieve its aims, provoking it to resort to extortion and impelling their own countries on to a path of vassal-like dependence on the United States of America.

This imposes a special task on the Communist Parties. They must take into their hands the banner of defense of the national independence and sovereignty of their countries. . . .

The principle danger for the working class today lies in underestimating their own strength and overestimating the strength of the imperialist camp.

II. THE U.S. NATIONAL SECURITY COUNCIL PROPOSES TO CONTAIN THE SOVIET UNION

In response to the control of Eastern Europe by Communist parties dominated by the Soviet Union and the occupation of these nations by Soviet troops, the U.S. government in 1950 adopted a policy of "containment" of the Soviet Union. This policy had been debated for many months and had been in effect since the declaration of the Truman Doctrine in 1947. It was formally set forth after a period of implementation in what became known as the National Security Council Paper 68, arguably the most important statement of American foreign policy of the mid-twentieth century. The paper presented the Soviet Union as a nation determined to pursue an expansionist foreign policy and ideological struggle and proposed a long-term policy of containing the influence of the Soviet Union diplomatically and militarily.

The fundamental design of those who control the Soviet Union and the international communist movement is to retain and solidify their absolute power, first in the Soviet Union and second in the areas now under their control. . . .

The design, therefore, calls for the complete subversion or forcible destruction of the machinery of government and structure of society in the countries of the non-Soviet world and their replacement by an apparatus and structure subservient to and controlled from the Kremlin. . . .

Our overall policy at the present time may be described as one designed to foster a world environment in which the American system can survive and flourish. It therefore rejects the concept of isolation and affirms the necessity of our positive participation in the world community.

This broad intention embraces two subsidiary policies. One is a policy which we would probably pursue even if there were no Soviet threat. It is a policy of attempting to develop a healthy international community. The other is the policy of "containing" the Soviet system. . . .

As for the policy of "containment," it is one which seeks by all means short of war to (1) block further expansion of Soviet power, (2) expose the falsities of Soviet pretensions, (3) induce a retraction of the Kremlin's control and influence, and (4) in general, so foster the seeds of destruction within the Soviet system that the Kremlin is brought at least to the point of modifying its behavior to conform to generally accepted international standards. . . .

One of the most important ingredients of power is military strength. . . . Without superior aggregate military strength . . . a policy of "containment"—which is in effect a policy of calculated and gradual coercion—is no more than a policy of bluff.

At the same time, it is essential to the successful conduct of a policy of "containment" that we always leave open the possibility of negotiation with the USSR. . . .

In "containment" it is desirable to exert pressure in a fashion which will avoid so far as possible directly challenging Soviet prestige, to keep open the possibility for the USSR to retreat before pressure with a minimum loss of face and to secure political advantage from the failure of the Kremlin to yield or take advantage of the openings we leave it.

SOURCE: (I) From United States Senate, 81st Congress, 1st Session, Document No. 48, *North Atlantic Treaty: Documents Relating to the North Atlantic Treaty* (Washington, DC: U.S. Government Printing Office, 1949), pp. 117–120, quoted in Katharine J. Lualdi, *Sources of the Making of the West: Peoples and Culture*, Vol. 2 (Boston: Bedford/St. Martin's Press, 2009), pp. 248–250. (II) From National Security Council, Paper Number 68, *Foreign Relations of the United States* (Washington, DC: U.S. Government Printing Office, 1977), Sections: III, IV, VI.

the Americans acted differently in the western zone. They concluded that if they followed the Soviet policy, the United States would have to support Germany economically for the foreseeable future. It would also cause chaos and open the way for Communism. They preferred, therefore, to try to make Germany self-sufficient, and this meant restoring, rather than destroying, its industrial capacity. To the Soviets, the restoration of a powerful industrial Germany, even in the western zone only, was frightening. The same difference of approach hampered agreement on reparations. The Soviets claimed the right to the industrial equipment in all the zones, and the Americans resisted their demands.

29.1.3.2 BERLIN BLOCKADE
When the Western powers agreed to go forward with a separate constitution for the western sectors of Germany in February 1948, the Soviets walked out of the joint Allied Control Commission. In the summer of that year, the Western powers issued a new currency in their zone. All four powers governed Berlin, though it was well within the Soviet zone. The Soviets feared the new currency, which was circulating in Berlin at better rates than their own currency. They chose to seal the city off by closing all railroads and highways that led from Berlin to West Germany. Their purpose was to drive the Western powers out of Berlin.

The Western allies responded to the Berlin blockade by airlifting supplies to the city for almost a year. In May 1949, the Russians were forced to reopen access to Berlin. The incident, however, was decisive. It increased tensions and suspicions between the opponents and hastened the separation of Germany into two states. West Germany formally became the German Federal Republic in September 1949, and the eastern region became the German Democratic Republic a month later. Ironically, Germany had been dismembered in a way no one had planned or expected. The two Germanys and the divided city of Berlin, isolated within East Germany, would remain central fixtures in the geopolitics of the Cold War until 1989. (See Map 29–2.)

29.1.4 NATO and the Warsaw Pact

Meanwhile, the nations of Western Europe had been moving closer together. The Marshall Plan encouraged international cooperation. In March 1948, Belgium, the Netherlands, Luxembourg, France, and Britain signed the Treaty of Brussels, providing for cooperation in economic and military matters. In April 1949, these nations joined with Italy, Denmark, Norway, Portugal, and Iceland to sign a treaty with Canada and the United States that formed the North Atlantic Treaty Organization (NATO), which committed its members to mutual assistance if any of them was attacked. The NATO treaty transformed the West into a bloc. A few years later, West Germany, Greece, and Turkey joined the alliance. For the first time in history, the United States was committed to defend allies outside the Western Hemisphere.

Map 29–2 OCCUPIED GERMANY AND AUSTRIA

At the end of the war, the victorious Allies occupied defeated Germany, including Austria, in the zones shown here. Austria, by prompt agreement, was reestablished as an independent, neutral state, no longer occupied. The German zones hardened into an East Germany (the former Soviet zone) and a West Germany (the former British, French, and American zones). Berlin, within the Soviet zone, was similarly divided.

A series of bilateral treaties providing for close ties and mutual assistance in case of attack governed Soviet relations with the states of Eastern Europe. In 1949, these states formed the Council of Mutual Assistance (COMECON) to integrate their economies. Unlike the NATO states, the Soviets directly dominated the Eastern alliance system through local Communist parties controlled from Moscow and the presence of the Red Army. The Warsaw Pact of May 1955, which included Albania, Bulgaria, Czechoslovakia, East Germany, Hungary, Poland, Romania, and the Soviet Union, formally recognized this system. Europe was divided into two unfriendly blocs. The Cold War had taken firm shape in Europe. (See Map 29–3.)

The strategic interests of the United States and the Soviet Union would not, however, permit the Cold War to be limited to the European continent. Major flash points would erupt around the world during the decades that followed, particularly in the Middle East and Asia.

The establishment of a Communist government in Cuba after 1959 would bring the conflict to the American hemisphere as well. In each case, the Cold War rivalry transformed what might otherwise have been regional conflicts into superpower strategic concerns.

29.1.5 The Creation of the State of Israel

One of the areas of ongoing regional conflict that became a major point of Cold War rivalry was the Middle East. Following World War I, Great Britain had exercised the chief political influence in the region under various mandates from the League of Nations. After World War II, both the Zionist movement, which sought to establish an independent Jewish state, and Arab nationalists, who sought to achieve self-determination, challenged British authority and influence.

Map 29–3 MAJOR COLD WAR EUROPEAN ALLIANCE SYSTEMS

The North Atlantic Treaty Organization (NATO), which included both Canada and the United States, stretched as far east as Turkey. By contrast, the Warsaw Pact nations were the contiguous Communist states of Eastern Europe, with the Soviet Union, of course, as the dominant member.

29.1.5.1 BRITISH BALFOUR DECLARATION

The modern state of Israel was the achievement of the world Zionist movement, founded in 1897 by Theodor Herzl and later led by Chaim Weizmann (1874–1952). In 1917, during World War I, Arthur Balfour (1846–1930), the British foreign secretary, declared in the **Balfour Declaration** that Britain favored establishing a national home for the Jewish people in Palestine, which was then under Ottoman rule. Between the wars, thousands of Jews, mainly from Europe, immigrated to what had become British-ruled Palestine. During this period, the *Yishuv*, or Jewish community in Palestine, developed its own political parties, press, labor unions, and educational system. Arabs already living in Palestine considered the Jewish settlers intruders, and violent conflicts ensued. The British tried, but failed, to mediate these clashes.

This situation might have prevailed longer, except for the outbreak of World War II and Hitler's attempt to exterminate the Jews of Europe. The Nazi persecution united Jews throughout the world behind the Zionist ideal of a Jewish state in Palestine, and it touched the conscience of the United States and other Western powers. It seemed morally right to do something for the Jewish refugees from Nazi concentration camps.

29.1.5.2 THE UN RESOLUTION

In 1947, the British turned over to the United Nations the problem of the relationship of Arabs and Jews in Palestine. That same year, the United Nations passed a resolution dividing the territory into two states, one Jewish and one Arab. The Arabs in Palestine and the surrounding Arab states resisted this resolution. Not unnaturally, they resented the influx of new settlers. Many Palestinian Arabs were displaced and became refugees themselves.

29.1.5.3 ISRAEL DECLARES INDEPENDENCE

In May 1948, the British officially withdrew from Palestine, and the Yishuv declared the independence of a new Jewish state called *Israel* on May 14. Two days later, the United States, through the personal intervention of President Truman, recognized the new nation, whose first prime minister was David Ben-Gurion (1886–1973). Almost immediately, Lebanon, Syria, Jordan, Egypt, and Iraq invaded Israel. The fighting continued throughout 1948 and 1949. By the end of its war of independence against the Arabs, Israel had expanded its borders beyond the limits the United Nations had originally set forth. Jerusalem was divided between Jordan and Israel. By 1949, Israel had secured its existence but not the acceptance of its Arab neighbors. As long as Egypt, Jordan, Syria, Lebanon, Iraq, and Saudi Arabia, to name those nations closest, withheld diplomatic recognition from Israel, the peace was only an armed truce. (See Map 29–4.)

The Arab–Israeli conflict would inevitably draw in the superpowers. The dispute directly involved Europe because many of the citizens of Israel had emigrated from there, and Europe, like the United States, was highly dependent on oil

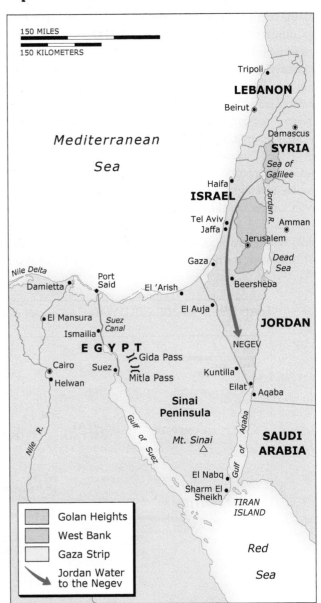

Map 29–4 ISRAEL AND ITS NEIGHBORS, 1949

The territories gained by Israel in 1949 did not secure peace in the region. In fact, the disposition of those lands and the Arab refugees who live there are the source of the region's unresolved problems to the present day.

from Arab countries. Furthermore, both the United States and the Soviet Union believed they had major strategic and economic interests in the region.

By 1949, the United States had established itself as a firm ally of Israel. Gradually, the Soviet Union began to furnish aid to the Arab nations. The bipolar tensions that had settled over Europe were thus transferred to the Middle East. Furthermore, the existence of the state of Israel would become one of the major points of contention between the United States and the governments of the various Arab states and later one of the chief complaints of radical political Islamists against the United States.

29.1.6 The Korean War

While early stages of the Cold War took place in Europe and the Arab–Israeli conflict developed in the Middle East, the United States confronted armed aggression in Asia. As part of a UN police action, it intervened militarily in Korea, following the same principle of containment that directed its actions in Europe.

Between 1910 and 1945, Japan, as an Asian colonial power, had occupied and exploited the formerly independent kingdom of Korea, but at the close of World War II, the United States and the Soviet Union expelled the Japanese and divided Korea into two parts along the thirty-eighth parallel of latitude. Korea was supposed to be reunited. By 1948, however, two separate states had emerged: the Democratic People's Republic of Korea in the north, supported by the Soviet Union, and the Republic of Korea in the south, supported by the United States.

In late June 1950, after border clashes, North Korea invaded South Korea across the thirty-eighth parallel. The United States intervened, at first unilaterally and then under the authority of a UN resolution. For the United States, the point of the Korean conflict was to contain the spread and halt the aggression of Communism.

Late in 1950, the Chinese, responding to the approach of UN forces near their border, sent troops to support North Korea. The American forces had to retreat. The U.S. policymakers believed mistakenly that the Chinese, who, since 1949, had been under the Communist government of Mao Zedong (1893–1976), were simply Soviet puppets. Accordingly, the Americans viewed the movement of Chinese troops into Korea as another example of Communist pressure against a non-Communist state, similar to what had previously happened in Europe. Today it is clear that Mao disliked Stalin and that tension existed between Moscow and the People's Republic of China but that was little understood at the time.

On June 16, 1953, the Eisenhower administration concluded an armistice ending the Korean War and restoring the border near the thirty-eighth parallel. (See Map 29–5.) Thousands of American troops, however, are still stationed in Korea.

The formation of NATO and the Korean conflict capped the first round of the Cold War. In 1953, Stalin's death and the armistice in Korea fostered hopes that international tensions might ease. In early 1955, Soviet occupation forces left Austria after that nation accepted neutral status. Later that year, the leaders of France, Great Britain, the Soviet Union, and the United States held a summit conference in Geneva. Nuclear weapons and the future of a divided Germany were the chief items on the agenda. Despite public displays of friendliness, the meeting produced few substantial agreements, and the Cold War soon resumed.

Map 29–5 KOREA, 1950–1953

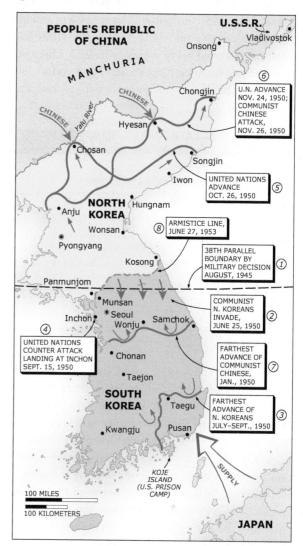

Shown here are the major developments in the bitter three-year struggle that followed the North Korean invasion of South Korea in 1950.

29.2 The Khrushchev Era in the Soviet Union

What domestic policies did Khrushchev pursue?

No other nation had suffered greater losses or more deprivation during World War II than the Soviet Union. Many Russians had hoped the end of the war would reduce the scope of the police state and redirect the economy away from heavy industry to consumer products. They were disappointed. Stalin did little or nothing to modify the character of the regime he had created. If anything, his determination to centralize his authority and a desire to undertake a new wave of internal purges continued until his death on March 6, 1953.

For a time, no single leader replaced Stalin. Rather, the *presidium*, or the renamed Politburo, pursued a policy of collective leadership. Gradually, however, power and influence began to devolve on Nikita Khrushchev (1894–1971), who had been named party secretary in 1953. Three years later, he became premier. Khrushchev's rise ended collective leadership, but he never commanded the extraordinary powers of Stalin.

KEY EVENTS OF THE EARLY KHRUSHCHEV ERA	
1953	Death of Stalin
1955	Austria established as a neutral state
1955	Geneva summit
February 1956	Khrushchev's secret speech denouncing Stalin
Autumn 1956	Polish crisis
October 1956	Suez crisis
	Hungarian uprising
1957	*Sputnik* launched

29.2.1 Khrushchev's Domestic Policies

The Khrushchev era, which lasted until the autumn of 1964, witnessed a retreat from Stalinism, though not from authoritarianism. Khrushchev sought to reform the Soviet system but to maintain the dominance of the Communist Party. Intellectuals were somewhat freer to express their opinions. Khrushchev also made modest efforts to meet the demand for more consumer goods and decentralize economic planning. In agriculture, he removed many restrictive regulations on private cultivation and expanded the area available for growing wheat. At first, this program led to record grain production, but inappropriate farming techniques soon reduced yields. The Soviet Union had to import vast quantities of grain each year from the United States and other countries.

29.2.1.1 THE SECRET SPEECH OF 1956
In February 1956, Khrushchev made an extraordinary departure from expected practice by directly attacking the policies of the Stalin years. At the Twentieth Congress of the Communist Party, Khrushchev gave a secret speech, later published outside the Soviet Union, in which he denounced Stalin and his crimes against Socialist justice during the purges of the 1930s. The speech stunned party circles, but it also enabled genuine, if limited, internal criticism of the Soviet government and many of the changes in intellectual and economic life cited earlier.

29.2.2 The Three Crises of 1956

Khrushchev's speech, however, had repercussions well beyond the borders of the Soviet Union. Communist leaders in Eastern Europe took it as a signal that they could govern with greater leeway than before and retreat from Stalinist policies. Indeed, Khrushchev's speech was simply the first of a number of extraordinary events in 1956.

29.2.2.1 THE SUEZ INTERVENTION
In July 1956, President Gamal Abdel Nasser (1918–1970) of Egypt nationalized the Suez Canal. Great Britain and France, who had controlled the private company that had run the canal, feared that this action would close the canal to their supplies of oil in the Persian Gulf. In October 1956, war broke out between Egypt and Israel. The British and French seized the opportunity to intervene militarily; however, the United States refused to support their action. The Soviet Union protested vehemently. The Anglo-French forces had to be withdrawn, and Egypt retained control of the canal.

The **Suez intervention** proved that without the support of the United States the nations of Western Europe could no longer impose their will on the rest of the world. It also appeared that the United States and the Soviet Union had restrained their allies from undertaking actions that might have resulted in a wider conflict. The fact that neither of the superpowers wanted war constrained both Egypt and the Anglo-French forces.

29.2.2.2 POLISH EFFORTS TOWARD INDEPENDENT ACTION
In the autumn of 1956 important developments in Eastern Europe demonstrated similar limitations on independent action among the Soviet bloc nations. When the prime minister of Poland died, the Polish Communist Party leaders refused to replace him with Moscow's nominee, despite considerable pressure from the Soviets. In the end, Wladyslaw Gomulka (1905–1982) emerged as the new Communist leader of Poland. He was the choice of the Poles, and he proved acceptable to the Soviets because he promised continued economic and military cooperation, and particularly because he continued Polish membership in the Warsaw Pact. Within those limits he halted the collectivization of Polish agriculture and improved relations with the Polish Roman Catholic Church.

29.2.2.3 THE HUNGARIAN UPRISING
Hungary was the third trouble spot for the Soviet Union. In late October, demonstrations of sympathy for the Poles in Budapest led to street fighting. The Hungarian Communists installed a new ministry headed by former premier Imre Nagy (1896–1958). Nagy was a Communist who sought a more independent position for Hungary. He went much further in his demands than Gomulka and directly appealed for political support from non-Communist groups in Hungary. Nagy called for the removal of Soviet troops and the ultimate neutralization of Hungary. He even called for Hungarian withdrawal from the Warsaw Pact. These demands were wholly unacceptable to the Soviet Union. In early November, Soviet troops invaded Hungary; deposed Nagy, who was later executed; and imposed Janos Kadar (1912–1989) as premier. (See the "Encountering the Past" sidebar, on the Soviet invasion of Hungary and the 1956 Olympics, which follows below.)

Encountering the Past

Blood in the Water

THE HUNGARIAN UPRISING WAS ALREADY underway when the national water polo team left for the Olympic games in Melbourne, Australia, in late October 1956. The players knew about the uprising, but they did not know the outcome until they

arrived in Melbourne. There they learned that the Soviet Union had sent 200,000 soldiers into Hungary to crush the revolt, killing at least 2,500 Hungarians in the process.

Tensions had always run high in water polo matches between Hungary and the Soviet Union, but as the two teams advanced toward a semi-final clash in Melbourne, it was clear that this match would be particularly brutal. Upon arriving in the Olympic Village, the Hungarian team had declared its loyalties by taking down the Hungarian flag with a hammer and cycle, and replacing it with one representing a free Hungary. Even as the Hungarian team won game after game, they worried about their families and friends in Hungary and about their futures. They brought that mix of anxiety and anger to the match with the Soviet Union.

HUNGARY VS. SOVIET UNION The water polo match between Hungary and the Soviet Union during the 1956 Olympics in Melbourne, Australia, was perhaps the most brutal in the sport's history. One casualty, Hungarian player Ervin Zador, left the pool after the match with blood streaming from a swollen eye.
SOURCE: Bettmann/Getty Images

The crowd for the match was overwhelmingly pro-Hungarian, and the Hungarian fans gave full vent to their feelings, shouting support for their team and hurling insults at the Soviets. In the pool, things were just as heated. Players threw punches and kicked and scratched their opponents below the water out of sight of the referee. The Hungarians cursed the Soviets for invading their country, and the Soviets called the Hungarians traitors. The Hungarians dominated the match, and as they built a 4–0 lead, Soviet frustration boiled over, culminating in a punch to the face of Hungarian team captain Ervin Zador that left him dazed and bleeding. The Hungarian fans poured out of their seats to confront the Soviet team. To prevent an all-out melee, the referee declared the match over and the Hungarians the winners.

The 1956 Olympic Games in Melbourne were not the only Olympics shaped by the Cold War. From 1952 to 1988, each Olympics was a proxy for the larger conflict between the United States and the Soviet Union. The Melbourne games, however, were unique. The Hungarian-Soviet water polo match, later dubbed the "blood in the water" game, was both political and personal. Whatever their ideological commitments, the Hungarian players were directly affected by the Soviet invasion of Hungary, and their antipathy for the Soviet team was fueled by deep emotions. Several of the Hungarian players would never return to their homeland, including Ervin Zador, choosing instead to defect to the West at the close of the games.

Questions

1. How did the Hungarian players respond to the Soviet invasion of Hungary in 1956?
2. How did the Olympic Games of 1956 reflect personally and politically the events of the Hungarian uprising and its aftermath?

The events of 1956 in the Middle East and Eastern Europe solidified the position of the United States and the Soviet Union as superpowers. In different ways and to differing degrees, the two superpowers had demonstrated this new political reality to their allies. The nations of Western Europe would be able to make independent policy among themselves within Europe but were generally curtailed from independent action on the broader international scene. For approximately twenty-five years, the nations of Eastern Europe would be permitted no autonomous actions in either the domestic or the international sphere.

way to demonstrate the Soviet Union's hard-line attitude toward the capitalist world.

KEY EVENTS OF LATER COLD WAR YEARS	
1959	Khrushchev's visit to the United States
1960	Failed Paris Summit
1961	East Germany erects Berlin Wall
1962	Cuban missile crisis
1963	Test Ban Treaty between Soviet Union and the United States
1964	Khrushchev falls from power
1968	Soviet invasion of Czechoslovakia
1972	Strategic Arms Limitation Treaty

29.3 Later Cold War Confrontations

How did the Berlin Wall and the Cuban missile crisis strain relations between the United States and the Soviet Union?

After 1956, the Soviet Union began to talk about "peaceful coexistence" with the United States. With the 1957 launch of *Sputnik*, the first satellite to orbit the earth, the Soviet Union appeared to have achieved an enormous technological superiority over the West. In 1958, the two countries began negotiations toward limiting the testing of nuclear weapons. By 1959, tensions had relaxed sufficiently for Western leaders to visit Moscow and for Khrushchev to tour the United States. A summit meeting was scheduled for May 1960, and President Eisenhower was to go to Moscow.

Just before the Paris Summit Conference, the Soviet Union shot down an American U-2 aircraft that was flying reconnaissance over Soviet territory. Khrushchev demanded an apology from Eisenhower for this air surveillance. Eisenhower accepted full responsibility for the surveillance policy but refused to apologize publicly. Khrushchev then refused to take part in the summit conference, just as the participants arrived in the French capital. The conference, as well as Eisenhower's proposed trip to the Soviet Union, was thus aborted.

The Soviets did not scuttle the summit meeting on the eve of its opening because of the American spy flights. They had long been aware of these flights and had other reasons for protesting them when they did. By 1960, the Communist world itself had split between the Soviets and the Chinese, who were portraying the Russians as lacking revolutionary zeal. Destroying the summit was, in part, a

29.3.1 The Berlin Wall

The aborted Paris conference opened the most difficult period of the Cold War. In 1961, the new U.S. president, John F. Kennedy (1917–1963), and Premier Khrushchev met in Vienna with inconclusive results.

Throughout 1961, thousands of refugees from East Germany crossed the border into West Berlin. This outflow of people embarrassed East Germany, hurt its economy, and demonstrated the Soviet Union's inability to control Eastern Europe. Consequently, in August 1961, the East Germans, with Soviet support, erected a concrete wall along the border between East and West Berlin, separating the two parts of the city. Despite speeches and symbolic support from the West, the wall halted the flow of refugees and brought the U.S. commitment to West Germany into doubt.

29.3.2 The Cuban Missile Crisis

The most dangerous days of the Cold War occurred during the **Cuban missile crisis** of 1962. In 1957, Fidel Castro (b. 1926) launched an insurgency in Cuba, which toppled the dictatorship of Flugencio Batista (1901–1973) on New Year's Day of 1959. Thereafter Castro established a Communist government, and Cuba became an ally of the Soviet Union. These events caused enormous concern within the United States.

In 1962, the Soviet Union secretly began to place nuclear missiles in Cuba. In response, the American government, under President Kennedy, blockaded Cuba, halted the shipment of new missiles, and demanded the removal of existing installations. After a tense week, during which nuclear war seemed a real possibility, the Soviets backed down and the crisis ended. This adventurism in foreign policy undermined Khrushchev's credibility in the ruling circles of the Soviet Union and caused other non-European Communist regimes to question Soviet commitment to their security and survival. It also increased the influence of the People's Republic of China in Communist circles and convinced Soviet military leaders to strengthen their forces so that they would be as strong as, or stronger than those of the United States in any future confrontation.

If the Cuban missile crisis had led to war, the United States could have launched missiles over Europe or from European bases into the Soviet Union. The crisis thus threatened Europe directly, but it was the last major Cold War confrontation to do so. In 1963, the United States and the Soviet Union concluded a nuclear test ban treaty. This agreement marked the beginning of a lessening in the overt tensions between the two powers.

29.4 The Brezhnev Era

What impact did Brezhnev have on the Soviet Union and Eastern Europe?

By 1964, many in the Soviet Communist Party had concluded that Khrushchev had tried to do too much too soon and had done it poorly. On October 16, 1964, Khrushchev was forced to resign. He was replaced by Alexei Kosygin (1904–1980) as premier and Leonid Brezhnev (1906–1982) as party secretary. Brezhnev eventually emerged as the dominant figure.

KEY EVENTS OF THE BREZHNEV ERA
1974   Solzhenitsyn expelled
1975   Helsinki Accords
1979   Soviet invasion of Afghanistan
1980   U.S. Olympic Games boycott
1981   Martial law declared in Poland in response to Solidarity
1982   Death of Brezhnev

29.4.1 1968: The Invasion of Czechoslovakia

In 1968, during what became known as the Prague Spring, the government of Czechoslovakia, under Alexander Dubcek (1921–1992), began to experiment with a more liberal Communism. Dubcek expanded freedom of discussion and other intellectual rights at a time when the Soviet Union was suppressing them. In the summer of 1968, the Soviet government and its allies in the Warsaw Pact sent troops into Czechoslovakia and replaced Dubcek with Communist leaders more to its liking.

At the time of the invasion, Soviet party chairman Brezhnev, in what came to be termed the **Brezhnev Doctrine**, declared the right of the Soviet Union to interfere in the domestic politics of other Communist countries. Whereas the Truman Doctrine of 1947 had supported democratic governments and offered help to resist further Communist penetration in Europe, the Brezhnev Doctrine of 1968 sought to sustain the Communist governments of Eastern Europe and prevent any liberalization in the region. No further direct Soviet interventions occurred in Eastern Europe after 1968, yet the invasion of Czechoslovakia showed that any attempt at greater liberalization could trigger Soviet military repression.

29.4.2 The United States and *Détente*

Foreign policy under Brezhnev combined attempts to reach an accommodation with the United States with continued efforts to expand Soviet influence and maintain Soviet leadership of the Communist movement.

Under President Richard Nixon (1969–1974), the United States began a policy of *détente* with the Soviet Union, and the two countries concluded agreements on trade and on reducing strategic arms. Despite these agreements, Soviet spending on defense and particularly on its navy grew, damaging the consumer sectors of the economy.

During Gerald Ford's presidency (1974–1977), both the United States and the Soviet Union along with other European nations signed the Helsinki Accords. The accords recognized the Soviet sphere of influence in Eastern Europe, but they also recognized the human rights of the signers' citizens, which every government, including the Soviet Union, agreed to protect. President Jimmy Carter (1977–1981), a strong advocate of human rights, sought to induce the Soviet Union to comply with this commitment, a policy that cooled relations between the two countries.

Throughout this period of *détente*, in addition to its military presence in Eastern Europe, the Soviet Union pursued an activist foreign policy around the world. During the 1970s, it financed Cuban military intervention in Angola, Mozambique, and Ethiopia. Soviet funds flowed to the Sandinista forces in Nicaragua and to Vietnam,

A DEFIANT CZECHOSLOVAKIA In the summer of 1968, Soviet tanks rolled into Czechoslovakia, ending that country's experiment in liberalized Communism. Defiant flag-waving Czechs rolled past a Soviet tank in the immediate aftermath of the invasion.
SOURCE: Hulton Archive/Staff/Getty Images.

which permitted the Soviets to use naval bases after North Vietnam conquered the south in 1975. The Soviet Union also provided funds and weapons to various Arab governments for use against Israel.

Each of these actions represented either Soviet support for what it viewed as its own strategic interests or an attempt to weaken the interests of the United States. Even more importantly, following its backing down in the Cuban missile crisis, the Soviet government was determined to build up its military forces. By the early 1980s, the Soviet Union possessed the largest armed force in the world and had achieved virtual nuclear parity with the United States.

29.4.3 The Invasion of Afghanistan

It was at this moment of great military strength in 1979 that the Brezhnev government decided to invade Afghanistan, a strategic decision of enormous long-range consequences for the future of the Soviet Union as well as the United States. Although the Soviet Union already had a presence in Afghanistan, the Brezhnev government, for reasons that remain unclear, determined to send in troops to ensure its

influence in Central Asia and to install a puppet Afghan government.

The invasion brought a sharp response from the United States. The U.S. Senate refused to ratify a second Strategic Arms Limitation agreement that President Carter had signed earlier that year. The United States also embargoed grain shipments to the Soviet Union, boycotted the 1980 Olympic Games in Moscow, and sent aid to the Afghan rebels through various third parties, as did Pakistan, Saudi Arabia, and other Islamic nations. The U.S. Central Intelligence Agency became directly involved with the Afghan resistance forces, some of whom were radical Muslims. China, which felt threatened by the invasion, also helped the rebels.

Eventually, the Soviet forces bogged down in Afghanistan and could not defeat their guerrilla enemies. The Afghans killed thousands of Soviet troops a year and inflicted many other casualties. The morale and prestige of the Soviet army plummeted. At first, few Soviets knew about the military failure in Afghanistan, but during the 1980s, it became common knowledge in the Soviet Union. Although the Afghan war did not make daily headline news in the Western press, it sapped Soviet strength for ten years and demoralized the Soviet Union not unlike the way the Vietnam conflict did the United States.

29.4.4 Communism and Solidarity in Poland

Events in Poland commencing in 1980—a time when the Soviet government was becoming increasingly rigidified and involved in Afghanistan—challenged both the authority of the Polish Communist Party and the influence of the Soviet Union.

After the events of late 1956, when the Polish Communist Party had accommodated itself to Soviet domination, chronic economic mismanagement and persistent shortages of food and consumer goods plagued Poland for twenty-five years. In 1978, the election of Karol Wojtyla, cardinal archbishop of Kraków, as Pope John Paul II (d. 2005) proved important for Polish resistance to Communist control and Soviet domination. An outspoken Polish opponent of Communism now occupied a position of authority and enormous public visibility well beyond the reach of Soviet or Communist control. The new pope visited his homeland in 1979 and received a tumultuous welcome.

In July 1980, the Polish government raised meat prices, leading to hundreds of protest strikes across the country. On August 14, workers occupied the Lenin shipyard at Gdansk on the Baltic coast. The strike soon spread to other shipyards, transport facilities, and factories connected with the shipbuilding industry. The strikers, led by Lech Walesa (b. 1944), refused to negotiate through any of the government-controlled unions. The Gdansk strike ended on August 31 after the government promised the workers the right to organize an independent union called Solidarity. In September, the head of the Polish Communist Party was replaced, the Polish courts recognized Solidarity as an independent union, and the state-controlled radio broadcast a Roman Catholic mass for the first time in thirty years.

The summer of 1981 saw events that were no less remarkable occurance within the Polish Communist Party itself. For the first time in any European Communist state, secret elections for the party congress were permitted, with real choices among the candidates. A single party continued to govern Poland, but for the time being, the party congress permitted real debate within its ranks.

This extraordinary Polish experiment, however, ended abruptly. In 1981, General Wojciech Jaruzelski (b. 1923) became head of the Polish Communist Party, and the army imposed martial law in December. The leaders of Solidarity were arrested. The Polish military acted to preserve its own position and perhaps to prevent a Soviet invasion similar to the one in Czechoslovakia in 1968. Martial law remained in effect until late in 1983, but the Polish Communist Party could not solve Poland's major economic problems.

29.4.5 Relations with the Reagan Administration

Early in the administration of President Ronald Reagan (1981–1989), the United States relaxed its grain embargo on the Soviet Union and placed less emphasis on human rights. At the same time, however, Reagan intensified Cold War rhetoric, famously describing the Soviet Union as an "evil empire." More important, the Reagan administration increased U.S. military spending; slowed arms limitation negotiations; deployed a new missile system in Europe; and proposed the Strategic Defense Initiative, dubbed **"Star Wars"** by the press, involving a high-technology space-based defense against nuclear attack. The Star Wars proposal, although controversial in the United States, was a major issue in later arms control negotiations with the Soviet Union. Star Wars and the Reagan defense spending forced the Soviet Union to increase its own defense spending when it could not afford to do so and contributed to the economic problems that helped bring about its collapse. Yet even during Reagan's first term (1981–1985), no major transformation of the Soviet Union seemed to be in the offing.

Meanwhile, throughout these four decades of the Cold War between the United States and the Soviet Union, extraordinary events had been occurring in Africa and Asia.

29.5 Decolonization: The European Retreat from Empire

How was World War II a catalyst for decolonization?

The transformation of much of Africa and Asia from colonial domains into independent nations was the most remarkable global political event of the second half of the twentieth century. The numbers of people involved alone reveals the magnitude of the change. At the founding of the United Nations in 1945, approximately one-third of the population of the world was subject to the government of colonial powers. Since that time, more than eighty of those then non-self-governing territories have been admitted to UN membership as independent states. (See Map 29–6.)

During the interwar years the European colonial powers had confronted a variety of revolts or nationalist movements, which they had been able to contain either by military force or modest reforms. The war and the opportunities it provided to indigenous nationalist movements within Africa, Asia, and the Middle East transformed the situation. World War II drew the military forces of the colonial powers back to Europe. The Japanese overran European possessions in East Asia and demonstrated that the European presence

Map 29-6 DECOLONIZATION SINCE WORLD WAR II

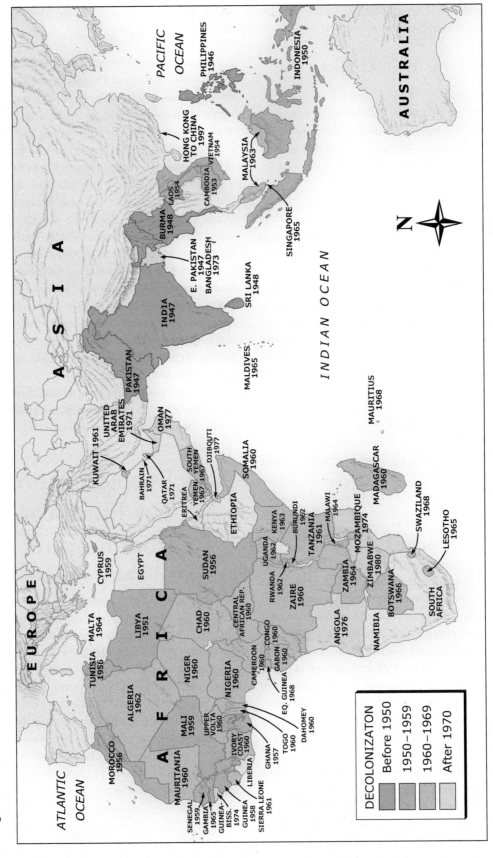

The Western powers' rapid retreat from imperialism after World War II is graphically shown here covering half the globe—from West Africa to the southwest Pacific.

there might not be permanent. After the dislocations of the war came the immediate postwar European economic collapse, which left the European colonial powers less able to afford their military and administrative positions abroad. Consequently, in less than a century after the great nineteenth-century drive toward empire, European imperialists found themselves in retreat around the globe.

The liberal-democratic war aims of the Allies had also undermined colonialism. It was difficult to fight against tyranny in Europe while maintaining colonial dominance abroad. The United States, and in particular Franklin Roosevelt, opposed the continuation of the colonial empires. This policy was, in part, a matter of principle, but it also recognized that both the political and economic interests of the United States were more likely to prosper in a decolonized world. The founding of the United Nations also ensured the presence of an international body opposed to colonialism.

The Cold War complicated the process of decolonization. Both the United States and the Soviet Union opposed the old colonial empires; but both also worried about the potential alignment of new nations, so they moved to create spheres of influence and, in some cases, alliances with newly independent states. Certain nations, such as India, fiercely pursued policies of neutrality in hopes of receiving aid and support from both sides.

29.5.1 Major Areas of Colonial Withdrawal

Decolonization was a worldwide event lasting throughout the second half of the twentieth century and beyond. It involved such dramatic moments as the Dutch being forced from the East Indies in 1949 to be replaced by the independent nation of Indonesia, the Belgian withdrawal from the Congo in 1960, the liberation of Portuguese Mozambique and Angola in 1974 and 1975, and the end of all-white rule in Rhodesia (Zimbabwe) in 1979 and most remarkably in South Africa in 1994.

Each of these events was important, especially to the peoples involved, but the two largest colonial empires were the British and the French. Their retreat from empire produced the most far-reaching repercussions not only in former colonial nations but also in both Europe and the United States as well.

29.5.2 India

No anticolonial movement so gripped the imagination of the Western world as that carried out in India under the leadership of **Mahatma Gandhi** (1869–1948), byname of Mohandas Gandhi. The British had solidified their rule

PRO-INDEPENDENCE LEADER MAHATMA GANDHI Mahatma Gandhi (1869–1948), shown here, in 1930, leading marchers against the repressive salt tax, was a key figure in India's struggle for independence. Part of his appeal was the simplicity of his life and dress.
SOURCE: PA Images/Alamy Stock Photo

of India in the mid-eighteenth century, extending and consolidating it throughout the nineteenth. The British administration required the Indians themselves to pay for British rule. India supplied the raw materials for the British cotton mills. Other British policies pushed many Indians to migrate to British possessions in East Asia, Africa, and the Caribbean. For decades, the religious, ethnic, linguistic, and political divisions among Indians permitted the British to dominate the country through a divide-and-rule strategy.

As early as 1885, politically active Hindu Indians founded the Indian National Congress with the goals of modernizing Indian life and liberalizing British policy. Muslims organized the Muslim League in 1887, which for a time cooperated with the National Congress but eventually sought an independent Muslim nation. After World War I, the Indian nationalist movement grew steadily in strength, in part because of British blunders but more importantly because remarkable leaders pursued effective strategies.

Chief among these leaders was Gandhi, who had studied law in Britain and there encountered the ideas of liberal Western thinkers, including the American Henry David Thoreau (1817–1862) from whom he learned the concept of passive resistance. After being called to the bar in London in 1891, he returned briefly to India and then in 1893 went to South Africa where for over twenty years he worked on behalf of Indian immigrants. During those years he continued to read widely and became convinced of the power of passive resistance. Gandhi returned to India in 1915 and soon distinguished himself as a leader of Indian nationalism by his insistence on religious toleration. From the 1920s to the mid-1940s, he inspired a growing movement of passive resistance to British rule in India. In 1930, he led a famous march to break the British salt monopoly by collecting salt from the sea. He was repeatedly arrested and jailed by the British authorities. To embarrass the British during these imprisonments and to gain worldwide publicity, he undertook long protest fasts during which he nearly died. In 1942, during World War II, Gandhi called on the British government to leave India. In 1947, the British Labor government, weary of the incessant agitation and uncertain of its ability to maintain control in India, decided to do so.

Gandhi became and remains the most famous anticolonial leader of the twentieth century. His career demonstrates how such a leader could use ideas taken from the West against colonial regimes. His use of passive resistance became a model for Dr. Martin Luther King Jr. (1929–1968) during the civil rights movement in the United States during the late 1950s and 1960s.

Gandhi and the Congress Party succeeded in forcing the British from India. However, they did not succeed in creating a single nation. Parallel to Gandhi's drive for an India characterized by diverse religions living in mutual toleration, the Muslim League led by Ali Jinnah (1876–1948) sought a distinctly Muslim state. When the British left India in 1947 there was a partition of the country into the states of India and Pakistan. Intense sectarian warfare and hundreds of thousands of deaths marked the partition. A Hindu extremist assassinated Gandhi himself in 1948. Despite partition a vast Muslim population remained in India. Pakistan was initially a nation of two parts separated geographically by hundreds of miles of Indian territory. In 1971, East Pakistan broke away to become independent Bangladesh.

The partition of India and Pakistan illustrates an often-neglected factor in the process of decolonization. In many colonial regions, the retreat of the colonial powers led to new or renewed conflicts among different ethnic and religious groups within the former colonial empires. For example, since partition, India and Pakistan have disputed the ownership of Kashmir in repeated armed clashes. Another example is the former Portuguese colony of East Timor whose people have asserted a right to independence against the government of Indonesia, which occupied it for twenty years after Portugal withdrew in 1975.

29.5.3 Further British Retreat from Empire

The British surrender of India marked the beginning of a long, steady retreat from empire. Generally speaking, the British accepted the loss of empire as inevitable. British decolonization sought first to maintain whatever links were economically and politically possible without conflict. Indeed, during the 1940s and 1950s, the British undertook various development programs in their remaining Asian, African, and Caribbean colonies. These investments paradoxically made the British government and public more aware of the actual costs of empire and may have led both to accept more easily the end of empire. Second, throughout decolonization the British hoped to oversee the creation of institutions in their former colonies that would ensure representative self-government once they had departed.

In 1948, Burma and Sri Lanka (formerly Ceylon) became independent. As already observed, the formation of the state of Israel and Arab nationalist movements forced Britain to withdraw from Palestine. During the 1950s, the British tried belatedly to prepare their tropical colonies for self-government. Ghana (formerly the Gold Coast) and Nigeria—which became self-governing in 1957 and 1960, respectively—were the major programs of planned decolonization. In other areas, such as Cyprus, Kenya, and Aden, now part of Yemen, the British withdrew under the pressure of militant nationalist movements. In many areas, violence between the British and the forces demanding independence hastened this retreat.

The development of these former colonies in the second half of the twentieth century has followed two distinct paths. In general, political instability and poverty have characterized the history of the independent states in Africa. By contrast, Asia has been an area of overall political stability and remarkable economic growth, challenging the economies of both the United States and Western Europe.

29.6 The Turmoil of French Decolonization

Why was France so reluctant to decolonize?

Although the British retreat from empire involved violence, at no point did the British "make a stand." Moreover, many groups in Britain, including the leadership of the Labour Party, had long been critical of colonialism. Such was not the case with France. Having been defeated by the Nazis and then liberated by the Allied forces, France believed it needed to reassert its position as a great power. This determination led it into two disastrous attempts to maintain its colonial empire, in Algeria and Vietnam.

29.6.1 France and Algeria

France had conquered the pirate's nest of Algiers in 1830 as Charles X (r. 1824–1830) futilely hoped the invasion would increase support for his monarchy. (See Chapter 20.) In late 1848, the French government made Algeria an integral part of France, establishing three administrative departments that were administered like those in France itself. Over the decades, as France consolidated and extended its position in Algeria, French soldiers and hundreds of thousands of Europeans from France and other Mediterranean countries settled there, primarily in the cities and on small farms. By the close of World War I, approximately 20 percent of the population was of European descent. Collectively these immigrants were termed the *pieds noirs*, meaning "black feet," a derogatory term. The voting structure was set up to give the French settlers as large a voice as the majority Arab Muslim population. Algerian Muslims were not given posts in the administration. Shortly after World War I, the French extended the rights of full French citizenship to Algerian Muslims who had fought in the war, who were literate in French, or who owned land, but this rewarded only a few thousands of them.

During World War II, the forces of Free France dominated Algeria after 1942 while the Vichy regime still governed metropolitan France. The Free French government did little to change the colonial status quo. Moreover, in May 1945, during celebrations of the Allied victory in World War II, a violent clash broke out at Sétif between Muslims and French settlers. Matters rapidly got out of hand, and people on both sides were killed, but the French repressed the Muslims with a considerable loss of life. It robbed the French administration of legitimacy and marked the beginning of conscious Algerian nationalism. Thereafter, many Algerian Muslims supported independence. To placate Muslim opinion, in 1947 the French established a structure for limited political representation of the Muslim population and undertook economic reforms. Not surprisingly, these steps proved ineffective.

Algerian nationalists soon founded the National Liberation Front (FLN). In late 1954, insurrections and soon open civil war broke out in Algeria as the FLN undertook highly effective guerrilla warfare. The government of the Fourth French Republic that had been founded in 1945 adamantly declared Algeria an integral part of France and refused to compromise with the insurgents. Thereafter a war lasting until 1962 continued between the Algerian nationalists and the French. Both sides committed atrocities; hundreds of thousands of Algerians were killed. The war divided France itself with many French citizens, often of left-wing political opinion, objecting to the war, and the French military, still smarting from its defeats in World War II and in Indochina, determined to fight on. The presence of more than one million European settlers in Algeria who saw settlement with the nationalists as a betrayal exacerbated the situation. The French government became paralyzed and lost control of the army, and there was fear of civil war in France itself or of a military takeover. In Algeria, violence was spreading.

In the midst of this turmoil, General Charles de Gaulle (1890–1970), who had led the Free French forces during World War II and had briefly governed France immediately after the war, reentered French political life largely at the urging of the military. His condition for taking office was the end of the Fourth Republic and the promulgation of a new constitution, which enhanced the power of the president and created the Fifth Republic. The voters ratified this, and de Gaulle became president of France in December 1958. He then undertook a long strategic retreat from Algeria. The process was neither peaceful nor easy. In 1962, however, de Gaulle held a referendum in Algeria on independence, which passed overwhelmingly. Algeria became independent on July 3, 1962.

Once the FLN took over Algeria under the presidency of Mohammed Ben Bella (b. 1919), however, a second factor came into play in French domestic life. Hundreds of thousands of pied noirs settlers fled Algeria for France, as did many Muslims who had supported the French and had good cause to fear reprisals. (Thousands of pro-French Muslims who did not flee were massacred.) The emigration of this latter group marked the beginning of a large, and largely unwelcome, Muslim population in France.

29.6.2 France and Vietnam

One of the reasons for the strong French stand against Algerian independence had been the loss of its south Asian empire in Indochina just before the Algerian insurrection broke out in 1954. Whereas the Algerian drive toward independence essentially involved only France and the populations of Algeria, the Indochina problem eventually drew the United States into war with Vietnam.

In its push for empire, France had occupied Indochina, which contained Laos, Cambodia, and Vietnam, between 1857 and 1893. By 1930, Ho Chi Minh (1892–1969) had transformed a nationalist movement against French colonial rule into the Indochina Communist Party, which the French for a time succeeded in suppressing. World War II, however, provided new opportunities for Ho Chi Minh and other nationalists as they fought both the Japanese who occupied Indochina in 1941 and the pro-Vichy French colonial administration that collaborated with the Japanese until 1945. The war thus established Ho Chi Minh as a major anticolonial, nationalist leader. He was a Communist to be sure, but he had achieved his position in Vietnam during the war without the support of Chinese or Soviet Communists.

In September 1945, Ho Chi Minh declared the independence of Vietnam under the Viet Minh, a coalition of nationalists that the Communists soon dominated. By 1947, a full-fledged civil war had erupted in Vietnam. Cambodia and, to a lesser extent, Laos remained quiescent under pro-French or neutralist monarchies.

Until 1949, the United States displayed minimal concern about the Indochina war. The establishment of the Communist People's Republic of China that year dramatically changed the U.S. outlook. The United States now saw the French colonial war against Ho Chi Minh as an integral part of the Cold War conflict. The U.S. support for France in Southeast Asia also gained French support for the establishment of NATO. Even though the United States supported the French effort in Vietnam financially, it was not prepared, despite divisions among policymakers, to intervene militarily. In the spring of 1954, during an international conference in Geneva on the future of Vietnam, the French military stronghold of Dien Bien Phu fell to Viet Minh forces after a prolonged siege. France lost the will to continue the struggle, which had become increasingly unpopular with the French people.

By late June, a complicated and unsatisfactory peace accord divided Vietnam at the seventeenth parallel of latitude. North of the parallel, centered in Hanoi, the Viet Minh were in charge; below it, centered in Saigon, the French were in charge. This was to be a temporary border. By 1956, elections were to be held to reunify the country. In effect, the conference attempted to transform a military conflict into a political one.

KEY EVENTS IN THE VIETNAM CONFLICT	
1945	Ho Chi Minh proclaims Vietnamese independence from French rule
1947–1954	War between France and Vietnam
1950	U.S. financial aid to France
1954	Geneva conference on Southeast Asia opens
1954	French defeat at Dien Bien Phu
1954	Southeast Asia Treaty Organization (SEATO) founded
1955	Diem establishes Republic of Vietnam in the south
1960	Founding of National Liberation Front to overthrow the Diem government
1961	Six hundred American troops and advisers in Vietnam
1963	Diem overthrown and assassinated
1964	Gulf of Tonkin Resolution
1965	Major U.S. troop commitment
1969	Nixon announces policy of Vietnamization
1973	Ceasefire announced
1975	Saigon falls to North Vietnamese troops

29.6.3 Vietnam Drawn into the Cold War

Unhappy with these arrangements, the United States, in September 1954, formed the Southeast Asia Treaty Organization (SEATO), a collective security agreement that somewhat resembled the European NATO alliance, but without the integration of military forces or inclusion of all states in the region. Its membership consisted of the United States, Great Britain, France, Australia, New Zealand, Thailand, Pakistan, and the Philippines.

By 1955, American policymakers had begun to think about Indochina, and particularly Vietnam, largely in terms of the Korean example. The U.S. government assumed incorrectly that, like the government of North Korea, the government in North Vietnam was basically a Communist puppet of the Soviets and the Chinese. That same year, French troops began to withdraw from South Vietnam. As they left, the various Vietnamese political groups began to fight for power among themselves.

The United States stepped into the turmoil in Vietnam with military and economic aid. Among the Vietnamese politicians it chose to support was Ngo Dinh Diem (1901–1963), a strong non-Communist nationalist who had not collaborated with the French. Because the United States had been publicly and deeply committed to the French, however, Vietnamese nationalists would view any government it supported with suspicion. In October 1955, Diem established a Republic of Vietnam in the territory for which the Geneva conference had made France responsible. Diem announced that the Geneva agreements would not bind his newly established government and that elections would not be held in 1956. The American government, which had not signed the Geneva documents, supported his position.

In 1960, the National Liberation Front was founded, with the goals of overthrowing Diem, unifying the country, reforming the economy, and ousting the Americans. It was anticolonial, nationalist, and Communist. Its military arm was called the Viet Cong and was aided by the government of North Vietnam. Diem, a Roman Catholic, also faced mounting criticism from Buddhists and the army. His response to these pressures was further repression and dependence on an ever-smaller group of advisers.

29.6.4 Direct United States Involvement

The Eisenhower and Kennedy administrations continued to support Diem while demanding reforms in his government. The American military presence grew from about 600 advisers in early 1961 to more than 16,000 troops in late 1963. The political situation in Vietnam became increasingly unstable. On November 1, 1963, an army coup in which the United States was deeply involved overthrew and murdered Diem. The United States hoped a new government in South Vietnam would generate popular support and looked

for a leader who could fulfill that hope. It finally settled on Nguyen Van Thieu (1923–2001), who governed South Vietnam from 1966 to 1975.

President Kennedy was assassinated on November 22, 1963. His successor, Lyndon Johnson (1963–1969), greatly increased the commitment to South Vietnam. In August 1964, after an attack on an American ship in the Gulf of Tonkin, Johnson authorized the first bombing of North Vietnam. In February 1965, major bombing attacks began. They continued with only brief pauses until early in 1973. The land war grew until more than 500,000 Americans were stationed in South Vietnam.

In 1969, President Richard Nixon began a policy known as **Vietnamization**, which involved the gradual withdrawal of American troops from Vietnam while the South Vietnamese army took over the full military effort. Peace negotiations had begun in Paris in the spring of 1968, but a ceasefire was not finally arranged until January 1973. American troops left South Vietnam, and North Vietnam released its American prisoners of war. In early 1975, an evacuation of South Vietnamese troops from the northern part of their country turned into a rout when they were attacked by the North Vietnamese. On April 30, 1975, Saigon, renamed Ho Chi Minh City, fell to the Viet Cong

U.S. COMBAT TRUMPS IN VIETNAM At the war's peak, more than 500,000 American troops were stationed in South Vietnam. The United States struggled in Vietnam for more than a decade, seriously threatening its commitment to Western Europe.
SOURCE: U.S. Army

and the North Vietnamese army. Vietnam was finally united. (See Map 29–7.)

The U.S. intervention in Vietnam, which grew out of a power vacuum left by French decolonization, affected the entire Western world. For a decade after the Cuban missile crisis, Vietnam diverted the attention of the United States from Europe. American prestige suffered, and the U.S. policy in Southeast Asia caused Europeans to question the American government and its commitment to Western Europe. Many young Europeans, people in the former colonial world, as well as many Americans came to regard the United States not as a protector of liberty but as an ambitious, aggressive, and cruel power determined to maintain colonialism after the end of the colonial era. Within the United States, the Vietnam conflict produced enormous divisions and debates over American involvement in the rest of the world that persist to the present day.

Map 29–7 VIETNAM AND ITS SOUTHEAST ASIAN NEIGHBORS

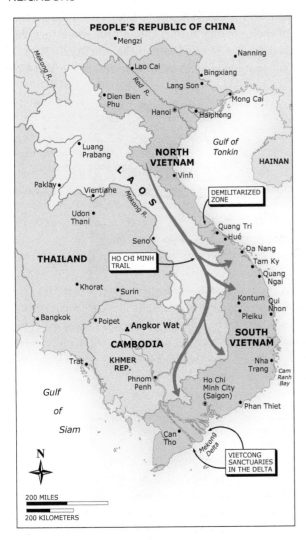

Shown in the map are the important locations associated with the war in Vietnam.

29.7 The Collapse of European Communism

Why did European Communism collapse?

The withdrawal of Soviet influence from Eastern Europe and the internal collapse of the Soviet Union are the most important European historical events of the second half of the twentieth century. They had virtually no parallel in modern European history. All the other major governments had fallen earlier in the century as the result of either domestic revolution brought on by military defeat, as in tsarist Russia, Germany, and Austria after World War I and Italy during World War II, or by military defeat and military occupation, as in Germany after 1945 and the Third Republic in France in 1940. By contrast, the Soviet Union essentially imploded and then divided into separate successor states. There was no foreign invasion, no military defeat, and no internal revolution. Many of the factors leading to the Soviet collapse remain murky, but here is a relatively clear narrative of what occurred.

Under Brezhnev, who governed from 1964 to 1982, the Soviet government became markedly more repressive at home, suggesting a return to Stalinist policies. This internal repression gave rise to a dissident movement. Certain Soviet citizens dared to criticize the regime in public and accused the government of violating the human rights provision of the 1975 Helsinki Accords. The Soviet government responded with further repression, placing some opponents in psychiatric hospitals and others under what amounted to house arrest. During the same period the structures of the Communist Party became both rigidified and corrupt, which increasingly demoralized younger Soviet bureaucrats and party members.

29.7.1 Gorbachev Attempts to Reform the Soviet Union

Although economic stagnation, party corruption, and the lingering Afghan war had long been undermining Soviet authority, what brought these forces to a head and began the dramatic collapse of the Soviet Empire was the accession to power of **Mikhail S. Gorbachev** (b. 1931) in 1985 after both of Brezhnev's two immediate successors, Yuri Andropov (1914–1984) and Konstantin Chernenko (1911–1985), died within thirteen months of each other. In what proved to be the last great attempt to reform the Soviet system, Gorbachev immediately began the most remarkable changes that the Soviet Union had witnessed since the 1920s. These reforms would, within seven years, force him to retire from office and would end both Communist rule

COLD WAR RAPPROCHEMENT President Ronald Reagan and Premier Mikhail Gorbachev confer at a summit meeting in December 1987.
SOURCE: Boris Yurchenko/AP Images

and the Soviet Union as it had existed since the Bolshevik Revolution of 1917.

29.7.1.1 ECONOMIC *PERESTROIKA* Gorbachev's primary goal was to revive the Russian economy to raise the country's standard of living. Initially, he and his supporters, most of whom he had appointed himself, challenged traditional party and bureaucratic management of the Soviet government and economy. Under the policy of *perestroika*, or "restructuring," they reduced the size and importance of the centralized economic ministries.

During these same years, Gorbachev confronted significant labor discontent. A major strike by coal miners occurred in July 1989 in Siberia. Gorbachev had to resolve their grievances quickly because the economy desperately needed their output. He promised them better wages and wider political liberties.

By early 1990, in a clear abandonment of traditional Marxist ideology, Gorbachev advocated private ownership of property and liberalization of the economy toward free market mechanisms. Despite many organizational changes, the Soviet economy remained stagnate and even declined. The failure of Gorbachev's economic policies affected his political policies. To some extent, he pursued bold political reform because he failed to achieve economic progress.

29.7.1.2 *GLASNOST* Gorbachev allowed an extraordinary public discussion and criticism of Soviet history and Soviet Communist Party policy. This development was termed *glasnost*, or openness. The contributions to Soviet history of such figures from the 1920s and 1930s as Nikolai Bukharin, whom Stalin had executed in 1938, received official public recognition. Workers were permitted to criticize party officials and the economic plans of the party and the government. Censorship was relaxed and free expression was encouraged. Dissidents were released from prison. In the summer of 1988, Gorbachev presided over a party congress that witnessed full debates.

Gorbachev soon applied *perestroika* to the political arena. In 1988, a new constitution permitted openly contested elections. After real political campaigning—a new experience for the Soviet Union—the Congress of People's Deputies was elected in 1989. One of the new members of the congress was Andrei Sakharov, the dissident physicist whom Brezhnev had persecuted. After lively debate, the Supreme Soviet, another elected body—although one the Communist Party dominated—formally elected Gorbachev president in 1989.

The policy of open discussion allowed national minorities within the Soviet Union to demand political autonomy. Throughout its history, the Soviet Union had remained a vast empire of subject peoples. The tsars had conquered some of those groups and Stalin had incorporated others, such as the Baltic states, into the Soviet Union. *Glasnost* quickly brought to the foreground the discontent of such peoples, no matter how or when they had been subjugated. Gorbachev proved inept in addressing these ethnic complaints. He badly underestimated the unrest that internal national discontent could generate.

29.7.2 1989: Revolution in Eastern Europe

Several Eastern European nations went through a revolution at the end of the 1980s. The fall of Communism in the Soviet Union linked all these upheavals. The Solidarity movement in Poland led the drive toward freedom in the Soviet-dominated states of Hungary, Czechoslovakia, and Romania. The reunification of Germany was perhaps the most dramatic outcome in this chain of events.

KEY EVENTS IN THE REVOLUTIONS OF 1989	
January 11	Independent parties permitted in Hungary
April 5	Solidarity legalized in Poland and free elections accepted by government
May 2	Hungary dismantles barriers along its borders
May 8	Janos Kadar removed from office in Hungary
May 17	Polish government recognizes Roman Catholic Church
June 4	Solidarity victory in Polish parliamentary elections
July 25	Solidarity asked to join coalition government
August 24	Solidarity member appointed premier in Poland
October 18	Erich Honecker removed from office in East Germany
October 23	Hungary proclaims itself a republic
October 25	Gorbachev renounces Brezhnev Doctrine
November 9	Berlin Wall opened
November 17	Large antigovernment demonstration in Czechoslovakia crushed by police
November 19	Czechoslovak opposition groups organize into Civic Forum and demand resignation of Communist leaders responsible for 1968 invasion
November 24	Czechoslovak Communist leadership resigns
December 1	New Czechoslovak Communist leaders denounce 1968 invasion; Soviet Union and Warsaw Pact express regret over 1968 invasion
December 3	Czechoslovak government announces ministry with non-Communist members
December 16–17	Massacre of civilians in Timisoara, Romania
December 22	Ceausescu government overthrown in Romania with many casualties
December 25	Announcement of Ceausescu's execution
December 28	Alexander Dubcek elected chairman of Czechoslovak Parliament
December 29	Václav Havel elected president of Czechoslovakia

29.7.2.1 SOLIDARITY REEMERGES IN POLAND

In the early 1980s, Poland's government relaxed martial law, and it eventually released all the Solidarity prisoners, although Jaruzelski remained president. In 1988, new strikes surprised even the leaders of Solidarity. This time, the Communist government could not reimpose control. After consultations between the government and Solidarity, the union was legalized. Lech Walesa again took center stage, as a kind of mediator between the government and the more independent elements of the trade union movement he had founded.

Jaruzelski began some political reforms with the tacit consent of the Soviet Union. He promised free elections to a parliament with increased powers. When elections were held in 1989, the Communists lost overwhelmingly to Solidarity candidates. Late in the summer, Jaruzelski, unable to find a Communist who could forge a majority coalition in Parliament, turned to Solidarity and appointed the first non-Communist prime minister of Poland since 1945. Gorbachev expressly approved the appointment.

29.7.2.2 TOWARD HUNGARIAN INDEPENDENCE

Throughout 1989, as these events unfolded within Poland, one Soviet-dominated state after another in Eastern Europe moved toward independence. Early in the year, the Hungarian government opened its border with Austria, permitting free travel between the two countries. This breach in the Iron Curtain immediately led thousands of East Germans to move through Hungary and Austria to West Germany. The Hungarian Communist Party changed its name to the Socialist Party, permitted other parties to engage openly in politics, and promised free elections by October.

29.7.2.3 GERMAN REUNIFICATION

In the autumn of 1989, popular demonstrations erupted in East German cities. Adding to the pressure, Gorbachev told the leaders of the East German Communist Party that the Soviet Union would not use force to support them. With startling swiftness, the East German government resigned, making way for a younger generation of Communist leaders who remained in office for only a few weeks. In November 1989, in one of the most emotional moments in European history since 1945, the government of East Germany ordered the opening of the Berlin Wall. (To know more about why the opening of the Berlin Wall was a great symbolic event, see the "Closer Look" sidebar, which follows below.) That week, tens of thousands of East Berliners crossed into West Berlin to celebrate, to visit their families, and to shop with money the West German government gave them. Shortly thereafter, free travel began between East and West Germany. (See Map 29–8.)

Within days of these dramatic events, West Germany and the other Western nations faced the issue of German reunification. Helmut Kohl (b. 1930), the chancellor of West Germany, became the leading force in moving toward full unification. Late in 1989, the European Economic Community accepted, in principle, the unification of Germany. By February 1990, some form of reunification had become a foregone conclusion, accepted by the United States, the Soviet Union, Great Britain, and France.

29.7.2.4 THE VELVET REVOLUTION IN CZECHOSLOVAKIA

Revolution in Czechoslovakia rapidly followed the breach of the Berlin Wall. The popular new Czech leader who led the forces against the party was Václav Havel (b. 1936), a playwright of international standing whom the Communist government had imprisoned. Havel's group, known as Civic Forum, forced Gustav Husak (b. 1913), who had been president of Czechoslovakia since 1968, to resign. On December 28, 1989, Alexander Dubcek became chairman of the Parliament, and the next day, Havel was elected president.

29.7.2.5 VIOLENT REVOLUTION IN ROMANIA

The only revolution of 1989 that involved significant violence occurred in Romania. There, in mid-December, the forces of President Nicolae Ceausescu (1918–1989), who had governed without opposition since 1965, fired on crowds that were protesting conditions in the country. By December 22, Bucharest was in full revolt. Ceausescu and his wife attempted to flee, but were captured, secretly tried, and shot on December 25.

POLISH SOLIDARITY In 1989 the Polish trade union "Solidarity" (*Solidarność* in Polish) successfully forced the Polish Communist government to hold free elections. In June of that year, Solidarity candidates, with the support of union newspapers and posters, won overwhelmingly.
SOURCE: Chris Niedenthal/The LIFE Images Collection/Getty Images

29.7.2.6 THE SOVIET STANCE ON REVOLUTIONARY DEVELOPMENTS None of the revolutions of 1989 could have taken place unless the Soviet Union had refused to intervene militarily, in contrast to 1956 and 1968. As events unfolded, it became clear that Gorbachev would not rescue the old-line Communist governments and party leaderships in Eastern Europe. In October 1989, he formally renounced the Brezhnev Doctrine. For the first time since the end of World War II, Eastern Europeans could shape their own political destiny without the fear of Soviet military intervention. Once they realized the Soviets would not act, thousands of ordinary citizens took to the streets to denounce Communist Party domination and assert their desire for democracy. The major question facing the Soviet Union became the peaceful withdrawal of its troops from Eastern Europe. The haphazard nature of that withdrawal and the general poverty to which those troops returned were other factors undermining the Soviet armed forces.

The peaceful character of most of these revolutions was not inevitable. It may, in part, have resulted from the shock with which much of the world responded to the violent repression of pro-democracy protesters in Beijing's Tiananmen Square by the People's Republic of China in May 1989. The Communist Party officials of Eastern Europe and the Soviet Union clearly decided in 1989 that they could not

offend world opinion with a similar attack on democratic demonstrators.

29.7.3 The Collapse of the Soviet Union

Gorbachev clearly believed, as his behavior toward Eastern Europe in 1989 showed, that the Soviet Union could no longer afford to support Communist governments in that region or intervene to uphold their authority while seeking to restructure its own economy. He also had concluded that the Communist Party in the Soviet Union must restructure itself and its relationship to the Soviet state and society.

29.7.3.1 RENUNCIATION OF COMMUNIST POLITICAL MONOPOLY In early 1990, Gorbachev formally proposed to the Central Committee of the Soviet Communist Party that the party abandon its monopoly of power. After intense debate, the committee abandoned the Leninist position that only a single elite party could act as the vanguard of the revolution and forge a new Soviet society.

29.7.3.2 NEW POLITICAL FORCES Gorbachev confronted challenges from three major political forces by 1990. One consisted of those groups—considered conservative in the Soviet context—whose members wanted to preserve

A Closer Look

Collapse of the Berlin Wall

NO SINGLE STRUCTURE illustrated the divisions of the Cold War as the Berlin Wall, which was erected in 1961 and where armed East German and Soviet guards had, for more than a quarter-century, prevented crossings except at a few heavily guarded checkpoints. The most symbolic moment in the collapse of Communism across Eastern Europe came in November 1989 when that wall was breached.

The sight of hundreds of Germans standing on top of the wall would have been unthinkable just days before.

English graffiti ensured that an international television audience, which was largely English-speaking, would understand the aspirations of those people who wanted the wall to come down.

The overwhelmingly youthful crowd indicates the repudiation of the Cold War divisions by the new generation of Germans and Europeans

THE WALL NO MORE

SOURCE: Régis BOSSU/Sygma/Getty Images

Questions

1. How did the vast numbers of photographs of this event, as well as amateur movies and videos, show that the dispersal of information could no longer be controlled by governments?
2. In June 1989, the Chinese government had violently suppressed a large rally in Tiananmen Square in Beijing. How does this picture from Berlin about six months later illustrate the decision of the Soviet and East German governments to react differently to popular opposition?
3. What does this picture both reveal and fail to reveal about the motives of East Germans who crossed the Berlin Wall in November 1989?

Map 29–8 THE BORDERS OF GERMANY IN THE TWENTIETH CENTURY

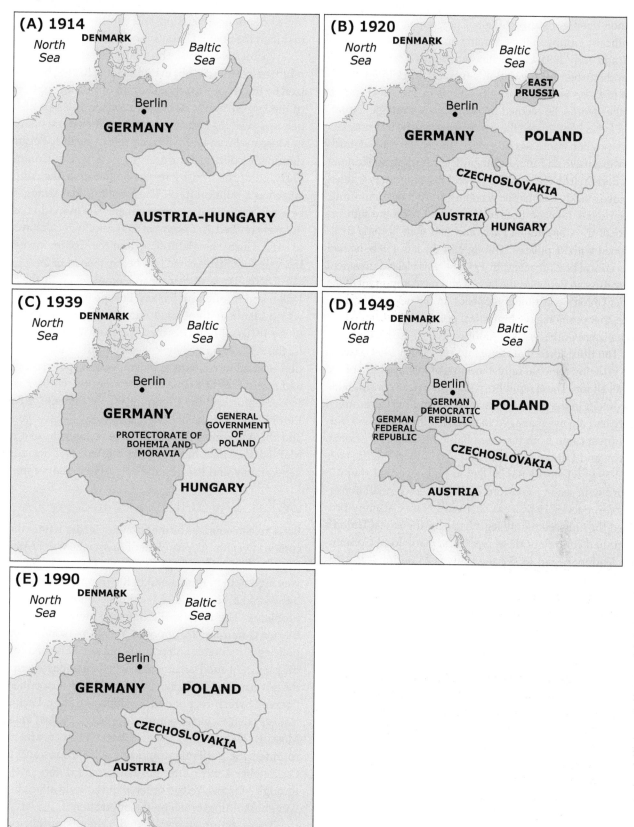

(A) The borders of imperial Germany at the outbreak of World War I. (B) German borders after the Versailles peace settlement. (C) German borders after Hitler's invasion of the Rhineland, the Anschluss with Austria, the Munich Pact, the invasion of Czechoslovakia, and the invasion of Poland. (D) Division of Germany into the German Federal Republic (West Germany) and the German Democratic Republic (East Germany) in the aftermath of World War II. (E) German borders after reunification in 1990.

the influence of the Communist Party and the Soviet army. The country's economic stagnation and political and social turmoil deeply disturbed them. They appeared to control significant groups in the economy and society. During late 1990 and early 1991, Gorbachev, who himself seems to have been disturbed by the nation's turmoil, appointed members of these factions to key positions in the government. In other words, he seemed to be making a strategic retreat.

Gorbachev initiated these moves because he was now facing opposition from a second group—those who wanted much more extensive and rapid change. Their leading spokesman was Boris Yeltsin (1931–2007). He and his supporters wanted to move quickly to a market economy and a more democratic government. Like Gorbachev, Yeltsin had risen through the ranks of the Communist Party and had then become disillusioned with its policies. Throughout the late 1980s, he had been critical of Gorbachev. In 1990, he was elected president of the Russian Republic, the largest and most important of the Soviet Union's constituent republics. In the new political climate, that position gave him a firm political base from which to challenge Gorbachev's authority and increase his own.

The third force that came into play from 1989 onward was growing regional unrest in some of the republics of the Soviet Union. These republics had experienced considerable discontent in the past, but the military and the Communist Party had always managed to repress it. Initially, the greatest unrest came from the three Baltic republics of Estonia, Latvia, and Lithuania, which had been independent states until 1940 when the Soviet Union had occupied them in accord with secret provisions of the Soviet–German nonaggression pact of 1939. That pact with Nazi Germany provided the only seemingly legal basis for the Soviet Union's continued control. In these republics, many local Communist leaders began to see themselves as national leaders rather than as party stalwarts.

During 1989 and 1990, the parliaments of the Baltic republics tried to decrease Soviet control, and Lithuania actually declared independence. Gorbachev used military force to resist these moves. Discontent also arose in the Soviet Islamic republics in Central Asia and the Caucasus. Riots broke out in Azerbaijan and Tajikistan, where the army was used as a police force against Soviet citizens. Throughout 1990 and 1991, Gorbachev sought to negotiate new constitutional arrangements between the republics and the central government. His failure to effect such arrangements may have been the single most important reason for the rapid collapse of the Soviet Union.

29.7.3.3 THE AUGUST 1991 COUP The turning point came in August 1991, when the conservative forces that Gorbachev had brought into the government attempted a coup. Troops occupied Moscow, and Gorbachev was placed under house arrest while on vacation in Crimea. The forces of political and economic reaction—led by people who at the time were associated with Gorbachev—had at last

tried to seize control. On the day of the coup, Boris Yeltsin climbed on a tank in front of the Russian Parliament building to denounce the coup and ask the world for help to maintain the Soviet Union's movement toward democracy.

Within two days, the coup collapsed. Gorbachev returned to Moscow, but in humiliation, having been victimized by the groups to whom he had turned for support. One of the largest public demonstrations in Russian history—perhaps even the largest—celebrated the failure of the coup in Moscow. From that point on, Yeltsin steadily became the dominant political figure in the nation. The Communist Party, compromised by its participation in the coup, collapsed as a political force. The constitutional arrangements between the central government and the individual republics were revised. In December 1991, the Soviet Union ceased to exist, Gorbachev left office, and the Commonwealth of Independent States came into being. (See Map 29–9.)

The collapse of European Communism in the Soviet Union and throughout Eastern Europe has ended the era in which Marxism dominated European socialism that began in the 1870s with the German Socialists' adoption of Marxist thought. The Bolshevik victory in the Russian Revolution seemed to validate Marxism, and the policies of Lenin and Stalin sought to extend it around the world. Now the Soviet Union and the Communist governments of Eastern Europe—heirs to the Bolshevik Revolution—have vanished, and the economies they built have collapsed. As a result, Marxist socialism has been discredited, and Socialism in general may find itself on the defensive in the future.

29.7.4 The Yeltsin Decade

Boris Yeltsin emerged as the strongest leader within the new commonwealth. As president of Russia, he was head of the largest and most powerful of the new states. His popularity was high both in Russia and in the commonwealth in 1992, but within a year, he faced serious economic and political problems. The Russian Parliament, most of whom were former Communists, opposed Yeltsin personally and his policies of economic and political reform. Relations between the president and Parliament reached an impasse, crippling the government. In September 1993, Yeltsin suspended Parliament, which responded by deposing him. Parliament leaders tried to incite popular uprisings against Yeltsin in Moscow. The military, however, backed Yeltsin, and he surrounded the Parliament building with troops and tanks. On October 4, 1993, after pro-Parliament rioters rampaged through Moscow, Yeltsin ordered the tanks to attack the Parliament building, crushing the opposition.

These actions consolidated Yeltsin's authority. The major Western powers, deeply concerned by the turmoil in Russia, supported him. In December 1993, Russians voted for a new Parliament and approved a new constitution. By 1994, the central government found itself at war in the Islamic province of Chechnya in the Caucasus. Under

Map 29-9 THE COMMONWEALTH OF INDEPENDENT STATES

In December 1991, the Soviet Union broke up into its fifteen constituent republics. Eleven of these were loosely joined in the Commonwealth of Independent States. Also shown is the autonomous region of Chechnya, which has waged two bloody wars with Russia in the last decade. Because the borders of Soviet republics were drawn not so much as to promote stability but instability among the many ethnic groups of the Soviet Union, long-simmering disputes flared up once the empire collapsed. The many conflicts Georgia has faced since it regained its independence in 1991 are representative: It fought unsuccessful wars in the early 1990s to keep the break-away regions of Abkhazia and South Ossetia, both of whose populations were heavily non-Georgian, under its control. In August 2008, when Georgia attempted to reassert its sovereignty over South Ossetia after Russian provocation, it was quickly repulsed by a massive invasion from Russia that resulted in hundreds of fatalities and billions of dollars of damage.

Yeltsin, Russian forces held off a rebel victory, but the war reached no clear conclusion.

During the mid-1990s, to dismantle the Soviet state and economy, former state-owned industries were privatized. This complicated process involved much corruption and opportunism by individuals determined to profit from the emerging economic organization. One result was the creation of a small group of enormously wealthy individuals, whom the press dubbed "the oligarchs." While these people amassed great wealth, the general Russian economy remained stagnant. In 1998, Russia defaulted on its international debt payments. Political assassinations occurred and have continued to the present time. The economic downturn contributed to further political unrest. In the face of these problems and in declining health, Yeltsin resigned the presidency in a dramatic gesture just as the new century began. His handpicked successor was Vladimir Putin (b. 1952), a relatively unknown figure at the time. Putin would lead the Russian Federation in new economic and political directions. Before considering Putin's role, it is necessary to examine the events that occurred during the 1990s in southeastern Europe.

29.8 The Collapse of Yugoslavia and Civil War

How did ethnic tensions lead to civil war in Yugoslavia?

Yugoslavia was created after World War I. Its borders included seven major national groups—Serbs, Croats, Slovenes, Montenegrins, Macedonians, Bosnians, and Albanians—among whom there have been ethnic disputes for centuries. The Croats and Slovenes are Roman Catholic and use the Latin alphabet. The Serbs, Montenegrins, and Macedonians are Eastern Orthodox and use the Cyrillic alphabet. The Bosnians and Albanians are mostly Muslims. Most members of each group reside in a region with which they are associated historically—Serbia, Croatia, Slovenia, Montenegro, Macedonia, Bosnia-Herzegovina, and Kosovo—and these regions constituted individual republics or autonomous areas within Yugoslavia. Many Serbs, however, lived outside Serbia proper.

Tito (1892–1980) had acted independently of Stalin in the late 1940s and pursued his own foreign policy. To mute ethnic differences, he encouraged a cult of personality around himself and instituted complex political power-sharing among these different groups. After his death, economic difficulties undermined the authority of the central government, and Yugoslavia gradually dissolved into civil war.

In the late 1980s, the old ethnic differences came to the foreground again in Yugoslav politics. Nationalist leaders—most notably Slobodan Milosevic (b. 1941–2006) in Serbia and Franjo Tudjman (b. 1922) in Croatia—gained authority. During the summer of 1990, in the wake of the changes in the former Soviet bloc nations, Slovenia and Croatia declared independence from the central Yugoslav government, and several European nations, including most importantly, Germany, immediately granted them recognition. The full European community soon did likewise.

From this point on, violence escalated. Serbia—concerned about Serbs living in Croatia and about the loss of lands and resources there—was determined to maintain a unitary Yugoslav state that it would dominate. Croatia was equally determined to secure independence. By June 1991, full-fledged war had erupted between the two republics. Serbia accused Croatia of reviving Fascism; Croatia accused Serbia of maintaining a Stalinist regime. At its core, however, the conflict was ethnic; as such, it highlights the potential for violent ethnic conflict within the former Soviet Union.

The conflict took a new turn in 1992 when Croatian and Serbian forces determined to divide Bosnia-Herzegovina. The Muslims in Bosnia—who had lived alongside Serbs and Croats for generations—soon were crushed between the opposing forces. The Serbs in particular, pursuing a policy called "ethnic cleansing," a euphemism redolent of some of the worst horrors of World War II, killed or forcibly removed many Bosnian Muslims.

More than any other single event, the unremitting bombardment of Sarajevo, the capital of Bosnia-Herzegovina, brought the violence of the Yugoslav civil war to the world's attention. The United Nations attempted unsuccessfully to mediate the conflict and imposed sanctions that had little effect. Early in 1994, however, a shell exploded in the marketplace in Sarajevo, killing dozens of people. Thereafter, NATO forced the Serbs to withdraw their artillery from around Sarajevo.

The events of the civil war came to a head in 1995 when NATO forces carried out strategic air strikes. Later that year, under the leadership of the United States, the leaders of the warring forces negotiated a peace agreement in Dayton, Ohio. The agreement was of great complexity but recognized an independent Bosnia. NATO troops, including those from the United States, have enforced the terms of the agreement.

Toward the end of the 1990s, Serbian aggression against ethnic Albanians in the province of Kosovo again drew NATO into Yugoslav affairs. For months, through television and other media, the world watched the Serbian military

DESTRUCTION OF SARAJEVO Years of siege and civil war left the city of Sarajevo in ruins. The war was fought not only on the battlefield but in the city streets as well.
SOURCE: Mark Milstein/Alamy Stock Photo

deport Albanians from Kosovo where Albanians constituted a majority of the population. The tactics closely resembled those the Serbs previously used in Bosnia. There were many casualties, atrocities, and deaths. Early in 1999, NATO again carried out an air campaign and sent troops into Kosovo to safeguard the ethnic Albanians. This air campaign was the largest military action in Europe since the close of World War II. In 2000, a revolution overthrew Slobodan Milosevic.

The disintegration of the former Yugoslavia took still another important turn in February 2008 when Kosovo, with its Albanian majority population, declared its independence from Serbia. The United States, a majority of the nations in the European Union, and all Kosovo's neighbors except Serbia have recognized the independence of Kosovo. The Russian Federation, a longtime supporter of Serbia, immediately and strongly condemned the independence of Kosovo. The issue of Kosovo's independence led to Russian military actions in the region of the Black Sea later in 2008.

KEY EVENTS IN THE BREAKUP OF YUGOSLAVIA	
June 1991	Slovenia declares independence; Croatia declares independence
September 1991	Macedonia declares independence
April 1992	War erupts in Bosnia and Herzegovina after Muslims and Croats vote for independence
April 1992	Serbia and Montenegro proclaim a new Federal Republic of Yugoslavia
November 1995	Peace agreement reached in Dayton, Ohio
March 1998	War breaks out in Kosovo, a province of Serbia
March 1999	NATO bombing of Serbia begins
February 2008	Kosovo declares independence

29.9 Putin and the Resurgence of Russia

What vision does Putin have of Russia's place in the world?

Vladimir Putin, who had become president of the Russian Federation in 2000, immediately moved to establish his position as a national and nationalistic leader of the federation. He vigorously renewed the war against the rebels in Chechnya, which resulted in heavy casualties and enormous destruction there, but also strengthened Putin's political support in Russia itself. By the middle of the decade, however, Russian forces had clearly established the upper hand over the Chechen rebels, and the drive toward independence was firmly checked at a very high cost in lives on both sides.

In the wake of the Chechen war and as part of his determination to have the central government dominate Russia's economy and political life, Putin has sought to diminish local autonomy and centralize power in his own hands.

The central government has also moved against leading oligarchs and other businessmen, with some being imprisoned. Putin used the attacks on these enormously wealthy and economically powerful figures to generate support from the broad Russian public who regard the oligarchs as thieves and one of the causes of the economic hardship of the 1990s. Putin also imprisoned political critics and opponents as well as moved against independent newspapers and television stations.

During Putin's presidency the Russian economy genuinely began to improve. Foreign debts were paid. The Russian ruble came to be regarded as a serious currency. Many more consumer goods were available. Much of this relative prosperity was the result of the oil resources available to the Russian Federation and the rising price of oil on the world market. Under Putin a clear trade-off occurred between political freedom and economic and political stability. In 2008 Putin left the elected presidency at the end of his second four-year term, turning the office over to his handpicked successor Dmitri Medvedev (b. 1965). At the same time, however, Putin assumed the office of prime minister and clearly remained the chief political figure in the country.

Putin both as president and prime minister has been determined to use the nation's economic recovery and new wealth to allow Russia to reassert its position as a major power on both the regional and world scene. After the terrorist attacks on the United States in September 2001, Putin supported the American assault on Afghanistan, largely because the Russian government was afraid that Islamic extremism would spread beyond Chechnya to other regions in Russia and to the largely Muslim nations that bordered Russia in Central Asia and the Caucasus. This period of cooperation proved short-lived. Putin became one of the leading voices against the American-led invasion of Iraq and has continued to criticize American policy in the region. Putin has also been sharply critical of the ongoing expansion of NATO, which has embraced nations directly bordering the Russian Federation. His government continued to attempt to exert influence in various new nations that came into existence with the collapse of the former Soviet Union, such as the former Soviet republics of Ukraine and Georgia. This determination to assert Russian domination over recently independent nations once part of the former Soviet Union dramatically displayed itself in August 2008. That month troops of the Russian Federation invaded the republic of Georgia. Georgia had shortly before sent troops into South Ossetia. Russian troops first drove the Georgians out of South Ossetia and then continued into Georgia itself. South Ossetia, itself a part of the former Soviet Union, had been divided into regions dominated by Russia and Georgia. Georgia sought to assert further influence, only to be immediately and overwhelmingly blocked by Russian forces. Russia eventually withdrew after a ceasefire but had

WHAT DOES PUTIN WANT? In 2017, Vladimir Putin invited Iranian president Hassan Rouhani and Turkish president Recep Tayyip Erdogan to Sochi to discuss prospects for peace in Syria. Their three-way handshake, with Putin positioned at center as the linchpin, symbolizes his leadership in trilateral negotiations.
SOURCE: Mikhail Metzel/ITAR-TASS News Agency/Alamy Stock Photo

succeeded in demonstrating its power in the region and in creating potential instability in postwar Georgia.

The Russian invasion of Georgia marked a new departure in post–Soviet Russian foreign policy and a resurgence of Russian international influence following the collapse of the Soviet Union nearly twenty years earlier. During that period both the European Union and NATO had moved to increase their memberships by expanding into Eastern Europe and into regions previously dominated by or part of the former Soviet Union. Discussions had taken place about the possibility of bringing both Ukraine and Georgia into NATO. The United States had indicated support for such inclusion. Putin and other leaders of the Russian Federation had witnessed how various regions of the former Yugoslavia, most recently Kosovo in February 2008, had broken away from Serbia and established their independence. The Russia Federation feared the international recognition of Kosovo's independence might inspire potential break-away regions in the Russian Federation. It also feared encirclement by NATO member nations where the United States might locate military bases. The action taken against Georgia served to demonstrate the ability of the Russian Federation to take military action on its borders and to give warning to other nations in the region of its capacity to intervene. At the same time the absence of any effective resistance to Russian actions in Georgia from either the United States or the European Union nations raised doubts about the capacity of either to influence of either in the region of the Black Sea. Therefore, though the Russian incursion into Georgia was relatively brief, it demonstrated that European great power politics remain alive in the new Europe. It also

demonstrated Russian willingness to take advantage of American involvement in Iraq and Afghanistan to reassert its potential authority in those regions it has dominated since the wars of Catherine the Great in the eighteenth century.

In late 2008 another question suddenly confronted Russia. As one element in the worldwide financial crisis commodity prices dropped sharply. These included the price of oil on the world market. As a result, Putin concentrated on overcoming the results of the world economic crisis during his second premiership. He also worked to end the demographic collapse that had taken place in Russia in the decades since the Cold War. During his third term as president of the Russian Federation, Putin invaded Ukraine several times and in early 2014, he annexed Crimea. Putin's actions were considered by many foreign observers as the start of a new foreign policy to recreate the Soviet Union, but his approval rating in Russia reached its highest levels in the two years following the annexation of Crimea.

29.10 The Rise of Radical Political Islamism

What forces gave rise to radical political Islamism?

On September 11, 2001, Islamic terrorists attacked the United States, crashing hijacked civilian domestic aircraft into the Twin Towers of the World Trade Center in New York City, the Pentagon in Washington, D.C., and a Pennsylvania field with a tremendous loss of life and property. These events and those following not only transformed American foreign policy toward the Middle East but also changed European relations with the United States.

In retrospect, we can see that those attacks were the result of forces that had been affecting not only the United States but also the Western world for at least a half-century. The end of the Cold War has been succeeded by a political world in which both the United States and the nations of Europe, including the Russian Federation, are endangered by terrorist attacks from nongovernmental or non-state-based organizations. These groups are guided by ideologies in the Islamic world that have filled a political and ideological vacuum left by the end of the Cold War.

Radical Islamism is the term scholars use to describe an interpretation of Islam that became significant in the Muslim world during the decades of decolonization. It is only one—and by no means the most popular—interpretation of Islam. The roots of radical Islamism extend back to the 1930s and resistance to British rule in Egypt, but for many years, those had little impact on the politics of the Middle East.

29.10.1 Arab Nationalism

Radical Islamism arose primarily in reaction to the secular Arab nationalism that developed in countries like Egypt and Syria in the 1920s and 1930s. Arab and other Middle Eastern nationalists, like nineteenth-century modernizers in the Ottoman Empire, believed that the path to independence and strength lay in adopting the technology and imitating the political institutions of the West. Advocates of radical Islam, however, rejected Western ideas and hoped to create a society based on a rigorous interpretation of Islam and its teachings.

In the wake of World War II, many of the foremost leaders of Arab nationalism against Western direct and indirect dominance, such as Gamal Abdul Nasser of Egypt, were sympathetic to Socialism or to the Soviet Union. Because Socialism and Communism were Western ideologies, left-leaning Arab nationalism was no less Western in its orientation than were nationalists friendly to the United States. Moreover, Soviet Communism was overtly atheistic and doubly offensive to devout Arab Muslims.

Nationalism forged by nondemocratic Middle Eastern governments, usually traditional monarchies or authoritarian regimes dominated by the military, had different results in the various Arab nations. Oil made Saudi Arabia wealthy and powerful and the small Gulf states, such as Kuwait, rich but not powerful. Other states, such as Jordan, Syria, and Egypt, which lacked oil, remained burdened by large impoverished populations.

Arab governments defining themselves according to nationalistic values worked out arrangements with local Muslim authorities. For example, the Saudi royal family turned over its educational system to adherents of a rigorist, puritanical form of Islam called *Wahhabism* while modernizing the country's infrastructure. The Egyptian government attempted to play different Islamic groups off against one another. These governments supported prosperous, devout middle-class Muslims while doing little about the plight of the poor. In general, Muslim religious leaders were hostile to the Soviet Union and its influence in the Islamic world.

29.10.2 The Iranian Revolution

The Iranian Revolution of 1979 transformed the Middle East. The Ayatollah Ruhollah Khomeini (1902–1989) united both the middle and lower classes of a major Middle Eastern nation to overthrow a repressive but a modernizing government that had long cooperated with the United States. For the first time, a religiously dominated government defining its mission in distinctly Islamic, as well as nationalistic, terms took control of a major state. Iran's revolutionary government was a theocracy, that is, there was no separation of religion and government or, in European terms, of church and state. The Iranian constitution gave the clergy, acting on behalf of God, the final say in all matters.

By challenging the Westernization of Iranian society, the Iranian Revolution shocked the world. It also challenged the largely secular presuppositions of Arab nationalists in states such as Egypt, Saudi Arabia, and Algeria that had failed to satisfy the needs of their own underclasses. In the mid-twentieth century, Arabs and other Middle Eastern peoples had turned to nationalism in reaction against European colonial powers. Those who grew up under nationalist leadership and still were economically disadvantaged, however, reacted against nationalism. The Iranian Revolution, which many thought would spread throughout the Islamic world, attracted them.

The Iranian Revolution both embodied and emboldened what is commonly called Islamic *fundamentalism*, but it is more correctly termed Islamic or Muslim *reformism*, the belief that a reformed or pure Islam must be established in the contemporary world. Most adherents of this point of view would emphasize personal piety and religious practice. However, a minority wish to see their states strictly governed, as way Iran purports to be, by Islamic law or the *Shari'a*. In fact, the Iranian clergy made numerous compromises to the practical demands of everyday government and the oil industry, but their public message was that Iran is a strict Islamic state hostile to the West in general and the United States—"the Great Satan"—in particular. The Iranian Revolution also opposed the state of Israel on both religious and nationalistic grounds.

The conservative Arab governments feared the Iranian Revolution would challenge their legitimacy. They consequently began to pay much more attention to their own religious authorities and cracked down on radical reformist or fundamentalist Muslims. In Egypt, such actions followed the assassination in 1981 of President Anwar Sadat (b. 1918) by a member of the Muslim Brotherhood.

29.10.3 Afghanistan and Radical Islamism

The Russian invasion of Afghanistan of 1979 introduced a major new component into this already complicated picture, illustrating the convergence of Cold War and Islamist politics. The Soviet Union sought to impose a Communist, and hence both Western and atheist, government in Afghanistan. Muslim religious authorities declared *jihad*, literally meaning "a struggle" but commonly interpreted as a religious war, against the Soviet Union. The Afghan resistance to the Soviets thus became simultaneously nationalistic, universalistic, and religious.

Thousands of Muslims, mostly fundamentalist in outlook, arrived in Afghanistan from across the Islamic world to oust the Soviets and their Afghan puppets. Conservative Arab states and the United States supported this effort, which succeeded when all Soviet forces withdrew in 1989. The conservative Arab states saw the Afghan war as an opportunity both to resist Soviet influence and to divert the energies of their own religious extremists. The United States saw the Afghan war as another round in the Cold War. The militant Muslim fundamentalists saw it as a religious struggle against an impious Western power.

29.10.3.1 THE TALIBAN AND AL-QAEDA The Soviet withdrawal created a power vacuum in Afghanistan that lasted almost a decade. By 1998, however, rigorist Muslims known as the *Taliban* had seized control of the country. They imposed their own version of Islamic law, which involved strict regimentation of women and public executions, floggings, and mutilations for criminal, religious, and moral offenses. The Taliban also allowed groups of Muslim terrorists known as *Al-Qaeda*, which means "Base," to establish training camps in their country. The terrorists who attacked the United States on September 11, 2001 came from these camps.

The ideology of these groups had emerged over several decades from different regions of the Islamic world but had been inculcated in Pakistan. The Pakistani government had long assigned considerable control over education to Islamic schools, or *madrasas,* that taught reformed Islam, rejection of liberal and nationalist secular values, intolerance toward non-Muslims, repudiation of Western culture, hostility to Israel, and hatred of the United States.

29.10.3.2 JIHAD AGAINST THE UNITED STATES Once the jihad against the Soviet Union had succeeded, radical Muslims, largely educated in these Pakistani schools, turned their attention to the United States, the other great Western power. The event that brought about this redirection was the Persian Gulf War of 1991. The occasion for that conflict was the invasion of Kuwait by Iraq, under Saddam Hussein (1937–2006). The conservative Arab governments, most importantly Saudi Arabia, not only supported the United States but also permitted it to construct military bases on their territory. Islamic extremists who had fought in Afghanistan, one of whom was Osama bin Laden (b. 1957), saw the establishment of U.S. bases in Saudi Arabia, which was the home of the prophet Muhammad and contains Islam's two holiest cities, Mecca and Medina, as a new invasion by Western Crusaders. The bases added a new grievance to the already long list of radical Muslim complaints against the United States.

The United States became a target because of its secular public morality, its international wealth and power, its military strength, its ongoing support for Israel, and its adherence to the UN sanctions imposed on Iraq after the Gulf War. Certain Muslim religious authorities declared a jihad against the United States, thus transforming opposition to American policies and culture into a religious war. Through the 1990s, terrorist attacks were directed against targets in or associated with the United States. These included bombings of the World Trade Center in New York City in 1993, of a U.S. army barracks in Saudi Arabia in 1996, of U.S. embassies in East Africa in 1998, and of the USS *Cole* in the Yemeni port of Aden in 2000. These attacks resulted in a considerable loss of life.

29.11 A Transformed West

How did the events of September 11, 2001, transform the West?

The attacks on the United States on September 11, 2001, transformed and redirected American foreign policy into what the administration of President George W. Bush (b. 1946) termed "a war on terrorism." In late 2001, the United States attacked the Taliban government of Afghanistan, rapidly overthrowing it. The defeat of the Taliban destroyed Al-Qaeda's Afghan bases but not its leadership, which survived, although it was dispersed and remained in hiding. By 2008 there was evidence that the Taliban had regrouped and again become active.

Following the Afghan campaign, the Bush administration enforced a policy of preemptive strikes and intervention against potential enemies of the United States. The administration argued that the weapons of mass destruction developed by governments such as that of Iraq falling into the hands of international terrorist organizations posed so severe a danger to U.S. security that the nation could not wait to respond to an attack but must take preemptive action. This argument, which aroused controversy both at home and abroad, marked a major departure from previous U. S. foreign policy. It is a direct result of the attacks on the United States that occurred on September 11.

In 2002, the Bush administration turned its attention to Saddam Hussein's government in Iraq. Since the defeat of Iraq in 1991 by an international coalition led by the United States, Saddam Hussein, contrary to widespread expectations, had remained in power and had continued to oppress his people. Throughout the 1990s, the Iraqi government had also resisted United Nations inspectors charged with discovering and destroying weapons of mass destruction found in Iraq or facilities capable of manufacturing such weapons. The Iraqis eventually expelled the United Nations inspectors in 1998, and the United Nations was unable to reinsert them for almost five years.

The U.S. government adopted a policy of regime change in Iraq during the last years of the Clinton administration (1993–2001), although it did little to carry out that policy. In the wake of the September 11, 2001, attacks, however, the Bush administration determined to overthrow Saddam Hussein and remove any threat from supposed Iraqi weapons of mass destruction. In late 2002 and early 2003, the United States and British governments sought to obtain passage of United Nations Security Council resolutions that would require Iraq to disarm on its own or to be disarmed by military force. These efforts failed. France and Russia threatened to veto the measure, and a majority of the Security Council voted against it. Nonetheless, the United States and Great Britain, backed by token forces or other support from over thirty other nations, invaded Iraq in late March 2003. After three weeks of fighting, the Iraqi army and with it the government of Saddam Hussein collapsed. The goals of the invasion, in addition to toppling the Iraqi regime, were to destroy Iraq's capacity to manufacture or deploy weapons of mass destruction and to bring consensual government to the Iraqi people. The latter goal has remained elusive as Iraq has been violently split by deadly internal political conflict.

The invasion of Iraq was undertaken in the face of considerable opposition from France, Germany, and Russia. It also provoked large antiwar demonstrations in the United States and throughout the world. Both the war and the diplomatic difficulties preceding it disrupted the long-standing Atlantic alliance. Moreover, French and German opposition to the war created strains within Europe and particularly within NATO and the European Union, as other European governments either strongly supported or opposed the United States and Britain. As a result, the war in Iraq marked a new and divisive era in relations between the United States and Europe and between the United States and the rest of the world.

Once the invasion of Iraq had been carried out and the occupation commenced, Al-Qaeda terrorists struck in Europe itself. On March 11, 2004, at least 190 people were killed in train bombings in Madrid, Spain. The terrorist attack occurred just before the Spanish election. The Spanish government, which had supported the American invasion of Iraq, unexpectedly lost the election. The new government then soon withdrew Spanish troops from Iraq. The Madrid bombings were the largest act of terrorism against civilians in Europe since World War II. The attack demonstrated that

TERROR IN LONDON Does the wave of newspaper headlines following terrorist attacks help or hinder those who would use violence to incite fear?
SOURCE: World History Archive/Alamy Stock Photo

terrorist attacks could directly influence European political processes.

The Iraq war and the bloody insurgency that followed generated enormous controversy. The coalition forces found no weapons of mass destruction in Iraq. Government commissions in the United States and Britain have criticized the intelligence information used to justify the invasion. In 2004, however, President Bush was reelected. In March 2005, thousands of Iraqis braved threats to vote in the first meaningful election held in Iraq since the 1950s; later in October 2005 they would vote to ratify a new constitution. In 2006 Saddam Hussein was tried and executed for crimes against humanity. Meanwhile in May 2005, the British government of Prime Minister Tony Blair was also reelected, though with a much reduced parliamentary majority. However, on July 7, 2005, terrorist bombings struck the London bus and subway system with a considerable loss of life. Once more, as in Spain, terrorism struck a major European city. The British government, unlike the Spanish, continued to retain its armed forces in Iraq.

The Iraq war, which witnessed the death of more than 4,000 American troops and thousands of Iraqis, continued to cause controversy in the United States and between the United States and its NATO allies. However, in early 2007 the Bush administration increased the number of troops committed to Iraq. The purpose of the increase in troops, called "the surge" in the press, was to bring about greater internal stability in the country and particularly in Baghdad. Over the months the level of violence did subside. By 2008 the United States under the Bush administration and the Iraq government were negotiating the future status of American troops in Iraq with the goal of significantly reducing their numbers in upcoming years. Somewhat surprisingly, issues of the economy more than those of Middle East dominated the 2008 U.S. presidential campaign. Early in 2009 after assuming the presidency, President Barack Obama undertook a policy to establish an orderly withdrawal of most American forces from Iraq by the late summer of 2010.

In the next year he announced that all American combat troops would be gone by the end of 2011. Critics argued that Iraq's government and society were ill-prepared to maintain themselves against the growing involvement of Iran, which seemed to be close to developing nuclear weapons. In the same year, Obama announced the deployment of an additional 30,000 U.S. troops to stabilize the worsening situation in Afghanistan. As a result, Al-Qaeda leader Osama bin Laden was killed in April 2011 by a commando raid of U.S. Navy SEALs.

In December 2014, the United States declared the end of major combat operations in Afghanistan, and NATO transferred full security responsibility to the Afghan government. But the Taliban made a resurgence in 2015. In 2017, the administration of U.S. President Donald Trump deployed an additional 5,000 marines to the Southern Helmand Province. As of May 2017, more than 13,000 foreign troops remained stationed in the country without any formal plans for withdrawal.

Terrorism has taken on new forms with the rise of a group known as the Islamic State of Iraq and Syria (ISIS), also known as the Islamic State of Iraq and the Levant (ISIL). This modern pan-Islamic group seeks to unify the Muslim world and establish a worldwide caliphate through violent action. ISIS has been especially active in Syria since establishing itself there in 2013. The group took advantage of the country's civil war, which broke out as part of the wider wave of 2011 Arab Spring protests. ISIS gained ascendency by using the chaos and societal collapse in Syria together with the Iraqi Civil War, thus creating a wider regional conflict. The spillover of the war in Syria has become known as the Arab Winter to express the loss of hope that the original protests, which took place in North Africa and the Middle East, might lead to more positive social and political change. Thus far, of all the countries that have experienced Arab revolutions, only Tunisia has witnessed the transition from an autocracy to a constitutional democracy.

The Chapter in Perspective

In 1900, the major European nations dominated the world. Their wealth in terms of manufacturing, investment banking, and consumer demand profoundly influenced the lives of millions of people on every continent. Their military power, particularly their navies, and their colonial administrators controlled most of Africa and much of Asia. Many Europeans were emigrating, especially to the Americas. Wherever Europeans traveled or governed, people on other continents would look to Europe as a model for industrial development, accumulation of wealth, and high culture in the arts and sciences. It was the apex of the European era that began at the close of the fifteenth century. In 1900, almost no one could have predicted the enormous human tragedies that would occur in Europe during the next half-century or the retreat from world dominance that would mark the European experience during the rest of the twentieth century.

World War II resulted in the political collapse of Europe. In the wake of the war, the United States and the Soviet Union emerged as two superpowers, both equipped with nuclear weapons. From that time until the collapse of the Soviet Union in 1991, the U.S.–Soviet rivalry dominated world affairs. Local flash points became regions for rivalry and conflict between the two nuclear powers.

While the Cold War profoundly influenced international relations, the process of decolonization spread around the globe. One nation after another in Africa and Asia became free of direct European colonial rule. Scores of new nations emerged. Both the Soviet Union and the United States frequently filled the political, economic, and military vacuum left by the departure of the European colonial rulers. This situation led each nation into major military interventions—the United States in Vietnam and the Soviet Union in Afghanistan—that had significant domestic consequences in each nation.

By the middle of the 1980s, the economy and political structures of the Soviet Union could no longer bear the burden of the Cold War. The effort to reform Soviet structures Mikhail Gorbachev began concluded with the surrender of political monopoly by the Soviet Communist Party. Simultaneously the Soviet Union retreated from Eastern Europe, and the states that the Soviet-controlled Communist Party formerly dominated achieved independence. By 1991, the Soviet Union had collapsed internally. The loosely structured Confederation of Independent States replaced it. Many former Soviet republics became completely independent states, some of which were hostile to Russia.

Since the collapse of the Soviet Union, the United States has remained the single superpower. Just after the turn of the new century, the United States suffered a major and unprecedented terrorist attack on its soil. Thereafter, the United States responded with unprecedented intervention in the Middle East. The political structures of that region were the result of the decisions the Western powers took after World War I at the Versailles peace conference in 1919. In that regard, the conflict between the United States and many Middle East groups, most prominently radical political Islamists, represents one more chapter in the long, unfolding twentieth-century story of the global interaction between regions of the world one dominated by European power and the West. The ongoing ramifications of decolonization have continued in the wake of the end of the Cold War.

The Chapter in Review

Review Questions

1. How did the United States and the Soviet Union come to dominate Europe after 1945? How would you define the policy of containment? In what areas of the world did the United States specifically try to contain Soviet power from 1945 to 1982? Why were 1956 and 1962 crucial years in the Cold War?

2. How did Khrushchev's policies and reforms change the Soviet state after the repression of Stalin? Why did many people consider Khrushchev reckless?

3. How did Gandhi lead India toward independence? How did French decolonization policies differ from Britain's? How did the United States become involved in Vietnam?

4. What internal political pressures did the Soviet Union experience in the 1970s and early 1980s? What steps did the Soviet government take to repress those protests? What role did Gorbachev's attempted reforms play in the collapse of the Soviet Union? What were the major events in Eastern Europe— particularly Poland—that contributed to the collapse of Communism? What are the major domestic challenges for the new Confederation of Independent States?

5. Was the former Yugoslavia a national state? Why did it break apart and slide into civil war? How did the West respond to this crisis?

6. What were the major difficulties that the Russian Federation faced in the 1990s and beyond? How did the policies of Yeltsin and Putin address them? How has Putin attempted to preside over a resurgence of Russian great power influence? How do his goals in part reflect concern over the example of the political disintegration of Yugoslavia?

7. How did the American response to the attacks of September 11, 2001 divide the NATO alliance? Why do some European nations feel able to dissent from the U.S. position in the Middle East when they rarely did so during the Cold War?

8. What were the major causes for the rise of radical political Islamism? In what ways is the present U.S. intervention in the Middle East a result of decolonization, and in what ways are other factors at work?

Key Terms

Balfour Declaration   Declared by Arthur Balfour, the British foreign secretary, in 1917; stated that Britain wanted to create a national home for the Jewish people in Palestine.

Brezhnev Doctrine   Statement by Soviet party chairman Brezhnev in 1968 that declared the right of the Soviet Union to interfere in the domestic policies of other Communist countries.

Cold War   The ideological and geographical struggle between the United States and its allies and the USSR and its allies that began after World War II and lasted until the dissolution of the USSR in 1989.

containment   The U.S. policy during the Cold War of resisting Soviet expansion and influence in the expectation that the USSR would eventually collapse.

Cuban missile crisis   Crisis in 1962 in which the United States, under President Kennedy, blocked Cuba after the Soviet Union placed nuclear missiles on the island in secret.

decolonization   The process of European retreat of colonial empires following World War II.

détente   Meaning "relaxation." The easing of strained relations, especially in a political situation.

glasnost **(GLAZ-nohst)**   Meaning "openness." The policy initiated by Mikhail Gorbachev in the 1980s of permitting open criticism of the policies of the Soviet Communist Party.

"Iron Curtain"   A phrase Winston Churchill used in a speech to refer to the division of Europe between a free and democratic West and an East under totalitarian rule.

jihad   Meaning "struggle." Commonly interpreted as a religious war.

Marshall Plan   The U.S. program, named after Secretary of State George C. Marshall, of providing economic aid to Europe after World War II.

Mikhail S. Gorbachev (MEEK-hail GORE-buh-choff)   The head of the Soviet Union from 1985 to 1991 who brought about the most remarkable changes the state had witnessed since the 1920s.

Mahatma Gandhi   (1869–1948) The most famous anticolonialist leader of the twentieth century who inspired a movement of passive resistance to British rule in India.

NATO   North Atlantic Treaty Organization. An alliance of countries from North America and Europe committed to fulfilling the goals of the North Atlantic Treaty signed on April 4, 1949.

perestroika **(pare-ess-TROY-ka)**   Meaning "restructuring." The attempt in the 1980s to reform the Soviet government and economy.

radical Islamism   The term scholars use to describe an interpretation of Islam that came to have a significant impact in the Muslim world during the decades of decolonization.

"Star Wars"   The U.S. Strategic Defense Initiative proposed by the administration of Ronald Reagan and involved a high technology space based defense against nuclear attack.

Suez intervention   The failure of British and French forces in 1956 to prevent Egypt from taking national control of the Suez Canal.

Vietnamization   The policy of President Richard Nixon in 1969 to withdraw U.S. troops from Vietnam while the South Vietnamese army took over the full military effort.

Warsaw Pact   An alliance of East European Socialist states dominated by the Soviet Union.

Chapter 30
Social, Cultural, and Economic Challenges in the West through the Present

EUROPEAN UNITY? The most important accomplishment of the European Community was the launching on January 1, 1999 of the euro, a single monetary unit that replaced the national currencies of most of its member nations. In Frankfurt, Germany, shown here, people crowded around a symbol of the new currency at its debut. The world financial crisis that commenced in 2008 placed many internal pressures on Europe and its single currency. More recent developments include the UK's vote to leave the EU and popular movements in other member nations, such as Italy, for greater independence from the EU bureaucracy.
SOURCE: Bernd Kammerer/AP Images

 Contents and Focus Questions

30.8 The Challenges of European Unification
What led to Western European unification following World War II?

30.9 New American Leadership and Financial Crisis
How did the year 2008 impact the relationship between the United States and Europe, and how have recent developments affected this relationship?

The Chapter in Brief

THE COLD WAR defined the life of the West during most of the second half of the twentieth century. This conflict affected not only political developments and military alliances but also the lives of millions of Europeans and Americans. For almost a half-century, the easy travel throughout the world that many people take for granted today and that enriches the lives of thousands of American students every year was impossible. Vast areas were closed off. The Iron Curtain separated families. Most of Eastern Europe developed separately from Western Europe, with consequences in the quality of life; approaches to the relationship between states and their citizenry; and attitudes about gender, social responsibility, the environment, and the future.

Nevertheless, European society in both Eastern and Western Europe changed remarkably after World War II, as did, of course, the United States. Western Europe enjoyed unprecedented prosperity, peace, and technological advances. During the same years, Europe also took unprecedented steps toward economic cooperation and political union.

30.1 The Twentieth-Century Movement of Peoples

How has migration changed the face of Europe?

In the twentieth century, the movement of peoples transformed European society and the character of many European communities. The most pervasive trend in this

THE FRIEDRICHSTRASSE IN THE HEART OF BERLIN Cityscapes such as the Friedrichstrasse in the heart of Berlin, where residents and tourists alike converge to shop and be entertained, reflect the fast-paced rhythm of contemporary urban life in Europe.
SOURCE: Sean Pavone/Alamy Stock Photo

movement of peoples was the continuing shift from the countryside to the cities. Today, except for Albania, at least one-third of the population of every European nation lives in large cities. In Western Europe, city dwellers are approximately 75 percent of the population.

Other forced movements of peoples by governments, however, were little discussed during the Cold War. During the twentieth century, millions of Germans, Hungarians, Poles, Ukrainians, Bulgarians, Serbs, Finns, Chechens, Armenians, Greeks, Turks, Estonians, Latvians, Lithuanians, Bosnian Muslims, and other peoples were displaced.

These forced displacements transformed parts of Europe. Stalin moved whole nationalities from one area of the Soviet Union and its satellite states to another. Millions of people were killed in the process. The Nazis first displaced the Jews and then sought to exterminate them. Throughout Eastern Europe, cities that once had large Jewish populations and a vibrant Jewish religious and cultural life lost any Jewish presence. The displacement of Germans from Eastern Europe back into Germany immediately after World War II transformed cities that had had large German populations into places almost wholly populated by self-identified Czechs, Poles, or Russians.

30.1.1 Displacement Through War

World War II created a vast refugee problem. An estimated 46 million people were displaced in central and Eastern Europe and the Soviet Union alone between 1938 and 1948. Many cities in Germany and in central and Eastern Europe had been bombed or overrun by invading armies. The Nazis had moved hundreds of thousands of foreign workers into Germany as slave laborers. Millions more were prisoners of war. Some of these people returned to their homeland willingly; others, particularly Soviet prisoners fearful of being executed by Stalin, had to be forced to go back, and many were executed. Hundreds of thousands of Baltic, Polish, and Yugoslav prisoners found asylum in Western Europe.

Changes in political borders after the war also uprooted many people. For example, Poland, Czechoslovakia, and Hungary forcibly expelled millions of ethnic Germans from their territories to Germany. This transfer of more than 12 million Germans "solved" the problem of German minorities living outside of Germany's national boundaries, one of Hitler's excuses for aggression against neighboring countries, but at tremendous cost for those involved. In another case of forced migration, hundreds of thousands of Poles were transferred from territory the Soviet Union annexed to Poland's new western territories, acquired from Germany. Other minorities, such as Ukrainians in Poland and Italians on the Yugoslav coast, were driven back into their supposed "homelands," although many had never set foot on the territory of Ukraine or Italy before. As one

historian has commented, "War, violence, and massive social dislocation turned Versailles's dream of national homogeneity into realities"[1]

30.1.2 External and Internal Migration

Between 1945 and 1960, approximately half a million Europeans left Europe each year. This was the largest outward migration since the 1920s, when around 700,000 persons had left annually. In the second half of the nineteenth century, most immigrants had been from rural areas. After World War II, they often included educated city dwellers. Immediately after the war, some governments encouraged migration because they were afraid that, as in the 1930s, their economies would not be able to provide adequate employment for all their citizens.

Decolonization in the postwar period led many European colonials to return to Europe from overseas. A dramatic example of this phenomenon was the more than one million French colonials who moved to France after the end of the Algerian war in 1962. Britons too returned to the British Isles from parts of the British Empire. The Dutch returned from Indonesia in the late 1940s; Belgians from the Congo in the 1960s; and Portuguese from Mozambique and Angola in the 1970s.

Decolonization also led non-European inhabitants of the former colonies to migrate to Europe. Great Britain, for example, received thousands of immigrants from its former colonies in the Caribbean, Africa, and the Indian subcontinent. France received many immigrants from its empire in Africa, Indochina, and the Arab world. This influx has proved to be a long-term source of social tension and conflict. In Britain, racial tensions were high during the 1980s. France faced similar difficulties, which contributed to the emergence of the National Front, an extreme right-wing group led by Jean-Marie Le Pen (b. 1928) that sought to exploit the resentment many working-class voters felt toward North African immigrants. Similar pressures have arisen in Germany, Austria, Italy, the Netherlands, Denmark, Switzerland, and elsewhere. Such tension did not result only from immigration from Africa and Asia; internal European migration—from the Balkans, Turkey, and the former Soviet Union, often of people in search of jobs—also changed the social and economic face of the Continent and led to a backlash. In recent years, internal immigration within the European Union has increased significantly. However, the growing Muslim presence in Europe has produced some of the most serious ethnic and political tensions.

30.1.3 The New Muslim Population

Well into the twentieth century the European relationship with most of the Muslim world was fraught with misinformation and misunderstanding. Muslims from the Ottoman Empire, the greatest Muslim state, rarely traveled in Europe, and few Europeans traveled in the empire. Europeans encountered Muslims mainly as subjects, in colonies such as Algeria, Egypt, the Indian subcontinent, sub-Saharan Africa, and the East Indies. In all these regions from at least the mid-nineteenth century onward, Christian missionaries often clashed with Muslim religious teachers.

At the same time, most Europeans, except for a few communities in the Balkans and the former Soviet Empire, regarded themselves and their national cultures as either Christian or secular. Indeed, until recently most Europeans paid little direct attention to Islam as a domestic matter.

That indifference began to change in the 1960s and had dissolved by the end of the twentieth century as a sizable Muslim population settled in Europe. This highly diverse immigrant community had become an issue in Europe even before the events of September 11, 2001.

The immigration of Muslims into Europe, and particularly Western Europe, arose from two chief sources: European economic growth and decolonization. As the economies of Western Europe began to recover in the quarter century after World War II, a labor shortage developed. To fill this demand, Western Europe imported laborers, many of whom came from Muslim nations. For example, Turkish "guest workers" were invited to move to West Germany—on a temporary basis, it was presumed—in the 1960s, and Britain welcomed Pakistanis. The aftermath of decolonization and the quest for a better life led Muslims from East Africa and the Indian subcontinent to settle in Great Britain. The Algerian war brought many Muslims to France. These Muslim immigrant communities shared certain social and religious characteristics. Originally, many Muslims came to Europe expecting they would eventually return to their homes, an expectation their host countries shared. Neither the immigrants nor the host nations gave much thought to assimilation. Moreover, except for Great Britain, where all immigrants from the Commonwealth may vote immediately upon settling there, European governments made it difficult for Muslim or other immigrants to take part in civic life. The Muslim communities have, therefore, generally remained unassimilated and self-contained. This segregation has provided internal community support for Muslim immigrants but has also prevented them from fully engaging with the societies in which they live. Many of their children have not learned European languages well, and Muslim women face challenges from both their own communities and the host communities when they try to become professionally or politically active outside the home.

Yet the world around these communities has changed. Many of the largely unskilled jobs that the immigrants originally filled have disappeared. Most of the Muslim immigrants to Europe, unlike many who have settled in the United States and Canada, were neither highly skilled nor professionally educated. As a result, they and their adult children who may have grown up in Europe have found it difficult to get jobs in the modern service economy. Furthermore, as European economic growth has slowed, European Muslims have become the target of politicians, such as Marine Le Pen in France, who blame the immigrants for a host of problems, from crime to unemployment.

The radicalization of parts of the Islamic world has also touched the Muslim communities in Europe. Although Turkish Muslims living in Germany come from a nation that has been secularized since the 1920s and thus tend to be less religiously observant than Pakistani Muslims dwelling in Great Britain, Muslims from both countries have been involved in radical Islamic groups. The July 7, 2005, suicide bombings in London were carried out by four young Muslims, three of whom had been born in the United Kingdom and one in Jamaica. By contrast, the French government has exerted more control over its Muslim population. However, that policy appeared to have failed badly when in the autumn of 2005 immigrant youth, largely Muslim, carried out riots in various parts of France. These were the most serious civil disturbances in France since 1968. Subsequent riots have occurred in Paris. There have also been sharp disputes in France over attempts by the government to forbid young Muslim women from wearing headscarves while attending secular government schools. (See the "Compare and Connect" sidebar, which follows below, for a debate over France's ban of the veil and its effect on feminism, Muslims, and human rights.)

Nonetheless, European Muslims are not a homogeneous group. They come from different countries, have different class backgrounds, and espouse different Islamic traditions. Many European Muslims and Muslim clerics disagree strongly with each other. At the same time, these Muslim communities, so often now marked by deep poverty and unemployment, have become a major concern for European social workers, who disagree about how their governments should respond to them. What has become clear, however, is that European governments cannot regard their Muslim populations as passive communities; rather, European governments and societies must engage with them as a permanent fact in the life.

30.1.4 European Population Trends

During the past quarter-century, the European birthrate has stabilized in a manner that has deeply disturbed many observers. Europeans are having so few children that they are no longer replacing themselves. Whereas in the 1950s European women on average bore 2.1 children (the minimum replacement level), that rate fell to 1.9 in the 1980s, 1.47 in the early 2000s, and has rebounded slightly to 1.6 at present. In some countries, including Austria, Germany,

Compare and Connect

Muslim Women Debate France's Ban on the Veil

IN APRIL 2011, a French law banning the wearing of certain types of veils in public went into effect. The ban applied to a covering that exposed only a woman's eyes, known outside of France as a niqab, but referred to as a burqa in the French debate. The 2011 law was only one further step in an extended debate about the place of public displays of religious piety, women's rights, the role of Muslims in French public life, and France's secular tradition. In 2004, France had already banned the wearing of veils in public schools. In June 2009, French president Nicolas Sarkozy explained his support of a more thorough ban: "We cannot accept to have in our country women who are prisoners behind netting, cut off from all social life, deprived of identity. . . . That is not the idea that the French republic has of women's dignity. The burqa is not a sign of religion, it is a sign of subservience. It will not be welcome on the territory of the French republic." In the months preceding and following the ban, France's public conversations about the veil, as in the two passages below, revealed a complex subject that involves feminists, Muslims, and advocates of minority rights in France, with representatives of each group often on both sides of the debate.

VEILED IN PUBLIC Kenza Drider, a French housewife from the town of Avignon, appears in public in a niqab, a face covering that reveals only her eyes, despite a 2011 ban on such veils in France.
SOURCE: Jean-Paul Pelissier/Reuters

Before Reading

- Consider the arguments Mona Eltahawy makes against requiring Muslim women to wear the head veil.
- Examine how Kenza Drider's defense of the veil reveals the larger issues at stake concerning the role of Muslims in France.

Questions

1. How and why is the debate about the veil particularly fierce in France? What elements of French history and identity are challenged by the veil?
2. How does Eltahawy distinguish between Muslims' rights and the right to wear a veil?
3. Why might feminists be divided over the issue of the veil? In what ways are women's rights involved in this debate, and who claims to speak on behalf of women?
4. What are the reasons cited for women's wearing of the veil? Are all of them related to religious piety?
5. What larger issues about the role of Muslims in France are exposed by this debate?

I. MONA ELTAHAWY ARGUES WOMEN'S RIGHTS TRUMP CULTURAL RELATIVISM

Defenders of the French ban of the veil include some prominent Muslim women. Mona Eltahawy, an award-winning columnist born in Egypt and currently living in New York City, calls herself a "proud liberal Muslim." Her opposition to the veil is based not on fear of Islam but on her belief that representing the veil as a necessary sign of Muslim feminine piety stems from a misinterpretation of the Koran. Her commentary encompasses topics as diverse as xenophobia, cultural relativism, feminism, secularism, and a deep conflict about the nature of individual freedom.

Some have likened this issue to Switzerland's move last year to ban the construction of minarets. . . .

Underlying both bans is a dangerous silence: liberal refusal to robustly discuss what it means to be European, what it means to be Muslim, and racism and immigration. Liberals decrying the infringement of women's rights should acknowledge that the absence of debate on these critical issues allowed the political right and the Muslim right to seize the situation.

Europe's ascendant political right is unapologetically xenophobic. It caricatures the religion that I practice and uses those distortions to fan Islamophobia. But ultra-conservative strains of Islam, such as Salafism and Wahhabism, also caricature our religion and use that Islamophobia to silence opposition. . . .

The strains of Islam that promote face veils do not believe in the concept of a woman's right to choose and describe women as needing to be hidden to prove their "worth." . . . There is no choice in such conditioning. That is not a message Muslims learn in our holy book, the Koran, nor is the face veil prescribed by the majority of Muslim scholars.

The French ban has been condemned as anti-liberal and anti-feminist. Where were those howls when niqabs began appearing in European countries, where for years women fought for rights? A bizarre political correctness tied the tongues of those who would normally rally to defend women's rights.

There are several ideological conflicts here: Within Islam, liberal and feminist Muslims refuse to believe that full-length veils are mandatory. . . . Feminist groups run by Muslim women in various Western countries fight misogynistic practices justified in the name of culture and religion. Cultural relativists, they say, don't want to "offend" anyone by protesting the disappearance of women behind the veil—or worse.

For example, French women of North African and Muslim descent launched Ni Putes Ni Soumises (Neither Whores Nor Submissives) in response to violence against women in housing projects and forced marriages of immigrant women in France. That group supports the ban and has denounced the racism faced in France by immigrant women and men.

Cultural integration has failed, or not taken place, in many European countries, but women shouldn't pay the price for it.

II. KENZA DRIDER DEFENDS HER RIGHT TO WEAR THE VEIL IN PUBLIC

Kenza Drider was an ordinary French citizen before the debate about the public wearing of the veil took over French politics and society. A housewife and mother of four, Drider insists that wearing the veil is an expression of her personal freedom, not a reflection of pressure from her husband, father, or religious authority. Her husband, Allal, told a reporter that when he first saw his wife in a full-body niqab he said, "Are you really going out dressed like that?" When two women were fined for violating the French ban in September 2011, Drider announced her largely symbolic candidacy for president against then-incumbent President Sarkozy.

I will be going about my business in my full veil as I have for the last 12 years and nothing and nobody is going to stop me. . . . This whole law makes France look ridiculous. . . . I never thought I'd see the day when France, my France, the country I was born in and I love, the country of *liberté, égalité, fraternité*, would do something that so obviously violates people's freedom.

I'll be getting on with my life and if they want to send me to prison for wearing the niqab then so be it. One thing's for sure: I'm not taking it off.

[Wearing a veil] is not a religious constraint since it is not laid down in Islam or the *Qur'an* that I have to wear a full veil. It is my personal choice. . . .

I would never encourage others to do it just because I do. That is their choice. My daughters can do what they like. As I tell them, this is my choice, not theirs. . . .

I never covered my head when I was young. I came from a family of practising Muslims, but we were not expected to even wear a headscarf. Then I began looking into Islam and what it meant to be a Muslim and decided to wear a headscarf. Afterwards in my research into the wives of the Prophet I saw they wore the full veil and I liked this idea and decided to wear it. Before, I had felt something was missing. Then I put it on and I felt serene and complete. It pleased me and it has become a part of me. . . .

When President Sarkozy said: 'The burqa is not welcome in France', the president, my president, opened the door for racism, aggression and attacks on Islam. This is an attempt to stigmatise Islam and it has created enormous racism and Islamophobia that wasn't there before. . . .

This is about basic fundamental human rights and freedoms. I will go out in my full veil and I will fight. I'm prepared to go all the way to the European court of human rights and I will fight for my liberty.

Fines? They don't bother me. What is the state going to do, send a policeman outside my front door to give me a ticket every time I go out? For me this is women's liberty, the liberty to wear what I wish and not be punished for it.

If women want to walk around half-naked I don't object to them doing so. If they want to wear tight jeans where you can see their underwear or walk around with their breasts hanging out, I don't give a damn. But if they are allowed to do that, why should I not be allowed to cover up?

SOURCES: (I) From Mona Eltahawy, "From Liberals and Feminists, Unsettling Silence on Rending the Muslim Veil," *Washington Post*, Saturday, July 17, 2010. (II) From Kim Willsher, " 'Burqa ban' in France: housewife vows to face jail rather than submit," *The Observer*, Saturday, April 9, 2011.

Hungary, Italy, Portugal, and Spain, the rate is even lower. In the early twenty-first century, the U.S. fertility rate reached its lowest level in a century, 2.0, but was still substantially higher than European rates. If the current rates hold, by the middle of this century, the United States will have more people than Europe for the first time in history.

There is no consensus on why the European birthrate has declined. One reason often cited is that women are postponing having children until later in their childbearing years. Another is that the economic crises of the past decade have made multiple children an indulgence some families feel they cannot afford. This demographic shift suggests that Europe may soon need new workers from outside its borders. Nevertheless, in response to public opinion, governments have been trying to limit immigration into Europe.

This falling birthrate means that Europe faces the prospect of an aging population, with fewer workers and more retirees. This puts tremendous financial stress on those European states that have traditionally provided strong state-funded support for retired persons. Postwar European prosperity has been tied to a strong welfare system, which the new demographics may make it impossible for states to continue to afford.

30.2 Toward a Welfare State Society

What effect did the Great Depression and World War II have on the way Europeans viewed the role of government in social and economic life?

In the second half of the twentieth century, the nations of Western Europe achieved unprecedented economic prosperity and maintained or inaugurated independent, liberal democratic governments. Most of them also confronted problems associated with decolonization and with maintaining economic growth.

The end of World War II led to vast constitutional changes in much of Western Europe, except for Portugal and Spain, which remained dictatorships until the mid-1970s. Before or during the war, Germany, Austria, Italy, and France had experienced authoritarian governments. The construction of stable, liberal, democratic political frameworks became a major goal of their postwar political leaders, as well as of the United States. All concerned recognized that the earlier political structures in those nations had failed to resist the rise of right-wing, antidemocratic movements. The Great Depression had shown that democracy requires a social and economic base, as well as a political structure. Most Europeans came to believe that government ought to ensure economic prosperity and social security. Success at

doing so, they hoped, would stave off the kind of turmoil that had brought on tyranny and war.

30.2.1 Christian Democratic Parties

Democratic Socialist parties faced challenges in the postwar era, in which they were opposed by both conservatives and Communists. Some were successful, including the British Labour Party, and Social Democratic parties in Germany, Austria, and Scandinavia. On the Continent, Social Democratic parties often shared power with various Christian democratic parties. Those Christian democratic parties, usually leading coalition governments, often introduced new policies that were also supported by Social Democrats.

Christian democratic parties were a major new feature of postwar politics. They were largely Roman Catholic in leadership and membership. Catholic parties had existed in Europe since the late nineteenth century. Until the 1930s, however, they had been conservative and had protected the social, political, and educational interests of the church. The postwar Christian democratic parties of Germany, France, Austria, and Italy, however, welcomed non-Catholic members. Democracy, economic growth, and anti-Communism were their hallmarks. After 1947, in a policy that responded to United States pressure as well as internal conviction, Communists were systematically excluded from Western European governments.

30.2.2 The Creation of Welfare States

The Great Depression, the rise of authoritarian states in the wake of economic dislocation and mass unemployment, and World War II, which involved more people in a war effort than ever before, changed how many Europeans thought about social welfare. Governments began to spend more on social welfare than they did on the military. This reallocation of funds was a reaction to the state violence of the first half-century.

The modern European welfare state was broadly similar across the Continent. Before World War II, except in Scandinavia, the two basic models for social legislation were the German and the British. Otto von Bismarck had introduced social insurance in Germany during the 1880s to undermine the German Social Democratic Party. In effect, the imperial German government provided workers with social insurance and thus some sense of social security while denying them significant political participation. In early-twentieth-century Britain, where all classes had access to the political system, social insurance was targeted toward the poor. In both the German and British systems, workers were insured only against the risks from disease, injury on the job, and old age. Unemployment was assumed to be only a short-term problem and often one that workers brought on themselves. People higher up in the social structure could look out for themselves and did not need government help.

After World War II, the concept emerged that social insurance against predictable risks was a social right and should be available to all citizens. In Britain, William B. Beveridge (1879–1963) famously introduced this concept in 1942. Paradoxically, making coverage universal, as Beveridge recommended, appealed to conservatives as well as Socialists. If medical care, old-age pensions, and other benefits were available to all, they would not become a device to redistribute income from one part of the population to another.

The first major European nation to begin to create a welfare state was Britain, in 1945 to 1951 under the Labour Party ministry of Clement Attlee (1883–1967). The most important element of this early legislation was the creation of the **National Health Service**. France and Germany did not adopt similar health care legislation until the 1970s because their governments initially refused to make coverage universal.

The spread of welfare legislation (including unemployment insurance) within Western Europe was related to both the Cold War and domestic political and economic policy. The Communist states of Eastern Europe provided their people social security as well as full employment. The capitalist states came to believe they had to provide similar security for their people in order to disarm a potential appeal of Communism within their populations.

30.2.3 Resistance to the Expansion of the Welfare State

Western European attitudes toward the welfare state have reflected four periods that have marked economic life since the end of the war. The first period was one of reconstruction from 1945 through the early 1950s. It was followed by the second period—almost twenty-five years of generally steady and expanding economic growth. The third period brought first an era of inflation in the late 1970s and then one of relatively low growth and high unemployment from the 1990s to the early twenty-first century. We are now in the midst of a fourth period, in which financial crises have led to unstable economies and a questioning of the safety of allowing the market to self-regulate. During each of the first two periods, a general conviction existed, based on Keynesian economics, that the foundation of economic policy was government involvement in a mixed economy. From the late 1970s, more people came to believe the market should be allowed to regulate itself and that government should be less involved in, though not completely withdraw from, the economy. Most recently, the financial crises of the twenty-first century have led many Europeans to question their earlier abandonment of Keynesian economics.

The most influential political figure in reasserting the importance of markets and resisting the power of labor unions was **Margaret Thatcher** (1925–2013) of the British Conservative Party who served as prime minister from 1979 to 1990. She cut taxes and sought to curb inflation. She and her party were determined to roll back many of the Socialist policies that Britain had enacted since the war. Her administration privatized many industries that Labour Party governments had nationalized. She also curbed the power of the trade unions in a series of bitter and often violent confrontations. Although her administration roused enormous controversy, she was able to push these policies through Parliament. Furthermore, over time the British Labour Party under the leadership of Tony Blair (b. 1953) largely came to accept what was at the time known as the Thatcher Revolution.

While Thatcher redirected the British economy, the government-furnished welfare services now found across continental Europe began to encounter resistance. The funding on which they were based assumed a growing population and low unemployment. As the proportion of the population consuming welfare services—the sick, the injured, the unemployed, and the elderly— has increased relative to the number of able-bodied workers who have paid for them, the costs of those services have risen.

The leveling off of population growth in Europe has thus imperiled the benefits of the welfare state. Furthermore, during the past two decades, significant levels of unemployment in major Western European nations have increased welfare payments. The low fertility rates across the Continent mean the next working generation will have fewer people to support the retired elderly population,

MARGARET THATCHER The daughter of a shopkeeper, Margaret Thatcher graduated in chemistry at Oxford in 1943 and later became the first female prime minister of Great Britain, serving in that office from May 1979 through November 1990. Known as the "Iron Lady" of British politics, she led the Conservative Party to three electoral victories and carried out extensive restructuring of the British government and economy.
SOURCE: PA Images/Alamy Stock Photo

challenging the system that has been the hallmark of postwar European prosperity.

30.3 New Patterns in Work and Expectations of Women

How has the status of women changed in Europe since the end of World War II?

Since World War II, the work patterns and social expectations of European women have changed enormously. In all social ranks, women have begun to assume larger economic and political roles. More women have entered the "learned professions," and more are filling major managerial positions than ever before in European history. Yet despite enormous gains during the second half of the twentieth century, and despite the collapse of authoritarian governments whose social policies inhibited women from advancing, gender inequality has remained a major characteristic of the social life of Europe twenty years into the twenty-first century.

SIMONE DE BEAUVOIR Simone de Beauvoir (1908–1986) was a French writer and philosopher whose work defined existentialism. Her book *The Second Sex* (1949) is regarded as a foundational text of European feminism.

SOURCE: Pictorial Press Ltd/Alamy Stock Photo

30.3.1 Feminism

Since World War II, European feminism, although less highly organized than in America, has set forth a new agenda. The most influential postwar work on women's issues was *The Second Sex*, published in 1949 by **Simone de Beauvoir** (1908–1986). In that work, de Beauvoir explored the difference being a woman had made in her life. She and other European feminists argued that, at all levels, European women experienced distinct social and economic disadvantages. Divorce and family laws, for example, favored men. European feminists also called attention to the social problems that women faced, including spousal abuse.

In contrast to earlier feminism, recent feminism has been less a political movement pressing for specific rights than a social movement offering a broader critique of European culture. This emphasis on women controlling their lives may be the most important element of recent European feminism. Whereas in the past feminists sought and, in significant measure, gained legal and civil equality with men, they are now pursuing personal independence and issues particular to women. In this sense, feminism is an important manifestation of the critical tradition in Western culture.

30.3.2 More Married Women in the Workforce

Throughout the postwar period, the number of married women in the workforce has risen sharply. Both middle-class and working-class married women have found jobs outside the home. Because of the low birthrate in the 1930s, there were fewer young single women in Europe in the years just after World War II. Married women entered the job market to replace them. Some factories changed their work shifts to accommodate the needs of married women. Consumer conveniences and improvements in health care also made it easier for married women to enter the workforce by reducing the demands child care and housekeeping made on their time. At the same time, surveys indicate that the need to provide care for their children continues to be the most important difficulty women face in the workplace. Where child care is inadequate, unavailable, or unaffordable, women are more likely to remain in part-time employment. This contributes to income inequality for women and limited career opportunities relative to men in the same occupations and with the same qualifications.

In the twentieth century, children were no longer expected to contribute substantially to family income. They now spend more than a decade in compulsory education. Many families need more income than one worker can provide. Such financial necessity led many married women back to work. Evidence also suggests that married women began to work to escape the boredom and isolation of housework. Most often, however, working women continue to be responsible for maintaining the household and caring for children, leading to what has been called the "double burden," or work inside and outside the home.

Women in some European countries, such as Norway, have demanded that the state provide support for working mothers that will guarantee sufficient child care for them to work with the same degree of flexibility and opportunity as men with children. Advocates of enhanced child-care provisions used campaigns, protests, and rallies to pressure parliament to address the issue in the 1980s. Some Norwegians demanded equal access to child-care facilities, while others wanted state-funded home care allowances to pay for women to stay home with young children. Many feminists consider such home-care allowances a threat to gender equality in the workplace and argue that they pressure women to stay home with young children.

30.3.3 New Work Patterns

The work pattern of European women has been far more consistent in the twentieth and twenty-first century than it had been in the nineteenth. Single women enter the workforce after their schooling and continue to work after marriage. They may stop working to care for their young children, but they return to work when the children begin school. For many women, however, returning to work is combined with fewer opportunities for professional advancement, limited hours, and unequal pay for the same work done by a male counterpart.

When women died relatively young, childrearing filled a large proportion of their lives. As a longer life-span has shortened that proportion, women throughout the West are seeking ways to lead satisfying lives after their children have grown. Decisions about when to have children and how many have also shaped the late-twentieth-century work patterns for women. Many women have begun to limit the number of children they bear or to forgo childbearing and childrearing altogether. The age at which women have decided to bear children has risen, to the early twenties in Eastern Europe and to the late twenties in Western Europe. In urban areas, women have fewer children and have them later in life than rural women do.

30.3.4 Women in Eastern Europe

Under communism, women generally enjoyed social equality, as well as a broad spectrum of government-financed benefits. Most women (normally well over 50 percent) worked in these societies, both because they could and because they were expected to. No significant women's movements existed, however, because Communist governments regarded them with suspicion, as they did all independent associations.

The new governments of the region are free but have shown little concern with women's issues. Indeed, the economic difficulties the new governments face may endanger their funding of health and welfare programs that benefit women and children. For example, a free market economy may limit the extensive maternity benefits upon which Eastern European women previously depended. Moreover, the high proportion of women in the workforce could leave them more vulnerable than men to the region's economic troubles. Women may be laid off before men and hired later than men for lower pay.

30.4 Transformations in Knowledge and Culture

How was cultural and intellectual life transformed in Europe?

Culture in Europe was rapidly transformed in the twentieth century. Institutions of higher education enrolled a larger and more diverse student body, making knowledge more widely available than ever before. Also, movements such as existentialism challenged traditional intellectual attitudes. Environmental concerns also raised new issues. Throughout this ferment, representatives of the Christian faith tried to keep their religion relevant.

30.4.1 Communism and Western Europe

Until the final decade of the twentieth century, Western Europe had large, organized Communist parties, as well as groups of intellectuals sympathetic to Communism. After the Bolshevik victory in the Russian Revolution and the subsequent civil war, the Western European Socialist movement divided into independent democratic Socialist parties and Soviet-dominated Communist parties that followed the dictates of the Third International. In the 1920s and 1930s, those two groups fought one another with only rare moments of cooperation, such as that achieved during the French Popular Front in 1936.

30.4.1.1 THE INTELLECTUALS During the 1930s, as liberal democracies floundered in the face of the Great Depression and as right-wing regimes spread across the Continent, many saw Communism as a vehicle for protecting humane and even liberal values. European university students were often affiliated with the Communist Party. They and older intellectuals visited the Soviet Union and praised what they saw as Stalin's achievements. Many of these intellectuals did not know about Stalin's terror. Others simply closed

GEORGE ORWELL George Orwell (1903–1950), shown here with his son, was an English writer of Socialist sympathies who wrote major works opposing Stalin and Communist authoritarianism.
SOURCE: Felix H. Man/Art Resource, NY

their eyes to it, believing humane ends might come from inhumane methods.

Four events proved crucial to the intellectuals' disillusionment: the great Soviet public purge trials of the late 1930s, the Spanish Civil War (1936–1939), the Nazi–Soviet pact of 1939, and the Soviet invasion of Hungary in 1956. Arthur Koestler's (1905–1983) 1940 novel *Darkness at Noon* recorded a former Communist's view of the purges. **George Orwell** (1903–1950), who had never been a Communist but who had sympathized with the party, expressed his disappointment with Stalin's policy in Spain in his 1938 *Homage to Catalonia*. The Nazi–Soviet pact damaged Stalin's image as an opponent of Fascism. Other intellectuals, such as French philosopher **Jean-Paul Sartre** (1905–1980), continued to believe in the Soviet Union during and after the war, but the Hungarian Revolution cooled their ardor. The Soviet-led invasion of Czechoslovakia in 1968 led to a general disillusionment with Soviet policies by left-wing Western European intellectuals.

Yet disillusionment with the Soviet Union or with Stalin did not mean disillusionment with Marxism or with radical Socialist criticisms of European society. Some writers and social critics looked to the establishment of alternative Communist governments based on non-Soviet models. During the decade after World War II, Yugoslavia was such an example. Beginning in the late 1950s, radical students and a few intellectuals found inspiration in the Chinese Revolution. Other groups hoped a European Marxist system would develop. Non-Soviet Communists became important to Western European Communist parties, such as the Italian Communist Party, that hoped to gain office democratically.

Another way to accommodate Marxism within mid-twentieth-century European thought was to redefine the basic message of Marx himself. During the 1930s, many of Marx's previously unprinted essays were published. These books and articles, written before the *Communist Manifesto* of 1848, were abstract and philosophical. They showed how the "young Marx" belonged more to the humanist than to the revolutionary tradition of European thought. They allowed people to separate Marxism from revolutionary violence or support of the Soviet Union. With the collapse of the Communist governments of Eastern Europe and the Soviet Union, Marxism's influence on European intellectual life seemed to wane. The financial crisis of the twenty-first century has led some intellectuals to revert back to Marx's critique of capitalism, even if they do not defend his vision of a Communist alternative. Whether doubts about the functioning of the free market will lead to a resurgence in Marxism's influence remains uncertain.

30.4.2 Existentialism

The intellectual movement that perhaps best captured the predicament and mood of mid-twentieth-century European culture was **existentialism**. Like the modern Western mind in general, existentialism, which has been termed the "philosophy of Europe in the twentieth century," was badly divided; most of the philosophers associated with it disagreed with each other on major issues. The movement represented, in part, a continuation of the revolt against reason that began in the nineteenth century.

30.4.2.1 ROOTS IN NIETZSCHE AND KIERKEGAARD
Friedrich Nietzsche (1844–1900) was a major forerunner of existentialism. Another was Danish writer **Søren Kierkegaard** (1813–1855), who received little attention until after World War I. Kierkegaard maintained that the truth of Christianity could be grasped only by those who faced extreme situations, not in creeds, doctrines, and church structures.

Kierkegaard also criticized Hegelian philosophy and by implication, all academic rational philosophy. Philosophy's failure, he felt, was the attempt to contain life and human experience within abstract categories.

The intellectual and ethical crisis of World War I led many to doubt whether human beings were in control of their own destiny. Its destructiveness challenged faith in human rationality and improvement. Indeed, the war's most terrible weapons—poison gas, machine guns, submarines, high explosives—were the products of rational technology. The pride in rational human achievement that had characterized nineteenth-century European civilization lay in ruins.

30.4.2.2 QUESTIONING OF RATIONALISM

Existentialist thought thrived in this climate and received further support from the trauma of World War II. The major existential writers included the Germans Martin Heidegger (1889–1976) and Karl Jaspers (1883–1969) and the French Jean-Paul Sartre (1905–1980) and **Albert Camus** (1913–1960). Although they frequently disagreed with each other, they all questioned the primacy of reason and scientific understanding as ways to come to grips with the human situation. Heidegger, a philosopher deeply compromised by his association with the Nazis, argued, "Thinking only begins at the point where we have come to know that Reason, glorified for centuries, is the most obstinate adversary of thinking."[2]

The romantic writers of the early nineteenth century had also questioned the primacy of reason, but their criticisms were much less radical than those of the existentialists. The romantics emphasized the imagination and intuition, but the existentialists focused primarily on the extremes of human experience. Death, fear, and anxiety were their themes. The titles of their works illustrate their sense of foreboding and alienation: *Being and Time* (1927), by Heidegger; *Nausea* (1938) and *Being and Nothingness* (1943), by Sartre; *The Stranger* (1942) and *The Plague* (1947), by Camus. The touchstone of philosophic truth became the experience of the individual under extreme conditions.

According to the existentialists, human beings are compelled to formulate their own ethical values and cannot depend on traditional religion, rational philosophy, intuition, or social customs for ethical guidance. The opportunity and need to define values endow humans with a dreadful freedom. The existentialists protested against a world in which reason, technology, and politics produced war and genocide. Their thought reflected the uncertainty of social institutions and ethical values in the era of the two world wars.

30.4.3 Expansion of the University Population and Student Rebellion

As rapid changes in communications technology expanded access to information, more Europeans received some form of university education. In 1900, only a few thousand people were enrolled in universities in any major European country and only rarely were women allowed access to higher education. By 2010, that figure had risen to hundreds of thousands. Over one-third of Europeans in their thirties have had a university education, and women are more likely to attend university than men.

One of the most striking and unexpected results of this rising post–World War II population of students and intellectuals was the student rebellion of the 1960s. Student uprisings began in the early 1960s in the United States and grew with opposition to the war in Vietnam. The student rebellion then spread into Europe and other parts of the world. It was almost always associated with a radical political critique of the United States, although Eastern European students resented the Soviet Union even more. The movement was generally antimilitarist. Students also questioned middle-class values and traditional sexual mores and family life.

The student movement peaked in 1968, when American students demonstrated forcibly against U.S. involvement in Vietnam. In the same year, students at the Sorbonne in Paris almost brought down the government of Charles de Gaulle, and in Czechoslovakia, students were in the forefront of the liberal Socialist experiment.

By the early 1970s, the era of student rebellion seemed to have passed. Students remained active in European movements against nuclear weapons and particularly against the placement of American nuclear weapons in Germany and elsewhere in Europe. From the mid-1970s, however, although often remaining political radicals, students generally abandoned the disruptive protests that had marked the 1960s.

30.4.4 The Americanization of Europe

During the past half-century, through the Marshall Plan, the leadership of NATO, the stationing of huge military bases, student exchanges, popular culture, and tourism, the United States has exerted enormous influence on Western Europe. **Americanization** a pejorative term, refers, in part, to this economic and military influence but also to concerns about cultural loss. Many Europeans feel that American popular entertainment, companies, and business methods threaten to extinguish Europe's unique qualities. Many American firms now have European branches. Large American corporations, such as McDonald's, Starbucks, Apple, and Gap, have outlets in European cities from Dublin to Moscow. American liquor companies and distilleries now sell their goods in Europe. Casual American clothing, such as blue jeans and baseball caps, is ubiquitous in Europe. Shopping centers and supermarkets, first pioneered in America, are displacing neighborhood markets in European cities. American television programs, movies, computer games, and rock and hip-hop are readily available. Furthermore,

AN AMERICAN IN PARIS The influence of American culture is pervasive throughout Europe. Notice the familiar Starbucks signage at this entrance to Arcades des Champs Elysees in Paris.
SOURCE: Hemis/Alamy Stock Photo

as Europe moves toward greater economic cooperation, English has become the common language of business, technology, and even some academic fields—and it is American English, not British.

30.4.5 A Consumer Society

Although European economies came under pressure during the 1990s and experienced high levels of unemployment, the consumer sector has expanded to an extraordinary degree during most of the last half-century.

The consumer orientation of the Western European economy emerged as one of the most important characteristics differentiating it from Eastern Europe. Those differences produced political results. In the Soviet Union and the nations it dominated in Eastern Europe and economic planning overwhelmingly favored capital investment and military production. These nations produced inadequate and low-quality consumer goods. Long lines for staples, such as food and clothing, were common. Automobiles were a luxury. Housing did not permit the luxury of privacy, and children were often forced to live with their parents well into adulthood.

By contrast, by the early 1950s, Western Europeans enjoyed an expansion of consumer goods and services.

Automobile ownership has soared. Refrigerators, washing machines, electric ranges, televisions, microwaves, videocassette recorders, cameras, computers, CD players, DVD players, and other electronic consumer items, such as smartphones, are taken for granted. Like their American counterparts, Western Europeans now have a whole gamut of products, such as disposable diapers, prepared baby foods, and a plethora of LEGOs to help them raise children. They take foreign vacations year round, prompting the expansion of ski resorts in the Alps and beach resorts on the Mediterranean. (For more about LEGO consumerism, see the "Encountering the Past" sidebar, which follows below.)

This expansion of consumerism, which began in the eighteenth century, became a defining characteristic of Western Europe in the late twentieth century in contrast to the consumer shortages in Eastern Europe. Yet through even the limited number of radios, televisions, movies, and videos available to them, people in the East grew increasingly aware of the discrepancy between their lifestyle and that of the West. They associated Western consumerism with democratic governments, free societies, and economic policies that favored the free market. Thus, the expansion of consumerism in the West, which many intellectuals and

Encountering the Past

Toys from Europe Conquer the United States

TODAY MANY EUROPEANS criticize what they term *Americanization*—the intrusion of popular American products and restaurant chains onto the European scene. Yet over the past half-century one European toy—LEGO building blocks manufactured in Denmark—has touched lives of children in the United States and the rest of the world, capturing their imaginations no less powerfully than the cartoon figures associated with the American Disney Corporation.

LEGO POWER Children the world over love LEGOs.
SOURCE: Stephane de Sakutin/AFP/Getty Images

In 1932, in the midst of the depression, Ole Kirk Christiansen opened a small business in Billund, Denmark, that manufactured household goods and wooden toys. The toys sold so well that two years later the firm renamed itself LEGO from the Danish *LEg GOdt*, meaning "play well." The company remained small, producing only wooden toys, until 1947 when it began to make molded plastic toys. It only sold its products in Denmark.

In 1955, LEGO introduced LEGO Bricks—plastic building blocks of the familiar stud-and-tube type—that it sold in sets under the name LEGO System of Play. That system, which the firm patented in 1958, allowed children to combine LEGO Bricks in endless number of ways, limited only by their own imaginations and that of their parents. Starting from 1961, the company extended its market across the United States.

Thereafter, the success of LEGO as a toy and as a company fed on itself. The company added many new features to the original concept of interlocking building blocks. For example, wheels enabled children to use LEGO kits to build their own trucks, trains, and similar mobile toys.

In 1968, the LEGO Company, no doubt following the example of the Disney Corporation in the United States, opened an amusement park in Billund in which the rides were designed to look like huge LEGO toys. By the end of the century, LEGO had opened similar parks in England, the United States, and Germany.

However, the company remained focused on making toys for children. It designed new toys, such as plastic figures with human heads to ride in LEGO vehicles, and whole LEGO villages, castles, and pirate ships. By the 1990s, LEGO had become the largest toy manufacturer in Europe and a part of modern culture. Museums displayed LEGO products and art built from LEGO blocks. Contests were held to construct the largest or most unusual LEGO structures. In 1999, *Fortune* magazine included the LEGO Brick among the "Products of the Century," and in 2002, LEGO persuaded European and American management consultants that working with LEGO blocks would help business executives think more clearly about corporate planning. Perhaps most astonishing is that during a half-century of tumultuous change, children around the world have continued to play with these little pieces of plastic.

SOURCE: Factual information derived from the official Lego Group Web site at www.lego.com/eng/info/history.

Question

1. How has LEGO been an example of the European effect on popular culture around the world?

moralists deplored, helped generate the discontent that brought down Communism in Eastern Europe and the Soviet Union.

30.4.6 Environmentalism

After World War II, shortages of consumer goods created a demand that fueled postwar economic reconstruction and growth into the 1950s and 1960s. In those expansive times, public debate about the ethics of economic expansion and efficiency and their effects on the environment was muted. Concerns about pollution began to grow in the 1970s, and by the 1980s, environmentalists had developed real political clout. Among the most important environmental groups at the time were the German Greens. The Greens formed a political party in 1979 that immediately became an electoral force. During these same years, concern for environmental issues, such as global warming and the pollution of water and the atmosphere, commanded the attention of governments outside Europe and of the United Nations.

Several developments lay behind this new concern for the environment. The Arab oil embargo of 1973 to 1974 pressed home two messages to the industrialized West: natural resources are limited, and foreign, potentially hostile, countries control critical resources. By the 1970s, too, the environmental consequences of three decades of economic expansion were becoming increasingly apparent. Fish were dying in the Thames River in England. Industrial pollution was destroying life in the Rhine River between Germany and France. Acid rain was killing trees from Sweden to Germany. Finally, long-standing worries about nuclear weapons led to concerns about their environmental effects, strengthening antinuclear groups and generating opposition to the placement of nuclear weapons in Europe.

The German **Green movement** originated among radical student groups in the late 1960s. Like them, it was anticapitalist, blaming business for pollution. The Greens and other European environmental groups were also strongly antinuclear. Unlike the students of the 1960s, the Greens avoided violence and mass demonstrations, hoping instead to become a significant political presence through the electoral process.

The 1986 disaster at the **Chernobyl** nuclear reactor in the Soviet Union heightened concern about environmental issues and raised questions that no European government could ignore. The Soviet government had to confront casualties at the site and relocate tens of thousands of people. Radioactive fallout spread across Europe. Environmentalists had always contended that their issues transcended national borders. The Chernobyl fire proved them right.

After Chernobyl, European governments, East and West, began to respond to environmental concerns. Some observers believed the environment would become a major political issue across the Continent. In Western Europe, environmental groups commanded many votes. Economic and political integration led to the possibility of transnational cooperation on environmental matters. As the European Economic Community solidified, it and its member nations will likely impose more environmental regulations on business and industry. The nations of Eastern Europe have been forced to face the cleanup of vast areas of industrial development polluted during the Communist era and to combine environmental protection with economic growth.

30.5 Art Since World War II

How did the Cold War shape Western art in the second half of the twentieth century?

It is impossible to cover even briefly the expansive and varied world of Western art since the end of World War II. However, we can note how both the Cold War and the memory of the horrors of World War II influenced Western art.

The stark differences between Soviet painter Tatjiana Yablonskaya's (b. 1917) sun-strewn *Bread* (1949) and the dizzyingly abstract *One* (Number 31, 1950) by the American **Jackson Pollock** (1912–1956) mirror the cultural divisions of the early Cold War.

Bread, measuring over six feet high and twelve feet wide, was a monumental example of **Socialist realism.**

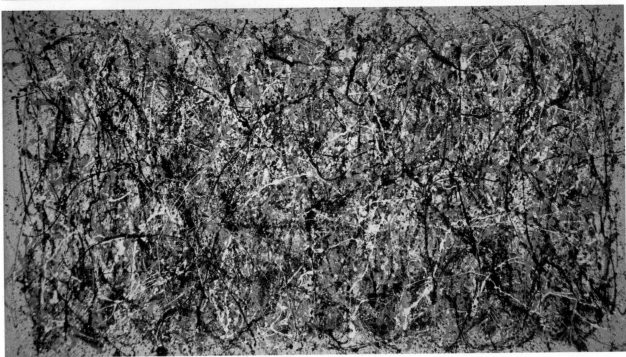

YABLONSKAYA VS POLLOCK Tatjiana Yablonskaya (1917–2005) painted rosy depictions of Soviet workers in a manner that exemplifies the style of Socialist realism popular during the Stalinist years. In the West, during the same period, Jackson Pollock (1912–1956) pioneered Abstract Expressionism. His "drip" paintings introduced a new dynamism into the creative process.
SOURCES: SPUTNIK/Alamy Stock Photo (top); Peter Horree/Alamy Stock Photo/Artists Rights Society (ARS), New York (bottom)

Established as the official doctrine of Soviet art and literature in 1934, Socialist realism created optimistic and easily intelligible scenes of a bold Socialist future, in which prosperity and solidarity would reign. Manual laborers and prominent historical and political figures were painted in a traditional and often rigid figurative manner. Social-ist realism became the dominant artistic model throughout the Soviet Union and Eastern Europe, only waning when Nikita Khrushchev liberalized Soviet cultural policy in the late 1950s.

Pollock's paintings were central documents of post-war American cultural life. Flinging paint from sticks and brushes onto his floor-bound canvas, Pollock freed his lines from representing figure or outline. The result, in *One*

(Number 31, 1950), which is more than eight feet high and seventeen feet wide, is a writhing tangle of pure visual energy. In the politically charged atmosphere of the early Cold War, critics saw Pollock's exuberant "drip" paintings as the embodiment of American cultural freedom and celebrated the Wyoming-born Pollock as a kind of artist cowboy.

As skeptical as many viewers might have been about the merits of abstract art (*Time* magazine, for instance, dismissed Pollock as "Jack the dripper" in 1947), many people in the West saw it as the antithesis of the restrictions that Socialist realism placed on individual creativity.

Indeed, New York City—not Paris—emerged as the international center of modern art after World War II. As the home of growing collections of twentieth-century art and dozens of European artists who had fled from the Nazis, New York became a fertile training ground for young artists such as Pollock. Just as American political and economic structures became models for the postwar redevelopment of Western Europe so did American cultural developments. By the time Pollock's first posthumous retrospective toured Europe in 1958, much European painting resembled an elegant imitation of his frenetic lines. (See "A Closer Look," for a poignant example of European minimalist art.)

Yablonskaya and Pollock together illustrate the two central poles of twentieth-century art: realism and abstraction. Although artistic style is no longer as closely associated with political programs as it once was, these two opposites still frame the work of countless artists today. (Art that can be seen as extending the idea of abstraction is present in the work of Rachel Whiteread whose *Nameless Library* is considered in the "Close Look" sidebar, which follows below.)

30.6 The Christian Heritage

How has the Christian heritage of the West been affected by events of the twentieth century?

In most ways, Christianity in Europe has continued to be as hard-pressed during the twentieth century as it had been in the late nineteenth. Material prosperity, political ideologies, environmentalism, gender politics, and simple indifference have replaced religious faith for many people. Still, despite the loss of much of their popular support and legal privileges and the low rates of church attendance, the European Christian churches continue to exercise social and political influence. In Germany, the churches were one of the few major institutions that the Nazis did not wholly subdue. Lutheran clergy, such as Martin Niemöller (1892–1984) and

Dietrich Bonhoeffer (1906–1945), were leaders of the opposition to Hitler. After the war, most especially in Poland but also elsewhere in Eastern Europe, the Roman Catholic Church opposed Communism. In Eastern and Western Europe, even in this most secular of ages, Christian churches have influenced state and society.

30.6.1 Neoorthodoxy

Liberal theologians of the nineteenth century often softened the concept of sin and portrayed human nature as close to the divine. The horror of World War I destroyed that optimistic faith. Many Europeans felt that evil had stalked the Continent.

The most important Christian response to World War I appeared in the theology of Karl Barth (1886–1968). Barth portrayed God as wholly other than, and different from, humankind. In a sense, Barth was returning to the Reformation theology of Luther, but the work of Kierkegaard had profoundly influenced his reading of the reformer. Those extreme moments of life Kierkegaard described were the basis for a knowledge of humanity's need for God.

This view challenged much nineteenth-century writing about human nature. Barth's theology, which came to be known as **neoorthodoxy**, proved influential throughout the West in the wake of new disasters and suffering.

30.6.2 Liberal Theology

Neoorthodoxy did not, however, sweep away liberal theology, which had a strong advocate in Paul Tillich (1886–1965). This German American theologian regarded religion as a human, rather than a divine, phenomenon.

Other liberal theologians, such as Rudolf Bultmann (1884–1976), continued to work on the problems of naturalism and supernaturalism that had troubled earlier writers. Another liberal Christian writer from Britain, C. S. Lewis (1878–1963), attracted millions of readers during and after World War II. This layman and scholar of medieval literature often expressed his thoughts on theology in the form of letters and short stories.

30.6.3 Roman Catholic Reform

Among Christian denominations, the most significant postwar changes have been in the Roman Catholic Church. Pope John XXIII (r. 1958–1963) initiated these changes, the most extensive in Catholicism for more than a century and, some would say, since the Council of Trent in the sixteenth century. In 1959, Pope John XXIII summoned the Twenty-First Ecumenical Council, which came to be called Vatican II. The council finished its work in 1965 under John's successor, Pope Paul VI (r. 1963–1978).

A Closer Look

Nameless Library, Vienna

BRITISH SCULPTOR Rachel Whiteread (b. 1963) is one of the leading artists of today's Europe. Her work illustrates European art breaking out of the modernist contours set at the beginning of the twentieth century. On the one hand, Whiteread's art depicts familiar forms; on the other, it forces us to view these forms in ways that are as new to us as cubism was to the public in its day.

The outline of books, whose spines turn inward, remain forever unread.

The locked library doors, like the books that can't be opened, symbolize the loss both of Jewish contributions to culture and of Jewish lives in the Holocaust.

NAMELESS LIBRARY
SOURCE: domonabikeAustria/Alamy Stock Photo

Whiteread's work is associated with minimalism in contemporary art. This movement, which originated in architecture and interior design, removes as many features as possible from the object being portrayed while retaining the object's form and the viewer's interest. Minimalist art aims to be as understated as possible. In Whiteread's hands, the minimal becomes the austere, and her work often exudes melancholy and loss.

One of Whiteread's most important public works and designed to endure is *Nameless Library,* at the Judenplatz Holocaust Memorial in Vienna. It commemorates the deaths of 65,000 Austrian Jews under the Nazis. The memorial, which resembles a huge haunting tomb, is cast in concrete.

Questions

1. Who is the intended audience for this piece of work? Viennese? Tourists? How do you imagine different people's responses to *Nameless Library*?

2. *Nameless Library* stands in Vienna's Judenplatz, in the center of its former Jewish district. It is surrounded by outdoor cafés and restaurants. What makes this an especially appropriate or inappropriate location for such a memorial?

Among many changes in Catholic liturgy the council introduced, Mass was now celebrated in the vernacular languages rather than in Latin. The council also encouraged freer relations with other Christian denominations, fostered a new spirit toward Judaism, and gave more power to bishops. In recognition of the growing importance to the church of the world outside Europe and North America, Pope Paul VI appointed several cardinals from the former colonial nations, transforming the church into a true world body.

POPE JOHN PAUL II Throughout his pontificate John Paul II maintained a close relationship with his native Poland to which he made several visits. The earliest of these, in June 1979, was important in demonstrating the authority of the church against Polish Communist authorities. Shown here is the Pope at one of several outdoor masses in Poland, this one in Czestochowa in southwestern Poland. In one of his sermons, he said, "Poland in our time has become a land called to give an especially important witness."
SOURCE: mw/stf/AP Images

In contrast to these liberal changes, however, Pope Paul VI and his successors have firmly upheld the celibacy of priests, maintained the church's prohibition on contraception and abortion, and opposed opening the priesthood to women. The church's unyielding stand on clerical celibacy has caused many men to leave the priesthood and many men and women to leave religious orders. The laity has widely ignored the prohibition on contraception.

John Paul II, the former Karol Wojtyla, archbishop of Kraków in Poland, pursued a three-pronged policy during his long pontificate. First, he maintained traditionalist doctrine, stressing the authority of the papacy and attempting to limit doctrinal and liturgical experimentation.

Second, taking a firm stand against Communism, he supported resistance to the Communist regimes in Eastern Europe. As a cardinal in Poland, he had clashed with the Communist government. After his election, he visited Poland, lending support to Solidarity. His Polish origins

made him an important factor in the popular resistance to Eastern Europe's Communist governments that developed during the 1980s. He thus began a new chapter in the relationship between church and state in modern Europe.

Third, John Paul II encouraged the growth of the church in the non-Western world, stressing the need for social justice but limiting the political activity of priests. The pope's concern for the expansion of Roman Catholicism beyond Europe and North America encouraged what appears to be a transformation in Christianity as a world religion. Whereas in Europe, Christian observance had declined sharply during the twentieth century, Christianity has grown rapidly and fervently in Africa and Latin America. By 2010, only about one-quarter of the world's Christians lived in Europe; another quarter lived in sub-Saharan Africa, and more than one-third lived in North and South America. Recognizing these changes, John Paul II appointed more cardinals from non-Western nations.

John Paul II died in 2005 and was canonized, together with Pope John Paul XXIII, on April 27, 2014, the festivity of the Divine Mercy Sunday that he instituted. His successor was his closest collaborator, the German cardinal Joseph Ratzinger (b. 1927), who took the name Benedict XVI. Benedict followed his predecessor in his rigorous defense of orthodoxy. Known as the main intellectual force in the church since the 1980s, he promoted the use of Latin and made the Tridentine Mass more prominent. Pope Benedict XVI also championed the role of religious freedom for Christians and other religiously observant peoples living in secular societies. In February 2013, Benedict resigned as leader of the Catholic Church citing his declining health from old age. At eighty-five, he became the first pope to resign since Gregory XII in 1415.

Following the retirement of Pope Benedict XVI, Jorge Mario Bergoglio was elected pope, the first from South America. He chose the name Francis in honor of Saint Francis of Assisi. A vehement critic of American capitalism, Pope Francis has emphasized God's mercy and concern for the poor. In striking contrast to Benedict, who reintroduced papal garments, Francis prefers a less formal approach to the papacy and is known for his simpler vestments without ornamentation. Also in contrast to Benedict's defense of orthodoxy, Francis has stirred controversy within the church for some of his stances on doctrine, such as allowing divorced and remarried people to receive communion.

30.7 Late-Twentieth-Century Technology: The Arrival of the Computer

What impact has the computer had on twentieth-century society?

During the twentieth century, technology crossed international borders the way popular culture did. As with other areas of European life and society, American technology had an unprecedented impact on the Continent, whether in the guise of the first airplanes or Henry Ford's method of producing affordable automobiles. However, no single American technological achievement of the twentieth century

THE FIRST GENERAL PURPOSE ELECTRONIC COMPUTER The earliest computers were very large. This photograph from 1946 shows the Electronic Numerical Integrator and Computer (ENIAC) built at the Moore School of Engineering at the University of Pennsylvania.
SOURCE: Science History Images/Alamy Stock Photo

will influence Western life on both sides of the Atlantic, and throughout the rest of the world, as the computer.

30.7.1 The Demand for Calculating Machines

Beginning in the seventeenth century, thinkers associated with the scientific revolution—most famously, French mathematician and philosopher Blaise Pascal (1623–1662)—attempted to construct machines that would carry out mathematical calculations that humans would find impossible because of the tedium and time they involved. Beginning in the late nineteenth century, the governments of the consolidating nation-states of Europe and of the United States faced new administrative tasks that involved collecting and organizing vast amounts of data about national censuses, tax collection, economic statistics, and the administration of pensions and welfare legislation. During the same years, private businesses required calculating machinery to handle and organize growing amounts of economic and business data. Such machines became technologically possible through the development of complex circuitry for electricity, the most versatile mode of energy in human history. Moreover, inventions that were dependent on electricity, including the telephone, the telegraph, underwater cables, and the wireless, created a new communications industry that also required large databases of customer information to deliver their services. By the late 1920s, companies like National Cash Register, Remington Rand, and International Business Machines Corporation (IBM) had begun to manufacture such business machinery.

30.7.2 Early Computer Technology

As has happened so often in history, warfare was the chief catalyst of change. After World War I and during World War II, the major powers developed new weapons that required exact mathematical ballistic calculations to strike targets with bombs delivered by aircraft or long-range guns.

The first machine genuinely recognizable as a modern digital computer was the Electronic Numerical Integrator and Computer (ENIAC), built and designed at Moore Laboratories of the University of Pennsylvania and used by the U.S. Army in 1946 for ballistics calculation. The ENIAC was an enormous piece of equipment with forty panels, 1,500 electric relays, and 18,000 vacuum tubes. It also used thousands of punch cards, and a separate tabulator had to print the data from them. Further computer engineering occurred at the Institute for Advanced Research in Princeton, New Jersey; in laboratories at the Massachusetts Institute of Technology; and in other laboratories the U.S. government and private businesses, especially IBM, ran. The other primary sites for computer development were laboratories in Britain.

30.7.3 The Development of Desktop Computers

During the 1950s, however, the transistor revolutionized electronics, permitting a miniaturization of circuitry that made vacuum tubes obsolete and allowed computers to become smaller. Computers still had to be programmed with difficult computer languages by persons expertly trained to use them.

By the late 1960s, however, two innovations transformed computing technology. First, control of the computer was transferred to a bitmap covering the screen of a computer monitor. The mouse, invented in 1964, eased the movement of the cursor around the computer screen. Second, engineers at the Intel Corporation—then a California start-up company—invented the microchip, which became the heart of all future computers.

The bitmap on the screen, operated through the mouse, in effect embedded complicated computer language in the machine, hidden from the user, who simply manipulated images on the screen with the mouse. Almost anyone could thus learn to operate computers. At the same time, the tiny microchip, itself a miniature computer or microprocessor, permitted computer technology to abandon the mainframe and move to still smaller computers. At the Xerox Corporation, engineers devised a small computer using a mouse, but the machine never achieved commercial success. By 1982, IBM had produced a small personal computer but temporarily lost the race for commercialization to a then small company called Apple Computer Corporation. The design features originally developed at Xerox informed the ideas of the Apple engineers, who in early 1984 produced a small, highly accessible, commercially successful computer, known as the Macintosh, that would fit on a desktop in the home or office. IBM soon adopted the Apple concept with different engineering and marketing approaches and manufactured a product called the Personal Computer, or PC. By the mid-1980s, for a relatively modest cost (and one that has continued to drop), individuals had available for their own personal use in their offices or homes computers with far more power than the old mainframes. The Apple Macintosh and the IBM PC transformed computers into objects of everyday life and in doing so, transformed everyday life itself. Nonetheless, the chief contemporary users of computers remained governments followed by the telephone industry, banking and finance, automobile operation, and airline reservation systems.

Despite the potential democratizing character of computer technology, the computer revolution has also introduced new concepts of "haves" and "have-nots" to societies around the world. Computers, whatever their possible shortcomings, enable users to do things that nonusers cannot do. Whether in poor school districts in the United States or in poor countries of the former Soviet bloc, students who graduate without computer skills have difficulty making their way in the world's rapidly computerizing economy. Some commentators also fear that boys are more likely than girls to receive technological training in computers. Nations whose governments and businesses become networked into the world of computers will prosper more fully than those whose access to computer technology is deficient. In that regard, the possession of computers and the ability to use them will probably determine future economic competition, just as they have determined recent military competition.

30.8 The Challenges of European Unification

What led to Western European unification following World War II?

The unprecedented steps toward economic cooperation and unity Western European nations took during the second half of the twentieth century were the single most important European success story of that era. The process originated from American encouragement in response to the Soviet domination of Eastern Europe and from the Western European states' own sense that they lacked effective political and economic power. Furthermore, leaders in France and Germany who recoiled from the disastrous peace that followed World War I were determined that the political collapse of Europe after World War II would have a different outcome. They understood that cooperation, rather than revenge, must inform the future of Europe.

30.8.1 Postwar Cooperation

The mid-twentieth-century Western European movement toward unity could have occurred in at least three ways: politically, militarily, or economically. Economic cooperation, unlike military and political cooperation, involved little or no immediate loss of sovereignty by the participating nations. Furthermore, it brought material benefits to all the states involved, increasing popular support for their governments. Moreover, the administration of the Marshall Plan and the organization of NATO gave the countries involved new experience in working with each other and demonstrated the productivity and efficiency that cooperation could achieve.

The first effort toward economic cooperation was the formation of the European Coal and Steel Community in 1951 by France, West Germany, Italy, and the Benelux countries (Belgium, the Netherlands, and Luxembourg). The community both benefited from and contributed to the immense growth of material production in Western Europe during this period. Its success reduced the suspicions of government and business groups about coordination and economic integration.

30.8.2 The European Economic Community

It took more than the prosperity of the European Coal and Steel Community to draw European leaders toward further unity, however. The unsuccessful Suez intervention of 1956 and the resulting diplomatic isolation of France and Britain persuaded many Europeans that only by acting together could they significantly influence the United States and the Soviet Union or control their own national and regional destinies. So, in 1957, through the Treaty of Rome, the six members of the Coal and Steel Community agreed to form a new organization: the **European Economic Community (EEC)**. The members of the Common Market, as the EEC was soon known, envisioned more than a free-trade union. They sought to achieve the eventual elimination of tariffs, a free flow of capital and labor, and similar wage and social benefits in all their countries.

The Common Market achieved stunning success during its early years. By 1968, well ahead of schedule, the six members had abolished all tariffs among themselves. Trade and labor migration among the members grew steadily. Moreover, nonmember states began to copy the EEC and, later, to seek to join it. In 1959, Britain, Denmark, Norway, Sweden, Switzerland, Austria, and Portugal formed the European Free Trade Area. By 1961, however, Britain had decided to join the Common Market. Twice, in 1963 and 1967, President Charles de Gaulle of France vetoed British membership. He argued that Britain was too closely tied to the United States to support the EEC wholeheartedly. Finally, in 1973, Great Britain, Ireland, and Denmark became members. Throughout the late 1970s, however, and into the 1980s, momentum for expanding EEC membership slowed. Norway and Sweden, with relatively strong economies, declined to join. Although in 1982, Spain, Portugal, and Greece applied for membership and were eventually admitted, sharp disagreements and a sense of stagnation within the EEC continued.

30.8.3 The European Union

In 1988, the leaders of the EEC reached an important decision. By 1992, the EEC was to be a free-trade zone with no trade barriers or other restrictive trade policies among its members. In 1991, the **Maastricht Treaty** made a series of specific proposals that led to a unified EEC currency (the euro) and a strong central bank. The treaty was submitted to referendums in several European states. Denmark initially rejected it, and it passed only narrowly in France and Great Britain, making clear that it needed wider popular support. When the treaty finally took effect in November 1993, the EEC was renamed the **European Union (EU)**. Throughout the 1990s, the union's influence grew. Its most notable achievement was the launching in early 1999 of the **euro**, which by 2002 had become the common currency in twelve of the member nations.

In May 2004, the European Union added ten new nations, raising the total number of members to twenty-five. (See Map 30–1.) Membership in the European Union indicated that a nation had achieved economic stability and genuinely democratic institutions. At the time, some older member states worried that several of the new member states from the former Soviet bloc were relatively poor and would require much economic support from the union.

Ironically, it was not states in Eastern Europe but mainly the sovereign debt crisis in Greece that plunged the EU into a debt crisis in 2010.

30.8.4 Discord over the Union

The 2004 expansion of the European Union marked for some the high point of European integration. During that year the leaders of the member nations adopted a new constitutional treaty for the union. This treaty, generally known as the **European Constitution**, was a long, detailed, and highly complicated document involving a bill of rights and complex economic and political agreements among all member states. It would have transferred considerable decision-making authority from the governments of the individual states to the central institutions of the European Union, many of which were located in Brussels, Luxembourg, and Strasbourg. To become effective, all the member states

Map 30–1 THE GROWTH OF THE EUROPEAN UNION

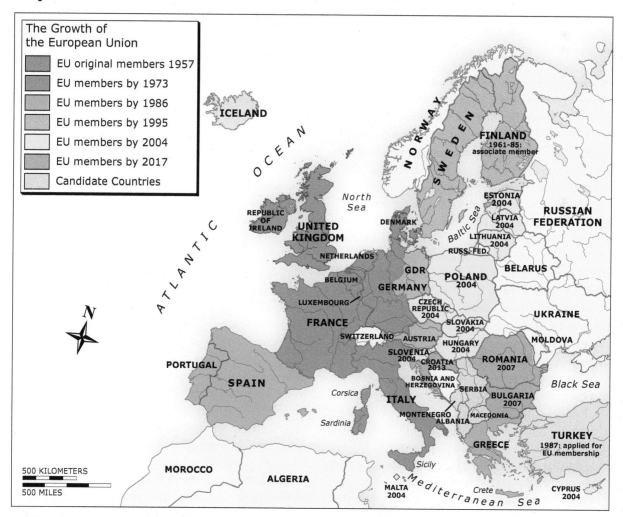

This map traces the growth of membership in the European Union from its founding in 1957 through the introduction of its newest members. Note that Turkey, though having applied for membership, has not yet been admitted and that by 2019, the UK will have withdrawn from the EU.

had to ratify the constitution either by their parliaments or through national referendums.

To the surprise of many in the European elite, in the spring of 2005, referendums held in France and the Netherlands heavily defeated the new constitutional treaty. Britain, where support for further European integration was lukewarm at best, immediately postponed holding its own referendum. Public opinion in other nations also soured on the constitutional treaty. Furthermore, immediately after these events, discord erupted over the union's internal budget. These events were an unprecedented crisis for the European Union and for the project of European integration. A similar crisis erupted in 2008 when a referendum in Ireland failed to support changes in the European Union that would create shared institutions of foreign policy formulation and military policy.

Several factors appear to have brought the European Union to this pass. First, for at least the previous fifteen years, a gap had grown between the European political elites who had led the drive toward unity and the European voting public. The former had either ignored the latter or had moved the project along with only narrow majorities. Second, the general Western European economy had stagnated for the previous decade with relatively high rates of unemployment, especially among the young. Voting against the constitution was a way to voice discontent with this situation. Third, many of the smaller member states of the European Union felt that France and Germany had either ignored them or taken them for granted. Fourth, some nations believed that they were at an economic disadvantage when the euro replaced their former national currencies because the rates of exchange were unfairly calculated. Fifth, many in the various states, large and small, had become reluctant to cede national sovereignty and the authority to make economic decisions to the bureaucracy in Brussels. The concern over national sovereignty was powerfully expressed when the United Kingdom voted to leave the European Union on June 23, 2016. The Brexit referendum was remarkable in demonstrating that membership in the Union was by no means irrevocable. In fact, independence initiatives have gained widespread popular support in countries such as France and Italy.

Finally, another large issue has informed the internal skeptics of the current European Union. Over the past several years, leaders of the major member states have grown more favorable to the eventual admission of Turkey as a member state. If Turkey were admitted, Europe would have to integrate into the union a state whose population is larger and much poorer than that of any other member state. This would place enormous social and economic burdens on the other states. Furthermore, although the Turkish government has long been seen as adamantly secular, the Turkish people are overwhelmingly Muslim. This "Islamic factor"

has become increasingly controversial among those Europeans who, whether they are religiously observant or not, believe European culture to be Christian. It is also a factor among secular Europeans who are deeply concerned about the political, economic, and social implications of the Continent's already significant Muslim population. The large number of people coming to Europe from African nations and the Middle East as part of the 2015 migrant crisis, the majority of entrants being Muslims, has become part of this issue. Syria's Civil War and the massive refugee crisis it has created have intensified these concerns. The reaction has been especially strong in Germany, which under the policies of Chancellor Angela Merkel, has accepted hundreds of thousands of Syrian asylum seekers since 2015.

30.9 New American Leadership and Financial Crisis

How did the year 2008 impact the relationship between the United States and Europe, and how have recent developments affected this relationship?

Much of the first decade of the twenty-first century witnessed considerable strain between the new post–Soviet Union Europe and the United States. The immediate European reaction to the attacks on the United States on September 11, 2001, was sympathetic. The events leading up to the U.S. Iraq invasion in 2003 and the violence occurring since that invasion caused considerable strain between the United States and Europe, especially in terms of popular opinion. Europeans, through their press and to some extent through their governments, voiced much criticism over what they regarded as U.S. unilateral action in its foreign policy.

Three events in 2008 may have begun to change this situation and possibly to lessen those tensions. The first was the Russian invasion of Georgia. The United States and the European Union agreed in condemning that action. Second, the American presidential election of 2008 brought the strong victory of Barack Obama, the Democratic Party candidate. Obama was the first African American to be elected to the presidency. He ran on a platform critical of the Iraq invasion and American unilateralism. Even though he also voiced strong support for the war in Afghanistan, Obama generated enormous popular support across Europe. Obama's victory in the presidential election and the expansion of Democratic Party majorities in Congress appeared to have persuaded many Europeans that their assumptions about American culture were incorrect and that a new era of American foreign and domestic policy was at hand. However, the announced "reset" in U.S. foreign relations with Russia and Europe ran into difficulty after Russia's invasion of Crimea in 2014 and its military intervention in Syria in 2015. In addition, Obama chose not to enforce the "red line" he pledged following the use of chemical weapons by the Assad regime in Syria.

It is difficult to predict what shape the foreign policy of President Donald Trump will take toward Russia and Europe. For example, during his campaign he was critical of NATO and suggested that, if elected, he might leave the alliance, but once in office, President Trump reaffirmed the U.S. commitment to NATO. On the other hand, his announcement on June 1, 2017 that the U.S. would withdraw from the Paris Climate Agreement has drawn censure in Europe.

Third, during the second half of 2008 a major international financial crisis potentially as damaging as that of the 1930s overwhelmed the American, transatlantic, and world economies. The crisis originated in the United States mortgage market where numerous major banks found themselves holding mortgages that could not be paid. Several major financial institutions in the United States failed, as did some banks in Europe. The United States and some European governments intervened deeply in areas of the economy where they had previously refrained from intervening. Stock markets around the world lost one-third or

more of their value. This new interconnectedness of world markets created financial panic around the globe.

30.9.1 European Debt Crisis

From the start, European states with strong economies knew that there was risk involved in sharing a common European currency with less affluent countries. The premise of the **Eurozone**, as the group of countries that shared the euro came to be known, was that each country would control its deficits and maintain a stable economy. Countries like Greece and Italy had to lower their inflation rates and deficits to qualify for the euro, and they had to promise to maintain those lower rates once they adopted the new currency. Participation in the euro made countries appear to be safer investments, and Greece, Ireland, Spain, and Portugal were able to borrow money at favorable interest rates. In 2009, the new Socialist government in Greece announced that the appearance of economic stability in Greece was based on the previous government's falsification of data: the deficit was, they announced, twice what it had been reported to be. Foreign investors withdrew not only from the Greek economy but from other potentially risky economies like Spain, Portugal, and Ireland, and

PROTEST AGAINST ECONOMIC AUSTERITY IN GREECE Outside the parliament building in February 2012, Greek citizens protest austerity measures aimed at reducing Greece's debt and securing loans from the European Union and other international organizations. This was just one battle in the fight to determine who should be responsible for rectifying the economic problems that had grown over the previous decade: the wealthy and big business through increased taxation or working people through reduced government services.
SOURCE: Aristidis Vafeiadakis/ZUMA Press/Newscom

those countries' governments had trouble refinancing their substantial debts. To prevent the crisis from spilling into other countries, Eurozone leaders like Germany insisted on strict and unpopular austerity measures designed to lower deficits in southern Europe. This has, in turn, raised issues over national sovereignty and the ability of individual member states to control their economies. As has been the case in response to the financial crisis in the United States, some commentators argue that austerity measures, which include freezing or drastically reducing government spending, punish working-class Europeans for unscrupulous or speculative behavior on the part of economists, investors, and bankers. Debates about whether increased or reduced government spending would be more effective in ensuring economic recovery in southern Europe are likely to continue for many years.

In ongoing debates about the wisdom of a common European currency, the fate of the euro has been linked to the fate of the European Union itself. The Brexit vote seems to mark a dramatic turning point for the future of the EU. The vote of the UK to leave the union has undermined confidence that in the face of a severe crisis such as the debt crisis in Greece, the members will stay together. The structure of the European Union—the instability of a monetary union without fiscal union—lies at the heart of the problem. Future negotiations will determine whether greater integration among its members is possible despite powerful resistance within individual nations.

The Chapter in Perspective

After decades of warfare and tension in the first half-century, European society developed peacefully in the postwar period. France and Germany became natural allies, both working toward the common cause of European integration. Migration and the economic growth of the second half-century reshaped the society of many European nations. Welfare systems provided an extensive social safety net. The role and opportunities for women in society expanded. More and more Europeans across the Continent attended universities. The end of Soviet domination began a process in which Eastern Europe increasingly came to participate in the affluence of the West with its myriad consumer goods.

By the close of the century, Europe, like much of the rest of the world, had entered a new technological revolution through the computer and advances in medical care. Economic growth slowed in the 1990s, but most of Europe outside the former Communist-dominated regions continued to enjoy some of the highest standards of living in the world under liberal democratic governments.

The efforts to unify Europe have transformed the Continent and the everyday lives of its citizens. The future of the European Union, however, now stands at a crossroads. The vote of the United Kingdom to leave the EU and concerns over migration and sovereignty among the populations of remaining members will only place new demands on the union.

Europe no longer dominates global cultural or economic forces as it did at the beginning of the twentieth century. In the twenty-first century, Europe is only one player in a global community of states that often look to their own traditions, rather than Europe, for models of how to organize societies, governments, and their interactions with one each other.

The Chapter in Review

Review Questions

1. How did migration affect twentieth-century European social life? What internal and external forces led to migration?
2. In what specific ways was Europe Americanized in the second half of the twentieth century? How do you explain the trend toward a consumer society?
3. How has Islamic migration into Europe affected social tensions on the Continent? How did the migration come about? What incidents occurring in Europe have raised resentment within the Islamic world?
4. How did women's social and economic roles change in the second half of the twentieth century? What changes and problems have women faced since the fall of Communism in Eastern Europe?
5. How did the pursuit and diffusion of knowledge change in the twentieth century? What have been the effects of the communications revolutions?
6. What were the technological steps in the emergence of the computer? What changes will computers bring in the next decade?
7. What were the major steps in the emergence of the European Union? Why is the union now facing a crisis?

Key Terms

Albert Camus (1913–1960) French existentialist author of *The Stranger* (1942) and *The Plague* (1947 whose work questioned the primacy of reason and scientific understanding as ways to come to grips with the human situation.

Americanization The economic and military influence exerted by the United States on Europe after the Second World War as a result of the Marshall Plan.

Chernobyl The 1986 disaster at the Chernobyl nuclear reactor in the Soviet Union that heightened concerns about environmental issues.

euro The common currency created by the European Economic Community in the late 1990s.

European Constitution The 2004 constitutional treaty for the European Union that involved complex economic and political agreements among member states and would have transferred decision-making authority from individual states to the central institutions of the union; heavily defeated by France and the Netherlands.

European Economic Community (EEC) The economic association formed by France, Germany, Italy, Belgium, the Netherlands, and Luxembourg in 1957; also known as the Common Market.

European Union The new name given to the EEC in 1993, which included most of the states of Western Europe.

Eurozone The monetary union of nineteen of the twenty-eight states of the European Union that have adopted the euro as currency.

existentialism The post–World War II Western philosophy that holds human beings are totally responsible for their acts and that this responsibility causes them dread and anguish.

George Orwell (1903–1950) English intellectual and writer who expressed his disappointment with Stalin's policy in Spain in *Homage to Catalonia* (1938).

Green movement A political environmentalist movement that began in West Germany in the 1970s and spread to some other Western nations.

Jackson Pollock (1912–1956) American abstract artist whose paintings are central documents of postwar cultural life in America.

Jean-Paul Sartre (1905–1980) French philosopher, author of *Being and Nothingness* (1943), and an existentialist who protested a world in which reason, technology, and politics produced war and genocide.

John Paul II (1930–2005) Karol Wojtyla, the former archbishop of Poland and the first non-Italian pope since the sixteenth century, who took a firm stand against Communism and supported resistance against the Communist regimes in Eastern Europe.

Maastricht Treaty Formally, the Treaty on European Union, or TEU, that was designed to integrate Europe first economically, with the introduction of the euro, and then also politically.

Margaret Thatcher (1925–2013) The first female prime minister (1979-1990) of Great Britain who led the British Conservative Party to three electoral victories and carried out extensive restructuring of the British government and economy.

National Health Service (begun on the "Appointed Day" of July 5, 1948) The most important element of the social welfare legislation passed by the Labour Party under the ministry of Clement Attlee.

neoorthodoxy The theology of Swiss pastor Karl Barth (1886-1968), which reemphasized the transcendence of God and the dependence of humanity on the divine.

Simone de Beauvoir (1908–1986) French philosopher whose writings are the most important postwar work on women's issues.

Socialist realism Established as the official doctrine of Soviet art and literature in 1934 that sought to create optimistic and easily intelligible scenes of a bold Socialist future, in which prosperity and solidarity would reign.

Søren Kierkegaard (1813–1835) Danish philosopher who criticized Hegelianism and, by implication, all academic rational philosophy and in whose work lay the foundations for existentialism.

Notes

1. Mark Mazower, *Dark Continent: Europe's Twentieth Century* (New York: Knopf, 1999), p. 218.

2. William Barrett, *Irrational Man* (Garden City, NY: Doubleday, 1962), p. 20.

The West and the World

Energy and the Modern World

NO SINGLE TECHNOLOGICAL factor so determines the social relationships and standard of living of human beings as energy. The more energy a society can command for each of its members, the stronger and more influential it will be. Throughout recorded human history, those societies that have found ways to improve their access to sources of energy, and have then effectively applied the energy, have dominated both their immediate environments and much of the world beyond. Indeed, the possession of, or the lack of powerful, inexpensive sources of energy in large measure determines which nations will be wealthy and which will be poor.

Animals, Wind, and Water

For civilization to advance technologically, energy had to be applied to tasks. The earliest source of such energy was animal power, which was used all over the world except among the peoples on the American continent prior to the arrival of the Europeans. Oxen, water buffalo, and horses were the major draft animals. Of these, horses were the most efficient.

Throughout the world until the eighteenth century, however, wind and water furnished most of the energy for machinery. Sailing ships had been used since ancient times for travel, fishing, and the transport of goods. The wind also worked mills that pumped water and ground grain. Water-wheels proved to be highly flexible machines and by the eighteenth century constituted the major sources of mechanical power in Europe and much of the rest of the world. But wind and water were uncertain sources of energy. The wind could cease; drought could dry up streams. Water-powered machinery had to be located near the stream furnishing the

FOURTEENTH-CENTURY WIND-POWERED SAILING SHIPS Until the eighteenth century, sailing ships were powered by manpower and by wind alone. In this fourteenth-century manuscript illustration, sailors navigate with the help of an astrolabe.
SOURCE: Bibliotheque Nationale, Paris, France/Bridgeman Images

water. Consequently, most of the mills employing such machinery were located in the countryside.

Although animals, wind, and water provided energy for relatively complicated machines capable of manufacturing and transporting high-quality goods, the economic and political transformations that have driven the history of the world for the past two and a half centuries could only have occurred through a qualitative as well as quantitative leap in the manner in which human beings commanded energy. The twin sources of this world-transforming energy have been fossil fuels and electricity.

Until the second half of the eighteenth century, fossil fuels—coal, petroleum, and, to a lesser extent, natural gas—contributed only a small portion of human energy requirements. Their use as meaningful sources of energy required a series of inventions that allowed the energy of heat to be changed into mechanical energy.

Steam Power and the Age of Coal

Although peoples living near coal deposits had used it as a household fuel for a very long time, only the invention of the steam engine, patented by James Watt in 1769, established a major industrial demand for coal. The steam engine first permitted the pumping of water from coal mines to increase production. But as the industrial uses for the steam engine grew, the invention itself drove the demand for greater quantities of coal as fuel.

Coal-fueled steam power changed the face of human society during the nineteenth century and in countries like China and India, it continues to provide the energy for the most powerful turbogenerators now. Steam-powered machines could be made larger and more flexible than those powered by wind or water, and as long as coal was available, they could run steadily day and night. Steam engines, in contrast to waterwheels, were transportable. Factories could be moved away from streams in the countryside to urban areas where a ready workforce existed. And goods produced in factories powered by steam engines could be carried around the world by steam-powered locomotives and ships. Those expanding markets in turn called forth more steam-powered factories and even greater use of coal. Furthermore, steam-powered factories could also produce military weapons that could be placed on steam-powered naval vessels constructed of iron and steel in vast coal-fueled blast furnaces. When Theodore Roosevelt sent the U.S. fleet around the world, it was a testimony to the power of coal and steam as well as to the power of the American navy.

The age of steam was the age of coal. The nations possessing large coal deposits dominated much nineteenth-century economic life as the nations that possess oil reserves dominate much contemporary economic life. For many decades, Great Britain dominated the world's production

and delivery of coal, which was transported over the entire world. Its domination was challenged only in the late nineteenth century as the United States and later Russia and China began to produce vast quantities of the fuel. Coal remained the chief fuel for the United States until after World War I and for Western Europe until after World War II. It remains the chief fuel for China.

Coal generated a rising standard of living in Europe and the expansion of European and later American power, but coal also generated a number of social and environmental problems. The most shocking conditions of exploited labor occurred in coal mines, where parliamentary reports of the 1840s described and illustrated half-clad women and children drawing coal carts from the depths of the mines to the surface. Throughout the nineteenth and twentieth centuries, thousands of miners died in mining disasters. Work in the mines injured the health of miners, as did the pollution sent into the atmosphere by coal fires from both factories and homes. By the early twentieth century, observers had begun to note the damage to the environment caused by strip mining of coal and the later abandonment of the regions.

The Internal Combustion Engine: The Age of Oil

As with coal, the impact of petroleum, the second major fossil fuel, also depended on the invention of machinery to use it. Originally, the use for oil was limited to kerosene, the fuel used for lighting around much of the world by 1900. It was based on the world demand for lamp oil that John D. Rockefeller founded the Standard Oil Company. The invention of the internal combustion engine in 1882 by Rudolf Daimler and the diesel engine in 1892 by Rudolf Diesel transformed the demand for oil. Toward the close of the nineteenth century, extensive oil production had begun in the United States, with Austria, Russia, Romania, Sumatra, Mexico, Iran, and Venezuela starting to tap their own oil resources before World War I.

Just as the steam engine had spurred the expansion of the coal industry, the internal combustion engine drove the oil industry. Fuel oil would begin to replace coal not so much because it was cheaper but because it was more efficient, easier to store and transport, and cleaner to burn. Initially, fuel oil tended to be used in those countries where it could be produced relatively near the point of use. Until the end of World War II, the United States was the primary world producer and user of oil. As fuel for the internal combustion engine, oil became the driving force of automobiles, locomotives, airplanes, ships, factory machinery, and electric generators. It revolutionized agricultural machinery and world food production, but as a fuel for transportation, it fostered a social transformation throughout much of the world.

Starting in the United States and then spreading elsewhere, automobiles introduced a new mobility factor to social relationships. People could move easily across long distances to join a new community or to start a new job. Inexpensive gasoline for cars and public transport buses permitted the development of suburbs ever farther removed from traditional urban centers. In turn, retailing moved away from city centers to shopping malls. At the same time, wherever the mechanization of farming through improved farm machinery took place, there usually followed a movement of people from farming communities to urban areas. The availability of cheap oil encouraged people to develop lifestyles that made them utterly dependent on that oil.

Cancel distance & conquer weather

A NEW MOBILITY Facing stiff competition from General Motors, Henry Ford turned out national advertisements to capture more market share. This ad, directed at women, highlights the independence and comfort that the Ford sedan would bring them.
SOURCE: Fotosearch/Stringer/Getty Images

Electricity Increases the Demand for Oil

The manufacture of automobiles and other forms of transport using the internal combustion or diesel engine was central to all modern industrial life. As those industries expanded so did the construction of extensive road systems. These in turn created new demands for fuel oil.

But the greatest demand for fuel oil arose from the application of electricity to the needs of everyday life. Electricity proved to be the most flexible and versatile source of energy for the twentieth century, and its generation provided the single greatest source of demand for both coal and oil. Electricity generation would also employ new modes of water power in the forms of hydroelectric generators.

The scientific basis for the production of electric energy was Michael Faraday's study of electromagnetic induction. In 1831, he demonstrated that mechanical energy under the proper conditions could be converted into electric energy. Even more important, the reverse was also true. Electricity could be generated in one location and applied far away wherever electrical lines could be extended. The applications of electrical power have appeared to be restricted only by the limitations of the inventive imagination.

During the second half of the nineteenth century, a host of inventors, such as Thomas Alva Edison, worked through the production and application of electrical power to service large regions. Electricity found applications across the spectrum of human society, actions, and enterprises. Access to electricity in the twentieth century became the key factor for an improved standard of living. A fundamental moment in the decision by Japan to modernize during the late nineteenth century was the construction of the Tokyo Electric Light Company in 1888. The extension of electrical lines into the American countryside was one of the major accomplishments of Franklin Roosevelt's New Deal. Electrical power transformed the workplace, but even more strikingly it transformed homes. Without access to electrical power, domestic households could not make use of any of the growing array of labor-saving appliances such as electric washing machines, electric irons, electric stoves, and electric vacuum cleaners. Electric lights brightened entire cities. Electricity replaced both coal and oil as the source of power for many locomotives; it powered public tram systems and opened the way for the telegraph, the telephone, the wireless, the motion picture camera, and television. It planted the seeds for the computer revolution in communication and information. Electricity allowed manufacturing plants and office complexes to be built wherever electric lines could be carried. Indeed, the access to electrical power has been the single best indication of economic advancement for any nation or region.

Yet within this era of ever-expanding electrification, coal and oil—the fundamental fossil fuels—would still provide the underpinnings of the world's energy. In fact, more oil and coal are used to generate electricity than for any other single purpose. Throughout the twentieth century, the demand for these fuels led to the refinement of their production techniques to permit the extraction of coal from ever-deeper seams and the strip mining of it from regions where previously it would have been economically unproductive to do so. The effort to discover, extract, and transport oil would have major consequences for the world's physical and geopolitical environment far into the twentieth and twenty-first centuries, with the effects of hydraulic fracturing—fracking—on public health and the environment being closely monitored.

Oil and Global Politics in the Twentieth Century

As the twentieth century began, the United States was by far the largest producer and exporter of petroleum. Yet by the 1920s, the American government began to worry about running out of oil. The British did too, as they depended on imported oil for their military and industrial needs. During the 1920s and 1930s, both governments encouraged oil companies to forge agreements for the drilling and export of oil from the Middle East. These arrangements fit into the pattern of formal and informal colonialism that still characterized the interwar period.

After World War II, Western Europe, the Soviet Union, and the nations of the Warsaw Pact turned from coal to oil as the basis for economic growth. Japan followed this course during the 1960s. By 1947, the United States had begun to import more oil than it produced. These two developments—a new dependence on oil by the industrialized nations and the expanded search for oil by the West—formed the basis for the new role that the nations of the Middle East would play in the world economy as the chief oil exporters. Simultaneously, as the world's industrialized

economies were growing dependent on Middle East oil production, nationalist leaders in that region were denouncing former colonial domination and rejecting relationships with the West and with Israel, a country that received strong political support from the United States and Western Europe. The stage was thus set for oil to play a new role in the geopolitical conflicts of the Cold War era.

Playing a major role in those conflicts was the Organization of Petroleum Exporting Nations (OPEC), founded in 1960. Regardless of their differences, OPEC members were united in two things: First, they deeply resented former colonial control of their oil supplies and second, they were determined that their own governments, not foreign oil companies, would control those vital resources. (Mexico had brought its own petroleum industry under state control before World War II.) In 1973, during the Yom Kippur War, OPEC acted, sharply raising oil prices to nations whose governments supported Israel. The action caused severe economic consequences in the West and led to new efforts to develop local oil reserves in politically safe locations such as in the North Sea. OPEC would attempt similar actions on other occasions, most successfully in 1979. In that year, a revolution in Iran overthrew the government, which had long been supported by the United States. OPEC cut off oil shipments to the West, causing severe dislocations. Concerns about securing oil supplies in the West were again sparked by the Persian Gulf War and other political tensions in the region.

In addition to the political problems associated with Middle East oil production, the industrial world's reliance on oil has had severe environmental consequences. Generally, when the United States dominated oil production, the oil refineries were located near the source of oil production. As the exploitation of oil reserves moved to the Middle East and then later in the century to Alaska and to the North Sea, oil refineries became separated from the drilling locations. Crude oil was shipped to refineries on enormous tankers. More than once, these supertankers have hit shoals or gone aground, causing large oil spills, calamitous to both animals and humans. Additionally, even when transported safely, the use of hydrocarbons like oil and coal contributes to air pollution and global warming, which scientists predict will have dire consequences for our planet's climate.

The Promise and Danger of Nuclear Energy

Following World War II, nuclear power became a new source for the generation of electrical energy. The power of the atom, first released in the 1940s for military purposes, held the promise of virtually infinite quantities of energy. The world would no longer be dependent on finite supplies of fossil fuel located in politically tense regions of the world.

CRUDE OIL In 1989, when a supertanker spilled 35,000 tons of crude oil into Alaska's Prince William Sound, rescue workers struggled to save the lives of seabirds and animals. Nevertheless, thousands died.
SOURCE: Gary Braasch/ZUMAPRESS/Newscom

The generation of such energy, however, required the most complex sets of machinery ever devised to produce electrical energy. France and Great Britain began to build nuclear reactors in the 1950s, with the United States, the Soviet Union, and various other European nations following in the 1960s. Nations outside the West, such as India and Pakistan, looked to the construction of nuclear power stations as a means rapidly achieving industrialization and a rising standard of living through extensive electrification. Nations with limited supplies of fossil fuel, such as Japan, hoped nuclear energy would solve their energy supply problem. During its postwar occupation of Japan, the United States also encouraged the dissemination of information about the benefits of nuclear energy, and strictly prohibited the linking of nuclear energy with the atomic bomb attacks on Hiroshima and Nagasaki. There was little or no discussion of the dangers of nuclear energy. The oil shock of the mid-1970s brought new enthusiasm to the adoption of nuclear

energy, but the economic downturn of the late 1970s and early 1980s slowed the construction of nuclear-generating stations. The construction of breeder reactors, which would produce their own fuel in the process of generating electrical energy, seemed to promise a world liberated from dependence on a finite supply of fossil fuels. Furthermore, unlike coal and oil, which have many uses besides that of fuel, uranium had no other economic use. Workers in the field of atomic energy were scientists and engineers rather than the industrial labor force that produced coal and oil.

Yet the technology of nuclear energy production proved to be exceedingly dangerous. The atomic reactors produced spent radioactive waste that would remain hazardous for hundreds of years. In 1979, a meltdown at the Three Mile Island plant in Pennsylvania raised the specter of massive human and environmental devastation. Although the reactor was brought back under control without any demonstrated effect on human populations, enthusiasm for nuclear energy in the United States diminished. In April 1986, a much more serious disaster at the Chernobyl nuclear-generating plant in the Soviet Union caused enormous, lasting damage. Most recently, in March 2011 an earthquake and tsunami caused a meltdown at the Fukushima nuclear power plant in Japan, although the plant was supposed to have been designed to withstand exactly that sort of environmental challenge. Both the promise and danger of nuclear power continue to inform the political life of nations using such power. It is unclear, for example, what will be done with the radioactive spent fuel. Furthermore, the construction of nuclear-generating plants has allowed nations that lack atomic weapons to train scientists and other experts who might be able to use that knowledge to develop atomic weapons. Whereas in the United States and Europe the military uses of atomic power came first and were followed by peaceful energy uses, in nations such as India and Pakistan the reverse has been the case. Despite its initial promise, nuclear power has contributed far less to energy production than originally imagined.

The Future of Energy Production

No less than 85 percent of the world's energy consumption today is supplied by fossil fuels such as oil, coal, and gas. Scientists and politicians continue to debate the degree to which global warming and climate change is a man-made problem. However, the consensus is that the rate at which the planet is warming is accelerated by the large volumes of carbon dioxide released into the atmosphere by the combustion of fossil fuels.

In recent decades, concern over climate change and global warming has created greater interest in renewable forms of energy. "Renewables" are sources of energy—such as wind, solar, geothermal, and hydroelectric power—that occur in nature and in theory are inexhaustible. Fossil fuels, on the other hand, are natural resources found only in a limited amount in different geographical areas around the globe. In both cases, countries that have fewer energy sources and less energy production must import their supply from countries that have more.

There are still many misconceptions about the so-called "green energy." For instance, some assume that it is called green because it does not pollute. Unfortunately, no source of energy today is completely green or without negative consequences for the environment; but every form of energy production has a disruptive impact on different natural ecosystems and on the entire planet. As a rule, when it comes to energy production and consumption, governments and industries can only deal with the lesser evil.

Another misconception is the idea that nuclear power may be a clean "alternative" to fossil fuels. In fact, nuclear power is not a clean source of energy because radioactive waste can remain toxic for hundreds of thousands and even several million years. Nuclear waste management involves several long-lived products of uranium fission, such as Iodine-129 (^{129}I), with a half-life of 15.7 million years, and Technetium-99 (^{99}Tc), which is responsible for the largest amount of the long-lived radiation emissions of nuclear waste, with a half-life of 211,000 years. These geological time frames clearly exceed the length not only of any human life but also of human civilization.

To mitigate the harmful effects of carbon dioxide (CO_2) released into the atmosphere, the use of sustainable, low-carbon sources of energy has been developed to help meet the world's increasing energy needs.

Although wind power accounts for only one percent of the world's energy production, it is now the fastest-growing form of alternative electrical power. Its technology has become at the same time less expensive and more reliable, as well as more capable of being integrated into an electric grid. On the other hand, finding suitable locations for wind turbines is still problematic, given that these can have a negative effect on the appearance and functionality of natural landscapes. Also, the fact that wind is variable and intermittent raises the question of how to store energy efficiently. For both these problems, the most promising solution might be trying to contain the costs of building wind farms offshore.

In many countries today, solar power accounts only for a fraction of a percent of the total energy consumption. Solar technology has been constantly expanding since it was first implemented in the United States in the 1950s. But it still has great challenges, such as the extremely high production costs of solar cells and solar panels. In addition, the intermittent and variable way in which sunrays reach the surface of the earth requires that solar power be stored as electricity to guarantee continuity and reliability of service.

Thanks to substantial governmental funding and private investment, renewable forms of energy are growing in importance around the world. Even so, they represent a fraction of the total energy output and consumption. In the foreseeable future and for decades to come, fossil fuels are likely to do the lion's share of energy production. For this reason, it is essential to understand how best to reduce the carbon dioxide emissions responsible for man-made climate change and pollution. This can be done at the supply end by using forms of renewable energy that in the long run constitute a viable alternative to fossil fuels, hence the term alternative energy.

Another way of reducing carbon dioxide emissions into the atmosphere is to develop technologies, such as Carbon Capture and Storage, or CCS, to effectively "capture" and "store" the liquefied gas deep underground. Over the last fifteen years our understanding of CCS has greatly advanced, but larger-scale projects are still necessary to properly assess the risks of slow leakages to the surface, as well as faster and more violent releases such as earthquakes.

Finding a definitive solution to carbon emissions on the supply side is ideal, but current technology does not allow it. Hence researchers are looking at demand as well, trying to lower energy consumption in many ways.

Industry uses by far the largest amount of energy in the world today. The main products are basic materials such as cement, steel, aluminum, plastic, and paper. In countries with the longest history of industrialization, these materials are already produced with great efficiency, as industries have been paying a high price for energy for hundreds of years. If the materials cannot be produced with less energy, therefore, it will be necessary to use less of them.

Fortunately, there are plenty of opportunities to reduce carbon emissions by reducing the amount of materials used. But to do so requires a mentality change and a change of behavior on the part of governments, businesses, and individuals. The car industry, for instance, can design cars that consume less. In the building sector, it is possible to recycle steel and other construction materials that can be used for new, more efficient homes and offices. Reducing carbon emissions on the demand end requires producing goods that are more efficient, can last longer, and can be used more intensively.

The problem of energy remains with us in the new century. Environmental pollution and the issues surrounding the nuclear generation of energy will demand increasing attention and expenditure of public funds. Similarly, the political tensions surrounding the oil supplies of the Middle East will not disappear, as advanced nations seek to secure energy reserves while the nations that possess those reserves seek to secure a higher standard of living. To realize the possibilities of renewable and alternative forms of energy and energy production will require great scientific innovation, effective governmental policies, and change in the behavior of individuals.

Questions

1. How did coal transform both the industry and the military power of the West?

2. How did inventions, such as the internal combustion engine, change the demands on sources of energy?

3. Why did the rise of electrical power increase the need for petroleum?

4. What opportunities and dangers has nuclear energy posed?

5. What possibilities do renewable forms of energy hold for the future?

Glossary

Academy Center of philosophical investigation and a school for training statesmen and citizens that was founded by Plato in 386 B.C.E.

Acropolis (ACK-row-po-lis) The religious and civic center of Athens. It is the site of the Parthenon.

Act of Supremacy The declaration by Parliament in 1534 that Henry VIII, not the pope, was the head of the church in England.

Act of Uniformity Imposed Thomas Cranmer's *Book of Common Prayer* on all English churches in 1549.

Adam Smith (1723–1790) A Scottish economist and moral philosopher and the author of *The Wealth of Nations*, a pioneering work of political economy.

Adolf Hitler (1889–1945) A German dictator and the leader of the Nazi Party, whose invasion of Poland in September 1939 led to the outbreak of World War II in Europe and who was a central figure in the Holocaust.

agape **(AG-a-pay)** Meaning "love feast." A common meal that was part of the central ritual of early Christian worship.

agora **(AG-o-rah)** The Greek marketplace and civic center. It was the heart of the social life of the polis.

Agricultural Revolution The innovations in farm production that began in the eighteenth century and led to a scientific and mechanized agriculture.

Albert Camus (1913–1960) French existentialist author of *The Stranger* (1942) and *The Plague* (1947) whose work questioned the primacy of reason and scientific understanding as ways to come to grips with the human situation.

Albigensians (Al-bi-GEN-see-uns) Thirteenth-century advocates of a dualist religion, who took their name from the city of Albi in southern France. Also called *Cathars*.

Alexander VI (1431–1503) Known as the Borgia pope, who openly promoted the political careers of Cesare and Lucrezia Borgia, the children he had had before he became pope.

Alfred Dreyfus (1859–1935) French Jewish artillery officer and a victim of violent anti-Semitism in France; convicted on charges of treason in 1894 based on false evidence; divided France as no other issue since the Paris Commune.

Americanization The economic and military influence exerted by the United States on Europe after the Second World War as a result of the Marshall Plan.

Amunhotep IV (r. 1353–1336 B.C.E.) Pharaoh of the Eighteenth Dynasty of Egypt, who promoted the worship of the Aten or "disk" of the sun above Re himself and the rest of the gods.

Anabaptists Protestants who insisted that only adult baptism conformed to Scripture.

anarchists Believed that government and social institutions were oppressive and unnecessary and that society should be based on voluntary cooperation among individuals.

Anschluss **(AHN-shluz)** Meaning "union." The annexation of Austria by Germany in March 1938.

anti-Semitism Prejudice, hostility, or legal discrimination against Jews.

Antitrinitarians A group of Protestants who were the strongest opponents of Calvin's belief in original sin and predestination.

apartheid (a-PAR-tid) An official policy of segregation, assignment of peoples to distinct regions, and other forms of social, political, and economic discrimination based on race associated primarily with South Africa.

Apostolic Succession The Christian doctrine that the powers given by Jesus to his original disciples have been handed down from bishop to bishop through ordination.

appeasement The Anglo-French policy of making concessions to Germany in the 1930s to avoid a crisis that would lead to war and that assumed that Germany had real grievances and Hitler's aims were limited and ultimately acceptable.

Archduke Francis Ferdinand (1863–1914) An archduke of Austria-Este, whose murder led to Austria's declaration of war against Serbia and resulted in the Central Powers and Serbia's allies declaring war on each other and starting World War I.

Areopagus The governing council of Athens, originally open only to the nobility. Named after the hill on which it met.

arete **(AH-ray-tay)** Manliness, courage, and the excellence appropriate to a hero. Was considered the highest virtue of Homeric society.

Arianism (AIR-ee-an-ism) The belief formulated by Arius of Alexandria (ca. 280–336 C.E.) that Jesus was a created being, neither fully man nor fully God, but something in between. It did away with the doctrine of the Trinity.

aristocratic resurgence Term applied to the eighteenth-century aristocratic efforts to resist the expanding power of European monarchies.

Ataturk (1881–1938) A Turkish army officer and the founder of the Republic of Turkey, who sought to modernize his country by forcing the Turks to adopt Western ways.

atomist School of ancient Greek philosophy founded in the fifth century B.C.E. by Leucippus of Miletus and Democritus of Abdera. Believed that the world consisted of innumerable, tiny, solid, indivisible, and unchangeable particles called *atoms*.

Attica The region of Greece where Athens is located.

Augsburg Confession (AWGS-berg) The definitive statement of Lutheran belief made in 1530.

Austro-Prussian War The Seven Weeks' War in 1866 provoked by Bismarck and that resulted in Prussia's decisive defeat of Austria and its allies at Königgrätz in Bohemia.

autocracy (AW-to-kra-see) Government in which the ruler has absolute power.

Avignon papacy (1309–1377) Known as the "Babylonian Captivity" of the church, refers to the time when Clement V moved the papal court to Avignon, an imperial city on the southeastern border of France.

Axis The alliance between Nazi Germany and Fascist Italy. Also called the Pact of Steel.

Balfour Declaration Declared by Arthur Balfour, the British foreign secretary, in 1917; stated that Britain wanted to create a national home for the Jewish people in Palestine.

banalités The feudal dues to which nearly all French peasants were subject, such as payment to grind grain at the lord's mill or to bake bread in his oven.

banalities Exactions that the lord of a manor could make on his tenants.

baroque (bah-ROWK) A style of art marked by heavy and dramatic ornamentation and curved rather than straight lines that flourished between 1550 and 1750, especially associated with the Catholic Counter-Reformation.

Bastille A great fortress in Paris once used to hold political prisoners.

Battle of Cannae (216 B.C.E.) Battle of the Second Punic War at Cannae in Apulia, in which Hannibal inflicted the worst defeat ever suffered by the Romans.

Battle of Crécy (1346) The culmination of a series of victories for Edward III against Normandy, ending with his seizing the port of Calais.

Battle of Gaugamela The decisive contest in 331 B.C.E. through which Alexander the Great beat Darius and proclaimed himself king of the Persian Empire.

Battle of Hastings Battle in 1066 in which William, the reigning duke of Normandy, defeated Harold's army to become king of England.

Battle of Kadesh Thirteenth-century battle in which the Egyptian Empire fought the Hittite kingdom to a draw in a massive chariot contest at the city of Kadesh on the Orontes River.

Battle of Lepanto (October 7, 1571) A Holy League of Spain, Venice, Genoa, and the pope that defeated the Ottoman navy in the largest naval battle of the sixteenth century.

Battle of Marathon A critical victory of the Athenians and the Plataeans over the forces of Persia in 490 B.C.E.

Battle of Salamis The naval contest in the narrow waters to the east of the island of Salamis that decided the fate of the victorious Greeks in 480 B.C.E.

Battle of Stalingrad A ferocious battle in summer 1942 that marked the turning point of the Russian campaign against the Nazis, in which Hitler lost an entire German army when he refused to allow a retreat.

Battle of the Marne (September 6–10, 1914) Battle in which the fighting resulted in an Allied victory over the German armies in the West to stop the German advance on Paris.

Battle of Trafalgar A naval conflict on October 21, 1805, that marked a great victory for the British against the combined fleets of the French and Spanish.

Beguines (bi-GEENS) Lay sisterhoods not bound by the rules of a religious order.

benefices Church offices granted by the ruler of a state or the pope to an individual. It also meant *fiefs* in the Middle Ages.

benefices Ecclesiastical offices for which holders receive incomes from endowments in return for services performed.

Benito Mussolini (1883–1945) An Italian politician and leader of the National Fascist Party, who ruled Italy as a dictator from 1925 to 1943; signed Lateran Accord with the Vatican, allowing the Roman Catholic Church and the Italian state to make peace with one another.

Benjamin Disraeli (1804–1881) Prime minister of the United Kingdom from 1874 to 1880, who believed in paternalistic legislation to protect the weak and ease class antagonisms.

bishop Originally a person elected by early Christian congregations to lead them in worship and supervise their funds. In time, became the religious and even political authorities for Christian communities within large geographical areas.

Black Death The bubonic plague that killed millions of Europeans in the fourteenth century.

Black Hand The political terror society, which killed Francis Ferdinand, also known as Union or Death.

Blaise Pascal (1623–1662) French mathematician and a physical scientist who sought to refute both dogmatism and skepticism.

blitzkrieg **(BLITZ-kreeg)** Meaning "lightning war." The German tactic early in World War II of employing fast-moving, massed armored columns supported by airpower to overwhelm the enemy.

Bloody Sunday At St. Petersburg on January 22, 1905, a massacre in which troops of Tsar Nicholas II fired on workers at the Winter Palace petitioning for better working and living conditions.

Boers Afrikaners, as the descendants of the Dutch in South Africa were known, who undertook the Great Trek during the 1830s and 1840s, moving north and east of the Cape; founded three states outside British control, two of which remained independent republics.

Bolshevik Party The Russian party led by Lenin, which seized power from the provisional government after the March Revolution.

Bolsheviks Meaning the "majority." Term Lenin applied to his faction of the Russian Social Democratic Party, which became the Communist Party of the Soviet Union after the Russian Revolution.

Bosnian crisis The crisis that erupted in 1908 when Austria annexed the Ottoman territories of Bosnia and Herzegovina.

Bouvines Site of decisive French victory over opposing Anglo-Flemish-German army on July 27, 1214, in what is known as the first great European battle.

Boxer Rebellion (1899–1901) The attempt by a Chinese group, the Righteous and Harmonious Society of Fists, better known as the Boxers, to resist Western incursions.

boyars The Russian nobility.

Brezhnev Doctrine Statement by Soviet party chairman Brezhnev in 1968 that declared the right of the Soviet Union to interfere in the domestic policies of other Communist countries.

Bronze Age The name given to the earliest civilized era, ca. 4000 to 1000 B.C.E. Reflects the importance of the metal bronze, a mixture of tin and copper, for the peoples of this age for use as weapons and tools.

Byzantine Refers to the culture that flourished in the East, was centered at Constantinople, and was known as the "New Rome."

Caesaropapism The direct involvement of a ruler in religious doctrine and practice, giving him powers of church as well as state.

cahiers de doléances The list of grievances drawn up in 1789 by each of the three estates in France to be presented to the king.

caliphate (KAH-li-fate) The true line of succession to Muhammad.

Canons Regular Independent groups of secular clergy (fd. 1050–1100) that adopted the *Rule of Saint Augustine* and practiced the ascetic virtues of regular clerics.

Cardinal Granvelle In 1561, tried to reorganize the Netherlands to tighten the control of the Spanish monarchy over the country.

Carlsbad Decrees Decrees issued by the major German states in 1819 to dissolve the student associations.

Carthusians The strictest of the new religious orders (fd. 1084) that resulted from the Gregorian reform, whose members lived in isolation and fasted three days a week.

categorical imperative According to Emmanuel Kant (1724–1804), the internal sense of moral duty or awareness possessed by all human beings.

Catherine the Great (1729–1796) Empress of Russia from 1762 to 1796; under her rule Russia became one of the great powers of Europe; she supported the local power of her nobles while promoting Enlightenment ideals and continuing the economic development begun under Peter the Great..

Catholic Emancipation Act   Act in 1829 that allowed Roman Catholics to become members of the English Parliament.

Catholic League   The league formed by Henry of Guise in 1576 to enforce absolute religious unity in France.

catholic   Meaning "universal." The body of belief held by most Christians enshrined within the church.

censor   Official of the Roman Republic charged with conducting the census and compiling the lists of citizens and members of the Senate and who could expel senators for financial or moral reasons. Two censors were elected every five years.

Charles Fourier   (1772–1837) French Socialist thinker who hoped to set up communities, called phalanxes, in which agrarian rather than industrial production would prevail.

Charles Louis de Secondat, baron de Montesquieu   (1689–1755) French political philosopher who argued that no single set of laws can apply to all peoples, at all times, in all places; his *Spirit of the Laws* is one of the most influential books of the eighteenth century.

Charles V   (1500–1558) The ruler of the Holy Roman Empire from 1519 until stepping down from the throne in 1556.

Charles X   (r. 1824–1830) French king who launched a military expedition against Algiers.

Chartism   The first large-scale European working-class political movement that fought for political reforms that would favor the interests of skilled British workers in the 1830s and 1840s.

Chernobyl   The 1986 disaster at the Chernobyl nuclear reactor in the Soviet Union that heightened concerns about environmental issues.

chiaroscuro **(kyar-eh-SKEW-row)**   The use of shading to enhance naturalness in painting and drawing.

Christine de Pisan   (1363–1434) Italian-born noblewoman and writer whose most famous work, *The Treasure of the City of Ladies*, chronicles the great women of history.

Cimon   The son of Miltiades, the hero of the Battle of Marathon, who dominated Athenian politics for nearly two decades after the Persian Wars. The leading general of the Delian League, he pursued a policy of aggressive attacks on Persia and friendship with Sparta.

Ciompi Revolt   A great uprising in 1378 of the poor in Florence, which established a chaotic four-year reign of power by the lower Florentine classes.

Cistercians   A reform wing of the Benedictine order (fd. 1098), known as the "white monks," a reference to their all-white attire, symbolic of apostolic purity.

civilization   A form of human culture marked by urbanism, metallurgy, and writing.

civilizing mission   The concept that Western nations could bring advanced science and economic development to non-Western parts of the world that justified imperial administration.

Claude Monet   (1840–1926) One of the leading French artists to transform painting and later sculpture through his use of light and color to represent modern life.

clientage (KLI-ent-age)   The custom in ancient Rome whereby men became supporters of more powerful men in return for legal and physical protection and economic benefits.

Clisthenes   The father of Athenian democracy who in 508 B.C.E. made the deme the basic unit of civic life and established the council of 500.

Cluny reform movement   Monastic reform movement of the tenth century based in Cluny monastery in east-central France; established the Western separation of church and state and the strict rule of celibacy for the clergy.

Cold War   The ideological and geographical struggle between the United States and its allies and the USSR and its allies that began after World War II and lasted until the dissolution of the USSR in 1989.

collectivization   The bedrock of Stalinist agriculture, which forced Russian peasants to give up their private farms and work as members of collectives, large agricultural units controlled by the state.

coloni (CO-loan-ee)   Farmers or sharecroppers on the estates of wealthy Romans.

Committee of Public Safety   A committee set up by the Convention in April 1789 to carry out the executive duties of the government.

Commonwealthmen   British political writers whose radical republican ideas influenced the American revolutionaries.

concentration camps   Camps first established by Great Britain in South Africa during the Boer War to incarcerate noncombatant civilians; later, camps established for political prisoners and other persons deemed dangerous to the state in the Soviet Union and Nazi Germany; term now primarily associated with the camps established by the Nazis during the Holocaust.

Concert of Europe   Term applied to the European great powers acting together (in "concert") to resolve international disputes from 1815 to the 1850s.

conciliar theory (con-da-TEE-AIR-ee)   The argument that general councils were superior in authority to the pope and represented the whole body of the faithful.

condottieri   Military brokers who furnished mercenary forces to the Italian states during the Renaissance.

Congregationalists   Put a group or assembly above any one individual and preferred an ecclesiastical polity that allowed each congregation to be autonomous, or self-governing.

Congress of Berlin   (June 13–July 13, 1878) The meeting of the six great powers following the Russo-Turkish War, which ended with the Treaty of Berlin replacing the Treaty of San Stefano and determined the territories of the Balkan states.

Congress of Vienna   A meeting of ambassadors from European states that took place from November 1814 to June 1815 and sought to prevent the recurrence of the Napoleonic Wars and arrange a lasting peace.

congress system   A series of international meetings among the European great powers to promote mutual cooperation from 1818 to 1822.

conquistadores **(kahn-KWIS-teh-door-hez)**   Meaning "conquerors." The Spanish conquerors of the New World.

conservatism   Support for the established order in church and state that, in the nineteenth century, implied support for legitimate monarchies, landed aristocracies, and established churches; favored only gradual, or "organic," change.

Consulate   French government dominated by Napoleon from 1799 to 1804.

consuls (CON-suls)   The two chief magistrates of the Roman state.

consumer revolution   The vast increase in both the desire and the possibility of consuming goods and services that began in the early eighteenth century and created the demand for sustaining the Industrial Revolution.

containment   The U.S. policy during the Cold War of resisting Soviet expansion and influence in the expectation that the USSR would eventually collapse.

Convention   French radical legislative body from 1792 to 1794.

Corn Law   Passed by the British Parliament in 1815 to maintain high prices for domestically produced grain by levying import duties on foreign grain; it was the first in a series of Corn Laws enacted in the United Kingdom from 1815 to 1846.

Corn Laws British tariffs on imported grain that protected the price of grain grown within the British Isles.

Corpus Juris Civilis Meaning "body of civil law." Three-part compilation and revision of Roman law ordered by Justinian.

Cosimo de' Medici (1389–1464) Florentine banker and statesman, the first of the Medici political dynasty, who used his great wealth as a patron of learning, the arts, and architecture.

Council of Lyons (1274) Church council that proclaimed a reunion of the Eastern and Roman churches, which lasted for only seven years.

Council of Trent (1545–1563) A general council of the church called by Pope Paul III to reassert church doctrine in response to the Protestant Reformation.

Count Alfred von Schlieffen (1833–1913) The chief of the German general staff whose ideas formed the basis for Germany's war plan for a quick victory against France in 1914.

Count Camillo Cavour (1810–1861) Italian statesman and a leading figure in the movement toward the unification of Italy.

Count Claude Henri de Saint-Simon (1760–1825) French Socialist pioneer who believed that the management of wealth by experts would ease poverty and dislocation.

Counter-Reformation The sixteenth-century reform movement within the Roman Catholic Church initiated in reaction to the Protestant Reformation.

courtly love A literary conception of love that involved married women pursuing married men. The poet recommended unconsummated love at a distance.

creed A brief statement of faith to which true Christians should adhere.

creoles (KRAY-ol-ez) Persons of Spanish descent born in the Spanish colonies.

Crimean War A military conflict from 1853 to 1856 that ended with the defeat of the Russian Empire by an alliance of the Ottoman Empire and the forces of France, Britain, and Austria.

Critias An Athenian oligarch and one of the more extreme Sophists whose ideas attacked the theoretical foundations of the polis. Member of the Thirty Tyrants.

Croesus The king of Lydia (r. ca. 560–546 B.C.E.) who subjected the Greek cities of Asia Minor under his rule.

Crusades Religious wars directed by the church against infidels and heretics.

Cuban missile crisis Crisis in 1962 in which the United States, under President Kennedy, blockaded Cuba after the Soviet Union placed nuclear missiles on the island in secret.

cubism A radical new departure in early-twentieth-century Western art whose name was first coined to describe the paintings of Pablo Picasso and Georges Braque.

culture The ways of living built up by a group and passed on from one generation to another.

cuneiform (Q-nee-i-form) A writing system invented by the Sumerians that used a wedge-shaped stylus, or pointed tool, to write on wet clay tablets that were then baked or dried (*cuneus* means "wedge" in Latin). The writing was also cut into stone.

Curia (CURE-ee-a) The papal government.

Danish War A successful conflict fought by Prussia against Denmark in 1864 under the leadership of Bismarck.

David Hume (1711–1776) Scottish philosopher best known for his empiricism, skepticism, and naturalism; in his *Inquiry into Human Nature*, he, argues that no empirical evidence supports the belief in divine miracles.

David Ricardo (1772–1823) British political economist who in his most famous work, *Principles of Political Economy*, argued for the "iron law of wages." Claimed that as wages increase, parents have more children, who in turn, enter the labor force and thus depress wages by increasing the number of workers.

deacon Meaning "those who serve." In early Christian congregations, assisted the presbyters, or elders.

Decembrist Revolt Crisis that took place on December 14, 1825, when Nicholas I ordered his cavalry and artillery to attack the Moscow regiment of the Russian army, which had refused to take the oath of allegiance to the new tsar.

Declaration of Indulgence Issued by Charles II in 1672 to suspend all laws against Roman Catholics and non-Anglican Protestants.

Declaration of the Rights of Man and Citizen The statement in August 1789 of broad political principles issued by the National Constituent Assembly before they wrote a new constitution.

decolonization The process of European retreat of colonial empires following World War II.

deism A belief in rewards and punishment for human actions after death; a belief in a rational God who creates the universe and allows it to function independently according to the mechanism of nature.

Delian League (DEE-li-an) An alliance of Greek states under the leadership of Athens that was formed in 478–477 B.C.E. to resist the Persians and, in time, was transformed into the Athenian Empire.

deme **(DEEM)** A small town in Attica or a ward in Athens that became the basic unit of Athenian civic life under the democratic reforms of Clisthenes in 508 B.C.E.

demesnes The landed property attached to a manor and retained for the owner's use.

Desiderius Erasmus (1466–1536) Most famous northern humanist who looked to combine the classical ideals of humanity and civic virtue with Christian love and piety.

détente Meaning "relaxation." The easing of strained relations, especially in a political situation.

Denis Diderot (1713–1784) A French philosopher and a leading figure of the Enlightenment who served as the chief editor of the *Encyclopedia*.

départements The eighty-three administrative units that the National Constituent Assembly set up to replace the ancient French provinces.

dialectic A negative, logical inquiry that seeks truth by finding the contradictions in the arguments against it.

Diet of Worms (1521) An imperial diet of the Holy Roman Empire over which Charles V presided, in which Luther expressed his views and refused to recant.

dioceses The twelve territorial units into which Diocletian subdivided the four prefectures of the Roman empire, each under a vicar subordinate to the prefect; in turn divided into a hundred provinces, each under a provincial governor.

Directory The five-person executive body in the Constitution of Year III, which governed France from November 1795 to November 1799.

divine right of kings A form of absolute rule that asserts that the monarch derives his right to rule directly from the will of God and is not subject to earthly authority.

domestic system of textile production Method of producing textiles in which agents furnished raw materials to households whose members spun them into thread and then wove cloth, which the agents then sold as finished products.

Dominicans A mendicant Order of Preachers founded by Saint Dominic and sanctioned by the pope in 1216.

Donatism The heresy that taught the efficacy of the sacraments depended on the moral character of the clergy who administered them.

Dorian invasion A group of Greek speakers that the Greeks themselves believed to have attacked the southern peninsula of the Peloponnesus at the end of the Bronze Age.

Duke of Alba Spanish general and governor sent by Philip II into the Netherlands to suppress the revolt in 1567 and root out heretics.

Dutch East India Company Founded by the Dutch to compete with the Portuguese in the spice trade of East Asia and chartered in 1602, it was the first company in history to issue bonds and shares of stock to the general public.

Dwight D. Eisenhower (1890–1969) American Army general and the commander of the allied forces who was responsible for the "D-day" landing of American, British, and Canadian troops on the coast of Normandy.

Edict of Nantes (April 13, 1598) A formal settlement announced by Henry IV to recognize minority religious rights in France.

Edict of Restitution (1629) An attempt by Ferdinand II, the Holy Roman Emperor, to reassert the Catholic safeguards of the Peace of Augsburg.

Education Act of 1870 For the first time in British history, government assuming responsibility for setting up and running elementary schools.

Edward III (r. 1327–1377) English king, the grandson of Philip the Fair of France, who may have started the Hundred Years' War by asserting his claim to the French throne.

ego One of the three entities in Sigmund Freud's model of the internal organization of the human mind; mediates between the id and superego and allows the personality to cope with the internal and external demands of its existence.

El Alamein A town on Egypt's Mediterranean coast where a decisive battle took place in 1942 between British and German forces and in which the Allied victory led to the German surrender in North Africa.

Eleanor of Aquitaine After divorcing her first husband, King Louis VII, became Henry II's queen in England from 1154 to 1170; a powerful influence on both politics and culture in twelfth-century France and England.

electors Seven German princes who had the right to elect the Holy Roman Emperor.

Emelyan Pugachev (1726–1775) The leader of the largest peasant revolt in Russian history, having promised the serfs land of their own and freedom from their lords.

émigrés (em-ee-GRAYS) French aristocrats who fled France during the revolution.

Émile The novel of Rousseau that presents his view on how the individual could lead a good and happy life uncorrupted by society.

Emmeline Pankhurst (1857–1928) Founder of the Women's Social and Political Union, a radical branch of British feminists.

Emperor Francis Joseph (1830–1916) Ruled Austria and then Austria-Hungary as king from 1848 till his death.

empiricism (em-PEER-ih-cism) The use of experiment and observation derived from sensory evidence to construct scientific theory or philosophy of knowledge.

enclosures The consolidation or fencing in of common lands by British landlords to increase production and achieve greater commercial profits, which also involved the reclamation of wasteland and the consolidation of strips into block fields.

encomienda (en-co-mee-EN-da) The grant by the Spanish crown to a colonist of the labor of a specific number of Indians for a set period of time.

Encyclopedia (1751–1772) One of the greatest monuments of the Enlightenment, a seventeen-volume work that included the most advanced critical ideas of the time on religion, government, and philosophy.

enlightened absolutism A form of monarchy in which the rulers in central and eastern Europe took inspiration from the ideas and outlooks of the Enlightenment to centralize their authority and to reform their countries.

Enlightenment The eighteenth-century movement led by the *philosophes* who believed that change and reform were both desirable through the application of reason and science.

Entente Cordiale A series of agreements in 1904 in which Britain abandoned its traditional antagonism toward France.

Epicureans (EP-i-cure-ee-ans) School of philosophy founded by Epicurus of Athens (342–271 B.C.E.). Sought to liberate people from fear of death and the supernatural by teaching that the gods took no interest in human affairs and that true happiness consisted in pleasure, defined as the absence of pain. Defined *ataraxia* as freedom from trouble, pain, and responsibility by withdrawing from business and public life.

equestrians (EE-quest-ree-ans) Meaning "cavalrymen" or "knights." In the earliest years of the Roman Republic those who could afford to serve as mounted warriors. Evolved into a social rank of well-to-do businessmen and middle-ranking officials, many of whom supported the Gracchi.

Erfurt Program The program in Germany of 1891 that insisted on the necessity of Socialist ownership of the means of production.

Erwin Rommel (1891–1944) German general and military theorist, known as the "Desert Fox" for his capable leadership of the German and Italian forces in the North African Campaign, and who also commanded the German forces opposing the allied invasion of Normandy.

Estates General The medieval French parliament that consisted of three separate groups, or "estates": clergy, nobility, and commoners. Last met in 1789 at the outbreak of the French Revolution.

Etruscans (EE-trus-cans) A people of central Italy who exerted the most powerful external influence on the early Romans and whose kings ruled Rome until 509 B.C.E.

Eucharist (YOU-ka-rist) Meaning "thanksgiving." The celebration of the Lord's Supper. Considered the central ritual of worship by most Christians. Also called *Holy Communion.*

euro The common currency created by the European Economic Community in the late 1990s.

European Constitution The 2004 constitutional treaty for the European Union that involved complex economic and political agreements among member states and would have transferred decision-making authority from individual states to the central institutions of the union; heavily defeated by France and the Netherlands.

European Economic Community (EEC) The economic association formed by France, Germany, Italy, Belgium, the Netherlands, and Luxembourg in 1957; also known as the Common Market.

European Union The new name given to the EEC in 1993, which included most of the states of Western Europe.

Eurozone The monetary union of nineteen of the twenty-eight states of the European Union that have adopted the euro as currency.

existentialism The post–World War II Western philosophy that holds human beings are totally responsible for their acts and that this responsibility causes them dread and anguish.

führer Meaning "leader." The title taken by Hitler when he became dictator of Germany.

Fabian Society Founded in 1884, Britain's most influential Socialist group that sought to educate the country about the rational wisdom of socialism.

family economy The basic structure of production and consumption in preindustrial Europe.

Fascism Political movements that tend to be antidemocratic, anti-Marxist, antiparliamentary, often anti-Semitic, invariably nationalistic and exalt the nation over the individual; supported the interests of the middle class and rejected the ideas of the French Revolution and nineteenth-century liberalism; first Fascist regime founded by Benito Mussolini (1883–1945) in Italy in the 1920s.

fealty An oath of loyalty by a vassal to a lord, promising to perform specified services.

feudal society The social, political, military, and economic system that prevailed in the Middle Ages and beyond in some parts of Europe.

fiefs Land granted to a vassal in exchange for services, usually military.

Florentine Academy An informal gathering of Florentine humanists devoted to reviving the works of Plato and the Neoplatonists.

foederati **(FAY-der-ah-tee)** Meaning "special allies." Barbarian tribes that enlisted as allies of the Roman Empire, in exchange for rights of settlement and material assistance.

Fourteen Points President Woodrow Wilson's (1856–1924) idealistic war aims.

Fourth Lateran Council (1215) Under the direction of Innocent III, sanctioned the doctrine of transubstantiation, and made annual confession and Easter communion mandatory for every adult Christian.

Francesco Petrarch (1304–1374) The "father of humanism," who celebrated Rome in his *Letters to the Ancient Dead*, imaginary personal letters to Cicero, Livy, Vergil, and Horace.

Francis Bacon (1561–1626) Englishman known as the father of empiricism and of experimentation in science.

Franciscans A religious order founded by Saint Francis of Assisi, who urged his followers to live a life of extreme poverty; recognized by Pope Innocent in 1210.

Francisco Goya (1745–1828) Romantic painter and the most important Spanish artist of the late eighteenth and early nineteenth century.

Franco-Prussian War Fought from 1870 to 1871 between France and Prussia led by Bismarck, which resulted in the defeat of France and the establishment of the German Empire.

Franklin D. Roosevelt (1882–1945) U.S. president who supported the British before the United States entered the war despite strong political opposition at home.

František Palacky (1798–1876) Czech historian and linguist who argued that the Czech people were not members of the German nation.

Frederick the Great (r. 1740–1786) Frederick II, king of Prussia; reorganized the Prussian army, initiated the Seven Years' War, and made Prussia one of the great powers.

Frederick William (r. 1640–1688) Became known as the Great Elector and established himself and his successors as the central uniting power in Prussia.

Frederick William IV (r. 1840–1861) Prussian king who declared his own constitution with a system of three-tier voting.

Friedrich Engels (FREE-drick ENG-ulz) (1820–1895) German philosopher who founded Marxist theory together with Karl Marx, with whom he co-authored *The Communist Manifesto.*

Friedrich Nietzsche (1844–1900) German philosopher who drew on the romantic tradition to question the adequacy of rationalism to address the human situation.

Fronde Refers to the series of rebellions among French nobles between 1649 and 1652.

Galileo Galilei (1564–1642) Italian mathematician and natural philosopher who used his observations of the heavens to argue in favor of the Copernican system.

Gallican Liberties The ecclesiastical independence of the French crown and of the French Roman Catholic church from papal authority in Rome.

Gaul (GAWL) Modern France.

Georg Wilhelm Friedrich Hegel (1770–1831) German philosopher. The most important philosopher of history in the romantic period and one of the most important thinkers in the history of Western civilization.

George Orwell (1903–1950) English intellectual and writer who expressed his disappointment with Stalin's policy in Spain in *Homage to Catalonia* (1938).

ghettos Separate communities in which Jews were required by law to live.

Giovanni Boccaccio An Italian who wrote a famous collection of tales of the plague, the *Decameron* (1358).

Giuseppe Garibaldi (1807–1882) Italian general, politician, and nationalist and one of the great figures in the history of Italy.

Giuseppe Mazzini (1805–1872) Activist for the unification of Italy and one of the leaders of romantic republican nationalism.

glasnost **(GLAZ-nohst)** Meaning "openness." The policy initiated by Mikhail Gorbachev in the 1980s of permitting open criticism of the policies of the Soviet Communist Party.

Glorious Revolution The overthrow of King James II in 1688 by the union of Parliament and William of Orange.

Golden Bull The agreement in 1356 to establish a seven-member electoral college of German princes to choose the Holy Roman Emperor.

Gothic Style of art and architecture that appeared first in mid-twelfth-century France, which evolved from the Romanesque, and includes distinctive features such as ribbed, crisscrossed ceilings, with pointed arches in place of rounded ones, and frequent exterior buttresses.

Gottlieb Daimler (1834–1900) The inventor of the internal combustion engine.

Government of India Act (1858) The British response to the mutiny within the Indian Army, which transferred authority from the East India Company to the British Crown.

Great Depression A prolonged worldwide economic downturn that began in 1929 with the collapse of the New York Stock Exchange.

"Great Fear" A wave of peasant riots and violence that swept through France in July and August 1789.

Great Purges The imprisonment and execution of millions of Soviet citizens by Stalin between 1934 and 1939.

Great Reform Bill A limited reform of the British House of Commons and an expansion of the electorate to include a wider variety of the propertied classes and that laid the groundwork for further orderly reforms within the British constitutional system.

Great Schism A split within the Catholic Church that lasted from 1378 to 1417. Three men simultaneously claimed to be the true pope. Driven by politics rather than any theological disagreement, the split ended with the Council of Constance (1414–1418).

Great Trek   The migration by Boer (Dutch) farmers during the 1830s and 1840s from regions around Cape Town into the eastern and northeastern regions of South Africa that ultimately resulted in the founding of the Orange Free State and Transvaal.

Green movement   A political environmentalist movement that began in West Germany in the 1970s and spread to some other Western nations.

guilds   Associations of merchants or craftsmen that offered protection to their members and set rules for their work and products.

gunboat diplomacy   The projection of Western force through steam power, which enabled warships to penetrate the inland rivers and shallow coastal waters of Africa and Asia.

Gustavus Adolphus II   The Swedish king who led the Protestant forces to a decisive victory at Breitenfeld in 1630.

hacienda **(ha-SEE-hen-da)**   A large landed estate in Spanish America.

Hammurabi   (r. ca. 1792–1750 B.C.E.) The sixth and most famous king of the First Babylonian dynasty, best known for the collection of laws that bears his name.

Harry S. Truman   (1884–1972) The U.S. president at the end of the war following the death of Franklin D. Roosevelt and who approved attacking Japan with atomic bombs to end the war.

Hatshepsut   (r. 1479–1458 B.C.E.) The fifth pharaoh of the Eighteenth Dynasty and one of Egypt's most successful monarchs.

Hegira **(HEJ-ear-a)**   Meaning "flight." The flight of Muhammad and his followers from Mecca to Medina in 622, marking the beginning of the Islamic calendar.

heliocentric theory (HE-li-o-cen-trick)   The theory, now universally accepted, that the earth and the other planets revolve around the sun. First proposed by Aristarchos of Samos (310–230 B.C.E.). Opposed the geocentric theory, dominant until the sixteenth century C.E., which held that the sun and the planets revolved around the earth.

Hellenistic   A term coined in the nineteenth century to describe the period of three centuries during which Greek culture spread far from its homeland to Egypt and deep into Asia.

Helots (HELL-ots)   Hereditary Spartan serfs.

heretics (HAIR-i-ticks)   People whose beliefs were contrary to those of the Catholic Church.

hieroglyphics (HI-er-o-gli-phicks)   Meaning "sacred carvings" in Greek. The complicated writing script of ancient Egypt. Combined picture writing with pictographs and sound signs.

Holocaust   The Nazi extermination of millions of European Jews between 1940 and 1945; also called the "final solution to the Jewish problem."

Holy Roman Empire   The revival of the old Roman Empire in the West, based mainly in Germany and northern Italy, that endured from 800 to 1806.

home rule   The advocacy of a large measure of administrative autonomy for Ireland within the British Empire between the 1880s and 1914.

Homo sapiens **(HO-mo say-pee-ans)**   Meaning "wise man." The scientific name for human beings. Emerged some 200,000 years ago.

honestiores **(HON-est-ee-or-ez)**   The Roman term formalized from the beginning of the third century C.E. to denote the privileged classes: senators, equestrians, the municipal aristocracy, and soldiers.

hoplite **phalanx (FAY-lanks)**   The basic unit of Greek warfare in which infantrymen fought in close order, shield to shield, usually eight ranks deep that perfectly suited the farmer-soldier-citizen who was the backbone of the polis.

Horatio Nelson   (1758–1805) The great British admiral responsible for the victory at Trafalgar against the French and Spanish, who also destroyed the French fleet at Abukir in 1798.

Houston Stewart Chamberlain   (1855–1927) British-born philosopher who championed the concept of biological determinism but believed that through genetics the human race could be improved and even that a superior race could be developed.

hubris **(WHO-bris)**   Arrogance brought on by excessive wealth or good fortune. Believed by the Greeks to lead to moral blindness and divine vengeance.

Huguenots (HYOU-gu-nots)   French Calvinists.

humanitas **(HEW-man-i-tas)**   The Roman name for a liberal arts education.

humiliores **(HEW-mi-lee-orez)**   The Roman term formalized at the beginning of the third century C.E. for the lower classes.

Hundred Years' War   (May 1337–October 1453) A great off-and-on conflict fought between England and France for control of territory and national identity.

Hussites (HUS-Its)   Followers of John Huss (d. 1415) who questioned Catholic teachings about the Eucharist.

Hyksos   A group of Asiatic invaders that took over the eastern Nile Delta to rule Egypt for nearly a century. Expelled by Ahmose, the first king of the Eighteenth Dynasty and founder of the New Kingdom.

iconoclasm (i-KON-o-kla-zoom)   A heresy in Eastern Christianity that sought to ban the veneration of sacred images, or icons, in worship.

id   One of the three entities in Sigmund Freud's model of the internal organization of the human mind; consists of the amoral, irrational instincts for self-gratification.

Il Duce **(DO-chay)**   Meaning "leader." Mussolini's title as head of the Fascist Party.

Iliad **(ILL-ee-ad)**   Epic poem by Homer about the "Dark Age" heroes of Greece who fought at Troy, and written down in the eighth century B.C.E. after centuries of being sung by bards.

Immanuel Kant   (1724–1804) German philosopher who argued that reason is the source of morality and criticized the European empires on moral grounds.

Imperialism of Free Trade   The advance of European economic and political interests in the nineteenth century by demanding that non-European nations allow European nations, most particularly Great Britain, to introduce their manufactured goods freely into all nations or to introduce other goods, such as opium into China, that allowed those nations to establish economic influence and to determine the terms of trade.

imperialism   The extension of a nation's authority over other nations or areas through conquest or political or economic hegemony.

imperium **(IM-pear-ee-um)**   In ancient Rome, the right to issue commands and to enforce them with fines, arrests, and even corporal and capital punishment.

indulgence   Remission of the temporal penalty of punishment in purgatory that remained after sins had been forgiven. The practice of selling pardons for unexpiated sins began under Clement VI (r. 1342–1352).

Industrial Revolution   Mechanization of the European economy that began in Britain in the second half of the eighteenth century.

Inquisition   A tribunal created by the Catholic Church in the mid-twelfth century to detect and punish heresy.

insulae **(IN-sul-lay)**   Meaning "islands." The multistoried apartment buildings of Rome in which most of the inhabitants of the city lived.

International Working Men's Association Founded in 1864 by British and French trade unionists, known as the First International; gathered statistics, kept labor groups informed of mutual problems, and provided a forum to debate Socialist doctrine.

Intolerable Acts Measures passed by the British Parliament in 1774 to punish the colony of Massachusetts and strengthen Britain's authority in the colonies, which provoked colonial opposition and led immediately to the American Revolution.

investiture controversy The medieval conflict between the church and lay rulers over who would control bishops and abbots, symbolized by the ceremony of "investing" them with the symbols of their authority.

Ionia (I-o-knee-a) The part of western Asia Minor heavily colonized by the Greeks.

"Irish problem" Under English rule in 1800, Irish nationalists who wanted independence or at least some measure of autonomy.

"Iron Curtain" A phrase Winston Churchill used in a speech to refer to the division of Europe between a free and democratic West and an East under totalitarian rule.

Isaac Newton (1642–1727) Englishman whose work on planetary motion established a basis for physics that endured for more than two centuries.

Islam (IZ-lahm) Meaning "submission." The religion founded by the prophet Muhammad.

Italia irredenta (1915) The territories (i.e., the South Tyrol, Trieste and some of the Dalmatian Islands) that the Allies agreed to deliver to Italy in exchange for Italian support in the war.

Jackson Pollock (1912–1956) American abstract artist whose paintings are central documents of postwar cultural life in America.

Jacobins (JACK-uh-bins) The radical republican party during the French Revolution that displaced the Girondins.

Jacquerie (jah-KREE) Revolt of the French peasantry.

Jacques Necker (1732–1804) The royal director-general of finances who issued a misleading report in 1781 to downplay France's financial problems.

James Watt (1736–1819) Scottish inventor best known for the improvements he made to the Newcomen steam engine that was crucial to the Industrial Revolution.

Jansenism A Roman Catholic religious movement that arose in the 1630s, which opposed the Jesuits and adhered to the teachings of St. Augustine.

Jean-Jacques Rousseau (1712–1778) A Genevan philosopher, whose political thought, claiming that society itself, not human beings, were the source of human evil, influenced the Enlightenment in France and across Europe.

Jean-Paul Sartre (1905–1980) French philosopher, author of *Being and Nothingness* (1943) and an existentialist who protested a world in which reason, technology, and politics produced war and genocide.

Jeremy Bentham (1748–1832) English philosopher and social reformer who created codes of scientific law founded on the principle of utility, namely the greatest happiness for the greatest number.

Jethro Tull (1674–1741) The Englishman whose ideas, such as using iron plows to turn the earth and planting wheat by a drill, helped bring about the Agricultural Revolution.

jihad Meaning "struggle." Commonly interpreted as a religious war.

Johann Gottfried Herder (1744–1803) German romantic writer and critic of European colonialism, who revived German folk culture by encouraging the collection and preservation of distinctive German songs and sayings.

Johann Joachim Winckelmann (1717–1768) A German archaeologist, whose books, *Thoughts on the Imitation of Greek Works in Painting and Sculpture* and *The History of Art*, fostered the rise of neoclassicism in art and architecture.

Johann Wolfgang von Goethe (1749–1832) Perhaps the greatest German writer of modern times, whose masterpiece, *Faust*, describes the pact with the devil.

Johannes Kepler (1571–1630) German astronomer who argued that the orbits of the planets were elliptical in a sun-centered universe.

John Calvin (1509–1564) The namesake of Calvinism who stressed the sovereignty of God's will over all creation and the necessity for humanity to conform to it.

John Eck A German Scholastic theologian and a defender of Catholicism during the Reformation; debated Luther in 1519.

John Locke (1632–1704) An English empirical philosopher whose political writings and contributions to social contract theory made him one of the most influential Enlightenment thinkers and provided the basis for later liberal thought in both Europe and America.

John Paul II (1930–2005) Karol Wojtyla, the former archbishop of Poland and the first non-Italian pope since the sixteenth century, who took a firm stand against Communism and supported resistance against the Communist regimes in Eastern Europe.

John Stuart Mill (1806–1873) English philosopher and political economist and one of the most important thinkers in the history of liberalism, whose idea of liberty endorsed the freedom of the individual as opposed to the unlimited control of the state.

Jonathan Swift (1667–1745) The author of *Gulliver's Travels*, considered the greatest prose satirist in the English language.

Joseph Mallord William Turner (1775–1851) English romantic artist who depicted the power of nature and the forces of the new industrialism.

Julian the Apostate (r. 361–363 C.E.) Roman emperor who attempted to stamp out Christianity and restore traditional pagan worship.

July Monarchy Following the abdication of Charles X, the proclamation in 1830 of the Chamber of Deputies that Louis Philippe was the "king of the French," thus ending the rule of the Bourbon Dynasty.

July Revolution The king and his ministers' attempt at a royalist seizure of power in 1830 in the wake of the stunning liberal victory in the French elections.

Junkers Members of the class of German noble landlords.

jus gentium **(YUZ GEN-tee-um)** Meaning "law of peoples." The body of Roman law that dealt with foreigners.

jus naturale **(YUZ NAH-tu-rah-lay)** Meaning "natural law." The Stoic concept of a world ruled by divine reason.

just price Imposed in place of the price set in the commercial marketplace when the urban crowd considered the market price unjustly high.

Ka'ba **(KAH-bah)** Meaning "the cube." Islam's holiest shrine in the city of Mecca that houses a sacred black meteorite.

Kaiser William II (r. 1888–1918) Came to the German throne in 1888 as an ambitious and imperious young man of twenty-nine, who believed he ruled by divine right; wanted a navy and colonies to rival Britain and establish Germany as the leading power of Europe; his aims ran counter to Bismarck's limited continental policy.

King Leopold II (r. 1865–1909) The Belgian monarch determined to acquire colonies in the Congo, despite the lack of interest by his government.

Klemens von Metternich (1773–1859) German diplomat who served as the Austrian empire's foreign minister and who took the lead role in a new system of cooperative conservatism that would become known as the Concert of Europe.

Kristallnacht (KRIS-tahl-NAHKT)   Meaning "crystal night" because of the broken glass that littered German streets after the looting and destruction of Jewish homes, businesses, and synagogues across Germany on the orders of the Nazi Party in November 1938.

Kulturkampf (cool-TOOR-cahmff)   Meaning the "battle for culture." The conflict between the Roman Catholic Church and the government of the German Empire in the 1870s.

laissez-faire (lay-ZAY-faire)   Meaning "allow to do." In economics, the doctrine of minimal government interference in the working of the economy.

Late Antiquity   The multicultural period between the end of the ancient world and the birth of the Middle Ages, 250–800 C.E.

latifundia (LAT-ee-fun-dee-a)   Large plantations for growing cash crops owned by wealthy Romans.

Latium   A region that included the small town of Rome, conquered by the Etruscan aristocracy in sixth century B.C.E.

League of Corinth   The federation of Greek states formed by Philip II in 338 B.C.E. to dominate Greece.

League of Nations   The association of sovereign states set up after World War I to pursue common policies and avert international aggression.

League of Venice   An alliance founded by Ferdinand of Aragon in 1495 to counter the French in Italy.

Lebensraum (LAY-benz-rauhm)   Meaning "living space." The Nazi plan to colonize and exploit the Slavic areas of Eastern Europe for the benefit of Germany.

Leon Trotsky   (1879–1940) Lenin's chief collaborator who organized a coup against the provisional government on November 6, 1917, which resulted in the establishment of Bolshevik rule in Russia.

levée en masse (le-VAY en MASS)   The French revolutionary conscription in 1792 of all males into the army and the harnessing of the economy for war production.

liberal arts   The medieval university program that consisted of the *trivium* (TRI-vee-um): grammar, rhetoric, and logic, and the *quadrivium* (qua-DRI-vee-um): arithmetic, geometry, astronomy, and music.

liberalism   Support for the protection and enhancement of individual rights; in the nineteenth century, shared the ideas of the Enlightenment as stated in the Declaration of the Rights of Man and Citizen.

Lionel Rothschild   (1808–1879) The British banker, politician, and philanthropist who was a member of the prominent Rothschild banking family of England.

Locarno Agreements   The seven agreements of 1925 designed to secure the territorial settlement after World War I between the Western European Allied powers and the new states of central and Eastern Europe.

Logos (LOW-goz)   Divine reason, or fire, which according to the Stoics was the guiding principle in nature and meant that every human had a spark of this divinity, which returned to the eternal divine spirit after death.

Lollards (LALL-erds)   Followers of John Wycliffe (d. 1384) who questioned the supremacy and privileges of the pope and the church hierarchy.

London Great Exhibition   The exhibition held in 1851 in the Crystal Palace that displayed the products and the new material life of the middle classes.

Lord Byron   (1788–1824) British romantic writer who rejected old traditions and championed the cause of personal liberty.

Lorenzo the Magnificent   (1442–1492; r. 1478–1492) The grandson of Cosimo de' Medici and one of the most powerful patrons of the Renaissance; brought great splendor to the city of Florence and was the model for Machiavelli's *Prince*.

Louis IX   King of France (r. 1226–1270), whose reign saw French society and culture become an example for all of Europe.

Louis Kossuth   (1802–1894) Hungarian nationalist who called for the independence of Hungary from Austrian rule.

Louis Napoleon   (1808–1873) The President of the French Second Republic (1848–1852) and the emperor of the Second French Empire (1852–1870).

Louis Pasteur   (1822–1895) French biologist, microbiologist, and chemist, whose discoveries led to the full acceptance of the bacterial theory of disease.

Lower Egypt   The Nile Delta.

Luftwaffe (LUFT-vaff-uh)   The German air force in World War II.

Lyceum   The name of the school founded by Aristotle when he returned to Athens in 336 B.C.E.

Maastricht Treaty   Formally, the Treaty on European Union, or TEU, that was designed to integrate Europe first economically, with the introduction of the euro, and then also politically.

maat   The Egyptian concept of truth, order, justice, law, and harmony, personified as a goddess.

Madame de Pompadour (Jeanne Antoinette Poisson)   (1721–1764) The mistress of Louis XV and a patron of the *philosophes* of the Enlightenment.

Maginot Line   Built in the 1930s on the French side of its borders with Switzerland, Germany, and Luxembourg and designed by the French with concrete fortifications, obstacles and weapons installations to deter invasion by Germany.

Magna Carta (MAG-nuh CAR-tuh)   The "Great Charter" limiting royal power that the English nobility forced King John to sign in 1215.

Magna Graecia   The area of southern Italy and eastern Sicily colonized by the Greeks starting in the eighth century and named "Great Greece" by the Romans.

Mahatma Gandhi   (1869–1948) The most famous anticolonialist leader of the twentieth century who inspired a movement of passive resistance to British rule in India.

mandates   The assigning of the former German colonies and Turkish territories in the Middle East to Britain, France, Japan, Belgium, Australia, and South Africa as de facto colonies under the vague supervision of the League of Nations with the hope that the territories would advance to independence.

Manichaeism   A syncretic religion named after its founder, Mani, a Persian who lived in the third century. Contained aspects of Zoroastrianism, and both Judaism and Christianity.

Mannerism   A style of art in the mid- to late-sixteenth century that permitted artists to express their own "manner" or feelings in contrast to the symmetry and simplicity of the art of the High Renaissance.

manors   Village farms owned by a lord, on which peasants labored.

March Revolution   The revolution of March 1917, in which the government of Tsar Nicholas II collapsed in the wake of popular protests against the war, its casualties, and the economic and social damage it caused to the country.

Margaret Cavendish   (1623–1673) English noblewoman renowned for her extensive writing on scientific subjects.

Margaret Thatcher   (1925–2013) The first female prime minister (1979–1990) of Great Britain who led the British Conservative Party to three electoral victories and carried out extensive restructuring of the British government and economy.

Maria Theresa (r. 1740–1780) Habsburg ruler who preserved the Habsburg Empire despite the Prussian seizure of Silesia.

Marius (157–86 B.C.E.) Roman general and consul who made important reforms to the Roman army.

Married Woman's Property Act Legislation in Great Britain in 1882 that allowed married women to own property.

Marshall Plan The U.S. program, named after Secretary of State George C. Marshall, of providing economic aid to Europe after World War II.

Marxism The theory of Karl Marx (1818–1883) and Friedrich Engels (1820–1895) that history is the result of class conflict, which will end in the inevitable triumph of the industrial proletariat over the bourgeoisie and the abolition of private property and social class.

Mary Godwin Shelly (1797–1851) English writer and author of *Frankenstein*, considered the first scientific fiction novel.

Mary Wollstonecraft (1759–1797) English author and feminist who wrote *A Vindication of the Rights of Woman* to oppose certain policies of the French Revolution that Rousseau had inspired, such as keeping the spheres for men and women distinct and separate.

Max Planck (1858–1947) German theoretical physicist who was the first scientist to articulate the quantum theory of energy.

Max Weber (1864–1920) German sociologist who saw the advent of rationalism, as shown in the rise of both scientific knowledge and bureaucratic organization, as the major advance of human history.

Maximilien de Robespierre (1758–1794) A French lawyer and one of the most influential figures associated with the French Revolution and the Reign of Terror.

Mein Kampf (MINE KAHMFF) Meaning "My Struggle." Hitler's statement of his political program, published in 1924.

Menander (342–291 B.C.E.) The leading playwright of New Comedy in Athens, who, in contrast with writers of drama in the fifth century B.C.E., abandoned mythological subjects in favor of domestic tragicomedy.

Mensheviks Meaning the "minority." Term Lenin applied to the majority moderate faction of the Russian Social Democratic Party opposed to him and the Bolsheviks.

mercantilism Close government control of the economy that maximizes exports and accumulates as many precious metals as possible in order to enable the state to defend its economic and political interests.

Mesopotamia (MEZ-o-po-tay-me-a) Modern Iraq. The land between the Tigris and Euphrates Rivers where the first civilization appeared around 3000 B.C.E.

Messiah (MESS-eye-a) The redeemer whose coming Jews believed would establish the kingdom of God on the Earth. Jesus considered to be the Messiah by Christians (*Christ* means *Messiah* in Greek).

Methodism An English religious movement begun by John Wesley (1703–1791) that stressed inward, heartfelt religion and the possibility of attaining Christian perfection in this life.

"Middle Passage" The stage of the Atlantic slave trade where millions of Africans were transported across the ocean to the New World.

Mikhail S. Gorbachev (MEEK-hail GORE-buh-choff) The head of the Soviet Union from 1985 to 1991 who brought about the most remarkable changes the state had witnessed since the 1920s.

Militia Ordinance A piece of legislation passed by the House of Commons in 1642 to give Parliament the authority to raise an army of its own.

Minoan (MIN-o-an) The Bronze Age civilization that arose in Crete in the third and second millennia B.C.E.

modernism The movement in the arts and literature in the late nineteenth and early twentieth centuries to create new aesthetic forms and to elevate the aesthetic experience of a work of art above the attempt to portray reality as accurately as possible.

monasticism Movement in the Christian church that arose first in the East in the third and fourth centuries in which individual hermits and later organized communities of monks and nuns separated themselves from the world to lead lives in imitation of Christ. In the West, dictated by the *Rule of St. Benedict* (c. 480–547).

Monophysites (ma-NO-fiz-its) Adherents to the theory that Jesus had only one nature.

monotheism The worship of one universal God.

Monroe Doctrine (1823) The policy of the United States that closed the Americas to European colonialism.

Mycenaean (MY-cen-a-an) The Bronze Age civilization of mainland Greece that was centered at Mycenae.

Napoleonic Code The Civil Code of 1804 through which Napoleon reformed and codified French law; confirmed the abolishment of all forms of property and privileges based on birth.

Naram-Sin (r. ca. 2254–2218 B.C.E.) The grandson of Sargon, the world's first emperor, who took the title "god of Akkad." The first Mesopotamian king to claim to be a living deity.

National Assembly The new legislative body created by the Third Estate during the French Revolution.

National Health Service (begun on the "Appointed Day" of July 5, 1948) The most important element of the social welfare legislation passed by the Labour Party under the ministry of Clement Attlee.

nationalism The belief that people are part of a nation, defined as a community with its own language, traditions, customs, and history that distinguish it from other nations and make it the primary focus of people's loyalty and sense of identity.

nationhood In the eyes of nineteenth-century nationalists, a concept of that would promote economic and administrative efficiency; enable nations to pursue their own destinies; distinguish nations as distinct creations of God; and allow nations to take their place in the divine order of things.

NATO North Atlantic Treaty Organization. An alliance of countries from North America and Europe committed to fulfilling the goals of the North Atlantic Treaty signed on April 4, 1949.

natural selection The theory originating with Darwin that organisms evolve through a struggle for existence in which those that have a marginal advantage live long enough to propagate their kind.

Nazis The German Nationalist Socialist Party.

neoclassicism An artistic movement that began in the 1760s and reached its peak in the 1780s and 1790s and was a reaction against the frivolously decorative rococo style that had dominated European art from the 1720s and on.

Neolithic Age (NEE-o-lith-ick) Meaning "new stone" in Greek. Also called the Age of Agriculture. The shift beginning 10,000 years ago from hunter-gatherer societies to settled communities of farmers and artisans. Included the invention of farming, the domestication of plants and animals, and the development of technologies such as pottery and weaving. First appeared in the Near East about 8000 B.C.E.

neolocalism The practice of young men and women leaving home to eventually marry and form their own independent households.

neoorthodoxy The theology of Swiss pastor Karl Barth (1886–1968), which reemphasized the transcendence of God and the dependence of humanity on the divine.

Neoplatonism (KNEE-o-play-ton-ism) A religious philosophy that tried to combine mysticism with classical and rationalist speculation. Chief formulator was Plotinus (205–270 C.E.).

Neville Chamberlain (1869–1940) The British prime minister who sought to prevent Britain going to war through the policy of appeasement with Hitler.

New Economic Policy (NEP) A limited revival of capitalism, especially in light industry and agriculture, introduced by Lenin in 1921 to repair the damage inflicted on the Russian economy by the Civil War and the policy of War Communism.

New Imperialism The extension in the late nineteenth and early twentieth centuries of Western political and economic dominance to Asia, the Middle East, and Africa.

Nicholas I (1796–1855) Emperor of Russia (r. 1825–1855); represented autocracy, with the use of censorship and surveillance by secret police throughout his reign.

Nicolaus Copernicus (1473–1543) Polish astronomer who challenged the Ptolemaic system by positing a heliocentric model of the universe.

nomes Regions or provinces of ancient Egypt governed by officials called *nomarchs*.

Odyssey **(O-dis-see)** Epic poem by Homer about the "Dark Age" heroes of Greece who fought at Troy, and written down in the eighth century B.C.E. after centuries of being sung by bards.

Old Regime Term applied to the pattern of social, political, and economic relationships and institutions that existed in Europe before the French Revolution.

Oliver Cromwell (1599–1658) The dominant military and political figure in England from 1649 to 1660.

Open Door Policy (1899) The policy of the United States designed to prevent formal annexations of Chinese territory and to allow all nations to trade in China on equal terms.

Operation Barbarossa The code name for the Axis invasion of Russia, which aimed to destroy Russia before winter could set in.

Opium Wars (1839–1842; 1856–1860) A series of wars waged by the British to impose a free trade in opium on China.

optimates **(OP-tee-ma-tes)** Meaning "the best men." Roman politicians who supported the traditional role of the Senate.

Orpheus The mythical poet and founder of the Orphic cult that believed in the transmigration of souls and life after death.

orthodox Meaning "holding the right opinions." Applied to the doctrines of the Catholic Church.

Otto I Holy Roman Emperor (r. 962–973) who defeated the Hungarians at Lechfeld to secure German borders and unify the German duchies.

Pacification of Ghent (November 8, 1576) The union against Spain of the ten largely Catholic southern provinces with the seven largely Protestant northern provinces of the Netherlands.

paedagogus A Greek slave who accompanied Roman boys from the ages of seven to twelve to school in the late republic and looked after their physical well-being and their manners.

Paleolithic Age (PAY-lee-o-lith-ick) Meaning "old stone" in Greek. The earliest period when stone tools were used, from about 1,000,000 to 10000 B.C.E.

Pan-Slavism The movement to create a nation or federation that would embrace all the Slavic peoples of Eastern Europe.

Panhellenic (PAN-hell-en-ick) Meaning "all-Greek." The sense of cultural identity that all Greeks felt in common with one another.

papal infallibility The doctrine that the pope is infallible when pronouncing officially in his capacity as head of the church on matters of faith and morals, enumerated by the First Vatican Council in 1870.

Papal States Territory in central Italy given by the Franks to the pope in 755 and ruled by the pope until 1870.

Paris Commune The new municipal government proclaimed March 28, 1871, elected by Parisians to administer Paris separately from the rest of France.

parlements A set of regional judicial bodies in France with which the crown usually conferred before making rulings that would affect them.

parliamentary monarchy A form of monarchy in which the sovereign has to govern according to a constitution.

Parmenides of Elea A philosopher of Elea who argued that change was only an illusion of the senses.

patrician (PA-tri-she-an) The hereditary upper class of early republican Rome.

Peace of Beaulieu (May 1576) Peace in which Henry III of France granted religious and civil freedom to the Huguenots.

peasants' revolt (1524–1525) A rebellion of the German peasantry against their landlords, which Luther condemned.

peerage A practice of the British aristocracy whereby the eldest son inherited the title of the father.

Peloponnesian Wars (PELL-o-po-knees-ee-an) The protracted struggle between Athens and Sparta to dominate Greece between 460 B.C.E. and Athens' final defeat in 404 B.C.E.

Peloponnesus (PELL-o-po-knee-sus) The southern peninsula of Greece where Sparta was located.

peninsulares **(pen-in-SUE-la-rez)** Persons born in Spain who settled in the Spanish colonies.

perestroika **(pare-ess-TROY-ka)** Meaning "restructuring." The attempt in the 1980s to reform the Soviet government and economy.

Peter Abelard (1079–1142). Brilliant logician and dialectician of the High Middle Ages, who promoted the new Aristotelian learning.

Peter Lombard (1100–1169). The learned churchman who wrote the *Four Books of the Sentences*, which every student of theology read and annotated.

Peter Paul Rubens (1577–1640) Flemish baroque artist and the leading religious painter of the Catholic Reformation.

Peterloo Massacre Response on August 16, 1819 to a mass meeting in the industrial city of Manchester, which demanded the reform of Parliament, in which royal troops and local militia fired on the crowd on the orders of local officials.

petite bourgeoisie **(peh-TEET BOOSH-schwa-zee)** The lower middle class.

Petition of Right A document recognized by Charles I in 1628 requiring that there should be no forced loans or taxation without the consent of Parliament, that no free-man should be imprisoned without due cause, and that troops should not be billeted in private homes.

pharaoh (FAY-row) Meaning "great house" or palace. The god-kings of ancient Egypt.

Pharisees (FAIR-i-sees) The group that was most strict in its adherence to Jewish law.

Philip II Augustus King of France (r. 1180–1223) who succeeded Louis VII; unified France around the monarchy after his victory at Bouvines in 1214.

Philip II of Macedon (r. 359–336 B.C.E) The king who united Macedon into a powerful state through both diplomatic and military means and who created a national and professional army with which he conquered the Greek world.

Philip V (r. 1700–1746) The first member of the Bourbon monarchs to rule as the king of Spain.

philosophes **(fee-lou-SOPHS)** The eighteenth-century writers and critics who forged the new attitudes favorable to change and who applied reason and common sense to the institutions and societies of their day.

Phoenicians (FA-nee-shi-ans) The ancient inhabitants of modern Lebanon. A trading people who established colonies throughout the Mediterranean.

physiocrats Eighteenth-century French thinkers who attacked the mercantilist regulation of the economy, advocated a limited economic role for government, and believed that all economic production depended on sound agriculture.

Pico della Mirandola (1463–1494) Author of *Oration on the Dignity of Man,* which gives perhaps the most famous Renaissance statement on the nature of humankind.

Pierre-Joseph Proudhon (1809–1865) French politician and philosopher who thought society should be organized based on mutualism, with peaceful exchange of goods and mutual recognition of the labor each area of production required.

Pisistratus The first tyrant in Athens (r. 546–527 B.C.E.) whose popular and mild rule lead to a golden age for the polis.

Platonism Philosophy of Plato that posits preexistent Ideal Forms of which all earthly things are imperfect models.

plebeian (PLEB-bee-an) The hereditary lower class of early republican Rome.

pogroms **(PO-grohms)** Organized riots against Jews in the Russian Empire.

polis **(PO-lis) (plural, poleis)** The basic Greek political unit. Usually, but incompletely, translated as "city-state." Thought of by the Greeks as a community of citizens theoretically descended from a common ancestor.

political absolutism A form of monarchy in which one person rules with absolute sovereignty and whose authority is not restricted by any laws or customs.

politiques Rulers or people in positions of power who put the success and well-being of their states above all else.

polytheists **(PAH-lee-thee-ists)** Those who worship many gods.

pontifex maximus **(PON-ti-feks MAK-suh-muss)** Meaning "supreme priest." The chief priest of ancient Rome. The title was later assumed by the popes.

Popular Front A government of all left-wing parties that took power in France in 1936 to enact social and economic reforms.

populares **(PO-pew-lar-es)** Roman politicians who pursued a political career based on the support of the people rather than just the aristocracy.

positivism The philosophy of Auguste Comte that science is the final, or positive, stage of human intellectual development because it involves exact descriptions of phenomena, without recourse to unobservable operative principles, such as gods or spirits.

Postimpressionism A term used to describe European painting that followed impressionism; applies to several styles of art, all of which to some extent derived from impressionism or were a reaction to impressionism.

Praemonstratensians A Roman Catholic religious order of canons regular founded in 1120 by Saint Norbert that practiced extreme austerity to recapture the life of the early church.

Pragmatic Sanction A document sought by Charles VI (r. 1711–1740) to provide the legal basis for a single line of inheritance within the Habsburg dynasty through his daughter Maria Theresa.

predestination The doctrine that God had foreordained all souls to salvation (the "elect") or damnation; especially associated with Calvinism.

Presbyterians Scottish Calvinists and English Protestants who advocated a national church composed of semiautonomous congregations governed by "presbyteries."

presbyters (PRESS-bi-ters) Meaning "elder." People who directed the affairs of early Christian congregations.

print culture A culture in which books, journals, newspapers, and pamphlets had achieved a status of their own.

proconsulship (PRO-con-sul-ship) In republican Rome, the extension of a consul's imperium beyond the end of his term of office to allow him to continue to command an army in the field.

proletarianization The process in the nineteenth century whereby artisans as well as factory workers became wage laborers and lost both ownership of the means of production and control over the conduct of their trades.

protectorates (pro-TEC-tor-ates) Non-Western territories administered by Western nations without formal conquest or annexation, usually de facto colonies.

Ptolemaic system (tow-LEM-a-ick) The pre-Copernican explanation of the universe, with the earth at the center of the universe, which originated in the ancient world.

Public Health Act of 1875 Reaffirmed the duty of the British state to interfere with private property to protect health and physical well-being.

Puritans A group of English Reformed Protestants who sought to "purify" the Church of England from the practices characteristic of the Roman Catholic Church.

putting-out system A method of producing clothing in which the manufacturer would purchase the material and then put it out for tailoring.

quadrivium **(qua-DRI-vee-um)** The liberal arts program made up of arithmetic, geometry, astronomy, and music.

Queen Isabella of Castile (r. 1474–1504) The monarch who commissioned Columbus's 1492 voyage to the New World.

Queen Victoria (r. 1837–1901) The British monarch who became empress of India in 1877 through an act of Parliament.

Qur'an **(kuh-RAN)** Meaning "a reciting." The Islamic bible, which Muslims believe God revealed to the prophet Muhammad.

racism The pseudoscientific theory that biological features of race determine human character and worth.

radical Islamism The term scholars use to describe an interpretation of Islam that came to have a significant impact in the Muslim world during the decades of decolonization.

realist The style of art and literature that depicts the physical world and human life with scientific objectivity and detached observation.

Reformation Parliament (1519) Established that the English monarch must consult with and work through parliament whenever fundamental religious changes are made.

Reformation The sixteenth-century religious movement that sought to reform the Roman Catholic Church and led to the establishment of Protestantism.

regular clergy Monks and nuns who belong to religious orders.

Reichstag **(RIKES-stahg)** The German parliament, which existed in various forms, until 1945.

Reign of Terror The period between the summer of 1793 and the end of July 1794 when the French revolutionary state used extensive executions and violence to defend the revolution and suppress its alleged internal enemies.

René Descartes (1596–1650) French philosopher who invented analytic geometry and developed a deductive scientific method.

Robert Owen (1771–1858) A Welsh social reformer and a founder of utopian socialism and the cooperative movement who believed that if human beings were placed in the correct surroundings, their character could be improved.

rococo An artistic style that embraced lavish, often lighthearted decoration with an emphasis on pastel colors and the play of light.

Romanesque Style of art and architecture of the High Middle Ages characterized by rounded arches, thick stone walls, and heavy columns that support their vaults or ceilings.

Romanitas **(row-MAN-ee-tas)** Meaning "Roman-ness." The spread of the Roman way of life and the sense of identifying with Rome across the Roman Empire.

romantic republicanism One approach used to unite the small, mostly absolutist principalities of the Italian peninsula into a single state.

romanticism A reaction in early-nineteenth-century literature, philosophy, and religion against what many considered the excessive rationality and scientific narrowness of the Enlightenment.

Royal Society of London Founded in 1660, the most famous of the institutions set up in the seventeenth century to allow information and ideas associated with the new science to be gathered, exchanged, and debated.

Rule of Saint Augustine A monastic guide dating from around the year 500.

Russo-Japanese War (1904–1905) War in which the empires of Russia and Japan fought over territories in Manchuria and Korea and in which the complete defeat of Russia changed the balance of power in East Asia and elevated Japan's status to that of world superpower.

Søren Kierkegaard (1813–1835) Danish philosopher who criticized Hegelianism and, by implication, all academic rational philosophy and in whose work lay the foundations for existentialism.

SA (*Sturm Abteilung*) The Nazi parliamentary forces, or storm troopers.

Saint Bartholomew's Day Massacre (August 24, 1572) The slaughter of thousands of Huguenots carried out during three days of coordinated attacks across France.

sans-culottes **(SAHN coo-LOTS)** Meaning "without knee breeches." The lower-middle classes and artisans of Paris during the French Revolution.

Sassanians An Iranian dynasty that seized control of Persia from the Parthians in 224 C.E. Recovered Mesopotamia in 260 C.E. and took the Roman emperor Valerian prisoner.

Scholasticism Method of study based on logic and dialectic that dominated the medieval schools. Assumed that truth already existed and that students had only to organize, elucidate, and defend knowledge learned from authoritative texts, especially those of Aristotle and the Church Fathers.

scientific induction Method of inquiry whereby scientists make generalizations derived from, and test hypotheses against, empirical observations.

scientific revolution The sweeping change in the scientific view of the universe that occurred in the sixteenth and seventeenth centuries, including new scientific concepts and the method of their construction that became the standard for assessing the validity of knowledge in the West.

scutage Monetary payments by a vassal to a lord in place of required military service.

Second Athenian Confederation Organized by Athens in 378 B.C.E. Sought to resist Spartan aggression in the Aegean and avoid the abuses of the Delian League.

Second Industrial Revolution The emergence of new industries and the spread of industrialization from Britain to other countries, especially Germany and the United States, in the second half of the nineteenth century.

Second Reform Act A reform bill introduced by the conservative ministry in 1867 in the United Kingdom; admitted large numbers of male working-class voters.

secular clergy Parish clergy who did not belong to a religious order.

Sejm A central legislative body of the Polish nobles, which excluded representatives from corporate bodies, such as the towns.

September Massacres The executions or murders of about 1,200 people who were in the Paris city jails (mostly common criminals) by the Parisian mob in the first week of September 1792 during the French Revolution.

serf A peasant tied to the land he tilled and subject to dues to a lord.

Sergei Witte (1849–1915) An economist in imperial Russia who led the country into the industrial age.

Seven Years' War (1756–1763) A global conflict fought between the kingdom of Great Britain and the kingdom of France, and involving all the great powers in Europe.

Shi'a **(SHE-ah)** Meaning "partisans of Ali." The minority of Muslims who trace their beliefs to the caliph Ali who was assassinated in 661.

Simón Bolívar (1783–1830) Venezuelan military and political leader and an advocate of both independence and a republic; crushed the main Spanish royalist forces at the Battle of Ayacucho.

Simone de Beauvoir (1908–1986) French philosopher whose writings are the most important postwar work on women's issues.

Sinn Fein An Irish political party that led the nationalist cause after World War I; its military wing, which became the Irish Republican Army, fought against the British army for the independence of the Free Irish State.

Sir Robert Peel (1788–1850) A British statesman and a member of the conservative party who sponsored legislation that placed police on London streets.

Sir Robert Walpole (1676–1745) The British statesman regarded as the first prime minister of Great Britain.

social Darwinism The application of Darwin's concept of "the survival of the fittest" to relate evolution in nature to human social relationships.

Socialist realism Established as the official doctrine of Soviet art and literature in 1934 that sought to create optimistic and easily intelligible scenes of a bold Socialist future, in which prosperity and solidarity would reign.

Solon The great statesman and lawgiver elected sole archon in Athens in 594 B.C.E. to reform the constitution.

spheres of influence Regions, cities, or territories where non-Western nations exercised informal administrative influence through economic, diplomatic, or military advisers.

spinning jenny A machine invented in England by James Hargreaves around 1765 to mass-produce thread.

Spiritual Franciscans A group of radical followers of Saint Francis of Assisi, who devoted themselves to extreme poverty.

Spiritualists A group of Protestant dissenters who believed that the Spirit of God was the only religious authority.

SS (*Schutzstaffel*) The chief security units of the Nazi state.

St. Ignatius of Loyola Organized the Society of Jesus in the 1530s to counter the Reformation and win many Protestants back to the Catholic Church.

Stamp Act (1765) An act of the Parliament of Great Britain that imposed a direct tax on the American colonies.

"Star Wars" The U.S. Strategic Defense Initiative proposed by the administration of Ronald Reagan and involved a high technology space based defense against nuclear attack.

Stoics (STOW-ick) A philosophical school founded by Zeno of Citium (335–263 B.C.E.) that taught that humans could only be happy with natural law; human misery was caused by passion, which was a disease of the soul; and that the wise sought *apatheia*, freedom from passion.

studia humanitatis **(STEW-dee-a hew-MAHN-ee-tah-tis)** During the Renaissance, a liberal arts program of study that embraced grammar, rhetoric, poetry, history, philosophy, and politics.

Sturm and Drang **(SHTURM und DRAHNG)** Meaning "storm and stress." A movement in German romantic literature and philosophy that emphasized feeling and emotion.

Suez Canal Opened in 1869, the canal that connected the Mediterranean to the Red Sea so that ships from Europe no longer had to sail around Africa to reach Asia.

Suez intervention The failure of British and French forces in 1956 to prevent Egypt from taking national control of the Suez Canal.

Suffragettes British women who lobbied and agitated for the right to vote in the early twentieth century.

Sunnis Those who follow the "tradition" (*sunna*) of the prophet Muhammad. The dominant movement within Islam to which the majority of Muslims adhere.

superego One of the three entities in Sigmund Freud's model of the internal organization of the human mind; embodies the external morality imposed on the personality by society.

symposium **(SIM-po-see-um)** The carefully organized drinking party that was the center of Greek aristocratic social life and featured games, songs, poetry, and even philosophical disputation.

syncretism (SIN-cret-ism) The intermingling of different religions to form an amalgam that contained elements from each.

Table of Ranks Published by Peter the Great to draw the nobility into state service, it equated a person's social position and privileges with his rank in the bureaucracy or the military.

taille **(TIE)** The direct tax on the French peasantry.

ten lost tribes The Israelites who were scattered and lost to history when the northern kingdom of Israel fell to the Assyrians in 722 B.C.E.

Tennis Court Oath The oath members of the National Assembly of France took at an indoor tennis court on June 20, 1789 after the king locked them out of their usual meeting place.

Tertiaries (TER-she-air-ees) Laypeople affiliated with the monastic life who took vows of poverty, chastity, and obedience but remained in the world.

Test Act An act of the English Parliament that required all civil and military officials of the crown to swear an oath against the doctrine of transubstantiation.

tetrarchy (TET-rar-key) Diocletian's (r. 306–337 C.E.) system for ruling the Roman Empire by four men with power divided territorially.

The Communist Manifesto (1848) The document in which Karl Marx and Friedrich Engels portrayed human history as developing from ancient times to the present through a series of economic class struggles.

Thermidorian Reaction The reaction against the radicalism of the French Revolution that began in July 1794. Associated with the end of the Reign of Terror and establishment of the Directory.

Third Dynasty of Ur (ca. 2125–2004 B.C.E.) The last ruling Sumerian dynasty based in the city Ur. Based on the foundations of the old Akkadian Empire, but much smaller. Produced earliest collections of laws.

Third Estate The branch of the French Estates General representing all of the kingdom outside the nobility and the clergy.

Third Reich (RIKE) Hitler's regime in Germany, which lasted from 1933 to 1945.

Third Republic The French republican form of government from 1870 to 1940 that came about after the suppression of the Paris Commune and the collapse of the Second French Empire.

Thirty Tyrants The oligarchic government that the Spartan Lysander installed after the Peloponnesian War in Athens, whose outrageous behavior, which included the slaughter of hundreds of Athenian citizens, earned them their name.

Thirty Years' Peace Treaty struck between Athens and Sparta in 445 B.C.E. that gave formal recognition of the Athenian Empire. An important clause in the agreement required that all disputes be resolved through arbitration.

Thirty Years' War (1618–1648) The culmination and the most destructive of the European wars of religion, which took place in the Holy Roman Empire.

Thirty-Nine Articles (1563) The official statement of the beliefs of the Church of England that established a moderate form of Protestantism.

tholos A large beehive-like chamber built of enormous well-cut and fitted stones and used as a burial chamber for kings in Late Bronze Age Mycenae.

Thomas Hobbes (1588–1679) The most original political philosopher of the seventeenth century, who argued that human society requires strong central political authority to overcome the perils of the state of nature.

Thomas Malthus (1766–1834) English cleric and scholar who argued in his book, *Essay on the Principle of Population*, that the human population grows at a geometric rate, thus outstripping the food supply, which expands at an arithmetic rate.

Thomas Paine (1737–1809) One of the Founding Fathers of the United States, who wrote *Common Sense*, one of the most influential pamphlets at the start of the American Revolution.

three-field system A medieval innovation that increased the amount of land under cultivation by leaving only one-third of land fallow in a given year.

Transubstantiation The doctrine that the entire substances of the bread and wine are changed in the Eucharist into the body and blood of Christ.

Treaty of Lodi (1454–1455) A political alliance that brought Milan and Naples, traditional enemies, into a union with Florence.

Treaty of Paris The peace agreement in 1763 that was signed at the close of the Seven Years' War between France and Great Britain, which recognized Great Britain as a world power.

Treaty of Pressburg The peace of December 2, 1805, that followed Napoleon's great victory over the combined forces of Austria and Russia at Austerlitz, in which Napoleon became recognized as king of Italy.

Treaty of Tilsit Peace of July 7, 1807, concluded by Russian tsar Alexander I and Napoleon I that confirmed France's gains and allied it with Russia.

Treaty of Utrecht The series of individual treaties in 1713 that established the Peace of Utrecht at the close of the War of the Spanish Succession.

Treaty of Westphalia (1648) Peace that ended all hostilities within the Holy Roman Empire, whose terms shaped the map of northern Europe and established the concept of sovereign states.

tribunes (TRIB-unes) Roman plebeian officials elected by the plebeian assembly to protect plebeians from the arbitrary power of the magistrates.

trivium (**TRI-vee-um**) The liberal arts program consisting of grammar, rhetoric, and logic.

Tycho Brahe (1546–1601) Danish astronomer whose observations helped advance the concept of a sun-centered system.

ulema (**oo-LEE-mah**) Meaning "persons with correct knowledge." The Islamic scholarly elite who served a social function similar to the professional priesthood or rabbinate.

Ulrich Zwingli (1484–1531) The leading figure of the Swiss Reformation; he opposed any belief that lacked literal support in Scripture.

Unam Sanctam (1302) The bull issued by Pope Boniface VIII, which declared royal, temporal authority to be "subject" to the spiritual power of the church.

University of Bologna The first important Western university; became the model for southern European universities and the study of law.

University of Paris Grew out of the cathedral school of Notre Dame and received its charter in 1200. The most famous college in Paris, the Sorbonne, was founded for students of theology.

Upper Egypt The part of Egypt that runs from the Nile Delta to the Sudanese border.

utilitarianism The theory associated with Jeremy Bentham (1748–1832) that the principle of utility, defined as the greatest good for the greatest number of people, should be applied to government, the economy, and the judicial system.

utopian Socialists Early-nineteenth-century writers who wished to replace the existing capitalist structure and values with visionary solutions or ideal communities.

vassals Meaning "those who serve." Persons granted an estate or cash payments in return for accepting the obligation to render services to a lord.

Vichy The French resort city where Marshall Pétain set up a dictatorial regime and collaborated with the Germans in hopes of preserving as much autonomy as possible.

Vietnamization The policy of President Richard Nixon in 1969 to withdraw U.S. troops from Vietnam while the South Vietnamese army took over the full military effort.

villa A fortified country estate that became the basic unit of life in the West during the fifth and sixth centuries.

Vittorio Emanuele II (1820–1878) King of Sardinia (r. 1849–1861) who became the first king of a unified Italy in the modern period (1861–1878).

Vladimir Ilyich Ulyanov (1870–1924) The leader of the Communist revolution in Russia who later took the name of Lenin.

Vulgate The Latin translation of the Bible by Jerome (348–420 C.E.) that became the standard bible used by the Catholic Church.

War Communism The economic policy adopted by the Bolsheviks during the Russian Civil War to seize the banks, heavy industry, railroads, and grain.

war guilt clause Clause 231 of the Treaty of Versailles, which assigned responsibility for World War I solely to Germany.

War of Jenkins's Ear (1739–1748) The conflict waged by Britain against Spain to prevent Spanish intervention in their trade.

Warsaw Pact An alliance of East European Socialist states dominated by the Soviet Union.

water frame A water-powered device invented by Richard Arkwright to produce a more durable cotton fabric that led to the shift in the production of cotton textiles from households to factories.

Weimar Republic (Why-mar) The German democratic regime that existed between the end of World War I and Hitler's coming to power in 1933.

William Gladstone (1809–1898) British prime minister from 1868 to 1874 whose ministry saw the culmination of classical British liberalism; looked to individualism, free trade, and competition to solve social problems.

William of Orange The leader of a movement for the independence of the Netherlands from Spain.

William Pitt the Elder (1708–1778) The British statesman best known as the leader in charge of Britain during the Seven Years' War.

William the Conqueror (r. 1066–1087) The duke of Normandy who defeated the English at the Battle of Hastings, in 1066, to become the first Norman king of England.

Winston Churchill (1874–1965) First lord of the British admiralty who, during World War I, proposed a daring plan to drive Turkey from the war and help the Balkan front by attacking the Dardanelles and capturing Constantinople; his poor execution of the attack forced the abandonment of the campaign.

Yorkshire Association Movement A popular attempt by property owners, or freeholders, to reform the government in Britain.

Young Turks A group of reformist officers in the Ottoman Empire who sought to modernize the empire.

ziggurat The most impressive religious structure in Mesopotamia. Consisted of a rectangular stepped tower meant to resemble mountains. Most likely inspired the biblical story of "the tower of Babel."

Zionist The movement to create a Jewish state in Palestine (the Biblical Zion).

Combined Index

William M. Anderson Library
West Shore Community College
3000 N. Stiles Road
Scottville, MI 49454
231-843-5529
library@westshore.edu